					SOCIATRY & GROUP DYNAMICS	APPLIED ANTHROPOLOGY						
1940	K. Mannheim		P. Landis E. W. Bakke						Lansburg & Spriegel		S. Hardwood Bingham & Moore A. Walton	1940
1941	J. Burnham	S. H. Slichter C. R. Daugherty R. A. Lester	W. F. Cottrell A. Jones				Roethlisberger	Follet & Metcalf				1941
1942	T. Arnold F. Graham J. A. Schumpeter	C. Golden & H. Ruttenberg	L. Wilson			Arensburg Richardson			Riegel	Yoder	J. Tiffin C. Rogers H. Hepner H. Moore	1942
1943	R. Brady	S. H. Patterson	E. Hughes	Jennings			Fox & Scott			Urwick		1943
1944	K. Polanyi W. Berge S. Chase	N. Chamberlain J. Dunlop P. Drucker					Mayo & Lombard				M. Smith R. McMurray	1944
1945	C. Whittelesey	Millis & Montgomery	B. B. Gardner	Lundberg Jacobs		Leighton	Mayo	M. Dimock	Tead	C. Northcott Walters S. Lewisohn	N. Cantor	1945
1946		F. Peterson	W. Moore W. Whyte	Rogers	Moreno French Bradford & Lippitt	E. Chapple & Donald					N. R. F. Maier	1946
1947		E. W. Bakke B. Selekman Harbison & Dubin Bakke & Kerr	W. L. Warner & Low	Zeleny	Bavelas		Mayo	J. Gaus H. A. Simon	Broaded	Pigors & Myers Jucius	T. Ryan C. Thomason	1947
1948	G. Stocking & M. Watkins G. Stocking & M. Watkins	W. H. Hopkins J. Barbash Lester & Shister A. Ross N. Chamberlain	W. Whyte Mills & Schneider		Lewin		Roethlisberger		Barnard	Ghiselli	H. Burtt R. Thorndike	1948
1949		E. Ginzberg J. Shister L. Reynolds	Richardson & Walker L. G. Reynolds & J. Shister		Lippitt	Leighton		P. Appleby	Niles	Thompson Pigors Bellows	M. L. Blum	1949
1950	V. Mund		P. Meadows E. W. Bakke							Hemphill		1950

KNOWLEDGE OF INDUSTRIAL RELATIONS

INDUSTRIAL SOCIOLOGY

HARPER'S SOCIAL SCIENCE SERIES

F. Stuart Chapin, *Editor*

INDUSTRIAL SOCIOLOGY

An Introduction to the Sociology of Work Relations

DELBERT C. MILLER

ASSOCIATE PROFESSOR OF SOCIOLOGY
UNIVERSITY OF WASHINGTON

WILLIAM H. FORM

ASSOCIATE PROFESSOR OF SOCIOLOGY
MICHIGAN STATE COLLEGE

HARPER & BROTHERS

PUBLISHERS : NEW YORK

INDUSTRIAL SOCIOLOGY
An Introduction to the Sociology of Work Relations
Copyright, 1951, by Harper & Brothers
Printed in the United States of America

All rights in this book are reserved.
No part of the book may be reproduced in any
manner whatsoever without written permission
except in the case of brief quotations embodied
in critical articles and reviews. For information
address Harper & Brothers

M-Z

TO OUR PARENTS

CONTENTS

PART FIVE. INDUSTRY, COMMUNITY, AND SOCIETY

PREFACE

This is a book about work with especial attention to the people who work and the social relations existing among them. The sociology of work relations is a study of people in jobs everywhere—in the factory, home, store, office, field, hospital, mine, and government.

Work has always been the major preoccupation of man. Most of his waking hours have revolved around the struggle to produce and sustain himself. This struggle has been the source of much of his happiness and despair. It is a theme of this book that both personal satisfaction and efficient production are mutually interdependent in work activity. Neither of these ends is possible without recognizing the total social situation in which people find themselves. The sociology of work relations becomes a study of the interrelations between work and the social milieu in which the worker moves.

In many ways it is unfortunate that most of the research in industrial sociology has been done on the factory. This has led to a semantic confusion —one of identifying research on the factory with industrial sociology. Already many of us are prone to look at the factory as the main locus of work. The fact is that not more than one-quarter of the workers in the United States are employed in factories. The workers in trade, transportation, government, and other services constitute significant proportions of the labor force.

We prefer to use the word "industrial" in its broader meaning: as referring to *all* forms of economic activity, including financial, commercial, productive, and professional enterprises generally. Industrial sociology includes the study of occupations, and all the social groups that affect work behavior. The field, so conceived, investigates the interrelationships between the work behavior of the individual and the other aspects of his social behavior. No hard and fast boundary lines can be drawn between work, play, worship, and family living. What the worker encounters in the social environment of his work has significance for him not only on the job but also in his participation within the local community. His family, his church, and his club all feel the repercussions of habits and attitudes acquired at work.

In modern times the relationship between work and other social activity has been obscured. The removal of work from the home or the neighborhood to the wide reaches of the industrial city has tended to block it off as a separate, distinct, and almost isolated social activity. In the past, work was not segregated as abruptly from other aspects of living as in the contemporary urban community. Then, work was geared more into a *way of life*. It

was differentiated only in part from resting, eating, worshiping, and playing. Medieval guilds recognized that occupations and industries draw people together because of similarity of interests. Guilds were the organizational reflections of the need for association, for learning of skills, for protection of position, for social participation in and out of work. It was only after the industrial revolution, accompanied by urbanization and specialization of occupations, that work began to differentiate itself from leisure and social life.

The focus of attention shifted away from the worker and his social relationships. Production, money, and profit became the ends of economic activity; not satisfaction, self-direction, and a sense of achievement. The worker became increasingly a commodity, another cost of production. He himself began to consider his income as the only purpose of his work.

Chapter I describes how this very emphasis on production, profit, and income finally led to a rediscovery that working cannot be divorced from living. It is now known that production, profit, and industrial peace depend in large measure on the recognition that industry is a complex of interacting groups and individuals. Technological progress alone does not solve the major problems in our work plants. These problems will be solved only by increasing knowledge and understanding of human relations in industry. Industrial sociology is a relatively new discipline dedicated to this end.

The field of industrial sociology has a steadily growing body of research studies and theory. This book seeks to introduce new research, integrate available materials, and provide a frame of reference for the study of work relations. Teachers, students, executives, personnel, and labor leaders will find reports of new developments as well as different perspectives regarding industrial relations. A glossary of terms is provided in the back of the book for those uninitiated in the field of industrial sociology.

The authors have tested this book in the classroom several semesters and have found that the book may be used for either a two-semester course in industrial occupational sociology, or for two separate courses. The instructor will, of course, decide how the book may be used for one or more courses. The writers have found that for a semester course in Industrial Sociology, Parts I, II, and III offer a suitable survey of the field. A course in Occupational Sociology or the Social Adjustment of the Worker will find Parts IV and V particularly fruitful. Much of the material in the second half of the book may also be valuable for a course in Industry and the Community.

ACKNOWLEDGMENTS

It would be impossible to acknowledge here all of the indebtedness the authors owe to colleagues, students, union and business leaders for their help and suggestions in making this book possible. Wherever possible we

have indicated in the text specific contributions of these people. We want to mention specifically several people who have helped us especially. Professor F. Stuart Chapin has critically read the manuscript and has given us many valuable suggestions. Professor C. P. Loomis provided us material aid for typing some of the manuscript, and has stimulated many ideas. We are indebted particularly to our wives: Rosemary Parisa Miller for assistance in drafting the illustrations and Mildred M. Form for typing many of the drafts. Both assisted us in the laborious task of editing the manuscript.

DELBERT C. MILLER
WILLIAM H. FORM

December, 1950

Part One

INDUSTRIAL SOCIOLOGY:
ITS RISE AND SCOPE

This introductory section traces in part the history and the beginnings of industrial sociology and defines the scope of its interests. The relation of industrial sociology to other fields is then described. Objectives and methods of industrial sociology are outlined. Finally, the educational training of an industrial sociologist is described so that the student may be guided more intelligently through his future study and vocational efforts.

CHAPTER I

The Rise of Industrial Sociology

THE LIGHT THAT FAILED!

THE ILLUMINATION EXPERIMENTS

The rise of industrial sociology may be identified with the failure of certain experiments in the Hawthorne Works of the Western Electric Company in Chicago between 1924 and 1927. It was in November, 1924, that the Western Electric Company, with the National Research Council of the National Academy of Sciences, planned to study the relation of illumination to work efficiency. Efficiency experts had long been trying to find the number of working hours, the manual methods and physical conditions which produce maximum daily output. Illumination experiments were designed to appraise the effects of lighting on output. Unknowingly, the researchers at Hawthorne were to discover something far more important than hours, wages, or physical conditions of work—*something which increased output no matter what was done about physical conditions.*

3

Search for the Mysterious Unknown

Stuart Chase in his graphic style describes the sixteen-year search for the unknown.[1]

This mysterious something is hidden deep in human nature. Fatigue experts did not find it. Stop watch boys overlooked it. Managers of factories have known intuitively that it was there, but they have not known what it was. Western Electric tried to find out.

Western Electric makes the equipment for the Bell Telephone system. It is a *progressive company* with pensions, sickness benefits, safety councils, recreation clubs, thrift plans. Yet this benevolent company, employing 30,000 human beings, of 60 nationalities, was rife with tension, even in the prosperous 1920's.

In 1924, Western Electric undertook to study the effects of lighting on work. It was assumed that the better the light the greater the output. Two groups of employees were selected. The "control group" worked under a constant amount of light. The test group was given increased light. And, under more light, its output went up. Good; that was to be expected.

But the output of the control group—without a candlepower of extra light went up too! This was completely screwy. But screwier results were to follow. Light for the test group was decreased below that of the control group. Its output went up again! So did that of the control group! What, in heaven's name, was going on?

Groping for an answer, the investigators pushed the research into one phase after another of working conditions at Hawthorne. It was not just a "company job"—it was carried on in close cooperation with M.I.T., Harvard, and the Rockefeller Foundation, and it is still going on. The fullest account of it is in a book[2] which the *Personnel Journal* calls "the most outstanding study of industrial relations that has been published anywhere, any time."

The lighting test was followed by a more ambitious experiment, which the researchers hoped would answer, besides more immediate questions, the fundamental question of what makes workers work.

The Test Room Experiment

The test room experiment about to be described by Chase has been called the first major social science experiment in industry.

A group of six girls who assembled telephone relays was chosen, or rather, two were chosen and allowed to pick the other four themselves, a point which later proved significant. A relay is a small gadget made up of some 40 separate parts. The girls' task was to take these tiny parts out of trays and put them together. It was a typical machine-age repetitive job. These six girls sat at one long bench in a special room. Their nimble fingers flew. Every minute or so, each girl

[1] From *Men at Work*, copyright, 1945, by Stuart Chase. Reprinted by permission of Harcourt, Brace and Company, Inc., pp. 9-27.

[2] F. J. Roethlisberger and W. J. Dickson, *Management and the Worker*, Harvard University Press, 1939.

finished a relay. As it dropped into a chute, it was counted by a little machine. For five years that machine recorded hourly, daily, weekly output.

An observer representing the research staff was also in the room. His job was to note everything of significance that happened. He was to be the counsellor and friend of the girls, telling them about the experiment, inviting their comments, listening to their complaints.

The idea was to let the girls work as they had been doing in the regular department, and count the relays. This would give a base rate of output. Then introduce changes, one by one. If fewer relays were produced, the change was bad; if more relays, the change was a good one and could be extended over the plant. It was all as clear as ABC.

If the investigators had been puzzled by what happened in the lighting experiments, they were knocked galley west by what happened in the relay room. Why didn't these girls do what efficiency books said they ought to do? As the weeks grew into months and years, the mystery became deeper. Being scientists, however, the investigators kept doggedly on, recording faithfully what happened even when they did not know what it meant.

Here is the story, divided into test periods of four to 12 weeks:

Periods 1 and 2. Normal conditions: a 48 hour week, including Saturdays; no rest pauses. Each girl produced about 2400 relays a week.

Period 3. The girls were put on group piecework. As one would expect, output went up.

Period 4. Two rest pauses of 5 minutes each were introduced. Output went up again.

Period 5. Rest pauses were increased to 10 minutes each. Output went up sharply.

Period 6. Six five minute rest pauses were tried. The girls complained that the rhythm of their work was broken. Output fell off slightly.

Period 7. Rest pauses were reduced to two, one with a hot snack provided by the company. Output went up.

Period 8. Same as Period 7, except that the girls were dismissed at four thirty instead of five. Output went up sharply.

Period 9. Same as Period 8, except that closing time was moved to four. Output remained on a level.

Period 10. Same conditions, but with closing time at *five*.

Were the girls discouraged by losing an hour a day of liberty? They were not. Weekly output went up with a rush! The research staff tore their hair. Their assumptions were disintegrating. Some unmeasured force was still pulling output up. So after trying Saturdays off for 12 weeks, in Period 11, and finding that output remained unchanged, they prepared for the greatest test of all.

In Period 12, every improvement of working conditions made over a year and a half was taken away, and the girls went back to the exact physical conditions of Period 3—no rest pauses, no company hot lunch, a full 48-hour week. According to all the rules of common sense and factory management, this should crush their spirits and reduce their output. Instead output jumped to an all-time high of 3000 relays a week per girl.

The staff swooned at their desks. They had thought they were returning the girls to "original conditions" but found that those original conditions were gone forever. Because of some mysterious X which had thrust itself into the experiment, the experiment had changed under them, and the group they now had was not the group they had started with.

The Discovery of X

This X wasn't in the production end of the factory. It was in the human end. It was an *attitude*, the way the girls felt about their work and their group. By asking their help and cooperation, the investigators had made the girls feel important. Their whole attitude had changed from that of separate cogs in a machine to that of a congenial group trying to help the company solve a problem. They had found stability, a place where they belonged, and work whose purpose they could clearly see. And so they worked faster and better than they ever had in their lives.

A factory performs two major functions: the economic one of producing goods and the social one of creating and distributing human satisfactions among the people under its roof. A great deal of study by efficiency experts had been devoted to the production function, but very little to the social function until the Hawthorne experiment came along and discovered that the two were insepa-rable. If a factory's human organization is out of balance all the efficiency sys-tems in the world will not improve the output.

The Big Idea

With this discovery, the results of the Hawthorne lighting experiment became clear. Both groups in the lighting test had been made to feel important. So their output went up regardless of the candlepower sprayed upon them.

The relay room showed other significant results. There was no cumulative fatigue. Periodic medical examinations showed that the girls worked at all times well within their physical capacity. If monotony was present it was blotted out in group interest, as output curves bore witness. There was an 80 percent decrease in absences. The girls were actually eager to come to work!

Each girl had her own technique of placing and assembling parts. Sometimes she indulged in little variations; the higher her I.Q. the more the variations. This helped to give her a real interest in the task. Beware, you stop-watch motion-study men, of destroying little ways like this. You may run into the paradox of decreasing output by saving motions.

The girls moved about as they pleased. Nobody shushed them. They discovered they were having a good time, and said so. They remarked also that they felt as if they had no boss.

With this sense of freedom came a sense of responsibility, and they began to discipline themselves. They worked as a team, helping each other, making up each other's work when one of the group was not feeling well, giving parties for one another outside the factory. They squabbled a bit but underneath they were members of the same gang. They had found here some of the clan unity which the machine age has stripped away from so many workers.

It must not be thought that the investigators concluded that hours, rates of pay, rest pauses, lighting, were without significance. But they did conclude that, when work was carried on well within the limits of human stamina, feelings counted more than hours of labor.

Other careful tests confirmed this: feelings not only counted more than hours of labor; they often counted more than wages. Indeed it was found that employees were more concerned about the relation of their pay to that of fellow workers than about the actual amount of cash they got. Even if their wages were high, they were burned up if somebody whose position they considered inferior received more. Some day factory managers are going to realize that workers are *not* governed primarily by economic motives. . . . Underneath the stop watches and bonus plans of the efficiency experts, the worker is driven by a desperate inner urge to find an environment where he can take root, where he belongs and has a function; where he sees the purpose of his work and feels important in achieving it. Failing this, he will accumulate frustrations and obsessions. "Fatigue" and "monotony" are effects of frustration rather than causes of it. For their neglect of the human function of production, managers have paid a high price in strikes, restricted output, and a vast sea of human waste. . . .

There is an idea here so big that it leaves one gasping.

WHAT IS WORK?

WORK AS GROUP ACTIVITY

The studies in the Western Electric Company have established the importance of the worker in-the-group. No longer can the worker be regarded as an isolated individual. The worker, whether doctor, business executive, barber, miner, farmer, or housewife, is a member of a number of groups. As such he has feelings and sentiments toward others which bind him to them in collaborative effort.

WORK AS SOCIAL ACTIVITY

Wherever men and women work they seek satisfactions based on needs and wants which arise and are nourished (or denied) in groups. The social world of the average adult is primarily patterned about work activity. One-half or more of his waking hours are devoted directly to the functions necessary for making a living.[3] The satisfactions of daily life are largely bounded by the rewards of work. And so, too, the dissatisfactions.

Both in and out of the work plant, the person expresses motives, desires, and interests conditioned by the definitions of success and failure assimilated from his social experiences at work. His vocational achievements are

[3] In some of the factories during World War II almost all of the waking hours were devoted to work. For example, Jack and Heintz, Inc., of Cleveland operated on a two-shift basis, with an $11\frac{1}{2}$ hour working day, seven days a week.

celebrated in the privacy of his home, the intimacy of his club, and perhaps in the spotlight of the annual honorary banquet. He is known in the community by the "work he does." From it he acquires a social position which like a cloak wraps around him and labels him. He is a "big shot," "laborer," "white collar," "flunkey," or "bum," depending on his job reputation. His community knows (if it does not it soon finds out) how successful he is at his job. For it is considered as important for a man to be successful at his job as he is in marriage. He cannot maintain his "place in society" if he consistently fails to "make good" on the job. His frustrations in the economic struggle may bedevil him day and night. Off work, the recreative expressions of hobbies, the freedom of play, or the escapes of liquor and fantasy may relieve the daily tensions of the job. Low status on the job may be compensated by status gained in the home, at the club, or at the beer garden. On the other hand, success at work brings him recognition in the home, neighborhood, community, and even at times in the society at large.

Thus the question, "What is work?" is really not simple to answer. Certainly it is naïve to imagine that work consists solely of operations on the job. Work is social as well as economic activity. It is a composite of skills, attitudes, habit patterns, status and power roles. It is an end in itself and yet a means to social ends both in and out of the work plant. It cannot be reiterated too frequently that jobs and human relations are always intertwined as social situations.

INDUSTRIAL SOCIOLOGY EMERGES

Social science research has only lately turned to the study of the social relations within work groups and the study of how the personality is affected by the nature of the social systems which arise in the factory, office, or store. The neglect of this field by sociologists was pointed out by Henry Pratt Fairchild in his presidential address to the American Sociological Society in 1936. At that time he said, "Business . . . is essentially a sociological reality, and should be clarified by sociological methodology. Yet most sociological writers seem to have caught almost no glimpse of its real meaning and to ignore it almost completely. . . . Out of twenty-one leading textbooks in sociology examined . . . there was not one that gave more than a passing discussion of business."[4]

These words were written more than a decade ago. In the intervening years much interest in industrial problems has been aroused among social scientists. Industrial relations research has increasingly employed sociological concepts and methods of investigation. Attention to this field has come from several sources within universities and industries.

[4] H. P. Fairchild, "Business as an Institution," *American Sociological Review*, February, 1937, pp. 4-5.

INDUSTRY AND UNIVERSITY

The hue and cry of business circles about the "impracticality" of academic men has not much validity in the field of industrial sociology. From the very beginning the university has assumed a leading role in bringing knowledge about man's social nature into business. Fortunately, far-sighted industrialists have been willing to coöperate in this effort.

The Harvard Studies

The great influence of the research studies from the Harvard Graduate School of Business has already been noted in the significant discoveries made at the Hawthorne Works of the Western Electric Company. Theory and research for industrial sociology have been suggested by a series of books and research monographs from the Department of Industrial Research of the Harvard Graduate School of Business Administration. Elton Mayo, long the director of the department, was a leading scholar of social problems in industry. His two most important books, *The Human Problems of an Industrial Civilization* (1933) and *The Social Problems of an Industrial Society* (1945), are important interpretations of the social forces which run through our industrial civilization. His departmental colleagues, T. N. Whitehead, F. J. Roethlisberger, and B. M. Selekman, have contributed many valuable additions.[5]

Contributions of the Social Sciences

Fortunately, the researchers in the different social sciences have been studying similar problems of human relations in industry. Sociologists and anthropologists, industrial and labor economists, psychologists and personnel researchers have often turned their attention to the same crucial problems of industrial and labor organization. A full portrayal of all the resources which have encouraged the growth of industrial sociology is almost too large an undertaking. However, the major outlines can be shown, and Figure 1 depicts the feeders which have developed the main currents of this new branch of sociological science.

THE PLACE OF SOCIOLOGY

The Harvard researches in the Western Electric Company brought to sociology a problem demanding decision. The research conclusions pointed to the importance of group life in determining work incentive, productivity, and work satisfaction. These conclusions pointed straight toward the field

[5] See T. N. Whitehead, *Leadership in a Free Society*, 1936, and *The Industrial Worker*, 1938; F. J. Roethlisberger and W. J. Dickson, *op. cit.* These and Mayo's books were all published by Harvard University Press. See also B. M. Selekman, *Labor Relations and Human Relations*, McGraw-Hill Book Company, Inc., 1947. A full list of the department publications may be found in E. Mayo, *Social Problems of an Industrial Civilization*, pp. 125-140.

of sociology. Scientific sociology has as its special field of social science the
investigation of matters relating to group life and the social development
of man. Was sociology willing to accept new research and teaching responsibilities?

At first only a few sociologists showed interest in turning their attention
to industrial and labor problems. The pioneers include Arensberg, Bakke,
Blumer, Chapple, Harbison and Dubin, Form, Gardner, Scott and Homans,
Hughes, Meadows, Miller, Moore, Warner, Whyte, and others.[6] These
research workers have been joined by many others. Interest reached such a
high level that the American Sociological Society created a Section on Industrial Sociology in 1946. Since then, the number of younger sociologists
attracted to the field has been rapidly growing.

Several research centers of industrial relations have been established.
One such center is the Committee on Human Relations in Industry at the
University of Chicago. The committee was organized early in 1943 to carry
on research in the social organization of industry and industrial society.
Experts from the social sciences combined their specialized knowledge with
those in business administration and education in the planning of research
work.[7]

The Massachusetts Institute of Technology followed a similar plan in
1944. Its institute for the study of group dynamics under the direction of
the late Kurt Lewin also combined the personnel and perspectives of the
social sciences in tackling the human problems of industry.

A school of industrial and labor relations was established by the state of
New York at Cornell University. Founded in 1944 and opened November 1,

[6] See Conrad M. Arensberg, "Industry and the Community," *American Journal of
Sociology*, July, 1942, pp. 1-12; E. Wight Bakke, *The Unemployed Worker*, Yale Uni-
versity Press, 1940; Herbert Blumer, "Sociological Theory in Industrial Relations,"
American Sociological Review, June, 1947, pp. 271-277; Eliot D. Chapple and Gordon
Donald, Jr., "A Method for Evaluating Supervisory Personnel," *Harvard Business Review*,
Winter, 1946, pp. 197-214; F. H. Harbison and R. Dubin, *Patterns of Union Manage-
ment Relations*, Science Research Associates, 1947; William H. Form, "Toward an
Occupational Social Psychology," *Journal of Social Psychology*, August, 1946, pp. 85-99;
Burleigh B. Gardner, *Human Relations in Industry*, Richard D. Irwin, Inc., 1945; Jerome
F. Scott and George Homans, "Reflections on the Wildcat Strikes," *American Socio-
logical Review*, June, 1947, pp. 278-287; Everett C. Hughes, Race Relations in Industry,"
in *Industry and Society*, edited by William F. Whyte, McGraw-Hill Book Company,
Inc., 1946; Paul Meadows, "Human Relations in Industrial Civilization," *Technology
Review*, April, 1947; Delbert C. Miller, "The Future Development of Industrial Soci-
ology," *Proceedings of the Pacific Sociological Society, Research Studies of the State
College of Washington*, April, 1947; Wilbert E. Moore, *Industrial Relations and the
Social Order*, The Macmillan Company, 1946; W. Lloyd Warner and J. O. Low, *The
Social System of the Modern Factory*, Yale University Press, 1947; William F. Whyte,
The Human Relations in the Restaurant Industry, McGraw-Hill Book Company, Inc.,
1948.
[7] The members of the Committee on Human Relations in Industry were: George
Brown and Burleigh Gardner of the School of Business, Allison Davis and Robert
Havighurst of the Department of Education, Neil Jacoby, Vice-President of the University,
and W. Lloyd Warner, Everett Hughes, and William Whyte of the Department of
Anthropology and Sociology.

1945, it became the first institution of its kind in the country. The purpose of the school is to provide both a general and an intensive training for those who look forward to a professional career in industrial and labor relations.

At Yale University E. Wight Bakke directs a labor and management center which focuses its resources on the critical issues in the field of industrial and labor relations. The activities of the center are fourfold: teaching, research, library, and community service.

Other research and teaching centers have been organized at California, Illinois, Michigan, Michigan State, Minnesota, Ohio State, Pennsylvania, Princeton, Washington, and many other universities.[8]

GOVERNMENT AND INDUSTRY

With the advent of World War II, far-sighted men in government realized that high production rates could not be achieved without some thought to the human relations within the work plants of the nation. Tried knowledge and techniques applied in a few industries had to be disseminated as rapidly as possible to other industrial organizations. The establishment of the Training Within Industry Service (T.W.I.) of the War Manpower Commission made it possible to bring together teams composed of university and industrial specialists in human relations. In January, 1941, Sidney Hillman, Commissioner of the Division of Labor in the Advisory Commission to the Council of National Defense, sent this question to the National Academy of Sciences: "What can be done to increase knowledge and improve understanding of supervision at the work level?"

The question was passed on to the National Research Council's Committee on Work in Industry. Dr. Lawrence J. Henderson, Director of the Fatigue Laboratory at Harvard, was made chairman. His committee recommended that training be directed toward "improving and accelerating the training of supervisors in handling the human situations under their charge so as to secure maximum cooperation." To Training Within Industry was delegated the responsibility of developing a training plan. F. J. Roethlisberger and John B. Fox were drawn in from Harvard and L. J. O'Rourke from the Civil Service Commission. At T.W.I. headquarters they met with four veterans of industrial training: C. R. Dooley of Socony Vacuum Oil Company, Walter Dietz of Western Electric Company, M. J. Kane of American Telephone and Telegraph Company, and William Conover of United States Steel Corporation. Out of their work came a ten-hour training unit called "Job Relations Training" designed to provide practice in handling human situations in industry.[9]

[8] Cf. Forest H. Kirkpatrick, "Labor Problems in the College Curriculum," *School and Society*, February 23, 1946, pp. 121-123.

[9] *The Training Within Industry Report*, 1940-1945, War Manpower Commission, United States Government Printing Office, September, 1945, pp. 203-204. Training Within Industry also developed Job Instruction Training, Job Methods Training, Union Relations Training, and a *Program Development Manual*.

Training Within Industry Service then set into motion its organizational machinery. In every major city, field representatives and institute conductors coached the training representatives sent by those companies desiring the service. These representatives then went back to their companies with their job relations manuals and within two years trained nearly a half-million leaders of industrial work groups in the "Foundations of Good Job Relations."[10] These leaders were plant foremen, office supervisors, plant superintendents, and business executives. They were from every kind of work plant—banks, stores, offices, and factories. No such mass training in human relations had ever before been attempted. T.W.I. programs developed a climate of opinion favorable to the future growth of industrial sociology. This is an asset of tremendous value to a new discipline.

THE FIRST TEXTBOOK OF INDUSTRIAL SOCIOLOGY

In this chapter we have described some of the historical developments that demonstrated the need for a science of industrial sociology. We also examined the origins of early basic ideas which recognized work as a social reality. A need for a systematic development of industrial sociology now emerges. Theory, research, and applied knowledge have reached a state which permits systematization. This book is the first to be entitled *Industrial Sociology*. As such it aims to define the major areas, concepts, and principles of a new discipline.

SUPPLEMENTARY STUDIES

FIELD INTERVIEWS: PLANNED AND CASUAL

1. Arrange an interview with a businessman and a union leader and discuss with him how human relations enter into his work and that of his associates.

2. Arrange an interview with a supervisor and a steward and discuss with him how human relations problems arise and how they are handled.

3. As informal contact occurs, with the bus driver, store clerk, barber, etc., ask him about his work life—what he has done prior to present job, how he got into his present line of work, what goals he has, if any, and what he thinks is important on the job. In short, attempt to acquaint yourself with the "raw material" upon which the field of industrial sociology is based.

LIBRARY: BOOKS AND ARTICLES

4. Browse on some of the published articles and books in industrial sociology shown in Figure 1. Try to get an appreciation of the different kinds of interest shown by sociologists who have studied work behavior.

[10] *Ibid*, p. 126. Between February, 1943, and August, 1945, 490,022 certifications of Job Relations Training were issued.

FIELD OBSERVATIONS: DIRECT OBSERVATION

5. Observe an organization or committee meeting. Try to discover the origin of conflicts, the manner in which these conflicts are expressed, the way compromise is attained, and the degree to which consensus is secured.

CHAPTER II

The Field of Industrial Sociology

WHAT IS INDUSTRIAL SOCIOLOGY?

WORK GROUP

The group is the elementary unit of observation for sociology. Whenever people congregate and interact, a structure of social relationships appears. Some people soon assume leadership, others become followers, friendships

are formed, and animosities are created. Relationships of superordination and subordination, antagonism and sympathy, coöperation and competition emerge and operate as social forces on the members of the group. The *work group* contains all of these social qualities. As workers interact with one another, common ways of behaving manifest themselves and become routinized into social habits. These social habits, as patterns of usages, soon acquire a degree of traditional sanction. The form of greeting, the manner of dress, the ways of speaking are familiar examples of customs which W. G. Sumner has called *folkways.*

Folkways are, then, the traditional and the expected ways of behaving in the group. A newcomer to the work group is expected to learn and adopt the prevailing folkways.[1] Examples of folkways in a work plant may be: giving the foreman a cigar for Christmas, greeting one's fellow workers in the morning, and helping the worker whose production is down. These patterns of behavior are not entirely compulsory, nor are they formally instituted. Yet they are group expectations which are regularly followed and observed. Some folkways must be observed by all members of the work group, but others specifically apply to certain individuals because of the work position which they occupy.

WORK ROLE

The part that the worker plays in the work group is called the *work role.* For example, the supervisor in his role is expected not to play favorites; he is supposed to be loyal to his men; he should be able to teach the skills of the jobs; he must not take "guff" from his subordinates; he should not lunch with the workers; and he must see that all of his workers get a personal greeting. Other workers have roles—there are the roles of the new worker, the old-timer, and the climber. Consciously and unconsciously the new worker develops attitudes and work roles which shape his personality according to the behavior expectations of the group. The success or failure of the worker depends not alone on his job performance but on how he plays his role in the work group. In playing his role he affects the attitudes and actions of those in his work group, and they in turn influence his work behavior.

WORK PLANT SOCIETY

Work plants enclose human organizations. Most of the work roles in the plant are performed in small, intimate, face-to-face groups. In fact, a study of the social organization of work plants shows that a network of primary group relations exists.[2] Other work roles, however, are performed in larger,

[1] Perhaps the best examples of folkways operating in the work group are to be found in F. J. Roethlisberger and William J. Dickson, *Management and the Worker*, Harvard University Press, 1947, pp. 459-510. See also William F. Whyte, *Human Relations in the Restaurant Industry*, McGraw-Hill Book Company, Inc., 1948.

[2] T. N. Whitehead, *Leadership in a Free Society*, Harvard University Press, 1937.

more impersonal, secondary groups. These small and large groups, with their folkways and work roles, overlap in every direction, for they are connected by mutual daily interaction. Thus the *work plant society* may be visualized as the complex pattern of social interrelationships that exists in any given work plant. The work plant society, as the social environment, fosters the growth of a variety of groups and work roles and sets limits to the social behavior which may be acceptable to members of that society.

THE STUDY OF INDUSTRIAL SOCIOLOGY

Among other things sociology studies group behavior, status positions, and roles that individuals play in groups. Industrial sociology merely applies the methods and concepts of general sociology to the field of work relations. The field of industrial sociology may be conveniently defined as the study of: (1) *work groups and work relations*, (2) *the role the worker plays in work groups*, and (3) *the social organization of work plant society*.

RELATIVES IN THE IMMEDIATE FAMILY

WORKER AS A BIO-PSYCHO-SOCIAL ORGANISM

After interviewing 21,000 employees in the Hawthorne plant, the Western Electric researchers concluded that the source of employee complaints could not be confined to one single cause. Rather, they agreed that the dissatisfaction of the worker is a response in most cases to many causes in complex situations. Adjustive behavior is no different from non-adjustive behavior in its origin. It too arises from many causes in complex situations. Figure 2 shows some of the types of influences which may affect the behavior of workers. The degree of job satisfaction and worker productivity results from three influences which exist both in and outside of the work plant. These are: (1) biological factors, such as nature of diet and health; (2) psychological modes of adjustment such as withdrawal, compensation, and rationalization; (3) social relations, such as leadership, rivalry, coöperation, and isolation.

The worker can be fully understood only by recognizing him as a bio-psycho-social organism. This may be illustrated by an account which a foreman related about one of his workers.

Joe was one of our best workers—a crack assembler in the portable compressor equipment department. Joe worked as a part of a team. Now a compressor is a complicated machine. Four men are assigned to the assembly of each machine. Joe's team was known as the fastest in the shop. They were young men, all eager to make as much money as possible. The company profit sharing plan gave them more money for every unit shipped. Joe was well-liked by his team because he worked fast and was always full of fun.

Last May Joe began to act queer. He became surly and started to loaf on the job. The men kidded him a little and he seemed to snap out of it. But later his work went down. He became slower and inspection began to catch errors in his work. Some of the men began to give Joe a hand on the more difficult parts, but the team continued to put out compressors as fast as ever.

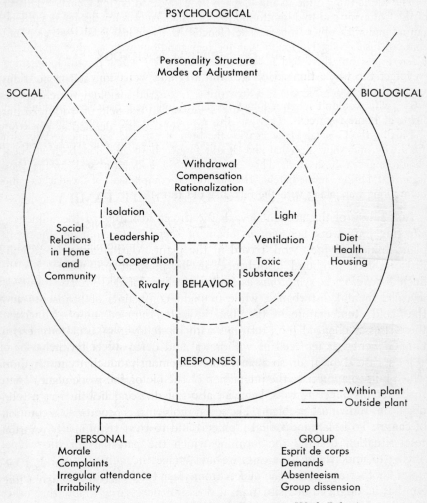

Fig. 2. In-Plant and Extra-Plant Influences on Work Behavior.

But Joe's work continued to fall off. He began to complain of headaches. He complained that it was too cold in the shop, and began to leave the job and spend more and more time in the toilet. He didn't kid much, and when the fellows asked him what was eating him, he told them to mind their own business. He told his best friend that no one gave a damn about him. The production of the crew began to fall off.

This went on for some weeks, with Joe's work getting worse. One day, he came in drunk. The men took him to the toilet and sobered him up. When he got back on the job, he was ashamed of himself. He told the fellows that he was having trouble at home. His wife accused him of running around with other women, threatened to leave him, and went to her sister's home for a week.

The whole thing came to a head when his wife called on the General Manager of the Company and told him to fire Joe. She said she was leaving Joe because he ran around with other women. The General Manager had a talk with Joe and some of his friends. He found that Joe had gone out with another woman for a few times; but there had never been anything but a few drinks. Joe wanted to forget the whole thing. He loved his wife and was deeply attached to his five year old son.

His wife wouldn't let him forget the affair and there had been nothing but fights at home for weeks. This was the period when Joe's work suffered most.

Finally, the General Manager with the help of a friend was able to talk with Joe's wife and show her that she should forgive him, and that both of them should make a fresh start. They agreed to this, and Joe's work at the shop improved almost immediately. He no longer complained of headaches, and before long was joking with the men like old times.[3]

An analysis of this account reveals the threefold nature of the influences affecting Joe's work behavior. A chain of *social factors* outside the work plant influenced Joe's work record in the plant. Marital discord and conflicts induced profound disturbances in his physical and mental health. Such *psychological symptoms* as futility, feelings of despair, and drinking revealed mental disturbance, while frequent complaints of headaches and the "cold" temperature of the shop indicated *physical upset*. Moreover, these stresses changed Joe's relations with his fellow workers. His cheerful temperament was replaced by withdrawal and defensive behavior.

Joe's case, typical of so many others, demonstrates that any analysis which fails to appreciate the interaction of the biological, psychological, and social factors affecting work behavior also fails to see the worker as a total organism. Individual problems, like social problems, are rooted in a complex of causes. To isolate individual problems and to treat them apart from the total situation destroys the meaning which the part has for the whole. Trying to understand Joe's case, we must trace the influence of one force upon another and assess the effects from their total interaction. If a problem has its origin in one situation, it does not necessarily follow that other situations will remain unaffected. In the above case the origin of the problem was marital discord. But this discord profoundly worsened the physical and mental health of the worker. In turn, the disturbances and stresses on the job accumulated and aggravated the relations with the family. This is what is meant by the statement that personal problems are rooted in a

[3] From a document secured by the authors from a supervisor in a midwestern compressor company.

complex of interacting forces. Thus we can diagram in Figure 3 the factors influencing Joe's behavior.

"Problem" cases may illustrate more dramatically the three sources of influences on the behavior of workers. One must remember, however, that the biological, psychological, and social factors also operate in normal and well-adjusted workers.

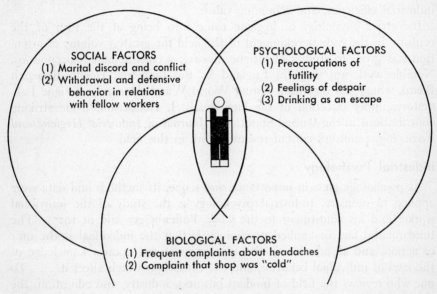

SOCIAL FACTORS
(1) Marital discord and conflict
(2) Withdrawal and defensive behavior in relations with fellow workers

PSYCHOLOGICAL FACTORS
(1) Preoccupations of futility
(2) Feelings of despair
(3) Drinking as an escape

BIOLOGICAL FACTORS
(1) Frequent complaints about headaches
(2) Complaint that shop was "cold"

FIG. 3. The Biological, Psychological, and Social Factors as Interacting Forces Affecting the Behavior of Workers.

THE TRIUMVIRATE OF INDUSTRIAL SCIENCES

A recognition of these interdependent factors has stimulated the development of three specialized fields of study. The basic sciences which are concerned with the understanding of the worker are industrial physiology, industrial psychology, and industrial sociology.

These sciences did not arise simultaneously. As applied sciences of man their history parallels the growth of physiology, psychology, and sociology.

Industrial Physiology

Each of these sciences, in turn, arose as man grew increasingly aware of the possibility of studying himself. Earliest interest developed in the fields of natural science. As knowledge about the biology and physiology of man accumulated, *industrial physiology* was born. Sometimes called industrial hygiene, it is the study of the health and physical efficiency of the worker.

Early in industrial operations the need for this applied science became

apparent. Accidents, illness, and industrial diseases plagued employers in their attempts to meet production schedules and increase their profits. Employers sought out physiologists to assist them in their drives to improve production and profits. Consequently, as a scientific aid to industry, industrial physiology tends to regard the breadwinner's health as a strategic commodity. The worker is looked upon as a machine which must be maintained at peak efficiency. His health is considered vital to his personal happiness, industrial efficiency, and economic value.

Industrial physiology or hygiene came into being at the turn of the century. In the early development of the field the greatest volume of attention was given to studies of fatigue, disease, accidents, and toxic poisons. Notable work was done in England by the Industrial Health Research Board, which was organized during World War I. Harvard's Fatigue Laboratory, under direction of the late Dr. L. J. Henderson, made striking contributions in the United States. The *Journal of Industrial Hygiene and Toxicology* publishes current research work in this field.

Industrial Psychology

As psychology grew in importance and scope, its methods and data were applied to industry. Industrial psychology is the study of the individual worker and his adjustment to the work. Poffenberger said in 1927: "The fundamental fact of applied psychology is that the individual is the unit of action, and all advance in this science must rest upon a knowledge of the laws of individual behavior, and the conditions which affect it. . . . To one who reviews the field of modern business, industry, and education, the striking thing is the emphasis that is being placed on the individual rather than the group."[4]

Moore has added, "The immediate concern of the psychologists is with those phases of business and industry that are uppermost in the minds of both employers and employees at the moment."[5] The most common applications of psychology to industry have therefore been made in employee selection and placement, merit rating, reduction of accidents, solution of visual problems, increasing the accuracy of inspection, improving training methods, and measuring and improving employee morale.[6]

Investigations for industry and a program for industrial psychology were first described in a series of lectures by Münsterberg during 1910-1911 at the University of Berlin. Since the publication of these lectures in 1912,[7] industrial psychology has advanced rapidly as a research discipline in both Europe

---

[4] A. T. Poffenberger, *Applied Psychology*, Appleton-Century-Crofts, Inc., 1927, p. 16.
[5] Herbert Moore, *Psychology for Business and Industry*, McGraw-Hill Book Company, Inc., 1942, p. 1.
[6] Joseph Tiffin, *Industrial Psychology*, Prentice-Hall, Inc., 1942, p. viii.
[7] Hugo Münsterberg, *Psychologie und Wirtschaftsleben*, Leipzig, 1912.

and America.[8] Applications of psychology are now being widely made in business and industry as quickly as management learns of its profitability.[9]

Industrial Sociology

Industrial sociology is the youngest of the three basic sciences to turn its focus on economic and work behavior. In the last decade attention has been moving from the worker as an individual to the worker as a group member. The impact of the large-scale industrial experiments at the Western Electric Company caused Elton Mayo and his staff to alter their entire axis of thought, from the proposition that all social problems are individual to the proposition that all individual problems are essential social. In July, 1925, after many years as a psychologist in industry, Mayo stated his thinking in positive terms. He wrote in *Harper's Magazine,* "When we talk of social problems, we are apt to forget that every social problem is ultimately individual. . . ."[10] By 1945 Mayo was writing, "In industry and in other human situations the administrator is dealing with well-knit human groups and not with a horde of individuals. . . . Man's desire to be continuously associated in work with his fellows is a strong, if not the strongest, human characteristic."[11]

While this transition in thinking was taking place, other changes were occurring in the political and economic order—changes which increasingly focused attention upon group relations. For example, while the framework of labor relations was set in the earlier pattern of individual bargaining, the individual worker remained the principal unit of attention. The growth of collective bargaining, with the passage of the National Industrial Labor Relations Act in 1935, emphasized the pressing need for knowledge of intergroup relations. This situation helped to stimulate the growth of interest in the application of sociology to industry and labor. Since then, industrial sociology has been seeking to develop a conceptual framework and a body of knowledge which will be helpful to students of labor and management.

THE RELATION OF SCIENTIFIC KNOWLEDGE TO ADMINISTRATION OF PERSONNEL, INDUSTRIAL, AND LABOR RELATIONS

The special task of the social sciences is to relate the human being to his social environment. This means that the worker must be understood not only as a bio-psycho-social *organism* but also as a *person* within a *social structure.* Industrial psychology, industrial sociology, and industrial and

[8] For a history of industrial psychology see Morris S. Viteles, *Industrial Psychology,* W. W. Norton and Co., 1932.
[9] H. E. Burtt, *Principles of Employment Psychology,* Harper & Brothers, 1942.
[10] See "The Fruitful Errors of Elton Mayo," *Fortune,* November, 1946, p. 238.
[11] Elton Mayo, *The Social Problems of an Industrial Civilization,* Harvard University Press, 1945, p. 110.

labor economics are the basic social studies which supply industrial and labor leaders with scientific knowledge about human relationships as they develop in work plants. Professional and research training for personnel, industrial, and labor relations takes place largely in these three social

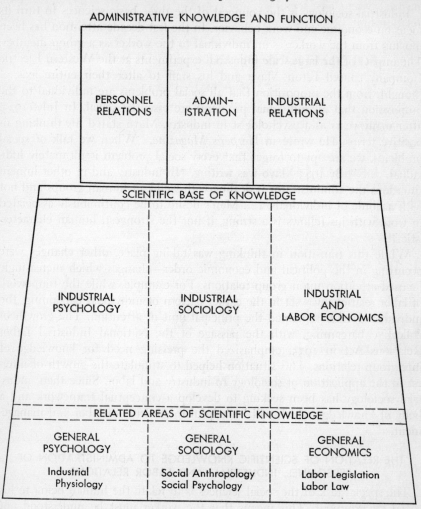

FIG. 4.   The Relation of Scientific Knowledge to Administrative Functions of Personnel Relations, General Administration, and Industrial Relations.

sciences. Such feeders as industrial physiology, social anthropology, labor legislation and law are exceedingly valuable sources of related knowledge. Figure 4 shows the relationship between the base of scientific knowledge and administrative functions. This figure also points out the applied or technical fields of personnel relations, administration, and industrial rela-

tions. These fields of study are concerned with the application of proved techniques for administering human relations. Technical fields contain knowledge of *how* to administer techniques. The professional fields of industrial psychology, sociology, and economics are largely interested in *what* relationships occur and *why* they exhibit themselves in different forms.

FOUNDATIONS OF INDUSTRIAL SOCIOLOGY

FIVE APPROACHES

Sociology has already developed within itself several areas that contribute to industrial sociology. Five major origins of sociological study of work groups and work relations are:

1. The factory as a social system.
2. Interpersonal relations in work situations.
3. The sociology of occupations and social classes.
4. The sociology of the city.
5. Social analysis of economic institutions.

Each of these approaches will be briefly described.

1. The Factory as a Social System

A social system is a complex pattern of social interrelationship which may be considered as a whole because each part bears a relation of interdependence to every other part. The concept of the factory as a social system has slowly emerged from several studies.[12] These studies use the techniques employed by social anthropologists in the observation of communities. Their approach is to observe the daily behavior of people toward each other until their patterns of interaction are identified. This may be done in the factory as well as in the community. Thus the factory is viewed as a community in which workers occupy different social positions and play the roles that are defined by their fellow workers.

Some of these social or status positions are clearly defined on the organization chart of the work plant. The president, superintendent, foremen, and the turret lathe operator have clearly defined duties and relationships with other workers. All of these prescribed statuses and relations, in addition to those found in the labor union, constitute the formal organization of industry.

However, much behavior is not the result of formal definition. Cliques, car pools, and friendships arise freely and spontaneously out of the inter-

[12] See especially F. J. Roethlisberger and W. J. Dickson, *op. cit.*, pp. 561-568; Burleigh B. Gardner, *Human Relations in Industry*, Richard D. Irwin, Inc., 1945, pp. 4-23; W. Lloyd Warner and J. O. Low, *The Social System of the Modern Factory*, Yale University Press, 1947; Wilbert E. Moore, *Industrial Relations and the Social Order*, The Macmillan Company, 1946; William F. Whyte, *op. cit.*

action of workers. Indeed, it has been pointed out that a work plant is composed of many small, intimate, face-to-face groups. The latter overlap in every direction and are connected by daily interaction. Thus a large factory is in reality a community or society of interrelated primary groups and not a number of separate individuals.[13] This unplanned structuring of work relations makes up the informal organization of a plant. The sentiments which members acquire from informal groups and the behavior of these groups have profound influence upon the formal structure of management and labor. Both formal and informal organizations as interacting entities comprise the social system within which the behavior of workers must be appraised.

2. Interpersonal Relations and Work Situations

J. L. Moreno has pioneered in the study and measurement of interpersonal relations.[14] He has called this area *sociometry*. His concern has been to reveal the feelings that people have toward each other, as *attraction, repulsion,* or *indifference.* These interpersonal feelings are looked upon as a dynamic psychosocial network which penetrates and encompasses all the formal and informal groupings within human society. To discover these feelings in a work group, the workers are asked to indicate the people with whom they prefer to work or not to work. Their choices are then paired and ranked, and work partners are regrouped in view of the expressed preferences. Charts of interpersonal relationships called *sociograms* are constructed which reveal the structure of interpersonal relations in any department, office, or plant. These charts make possible a planned grouping of workers so that highest morale may result.

In applying sociometry to the field of marketing, Lundberg found that there is an informal network of social relationships in a neighborhood that may be related to the occupational world. For example, a wife of a skilled worker in a neighborhood largely composed of unskilled workers was found to be a "key" or "natural" leader. She exerted much influence on the actions and attitudes of the other wives.[15]

The practical applications of this idea are great. The Curtis Publishing Company has recently sought to discover the key leaders in a community to ascertain their influence over others in the choice of grocery stores and brand purchases.[16] This research has shown that the "centers" of advertising power reside in the natural leaders of a community. Just as natural

[13] Whitehead, *op. cit.*

[14] J. L. Moreno, *Who Shall Survive?* Nervous and Mental Disease Publishing Company, 1934; John H. Jacobs, "The Application of Sociometry to Industry," *Sociometry,* May, 1945, pp. 181-198; Helen Jennings, *Leadership and Isolation,* Longmans, Green and Company, 1943, pp. 226-232.

[15] George A. Lundberg, "Marketing and Social Organization," Charles Coolidge Parlin Memorial Lecture, Curtis Publishing Co., 1945.

[16] "Grocery Dealers Survey of Kent, Ohio," Curtis Publishing Co., Research Department, 1946.

leaders can be identified in communities, they may also be located in work groups. The application of sociometric techniques makes possible both improved selection of supervisor, personnel, and labor leaders as well as the building of greater coöperation within the work group.

Moreno has also devised a way of reducing tension in work situations. Essentially, this technique requires that each person replay on a stage his role and the roles of others in his group. This is called the *psychodrama*. When carried on in a group setting the process is commonly called *sociodrama* or *group dynamics*. It has been found effective in reducing tension, as well as gaining insight into the causes of group conflict and the ways of group coöperation. The role-playing methods of the sociodrama are now being applied to the study and training of workers and supervisors.[17] Current reports of research efforts are published in a new journal of group therapy first called *Sociatry* and now titled *Group Psychotherapy*.[18]

The late Kurt Lewin and his associates conducted experiments that have implications for leadership in work groups.[19] Their studies were directed toward finding and describing behavior found in various "social climates." They set up experimentally created "climates" (situations) of democratic and authoritarian character and then observed the significant differences in the behavior of the group members and the leaders in each of these climates. The success they achieved in the retraining of leaders for democratic participation is promising.

3. The Sociology of Occupations and Social Classes

During the past twenty-five years sociologists have been building a growing body of literature on the sociology of occupations. Their approach has been unique and challenging. The usual procedure of studying a group is somewhat as follows: A sample of workers in an occupation or profession is carefully selected at all stages and ages in their occupational careers. Extensive case histories are gathered which provide clues to the selective social forces typically operating to induce people to enter a given occupa-

[17] Psychodramatic training of foremen in industry has been conducted by John R. P. French at Hardwood Manufacturing Company in Marion, Virginia; a psychodramatic course was also given for the training of sales and restaurant personnel at O. P. Baur Confectionery Company, Denver, Colorado. For a report of additional work see *Sociometry*, May, 1945. An excellent report is made by John R. P. French, Jr., "Role Playing as a Method of Training Foremen," in S. D. Hoslett (ed.), *Human Factors in Management*, Park College Press, 1946, pp. 99-116.

[18] Cf. Ronald Lippett, Leland P. Bradford, and Kenneth D. Benne, "Sociodramatic Clarification of Leader and Group Roles," *Sociatry*, March, 1947, pp. 82-91; Alex Bavelas, "Role Playing and Management Training," *Sociatry*, June, 1947, pp. 188-191.

[19] Kurt Lewin, *Principles of Topological Psychology*, McGraw-Hill Book Company, Inc., 1936; Kurt Lewin, K. R. Lippett, and R. D. White, "Patterns of Aggressive Behavior in Experimentally Created Social Climates," *Journal of Social Psychology*, May, 1939, pp. 271-299; Alex Bavelas and Kurt Lewin, "Training in Democratic Leadership," *Journal of Social and Abnormal Psychology*, January, 1942, pp. 115-119; Kurt Lewin, *Resolving Social Conflicts*, Harper & Brothers, 1948.

tion. From these data the social characteristics of the workers are described. This is then followed by a detailed analysis of the modal career patterns of the group. The social background of the workers, such as father's occupation, education, and income, are investigated to indicate their effect on the occupational choices of the workers.[20]

Other social phenomena related to the occupation are examined. Included may be an analysis of the effect of occupational routines on social life, the impact of technological and social change on the group, the way in which the social customs and rituals of the occupation affect the social life of its members. Special attention is devoted to the dominant social, political, economic, religious, and other prevailing ideals, values, and beliefs of the group members. These are, in turn, explained by the typical life experiences they encounter.

Several interesting occupational groups have been studied—the academic man, hobo, teacher, waitress, professional thief, taxi dancer, railroader, musician, and salesgirl.[21] The sociologist does not make any distinctions between the so-called legal or extralegal vocations, for more knowledge is needed about the social origins and behavior of people in all occupations.

Social classes are differentiated among other things by differences in income, education, and occupations of their members. Because of the high correlation of occupation and social class, social stratification is largely a study of occupational stratification. Such similarities in background as manners, tastes, recreation, and dress grow out of habits of living fostered by socioeconomic groups. Sociologists in studying all levels of class and caste have gathered a great amount of occupational information which clarifies the structure of classes and the effect of class position on personality development. Since industry brings together workers from all social classes, knowledge in this area is necessary background for the study of social life within the work plant society.[22]

[20] William H. Form and Delbert C. Miller, "The Occupational Career Pattern as a Sociological Instrument," *American Journal of Sociology*, January, 1949, pp. 317-329.

[21] M. Anderson, *The Hobo*, University of Chicago Press, 1923; E. Wight Bakke, *The Unemployed Man*, Nisbet and Company, 1933, and *The Unemployed Worker*, Yale University Press, 1940; W. Fred Cottrell, *The Railroader*, Stanford University Press, 1939; Paul Cressey, *The Taxi Dance Hall*, University of Chicago Press, 1932; F. R. Donovan, *The Woman Who Waits*, R. G. Badger, 1920, *The Saleslady*, University of Chicago Press, 1929, and *The School Ma'am*, Stokes and Company, 1938; C. L. Lastrucci, "The Professional Dance Musician," *Journal of Musicology*, Winter, 1941, pp. 168-172; A. M. Carr-Saunders and P. A. Wilson, *The Professions*, Oxford University Press, 1933; C. R. Shaw, *The Jack Roller*, University of Chicago Press, 1930; E. H. Sutherland, *The Professional Thief*, University of Chicago Press, 1937; Logan Wilson, *The Academic Man*, Oxford University Press, 1942; Florian Znaniecki, *The Social Role of the Man of Knowledge*, Columbia University Press, 1940.

[22] Robert S. Lynd and Helen M. Lynd, *Middletown*, Harcourt, Brace and Company, 1929; John W. McConnell, *The Evolution of the Social Classes*, American Council of Public Affairs, 1942; P. A. Sorokin, *Social Mobility*, Harper & Brothers, 1927; W. Lloyd Warner and Paul S. Lunt, *The Social Life of the Modern Community*, Yale University Press, 1941.

Public opinion polling has demonstrated that occupational and economic status greatly influences attitudes on many public and personal issues. As a result a wealth of attitude and opinion data classified by major occupational groups is now available.[23] While the amount of polling has been relatively great, not much has been done to explore the process whereby attitudes become incorporated into personality patterns. Sociologists have therefore proposed a more systematic study of the social psychological attributes of each occupational level.[24] Some reseach projects are now being conducted in this direction. They seek to discover how attitudes are connected with each other into patterns or ideologies, for different occupational groups.

4. The Sociology of the City

Roughly three-fifths of all workers are in urban areas, where occupational specialization has developed most extensively. Almost inevitably the study of occupations pushes the investigator into a study of city life in general. The history of urban development has been intimately associated with the rise and expansion of large-scale industry. Sociologists have studied this intimate relationship in a sub-field known as urban sociology. Much of the literature in this field is devoted to an analysis of the forces which create and produce social changes in cities. Since change in the economic institution usually instigates most of the social changes, urban sociologists have studied changes in economic life in considerable detail.[25]

Problems of industry have their repercussions in the social life of the entire city. Urban sociologists have studied the effect of industrial growth on the physical, ecological, and social development of the city. They have been especially interested in the clashes of different economic interest groups as they seek to control the political and social life of the community. They have described how technological change and shifts in industrial policy have produced problems which the entire city has to solve.

How does the strike affect the community? What are the problems faced by the industrial worker? How is the culture of cities affected by industrial changes? What groups align themselves with management and with labor? These and similar questions have been asked and answered by urban soci-

[23] See *Public Opinion Quarterly* for periodic summaries of public opinion polls; see also Richard Centers, *The Psychology of Social Classes*, Princeton University Press, 1949.

[24] William H. Form, "Toward an Occupational Social Psychology," *Journal of Social Psychology*, August, 1946, pp. 85-99. See C. Wright Mills, *The White Collar Worker*, (forthcoming).

[25] Consult: Lewis Mumford, *The Culture of Cities*, Harcourt, Brace and Company, 1938; Conrad M. Arensberg, "Industry and the Community," *American Journal of Sociology*, July, 1942; Lynd and Lynd, *op. cit.*; Ruth McKenny, *Industrial Valley*, Harcourt, Brace and Company, 1939; Liston Pope, *Millhands and Preachers*, University of North Carolina Press, 1942; W. Lloyd Warner and J. O. Low, *The Social System of the Modern Factory*, Yale University Press, 1947.

ology. Here is an abundant source of information on the social and industrial life of the city. Industrial sociology will find many of these materials useful.

5. Social Analysis of Economic Institutions

Another source of materials for industrial sociology is the study of economic institutions. An institution has been conceived as all of the folkways, mores, and organizations that revolve about the satisfaction of a need—in this case, the need or function of self-maintenance. The institutional approach to economics focuses its attention on all work plants and work groups, as well as those organizations that seek to control economic life. It regards economic organization as a system of social relationships which impinges on all social life. It studies the economic behavior of people as revealed by their attitudes, ideologies, social habits, and sentiments. Chapin's concept of an institution as "a defined need and the culture surrounding it" embraces the wide sweep of social relations which constitute the economic institution of our society.

One of the central facts about any economic organization is the way in which it defines property. The definition of private and public property, the rights of property ownership, and the effects of ownership and rights upon economic behavior are guides to the understanding of work behavior.[26] Questions concerning the influence of economic groups have been the center of much thought and study since the industrial revolution. The powerful effect of the economy upon political organization, the church, the family, and the school is now well known. Economic organization is seen as a system of power affecting all phases of social life.[27] The rise of trade associations has been matched in latter days by the rise of labor organizations. Big economic organizations have grown into powerful pressure groups, which affect the economic and social behavior of everybody.

Penetrating analysts like Thorstein Veblen have been able to show how the economic position of an individual determines his group membership, establishes his ideological perspective, and influences his entire style of living. Data drawn from social investigations of property, power, and ideology have provided the industrial sociologist with rich materials to assess the relation of industry to society.

[26] Alfred W. Jones, *Life, Liberty, and Property*, J. B. Lippincott Company, 1941; Thorstein Veblen, *The Theory of the Leisure Class*, B. W. Huebsch, Inc., 1918. See also the *Journal of Legal and Political Sociology*.

[27] Thorstein Veblen, *The Theory of Business Enterprise*, 1918, *Absentee Ownership and Business Enterprise*, 1923, and *The Vested Interests and the Common Man*, 1918, all published by B. W. Huebsch, Inc.; Robert Brady, *Business as a System of Power*, Columbia University Press, 1943; Karl Mannheim, *Man and Society in an Age of Reconstruction*, Harcourt, Brace and Company, 1940; Stuart Chase, *Democracy Under Pressure*, The Twentieth Century Fund, 1945.

ORIENTATIONS TO THE FIELD OF INDUSTRIAL SOCIOLOGY

Five basic sources of research and theoretical development have been enumerated and described. The integration of these sources is now in process. This book provides a structure for this synthesis.

The basis of the synthesis corresponds to the general approach of sociology itself. The main tasks of sociology are (1) to describe the nature of social organization and (2) to analyze the process by which the individual becomes socialized within a given society. Therefore, the area of industrial sociology undertakes to study (1) the social organization of the work plant and (2) the socialization of the worker. In the analysis of actual work situations the interrelationship between the social organization of the work plant and the worker's social adjustment becomes a living reality. This is true because social organization is finally the feelings and attitudes which the workers have toward each other. Thus the *unity of the work situation retains vitality only as the worker can be observed in dynamic interactions*: the work group compelling its members to adopt common ways of behaving; the worker seeking to express his needs and wants by attempting to pull the group into conformity with him.

The work group functions inside a social network, which is a framework of dynamic but relatively stable relations. Folkways and technicways, composing the customs of the work plant, exist prior to the induction of the individual worker. He bumps against them from time to time. His reactions are recorded in the defenses and compensating adjustments which he makes. Underneath the flow of work behavior there is an unending struggle for self-expression and security. Here, the young worker flounders and gropes, trying to find the work position which will satisfy his ambitions. There, the older worker can be seen moving along the channels of a stable work life. Yet he has no mature peace, for over the work plant a confusion and turbulence threatens the work patterns of both young and old. Such is the social setting of our time that no work plant can escape the insecurities of the larger society.

The interrelation of social organization and social adjustment provides the central focus for different levels upon which the social analysis of work plant society may proceed.

The first level describes the structure of the work plant society. On this level the society is viewed as semiautonomous, capable of being judged in terms of its own purposes. It governs by formal and informal controls of its own making, providing guides to behavior and creating roles expected of the worker.

The adjustments which the worker makes—or fails to make—in his efforts to win status and security within the work plant form another level of social analysis. This approach relates individual needs to the structure. It is con-

cerned with the socialization of the worker and the typical problems confronting him in work plant society.

The recognition of significant interrelationships between the local community and the work plant provides yet another level of study. The institutions of the local community are the training grounds for the customs and traditions which are carried into the work plant as an integral part of the work behavior. As the community places the burden of its economic needs upon the local work plants, they, in turn, make many demands upon the institutions and groups of the community.

Finally, the link which ties the work plant and the community into the state, nation, and world of nations grows stronger year by year. The reverberations of the outer or what Walter Lippmann once called the "unseen" world flow into the local community through the radio, newspaper, and motion pictures. Government controls reach into and regulate the daily routines of employers and employees. The latter in turn, through political activity, try to exert influence on the state. In this manner political and social ideologies are crystallized and transmitted outward. The stresses and strains of a transitional society press upon the local community and its work plants. Even the events in Paris, Moscow, London, and Chunking jar and jolt the workers, unhitching feelings and emotions that sweep through local work plants and affect the day's behavior.

These are levels which we shall recognize in our analysis of industrial society. They provide the basis for major parts of our book and suggest a framework for industrial sociology.

THE FRAMEWORK OF INDUSTRIAL SOCIOLOGY

FIVE MAJOR PARTS OF THIS BOOK

This book is divided into five major parts:
  I. Industrial Sociology: Its Rise and Scope
  II. The Social Organization of the Work Plant
  III. Major Problems of Applied Industrial Sociology
  IV. The Social Adjustment of the Worker
  V. Industry, Community, and Society.

I. Industrial Sociology: Its Rise and Scope

The reader is in the midst of this section of the book. He will have observed that the writers are trying to describe what industrial sociology is, how it came into being as a scientific discipline, and how it is related to other closely allied sciences and applied fields of study. As he proceeds he will discover a chapter which sets forth a brief history of scientific experiments in work group behavior conducted within industry. This will be followed by a discussion of the educational training which the student

of industrial sociology is expected to acquire. It is hoped that the student upon completion of this section will understand the nature of industrial sociology, how the sociologist thinks about the data which he observes, and what his goals are.

II. The Social Organization of the Work Plant

Part Two describes the social world of work. It begins with such questions as: Why do men and women work? What do they want from their work? What does the work plant demand of people? The answers workers give reflect in part the nature of the social structures in which they work. These structures are seen as social organizations within which each worker has a "place." His "place" is to be found in both formal and informal organizations that compose the work plant society. The work position becomes a base from which radiates a network of social relations tying him to many groups within the work plant. These groups train him in the work roles which they expect of him. In this social world of work (and each worker has such a world) social "know-how" is much more than knowledge of machines and materials. Social insight and social skill come forth as important determinants of "making good" on the job.

III. Major Problems of Applied Industrial Sociology

Part Three emphasizes the applied aspects of industrial sociology. It suggests the role of a professional sociologist in a work plant, and this includes a union organization as well. Inside a going concern the professional sociologist must be an observer, a researcher, a teacher, and sometimes an administrator. He is called upon to deal with many practical problems involving social behavior. Most of these problems will center about worker placement and the adjustment problems of workers. He will be expected to provide knowledge and counsel for the complex task of building industrial morale and teamwork.

IV. The Social Adjustment of the Worker

Part Four considers the worker and his adjustments. The worker plays his roles in work situations. His adjustments over a lifetime ordinarily fit a pattern. As a child he is initiated early to chores, the school, contacts with maintenance and service workers around the house and in the community, and to the talk of parents and friends about work. As a youth he may secure his first part-time jobs that are rewarded with "pay." Later he graduates to full-time work as he leaves the school and begins his search for a steady job. The period that follows is usually one of trial. Various jobs are attempted until the worker finds the position in which he finally remains. Then, as he finds a permanent job and becomes an integral part of a community, he enters a period of occupational stability. With retirement comes with-

drawal from active work life and preoccupation with home and community life. These work experiences constitute a common lifework pattern.

V. Industry, Community, and Society

Every community acquires character from the nature of its work and its workers. The sex, age, education, and ethnic composition of communities influence their vitality and group morale—those subtle qualities underlying "good" communities. The stability of work plants affects the fortunes of other institutions such as the school, church, and government. And the business and labor leaders of a community can either provide roots for a growing and enriched community life or lay waste its human and natural resources.

The average worker within a peaceful society divides the bulk of his living in approximately equal proportions between the work plant and the community. Of his sixteen waking hours, perhaps eight are spent at work and eight in home and community. The patterns of family and community life precondition attitudes and feelings which workers bring into the plant, and, in turn, the work plant profoundly affects community life.

Whereas the local community defines the range of social movement, the society provides the frame of values and conditions the thinking of modern man. In a dynamic and free society the range of movement and thought widens out with ever greater alternatives. The worker can feel these forces which he perhaps cannot see or understand. He makes new demands on his employers even as they are pressing their claims upon him. Both know that their needs are real; both feel that "right," "justice," and "survival" are at stake. These are not just local matters. The conflict of values is widespread. The final decisions reach out beyond the worker, beyond the community, to the larger society. In this final section we deal with the impact of industry upon the community and upon the society.

SUPPLEMENTARY STUDIES

FIELD INTERVIEWS: PLANNED

1. Arrange interviews with the professors in your college or university who teach industrial psychology, industrial physiology, industrial economics, labor economics, and applied anthropology. Discuss the kinds of problems which are studied in their field. Compare the problems and the way in which each specialist seems to think about them.

LIBRARY: BOOKS AND ARTICLES

2. Examine carefully: F. J. Roethlisberger and William J. Dickson, *Management and the Worker*, Harvard University Press, 1939; Elton Mayo, *The Social Problems of an Industrial Civilization*, Harvard University Press, 1945.

3. Browse on the three leading texts in industrial sociology, which are: William F. Whyte (ed.), *Industry and Society*, McGraw-Hill Book Company, Inc., 1946; Burleigh B. Gardner, *Human Relations in Industry*, Richard D. Irwin, Inc., 1945; Wilbert E. Moore, *Industrial Relations and the Social Order*, The Macmillan Company, 1947.

4. Read the following articles to secure different views of sociologists as they seek to define the field of industrial sociology: Wilbert Moore, Robert Dubin, Delbert Miller, Alvin Goulder, and Paul Meadows, "Industrial Sociology: Status and Prospects," *American Sociological Review*, August, 1948, pp. 382-400; Herbert Blumer, "Sociological Theory in Industrial Relations," *American Sociological Review*, June, 1947, pp. 271-277; Wilbert E. Moore, "Current Issues in Industrial Sociology," *American Sociological Review*, December, 1947, pp. 651-661; Delbert C. Miller, "Future Development of Industrial Sociology," *Proceedings* of the Pacific Sociological Society in *Research Studies of the State College of Washington*, June, 1947, pp. 155-161.

5. Browse through a number of copies in some of the journals listed below. Examine to see how the various articles are related to problems and concerns of the worker, management, or unions.

Advanced Management
American Journal of Sociology
American Sociological Review
Factory Management and Maintenance
Fortune
Harvard Business Review
Human Organization (formerly *Applied Anthropology*)
Human Relations
Industrial and Labor Relations Review
Industrial Medicine
Industrial Nursing
International Labor Review
Iron Age
Journal of Applied Psychology
Journal of Industrial Hygiene and Toxicology
Labour Monthly
Management Record
Management Review
Monthly Labor Review
Occupations
Personnel
Personnel Administration
Personnel Journal
Sociatry
Sociometry

CHAPTER III

A Brief History of Scientific Experimentation in Industry

GENESIS OF INDUSTRIAL SOCIOLOGY

THE THOUGHTWAYS OF ELTON MAYO

Like many discoveries, industrial sociology was discovered largely by accident. It might be said that the Harvard psychologists and engineers in the Industrial Research Department *backed* into the substantial fact that work behavior is group behavior. Only sociologists seem to have been left without surprise when George Elton Mayo and Fritz J. Roethlisberger announced that their research studies showed that in every work activity the workers do not perform as individual workers but always as working groups. Mayo said, "The workers, whether aware of it or not—formed themselves into a group with appropriate customs, duties, routines, even rituals; and management succeeds (or fails) in proportion as it is accepted without reservation by the group as authority and leader." Roethlisberger added, "If this is true—and all the evidence of the Western Electric researches points in this direction—have we not a clue as to the possible basis for labor unrest and disputes? Granted that these disputes are often stated in terms of wages,

hours of work, and physical conditions of work, is it not possible that these demands are disguising, or in part are the symptomatic expression of much more deeply rooted human situations which we have not as yet learned to recognize, to understand, or to control?"[1]

Mayo and his colleagues have been rightly hailed as opening up a new world and a new point of view which they have confirmed by numerous studies. Yet what they discovered was not so new in theory as in fact. Sociological theory had long anticipated the Harvard researches into work behavior.[2] It remained for Elton Mayo to verify this theory in the realm of work activity and to awaken businessmen, labor leaders, and research workers throughout social science to the compelling importance of the group. *Fortune* magazine presented this remarkable man to its readers in November, 1946, as follows:

One of the most challenging views in the turbulent field of industrial relations today is held by Elton Mayo, diminutive chain-smoking professor of industrial research at Harvard's Graduate School of Business. Scientist and practical clinician, Mayo speaks with a rare authority that has commanded attention in factories as well as universities. His erudition extends through psychology, sociology, physiology, medicine, and economics, and his experience comes from a lifelong, firsthand study of industry. At the end of twenty years incubation at Harvard, on the eve of his retirement, Mayo's view gives promise of exerting through the field of business administration a significant influence in the future relations of United States management and labor. Indeed, many believe that Mayo holds the key to industrial peace.[3]

Whatever his influence may be upon industry there is no doubt about his influence upon industrial sociology. His mind is like a mirror reflecting the dominance and change of compelling ideas which stamped the thoughtways of his time. To watch Elton Mayo learn from his experiments is to look upon the metamorphic growth of industrial sociology. For this reason we have chosen to follow chronologically the research life of this man.

George Elton Mayo was born in 1880 in Adelaide, Australia. After graduating from Adelaide University he spent a number of years in Australia

[1] "The Fruitful Errors of Elton Mayo," *Fortune*, November, 1946, pp. 183, 238.
[2] Cf. Lester F. Ward, *Dynamic Sociology*, D. Appleton Company, 1833, Vol. I, pp. 468-471. See W. I. Thomas and Florian Znaniecki, *The Polish Peasant in Europe and America*, Alfred A. Knopf, 1927. Also cf. Whiting Williams, the perambulate, participant observer, who wrote in 1925, "Anyone who tries to understand his fellows by observing them in action on a wide range of platforms will, surely, understand how my 'over alls' experiences of the past few years brought me these . . . outstanding impressions:
"The unbelievable importance of the worker's feelings and experiences rather than his logic or reason as a factor in all his viewpoints and attitudes.
"The unity of life and labor—the complete impossibility of walling off the factory from home, the workers from the citizen, of dividing the hankerings of a man's working hours off from those of his hours of leisure." *Mainsprings of Men*, Charles Scribner's Sons, 1925, pp. 3-4.
[3] "The Fruitful Errors of Elton Mayo," *Fortune*, November, 1946, p. 181.

engaged both in industrial work and in teaching logic and psychology at Queensland University. Mayo came to the United States to continue his studies under a grant of the Laura Spelman Rockefeller Foundation. For three years he was a research associate in the Wharton School of Finance and Commerce at the University of Pennsylvania. When the Department of Industrial Research was organized at Harvard University in 1926, Dean Wallace B. Donham of the School of Business Administration appointed Elton Mayo as its first head, and he remained at this post until his retirement in 1947.

Mayo has characterized explanations of human behavior in industry at the time his work began as follows:

The industrial area was haunted by individuals each of whom seemed assured that the abstractions he expressed—economics, politics, psychology of efficiency—were adequate to the special problem he studied. All these logics had to be tentatively set aside on the ground that they might be derivations rather than the achievement of logico-experimental investigation. In every instance *the particular situation* had to be studied, and without preconceived determination. In every instance care had to be exercised to account for the *simple and the obvious*, for the simple and obvious facts are so firmly established in the awareness of industry that they are apt to be disregarded.[4]

It cannot be assumed that Mayo achieved purification from all bias by this attitude. On the contrary, he was repeating his best psychological training when in 1925 he wrote the terse statement, "When we talk of social problems we are apt to forget every social problem is ultimately individual . . ." It was as a psychologist that Mayo entered upon his first research studies in America. However, it is a tribute to his openness of mind that this man could "alter the entire axis of his thought from the proposition that all social problems are individual to the proposition that all individual problems are essentially social."[5] The transition of Mayo's thinking from a psychological to a sociological frame of reference is well shown in 1945 when he wrote,

Unfortunately . . . the economist talks of wage rates and prices: the collective bargainers follow this lead and import lawyers into the discussion. The psychologist speaks of vocational guidance and tests. The physiologist thinks in terms of fatigue and nutrition. But none considers the group and its function in society as a constituent unit of integrity. Yet the group has an impulse to self-preservation as strong as, or stronger than, that of the individual; and many strikes are actually symptomatic of the attempt of a group to hold together. Economics, psychology, physiology, all . . . ignore the fact that complex group association is the distinguishing character of the human being.[6]

[4] Elton Mayo, "Industrial Research," *Harvard Business School Alumni Bulletin*, 1940, p. 87.
[5] "The Fruitful Errors of Elton Mayo," *Fortune*, November, 1946, p. 241.
[6] *Ibid.*, p. 242.

THE FIRST INQUIRY: LABOR TURNOVER IN A PHILADELPHIA TEXTILE MILL

The first research study Mayo conducted in America was an investigation which he began while he was at the University of Pennsylvania. In 1923 he began an inquiry into the causes of high labor turnover in the mule-spinning department of a textile mill near Philadelphia. The general labor turnover in other departments was estimated to be approximately 5 per cent or 6 per cent per annum; in the spinning department the turnover was estimated at approximately 250 per cent.

Four incentive plans had been tried to reduce the high turnover of the mule spinners but all failed. High labor turnover continued and productive efficiency remained low. It was almost as a last resort that the firm consulted the university.

An inspection of the mule-spinning department showed that conditions of work seemed much the same as those in the other departments. The workers had a fifty-hour working week—five days of ten hours, two shifts of five hours each separated by a forty-five-minute lunch period. The mule-spinner attendant was called a piecer. He walked up and down a long alley about thirty yards or more on either side of a machine head which operated spinning frames. The piecer was responsible for tying together the threads, which instantly broke and had to be pieced together. The work appeared to be monotonous. The noise and the distance separating the workers combined to make communication well-nigh impossible.

When the piecers talked to the nurse they complained of neuritis in arms, shoulders, or legs. To the researchers they spoke discouragingly of the lowly place which their work occupied in their opinion. They said everybody knew "it don't take any brains to be a piecer—just strong legs." Many spoke of the solitary nature of the job and of the fatigue they experienced when the day was done. It was not uncommon for a worker to flare up in anger on the job and abruptly announce his leaving and walk out. These were the conditions observed prior to October, 1923.

The operation of the mule-spinning room was so far under its production quota that the workers never received any of the bonus which was supposed to motivate them to higher production. It was necessary for a department to exceed 75 per cent of a carefully calculated quota in order to participate in a monthly bonus. Every spinner was to be paid an excess percentage of his flat-rate wage equivalent to the average excess percentage of production over 75 per cent. An efficiency of 80 per cent meant a 5 per cent bonus on his monthly wage to every employee in the department, but the mule-spinning department had never been above an approximate 70 per cent.

The experimental changes that were made were to lift the mule-spinning department to higher levels of efficiency than had heretofore been attained. But the changes which occurred in the mule-spinning room and in the

TABLE 1. Production Efficiency Records Established Under Five Different Working Conditions

Nature of Change in Working Conditions	Date	Production Efficiency in Percentage
1. Initiation of rest periods (experimental change)	Pre-October, 1923 October, 1923 November, 1923 December, 1923 January, 1924 Feb. 15, 1924	70 (Maximum) 79½ 78¾ 82 78¾ 80¼
2. Rest periods abandoned (administrative change)	Feb. 15-Feb. 25, 1924	Swift drop below 70
3. Rest periods reinstated with earned rests (administrative change)	Feb. 25-March 31, 1924	70
4. Rest periods with assured rests and with machines stopped (experimental change)	April, 1924	77½
5. Alternate rest periods assured and set by group decision (administrative change)	May, 1924 June, 1924 July, 1924 August, 1924 September, 1924 Post September, 1924	80¼ 85 82 83½ 86½ 80 and above

textile mill generally during the time span from October, 1923, to September, 1924, were not all experimental in nature. Some were introduced by the decisions of executives who acted independently of the researchers. The experimental and the administrative changes provide five distinct periods for scientific study. Table 1 shows these periods as changes in the introduction of variables and the subsequent production record which resulted.

1. Initiation of Rest Periods

Period 1 begins with the introduction of rest periods, two of 10 minutes' length in the morning and two again in the afternoon. These were arranged so that the work period in the morning would be divided thus: 2 hours of work, 10 minutes rest; 1½ hours of work, 10 minutes rest; and a final work period of 1 hour and 10 minutes. The schedule was repeated in the afternoon. During the rest period the workers were permitted to lie down and were encouraged to sleep for ten minutes. At first only one-third of the piecers were used in the experiment. The results were encouraging from the outset. The men were agreeable and interested. Morale improved,

symptoms of melancholy preoccupation almost disappeared, and labor turn-over came to an end. But there was a curious, unanticipated effect. *An almost equivalent improvement showed itself in the work of the other two-thirds of the piecers although they had been given no rest periods.* In 1923 Elton Mayo was not able satisfactorily to account for this effect. It was not until later that the full significance became known.

The president of the firm was pleased with the results of the experiment and asked that the rest periods be extended to the entire department. This extension made it possible to measure the effect of rest periods upon the productivity of the department. The researchers eagerly awaited the tally of production for the first month. When the result was announced everyone was surprised. Production efficiency had hit 79½ percent and the first bonus ever received in the spinning room was distributed. According to the incentive plan each man received 4½ percent more in his pay check. All through the fall and winter productive efficiency remained high. In December a high rate of 82 percent was achieved. Labor turnover had all but disappeared. The physical and mental condition of the men continued to improve. Morale had never been higher.

The researchers were pleased with the operation of the experiment except for the attitude of the immediate supervisors. They had never liked the sight of workers lying asleep on the sacks while the mules were running. They felt the men should be made to "earn" their rest by completing certain tasks before a rest period was authorized. But for the most part the men received their rests and the system seemed to be working well.

2. Rest Periods Abandoned

The second phase of the experiment occurred when the supervisor who had introduced the idea of earned rest periods ordered abandonment of the rest periods in order to meet a deadline on a rush order. It was Friday, February 15—a black Friday for human relations in the mule-spinning department. Within five days production was down to a point lower than it had been for months. The pessimistic preoccupations returned.

3. Rest Periods Reinstated with Earned Rests

Another administrative change introduced phase 3. The supervisor in charge ordered resumption of rest periods but strictly on an earned basis. The men failed to respond and production fell to the old 70 per cent point. The president of the company took charge. He called a conference in his office which included supervisors and researchers. His question was blunt. Why had there been such a sudden drop in production from 80 percent to 70 percent?

The researchers pointed out that the whole rest period system had never been given a fair trial. The workers had never been assured that they were

going to receive four rests in the day. Mayo pointed to a chart showing a marked increase in absenteeism. He said that this meant men were taking their rest periods in the form of "missed" days. Neither worker nor plant was being helped by this procedure. What was needed was assured rest periods on the job.

4. Rest Periods with Assured Rests and with Machines Stopped

The president made a quick decision. He ordered that during the month of April the spinning mules should be shut down in order that everybody —he repeated—everybody from the floor supervisor down should rest as he had been instructed to do. The supervisors left the conference room dazed and bewildered. Was the president losing his sense of good judgment? How could he possibly believe that the forty minutes lost by forty men per day during a whole month could ever be recovered? The machines could not be speeded up and there seemed to be no other way of making up the lost time. In spite of this belief production under the new plan came back up during April, reaching 77½ percent. A 2½ percent bonus appeared in the pay envelopes of the workers. Morale improved and absenteeism diminished.

5. Alternate Rest Periods Assured and Set by Group Decision

In the month of May the president ordered a system of alternating rest periods with each group of three men in the alley deciding when they should take their rest periods. When they decided upon one of their four assured rests, they stretched out on cots which had now been provided and went to sleep while the machines continued running. This initiated the final phase of the experiment. From May to September production continued to reach new highs. The record high occurred in September with an efficiency of 86½ percent. The labor turnover problem was licked. Several years later the president reported that the company had never experienced any higher turnover in the mule-spinning department than approximately 5 percent or 6 percent per year.

THE PSYCHOLOGICAL EXPLANATIONS OF 1924

The Mayo of 1924 had a perfectly good psychological explanation for the experimental results. He wrote in the *Personnel Journal* his summary of findings:

1. As ordinarily carried on, the operation of spinning-mules tends to produce physical-postural fatigues. Its relative monotony also induces dispersed thinking and states of revery which are apt to be pessimistic.

2. The introduction of rest pauses relieves this condition and greatly increases production by (a) restoring normal circulation and relieving postural fatigue, and (b) effectively interrupting pessimistic revery.

3. In the instance described, the rest pauses are chiefly effective because they eliminate pessimistic revery.[7]

Mayo obviously thought that he had correctly diagnosed the industrial case and that the introduction of rest periods would prove the proper therapy for a number of mentally preoccupied individuals. He elaborated a *worry* theory to explain the reverie states of the workers.

The investigation of revery seems to show that the essential problem is that as to the *mental preoccupations induced in the workers by the condition of their work.* Speaking generally it may be said that an individual's daily work or avocation may serve to minimize or to intensify any preexisting tendency to pessimistic or paranoid meditation. Everyone, worker or executive, probably carries with him a private grief or discontent. Wherever the conditions of work are unsuitable, physically or mentally, the immediate effect seems to be an increase of pessimistic or bitter reflection. The opinion of the worker as to the suitability or otherwise of his working conditions is apparently of no value in this respect. . . .[8]

THE SOCIOLOGICAL EXPLANATIONS OF 1945

In 1945 in *The Social Problems of an Industrial Civilization,* Mayo reinterprets the data of this first investigation. This time he seeks to find influences which may have affected the workers as a group. He observes that the interest which the researchers and the president had expressed in the workers' welfare may have been highly significant. For example, they had listened carefully and with full attention to anything a worker wished to say, whatever the character of his comment. The loyalty of the workers to their president is noted. The president was a former army colonel who had commanded many of his own workers in the trenches of France and held their highest respect. The president himself had swept aside the supervisor who had instituted the much disliked system of earned rest periods. Mayo says, "But in addition to this—and we did not see this clearly at the time— the president had effected another important change. He had helped to transform a horde of 'solitaries' into a social group. In May, 1924, he placed the control of rest periods squarely in the hands of the workers in an alley with no one to say them nay. This led to consultation, throughout the group—and to a feeling of responsibility directly to the president. And the general social changes effected were astonishing—even in relationships outside the factory."[9]

What changed the thinking of Elton Mayo between 1924 and 1945? The answer to that question begins with the now famed social experiments in the Hawthorne plant of the Western Electric Company. The reader is already aware of the major finding on the relay test room as reported in

[7] Elton Mayo, "Revery and Industrial Fatigue," *Personnel Journal,* December, 1924, pp. 273-281.
[8] *Ibid.,* p. 279.
[9] Elton Mayo, *The Social Problems of an Industrial Civilization,* Harvard University Press, 1945, p. 67.

Chapter I. However, the story which bridges Mayo's life from 1924 to 1927 is an extremely interesting one, for it describes the step which took him out of a strictly psychological frame of reference to a new awareness of the sociological implications of work behavior.

HAVOC AT HAWTHORNE

THE ILLUMINATION EXPERIMENTS

One night in 1927 in New York City Elton Mayo met George A. Pennock. Mayo had come down from Harvard to give a talk at the National Industrial Conference Board. Pennock was then a Western Electric engineer. As Mayo talked, he was struck by certain similarities between a project on which he was working and that which Mayo described. After the talk he discussed some of the features of his project which had puzzled him. On the strength of the conversation he entreated Mayo to come out to the Hawthorne plant at Chicago and look it over.

In the Western Electric plant, Mayo was shown the results of a simple experiment which had been set up to test the effect of illumination on the productivity of workers. For 2½ years—between November, 1924, and April, 1927—the Western Electric Company in connection with the National Research Council had been studying the relation of quality and quantity of illumination to efficiency in industry. A group of engineers had designed an experiment with rigorous controls. An experimental room operated under variable conditions, a control room with constant conditions. Changes were brought in one at a time while other conditions were held steady. In the beginning it was assumed that the greater the light the greater would be the output. This seemed to be a feasible assumption since most studies had demonstrated that increasing the amount of illumination increased worker efficiency. And indeed, Engineer C. E. Snow reported that the efficiency of the experimental room was higher under increasing illumination. But so was the efficiency of the control group! In fact he says, "This test resulted in very appreciable production increases in both groups and of almost identical magnitude. . . . We were . . . unable to determine what definite part of the improvement in performance should be ascribed to improved illumination."[10]

At this point the engineers put the experiment in reverse. Lighting was diminished in the experimental room; in the control room it was held constant. According to the books, production should have declined in the experimental room and remained constant in the control room. This did not happen. Snow reports: "After the level of illumination in the test group enclosure changed to a lower value, the efficiencies of both the test and control groups increased slowly but steadily. When the level of illumination

[10] C. E. Snow, "A Discussion of the Relation of Illumination Intensity to Productive Efficiency," *Tech Engineering News*, November, 1927.

for the test group finally reached 3 foot candles, the operatives protested saying that they were hardly able to see what they were doing, and the production rate decreased. The operatives could and did maintain their efficiency to this point in spite of the discomfort and handicap of insufficient illumination."[11]

Failure at the Controls

George Pennock in his interpretation of the illumination experiments drew two conclusions:[12] (1) that light is only one, and apparently a minor, factor among many which affect employee output; (2) that the attempt to measure the effect of one variable had not been successful because (a) the various factors affecting the performance of the operators had not been controlled, and hence the results could have been influenced by any one of several variables, and (b) in studies conducted in regular shop departments or on fairly large groups of people there were so many factors affecting the reactions of the workers that it was hopeless to expect to evaluate the effect of any single one of them.

These results from the illumination experiments aroused a desire to go on and find out what would be the effect of making certain changes in working conditions. Moreover, the necessity of setting rigid controls seemed to be of paramount importance. The lighting experiment suffered, it was believed, because the controls were not rigid enough. Now, the researchers said, the need is to wall off every interfering variable. When a specific change in the working conditions is introduced, the effect due to the change will be precisely accounted for by the change deliberately inserted by the researchers themselves into the working conditions.

Mayo took a good research team to Hawthorne. His colleagues, F. J. Roethlisberger and T. N. Whitehead, were called in. At the Hawthorne plant they worked with William J. Dickson, Chief of Employee Relations, and Harold A. Wright, Chief of Personnel Research. Their combined thinking led to the design of the relay assembly test room experiment. It is called by many observers the first great scientific experiment in industry.

THE RELAY ASSEMBLY TEST ROOM

DESIGN FOR EXPERIMENTS

The first step in the design was the isolation of a small group of workers in a separate room somewhat removed from the regular working force where their behavior could be studied carefully and systematically.

This decision to use a small group was based on a desire to keep the number of variables that might creep in to an absolute minimum. It was

[11] *Ibid.*
[12] G. A. Pennock, "Industrial Research at Hawthorne," *Personnel Journal,* January, 1930, pp. 298-290.

believed that it would be much easier to keep a close watch over a small group than over a large one, and to observe and record the changes which took place both within and without the individual. Moreover, the investigators believed they could more easily establish confidence between the work operatives and themselves. To establish adequate control over the experiment it was felt necessary to eliminate such variables as (1) amount of work ahead of the operator, (2) changes in type of work, (3) introduction of inexperienced operators, and (4) shifting of personnel because of fluctuations of work schedules.

In order to do this it would be necessary to take into account the kind of job that should be observed and also the kind of operators who should be selected.[13]

The Kind of Job Selected

Certain criteria were laid down to find the kind of job best suited to the demands of the experiment. There was agreement on the following criteria of selection.

1. Job should be a repetitive one, for the repetitive tasks are increasing in industry and the effect of such processes upon those engaged should be assessed.
2. All operators should be engaged in the same operation in order to make accurate comparisons between individuals.
3. A complete operation that can be performed in a relatively short time should be secured. Operation should not require more than a minute in order to secure a large statistical count sensitive to any change in operator productivity.
4. The job should be one on which employment will continue for a considerable length of time so that there shall be no change in the work routines.
5. The speed of the operation should be wholly controlled by the operator. This meant that machine work must be excluded.

The job finally chosen to meet these requirements was the assembly of telephone relays, an operation performed by women, who placed thirty-five small parts in an assembly fixture and secured them by four machine screws. The operator, using both hands, picked up the parts in front of her and completed the assembly in about one minute. Repeating these operations each operator was able to assemble approximately 500 relays each day.

The Kind of Operators Selected

There were two criteria established for the selection of the operators:
1. Only experienced operators should be used in order to avoid the influence of "learning" upon the results.

[13] F. J. Roethlisberger and W. J. Dickson, *Management and the Worker*, Harvard University Press, 1939, pp. 19-21.

2. The operators that were selected should be willing and coöperative in order that normal reactions to the changing conditions of the experiment might be secured.

These conditions were met by selecting two experienced operators who were known to be friendly with each other and inviting them to choose

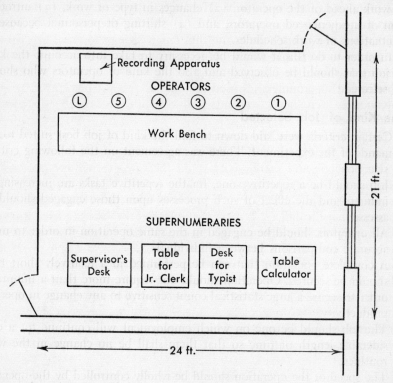

Fig. 5. The Relay Assembly Test Room. (Reprinted by permission of the publishers from Thomas North Whitehead, *The Industrial Worker*, Cambridge, Mass.: Harvard University Press, 1938, Vol. II, pp. A-2.)

four other girls with whom they would like to work. This manner of selection seems to have had a most significant influence on the course of the experiment although this fact was not recognized at the time.

Functions of a Skilled Observer

A final part of the design was the assignment of a skilled observer to the test room charged with a twofold function: (1) to keep accurate records of all that happened and (2) to create and maintain a friendly atmosphere in the test room.

The Physical Setting

All now was in readiness. The test room was partitioned off from the main relay assembly shop and was placed under the general supervision of the shop foreman. Figure 5 shows the position of the five relay assemblers and the layout operator working at the large bench. The supernumeraries refer to the supervisory and clerical staff. The main thing to notice is that the operators and supernumeraries each sat in a row, and the two rows faced each other across the floor of the room, thus emphasizing the social gap between the bench workers and the white-collar group. As a matter of unwritten custom, the foremen usually used the door at the right top of the plan, whereas the supernumeraries used the door at the left bottom of the plan. Interviewers were never residents and they interviewed the operators in another room.[14]

The reader will recall that the plan was to introduce one change in working conditions at a time. The belief was that any observed effects in the workers' morale and productivity could then be precisely assigned to the influence of the variable which had been inserted by the researchers. The test room experiment had been designed so rigorously that it could not be imagined that the difficulties which had plagued the illumination experiment would reappear. The illumination experiment had taught that uncontrolled variables could creep in; the test room was to be a triumph of scientific control and measurement. In spite of the elaborate and skilled preparations, Mayo was to make another one of what *Fortune* magazine called the "fruitful errors of Elton Mayo." The great error of the test room experiment was the inability to foresee the sociological nature of a work group. None of the researchers seemed to have had the slightest inkling that the importance of group relations was to be established in the test room.

EXPERIMENTAL RESULTS

The reader may at this point wish to refer again to the account of the test room experiments as given by Stuart Chase in Chapter I. We shall merely summarize the record of these experiments here.

The introduction of such changes as rest periods and hot lunches in midmorning and changes in the length of the working day all increased productivity, but there was never any way to return to original conditions. Periods 7, 10, and 13 had nominally the same working conditions—fifteen-minute rest and lunch in midmorning, ten-minute rest in the afternoon. But the average weekly output for each girl was:

Period 7—2500 units.
Period 10—2800 units.
Period 13—3000 units.

[14] T. N. Whitehead, *The Industrial Worker*, Vol. II, Harvard University Press, 1938, pp. A-1, A-2.

Periods 3 and 12 had similar experimental conditions. In these periods the
workers were required to work a full day without rest periods. But here also
the difference of average weekly output for each girl was:

Period   3—less than 2500 units.

Period 12—more than 2900 units.

The researchers came to the conclusion that this amazing result was due
to the fact that "Six individuals became a team and the team gave itself
wholeheartedly and spontaneously to cooperation in the experiment." The
workers acquired a feeling of participating freely and without coercion from
above or limitation from below. Yet before this conclusion was reached,
many other hypotheses were carefully tested. It was almost as a last resort
that the researchers were forced to face the fact that group relations developed during the course of the experiment and that they were more
powerful than specific working conditions in determining morale and productivity. The recognition of such group relations emerges from the conclusions of the fourth confidential report, issued on May 11, 1929, to the
officials of the Western Electric Company. From this document one can
gain some idea of the contemporary attitude of those who were directing
the studies.

1. There has been a continual upward trend in output which has been independent of the changes in rest pauses.

2. The reduction of muscular fatigue has not been the primary factor in
increasing output. Cumulative fatigue is not present.

3. There has been an important increase in contentment among the girls
working under test-room conditions.

4. There has been a decrease in absences of about 80 per cent among the
girls since entering the test room group.

5. Output is more directly related to the type of working day than to the
number of working days in the week.

6. The changed working conditions have resulted in creating an eagerness on
the part of operators to come to work in the morning.

7. Important factors in the production of a better mental attitude and
greater enjoyment of work have been the greater freedom, less strict supervision
and the opportunity to vary from a fixed pace without reprimand from a gang
boss.

8. The operators have no clear idea as to why they are able to produce more
in the test room; but as shown in the replies to questionnaires . . . there is the
feeling that better output is in some way related to the distinctly pleasanter,
freer, and happier working conditions.[15]

The researchers checked upon the possibility that the influence of physical

[15] Elton Mayo, *The Human Problems of an Industrial Civilization*, The Macmillan
Company, 1933, pp. 67-69.

circumstances might operate to produce marked variations in output. Some of the records maintained for the test room were:

1. Temperature and humidity of the room, which were recorded each hour and then averaged.
2. The number of hours each operator slept at night.
3. The wind, sunshine, precipitation, and temperature of Chicago.
4. Physical examination records of the operators, who were examined every five or six weeks.
5. Work rates for different days of the week.[16]

Literally tons of material were collected. Probably nowhere in the world has so much material been collected about a small group of workers for such a long period of time.

T. N. Whitehead spent several years with a statistical staff trying to relate variations in output with variations in the physical circumstances and found "not a single correlation of enough statistical significance to be recognized by any competent statistician as having any meaning."[17]

The meaning of work behavior becomes clear. Mayo begins to use a new vocabulary to explain his fresh perspective:

The consequence was that the group had to readapt themselves to a new industrial milieu, a milieu in which their own self-determination and their social well-being ranked first and the work was incidental. The experimental changes—rest pauses, food, and talk at appropriate intervals—perhaps operated at first mainly, to convince them of the major change and to assist the readaptation. But once the new orientation had been established it became proof against the minor experimental changes. At Hawthorne, as the situation developed *the experimental changes became minor matters in actuality—whatever the operatives thought.*[18]

SIGNIFICANCE OF THE RESULTS

What is the significance of this first experiment? Some reviewers have expressed no surprise at the results. Indeed, one writer said:

Big Business has a way of inveighing against government expenditure. Some day a study should be made of "Researches in the Obvious Financed by Big Business." But maybe that too will turn out to be a set of tables and charts and mathematical formulas to prove what we already know. In any case the originator of the Western Electric experiment, Elton Mayo, modestly states that the authors of *Management and the Worker* do not claim that the enlightenment the many collaborators of the scheme got from their researches was "either very extensive or very profound." With this I am in complete agreement. That what they

[16] For a complete statistical treatment see T. N. Whitehead, *op. cit.*
[17] Quotation is attributed to F. J. Roethlisberger in "Fruitful Errors of Elton Mayo," *Fortune*, November, 1946, p. 182.
[18] E. Mayo, *The Human Problems of an Industrial Civilization*, p. 73.

learned was "novel and unexpected" seems to me an acknowledgement of inexperience in the field of industrial practice.[19]

In contrast to this statement, the reviewer for the *Personnel Journal* called the research "the most outstanding study of industrial relations that has been published anywhere, anytime."

A sociologist trying to weigh the merits of the test room experiment must confess the result is no surprise. The knowledge of group life that has accumulated during the last fifty years points toward the importance of feelings and attitudes which are developed in and through group participation. Mayo by scientific design made the demonstration of this fact so convincing that the Hawthorne relay assembly room yielded much more than the mere "obvious." In that room old ways of thinking were forced to give way to new ways of thinking. What transpired there as the researchers tried to raise productivity by mechanical changes of working conditions was a triumph for a simple fact. It became indisputable that men and women live in groups—at work, at play, at home, and in the community. Mayo expresses this by pointing out that the *rabble* hypothesis so long held as the basis of economic thinking cannot now be presumed tenable. The rabble hypothesis, according to Mayo, had been built around three postulates of economic theory held by Ricardo:

1. Natural society consists of a horde of unorganized individuals.

2. Every individual acts in a manner calculated to secure his self-preservation or self-interest.

3. Every individual thinks logically, to the best of his ability, in the service of this aim.[20]

On these postulates modern business administration rose and developed, but at Hawthorne they did not work.

In the test room poorer working conditions had brought about under certain group definitions of the situation improved morale and productivity. Even the financial incentive of the bonus proved to be pretty much of a fizzle. Mayo, eighteen years after he first participated in the experiment, was able to see most clearly and to explain best the meaning of Hawthorne. He said: "The desire to stand well with one's fellows, the so-called human instinct of association easily outweighs the merely individual interest and the logical reasoning upon which so many spurious principles of management are based."[21]

The Labor Committee of the Twentieth Century Fund has said that the new emphasis transforms the question "What makes a worker more produc-

[19] Mary B. Gilson, review of *Management and the Worker* in *American Journal of Sociology*, July, 1940, p. 101.
[20] Elton Mayo, *The Social Problems of an Industrial Civilization*, p. 40.
[21] *Ibid.*, p. 43.

tive?" into the question, "What makes a worker more willing?"[22] This emphasis is sending repercussions through business management, economic theory, time and motion study, industrial psychology and physiology. It has fortified sociologists with new confidence in their theoretical and methodological approach toward group relations in industry. It may be safe to say that the field of industrial sociology was born in the test room and that Mayo and his colleagues, in many ways obliquely trained for the task, have made sociological problems the new frontier of industrial research.

THE INTERVIEWING PROGRAM

EARLY DISCOVERIES

Since "all attempts to relate the experimentally introduced changes to the operator's performance apart from their effect upon the operator's attitudes had been inconclusive, management decided therefore, that everything pointed to the need for more research on employee attitudes and the factors to which they could be related."[23] This decision opened the interviewing program.

The interviewing program started essentially as a plan to improve supervision. The test room studies had shown that there was a close relation between employee morale and supervision. The operators worked better after they had been released from "apprehension of authority." Their feelings and behavior suggested that some of the supervisory methods being employed in the regular shop departments were unsatisfactory. The researchers decided to gather essential facts by approaching the employees themselves and asking them to express freely their likes and dislikes about the working environment.

In September, 1928, the interviewing program began in the inspection branch and was later extended to the entire plant. From the very beginning the program was well received. One of the most interesting observations made by the researchers was the way in which real and imagined improvements were attributed undeservedly to the interviewing program. There was, for example, the woman worker who complained at great length about poor food in the restaurant cafeteria. A few days after her interview she chanced to meet the interviewer and thanked him for taking her grievance to management and securing such a great improvement in the food. And yet the interviewer had done nothing but give the worker an opportunity to talk!

Careful description of many varied situations within the interviewers' experience showed that a grievance or complaint was almost always a *symptom* of some underlying discomfort and not the real cause. To under-

[22] Labor Committee, *Partners in Production*, The Twentieth Century Fund, 1949, p. 141.
[23] Roethlisberger and Dickson, *op. cit.*, p. 186.

stand a grievance it became necessary to study the situation anew to gain knowledge of its source. This discovery did not come to the researchers immediately. On the contrary, it came only after many interviews were made, during the course of which an entirely different method of interviewing was adopted.

Direct Question Interviewing

At the beginning direct question interviewing was undertaken. The aim was to ask the employee about his likes and dislikes, first about supervision and then about his working conditions and his job. The interviewer had certain questions which he was mentally equipped to ask, such as:

> How does your boss treat you?
> Does your boss ever bawl you out?
> Has he any favorites?
> Is your boss a slave driver?
> Do you consider your boss to be reasonable?

The interviewer led the conversation, the employee followed. It was soon found that direct question interviewing was unsatisfactory for at least four reasons:

1. It put the interviewee in a yes-or-no frame of mind.
2. It tended to arouse a reaction of antagonism or stereotyped response instead of spontaneous and real conviction.
3. The direct questions suggested answers.
4. The questions elicited opinions on topics which interviewers felt important but which the employee may never have thought of.

The interviewers came to discover the unsatisfactory nature of direct question interviewing by reporting back that they were having difficulty holding their interviews to a given topic. They claimed that the employee would start responding to a topic and then shortly talk off the subject. If he was brought back to the original topic, he would soon leave it to talk about something else. Every interviewer began to give cases citing this difficulty. One interviewer told of a worker who would wander off the topic to explain his personal life, his experiences, and other "irrelevant" topics. Another interviewer said he had a worker who was hipped on one subject and couldn't be persuaded to talk about anything else. A third interviewer told of a very reticent worker he had interviewed. This worker just wouldn't talk until they got on a given topic and then he became remarkably communicative.

Adoption of Indirect or Non-Directive Interviewing

In July, 1929, the method of interviewing was changed from direct to indirect or what has become more commonly called non-directive interviewing. The employer is led to his own center of interest and is permitted to talk

freely. This decision soon revealed that most workers have something "on their minds" about which they wish to talk freely to a competent observer. The research group became more certain that the chief value of interviewing as a method of industrial research lay in the fact that such a method could obtain the *emotional significance* to the worker of particular events and objects in his experience. It was clearly shown now that a complaint is not necessarily *an objective recital of facts*; it is a symptom of personal disturbance, the cause of which may be deep seated.

LATER DISCOVERIES

It was discovered that the talking-over process served as an *emotional release* to the employee and seemed to be of great advantage to him in achieving a more satisfying mental state.

In trying to diagnose the *emotional significance* to the worker of certain critical experiences it became apparent that the interviewer must somehow come to understand the *personal situation* of each worker. Certain rules for conducting the interview were devised with this end in mind. They were:

1. Give your whole attention to the person interviewed and make it evident that you are doing so.
2. Listen—don't talk.
3. Never argue; never give advice.
4. Listen to:
   (a) What he wants to say.
   (b) What he does not want to say.
   (c) What he cannot say without help.
5. As you listen, plot out tentatively and for subsequent correction the pattern (personal) that is being set before you.
6. Everything said must be considered a personal confidence.[24]

Exploration of the Personal Situation

When complaints became the signal to explore personal situations the attention was directed toward the personal and social reference of the individual. Figure 6 shows the configuration of relationships which the interviewer came to take into account. The verbal and overt acts (A and B) of the interviewee are to be kept in their contexts, the meanings of which are to be sought in terms of the sentiments which such contexts express (personal reference, C). These sentiments, in turn, are to be seen in relation to their social reference: the speaker's past social conditioning (social past, D) and the present personal interrelations he has with the groups in which he is now living and working (social present, E).

[24] E. Mayo, *The Social Problems of an Industrial Civilization*, pp. 73-74. The method of non-directive interviewing has been studied most intensively by Carl R. Rogers, *Counseling and Psycho-Therapy*, Houghton Mifflin Company, 1942. The application of this method of employee counseling in industry is best described by Nathaniel Cantor, *Employee Counseling*, McGraw-Hill Book Company, Inc., 1945.

This configuration forces attention upon personality organization, social background, and social participation. The sentiments, desires, and interests —the value system of the person—are a latent pattern lying under his verbal and overt behavior. It is implicit rather than explicit. It is inferred

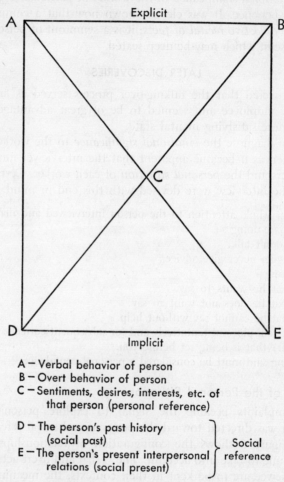

A – Verbal behavior of person
B – Overt behavior of person
C – Sentiments, desires, interests, etc. of
    that person (personal reference)

D – The person's past history
    (social past)   Social
E – The person's present interpersonal   reference
    relations (social present)

Fig. 6.   Configuration of relationships to Be Taken into Account by Interviewers. (Reprinted by permission of the publishers from F. J. Roethlisberger and Wiliam J. Dickson, *Management and the Worker*, Cambridge, Mass.: Harvard University Press, 1939, p. 282.)

rather than observed. Once the value system is identified it is important to understand it. In the search for understanding the researchers came to recognize that *the worker is a person whose attitudes and work effectiveness are conditioned by social demands from both inside and outside the work plant.*

Interpretation of Social Demands Affecting Employee Satisfaction Inside the Work Plant

The social organization of the group and the position of the worker in the group form a reference from which the emotional significance to the worker of an event, object, or person can be fruitfully viewed. Figure 7 is reproduced from Roethlisberger and Dickson to summarize the conceptual scheme for understanding employee satisfaction or dissatisfaction.

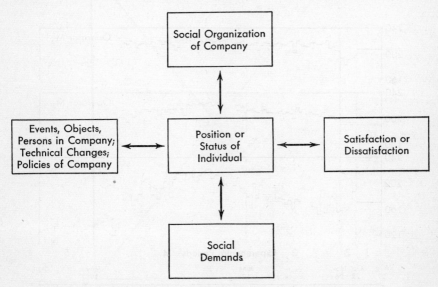

FIG. 7. Scheme for Interpreting Complaints Involving Social Interrelationships of Employees. (Reprinted by permission of the publishers from F. J. Roethlisberger and William J. Dickson, *Management and the Worker*, Cambridge, Mass.: Harvard University Press, 1939, p. 375.)

This figure recognizes that material goods, physical events, wages, and hours of work do not in themselves act as stimuli for social behavior. Rather they are carriers of social values. For the worker the whole working environment is a social environment. The significance of each aspect depends upon his social relationship to it. To understand the meaning of any employee's complaint or grievance, it is necessary to take account of his *position or status* in the company. The worker when preoccupied with expectations based upon personality, education, loyalty, or length of service critically appraises those values of the social organization on which his own personal integrity and position depend. The young worker with a high school education and short service, unmarried and ambitious, stresses the need for an organization in which advancement is dependent on education and personality rather than time, age, and experience. The middle-aged worker

with a grammar school education, long service, and a number of dependents talks about the importance of service, experience, and loyalty. Any action on the part of the social organization to lower the importance of these values is viewed by the worker with apprehension, frustration, and disillusionment. His dissatisfaction had its roots in the jeopardy or destruction of values on which he comes to rely for his source of dignity and security. Slowly but surely research is demonstrating that *one root of much serious labor trouble is not wage demands but status demands.*

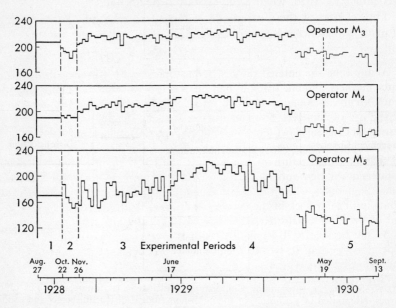

FIG. 8.   Average Hourly Output per Week of Operator M₃, M₄, and M₅ in the Mica-Splitting Test Room. (Reprinted by permission of the publishers from F. J. Roethlisberger and William J. Dickson, *Management and the Worker*, Cambridge, Mass.: Harvard University Press, 1939, p. 147.)

Equally significant in gaining understanding is awareness of the significance of the social demands which the worker is making of his work. The ultimate significance of his work is defined not so much by his relation to the company as by his relation to the whole of life itself. This fact forces recognition of social experiences and of the position of the worker in his family and community.

Interpretation of Social Demands Affecting Employee Satisfaction Outside the Work Plant

Whiting Williams had as early as 1925 pointed out the "unity of life and labor—the complete impossibility of walling off the factory from the home, the worker from the citizen, of dividing the hankerings of a man's

working hours off from those of his hours of leisure." The researchers were able to trace the influence of out-of-plant experiences and to read their effect in the output records of the workers.

Figure 8 shows the average hourly output of three operators in the test room. During the first five months in the test room operator 5 showed an irregular output and complained of a headache. Then her output began to rise. At about the twelfth month, on September 7, 1929, her production reached the highest point. For fourteen weeks it remained high, until about December 14, 1929, when again it started to decline.

The relation of these variations in output correspond to significant out-of-plant experiences. Roethlisberger and Dickson describe the operator as follows:

At the time she entered the test room Operator M 5 lived with her parents, three brothers, and one sister. When she was two years old, her family had moved from Vienna to America. She had attended grade school and had gone to work at the age of fourteen. She had worked at many different jobs for three years, finally coming to Hawthorne in January, 1927. Her mother, a nervous, easily irritated, and penurious woman, whose chief desire was to lay aside every cent so that she could return to Europe, was constantly finding fault with her husband and children and on occasions did not speak to them for a week at a time. Sometimes when the oldest daughter had been out and did not return home until 11 o'clock in the evening, she found that her mother had locked her out of the house. Naturally, Operator M frequently talked about leaving home.

As she became well acquainted with the other operators in the test room, Operator M began to talk to them about home difficulties. Comments such as the following were typical:

"My mother bawled me out for coming home early Monday. She said it was too bad that overtime was discontinued, as I would be more of a bother around the house."

"My mother was sore this morning. She wanted to know how much money I was going to bring home today and why I didn't bring home as much as I used to. She knows I haven't been working overtime and I have been working hard lately. She said I had too much taken out of my pay. The more money she gets, the more she wants. My brother, my dad, and I give her our pay checks, but when I want a new dress or a new pair of stockings she won't give me the money. She says I don't need it. She's told me before that if I don't like it at home I can pack up my things and go. The next time she tells me that, I am going."

"My mother is always hollering at me not to go out and that I ought to stay home nights. She knows where I go and I don't stay out late. She makes me sore."

On August 17, 1929, she finally decided to leave home and go to live with a girl friend, which she did for a period of four months. On December 28, 1929, because of her mother's illness she was forced to return home and help take care of her mother.[25]

[25] Roethlisberger and Dickson, *op. cit.*, pp. 175-177.

It was interesting to note that this operator's production in the test room began to increase as soon as she was able to express more freely her preoccupations with regard to her home situation. Since she was the youngest girl in the group, she was mothered by the older women, who listened to her troubles and gave her advice. Her output reached the highest point when she decided to leave home, and it remained at this high level practically the entire time she was living in more congenial surroundings. With the return home, however, her output began to fall.

This case shows what has been so often observed—namely, the effect of out-of-plant experiences upon worker morale and productivity. This fact emphasizes that *the worker is a social organism and must be viewed as a member of many groups both inside and outside the work plant.*

Summary of Findings

The Western Electric interviewers talked with over 21,000 people in three years. They found that employee dissatisfaction could seldom be referred back to the sole influence of the physical environment. People working in similar surroundings did not react in the same way to those surroundings. A number of generalizations can now be formulated from the data.

1. A complaint is not necessarily an objective recital of facts; it is a symptom of personal disturbance the cause of which may be deep seated.
2. Objects, persons, and events are carriers of social meanings. They become related to employee satisfaction or dissatisfaction only as the employee comes to view them from his *personal situation.*
3. The personal situation of the worker is a configuration of relationships composed of a personal reference involving sentiments, desires, and interests of that person and a social reference constituting the person's social past and his present interpersonal relations.
4. The position or status of the worker in the company is a reference from which the worker assigns meaning and value to the events, objects, and features of his environment, such as hours of work, wages, etc.
5. The social organization of the company represents a system of values from which the worker derives satisfactions or dissatisfactions according to his conception of his social status and the expected social rewards.
6. The social demands of the worker are influenced by social experiences in groups both inside and outside the work plant.

THE BANK WIRING OBSERVATION ROOM

SEARCH FOR INFORMAL GROUP STRUCTURE

The final phase of the research program in the Hawthorne plant consisted of a detailed study of a shop situation from a sociological point of view. This study is significant in recording the changing thoughtways of the research group. The test room had shown the importance of feelings and attitudes;

the interviewing program had confirmed the importance of such data. T. N. Whitehead was discovering underneath his voluminous statistical compilations that it was the social organization among the test room operators which caused the differences in productivity. All the weather changes in Chicago, all the changes in temperature and humidity, all the variations in rest pauses, hours of sleep, and diet did not explain as much as the social relationships formed in the test room. Likewise, the interviewers who talked with the 21,000 found it impossible to catch the more subtle and spontaneous aspects of the employees' social organization. They recognized that "there was every indication that more intensive studies of small groups would have to be made before an adequate understanding of the social situation in which employees functioned could be obtained."[26] The bank wiring observation room study was projected to achieve this objective.

The interviewing staff discovered early in 1931 that social groups in shop departments were capable of exercising very strong control over the work behavior of their individual members. Interviewers were assigned to departments in the belief that concentrated interviewing might maximize the therapeutic values. Their reports showed that there were problems of employee interrelations and group organization which had escaped them before this time. Chief among these was restriction of output. The evidence obtained suggested that the wage incentive systems under which some of the groups worked had been rendered ineffectual by group pressure for controlled output.

The bank wiring observation room study then was planned to obtain more exact information about social groups within the company. It was conducted with a group of fourteen male operators who were working as they were accustomed to work, under standard shop conditions. The investigators spent the period of six and one-half months between November, 1931, and May, 1932, observing the work situation before them.

The Method of Study

The investigators were quite aware that the bank wiring observation room was to impose new problems of research method. Direct observation of the work group had not seemed to be of central importance in the test room although the test room observer did keep a record of important events that transpired.

In the interviewing program the interviewers had worked only with statements of how the employees said they acted. They had no means of relating these statements to what actually transpired. What was now needed was a means of observing and recording overt behavior as well as verbal behavior. This demand led to an innovation in method which distinguished the bank wiring room study from all the others dealt with so far, namely, supplement-

[26] *Ibid.*, p. 376.

ing the interviewing method with carefully controlled methods of direct observation. In planning their experimental design the researchers were fortunate in having the counsel of William Lloyd Warner, at that time Assistant Professor of Social Anthropology at Harvard University and now Professor of Anthropology and Sociology at the University of Chicago. The general methodological concepts employed were chiefly derived from Mr. Warner. The responsibility for their detailed application rests with the investigators, who made a number of initial decisions. They decided to:

1. Concentrate on one small group engaged in one type of work rather than to spread their efforts over a number of groups with dissimilar jobs.
2. Place the group to be studied in a separate room in order for the observer to keep adequate records without interfering with production in the shop.
3. Make base period studies before supervisors or workers knew anything about the study in order to assess the effect of placing the group in a separate room.
4. Say nothing in selecting the group to be studied which might alter their status in any way, either in explaining the study to them or in removing them from the department.
5. Make no records which might tend to make the workers apprehensive or consciously aware that they were being studied.

The investigating work was divided between an observer and an interviewer in the belief that the type of material to be gathered was quite different and that both types of material could not be gathered equally well by one person.

The Observer's Task

The observer was stationed in the group as a disinterested spectator; he was to establish friendly relations with everyone in the group. The observer was given certain general rules to guide him in playing an objective role.

1. He should not give orders or answer any questions which necessitated the assumption of authority.
2. He should not enter voluntarily into any argument. If forced to do so, he should be as noncommittal as possible.
3. He should not force himself into a conversation or appear to be either anxious to overhear what was going on or overinterested in the group's behavior.
4. He should never violate confidences or give any information to supervisors, whatever their rank.
5. He should not by his manner of speech or behavior set himself off from the group.

While playing a friendly but detached role it was the observer's job to secure a record of significant events in the behavior of the workers. But what is a significant event? Observation, if it is to be scientific, must be guided by a working hypothesis which enables the researcher to select

relevant events from a welter of irrelevancies. The investigators agreed upon certain hypotheses. These were:

1. There is a difference between the way the formal and technical organization is supposed to operate and the way it actually operates.
2. A strong informal organization of workers will be found.
3. The informal organization fulfills functions both for the people participating in it and for the larger structure of which the group is a part.

With these hypotheses as guides to observation the observer was instructed to look for and record the following:

1. Every item which indicated a similarity or difference between the actual situation and the way it was supposed to be recorded.
2. Evidences of any informal organization which the employees in their face-to-face relations consciously or unconsciously found, such as:
   a. Recurrent verbal utterances or overt acts indicative of the relations between two or more people.
   b. Manifestations of the kind and extent of a person's participation in the immediate group situation.
   c. Evidences of the existence of a group solidarity.
   d. Evidences, if group solidarity existed, of the occupational groups to which it extended and how it was expressed.
3. Evidences of the functions which the informal organization fulfilled in the lives of the workers.

Needless to say, the observer was aware of the necessity of avoiding personal judgments. His task was to ask such questions as, "Why does he act this way? What do his actions indicate his position in the group to be? How do his actions affect the interpersonal relations of others in the group?"

The Interviewer's Task

The interviewer was to remain outside the group. Although he was to remain in daily touch with the observer, he was not to enter the bank wiring observation room. This stipulation was made in the belief that the workers would feel more like telling the interviewer about themselves, their work, and occurrences in the observation room. The interviews were held by appointment and conducted in privacy.

The interviewer was to secure a maximum of insight into the attitudes, thoughts, and feelings of the workers. He was to discover the personal situation of each worker, which is to say, his personal values and the way they were related to personal history, family situation, and social life outside the plant.

Selecting the Department to Be Studied

It was determined that the department to be selected should contain jobs fulfilling the following requirements:

1. Operators engaged in the same task.
2. Output for each operator capable of being exactly determined.
3. One unit of output completed in relatively short time, not more than a minute.
4. Work pace of operator determined by his own effort and not controlled by a machine or conveyor.
5. Assurance of reasonable continuance of employment of those selected.
6. Work group to be removed from the department without inconvenience.
7. Removal to a separate room not to require the installation of bulky or costly equipment.
8. Male operators to be experienced at their work.

The department best fitting these requirements was one engaged in the assembly of large electrical switches. One operation performed in the department, that of connector and selector bank wiring, was particularly suitable, and the men performing this operation were chosen for the study.

Three groups of workers—wiremen, soldermen, and inspectors—were necessary to perform the task of selector and connector bank wiring. Each of these groups performed a specific task and collaborated with the other two in completion of each unit of equipment. The work rate of one workman in any one of these groups was related to the rates of the two other workmen.

The Composition of the Bank Wiring Observation Group

Some of the more important facts relating to the composition of the bank wiring group are shown in Table 2. All operators except one ranged from twenty to twenty-six years of age. Half of them had an eighth-grade educa-

TABLE 2.   Composition of the Bank Wiring Observation Room

Operator	Age	Birthplace	Nationality	Marital Status	Education	Service—Yrs., Mos.	
Wireman 1	22	U.S.A.	Polish	S	7 G.S.	2	2
Wireman 2	25	U.S.A.	German	S	2 H.S.	5	5
Wireman 3	26	U.S.A.	American	M	8 G.S.	2	5
Wireman 4	20	U.S.A.	Irish	S	2 H.S.	3	7
Wireman 5	24	U.S.A.	Bohemian	M	4 H.S.	2	8
Wireman 6	21	U.S.A.	Polish	S	2 H.S.	3	1
Wireman 7	22	U.S.A.	Bohemian	M	8 G.S.	3	2
Wireman 8	22	U.S.A.	German	S	4 H.S.	3	8
Wireman 9	21	U.S.A.	American	S	8 G.S.	2	10
Solderman 1	21	U.S.A.	German	S	8 G.S.	5	4
Solderman 2	26	Yugoslavia	Bohemian	S	6 G.S.	9	8
Solderman 4	20	U.S.A.	Bohemian	S	8 G.S.	8	0
Inspector 1	23	U.S.A.	American	S	4 H.S.	3	0
Inspector 3	40	Turkey	American	M	3 Col.	7	0

tion or less. Most of them were single men, but all fourteen, except one, had some person in their families dependent upon them.

OBSERVATION IN THE BANK WIRING ROOM

The work of the bank wiring group took place in an observation room approximately 40 feet long and 20 feet wide and located about 200 feet from the regular department. The observer's desk was placed at the rear of the room. When he was seated, he faced a side wall and could not look directly at the group without turning to one side. It was believed that this position would minimize any feeling the operators might have of being watched.

Such considerations are not without importance, as the first weeks soon revealed. During the first week the men were under considerable strain. They behaved quite differently from the way they worked in the department. The observer was regarded with distrust. It was not until the end of the third week that the observer was on fairly good terms with everyone and was included in freely expressed conversations. The observer mingled and talked. He listened to complaints and occasionally asked for suggestions, but each time explained that he could do nothing to correct the conditions complained about. The interviewer discovered that all of the workers had misinterpreted the purpose of the study and he was able to help dispel the fears and uncertainties.

As the group settled down in their normal pattern of work, the observer and the interviewer kept gathering records. Records were made of output for each man at noon and at night. The quality rating of the work of each wireman for each day was recorded. The observer kept a daily record of significant happenings in the observation room, of conversations, and of his own impressions. Interviews were held with each man before the study began and two or more times during the study itself. Each person was given a thorough physical examination, which showed that all the men were in good health and had no interfering physical disabilities. Mental and dexterity tests were administered by a psychologist.

SIGNIFICANCE OF THE BANK WIRING ROOM EXPERIMENT

The full account of the informal organization of the bank wiring workers can be found only in *Management and the Worker*. In Chapters 20-25 the informal organization of workers is discussed and many observations from this experiment are reported. At this point only a few significant conclusions will be drawn.

1. It was discovered very early that each individual in the group was restricting output in spite of the fact that the group piecework incentive plan in opera-

tion provided for a larger wage return the greater the number of units completed.

2. The working group as a whole actually determined the output of individual
   workers by reference to a standard predetermined but never clearly stated, that
   represented the group conception of a fair day's work.

3. The group output standard is only one of many social norms defined by
   the informal organization of the workers. Workers formed themselves into
   strong social groups with appropriate customs, duties, routines, even rituals.
   Strong social controls were constituted to command conformity to the
   group definitions and expectations.

4. In the contest between a management expectation and the group standards,
   the informal organization of the workers is most likely to prevail in determining conduct.

5. The power of the group controls is attested to by the fact that no relation was
   found between individual scores on dexterity or output or between intelligence
   test scores and output. The lowest man in output, for example, ranked first in
   intelligence.

STUDIES OF ABSENTEEISM IN THE EAST COAST METALWORKING SHOPS

FROM RECORDS TO SUPERVISORY RELATIONSHIPS

During the war years, 1941-1945, absenteeism increased and leaders in
government, labor, and industry became seriously concerned about its effects
on war production. The concern was not without substance. When absenteeism reached the 10 percent level, as it did in some plants, it meant that
many more workers were needed to carry the productive load. A company of
35,000 workers would require 3500 more employees to maintain a production schedule based on the original labor force. This procedure was expensive not only in money but in man power. The alleged reasons for the
increased number of absences were many—the difficulties of transportation,
the strain of long workdays, the special family and health problems of
women workers, and the like. Some observers claimed that much of the
absence was willful and caused by "more money in the worker's pockets
than they had ever had in their lives." There was no doubt that many
workers were taking a long week end, for absences on Saturday and Monday
reached weekly peaks. What was the cause of absenteeism? How could it
be remedied?

The industrial research staff at Harvard was asked by a government agency
to investigate absenteeism in three metalworking companies located in the
same industrial district of a small east coast industrial city.[27]

[27] The detailed account of the research is by John B. Fox and Jerome F. Scott,
Absenteeism: Management's Problem, Harvard Business Research Studies, No. 29, Harvard
University Press, 1943.

The first step the researchers took was to examine the official statistics of the three companies. The records were not immediately of great help since absence had been recorded in man-hours of work lost. The amount of total absence was shown for the company and for the departments but the total did not reveal to *whom* the absences were charged. In addition, the records of reasons for absence were unreliable. However, attendance data were available for each worker and this permitted an immediate attack on the problem. A significant decision was made. The investigators determined to discard the man-hour tables as being useless for purpose of analysis and to construct a simple index of regular attendance. The index was constructed by deciding to count any absence of a number of consecutive days as *one* absence. The reason for this decision was based on the fact that the greatest single reason for absence in the United States is sickness or injury.

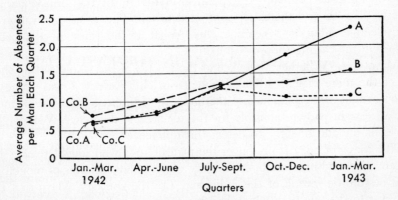

FIG. 9. Absences of Veterans by Quarters, January, 1942, Through March, 1943: Casting Shops of Companies A, B, and C. (From Elton Mayo, *The Social Problems of an Industrial Civilization*, Harvard University Press, 1945, p. 96.)

The real difficulty in the present situation was to distinguish between real sickness and alleged sickness. There was no way to do this quickly and accurately. But the counting of consecutive absences as one absence would have the effect of minimizing successive days of absence and maximizing frequency of absences. The underlying assumption was that the successive days of absence probably represented a high proportion of real illness or injury, the frequent absences probably represented a high proportion of willful absences. For example, two male workers were absent for twenty-two days in 1942. One was out for twenty-two successive days with appendicitis and was not otherwise absent; the other was absent eleven times for two days, mostly over the week end. The first was scored for one absence, the other for eleven absences. This device now made possible a meaningful interpretation of the group attendance pattern.

The records of men who had been continuously employed throughout 1942 were set aside in one group. In mid-1943 the majority of these men were still with the company. They were called the veterans. As a group their attendance record was good in all three companies. Many workers were not absent at all and most workers not more than a few times. However, there was striking variation between individuals and between some departments. The bulk of the absences could be charged to a small minority of persons whose records showed high frequencies. When the casting shops of the three companies were compared, significant variations were observed between those departments. The differences in attendance patterns can be seen in Figure 9.

This figure shows that company A has experienced a steadily rising rate of absences which tops all of the other shops; in company B absenteeism rose steadily; in company C, absenteeism rose until the July-September quarter of 1942 and thereafter continued to fall. This is an observation of considerable interest—a genuine clue. What is the cause of the better record in the casting shop of company C?

Mayo says, "Whether we looked at the records of the whole casting shop or of the more regular attendants in it—in either event it was borne in upon us that some difference of method and of internal organization must be, at least in part, responsible for the remarkable difference. Was it possible, simply and directly, to detect this difference?"[28]

The Mayo of 1943 is no longer the man of 1933 who sought reasons for absenteeism and turnover by looking for explanations in terms of monotony and pessimistic reverie of the individual. On the contrary, Mayo says the "answer to the question, which had become clear and specific, was not far to seek." Three findings are used to interpret the cause of lower absence in company C:

First: Foremen in company C had been trained to handle human situations. The company had supported a training program for twenty years which instructed supervisors not only in the technical details of their job but also in human relationships on the job.

Second: The delegation of routine technical responsibilities to certain qualified technical assistants gave the foremen the time required for the responsibilities involved in team leadership. This improved communication from above down. In addition, payment of the three shifts for their twenty-four-hour output on a furnace built up a team spirit. No shift tended to slack off as the end of its period of work approached. "Teamwork and no buck passing" became a meaningful slogan.

Third: Foremen and individual workers on the shift arranged every week which day off each worker should have. Unlawful failure of one worker to appear

[28] E. Mayo, The Social Problems of an Industrial Civilization, p. 100.

caused an upset in the whole arrangement. As a consequence the workers put pressure on the individual of a severity that management could not have exercised.

TEAMWORK AND LABOR TURNOVER IN THE AIRCRAFT INDUSTRY OF SOUTHERN CALIFORNIA[29]

SIGNIFICANCE OF THE WORK TEAM

Late in 1943 Mayo and certain members of his staff were asked to study the problem of labor turnover in the aircraft industry in Southern California. The social setting was full of dynamic changes. The small airplane plants had grown to large industries in a few years. The drafting of workers into the army was a constant drain on the labor force for the industry and necessitated a constant induction of new workers. These new workers migrated into California by the thousands. Officers of the Los Angeles War Manpower Commission estimated that every month during 1943 approximately 25,000 people moved into Southern California and between 12,000 and 14,000 moved out. In this social setting it is not surprising to learn that labor turnover in the industry was running between 70 and 80 percent. Mayo refused to believe that this unsettlement was in itself a sufficient explanation of the turnover. It is a large tribute to the acumen of this superb research man that he has looked for prime determinants of work behavior within the *social organization* of a specific work situation. He has been particularly emphatic in pointing out that no remedies external to a specific work situation can change a fundamental defect of organization within it. The reference here is to the application of rest periods, music, vitamin pills, free life insurance, steam baths, pretty entertainers, war heroes, dance pavilions, or other bread and circus measures which avoid the essential problems arising in face-to-face association in work groups. In place of these palliatives Mayo holds that if an organization is to achieve its material and economic purpose it must secure the spontaneous coöperation of its workers. Three types of problems are continuously posed for management study:

    1. The application of science and technical skill to a material product.

    2. The systemization of operations.

    3. The organization of sustained coöperation.

The labor turnover problem in the southern aircraft industry seemed to prove the validity of this theme just as all the other experiments had done. It showed that management had done an excellent job of applying scientific-engineering knowledge and organizing operations, but the organization of teamwork had received scant attention.

[29] Elton Mayo and George F. F. Lombard, *Teamwork and Labor Turnover in the Aircraft Industry of Southern California*, Business Research Studies, No. 32, Harvard University Press, 1944.

It soon became apparent to the researchers that it would be necessary to ignore the larger groups—departments or shifts—and to center attention upon smaller groups of persons actually in daily intimate working association with each other. Seventy-one such groups were identified; among them were good and bad groups from the standpoint of attendance. They ranged from 100 percent regularity to no regularity at all.

One of the groups with excellent attendance came under observation. It had a reputation for "working like beavers." Their foreman said their efficiency ran 25 percent above that of the average of the plant. The group itself was thought by others to be somewhat clannish; members of it quite definitely thought of themselves as a group and in some degree different from other workers in the plant.

The teamwork which had obviously developed there could be definitely traced to key persons. The foreman of the department rarely visited this work group; his senior assistant visited it once daily. The work was actually in charge of a "leadman," who was a college man with considerable experience in steel mills. He did not have supervisory rank and in many ways was just another worker with the extra job of taking care of minor hour-to-hour interruptions in the operations of the group. Nonetheless, this leadman, with the support of the senior assistant foreman, placed the importance of group solidarity above other considerations. He functioned in three important ways to strengthen job relations.

First: He introduced new employees, always first getting acquainted with a new man as a person and then trying to get him congenial work associates. After a few days he would take the new employee to the assembly line and show him where the part he made was installed in the completed machine. He always listened to complaints and when he could not settle them would discuss them with the senior assistant foreman.

Second: He served as a trouble-shooter, anticipating emergencies and shortages. When troubles arose he worked hard to get materials for his department.

Third: He became a buffer against and an effective link with the plant, the "outside world." The leadman handled inspectors, efficiency men, and the like; requests for raises went through him to the foreman.

This leadman made his chief self-imposed task that of securing for the individual worker an effective and happy relationship with his fellow workers and his work. The result was a well-knit human group superior in morale and efficiency to the disunited collections of workers scattered in so many other departments.

The problem of absenteeism, turnover, low morale, and poor efficiency reduces to the question of how groups may be solidified and collaboration increased in the large as well as the small work plant. The problem, as the famed sociologist, Charles H. Cooley, would say, is how to build primary

group life. Mayo has a theory that the building and extension of group solidarity may be observed in three recognizable units. These he has called the "natural" group, the "family" group, and the "organized" group, all of which were identified among those having high attendance records.

The "Natural" Group

The "natural" group is a very small group varying from two to three to six or seven workers (see Fig. 10). Twelve such groups were identified having almost perfect attendance records. The small group is apparently conducive

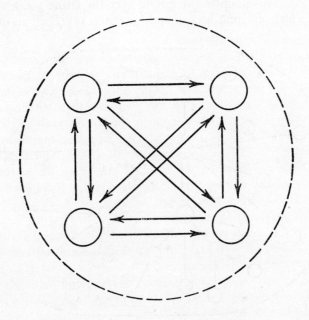

Fig. 10. A "Natural" Group. (After Mayo.)

to the development of intimacy and cohesiveness. Such groups stand as the strongest evidence that human beings like regular association with others at work. These groupings of human beings are normal products of social interaction and should be expected unless interferences occur. However, unless there is a deliberate effort made to nourish and support such associations numerous interferences may distort the social process or never give it a chance to develop.

The "Family" Group

The "family" group is merely an arbitrary name given to denote a larger group with a central core of regulars (see Fig. 11). This core of regulars may if they have prestige determine the standards for the group. These groups

contain from eight to thirty members. It is estimated that a minimal period necessary for the formation of a work team of this size may be from six months to a year of continuous association. This assumes no explicit organization of human needs by management. Skilled management, by establishing a favorable organizational "climate," can shorten the time necessary for the formation of such a group. Under conditions of emergency or unusual stress even large teams may form almost overnight.

The "Organized" Group

The "organized" group might extend over the entire plant and include persons of widely different backgrounds (see Fig. 12). Such an organization

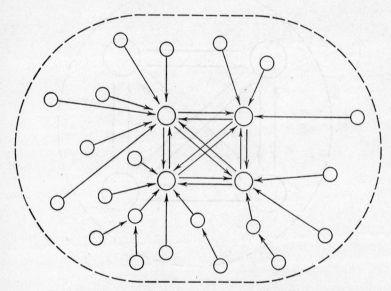

FIG. 11. A "Family" Group. (After Mayo.)

envisages a community organization in which all or most individuals are members and participants of well-knit "natural" groups, with each of these groups linked together in common purpose. It requires administration with experience, intelligence, and skill *deliberately* setting itself the task of creating group integrity of association. And above all, the planning for a work plant community requires new knowledge. Sociologists will be expected to supply an ever greater volume of basic and applied knowledge to the problem of group formation and collaboration. Industry, government, and community organization are equally concerned with the formation of effective groups. The basic questions are: How can the formation of groups be stimulated? What conditions make for the growth of solidarity? How are leaders of teams found and trained? How can the purposes of a large organ-

ization be transmitted and effectively introduced into component groups in such a way that the entire organization actually strives for similar ends? To seek answers to these questions a growing body of researchers is studying group processes under such assorted titles as "group dynamics," "sociometry," "group discussion," and "group work."

Vital as group processes are, still another large consideration intrudes. This is the impact of social changes upon the internal structure of industry. Mayo wrote in 1945 that he

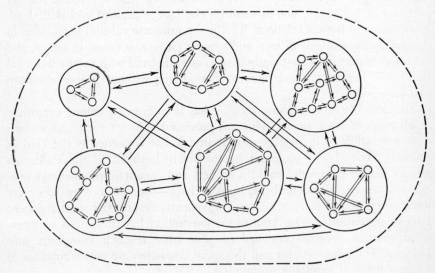

FIG. 12. An "Organized" Group. (After Mayo.)

had not fully realized in 1932 . . . how profoundly the social structure of civilization has been shaken by scientific, engineering, and industrial development. This radical change—the passage from an established to an adaptive social order—has brought into being a host of new and unanticipated problems for management and for the individual worker. The management problem appears at its acutest in the work of the supervisor. No longer does the supervisor work with a team of persons that he has known for many years or perhaps a lifetime; he is a leader of a group of individuals that forms and disappears almost as he watches it.[30]

In the Southern California aircraft companies loans and transfers of workers caused by technical demands of production were constantly ripping work teams apart. On top of these internal changes, labor turnover continued to disrupt group formation with a vengeance.

These problems, which have diminished with the war, still exist with such intensity that they pose the severest obstacle to group formation and

[30] Elton Mayo, *The Social Problems of an Industrial Civilization*, p. 75.

solidarity. The separation rate in manufacturing industries in 1948 averaged 4.52 percent monthly or 54.3 percent for the year. It becomes difficult for the small "natural" group to form under these conditions; "family" groups do not have a chance to form without a central core of regulars; and the "organized" group which means a real work plant community is well-nigh impossible unless the plant is small. Loose, amorphous social relationships become the rule. Moreover, this lack of work teams inside work plants becomes all the more serious when it is realized how few of the essential leadership posts are manned by men and women who appreciate the importance of teamwork, not to mention the lack of trained and skillful administrators of human relations. This is the immense cultural lag as seen in the day-by-day contacts of men and women on factory floors, in offices, and in stores. Superb technical equipment is administered with expert technical skill while human relations are left floundering without proper attention and knowledge.

The desire to do something about it has been growing among executives in all types of work plants. This has produced calls for men and women with new kinds of knowledge and ability. What is needed is the kind of precious "know-how" possessed by the lowly leadman in the California aircraft factory who could hold his workers and "maintain production in the midst of a scene of indescribable human chaos—thousands of workers every week entering and leaving factory employment despite the most stringent Federal regulations." This kind of demonstration has stimulated an intensified research program designed to pour basic research knowledge into industry. The administrator and the social researcher are drawn together in a closer bond of common aspiration.

A SOCIOLOGICAL ORIENTATION TO WORK RELATIONS

A sociological orientation to work relations has emerged from these experiments to guide accumulated research knowledge. This orientation is characterized by the following generalizations, which have been verified by the experimental findings:

Generalization	Drawn From
1. Work is a group activity.	All Harvard industrial research studies.
2. The social world of the adult is primarily patterned about work activity.	Textile mill; relay assembly test room.
3. The need for recognition, security, and sense of belonging is more important in determining worker's morale and productivity than the physical conditions under which he works.	Relay assembly test room.

Generalization	Drawn From
4. A complaint is not necessarily an objective recital of facts; it is commonly a *symptom* manifesting disturbance of an individual's status position.	Interviewing program.
5. The worker is a person whose attitudes and effectiveness are conditioned by social demands from both outside and inside the work plant.	Relay assembly test room; bank wiring observation room.
6. Informal groups within the work plant exercise strong social controls over the work habits and attitudes of the individual worker.	Bank wiring observation room; metalworking companies.
7. The change from an established to an adaptive society tends continually to disrupt the social organization of a work plant and industry generally.	Southern California aircraft companies.
8. Group collaboration does not occur by accident; it must be planned for and developed. If group collaboration is achieved, the work relations within a work plant may reach a cohesion which resists the disrupting effects of adaptive society.	Southern California aircraft companies.

This is the story and the implication of modern scientific experimentation in industry. It has been almost completely a story of Elton Mayo or his colleagues. One writer asserts that the "most important accomplishment of these studies is that in their course more researchers have talked to more workers and explored more factory situations than in any other investigations in fifty years."[31]

However, these men are not the only researchers who have new knowledge about the formation of groups and the problems which beset them. Social scientists have amassed a vast store of useful knowledge about the processes of group life. Although the record of research which has been chronicled in this chapter is an enduring monument to Mayo's achievements, these researches are not without some shortcomings. As a matter of fact, it is obvious that Mayo had to outgrow his biases, which sprang from a point of view based only on an individual psychology. It took many years of research education to reorient him. To the critical sociologist his failure to grasp the significance of groups in his initial efforts seems somewhat naïve, and his subsequent interpretations reveal a man who must, of consequence, learn through his errors. Mayo gained the entry of a scientist to the group life of work plant societies and rose to greatness by the open-minded and hard-headed appraisal of facts which he found there. It is important for the forward push of science that a similarly open-minded

[31] Daniel Bell, "Exploring Factory Life," *Commentary*, January, 1947, p. 86.

and hard-headed appraisal be made of the work of Elton Mayo and his colleagues.

A CRITIQUE OF MAYO AND HIS RESEARCH GROUP

The weight of criticism directed against Mayo and his collaborators can be assembled from two directions. First, the omission of certain critical factors in his interpretation of the situations which he observed detracts from a full appreciation of the meaning of the results. Second, the biases of his own personal situation, or better, what V. F. Calverton once called cultural compulsives, color his views at many important points.

These criticisms grow out of Mayo's interpretations of the experimental findings as well as from many of his personal views concerning education and society. The criticism made here is to be construed not as depreciation of the achievements but as a basis for future growth. The student is particularly urged to follow the argument in order that the next chapter, on the educational training of the industrial sociologist, may take on more constructive meaning for him.

GAPS IN THE THOUGHTWAYS OF THE HARVARD INDUSTRIAL RESEARCH GROUP

1. There Is no View of the Larger Institutional Framework of Our Society

One critical reviewer of the Hawthorne studies is struck by the paucity of conclusions drawn from the mass of material collected. "The reason for this, one feels, is that no one has approached this material armed with basic hypotheses about the nature of our industrial system. Without general hypotheses, the researchers merely 'psychologize,' asserting that workers 'feel' this, or that management 'feels' that. There is no view of the larger institutional framework of our economic system within which these relationships arise and have their meaning."[32]

This omission shows up in "failure to grasp the significance of changes in the class and occupational structure of America." In the white-collar classes the growth of service, research, and commerce has produced new social strata of technical and managerial employees. In the working classes the rise of semiskilled machine operatives has accelerated as technological advances have tended to de-grade the skilled worker and to replace the purely manual worker.

Warner and Low describe the effect of this leveling of jobs in the modern factory and show how the breakdown of skills causes a collapse of social structure in the work plant. Figure 13 is a diagram showing the leveling of technological jobs in a shoe factory. The picture of the old skill hierarchy

[32] *Ibid.*

in the days of handicraft shoemaking can be seen. This was more than a job structure; it was a social structure in which each worker had a clearly defined status. Warner and Low often call it an age-grade structure. The young apprentice was assigned job A at the bottom of the hierarchy. After years of training he could look forward to an increase of security and prestige as he was promoted to journeyman. The highest rank of all, master craftsman, was the coveted achievement available only to the older worker who had faithfully served his time as apprentice and journeyman. Then came the introduction of the machine into all parts of the production processes of the factory. The skill hierarchy was largely destroyed. Today

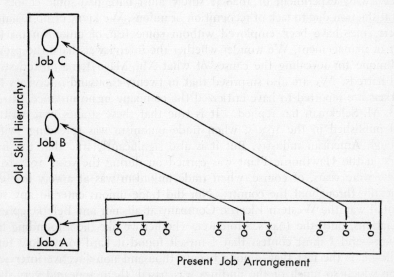

FIG. 13. The Results of the Leveling of Technological Jobs in the Shoe Factory. (From W. L. Warner and J. O. Low, *The Social System of the Modern Factory*, Yale University Press, 1947, p. 81.)

many skilled jobs have been divided into a number of simple, low-skilled ones, and machines are performing most of the actions necessary for each job. Now jobs formerly at the top and the bottom of the skill hierarchy that were separated by differences in prestige and pay are in the same category of prestige and pay. A master craftsman works beside a machine, his skill useless and his prestige stripped away. Beside him work young men and women at the same task who say that there ought to be equal pay for equal work. The age-grade structure has broken down and a class of interchangeable factory hands has almost become a reality. The informal and formal organizations of workers arise like reflex actions to protect them in the midst of their new insecurity.

Mayo does not acknowledge the dynamic changes in the status of workers.

In fact, he carefully excludes organized labor from his report. This seems exceedingly strange to Mary B. Gilson, who reports, "In all the more than six hundred pages describing the Western Electric experiment, costing hundreds of thousands of dollars and supported by some of the wealthiest groups of this country, no reference is made to organized labor except a short statement, unindexed, that it was so seldom mentioned by any workers that it was not considered sufficiently important to discuss. . . .

"From 1933 to 1936 the Western Electric Company paid out $25,825.73 for espionage."[33]

"The interviewers who engaged in 'counseling' service subsequent to the interviewing experiment of 1928-31 surely must have had some echoes of dissatisfaction due to lack of recognition of unions. We know of no instance where spies have been employed without some fear of unionism on the part of management. We wonder whether the interviewers have the proper technique for revealing the causes of what Mr. Mayo terms 'futile strife and hatreds.' We are also surprised that in twenty thousand interviews the workers are reported to have criticized the company in no instance."[34]

B. M. Selekman has replied: "It is true that these studies were written and published in the 1930's, when trade unionism was spreading swiftly through American industry. But it is also significantly true that the field work in the Hawthorne Plant was carried on during the years 1927-1932. These were years, of course, when trade unionism was at a very low ebb generally throughout the country. Nor did trade unions enter in any substantial way the Western Electric Company at all, nor any Bell Telephone operations, until the 1940's. Moreover, whether we like the astounding fact or not—and I must confess that I myself found it hard to swallow for a while—it is the fact that, among twenty thousand non-directive interviews upon which so much of the findings was based, there appeared very little articulation on trade union matters among the workers."[35]

It is understandable that Mayo did not regard an interpretation of an entire society as his task when he helped design the Hawthorne experiments. However, failure to pose certain hypotheses regarding the nature of the interacting forces has left him peculiarly exposed to the kind of devastating criticism which both Daniel Bell and Mary Gilson have made.

C. W. M. Hart pounds away at the same theme. "Since all the in-plant research approaches the worker through his activities and preoccupations *upon the job*, it gives little or no indication of the importance of large, strong, well-run unions. . . . It would appear obvious then, that in addition

[33] Report of the [U. S. Senate] Committee on Education and Labor (2d session, 75th Congress), Report No. 46, Part 3, United States Government Printing Office, 1937, p. 88.
[34] Mary B. Gilson in a review of *Management and the Worker* by F. J. Roethlisberger and W. J. Dickson, *American Journal of Sociology*, July, 1940, p. 101.
[35] *Proceedings of the Industrial Relations Research Association*, December, 1948, p. 231.

to economic studies of labour, such as the older literature provides, and the psychological studies of the worker which the Mayo school has given us, we are badly in need of empirical data upon the sociology of labour unions and their place in the industrial community. The central problem of industrial society appears to be the impact of the new institutions upon the older equilibrium of institutional forces."[36]

2. There Is a Failure to See Social Skills in Modern Society

Mayo asserts that technical skills have grown apace but that "social skill (that is, our ability to secure cooperation between people) has disappeared."[37]

Nowhere, it is asserted, is anyone training people in social skills. "The so-called social sciences encourage students to talk endlessly about alleged social problems. They do not seem to equip students with a single social skill that is usable in ordinary human situations."[38] This charge is leveled at a time when modern educational philosophy and educational practice have been steadfastly pursuing a program of education designed to increase social knowledge and skills. Can Mayo be unaware of Dewey, Kilpatrick, Bode, Tyler, and other modern educational philosophers? Or the teachers of America? Perhaps at no time in the history of education has such concentrated time and energy been given to the improvement of social skills. Curricula have been examined and reëxamined; new kinds of curricular and extracurricular activity have been introduced and encouraged to develop abler personalities and better citizens. It is the aim of every youth organization that the writers know how to give each of its members an increasing number of opportunities to participate in groups. Some observers have asserted that Americans of all ages are among the greatest of joiners and participators in group organizations. It may very well be true that more and better skills might be developed, but this is a far different view from the blind assertion that social skill has disappeared.

Two serious omissions in the thoughtways of Mayo and his Harvard research group have been pointed out. Each bears a relationship to the design and the interpretation of the industrial experiments that have been reported in this chapter. No observer looks at any section of the social world and comes away with meaning unless he has taken some kind of hypotheses or concepts with him. It is not too surprising that the psychologist, Mayo, and the engineer, Roethlisberger, have revealed their weakness in knowledge of social structure. They did not start as students, or as scholars, or as researchers to train themselves in this direction. They are self-educated

36 C. W. M. Hart, "Industrial Relations Research and Social Theory," *Canadian Journal of Economics and Political Science*, February, 1949, pp. 72-73.
37 E. Mayo, *The Social Problems of an Industrial Civilization*, p. 2.
38 *Ibid.*, p. 20.

social scientists who rose to the implications of their experiments. Their growth has been great and their omissions are not the more serious deficiencies. The gravest charge that can be leveled against their research is that they allowed two kinds of bias to color their interpretation. These are a pro-management bias and a clinical bias.

TWO KINDS OF BIAS

1. The Pro-Management Bias

It must be remembered that all of the industrial researches which Mayo directed were by permission and subsequent arrangement with management. It is also a well-known fact that professors as well as researchers in "good" colleges of business administration do not displease the business community. If Mayo, out of a lifetime of service in the interest of industry, should carry either consciously or unconsciously a pro-management bias it should not be considered surprising. These researches were conducted to help *management* solve its problems. Therefore, the *status quo* is accepted. Bell has said that the Harvard industrialists "uncritically adopt industry's own conception of workers as *means* to be manipulated or adjusted to impersonal ends. The belief in man as an end in himself has been ground under by the machine, and the social science of the factory researchers is not a science of man, but a cow-sociology."[39]

This charge, although serious, should be tempered by appreciation of the fact that the experiments were guided by the scientific method which is not *in itself* subject to modification by political or economic values.[40]

What should be of concern is whether the *interpretation* of the experiments is colored by biases not clearly revealed to the reader. Evidence for such bias can be found. For example, Roethlisberger and Dickson propose that there are two major parts to the social organization of industry, a formal organization and an informal organization. These we are told exist for both managers and employees. The formal organization refers to patterns of interaction prescribed by the rules, regulations, and policies of the company. (Note that a formal organization of workers is ignored.) In the formal organization of management the logics of cost and efficiency are said to apply. The logic of cost refers to the system of ideas and beliefs by means of which the common economic *purposes* of the total organization are evaluated. The logic of efficiency refers to ideas and beliefs by which the *efforts* of the members of the organization are evaluated.

The informal organization refers to all personal relationships which are not represented by the formal organization. Although the informal organization is known to exist among both managers and employee groups, no

[39] Daniel Bell, *op. cit.*, p. 88.
[40] George A. Lundberg, "Sociology Versus Dialectical Materialism," *American Journal of Sociology*, September, 1947, pp. 85-95.

data is made available on the informal organization of managers. (But a great mass of data for informal organization among employees was gathered.) In the informal organization of workers the logic of sentiments in contrast to the logics of cost and efficiency is supposed to dominate. It is explained that the logic of sentiments grows from feelings and emotions derived by values held by members of the informal organization. The only data given on feelings and emotions are those made available for worker groups. The implication that emerges, whether intended or not, is that managers are guided by a logic of reason whereas workers are largely creatures of feelings and emotions. From the test room to the interviewing program and on to the bank wiring observation room the researchers are amazed that workers have feelings and emotions that contradict the logics of management—namely, cost and efficiency. It is implied that they are acting on sentiment; management men on logic. It does not seem to appear to Mayo and his colleagues that the social organization of a factory contains diverse and conflicting *interests* and that real differences in "logic" are held with as cold rationale among workers as among managers. Indeed, as Miss Gilson stated, the area of conflicting interest is so completely skirted that almost nothing appears anywhere to indicate that the workers ever considered or even talked about a labor organization!

Evidence of a pro-management bias appears in the repeated emphasis on social skills to improve production. This oriented-like management view makes it impossible for Mayo to conceive of other ends. Thus, social skills become good since he relates the achievement of social skills to the improvement of production and the maintenance of the *status quo*. All conflict, including war, can only be seen as the absence of social skills. Again, Mayo's inability to see a conflict of interest in a dynamic society involves him in a limited perspective. The "logics" of his world remain so fixed upon management goals that he is shocked to find the new world is full of "emotional" or "radical" ideas. If Mayo could remove his glasses he might find that these revolutionary currents are not moved in the absence of social skills but with a high degree of coldly calculating social skill.

2. The Clinical Bias

The second bias grows from Mayo's view of the scientific method. He claims that the "scientific method has two parts, represented in medicine by the clinic and the laboratory. The two are interdependent, the one unfruitful without the other. The characteristic of the clinic is careful and patient attention to a complex situation any part of which may suddenly discover unanticipated importance; that of the laboratory is experiment and logical construction. . . . Observation—skill—experiment and logic—these must be regarded as the three stages of advancement."[41]

[41] Elton Mayo, *The Social Problems of an Industrial Civilization*, pp. 19-20.

Research workers would probably agree with Mayo upon inclusion of these steps within scientific method, but they would certainly want to relate theory and accumulated knowledge to any research undertaking. Of theory Mayo has acquired a high disdain. He says, "Science did not begin with elaborate and overwhelming systems and thence proceed to study the facts." On the contrary, the researcher is urged just to gain "intimate, habitual, intuitive familiarity with things."[42]

A careful reader of *Management and the Worker* will come to wonder what happened to teammate Roethlisberger, who wrote such heresy as: "The point is that observation, if it is to be at all scientific, must be guided by a working hypothesis which enables the observer to make active discriminations in the complex interplay of factors before him. Without such guidance he is likely to miss much of significance and become lost in a welter of irrelevances."[43]

This view places research back into a theoretical setting, for it is patent that no hypothesis should be investigated until a thorough knowledge of previous theory and research effort has been examined. Not so obvious but nonetheless essential is the need to know all theory relevant to the problem in order to pose a fruitful hypothesis. Failure to grasp these essentials has led the sociologist Wilbert Moore to write,

Professor Mayo's views as to the proper course of social science inquiry may be most succinctly summarized as radical empiricism. This position rests on two fundamental misunderstandings: (1) The author is ignorant of the role of theory in social research. Rather, he advocates amassing observations, apparently at random. At no place does he indicate how it is that one knows where to begin observing the infinite phenomena of the universe. (2) He is ignorant of the difference between science and technology, and thus is insensitive to problems of ends or values. He pleads for knowledge of the techniques of cooperation, which will settle all issues from those in industry to those in international affairs. Cooperation, toward what goals, with what inducements, under whose direction, with what safeguards for participants? The direction and use of research in industry is not so simple as in the case of medicine, to which the author frequently and mistakenly refers as a science rather than as a useful art.[44]

Mayo's ignorance and disdain of theory lead him to proclaim a new educational method, which he explains by making a false bifurcation between knowing and doing. He talks of knowledge-about and knowledge-of-acquaintance. Knowledge-about is the product of reflective and abstract thinking; knowledge-of-acquaintance comes from direct experience of fact and situation. In essence, there has been too much knowledge-about, not

[42] *Ibid.*, p. 18.
[43] F. J. Roethlisberger and W. J. Dickson, *op. cit.*, p. 389.
[44] Wilbert Moore, review of Elton Mayo, *The Social Problems of an Industrial Civilization*, in *American Sociological Review*, February, 1947, p. 123.

enough knowledge-of-acquaintance. What is needed is to give students direct experience because, it is argued, knowledge-about does not develop useful and effective skill. Chemistry, physics, and physiology are proclaimed successful sciences because they take students to a laboratory where they can manipulate equipment and store up knowledge-of-acquaintance.

But the social sciences, sociology, psychology, and political science are labeled "unsuccessful" because they transmit knowledge-about, which does "not seem to equip students with a single social skill that is usable in ordinary human situations." Mayo seems to forget that men for generations have written that education is power because great ideas have given men and women social skills of unparalleled significance. It is knowledge-about that lights the way and gives meaning to every facet of human living. Moreover, since the world to which modern man must adjust is increasingly a symbolic environment, it follows that knowledge-of-acquaintance comes also by reading, listening, talking, and doing.

It is a new and limited view which holds as Mayo does that the training of a student in social science begins with crude experience. He says,

> There is no way of dealing effectively with these international or intranational situations other than the way that all the sciences have trod. The first step is the patient, pedestrian development of "firsthand knowledge" or "knowledge-of-acquaintance." The second step is that of the administrator, the clinician, the artisan—intimate acquaintance with the facts gives rise to skill in handling them. The demonstration of an unquestionably effective skill is immensely important, for it provides the justification, and at first the only justification for the third step. The third step is the clear statement, for laboratory, test and development, of the logical implications of the effective skill. All skill—administrator, clinician, artisan—is based upon the capacity of the operator to select from the mass of facts offered for his inspection two or three that are especially significant for action in the situation.[45]

In this statement it can be seen how this radical empiricism cast loose from theory is proposed not only as a research method but as an educational method. Mayo, unfortunately, misinterprets progressive education when he sees the laboratory as the beginning of knowledge. "The first really important training of a student of physics, chemistry, or medicine," he says, "is in the clinic and laboratory; it is thus that he develops intuitive familiarity with the materials of his study and manipulative capacity with respect to these materials. Only upon the basis of skill thus acquired can he build a systematic logic and slowly acquire the further insight that a developed science gives him."[46]

This statement is not only poor educational method; it is unsafe. Any

[45] Mayo, *op. cit.*, p. 115.
[46] *Ibid.*, pp. 15-16.

teacher of chemistry who took his students to the laboratory without carefully explaining the pertinent facts regarding the behavior of the chemicals involved would be exposing the students to serious risks. There are first things to do before gaining intimate familiarity with things. The initial steps, from the standpoint of health and learning, require instruction in the behavior of matter and the best theoretical research explanations for that behavior. Only then can the student observe fruitfully and relate observations meaningfully to larger frames of reference. This is as true in human relations as in chemical relations. However, Professor Roethlisberger has taken an opposite view. In a recent article he defines the outlines of a "new" field, which he names "human relations." It is a field dealing with problems in the spirit and method of science but divorced from science. He writes that *"human relations"* has no "principles." "It is a clinical approach, and in the development of 'science' generally *precedes* the experimental or laboratory orientation. It leads to skills of diagnosis and judgment derived from long experience and intuitive familiarity with the facts. . . . Just what are *these* holy and sacred entities for which each author seeks and which at times are made to appear as the only justification for practice? In modern science, principles like all the other holies—theories, generalizations, and so on—are subordinate to facts. . . . What is needed is more practice of human relations skills and less talk about verbal principles."[47]

There is no dispute with Professors Mayo and Roethlisberger over the need to develop social skills. The clinical approach is a mature test for the well-trained man. The modern medical student is permitted to engage in clinical work only after many years of training in the basic physical and biological sciences. Surely most human problems are as complex as most health problems. The argument then, is all over the effective way to develop the skills of social diagnosis, prognosis, and administration. Social scientists and educators have fairly well agreed that knowledge and skill walk hand in hand. The best-tested area of knowledge is scientific knowledge. Such knowledge grows in both pure and applied sciences and represents the accumulated experience of mankind. Unless this is to be thrown out as a collective body of wasted effort, it must be used. The principles are as useful as they are relevant to the realities which they assert. For men who assert that human relations can develop only "simple theories and hypotheses" Mayo and Roethlisberger have laid down an amazing number of principles. Those tested principles of group formation and collaboration which have emerged from the Harvard Industrial Research Department now take their place in the larger body of social science. Here as well as in business admin-

[47] F. J. Roethlisberger, "Human Relations: Rare, Medium or Well Done?" *Harvard Business Review*, January, 1948, pp. 89-107.

istration they will continue to challenge research workers, businessmen, and students for many years to come.

SUPPLEMENTARY STUDIES

LIBRARY: BOOKS AND ARTICLES

1. Read the following criticisms of the Mayo-Roethlisberger researches:

    Bell, Daniel, "Exploring Factory Life," *Commentary*, January, 1947, pp. 79-88.

    Bendix, Reinhard, "Primitism, Authority, and Human Relations," *Proceedings of the Pacific Sociological Society*, March, 1949, pp. 29-34.

    "Deep Therapy on the Assembly Line," *Ammunition*, The Magazine of the United Auto Workers, C.I.O., April, 1949, pp. 47-51.

    Gilson, Mary B., "Review of *Management and the Worker*," *American Journal of Sociology*, July, 1940, pp. 98-101.

    Hart, C. W. M., "Industrial Relations Research and Social Theory," *Canadian Journal of Economics and Political Science*, February, 1949, pp. 53-73.

    C. Wright Mills, "The Contribution of Sociology to Studies of Industrial Relations," *Proceedings of the Industrial Relations Research Association*, December, 1948, pp. 199-222.

    Moore, Wilbert E., "Review of E. Mayo, *The Social Problems of an Industrial Civilization*," *American Sociological Review*, February, 1947, pp. 123.

    Sheppard, Harold L., "The Treatment of Unionism in 'Managerial Sociology,'" *American Sociological Review*, April, 1949, pp. 310-313.

2. Read Elton Mayo and George F. F. Lombard, *Teamwork and Labor Turnover in the Aircraft Industry of Southern California*, Harvard University Graduate School of Business Administration, 1944. Graduate students should examine carefully the research questions indicated by Mayo on p. 29. These research questions could become the basis of valuable graduate theses in industrial sociology.

3. For a review of American research in industrial sociology as evaluated by a British point of view see "The Human Factor in Industry," *Political and Economic Planning*, March 5, 1948, pp. 249-267.

CHAPTER IV

The Educational Training of an Industrial Sociologist

THE PURPOSES OF INDUSTRIAL SOCIOLOGY

The field of industrial sociology can be at once a base to nourish general education and a training ground for specialists. It is not unusual to find students assembled in introductory courses in industrial sociology for at least three different reasons. There are some who wish to pursue such a course of study in order to broaden their knowledge and understanding of work behavior. These students come from curricula emphasizing the general education of the student.

A second group is perhaps searching for specialized training that may be applied to later occupational pursuit in a personnel, labor, or managerial post. These students are particularly anxious to find practical tests and techniques that will enable them to sell their services more readily to the industrial world.

Members of a third group may have determined that they will seek to enter industry and wish to secure their basic training in sociology. Their interest is both broad and specific. They desire to increase their knowledge and understanding of work behavior but at the same time want to know what specific contributions and challenges are offered by industrial sociology as a specialized branch of sociology. Teachers soon come to realize that three purposes are constantly operating as expectations in students. They become evident as demands for both general education and specialized training. Students expressing these demands will ordinarily come to the teacher as majors in sociology, psychology, economics, or business administration. The teacher, if he is to satisfy these felt needs, must somehow furnish the intellectual food which will either resolve the different interests or supply the required materials. This is not an easy problem and it grows no easier as general education and vocational-professional education try to live together in the same ferment. It is important, therefore, for the teacher to locate the different expectations of the students and come to terms with them.

The writers of this book are teachers. They have been stimulated to develop a course which could be of greatest value to all their students. This has required some fundamental decisions about learning, personal growth, and professional practice. In the first place, it is presumed that the aims of the student, whether general or specific, will be met in part by an explanation of the social structure and processes which characterize work plants and work behavior. This decision rests upon the belief that mature judgment in the future worker, citizen, or specialist requires the fullest awareness of all the pertinent uniformities which characterize social phenomena in work activity. In other words, in an introductory course which at best can only be preprofessional in nature the aims of general education must become the central guide. However, this does not limit the course content and requirements to reading or listening. On the contrary, the use of observational instruments, interviewing, sociodramatic performance tests, and role-playing methods of leadership training can be utilized to introduce the student not only to basic uniformities in work behavior but also to methods which are distinct contributions of sociology and valuable instruments in industrial practice. At the end of some of the chapters the attention of the student and teacher is directed to specific projects and also to relatively unexplored areas of research. It has been our experience as teachers that the combining of reading, lecture, and observational material pro-

vides for the full development of the student and meets the different expectations which are brought to the industrial sociology classroom.

THE CURRICULUM FOR THE TRAINING OF AN INDUSTRIAL SOCIOLOGIST

There is no single curriculum approved for the training of persons interested in industrial relations or in industrial sociology specifically. Each university will have offerings with more or less application to industrial relations. Some have specially designated industrial relations curricula and faculty brought together in an industrial relations center. Others offer courses in the separate departments of the university. In any event there is a growing consensus that the resources of at least four major social sciences

	Lower Division: Basic Training	Upper Division: Specialized Courses	Graduate Division: Specialized Courses
BUSINESS ADMINISTRATION	Introduction to Business Administration	Human Relations in Business and Industry Personnel Management	Seminars in Human Relations and Personnel Management
ECONOMICS	Introduction to Economics	Labor in the Economy Union-Management Relations American Labor History	Seminars in Labor Relations, in Labor Economics, and in Distribution Theory
PSYCHOLOGY	General Psychology	Vocational Psychology Industrial Psychology	Occupational Analysis Employment Psychology Proficiency Training Industrial Training Motivation and Morale in Industry
SOCIOLOGY	Survey of Sociology	Industrial Sociology Social Adjustment of the Worker Industry and Community	Industrial Sociology seminars
ANTHROPOLOGY	Principles of Anthropology	Early Economic Systems Primitive Social and Economic Institutions	Seminars
GENERAL STUDIES	Courses from above fields	Courses from above fields This is required	

FIG. 14.   Curricula for the Study of Industrial Relations at the University of Washington.

should be utilized. These are sociology, economics, psychology, and anthropology. Professional formulation and practice of human relations in industry takes place in three areas. These are administration, personnel relations, and labor relations. Wherever applied courses are found that relate to these functions, managerial or specialist training can be obtained. Courses in these areas are most often offered in a college of business administration, although labor courses may be found in economics, political science, and sociology as well.

Figure 14 shows the six common pathways to the study of industrial relations at the University of Washington. Here a student may elect to enroll as a major in sociology, economics, psychology, anthropology, business administration, or in the industrial relations curriculum of the general studies program. The undergraduate on the lower division seeks broad, general training in his major and in as many allied fields as he may elect. This gives him a range of points of view and body of knowledge which are basic to any of the specific or applied courses that he may wish to take when he reaches upper division standing. This level offers him an opportunity to enroll in courses directly concerned with human behavior in industry. The requirements of his major become the student's first consideration, but he is encouraged to seek the greatest possible training in the special courses of the allied fields. Some students find that the general studies program offers them an opportunity for a greater breadth of training since they take all of the special courses in industrial relations. This is facilitated by the withdrawing of certain curricular demands that are made upon students who major in a given field. These students undoubtedly gain in breadth; they possibly lose something by the lack of concentrated training in one field. Each student in every field must be carefully guided in terms of his interest, capacity, and vocational goal.

The graduate school offers advanced study and research training in business administration, sociology, economics, psychology, and anthropology. Theoretical and research attacks upon advanced problems constitute the core of graduate training.

The curricula of the University of Washington have been used as examples of the pathways which students take when they are interested in studying industrial relations. Undoubtedly, most of these pathways are open to students in all American colleges and universities. Whatever differences there are in the quality of training available will most often be located in the quality of faculty and not in any particular arrangement of curricula.

THE METHOD OF INDUSTRIAL SOCIOLOGY

THE APPLICATION OF SCIENTIFIC METHOD TO INDUSTRIAL BEHAVIOR

Industrial sociology is a sector within the larger field of social science. Therefore, an industrial sociologist is first of all a social scientist. He shares the belief of all social scientists that the problems which confront a society

can best be solved by systematic observation, verification, classification, and interpretation of social phenomena. In his search for "answers" he sets up working hypotheses and attempts to find underlying uniformities which may eventually be applied to predict kinds of social behavior under given conditions.[1] Lundberg puts it this way: "Science, then, is fundamentally a technique of deriving reliable knowledge about any type of phenomena in the universe and then applying this derived knowledge for the purposes of prediction and control."[2]

Within industry the scientific habit of thought, especially about personnel and industrial relations, has not penetrated very far. A typical attitude is that people are unpredictable and that a science of human behavior does not now exist and cannot conceivably be established. Another mind-set which is in contradiction to science may be described as belief in the uniqueness of every situation. It is a common saying that you must always consider every problem a unique case. Such thinking tends deliberately to ignore the knowledge which has accumulated about *similar* problems. The so-called practical man often feels he has risen to new effectiveness by depreciating the theory which other men have tested on similar observations. If scientific knowledge is cast aside, then reliance is placed upon the unique intuitive experiences of a single individual. Although a seasoned woodsman may become quite an "expert" in predicting the next day's weather by the drifting smoke of his campfire, the weather forecaster with his larger store of accumulated knowledge and more rigorous observations can easily excel in the accuracy of his predictions. The weather forecaster builds his score of correct predictions to a more accurate level by comparing the "unique" weather conditions of a given day with the kinds of weather which have *uniformly occurred* in the past as a consequence of such *similar* conditions. In so doing he cuts down time and effort. Training in science even as it grows longer is still a shorter and more accurate training than the experiencing of uniqueness which is required to build intuition. In spite of these superiorities of science, deprecation of scientific knowledge and theory about social behavior by so-called practical men in industry continues as one of the larger obstacles to the advance of science in industrial relations. And belief in intuition grows as deficiencies in scientific knowledge are revealed. In many important areas of social behavior in industry the social scientist must frankly confess that he does not have a store of scientific knowledge to draw upon. This is largely because of the relative newness of social science; it is partly due to the difficulty which the scientist has in gaining entry into industry to conduct scientific investigations. Like the administrator who equally lacks scientific knowledge the scientist must

[1] Cf. George C. Homans, "The Strategy of Industrial Sociology," *American Journal of Sociology*, January, 1949, pp. 330-337.
[2] George A. Lundberg, *Social Research*, Longmans, Green and Company, 1942, p. 5.

begin with intuition or a hunch. Here the analogy ends, for the scientist calls his hunch a working hypothesis. He is not preoccupied with what he considers a unique case. On the contrary, he begins to search for uniformities, to compare similarities and differences of the case with those of other cases he has observed, and finally to record any generalization which may be applicable to future cases. When he succeeds he transmits a segment of knowledge which has been tested under given conditions with such rigor that it can be verified by *anyone* who repeats the methods of observation and measurement that have been carefully recorded. The need for more knowledge about the constants of work behavior is apparent. Problems of human relations must be solved. No other method has the accuracy and power inherent in the scientific method. The increasing application of science may be expected to reap rewards as great in human relations as in the older natural sciences. In this advance industrial sociology should assume a large responsibility.

STEPS IN THE DEVELOPMENT OF INDUSTRIAL SOCIOLOGY

The industrial sociologist, we have said, is first of all a scientist. The scientific method requires that he follow certain well-defined steps when he is investigating any problem. These may be defined as:

1. Setting up a working hypothesis.
2. Observing and recording data.
3. Classifying and organizing data collected.
4. Drawing generalizations.
5. Verifying by repeated experimentation.[3]

These steps become distinguished by the scientist through the degree of rigorousness which he imposes over all of the steps. The steps tend to become equally applicable as his guides to thought and appraisal of his formal procedures in the laboratory. Every student can equally strive to improve his thinking so that it tends to conform to the scientific method of thought even though he should never perform a scientific experiment.

The steps in the scientific procedure can be much more easily explained and taught than can the *art* of scientific research. This *art*, like any other, requires high imagination and originality.

Inquiry—The Art of Raising Questions

From imagination and originality the art of raising questions originates. Inquiry is the first step in the growth of any research project, and the excellence of the contribution will depend in large part on what question was raised and how it was asked. This precious skill of raising questions does not spring from sheer intelligence. On the contrary, the best questions are raised when there is a large mastery of accumulated thought and research.

[3] Cf. *ibid.*, p. 9.

In fact, originality and imagination become valuable to the advancement of research only as they represent leaps away from the accumulated body of knowledge. The second step in the growth of a research project is appraisal of the literature. Perhaps others have raised the same question and designed an experiment or formulated a theory to provide an answer. When appraisal is complete the researcher is ready to state his working hypothesis and plan his procedure for testing it.

Four Levels of Observation

Four levels or degrees of rigorousness may be utilized in making observations:

1. The first level might be called *common-sense observation*. The observer looks around in areas where he believes he may find events which will serve as evidence. He takes with him the everyday concepts of folk language and records what he sees in "simple" language. This gives him an account which can be easily understood by others but it lacks the precision and insight into social processes that can be transmitted clearly only by a more rigorous body of concepts. This common-sense level is the one which the layman uses constantly to gather information. In the hands of a literary artist it reaches its highest development. The penetrating social insight of a superb novelist can furnish many fruitful hypotheses and illustrations of social process. But, again, the difficulties of this level as seen by a scientist are the limitations upon precision, interpretation, and verifiability. The literary artist or the layman can tell what occurred as he saw it but he usually is not able to describe the fundamental why or explain the method by which his observation may be verified. His attention has been preoccupied by the uniqueness of the case and has not caught the uniformities.

2. A second level or degree of rigorousness is achieved by *systematic or conceptual observation*. The observer asks in advance how his observations may be most meaningfully discerned and recorded. He defines explicitly the units of observation in such a way that other observers may be able to use them with a high degree of reliability and validity. He checks to see that his observations are made upon a representative sample of cases within a carefully designated population. This level is of greater aid to scientific advance because it supplies data that may reveal uniformities and patterns of deviation. The resulting report is open to independent verification because by following the method originally used subsequent observations may be made and checked against the first. The research methods commonly used at this level include interviewing or observing of "cases" and use of simple observation schedules.

3. A third level may be described as *measured observation*. The observer uses mathematical language to aid him in making precise quantitative measurements of his observations. He usually develops or uses a standardized

sociometric scale or he may utilize carefully defined units of measurement such as have been constructed for observation in human ecology, sociometry, or public opinion analysis. Often he will develop or use a standardized sociometric scale in order to increase his ability to record not only the presence of social data but the intensity of the data in standardized units.

4. The most rigorous level of observation is the *social experiment conducted under strictly controlled conditions*. The objective of the social experiment is to observe the effect of one or more independent variables upon a dependent variable or criterion. Thus, in the relay assembly test room perhaps the first social experiment in industry was performed. The dependent variable was output; the independent variables were rest periods, hot mid-morning lunch, and shortened working hours. Great care was taken to exclude all other variables that appeared to have some possibility of interfering with the relationship of the chosen independent variables. In the test room what was hoped for did not occur. No relationship in output could be shown to be due to the independent variables alone. Rather, the new *esprit de corps* of the group proved an "interference" that could not be removed.

Although it was apparently not possible at the Hawthorne plant, the ideal design for a social experiment includes the use of a control group as well as an experimental group. The aim is to equalize the controls over both groups but withhold the introduction of the independent variable of treatment from the control group. If effects of the independent variable are observable in the experimental group and no similar effects are observed in the control group, it follows that such effects are probably due to the independent variable of treatment.

The social experiment requires carefully defined units of measurement, and these are in best form when standardized scales are used. Such scales should have high reliability and validity in order to secure precise and accurate measurements.[4]

Validation and Prediction

If science is to move forward to its greatest advances the social experiment must be repeated under the given conditions often enough so that its results are shown to be valid beyond any question of doubt. In agricultural experimentation, for example, it is a common practice to repeat the testing of seeds and fertilizers under given conditions to determine their qualities. The chemical researcher is quick to repeat new experiments which are reported in his field. Increasingly, the social experimenter is learning the lesson of repeating the significant social experiments that have been reported.

[4] See F. Stuart Chapin, *Experimental Designs in Sociological Research*, Harper & Brothers, 1947.

When valid results are available the factors which are related to important social criteria may be set up into a prediction scale.

With the effect of independent factors accurately determined, weights can be assigned and the probability of occurrence of future acts within the criterion may be predicted with a stated accuracy. Sociologists have learned how to predict the individual probability of success or failure of probation or parole. The prediction of the probability of success or failure in marriage is an achievement of family sociologists. The prediction of morale and job satisfaction has been accomplished by industrial sociologists.

THE STUDENT AND RESEARCH

The student of industrial sociology is introduced in this book to the methods which social scientists use in their work. At the end of some of the chapters the student will find projects which he is encouraged to undertake. Instruments of observation and interview have been developed for his use. He will observe that most of these represent early steps in scientific development. If the student will utilize these experiences, they will provide him with practice in the scientific method of thinking and give him the early training which he needs for any future growth in industrial sociology.

EDUCATIONAL ORIENTATION OF THE STUDENT OF INDUSTRIAL SOCIOLOGY

THE ROLE OF THEORY AND PRACTICE

A student of industrial sociology must clarify for himself the role which theory and practice shall play in his education. If he fails to do this, he will find himself caught in a confusion of motives and cross-purposes that will weaken his efforts to grow. This problem can easily exist because the controversial muddle over theory and practice is so prevalent in industry and in education that the student is almost certain at some time to be in the middle of it.

L. Urwick, the Director of the International Management Institute at Geneva, Switzerland, says:

One of the greatest obstacles to the creation of any really satisfactory scheme for the training of future business leaders is the persistence of an artificial distinction between what is called "theoretical" and what is called "practical." This is largely due to the character of the change which comes in a student's life, when he leaves school or college and "goes out into the world." The moment is dramatized, both to the student and by his new superiors. He is thus led to distinguish sharply between his academic life and his new experiences. Because, in the majority of cases, examinations are behind him, he is only too prone to imagine that the whole standards and apparatus of conscious intellectual endeavor should be jettisoned. The illiteracy of many successful business men

in their own subject is remarkable. They are successful despite it—not because of it. But they help to maintain the myth that there is a dividing line—on one side of it "practical" life and on the other the "mere theories" of schoolmen. And as long as that myth persists it will be impossible to treat the subject of training for leadership as it should be treated—namely, as a whole, including both the academic education of those concerned and the earlier stages of their careers in business.[5]

This hiatus poses a severe problem for the teacher. The myth of division between theory and practice prejudices not only the attitudes of his students but also those of business and union leaders with whom he seeks to develop closer academic ties. But this is not the end of the dilemma. It intrudes in still another way. Urwick says:

The tendency towards the specialization of function within the structure of business . . . places the educationalist in a dilemma. In a practical world his pupils expect to leave him equipped to start earning a livelihood immediately. On the other hand, in a world which is also competitive that demand tends to emphasize a form of training which is itself highly specialized and vocational in character. The young graduate must possess a store of marketable knowledge adequate to enable him to fill a subordinate position in some single one of the many sharply differentiated functions of a modern business.

At the same time the "educationalist," if he is worthy of the name, knows very well that such vocational training if carried to extremes, is, whatever its immediate utility, unlikely to be the most suitable form of education taking the long view. Whatever the proficiency of his pupil in the immediate field it will have been dearly bought unless at the same time he has acquired a balanced view of the general contribution of other departments of knowledge to the common stock, not to mention intellectual habits which will enable him to approach tasks outside his own special field with intelligence and insight.[6]

Two forces can be seen to press down hard upon the teacher. The myth that divides theory and practice into separate compartments prejudices thought and action. Theory is castigated by so-called practical men. The student is thus led to believe he is being forced to attend to "impractical stuff" and demands a more "practical" approach. This demand becomes reinforced by the awareness that he must have a "store of marketable knowledge" which is vocational in character if he wishes to get a "good" job in industry. Both of these demands are based on short-run considerations. It is important for the student to understand that these demands are short-run considerations and represent a poorer educational investment than one which stresses the fullest development of outlook and a working acquaintance with industrial functions other than the one he may first come to perform. In order to see this clearly it is desirable to describe the nature of this clash between theory and practice.

[5] L. Urwick, *Management of Tomorrow*, Nisbet and Company, Ltd., 1933, pp. 165-166.
[6] *Ibid.*, pp. 164-165.

THE CLASH BETWEEN THEORY AND PRACTICE

1. How the "Practical" Man Views Theory and Practice

The "practical" man is for our purposes an ideally constructed type. He may be found anywhere in institutional life but usually is a product of the business institution. He represents a special philosophy of practicality. He views certain ideas and labels them theoretical and impractical for one or more of the following reasons:

1. Their application makes them too costly.
2. They overlook the unique conditions of a given situation.
3. Their application will not yield a profit.
4. They are untried.
5. They are not easily understood by a "practical" man.
6. They failed to work in another situation.

If these reasons are examined carefully, it is easy to see that ideas become "practical" as they are considered to be immediately useful. Usefulness means they must meet criteria of cost, specificity, profitability, workability, and understandability. In other words, they must meet the strictly defined patterns of thought prevalent in business institutions at a given time.

2. How the Man of Knowledge Views Theory and Practice

The man of knowledge is again, for our purposes, an ideally constructed type. He may be found in industry, in government, and in educational institutions. He views ideas neither as theoretical nor as practical. His unwillingness to separate ideas into two compartments grows out of a belief that ideas which fit observed or carefully stated conditions represent sound theory and those that fail this test constitute bad theory and should be discarded. He is continually searching for some underlying uniformity, for some principle. He believes that by examining all ideas that fit stated conditions he has a power of analysis and comparison enabling him to consider new approaches to problems and to have a wider appreciation of the consequences of action. He is convinced that this emphasis upon the principles of social relationships promises a fuller development of leadership ability, whether such ability is employed in industry, social service, public service, or any one of the 7,000,000 executive positions of leadership in the United States.

Practical ideas are, in this context, seen to be those which fit *some* theoretical framework. Thus, all self-styled "practical" men embrace *a theory* whether they acknowledge it or not. All too often they are unaware that their ideas are embedded in a theory and have failed to consider the origin, history, and implications of their theory. Such endeavor is, of course, pre-

sumed to be "impractical" because a practical man accepts the thoughtways of institutions as he finds them.

3. How This Hiatus Between the Practical Man and the Man of Knowledge Develops

The practical man develops his thinking by *direct* experience with many events and problems within a given institutional setting.[7] Elton Mayo likes to call this knowledge-of-acquaintance. The man of knowledge relies more heavily upon mastery of accumulated knowledge, or knowledge-about. He is thus removed from the on-the-spot experiences of the "practical" man. Table 3 shows the differences in the knowledge, experience, and thinking of

TABLE 3. The Contrasting Characteristics of the Man of Knowledge and the Practical Man

	The Man of Knowledge	The Practical Man
Content	Principles and Concepts	Specific cases, routines, and established techniques.
How acquired	Theoretical and scientific investigation. Innovative, unorthodox, abstract thinking.	Practical experience, drill in routines, and special skills. Routine, orthodox, concrete, intuitive thinking.
Advantages	Increases power to see all cases in perspective. Awakens new possibilities. Principles can be acquired with relative rapidity.	Easier to understand. More immediately useful. Provides quick and skillful appraisal of a concrete situation.
Disadvantages	Often fails to be immediately applicable. Often fails to fit the conditions of a given situation.	Limits view and perspective. Relies upon lengthy accumulation of intuitive experience.

these two social types. Note how the man of knowledge is filled with principles and concepts as he acquires scientific knowledge, whereas the practical man absorbs the lessons of specific cases and builds up routines and established techniques. The resultant thinking tends to be distinguished in the man of knowledge by the display of innovative, unorthodox, abstract thinking, and in the practical man by routine, orthodox, intuitive, and concrete thinking. Each has certain skills and certain weaknesses. The man of knowledge has a wider range of perspective and can bring more facts to bear upon the problem but he may not be able to understand or appreciate the limitations of his views under limiting conditions. The practical man does not lack this appreciation. He has learned through practical experience the kinds of action which fit the thoughtways of a given structure. He has

[7] Cf. William E. Henry, "The Business Executive: The Psychodynamics of a Social Role," *American Journal of Sociology*, January, 1949, p. 290.

acquired and perfected many routine and special skills which apply to given situations. His power lies in his ability to appraise and execute programs or techniques on immediate problems. However, the very experience which provides this ability may limit the materials upon which to gain wider views and richer alternatives to action.

Ideally, every man should combine the best qualities of knowledge and experience. But specialization of function makes this difficult. In the field of education the schism is brought into sharp focus by our system in which the student is supposed to be educated by a relatively long period of isolation in the academic world and then the gaining of practical experience in later stages of his life. The intermingling of work and academic life requires an interpenetration of business and education which has never been encouraged to the point that a comprehensive revision could be effected. Urwick points out that "the educationalist must content himself with the present bisected system, where the student sits like Humpty Dumpty on an academic wall till the end of his school or university career, and then falls with a crash into practical life only too frequently, alas, to renounce its intellectual consideration for evermore. But the educationalist would be wise to keep in mind the possibility of a more balanced arrangement."[8]

4. How This Hiatus Between the Man of Knowledge and the Practical Man Leads to Conflict

The difficulty of the present system is that it induces tensions both in business and in education. They become particularly acute as business makes demands for educational products that fit its immediate needs. The tension may be diagrammed something like this:

	Men of Knowledge	Liberally Educated, Specialists	Men of Specialized and Routine Skills
Industry: Goals of efficient, satisfied workers	Wants few of these	Wants a limited pool of leadership potential	Wants a great number of these. Urges the development of vocational and technical training
TENSION			
Education: Goals of personality development and citizenship training	Wants to produce a maximum number of these	Wants to produce a great number	Terminates or sets up a special curriculum for these. Tries to develop meaningful general education as far as possible

[8] L. Urwick, op. cit., p. 173.

The goal of industry is to obtain productive, satisfied workers. The goal of education is to develop the person in the fullest sense of the term, as worker, parent, and citizen. The result is that industry puts a high premium upon effective skill and satisfied workmanship for it needs a large population with such qualities. It wants a core of leaders who combine knowledge and practice. Strict men of knowledge are commonly called "geniuses" in industry. Few "geniuses" are required, and such as are employed are placed in laboratories or isolated offices. Education, on the other hand, is busy trying to produce as many "geniuses" as it can. They are ordinarily rare, and the institution proceeds to work with what it has but tries to produce the highest level of liberally educated persons. It encourages extracurricular activity, part-time work, field trips, specialized courses, laboratory work, and other kinds of activity to build practical experience. For those who show themselves incapable of development except by improvement of routine skills curricula are developed and made available.

HOW THE SCHISM BETWEEN THEORY AND PRACTICE INTRUDES INTO EDUCATIONAL AND RESEARCH METHOD

Both the educational and the business institution have tried to find a common solution to the problem of equipping students with work experience to accompany their classroom experiences. The failure to make much headway on this problem has intensified the pressure from students and employers for a more "practical" curriculum and method. Elton Mayo has proposed what he calls the clinical approach and what the Harvard Business School calls the case method of teaching in order to train students in effective skills. Case studies represent interesting and efficient devices when used to illustrate principles. However, Roethlisberger says there are no *principles* of human relations. He claims that "what is needed is more practice of *human relations* skill and less talk about verbal principles."[9] In proposing to rid the groves of academicia of purely verbal abstraction it appears that he would throw out the baby along with the bath. Let us investigate the thought processes by which "cases" effectuate new skills.

John Dewey has stated that "all reflective thinking is a process of detecting relations; . . . good thinking is not contented with finding 'any old kind of relation' but searches until a relation is found that is as accurately defined as conditions permit."[10]

He states that the flow of reflective thinking involves:

1. A felt difficulty
2. Its location and definition
3. Suggestion of possible solutions

[9] F. J. Roethlisberger, "Human Relations: Rare, Medium or Well Done?" *Harvard Business Review*, January, 1948, p. 107.

[10] John Dewey, *How We Think*, D. C. Heath and Company, 1933, p. 77.

4. Development by reasoning of the bearings of the suggestions
5. Further observation and experiment leading to its acceptance or rejection.[11]

If we trace through the case method of instruction in human relations we can identify the steps which must be taken if the case is to provide a genuine exercise in reflective thinking. The student is trained to look at problem cases with an objective point of view. No judgment of moral rightness or wrongness is to intrude. After the difficulty is located and the facts of the problem are determined, the student begins to locate the causes of the difficulty. He relies upon his *accumulated store of knowledge* as it pertains to similar cases which he has encountered. He considers the trouble spots which he has come to observe repeat with regularity under certain conditions. Now, he turns over in his mind various solutions to the problem. As he does so he must consider *why* the problem arose and *what possible consequences* each of his proposed solutions may have. At this point all knowledge-of-acquaintance and knowledge-about must be brought into play. Here excellence of thought depends upon the range of scientific knowledge. The student who has the largest and best-organized store of sociology, economics, psychology, and anthropology combined with experience in reflective observation of similar problems is armed with the richest body of understanding to direct upon the problem. The poorly trained student has only unsystematic folk experiences to rely upon and these are often highly unreliable.

Each student will finally submit his solution. If, when this step has been completed, experience is to be a teacher of greater skill, then the solution must be carefully watched to see what the consequences are under the given conditions. Unfortunately, this cannot be done with the case method. However, if real cases have been studied and certain steps were taken to solve the problems, the consequences under the given conditions can be ascertained.

The case method emerges as a teaching device with an effectiveness which depends upon its ability to train the student in the underlying uniformities or principles of social relations as they operate within a concrete situation. If the importance of theory is denied, the student is cast adrift from the experience of men and women who have transmitted their tested and verified observations for the use of mankind.

The objective of this discussion is to stress the role of theory in any practice to gain "social skill." The challenge to the clinical approach is to weld scientific knowledge and practice into the highest level of administrative skill. Whether learning proceeds by lecture, movies, group discussion, case analysis, or any other educational method, its excellence depends upon its

[11] *Ibid.*, p. 72.

ability to provide greater insight and understanding of the social structure of work plants and the social behavior of workers.

THE SCIENTIFIC APPROACH TO THE STUDY OF HUMAN RELATIONS

Science recognizes two major types of inquiry. There is the kind of inquiry that asks only why and has no concern with practical, ethical, or social ideals. This is called pure scientific research.

Applied scientific research is directed toward some practical end. The development of the atomic bomb is often pointed to as a great achievement of engineering made possible by applying scientific research. This invention, like all others, rested upon the achievements of pure research.

The social sciences are like the natural sciences in their quest of pure and applied knowledge. The early American sociologist, Lester Ward, made a clear definition of pure and applied sociology:

By pure sociology, then, is meant a treatment of the phenomena and laws of society as it is, an explanation of the processes by which social phenomena take place, a search for the antecedent conditions by which the observed facts have been brought into existence, and an aetiological diagnosis that shall reach back as far as the state of human knowledge will permit into the psychologic, biologic, and cosmic causes of the existing social state of man. But it must be a pure diagnosis, and all therapeutic treatment is rigidly excluded. All ethical considerations . . . must be ignored for the time being, and attention concentrated upon the effort to determine what actually is. Pure sociology has no concern with what society *ought* to be or with any social ideals.

. . . The pure method of treatment keeps aloof from all criticism and all expressions of approval, from all praise or blame, as wholly inapplicable to that which exists of necessity. . . . This strictly objective treatment also necessitates the looking of facts in the face, however ugly they may be. It is no more the part of pure sociology to apologize for the facts, than to extol or condemn them. Still less can it afford to deny what really exists, or attempt to minimize it or explain it away, merely because it is abhorrent to certain refined perceptions of highly developed races.[12]

Just as pure sociology aims to answer the questions, what, why, and how, so applied sociology aims to answer the question, what for? The former deals with facts, causes, and principles, the latter with the object, end, or purpose. The one treats the subject matter of sociology, the other its use. However theoretical pure sociology may be in some of its aspects, applied sociology is essentially practical. It appeals directly to interest. It has to do with social ideals, with ethical considerations, with what ought to be. . . . Applied sociology is not government or politics, nor civic or social reform. It does not apply sociological principles; it seeks only to show how they may be applied. It is a science, not an art. The most that it claims to do is to lay down certain general principles as guides to social and political action. But in this it must be exceedingly cautious. The principles

[12] Lester F. Ward, *Pure Sociology*, The Macmillan Company, 1903.

can consist only of the highest generalizations. They can have only the most general bearing on current events and the popular or burning questions of the hour. The sociologist who undertakes to discuss these, especially to take sides on them, abandons his science and becomes a politician.[13]

These definitions of pure and applied sociology provide the guides to scientific inquiry. When the lines they draw are transgressed, scientific inquiry gives way to social philosophy and social action. This book attempts to take the student along the pathways of science as they lead into sociological problems of industry. *Sociological* problems should not be confused with *social* problems. The first deal with problems of scientific inquiry and the latter with problems requiring social reform. Such division is not picayune. Nor is it ostrich-like. It is a deliberate division of labor made in order that the greatest advance may be accomplished in the solution of the burning questions of social action. Lundberg expressed this point most succinctly when he wrote, "Whatever the immediate practical problems on which scientists find themselves compelled to work, we know that *scientific* inquiry cannot proceed very far without becoming involved in the *general underlying principles governing all behavior, or at least all behavior common to multitudes of particular problems.*"[14]

The industrial sociologist is anxious to be of service to industry and labor in providing knowledge and techniques that may assist in resolving current conflicts. He believes, however, that through scientific inquiry which often seems slow and far from the practical need the most effective advance can be made.

To hold fast to science is difficult. It requires patience and vision. It becomes an exciting adventure only to those who can and will develop these qualities. A special appeal is made to the student of industrial sociology, for ordinarily he comes to this field with high hopes of learning about practical solutions for practical problems. When he finds inquiry and analysis moving along broader and seemingly more detached lines, he is often disillusioned. This discussion was written to prepare (or strengthen) him for the demands made by scientific work in the solution of problems in industry. Every great scientist in the world, regardless of field, knows that out of pure or basic research the large advances in applied research are made possible. This fact is ultimately as important for the practitioner as for the scientist.

A most succinct summary of this point of view is made by T. E. Allbutt: "The man of affairs without science is like the physician who has fallen out of the anatomy and physiology he may once have known; within limits he may be a shrewder and abler practitioner than an academic professor; but this he will be at the cost of being stationary. . . . To principles sooner

---

[13] Lester F. Ward, *Applied Sociology*, Ginn and Company, 1906, pp. 5-6, 9-10.
[14] George A. Lundberg, "Sociology versus Dialectical Materialism," *American Journal of Sociology*, September, 1947, p. 94.

or later, the subtlest craftsman has to bow his head, or be left behind; for, even while his hand is on his tools, by theory contingencies and complications are being detected and eliminated, and processes shortened and economised."[15]

RESEARCH TRAINING OF THE STUDENT

In addition to the classroom, the library, the laboratory, and the field are ordinarily available for research training. For directed use of the library a selected bibliography is appended to almost every chapter of this book. Role playing and interview projects are designed for the sociological laboratory. Observation and interview instruments have been devised for field work. Unexplored areas of research have been designated in order that the student may be challenged now or in the future to undertake the adventure of research into unknown or partially investigated areas of industrial sociology. Whether the motive is only general understanding or ultimately a position as specialist or administrator of social relationships, it is by the highways of library, classroom, laboratory, and field that development of the person comes to its largest promise.

SUPPLEMENTARY STUDIES

LIBRARY

1. Read George A. Lundberg, *Can Science Save Us?* Longmans, Green and Company, 1947, especially chap. 1, 2, 3.
2. Karl Mannheim, *Ideology and Utopia*, Harcourt, Brace, and Company, 1936.

FIELD INTERVIEWS: PLANNED AND CASUAL

3. Arrange an interview with the Dean of Liberal Arts (or his assistant) and also with the Dean of Business Administration. Discuss with each of them how the curricula in their colleges fit the student for occupations in the field of personnel or industrial relations.
4. Arrange an interview with a business executive and ask him what educational training and occupational experience some of his most effective supervisors possess.
5. Casually introduce to a student or older adult group the idea that a liberal education is a better training for a career in business and for general living than a specialized training in an applied business field. Watch for the different ideas that are expressed.

[15] T. E. Allbutt, *On Professional Education*, as quoted by L. Urwick, *op. cit.*

Part Two

THE SOCIAL ORGANIZATION
OF THE WORK PLANT

The people who live and work inside the factory, store, or office become participants in many social groups. They become of necessity members of a social structure and take their place in a work plant society. This society commonly contains a House of Labor and a House of Management. In one sense, all workers live in both houses but their interests and loyalties tend to be concentrated in one direction or the other. Both houses are distinguished by separate and overlapping organizations.

In this section we shall examine in detail the Houses of Management and Labor—their major organizations and their largest problems. We shall be centering our attention on the roles which different people play in the work plant. Finally, we shall try to discover what satisfactions they derive from this fundamental social institution.

CHAPTER V

Work, Workers, and Work Society

AN OVERALL VIEW OF A CONTEMPORARY WORK PLANT

What are the essential characteristics of modern industry? This question is broad and complex. Most persons would find it difficult to answer. They would describe the machines, the policies, and the procedures of the work

plants they were acquainted with. If they failed to discover the universal features of industry which have so drastically altered modern life, their omission would not be uncommon. We all tend to be blind to our immediate environment. Often a person from another culture can see things which the inhabitants fail to observe in their very midst. To get such an outsider's view let us try to imagine the kinds of things a skilled craftsman from the eighteenth century would observe in our industrial culture. He is not totally ignorant of our culture, for he is familiar with our language and some of the elements of modern technology. Let us try to imagine how modern industry might appear through his eyes.

MATERIAL CULTURE AND TECHNICAL ORGANIZATION

Probably the first thing to impress him would be the abundant material culture of industry. He would be amazed at the amount and variability of such artifacts as giant boring mills, cash registers, and assembly lines. He would soon notice that some people are making things, others are carrying things, and others are exchanging things. He would be most intrigued, perhaps, by the place in which things are made.

Let us take him to a typical factory in America in 1950. His first perceptions will be of material objects. As he approaches the factory, he observes that it is a low one- or two-story building covering a relatively large area. He notices that it is a large building which houses many different kinds of objects. Figure 15 shows what he sees. We shall try to describe some of his reactions.

As he enters he sees a honeycomb of rather small cells or rooms in which are found tables, storage boxes, contraptions that make marks on paper, black horns into which people speak, and innumerable large and small sheets of paper with some strange and some familiar markings. The rooms appear light and clean, and there is an underlying murmur of voices mixed with an incessant clatter from the marking and other contraptions.

As the observer enters the adjacent area, he sees a vast shed from which emerges a continuous clang and clatter of metal. The room is filled with large and small machines, each of which emits its peculiar cacophony. On closer observation he notes that similar machines are grouped together in different parts of the shed. The chorus of noise is a record of what the machines are doing to the resistant metal—shaping, drilling, stamping, grinding, and milling. He is amazed at the abundance of steel and iron. In a nearby area he finds the source of these materials. He sees caldrons brimming with shimmering, molten metal. Huge ladles and pans filled with the liquid travel around the shed spilling their contents in designated places.

He wanders off to another section of the factory and enters another vast room. It appears more quiet, somewhat lighter, and more airy. There are many more people here. They are lined up rather close together. Some of

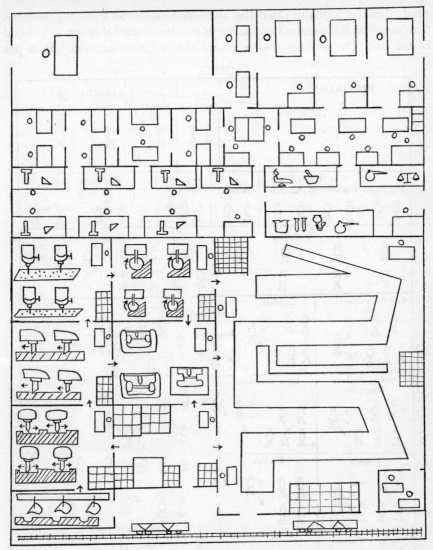

FIG. 15. The Material Culture of a Modern Factory. Can you identify the artifacts and basic social divisions?

them are running machines, but most of them are working with hand tools. Some of the workers have huge shallow trays before them. Inside the trays are many small pockets or compartments filled with different-shaped pieces of metal from which workers are picking out pieces at a rapid rate.

Other people are seen lined up alongside a moving counter. All kinds of metal pieces are found on the counter. The workers pick off the pieces they

need, then occasionally place the assembled pieces back on the counter. The pieces on the counter become larger and larger until they get to the end of the line. The product is now completed or "manufactured." It is put

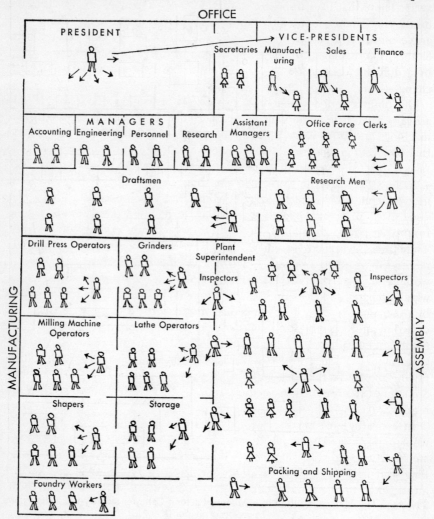

FIG. 16. The Social Organization of a Modern Factory.

into boxes by other machines and loaded into contrivances by still other machines.

SOCIAL ORGANIZATION

As our observer continues to study the plant, its physical layout and machines hold less interest for him. He wants to know more about the people in the factory. He begins to study their behavior, as shown in Figure

16. This figure describes the social organization of the factory. He watches the workers come to the plant in the morning. He notices that they all live away from the plant. Some of them live close by, and others live farther away. Those that live closer enter one side of the sheds. As soon as they are inside, they change their clothes and put on darker garments. A few workers arrive already dressed in darker garments, and they do not change their clothes. Those who live farther away come to the plant later. They enter it by a different door. Although their clothes are light in color they do not change them.

Our observer notices that these two classes of workers, the early and late arrivals, have little to do with each other. The early arrivals work with the machines and other large objects; the others work with paper. He is told that the clean group works in the "office" and the dirtier group works in the "shop." This distinction he discovers is very important.

As he scrutinizes the workers in the shop, he notices that those who are near one another do much the same thing. Most of the workers stay at the same place all day long tending machines. A few, however, wander around from place to place, talking to other workers who are doing similar things. These men are called "foremen." The areas they cover or their routes are referred to as "departments." Only men are allowed to work in the metal-working departments in this society. There is the foundry department, which prepares and casts the metal. The metal is then cut up and processed by other departments. It is shaped in one department, milled in another, drilled in another, ground in another, and finished in another. These departments are more closely related to one another than to any other department. One man, the "superintendent" walks around all of these departments, talking mostly to the foreman as they walk around in their smaller areas. Sometimes the foremen leave their areas and go to the superintendent for a talk.

In a nearby area are the moving counters. Here the workers, including women, put together the pieces made in the other part of the factory. They are sometimes called "assemblers." The assemblers stay in one place all day long. But here again there are a few men who walk around in designated areas. Some of them only look at the products, and put marks on them. They are the "inspectors." Foremen are also walking about talking here and there to the workers. At the end of the counters, the products are boxed, put into trucks or freight cars, and taken away. Pieces of paper are sent to the "office" periodically to inform the people "up" there of these movements.

As the observer looks at the office, he notices that it, too, is subdivided into sections or departments. Here it is more difficult to tell who the foremen are because many people are moving around. Everybody seems to be doing the same thing because they all are making marks on paper and talking. However, he notices that there are more women working here than in other parts of the plant. The women have smaller places on which to

put their papers than the men. The men generally tell the women what to do. None of the workers seem to be making anything—all they do is write and talk. Despite this it appears that they regard themselves as better than the people in the shop.

The functions of the office slowly become clear. The office, it seems, is closely related to activities in the shop. Some of the workers order the materials for the shop, others sell the products made. Some of the men are constantly planning to improve the machines in the shop. Others are concerned with coördinating the work of the departments. Then there are "specialists" who keep track of green pieces of paper and put them into envelopes. Everything done must be recorded, and this is the job of the younger women in the offices.

POWER GROUPINGS

The longer the observer stays in the office the more he realizes that it is the place where decisions are made which change things in the plant. Much of the activity of the "walkers" in the shop is in obedience to orders from the large-desk men in the office. The observer notes that the large-desk men in the large empty rooms have more authority over other workers. The smaller-desk men in small rooms have less authority. The largest-desk men have jurisdiction in general over the entire work plant. They delegate specific power over smaller groups to smaller-desk men. On the plant floor, the smaller the area of the walkers, the more specific and smaller is their authority. Finally, all the way down the "line," there are persons who obey everybody and give orders to nobody. The observer is not surprised when he learns that these are the "workers." The walking men he identifies as the "bosses." Everywhere he sees the bosses busily observing the behavior of others and reporting it to people with the bigger desks. The big-desk workers then give commands. When they are carried out, reports are given to them and the process is repeated over and over.

Much of the activity in the plant is concerned with the giving of orders, carrying them out, and reporting on them. Occasionally the workers in the shed object to the commands of the large-desk men. Then they meet together in small groups on the plant floor. Sometimes all the plant workers are called together outside the plant. Their representatives from these meetings, called stewards and union officials, meet with the desk men and tell them what the workers want. Only by these means do the workers have any influence on the large-desk men. Working, obeying, reporting, and holding meetings seem to be the main activities of the workers. These things are related to the accumulation of green pieces of paper in envelopes at the end of the week.

However, there are other things the workers do that are not immediately related to making things, obeying, reporting, or holding meetings. In the

middle of the day they eat a meal. The observer notices that the men eat by themselves and so do the women. He also notices that clean workers eat only with clean workers. Sometimes a man will eat with a woman, or a clean worker with a dirty one. Nobody seems to like this especially. No paper says this should not be done, but gossip among the workers seems to prevent it.

Many other types of activity are present which bear only indirect relation to work. In one department five of the men are in a bowling league, six other workers play "baseball," and four others do not enjoy athletics. The observer notices that the bowlers do not associate with the baseballers. The bowlers ride together in the same wagon contraption to and from work. They eat by themselves and play cards during lunch time. The non-players think they are superior to the players. They frequently argue with the players. The foreman of this department is currently in disfavor with the "big-desk boys" because the production of his workers is low.

As the observer looks at the office he finds that there, too, people are engaged in activities not directly related to the work. Some people prefer to work and play with others, both in and out of the plant. Some people avoid one another. With further study he finds that these likes and dislikes have an appreciable effect on the entire operation of the plant.

SOCIAL ATTITUDES

Up to this point our observer has only incidentally listened to people talking, for he was concerned with their work. Now he begins to listen to conversations, and in a few cases asks some questions.

One thing he notices is that the workers do not buy and sell their products. The purpose of work is to get paper. The dirty workers get green paper once a week, the clean girls get white paper once every two weeks, and the desk men get a piece of paper every month. This paper or money certifies that they can get food and other things at stores. In general, the dirtier the worker the less his paper can buy.

As our preindustrial man listens to the conversations, he notices that there is much talk about this paper. Everybody seems to want more of it. Sometimes the workers ask each other, "How much (paper) do you get?" This question sometimes leads to trouble, because some workers won't answer it. Many people brood about paper all day long. When they go home they talk about "how much" of the paper so-and-so must get. They notice about how much and what so-and-so buys and imagine how much paper he probably gets for himself. People look for two or three items of purchase —the living accommodations, the size and type of "auto" he drives, the amount and type of clothing he wears. If a man gets a small amount of paper and has a big "auto" and a large home, the workers get suspicious. But if he gets a lot of paper and doesn't have these things people ask, "What does he do with his paper?"

It is difficult for the observer to discover why workers in some jobs get more paper than workers in other jobs. He is told that the more difficult the job, the more the worker gets. But which jobs are more difficult? Some jobs do not require much exertion. They appear to be healthful, clean, and easy. The workers in these jobs receive much paper. Other jobs appear difficult, dirty, and exhausting. The people in these jobs receive very little paper. Some men and women who have clean desk jobs do not earn as much as the men in dirty jobs. Despite the fact that everyone says that the *paper* is the most important thing you get from the job, the lower-paid clean workers will not under any circumstances accept higher-paid dirty jobs. This is all very puzzling, especially when it appears that people want better-paying jobs. Many workers go to school to learn how to do "hard" jobs. But mostly they learn how to handle paper and talk. It doesn't matter sometimes if they don't use what they learn in school. They get more paper anyway. The observer decides that perhaps one of the myths of this society is that the more paper a person makes, the more difficult his job is; or vice versa. He's not sure.

He is sure, however, that the workers have strong feelings about paper. In reference to paper, certain questions are asked repeatedly, "What does he do?" "How long has he been here?" "What kind of record does he have?" These questions are asked because workers feel that hard jobs should be rewarded with more paper. They also believe that a worker who has been in the shed or office longer than others should get more paper. But the "bosses" add that to get more paper one must have a "good record." By this the bosses mean that a person must arrive at work on time, produce many things, learn new jobs, and obey the walking men or the men with the big desks.

From the legends, stories, and histories it seems that some men have gotten more money and "better jobs" by doing these things. The bosses continually repeat these stories to the workers. But some workers complain that although they have "good records" they have not been rewarded. They get very angry when other workers with only "average records" get rewarded. The observer hears such remarks as, "You've got to have 'pull' around here to get any place"; "Only people with influence get rewarded"; "You've got to have money to make money"; "You've got to kowtow to the big boys to get any place."

These assertions are denied by the bosses. They say, "There is plenty of room at the top"; "The workers should be ambitious and work harder to succeed"; "The problems of management are very difficult"; "The workers do not appreciate the favors bestowed on them." The observer notices that the workers and bosses do not really understand each other. Promotions are often based on personal and social qualities of a man and not altogether on his work record. Management says, "A boss must meet people. He must

have poise, and ability to persuade people. He must be well-dressed, confident, and dominant. He must be able to express himself clearly, and make good impressions on people. Above all, he must be loyal to the company." The workers, on the other hand, say, "A boss must first know the jobs of his men. He must be kind and understanding. He should be a regular guy, and not the snooty type. He's got to be a man the fellows can respect. He should be loyal to his own men."

In general, what the bosses say has more influence on the workers. Everybody is concerned with what his boss says, doesn't say, likes, or dislikes. They know what irritates him and what pleases him. By experience, they find that bosses, too, must have good records to show their bosses. Everybody wants to please the big boss, who is most pleased when he is making more paper for himself and for some people called stockholders, who live far away and never come to the plant.

But sometimes the workers feel that the more paper the big boss makes, the less they make. Or they feel the boss should give them more of his paper. When the boss and workers cannot agree on how to divide the paper and other things, workers begin to talk about their organization, the union, "doing something about it." Only the dirty workers talk about the union. If the union cannot convince the bosses, they begin to talk about a "strike." The observer hears such remarks as "They can't push us around"; "We'll close down the plant"; "Solidarity forever"; "We'll have to hold a strike meeting"; "We haven't much dough for a strike." Finally, a meeting is held. When the men decide on a strike, they do not go to work. The vast sheds remain empty unless the bosses relent a little. Sometimes the bosses try to get new workers in the plant, and a fight ensues. But usually an agreement is reached after a while, and the men go back to work.

Our observer asks, "Why does everybody want more paper?" He finds that the obvious answer, "To have more things," does not always apply. He finds that those making more money are looked up to by others. He wants to associate with people who are looked up to. He wants people to hold him in high regard, and to honor his family. For this he usually feels he must make more paper.

The worker also finds that the big-paper men have more independence. They don't have bosses over them all the time. In fact, they often are bosses themselves, and they tell other people what to do. The less one makes in society the fewer decisions he can make for himself. In fact, sometimes workers accept jobs which do not give them more money. But they are jobs which people respect, jobs which give them some independence. These are usually non-machine jobs.

Everybody in the factory seems worried. The big boss is afraid of his competitors. He fears that some day people will not be able to buy his products. The clean people below him are afraid that they won't climb into

better and bigger jobs. The bench workers are afraid that a machine will be invented that can do their work and they will be without a job. They fear they may not be able to buy food and clothing. Each group blames the others for its problems.

Our observer decides he still doesn't know too much about these strange people and their factories. He decides to visit some other factories and businesses. He wants a broader view of the country and its people. What does work mean to these people? How many different kinds of work are there in this vastly changed land? After he answers these questions he will return to the factory and study it more in detail.

WORK IN INDUSTRIAL SOCIETY

The composite picture of the social organization of a modern factory just given emphasizes the part-whole relationships within a work plant. To understand the operation of a machine, the operator must know the number and functions of its parts. So it is with the social organization of work; one must know how each part fits into larger patterns. When many different work plants are examined we are impressed by the vastness and heterogeneity of their activities. What factors need to be examined to appreciate the structure of work institutions in western society? Three basic areas are arbitrarily selected for study. They are: (1) the nature of work in general, (2) the occupational and industrial distribution of the workers, and (3) the type of work environment in which people work.

WHAT IS THE NATURE OF WORK?

1. Subsistence Activity

The most common conception of work is that it is any activity which is directly or indirectly centered around the goal of subsistence. It is comprised of the activities one performs to make a living. These may be clipping coupons, digging a ditch, operating a machine, writing a book, or robbing a bank.[1] Work, however, has no necessary relationship to a market, and payment is not a necessary criterion. Thus, the housewife is a worker, even though she receives no direct payment. This is also true of an unpaid worker on the farm. The general activity centering around subsistence is called work, and the specific routines of this activity are usually referred to as occupations.

2. Work as Social Activity

To the sociologist, economic and technological definitions of work are incomplete because they omit the important fact that work is centered

[1] See Arthur Salz, "Occupation," *Encyclopaedia of the Social Sciences*, The Macmillan Company, 1933.

around social activity. Work, like religious, recreational, or family behavior, is pursued for its social rewards.

Almost every aspect of work is social. The production, servicing, and handling of goods is essentially a coöperative or group process. In addition, the nature of our industrial economy makes all workers dependent on one another for the goods or services they buy or sell.

In a narrower sense work is social activity, for it is often done in the presence of others. Work plants bring many people together; and when people are assembled they inevitably interact. Anything done in a social atmosphere becomes defined as social activity. Thus the behavior or operations of work are soon evaluated for their prestige or social importance. The motives for working cannot be assigned only to economic needs, for men may continue to work even though they have no need for material goods.[2] Even when their security and that of their children is assured, they continue to labor. Obviously, this is so because the rewards they get from work are social, such as respect and admiration from their fellow men. For some, work becomes an avenue for securing ego satisfactions by gaining power and exerting it over others. For all, work activity provides fellowship and social life.

3. The Social-Psychological Importance of Work

Many young people do not fully appreciate the fact that work is the unescapable fate of the overwhelming majority of men and women. Despite a recent cultural tendency to deëmphasize hard work and to accentuate "having a good time" (presumably, the antithesis of labor), work still remains the most important segment of adult life. The impact of work routines is found in almost every aspect of living and even in the world of dreams and unconscious fantasies. During "vacations," for example, many people find the departure from work routines a disturbing thing. Others find rejuvenation in being released from occupational duties. Both instances demonstrate the importance and pervasiveness of work. It is not an overstatement to suggest that work is not a part of life, it is literally life itself.

Studies of the effect of work on the person and especially on his social behavior are few and fragmentary. This subject may be studied on four levels.

1. The impact of specific work routines on the workers.
2. The social atmosphere of the work plant as it affects all workers, irrespective of occupational habits.
3. The consequence of occupational and industrial routines on the extra-work adjustment of the person.
4. The attitude of the worker toward his job, as it affects his outlook on life.

[2] E. Wight Bakke, The Unemployed Worker, Yale University Press, 1940, chap. 1-4.

IMPACT OF WORK ROUTINES

The best way to study the impact of work on general behavior is to examine specific occupations or closely related occupations. Since space does not permit this, we may suggest how some work routines affect the general adjustment of the worker. The things that need to be studied in relation to this are: the social factors which operate to select some types of recruits for certain occupations, the kind of formal or informal training that different occupational groups receive which encourages or discourages the development of certain capacities, and the effect of job routines on personality organization. A model study constructed along these lines was made by W. Fred Cottrell. He describes how the importance of time to the railroader arises from his occupational orientation.[3] Some novelists have been able to capture the molding influences of the job routine on personality. Kauffman's novels show insight of the influence of the job on personal development. In one of his books he describes the life of a clerk in a department store.

Kate Flanagan arrived at the Lennox department store every morning at a quarter to eight o'clock. She passed through the employees' dark entrance, a unit in a horde of other workers, and registered the instant of her arrival on a time-machine that could in no wise be suborned to perjury. She hung up her wraps in a subterranean cloak-room, and hurrying to the counter to which she was assigned, first helped in "laying out the stock," and then stood behind her wares, exhibiting, cajoling, selling, until an hour before noon. At that time she was permitted to run away for exactly forty-five minutes for the glass of milk and two pieces of bread and jam that composed her luncheon. This repast disposed of, she returned to the counter and remained behind it, standing like a war-worn watcher on the ramparts of a beleaguered city, till the store closed at six, when there remained to her at least fifteen minutes more of work before her sales-book was balanced and the wares covered up for the night. There were times indeed, when she did not leave the store until seven o'clock, but those delays were caused rather by customers than by the management of the store, which could prevent new shoppers from entering the doors after six, but could hardly turn out those already inside.

The automatic time-machine and a score of more annoying, and equally automatic, human beings kept watch upon all that she did. The former, in addition to the floor-walker in her section of the store, recorded her every going and coming, the latter reported every movement not prescribed by the regulations of the establishment; and the result upon Katie and her fellow workers was much the result observable upon condemned assassins under the unwinking surveillance of the Death Watch.

If Katie was late, she was fined ten cents for each offense. She was reprimanded if her portion of the counter was disordered after a mauling by careless customers.

[3] *The Railroader*, Stanford University Press, 1940.

She was fined for all mistakes she made in the matter of prices and the additions on her salesbook; and she was fined if, having asked the floor-walker for three or five minutes to leave the floor in order to tidy her hair and hands, in constant need of attention through the rapidity of her work and the handling of her dyed wares, she exceeded her time limit by so much as a few seconds.

There were no seats behind the counters, and Katie, whatever her physical condition, remained on her feet all day long, unless she could arrange for relief by a fellow worker during that worker's luncheon time. There was no place for a rest save a damp, ill-lighted "Recreation Room" in the basement, furnished with a piano that nobody had time to play, magazines that nobody had time to read, and wicker chairs in which nobody had time to sit. All that one might do was to serve the whims and accept the scoldings of women customers who knew too ill, or too well, what they wanted to buy; keep a tight rein upon one's indignation at strolling men who did not intend to buy anything that the shop advertised; be servilely smiling under the innuendoes of the high-collared floor-walkers, in order to escape their wrath; maintain a sharp outlook for the "spotters," or paid spies of the establishment; thwart, if possible, those pretending customers who were scouts sent from other stores, and watch for shop-lifters on the one hand and the firm's detectives on the other.

"It ain't a cinch, by no means"—thus ran the departing Cora Costigan's advice to her successor—"But it ain't nothin' now to what it will be in the holidays. I'd rather be dead than work in the toy department in December—I wonder if the kids guess how we that sells 'em hates the sight of their playthings?—And I'd rather be dead an' damned than work in the accounting department. A girl friend of mine worked there last year,—only it was over to Malcare's store—an' didn't get through her Christmas Eve work till two on Christmas morning, an' she lived over on Staten Island. She overslept on the twenty-sixth, an' they docked her a half-week's pay.

"An' don't never," concluded Cora, "don't never let 'em transfer you to the exchange department. The people that exchange things all belong in the psychopathic ward at Bellevue—them that don't belong in Sing Sing. Half the goods they bring back have been used for days, and when the store ties a tag on a sent-on-approval opera cloak, the woman wriggle the tag inside, an' wear it to the theatre with a scarf draped over the string. Thank God, I'm goin' to be married!"[4]

Upton Sinclair in *The Jungle* vividly portrays how work routines of a fertilizer man affect his entire being and that of his family.

His labor took him about one minute to learn. Before him was one of the vents of the mill in which the fertilizer was being ground—rushing forth in a great brown river, with a spray of the finest dust floating forth in clouds. Jurgis was given a shovel and along with half a dozen others it was his task to shovel this fertilizer into carts. That others were at work he knew by the sound, and by the fact that he sometimes collided with them; otherwise they might as well not have been there, for in the blinding dust-storm a man could not see six feet in front

[4] Reginald Wright Kauffman, *The House of Bondage*, 1910, pp. 151-153.

of his face. When he had filled one cart he had to grope around him until another came, and if there was none on hand he continued to grope till one arrived. In five minutes, he was, of course, a mass of fertilizer from head to feet; they gave him a sponge to tie over his mouth, so that he could breathe, but the sponge did not prevent his lips and eyelids from caking up with it and his ears from filling solid. He looked like a brown ghost at twilight—from hair to shoes he became the color of the building and of everything in it, and for that matter a hundred yards outside it. The building had to be left open, and when the wind blew Durham and Company lost a great deal of fertilizer.

Working in his shirt-sleeves, and with the thermometer at over a hundred, the phosphates soaked in through every pore of Jurgis' skin and in five minutes he had a headache, and in fifteen was almost dazed. The blood was pounding in his brain like an engine's throbbing; there was a frightful pain in the top of his skull, and he could hardly control his hands. Still, with the memory of his four jobless months behind him, he fought on, in a frenzy of determination; half an hour later he began to vomit—he vomited until it seemed as if his inwards must be torn into shreds. A man could get used to the fertilizer-mill, the boss had said, if he would only make up his mind to it, but Jurgis now began to see that it was a question of making up his stomach.

At the end of that day of horror, he could scarcely stand. He had to catch himself now and then, and lean against a building and get his bearings. Most of the men, when they came out, made straight for a saloon—they seemed to place fertilizer and rattlesnake poison in one class. But Jurgis was too ill to think of drinking—he could only make his way to the street and stagger on to a car. He had a sense of humor, and later on, when he became an old hand, he used to think it fun to board a streetcar and see what happened. Now, however, he was too ill to notice it—how the people in the car began to gasp and sputter, to put their handkerchiefs to their noses, and transfix him with furious glances. Jurgis only knew that a man in front of him immediately got up and gave him a seat; and that half a minute later the two people on each side of him got up; and that in a full minute the crowded car was empty—those passengers who could not get room on the platform having gotten out to walk.

Of course Jurgis had made his home a miniature fertilizer-mill a minute after entering. The stuff was half an inch deep in his skin—his whole system was full of it, and it would have taken a week not merely of scrubbing, but of vigorous exercise, to get it out of him. As it was, he could be compared with nothing known to man, save that newest discovery of the savants, a substance which emits energy for an unlimited time, without being itself in the least diminished in power. He smelt so that he made all the food at the table taste, and set the whole family to vomiting; for himself it was three days before he could keep anything upon his stomach—he might wash his hands, and use a knife and fork, but were not his mouth and throat filled with the poison?

And still Jurgis stuck it out! In spite of splitting headaches he would stagger down to the plant and take up his stand once more, and begin to shovel in the blinding clouds of dust. And so at the end of the week he was a fertilizer-man for life—he was able to eat again, and though his head never stopped aching, it ceased to be so bad that he could not work.[5]

[5] Upton Sinclair, The Jungle, The Viking Press, Inc., 1946, pp. 129-131.

Other factors in job routines need to be studied systematically, such as the amount of energy required by the job, kind of faculties exercised, the postures assumed, the amount of light, ventilation, or noise, presence or absence of people, type of social contacts, hours and time of labor, and others.

THE SOCIAL ATMOSPHERE OF WORK

In addition to specific work routines, the physical and social atmosphere of the work plant influences the worker's adjustment. Even the untrained observer, for example, feels that the physical-social-cultural atmosphere of the coal mine is in striking contrast to that of the hospital, office, or school. All workers in the mine—foremen, diggers, counter-men, weighers, time-keepers, engineers, and water boys—are affected by the same work environment. If the mine is underground, darkness, dampness, dust, noise, and turmoil prevail. The mine is a physical world where the materials handled are bulky and heavy and the labor is strenuous and manic. It is a male world, a world where the sounds of voices and machines resound against the tunnel walls. Everyone is dressed in dark, serviceable clothing. Everyone has a constant if hidden fear of the possibility of an explosion, a cave-in, or other dangers. The combination of physical environment and the dominant social and cultural atmosphere we shall call the *ethos* of the work plant.

The contrast between the ethos of the mine and of the hospital is striking. The white, gleaming, silent halls, the smooth stone floors, the mild antiseptic aroma, the brisk pace of the nurses, the stiff-starched uniforms of the workers, the patient-centered attitude, the autocratic nature of the staff, their mechanical cheerfulness, their satisfied self-awareness, the systematic and precise regulation of feeding, sleeping, and medication—all blend to produce a unique atmosphere, which leaves a lasting impression on workers and patients alike. All of the hospital workers, from part-time voluntary aides through orderlies, clerical workers, cooks, nurses, doctors, and administrative heads, are steeped in this atmosphere. They all assimilate in some measure a similar mental and occupational outlook.[6]

Space does not permit an extended description of the ethos of other types of work plants. Although sociologists have not yet perfected techniques of describing and measuring work ethos, its reality cannot be ignored. It must be recognized as one of the main sources of influence on the worker's behavior. Many novelists are sensitive to the ethos of the job. Few have written about it as dramatically as Di Donato when he describes a concrete worker:

Whistle shrilled Job awake, and the square pit thundered into an inferno of sense-pounding cacophony. Compression engines snort viciously—sledge heads punch sinking spikes—steel drills bite shattering jazz in stony-stone excitedly jarring clinging hands—dust swirling—bells clanging insistent aggravated warn-

[6] Nancy McDonald, "Are Hospitals Made for People or Vice Versa?" *Politics*, October, 1945, pp. 306-308.

ing—severe bony iron cranes swivel swing dead heavy rock high—clattering dump—vibrating concussion swiftly absorbed—echo reverberating—scoops bull ing horns in rock pile chug—shish—clug—chug aloft—hiss roar dynamite's boomdoom loosening pertrified bowels—one hundred hands fighting rock—fifty spines derricking swiveling—fifty faces in set mask chopping stone into bread— fifty hearts interpreting Labor hurling oneself down and in at earth planting pod-footed Job.[7]

THE EFFECT OF WORK ON EXTRA-PLANT ADJUSTMENT

The study of how the job affects the social life of the worker and his family has received only incidental attention. The worker tends to accept as inevitable the mode of life that his job forces upon him. Two important conditions of work demonstrate how the job affects off-the-job living. They are the daily cycle of work and the seasonal rounds of the industry. The daily cycle of work refers to the hours of the job (including time of arrival and departure), the length and time of the lunch hour, and the number of working days in the week. The seasonal round of the industry refers to the changes or accommodations that the industry must make over the year as a response to traditions, market conditions, changes in production, inventory, climatic and other changes.[8]

Work Routine and Style of Living

How daily routines and seasonal rounds alter the style of living is evident when we compare such diverse jobs as the insurance agent, teacher, coal miner, jazz musician, business executive, or professional thief. The college professor may be taken as the first illustration. He may teach only twelve hours a week, four hours a day for three days a week. Presumably, he may arrange his remaining work hours as he sees fit. He has periods when he has no teaching duties—summers, extended holidays, registration, and other periods. He may prefer to study, write, read, hold conferences almost any time he sees fit. He may work hardest and longest after 9:00 P.M. by which hour the coal miner is contemplating bedtime. A few hardy professors may even prefer to study in early morning hours from 4:00 to 9:00 A.M. Contrast this to the miner, who enters the pit every morning at 7:30 and leaves at 4:30. Or the jazz musician, who plays from 10:00 P.M. to 3:00 A.M.; or the nurse, who may work on day, night, or "swing" shift; or the executive, who works from 9:30 A.M. to 4:00 P.M.

The nature of the industry may be such that some workers must work long hours during some seasons and have little or nothing to do in other

---

[7] From *Christ in Concrete*, by Pietro di Donato, copyright 1937, used by special permission of the publishers, The Bobbs-Merrill Company.

[8] There are, of course, other factors associated with jobs that will not be examined here. For example, the amount and type of income affects what people eat, how much they eat, how they dress, where they live, how much they save, how much they spend on various items.

seasons. This is the case with clothing, canning, and building. Other industries require work around the clock, as steel[9] and transportation. Others operate during different periods of the day, such as night clubs and theaters, which require work in the evening, milk delivery in early morning, restaurants in afternoon and evening, and retail trade during daylight hours.

Such daily routines and seasonal rounds imposed by industry regulate the non-work life of the worker and his family. Let us consider recreation. Night baseball and night-clubbing are unavailable to the milkman. Almost no recreation is available to those working on swing or night shifts, while almost all forms of recreation are available (in terms of time schedule) to the executive and white-collar worker.

Intimate family life is affected by the work routines of the chief breadwinner. The time the wife arises, shops, prepares meals, participates in neighborhood or community life is influenced by her husband's work routine. The amount of family social life is likewise affected. The suburban insurance salesman leaves his home before his young children arise and returns about their bedtime. In many cases he is literally a strange weekend guest whom the children are told is their father. The reverse is the case for those grocers who have their shops at the front of the house. The minister or teacher may spend much time at home if he wants to.

Work Routine and Community Participation

The influence of work schedules extends to the field of community participation. Sociologists have observed that only a small proportion of people are the community leaders, and these tend to be the middle-class men and women.[10] This is largely explainable in terms of the nature of the jobs and the type of job routines held by white-collar workers and businessmen. Those who participate in community activities and become its leaders are those who have higher income, prestige, and power in the community. The income, status, and influence that a person has are set largely by his job or by that of the chief breadwinner in his family.[11]

The cost of community participation affects the type of participants. The Bowling League, P.T.A., Boy Scouts, Girl Scouts, Hi-Y, Christian Endeavor, Republican party, bridge club, Red Cross, and many other organizations have fees or contributions connected with them. The higher these fees, the less those in lower-paid occupations (and their families) can participate. Also, the higher a person climbs up the officer ladder of organizations, the greater his expenses will be.

[9] For an intimate picture of how the steel industry affects the worker's life, see C. R. Walker, *Steel: The Diary of a Furnace Worker*, The Atlantic Monthly Press, 1922.

[10] W. Lloyd Warner, Robert J. Havighurst, and Martin D. Loeb, *Who Shall Be Educated?* Harper & Brothers, 1944.

[11] Chapter XXI, "Industry and the Community," demonstrates the status and power relations in the work plant and compares them to those in the community.

Time, like money, also bears on community participation. Time is a limited commodity, which can be bought or sold. The middle-class housewife can afford to buy time in the form of hiring someone to attend to her household or child-rearing duties. This frees her to participate in the church, neighborhood, and social life of the community. Her husband can afford, owing to the nature of his job, to lose time. He is not tied down to his desk as the worker is to his bench. The businessman can take two hours off for lunch to attend Rotary, Kiwanis, Lions, or the Chamber of Commerce. He has the economic power and the time schedule to enable him to take time off from his work to devote to the Red Cross drive, the Community Chest, the country club, the Boy Scouts, or other organizations. He may attend meetings late in the evening because he can postpone or delay his work, or assign it to someone else.

The wife of the manual worker cannot be released from domestic duties. She must cook *all* of the meals for *all* of the family. She is geared to the time schedules of her children *and* her husband. In short, she is tied down to the neighborhood, in the physical as well as the social sense. Her husband is likewise tied to his job in a time-space sense. His extra-work activities are limited, as are those of the children. The income, social status, and job routines of the father limit the participation of his children in and out of school. His work schedule has the effect of decreasing everyone's formal community contacts and increasing informal neighborhood ones.

The result is that community events tend to be geared to the money levels and time schedules of the middle classes. With different cultural groups excluded from participation, the middle classes further solidify their values and activities. Even when they make a conscientious effort to integrate lower-class people into their organizations, it is not possible. The cultural values of the two groups are no longer compatible. With this background in mind it is possible to understand the importance and the role of the week end and the holiday to lower-class workers and their families. To many of them that is all the release and expression they may have to make work and living more than a dull routine.

ATTITUDE TOWARD WORK

The attitudes that workers have toward their labor basically affect their outlook on life. Work may be the activity that gives interest and purpose to life. It may, on the other hand, bring only irritation and pain. How the worker feels about his work bears not only on his adjustment but on that of his family. The person who finds fulfillment in his job need not use the family as the object of his frustrations. The maladjusted worker has problems on many fronts.

The worker's attitude toward his job is not altogether a matter of individual adjustment. Orientation toward work is also culturally defined. For

example, work occupied a central position in the value scheme of the Puritans. A person could not be considered a proper member of the community if he did not regard work as his main goal in life. Indeed, his religious salvation was in some measure reflected by his work achievement. This glorification of work still survives as a value in American culture. The Puritanical aphorisms are tightly packed in a poem called "Work" by Henry Van Dyke.

> Let me but do my work from day to day,
>   In field or forest, at desk or loom,
>   In roving market-place or tranquil room;
>
> Let me but find it in my heart to say,
>   When vagrant wishes beckon me astray,
>   "This is my work; my blessing, not my doom;
>   "Of all who live, I am the only one by whom
> "This work can best be done in the right way."
>
> Then shall I see it not too great, nor small,
>   To suit my spirit and to prove my powers;
>   Then shall I cheerful greet the labouring hours,
> And cheerful turn, when long shadows fall,
> At eventide, to play, and love and rest,
> Because I know for me my work is best.[12]

Although we may smile at these verses, nevertheless the sentiments in them express for our society the ideals of what work attitudes should be. They are the joy of working and the orderly adjustment of work to family living. It is to be noted that Van Dyke makes no allusion to work as play. Work is a serious activity of primary importance. Such work attitudes are not those of many people in contemporary Western culture. The contrast between ideal attitudes toward work and prevailing ones is probably a source of much frustration and anxiety today.

A much more common feeling is that work is a harsh, monotonous, enervating, and endless activity. Far from constituting a source of happiness, it brings only misery.

The following remarks of a housewife made in the union commissary during the 1937 Flint sit-down strike illustrate sentiments which are the reverse of those expressed in the poem "Work." Work here is the source of much suffering and anguish, not only to the worker but to his family.

"I'd like to shout from the housetops what the company's doing to our men. My husband, he's a torch solderer, they call them welders, but that's not what he is; he solders. You should see him come home at night! So

[12] Reprinted from *Music & Other Poems* by Henry van Dyke; copyright 1904 by Charles Scribner's Sons, 1932 by Henry van Dyke; used by permission of the publishers.

tired, like they was dead and irritable. My John's not like that. He's a good
kind man. But the children don't dare go near him, he's so nervous and his
temper's bad. And then at night in bed, he shakes his whole body he shakes.
They're not men any more, if you know what I mean, and unless we have
the union things will get worse."[13]

Although this outburst may not be a typical one, it does demonstrate a
sentiment pattern toward work and how these sentiments affect the workers'
adjustment and that of their families.

Perhaps the most common attitude toward work today is one of ambiv-
alence. Work is both sought and avoided; it is at the same time good and
bad; it is at once a source of satisfaction and sorrow. This composite contradictory sentiment toward work has been captured by Di Donato.

Paul laid brick for brick with some men. He worked next to La Lucy and at
one time kept up with him for a few courses. He ran his stretch of wall right up
to La Lucy's part, and it thrilled him. It felt like one of his dreams where he
had raced an incredible distance at terrific speed on a road that stretched beyond
the earth. Quickly he sweated, and human water mingled with lime-mortar and
brick. This is the fresh stink of Job, this is the eight-houred daily duel, this is
the sense of red and gray, and our bodies are no longer meat and bone of our
parents but substance of Job.

Job became noisier expanding organism—banging, growing, thudding, and
pushing UP.

Brick and mortar was to become for Paul as stuff he could eat, and the constant cycle from brick pile and tub to wall was to become a motion that fed upon
itself.

With the beginning of each Job men, though knowing one another and
having raised Job for years, wed themselves to Job with the same new ceremony,
the same new energy and fear, the same fierce silence and loss of consciousness,
and the perpetual sense of their wrongness . . . struggling to fulfill a destiny of
never-ending debt. These men were the hardness that would bruise Paul many
times. These were the bodies to whom he would be joined in bondage to Job.
Job would be a brick labyrinth that would suck him in deeper and deeper, and
there would be no going back. Life would never be a dear music, a festival, a gift
of Nature. Life would be the torque of Wall's battle that distorted straight limbs
beneath weight in heat and rain and cold.

No poet would be there to intone meter of soul's sentence to stone, no artist
upon the scaffold to paint the vinegary sweat of Christ—and in correspondence
with red brick and gray mortar, no composer attuned to the screaming movement
of Job and voiceless cry in overalls.

Sugar and shine would ride high in state and wave a wand. . . .

And blood and stone would go on creating World.

Unseen would be the pushing hands and driving shoulders, the ripple-strained
stomachs, and gripping feet.

[13] Henry Kraus, *The Many and the Few*, The Plantin Press, 1947.

Unsmelled and untasted would be Tenement and manager of worker.
And Paul was now bricklayer-worker . . . welded to the hands whose vibra-
tions could shatter the earth.[14]

The satisfactions and dissatisfactions derived from work are a fruitful area
for sociological inquiry. One of the variables that must be considered in
such a study is occupation. Probably the greater the skill associated with a
job, the greater the satisfactions derived from it. The problem of adjustment
may be most widespread among repetitive workers.[15] Other variables besides
occupation may have a bearing here, such as the worker's ability and his
general psychological adjustment.[16] We shall now turn our attention to the
first of these variables, the occupational composition of the American labor
force.

OCCUPATIONAL AND INDUSTRIAL COMPOSITION OF THE LABOR FORCE

This section outlines some of the basic characteristics of the American
labor force. The description provides answers to three questions: Who are
the workers? What do they do? Where do they work? Answers to these
questions reveal the structure of modern work society.

If the work activities of the entire population are to be properly surveyed,
then no kind of work must escape us. It will be useful to imagine the people
of the United States within a giant work plant all engaged in their various
occupational pursuits. There are white-collar workers, workers in overalls,
workers in white, gray, blue, and khaki uniforms, housewives, school pupils
and college students, children at their chores, and seamen on their ships.
What, more specifically, are all these different kinds of work? What proportion of all activity is "paid" activity? What changes are taking place in
these work activities?

ACTIVITY PATTERNS OF THE POPULATION

Table 4 shows that the largest activity group in the nation is "persons
gainfully employed," or what economists call *"the labor force."*[17] They con-

---

[14] From *Christ in Concrete*, by Pietro di Donato, copyright 1937, used by special permission of the publishers, The Bobbs-Merrill Company.

[15] A penetrating sociological analysis of occupational adjustment of factory workers is
made by Simone Weil, "Factory Work," *Politics*, December, 1946, pp. 369-375.

[16] An extensive study of factors in work adjustment has been made in an older idiom
by Henri de Man, *Joy in Work*, George Allen and Unwin, Ltd., 1929, translated from
the German by Eden and Cedar Paul. See also Henry Durant, *The Problem of Leisure*,
George Rutledge and Sons, Ltd., 1938, and Max Weber, "Science as a Vocation," *From
Max Weber: Essays in Sociology*, translated by C. Wright Mills and H. H. Gerth,
Oxford University Press, 1946.

[17] Much of the data in the following tables have been derived from the census reports
of the United States. Since the Census Bureau does not collect and arrange its data the
same way in every census, care must be taken in the interpretation of its data. It is also
unfortunate that the activity groups are not singled out in greater detail by the census.

stitute slightly over two-fifths of the population, who support the remaining three-fifths of the people. The supported are made up primarily of (1) non-

TABLE 4. Estimated Primary Activity Distribution of the Total Population of the United States: 1870–1947[18]

Activity Group	1870	1880	1890	1900	1910	1920	1930	1940	1946–1947
Children under 5 yrs.	14.3	13.8	12.4	12.1	11.5	10.9	9.3	8.0	8.7
Children 5 to 15 yrs. not at school or gainfully occupied	10.7	6.8	6.8	6.7	3.8	3.7	2.9	1.7[a]	1.5[a]
Persons attending school	16.6	19.8	18.6	17.7	19.6	20.6	22.7	20.3	19.0
Housewives not gainfully employed	21.3	21.9	21.7	21.6	21.2	21.5	21.3	22.0	21.2
Persons gainfully employed	32.4	34.7	37.2	38.3	40.6	39.6	39.8	40.1	42.5
Adults in institutions	.3	.4	.4	.5	.5	.6	.6	.9	.8[a]
Not accounted for	4.4	2.6	2.9	3.1	2.8	3.1	3.4	7.0[b]	6.3[a, b]
Totals	100.0	100.0	100.0	100.0	100.0	100.0	100.0	100.0	100.0

a. Estimated.

b. Includes those unable to work. In earlier censuses these were partially included in the labor force.

working wives, who are about one-fifth of the population, (2) students attending school, who compose another fifth, and (3) preschool children, those unable to work, and others, who constitute the remaining fifth. Those unable to work are the sick, the indigent, patients of mental and penal institutions, retired persons, and others.

At least three important trends may be noted in relative size of the activity groups. The first is the relative increase in size of the labor force. Since 1870, the paid working population has grown from less than one-third to over two-fifths of the total population. The second trend, the relative decrease in number of children under five years, is linked with the first trend. With the falling off of the birth rate and the lowering of the death rate the population has grown older. This means that the proportion of those in the "working ages," 16–55 years, has increased. The third trend is the increasing proportion of children going to school in the age range of five to twenty-one years. If it were not for this latter trend, the proportion in the labor force might be still higher.

THE LABOR FORCE

The Problem of the Aged

Barring unforeseen changes, these three trends will continue for another three decades. After that we may see a growth in the proportion of retired

[18] Data from 1870 to 1930 were taken from Ralph G. Hurlin and Meredith B. Given, "Shifting Occupational Patterns," *Recent Social Trends*, Whittlesey House, 1934, Table 1, p. 274. Data for 1940 and 1946–1947 were computed from various releases of the U.S. Census Bureau.

people and old people, and perhaps a relative decrease in the size of the labor forces. In fact, our society is already facing the "problem of the aged."

Table 5 indicates to some extent what is happening to the age structure of the working force. For both sexes, and especially for the females, the

TABLE 5. Percent Distribution of Gainful Workers by Age and Sex for the United States: 1900–1940[19]

Age Ranges	Male				
	1900	1910	1920	1930	1940[20]
10–15	5.3	4.0	3.1	1.2	.5
16–44	68.4	69.6	66.9	66.0	65.2
45–64	21.5	22.0	25.3	27.6	29.6
65 and over	4.5	4.2	4.5	5.1	4.6
Unknown	0.3	0.2	0.2	0.1	—
Totals	100.0	100.0	100.0	100.0	99.9

Age Ranges	Female				
	1900	1910	1920	1930	1940
10–15	9.1	5.8	4.2	1.9	.4
16–44	74.9	78.1	77.6	77.7	77.9
45–64	13.1	13.6	15.7	17.8	19.6
65 and over	2.6	2.3	2.3	2.5	2.1
Unknown	0.3	0.2	0.2	0.1	—
Totals	100.0	100.0	100.0	100.0	100.0

Age Ranges	Total, Male and Female				
	1900	1910	1920	1930	1940
10–15	6.0	4.3	3.3	1.4	.5
16–44	69.6	71.2	69.1	68.6	68.2
45–64	20.0	20.4	23.4	25.4	27.2
65 and over	4.1	3.9	4.0	4.5	4.0
Unknown	0.3	0.2	0.2	0.1	—
Totals	100.0	100.0	100.0	100.0	99.9

[19] Adapted from *Sixteenth Census of the United States. Comparative Occupation. Statistics for the United States, 1870 to 1940.* United States Government Printing Office, 1943, Table XVII, p. 95.

[20] Adapted from *Sixteenth Census of the United States. Population.* Vol. III, *The Labor Force,* Part I, U.S. Summary, Table 5, p. 19. Only ages fourteen and fifteen are represented in age range of ten to fifteen years.

proportion of workers between ten and fifteen years has shrunk rapidly. The percentage of workers in the range of sixteen through forty-four years has, on the other hand, remained fairly constant. The age range from forty-five to sixty-four shows a slow, steady increase for both sexes, and the proportion sixty-five years and over remains relatively constant. Table 5 does not show the increasing proportion of aged persons retiring from the labor market. Before World War II industry showed great reluctance to hire older people. In the future it must do so or face the problem of indirectly supporting the aged through social security or other means. If industry retains more older workers it must make numerous adjustments of a technical and social nature. For example, operations must be redesigned for the more feeble workers, and the problem of induction of older workers into lower-status jobs must be considered.

Women in the Labor Force

The failure of the census to include the "nonworking" housewife in the labor force is very unrealistic. Women probably contribute more than their share of labor to any society. Even among the gainfully occupied they constitute a significant section. During World War II they undoubtedly constituted over one-quarter of the gainfully employed. This was in part the manifestation of a long-term trend. Breckinridge reports that since 1870 the number of working women has increased over six times, whereas their numerical increase in the population was four times.[21] Table 6 gives the sex ratios of the labor force since 1870. At that time women were 14.8

TABLE 6. Sex Composition of the Labor Force of the United States by Percentages: 1870–1940[22]

	1870	1880	1890	1900	1910	1920	1930	1940
Male	85.2	84.8	82.8	81.7	79.1	79.6	78.0	75.8
Female	14.8	15.2	17.2	18.3	20.9	20.4	22.0	24.2
Totals	100.0	100.0	100.0	100.0	100.0	100.0	100.0	100.0
Total in millions	13	17	23	29	37	41	49	52

percent of the labor force; in 1940 they constituted about one-quarter of the total.

The increase in women workers has been occurring at all ages above sixteen,[23] for both single and married. As might be expected, the proportion of married women working has grown faster than the proportion of single

[21] S. P. Breckinridge, "The Activities of Women Outside the Home," *Recent Social Trends*, Whittlesey House, 1934, p. 712.
[22] Computed from data of *Sixteenth Census of the United States.* For 1910–1940, see *Comparative Occupation Statistics . . . 1870 to 1940*, Part I, U.S. Summary, Table XXI, p. 100.
[23] Breckinridge, *op. cit.*, p. 713.

working women. In 1900, for example, married women were only 15 percent of all working women. Their proportion steadily increased until in 1940 they constituted over 36 percent of all working women. This fact reflects the general aging of the population and the growing proportion of married people. But it also reflects a change in cultural definition of the role of married women in our society.

The social consequences of women working both in the work plant and in the home are enormous. The engineer has had to make adjustments in manufacturing processes; the occupational status structure has been jarred; the unions have had to alter their organizing techniques; the behavior of mixed groups in the plants has been altered. Such "problems" will increase rather than decrease in the future.

Occupational Classifications

Occupational statistics are the basic data for answering the question of what people do in a particular society. Heretofore, the job of describing occupational trends was well-nigh impossible for two reasons. First, the manner in which the Census Bureau presented data made the segregation of occupational and industrial statistics very difficult. Second, the occupational definitions and classifications were changed from census to census. Fortunately, Alba Edwards of the U.S. Census Bureau has done a magnificent job of segregating industrial from occupational statistics and making these data comparable for the different census periods.[24]

It is difficult to defend the use of any occupational classification, because every one emphasizes some aspects of occupations at the expense of others. Alba Edwards' classification purports to be a socioeconomic scale in which occupation is highly related to social status and income differences. It is usually agreed that the general level of education of a group reflects its general social and status position in the society. Similarly, the income received indicates general economic status. Table 7 (p. 130) presents some evidence to support Edwards' contention that his occupational classification constitutes a socioeconomic scale. There is a rather close relation of educational attainment to the socioeconomic ranking of the occupations. The professionals have the most education; then come the clerical workers, followed by proprietors, skilled operatives, servants, and unskilled workers, in that order. Although proprietors, farm owners, managers, and officials have less education than the clerks, they are placed in higher socioeconomic positions. This is due to the fact that proprietors usually receive higher incomes, as well as higher prestige because they own and control property. Since this scale tries to take both social and economic factors in considera-

[24] See *Sixteenth Census of the United States: 1940. Population. Comparative Occupation Statistics for the United States, 1870 to 1940*, United States Government Printing Office, 1943.

tion simultaneously, proprietors, managers, and officials rank higher than clerical workers.

The compromise of social with economic factors in occupational ranking may be seen in Table 7. Despite the spotty nature of income data, we note

TABLE 7. Median Number of School Years Completed[25] and Median Annual Income[26] by Major Occupation Groups for the United States, 1940

Occupational Group	Median Years of School Completed	Median Annual Income
Professional and semiprofessional workers	15.6	$1803.05
Farmers and farm managers	7.6	
Proprietors, managers, and officials	10.9	
Clerical, sales, and kindred workers	12.2	1275.17
Craftsmen, foremen, and kindred workers	8.5	1551.69
Operatives and kindred workers	8.5	1142.14
Domestic service workers	7.9	
Protective service workers	8.8	
Service workers, except domestic and protective	8.7	
Farm laborers and foremen	7.4	362.93
Laborers, except farm and mine	7.7	979.76

that white-collar workers generally have greater incomes than manual workers. Although clerks have lower incomes than skilled manual workers, the superior social position and education of white-collar workers usually give them a higher general ranking. Within the manual-labor category, the relationship of income to socioeconomic status is clear. The skilled workers have highest income, then come the semiskilled, and last the unskilled. Thus an occupational description is something more than a cataloguing of people who perform roughly similar tasks. It is a ranking of people in the economic and social sense. With this in mind one may interpret occupational data more meaningfully.

Occupational Composition of the Labor Force

Table 8 reveals the occupational composition of the labor force in 1940, and Figures 17, 18, and 19 portray the occupational trends since 1910.[27]

[25] U.S. Census, *Comparative Occupational Statistics . . . 1870 to 1940*, Table XXV, p. 181.

[26] *Ibid.*, Table XXIV, p. 181.

[27] The student should consult Edwards, *Comparative Occupational Statistics . . . 1870 to 1940*, for an excellent and detailed discussion of occupational trends. Much of the data here are obtained from that source.

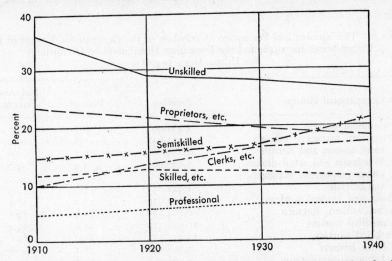

FIG. 17. Occupational Trends of American Workers. (From Alba M. Edwards, *Comparative Occupational Statistics for the United States, 1870-1940*, United States Government Printing Office, p. 185.)

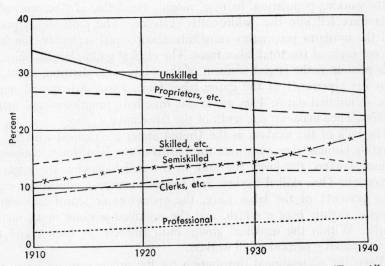

FIG. 18. Occupational Trends of Male Workers in the United States. (From Alba M. Edwards, *Comparative Occupational Statistics for the United States, 1870-1940*, United States Government Printing Office, p. 185.)

Several interesting observations may be made of the occupational picture in 1940.

TABLE 8.   The Number and Percentage Distribution of the Occupational Groups of the
United States for 1940; and the Percentage Distribution of Occupations
for Urban Areas, 1940[28]

Occupational Groups	Number	Percent	Urban Areas Percent
1. Professional persons	3,381,993	6.5	7.8
2. Proprietors, managers, officials	9,233,643	17.8	9.2
a. Farm owners and tenants	5,274,706	10.1	—
b. Wholesale and retail dealers	2,037,900	3.9	4.7
c. Other proprietors, managers, and officials	1,921,037	3.7	4.5
3. Clerks and kindred workers	8,923,939	17.2	20.8
4. Skilled workers, foremen	6,104,985	11.7	14.1
5. Semiskilled workers	10,918,312	21.0	25.4
6. Unskilled workers	13,457,151	25.9	22.6
a. Farm laborers	3,708,191	7.1	—
b. Laborers except farm	5,566,493	10.7	12.9
c. Servant classes	4,182,467	8.0	9.7
Total	52,020,023	100.1	99.9

Two basic groups into which the working population is often divided are "white-collar" and "manual" workers. They are sometimes referred to as "the business class" and "the working class." Although this segregation is somewhat arbitrary and unrealistic, it does denote a basic status demarkation of the working population. In 1940, roughly two-fifths, 41.5 percent, of the labor force fell into the "white-collar" category. The professional persons and the nonfarm proprietors constitute about equal segments, roughly 7 percent each, of the total labor force. The clerical group, largely office and sales persons, is the largest segment of the white-collar division, about one-sixth (17.2 percent) of the entire labor force. Farm owners and tenants have an unusual status. They are at one time both proprietors and manual workers. They make up one-tenth of the labor force.

The bulk of the workers in the United States are manual workers. Not counting farmers, they constitute three-fifths of the labor force. Among the manual workers, the lower the rank in the skill hierarchy, the larger the proportion. Thus skilled workers and foremen comprise almost one-eighth (11.7 percent) of the labor force, the operatives or semiskilled workers compose slightly over one-fifth, and the unskilled workers make up one-quarter. Within the unskilled group, farm laborers are found, and they number about 7 percent of all workers.

When the occupational distribution for the *urban working force* is ex-

[28] See *ibid.*, Table XXVI, p. 186. Urban percentages are estimates obtained by recomputing proportions in the major occupational groups, after excluding farm owners, tenants, and laborers.

amined, we find that the proportions in most of the occupational levels are increased somewhat. Two important changes must be noticed, however: (1) The proportion of proprietors, managers, and officials is decreased by half—from nearly 18 to 9 percent; (2) the unskilled laborers decline in percentage from about 26 to 23 percent of all workers. Perhaps the most important urban statistic is the proportion of workers who are dependent upon others for a livelihood. The census estimates that over 85 percent of the employed workers are wage or salaried employees.[29] Thus the chances

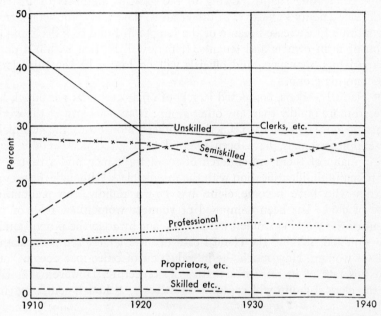

Fig. 19.   Occupational Trends of Female Workers in the United States. (From Alba M. Edwards, *Comparative Occupational Statistics for the United States, 1870-1940,* United States Government Printing Office, p. 185.)

are small for an average worker entering the labor market to fulfill his aspirations for economic independence.

Occupational Trends

With the general picture of the occupational structure in mind, let us examine the trends occurring within it. These may be seen in Figures 17, 18, and 19. Professional workers have increased gradually since 1910, from 4.4 percent of the total to 6.5 percent. Much of this growth resulted from the increasing number of women professionals, who entered the labor market as teachers, nurses, and social welfare workers. As late entrants in the professional field both women and men have become "dependent or salaried"

[29] U.S. Census, *Population*, Vol. II, Part I, Table X.

workers. The prospects are that the proportion of professionals in both sexes will continue to increase.

The trend among proprietors, managers, and officials is rather complex. Figures 17-19 reveal a general decrease in this group since 1910. However, most of the decline is due to the precipitous shrinkage in the proportion of farmers, from one-sixth to one-tenth of the labor force. The percentage in the category of nonfarm proprietors, managers, and officials, on the other hand, increased from 6.6 to 7.6 percent of the total.[30] This category will continue increasing slightly, owing to the growing numbers of managers and officials (nonproprietors), in urban areas. The total proprietary groups will continue to decrease because of the long-term trend of a declining proportion of farm owners and tenants. It may well be that within a decade the proprietors, managers, and officials will no longer be the third largest socioeconomic group.

The clerical workers, composed largely of office and sales personnel, have increased more rapidly than any other group: from one-tenth of the workers in 1910 to one-sixth in 1940. Clerical workers, along with the technicians and semiprofessionals, have been referred to as "the new middle class," because many of them are children of small tradesmen and artisans, who want to maintain identification with the middle class. Although the segment of males who have become clerks has grown rapidly, the predominant source of clerks has been composed of younger women. In 1910 only 14 percent of the working women were clerks, but by 1940 the proportion had about doubled, making the clerical category the largest source of employment for women. How much the introduction of office machines will slow down this rate of increase is a matter of conjecture. However, it is likely that the clerical group will continue to increase, although somewhat more slowly.

The relative proportion of skilled workers increased somewhat between 1910 and 1920, and then gradually decreased. However, the percentage of skilled women workers has decreased steadily since 1910. This trend is the result of the relentless pressure to replace hand labor with machine labor. World War II found this country with a shortage of skilled workers. Although many skilled workers were trained during the war, probably their relative proportion in the labor force will continue to decrease slowly.

Since 1910 the percentage of workers who are semiskilled operatives has increased more rapidly than any other group excepting the clerks. The increase was gradual in the second decade of the twentieth century, stabilized in the third decade, and accelerated rapidly again in the fourth. The growth from 17 to 21 percent in the thirty-year period resulted from the large influx of male workers in the group. The relative increase of operatives was realized somewhat at the expense of skilled workers, but more at the

[30] Edwards, *op. cit.*, p. 183.

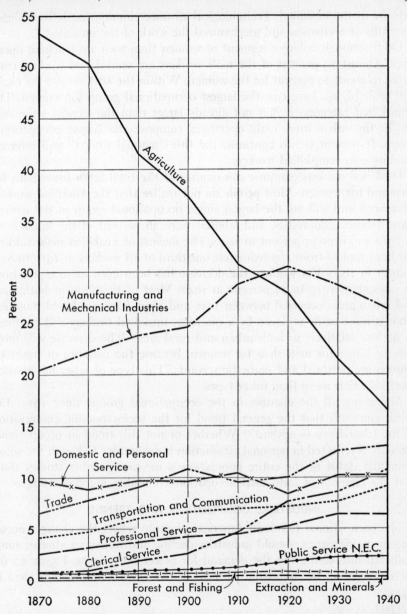

FIG. 20. Trends in the Distribution of Gainful Workers by General Divisions of Occupations for the United States, 1870-1940. (Adapted from Alba M. Edwards, *Comparative Occupational Statistics for the United States, 1870-1940*, United States Government Printing Office, p. 101, and reprinted from *Occupational Trends in the United States*, by Percy E. Davidson and Dewey Anderson, with the permission of the authors and of the publishers, Stanford University Press; 1940, p. 33.)

expense of the unskilled. Technological advance simultaneously has diluted the skills of craftsmen and mechanized the work of the unskilled.

Oddly enough, a larger segment of women than men are machine operatives. Almost 19 percent of the male workers are semi-skilled workers compared to about 29 percent for the women. Within the next decade the clerks will probably no longer be the largest occupational group for women. The semiskilled category, if it is not already larger than the clerical, soon may be. In the urban area, male operatives compose the largest occupational group. If present trends continue, the title "manual worker" will refer increasingly to semiskilled workers.

Unskilled workers comprise one-quarter of the total labor force both for men and for women. Most people do not realize that the unskilled workers have been and still are the largest single occupational group in the nation. Farm laborers, domestics, and laborers were 36 percent of the labor force in 1910 and over 25 percent in 1940. The decline of unskilled male workers has been rapid—from approximately one-third of all workers in 1910 to one-quarter in 1940. For women, the decrease has been even more rapid, from 42 percent in 1910 to 25 percent in 1940. Most of this drop in both rural and urban areas occurred between 1910 and 1920. Since unskilled muscular labor is most easily replaced by a machine, unskilled workers will continue to decline relatively in both urban and rural areas. The decrease will probably be larger for men than for women, because the majority of unskilled women are personal and domestic servants. This type of labor has resisted mechanization more than other types.

Appraising all the changes in the occupational groups since 1910, Edwards contends that the general trend for the socioeconomic composition of the labor force is upward.[31] Whether or not this trend in occupational mobility is reflected in personal satisfaction is debatable. Although the socioeconomic status of the entire population is increasing, other studies show that the chances of individual occupational mobility are decreasing.

INDUSTRIAL COMPOSITION AND TRENDS

The occupational trends in America primarily reflect the changes occurring in its industries. As old industries decline and new ones appear, some skills fall into disuse but the demand for newer skills arises. Figure 20 depicts changes in the industrial patterns of the United States from 1870 to 1940.[32]

[31] *Ibid.*, p. 186.

[32] No completely satisfactory classification of industries has been made. One continually runs into the difficulty of segregating occupational from industrial data. Some industrial classifications refer primarily to industries, irrespective of the occupations that comprise them; others refer almost solely to occupations. For example, the "manufacturing and mechanical industries" contain several occupational groups, as skilled, semiskilled, and unskilled. For the industrial classification of clerical service, however, only lower white-collar workers are included.

The most conspicuous trend seen in Figure 20 is the movement of agricultural workers to nonagricultural pursuits. The decline of the relative importance of agriculture since 1870 is spectacular. In that year the industry occupied 53 percent of the workers. By 1940 it employed only 18 percent. This decline reflects not only the mechanization of agriculture but also the exodus of rural workers to urban areas. The process of urbanization is documented by the fact that up to 1930 almost every industrial group showed a relative increase. This was only possible because of the continual release of agricultural workers.

Up to the beginning of World War I agriculture employed more workers than any other industry. In 1915 manufacturing and mechanical industries replaced agriculture in first place. The growth of manufacturing industries proceeded steadily upward from 1870 to 1920 and then declined gradually. Although still hiring more workers than any other industry, manufacturing has been steadily losing workers to the service industries.

Concurrent with the growth of mechanical industries was the gathering together of workers in increasingly larger plants. Thus in 1939, manufacturing plants hiring 100 or more workers comprised only 8.3 percent of all plants. Yet they employed 70 percent of all wage earners in manufacturing.[33] The process of industrial growth was also a process of building increasingly larger work plant societies. New problems of social organization and administration arose. The job of coördinating the activities of men was as gigantic and as new as the technical and engineering problems that were being faced. The social history of industrial expansion is an interesting sociological problem awaiting further attention and analysis.

The Basic Industries

The industries that produce the material goods of the economy are agriculture, forest and fishing, extraction or mining, and manufacturing and mechanical. In 1870 over three-quarters of the workers were engaged in these industries. By 1940 less than one-half of the workers were so engaged. With the advances in mechanization, a smaller and smaller segment of the work force was needed to produce the physical goods. A growing proportion of workers was needed to transport, distribute, and service the goods. Others were needed to record what was going on in the vast, complex industrial and commercial organizations.

These facts are portrayed in the trend lines of the white-collar industries in Figure 20. The largest "nonproductive" industry is trade. Edwards says, "The relative importance of trade and of transportation and communication as fields of employment of gainful labor, especially female labor, increased considerably from 1870 to 1930. . . . [In this period] the numbers engaged

[33] *Statistical Abstract of the United States, 1946*, United States Government Printing Office, Table 925, p. 810.

in transportation and communication increased over 600 percent, and the number engaged in trade increased nearly 600 percent as compared with an increase of 278 percent in the numbers engaged in all occupations."[34]

The domestic and personal service industry exhibited less change than any other. During the last seventy years it has absorbed about 10 percent of all workers. The industry has a greater percentage of women than any other field of employment.

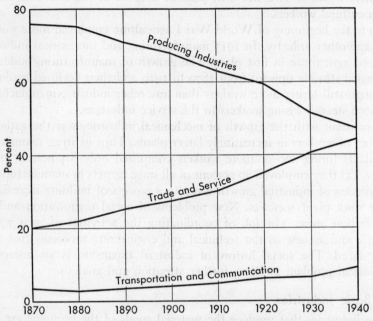

FIG. 21. Functional Groups as Percentages of Gainfully Employed. (Reprinted from *Occupational Trends in the United States*, by Percy E. Davidson and Dewey Anderson, with the permission of the authors and of the publishers, Stanford University Press, 1940, p. 35.)

Clerical service and professional service have experienced large relative increases. Clerical service has risen in importance faster than other industrial groups. As in the case of professional service, the entrance of large numbers of women into the field accounts for much of its growth.

Public service workers constitute a small but growing section of industry. Unfortunately, all persons working for government are not included by the census in this group; only government workers not elsewhere classified are included. For example, the million teachers in the United States are listed under professional service; so are judges, lawyers, librarians, physicians, nurses, and others. The 200,000 government clerical workers are counted in

[34] Edwards, *op. cit.*, p. 102.

clerical service. The utility, service, and maintenance workers of municipalities are also listed elsewhere. With this group excluded, public service
employed 2 percent of the workers in 1940.

The general changes in the industrial make-up of the nation are revealed
in Figure 21. The producing industries are falling rapidly in relative importance. Since 1870 the proportion of workers in trade and service industries has more than doubled, until these groups now employ as many workers as the producing industries. Transportation and communication has
doubled in percentage and now employs about one-tenth of the labor force.
The workers in the producing industries are now a minority, and will continue to be so in the future.

This chapter presented a preview of the social organization of the work
plant. It also examined the social importance of work in our society. An
effort was made to give the student a feeling for the occupational composition and changes occurring in the vast industrial plant of the country. In
the next chapter we shall enter specific work plants and study their social
organization intensively.

SUPPLEMENTARY STUDIES

FIELD OBSERVATION: DIRECT OBSERVATION OF A SELECTED WORK PLANT
(A PROJECT TO ACCOMPANY THE CHAPTERS IN PART TWO)

Select a work plant you will observe as you study the chapters in Part Two of
this text. In making your choice it will be important to consider whether you
will have convenient access to the work plant and the workers you wish to
observe. It would be helpful to choose a work plant which is easily available from
your home or your campus. A work plant is simply a place where people work,
whether such work commands pay or not. Therefore, your choice of a work
plant may be a store, a warehouse, a factory, a fraternity, a home, a dormitory,
a church, a construction site, a restaurant, a school, or any other place where
work is performed. It may be well to select a work plant in which you are now
working or one in which you have worked. It is acceptable to select a work plant
in which you have never had any previous contacts as long as you can find a
vantage point for observation. It is important that the workers do not know they
are being observed, for this information may affect their behavior. It is also
important that you either select a small work plant (under 100 workers) or
narrow the range of your observations so that no more than 100 workers are
involved. A useful approximation would be to consider no more of a work area
than can be accurately observed within a full circle of your vantage point or
points. A vantage point from which your observations may seem casual and
unobtrusive is greatly to be desired.

When you have selected a work plant describe:

Orientation Detail

1. The type of work plant.
2. The relation of the work plant to the community.
3. Your personal experience and present relationship to the plant.

Culture Content

1. Make an inventory of the *material traits*. Identify the *core traits* and the *culture complexes* formed about them.

    Note: A culture trait is the smallest functional unit of culture. It may be a unit of material culture such as a hammer, micrometer, a uniform, blueprint, or stamping machine. It may be a unit of nonmaterial culture such as a folkway, *mos*, rule, or law.

    A culture complex is a combination of two or more culture traits that functions as a unit. Culture traits tend to function around core or central traits. A college classroom often revolves around the professor's lecture notes. Every other material trait tends to assume meaning as they cluster about this core trait. Therefore, the "lecture complex" includes blackboard, chalk, notebooks, pencils, chairs, desks, walls, windows, etc.

2. Describe the *physical* and *social atmosphere* of your work plant.

    The physical atmosphere refers to such qualities as noise, odor, color, heat, volume and intensity of activity. The social atmosphere refers to the culture traits and the patterns of activity which influence the worker's pace, his work outlook, his sentiments, and culturally prompted observable acts.

3. Describe the *jargon* and *argot* of the members in the work group or groups in your work plant.

    Jargon refers to the technical or secret vocabulary of a science, art, trade, profession, or other special group. The aim is to identify the terms which constitute the language of the trade as you hear them and to record them with meanings if you can ascertain them.

    Argot refers to the conventionalized slang of the group. College students speak of taking "soc," "econ," and "P. E." courses. They make appointments with professors or go to their committee meetings during a "float." Every work group tends to adopt a slang. To be able to speak it identifies the worker as assimilated, i.e., one who understands the trade and one who may be quickly accepted. Failure to understand or to speak the jargon or the argot stamps the worker either as a "greenhorn" or as one who is inexperienced and not practical.

4. Invoice *folkways, mores,* and *rules* in the work group you are observing.

    Folkways are simply habits of action common to the members of the group. They have some degree of traditional sanction for their persistence. The greeting "good morning," the handshake, the eating of three meals a day, taking rest periods are familiar examples.

    Mores are folkways which come to be defined by the group as the "right" ways. Group members are more conscious of the mores and they are always in some degree emotional. The violation or threatened violation of the mores causes concern or resentment. The mores need not be written down. For example, college students may have different definitions of cheating but there is common agreement that the professor should not have "favorites" and give better grades to "apple polishers." That is not "right."

Rules refer to explicity prescribed standards of conduct, usually written, and often imposed upon a group without prior agreement of the members.

5. Identify the *public values* and *ideals* of the work plant.

The public values and ideals of the work plant refer to the rationalized purposes of the activity which are presented to outsiders to justify morally the service of the work plant. Examples of such public or service ideals are "Safe milk for your baby," "Boeing builds the finest bombers," "We build poise and confidence in your personality."

6. Describe the *style of life* induced by the various work positions in the work plant.

Style of life refers to the particular mode of living which the work position tends to establish for a worker.

It may be useful to describe the salient features of the daily routine for a typical member of the work group starting when the worker rises and tracing through a full twenty-four-hour cycle. It is important to describe the major habits, the attitudes, bearing, dress, and manner of the worker.

A thorough description when you can get the data will include the way in which the work role affects the lives of family members, and contacts in the neighborhood and community as well as other members in the work group.

Grouping and Contacts

1. Make a rough floor plan of the work plant showing the arrangement of workers at their *work stations*. If they move about in their work activity indicate *work routes* that they take in the course of their daily routines.

2. Describe the *size* and *number* of the separate working groups.

3. Identify the kind of interaction (primary, quasi-primary, and secondary).

Primary group interaction is characterized by (a) face-to-face association, (b) small numbers, (c) unspecialized purpose, (d) comparative intimacy, and (e) relative permanence.

Quasi-primary group interaction is characterized by (a) face-to-face association and (b) small numbers but is limited in some degree by special purpose and (c) tends to be more formal and less intimate.

Secondary group interaction is characterized by (a) formal association, (b) large numbers, (c) specialized purpose, and (d) communication by such devices as telephone, letters, bulletins, etc.

4. Describe the workers. List such characteristics as *age, sex,* and *background*. Indicate if possible where they live and some of the characteristics of their *paths to work*.

5. If there are customers who make a contact with the work plant, explain the kind of contacts made with customers.

(Supplements to this project accompany each of the following chapters in Part Two.)

Library: Books and Articles

Read:

Drucker, Peter F., "The Corporation as a Social Institution," in *Concept of a Corporation*, The John Day Company, 1946, chap. 3, pp. 130-208.

Roethlisberger, F. J., "A Disinterested Observer Looks at Industry," in *Management and Morale*, Harvard University Press, 1947, Chap. 5, pp. 67-87.

Williams, Whiting, *What's on the Worker's Mind*, Charles Scribner's Sons, 1920.

Browse on:

Edwards, Alba M., *Comparative Occupation Statistics for the United States, 1870-1940. Sixteenth Census of the United States: 1940. Population,* United States Government Printing Office, 1943. See especially Part III, "A Social Economic Grouping of the Nation's Labor Force, 1910-1940," pp. 175-182.

RESEARCH GAPS

Comparative analysis of styles of living associated with different occupations over the full socio-economic range.

The effect of work routines in facilitating or impeding civic participation.

Attitude syndromes associated with occupations.

The effect of changes in the occupational composition of the labor force on the class structure in America.

CHAPTER VI

The Formal Organization of Management

WHAT IS ORGANIZATION?

The question of organization brings up a variety of images to different people. To some it means a kind of group—as a union, lodge, or church. To others it calls to mind a number of offices in an association or society. Still others think of it as the means of introducing system or order into lifework.

To the labor leader or business executive, organization is a much more specific concept. It refers to a method of arranging men and materials. It represents an effective way of getting things done most efficiently. Organization is needed as the efforts of more and more people must be coördinated. It means, therefore, allocating authority to some individuals, delegating it to others, dispersing functions to still others, and keeping records of all activities.

No one will quarrel with these concepts of organization as far as they go. The scientist, however, is not content to use the specific definitions of particular groups. He is interested in the general phenomenon of organization and its manifestations everywhere. From a sociological point of view, social organization arises whenever people interact on a continuous basis in pursuit of common goals. Organization consists of the routines which group members display in their behavior toward each other. More exactly, organization consists of the behavior expectations that the people have toward each other as group members. The actual behavior of the members may not conform to these ideal expectations because many factors may intrude. The latter may include unusual events, individual differences, and interaction with other groups.

The sociological concept of organization is, then, simple and concrete. It consists of records of "observing the behavior of individuals in groups." All the uniform, routine, or conventional ways of group action constitute social organization. When these expected patterns of behavior are not observed, disequilibrium, disorganization, or social change ensues.

FORMAL ORGANIZATION

This approach to organization is not commonly utilized by all social scientists. When the economist speaks of the organization of business, or when the political scientist describes the organization of government, each is referring to only one aspect of social organization, namely, *formal organization*. Urwick's definition is typical of business administrators. He says

organization is "dividing up all of the activities which are necessary to any purpose and arranging them in groups which are assigned to individuals."[1] Although this idea is drawn with an eye on practical problems of administration, it contains the essential elements included in formal organization. Among the things included would be all written specifications of individual relationships in the group, all rights, duties, and privileges that are formally assigned to personal and group roles, and all rituals and regulations that are created as models of personal and group activity. C. I. Barnard in his book, *The Functions of the Executive*, summarizes the characteristics of formal organization in a pithy definition: "The central hypothesis of this book is that the most useful concept for the analysis of cooperative systems is embodied in the definition of formal organization as a *system of consciously coordinated activities of two or more persons.*"[2]

Barnard specifically emphasizes that his definition of formal organization *excludes* the physical environment (as a plant), the particular social situations, and the specific members of the organization.[3] Formal organizations are: (1) impersonal or nonpersonal in nature, (2) composed of members who bear ideal *relationships* toward each other, and (3) usually parts of larger coöperative systems.[4]

The reader may think it contradictory that people are necessary to organization and yet specific individuals and social situations are excluded in the definition of organization. The distinctions between "office" and person may clarify the point. The judge, the teacher, the priest may be thought of as offices or statuses that particular individuals hold. The judge must act toward the violator of the law in accord with formally constituted specifications. His relationship toward the violator is impersonal. In the capacity of a judge, a husband may have to pronounce sentence on a traffic violator, who may happen to be his wife. In the formal organization of the court, *the persons are incidental to their defined relationships.* So it is with formal organization generally.

The specific social situation is not included in formal organization for similar reasons. To elaborate our illustration: On a particular morning our judge may have a "hangover"; his wife may have just told him she must have an operation. Certainly these unusual circumstances will alter the operation of the court, yet such situations are too fluid to be considered as part of a system of relations that typically govern the behavior of the court.

When we describe the formal organization of business or labor, then we are concerned with the relations as specified in the organizational charts. Some of these relations are: (1) the authority relations, or what offices

---

[1] L. Urwick, *Management of Tomorrow*, Nisbet and Co., Ltd., 1933, p. 53.
[2] C. I. Barnard, *The Functions of the Executive*, Harvard University Press, 1947, p. 73.
[3] *Ibid.*, p. 64.
[4] *Ibid.*, *passim*, pp. 74-80.

appear to have authority over other offices, (2) what offices or groups are responsible to what other offices, (3) what groups have what specific functions (auditing, cleaning, managing), and (4) who reports what to whom (the communication system).

These relations are found universally in formal organizations everywhere. They are present in labor, business, political, educational, religious, and other organizations. The specific relations may be structured differently in different organizations, but the types of relations themselves are universal, and therefore noncultural.

This view of formal organization is valuable, but, as the reader is already aware, it is not concerned with the person *in the act of fulfilling his role*. When one begins to examine formal organization in actual operation, one notes that people do not altogether live up to the specific definitions of their offices. And this is to be expected because formal organization cannot take into account the individual attributes of the person in an office and in changing situations. In fact, it may be stated as a principle that "whenever persons are placed in continued formal contact, in whatever circumstances, their relationships become characterized by actions and reactions over and above formal expectations."[5] To assume that the big boss's secretary, especially if she's pretty, has no influence on his job is naïve. It is also naïve to assume that such personal relations as might develop are totally unpatterned or inconsequential. In fact, the sociologist believes that the personal relations existing among members of an organization which are not represented by the "blueprint" constitute another aspect of organization, namely, informal organization. This informal organization plays as important a part in the functioning of social organization as formal organization itself.

INFORMAL ORGANIZATION

Informal organization consists of a number of things. It is composed of the animosities and friendships among the people who work together. It contains the primary groups, cliques, and congeniality groups that develop in shop or office. It further consists of the folkways, mores, norms, and values which guide the behavior of workers, sometimes in the fulfillment of the goals of formal organization and sometimes in the blockage of those goals. Informal organization is a source of much social control. In it a prestige and power structure evolves which may be at variance with similar structures in the formal organization. In fact, the relation of the informal organization to formal organization determines how effectively the latter will function.

THE CONSTITUENT SEGMENTS OF THE WORK PLANT

The distinction between formal and informal organization is made only for analytic purposes. The functioning of informal organization may be

[5] Wilbert E. Moore, *Industrial Relations and the Social Order*, The Macmillan Company, 1946, p. 314.

meaningless without knowledge of the formal structure to which it is associated. The reverse may be equally true. The study of the "invisible" informal aspect of organization is a primary contribution of sociology to the

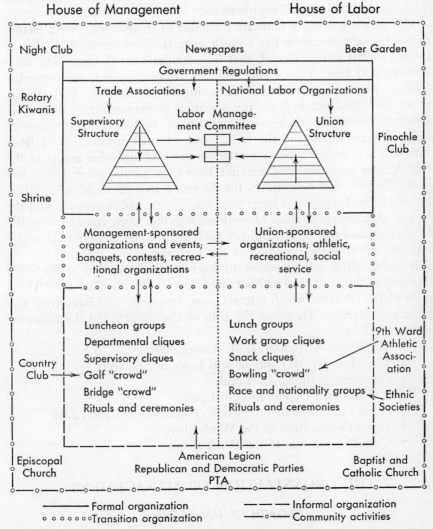

FIG. 22. Simplified Diagram of the Social Organization of Work Plants in Their Community and Society Setting. Only the major social segments are presented so that their interactive relations may be emphasized.

field of organization and administration, as is the study of the interrelations of informal and formal organization.

Figure 22 portrays the constituent parts of the social organization of a work plant. In the diagram the basic vertical line divides the "House of

Management" from the "House of Labor." In the management section the supervisory structure comprises most of the formal organization. In the workers' section the labor union represents the formal aspect of organization. The houses of labor and management are divided internally into formal, informal, and "transition" organizations.

This diagram serves to illustrate a number of things: first, that a factory or any business enterprise has a much more complex organization than is evident at first glance; second, that the organizational divisions into management and labor, formal and informal, although useful, are somewhat arbitrary. Social organization is a functioning interacting whole. For example, as we shall demonstrate later, the operation of management's supervisory structure cannot be understood without an analysis of management's informal organization and the formal and informal organization of labor with which it interacts. Nor may the operation of any other aspect of the organization be appreciated without knowledge of the other interacting parts. The third fact indicated by the diagram is that the social organization of a work plant is part of a larger complex, namely, the community and the society. A complete analysis of work organization must consider how the community and the society, through their own formal and informal organizations, influence the operation of the work plant.

It is difficult if not impossible to describe the interaction of the main segments of the work plant without first analyzing its individual parts. Those parts of the structure which interact more frequently and intensively will be treated together. Therefore, the plan of this chapter and the following chapters will be:

1. The Formal Organization of Management.
2. The Major Work Positions and Roles of Managers.
3. Operation of the Union Local.
4. The Informal Organization of Labor.
5. Power Organization: Interaction of Management and Labor.
6. Status Organization of the Work Plant.
7. Class Organization of the Work Plant.

THE ORGANIZATION OF MANAGEMENT

GROWTH OF MANAGEMENT

Very few occupational groups are as self-conscious as modern executives and managers. This narcissism has not always existed; it is the product of particular historical changes occurring in the economic system. The evolution of modern management organization has accompanied the growth and expansion of business and industry. This growth probably could not have occurred without two accompanying social movements. The first of these

was the development of the natural sciences. The second was the growth of a vigorous capitalistic economy which employed the discoveries of science for private profit. Under the twin stimulations of applied science (technology) and capitalistic enterprise the size of businesses grew. The advantage of large-scale production was soon apparent for both technological and financial reasons. The ability to expand production on the basis of technical improvements grew faster than the ability of private individuals to finance plant expansion. Under these conditions, the corporative form of business enterprise was invented and diffused.

The growth of the corporation had two important consequences. One was the dispersion of owners (or stockholders), who had little or no contact with the actual operation of business. The extent of the separation of owners from workers was documented in a study by Berle and Means. They discovered that as early as 1929, 94 percent of all manufactured products were made by corporations.[6] The second consequence of corporate growth was the impetus it gave to the occupational division of labor. As finance was made available to introduce new machines and new operations, the growth of specialized occupations increased enormously. Data from the census and the *Dictionary of Occupational Titles* present graphic evidence of the proliferation of occupations in America today. Admitting an incomplete enumeration, the latter publication in 1939 defined 29,744 different occupational titles.[7]

FUNCTIONS OF MANAGEMENT

With owners dispersed and unable to attend to the direction of business, and with industry growing in size and complexity, there was a pressing need to *coördinate more effectively the activities of many people*. This is the management or executive function. As industry grew larger and more complex the executive process became more crucial. Barnard, who has made an important study of the management process, indicates that its three main functions are:

1. To provide a system of communication.
2. To promote the securing of essential efforts.
3. To formulate and define purpose for the organization.[8]

Although Barnard has substituted a vocabulary of coöperation for a vocabulary of command in his analysis of executive functions, he is nonetheless correct in suggesting that management's duties are essentially devoted toward coördination of human, not technical, activity. It is difficult to over-

[6] See Adolf A. Berle, Jr., and Gardiner C. Means, *The Modern Corporation and Private Property*, The Macmillan Company, 1933, p. 39.
[7] *Dictionary of Occupational Titles*, United States Employment Service, United States Government Printing Office, 1939.
[8] Barnard, *op. cit.*, p. 217.

stress the role of management as one which is directed toward people and the integration of their efforts.

Figure 23 depicts how the functions of management grow as a response to large-scale organization. As the number of persons in an organization increases, their relationships expand geometrically. Since it is management's task to coördinate people, management activities increase tremendously with

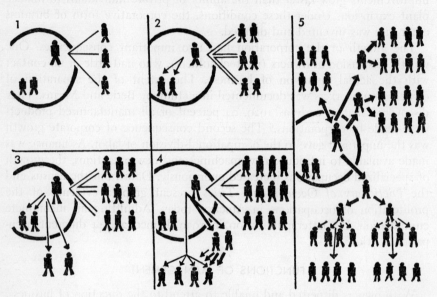

FIG. 23.   The Expansion of a Work Plant and the Rise and Change of Management Function. (1) The craftsman sells to a few customers. (2) As the volume of his business increases, his sons begin to work under his direction. (3) With further increase in sales, he employs apprentices outside the family. (4) With a larger volume of business, all the manufacturing is done outside of the family, and a factory hierarchy develops with foremen supervising the workers under his direction while he continues to sell directly to his customers. (5) With further expansion he invites others to buy shares of his business. He delegates his sales duties to others, delegates his supervision over manufacturing to another, and spends most of his time integrating the activities of everyone. (Adapted from Eliot D. Chapple and Carleton S. Coon, *Principles of Anthropology*, Henry Holt and Company, 1942, p. 369.)

expanding size of organization. The functions of management are of course performed in the smallest enterprises; even if the business consists of two individuals, the functions of coördination must take place. As a small business grows, the duties of the manager become more pressing until all his energy must be devoted to them. With further expansion of business, the management functions must be subdivided, for they become too burdensome for one person. Thus management becomes a specialized occupation with many subclassifications.

FORMAL ORGANIZATION: A THEORY OF SUPERORDINATION

Figure 24 portrays the skeletal social organization of management. Perhaps the most important idea shown in the figure is that formal management

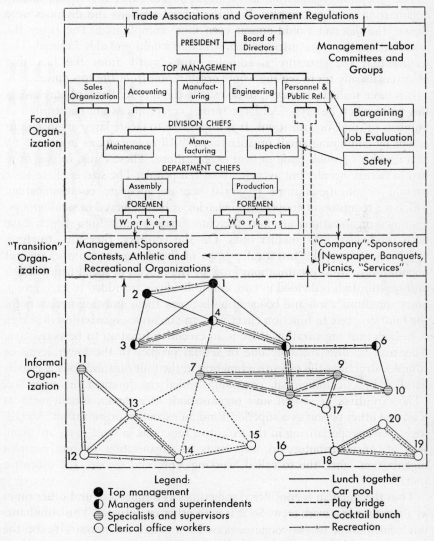

FIG. 24. The Social Organization of Management.

organization is only a segment of an integrated work organization. For purposes of analysis we shall examine formal or "blueprint" organization separately. The upper portion of Figure 24 depicts that structure in a factory.

Although much variability may be found in the formal structures of factories, department stores, labor unions, governments, or other enterprises, the principles of organization are much the same almost irrespective of the function or the size of the organization.

The blueprint organization in Figure 24 suggests that the typical factory organization is rather complex. If *all* the formal relations and divisions were shown, the diagram would appear even more complicated. The larger the organization, the more intricate this structure would probably become. The feeling that the structure is complex arises partly from the fact that observers usually try to see the *whole organization from the top down*.

It is more realistic, however, to do exactly the reverse. Barnard emphasizes this point when he says, "All large formal organizations are constituted of numbers of small organizations. It is impossible to create large organizations except by combining small organizations."[9] *All organizations are made up of a number of small basic or unit organizations.* These range in size from two to twenty people, but average about ten people. The size of these basic or unit organizations must be small because adequate communication, which is a requisite for coöperative behavior, is best achieved in small groups. Complex organizations are *not*, therefore, mass organizations which have been subdivided into smaller ones. On the contrary, they are structures which result from the historical process of increasing the number of unit organizations. Most organizations grow by the process of social fission. Each unit organization is divided in two, and individuals are added to each group. Since communication and coöperation between these units are necessary for the total structure to function effectively, an executive organization develops.

In each unit organization there is an executive function to be performed. This may be discharged by one or several people. In the lower levels of complex structures the executive function in the unit organizations is usually handled by one individual, commonly called the foreman or supervisor. "The executives of several unit organizations as a group, usually with at least one other person as a superior, form an executive organization. Accordingly, persons specializing in the executive functions in most cases are members of, or contributors to, two units of organization in one complex organization—first, the so called 'working' unit, and second, the executive unit."[10]

Thus the foreman is considered sometimes as a supervisor and other times as a member of a work crew. So it is with other executives. "This simultaneous contribution to two organizations by a single act appears to be the critical fact in all complex organizations; that is, the complex is made an organic whole by it."[11]

[9] *Ibid.*, pp. 104-105.
[10] *Ibid.*, p. 111.
[11] *Ibid.*, p. 112.

The work plant, and especially its formal organization, is like an organism composed of many cells and coördinated by a nervous system which reaches every cell. This nervous system is the executive organization, which is sketched out in the organization chart.

Another attribute of complex structures is that they grow *from the bottom to the top by the process of superordination; or, looked at in reverse, organization grows by waves of subordination.* Both processes are needed if the rights, duties, and limitations of the unit organizations are to be properly circumscribed. By their very nature unit organizations perform only part of the work. Therefore, their activities must be controlled by other organizations if teamwork is to be achieved. We shall now proceed to detail the ways in which the basic units are related to each other in the formal organization.

HOW THE COMPONENTS OF FORMAL ORGANIZATION ARE SUPPOSED TO OPERATE

BUREAUCRACY: A SOCIETY OF UNEQUALS

Bureaucracy may be defined as the pyramiding of unit organizations. As such, it is the typical form of large-scale organizations. The term "bureaucracy" has been unfortunately abused by businessmen and others when they want to refer to governmental inefficiency. But as one businessman said after serving in government, "We in business have bureaucracy just like the government. Only we call it 'system.'" Of course, he was correct, for bureaucracies grow when any enterprise begins to expand, whether it is a factory, department store, government, hospital, university, labor union, or coöperative.

A manager in a nation-wide grocery chain relates his first-hand experiences with the growth of bureaucracy: "When I first came to work for this organization about ten years ago, my boss handed me a guide, which was about a half-inch thick. He told me, 'You'll find the answers to some of your questions in this guide. Half of the instructions in it are useless. But if you get stuck, just give me a ring, and we'll talk your problem over.' Mind you, today every manager is given a thirteen volume library to guide him in his work. And furthermore, there is a guide index for the guide."

As suggested, bureaucracy is simply a hierarchical arrangement of unit organizations. It is, or should be, an orderly arrangement of units based on division of function and authority. This means that a bureaucracy is an organization or a society of unequals. The basic inequalities are exemplified in the *supervisory hierarchy,* which forms a pyramid of authority. The hierarchy may be visualized as several layers of authority. At the top is the president, who has greatest power. His subordinates are the managers,

division chiefs, department chiefs, foremen, and workers, in that order. Although variations exist in the names given to offices in the layers, everywhere the structure is coördinated by a series of superior-subordinate or man-boss relations.[12] Figure 25 shows that in such a structure the man on the top presumably directs and controls the entire organization. Excepting him and the workers in the lowest layer, everybody in between reports to a boss and is in turn a boss over several other people. Thus the big boss *looks down* the supervisory structure, the workers fret about the bosses *above* them, and division chiefs, department heads, superintendents, and managers worry *both* about their bosses and about those whom they boss. Each rank is responsible for doing a specific job and is accountable to someone who wants it done.

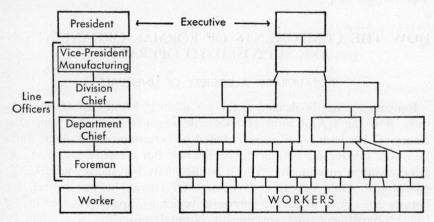

FIG. 25.   Line Organization Shown as a Straight Line and as a Pyramid.

THE LINE ORGANIZATION

The part of the structure which is dedicated to getting the work out is called the *line organization*. Theoretically, there is a direct line from the man at the top of the hierarchy to the worker who actually makes the product or provides the service. Obviously the top officer or the big boss cannot oversee everyone's work in the plant. Hence he issues some orders to the vice-president, who is then responsible for their execution. To facilitate this the president presumably delegates some of his authority to the vice-president. The vice-president in turn issues orders to the division chief, and subdelegates enough authority to enable him to carry out orders. This process is continued down the line to the actual workers. Obviously, the larger the organization, the longer is the line of authority and the greater

---

[12] Burleigh B. Gardner, *Human Relations in Industry*, Richard D. Irwin, Inc., 1945, p. 4.

the social distance between the worker and the big boss. All the intermediaries from the big boss to the workers are necessary because the number
of persons a boss can properly supervise must remain relatively small.[13]

The greater the number of layers in a structure, the less do the people in
each layer know of the activities of people in other parts of the work plant.
Higher executives do not have a complete or reliable picture of what is happening on the plant floor. Indeed, they do not need complete information.
Their job is to formulate general objectives and policies. Each intermediary
translates these objectives into more concrete and specific commands to the
level below, until the worker is given specific instructions to punch a half-
inch hole into this piece of metal.

Of course, other things must be done besides punching holes. The fantastic amount of division of labor and specialization in the modern factory
points to the multitude of tasks that are done. The greater the number of
tasks, the more complex the line organization becomes. A proliferation of
offices occurs. The president is now assisted by more than one vice-president.
Each vice-president is assigned special tasks and is given a *different* area of
authority. Each vice-president has under him *several* division chiefs, each of
whom has specific duties. As seen in Figure 25, this process of subdivision
is repeated down the line, with the end result that the organizational chart
looks like a pyramid.

FUNCTIONAL ORGANIZATION

The second basic division in the work structure is the functional organization. Each vertical segment in Figure 25 represents a group which has a
distinct function to perform. In an automobile plant, for example, a different department manufactures the ignition system, and so on. A plant may
be functionally divided in various ways. The division may correspond to
items, as in the auto plant. Divisions may be based on a process rather
than a product. For example, one department may do all the wiring for
any product manufactured, another may do all the printing, drilling, or
packing for all other departments. Functional divisions or departments may
be based on other principles—the use of similar materials, the need for
similar skills in different processes, or the most efficient handling of bulk or
materials. Efficiency is *supposed* to determine how the departments are to
be organized. However, this is not always the case, and how work is divided
may reflect the tastes of those who have power.

Since specialization has proceeded so far in our industrial organizations,
functional charts of large organizations are extremely complicated. In fact,
it is almost impossible to picture clearly all of the functional divisions,
departments, subdepartments, and units in such an organization as the Ford
Motor Company. Some segments are too minute; others overlap in several

[13] Moore, *op. cit.*, p. 97.

directions at once. Since functional divisions are not as clear as authority divisions, squabbles tend to develop over them. We shall treat these problems in another section.

STAFF ORGANIZATION

We have indicated that authority not only may be delegated but may be divided into spheres of specialization. Since policy-forming executives in larger organizations do not always have the technical competence to translate general policies into specific orders, they must integrate into their organization people who do have the technical competence. In addition to these advisers, other specialists who have little to do with production are

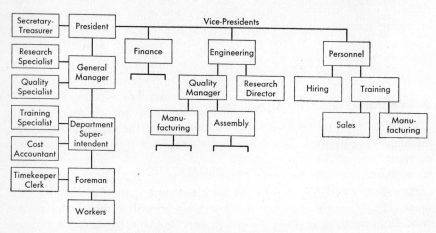

F‌ig. 26.   Ideal-Typical Organizations of Staff: Horizontal Staff and General Staff.

needed. For example, research, hiring, training, keeping financial records, and selling are all specialist services that are not involved directly in the main purpose of the organization. The technical advisers and people who provide specialist services are considered to be part of the *staff* organization. Strictly speaking, although staff members have no authority over line organization, they must be integrated into that organization. Moore suggests that the staff may be integrated into the line organization in three ways.[14]

1. Integrating Specialists in Advisory Capacities

With the line still representing the supervisory structure, the specialists or *staff* people may be integrated into it in an advisory capacity. This is done in two ways. The first technique is to place them into a "horizontal" relationship at any level where their skill is needed. Thus a *staff* man may be integrated at any level from the top to the bottom. The other technique is

[14] *Ibid.*, pp. 101-104.

to bring all staff people under one or several high *line* or *staff* officials. The latter provide specialist staff service to any line official who may need it. Figure 26 shows the first alternative on the left and the second alternative on the right. Actually these alternatives rarely exist in pure form. Usually both techniques of incorporating staff services are used simultaneously.

2. Integrating Specialists Directly into the Line Organization

According to F. W. Taylor, the functional specialization of management should ideally extend throughout the organization from top management to foremen. Thus all managers would always be specialists, and would have authority over others only in their area of competence.[15] In such an organization, a single worker might be under the supervision of several managers, including trainers, inspectors, planners, researchers, expediters, and so on. Obviously such a plan is difficult to operate. It creates problems of coördination which are very difficult to solve. For this reason this kind of direct integration of specialists is rarely used in pure form.

3. Integrating Staff in All Capacities

Within the same establishment all the techniques of integrating staff members may be used. For example, the president may have several staff assistants who advise him on policy. These advisers are not at the head of an organization; they are only consultants on policy. Within the same organization specialists may be found who occupy positions as line managers. They may direct research, labor relations, engineering, and at the same time supervise a production department. Yet in another part of the plant a high staff official may have under him an extensive staff organization. The latter may include several departments and sections and a small supervisory structure.

Still another method of integrating the staff is to give it authority under certain conditions to insert orders directly into the line organization. Thus in actual cases line-staff distinctions may be somewhat hazy. The fact that there is no agreement on the best way to integrate the staff into the line organization is the occasion for many conflicts. These conflicts are sometimes heightened because staff people not only consider themselves to be part of management but also feel a status superiority over some line officials.

THE COMMUNICATION ORGANIZATION

A generally recognized sociological maxim is that the larger and more complex the social organization, the greater the need for coördinating it. The modern factory, with its extensive specialization, is subject to this principle. Ideally speaking, a properly functioning organization should be

[15] F. W. Taylor, *Shop Management*, Harper & Brothers, 1911.

self-coördinating. If the supervisory structure, functional divisions, and staff organizations dovetailed perfectly, little coördination would be needed. Orders would go down the line, functions would be parceled out, advice would be given where needed, and jobs would be completed.

But this is rarely the case because social organization is not a machine. Human elements insert themselves. Goals may be inescapable of fulfillment. Orders may not be clearly expressed; new problems arise which require special attention. Financial emergencies must be solved. Certain managers may be incompetent. Executives feel that whenever possible they should reduce these problems. One way of doing this is to make sure that communication flows freely. To minimize the possibility of misinterpretation orders are issued down the line in *written* form whenever possible. Written orders issued by top management are quite general. They become more detailed as they go down the line.

In order to know what is going on, top management expects daily, weekly, monthly, semiannual, and annual reports from subordinates. Daily reports flow up the line, usually in written form. They contain information on the general problems encountered as well as the achievements. The lower the supervisory level, the more detailed are the reports. As they flow up the line, they become more general and less technical. On the bases of these reports managers on all levels issue new orders to meet both the new and the older problems.

All kinds of commands and reports flow up and down the line. These may be classified into four categories: technical, financial, inspectional, and attitudinal. The first three are formally recognized by management. The last, although not so recognized, is nonetheless present. The ideas, feelings, sentiments, and gossip of all groups travel up and down the line.

Although communication between departments on the same level occurs, theoretically it is not supposed to be direct. Reports, desires for service, or criticisms that one department has of another are supposed to be sent up the line until they reach an executive who heads the organizations involved. They are then held, revised, or sent directly down the line to the appropriate officials and departments. The reason for this circuitous route is to inform higher officials of things occurring below them.

An illustration demonstrates the degree to which the channels of communication can become formalized. In a nation-wide wholesale grocery business each executive has a printed list of the kinds of things he may discuss with executives in different divisions of the organization. If a matter arises which has not been anticipated in the printed list, the individual must seek permission from his superior two levels up the line to discuss it with the appropriate official in another division. If the request is approved, a high official in the appropriate division is contacted, from whom permission to

communicate is sought. This request is passed down the line and acted upon. If approved, it must go back up the line, over to the original division, and down the line to the initiating person. Then direct communication is authorized. This process is called observing the channels, and it consumes a lot of time. It is especially frustrating when the communicants are located just across the hall. In such cases direct contacts are resorted to and formal requests for communication are initiated to be on the safe side. Frequently, however, the individual may not know whom he should contact. All he knows is that he must seek permission from his immediate boss and wait. Going directly to the person or office up or down the line without attention to procedure is called *short-circuiting* the line. This is usually frowned upon, for everyone wants to know all the important information. To be caught without knowledge by a superior is a source of embarrassment.

In summary, the *theory* of formal organization is in itself quite simple. It holds that throughout the organization there is a strict definition of authority and responsibility. Similarly, there is an equally precise definition of the functions of every department. Free and accurate communication flows from every part of the organization to every other part. Every action is guided by the principle of what is best for the organization as a whole.

IMPLICIT ASSUMPTIONS OF FORMAL ORGANIZATION

In addition to the described attributes of formal organization there are several implied assumptions. The first of these is that formal organization is necessary to achieve organizational goals. It is necessary because it is by nature impersonal, logical, and efficient. An organization can function best when individual idiosyncrasies, sentiments, and prejudices do not interfere with official activities. Thus, by defining offices and roles as a series of rights and duties, the individual element in social interaction is reduced.

The second assumption of formal organization is that it is the only organization. In the literal sense many managers believe the only organization that exists is that portrayed on the blueprints. To them, good organization is simply that which duplicates the blueprint structure.

A third assumption is that formal organization is flexible, and that it can meet problems readily. If, for example, a factory department needs more men, it may borrow them from another department which has a temporary excess. The men and departments involved will agree to such an expediency for it is to everyone's benefit. Underlying the thinking here is the idea that the chief aim of organization and personnel is to achieve organizational goals. When the enterprise achieves this end, the employees automatically achieve their individual aims. In other words, efficient workers make an effective organization, and vice versa. What is best for the organization in the immediate and distant future is best for the individual workers.

THE OPERATION OF MANAGEMENT ORGANIZATION

FORMAL ORGANIZATION AS HUMAN ORGANIZATION

We have briefly described the theory of formal organization and some of the assumptions underlying it. Although formal organization is designed to subject production to logical planning, things never seem to go "according to plan." This is evidenced by the many "problems" managers encounter. They find that no matter how carefully they organize, despite the concern in anticipating problems, unanticipated ones always arise: (1) Some parts of the organization function better than others. (2) The line may not follow suggestions of staff. (3) New recruits may be difficult to secure. (4) Central management may be in conflict with divisional management. (5) Community relations may be disturbing. (6) Disagreements arise in the interpretation of orders.

For these kinds of eventualities formal organization offers little guidance because it is created as a guidepost for the routine, the typical, and the foreseeable. Although it provides the framework for dealing with new problems, these are foreseen as capable of routine treatment. This does not mean that formal organization is sterile and useless. On the contrary, it is both necessary and inevitable, to realize sustained coöperation of many people and groups. Even though an organization cannot be understood without knowledge of its formal structure, it is equally true that the most complete knowledge of formal organization does not tell us how the enterprise actually functions.

The reason this is so is quickly identified. The most important variable in the organization chart has been absent, namely, people. Formal organization looks on the people that inhabit the different offices or positions as constants. It assumes that all of the workers in a plant are unrelated individuals, or that their relations are only those which are specified on the chart. As individuals, they think and act logically in a manner calculated to promote their economic self-interest. The motive of this individualistic, rational, and selfish behavior is to promote the economic well-being of themselves and the enterprise.[16]

THE PERSPECTIVES OF THE SOCIOLOGISTS

Sociologists not only deny the reality of these assumptions; they suggest alternative ones. Whenever they examine organizations, economic, political, religious, educational, or others, they do so with a special set of tools, concepts, or ideas. One of the most fundamental ideas is that people can only be understood in their social relations with each other. *Social relations, not*

[16] Elton Mayo has referred to these assumptions as "the rabble hypothesis." See his *The Social Problems of an Industrial Civilization*, Harvard University Press, 1945, p. 40.

individuals, are the basic units of observation. Since social relations constitute the essence of groups, sociologists begin looking for social relations or groups whenever they examine human activity. This is what we shall do as we study the social organization that develops around the formal organization of management.

The sociological point of view does not demand an examination of the relations of specific individuals and situations. Rather, it seeks to find the kinds of social relations that may be expected to develop under certain stable conditions. It proceeds by applying what is already known about human relations in general to typical and recurrent situations—in this case, work situations.

The major generalizations that the sociologist applies to the study of work organization may be stated as follows:

1. Individuals who are in physical and social contact almost invariably form groups which have structure and permanence.

2. Specific relations tend to become social relations. Thus, economic, political, or educational relations between people tend to become more widely defined as general social relations.

3. Social relations may be examined in their static and dynamic aspects. In the static sense the sum total of a worker's specified relations to others in the structure is called his *work position*. It is composed of a number of rights, duties, functions, and obligations. In the dynamic sense, the carrying out of these rights, duties, and responsibilities is the *work role*. All people in every stable group have positions and roles, and all groups may be analyzed as coördinated series of positions and roles.

4. Interaction between people always *involves communication* of meanings through symbols. To understand group structure one studies the amount, direction, frequency, intensity, and content of communication.

5. Every group shares a number of ideas, beliefs, customs, values, and sentiments. Sometimes these are integrated into a system or an ideology. Individual and group behavior cannot be fully comprehended without knowledge of the prevailing ideologies.

6. Whenever people in a group have different social characteristics or functions, social stratification invariably ensues. In our society stratification is, among other things, based on money, prestige, and authority. In turn, class, status, and power organizations arise in society which reflect these bases of stratification.

7. All groups tend to regard themselves as somewhat separate and superior to all other groups. Ethnocentrism, social distance, and segmentation develop between groups.

8. Formal structure never describes completely the relations among people. Friendships, cliques, and small informal groups develop which often function contrary to the expectations of formal structures.

9. All groups may be thought of as representing an equilibrium of integrative and disintegrative forces. The group always is in a dynamic process of being built up or torn down.

COMMUNICATION AND SEGMENTATION PROBLEMS

Work organizations also exhibit these principles. In work plants the same two contradictory pressures or tendencies may be found. One is to coördinate small groups so that their individual identity is reduced; the other is to preserve as much individual identity in the small group as possible. The tendency of a larger group to divide into smaller ones is called *the segmentation tendency*. When these small groups subordinate their purposes to the larger organization, effective coördination is attained and there are no organizational problems. When different parts struggle to dominate each other or retain independence, segmentation tendencies are greater than the coördination or integration tendencies. Sociologists speak of this state as a disequilibrium of forces. The theory of formal organization seems to ignore these segmentation and integration forces.

This is unfortunate because the division of a large organization into many smaller parts introduces problems of communication. People in one segment fail to understand what people in another segment are doing or trying to accomplish.

This creates an entirely new problem of communication. Elton Mayo has emphasized the importance of communication in strong terms. He says, "I believe that social study should begin with careful observation of what may be described as communication: that is, the capacity of an individual to communicate his feelings and ideas to another, the capacity of groups to communicate effectively and intimately with each other. This problem is, beyond all reasonable doubt, the outstanding defect that civilization is facing today."[17]

The Relation of Communication and Segmentation

Communication is basic to the understanding of human relations in a work plant whether it is large or small. In a large plant the many segmented parts tend to multiply the difficulties of securing clear and accurate communication.

Theoretically the line is supposed to carry all communication, orders going down and reports going up. Orders are never supposed to flow up the line, and reports about the "big boys" are not supposed to go down the line. Apart from orders and reports, a third type of communication, though acknowledged, is often neglected. It may be called "peer" communication, because it is horizontal in nature. When equals or peers consult and advise with each other, there are no orders or reports in the strict sense. Peer com-

[17] *Ibid.*, p. 22.

munication is important because it provides an excellent index to the processes of segmentation and integration. For example, the fact that foremen of two departments frequently consult with one another and are friendly, whereas they rarely consult or have social contacts with other foremen, provides a clue to the relative integration or segmentation of the departments of the work plant.

Segmentation of groups does not occur accidentally. It develops naturally in the manner that communication travels up and down the line. The very nature of the man-boss linkage affects the accuracy, speed, and content of communication.[18] Obviously, the more levels communication must travel, the less complete and accurate it will be. A superior is only kidding himself if he thinks he has comprehensive knowledge of what is going on as close as two levels below him. He is largely dependent for what knowledge he does have on what the intervening supervisors want to tell him. Supervisors presumably report all the information which their bosses need to make decisions. This ideal is seldom achieved, however. More frequently bosses do not get the important information; indeed, irrelevant details often clutter their desks, making efficient administration an impossibility.

DISTORTION UP THE LINE

Gardner points out that each supervisor wants to have a good record for himself and for his department. In his efforts to make a good impression the communication he sends up the line is distorted. There is the tendency to give the boss what he wants to hear, namely, that "operations are going according to plan." Also, subordinates are likely to "cover up" when things do not so move.[19] This is done in the hope that the job will soon be straightened out and the boss won't find out what the situation really is.

Thus, each responsible person up and down the line acts as a *sieve* or *filter*. Orders going down the line should be concise, accurate, and complete. In the process of interpretation, and making orders increasingly specific, errors or omissions sometimes intrude themselves. Orders may be issued too late; they may be incomplete, inaccurate, or ambiguous. Sometimes information which should not be released is accidentally circulated. Thus communication going down the line can become as distorted and filtered as information traveling in the reverse direction.

From these observations it is apparent that formal communication does not travel evenly, freely, and accurately from each section to all other sections of the work plant. There may be little or no interchange of information between some departments of the organization. This isolation may be the result of previous friction, physical segregation, or other factors.

[18] See Gardner, *op. cit.*, chap. 2, "The Line of Authority and Communication," for an excellent discussion of this problem.
[19] *Ibid.*, pp. 25-28.

On the other hand, there may be frequent, rapid, and accurate communication between two or more sections of the organization. Or communication may travel rapidly, but it may be inaccurate or antagonistic in content. The communication flow among the segments of an organization may be accurately charted. It should be recorded in terms of its source, frequency, duration, direction, intensity, and content. Such a diagram for a particular plant would be of invaluable aid in examining its problems.

Even with such a diagram, however, all problems would not be solved. Some writers have asserted that if there is free and open communication in a work plant people will understand each other and problems will be automatically solved. Although many problems may be reduced by good communication, all of them cannot be erased, for several reasons. First, it is impossible for any group to anticipate all the information another wants. Even if this were possible, some would not regard it as desirable. To withhold information is sometimes as vital as to release it. Yet withholding communication may arouse resentment in other groups. Even when there is no restraint on releasing facts, people will interpret them differently and act upon them differently. This is especially important when different segments of an organization do not share the same values. Further, when groups do not want to coöperate, free communication between them does not necessarily reduce the friction. In fact, *it may increase it*. In the following sections we shall demonstrate how organizations develop internal ruptures which increase rather than decrease the friction within them.

Time Segmentation

Sometimes segmentation develops within organizations because of the difficulty in synchronizing activities. Strains develop particularly in an industry which has two or more shifts.[20] In the first place, the "regular shift" regards itself as the most important shift. Most of the staff is present during the day. Problems of the regular shift are met and solved, with the expectation that the following shift will merely follow precedent. The regular shift is frequently regarded as the big moneymaker; the others as secondary. They keep the plant going and, by doing so, keep costs down. The members of the second and third shift, however, do not regard themselves as secondary. They are quick to feel slights and insults.

All too frequently, there is little or no face-to-face communication up and down the line between the people in the various shifts. The sum total of communication is often no more than hastily scribbled "memos" pointing out the difficulties of the last shift and setting the quotas for the next shift. Rarely is there social or recreational contact between shifts. Obviously, this incomplete and impersonal communication is the source of irritation.

On paper little distinction is made between the shifts. They are all part

[20] Paul and Faith Pigors, "Human Aspects of Multiple Shift Operations," Publications in Social Science, Series 2, No. 13, Massachusetts Institute of Technology, 1944.

of the organization. Theoretically each shift's performance should dovetail neatly into the others'. Since the interdependence of the shifts is real, anything that interferes with the fulfillment of expectations is a source of frustration. Problems between the shifts cannot be as adequately met as those arising within a shift, for the physical presence of people is often needed to meet problems on the spot.

Since no shift has complete dominance and advantage over the other, each shift can make the life of the next miserable. When poor relations develop between shifts, the irritations are cumulative. Each shift tries to outdo the other in inconveniences it can concoct for the other. The causes for intershift tensions may appear petty and unimportant to outsiders. To the workers themselves these irritations seem to mount to obsessive proportions. The ravings of a foreman in a tube-making department of a New York factory demonstrate this obsession:

> We're in a hell of a fix tonight. Everything's gone wrong from the first minute. But what can you expect from Krieger and his bunch? Krieger scribbled me a note to keep on making ⅜″ tubing. His men as usual stopped the machines with the whistle, leaving the stock inside of the machines. Naturally we thought they was making ⅜″. So for two hours we've been making half-inch. We're supposed to turn out thirty thousand feet of ⅜″ tonight, but we'll never make it. . . . I'll catch hell for not checking the dies first. So we looked for the dies in the cabinet. The cabinet was locked and Krieger had the keys. So while I send Charlie to get the keys I ask the men to clean up the machines and sweep up. I get the lip from them because they claim that Krieger's men always leave them the dirty work. 'Course my boys ain't angels exactly. Krieger blowed off the other night on account of my men put so much grease on the stock that it was almost impossible to handle. I tell you, half of this trouble wouldn't happen if the chief took an interest in this department and in this shift. I usually see him leaving as I come in, taking off like a bat out of hell, to play golf or something.

Similar problems of time segmentation occur within a shift, especially when work teams are dependent on other teams for supply of materials. When one group in an interrelated work flow organization fails to meet a time schedule, total production is affected. Antagonisms which arise out of a failure to integrate work teams and plans to improve work flow will be examined in one of the later sections of this chapter.

Space Segmentation

The organization chart does not reveal a common occurrence, namely, the spatial segregation of parts of a division or department. During World War II, especially, the pressing demand for space resulted in the physical separation of closely interdependent unit organizations. For example, the Sperry Gyroscope Company operated its main Brooklyn plant, rented large terminal buildings in Brooklyn, built a plant on Long Island, and maintained an office in Manhattan, New York. The work of numerous plants

spread over a fifty-mile radius had to be organized. Problems of coördinating the different units of the factory naturally arose.

There are several ways in which units of an organization may be physically segregated. Sometimes the offices of executives, staff, and clerical workers are distant from the operational divisions. Such a split increases the segmentation of office and plant organizations. This is to be avoided if at all possible for even under normal conditions the relations between office and plant tend to be touchy. Another common device is to segregate the central plant from the subsidiary plants, which perform specialized services. Still another technique is to create as many self-sufficient organizations as possible, with the central organization exercising a minimum of control. This is the case in the headquarters-field arrangement.

Irrespective of the method of spatial segregation, each section tends to regard itself as more important than any other unit, or as having problems which are unique or more pressing than those in other parts of the organization. This is understandable, because physical segregation reduces free, direct, and personal communication. As a principle, the greater the physical segregation of component units of an organization, the greater are the problems of coördinating activity. The greater the segregation in physical space, the greater the tendency to be divided by social space.

To lessen this social distance, to increase communication, and to promote the feeling of interdependence single-story plants with few or no partitions between and within departments are being built instead of multi-story buildings.

An interesting illustration of spatial segmentation was evident in a banking firm in Lansing, Michigan. The job of processing checks was done by two groups of girls under the same supervisor. Half of the girls in this department worked on the main floor and the second half worked upstairs. To all intents and purposes their jobs were identical. When new girls were hired they went to work on the ground floor. When vacancies occurred upstairs, girls were taken from the downstairs group. An antagonism developed between these two groups, each regarding the other as aloof, unfriendly, and troublesome. By informal agreement each group ate lunch at a different time, and even used the rest rooms at different times. When a girl from downstairs joined the upstairs crew, she was soon accepted, but the downstairs crew would have very little to do with her. Such social distance and ethnocentrism has been known to develop even between junior executives who occupied different sides of the same room. Of course, spatial segregation alone does not produce cleavages. Other factors are equally important.

Organizational Strictures

The places where cleavages are most likely to develop in work plants are along the "natural" divisions of the structure. That is, wherever there are

breaks, as between supervisory levels or between functional units, there is a greater likelihood of segmentation. This should be expected since it is usually more difficult to coördinate disparate units than similar ones. Within an organizational unit there usually is more communication, similarity of function, and commonness of purpose. Although it is true that organizational divisions increase the interdependence among the divisions, machinery to effect coördination does not grow automatically to meet the problem.

The organizational breaks where cleavage or segmentation is likely to be highest are:

1. At the divisional, subdivisional, and department breaks.
2. Between the supervisory levels.
3. Between the line and staff organizations.

DIVISIONAL AND RELATED CLEAVAGES

It is scarcely necessary to demonstrate that antagonisms exist between divisions, departments, sections, and other units. The mere creation of an organizational unit creates cleavage, but other factors operate. The coördination of segments is seldom perfect and the defects add to the difficulties. Assembly, for example, is dependent on manufacturing for its materials; manufacturing is in turn dependent on the purchasing division; the latter in turn has to operate within a budget, and so on.

Each section, division, or department wants a "good record." Each is trying to impress top management with its performance. *Yet its performance depends on the perfect coöperation of the other sections.* This is next to impossible. Assembly may be held up because manufacturing is not supplying the needed items. When the supply is good, quality may be low. As a result, assembly may be slowed up. The chief of assembly then puts pressure on manufacturing to keep up supplies, and quality. His organization becomes aware of his impatience. The assembly chief may use manufacturing as a scapegoat for his own inadequacies or for his bad luck. On the other hand, he will take the credit when his section is performing better than the others.

Other less formal factors may augment distance between units of the structure. Some division heads are the "fair-haired boys" of the big boss. They get most of the breaks. In addition, the personnel of a department may be more skilled, more highly educated, more experienced than another; its members may flaunt their superiority feelings in their relations with people of other departments. Members of other departments resent the advantageous position of their fellow workers and begin to look upon them as deadly rivals. Thus, in-groups are formed which develop insulation against communication with other divisions. A number of protective rituals are soon evolved which make group members more self-conscious and pro-

vincial. These tendencies are sometimes encouraged by supervisors. Loyalty toward the division is rewarded. But loyalty is a two-edged sword. Although it may increase *esprit de corps* within the department, it may also reduce coöperation with the entire organization. Whereas it may be pursued at first for the purpose of increasing output, it later may be pursued as an end in itself.

SUPERVISORY LEVELS

In the next chapter we shall explain in some detail the functions and problems in various supervisory levels. Here we shall deal with some of the general reasons that cleavages appear between the levels. Tensions arise between the supervisory levels because the different functions, identifications, authority, and responsibilities of each level inevitably come into conflict. This is true because each level feels it could do a better job if the other levels would coöperate with it in its every problem.

It is the human tendency of every executive to see the total organization from the peculiar perspective of his level. Obviously, the image of each is a product of his unique experiences and problems. Since the perspectives of each level cannot be the same, the problem of communicating desires and achievements arises. On the basis of this kind of partial and incomplete communication segmentation tendencies increase. No supervisory level —or better yet, no section of the organization—has a completely accurate view of the whole structure. Nor can the whole be seen accurately from a partisan point of view. Only the outside observer can approximately gain such a perspective.

The feeling of each level is very strong that its problems are unique and that no one can really understand them unless he is physically on the spot. Supervisors not only feel that their problems are unique, but also think that their problems are of greater magnitude. Listening to the "gripe session" of supervisors is a good way to observe the pervasive belief that each level has problems that are unique and difficult. The participants of these sessions don't communicate or inform. They just release tensions in the hope that they will get sympathy.

In addition, each supervisory level is at the same time subordinate and superordinate to others. On each, there is a pressure from above to produce. Authority, with all its incipient threats, accompanies this pressure and promotes feelings of insecurity. The supervisor often feels that his chief has too much authority to expect so much of a man who has limited authority. Among supervisors the sentiment universally persists that one should have more authority to resist pressure and to enlist coöperation. Subordinates often complain that their chiefs "pass the buck" to them; that they get only the tough problems or the dirty menial tasks.

Supervisors make the same demands on their subordinates that their

chiefs make on them. As chiefs they feel their performance depends on the coöperation of those below them. Their reaction to this kind of dependency results in pressure and demands. Overweighted with work, they pass down the menial and difficult jobs. They cannot understand why they do not get all that they expect. Thus, how a supervisor feels and acts depends upon whether he is looking down or looking up the structure. The different way he acts does not strike him as contradictory or unreasonable. Yet this contradiction makes for segmentation in the structure.

STAFF AND LINE

The cleavages between supervisory levels are paralleled by those arising between line and staff organizations. The line organization is concerned with manufacturing the product or providing the service. Staff organization includes all the remaining functions, such as sales, engineering, personnel, and accounting. Theoretically, the staff organization is supposed to advise and assist the line organization on its problems and provide such services as hiring, training, and research.

Antagonisms between the line and staff exist in almost every organization. This does not mean that the whole staff has antagonistic feelings toward line. As a matter of fact the watertight distinctions between staff and line are not always found in industry. Cleavages between these two parts of the organization generally occur over specific functions at specific times. Since we cannot survey all of the specific situations leading to cleavages, we shall examine the general cause of segmentation.

The line organization is a united organization with one supervisory hierarchy. It is well aware of its central position in the organization and of the subsidiary position of the staff. The staff, on the other hand, is often composed of several organizations, each having its own supervisory structure. The fact that the staff is not a united structure, plus the fact that its role is considered secondary, decreases the possibility of unrestrained coöperation with the line.

The staff finds it difficult to prove to the line that it is worth its salt. Line officers often comment that they make the money for the organization while the staff spends it in nonessential ways. Line men often feel that the plant can partly dispense with many staff functions. To them staff people often appear impractical and theoretical. Their services might be more useful if they were under the dominance of line officers. In difficult times, staff funds are cut and line people do take over some of their functions.

Thus the staff is often put on the defensive. It must prove *the need for and profitability of* large sales, research, personnel, and accounting organizations. It can do this largely at the expense of the lower parts of the line organization. For example, the cost accounting officials can "prove" to top management that a particular line division is losing money. The research

division can "prove" that antiquated methods are responsible for this loss. Personnel can "prove" that it can repair the situation by introducing new training and selection methods. Thus all the staff groups can justify their existence by *criticizing the line*. Nobody loves a critic.

The frustrations of the staff are increased by the fact that it has no power to enforce its recommendations. Since it cannot, excepting in unusual situations, insert commands into the line organization, it seeks more authority. The line resists this because it does not want its routines broken by every new idea the staff concocts. Under these conditions the staff seeks to influence top management to insert its recommendations into the line. It is successful in this regard because its members are in continual physical and social contact with top management. Whereas the attention of the line is on the departments that produce the goods or provide the service, the focus of the staff is on top management.

On the other hand, only the upper levels of line officers come into close contact with top management. In general, staff people are more highly educated than line people.[21] The specialist or professional training of staff members makes them feel superior to the less formally trained line officers. In addition, staff feels a sense of superiority because its members are and always have been white-collar people. Many line officers, on the other hand, have risen through the ranks. They have ambivalent feelings concerning their social origins and their present social position. Consequently they sometimes feel antagonistic toward staff people *per se*.

Social and Cultural Differences

The existence of social and cultural differences among various segments of work organization is infrequently recognized. Although the formal structure is designed to minimize the influences that arise from differences in personality, social experiences, and cultural backgrounds, it cannot do away with them altogether. It is almost impossible to keep interhuman contacts within formally defined limits. The economic, political, and religious sentiments of people sooner or later are expressed. Cliques, friendships, enemies, and allies invariably arise on the basis of sentiment agreement or disagreement. The appeal made to the slogan "business is business" points to the sociological reality that business is often mixed up with other sentiments.

The work plant is one of the major areas where the sub-cultures meet and interact. Foreign cultures and lower-class culture are expressed in the behavior of the workers on the plant floor. Some of the difficulties that arise between supervisory levels reflect the cultural differences between workers and managers. Managers are usually native Americans, imbued with the values of time, profit, success, and ambition. If their workers do not share these values, as is often the case, managers sometimes feel that the workers

[21] Melville Salton, "Conflicts Between Staff and Line Managers," *American Sociological Review*, June, 1950, pp. 342-350.

are stupid or even subhuman. Tardiness, absenteeism, and the observing of certain rituals may be anathema to supervisors, but it may be customary behavior to many workers. Such differences in cultural backgrounds tend to restrict the communication and understanding between groups. Indeed, cultural differences often promote antagonism, for intolerance seems to be almost a universal trait.

Other areas of cultural conflict are exhibited in factory life. The antagonisms between office and factory reflect the middle class-lower class antipathy in our society. Sometimes conflicts occur because men and women compete over the same jobs. Departments which interact may have members representing different educational levels, different national origins, different religions, and so on. The cultural differences in the work plant should be known and plotted, to enable the analyst to assess some of the sources of segmentation there. What seems at first to be segmentation based on spatial, organizational, or functional divisions may in reality be due to cultural differences.

Ideological Contradictions

In addition to the cleavages caused by cultural differences, cleavages may arise from contradictory traits within the culture. One contradiction, especially, inherent in business thinking is the conflict between teamwork and individualism. One primary ideal in business organization is the desire for a smooth-functioning team. Many of the ideals of sports pervade the idea system (ideology) of management. Among them are: Business is a competitive affair; to win out, teamwork is necessary; each man not only should be an expert in his position but should be loyal to the team; coöperation is essential to victory; the team is more important than the individual; no man should play for the grandstand.

A conflicting ideal is that every worker should be personally ambitious to make a good record. Rewards are distributed according to the achievements of the individual in the competitive struggle inside and outside of the organization. The success of the worker is measured in his ability to outperform his fellow workers. This *individualistic, competitive, struggling* ideology sets individuals against individuals. Every worker is urged to do his best no matter whom he may hurt in the process. Everyone is encouraged to entertain the thought that he can do a better job than his boss. Indeed, he may even aspire to replace his boss if his performance is unusually good. If he can demonstrate that a person, group, or department is not doing a good job, and further, if he can point the way to doing a better job himself, he is rewarded. The other person, group, or department will be punished, reprimanded, or demoted, as the case may be.

Coöperation and competition, group-consciousness and individualism, loyalty and mobility are not necessarily compatible. It is quite possible that such a contradictory atmosphere breeds insecurity feelings rather than high

teamwork and morale. When a worker feels that at any time one of his subordinates or colleagues may threaten his position, he is filled with distrust and suspicion. Far from developing an atmosphere of uninhibited, spontaneous coöperation, this system breeds a structure of strange contradictions.

Managers of some concerns accept tensions as a normal, if not desirable, aspect of business life. One of them bluntly admitted that he was suspicious of subordinates who genuinely liked their superiors. When this is the case, he contended, the superior is not doing a good job. The job of the executive is to find something wrong with the work of subordinates. People who find things wrong should not be liked by subordinates. Thus it is necessary for him to be feared, so that he can constantly keep workers alive to the necessity of improving their work.

Two illustrations may demonstrate the unintended consequences of the contradictory elements in management ideology.[22] During World War II, the Treasury Department in Washington, D.C., hired many girls to sort canceled checks. A bulletin board was erected which showed how many checks each girl had sorted during the month. The objective was to stimulate the girls to do more work. Promotion was to be based on the number of checks sorted. At first the girls were anxious to know where they stood. At the end of each month they would anxiously scan the bulletin board to find their positions. The girls at the lower end of the scale soon began to hate this system. They indicated that it did not take into account absences and other eventualities. Far from stimulating them, it seemed to encourage squabbling and absenteeism. Those at the top of the scale soon found that increases in salary were limited by the salary scale. After reaching the top rung of the scale they no longer tried to produce more. This case illustrates the fact that management ideology is not always accepted, and when accepted often has unanticipated consequences by causing cleavages.

A national grocery chain evolved a complex method of evaluating the managers of the individual stores. Each manager is constantly stimulated to improve his rating. He is told that promotions are based on his competitive position with other store managers. The company lets him know when he is not doing well, but it never tells him where he stands in reference to other store managers. A manager never knows how "good" he really is. A high executive justified this "keep them in the dark policy" by suggesting that it was a good incentive device. He said, "If a man knows that he is on top or close to the top, he will not continue to improve. If he doesn't know how he stands he will try to improve continually."

In this case top management operated under the assumption that all men have the same motives. It imputed to the store managers a restless ambition to operate in an ill-defined or undefined situation. As it happened, many

[22] Robert Merton, "Unanticipated Consequences of Purposive Social Action," *American Sociological Review*, December, 1936, pp. 894-904.

local managers were discouraged by the lack of information. Some of them went to other organizations where they would know where they stood. Those that remained got together informally to compare their performances. Thus the inconsistent ideology of management promoted a conspiracy among the workers. This conspiracy was motivated by the desire to lessen some of the pressure from the top.

We have seen in this section that the social organization of the work plant is an interactive system composed of many parts. The *formal* and *informal* organizations of labor and management constitute major divisions. These organizations split into many smaller segments. Management's main role in industry is to secure coöperative effort among its unit organizations. This is difficult because of the inherent and persistent tendency of large enterprises to become fragmented into smaller groups having a separate identity. *Such tendencies toward segmentation in the structure interfere with the free flow of communication between sections of the larger organization.* The main blocks to free communication flow tend to occur between all the different sections of the structure. Among these are *line and staff, office and plant, different supervisory levels,* and *functional divisions.* Cleavages between groups are emphasized by the *social* and *cultural differences* that exist among work groups in the plant. Contradictions in *management ideology* also punctuate the natural cleavages that arise.

WORK FLOW AND SEGMENTATION

Everyone in a work plant may be considered as either directly or indirectly concerned with making the work flow. Some workers are obviously directly concerned with processing the flow of goods. Others are indirectly concerned when they service people or machines that actually move the work or the services. There is a growing awareness that work flow is both an index of coördination and the state of human relations. When jams occur in work flow, production drops, tempers flare, and frantic efforts are made to disentangle the bottlenecks. What connections exist between the smooth and efficient flow of work and "good" or "bad" human relations, and why?

THE LINE OF PRESSURE

When William Whyte studied the restaurant industry, he observed that the fluctuating flow of customers introduced some serious problems of work flow and human relations. The surge of hungry customers at the conventional mealtime hours set up pressures which affected almost every worker. The customer originates every action which sets into motion the complex organization of a large restaurant. With the placing of his order a *line of pressure* is initiated, and it lengthens as the worker is directed to produce

food or accompanying service. Figure 27 portrays the *line of pressure* in a large restaurant. Here it can be seen how pressure is transmitted from customers to waitresses and then onward to pantry workers, runners, cooks, and food preparers. Meanwhile, the supervisors "breathe down the necks" of the various workers for whom they are responsible. The cry is hurry! hurry! hurry! The strain on human relationships grows as the pressure mounts. At times, the strain becomes too great and taut nerves can take no more. Crying and emotional upsets on the part of the waitresses are common problems. Antagonistic feelings tend to surge up among all workers. The supervisor needs social skills of a high order to meet these problems. Improvement in the work flow also helps morale and heads off human relations problems. Whyte has studied this work flow and has identified

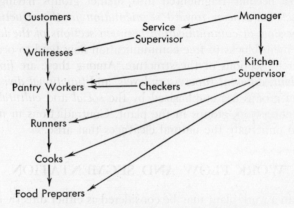

FIG. 27.   Line of Pressure in a Large Restaurant.

the points at which friction develops. One example will illustrate how important small details can be.

The point of contact between waitresses and pantry people also deserves supervisory attention. In Jessup's restaurant, when supplies did not come up, the waitresses felt frustrated not only because they were delayed but also because they could not understand what was going on. When they demanded the attention of the countermen, this only created friction. If the pantry supervisor had been able to step in between the two groups, explain the situation to the waitresses, and let them blow off steam to her, it seems likely that the flood of tears could have been avoided. It may be worth while to experiment in developing a go-between role for the pantry supervisor.

Before we leave the service pantry, we should look at the social role of the insignificant-looking spindle. It serves to fend off from pantry people a good deal (but not all) of the pressure exerted by waitresses. Where we have men (unaccustomed to taking orders from women) behind the counter, it seems likely that the spindle makes the difference between a workable system and one that would blow

up. . . . The spindle is also of great importance where we have middle-aged counterwomen and young waitresses. . . .

To sum it up, wherever the people on the receiving end of the orders are related to the order givers as males vs. females, or older vs. younger, then it is important for the pantry people to have some impersonal barrier to block the pressure from themselves. Even when such differences are eliminated, the use of spindles makes the job easier for the pantry people.[23]

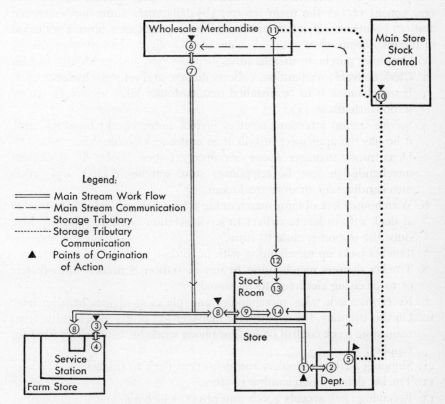

FIG. 28. Sociographic Map of Work Flow in an Auto Accessory Department.

This illustration, in which the lowly spindle plays such a major role, verifies the importance of small details in the flow of work.

THE SOCIOGRAPHY OF WORK FLOW

The work flow in any work plant may be compared to a river. Initial actions at the headwaters of the main stream start the flow of goods or services. Unfinished parts flow downstream from worker to worker. Tribu-

[23] From *Human Relations in the Restaurant Industry*, by William F. Whyte, 1948. Courtesy of McGraw-Hill Book Company.

tary services flow into the main stream, and the work nears completion at the river's end. This stream concept and image has several advantages. It enables an observer to visualize clearly and to plot graphically whatever a department or an individual contributes to the work flow at the physical spot where his contribution is made.[24]

Figure 28 is a sociographic map of work flow in an auto accessory department in a Sears, Roebuck and Company retail store. The elements of work flow consist of (a) the main stream, (b) tributaries (into main stream), and (c) points of origination of action. The sequence of actions represented in the map begin when:

1. Customer purchases merchandise.
2. Clerk delivers merchandise, collects money, and returns change.
3. If merchandise is to be installed free, customer takes invoice to service station attendant (4).
4. Service station attendant receives invoice order, checks his stock, and, if he has the appliance, installs it in customer's automobile.
5. Department manager keeps inventory control books. If stockroom merchandise is low, he telephones store warehouse clerk and orders merchandise sent to store stockroom.
6. Warehouse clerk obtains merchandise from stock and delivers to trucker at dock with orders to deliver to service station or store. (Overlap here since the station is close to store.)
7. Trucker picks up merchandise with his orders.
8. Trucker delivers merchandise to service station if needed immediately or to receiving clerk (9) to be stored.
9. Receiving clerk takes merchandise and places it in merchandise bins.
10. On this tributary, the department manager (5) orders merchandise from main store stock control by mail or phone when his books show need for supplies.
11. Shipping clerk takes orders and delivers at dock to trucker.
12. Trucker delivers merchandise to store.
13. Receiving clerk accepts goods and places it in bins.
14. When counter stock is low, clerk fills it from store stockroom.[25]

Smooth work flow is important in the operation of this department. For example, the type of relationship between the shipping clerk and the truckers can save or lose money for the company. The truckers are not Sears employees since the trucks are contracted from a trucking concern. This often means that the driver is not too coöperative in minimizing damage in transport or in creating good customer relations. The shipping

[24] We are indebted to F. L. W. Richardson, Jr., and Charles R. Walker for this concept as described in *Human Relations in an Expanding Company*, Yale University Labor and Management Center, 1948, pp. 54-85.

[25] The data for this map were collected by Douglas M. Allan, a senior student in the University of Washington.

clerk, by creating friendly relations with the truckers, can help this situation. A good shipping clerk "kids" the drivers, never demands a delivery, but secures their coöperation by including them in his work group and getting

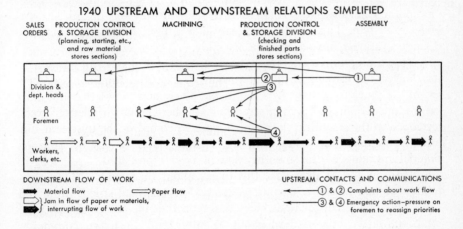

1940 UPSTREAM AND DOWNSTREAM RELATIONS SIMPLIFIED

SALES PRODUCTION CONTROL MACHINING PRODUCTION CONTROL ASSEMBLY
ORDERS & STORAGE DIVISION & STORAGE DIVISION
(planning, starting, etc., (checking and
and raw material finished parts
stores sections) stores sections)

DOWNSTREAM FLOW OF WORK UPSTREAM CONTACTS AND COMMUNICATIONS
Material flow Paper flow (1) & (2) Complaints about work flow
Jam in flow of paper or materials, (3) & (4) Emergency action—pressure on
interrupting flow of work foremen to reassign priorities

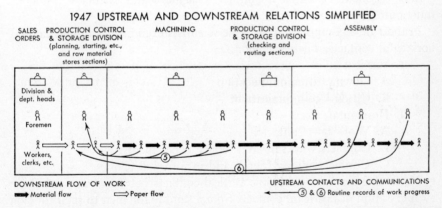

1947 UPSTREAM AND DOWNSTREAM RELATIONS SIMPLIFIED

SALES PRODUCTION CONTROL MACHINING PRODUCTION CONTROL ASSEMBLY
ORDERS & STORAGE DIVISION & STORAGE DIVISION
(planning, starting, etc., (checking and
and raw material routing sections)
stores sections)

DOWNSTREAM FLOW OF WORK UPSTREAM CONTACTS AND COMMUNICATIONS
Material flow Paper flow (5) & (6) Routine records of work progress

FIG. 29. Upstream and Downstream Relations at International Business Machines Manufacturing Corporation. (From F. L. W. Richardson, Jr., and Charles R. Walker, *Human Relations in an Expanding Company*, Yale University Press, 1948, pp. 82-83.)

them to respect him as a man. The truckers are usually strong men physically, and if the shipping clerk can "hold up" his end of a refrigerator they learn to include him in their group. Similarly, it is necessary to bring the truckers into the store organization so that they will realize some of the clerks' problems and come to coöperate with them.

WORK FLOW IN THE FACTORY

Richardson and Walker have made a sociographic analysis of work flow in the factory of the International Business Machines Manufacturing Corporation at Endicott, New York. In 1940 the company was organized on a job shop system. This system had many advantages, but as the company expanded various jams occurred in assembly.

In 1947 a progressive assembly system was adopted. Parts and assemblies now flowed downstream without returning to a central storeroom, as they had in the previous system. As a result, the researchers report that not only was a more economical plan effected but also better human relations were developed in the smoother work flow. Figure 29 compares the upstream and downstream relations in 1940 and 1947. As the jams in flow of paper or material are removed the smoother flow of 1947 is produced.

Richardson and Walker have this to say about their study: "The introduction of new assembly operations are seldom analyzed strictly from the standpoint of human relations. This has been the sole object of this presentation. Matters of work flow, layout, assembly, and control are commonly considered the sole province of the engineer. This study demonstrates that they are of equal concern to the student of human relations in the modern factory. . . . In a large factory, it is one thing to install a new layout and plan new schedules, but it is another to achieve and maintain a smooth functioning operation."[26]

In the I.B.M. Corporation the Yale scientists examined both vertical and horizontal contacts. These include:

    I. Vertical
        A. Downward communication.
        B. Upward communication.
    II. Horizontal
        A. Work flow contacts.
        B. Contacts with staff and service departments.
        C. Contacts among friends and in informal cliques.[27]

Three changes occurred in the vertical contacts between 1940 and 1947:

1. A cessation of upstream contacts from assembly foremen to their division heads regarding work flow complaints.
2. Cessation of downstream contacts from machining foremen to their men: cessation of interrupting and reassigning jobs because of holdups.
3. Increased opportunity for worker-foreman contacts, arising out of availability of more time to foremen because of better work flow.

Changes in horizontal and oblique contacts also took place:

[26] Richardson and Walker, op. cit., p. 81.
[27] Ibid., p. 4.

1. The downstream flow of work from employer to employee became far smoother.
2. In the paper flow sections (office) near the head of the work stream production planners now had better communication with employees downstream in the material flow sections.
3. Many upstream complaints and emergency contacts were greatly diminished.
4. Contacts between assembly foremen with contiguous positions along the work stream increased considerably.[28]

Such dramatic results promise a fruitful future for the study of work flow and segmentation problems. Large organizations do not have to stand by and watch communication lines become jammed and human relations made worse. The trend toward greater centralization, longer lines of communication, multiplication of staff functions, and greater segmentation reaches a point of diminishing returns. The scientific study of work flow and communication can lead the way to an intelligent counter-trend with emphasis on better communication and integrated work teams.

SUPPLEMENTARY STUDIES

FIELD OBSERVATION: DIRECT OBSERVATION OF A SELECTED WORK PLANT
(continued from Chapter V)

In the work plant you have selected for observation chart:
Formal Structure of Management
1. Diagram the *chain of command* showing line and staff.
2. Describe the segmentation of the structure. Look for
    a. Time segmentation.
    b. Space segmentation.
    c. Divisional, subdivisional, and department breaks.
    d. Breaks between supervisory levels.
    e. Breaks between line and staff.
Communication
   Analyze:
1. Communication down the line.
    a. Procedures and channels of written and verbal communication.
    b. Indicate effects and defects.
2. Communication up the line.
    a. Procedures and channels of written and verbal communication.
    b. Evidence of filtered information and short-circuiting.
3. Horizontal or Oblique communication.
    a. Contacts with staff and service groups.

[28] *Ibid.*, pp. 84-85.

    b. Operation of grapevine.

    c. Secret-sharing communication.

Work Flow

1. Diagram the main stream of work flow.
2. Diagram the tributaries of work flow.
3. Mark the points where action originates.
4. Chart the line or lines of pressure.
5. Describe the way in which workers transfer pressure such as buck-passing, joking, laughing, crying, etc.
6. Describe the human relations problems and tensions induced.
7. Submit suggestions for reduction of tensions.

FIELD OBSERVATION: DIRECT OBSERVATION BY THE CLASS

Arrange to visit a relatively large work plant. Ask a company official to tell and show how the large working force is broken into small working groups. Discuss with him management's organization plan for all of the operations. Ask him for examples of the way human factors enter in and disrupt organization planning.

LIBRARY: BOOKS

Archibald, Katherine, *Wartime Shipyard,* University of California Press, 1940, pp. 1-14, 185-237.

Barnard, Chester I., *The Functions of an Executive,* Harvard University Press, 1947, Part II, "Theory and Structure of Formal Organization," pp. 65-123.

Gardner, Burleigh B., *Human Relations in Industry,* Richard D. Irwin, Inc., 1945, chap. 4, "Segmentation of the Structure," pp. 65-95.

Pigors, Paul, *Effective Communication In Industry,* National Association of Manufacturers, Lt. Toland Memorial Fellowship Study No. 1, 1949.

Research Report Series No. 79, *Transmitting Information Through Management and Union Channels,* Princeton University Press, September, 1949.

Richardson, F. L. W. and Walker, Charles R., *Human Relations In An Expanding Company,* Yale Labor and Management Center, 1948.

Shartle, Carroll L., *Leadership and Executive Performance,* Pamphlet of American Management Association, 1949; also published in *Personnel,* March, 1949.

Worthy, James C., "Organizational Structures and Employee Morale," *American Sociological Review,* April, 1950, pp. 169-179.

RESEARCH GAPS

The measurement of tensions and lines of pressure set up in the social relations of a work plant.

The measurement of the efficiency of communication systems in the work plant.

The correspondence of sociometric patterns to the formal organization.

CHAPTER VII

The Major Work Positions and Roles
of Managers

WORK POSITIONS AS SOCIAL PATTERNS

THE GAP BETWEEN MANAGEMENT THEORY AND MANAGEMENT PRACTICE

In the last chapter we discussed the formal organization of management and described the theory of formal organization. It will be remembered that the theory of formal organization created a model which classical economists would be likely to call "pure" and "perfect" management. Inside such a model managers would always get high production and the smoothest of human relations. These are the things managers *would like to achieve* through the formal structure. But problems are always arising and something is always going wrong. The problems of communication and segmentation already examined indicate that the gap between theory and practice grows fairly wide. And this breach tends to widen in spite of the best efforts which intelligent and experienced managers can give. Why is this so? Let us explore in more detail the reasons for this breach.

To begin with, we have seen that human factors do intervene and affect the operation of formal management structure. Organizational cleavages which are unanticipated arise within the formal structure. Far from being a well-integrated organism, industry tends to be divided into a number of parts or groupings which have a quasi-independent existence. The process by which a larger organization separates into smaller segments is called,

appropriately, segmentation. The forces which facilitate segmentation arise from the nature of the structure and from the motives of its occupants, and so do the forces for organizational integration. Industry, like any human organization, contains an equilibrium of forces which simultaneously integrate and divide work groups. The processes of integration and segmentation are neither "good" nor "bad." They are natural processes which may be used to promote one end or another. The problem of administration requires that these processes be recognized and kept in balance.

In actual function, an organizational segment is composed of a number of people interacting according to expected patterns. It is unrealistic to ignore these specific behavior patterns. In order to get a more complete picture of the operation of management, we shall focus our attention on some of the more important managerial jobs and the problems that are tied to them. The technical duties connected with management's jobs are not the concern of the sociologist.

From a sociological point of view, technical job descriptions contain only a partial definition of the worker's behavior. The sociologist approaches the job with four major assumptions: (1) Every worker is a group member; (2) every group has a number of more or less well-defined patterns of behavior for each of its members; (3) the work plant is a conglomeration of work groups; and (4) a worker interacts and participates in these groups. Under these assumptions the job must be considered as a social element.

THE MEANING OF WORK POSITION

When "job" is approached in this social sense, we call it a *work position*. The work position does not refer to an actual individual performing his job. Rather, it describes a series of typical functions and social relations which any person in the work position must observe. Irrespective of the occupant, the work position has three major aspects:

1. The technical operations of the job.

2. The physical locations of the worker on the job and all of the physical objects which compose and surround a given work position.

3. The social demands which must be fulfilled by anyone who is to perform adequately in the position. The demands include:

a. The circumscribed round of activities, or the sequence of activities, demanded of the job.

b. The number and nature of the worker's contacts with other people or objects while on the job.

c. The way in which the worker's activities fit into those of other workers and are viewed by other workers in their jobs.

If the observer gathers descriptions of all the main work positions in the plant and then relates them, he has a complete picture of the organization of the work plant. However, he does not have a picture of the plant in operation, but a good structural or static view of plant organization. To

know how the organization functions from day to day he would have to observe people acting in their work positions.

WORK ROLE

When workers are actually engaged in fulfilling the expectations of their work positions, they are playing their *work roles*. The work role is the dynamic aspect of position. It is difficult to make concrete generalizations about roles because they are so dynamic. This is why work position and work role never coincide exactly. Role playing is affected by individual personalities acting in specific situations at designated times. However, much of the role may be understood and even predicted by studying the work position. This is possible because position defines the framework within which the role is played.

WORK-ORIENTED GROUPS

Work position and work role are both group-oriented concepts. They differ from the usual concept of "job" because they consider the worker in *all* of his social relationships. Obviously the worker participates in formal and informal groups both inside and outside of the plant. The definition of his work position and work role demands an enumeration of all the work groups in which he participates and a description of the part he plays in each of them. We may classify the groups in which the worker is attached as nuclear, satellite, and societal work groups.

1. Nuclear Work Groups

The nuclear work group, containing people who interact daily on a face-to-face basis on the job, is usually composed of work positions that are physically adjacent and functionally interrelated. The contacts and interactions which are necessary to perform the job define the person's nuclear work group. Occasionally the contacts among members of a nuclear work group may be indirect—as reporting to the boss daily by telephone or by mail. Generally, the group may be identified by observing the interaction of people on the job. Frequently, many workers belong to the same nuclear groups, as in the case of a telephone repair crew. Identifying such groups for other workers may be more difficult because some work positions do not dovetail neatly into each other.

2. Satellite Work Groups

There are other groups to which a worker belongs by virtue of his being an employee of a work plant. Contacts in these groups may be incidental to the job. For example, participation in the labor union, picnic committee, or safety committee is not part of the job. Although contacts in such groups may be occasional, the worker may be highly involved in them and derive

considerable satisfaction and prestige from membership. Many satellite groups are informal in nature, as the lunch group, the car pool, cliques on the job, the informal recreational groups, the company-sponsored teams, and clubs. Even though participation may occur outside of the plant, the fact

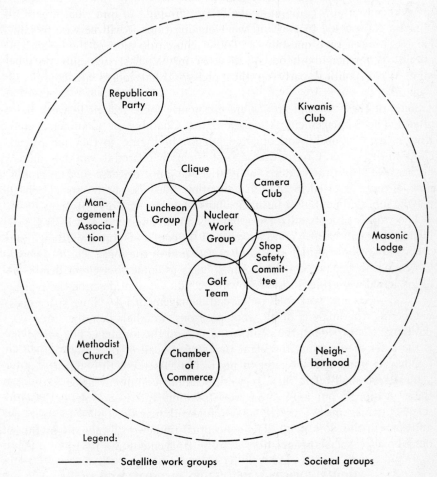

Legend:

———·——— Satellite work groups   ——— ——— Societal groups

FIG. 30.   The Nuclear, Satellite, and Societal Group Affiliations of a Business Executive.

that the members are employees of the same plant satisfies our definition of satellite work group. It is difficult to overstress the importance of these groups, for they may affect the worker's role and job performance.

3. Societal Groups

Figure 30 portrays the group affiliation of an executive. His nuclear and satellite groups can be seen in the inner circles. The reader will note that the

third concentric circle contains some groups which do not appear to be directly related to work or the work plant. Yet the church, neighborhood, and political party are included because they may bear significantly on work activity. Although the relation may not be obvious, many workers appreciate the importance of these societal groups. Not infrequently, when an executive comes to a new community, he "shops around" to find what organizations he is expected to join and what organizations it will be wise to join. He asks himself such questions as: What church do most of the executives attend? What neighborhoods do they live in? What service clubs do they join? What political party do they prefer? What lodges are considered "right"?

Some of these societal groups are apparently more related to work than others. The Management Association, the Chamber of Commerce, and Kiwanis are obviously work-oriented groups. In Figure 30 they are placed closer to the center. Groups that are not as closely related to work are drawn farther away from the center. The relative relevance of these societal groups may be quite reversed in an actual situation. That is, purely "social" clubs may be more influential in business affairs than business organizations.

The worker accepts all these groups as an integral part of working and living. Although he may consider some of his contacts more important than others, his *group relations as a whole locate him in the social world of work.* Observing his behavior in these groups helps us come to a closer definition of his actual work role. In the following section we shall describe the typical work positions and work roles for several management jobs. Since space does not permit the analysis of all work positions, we shall describe three key positions: the president, the plant manager, and the foreman. The president is the chief of planning, the plant manager is head of operations, and the foreman is immediate overseer of production. As these three positions are analyzed we shall relate them to work positions commonly associated with them. Although our analysis of work position and work role deals with selected management jobs, the same framework may be applied to positions and roles in the work plant. The conceptual framework is equally useful in describing the social organization of both management and labor.

WORK POSITIONS AND WORK ROLES OF MANAGEMENT

THE BIG BOSS

Formal Functions

The work plant is generally directed by a chief executive officer or by the big boss. His title may be president, chairman, director, commissar, secretary, or leader. Irrespective of title, he is the executive head of the organization. It is difficult to describe his position and role in detail because

they differ somewhat with different sizes and types of enterprises. For our purposes we shall place the big boss in an organization large enough to need a layer of top managers, composed of vice-presidents or directors.

The duties of the big boss tend to be the same in all work plants. If he is not an honorary head, his primary job is to make the policy and see that "policy" is carried out. Several functions are ordinarily considered a part of his policy-making duties. He is primarily concerned with maintaining and improving the position of his enterprise. He must do everything possible to enable the organization to grow and survive. Even if he is head of a government department or bureau, he must be concerned with the survival and future growth of his organization. For in all large enterprises, departments are in a desperate struggle with each other to obtain funds, stay in favor with the super-chief, and justify their existence. Survival activities may occupy most of the time of the big boss. In a monopolistic business, less attention needs to be paid to struggle for survival. However secure his organization, the big boss spends considerable time keeping abreast of financial reports, newsletters, market and business conditions. Central to the work position of the big boss, then, is the job of coördinating all parts of the enterprise, so that it will be able to survive foreseeable social, political, economic, and other changes.[1]

A closely related function of the chief executive is to maintain equilibrium within the organization so it functions smoothly. In well-balanced organizations this role will be minimal, because the functions of the various segments dovetail nicely. But as we have noted, all organizations display segmentation tendencies, such as factional disputes between levels and departments, jealousies, and other problems. One major function of the big boss is to make and to keep the balance within the organization, by adjudicating these disputes.

On occasion, important problems of a technical nature require the attention of the chief executive. Or, as is more frequently the case, timid subordinates, afraid to make major decisions, push them up the line until they appear on the chief's desk. Many of the problems that reach the chief are exceptional and unusual ones. Most problems arising in a business should be anticipated and solved by the formal organization down the line. If this is the case, the job of the big boss is to deal with the unanticipated or the exceptional problems. Some bosses then conceive of their jobs as "governing by exception." Although others will not admit this as their primary function, it is nonetheless present in the jobs of all chief executives. Ideally, each exception which is ruled upon becomes a precedent, guiding behavior of subordinates in similar future cases. More frequently, however,

[1] Burleigh B. Gardner, *Human Relations in Industry*, Richard D. Irwin, Inc., 1945, p. 58.

the big boss insists upon handling certain kinds of problems whenever they arise.

Another function of the chief is to stimulate his organization to do more effective work. He tries to "keep tabs" on operations by reading reports on production costs, turnover, absenteeism, and other things. In addition, he attempts to stimulate each section to do better. On rare occasions, especially in the smaller plant, he may make a "tour of the plant," to see what is "really" going on. This usually is a pretense to show that he takes an interest in the plant. Since nobody likes this practice very much, the big boss usually retreats to his office and stays there. He feels his time is too valuable to spend on petty details.

The president's orientations, then, are off the floor and often outside of the plant itself. He feels that it is important to keep up his business and social contacts in the community. He may spend considerable time attending meetings of the Chamber of Commerce, Rotary Club, Red Cross, and the Management Association.

A Typical Day

Before the big boss arrives, his mail is sorted by his secretary. Reports from the managers and directors of the various departments are read, processed, and summarized by his staff assistants, with notations of the decisions that might be made. Around nine o'clock the big boss enters his office. He is usually above average in build, around fifty years old, and neatly dressed. He calls in his secretary and one of his staff assistants. He and his assistant discuss the important mail and the routine reports. The secretary makes a record of the letters to be sent out, of the orders to the assistant, and of decisions which must be carried out.

The chief then calls in the general manager or some other high line official. They review reports of the operating departments. The main problems arising in the departments are discussed, and whenever possible, decisions are made on how to proceed. But this session is for the most part an informative one for the big boss. Some routine decisions may be made, as well as some "exception" decisions. On the basis of this conference, if the boss really knows the business, he schedules meetings with operating chiefs, financial officers, personnel people, and others. The balance of the day is consumed with conferences that were arranged or scheduled for that day. In between the conferences are sandwiched short meetings with big customers, important visitors, and other influential people.

The day of the big boss is a day of conferences with small groups. At most four or five officials meet with him in his office or in one of the conference rooms. The men that participate in these conferences are officials on the next lower level—vice-presidents, directors, and managers. Each vice-president may bring to the conference three or four subofficials who

do not participate in discussions unless they are asked to provide information. These assistant managers would not consider dropping in on the big boss unescorted by their superiors.

Occasionally, the chief eats near one of the assistants at lunch time in the executive dining room. More likely than not, however, he will be surrounded by vice-presidents. Lunch may be served in his office, while a conference is being conducted. Probably once or twice a week he lunches uptown with high executive officials of other companies.

The afternoon is occupied with more conferences. Some time late in the afternoon there is a period of relaxation when no conferences are scheduled. At this time, staff assistants or the other high officials drop in for a chat. Problems arising during the day may be discussed, if it is not too inconvenient. If they involve getting more information, they are put on tomorrow's calendar. The big boss leaves the office exhausted, perhaps with the thought that conference work "takes more out of you than physical labor."

The big boss's range of social contact on the job is relatively small. He probably sees the same fifteen or twenty people every day. These people represent the upper two or three levels of management. The big boss's spatial mobility is also limited to his office and conference room. Although he may have a "feel" for his organization derived from inspecting its blueprints, his own job perspective is rather narrow. His world is an office world of appointments, official papers, and conferences.

The Big Boss and Top Managers

In a large organization there may be several vice-presidents, or managers, under the president. They represent, perhaps, manufacturing, engineering, sales, industrial relations, public relations, and finance. In smaller organizations two or three of these offices may be combined in one. On paper all of these officials appear equally important. They may even receive very similar salaries. *The problem of knowing the social situation at the top levels is one of arranging these officials in terms of their relations to the president, who is the big boss. It is also a problem of analyzing what kind of resources these top officials have in their struggle with each other to gain the attention and confidence of the big boss.*

Each of these officials is a big boss over a section of the organization. His daily schedule and duties are not unlike those of the big boss. He, too, has subofficials under him. The larger the organization the more the jobs of the top managers approach that of the president. Only their preoccupations are somewhat different. Each of them heads something like a political machine —a public relations machine, a sales machine, or a production machine, as the case may be. Each machine wants to protect or promote its security. Since each boss has some sovereignty over an area, he is jealous if someone interferes with his autonomy.

Generally speaking, the president does not want to interfere in the internal affairs of these sub-organizations. He hesitates to order changes in their structure or functions unless he thinks it absolutely necessary. He likes to have harmony (often defined as lack of open conflict) between the sections of the enterprise. Therefore he gives the vice-presidents freedom to run their organizations as long as they are doing satisfactory jobs.

The president, however, shows greater interest in the operation of some departments than of others. Finance, production, and industrial relations attract his attention. Normally he spends much of his time with the secretary-treasurer of the organization. In fact, it is not unrealistic to think of the president as the chief financial officer, because the board of directors and stockholders hold him responsible for profit and loss. So the big boss must spend time with his chief financial officer, whether or not their interpersonal relations are pleasant.

The relations between president and head of production are also close. Since profits depend upon the performance of the line organization, it is to the president's interest to keep informed on production schedules, bottlenecks, and achievements of the production organization. Not infrequently the president has been chief of production, so he is in a position to give advice.

If the president is not himself the informal head of industrial relations, he spends a great deal of time with the manager of this division during periods of labor strife. Although he does not ordinarily concern himself with industrial relations, a strike or threat of strike means that the finances and profit will be affected. During a strike, then, he spends most of his day with his industrial relations manager.

Emergencies may appear in other sections of the organization, requiring the president to spend more of his time with the appropriate officials. Thus the work positions of the president and of top management are in part traditionally defined and in part situationally defined. It is important to know how close the relations of the boss and his satellites are "normally" to evaluate the social situation of the moment.

Irrespective of situations, however, the president has two roles which he constantly plays. One is *instigation*, to stimulate all parts of his organization to do a better job. He must never allow his interest and attention to flag to the point that one part of the structure lags behind others. His second role is the *veto*. Each vice-president or manager wants his organization to be tops. For example, the head of manufacturing demands new and expensive machinery, the personnel director wants to institute a training program, the sales manager desires to step up advertising, the financial officer wants to institute better cost analysis methods. The president must learn when, to whom, and how to say *yes* and *no*. Getting knowledge to back his *no* occupies much more time than saying yes.

The social relations of the big boss in an actual work situation are portrayed in Figure 31. The three concentric rings around the president connote the varying degrees of interaction. In the first ring are found the president's private secretary and his two staff assistants. They form a tight primary group because they are in daily contact with the boss. In the second ring are

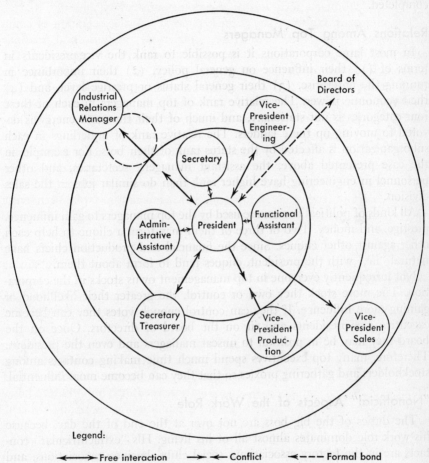

Legend:

⟵——⟶ Free interaction   ⟶ ⟵ Conflict   ⟵--- Formal bond

FIG. 31. The Social Atom of a Company President.

found the secretary-treasurer and the vice-presidents of production and engineering. The big boss does not interact with these three as extensively or intensively as with those in ring 1. In this case some antagonism exists between the big boss and the vice-president of production, whereas free interaction characterizes relations with the secretary-treasurer and the vice-president of engineering. In the third ring are found the vice-president of sales and the industrial relations manager. The big boss interacts with the

sales executive only when necessary. Close interaction between the boss and the industrial relations manager depends upon the state of labor-management relations. Relations between the boss and the board of directors are formal and most distant. This kind of positional analysis should be made in reference to many positions before the social analysis of a work plant is completed.

Relations Among Top Managers

In most large corporations it is possible to rank the vice-presidents in terms of (1) their influence on general policy, (2) their importance in running the enterprise, (3) their general status or prestige level, and (4) their economic power. The relative rank of top managers in each of these four categories is not stationary, and much of their time and energy is devoted to moving up these ladders. The relative rank of underlings in each suborganization is affected by the status rank of their boss. For example, in the case presented above, the assistant managers, secretaries, and other personnel in engineering have higher rank than do similar jobs in the sales division.

All kinds of political devices are used by the top managers to gain influence, prestige, and money. Two or three of them may form a clique to help each other against other cliques. Since the financial and production chiefs have natural "ins" with the president, cliques tend to form about them.

Not infrequently everyone in top management owns stocks in the corporation. The more stock they own or control, the greater their likelihood of gaining more influence. If they can control enough votes they can become executive vice-presidents and sit on the board of directors. Once on the board they may be in position to unseat managers and even the president. Therefore, many top executives spend much time making contacts among stockholders and gathering proxies so that they can become more influential.

"Nonofficial" Aspects of the Work Role

The duties of the big boss are not over at the end of the day, because his work role dominates almost all of his living. His "extracurricular" contacts are in the factory associations, social clubs, business associations, and the community.

"DUTY" CONTACTS

There are certain "duty" contacts which the big boss must develop and sustain. Frequently, the lower executives of businesses organize occupational and recreational groups. The Supervisory Association is an example of the first, and the Bowling League illustrates the second. The president may be asked to preside over the association or to give a talk; he is also expected to make an occasional appearance at the social affairs of lower executives. On

the average of once a week, he has one of these "duty" calls to perform. He rationalizes that, "It is time well spent in personnel relations. It's a good idea to mix with the men and let them know you're a human being."

The vice-presidents and managers also have duty contacts, although they may not be as pressing as those of the president. Generally speaking, the further down the line, the less time is spent on these duties and social functions. But even the foreman has to spend some time on them. Each department, such as engineering, materials, production planning, and manufacturing, may have an annual picnic, athletic teams, and other clubs. The managers may be asked to encourage these organizations with their presence. They may also be requested to attend the company-wide picnic, the monthly dance, and other events, to impress on everyone that they take an interest in the whole organization.

SOCIAL CLUBS

Apart from internal duty contacts, high officials spend much of their time developing contacts. Some of these contacts are closely connected to their work positions. The president, for example, may endeavor to develop social contacts with members of the board of directors and important stockholders. Not infrequently high officials must maintain enough stock votes or strength to stay in office. Therefore time and energy is consumed entertaining people who can help their positions. One way to meet these people is to join their clubs and organizations. The country club, boating club, university club, and fraternity are just a few sources of social contacts. The reader may review a few "social participation profiles" of businessmen in *Who's Who*. For example,

Seary, Harry Lauderdale, life ins.; *b.* Galatin, Tenn., Nov. 25, 1872; *s.* George Edward and Mary (Lauderdale) S.; student, Vanderbilt, 1890-1893; LL.B., Georgetown U., 1894; *m.* Margaret Ballentine, Dec. 17, 1902; 1 son, Harry L. In practice of law, Dallas, Tex., 1894-1915; pres. Southland Life Ins. Co. since 1915; res. Am. Rio Grande Land & Irrigation Co. since 1902; v. p. Dallas Power & Light Co.; dir. Tex. Power and Light Company. City Commissioner, Dallas, Tex., 1907-1911; mem. Nat. Council Defense, World War; Pres. Amer. Life Conv., 1917-1918; dir. Tex. State Fair Assoc.; member, Kappa Alpha. Democrat. Mem. Christian Church. Mason (32, Shriner). *Clubs:* Dallas Athletic Fincastle Lake, Little Sandy Lake (Dallas); Shary Yacht (Point Isabel, Texas). *Home:* 3707 Beverly Drive, Highland Park, Dallas. *Office:* Southland Life Bldg., Dallas, Tex.

BUSINESS ASSOCIATIONS

Business associations are also part of the extra-plant social life of the top executives. The Chamber of Commerce, Management Association, Society of Engineers, City Club are just a few of these. Business organizations shade

off into semi-business groups such as Kiwanis, Rotary, and Lions. Participation in these clubs often constitutes the "community" activity of many business leaders.

COMMUNITY ACTIVITIES

However, some of the presidents urge their executives to get out into "genuine" community activities. They are urged to work for the Red Cross, political organizations, Planning Commission, Community Chest, and others. Indeed many of these organizations have the same social members as the service clubs. Industrial and business leaders feel that this kind of work is a "contribution" of their organization to the community. Men are released from their official duties to participate in these "worthy" activities. It is a principle that the lower down the line one is, the less are his chances of being released from work routine to participate in community life.[2]

Motives that impel community participation are mixed. There is a tradition that businessmen should serve their communities, and most executives follow this tradition. But participation may also be considered an unofficial part of public relations. Since the relations between industry and community are frequently intimate and important, it pays to have the good will of prominent people in the community. Not to be neglected is the fact that such participation is another channel for making business contacts. Apart from the fact that business people think and act alike, and therefore find their own company congenial, community organizations are a good place to develop business contacts.

Ideology of Top Management

As a result of the similar backgrounds, experience, social participation, and frequent contacts, the big boss and his top executives think very much alike on social, political, and economic issues.

Top management is a *highly self-conscious* group, widely separated from the mass of people. The adulation that many people have for the captains of industry understandably affects their self-conception. Like other occupational groups, top executives are not only self-conscious but conscious of their *self-importance*. Their ethnocentrism leads them to believe that they have special gifts and attributes not generally shared by the population. The greatest of these is the ability to manage and organize people. They feel that good management is the biggest asset of any organization; without it, a business community or nation could not progress. Other virtues they honor, apart from occupational knowledge, are energy, dynamic ambition, initiative, leadership, and "personality."

During the recent war, the esteem that management had for its own skills was sloganized as "know-how" and "can do." Technical knowledge

[2] See Chapter XXI, "Industry and the Community."

and organizational skill are considered absolute requisites for executive success. The intense admiration for skills and achievements leads to the questions "What can he do?" "How good is he?"

A common question managers ask is, "What kind of fellow is he?" They are very preoccupied with the personal and social attributes of a man. Although they consider technical skill more important than all other factors, they are also concerned with "developing" personality and social "know-how." The veritable deluge of books and pamphlets in recent years on how to make friends and develop personality reflects the faith that "personality and social success" are learnable. A tightening of the channels of upward mobility may be no small factor in the sale of such "success" books.

Top management is an *authority-conscious* group. Men at the top of the supervisory structure are consumed with decision making and commanding. Yet they do not like to believe that men obey them because they have power. This thought derives from a wish to be appreciated both as persons and as officials. In meetings of business executives one or two speeches are invariably devoted to the *importance of leadership*, the *development of leadership*, the *techniques of leadership* and the *role of leadership* in industry.[3] Perhaps the American political ideal of democratic leadership is so powerful that executives want to realize it in business. Obviously they want to be and like to be thought of as leaders. They want to feel that they command because they are gifted to lead; that others obey because they recognize this ability. This cult of leadership may be an integral part of the larger American tradition of individual mobility in a free society.

Another facet in the ideology of management is *social responsibility*. Chief executives do not like to believe that their only motive in business is profit. They like to feel that as leaders of industry they must assume the responsibility of directing the community. Since many workers and investors are dependent upon them for their livelihood, they feel obliged to do a good job.[4] Unions and other such organizations interfere with this responsibility. The business leader likes to look at himself as a man who has dedicated his life to the *service* of investors, employees, and customers. He feels that his salary includes a payment for a stewardship which he owes to the community. He derives much satisfaction from the knowledge that he is serving his stewardship well.

In exercising his calling, the business leader feels that the *good of the organization* is paramount. Unlike other people, he must be concerned with the entire enterprise. It is his duty to think of the requirements of the *whole* organization. Although he may hurt people in the process, he feels that this

[3] See Schuyler Dean Hoslett, *Human Factors in Management*, Park College Press, 1946, Part I.

[4] J. David Houser, *What People Want from Business*, McGraw-Hill Book Company, Inc., 1938.

hard-heartedness is really hard-headedness, for the entire organization would suffer if he did not play this role.

The good executive feels that a good business is one that is *making money*. Money is an indicator of efficiency, as well as a goal. It is simultaneously an incentive and a yardstick. Without it, business would flounder in a sea of inefficiency. Another element in the thought system of managers is concerned with costs. The causes of inefficiency are thought to be almost invariably *internal*, and the cure of inefficiency must start from *within*. The first step in this cure is to *cut costs, by whatever means are available*. Cutting costs and keeping them down is one of the major jobs of executives, for costs and profits are very closely related. Any organization that doesn't keep costs down is not a good organization. That is why government is inefficient. It costs too much, and the way to make it efficient is to cut its budget. It will, like business, find ways to be more efficient.

The thinking continues: A good business cannot prosper without *good organization*. Any business can be better organized; and poor business can often be saved by reorganization. Many businessmen falsely believe that organization is a science and should be applied like a science. The executive feels that he cannot be queasy about the application of his science. Personality and sentiment should not enter into the science of business administration. The more this happens, the more inefficient business will be.

Obviously there are differences in the ways different executives think their businesses should be run. Some believe they should rule with an iron hand, others believe in more permissive methods. Some feel that money is the chief object, others think it is satisfaction from a job well done. We have tried to describe just a few traits in the idea system of men who generally play the roles of top management.

As far as production goes, top management thinks that this depends on a *good plant manager*. If things are not going right, the plant manager is probably blamed. Let us inspect the position and role of the plant manager.

PLANT MANAGER AND HIS SATELLITES

There are many titles in vogue for the official who is head of operations. He may be called the executive vice-president, plant manager, bureau head, general superintendent, or chief of production. In larger organizations he is usually vice-president in charge of production; in smaller plants he is usually called plant manager. Irrespective of his title, his position, functions, and duties are very similar.

Functions of the Plant Manager

The plant manager occupies an important and strategic position. Everyone, including his supervisors, recognizes that he is the head of the most important section of the plant. In a sense, all other departments are supposed

to help his department function more effectively. On the success or failure of the line rests the financial position and the very survival of the entire plant. Therefore, hardly any decision of consequence can be made without at least consulting the head of operations.

Plant managers are top managers, and one of their functions is to participate in making plant policy. Since policy affects the operation of the line most directly, the role of the chief of operations in planning sessions is critical. If he is an unwilling party to major decisions, trouble may be expected. As a matter of fact, when the plant manager does not concur in general policy, the policy is usually altered in line with his wishes or he is fired.

To avoid continuous bickering with top management, the plant manager is often given a considerable amount of autonomy in planning. He spends a great deal of his time in planning production or services for the organization. Frequently he heads a large staff which does little else but plan production. Thus the plant manager is engaged in planning at two levels: overall plant policy planning, and production or service planning.

Aside from planning, the chief responsibility of the plant manager is to oversee production or service. Of course, he is too far removed from the plant floor to supervise production directly. In fact, it is not unusual for him to stay out of the plant and work entirely with his office staff. However, he must keep close tabs on the production schedules of the various departments or sections. He and his staff are occupied with production goals or schedules, designing work flow, and *coördinating* the work of the departments. With the growth of organizational size, coördination becomes increasingly complex and difficult. The process of coördination is dependent upon (1) carefully drawing up the large overall production plans, (2) scheduling the plan into definite time periods, (3) breaking down the overall plan and schedule into smaller component parts, (4) obtaining periodic reports of the progress of the smaller plans and the overall plan, and (5) readjusting plans and schedules of the whole and the parts in the face of restricting circumstances.

The daily behavior of the plant manager is not unlike that of the president. He begins his day by reading a series of *reports* from engineers, staff officers, and foremen. Unlike those which the president receives, these reports are much more specific and technical. They deal with the progress of plans and problems that arise on the plant floor. Besides going over written reports, the plant manager engages in a number of formal and informal conferences, the purpose of which is to gain additional information that he wants. On the basis of these reports and conferences, further meetings are held with key individuals—accountants, engineers, inspection supervisors, and others—to iron out problems and project further plans.

The plant manager, if he is going to be effective in conference work, not

only must be a good coördinator but must have technical knowledge. Like top management he must be a good executive, but he must also have the knowledge to understand the problems that arise, and suggest paths to solve them. For this reason he must be either (1) a professionally trained person —an engineer, scholar, doctor, chef (depending on the industry)—or (2) a person who has had wide practical experience by working up from the plant floor. The greater his capacity to *follow up reports* with detailed suggestions on what needs to be done, the better he is. Top management expects him to do a good job, irrespective of the kind of men he has under him.

Some of the functions that we have listed for the plant manager may be performed by two or three line officials in larger organizations. For example, participation in overall company policy may be the job of the executive vice-president, production planning may be the job of another vice-president, and technical supervision may be given to the plant superintendent. In this section we are *not* concerned with the general policy planner. He is oriented too much like the president to be considered on a genuinely different level. We are concerned with the manager who is oriented downward to the actual problems of the production organization.

Work Position of the Plant Manager

The plant manager's work position may be analyzed by studying his relationship to (1) the top management of the plant, (2) the various staff departments and their members, and (3) his own organization. We shall consider each of these relations.

1. RELATION TO TOP MANAGEMENT

A strong cleavage exists between top management and the plant manager who is oriented downward. The latter feels that he heads the most important section of the organization and should be master of his own bailiwick. His ever present thought is to *get out the production.* Top management may make demands that interfere with his production schedules and the rate of output. Since many of the top executives have entered the organization through such channels as sales, accounting, and personnel, they do not share the attitudes and background of the plant manager. Such contrasts are especially noticeable if the plant manager has risen through the ranks and has not had much formal education. He is likely to regard management's ideas as criticisms. Impulsively he tends to ward off interaction with the top by taking the attitude that he is boss of his organization. Gardner's illustration demonstrates the irritation of top management over this situation. A top executive said:

"For all the influence I have you would never know that the plant is part of the company. Why, if I go into the plant for anything, I hardly get to the door before the superintendent is standing by my side, and he stays with

me until I leave. And I know that I only get to see the things he wants me to see. And trying to introduce any changes is a hopeless task; it's like pushing against a stone wall. Even when he seems to agree to something, it goes only slowly and half-heartedly, and there are dozens of things wrong with it."[5]

2. RELATIONS TO THE STAFFS

Many of the pressures that top management exerts on the plant chief are usually changes desired by the various staff departments. In theory, the staff departments are at the service of the line organization. Although the line should consult the staff on its problems, it frequently feels that it needs only minimal services. If the staff organizations acquiesce in this feeling, they are signing their own death warrants. Organizations which are to survive must justify their existence and their right to be useful in the scheme of things. Since the staff has representatives in top management, it can literally demand that the shop organization use its services. Many of the squabbles in industry may be understood with this situation in mind. We shall examine several sources of pressures on the shop manager and his staff.

a. Pressure from Finance. In the discussion of the work role of the president, the importance of the finance organization was emphasized. This organization parallels the entire work plant from top to bottom. It is concerned with company profits, but it is equally concerned with costs in every nook and cranny. Especial concern is shown in the financial status of the line department. To evaluate this status, finance organizations have evolved accounting systems which can theoretically measure the costs of every operation, in every section, in every department of the entire plant. At almost any time, the accounting division can give top management the prevailing cost-profit picture of the line and its departments. It can also compare this record with past performance.

The plant manager and his organization are bothered by the accounting staff in two ways. First, the accounting activities disrupt the relations among the departments in the line. Second, the accounting process naturally restricts the freedom of the line organization. In the first instance, the finance organization prepares cost reports for each department in the line. Since previous reports become standards for present performance, each foreman or division chief is concerned with his record. Instead of trying to improve his section irrespective of anything, he operates in terms of what will look good on the record. Every supervisor keeps an informal check on his cost picture, with the end result that the *line organization is running informally a parallel* finance organization. Thus, much of the time and energy of the supervisor is occupied in duplicating the functions of another organization.

[5] Gardner, *op. cit.*, p. 57.

The plant manager is affected by the financial preoccupation of his under-lings in an indirect way. For example, a poor record in assembly may be due to slipshod work in manufacturing, failure of the supply organization to pro-vide requisite materials, the fact that maintenance fell down on its job of repairing machinery, high absenteeism rate, or other factors. Since the accounting reports do not reflect these extenuating circumstances, the head of assembly is called on the carpet. He naturally feels a resentment against other department heads who may be responsible for his poor record. Recrim-inations against other departments are brought to the plant manager. The latter would not have to play a mediating and repressive role if he were not subject to pressure from the accounting organization.

The animosities that the plant manager builds against the finance organ-ization are more direct in matters of general policy. In order to keep up production schedules, he needs better materials, new machines, higher-skilled workers, and more space. All these may entail expenditure of money and reduction of profits. Usually the treasurer is a conservative individual who dislikes disbursing large funds. Plant managers see this as resistance to pro-duction, and they get angry, and relations between these two officials are not usually cordial.

b. *Pressure from Inspection.* Sometimes the inspection organization is separate from the line. Since it is the job of inspection to pass on the quality of work, it plays a critical role. Aside from the fact that nobody loves a critic, over-critical inspection can affect the cost adversely. Wastes and rejects do not look good on a department's records. Consequently *the line organ-ization sets up informally its own parallel inspection system* when the regular inspectors get too rigid. Bad parts do not reach inspection points.[6] If inspec-tion discovers this ruse, the inspection head "beefs" about it to the plant manager, who berates his men while informally backing them up. The pre-occupation of the plant manager is to get out production, even if quality must be lowered. The head of inspection will fight this, especially if his relations to the plant manager are strained. Therefore, the plant manager must spend some time either fighting inspection or courting its good will. It is desirable to have the good will of inspection because inspection stand-ards are often flimsy and dependent on the personal judgment of the inspectors. "Rough" or "easy" inspection depends on the social relations between the heads of inspection and line organization. One of the sources of irritation that the heads cannot overcome is the antagonism between inspectors and workers. The former are white-collar workers who feel superior to the manual workers. This does not make for cordial relations.

Sometimes inspection is under the control of the plant manager. Inspection foremen then feel like a tool of the boss because they cannot perform honest

[6] *Ibid.,* p. 93.

functions. Their craving for independence does not make the manager's job easier.

c. Pressure from Engineering. If inspection feels superior to the shop organization, the engineering and research people feel like Brahmin. Research people have generally had professional and technical training to find new ways of improving the product and its manufacture. Consequently, engineering or research organizations continually exert *pressure to change the prevailing methods of operation.*[7]

Presumably both line and engineering are interested in improving the product or service. However, the plant manager and his assistants hate to disrupt production and delay work schedules. Further, if they have risen from the ranks, they have an almost religious belief in the traditional methods of operation. Untrained in theory, they can only visualize small changes that bring immediately visible results.

For these reasons the plant manager may not consult engineering frequently. But engineering justifies its existence by the number of "advances" it introduces in manufacturing. A research organization is expensive to support. If it does not "pay off," its funds may be curtailed, or it may even be liquidated. On the other hand, if research is constantly finding something wrong or something to improve, the head of production begins to feel that his organization "is being shown up." He puts pressure on his men to anticipate changes which engineering may find, thus getting credit from top management. In fact, the intimate acquaintance that the line has with production often enables it to find improvements which engineers overlook. If the shop does this too effectively, the research organization feels it is not earning its way and is being "shown up" by less-trained people. It seeks to offer more basic suggestions for improvement.

These are frequently resisted because they are too "theoretical," "harebrained," or "textbookish." Research cannot institute its ideas unless its gets management support. In the face of resistance from line officers, it seeks *more authority* from management to put its ideas into practice. To demonstrate this need, it criticizes and never praises the line. Backed up by the president, the "prima donnas" usually get what they want. Animosity arises and the line resists giving staff any more authority.

An executive vice-president of a clay products company in Ohio and Pennsylvania writes of his problems of inducing changes in tradition-bound plants dominated by old-line superintendents:

I have at present the job of filling certain key spots such as that of chief engineer, sales manager of the pottery division, and unfortunately, the replacement of certain other key men as they have not been functioning for quite some time. I have finally gotten the production superintendent to cooperate with the sales department to produce what the market requires, and have gotten the sales de-

[7] *Ibid.,* p. 77.

partment to start to plan by making market analysis, on a logical basis. Despite some resistance from an old line superintendent, I am installing material handling equipment in our plants and directing other purchases to reduce manual labor in quantity, and to make certain jobs easier to perform so that we can attract good workers. Most of our operations were of the hand labor type, as our base rate for common labor in 1933 was 37 cents per hour and in 1947 is $1.01 per hour. It would have taken perhaps ten years to pay for a new piece of labor saving machinery then, but the same piece of machinery or material handling equipment would now pay for itself in about six months or a year. Due to the low labor rate, *the incentive to modernize was not strong,* and . . . over the past ten years, little was done. Our company apparently recognized the trend as we started to build a plant about six years ago which I am just getting into operation. It is completely modern, and shows that our stuff can be manufactured as other things can be. Most of our other plants should be torn down in part, at least, and started over again. But our investment in each plant represents about $500,000 or more, or a total of four million in the eight plants and branch warehouses, which also should be modernized with material handling equipment. We do not have enough money to do all of this right now, although each step will pay for itself and give us a working set-up that will enable us to compete in the competitive market now here. We are as well off as anyone in our business. Our low production and the up-to-date aggressiveness of such companies as Johns-Manville Corporation, with transit pipe and others with concrete pipe and cement pipe manufacturers, fibre pipe, cast iron pipe, aluminum pipe, etc., have made heavy inroads on our market and will continue to do so if our price gets out of line or our merchandising policy lets the public forget about the superior quality of our products. We are trying to get younger men into our business and desperately trying to get a better caliber of employees in our plants. Unfortunately, due to our reputation for low pay, and disagreeable work we can't get them, even though our rates are up and working conditions so much better.

d. *Pressure from Industrial Relations and Personnel.* Most plant man agers and superintendents want an experienced and highly skilled labor force. They also want power to use this labor as they see fit. In the past, they hired, trained, transferred, promoted, and paid workers as they wished. With the advent of unions, personnel and industrial relations departments evolved which absorbed some of their functions. The attitude of plant supervisors toward this development has been mixed. On the one hand, they were glad to get rid of functions which occupied much of their time; on the other hand, they resented the new departments because they restricted their freedom in the treatment of workers.

For example, when the personnel department chooses workers according to job specifications, it limits the range of job transferability. Plant managers, on the other hand, like workers who can be easily shifted around. But shifting can only be done by consulting the personnel organization, which then changes pay rate, withholding tax, seniority provisions, and so on. The extra paper work and the delays involved hamper the plant manager. In fact,

anything that slows down production schedules incurs his ire. Similarly, when unions cannot agree with management on wages and other provisions, shop heads get impatient. They are likely to agree to almost anything, as long as it does not interfere with production.

Top labor relations and personnel people are part of management and have an influence on policy formation which plant people must follow. When the plant manager dislikes a directive, he and his subordinates may sabotage it by various indirect means. The effect is to make the work of the staff appear ineffective and even ludicrous.

Top management of a New York precision instrument company decided

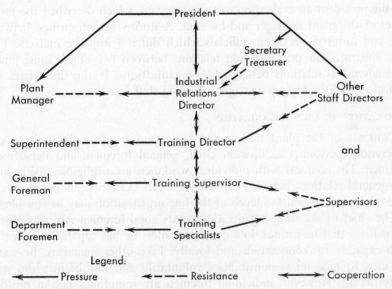

FIG. 32. Internal Pressures and Resistances Around a Supervisory Training Program.

to institute a supervisory training program. The industrial relations director, with the strong support of the president, inaugurated a series of training meetings for supervisors and foremen. The director asked for a half-million dollars to make the program work. Resistance arose from all sides. In the first place, the secretary-treasurer balked at the sum. He complained that the company could not afford such an extravagant program. His advice for a trial on a reduced scale received backing from other staff departments, which did not want to see Industrial Relations grow so powerful. Although the program was primarily designed to help the line, the plant manager gave it only silent approval. A limited program was finally installed.

Figure 32 shows what actually followed. The plant manager as head of the line let it be known to his subordinates that the training scheme was not

to be taken too seriously. They should coöperate, but not spend too much time at the training sessions. In addition, the foremen were reminded that their presence at the training sessions was voluntary, and that their primary job was to get out production.

Thus, at every point along the supervisory hierarchy the training staff confronted resistance. Attendance at training sessions was good at first but then began to slacken in the face of pressing production schedules. Supervisors in other staff departments, who were also participating in training sessions, complained that the program was oriented to factory supervisors and had little application to office problems. The training supervisors and specialists encountered increased resistance. In desperation they prepared for the president an evaluation of their program, which described the resistances of the plant manager and his staff. A stormy session ensued between line and industrial relations officials which did not improve matters. This case illustrates the principle that relations between two offices must finally be analyzed as relations between two organizations. It also dramatizes the typical role of the factory manager regarding staff functions.

3. RELATION TO OWN ORGANIZATION

Contacts of the plant manager in his organization are limited to such supervisory personnel as division chief, general foremen, and department foremen. His contacts with individual workmen are negligible. Aside from the general relations between supervisory levels examined above, other specific relations between the levels of the line organization may be considered.

The chief of the shop organization wants good foremen and supervisors. He realizes that he cannot do a good job unless he has capable men with a high capacity for coöperation and loyalty. Like other managers, he wants his men to take up responsibilities voluntarily and not bother him with petty details. However, individual foremen are sometimes not in position to know what a petty detail is. Consequently, when they consult him, he becomes somewhat impatient. One reason for his impatience is that he is often unable to give help on problems with which he has little intimate acquaintance. He sees his organization as a number of integrated parts and not as a series of minute problems.

The superiority attitudes that plant managers display toward their foremen and supervisors derive from the fact that they are better educated and have had broader factory experience. From his vantage point, the manager can see the operation of his entire organization, so that he appears omniscient to those who can see only part of it. In addition, he is definitely marked as part of management by his spatial segregation from the plant floor, his office surroundings, his clerical staff, and other management paraphernalia.

Foremen and supervisors bring to the plant manager many of their prob-

lems. They complain that operation sheets are too technical and far removed from the practical conditions in the shop. Engineers are then called in to revise and simplify these sheets and schedules. Subordinates may also complain about men, materials, and machines. Although the plant manager may not have the power to remedy these problems, he does not want to admit this to his men. An example will clarify this situation.

Foremen frequently complain about their workers; they need more help, some men should be dismissed, others should be transferred. The manager promises to rectify the situation. He goes to the personnel department with these problems and gets promises of action. Inevitably, delays occur and foremen get impatient. The plant manager becomes irked by their impatience because he has little control over hiring, firing, and transference of men.

Other problems are brought to the manager which he cannot deal with directly. New machines! Better maintenance! Better materials! More materials! Prompt delivery! More authority!—are continual demands of the foremen. The chief has little responsibility or control over some of these demands. He can only say that he will "see what he can do," and insist that the men do a better job with what they have.

Social Orientations of the Plant Manager

The social life of the plant manager depends to a large degree on his job orientations and work history. If he is a professional engineer, he probably has aspirations to belong to the top echelons of management. In a large plant, he wants to become executive vice-president or perhaps even president. Therefore, he seeks to develop social contacts with the men who are now filling these offices. Despite the fact that he may be having some difficulties with the finance officer, head of industrial relations, and others, he cannot afford to alienate himself from their good graces. He will try to join their social clubs and participate in their social activities.

Difficulties usually confront the plant manager who tries to join in the social circle of top management. He is tied down to his office and the plant to a far greater degree than other managers. It is hard for him to take two or three hours out of the middle of the day to attend a meeting of a business and social club downtown. Problems within the plant demand his constant attention and cannot be as easily postponed as can other staff problems.

The plant manager who has risen from the ranks has a different orientation. He has probably climbed as far as he can go. His limited formal education and the cultural attributes of his working-class background make him feel insecure among business-class people. His use of slang and factory argot especially tends to mark him off somewhat from other executives. If he prefers not to climb to the top, he has a secure position in his own organization. Under him there are usually several well-trained men who cultivate

his good graces. He can "lord it over" the college boys by showing them insights gained from practical experience.

The social life of the downward-oriented plant manager is spent with his assistants, the heads of divisions, and some old cronies in the shop. He also spends some time with staff people with whom he has contacts on the job. They tend to be those who are second-in-line in the accounting, industrial relations, engineering, and other departments. *They compose the social links between top management and operating heads in the line.*

The social life of the line organization is often quite elaborate. Since the organization often feels somewhat autonomous compared with the rest of the plant, it often creates parallel social organizations. Because the line is the largest segment of the plant, its social program is likely to be impressive. A separate picnic is held, a separate bowling league is instituted, a separate paper is published. The plant manager who attends many of these events takes off his vest and is really "one of the boys" for a day.

The informal social contacts of the plant manager and his associates are with white-collar people. However, they do not as a rule take as active a role in community and civic organizations as does top management. Although the plant manager may be encouraged to "get into the community," he cannot give it the requisite time and energy. Public relations are not as important in his job as with top management.

Ideology[8]

The prevailing social ideas of plant managers are not significantly different from those of top management. Both groups feel that they occupy high positions by virtue of their abilities; both believe in the importance of managerial responsibility; both have an ardent faith in free-enterprise capitalism; both are highly conscious of costs and profits; both are highly self-conscious; and both support the dominant values in the community.

In one or two ways the values of the two groups differ. Plant managers agree that top management may be necessary, but they firmly believe plant people are more important. In some instances operating chiefs feel that they could run the organization better without the "help" of the big boys. Underlying this notion is the thought that technical knowledge is more important than organizational knowledge. All the community participation, planning, labor relations, cost accounting, research, and public relations are almost parasitical because they do not contribute income to the enterprise. Plant managers regard much of the activity of top management as political and wasteful. They feel that the public misplaces respect, because the people who *do things*, who actually plan and supervise production, should receive highest esteem. They feel that there wouldn't be labor, public relations, and other problems if the people who were supervising the actual work had more

[8] See Thorstein Veblen, *Engineers and the Price System*, The Viking Press, Inc., 1940.

authority. Some deep-rooted ideas are that plant people are guided by science and reason, that they are accustomed to solving practical problems in a practical way, that there is no room for politics and sentiment among practical people. Therefore, they contend, everybody's economic and social welfare would be increased if plant people were given more power to exercise their practical knowledge and experience as they see fit.

FIRST-LINE SUPERVISORS

The man behind the man behind the bench has become a critical figure in American industry. He has been called "the forgotten man," a "stooge" for management, and the man in the middle. He is the first-line supervisor or foreman. He has been called alternately the most important and the least important part of management. But he has not been ignored.

The first-line supervisor constitutes the third basic level in the supervisory hierarchy. He is the man who is supposed to do the actual job of supervising production or service. This involves daily face-to-face contact with the workers. Various titles are current for his office, including supervisor, foreman, chief, leader, and straw boss. The variety of nomenclature is somewhat disturbing because sometimes the designations are used synonymously and sometimes differently. The definition of first-line supervision varies from plant to plant and from industry to industry. Apart from this confusion, the distinctions within the ranks of first-line supervision are not always drawn.

In large-scale industry the designation of foreman, supervisor, and chief extends from superintendent to the leading hand in a small working group. For example, in the Hawthorne plant, the general foreman is five levels above the worker. Below him in the supervisory ladder are the foreman, assistant foreman, section chief, group chief, and finally the operator.[9] In smaller plants, the foreman may be the only official between the superintendent and the worker. In the office common titles for this level are supervisors and chiefs, never foremen.

The work position of a foreman or supervisor must be more clearly defined. For our purposes this position is an office that requires supervision of the actual production or service as a full-time job. The person filling this office must have official contacts with both supervisory officials and the operators or clerks on the job. He must spend most of his time on the plant floor supervising personally, or supervising people who are part-time supervisors and part-time workers. Paper work must not occupy so much of his time that he has to have a secretary. He does not spend more than one-third of his day on it. In fact, paper work irritates him and keeps him off the floor. Further, he does not participate in policy making. In short, his orientation

[9] F. J. Roethlisberger and W. J. Dickson, *Management and the Worker*, Harvard University Press, 1947, p. 11.

is downward toward the workers and their problems. He must have enough authority so that workers obey his technical commands. For purposes of convenience we shall use the term "supervisor" or "foreman" for the work position having these characteristics. In an actual plant two or three positions may together fulfill our requirements. They shall be treated as a single position here.

The Supervisor's Functions

Listing the supervisor's functions is precarious because there is no general agreement on what they are or ought to be. For no other work position is there as much controversy on role, position, and function as for the supervisor or foreman. In addition to the fact that his role, position, and functions vary with plants, the definition of his position is in a state of transition. Drucker points out that two generations ago "There were a few plants in this country where the foreman was a semi-independent contractor who had undertaken to supply a certain product or to do a certain process at a stipulated rate. If he could do the job more cheaply, the difference was his profit; . . . if he lost out on the transaction the loss was his. In other words, the foreman was close to being an independent businessman, except that he did not own his capital equipment."[10]

Obviously this is not the situation today. The supervisor is at the bottom of the management hierarchy. There are some who would even debate this. They feel that supervisors are mass-production workers, whose occupation is to hound other workers to produce more. Without entering this debate directly, we can state that the main task of the supervisor is to oversee production. *His job is to insure that the production or service schedules set up by higher executives are actually fulfilled.* While performing this function he must handle any on-the-spot eventualities which may interfere with schedule fulfillment. This is a more difficult job than it sounds because many kinds of contingencies may arise which, because of his peculiar role, he may not be able to resolve.

F. J. Roethlisberger, in a penetrating article on the foreman's position, states that his job is much more difficult than it was a generation ago.[11] The foreman, he contends, must know more than his old-time counterpart. This fact is revealed in the foremanship training programs of modern industry. According to these he must know

. . . not only (1) the company's policies, rules, and regulations and (2) the company's cost system, payment system, manufacturing methods, and inspection regulations, in particular, but also frequently (3) control, and time and motion study

[10] Peter F. Drucker, *The Concept of the Corporation,* The John Day Company, 1946, p. 163.
[11] Fritz J. Roethlisberger, "The Foreman: Master and Victim of Double Talk," in Hoslett, *op. cit.,* p. 56.

in general. He also has to know (4) the labor laws of the United States, (5) the labor laws of the state in which the company operates, and (6) the specific labor contract which exists between his company and the local union. He has to know (7) how to induct, instruct, and train new workers; (8) how to handle, and where possible, prevent grievances; (9) how to improve conditions of safety; (10) how to correct workers and maintain discipline; (11) how never to lose his temper and always be "fair"; (12) how to get and obtain cooperation from the wide assortment of people with the shop steward. And in some companies he is supposed to know (13) how to do the jobs he supervises better than the employees themselves. Indeed, as some foreman training programs seem to conceive the foreman's job, he has to be a manager, a cost accountant, an engineer, a lawyer, a teacher, a leader, an inspector, a disciplinarian, a counselor, a friend, and above above all, an "example."[12]

The Foreman's "Little" Helpers

One would imagine that a job requiring all this knowledge would make its holder the cock of the roost. It may be true that all the knowledge the foreman is supposed to have does him no harm. However, in view of his actual position, all these requisites turn out to be double talk because the foreman cannot use his knowledge as he sees fit. On the contrary, he is ordered what to do, when to do it, and how to do it. If a problem arises in his department he cannot solve it with his knowledge. Someone else (usually on the staff) knows more about it than he does; someone else has had a role in formulating policy on that problem; someone else expects to be consulted about it.

Is there a question of changing machines around? "Call in engineering." Should an operator be promoted, transferred, or fired? "Call in the boss, personnel office, and the union!" Is the product good enough to go through? "Call in cost and quality control!" Is operator Y falling down on the job? "Call the steward!" The foreman is responsible for technical efficiency, personnel relations, quality of production, keeping costs down, labor relations, and other things. Yet he has little or no authority to fulfill his responsibility. All kinds of staff people are anxious to "help" him.

Relations to the Staff

Possibly, modern industry could not function without staff participation in the problems of first-line operations. But this does not solve the foreman's dilemma, because staff men not only participate in the foreman's job but are responsible for the stream of unending changes that bombard him and his workers. Engineers, technologists, and accountants are responsible for changes on the plant floor. Before one set of technical and financial codes becomes the *modus vivendi* of the shop, other codes are proposed and installed. The foreman cannot protest for he has no authority

[12] *Ibid.*, p. 54.

or specialized knowledge. And the staffs keep justifying their worth to the organization by the new techniques and financial checks that they introduce.

All eyes are on the plant floor, where the money is made. Almost all changes proposed by management and the staffs are aimed at the foreman and his workers. In a sense everybody is a threat to any security or status the foreman may have. What is more important, his performance and that of his workers is being made increasingly measurable. Production by nature is more measurable than are other types of labor. The number of workers, units produced, the cost of items, and scrap are all measurable. The work of the plant manager, president, engineer, and accountant is not measured partly because it is more difficult to measure, but, more important, *these people are in a better position to resist measurement of their performance.* The measurement of his performance increases the foreman's insecurity. The fact that his position may be short-circuited makes the position even more insecure. If the foreman just had to report to his boss, he could cover up and report only favorable things. After all, this is what everybody else does. However, many staff people can report the foreman's activities to his boss and higher management. The union can and does go over his head. So do inspection, cost control, engineering, and other organizations. Down to the foreman comes the question, "Why didn't you inform us?" Down come commands to coöperate with the staff people. Down come new people and new studies of his workers' performance. A foreman's life is not a happy one.

The Foreman and the Union

To the foreman the union is like another staff organization which limits his functions and authority. The union does not, as Roethlisberger would have us believe, remove "the last vestiges of initiative, judgment, and what is more important, personal relations with his subordinates."[13] True, it does introduce a new set of rules which the foreman must observe in his conduct toward the workers. But the volume, mass, and complexity of these rules are not greater or more disturbing than those imposed by the staff organizations. On the contrary, union rules, being fixed by contract, define precedents and relationships that create order and stability on the plant floor. Management directives tend to introduce more changes in the foreman's activities. In fact, as Gardner points out, the foreman on occasion uses the union as a means of short-circuiting his line. When he feels that his department has needs which his boss has failed to attend to, he may resort to the artifice of urging the union to ask top management to do something about the situation.[14] However, this technique is not very commonly used.

The attitude of the foreman toward the union may be hostile or friendly,

[13] *Ibid.*, p. 64.
[14] Gardner, *op. cit.*, pp. 106-107.

depending on his past experiences with it. If he has been a union man, he may not resent union restrictions on his activities. If he considers his job a step up the management ladder, he may resent the union's restrictions. In any case, it is another organization which limits his freedom of action.

Figure 33 summarizes the changes that have occurred in the foreman's role in the last generation or two. The diagram on the left portrays the functions he once had; the other diagram names the staff organizations that have absorbed each function. The sizes of the pieces of the pie are only crude approximations of the time spent on each function. In summary, the problems the plant manager has in his relations to staff organizations are

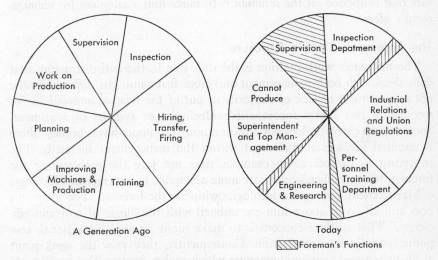

FIG. 33.   The Foreman's Functions: A Generation Ago and Today.

but a part of his daily routine. The foreman, however, is deprived of the prestige which comes with social distance. "He is an ideal scapegoat for the expression of any disturbances in the social equilibrium."[15]

The Foreman and His Boss

Every worker in each level of the supervisory structure is preoccupied with what his boss thinks of him. The foreman is no exception. If superiors are displeased, they can make his life miserable. Indeed, they can take away his job. Just as the worker spends a great deal of time worrying about how his performance affects the attitudes of his foreman, the foreman, in turn, worries about his relations to his boss.

There is some evidence to support the idea that the foreman's position exposes him to the strongest kind of worker-boss cleavage. It is necessary to explain the tensions arising between the supervisor and his boss to under-

[15] Roethlisberger and Dickson, *op. cit.*, p. 368.

stand the former's position. Although the foreman is at the bottom of the supervisory hierarchy, he has little or none of management's prerogatives. In the literal sense, if not in the organizational sense, *the management ladder ends with the foreman's boss*. Supervisors are left with the role of urging workers on so that production schedules materialize. Under this situation the pressure from top-level executives is on the lowest management official who has *authority as well as responsibility*. He, of course, is the supervisor's boss: the superintendent, division chief, or some such official. The pressure of all management levels focuses upon him because he, not the foreman, is the culmination of a series of management links. *The pressure that is applied on the foreman is to make him a salesman for management's ideas.*

The Foreman's Double Exposure

The foreman's work position is the only one in the entire structure that daily deals with *both* management and labor first-hand. His *difficulties arise not so much out of lack of authority as out of the relative impossibility of reconciling two rather incompatible ideologies or systems of sentiment.* Such a sharp cleavage does not appear among the upper levels because there is essential ideological agreement *within* the management hierarchy. The supervisor in the office, for example, does not face the problems of the foreman because office workers are more amenable to management ideology.

Management and worker ideologies whipsaw the foreman. The foreman's boss and all levels above him are imbued with the "logic of cost and efficiency." That is, their concern is to make profit by applying rational, economic principles to production. Consequently, they view the work plant as an impersonal economic machine which makes money. The workers are also units to be considered in this process of moneymaking. Although managers do not regard relations among themselves impersonally, they do think of problems on the plant floor as impersonal, financial ones.

The foreman's boss has assimilated this ideology of cost and efficiency,[16] and tries to imbue it in his foremen. The latter, however, have to deal with workers who usually do not share management's conception of their role as cost items. Workers do not consider themselves as machines to be moved about and used according to the best logic of efficiency.[17] They have emotional stakes in their work and want to be considered accordingly. Management is sometimes aware of this fact on its own level but does not seem to see it on the worker's level. The superintendent's view of the men below the foremen is impersonal.

The foreman, like any worker in the structure, does not want to incur the disapproval of his boss openly by violating norms of efficient economic

[16] See section on ideology of the plant manager above.
[17] See Chapter VIII, "Operation of the Union Local."

behavior. Yet he must deal with the workers as people. He must meet situations which clear economic thinking cannot predict. He knows that he cannot disregard workers' sentiments about jobs, rates, profits, and procedures. He knows "it is impossible to uphold strictly the logic of efficiency without sometimes demoralizing the group."[18] If he informs the superintendent of all of the workers' resentments to management ideology, his boss will berate him for having so much dissension in his section. If he does not report these matters, his boss discovers them through other channels. Either path is dangerous.

Orientations of the Foreman

Gardner indicates that foremen tend to solve these problems by making an identification in one of three directions:

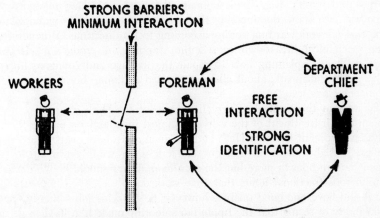

FIG. 34. Foreman Identified with Department Chief. (Adapted from Burleigh B. Gardner, *Human Relations in Industry*, Richard D. Irwin, Inc., 1945, p. 44.)

1. Identification with department chief and management.
2. Identification with the workers under him.
3. Isolation, or identification with other foremen.

IDENTIFICATION WITH DEPARTMENT CHIEF

When the foreman identifies with his superior, he embraces management ideology. He tends to be critical of his workers, finds fault with their work, and presses them for ever greater output.[19] This often occurs when the foreman is brought in from the outside with the expectation that he will be moved up into an executive job. Even if this is not the case, the foreman who identifies upward develops social distance toward his workers. The

[18] F. J. Roethlisberger, *Management and Morale*, Harvard University Press, 1943, p. 38.
[19] Gardner, *op. cit.*, p. 43.

latter will not confide in him or have much to do with him outside of work. On the contrary, they will withhold information, restrict their work, and use the union to make his life uncomfortable. Gardner has illustrated this situation in a diagram which is reproduced as Figure 34. Drucker believes that this type of identification must exist if the present economic system is to survive in America.[20] Below is a worker's view of a boss dominated by management ideology.

Before the war I was employed at the tipple of the Rice Brothers Coal Company, and it was there that I came in contact with this man whom I shall never forget.

Herbert Dias, better known as Herb, was a nervous, wizened, little man with coal black eyes that peered out from behind a pair of thick-lensed glasses; those same peering eyes seemed never to miss a thing that went on around him. Herb was the proud possessor of the title of tipple boss, and to know that meant he was lord and master over all his domain, the tipple. No king ruling from his throne was ever more domineering than Herb as he nervously paced the floor seeing that all work was functioning according to his directions. Whenever some minor mechanical breakdown caused the stoppage of production, Herb was always on hand explaining how to repair the damage and trying to hurry the mechanics in their work; about all he succeeded in doing, however, was getting in someone else's way.

The men in the tipple had very little respect for Herb when it came to a problem of fair treatment of the workers. Almost invariably on payday there was always an argument between Herb and the men as to how many hours of overtime pay was due them on that check. Herb never wrote down any overtime unless it was an hour or more but the men figured they should be reimbursed for the numerous fractional hours that they worked.

Herb did have one good quality, however; he took his job seriously. But the responsibility of seeing that the tipple ran smoothly made him hard to get along with at times.

IDENTIFICATION WITH THE WORKERS

When the foreman is sympathetic with his workers he tends to accept the ideology of labor. A foreman in this situation considers the sentiments of his men, is friendly toward them, and has social contacts with them on and off the job. Identifying with his men tends to increase social distance toward his chief. Free communication with his chief is reduced, for the foreman tries to cover up for his men, resist changes imposed from above, understand the union's demands, and modify his orders to fit the local situation.

This type of identification probably occurs more frequently when the foreman has risen from the ranks and has no aspirations to climb the management ladder. Since upward mobility from the plant floor to managerial

[20] Drucker, *op. cit.*, p. 174.

positions seems to be diminishing, downward foreman identification may be increasing. The rewards the foreman obtains from this type of identification are those of leadership, for both management and workers regard him with respect.

A student describes how a boss identified with his workers behaves:

His name was Sullivan, a plain, ordinary Irish name. His looks could have been anyone of those of the several million Irishmen living in this country. But to me, he was more than any other boss for whom I have worked. These past few years in which I have not seen him have made me appreciate him more than ever before. There have been countless times when I have tried to analyze his being liked so much.

There was no doubt in anyone's mind that he was capable. But how many hundreds of bosses have we encountered who have been capable but disliked very much? He had a cheery disposition, a good sense of humor, a straightforward way of speaking, and an ability to keep the employee interested in his job.

But those qualities I have just mentioned sound more like platitudes copied out of a textbook. They seem old and rather worn and do not find the real character of my boss' personality.

The thing I am going to say is something we have all heard thousands of times. It is a thing that must be said this way because I have not uncovered a better way of saying it. It is a word that has been battered back and forth from the mouths of laymen to those of the wealthy.

That word is *respect*. Sullivan respected his employees. He respected their feeble excuses for coming in late to work. He respected their rights to ask for more pay and less hours. He respected their right to go home when not feeling well. He respected the fact that these men were human beings and not mere animals. And in that man I not only discovered the best boss for whom I have ever worked, but I have also discovered the core of happiness.

HORIZONTAL IDENTIFICATION

The third type of identification refers to an attempt to straddle both management and labor and maintain a loyalty to both. Horizontal identification is most difficult, because very few people have the ability to satisfy both management and labor at the same time. However, such an identification can occur where foremen or managers have risen from the ranks, and retain a certain sympathy for the worker's way of life. Climbing, however, has a way of eliminating most of these sympathies, and a foreman tends to accept his role as a part of management.

Horizontal identification is commonly observed among newly appointed foremen. Their recent and perhaps long experience as workers and union members has given them both friends and sympathies for the working man. Moreover, there is always the prospect that the road they have taken into foremanship may lead back, at the first drop in sales, to the machine and the worker status from whence they came. In such an eventuality the ques-

tion is always whether the union will receive them and restore the seniority which they gave up when they became foremen. Meanwhile, as new foremen they are told that they now represent management. One plant manager described his method of inducting new foremen. He said, "Well, I get the new foremen together in the conference room and I tell them that they are now part of management and that they must think and act like managers. I tell them that managers have four big responsibilities. I draw a small square. At the base I write PROFITS. This is the most important because none of us, I say, can be sure of our jobs unless business can make a profit. Then on one side of the square I place COSTS, on the other side, QUALITY, and on the top, SAFETY or SECURITY of your men. I give them about fifteen minutes of lecture on these responsibilities, ask them if they have any questions and send them back to the floor."

With these instructions ringing in their ears foremen must decide upon their future role. Those who attempt to ignore the conflict of sentiments between management and labor isolate themselves from both. By keeping their contacts minimal and formal, they may be able to operate like a "mugwump" as long as no issue arises which demands a showdown. In the case of a showdown the foremen are likely to side with management. From then on they are identified as management-oriented.

Horizontal identification is at best an unstable position for the foreman. In reality it turns out to be an ostrich reaction. In the long run it puts him in the middle of a tug of war as his sympathies seesaw and he "gets hell" from both his superiors and the union.

Another and more unusual adjustment for the foreman is for him to attempt to become a third power in the struggle. By forming a labor union with other foremen he can refuse to be pushed around by either management or labor. Although foremen have been prohibited by law from forming labor unions, this type of adjustment may be used informally. That is, foremen may get together with each other and decide to "get tough" with any who threaten their position. Under present conditions, however, this course would be based more on courage than on strength. It does reveal, however, a feeling on the part of foremen that although they are neither fish nor fowl they do not intend to remain the "men in the middle" very long. Any redefinition of their status will probably place them with organized labor. At least, the European experience reveals a tendency for foremen and technicians to become unionized.

Social Life of the Foreman

The informal associations of the foreman in and outside the work plant depend upon the type of identification he makes. If he identifies with management he seeks to lunch, confide, and associate with other foremen and people in the stratum above him. Unless he can climb the management

ladder, however, it is unlikely that his "advances" will be entirely reciprocated. Even when the superintendent makes it his business to visit his foremen, he is usually too preoccupied with technical work and social contacts within his "set" to spend much time with them.

On occasion, foremen's "clubs" are organized by management to promote solidarity among foremen and to make them feel a part of management. The typical routine in these clubs is to have dinners periodically, listen to speeches by a high management official, be exposed to supervisory training, and be encouraged to be loyal to the business. Without such an organization, foremen will seek social contacts according to their individual inclinations.

We have examined the work positions and work roles of three levels of management. In the analysis of work roles especially, it was necessary to consider the social relations between two or more jobs. The formal theory of management which ignores these social relations omits an important segment of work organization. To understand the dynamic life of a work plant it is necessary to examine these relations as they fit together in informal organization.

INFORMAL ORGANIZATION OF MANAGEMENT

Informal organization is a system of personal and social relations which develop among people as they interact in formal structures. It consists of congeniality groups, cliques, rituals, ceremonies, and sentiments which control the behavior of group members. The tendency for informal groups to grow in formal structures is found everywhere, but literature on the informal organization of management is very scanty.[21]

WHY IGNORED

The reasons why this subject has been ignored are not difficult to find. In the first place, managers have initiated most of the studies of work organization. They have followed the natural tendency to see their problems as caused by other groups. In the attempt to account for "resistance" to orders, "restriction" of production, absenteeism, and other problems, management-oriented students discovered that an informal organization exists among workers that sometimes runs contrary to management's plans. They imputed the rise of informal organization to the nonlogical, emotional, and sentimental nature of the workers. On the other hand, they conceived management's behavior to be guided by the logic of cost and efficiency. They came to the conclusion that the conflict between sentiments and efficiency norms is responsible for many tensions in work rela-

[21] For a good analysis see Alexander Leighton, *The Governing of Men*, Princeton University Press, 1945.

tions.[22] This thinking leads them to the thought that sentiment-bound informal organization does not exist in management, or if it does exist, it is negligible and unimportant.

Another reason for not seeing informal organization in management lies in the fact that office jobs are not as physically circumscribed as plant jobs are. If a machine operator is not working at a specific rate, this can be noted and measured. It is much more difficult to observe restrictions of output in office jobs, because moving about and talking to people may be part of the job. It is difficult to distinguish official and nonofficial behavior. If the machine operator talks at all, it is labeled unofficial behavior. Moreover, since workers are on hourly rates and office workers are on salary, a double standard is rationalized. Hourly workers are not expected to be off the job except at stated periods. Most managers may leave their desks at any time. The managers, particularly, regard themselves as on call. Since they give "extra" work to the company after regular hours, they can justify (to themselves) the length of almost any lunch hour or rest period they wish to take.

The more reserved behavior of middle-class people is also a good smoke screen for their nonofficial work activity. Their loafing is more restrained, whereas on the plant floor horseplay, joking, razzing, bottom slapping, and swearing are visible expressions of impulsive behavior. Middle-class researchers recognize more readily such overt conduct, which seems to be a departure from their work norms.

LOCATING INFORMAL ORGANIZATION

The task of finding informal groups must be concerned with locating nonofficial social relations among workers.[23] The basic question one asks is, "What kinds of activities not dictated by the job do people who work together indulge in?" The resulting inventory may include gossiping, lunching, driving to work together, playing bridge, entertaining, playing together, and undermining the boss's position. It is important *not* to regard these activities as random incidences, but as behavior initiated and transmitted by informally organized groups. A study of informal organization is a study of group life as congeniality groups and cliques.

Management Cliques

Anyone who has observed executives in action realizes that they are as clique-ridden as any group. Moore defines a clique as "an informal grouping of persons representing common interests which are at variance with their official capacities and relations, and which cut across formal patterns

[22] These findings by Roethlisberger and Dickson are examined in Chapter III.
[23] See Chapter IX, "The Informal Organization of Labor," for a detailed procedure for studying informal organization.

of contact and authority."[24] He further suggests that management cliques tend to arise in organizations whenever there is a highly interactive competitive situation for higher positions, and where the criteria for advancement are poorly defined.[25] Moore conceives a clique as a group whose main function is to protect incompetent workers in a competitive situation. Certainly this is one of the functions of a clique, but, as we shall show, it has other functions, the most important of which is providing patterns of conduct for the group. Managers accept these patterns so completely that they do not recognize their informal nature. "This is the way we do things

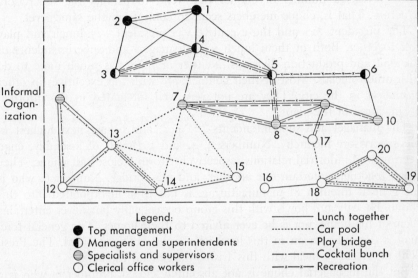

Legend:
- ● Top management
- ◑ Managers and superintendents
- ⊜ Specialists and supervisors
- ○ Clerical office workers

——— Lunch together
·············· Car pool
— — — Play bridge
—·—·— Cocktail bunch
—×—×— Recreation

FIG. 35. Informal Organization of Management in a Midwestern Manufacturing Concern.

in our company" is a recurrent phrase uttered in all supervisory levels. The more frequently it is heard, the more ingrained is informal organization.

INFORMAL ORGANIZATION AND THE SUPERVISORY STRUCTURE

Almost every person in management structure is involved in social activities not prescribed by the job. Some of them participate in many activities of well-knit groups; others have less intensive and extensive social contacts. Some of the informal groups and cliques are concerned with promoting their common welfare and the position of the department. Others, based upon congeniality, are knit together by social and recreational activities.

[24] Wilbert E. Moore, *Industrial Relations and the Social Order*, The Macmillan Company, 1946, p. 152.
[25] *Ibid.*, p. 153.

Preliminary studies made by the authors seem to indicate that the informal organization of management closely parallels the supervisory structure to an amazing degree. In fact, with the exception of a few individuals who participate in the social life of different levels, the membership of informal groups is limited to people having similar jobs on the same supervisory level.

Figure 35 portrays part of the informal organization of management in a midwestern manufacturing concern. The social relations among all of the members are charted for five types of activities. The workers are also identified for their position in the supervisory hierarchy. A brief glance at the figure reveals a number of cliques that tend to parallel the supervisory structure. That is, clique members seem to come from the same level.

The president (1) and the executive vice-president (2) lunch and play golf together. Both of them lunch with managers and superintendents of the staff and production divisions. Neither of them has much more to do with other officials. Most of their contacts are with top executives in *other businesses* in the city. They are not very well integrated in the informal organization of the plant.

The manager and superintendents (3, 4, 5, and 6) are next highest in the supervisory hierarchy. Numbers 3, 4, and 5 (heads of assembly, engineering, and industrial relations respectively) form a close-knit clique. They lunch together, entertain one another, and play bridge. Number 6, who is the general foreman of manufacturing, is not fully incorporated into this clique. He eats and bowls with this group occasionally but never entertains them at his home, nor is he ever invited to their homes. The general foreman is the only person in this level who is not college trained. The President never eats a meal with this Irish-born general foreman.

But the managerial clique is not absolutely closed. Number 7, who is a young, inexperienced engineer, entertains his boss at his home and is entertained in return. Sometimes he is invited by his boss's friends to a cocktail party. Number 7 has an unusually attractive young wife whom others consider an extremely "gracious" person. She will play an important role in her husband's career. Number 8 is the son-in-law of the industrial relations director. His father-in-law provides him contacts into the higher levels.

The young engineer (7) and his wife are in the center of a clique of supervisors and junior executives (7, 8, 9, and 10). The men not only eat together at work but with their wives form the nucleus of a bridge club. Note that the aggressive young engineer entertains only the son-in-law of the public relations director. In an effort to be popular with the office staff, he drives three of the female clerks to a bus line which is a mile from the factory. There is only one office girl who participates in the social life of the junior executives. She is a college-trained clerk (17) who is engaged to a supervisor in the accounting division (9). They are invited to play bridge with the clique.

The strongest clique (18, 19, 20) is composed of single girls who work in the office. These girls eat lunch together, are members of a car pool, and go to the movies together. Number 16 is a new girl who lives in another part of town. She is not yet fully inducted into the group. Although the clerical force is not a part of management, its physical proximity to management provides some of its members an opportunity to be tied into their informal organization. It is obvious from the diagram that this does not occur often. Neither the clerical clique nor the other clerks (12, 13, 14, 15) have much to do with management. The one exception is number 11. She is a divorced woman who heads a group of girls in the clerical pool. Although she lunches with her girls and participates in their recreation, she has nothing to do with the other supervisors and junior executives.

SOCIAL INDUCTION

Fraternal organizations have typically developed ceremonies and rituals to initiate new members. On the factory floor the resemblances of social induction to formal initiation ceremonies is very apparent. Neophytes are razzed; they are "given a hard time"; they are asked to do absurd things. Although initiation in management informal groups is not so conspicuous, it is present nonetheless. The formal ceremony of induction is usually centered about the dinner or cocktail party at the home of the boss. The newcomer learns to keep careful account of the invitations he receives and compares them to the expected pattern of invitation. When the newcomer observes that the boss has had everyone over to dinner excepting himself, he is insecure. Until he is invited, he is not considered a fully accepted member of the group. Similar initiations and passage rituals (for promotion and transfer) among white-collar workers need to be studied. Of course, induction also occurs in the plant itself. It includes inviting the new man to lunch, exchanging gifts, placing him on "social" committees, and, above all else, testing his ability to "take it."

"Let's summer and winter with the guy," Kaiser men say as they look a candidate over. And " 'Mother,' Mrs. Kaiser, has a blackball too. The group of about twenty men has seen no new face for ten years."[26]

CLIMBING AND INFORMAL ORGANIZATION

Many of the informal activities in management organization are understandable, if the observer is aware of the climbing mania existing among the supervisory staff. The strength, discontent, or esprit de corps of cliques depends in great measure on the ability of group members to fulfill their climbing aspirations.

American ideology insists that climbing depends upon ability and performance. An analysis of clique formation may begin with the questions, Who climbs? Who doesn't climb? Why do they climb or fail? What is

[26] "The Truth About Henry Kaiser," Collier's, August 3, 1946, p. 26.

the effect on clique formation of climbing? Or the failure to climb? The following case suggests what can happen when a clique struggle is instigated.

John M. was offered an appointment as head of a staff of thirty librarians. As a condition of acceptance he made the stipulation that the institution also hire two librarians who were his assistants in the library in which he was then employed. This was done. Upon accepting the job, M. appointed a third librarian who was recommended to him by a friend. These three new appointees were invited to M.'s home rather frequently; the rest of the staff was invited on one formal occasion. The new appointees came to be regarded as "M.'s group." The rest of the staff talked about themselves as the defeated "Old Guard." After certain promotions and merit raises went to members of "M.'s group," a basic social cleavage developed between the two cliques. M., who was personally accepted by the entire staff, had to spend much of his time soothing crying librarians and attempting to patch up "conflicts in personalities."

An analysis of the situation showed that the older workers on the staff had ambivalent feelings toward M. for three reasons. Although they liked him as a person, (1) he had violated the system of expectancies of promotion; (2) his new appointees violated line of authority by going to him directly with their problems; (3) he played favorites in the informal life of the library.

Other factors interfere with the operation of the climbing ideology. Not infrequently kinship relationships disturb the social equilibrium of the plant. Children and relatives of the executives violate the merit code by climbing ahead of people with greater ability, seniority, and experience. "Drag," "good looks," and "social background" are additional factors that violate the merit code. In Chapter XI, "Status Organization of the Work Plant," an analysis is made of the social factors responsible for informal cleavage along status or prestige lines. Other sentiments besides climbing and status are evident in management structure. Some of these powerful emotional forces deserve our further consideration.

SENTIMENTS IN MANAGEMENT ORGANIZATION

In the discussion of work roles and positions, the ideology of managers was described. Other ideas and sentiments, however, are present in all management levels. One of the most important sentiments, pervading the entire informal social life of the supervisory structure, is *loyalty*. A person not only must be loyal to his department, division, or section, he must also be loyal to his chief. Irrespective of personal antagonisms within the plant, a good supervisor defends the enterprise to outsiders.

A plant worker may also share this sentiment, but he is not ostracized if he thinks and says, "This is a hell of a company." Since managers are part of the controlling agency, they are expected to endorse the organization all the time. They must act as if their "future" rests with the company.

Other sentiments revolve around the business of climbing. There are proper and improper methods of climbing. Although aggressiveness is an ideal attribute, "overaggressiveness" is not. The overly ambitious social climber is looked down upon by fellow managers. The number of times the boss and his family may be entertained is fairly well defined.

Overaggressiveness in other areas is also discouraged. An example illustrates this point. Lane and Briggs had charge of a section of insurance agents. Briggs complained about overaggressiveness in Lane. Previous to this charge, a higher executive had stimulated rivalry between these two men and between their organizations. Lane's section consistently sold more insurance than Briggs's. Despite the better performance of Lane's section he was not in rapport with the big boss. The latter had received many complaints to the effect that Lane and his boys were too aggressive. The friendly rivalry that existed between the two sections turned into bitter factionalism. The losing section complained that Lane, among other things, had advised his agents to invade the Briggs territory to revive lapsed cases. Although regulations were in effect which stated that all collecting and soliciting of new business should be pursued on an assigned area basis, no rule covered lapsed policies. In the past, lapsed cases had been left to the discretion of the collectors in the areas. If they cared to revive them they might. If not, they were neglected. This breach of a poorly defined procedure was defined as overaggressiveness, and Lane was asked to discontinue it.

In this chapter we have introduced the concepts of work position and work role because they improve our picture of the social organization of the work plant. A study of the latter is not complete until the main work positions and roles are selected and described. Despite the wide range of personality types occupying these work positions, their behavior is very similar because they are subjected to similar institutional pressures. The position of the big boss, for example, is dependent on his relations to top executives. His performance in community affairs is also prescribed, as are his business ideals and sentiments.

The plant manager's performance is circumscribed not only by his official duties but by his relations to the chiefs of the staff departments. His behavior differs from that of top executives because his orientation is primarily on plant operations and not on policy formation. The ideology of this position derives from the fact that its occupants are immersed in a physical world of production.

The foreman's work position is in a state of transition because staff organizations are gradually liquidating many of his historical functions. The foreman's role is difficult to play because it involves mediation of the management and labor ideologies. The orientation of the foreman sets the tone of management-labor relations in his department.

The way in which work roles are played depends partly on the informal organization in the management structure. It seems that the cliques and informal groupings in management parallel those on the supervisory levels. The dynamics of informal group life revolve around the ever pressing desire of its members to climb in the organization. Resistances toward this impulse create many personality problems and problems of group morale.

In summary, the analysis of work positions and work roles of managers has revealed a tremendous range of social influences which affect conduct and decision. No wonder the formal theory of management fails to describe "what really goes on inside a work plant." It is only as social factors are recognized that the operation of management can be understood realistically. In so far as an analysis penetrates into the social structure, to that extent it provides a guide to managerial behavior.

Before the picture of the social life of the plant is completed, the formal organization of labor must be analyzed. Since the union is the formal organization of labor, we shall begin by examining its operation.

SUPPLEMENTARY STUDIES

FIELD OBSERVATION: DIRECT OBSERVATION OF A SELECTED WORK PLANT
(Continued)

In the work plant selected describe:

Work Positions and Work Roles

1. List the work positions and analyze the work roles which are observed.
2. Examine the manner in which workers with authority exercise their power or influence over their work associates.
3. Indicate any cleavages and conflicts (a) in the line, (b) in the staff, (c) between line and staff.
4. Describe the informal organizations of managers. Look for
   a. Talk patterns.
      Who talks.
      Amount of talk.
      Content of talk.
   b. Sociometric patterns.
      Cliques.
      Lunch association.
      Recreation association.
      Club and lodge association.
      Cliques of managers' wives.

FIELD INTERVIEWS: PLANNED

If possible secure a top management executive, a plant manager, and a foreman to make up a panel. The chief assistants to each of these officials are useful

resource persons if the major line officials are not available. Ask them to speak on the following:

1. Describe your day from the time you awake until you retire.
2. Describe any "off-the-job" or "duty" contacts your work imposes or encourages.
3. What social clubs and other community activities do you engage in? Do you regard these as important to the company? Do you regard these as useful to your advancement in the company?
4. What are the pressures that your job induces?
5. What cleavages and conflicts between departments and groups must you recognize and live with? What successes have you had in reducing any of these conflicts?
6. What are the most effective ways to get production from people? (a) short run; (b) long run.
7. Do you think the basic interests of management and the basic interests of workers are directly opposed, identical, irreconcilable?
8. What advice would you give a college student who is seeking a career in the business world?

LIBRARY: BOOKS AND ARTICLES

Chamberlain, Neil W., *Management in Motion*, Yale Labor and Management Center, 1950.

Henry, William E., "The Business Executive: The Psychodynamics of a Social Role," *American Journal of Sociology*, January, 1949, pp. 286-291.

Moore, Wilbert E., *Industrial Relations, and the Social Order*, The Macmillan Company, 1947, chap. 7; "Managerial Functions: Executives," and chap. 8, "Specialists and Supervisors," pp. 119-164.

Roethlisberger, Fritz J., "The Foreman: Master and Victim of Double Talk," *Harvard Business Review*, Spring, 1945.

Selekman, Benjamin M., *Labor Relations and Human Relations*, McGraw-Hill Book Company, Inc., 1947; chapter 7, "Wanted Mature Managers," pp. 141-172.

Ulrich, David H., Booz, Donald R., and Lawrence, Paul R., *Management Behavior and Foreman Attitude*, Howard University Press, 1950.

Wray, Donald E., "Marginal Men of Industry: The Foremen," *American Journal of Sociology*, January, 1949, pp. 298-301.

RESEARCH GAPS

1. Assessment of authoritarian and democratic leadership in business organization upon morale and productivity.
2. Definition of a good supervisor as secured by performance analysis.
3. The foreman as a marginal man.

CHAPTER VIII

Operation of the Union Local

This chapter will present a sociological interpretation of the labor union in the contemporary work plant. In the following chapter, the informal organization of workers will be examined.

The plans for these two chapters are to make an analysis of the House of Labor along the lines which were followed in describing the House of Management. The focus of attention will be on union organization as it operates on the local level. We shall look upon the union local as a social institution. Our interest will be centered on its structure and function with particular attention to the roles of union leaders and union members.

We have chosen to make the union local the center of study because most union members and officials live out their lives in work plants. Although it is true that the national or regional leaders of large unions are spearheads of union power and capture headlines in the daily press, it is also true that the real strength of a national union resides in the support of its constituent locals. The origin of the union, no matter what its size or affiliations, is to be found in the men and women who work inside the work plants. For this reason, we have elected to study at the "grass roots" of union organization. Before we can begin, we must ask first of all, Who is organized?

WHO IS ORGANIZED?

Every work plant containing more than a score of workers has some kind of formal management organization. This is not true of labor, for probably not more than sixteen million workers were unionized in 1950. At that time about 40 percent of urban nonproprietary and nonprofessional workers were unionized. Although the proportion of work plants that are unionized is unknown, some estimates exist of the proportion of workers covered by union agreements.

Peterson reports that 65 percent of the wage earners in manufacturing are covered by union agreements.[1] However, in such "industries" as aluminum

[1] Florence Peterson, *American Labor Unions*, Harper & Brothers, 1945, p. 189.

fabrication, automobile and air frame, men's clothing, nonferrous metal smelting and refining, shipbuilding, steel, coal mining, theatrical (professional actors and musicians), ship loading, and railroads over 90 percent of the workers are covered by union agreements.

Over 80 percent of workers in the construction, maritime, local bus and street railway, trucking, and telegraph industries are union members; and about one-half of the workers in the baking, grains, leather, lumber, petroleum, pottery, shoe, concrete, and woolen textiles industries are unionized.

Less than one-half of the workers belong to unions in the canning, chemicals, cotton, textiles, paper, athletic goods, barbering, fishing, hotel, and laundering industries. Only one-quarter or less of the workers are under collective bargaining agreements in the service trades (other than domestic), and in clerical, technical, and professional occupations of businesses classified under manufacturing, finance, and wholesale and retail trade.[2] About 50,000 union contracts are in operation in all these industries.

Only crude estimates can be made of the financial power and social importance of the unions. The moneys that unions get from dues, initiation fees, special assessments, and other sources probably amounts to *one billion dollars* a year. Approximately a million persons are actively engaged in union affairs by virtue of being union officers or committee members. The money and energy spent in this business of promoting and protecting the interests of workers are considerable.

Thus, although less than half of the urban workers are organized, unions are heavily represented in many industries. In others, where their representation is smaller, they often exert influence by setting the pattern for wages, hours, and working conditions which most nonunionized plants follow.[3]

Those workers who benefit from gains made by unions but who will not become members are called "free riders." We shall ignore both "free riders" and nonunionized plants in this chapter, because any formal organization among wage or salary workers which is not part of the labor union movement is usually weak or management-oriented. Company unions, labor-management committees, and other formal structures not buttressed by labor unions are usually best considered a part of management organization.

THE SETTING OF UNION ORGANIZATION

The figures on union strength given above may be somewhat misleading. They appear big because they are national figures. But most union activities take place on the local level. Powerful as some local unions may be, it would be an error to place them in a coördinate power position with management.

[2] *Ibid., passim*, pp. 189-191. See also *Monthly Labor Review*, April, 1945, and *Collective Bargaining Agreements with Associations and Groups of Employers*, Bulletin No. 897, U.S. Department of Labor, United States Government Printing Office, 1947.
[3] F. H. Harbison and R. Dubin, *Pattern of Union-Management Relations*, Science Research Associates, 1947.

The latter has active jurisdiction over all workers during the entire working day. One supervisor or another is directing the activities of the workers most of the time. Consequently, workers are usually more preoccupied with *doing their job* and *worrying about the boss* than they are with union matters. Probably not more than 5 percent of the workers' time is consumed with thoughts and conversations about union affairs. They may attend union meetings once a month; read the union paper; on rare occasions contact their stewards; vote periodically for union officers; and pay their dues.

Of course, there is variation in preoccupation over union affairs. During the organizing phase of unionization, or during a wage demand, strike, or grievance, union matters are of dominant interest. At such times workers discuss union business incessantly—while going to work, at mealtime, and during union meetings. For days most of the workers' waking hours may be preoccupied with union matters. When crises are over, however, the union preoccupation and participation of the average worker is limited to an occasional (often compulsory) monthly or bimonthly meeting of the local. The apathy of the rank-and-file union member in noncritical periods is common knowledge.

As in all associations, there are active leaders, enthusiastic followers, and apathetic followers. The steward, the local officers, the leaders of regional and international union organizations, and members of committees spend a great deal of energy on union affairs. Like their management counterparts, these executives live their union business in and out of the plant—in their work as well as in their social life.

It would be a mistake, then, to measure the importance of the union in terms of the amount of time and energy that the average member or officer gives the organization. The union is an institution and a social movement whose structure comes into action when the need arises. We may think of the union much as we think about the religious institution and churches. To gauge the influence of religion by counting the number of hours members spend in churches would be most unrealistic. Moral, ethical, and religious values underlie daily conduct. That these values come into sharp focus only infrequently does not detract from their pervasive importance. The rituals of baptism, marriage, and burial are not unimportant because they occur infrequently. The churches, their dogma and rituals, play a role out of all proportion to the amount of time the ordinary member spends in formal religious participation. So it is with the unions.

THE UNION AS A SOCIAL INSTITUTION

INSTITUTIONAL CRITERIA

The union organization in a work plant is part of the institution of unionism, just as a particular industry is part of the institution of business. In fact, union locals are often tied together to a far greater degree than are

many individual businesses. To understand the operation of local unions
one must know something about the institution and the social movement
of which they are an intimate part.

Sociologists have traditionally defined an institution as "a defined need
and the culture surrounding it." Chapin has refined this conception by de-
tailing four type-parts of institutions. They are:

1. Dominant attitudes and behavior patterns.
2. Symbolic culture traits.
3. Utilitarian culture traits such as real property.
4. Written or oral codes that specify conduct.[4]

1. Some of the dominant attitudes in union organizations are solidarity
in economic and social action, the belief in coöperative rather than individual economic action, loyalty to the traditions of unionism, suspicion
toward employers' tactics, and the right of workers to organize for the advancement of their material and social goals. These attitudes are reflected in
members' attendance at union meetings, paying of dues, participation in
strikes, and defense of the unions' economic and social philosophies.

2. Symbolic culture traits are found in all unions from the smallest local
to the largest federations and congresses. Over a period of time the unions
have built up an elaborate folklore and ritual not unlike those found in
the Masons, Elks, and Knights of Columbus. In fact, many of the older
craft unions were founded as fraternal orders. They clothed themselves with
such ceremonial trappings as initiations, pledges, secret oaths, handclasps,
uniforms, and expulsion rites.

3. Unions also have utilitarian culture traits. The investment that unions
have made in material goods is incalculable. Some of the material manifestations of unionism are the countless union halls, labor lyceums, schools,
international headquarters, camps, printing presses, amplifying equipment,
books, movies, credit unions, health resorts, and even night clubs.

4. Unions have elaborate oral and written codes that relate the dominant
attitudes and the symbolic and utilitarian culture traits. The whole institution is prescribed by a set of relations found in the constitution, bylaws,
and contracts with the employers. In addition, there are written and unwritten models of what constitutes good or bad unionism. Unions also
establish a system of punishments and rewards to keep the codes and models
alive and effective. Bakke grasps the institutional nature of the union when
he says,

They develop an institutional life of their own beyond the lives of individual
members. A basic objective of that development is strength and power and prestige as such. Internal conflicts must be ironed out. The membership must be
bound together by a common philosophy and achievement. Power of many sorts

[4] F. Stuart Chapin, *Contemporary American Institutions*, Harper & Brothers, 1935,
p. 16.

has to be acquired. Protection against other unions must be sought. A strong internal government and leadership must be developed. . . . Every demand, every counter proposal, every compromise, must be measured against the need for survival and the growth of the union itself. Even the degree to which the clearly expressed wishes of the employees themselves can be followed by union leadership must face that test.[5]

FUNCTIONS OF THE UNION LOCAL

To understand the functions of an organization is to know the social needs to which it responds. Since the local is the basic unit of unionism, its functions do not differ substantially from those of unionism generally. Although singular circumstances may make the functions of a particular local unique, locals generally meet similar social needs or motives. Consequently their functions are similar.

Economic Security

The basic function of the locals and unions generally is to maintain or increase wages. For a long time this was conceived to be their *only* function. Labor economists evolved a theory that the union is *merely* an organization which sells labor to the employer. Dunlop has advanced the most sophisticated view of this theory when he suggests that the union is primarily devoted to maximizing wages. So conceived, the union is a business enterprise selling labor, and it behaves as a wage-maximizing business organization.[6] Taken by itself this theory is too narrow. Even competitive businesses are something more than profit-maximizing enterprises, let alone unions. Unions have other functions which we shall soon describe. Narrow as the wage-maximizing theory is, it would be more unrealistic to underestimate the economic functions of the labor union. For example, since the discovery of the social importance of work, it has been fashionable for writers to claim that wages in themselves are not important to workers. Rather, the theory goes, the *relations* among wages are important. It is suggested that the worker is really concerned with how his wages *compare* with those of other workers doing the same or similar jobs. When the worker feels that there is a wage imbalance, a sense of unfairness drives him to use the union to correct this disequilibrium. The union thus conceived is a mechanism to adjust wage inequities.[7]

This is no doubt an adequate explanation under some conditions. By itself the theory is as inadequate as the wage-maximizing theory. Obviously unions, like all institutions, have many functions. Economic motives, like

[5] E. Wight Bakke, *Mutual Survival: The Goal of Union and Management*, Yale University Press, 1946, pp. 3, 4.

[6] John T. Dunlop, *Wage Determination Under Trade Unions*, The Macmillan Company, 1944, pp. 32-34, 119.

[7] Burleigh B. Gardner, *Human Relations in Industry*, Richard D. Irwin, Inc., 1945, p. 124.

all others, operate in a system of interacting values. Describing single motives, like discussing separate institutional functions, is necessary only for analytic and descriptive purposes. In actuality, neither personal motives nor the institutional functions which derive from them exist in isolation. Weighing the relative importance of motives and functions is always a precarious affair.

In American society, economic motives are fundamental. The union cannot ignore this fact. As many union organizers can testify, the American wage worker measures the effectiveness of the union in terms of the size of his pay envelope. He believes that union idealism has its place, but it does not buy the necessities and luxuries of life. He constantly exerts pressure on the union leader to *raise wages* to the level possessed by the most favored of his customary associates in the community.[8] However, the far-sighted union leader tries to convince the rank and file that this single demand for high wage rates is short-sighted. He attempts to convince union members that their most important goal is to gain control over those factors which make their economic position *insecure*. He stresses the importance of a contract which controls (1) entrance into the trade, (2) hiring, (3) layoffs, (4) seniority, (5) amount of work, (6) effects of technological change, (7) wages and hours, and (8) unionized and nonunionized competitive situations.[9] The leader points out that the union succeeds best when it keeps such achievements in mind. He sometimes goes beyond this and urges that attention be directed toward election of political leaders who will be favorable to labor. He urges members to get behind pending legislation and put pressure on the local representatives. It is apparent that a major task of a labor leader is to raise the level of thinking among members so that they come to grasp the importance of overall policies rather than the single urgency of wage rates. The thoroughly assimilated union member shares the larger goals with his leaders.

Resistance and Independence

In the preceding chapters the "logic" and sentiments of management were discussed. Foremost among these is the tendency of management to regard workers as tools to be used according to the "best" canons of efficiency. Since managers are mostly concerned about getting the job done, they split workers from their work groups, promote, demote, and rearrange or release them according to the demands of the situation. The problems and attitudes of workers are treated as secondary to the job that must be done. Workers are at the bottom of the structure and know they have no power to convince management of the importance of their aspirations, feelings, and desires.

[8] E. Wight Bakke, "Why Workers Join Unions," *Personnel*, July, 1945, pp. 2-11.
[9] See Sumner H. Slichter, *Union Policies and Industrial Management*, The Brookings Institution, 1941.

The union changes this situation. It considers the worker first as a person with rights. The union can communicate to higher management the personal hurts and grievances of the worker by going over the foreman's head to the very top. See Figure 36. The union does not have to wait for things

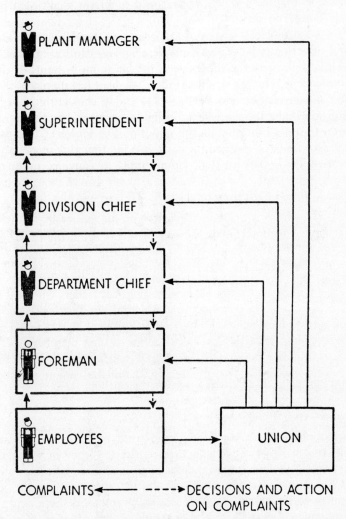

COMPLAINTS ←——— - - - - → DECISIONS AND ACTION ON COMPLAINTS

Fig. 36. Communication Through the Union. (From Burleigh B. Gardner, *Human Relations in Industry*, Richard D. Irwin, Inc., 1945, p. 102.)

to move up the line through the normal management channel but can go directly without waiting at any level. The individual worker feels he can stand up to his boss because he has the power of the group behind him. Thus, a primary function of the union is to *resist* pressures from management. The local union is the instrument which informs bosses that they

cannot push workers around. Even the least ardent union man appreciates this role of the union.

This negative role of resisting management's aggression is supplemented by a positive role. The union takes advantage of a strong cultural compulsion among its members to act. Americans say, "If you don't like your position, why don't you do something about it?" Passive acceptance is disapproved in our democratic society. Joining and supporting a union is a way of "doing something about work conditions." The worker can complain to his steward. If the latter demurs, he can go over his head with impunity. At the next election he can vote to oust the steward or other officers who he feels have not given him a square deal. The union offers other vehicles of action to the worker. He can vote on strike issues, he can be on committees, he can run for office, he can educate himself on union and economic problems, he can form a faction within the union, he can even fight against the union. All these give the worker a feeling that he can make his way in the world.

Golden and Ruttenberg report this reaction of workers in a Pennsylvania cork plant. During organization meetings for the proposed union, several people gave vent to their desires for independence from the company. Said a comely girl: "It's about time something like this happened. We have to stand on our own feet. They do everything for you but provide a husband, and I even know girls they got husbands for. And they what ain't got time to get pregnant, they get foster kids for."[10] And a middle-aged man complained: "They lay out my work with so many instructions that there's nothing left for me to figure out for myself. The only reason they keep half of us is 'cause they ain't discovered a machine yet that would take our places."[11]

A radio wireman, in an interview with the authors, made this statement about independence fostered by the union:

You ask me about the union. Three years ago, we finally got the CIO in here. All during the depression we had no union. The company increased our quotas up and up. Finally they broke down our jobs and brought the girls in the department. The union hasn't brought up the rates to where they used to be, but it has helped a lot. The best thing that happened is that the fellows don't feel they've got to play up to the foreman any more. If we got gripes, we take 'em up with the union. Sometimes something is done and sometimes it isn't. But at least we feel we're getting some place. . . . Of course, we get all kinds of fights in the union; but you get the feeling that we're all after the same things, and that's what really counts.

[10] Clinton S. Golden and Harold J. Ruttenberg, *The Dynamics of Industrial Democracy*, Harper & Brothers, 1942, p. 15.
[11] *Ibid.*, p. 15.

In an authoritarian structure those who obey orders build up aggressions against those who give orders. This is especially true in our culture, where there are general impulses toward independence and equality. The protection of the union allows the worker to voice his feelings against individual supervisors and against the business as a whole. At union meetings and in the community he can decry the "injustice," "unfairness," "inhumanity," and "tyranny" of his bosses. He can even participate in direct action against his employer by resort to the strike, slowdown, and even violence.

Middle class-citizens and scholars have not been able to understand, let alone sympathize with, the aggression of workers against their employers. Parker expresses this unrealistic middle-class analysis of worker violence when he says of the worker, ". . . He strikes or brings on a strike; he commits violence, or stays on the job and injures machinery, or mutilates the materials. He is fit food for dynamic conspiracies. He is ready to make sabotage a part of his regular habit scheme. His condition is one of mental stress and unfocused psychic unrest, and could in all accuracy be called a definite industrial psychosis. He is neither willful nor responsible, he is suffering from a stereotyped mental disease."[12]

Apart from the fact that Parker's social psychology was bad, he did not realize that the union more or less institutionalizes workers' antagonisms. Without the union, aggression tendencies might, under certain circumstances, know no bounds.

Personal Recognition and Social Life

Many thinkers have considered the trade union as an instrument of class solidarity, that is, as an expression of the common values and ideals of the working class. They feel that the union must play a political role in national and international affairs until the working class obtains control over the economy and the society. This socialist view of the union's function has not been generally accepted in the United States. In Europe and elsewhere, the theory not only has been accepted but has been realized "according to plan."

The trade union philosophy dominant in the United States is an outgrowth of the thinking of Samuel Gompers, first president of the American Federation of Labor. He felt that since American unions would not support any society-saving or society-destroying schemes, they should concern themselves with immediate day-to-day improvements in the economic and social life of working people. The union had no ultimate ends as such, excepting the vague goal of "securing a better life for all."[13]

Such a position was well calculated to appeal to the American wage

[12] Carleton H. Parker, *The Casual Laborer and Other Essays*, Harcourt, Brace and Company, 1920, pp. 161-163.

[13] Samuel Gompers, *Labor and the Common Welfare*, E. P. Dutton and Company, Inc., 1919, pp. 7, 8, 20.

earner. Traditionally, he did not conceive of himself as a member of a class, for he shared the prevailing ideal that his station in life was temporary. He or his children would become "successful" by achieving an independent entrepreneurial status. As long as a considerable number of workers rose in the occupational scale, the appeals of unions to the working "class" had to be soft-pedaled.

As a more or less hereditary working class arises in the United States, the possibility of obtaining middle-class respectability decreases. Respect or prestige on the job is also diminishing owing to the mechanization tendencies in industry. For many workers, then, prestige is obtained not by getting out of the working class but by becoming an active part of it.[14]

Bakke has enumerated some of the ways of achieving a socially respectable role through union participation. The union, for example, provides a scale of offices which ambitious people can climb. Prestige may be secured from playing the role of steward, officer, or committee member. Other roles which lead to recognition are open, such as standing up to the foreman, fighting for better working conditions for the gang, attending union meetings and conventions, *making real decisions and policy for* the union, and exerting authority in the union.

The stairways to recognition in the union should not be considered solely as a sour-grapes reaction to mobility blockage in the management ladder. In the past this may have been the case for many aspiring union leaders. However, as the labor movement developed, it has become a normal channel of mobility and recognition.

Channels of upward mobility are quite small even when the avenues of both management and labor are combined. Most workers are destined to stay on the same job level the rest of their lives.[15] What role does the union play for them? It defines for them an area of participation which is not only acceptable but respectable *in the eyes of the peer group*. To be considered a good union man, to be loyal, to represent the organization with dignity in the community are sources of gratification. Many workers join unions and remain loyal to them because membership is the way of obtaining and securing respect in their class. "To be a regular guy," "to show you're on the right side," "to be with the workingman" constitute strong goals as long as the workers' recognition is in his own class level.

But even to the middle-class public the status of the union is undergoing a change. The union has moved in public definition from a semicriminal conspiracy to a respectable social institution in the organizational life of the community. Some union officers are even members of Rotary and the Chamber of Commerce! The union has gained general respect as it has gained power and numbers. Its participation in community events like the

[14] Bakke, "Why Workers Join Unions," *op. cit.*, p. 4.
[15] See Chapter XIX, "The Stable Work Period."

Red Cross, bond drives, Civic Improvement Association, and Community Chest is now actively sought.[16] The union has given the working class a position of dignity and importance in the community. Membership in the union tends to strengthen working-class ties by giving them organizational direction.

As a social movement the union is filling a gap felt by its members. It has become an overall social organization to do whatever its members want it to do. Do they want education? It furnishes a school with all necessary paraphernalia. Do they need advice on personal and family problems? It provides counselors and welfare workers. Do they want recreation? A program of athletic contests, picnics, singing, and hobbies is instituted. Is material help needed? The local becomes a welfare organization. Are community services being provided? The union becomes a pressure group in local politics. Is Congress looking out for the workers' interest? The union acts as a lobby.

The union promises to extend rather than curtail its functions in the future. Although other agencies are competing with it to provide services— as employers, the community, and the state—the union will continue to play a dominant role. For it is close to the members, controllable by them, and sympathetically sensitive to their needs. More than any other organization, it acts in terms of experiences that workers understand. Whitehead believes that the past failure of American unionism was due to the fact that it ignored its primary function as an organ of social living. Indeed, he suggests that "the future of unions will depend on the degree to which social living is made a first concern of those who are in a position to lead."[17]

THE LOCAL: ORGANIZATION AND STRUCTURE

THEORY OF FORMAL UNION ORGANIZATION

The theory of union organization is essentially a democratic theory of organization. The reader is no doubt aware of the organizational skeleton of democracies and unions. The central fact in a democratic organization is that the ultimate source of authority resides in the people—in this case, in the union members. The union exists for its members, not members for the union. Although responsibility is vested in the members, the exercise of that responsibility is a matter of individual discretion. Presumably the union citizen will take interest in his organization, inform himself on its activities, and become a factor in its operation.

Since all union members theoretically have equal power by virtue of their ballot, the union is supposed to be concerned with the welfare of all its

[16] See Chapter XXI, "Industry and the Community."

[17] T. N. Whitehead, *Leadership in a Free Society*, Harvard University Press, 1936, p. 146.

members, irrespective of sex, color, creed, or occupation. Each group has the right to expect fair treatment within the union and in the union's dealings with the employers.

The position of leaders in a democracy is precarious. Union officers are elected for short terms and may be removed from offices by vote of the electorate. A few offices are appointive, but even here tenure depends on satisfactory performance and not on any inherent right to the office. As a matter of fact, any office is available to any member in good standing. Presumably any member is capable of understanding and handling the issues and problems inherent in any office. The duties and responsibilities of offices are defined, not by logic, but by constitutional provisions and laws. Thus, the functions of any union job may be changed at any time the members want to change them. In addition, all major decisions (such as the calling of a strike) are ultimately made or approved by the members, irrespective of their knowledge, or the recommendations of their officers.

The techniques of settling issues in unions are those commonly used in democratic bodies. Anybody in the meeting may raise an issue; anyone may declare his feelings on the issue; and everyone may vote on it. The minority must, of course, abide by the decisions of the majority. By actively campaigning, however, the minority may influence enough members to reverse the policy.

Thus, the union is theoretically an organization responsible to and run by amateurs who believe in democracy and hold office by election of the members. This structure is pitted against an organized bureaucracy run by professional managers who are appointed and responsible to the president, who is himself an appointive official. This contrast between management and union organization is important enough to merit separate attention.

COMPARING UNION AND MANAGEMENT ORGANIZATIONS

Arthur Ross has made a penetrating comparison of similarities and dissimilarities in union and business organizations.[18] Such a comparison is necessary to understand the interaction of these two groups.

Similarities

Both trade unions and business firms have formal purposes and official rationales. Both groups seek to maximize the formal aims of the organizations. The policy of managers is guided by the goal of profit maximization. To union officials maximization of the economic welfare of union members is presumably the guide to policy and behavior. Actually, the ends of both groups are loosely defined, as are the means they use to attain their ends. It is the job of management and union officials to define ends in the

[18] Arthur Ross, *Trade Union Wage Policy*, University of California Press, 1948, chap. 2, "The Union as a Wage Fixing Institution."

situational sense, and manipulate conditions to realize diverse goals. Thus, managers must decide: How much profit is to be attempted? How immediately must profit be realized? Should it come from expanded markets, decreased wages, or new products? Labor executives must decide what kind of "welfare" to pursue in the situation: higher immediate wages, vacations with wages, a good seniority system, or a closed shop? They also must decide which procedure to employ to attain a specific goal. What stratagem will work best? Promises, threats, cajoling, a slowdown, or a strike?

Both labor and management officials are subject to pressures from those who want the formal ends of the institution to be defined for their welfare. The "lobbies" which try to influence corporate executives are the bankers, stockholders, the union, the trade association, employees, customers, and government agencies.[19] The pressures on union executives emanate from the rank and file, the employers, international officials, other unions, the federations, and agencies of government.

One of the managerial functions of both sets of leaders is to reconcile their respective pressures. In vigorous structures the executives make decisions which are calculated to foster the growth and survival of the organization and not any one group. Foremost in their minds is the survival of the business and their jobs. There is usually a close identification between the personal ambition of the leaders and organizational growth. A good "company man" fosters his organization, as does the good "union man."

Dissimilarities

The formal purpose of the union is vaguer than that of business. The latter has a rather precise measuring instrument of its effectiveness, namely, profit and growth. For the union, "betterment" may mean almost anything, such as union recognition, higher wages, closed shop, shorter hours, improved working conditions, or job security.[20] Some observers feel that both union and management are engaged in selling—the former, its goods; the latter, its labor. This is not strictly true, for the union only bargains for wages; it does not determine wage fixing.

The relation between the union and its members differs from the relation between stockholders and the corporation. Stockholders buy and sell their shares in the company with little effect on capital strength. In contrast, the acquisition or loss of members in the union greatly affects its strength.

Stockholders leave the operation of business in the hands of managers. But *survival* is a much more serious problem to the union and its leaders.[21] Business needs capital and customers to survive. Labor unions need not only economic strength but political approval or tolerance. Although legis-

[19] *Ibid.*, p. 25.
[20] *Ibid.*, p. 27.
[21] Benjamin M. Selekman, *Labor Relations and Human Relations*, McGraw-Hill Book Company, Inc., 1947, p. 176.

lation can only restrict business operations, it can actually threaten the survival of unionism. When hostility of powerful employers and their organization is added to legislative threats, the survival of unions is more tenuous.

Both *apathy* and *participation* of the rank and file present problems of security and stability to unions and their leaders. Perlman and Taft state, "The overshadowing problem of the American labor movement has always been the problem of staying organized. No other labor movement has ever had to contend with the fragility so characteristic of American labor organizations."[22] Union leaders are neurotic about participation. Unlike business managers, their tenure in office is dependent upon those below them, not those above them. As elected officials, their future depends upon voters who are often apathetic and uninformed. When aroused, the rank and file may throw a man out of office for a picayune matter, so the union leader must be a politician as well as a manager to stay in power. When members are not aroused, leaders may stay in office indefinitely no matter what they do. Another threat to survival is the encroachment of rival unions. Unions not only must guard against business and government, they must also guard against their own kind.

A democracy, like any other organization, is supposed to get things done. But restrictions are placed on the means that leaders can use to get things done. If the members trust their leaders implicitly, they may give them almost autocratic powers. If the members do not trust their leaders, the latter are almost powerless. The tension in democratic organization arises from the conflict between the two wishes of efficiency and responsibility. All types of compromises between these two ideals are represented in union local and international structures. Therefore, it is impossible to describe typical organizations. At best, several models may be selected which represent recurring structures.

TYPES OF UNIONS

There are four main types of union structures in the United States.[23] In the first, unions are organized around a craft or group of crafts. All union members in any work plant of a particular community or region having these skills are members of a union local. This is the situation in many A.F. of L. unions. Secondly, unions may organize workers in all factories which manufacture a product or series of products. Thus, all workers employed in garages, in restaurants, or in clothing factories in an area, irrespective of occupation, belong to the individual unions. A third type appears when a dynamic labor leader in a strategic industry organizes the workers in a region

[22] Selig Perlman and Philip Taft, *History of Labor in the United States, 1896-1932,* The Macmillan Company, 1935, p. 7.
[23] E. Wight Bakke and Clark Kerr, *Unions, Management, and the Public,* Harcourt, Brace and Company, 1948, pp. 150-151.

regardless of their occupation or industry. The United Mine Workers' District 50 and the Teamsters' Union are cases in point.[24] The ability to tie up coal production or transportation gives these unions strategic power to organize workers in unrelated occupations and enterprises. Fourth, unions are organized on the plant basis. All workers in a particular plant or company may be in one local. Such industrial unions as the United Automobile Workers of America (C.I.O.), in Ford, Chevrolet, and General Motors plants, are cases in point.

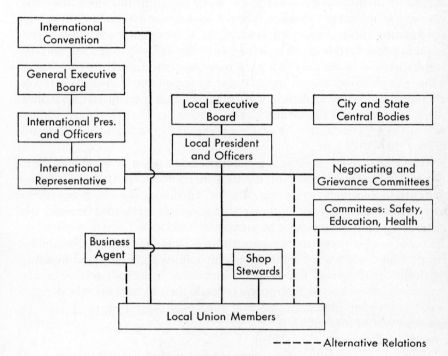

FIG. 37.   The Formal Structure of a Union Local.

Union locals range in size from a half-dozen to over 100,000 members. The large majority of locals have less than two or three hundred members, and only 10 percent have more than a thousand members.[25] The type of union whose local structure we shall describe has about five hundred members and contains workers in several occupations who are employed in one or two plants in the locality. Figure 37 presents a typical structure for this kind of a local. Certain parts of the structure are omitted for purposes of clarity. The staff, organizers, and committees of the local and the international are not included.

[24] *Ibid.*
[25] Peterson, *op. cit.*, p. 76.

When Figure 37 is compared to the typical management structure, two main differences are revealed. The first is that the local union organization is intimately tied into its parent structures, the international union and the congress or federation. Secondly, more lines emanate from the workers, which means that more officials are responsible to them.

FUNCTIONS AND ROLES OF LOCAL UNION OFFICIALS

The union local has about twenty elective offices. There are five to seven members of the executive board and about an equal number of executive officers. In addition, two important committees are sometimes elected, the negotiating and the grievance committees. The two most important officers who are usually not elective are the business agent and the international representative. Countless other committees—as health, safety, sickness, picnic, education, flower, entertainment—are usually appointed by the president. Whether elected or appointed, most of the officials are theoretically responsible to the members.

The President

The president is sometimes a full-time paid official in the larger locals. More frequently, however, he is a regular employee and is paid for each meeting over which he presides. His formal duties and functions are not very clearly defined. Like most chief executive officers, he is concerned with organizing and strengthening his charge. How he actually exerts his influence depends on his personal ambitions and the local political and social situations. In old and mature locals his role may be as perfunctory as the constitutional stipulations of the office. He presides over the bimonthly meetings, represents the local in interunion councils, attends sessions of the local executive board, and participates in the business of bargaining with the employers. But most of his time is preoccupied with the day-to-day administration of the contract agreement.

In newer, less stable locals, the president's role is more dynamic and difficult. When the union is insecure, his job is to keep the membership girded for battle, by inspiring morale and solidarity through the use of anti-employer propaganda. Yet he must secure discipline if impetuous groups are not going to wreck the inexperienced union. It is his business to (1) assess the employers' ability to pay, (2) gather data needed for bargaining, (3) foresee employer tactics, (4) conceive counter-tactics, and (5) gauge the frame of mind of the membership and their proclivity to strike. In addition, he must protect his position against those who want it as a stepping stone to professional careers in the international organization.

When political or factional disputes infest the local, the president may play one of two roles. If he believes in business unions, he tries to suppress political ruptures in order to make the local effective in its struggle with

employers. If he heads a faction, he tries to crush or neutralize the opposition by controlling appointive positions and achieving a good record. In either case he attempts to pacify the articulate minorities, so that the organization is not imperiled. Sometimes he devotes time to politics in the international.

The Executive Board

The executive board, an elective body, usually has a great deal of authority in the union. The president, who sits with the board, presents all major matters to it for clearance before bringing them up before the membership. A union member or group may request the board to bring up particular problems at subsequent meetings of the local. Although the board cannot refuse to do this, it may present its recommendations along with the requests. However, the main function of many boards is the preparation of the next contract. In such a capacity it serves as a contract committee.

The subjects the board may discuss and recommend to the membership include almost everything. It may recommend a change in the dues and fees, make reports on the operation of the seniority system, study grievances, consider local relations with unions in the district or region, act as a jury on membership status, suggest the addition or removal of union services, urge political action, make investigations of expenditures, and many other things. Membership on the board gives a man or woman opportunity to exercise leadership. A board member often runs for such offices as business agent or delegate to conventions of the international, because he can exploit the contacts he makes with union members and officials.

The Secretary-Treasurer

The secretary-treasurer, who is elected, has the duties usually associated with the office. He is paid a few hundred dollars a year to keep the accounts, preserve records of meetings, and maintain membership rolls. In addition, he keeps records of the dues, the expenditures of the local, and moneys sent to the international. Since he can draw on accounts, he is in a position to exert considerable influence. One source of his power flows from his right, under certain conditions, to refuse sanction of expenditures. Some locals are beginning to hire a bookkeeper or an accountant to assume some of the duties of this office.[26] However, in middle-sized unions, the secretary-treasurer is often the only full-time paid official. When this is the case he has considerable influence because he can concentrate all of his energies on union affairs. His intimate knowledge of union operations puts his services at a premium. Consequently, his reëlection provides continuity to union organization.

[26] *Ibid.*, p. 79.

The Business Agent

The business agent is usually found in highly competitive and relatively small-scale industries rather than in large manufacturing enterprises such as steel, auto, and rubber.[27] This may be an elective or an appointive office. Thus, in smaller unions the business agent is usually the only full-time paid official who provides continuity to the local's activities. Not uncommonly he is the most powerful officer in the union. This condition derives from two facts.[28] First, most agents have spent a long time as workers in the plant and have an intimate knowledge of the problems of unions. Second, their functions in the local cover the whole range of union activities.

The business agent is a jack-of-all-trades. His main job is to represent the union in the administration of the contract. He polices the activities of both employer and union. He checks the working conditions in the shop. He scrutinizes the operation of the seniority system. He is on guard against nonunion employees working in the shop. He assures himself that other unions are not overstepping jurisdictional lines. Sometimes he even acts as an employment agency.

In many unions the business agent is a grievance officer. He hears complaints from workers about unjust treatment, discrimination, and severe discipline.[29] When grievances cannot be settled at the lowest level, he accompanies the grievance chairman in sessions with higher management. At times the agent has some of the responsibilities of the secretary-treasurer. He may maintain the union's office, preserve records, and even collect dues. Sometimes he has charge of union publicity and the local's newspaper.

The business agent is usually an experienced and clever negotiator. Although unable to vote in contract sessions, he meets with the executive board and advises it how to act. During negotiations with employers he gives advice to the bargaining and contract committees. As a professional union man with wide experience, he has influence out of proportion to his formally assigned duties.

The International Representative

The international representative, or organizer, is a full-time paid official of the international organization. He is appointed by the international to represent it in the local's affairs. Sometimes he has a circuit of locals which he visits. Not uncommonly he is attached to a large local. The duties of the international representative vary with his aggressiveness and the amount of control the international has over the local. In general, his duties are growing because the internationals are not only increasing their influence over

[27] Jack Barbash, *Labor Unions in Action*, Harper & Brothers, 1948, p. 113.

[28] Peterson, *op. cit.*, p. 29.

[29] Harry A. Millis and Royal E. Montgomery, *Organized Labor*, McGraw-Hill Book Company, Inc., 1945, p. 251.

the locals but also supplying them with more services.[30] Some of the controls commonly exerted by the international over the local have to do with the conditions under which locals shall be chartered, the amount of dues and initiation fees locals may charge, membership specifications, procedure of dealing with employers, and even work rules which must be observed.[31]

The job of the international representative is to insure that these controls are enforced. Among other things, he examines the books of the local and sends reports to headquarters. He is more than policeman, however, because he provides many needed services. He is usually a seasoned union man who sees union problems in a broad perspective. For example, he knows or can obtain the data on the economic state of the whole industry. He can secure statistics on wages, living costs, and profits in all localities in which the union is represented. This information is vital because internationals seek to maintain uniform working standards.

In negotiations with top management, the international representative carries the weight, influence, and prestige of the larger union organization. If occasion demands, he invites the international's lawyers, other organizers, statisticians, economists, and strategists on the local's case. Especially in unions where industry-wide bargaining is the rule, local inexperienced officers need the advice of the representatives. Not infrequently, the representative has a stabilizing influence over the local. The latter may select an inopportune time to strike or make demands. The representative can discourage rash action by threatening the local with withdrawal of the financial or other support of the international. If the local is still adamant, he tells it, "O.K. You're on your own. Don't come begging to us for help." This is usually enough to bring the local back in line with international policy.

Committees

Committees in the local may be separated according to their functions. The grievance, negotiation, and contract committees are concerned with *bargaining* relations with employers. Other committees *represent* the local in city, state, and regional union bodies. Health, safety, education, recreation, and other committees carry on many of the *internal social functions* of the union.

The committees on grievances, negotiations, and contracts are by far the most important. Their members are either appointed or elected. During bargaining sessions and other crises, these committees determine the fate of the union. Ordinarily, a committee post does not offer the individual member much of an opportunity for leadership. However, membership on these business committees may provide the stepping stone to higher union jobs.

Members of the city centrals and large union bodies are usually officers

---

[30] Barbash, *op. cit.*, p. 57.
[31] Peterson, *op. cit.*, p. 58.

of local unions. These thankless jobs are accepted by only those who fervently believe in the union movement. The internal social committees of the union function perfunctorily and often dismally. Officers try to get many members on these committees, in an endeavor to integrate them into active union affairs.

Stewards

Stewards or shop committeemen are usually elected by workers in a department of a plant. Strictly speaking, stewards are not union officers but departmental or occupational *representatives* of the workers. A union member who feels he has a grievance usually gets in touch with his steward. The problem may be one of seniority, promotion, favoritism, rate cutting, or job jurisdiction. The steward, if he feels that the worker has a case, goes to the foreman and attempts to adjudicate the dispute on the spot. If they cannot come to an agreement, the case is turned over to the chief steward or grievance committee, who goes to a higher management official for settlement. Another function of the steward is to make sure that union agreements are lived up to in the shop. His only reward for the thankless task of handling grievances is seniority and his regular wages during the time spent on cases.

Workers

Workers are a definite part of the structure of the union local. Theoretically, they occupy the highest rung of the structure because all union officials are directly or indirectly responsible to them. If the workers are determined and organized, they can control the behavior of their officers and the policies of their union. The fact that unions do not live up to the highest expectations of democracy may be the result of the vague distribution of power in their structure.

There are several reasons for the loose structuring of power in the union local. For one thing, power, authority, and jurisdiction in democratic organizations are often poorly defined. The mass of the membership of the union cannot exercise all of its authority. It cannot rest assured that officers will not overstep their assigned powers. The fact that the union deals with emergencies means that officials must have power to act quickly. Different officials must have power at different times. The grievance committee or executive board may occupy the focus of attention during some periods. Its members must have almost independent power during bargaining sessions. In another situation, the business agent or international representative must have power. Power in management organization, on the other hand, resides among the same officers, almost irrespective of situations.

Three officials have the power to guide the daily routine business of the local: the president, business agent, and international representative. Since

the latter two are often appointive officials, they are not subject to the whims of the rank and file. Therefore, if they act in concert with the president, they can run the organization even in the face of considerable opposition.

No attempt has been made in this section to portray how the union local actually functions. We have presented the formal structure of the union and its theory of formal organization. The gap between union theory and practice is as great as the contrast between the theoretical and actual operation of management organization. This does not mean that formal structure of unions is unimportant. It does mean that the formal structure must be examined in the light of the typical situations which confront it and the common tensions that arise within it. This we shall do in the following section.

UNION LEADERS AND UNION MEMBERS

UNION MEMBERS LOOK AT THEIR LOCAL

A college freshman gives his impression of his first union meeting:

I had just started working for the City Coal and Ice Company when I was asked to attend a union meeting. Our union was no large organization, but had unity. We had our meeting over the ice plant which we called the "union hall." The room was small, but large enough for our small group.

The minutes of the last meeting were read. The chairman, "Fat Bowman" by name, asked for any problems or difficulties that had recently developed. Since no reply was given, the formalities of the meeting were over. Four men immediately went below to the ice house and returned with two kegs of beer. At this time the organization of our union broke loose. The two kegs of beer lasted no time, but we didn't mind. There were more kegs below ready any time. The climax of the meeting was a little "stage" show of our own. At the end of our meeting everyone proceeded home, or in that general direction. Everyone enjoyed that union meeting.

A rubber worker wrote:

I attended my first union meeting at the unusual hour of one o'clock in the morning. The committeemen went around to the third shift workers and told us there was a meeting scheduled after work. We went to the local union hall, where the talks were going to be given. The hall wasn't very large, and smoke filled the room for most of the men were smoking. There was quite a noise coming from the scraping of chairs and the murmur of everyone's voices.

The meeting was finally called to order; the president and secretary took their seats, and the meeting was started. The president of the union explained why we were called together. He was asking tire builders to drop one operation of their piece work rate, for they were running too high. He gave us data on the number of machines that were idle in the plant, and he said this was due to the high rate of production we were giving the company. The union had found that

the company planned to move this idle machinery to a new plant they were building. This would remove a source of employment away from Akron, and the union planned to fight this action. The lowering of production was part of the plan to force the company to hire more men and fill the places on the empty machines. Another reason for dropping an operation was the amount of pay was exceeding the ten per cent over base rate; the union was afraid the company would cut the rate, thereby getting more production for less money. The increased production might lead to lay offs of some of the employees whose length of service was short. The president and older members gave examples and dates of the times they had seen this done.

The men in the audience agreed that this was the course to follow, but one argument came up. It was stated that we were but one shift and we wanted to know if the other shifts would also do the same. It was agreed, then, that each of the other shifts would hold separate meetings, and they would decide on the issue too. It was recorded that the third shift agreed with the issue and the meeting was adjourned.

A working girl inadvertently tells about her mystification of union functions:

I'd been working at Lamson and Sessions for about two weeks when a girl in my department comes around to me and says that it was necessary for a new employee to attend their first union meeting at the next one scheduled. I didn't care for the idea because I was only going to work three months.

It was on a Sunday and it took place above Wright's store. We were told to wait out in the hall while some kind of ceremony took place. About five minutes later they called us in and told us to repeat after the president of the union the oath. (There were about ten people in the whole room.)

Then we sat down in the back and the meeting got underway. There was one man who elected himself spokesman. He kept putting up new business which was turned down. He did, however, get a new typewriter for the secretary of the union. He was the most boring talker I had ever heard. He was the type that droned on and on while everybody slept.

He finally said something of interest and everybody started arguing. That lasted about half an hour. Then a man with one eye got up and said that he motioned the meeting be closed and some woman seconded the motion.

They put your clock number in a hat and had me (of all people) pick a number out of it. I picked out number five-eighty-two. That was my own number. Naturally everybody got a big kick out of that including myself, because I was made the proud owner of a five dollar bill. The man with one eye comes around and slaps me on the back and says, "You're the second one that's done that."

Another worker relates how his attitude toward unionism changed:

I started on my first job with the idea in my mind that all unions were just racketeering organizations that innocent citizens like myself were forced to join. This thought had been carefully planted in my mind since the time when I was old enough to understand anything at all. Since that time, the idea had been

cultivated and kept alive by the constant bombardment of propaganda by the newspapers, radio, and news magazines. For this reason, I was more than a little skeptical when told that I would have to join a union. However, I needed a job, so I thought it would pay me to join even if I did have to give part of my pay away to the union.

My first surprise came when I was asked for the initiation fee and the first month's dues. I found these to be reasonable and no more than one would pay to join any fraternal organization. I had imagined that all the officers would be the gangster type, especially the business agent. Therefore I was very much surprised to find that my immediate superior on my job was the president of the union and that the business agent was a mild, intelligent man who held down the same job that I had, only for a different company.

When I attended the first union meeting, which was well advertised, and to which all members were invited, I found that things were run in a very orderly fashion, by parliamentary rules. By this time my views on unions were beginning to change and I decided to find out more about the whole matter. I discovered that most of the people were just common ordinary citizens like myself. They spoke the same language, had the same ideas, and shared my likes and dislikes. When I asked what happened to the money that was collected as dues and initiation fees, I was told that, since I was now a member, I was free to inspect the books any time I wanted to.

All the time I worked on that job, I found the union to be the protector of the worker. If the union member was in trouble, and the union decided he had a just grievance, every member would stand behind him until the matter was taken care of. The union also sponsored a social life which included dances, outings, and other events which took some of the drudgery out of our everyday life.

At this time, my views concerning unions have changed completely from what they had been when I started working. I cannot speak for all unions, but if they are at all similar to the one I belonged to, I say "let there be more and stronger unions!"

Most people are not shocked or indignant to learn that the operation of management organization does not adhere entirely to the formal requisites of bureaucracies. Yet they are wrathful at the thought that unions do not always function according to their image of a democratic model. There is no more reason to expect a democratic structure to operate according to its formal expectations than a bureaucratic one. Both types of organization inevitably develop internal strains and inconsistencies when confronted with daily human situations. No functioning organization with changing personnel and situations will conform completely to its formal organizational expectations. Formal organization limits and conditions behavior but it cannot force all behavior into a rigid mold.

UNION LEADERS AND THE RANK AND FILE

The nature of union organization is such that the rank and file does not and cannot give much attention to union affairs. The union, like most

democratic organizations, is not a mobocracy or a perpetual town meeting. Ordinary members attend occasional meetings but leave the operation of the local in the hands of the officers. Thus, the union is run by its officers. Only when the union organization is weak does the rank and file take over. Conversely, the union is strong and successful when officers effectively perform the function of "delivering the goods" in terms of higher wages, shorter hours, and better working conditions.[32] This does not mean that the union is not devoted to democratic ideals and principles. On the contrary, union democracy is usually idealized and provisions are made to realize it. Ross says, in this regard, that "there are few institutions in the economic and social life of the nation with so many channels of communication between the rank and file and the leadership."[33] Yet most unionists recognize that considerable discretion must be given to the leaders if they want a permanent and effective organization.

Therefore, in discussing trade union wage policy, Ross emphasizes the dependence of the rank and file on the officers. He says, "The wage policy of a union, like the foreign policy of a nation, is poorly suited to the methods of primitive democracy."[34] The workers are dependent on the leadership for defining what is equitable, possible, and acceptable in reference to wages. It follows that when members reject a decision urged on them by their leaders, vigorous democracy is not at work but rather internal demoralization. It is also true, then, that revolts of the rank and file against the leaders occur only when organization is functioning poorly.

The following section will examine the operation of the union by observing the ordinary roles of union officers. The day-to-day functions of the leaders will be discussed, rather than spectacular crisis situations. Similarly, attention will be focused on internal problems of local organization, rather than on relations with employers. This subject is dealt with in another chapter.[35]

Ideally, the role of each important union official should be examined separately. Owing to the diversity of local structures, this is difficult to do. We shall consider all officials who have something to do with the formation and execution of policy as a group.

In some ways, the officers of the local may be studied better as a group than as a number of individual leaders. Since most of the officers are elected, they are responsible not to each other but to the membership. In management organization, each level in the supervisory structure is clearly responsible to the level above it and has authority over the level below it. Thus,

---

[32] Robert F. Hoxie, *Trade Unionism in the United States*, Appleton-Century-Crofts, Inc., 1923, p. 177.

[33] Ross, *op. cit.*, p. 38.

[34] *Ibid.*

[35] See Chapter X, "Power Organization: Interaction of Management and Labor."

the relations of each level in management are different and must be studied separately. Since union officials do not stand in a hierarchical relationship to each other, they can be distinguished as a group from the rank and file. This basic division is recognized by the members. All officers, irrespective of importance, are lumped into "they," and all non-officers into "we."

This segmentation or cleavage between officers and members is reinforced by the fact that officers are relatively few in number. Consequently, they get to know one another rather well. The interaction among them between meetings is much higher than their interaction with the rank and file. As full-time paid officers, their isolation from the rank and file may be almost complete. Under these circumstances union officers tend to support each other and stick together as a group.

The cleavage between union officers and members usually does not develop as sharply as it does between management and the workers. Several factors are responsible for this. First, the chains of man-boss relations that typify management organization are absent in the union. Second, communication between members and officers is freer, more frequent, and more direct. Third, the thoughtways of both groups are very similar since union officers are almost universally recruited from the rank and file.

ROLES OF UNION LEADERS

Selekman points out that most union leaders perform four main roles. They are:[36]

1. As commander of a fighting organization.
2. As administrative head of a fraternal society.
3. As business administrator of a labor marketing coöperative.
4. As democratic leader of a political association.

All of these roles concern policy determination and administration. Only in theory do the rank and file fix policy. If the members have confidence in their leaders, they will accept recommendations or policies. The mass of union members do not have the time, capacity, or inclination to inform themselves on policy matters. Their acts are in the nature of plebiscites; they vote "yes" or they veto.

When roles of union leaders are contrasted with managers' roles, an important difference is revealed. The roles of union leaders concern themselves almost entirely with human elements, whereas management roles deal with human *and* technical *and* financial elements. Both leaders must deal with people, but the effectiveness of union leaders is measured in terms of their ability to *satisfy* the motives of workers, while the effectiveness of managers is measured by their ability to *coördinate* people for production.

The four roles which union leaders are expected to play are not equally

[36] Selekman, *op. cit.*, p. 180.

important at all times. The age of the local, the nature of its relation to the international, the kind of problems it currently faces, its degree of maturity, and the nature of its structure call for the emphasis of different roles. Leaders are rare who perform each role equally well. We shall examine how union leaders attempt to play and integrate each of these roles.

FIGHTING LEADER

Union members evaluate the performance of their leaders by the kind of contract they secure. Even though bargaining may occur on an industry-wide basis, local leaders must take some responsibility for the kind of contract the union gets.[37] The worst accusation that may be hurled against leaders is that they "sold out" to the employers, or that they were handed a "bill of goods." To avoid this charge officers try to convince the members that they are *fighting hard* for them. They remind the members of the great strength of management and how hard they are struggling to get a few concessions. They tell them that they cannot fight management alone; that all the workers must stick together and fight together.

Although the union leader is supposed to be head of a militant organization, many things conspire to make his role ineffective. Foremost is the fact that he has to fight management with a voluntary army over which he has no final authority. Indeed, as Muste suggests, the union leader is put in the anomalous position of being a democratic generalissimo. He is elected to office by his soldiers often on the eve of battle. His army votes on issues of war, peace, or armistice. The plan of attack is discussed in public debate by the soldiers! Secrecy, obedience, and loyalty, the heart of a military organization, are at low ebb.[38]

Other restrictions hamper the skillful execution of the role of the fighting leader. The international organization may send in negotiators (generals and diplomats) who do not know the local situation. The international may refuse permission to war, or to negotiate. It may insist on approving the terms of the armistice (contract). It may denounce the general to the soldiers and ask them to throw him out.

The enemy, or employer, is never an "easy" opponent. In the first place, his army is an efficient bureaucracy run by autocratic generals. Secondly, it is not the purpose of battle to destroy the enemy but to make him treat the soldiers better. In fact, if the enemy perishes in the conflict, the soldiers will starve. Therefore, he must be treated with some consideration, for after the battle coöperation with him is expected. Furthermore, the armistice (contract) binds the union and the enemy together. If the union violates

[37] In cases of industry-wide bargaining, officers of locals are consulted or get representation on the negotiating committees. The local abides by the majority decision of the committees.

[38] A. J. Muste, "Factional Fights in Trade Unions," in *American Labor Dynamics*, edited by J. B. S. Hardman, Harcourt, Brace and Company, Inc., 1928, pp. 332-337.

the armistice, the employer may call in the government to make the union behave, or vice versa.

These alignments present a difficult situation for the union leader. He tries to be a democratic general but finds he is accused of being too timid or too autocratic. He worries about the kind of attack he should make. If he decides to take the course of the diplomat, he tries to collect all the economic data he can in preparation for negotiations. His intelligence organization, however, may not be very effective. Moreover, the employers may have decided to fight. Therefore, he must revise his plans and convince his men that they must gird for battle. Depending on their mood, he is called courageous, alert, stupid, ineffective, or bungling.

The kinds of policy decisions that union leaders must make in their relations with employers are many and recurrent. The membership may have instructed them on such areas as the closed shop, jurisdiction, the training and recruitment of workers, union recognition, higher wages, or shorter hours. Yet they may have to make policy decisions independent of member endorsement. They never are certain that they will get backing on these private decisions.

Perhaps the military role of the union leader has been overdrawn. Nonetheless, it suggests the contradictions that exist within the role.

FRATERNAL EXECUTIVE

Union officers are also supposed to act as leaders of a fraternal association. They are supposed to build in the members a feeling of loyalty and devotion toward one another and toward the local. Such *esprit de corps* is essential if an organization is to function during such crises as unemployment, strikes, and jurisdictional disputes. To be effective in this role, union officers must be genuine democratic leaders, who know the sentiments and everyday problems of the group. Leaders who want union solidarity must know how to make members aware of their common bonds and purposes. They must instill in the workers a willingness to endure hardships for the sake of the organization.

Even with excellent leadership capacities, the union leader finds difficulty in playing the role of the head of a fraternal order. If he is a full-time officer, he cannot spend much time with workers on the plant floor. The longer he stays in office, the less acquainted he is with the workers' intimate problems and ideas. In the midst of high labor turnover he knows fewer and fewer members personally. If he is not warm and friendly toward them, he is called "stuck up." If the word gets around that a leader can't relax with the boys, that he hasn't time for a beer or a hand of poker, he loses popularity. If he plays his fraternal role well, the union leader will not depart very far from the language, dress, ideas, and sentiments of the workers.

Yet the very nature of his job exposes him to new experiences not shared

by the members. As he comes in contact with management he may for the first time see management-labor relations in their totality. Unless he is ideologically frozen, he changes and adjusts to his new perspective. Yet he must not depart too far from his earlier sentiments about management, for they are closer to those found among the workers. If he does, he is considered a "sellout" and no longer a brother who knows the problems of the working "stiff."

There is still another problem that makes the fraternal role a difficult one to play. It is the job of welding a heterogeneous group into a fraternal society. Union members represent many political groups, occupations, nationalities, races, industries, religions, age groups, and interests. The union is not a solid corps of workers who have the same social background, experience, and expectations. The Negro members may be concerned with equal treatment, females with equal pay, nationalities with the use of their native tongue, older men with security, younger men with high wages, politicians with votes, and so on.

To build *esprit de corps* with such a mixed group is difficult. To a degree, cohesiveness is built with the energy, drive, and enthusiasm of the leader and his cohorts. There is a limit, however, to what their resources can accomplish. The consolidation of a heterogeneous group is made easier by creating meaningful rituals and ceremonies around initiation, suspension, reinstatement, and expulsion. Shop codes, emblems, and songs may also help in this connection.

But men do not live by ritual alone. Solidarity grows to the extent that the group satisfies different physical, psychological, and social needs. In their fraternal role, then, union officers must try to create a program to satisfy these needs. That they have met with partial success is evidenced by the many activities that unions have inaugurated. The union has attempted to assume functions in areas where other institutions have failed to develop them according to the needs of the workers. Some of these deal with worker education, including union history and techniques, counseling, banking, credit facilities, medical care, insurance, coöperative housing, legal advice, recreation, vacation facilities, coöperative buying, and political action.[39]

These activities underscore the role of the union leader as he tries to push a policy which will make the union a vital part of the workers' lives. The more needs it meets, the closer it comes to the objective of being the workers' community. This is one of the main reasons union leaders often fight employer welfare efforts. They argue that union paternalism must take precedence over employer paternalism, if loyalty to the union is to flourish.

The furthering of fraternal feeling by expanding services is difficult because the resources of the local are limited. The cost of services must

[39] Mark Starr, "Role of Union Organization," in *Industry and Society*, edited by William F. Whyte, McGraw-Hill Book Company, Inc., 1946.

be borne by union members. With limited funds, a struggle over which service should come first is inevitable. The leader must decide which service will bring the greatest union identification. Actually, the limited resources of the union have pushed union leaders into the political arena. Many of them believe that what the union cannot afford perhaps the government should provide. This is especially the case with social security. So vital is this issue becoming that conflicts will surely arise as unions decide that economic security may be more important than level of wages.

BUSINESS ADMINISTRATOR

The business role of the local union leader is often neglected. The union is in one respect a business organization which sells labor. As such it has some of the paraphernalia of business. Records must be kept, funds must be accounted for, contracts must be made, investments need scrutiny, and the staff must be directed. The larger the local, the greater the preoccupation with business functions. Accountants, auditors, secretaries, treasurers, economists, lawyers, typists, and others may be on the union pay roll.

Union leaders who are put in business situations are constrained to act as businessmen. They become aware of their position as head of a supervisory hierarchy. They become imbued with the logic of cost and efficiency. They want a sound financial union. They worry about the size of the treasury and about useless expenditures. They insist on honoring agreements and contracts.

The primary business function of union officers is to negotiate and administer the contract. This takes as much skill on the part of labor officials as it does on the part of businessmen. To perform the role efficiently, the labor leader needs to know business. He has to understand the economics of the industry. He needs to know something about the business condition of the company and its competitors.

To accumulate this business knowledge, the union official requires long tenure in office. This fact is not generally appreciated by the rank and file. Many believe that the offices should be passed around, and that terms of office should be short. Some older and experienced unions which recognize the need for experienced leaders often reëlect their officials. Other leaders manipulate the rank and file to stay in office. In either case the ability of the official to stay in office depends upon his capacity to play his political role.

POLITICAL CHIEF

An elected official who wants to stay in office must "play politics." Politics, the art of manipulating people, is found in all groups where there is competition for leadership. It is found in government, social clubs, business, and labor. It is not inherently good or bad but the normal and inevitable accompaniment of group life.

The political life of the union may be analyzed around the process of the "circulation of leaders." This process has two phases: getting into office and staying in office. Both depend upon the ability of the officer or prospective officer to get sympathetic support from the general membership. For ultimately, the approval of the rank and file is needed to get into office or stay in it.

Usually, getting or staying in office in many unions is not very difficult. The number of members who aspire to office is small. In fact, in most locals any energetic, ambitious, and moderately intelligent person can, if he wishes, play at least a secondary leadership role. The paucity of political candidates derives from the fact that some workers consider themselves only temporary union members. They aspire to climb into management. Then there are those who are apathetic to unionism, and those who are actively anti-union. In addition to these, a large number of workers are not qualified by temperament or experience to hold office.

In some of the older unions, officers need do little to stay in office. Apparently, the members are satisfied with their performances, for they are perfunctorily reëlected. In newer unions, staying in office is more difficult. The techniques incumbents use to remain in office depend somewhat on the history of the local, current issues, and performance in office. Irrespective of these conditions, however, the candidates must be articulate enough to convince the rank and file that they are doing a good job. Inexperienced and insecure leaders exhibit violent militancy toward employers. By vilifying businessmen and using them as scapegoats, they hope to take advantage of the latent hostility of workers toward employers. Thus, it is difficult to distinguish when attacks on employers are genuine and when they are motivated by "political" expediency. An element of both is probably always present. In any case, the technique is useful in calling attention to oneself, and sometimes this is all that is needed to get into or to stay in office.

A mechanic, recently defeated in a local union election, complained, not without some justification, that "It's not what you know or do that counts here. Most of the fellows vote for the guy who makes the most noise. They hear 'Joe Smith,' 'Joe Smith,' 'Joe Smith.' When time comes to vote, they don't know the records of the candidates. They see 'Joe Smith' and think, 'Oh, yeah, I know him.' So they vote for him. The next day, they hear something about Smitty and remember him as the guy that did them dirt. And they say to themselves, 'I voted for the wrong guy.' See what I mean?"

However, attention-getting devices have limited usefulness. If officers don't deliver something substantial eventually, they get the reputation of being "loud mouths." An ex-union official commented on this situation: "In the long run, the quiet efficient guy makes the best officer. At first the members like the extrovert who wants to be in front. He gets elected to a small committee by making lots of noise. He develops a clique around him which

puts him in office. Once there he keeps on making lots of noise to be reelected. Come the negotiations, he doesn't know what to do. So he tells 'em (the bosses) off. After a while the members get sick and tired of these blow-mouths who go in, and tell-'em-off, and come out with nothing. I always say, it's what you come out with that counts. The membership learns that the hard way."

The techniques of getting and staying in office are many and varied. An individual must gain popularity to get into office, and he must retain it to stay in office. Getting and retaining popularity takes time and effort. In large locals particularly, no individual can make himself known to all members. He needs someone to help him and to sell him. In short, he needs a political machine. The machine is so important that the operation of the union cannot be understood without an appreciation of its rise and function.

Regardless of the importance he himself assigns to his roles as *fighting leader, fraternal executive, business administrator,* and *political chief,* the union officer cannot survive to play any of them unless he becomes adroit in building and using a political machine.

THE POLITICAL MACHINE

NATURAL HISTORY OF A MACHINE

There is nothing unusual or insidious about a political machine. It arises regularly whenever an office is dependent on the consent of large numbers. A machine in the union comes into being and functions in much the same way as the machine in a city precinct or ward. Let us take an illustration to see how a machine grows.

Sam Gibson is a toolmaker in Department 34 of Acme Manufacturing Corporation. Sam is a likable fellow who has the respect and confidence of his fellow workers. He attends union meetings regularly and shows an interest in union affairs. Some of his friends in Department 34 decide that he would make a good steward. He is elected with little opposition. As he makes the rounds as a steward, he sees more people. He discusses union affairs with them and lets them know that he is available for office. An informal committee of his co-workers and friends starts to talk about running Sam for a union office. They point to his good record as a steward and get others to "talk up" Sam.

Soon an organized drive is under way. Sam and his group draw up an informal program or platform which makes promises of different things to different groups. They gather a list of the promises and unfulfilled promises of incumbents. Armed with literature, speeches, and informal arguments, Sam's clique goes to work. They buttonhole as many of their friends as possible and ask them to support Sam for office. All the tactics and appeals

of local precinct politics are used. If a good job of electioneering is done, Sam and his group are elected to office.

Once in office, Sam naturally appoints his friends and other ardent supporters to important posts and committees. If Sam likes his job, he may want to stay in office. In the meantime, another group is booming a rival. Sam gets his "heelers" in the plants to campaign for him again. They distribute literature make new promises, and advance arguments against new candidates. Here is a typical sales talk of a heeler:

"You know Sam Gibson has done a fine job in office. He's got a lot of valuable experience. It'd be a shame to change presidents at this critical time. . . . Paul Miller is a good candidate, but he's green. I think he needs more experience. Besides, you know how those guys are in Miller's gang. If they got in power, they'd shove shop 34 around, and you know I'm not kiddin'."

STAYING IN POWER

Obviously, a machine needs fuel and lubrication to keep running. In the union the loyalty of political supporters must be rewarded. Sometimes the machine uses graft, patronage, and threats to stay in power. But in most cases it feeds on the normal motives of its heelers. Some of the latter are ardent unionists, who believe that their candidate and his program will do the most for unionism. They give unstintingly of their time and energy. Other heelers have aspirations for a high appointive job in the union hierarchy. Lacking the personality qualification for leadership, they work for a machine with the hope that their service and loyalty will be rewarded.

Others are motivated to support a machine by money. They may get a job on the election committee, which pays them a few dollars on election day. The only reward that most machine workers get is recognition in the form of an office or committee post. A few like to bask in the limelight of their champion, especially if he is rising in the union hierarchy: "Yes, I know Gibson well. He used to work right next to me as a welder. About once a month some of the boys who put him where he is get together for a little poker. Sam's a great guy. He's still one of the boys. His job hasn't gone to his head."

Any group in power has advantages over others aspiring to get into power. One of these advantages is a quasi-monopoly of officers over communication and attention. During membership meetings, officers can play up those things that make their administration seem efficient. They may refuse to recognize dissident "agitators" on the floor. They can pack committees with workers who are sympathetic to them. They can time the presentation of "bad" reports so that they do little damage. They can use delaying tactics, call meetings at peculiar hours, and take arbitrary actions. In sort, they can and do use all the parliamentary tricks known to democratic groups.

An important advantage of a machine is the union newspaper. Since many members rarely attend union meetings, the paper is their only source of official information. The editor of the paper is often hired from the outside and is responsible to the president. It is not unusual for the editor to play the role of publicity man for the president. For example, the president may request "fuller coverage" of his activities in the paper. If he senses a rival for office, he may be able, by a well-placed editorial, to nip a boom in the bud. A typical editorial might read: "I have been very gratified with the work that brother John Beagle has been doing on the grievance committee. During the year we have settled 138 grievances amicably. The membership may not realize the amount of time and energy we have had to spend on settling grievances. John Beagle has been of invaluable assistance to me in this work. The job of chairman of the grievance committee is going to continue to be critical. We need the skill, energy, and experience of John Beagle on this job."

Using the International

The ordinary worker has little or no direct contact with the international union organization. The officers of the local usually have all of the contacts with it. This enables them to further their political ambitions both in the local and in the international union.

The formal relations of the local to the international range from almost complete autonomy to complete dependence. Although the local is becoming increasingly dependent, its leaders can either facilitate or discourage this trend, depending on their personal motives and aspirations. Political-minded local officers may be divided into two groups: those who want to remain in power in their locals and those who want offices in the international.

The prestige and power of the international can be used to advantage by the local officers who want to stay in power. This is so because the tenure of international officers depends in part on what officers of locals think of them. The latter, or their representatives, are usually the delegates at the international's conventions. If international officers lend their prestige to the fight of local officers to stay in power, they also stand a greater chance of being reëlected at conventions.

If the job of a local officer is threatened, the international may give him a "favorable spread" in the international newspaper. International officers may visit the local and make speeches on the "good job brother Smith is doing here." The international office may furnish the local its best legal talent and negotiators in bargaining sessions, and it may appoint local members to jobs in the international.

But apart from these motives, international officers generally encourage long tenure of local officers. They like to deal with experienced local leaders, for it is an arduous job to keep teaching new leaders their duties and re-

sponsibilities toward the international. International officers also find it difficult to keep track of shifting local situations. Like most executives they prefer stability in their organizations.

Although international officers have longer tenure than local ones, they are also threatened by rivals. Since international leaders soon lose touch with the rank and file, they depend on their reputations or on a political machine to keep them in power. An aggressive head of a large local commands a large number of votes at the international convention. He can, therefore, threaten the security of international officers or exert pressure on them to change their policies, or both. The local leader can report to the members that there is "bureaucratic dry rot" in the international, that the international is dominated by the locals in which the officers were former members, that the international is threatening the autonomy of locals by dictatorial and autocratic tactics, that there is waste, corruption, and plundering of the international treasury.

These attacks may be used as a cry-wolf technique by local officers to remain in power. Or they may be used to get into offices of the international. Luckily, most local officers are sincere and hard-working. They do everything they can to coöperate with the international. They take defeat on local and international elections as part of the game. They really make continuity and order possible by their devotion to unionism.

What is a good union man? What are the basic elements in the union leader's ideology?

UNION LEADER'S IDEOLOGY

The thought patterns of local union officers are conditioned by the ideological position of the union and its history with management. In general, the dominant outlook of unions has been the business policy of getting "more here and now," in the form of wages, hours, and working conditions. The techniques to obtain "more here and now" have varied—from general coöperation with management to a rugged "get tough" policy. For example, the Amalgamated Clothing Workers of America have used coöperative techniques whereas the American Federation of Musicians has been militant. The former union insists that labor must do all it can to make the industry efficient and prosperous; the latter has demanded union security before technological change, profit, or anything else. Both have been business unions in the strict sense of the word.[40]

Other unions are less business-oriented and more ideologically conscious. They consider the labor movement as part of a working-class movement, which should be to further the well-being of all workers and not of union members only. This should be done even at the expense of better wages, hours, and working conditions. Such ideological unionism varies from a social welfare philosophy of the New Deal variety to the class-conscious

[40] Barbash, *op. cit.*, chap. 10, "Union Leadership."

idealism of socialism and communism. These ideological unionists are more concerned with "extracurricular" functions, such as public ownership, political action, public housing, socialized medicine, and international politics, than with the immediate issue of a ten-cent-an-hour raise in plant X in the fall of 1950.

Sometimes a union local whose international policy is business-dominated seems to act like an ideological union, and vice versa. In these cases the historical relations with local employers may be so different as to make reversals of position imperative. For example, a local may find it difficult to coöperate with plants that wish to destroy the union. Consequently, it becomes defiant, aggressive, and militant. On the other hand an understanding and coöperative employer may, by his sincerity, temper the ideological rapacity of the local.

The ideology of the typical local union leader is not systematic and organized. It is made up of a number of pragmatic principles which he has learned through daily contact with management and the workers. These principles usually embrace (1) some democratic dogma concerning the ends of union organization, (2) the means best suited to obtain these ends, (3) guides to relations with employers, and (4) techniques to keep the union strong. Barbash reports a list of the attributes of the good trade unionist.[41] The reader is invited to label which attributes are associated with each of the four principles listed above.

The good trade union leader:
1. Recognizes a picket line.
2. Does not discriminate between color, race, creed, sex, or minority group.
3. Patronizes union labor by
   a. Advertising to other workers the benefits of belonging to a labor organization.
   b. Acting to unify the labor movement.
   c. Showing spirit of mutual aid.
4. Shows management it profits from unionism.
5. Does not report another worker to employer.
6. Abides by majority decision.
7. Does not carry internal disputes to the public.
8. Keeps union affairs from management.
9. Is sure that information about union is complete and correct before it is released to members.
10. Settles disputes and grievances between members within the union.
11. Organizes the unorganized, for every unorganized worker retards the progress of organized workers.
12. Participates in civic affairs.
13. Brings the principles of unionism to the public.[42]

[41] *Ibid.*, pp. 181-182.
[42] *Ibid.* Taken from National Federation of Telephone Workers. "Wisconsin Stewards Training Program" (unpublished report), 1946.

These guides to activity are easily understood by union members and leaders. Although they deal mostly with the problems of maintaining the internal solidarity of the union, the roles of the union leader are also outlined. In the above sections we described how leaders are blocked from playing their roles well by the contradictory pressures in union organization. Union leaders are expected to play certain roles, yet the nature of the organization almost prevents them. In addition to these difficulties, leaders have more trouble in integrating roles. Almost invariably, one role is overplayed at the expense of the others. The president of a local may be an excellent business organizer but a poor fraternal leader or political boss. This failure on the part of union officers to play all roles equally well is an indirect cause of their short tenure. Incumbents are replaced by those who can assume roles which were underplayed. Fortunately, the union does not depend for its survival on the day-to-day work of its officers. The steward is the "work horse" who keeps the organization going. The next section examines his functions and roles.

THE STEWARD AND THE WORKERS

DUTIES OF THE STEWARD

The union contacts that are most meaningful to the workers are those which they experience on the job. Just as "management" in the eyes of the workers refers mostly to foremen, similarly, the "union" is really the steward and the grievance committee. The steward is a union member who is elected by the members of a department to represent them in their dealings with management. Whether elected or appointed, he is not, strictly speaking, a union official but a union representative. With rare exceptions, the steward works full time at his job like any other worker. He is subject to his foreman's commands just like any other worker. Usually, in case of a controversy between workers and the foreman the steward may leave his work to represent the worker. If any employee has a grievance, he generally expresses it to his steward.[43] The latter, theoretically, decides whether the grievance is just—that is, whether it is a violation of the contract or a discrimination against a union member. If he thinks it is, he takes the matter up with the foreman and an attempt is made to settle the controversy immediately. If they cannot come to an agreement, the case is taken up the line to the grievance committee, which meets with higher management. The parties usually come to an agreement or submit the case to arbitration.

The union recognizes the importance of the steward in the minds both of the workers and of management. He represents the first line of the union

[43] This depends somewhat upon the contract. In the General Motors-U.A.W. contract the grieved must always inform his foreman first. This tends to cut down grievances because of the inequality of the two parties.

just as foremen represent the first line of supervision. The steward manual of the Textile Workers Union of America admonishes its stewards:

As a shop steward, yours is the job and the opportunity to make this industrial democracy function. You represent your fellow workers in the shop. You are the non-commissioned officer in the union army. As you carry out your duties effectively, you will represent your fellow unionists well, and the union will have value and meaning for them, and will flourish.

You are the representative of the union in the shop. It is within your power to turn a contract from a document of words and clauses into a living protection for the rights of workers. Without you, and others like you, even the best contract is meaningless. You put life in its veins. You make it work. Because you are in the shop, in immediate contact with both workers and management, you become the basic foundation of the union. The wisest union leader, the most efficient business agent, cannot build the union and make it function effectively without your help. You must deal with management relating to conditions of work, while at the same time you keep the union strong within the shop so that the boss knows that you represent the workers.[44]

The duties of the steward fall into three categories.[45] First, he must see that the general union guarantees provided by law are not violated by the employer. Second, he must insure that specific clauses in the contract with the employer are not violated, including grievances. Third, he is the work horse of the union. That is, he educates workers in their union obligations, sells them on union policies, and sets a good example for them to follow.

Actually, most of his time as a steward is spent in his second duty—seeing that the contract is carried out and that grievance cases are properly handled. The kinds of problems that stewards must deal with are many and varied. Some are plant-wide, involving basic policies, and others are imaginary, petty grievances of individuals. Each must be considered, evaluated, and acted upon, for nobody believes that his grievance is unimportant.

The contract, with its legal phrases and clauses, means little to the average worker. He wants the union to do things for him irrespective of the contract. The kinds of problems he brings to his steward represent his aspirations and his fears concerning his position. For example, he wants good working conditions in terms of light, ventilation, and safety. The union's ability to do something about these is vital, as the following illustration proves. A young worker reported: "When I was working at the factory, the foreman put a bunch of us to work, piling up boxes containing the finished product. Above our heads was a conveyor belt carrying steel from one department to another. Because of the danger of this steel slipping off the conveyor belt and falling on us, we refused to work. We reported this

[44] "So You're a Steward," Textile Workers Union of America, C.I.O., New York.
[45] Glenn Gardiner, *When Foreman and Steward Bargain*, McGraw-Hill Book Company, Inc., 1945, pp. 19-40.

to the steward who reported it to the foreman. Action was swift. A group
of maintenance men arrived and soon a steel screen was built to catch any
steel which might fall from the conveyor belt. We resumed our job of
piling boxes."

Probably the most frequent complaints the steward must handle concern
income, job rates, and promotions. Although there may be nothing in the
contract stipulating an advance in pay after a specific length of service,
workers may ask the steward to do something about this. Workers get to
know the informal pattern of advancement in pay and position. They are
constantly comparing their *relative* pay with that of other workers. If they
are not advanced as rapidly as they believe proper, they feel a sense of
discrimination. Thus, the steward is asked to do something for which he
has no legal power. A steward summarized his peculiar position in such a
case: "Pete Fisher asked the foreman twice for a raise but got nowhere. He
asked me to file a grievance because his brother-in-law in department 14
has been with the company less time and he's making more money. Pete's
got a right to gripe because they're both doing the same kind of work. But
there's nothing I can do. The foreman hasn't violated the agreement. Pete's
just unlucky. Yesterday I told him the situation, and now he's sore at me.
You just can't win with these guys."

More common grievances concern a change of rate which affects the
entire department. Here, too, the steward is placed in a difficult position
because he is pitted against managers and engineers who bombard him with
a mass of technical evidence that new rates will be actually better than the
old ones. At the same time the workers have a deep-seated suspicion of any
change in wage rates. To be reasonable with management and to protect
the men at the same time is a difficult task.

Workers develop a sense of proprietorship around their jobs. They resist
being moved from one job to another because they then feel that they
don't belong to a job. They want to feel that they are indispensable to a
particular job or machine. In short, they want security, and they press this
fact on the steward. In some industries transferability is necessary because
of rapid changes in operations. This makes the steward's job a trying one.
The following complaint illustrates how the position of the steward may be
undermined when he cannot deal with the problems of job security:

Our union was very weak in taking care of grievances on the job. It seemed
as if our grievance committee was afraid of the company officials. I'll take my
case as an example. I was an automatic screw machine operator. I was not supposed to whell chips as a regular job; however this was the kind of work that I
did for two months. I took my complaint to the steward, and after fumbling for
words, he said that there was nothing that could be done about the situation.
This was the first and the last time I ever took up a grievance through the union.
Other complaints which I placed directly before the company officials got much
more satisfactory results.

In such cases, where workers get action from management rather than from the union, the security of the union is threatened. Even when management offers the workers something they deeply desire, the union is suspicious. It may interpret employer welfare efforts as a wedge to separate the worker from his union. It wants the worker to think of the union as the only source of his welfare. Therefore it is important for the steward to be successful in workers' causes.

Another goal of the union steward is securing uniformity of working conditions. The union is thoroughly suspicious of differential treatment because it, too, can become a weapon to separate the union from its members. Securing uniformity in the treatment of workers is based on the notion that employers should be related to workers as a group and not as individuals. It is the steward's job to see that even minute violations in this code do not occur, for workers are not immune to accepting favored treatment.

Uniformity in practice covers such areas as wages, methods of upgrading and transferring, rest pauses, starting and quitting time. Insistence on uniform treatment of workers means that companies are reluctant to introduce new changes, even on an experimental basis. If they want to adopt a new practice, it must be adopted in all departments simultaneously with union consent.

ORIENTATIONS OF THE STEWARD

How the steward performs his duties depends upon his orientation, how he interprets his role, and the social situation in his department.

The Job- or Management-Oriented Steward

Some workers are not stewards by choice. The men in a department may regard the steward's job as a thankless one and as one that is forced upon an individual. Frequently, this person is not an ardent unionist. In fact, sometimes he hopes to leave the union by getting a foreman's job. But in the meantime he must be "one of the boys" and must demonstrate to management his ability to get along with people.

The job-oriented steward may play his role in one of two ways. First, he may do as little as he can for the union, yielding only to strong pressure from the workers. When conferring with the foreman or management, he may impress them with his "reasonableness, fairness, and intelligence." Stewardship for him is an avenue for meeting and conferring with management officials. If astute enough, he can impress both management and the workers with his ability. However, he may arouse the suspicion of both. A punch press operator who suspected his steward complained, "Ed won't do nothin' for us on da rate. He's got his eye on da foreman's job I betcha. D' odder day I was called before da board to testify. Ed was sittin' dere all slicked up and talkin' smooth an fast. Dere's no tellin' what he's up to.

He's got us all buffaloed. He's gotta way of smilin' at everybody and talkin' smooth so ya can't tell what he says or means. Ya notice we din't win, but nobody gets sore at Ed. But I sees tru him and his yak, yak, yak. Onct I heard 'im say that he'd quit the steward's job tamarra if he taught it'd hurt his chances on da job. I tell ya, I don' trust 'im."

The job- or management-oriented steward may play a very vociferous role. So concerned is he with convincing management of his ability that he presents workers' grievances with special zeal. He hopes to impress management with the idea that he could do an equally good job if he were a foreman and had to fight grievances. This type may regard the steward job as a game, as a battle of wits with management. He does not get angry, or even believe in his own tactics. His purpose is to do such an effective job that management feels it cannot do without his services.

A sales manager reminisced on his days as a union man:

I had a lot of fun in the union. I wanted to be a mechanic but I really wasn't any good. As a joke the fellows elected me their steward. But I surprised them by being one of the best stewards they ever had. I guess I have the gift of gab, and that's what a steward needs. Anyway, I remember one time on an almost hopeless grievance case, I bet the superintendent ten dollars I'd win. And I even told him the way I'd do it.

Of course, he wouldn't believe me. When we met I gave it to the board just as I said, and the superintendent wasn't prepared for a defense. Of course, I was ready for an entirely different attack if he did believe me. But there was no bad blood. Not long after that he recommended me for a job in personnel.

The Union-Oriented Steward

Other stewards are certain that their future rests not with the company but with the union. By being effective stewards they hope to build a machine that will boost them into an office of the local. They also may hope for a full-time paid job in the international organization.

This type of steward is immersed in union ideology. He takes up many doubtful cases and does his best to win them. The image he wants workers to have is that he is willing to do everything in his power to help anyone who needs it. Frequently, he is a vocal and colorful person. He tends to take his job seriously. He gets steward training, reads union literature, attends union meetings, and practices the philosophy that the union is always right.

Sometimes this philosophy yields unforeseen problems. Gardner describes the case of an overly zealous steward who not only increased tension in the union but got into a difficult personal position.

... In a department working on shifts, the morning shift started at 6:00 A.M. and the second shift ended at midnight. Some of the people on the first shift complained that they had to get up too early in the morning and wanted to

change their starting hour to 7 o'clock. This seemed reasonable until the steward discussed it with workers on the second shift. They were strongly opposed to the change because they would not get through work until 1 o'clock instead of midnight. If the steward then officially requested the change, the second shift would be down on him; but if he did not, the first shift would feel that he was not representing them properly.[46]

Ambitious stewards as they climb the union ladder tend to regard each job as a stepping stone to another. Consequently, as is the case with climbers in management organization, they tend to lose touch with the problems and sentiments of workers at the lower levels. They also tend to unsettle the fabric of social relations, by emphasizing existing antagonism between officers and the rank and file. Career-bent unionists become known as "porkchoppers," i.e., career men who are concerned primarily with their jobs and not the welfare of the workers.

The Worker-Oriented Steward

Most commonly the steward is an ordinary worker who has the confidence of the men in his department. He is secure in his job and has no burning ambition to climb either the management or the union hierarchy. The job of steward usually doesn't consume too much of his time because he has worked out an adequate adjustment to it.

Worker-oriented stewards interpret their role as one of "helping out the boys." They know how to handle the chronic complainers, how to push a case which has merit, and how to deal with the foremen. This kind of steward is frequently reëlected because the men have confidence in him. Also, management would rather work with him than with a new steward every year. This is understandable because being a steward means learning some of management's problems. Irrespective of his attitude toward management, the steward comes to see that some of management's problems are real and not susceptible of easy solution.

The men, on the other hand, also prefer the worker-oriented steward who is reasonable and who at times even resists mandates from union officials. Workers sometimes suspect *both* management and union officials. Therefore, a steward who works for them against management and sometimes against the union is trusted, for he represents both the beliefs and the fears of his men.

The worker-oriented steward is not necessarily the most effective steward. But he is more acceptable because he does not threaten anyone's status, and he does not disturb the working relationships. Since he tends to be the kind of stable "work horse" who is reëlected year by year, the problem of adjusting to a continuous change of stewards is avoided by the workers in his department. The men are unsure of a new steward until they test him out. Being on trial tends to make the steward overplay his role, to the

[46] Gardner, *op. cit.*, p. 115.

irritation of the foreman. Since all work relations have a strain toward stabilization, foremen and workers prefer to deal with the same steward, who, whatever his shortcoming, is sincere and reliable.

A poem from the *CIO News* glorifies the steward.[47]

The Steward

Who's the guy that gets the grief,
Takes abuse beyond belief,
Bends the ear without relief?
  It's the steward!

He tries to keep the group intact,
Sifts the rumor from the fact;
In a pinch, who has to act?
  It's the steward!

When the opposition's tough
And the going's plenty rough.
Does he say he's had enough?
  Not the steward.

With a cheer they pick him out,
But let one judgment be in doubt,
Comes the cry, "Let's kick him out!"
  The poor steward.

When he's hammered out a raise
After sweating nights and days—
Does he get a bit of praise?
  Ask the steward.

When St. Peter swings the gate
Stand aside and let us wait,
There's one guy that ought to rate—
  It's the steward.

REWARDS OF STEWARDSHIP

The job of steward is a thankless task because it is almost a continuous mediation process. The steward is constantly trying to adjust conditions which are irritating to one or more workers. Since he cannot be uniformly successful, he bears the antagonism of some of his fellows. In plants where unionism is not fully accepted, he may be disliked by the foremen including his own. We have already signified that his reward depends on his orienta-

[47] *Michigan CIO News*, December 15, 1948.

tion. If he seeks to climb in the management or union hierarchy, he realizes that he must make sacrifices to impress officials.

One reward automatically granted to the steward is seniority. He is last to be released and first to be hired. This is not an inconsiderable reward especially during depressed times. Other rewards make the position attractive to some. For one thing, the steward receives special attention from workers and management alike. In a mass-impersonal situation attention may provide considerable gratification. The prestige and respect the steward receives from his fellow workers may be an adequate substitute for occupational mobility. A more simple reward, especially where the job is routine and monotonous, may be the welcome release from ennui and boredom. For one or more of these reasons, stewards continue to be recruited from among the workers. Thus, the first line of the union develops its strength by appealing to different motives and different satisfactions. Management and the union are equally challenged to find good first-line leadership, to attract it to their organization, and to retain its loyalty.

CONCLUSION

The union local is the basic unit of the formal organization of labor. It is a part of a larger institution which seeks to satisfy both economic and noneconomic needs of the membership. The local, like the union movement in general, arises from the need for group protection in an insecure environment.

The formal organization of the local theoretically follows a democratic model. Election, voting, responsibility—all the paraphernalia of democracy are part of the organizational machinery of the local. It follows that unions will inevitably find themselves in the midst of many political problems which confront any democratic organization. Cleavages develop between members and elected officials, machine organizations evolve, and politics is played. As in large democratic structures, much of the direction of union affairs is left in the hands of elected officials. The latter have many roles to play. The organizational setting of the union makes it difficult for leaders to play these roles as they are formally prescribed. Not only are the roles internally contradictory; they also operate at cross-purposes. The strength and weakness of union organization flow from the problem of mass democracy inherent in it and from the contradictory roles officers must play.

The everyday activities of the union on the plant floor are carried on by the steward. How he plays his role depends on his orientation. His activities, like those of the chief officers of the organization, are delimited by the dictates of democratic organization and the particular situations in his department. These situations develop around the work group and the social

expectations which are peculiar to it. In the following chapter we shall investigate the factors that are important in the social life of workers in the plant.

SUPPLEMENTARY STUDIES

FIELD OBSERVATION: DIRECT OBSERVATION OF A SELECTED WORK PLANT
(Continued)

In the work plant selected analyze:
Structure and Operation of the Union Local
Describe:
1. Chain of command (a) line, (b) staff.
2. Segmentation of the structure.
3. Work positions and work roles.
4. Exercise of power and influence.
5. Cleavage and conflicts.
6. Relations with union members.
7. Relations with management.

FIELD INTERVIEWS: PLANNED

If possible secure a top labor executive, a business agent, and a steward to make up a panel. The chief assistants to each of these officials often prove to be useful resource persons if the major line officials are not available. Ask them to speak on the following:
1. Describe your day from the time you awake until you retire.
2. Describe any "off-the-job" or "duty" contact your work imposes or encourages.
3. What social clubs and other community activities do you engage in? Do you regard these as important to the union? Do you regard these as useful to your advancement in the union?
4. What are the pressures that your job induces?
5. What cleavages and conflicts between members and groups must you recognize and live with? What successes have you had in reducing any of these conflicts?
6. What are the most effective ways to get loyalty from membership? (a) short run, (b) long run.
7. Do you think the basic interests of management and the basic interests of workers are directly opposed, identical, irreconcilable?
8. What advice would you give a young college man or woman who seeks a career in a union organization?

FIELD INTERVIEWS: CASUAL

Talk with some union members you know. Ask them why they are members, how their union operates, and what they get out of their membership in the union.

LIBRARY: BOOKS AND ARTICLES

Archibald, Katherine, *Wartime Shipyard*, University of California Press, 1947, chapters on "Unions" and "Class Consciousness," pp. 128-184.

Barbash, Jack, *Labor Unions in Action*, Harper & Brothers, 1948.

Ginsberg, Eli, *The Labor Leader*, The Macmillan Co., 1948. See Chapter, "The Parkiston Local."

Goulder, Alvin, "Attitudes of 'Progressive' Trade Union Leaders," *American Journal of Sociology*, March, 1947, pp. 389-392.

Mills, C. Wright, and Schneider, Helen, *New Men of Power: America's Labor Leaders*, Harcourt, Brace and Company, 1948.

Selekman, Benjamin M., *Labor Relations and Human Relations*, McGraw-Hill Book Company, Inc., 1947, chap. 8, "Wanted: Mature Labor Leaders," pp. 173-210.

Ross, Arthur, *Trade Union Wage Policy*, University of California Press, 1948, Chapter 2, "The Union as a Wage Fixing Institution."

Shepard, Herbert A., "Democratic Control in a Labor Union," *American Journal of Sociology*, January, 1949, pp. 311-316.

Starr, Mark, "Role of Union Organization," in *Industry and Society*, edited by William F. Whyte, McGraw-Hill Book Company, Inc., 1946.

Whyte, William F., "Who Goes Union and Why," *Personnel Journal*, December, 1944, pp. 215-230.

RESEARCH GAPS

1. Informal social structure in the union local.
2. The career pattern of the union leader.
3. Role problems of the steward.

CHAPTER IX

The Informal Organization of Labor[1]

[1] Although the informal organization of labor is treated in more detail than the informal organization of management, the principles which underlie both are the same. Unfortunately, there is more data available on this subject in labor than in management. We do not concur that informal organization is more fully developed in labor than in management.

INTRODUCTION

MANAGERIAL MYOPIA

Many American businessmen operate with a rather simple picture of work life. The objective of life is "success," that is, the maximization of production and profit. The ingredients of success (apart from individual ability) are improved technology, trained personnel, and good organization. If success is not forthcoming, one of these ingredients is lacking. The prescription in any case is simple and obvious. Get new machinery, get better-trained people, and undergo a thorough reorganization.

Administrators have clung to this simple view of their universe despite mounting contrary evidence. For example, many plants with antiquated machinery, untrained personnel, and haphazard organization seem to defy dire predictions of doom.[2] How can one explain the fact that plants with modern equipment, highly trained engineers, and model organizational schemes sometimes flounder in the economic struggle? During World War II some of the new defense plants which had the best equipment, personnel, and administrative organization had poor production records. What is more remarkable, people often preferred to work in older, poorly lighted, poorly ventilated, and ill-kept plants.[3] The literature is replete with instances of industrial strife in plants that were considered technical and organizational models.

To explain such occurrences executives have examined "intangibles" like morale, teamwork, and coöperation. Characteristically, they defined these intangibles largely in terms of production and profits. Thus, they conceived morale as a willingness to work hard and produce. However, what is morale in one organization is not morale in another. Workers may have high

---

[2] William J. Goode and Irving Fowler, "Incentive Factors in a Low Morale Plant," *American Sociological Review*, October, 1949, pp. 618-623.

[3] E. Mayo, *Social Problems of an Industrial Civilization*, Harvard University Press, 1945, p. 96. Cf. Peter Drucker, "Why Men Strike," *Harper's Magazine*, November, 1946, p. 391.

internal morale when they participate in a slowdown or strike. That many businessmen do not consider this morale testifies to their inability to deal with human and social problems.

To be sure, executives believe that they have attended to "human problems" when they study supervision, wage rates, and incentive schemes. In previous chapters we have signified that these are primarily human problems in formal organization. Businessmen and labor officials have devoted too much thought to this kind of organization and not enough to the sum total of social organization in the plant, including informal organization.

Informal organization constitutes that network of personal and social relations which are not defined or prescribed by formal organization. It may be thought of in a residual sense, as including every aspect of social life that is not anticipated by technological and formal relations.

SEGMENTS OF INFORMAL ORGANIZATION

Informal organization is a rather complex structure, made up of the following interrelated items:

1. Congeniality groups, as gangs, friendships, and cliques.
2. An organization and structure which defines the relations between these groups, in terms of rights, obligations, prestige, and influence.
3. Codes of conduct for group members, including customs and norms. These may be arbitrarily divided into two sections:
   a. *Internal* codes, which regulate activities within the informal social organization.
   b. *External* codes, which regulate activities toward formal organization (management and union) and other formally or informally organized out-groups.
4. Scheme of ideas, beliefs, and values which underlie and support the code of conduct and group activities, such as "folk" knowledge, prejudices, stereotypes, myths, and ideologies which give meaning to occurrences.
5. Informal group activities, related to or independent of formal work behavior. Ceremonies, rites, gambling, recreation, swearing, and joking.
6. Communication systems which inform members of ideas, sentiments, and occurrences vital to group solidarity and action.

Since organization is an interrelated functioning organism, the division of informal organization into these six sections is an arbitrary, but convenient, way to understand the subject. Each aspect of informal organization will be described below in detail.

ILLUSTRATIONS OF INFORMAL ORGANIZATION IN OPERATION

One apparent reason why informal social organization has been infrequently recognized is that it is often invisible to the untrained observer. When any organization is running smoothly, it is natural to assume that

the formal structure is in control. However, unusual things do happen in work plants which cannot be explained by analysis of the formal organization alone. Some of these "unexplainable" events include the following:

A wildcat strike occurs without forewarning.

Union members will not respond to the discipline of their officers.

A union is "suddenly" organized without apparent aid from organizers, in a situation where "unrest" was unknown to managers.

Absenteeism rises suddenly without apparent cause.

There is a rash of stealing, destructiveness, and sabotage.

A brawl occurs during an executive conference between two groups which had shown no evidence of antagonism in previous meetings.

One department excels another comparable department in production, earnings, and performance without apparent cause.

A group inaugurates a number of social functions—as dances, athletics, and picnics—whereas another group never engages in social affairs.

A rumor sweeps through the plant like wildfire: The plant is going to close down or move away, a big bonus is coming through, Negroes are going to be hired, and so on.

As long as events such as these are regarded as irregularities, the observer is not fully aware of existent informal social organization. He is likely to explain occurrences in terms of the personalities involved, their insidious motives, or unusual circumstances.

IMPORTANCE OF INFORMAL ORGANIZATION

Everyone has at one time or another recognized that his interpersonal relations are critical to his success or failure. Sometimes these relations take the form of "pull," "drag," "prejudice," and "favoritism." In America such things are regarded as unfortunate, undemocratic, and perhaps somewhat inevitable. They are considered private problems outside the realm of scientific investigation.

As a matter of fact, pull, favoritism, and prejudice are group phenomena capable of sociological investigation. They occur in work plants as an extension of friendships, clique life, and personal antagonisms. Anyone who studies friendships, cliques, and hostilities of a group will find that they constitute an integrated system of relationships. As such, they are as much a part of the social organization of industry as the supervisory and the union structures. Thus, informal relations are not accidental, incidental, or tangential to the operation of industry. On the contrary, no organization can function effectively if it does not contain a parallel spontaneous network of interpersonal relations.

The study of informal organization is important if for no other reason than that it is needed to get the *entire* picture of organization. The student

of industry needs to know how *both* formal and informal organizations operate. The relationship between these two types of organization is not supplementary but interactive. In a very real sense, then, it is impossible to understand how the supervisory structure actually operates without systematic knowledge of the ongoing informal social organization in it. It is equally true that knowledge of informal organization is made more meaningful when it is considered in relation to the formal structure with which it is interacting.

To understand informal organization it is helpful to get down to cases. True, a theory of informal organization can be applied anywhere, just as the theory of formal organization can be applied in any large work plant. The fact that peculiar conditions exist in specific work plants and situations means, however, that "local" knowledge is needed to interpret the operation of both structures. Although there is consensus on how formal structure should operate, there is no such normative conception for informal organization. Therefore, it is useful to study informal organization by the case method to see what forms it takes.

Such knowledge may be used to bridge gaps between divergent groups; it may likewise be used to promote cleavages and antagonism between them. The sociologist is not concerned with how knowledge should be applied. His job is to find out why people behave as they do in the spontaneous groups which they build. A considerable body of data has been developed on this process. Perhaps by outlining the technique of studying informal organizations we can show how it arises.

HOW TO STUDY INFORMAL ORGANIZATION

THE NEED FOR GROUP MYOPIA

To study informal organization or any kind of organization one must study existing social relations. This simple and obvious fact is more often ignored than recognized. Even social scientists sometimes forget that their *unit of observation is the social relationship* and not the individual.

Roethlisberger and Dickson, who pioneered in the study of informal organization in industry, suffered from the common misconception of the nature of the group. They felt that it was necessary to study each individual to get a picture of the group. Finally, by examining every person's relations to others, they concluded that they were actually observing a group and not a number of individuals.[4] In other words, they ended where they should have begun—with a hypothesis that individuals reflect the previous existence of a group.

[4] F. J. Roethlisberger and William J. Dickson, *Management and the Worker*, Harvard University Press, 1947, chaps. 7 and 17.

The conception of the group as an additive phenomenon is difficult to erase. It is pictured thus:

$$\text{Individuals } A + B + C + D = \text{Group}$$

The sociologist begins with a different approach. He recognizes that the individual can be understood only in process of *interacting* with other people. He is less interested in persons than in their interrelations. *Inter-relationship defines the group, not a mere collection of individuals.* Thus a number of women shoppers crowding the street on a Friday afternoon do not compose a group. A diagram showing the interactive and sociological conception of a group follows.

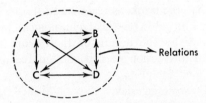

If a person wants to study informal social life in a work plant he must almost slavishly follow a few simple rules. They are:

1. Keep your eye *primarily* on people, and secondarily on what they are producing or servicing.
2. Observe how they *react to each other.*
3. Listen to what they say and don't say; observe what they do and don't do in reference to each other.
4. Note the degree to which saying and doing jibe with each other.
5. Find the ideas, beliefs, and attitudes on which they generally agree or disagree.
6. Appraise how stable or unstable your findings are as situations change.
7. Do not become a factor in the situation you are observing. If this is impossible, try to analyze your relations to the group as you would analyze any other person's.[5]

Moreover, as the observer moves into a specific work situation, he should have some questions which he wants answered, some hunches that he wants to test, and some ideas on how to get the best answers. Although questions, hypotheses, and methodology will vary with research interests, a few basic guides to research in informal organization will be helpful.

TECHNICAL, SOCIOTECHNICAL, AND SOCIAL BEHAVIOR

The first thing an observer should determine is which behavior is *essentially* technical, which is sociotechnical, and which is social. These three

[5] This difficult problem is discussed in an important article by Burleigh B. Gardner and William Foote Whyte, "Methods for the Study of Human Relations in Industry," *American Sociological Review*, October, 1946, pp. 506-512.

types of behavior should not be confused, and the relations between them should be ascertained.

Behavior which is essentially technical is usually referred to as "skill." The tailor cutting his cloth, the draftsman drawing his plans, the researcher conducting an experiment are largely engaged in technical behavior. Thus, a drill press operator can do his job whether he is an introvert or an extrovert, single or married, Negro or white, Protestant or Catholic, in the presence or absence of other people. Much of this behavior may be thought of as nonsocial. It is the chief interest of the engineer and the apprentice, not of the social scientist. The only social aspect to technical behavior is the social rank or meaning that others assign it. Thus the performance of the job may be affected by the worker's reaction to its social rank.[6] Not much work activity begins and ends on the technological level, for workers are also forced to interact by the nature of their work. Technical behavior which involves social interaction may be designated as *sociotechnical behavior*.

Let us examine the sociotechnical behavior of an "isolated" cloth cutter in a mill. In the morning he goes to the supply depot to get his cloth, or the buggyman delivers it to him. The cutter must give the supply clerk a check or receipt. A few times a day a foreman checks his work, complains about the wastages and bad cuttings. Occasionally he is handed company notices. At the end of the week someone gives him a pay check or his wages. Once in a while he is asked to teach his job to a new worker. Once a month he attends a union or company meeting. All these are social acts that are incumbent on him as a cloth cutter and worker. In short, some social behavior is a necessary component to technical behavior and cannot be totally separated from it. It is as much a part of the job as are the manual skills.[7]

Jobs vary in the amount of sociotechnical behavior they contain. Members of a repair crew or assembly team, foremen, salesmen have jobs with considerable sociotechnical behavior. The point where sociotechnical behavior may be distinguished from purely technical on the one hand and purely social on the other is difficult to make. In some occupations the purely technical and sociotechnical behaviors overlap and coincide almost completely. This is especially the case for the personnel director, the interviewer, the industrial relations expert, and others. Human relations are their business. Their technical skills are skills in interpersonal relations.

The third level of work behavior is purely social. Whenever people interact in formal organization they tend to develop interests in each other as persons. Any behavior which is not a function of formal organization is

---

[6] See William Foote Whyte, *Human Relations in the Restaurant Industry*, Mc-Graw-Hill Book Company, Inc., 1948, chap. 4, "Status in the Kitchen."

[7] See F. L. W. Richardson, Jr., and Charles R. Walker, "Work Flow and Human Relations," *Harvard Business Review*, January, 1949, pp. 107-122.

social. Joking, razzing, eating lunch together, playing cards, cutting down on production are examples of social behavior. Of course, it is necessary to realize how each type of behavior affects the other. Razzing may arise out of the inability to practice the technical skills correctly, and interpersonal tensions may arise out of contacts which are sociotechnical in nature.

Technical organization and sociotechnical behavior must be analyzed in order to have a bench mark with which to compare social behavior. Technical organization throws some workers together, keeps others segregated, permits others to have contacts. The formation of many informal groupings may be largely explained in terms of the formal and technical organization of the work plant. If it develops where one would *not* expect it (because of sociotechnical differences in occupational routines), one is impelled to look for the motives of such behavior.

In addition to the effect of technical organization on social contacts, there are a number of *shop rules*, policies, and practices that affect social life in the plant. They may deal with the amount of talking permitted on the job, the routine to follow in case of an accident, how to contact the steward, whom to see about a suggestion, complaint, or assistance. These data must be known beforehand to enable the investigator to evaluate whether the behavior of workers happens to be formally or informally prescribed. When the total amount of interaction is compared with that made necessary by sociotechnical behavior and shop rules, we have an index of the degree to which informal organization has grown. In some cases it may even be useful as an index of union or company morale.

SHOP TALK

Talking is an important part of social behavior. "People have ears but they hear not," applies to the world of work as well as to other areas. A complex theory is not needed to analyze the role of talk in informal organization. To assume that most shop talk is unimportant is to ignore an area of great social significance. Largely by listening to what people say one can learn their attitudes, values, sentiments, and idea systems. Once these things are known, it is possible to give meaning and interpretation to behavior and social events.

Amount of Talking

Many executives who prohibit talking believe that it interferes with work. This may be true for some jobs but not for others. In fact, in many routine jobs, conversation not only may improve performance but indicates a degree of adjustment to the job. In other circumstances the absence of talking may point to explosive situations in the making. Compatible workers with similar backgrounds and interests may be expected to be garrulous, and incompatible workers with different backgrounds may not communicate.

In some cases, then, concern should be felt because there is little talking among workers.

Preliminary observations on informal organization may be made by noting the amount of talk. The questions that should be raised are: How much talking is possible in this kind of work situation? How much conversing is necessary for these jobs to get done in the technical sense? How much talking is permitted by foremen and others? During what time of day is talking at its highest peak and its lowest ebb? What kinds of events in the shop occasion most discussion? Does the amount of talk vary with the presence or absence of the boss?

Answers to these questions provide the first crude notions of normal behavior on the job, amount of solidarity among workers, attitude toward supervisors, and amount of group morale.

Who Talks?

Obviously some people will talk all of the time, some people part of the time, and others very little. In and of itself such observation has little meaning except to suggest personality differences. When data of who talks and how much are related to action, they become more meaningful. For example, the person who chatters endlessly may be assigned by the group the informal role of "scatterbrain." When careful attention is given to the comments of one person, he may be playing the role of the informal leader or educator. Analysis of who is allowed to "hold the floor" may indicate status and deference patterns in the work group.

Content of Talking

The content of conversation must be analyzed to understand informal organization of the group. If a group is organized it must share a minimum of common ideas, ideals, sentiments, and attitudes. A long interview or questionnaire is usually not needed to obtain the basic thoughts and feelings of a group. A content analysis of their conversations correlated to group behavior is a more naturalistic and realistic way to get a picture of group life.

From a content analysis of conversation we can obtain vital information on the group's interests. Does the worker talk mostly about production, baseball, sex, job climbing, or the union? What kinds of incidents that occur seem to be systematically avoided in the conversations? Do they concern the foreman, the size of the take-home pay, or the conduct of union leaders? Thus, basic data on informal group life would contain an analysis of interest and avoidance subjects ranked in order of the amount of talk. A ranking of interest-avoidance subjects such as appears below provides a basis for understanding the context of informal organization. These subjects may be rearranged along different axes, such as the priorities of

worry, the priorities of changes desired in the department, the priorities of job aspirations, and so on.

Interest Subjects	Avoidance Subjects
Baseball and sex	New foreman
The change of the work rate	Foreman training program
The Proposed medical plan	Union election

Talk and the Sentiment-Value System

From a content analysis of conversation, the basic sentiment and value system of the group under observation may be discerned. When the primary ideas, ideals, symbols, stereotypes, myths, folklore, and ideologies are uncovered, group activities and processes are capable of being fully understood.

It is particularly important to know the value system because it furnishes knowledge of the basis of group integration or lack of it. Although the group may be located in an economic organization, its cohesion may derive from noneconomic ties in ethnic, religious, political, or other associations. Of course the observer should be especially aware of the values which directly affect behavior in the plant. Sentiments about property, supervisors, taking orders, security and unemployment, savings and investment, politics and government, superior and inferior classes are some of the basic items to study.

In addition, it is vital to segregate which values, sentiments, and behavior patterns are held by the entire group, which are shared only partially, and which are divergent in nature. In a later section of this chapter we shall demonstrate how the value-sentiment system not only provides the basis for informal organization but also explains the unpredictable occurrences in the formal and technical organizations.

OVERT BEHAVIOR

Data on informal organization may also be gathered by direct observation of overt behavior. First it is desirable to locate people socially with respect to certain basic categories of occupation, sex, seniority, age, prestige, and authority. When groups are examined according to these and other factors, the social composition of the participants of each activity may be known.

At first, simple things may be observed, as who eats lunch with whom, who exchange jobs, who participate in horseplay, who are members of a car pool. Which people play together in and out of the plant? Who entertains whom? What groups form before, during, and after working hours? How persistent are they? What customs are developed for amusement, to display social solidarity or hostility? What folkways and rituals arise to express group attitudes toward "superiors" and "inferiors"? How is a new worker inducted into an informal group? How are informal groups tied together?

Other interesting things may be learned by posing simple questions. The stratification in informal groups may be obtained by observing who defers to whom in *any* kind of activity. Other patterns may be found by noticing who initiates action, who follows, and who assumes *what roles* in what activities. In a later section we shall suggest some answers to these questions. Before this is attempted, however, a basic problem must be explored: the factors responsible for informal group formation and persistence. This may best be done by selecting an actual illustration for analysis.

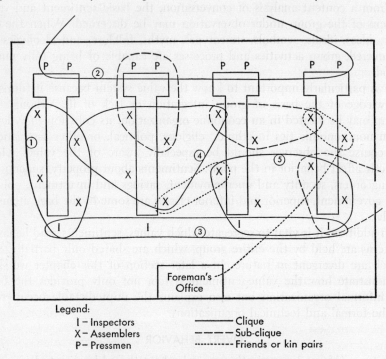

Legend:
I – Inspectors   ——— Clique
X – Assemblers   – – – Sub-clique
P – Pressmen   ·········· Friends or kin pairs

FIG. 38.   The Informal Clique Structure in a Small Department.

SOCIAL BASES OF INFORMAL NUCLEATIONS

Figure 38 pictures the informal clique structure in a department of a small Ohio airplane headlight factory. Obviously this structure differs from the formal structure. The latter recognizes only occupational distinctions among the workers. They are: foremen, inspectors, pressmen, assemblers. The informal organization, on the other hand, is much more complex. It is an unplanned structure that arises out of the spontaneous interaction of people. No doubt occupation and position in the supervisory structure play a role in the creation of informal groupings. However, other personal and social characteristics of workers play an equally important part. Together

these formal, personal, and social factors provide the basis for group and clique formation.

CLIQUES

Figure 38 shows a number of overlapping groups. For arbitrary purposes these groups are labeled cliques, sub-cliques, and friendships. Informal groups are located by finding patterns of congeniality, social interaction, and consensus. For our purposes a clique includes several members who commonly associate, and a friendship group reflects *closer* association and compatibility of two or three work associates. The interlocking of these cliques, sub-cliques, and friendships throughout the entire work plant constitutes the plant's informal organization. Although informal ties connect management and labor groups, such connections are not as numerous as the ties within these groups. Two separate informal structures tend to develop, especially in the larger unionized work plants. In this chapter we shall describe the informal relations existing among the workers.

Obviously these spontaneous, unplanned groups are very important to the worker. They are responsible for his social satisfactions on the job. From them he derives prestige and recognition of his personal qualities and problems. His ideas, ideals, and sentiments are forged within these groups. In short, he is a member of many groups, and his behavior is largely explained in terms of group pressures and customs.

The job of the sociologist is to explain how these spontaneous groups arise, what their social basis of membership is, what functions they serve, and what behavior typifies them. We shall first turn our attention to their social basis of membership.

Occupational Bases

The formation of cliques in a work plant may often be explained in terms of occupational or technical distinctions among the workers. Those who have similar occupations tend to form status groups with informal membership rules. This is especially the case where workers have highly developed skills or crafts. Cottrell's study of the railroader documents the importance of occupation in the informal groupings and work relationships on the job.[8] He describes how a regular status hierarchy, from firemen, engineers, and brakemen down to repairmen and section hands, controls group membership and customary behavior on the job. Although the clerks, station agents, and traffic department representatives have high white-collar status, they are not considered by others to be in the railroad craft. Pullman conductors, although in the craft, are not considered to be "regular" trainmen.

[8] W. Fred Cottrell, The Railroader, Stanford University Press, 1940, especially chap. 3, "Technological and Social Groupings."

Sometimes very small job distinctions are singled out as the basis for group identification. Whyte's study of social groupings within the restaurant industry indicates that those who work with fish have lower rank than those who work with meat. Workers who specialize very slightly in the preparation of certain foods form cliques which are antagonistic toward cliques of other food "specialists."[9] The differences in function between professional ranks in colleges are minimal, yet sufficiently large to furnish bases for group affiliation.

In addition to occupation, or in place of it, the social bases of informal group membership may be age, nationality, seniority, regional origin, or other factors. Solidarity arising from these ties may then be expressed through occupational pride, exchanging jobs, and mutual aid.

Let us examine the role of occupation in the formation of the informal groups portrayed in Figure 38. There we have located five major cliques, three sub-cliques, and three friendship pairs. The inspectors, pressmen, and clique 4 (assemblers) form occupationally homogeneous groups, and so do one sub-clique and two friendship pairs (assemblers). However, cliques 1 and 5 and two sub-cliques cross job lines. Other factors besides technical distinctions on the job are responsible for social groupings because people in the same occupation often belong to different groups.

Spatial or Ecological Factors

Space may be an important factor in the formation of cliques. The first requisite of a group is communication, and the most rapid communication arises from face-to-face contact. Although daily face-to-face contacts need not occasion intimacy, they will lead to interaction over and above that required by sociotechnical relations. This is especially the case where physical mobility on the job is limited. If those who work next to each other perform similar jobs, interaction is facilitated, but it will usually occur regardless of occupational specialization.

Thus in Figure 38 the inspectors regarded themselves as socially superior and expressed their solidarity by eating together, going to movies, riding to work together, and going to the washroom in pairs. However, they also participated in cliques 1 and 5 as well. These two cliques, clique 4, and the sub-cliques and friendship pairs appear to be based on proximity.

Since sociotechnical interaction was necessary between inspectors and assemblers, cliques containing both assemblers and inspectors developed. In these, inspectors tended to become the informal leaders for they initiated such activities as birthday parties, lunch trading, shopping sprees, and mutual aid.

It is difficult to ascertain what groups would form naturally on the basis of physical proximity alone. The arrangement of walls, machines, and pro-

[9] Whyte, op. cit., chap. 4, "Status in the Kitchen."

duction technique is rarely so constituted as to force a particular nucleation. In Figure 38, for example, some of the members in the pressmen's clique and the sub-clique of clique 5 belonged in other departments. The pressmen were the only men in the department in question. They received higher pay and had more status than the women. They ate lunch together and engaged in recreation activities with men in other departments.

Where status and other social differences are not great, spatial proximity plays a more important role in the process of group making. Over a period of time, spatial recognition may be granted to social cohesion. Thus, the older workers tend to locate near each other, as do members of ethnic groups, races, neighborhood cliques, and others. Once recognition is attached to a given location ("that's where the old-timers hang out"), space becomes an important social item around which sentiments and attitudes are formed.

Status or Prestige Elements[10]

It is characteristic of prestige to adhere to almost any personal or social attribute in or out of the plant. As a consequence, informal groups tend to be ranked in terms of their prestige differences. The cliques in Figure 38 were ranked in prestige in the following order. From high to low:

> Pressmen—clique 2
> Inspectors—clique 3
> Old girls—clique 1
> Italian girls—clique 4
> Love-doves—north center sub-clique
> High school crowd—clique 5
> Old hens—northeast sub-clique

Extra-Plant Indices

The bases of status distinctions arise from both internal (plant) differences and external (extra-plant) factors. In the headlight factory occupational rank, an internal plant factor was the basis of the prestige of the two highest cliques. Seniority was the basis for solidarity in clique 1. Nationality, being in love, coming from the same high school, and being old married women seem to be the ties in the remaining cliques. Although these social characteristics are not directly related to plant operation, they are important in determining status groups within the plant. The workers themselves do not distinguish between plant and extra-plant personal and social attributes when they rank one another informally. This fact may be documented with an illustration:

General Motors has a large parts plant located in the outskirts of a

[10] This subject is treated in detail in Chapter XI, "Status Organization of the Work Plant."

middle-sized city in New York State. Its workers are recruited from the city and from the rural fringe. Residence seems to be fundamental in the formation of cliques in the plant. Those from the rural fringe associate with each other, discuss their farms, sell the produce they raise, vote Republican, and avoid criticism of management. They are regarded as "squares" by the urban cliques. The latter engage in recreational activities, sports talk, and drinking. There is no union in this plant, and questions of raises, promotions, and other squabbles are more closely related to the rural-urban origin of the participants than to other conditions.

Other "outside" factors may underlie nucleation or cleavages in the informal organization of industry. Some of these factors include membership in a car pool, personal compatibility, religious or organizational affiliation, political beliefs, social class origin, occupational aspiration, ethnic or racial background. Several studies have been made which demonstrate the force of special social factors in formation of informal groups.[11]

Multiple Factors

More than one factor usually underlies group formation or cleavages. Nationality, seniority, technical skill, and attitude toward unions may operate simultaneously to form a group. Group members are rarely homogeneous in respect to all social indices. Thus, in Figure 38 one girl in the Italian clique was of Scotch origin, a "new" girl was included in the "old bunch," and so on.

Common social background may be important in bringing people together, but the common experiences which mold a set of attitudes, sentiments, and customs on the job become increasingly important with time. After a group is formed, a person is admitted or expelled from it depending on his acceptance or rejectance of the group's sentiments and customs. The demographic characteristics of the group may change, but it is still the same group as long as the sentiments and customs persist in an atmosphere of personal and social compatibility. A group may remain intact despite the incompatibility of some of its members, but it is no longer a clique in the strict sense of the word.

RELATING CLIQUES

If the above view of informal organization were abandoned at this point we would have a distorted and biased picture of it. Many students have tended to equate clique organizations with informal organization. They have been so engrossed with the importance of the small group that they

[11] Everett C. Hughes, "Knitting of Racial Groups in Industry," *American Sociological Review*, October, 1946; Orvis Collins, "Ethnic Behavior in Industry," *American Journal of Sociology*, January, 1946; Leslie O. Zeleny, "Selection of Compatible Flying Partners," *American Journal of Sociology*, March, 1947.

have become small-group cultists. One almost suspects that they crave to rediscover the small sentiment-bound groups that may have been more extensive in a bygone era. Some "progressive" managers, when informed about the pervasiveness of clique organization, have considered reordering production to encourage small groups at the expense of large ones. Their thought is that it may be easier to manipulate smaller cliques than large formal groups, such as the union.

Both students and administrators should realize that a giant sociogram of the clique structure of a plant would still constitute an incomplete picture of the plant's informal organization. Although the diagram would show that groups and cliques were related, it would not show *how* they were related. The social bonds or lack of them among the cliques must be *qualitatively* studied to determine their significance.

In Figure 38 several cliques were located. They might have been located quickly by merely asking people whom they preferred to work with, and then plotting all of their choices. But this would not have meant much without knowledge of the existing social situation. Cliques may reflect antagonistic relations between groups. They may, on the other hand, merely point to a haphazard distribution of congeniality groups. After all, there is a limit to the number of people that can go to lunch together, converse, or play cards.

When cliques do not reflect rivalry, antagonisms, or divisions of sociability, greater significance may reside in inter-clique relations. The important social fact is that cliques may be segments of larger groups which remain unrevealed by typical sociometric questions. Thus a sociogram of the clique structure of a plant may not reveal the presence of larger informally organized publics. The significances of cliques in a particular factory may be that they represent the cell structure of a nascent labor union. In this case clique integration is more important than the knowledge of independent cliques, for the cliques here represent a communication system and not internal group cleavages. The question must always be raised, Do cliques represent cleavages or integration? If no sentiments tie the cliques together, a plant does not have an informal organization in the full sense of the term. It has only a bunch of cliques incapable of uniting for or against management or labor on any issue. Administrations need not "worry" so much about the existence of cliques as they might about the integration of cliques.

Cliques and Issues

The technique of locating cliques is based upon knowledge of association patterns such as eating, work trading, car pool participation, talking, friendship, and visiting. An intensive analysis of cliques may show that in some cases these indices are not sensitive to other social relations within the

cliques. Many people who eat together, ride to work together, and trade jobs are not congenial or compatible. In fact, they may despise each other, argue incessantly, and fight over many issues. Such nucleations, then, are not congeniality groups but patterns of association.

An over-intensive concentration on cliques may blind the investigator to issues which are broader than locality cliques. The important issues in the plant may be union organization, seniority systems, retirement plans, and recreational programs. Some cliques may be split internally on these issues, some may be internally united, some people from various cliques may unite on an issue. In the last case the workers are part of a *public* scattered all over the plant. They would not appear as a clique in a sociogram. Publics may be more important in some instances than congeniality groups or cliques. The activities of the public may explain what happens both within the plant and within the cliques.

This is especially the case when cliques are amorphous nuclei which break and re-form with changing issues and problems. Cliques form and shatter quickly when large numbers of people are being formally organized into a union or a pressure group. After a period the cliques may stabilize and become polarized. They then may exhibit social stratification, division of labor, "foreign" relations, and other attributes. Cliques should be analyzed also for their degree of integration and persistence. They may be tightly knit all-purpose cliques, tightly knit one-purpose cliques, or loosely knit all- or one-purpose cliques.

The study of cliques within formal organizations is important because it is the operation of the formal structure that may give meaning to clique *functions*. Many cliques and publics would not be created were not the "need" for them inherent in the formal policies of union and management leaders. Poor formal organization often forces cliques to arise, so that the job may be done. In addition, cliques may communicate with each other through the channels provided by formal organization. The interaction of formal and informal organization is as critical a study as are the activities of either organization.

THE TOTAL PICTURE

From an organizational point of view, informal organization may be perceived on five levels:
1. The general overall system of interlocking groups of all kinds.
2. Major publics, which may include interrelated cliques arising out of major local plant issues. These are often referred to as "crowds" or "bunches" or "gangs."
3. Cliques and congeniality groups formed more or less on the locality basis and engaging in common activities, as eating, joking, and work exchange.

4. Very intimate friends who may be part of larger cliques.
5. Isolated individuals who participate rarely in any kind of social life in the plant.

THE WORK CULTURE OF INFORMAL ORGANIZATIONS[12]

Every persistent group, including occupational and industrial groups, tends to develop a peculiar pattern of behavior. A newcomer to a work group is often made painfully aware of the fact that learning the job is only part of what he has to know to get along. He's got to learn "who's who" (informal status system), "what's what" (the local situation), "the ropes" (the way of doing things), and even how to talk. The mature worker has assimilated the local culture so completely that he is often unaware that new workers are expected to conform to a rigid set of behavior patterns. Only the "greenhorn" and the individualist make him aware that he has learned something that others need to know.

The culture of informal work groups is varied, and may be learned only by studying local situations. However, an outline of the content and structure of work culture may be made for groups of similar social background. In this section we shall focus primarily on the work culture of manual employees. One thing that is a constant in work culture, irrespective of situation, is the culture and customs surrounding particular occupations.

OCCUPATIONAL CULTURE

Each new job does not require the worker to learn a new set of customs, traditions, rituals, and beliefs. Many of the customs practiced in particular work situations may be found existing elsewhere. An experienced railroader, carpenter, thief, or college professor has learned the folkways of his group. He knows how a "proper" railroader, thief, or carpenter should behave, and acts accordingly. His induction into a new work situation will be relatively rapid and easy, for "he knows the ropes and the score."

Apart from the fact that the experienced worker knows the occupational culture, he is also aware that no two work groups are exactly alike. On entering a new one, he is careful to find out "the way things are done here." He does not act without thinking; he asks leading questions; he "feels out" the group until he finds out or is told what the local culture is. The neophyte, on the other hand, must learn not only the occupational culture but local culture as well.

Much of occupational culture concerns technical operations on the job. A novice may be noticed because he does his work exactly as he was taught.

[12] All the material in this section applies equally well to management organization. The subject is treated here merely for the sake of convenience.

An experienced worker often violates the theoretical pattern of work routines. He has learned, or was taught on the job, certain short cuts, acceptable alternative routines, needless elaboration or refinement on some parts of the job, older manual processes now only rarely used, skills of closely related jobs, and other things.

OCCUPATIONAL LANGUAGE

Part of the occupational culture is the development of jargon and a technical language and argot. Jargon is developed more extensively among highly skilled workers because "everyday language" does not contain words that refer to objects and occurrences at work. Listening to chemists, sociologists, toolmakers, or auto mechanics "talking shop" soon convinces the observer that he has to learn a new language to understand them.

The words that are substitutes for ordinary traditional words constitute an occupational argot.[13] Sometimes the argot has a semitechnical use—as an abbreviation for a longer phrase—but it also has a social function of identifying group members and creating social cohesion. The armed services have developed both a technical vocabulary and an argot. The words "floor," "ceiling," "walls," "toilet," "right and left hand" are common words with rather exact referents. But the navy insisted its argot be used: "deck," "overhead," "bulkheads," "head," "starboard" and "port." All cohesive groups tend to develop an argot, and work groups are no exceptions.[14]

Railroadmen have a colorful occupational language. Below is a sample. How much of it can you translate?

At 3 P.M. Mott Haven Yard was a busy place. A crew of gandy dancers tamped methodically on a frog near the switching lead. L.S. 3 was all made up and ready to be doubled over. She had forty-six hog racks on the head end and sixty-five empty reefers on the hind end. Her crew were all new men on the run. Mike Madigan, the hog-head, had just been set up. Bill Blanchard, the fire-boy, was a boomer who had recently hired out. Jack Lewis, the brains of the outfit, had been a no bill since he was fired out of the Snakes for violating Rule "G." Brady Holms, the flagman, used to work the high iron in a monkey suit, and J. B. Wells was a "stu" brakeman, right off the street. Over on the hump lead, the yard rats were riding 'em in the clear and tying 'em down. The east side switcher was kicking loaded hoppers around, despite the violent washouts of the yardmixer who had discovered a hot box. Two Malleys were on the plug and three more were at the coal pocket. Our train, Number B.D. 5, was all ready to pull out. We were running light today with a few gondolas and twenty loaded

[13] Wilbert E. Moore, *Industrial Relations and the Social Order*, The Macmillan Company, 1946, p. 324.

[14] Teen-age "jive talk," student lingo, and talk of fraternal societies exemplify this fact. For collections of occupational argots see Cottrell, *op. cit.*, chap. 7, "Railroad Language," and Glossary; Edwin H. Sutherland (ed.), *The Professional Thief*, University of Chicago Press, 1937, especially Glossary.

westerns next to the buggy. Old Yellow Light gave us a highball and the tower gave us a ninety board on the high road. We slowly rolled out of Mott Haven.[15]

Some students have mistakenly included swearing or obscene language as part of the occupational language. Abundant blasphemy tends to be characteristic of male lower-class workers irrespective of occupation. Swearing is normal in their speech patterns both at work and outside of work. Although schools train students in the middle-class mode of non-swearing, swearing is consistent behavior outside of school and at work. However, it soon loses much of its emotional context. It becomes a class mark, or a mark of social acceptance.[16] In the army, lumber camp, men's club, and in other all-male groups swearing is an intimate part of communication.

Each class tends to develop a characteristic vocabulary which it uses in many situations. It is easy to overestimate the meaningfulness or importance of this class vocabulary. In many instances swearing has no emotional connotations, just as polite language among middle-class working people may have little significance. "Thank you," "You're welcome," "please," "if you don't mind," "I beg your pardon" are hackneyed, well-worn middle-class phrases which serve as convenient bridges or terminations to conversation. Being courteous is part of middle-class culture, just as swearing tends to be characteristic of lower-class male culture. The meaning of politeness or swearing depends upon the situation. Being icily polite may convey as much aggression as swearing violently.

The hypothesis of Whiting Williams, that swearing on the part of lower-class people is a form of aggression against prescribed moral vocabulary of

[15] From a report from Fred A. McGlone, a student at Michigan State College. The translation runs as follows:

At 3 P.M. Mott Haven Yard was a busy place. A section crew worked methodically on a frog near the switching track. A frog is the point where the two rails come together on a crossover track. A westbound freight train, Number L.S. 3, was made up on two tracks and was getting ready to double over. It had forty-six hog cars next to the engine and the rest of the train consisted of sixty-five empty refrigerator cars. Its crew consisted of all new men on the run. Mike Madigan, the engineer, had recently been promoted from fireman to his present job. Bill Blanchard, the fireman, was a seasonal worker who had only three months' seniority. Jack Lewis, the conductor, had not belonged to the Brotherhood since he had been fired out of the Switchmen's Union for drinking. Brady Holms, the flagman, worked on the main line as a passenger brakeman at one time. J. B. Wells was a student brakeman and this was his first run. Over on the hill track, the yard brakemen were riding the cars and putting hand brakes on them. The east side switcher was shuffling loaded coal cars around, despite the stop motions of the yardmaster, who had discovered a smoking wheel. Two freight engines were on the water plug and three more were at the coal pocket. Our train, Number B.D. 5, was all ready to pull out. We had a small train today that consisted of twenty loaded cars next to the caboose, plus a few low-sided gondolas. The switchman gave us a "go ahead" motion, and the towerman gave us a clear signal for the main line. We slowly rolled out of Mott Haven.

[16] This is an explanation offered by Whiting Williams. See his *What's on the Worker's Mind*, Charles Scribner's Sons, 1920.

the community, needs to be tested. The same applies to the hypothesis that swearing is a response to conditions of tension and frustration.[17]

Technical language, argot, and class vocabulary are inextricably woven into a pattern of speaking. A worker who is fully integrated into the work group and its culture must literally know how to talk to be fully acculturated in the group.

There are other aspects of occupational acculturation, as the development of a distinctive garb, sharing specific attitudes toward other occupational groups, engaging in unique initiation devices, sharing similar economic, political, and social sentiments. Wherever members of a particular occupation go, they carry this culture with them. Knowing the culture of a particular occupational group enables the scientist to predict large areas of informal behavior in many work situations.

Data on occupational cultures do not provide complete information on work culture for at least two important reasons. First, many work groups are composed of members of different occupations. When they interact, new behavior patterns arise. Occupational cultures seem to flourish best in relative isolation. Second, the occupational culture of semiskilled workers is not as unique or as clearly demarcated as those of the crafts and the professions. Both of these factors push the investigator into a study of specific work groups in specific social situations. Here the student should concentrate on the local culture, which contains the ceremonies, myths, rituals, and informal activities of the group.

CEREMONIES AND RITUALS

Rituals and ceremonies are a form of prescribed and elaborated behavior which occur as culture traits and which are extraneous from the technological point of view.[18] Sometimes they are formal in nature, such as the presentation of awards at company banquets. However, many ceremonies and rituals arise informally in local work groups. They are important because they may reveal the basic ideas and beliefs of the group better than do other cultural traits.

Initiation rites are not restricted to primitive people and fraternal orders. The novice to a work group may be asked to get a left-handed monkey wrench, a glass saw, a diamond sharpener, or other nonexistent tools. This is done to impress him with his ignorance and "greenness" on the job. The new worker is often required to run errands and to do favors for the group members. At the same time he may be subjected to continual verbal abuse, as "ribbing" and "razzing." Even the experienced worker is ridiculed and

[17] *Ibid.* See also Norman Mailer, *The Naked and the Dead*, Rinehart and Company, Inc., 1948, for a realistic presentation of swearing in the army and the relation of swearing to conditions of tension.

[18] Ruth Benedict, "Ritual," *Encyclopaedia of the Social Sciences*, The Macmillan Company, 1930.

razzed sometimes. The object of this abuse is to test the individual's resourcefulness, his attitude toward the group, and his willingness to share group sentiments. It is part of the process of social induction which, if successful, marks the group acceptance of the individual. The induction process is complete when the individual practices with no self-consciousness the rituals of the group, when he believes in its myths and sentiments, and above all when he participates in the induction of other newcomers.

When workers change jobs (promotion, demotion, or firing) or when they retire, they often participate in a *rite of passage*. The rite may be nothing more than shaking hands with all members, receiving a gift, making a speech, or having a party. It may take the form of joking, giving advice, or backslapping. Nonetheless, there is a group compulsion to do something to indicate the termination of a relationship. The significance of the ritual varies somewhat with the situation. The function of the ritual may be to manifest group identification and loyalty, to ease the process of separation from the group, to emphasize the finality of the social rupture, or merely to indicate that all past animosities are forgiven and forgotten.

The rites of passage that occur in the community are often also observed in the office or factory. Engagement, marriage, birth of children, and death are observed with appropriate ceremony. Holidays and other events which occur periodically are the occasion for rites of intensification.[19] These rites are very important for they maintain, reinforce, and express feelings of solidarity in the group. They also symbolize the common values.

Rites of intensification are ceremonies which demonstrate the essential unity of the group. They may be quite simple, as the custom of meeting before work in the locker room, exchanging greetings, pleasantries, and gossip. Other rites which are less frequently observed may provide greater emotional satisfaction. These may be the annual picnic, going to the opening night baseball game, stopping for a beer on the way home, celebrating Christmas or New Year's by holding a "spontaneous party" in the plant.

An inspector in an eastern radio factory, who was not fully accepted into his work group, inadvertently explained the function of such a rite when he said,

You know, I cannot understand the fellows at the plant. All year long they argue and stab each other in the back. You can't imagine the swearing, fighting, and arguing that goes on all year long. Come the day before New Year's and everything is lovey-dovey. Today we didn't do more than two hours' work. About ten o'clock the bottle was passed around. It was gone in no time. Then somebody sneaked out and got a couple of fifths. By noon everybody was happy. Where the food came from I don't know—but everybody spent the rest of the day eating and drinking, and having fun I suppose. . . . About an hour before

---

[19] See Eliot D. Chapple and Carleton S. Coon, *Principles of Anthropology*, Henry Holt and Company, 1942, chap. 21, "Rites of Intensification."

quitting time everybody started to walk around and shout. Everybody was kissing everyone else. Old enemies were shaking hands and wishing each other Happy New Year. Come Monday everybody will feel pretty good toward the other fellow. Inside of a week they'll be cussing and stabbing each other in the back. I can't stand that kind of hypocrisy. Either a guy is your friend all the time or he isn't. The hell with this, "Happy New Year's, George" one day and "You s.o.b." the next.

The function of this ceremony was to restore the equilibrium of the group that had been disturbed by conflicts during the year. It was an expression of fundamental unity and belongingness. This and other rites reinforced the habitual relations within the group.

CONVERSATION AND GOSSIP

A great deal of the time of an integrated work group is spent in talking and gossiping. As suggested above, talk should be analyzed to know the interests and sentiments of the group. The content and variety of gossip depends upon the sociocultural background of the group and its own peculiar traditions.

All groups spend some time talking about work itself—quality of materials, technical problems, bottlenecks, production quotas, pay rates, qualities of the supervisors, union and company issues. The generalization may be made that the higher the skill, the more talk about technical problems of work. Skilled workers and professionals tend to talk more about their work than semiskilled and unskilled workers.

Although the manner in which it is discussed varies, sex is a common subject of conversation among all groups. Managers and executives often tell sex jokes of different degrees of sophistication. Personal sex experiences and relations are tabooed subjects for most middle-class people. Female white-collar workers also discuss sex problems and sexual irregularities, but crude sex jokes and personal experiences are kept at a minimum. Male manual workers discuss sex more freely and openly than other groups. They hold sex jokes at a premium, and often relate their own intimate sexual affairs with wives or paramours. Their sophistication about sex amazes some observers, but it is merely the extension of street-corner life and conversation into the plant. The hypothesis that "poverty of social experience" and general dissatisfaction with working conditions is responsible for this preoccupation with sex,[20] is untenable. Other subjects of conversation compete successfully with sex in all social levels of the plant.

For example, in management circles much of the talking concerns politics of promotion, household purchases, material acquisitions, and achievements of children. Women workers discuss clothing, family problems, dates, and the usual gossip. Manual workers, on the other hand, discuss politics, parties,

[20] Williams, *op. cit.*, pp. 303-305.

drinking, and above all, recreation and sports. Interest in the latter arises naturally from the sports activities of the younger members outside the plant. But interest is also exhibited by non-players and by older members as well. "How did they do?" "How did they come out?" These questions can only refer to one thing—the performance of the home team in the last game.

All day long the discussion of sports continues—which is the best team in which league, the prospects of rookies, comparative scores, past glories of heroes and teams, the prospects of the coming season, and personal sports experiences. The amount of lore and knowledge about sports that many workers have is encyclopedic. Some employers have capitalized on this interest by providing sports and recreational facilities at the plant.

MYTHS AND BELIEFS

An analysis of the content of the conversations reveals that workers create myths, folklore, and fictions about their work situations. This is not surprising, since man is a myth maker wherever he is.[21] He mixes freely and unconsciously his factual knowledge, ideas, opinions, beliefs, and mythology into a system of thought (ideology) which guides his perception of all social situations. In order to understand and predict his behavior, then, the observer should be aware of this system of thought. An exploration of the content and function of folklore and mythology is especially useful because it discloses the basic ideals and sentiments which motivate and make meaningful daily behavior.

An analysis of the thought system of people in all levels of the supervisory structure reveals that all are about equally suggestible to myth thinking and making. Nowhere is there more mythology in management thinking than in the area of human relations. Any serious student of industry is conversant with some of these fictions of management. For example: workers are indolent, lazy, and try to get away with everything; they respond only to economic motivations; they are emotional and animal-like; they will follow any rabble-rousing leader. Workers in turn maintain fictions about bosses: they care only for profits; they are heartless; they resort to subterfuge whenever possible. These fictions become part of the tradition which guides behavior.

Since myths and folklore are elaborate and enduring, they must have an important function to serve. One such function is the dramatic symbolization of group ideals and values. Tales about the tremendous output or production of a mythical character persist among many skilled groups. One young bricklayer perpetuated such a myth when he mused,

You know I'm not much good in the afternoons. None of us are, I guess. We're not as tough as the old folks. I can remember as a kid when old John

[21] Read Bain, "Man, the Myth Maker," *Scientific Monthly*, July, 1947, pp. 61-69.

Kiddy was building a house next door to us. One Saturday morning him and his old lady decided to lay the north wall of the house. The old lady mixed the mud and John laid the bricks. You should of seen the old man work—he was 70 years old then. He was a demon—not a useless move—just laying row after row without a minute's rest. The old lady kept right up with him. By two o'clock they had her done. After cleaning up they went to a square dance. Yes sir, John Kiddy worked with my father's gang until he was eighty-five. Guess we ain't like the old folks. Just too soft.

Such a myth serves to fortify the important value of skill and individual achievement. When other values threaten the place of skill in determining status, the story is repeated, especially by those who want to abide by the old order. Myths of this type may even be fabricated to perpetuate a desired end.

The myth is an important factor in social adjustment. To know what role it plays in the group one must know the values and aspirations of the members, as well as their problems and frustrations. For example, in an industrial structure where individual achievement is glorified but where promotion is rare, the myth may provide rationalizations for failure to climb. In such cases the myth may play a therapeutic role. Richard R. Myers has presented several illustrations in an important article.

In a Grand Rapids furniture concern, among the furniture craftsmen where the Dutch-Americans constitute a dominant group, the myth has it that one cannot become a supervisor without a good Dutch name. However, the records show supervisors with Jewish and South European names, some of long standing and some of more recent promotions. Similarly, interviews in a Detroit automotive parts manufacturing concern indicated a well developed belief among workers of Polish extraction that management regards "Hamtramck Poles" as trouble-makers and undesirable as supervisory types. Careful check, however, indicated that management proportionately employed more foremen of Polish background than of any other ethnic antecedents. *This myth is a reflection of the general self-consciousness and a sense of persecution which many Polish-Americans have in Detroit, and represents a device for easing personal frustration in a competitive situation.*[22] [Italics are ours.]

All work groups have myths about themselves and about other groups with which they interact. Some myths function to preserve group values, some "explain" the social system, some maintain morale; others are fabricated consciously by leaders to achieve certain ends.[23]

INFORMAL ACTIVITIES

Much activity of an informal nature goes on in most work groups. Apparently technical behavior and union participation are rarely so arranged as

[22] "Myth and Status System in Industry," *Social Forces*, March, 1948, p. 335.
[23] *Ibid.*

to provide people with sufficient and satisfactory social relationships. They invariably devise social activities of all kinds to relieve the boredom of monotonous work, to obtain release from job tensions, to compensate for unsatisfactory social relationships, or to fulfill an endless variety of social demands.

The range of informal activities is enormous, for it varies with the cultural background of the workers. Much of it seems to be recreational in nature, such as gambling, horseplay, practical joking, smoking, and singing. However, conflict behavior is also evident, as fighting, politicking, and sabotage. Other behavior seems to be merely an expression of group living, such as lunching, trading jobs, loaning money, and forming a car pool. At first most of this activity may appear as random, haphazard responses of individuals to chance situations. Closer observation reveals that much of it is organized by the group to satisfy the recurrent demands in the work culture.

An illustration may be presented to elaborate this idea. A research committee in a college faculty group held weekly meetings to criticize the work being done and to develop plans for future research. Owing to the nature of the work, it was difficult for individuals to take full credit or blame for group achievements. Yet criticism and responsibility had to be placed somewhere if a good research report was to be issued. Although each member held all of the others in high respect, differences in opinion did develop. Incessant arguments occurred over the future direction of research, the interpretation of data, and the division of labor.

Two quasi-recreational activities arose as a response to the tension in these situations. The first occurred before the meetings. It took the form of verbal repartee, joking, razzing, humorous threats, boasting, and general hilarity. In the midst of this hilarity the chairman would suggest that the group get down to work. After a few jibes in his direction, work would actually begin in earnest.

At the end of the often exhausting and sometimes bitter sessions, the group would adjourn for an hour to a coffee shop across the street, where they would eat a snack, smoke a cigarette, and drink coffee. At the tables the antagonists would usually sit next to each other and continue their discussion. After a time attention turned to stories, daily incidents and jokes. Invariably, by the time the group left the coffee shop differences were settled and agreements were made.

The functions of these quasi-recreational activities before and after the meetings were to maintain and restore group equilibrium. The joking had the effect of setting an atmosphere conducive to good will for the following period of tension. The coffee ritual had the effect of restoring mutual confidence and respect among the antagonists. As long as the group engaged in these activities it remained an effective research team.

Variations in this ritual are common. Among manual workers horseplay,

work play, and practical joking are substitutes for verbal repartee. Giving the hot-foot, squirting water, and putting salt in coffee are examples of such work play. More techniques are developed to fit the situation. Machines are jammed, meters are decalibrated, tools are broken, and materials are hidden.

Although everyone, at one time or another, may be subjected to practical joking, some individuals are more frequently elected than others. The man who cannot "take" it, the member who gets "too big for his britches," and the low-status person often lead a miserable existence until they conform to group standards or leave. Occasionally standardized punishments are evolved for those who violate group customs. In the bank wiring room of Western Electric workers "binged" (struck a hard blow on the shoulder) each other for swearing, overproducing, and telling poor jokes.[24]

Many other informal activities occur in work groups. Gambling, card playing, horse betting, lotteries, football pools, and dice attract largest participation. Various explanations have been offered for widespread gambling. To be sure, gambling may relieve monotony on the job, but so do other activities. Since not much money is exchanged in card playing, the economic incentive in gambling is not great, as it is in the lottery and pools. Loyalty to the latter may be explained by their integration of workers in the racketeering and gambling interests in the community.[25] Gambling is not generally considered immoral among workers because it is a part of their tradition, like smoking, drinking, and joking. The campaigns of management to eliminate such activities thus face resistances of all kinds. Elaborate systems of secret signals are created to warn gamblers of approaching bosses. In many instances foremen make only a pretense of enforcing company rules. In fact, they may even collaborate with the men, for they realize that enforcement of rules may be more trouble than it's worth. In the following section we shall explore in greater detail how informal groups adjust to the rules and regulations of management and labor.

In summary, the culture of informal groups is made up of occupational culture and the culture of the local groups. Beliefs, myths, folklore, and rituals occupy a central place in the work culture, for they provide clues to the dominant sentiments and attitudes of the groups. Activities such as gambling, recreation, and ceremonies not only express group sentiments but also serve as social control devices.

FUNCTIONS OF INFORMAL ORGANIZATIONS

Social scientists have been intrigued with the question of why informal organization arises and persists. They have also wondered why it is so well organized and powerful in some situations and so loosely organized and

[24] Roethlisberger and Dickson, op. cit., pp. 421-423.
[25] William F. Whyte, Street Corner Society, University of Chicago Press, 1943, Part II, "Racketeers and Politicians."

powerless in other situations. It is easier to explain the rise and persistence of informal groups than to account for their solidarity.

PERPETUATION OF CULTURE

Groups arise and persist because they satisfy the social needs of their members. These "needs," of course, are culturally defined by the group and are only indirectly related to biological and psychological mechanisms. Thus anything may be a need if it is so defined by the group. Needs may include accumulation of wealth, glorification of service, continuation of hostility, and sacrifice to maintain group traditions. In addition, all groups feel a need to perpetuate themselves. This is so fundamental that it is only very rarely

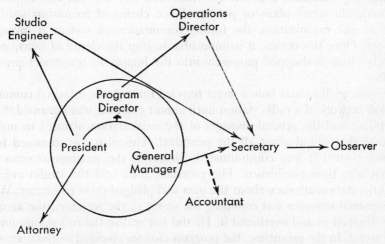

FIG. 39. How a Secret Traveled Through the Informal Communication Network of a Radio Station.

questioned. It is "natural," essential, and almost inevitable that, once groups arise, they do everything they can to perpetuate themselves. All customs, folkways, mores, rituals, traditions, folklore, and mythology are assumed to be important and necessary for the survival of the group. Nobody questions why a custom should persist; and if they do, the answer usually is, "Because we've always done it this way and there's no need to change."

Thus one of the main functions of informal work organization is to maintain whatever its members have found satisfying. This means that new members must be inculcated with the group's prevailing sentiments and traditions. Only an adequate system of communication can achieve this end.

MAINTENANCE OF A COMMUNICATION SYSTEM

Once a group is established within an organization it wants all the information that might affect its welfare either positively or negatively. Not infre-

quently informal groups suspect that managers will act in such a way as to
harm their members. They want to know ahead of time what those acts
will be so that plans may be made to counteract them. Thus informal
groups that are not apprised of the policies, motives, and intentions behind
specific orders are not only suspicious but anxious to get information. They
try to tap the formal line of communication. Once this is done, information
spreads like wildfire through the informal network of communication. If
information is unavailable, the workers conjure up motives and discuss them.
After this a pattern of action is planned to resist or encourage the anticipated policies of union or management administrators.

Since the informal communication system is so intimately connected with
formal organizations, it is easy to understand why it is virtually impossible
to maintain secret plans or policies. Since chains of friendship span the
entire work organization, the formal communication system is invariably
tapped. Once this occurs, it is impossible to stop the spread of news, unless
another item is dropped purposely into the hopper to counteract previous
leaks.

Figure 39 illustrates how a secret traveled through the informal communication network of a radio station until almost everyone was informed.[26] The
president and the general manager of the radio station planned to make a
change that would affect all the personnel. This plan was supposed to be
a secret until it was consummated. However, the program director was
taken into their confidence. The president then told the studio engineer
and the station attorney about the plan and pledged them to secrecy. While
the general manager was confiding the secret to the secretary, the accountant dropped in and overheard it. He did not realize the full significance of
the secret. In the meantime, the program director confided in the operations
director, who told the secretary, who already knew. The studio engineer also
told the secretary, who later reported it to the participant observer. The
complete circuit of secret sharing may be traced in Figure 39.

It is as important to know who doesn't participate in secret sharing and
why. In the radio station, the general manager and the studio engineer did
not like each other. For this reason the president did not tell the general
manager that he had confided in the studio engineer. As a matter of fact,
the president and the studio engineer always share secrets, as do the general
manager and the secretary, as well as the program director and the operations director. The operations director only occasionally shares secrets with
the secretary. The studio engineer shares secrets with the president. He rarely
shares with anyone else, and on these rare occasions he tells the secretary.
The latter usually shares secrets with the observer. The secret was, by the
way, that a new general manager was being appointed.

A communication system, once it is established, functions to convey any

[26] From a student report by Robert M. Hallberg, University of Washington, 1948.

information of interest to its members. Not only are official policies trans-mitted, but any news of interest. Baseball scores, results of horse races, news of sickness or death, political news, jokes, incidents, and just plain gossip circulate freely. It is the channel which functions to make and maintain public opinion in the plant. The "sudden resistance" that management often encounters when it makes "new" proposals on wages, hours, pensions, sen-iority, recreation, or other plans may be explained by the fact that these proposals have already leaked out and been thoroughly discussed. Thus it is often unnecessary for management or labor leaders to discuss things and "reason" with the workers. The latter have already discussed the matters and arrived at a consensus.

SOCIAL CONTROL

One of the primary functions of informal social organization is social control. It is commonplace knowledge that even the mere presence of other people influences or constrains the behavior of individuals. Whenever informal organization exists (and only in very rare cases is it absent), every-one feels some constraint on his freedom of action. Indeed, as Moore suggests, "the whole of informal organization seems to imply a substitution of group ends for competitive individual ends."[27] Since informal organization extends from the top to the bottom of the structure, it follows that every-one's behavior is somewhat informally controlled.

Informal organization is made up of many small though interconnected groups, operating within a formal structure. Therefore, from the point of view of the small individual groups social control is exerted (a) inwardly toward its own members, and (b) outwardly toward other informal groups and toward the formal organizations.

Internal Control

In general, social control is directed inward to make members conform to the culture of the group—its customs, ceremonies, rituals, and mythology. Conformity to the occupational and local work group culture is enforced by all the common techniques of ridicule, ostracism, and violence. Violation of even small rules may arouse a reaction against recalcitrant members.

An illustration will demonstrate this point. A straw boss of a gang of laborers wore an old cloth cap on the job. One day he appeared wearing a light-gray Stetson. The workers "razzed" him and asked him if he thought he was a big boss. He offered some excuse, but reappeared the next day with the Stetson. Again the workers reacted, but more violently than on the previous day. On the third day the straw-boss arrived on the job with his old hat. A similar negative reaction was directed against truck drivers who began to wear white shirts and ties on the job. In both cases, the workers accused

[27] Moore, *op. cit.*, p. 331.

the violators of going "high-hat." It is always possible for workers to impute motives to deviant behavior and find reasons why a custom should not be abandoned. It does not matter if these motives are incorrect because group members feel that customs should be preserved.

Several rules of internal social control are found in almost all groups in industry. The most basic of these is the notion that each member should do his fair share of the work, especially where there is joint responsibility for output or service. In fact, where strong informal groups are present, there is no need for the foreman to enforce minimum standards of work. The group will do it for him, and much more effectively.[28]

A broader interpretation of this concept of doing a fair share of work is found in the idea that no group member should profit at the expense of another member. Many specific informal rules demonstrate this principle. In seeking job advancements, for example, the group exerts pressure on its members to observe legitimate channels of promotion. Resort to favoritism, drag, or pull is regarded as disloyalty. In fact, any action is censured which operates to the detriment of the group.

It follows that reproach will be directed toward anyone who reduces a temporary or permanent advantage of the group, no matter how unfair that advantage may seem to be. Group loyalty is so highly valued that anyone who "squeals" is censured. This is particularly the case when someone gets away with violating a company policy. For example, the no-smoking rule is violated often by some groups, but not by others. Anyone, including the foreman, who reported this temporary or unfair advantage to higher management would be immediately censured, even by the nonsmokers.

This protection of the individual does not apply when the informal standards are violated. Vulnerable individuals and group advantages are protected only when the group interacts with the formal system. But the advantages that individuals or cliques have within the informal structure are generally disapproved.

External Control

The control that informal groups exert over their members may be seen in their efforts to control the formal structures of management and labor. Management and union officers recognize that their plans, however carefully laid, are often violated or modified by the workers. Students have considered the problem of managing men, but they have neglected the problem of how the managed adjust to the efforts to manipulate them. It is inevitable that workers will try to adjust to or manage their managers.

One of the problems that interest administrators is the efforts of the workers to restrict production. Although management's preoccupation with this subject is understandable, it displays their general ignorance of the

[28] Roethlisberger and Dickson, *op. cit.*; Williams, *op. cit.*

total function of informal organization. That is, they see informal organization largely in the form of resistance and rarely in the form of assistance. Without the assistance of informal organization, formal organization would often be ineffective.[29] This is frequently the case when managers try to determine every detail in production. They are too far removed from production to envision many of the problems that arise. Yet frequently they give orders on the basis of presumed knowledge. If their orders were completely obeyed, confusion would result and production and morale would be lowered. In order to achieve the goals of the organization workers must often violate orders, resort to their own techniques of doing things, and disregard lines of authority. Without this kind of systematic sabotage much work could not be done. This unsolicited assistance in the form of disobedience and subterfuge is especially necessary to enable large bureaucracies to function effectively.

Restriction of production is commonly found in all levels of industry, irrespective of occupation.[30] It may be direct or indirect, sporadic or persistent, boss-ordered or spontaneous. In almost all cases it is related to the concept of a *fair day's work*. There is a group tendency to keep observable production within the capacity range of the average worker. Two important rules are, therefore, that the worker should not overproduce and be a "rate buster"; neither should be underproduce and be a "chiseler." Many illustrations may be found to demonstrate these group norms.

"In a Michigan lumber yard the handling of lumber was standardized by the men. . . . The worker soon learned that he was expected to lift two pieces of a certain kind, one piece of another size, and so on. He felt that the standards specified about half what could have been handled comfortably. When pieces were small enough to handle alone he found that the other workers frowned on his picking a normal load. He was expected to handle about half the number of pieces which, when left to himself, he would have taken as a matter of course. This manner of handling was clearly a restrictive device worked out by the men themselves."[31]

Why restrictive productive practices persist even under almost perfect working conditions has puzzled many businessmen. Restriction in the face of good wages and adequate security provisions has led many researchers to conclude that workers are motivated by nonrational sentiments rather than logic. This position may appear reasonable to those unacquainted with the social and cultural life of workers.

In the first place, it is erroneous to feel that restriction is typical of manual workers alone. It is found among all workers. Secondly, workers

[29] We are indebted to A. T. Hansen for the precise conceptualization of this problem.
[30] See Stanley B. Mathewson, *Restriction of Output Among Unorganized Workers*, The Viking Press, 1931.
[31] *Ibid.*, p. 25.

restrict production because this is a part of their cultural tradition. Their collective experiences have taught them that it is not judicious to produce as much as they possibly can. Folk knowledge also provides reasons why they should restrict production.

The suspicion that workers have toward speed-up schemes is a rational response to the tactics many employers have used in the past. The folklore of workers contains many stories of financial incentive plans that resulted in increased production with no increase in income. These stories are reinforced by the common notion that the employer profits from labor under any circumstances. Thus the worker feels that the more he puts out, the more the boss makes in proportion. Further, he believes that he always loses in the long run, because the boss's only motive is to have greater production for greater profit. Those ideas persist whether or not a labor union exists. Of course the presence of an organization functions to keep sentiments alive in a more systematic way.

To maintain his place in the group the worker must conform to these sentiments. The fear of being unemployed or underemployed further encourages restrictive practices. Even where there is plenty of work to do, the fear exists that this may not be the case in the future; so it is best to act in a uniform way. All efforts must be made to protect the job. The following illustrates a common occurrence in many factories:

In a tube-making plant in New Jersey it ordinarily took the machinists four days to set up a new job. One particular job was not completed after a full week's work. Scrap and other costs were running high. The night foreman casually asked McCarthy if he wanted to try his hand on the problem. Inside an hour and a half he had the machine set up. Although the day foreman was happy to hear that the problem was solved, he asked the night foreman not to allow McCarthy to do such work in the future. Although the plant was not unionized the regular setup men threatened to quit as a group if a man with only a month and a half of experience in the plant was allowed to do their work. The fact that McCarthy had thirty years' experience on Brown and Sharpe automatic machines did not impress them.

Mathewson reports a similar case of slowdown to stretch out work. "The men in a stock room of another firm checked up every morning the available work. When it appeared slack, they passed the word around, 'Take it easy, not many orders on hand this morning.' This always gave the signal for slow work for the group of four men involved."[32]

Regulation of production takes many forms. It almost always appears whenever time setters are used. Sometimes it takes the form of sharing work when it is unevenly distributed. The pace of work may be regulated, so that most of the work is done in the morning and visiting takes place in the after-

[32] *Ibid.*, p. 26.

noon. Regulation may come at the behest of foremen, the union, or the men themselves.

The attempt of workers to control the formal organization of the union through internal group pressures also occurs. If union officials and stewards displease workers the same pressure devices are used on them that are used on managers and foremen. The life of the steward may be made very uncomfortable by making too many requests for his services and by accusing him of improper motives. Union officials may be embarrassed by a refusal of the workers to participate in union-management committees, by violations of contract stipulations, and by resort to a wildcat strike against union officials. Playing politics, building pressure groups and machines are activities that occur mainly in the informal groups of the plant.

SOCIAL LIFE

Obviously informal social organization provides interest and fun in work life. Many jobs are so monotonous that they cannot occupy the attention and interest of the workers. In addition to being humdrum they offer no bright future. Therefore, all of the satisfactions at work must derive from the interpersonal associations, and the activities are spontaneously invented.

For example, the singing, gambling, playing, drinking, and smacking might conceivably be reduced if the job required the full attention of the worker and gave him satisfactions in return. When this does not occur achievement is sought as the best storyteller, drinker, and practical jokester. It is difficult to overestimate the entertainment value provided by informal activities, just as it is easy to ignore the personal recognition and attention they provide for people who would otherwise be in anonymous surroundings.

In many instances the social life of informal groupings gives people their only social satisfactions. The amount of social participation for many urban people is so small that the work group functions to provide practically their only social outlet. This situation is exemplified in the pathetic case of an unemployed woolen mill worker who went to the factory every day at noon so she could have lunch with the girls.

CONCLUSION

Informal organization is observed when personalities and situations are considered apart from the formal operations of groups. Informal structures are more than a number of congeniality groups—they are composed of a network of spontaneous group relations that pervade the entire work plant. The morale or lack of morale in a plant is a result of the relation of informal group to managers and their policies.

Cliques and other informal groups have a culture of their own. It is made

up in part of the occupational cultures of the members and the peculiar social heritage in the plant. Myths, ceremonies, rituals, and ideologies—all the components of culture—are found in informal groups. One of the main functions of informal groups is to perpetuate this culture. But equally important, informal group life gives the worker an additional channel to secure recognition and prestige from his fellow worker.

Many of the activities and ideas that find expression in informal organizations are set by the climate of labor-management relations. As these two houses jockey for power and prestige, local work groups come to decisions that influence the ongoing struggle. These processes will be examined in detail in the following chapter.

SUPPLEMENTARY STUDIES

FIELD OBSERVATION: DIRECT OBSERVATION OF A SELECTED WORK PLANT
(Continued)

In the work plant selected, analyze:

Informal Group Structure

Describe:

1. The kinds of technical, sociotechnical, and social behavior in which the worker engages.
2. Talk Patterns.
   a. Who talks.
   b. Amount of talk.
   c. Content of talk—interest subjects and avoidance subjects; patterns of ideas and sentiments.
3. Sociometric patterns.
   a. Cliques.
   b. Car pools.
   c. Lunch cliques.
   d. Recreation groups.
   e. Interpersonal feelings and relationships.
   f. Reciprocating behavior patterns such as job trading, helping one another, etc.
4. Initiation, ceremonies, and rituals.
5. Work play such as gambling, horseplay, practical joking, singing, joking relationships, etc.
6. Conflicts such as fighting, "politicking," and sabotage.
7. Informal group code.
8. Social controls used to enforce the informal code.
9. Race and ethnic relations.

FIELD OBSERVATION: PARTICIPANT OR DIRECT OBSERVATION

Make a record of the content of talk of workers in different occupations. If possible, try to secure such contrasting groups as professional, managerial, skilled,

and unskilled workers. Wire or tape recordings would provide excellent data for analysis.

LIBRARY: BOOKS AND ARTICLES

Archibald, Katherine, *Wartime Shipyard*, University of California Press, 1947, chapters on "Negroes" and "Lesser Minorities," pp. 58-109.

Cottrell, W. Fred, *The Railroader*, Stanford University Press, 1940.

Hughes, Everett C., "The Knitting of Racial Groups in Industry," *American Sociological Review*, October, 1946, pp. 512-519.

Roethlisberger F, J., and Dickson, W. J., *Management and the Worker*, Harvard University Press, 1939, chaps. 20-22, pp. 459-548.

RESEARCH GAPS

1. Operation of the grapevine in different work plants.
2. Secret-sharing relationships in different work plants.
3. The influence of satellite work groups (car pool, snack groups, bowling league, etc.).
4. The study of dissension in the work group.
5. Management cliques.
6. Management and supervisory insecurity.
7. The role of the manager's wife.
8. Social processes operating in and through the associations of managers' wives.

CHAPTER X

Power Organization: Interaction of Management and Labor

ELEMENTS OF POWER IN INDUSTRIAL ORGANIZATION

THE ORIGIN OF POWER, STATUS, AND CLASS ORGANIZATION

Up to this point, the social organization of a work plant has been a study of what we have called the House of Management and the House of Labor. These structures have been shown to be both separate and overlapping. Each house has a formal and informal organization. People in both management and labor have both formal and informal roles to play. We have described these roles in fairly complete detail.

Other rather enduring patterns of relationships, or *social organization*, cut through the formal and informal organizations of industry. Max Weber early pointed out the critical importance of such organizations as power, status or prestige, and class. These organizations represent both formal and informal patterns of stratification as people seek to control others, gain status or prestige, and secure economic superiority.

The evidence of the organizations of control, prestige, and economic superiority have already been suggested. We shall describe them in detail in this and the two following chapters. In particular we shall identify workers and work groups in reference to rankings of power, status, and economic position. All persons in work plants have such positions in various organizations, but the way they play their roles may vary widely. Some are consumed

with power, some want social status more, and others want the material satisfaction which money can command. Still others want to be at the top of all three structures.

Whatever the motives of individual workers and groups all are ranked as to power, prestige, and class positions. The social significance of these three factors, the ordering of people according to them, and the social process of ranking constitute the power, status, and class organizations. This chapter offers a partial description of the social organization of power in industry.

WHAT IS POWER?

The concept "power" has an unpalatable flavor to those reared in democratic ideology. To many it conveys the repugnant suggestion of "pushing people around." This feeling has somewhat obscured our ability to see the functioning of power and all of its manifestations. The fact that people are being forced to obey others may not always be obvious. However, this does not deny the fact that ordering and obedience are widespread organizational realities. For this reason, therefore, we have purposely chosen the word "power" rather than some other more neutral designation, such as "social control."

In some folk societies which have a well-integrated and stable social order, the concept "social control" may be more useful than "power." The folkways and the mores provide the unconscious and informal authority. In contemporary, heterogeneous, and complex societies law, contract, and regulations increasingly play the role of social control. Industrial organization of today shares, if it does not actually determine, the trend toward rational, consciously derived regulations of group behavior. For this reason it is more appropriate to employ the concept of power, for it has the element of rationality, and consciously determined relations.

Max Weber's concept of power is one which we shall find useful. Power may be defined in broadest terms as the probability of securing obedience.[1] A power situation exists whenever individuals or groups compete for control of a larger group to promote their desired ends.[2] The power of groups is measured in terms of the probability that others will obey them. Thus a power situation can exist only in groups, for it presumes some amount of socialization.

Obviously, the concept of power and politics are closely related. Lasswell defines politics as "who gets what, when, and how."[3] The exercise of power,

[1] See H. H. Gerth and C. W. Mills, *From Max Weber: Essays in Sociology.* Oxford University Press, 1946, p. 180.
[2] See R. M. MacIver, *The Web of Government,* The Macmillan Company, 1947, p. 82. "By social power we mean the capacity to command the service or the compliance of others."
[3] H. D. Lasswell, *Politics: Who Gets What, When, How,* McGraw-Hill Book Company, Inc., 1936.

then, need not be conceived invariably as conscious, rational, purposeful, scheming, autocratic behavior. On the contrary, people get things by using indirect, amorphous, and even benevolent or democratic methods. But irrespective of how power is exercised, its core is clear. It is group manipulation for desired ends.

Power used in this sense includes many phenomena which parade under such words as "influence," "leadership," "collaboration," "authority," "coordination," "adjustment," "realignment," and "reorganization." All of these notions are concerned with the distribution of power. True power may be distributed in many different ways—and some of these concepts suggest this fact. How power is used, disseminated, or concentrated is a basic and fundamental problem of industrial society. But the first task of the social scientist is to recognize the phenomenon everywhere it exists. Then he may study the social patterns which it assumes.

The Interaction of Labor and Management in a Power Framework

Obviously, the existence of power and the patterns it assumes are clearly found in management and union structures. The supervisory hierarchy is a formal power arrangement or organization. It is a hierarchal structure which has been institutionalized. To be sure, struggles for power occur within and between the levels of management.[4] However, the general outlines of power are rather clearly defined and parceled out. In like manner the local labor union has its own organization of power. We have seen that many of the internal attributes of unions may be understood only if the union is conceived as a political system which represents a more or less temporary arrangement of groups struggling for power. The union's constitution and procedural conventions define the type of political adjustments which can be made.[5]

A picture of the organization of power in industry is more than the combined descriptions of the power structures in management and labor. It must also include the nature of the power arrangements between these two groups. The interaction of management and labor is best understood if that interaction is interpreted as a struggle of each group to extract from the other its desired ends—that is, as a power struggle. Even the existence of a seemingly perfect coöperative relationship between management and labor does not belie the existence of a power relation between them. The belief in coöperation and mutual survival merely represents a power settlement more or less temporary in nature. As long as workers feel they need their union, complete coöperation is not present. The power is kept in reserve.

In any case, when efforts to extract concessions from the other become

[4] See Chapter VII, "The Major Work Positions and Roles of Managers."
[5] See Chapter VIII, "Operation of the Union Local."

somewhat routinized or patterned, we may speak of an existent power organization. That the interaction between management and labor may be best analyzed as a power relation is apparent when the historical shifts in their relations are known.

TWO CASES: A CONTRAST IN AUTHORITY RELATIONS

I'm over seventy years old, do you know that? I don't look it, do I? It's not because I've had an easy life. You young Americans do not know what it is to work. Yes, I've worked all but the first ten years of my life. My father was a mule trader in the old country; he traded in mules and other animals. I was the oldest boy in the family, and my folks had plans for me to go to school, and then take care of my father's business. They were cautious people, so they took care of all eventualities. It was decided that first I should get an education, but also to be on the safe side, I should learn a trade.

I went to school for four years, and I loved it. You know, in the old country you get a real education. I know more astronomy than most college graduates in America, do you know that? But to get back to my story. Father's business was going bad, and education was expensive, so I was taken out of school.

I can still remember the day when my father took me to the shop of the master cabinet-maker in the little town in which we were living. My father said to the old master, "Here he is. Make him learn and obey. Do not be afraid to apply the switch." These admonitions were not necessary. The master knew how to control the boys and to get most out of them. I soon learned that one must obey and honor the master just like your own father. He was always to be addressed "Teacher" or "Master."

Since I was the youngest boy, I did little but sweep and clean around the shop. Later I was asked to look at somebody working, to hold a piece of wood, and so on. If my attention lagged, Teacher flicked my ears; if I spoiled the stain, he gave me a flogging; if I tarried on the way back from the apothecary (where we bought our dyes for the stains), he gave me a tongue lashing; if I complained of being tired, he might relent, but more often I received silent censure.

Day after day, I sanded wood, rubbed in finishes, polished and waxed until my arms ached. I despaired of ever learning anything. The days were long, for we worked from twelve to fourteen hours a day. And for all this backbreaking labor, we received fourteen cents a week, an occasional whipping, and continual remonstrations.

But it wasn't much better for the older boys and young men in the shop. They had to knuckle down to the Master, address him respectfully, and carry out his orders to the letter. Despite his severity, nobody disliked him. He was a kindly man underneath, perhaps better than most others. The important thing was that he turned out excellent craftsmen, who would never do a shoddy piece of work. We turned out real craftsmen in the old country. I know everything about cabinet making; from cutting down a log to putting on the final finish on a piece of furniture.

When I came to America I got a job in a furniture factory, and after a few years I became the foreman of the veneer department. Things were bad in the

old country, and my master came to this country. I got him a job working in my department. Although I was his boss, I usually took his advice, and dutifully called him "Master" until the day he died. My children used to call him "Uncle Master" and his wife "Aunt Master," just like natural aunts and uncles, and obeyed them like they do me.

The following description was given by a nineteen-year-old boy.

Yeah, this is the first full-time job I ever had. A year ago June when I finished school, I got a job at Acme Radio Corporation. I polish up the radio cabinets when they come off the line. I don't like the job so much. It's not the kind 'a job I want, because you can't use your intelligence and initiative. It's kind 'a easy though. You put in your eight hours, and the pay is pretty good. The union's gonna try to get us a fifteen cent increase. So I'll stick at it for a little while.

You know, that place would be a hell of a lot better if there wasn't so many guys tellin' you what to do. Bob, our foreman, is a nice kind of guy, but every once in a while he flies off the handle. I guess they have meetings about production or somethin', and after them meetin's, Bob starts to yell for more and better work. I suppose you can't blame him though. The superintendent gives the general foreman hell, the general foreman gives Bob hell, Bob gives us hell, and we raise hell among ourselves. Finally, Ralph (the steward) tells Bob off, and things are better for a little while.

It isn't so bad taking it from Bob, but then those inspectors think they're big cheeses. They ain't got any control over us, but every once in a while they tell us we ain't doing things right. They even get Bob worried. Then there's them rate setters and efficiency experts. They come snoopin' around and tell us how we are supposed to do our jobs. You should hear Ralph blow steam when they come around. I tell you if they would only leave Ralph and Bob work things out, everything would be all right. The company newspaper is always talkin' about loyalty. But how can you be loyal when everybody is on your neck all the time, and you don't have any chance for advancement?

Historical Changes in the Organization of Power

These two cases exemplify two different systems of production and, what is more important, different types of power relations that attend them. The first case illustrates a system in which the production units were small. The division of labor was based on a skilled hierarchy. All neophytes were expected to go through the same steps as the others in attaining higher skill. The authority structure was clear cut. All workers were directly and personally responsible to the master. Custom defined the authority, which was self-endorsed by a system of generally approved norms and conventions. Another important feature was the broader nature of authority in the system. Not only did the master craftsman have control over his workers and their labor, but he had the right to exert other kinds of discipline. He taught his boys to respect not only him but older people in general. Thus, he shared the responsibility for rearing his wards. He was expected to see that they went

to church on religious days, that they did not become exposed to corrupting influences, and that their parents were informed of their progress. In short, he acted the father surrogate to his apprentices.

The master himself was subject to indirect controls. The very fact that he knew the parents of his apprentices rather intimately, plus the fact that his apprentices were economic assets, curbed his exploitative tendencies. His status in the community was largely dependent on how he ran his business. He had to be fair to his boys or they might be apprenticed to his fellow craftsmen. He had to sell his goods at a fair price, because he sold in a personal market. (The customer is always right where the customer knows the seller, and when customers know one another.) Custom and tradition defined the authority relations by defining relations in general. Few if any formal organizations were needed to enforce regulations. Custom defined behavior as well as the means of its enforcement.

This system worked well mainly because it was not challenged by other systems. The family, the church, the school, the workshop, and the community all reinforced one another. One must not assume that this was an ideal system exemplified by harmony, reason, and balance. The fact that a system is generally accepted need not imply that all its members are well adjusted to it. Tension and frustration existed in the authoritarian system. The student must avoid the unrealistic conclusion that because authority was clearly defined and unchallenged it operated to everyone's satisfaction. The efficiency of enforcement, however, was a reality. Although intimate and personal relationships existed, the system was strongly institutionalized, and authority relations reflected these conditions. The system was seldom challenged.

The contrast of the older structure of authority to the authority structure in our modern work plant is striking. The most obvious trends in modern industry are its increase in size and the changes this brings in the nature of authority relations. Obviously, the larger the enterprise, the less the employer is able to oversee all those below him. He necessarily must concentrate on his economic relations with his employees and less on his noneconomic relations. This situation produces a reaction among the workers. Since they see less of the big boss, they tend to react to him largely as a bargaining opponent. The personal relation of the owner-operator to the individual worker has been almost completely desiccated, and consequently, the impersonalization of authority is now rapidly nearing completion.

In bureaucracies many workers do similar tasks. When they become aware of this they can be organized rather easily to think in group terms. In conditions involving power relations, therefore, they tend to associate authority with groups and not with individuals. The shift is from personal to impersonal power, from informal, sympathetic relations to formal, contractual ones.

This change in power relations places the modern work plant in an entirely different setting.

THE SETTING AT THE LOCAL LEVEL

Both management and labor have discrete organizations, each with its own structure and culture, each the subject of internal and external forces and strains. The Houses of Management and Labor have been separately described above. Discrete descriptions of these two groups are somewhat arbitrary because there is, in reality, an immense amount of interaction between them. It would be just as arbitrary, however, to study the inter-relations of management and labor without analyzing the separate characteristics of each. In some areas each stands apart, in other areas each directly affects the behavior of the other. Thus, it is necessary and important to study the two houses both in *relative isolation and in interaction*.

In keeping with the plan of this book, the primary focus of attention will be on the local work plant. We are well aware that the power setting and general interaction of the union local and of local managers are conditioned by the community, the employers' associations, the international, and even by labor congresses. These influences will be described in later chapters. Here we are interested in the daily and periodic adjustments and conflicts which face the officers of the local union and the plant managers. Attention will be primarily devoted to the patterns of interaction that arise between the two groups.

THE STUDY OF LABOR-MANAGEMENT INTERACTION

One of the difficulties facing the sociologist who wants to describe the interaction of labor and management is the almost endless diversity of their patterns. For example, some large plants must bargain with several different union locals, each of which has evolved a different relationship with management. On the other hand, a particular local may have members in several plants, each of which has different problems. Another factor introducing variability in relations is the different attitudes that employers and unions have toward each other. These range from complete acceptance to absolute distrust. An organizational difference between the two houses may exist. For example, many union locals have almost no autonomy from the international to deal with their local employers, who may have complete independence. Similarly, a subsidiary plant may have no latitude in its union relations. In other cases, both may represent highly centralized or decentralized organizations.

Obviously, all these patterns will not be described in detail, and this is not necessary in any case. The student of industry is more interested in describing *patterns* of relations than their endless diversity. He is concerned

more with the emerging similarities in the processes of adjustment than in a particular adjustment to a specific situation. He believes that *understanding the dynamics* of many situations is superior to an intimate acquaintance of a unique situation.

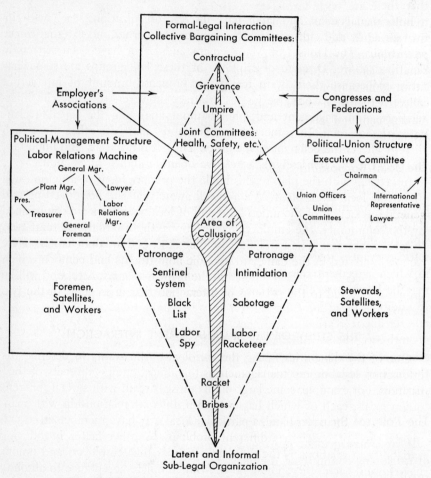

FIG. 40.   The Power Structures of Management and Labor.

In keeping with this principle we shall use as our model a middle-sized plant which deals with a single union. The latter represents most of the workers. Although the union is well entrenched among the workers, it has not evolved a stable relationship with management. Each group has had enough experience with the other to be able to anticipate in some measure the strategy and tactics of the other. Yet both are aggressive—each is trying to enlarge the area of its influence.

LABOR-MANAGEMENT ORGANIZATION

The organizations which labor and management build in the process of interaction are really a complex of several substructures. Figure 40 shows that there are both formal and informal power structures which emerge to influence labor-management interaction. The peak of joint formal activity is observed in the *collective bargaining committees*. The composition of a *political-management structure* and a *political-union structure* is also detailed. Finally a *latent and informal structure* of sub-legal activities is shown. This entire configuration may be regarded as a culture pattern which surrounds collective bargaining and all the other activities involving interaction between management and labor. We shall describe each of these structures and their interaction.

The Joint Bargaining Structure

Periodically (every year or two) representatives of labor and management meet as a committee to determine the conditions of their relationship for a period set by the contract. This committee, in addition, creates or is responsible for other formal organizational machinery. A procedure is set up to settle grievances that will arise during the period of the contract. For cases in which agreement cannot be reached on issues or grievances, an umpire may be hired, or arbitration and mediation machinery may be instituted. In addition, other joint committees may be established—for health, safety, rate setting, recreation, and welfare. These committees have varying degrees of authority. Taken altogether, the collective bargaining committees, the grievance committees, and other joint miscellaneous committees embrace the area of legalistic interaction which characterizes the joint bargaining structure.

The Political Structures of Management and Labor

If labor-management relations were limited strictly to joint participation of bargaining committees, the machinery of negotiation would be relatively small. However, a large part of the organization of both houses is maintained to *support, buttress, or improve their positions* in the bargaining room. In management structure, for example, the position of labor relations director is made necessary by the presence of a labor union. Many of the activities of other managers are also fashioned by the existence of a union. Of course, much of the labor union structure is designed to give support to its representatives in joint bargaining sessions. A large part of the political structure from the House of Labor is drawn into the preparations for the periodic battle over a new contract. At these junctures the relative positions of both union

and management are at stake. A new balance of power may be struck, and this possibility becomes the largest concern of both houses. Both houses gird for the next battle almost as soon as the last one is completed.

The political structures of management and labor should be distinguished from other parts of their organizations. In management structure, the personnel of the structure does not necessarily correspond to the supervisory hierarchy. Often the president and other vice-presidents have nothing to do with labor relations. Very commonly, the bulk of labor relations planning, negotiation, and execution is carried on by a small group composed of the executive vice-president, plant manager, company lawyers, labor relations director, treasurer, and superintendent. Other officials are called in to supply information and advice as they are needed. After the contract is finally written the execution of the labor policies is carried on by the labor relations director and the supervisors. This execution phase is very important for the general atmosphere of labor relations. It will be discussed in detail later in this chapter.

The political corps of labor is composed of a small group of union officials. Unlike the labor relations officials in management, the labor members occupy coördinate positions in reference to each other. Usually, the formal bargaining machine is made up of the executive committee, the elected officials, the international representative or business agent, and heads of important committees such as the contract committee. The composition of this group is not fixed—it is flexible and can be changed as conditions warrant. Once the final contract terms are fixed, the stewards, their satellites, and other workers have the responsibility of executing the agreement.

The political structure of the union does not have the organizational advantages of the management structure. The membership, through the contract committee, designates the kind of agreement it wants. The bargaining committee must report on the progress of negotiation. When a settlement has been reached, it must be submitted to the membership for approval. Such is not the case with management. It fixes its own goals and bargains to get them.

In some cases, both houses are subject to approval of their activities by outside agencies. Whereas management may have to heed the dictates of industry-wide associations, labor locals may have to follow policies of their international or federations. Both the business associations and labor congresses exert pressure on each other as well as on their own local representatives. The large business and labor associations may enter directly into the power struggles of local groups. This is particularly true in the case of the steel, coal, automobile, and transportation industries. In these cases, parent bodies are so directly involved in fixing power relations that individual plants and locals merely execute the directives of the parent groups.

The Latent Informal Structure

In addition to the joint organizations of labor and management and the political structures of each, there exists an informal latent structure that has not received much attention. Figure 40 shows how this structure is intimately tied into the political organization of both groups. Informal agreements are made through the latent structure which may see ultimate realization in the contract. The methods of persuasion or pressure used in this area are not formally recognized by either group. Occasionally, agreements are sub-legal in character, involving bribery, threats, and intimidations on both sides. A patronage system may be in operation in which each side pays the other for information and unofficial help. This is usually in addition to a spy or sentinel system which both groups set up to get information on the strategy and tactics which are being used or will be used to secure advantages in power struggles. These sub-legal and informal tactics permeate the entire organization, from top to bottom. They even reach into the mediation and arbitration machinery.

THE STRATEGY AND TACTICS OF GRIEVANCE BARGAINING

TWO LEVELS OF BARGAINING

There are two major levels or areas in which management and labor struggle to gain advantage or hold advantage over each other. The first level is *contractual* and the other is *grievance* bargaining. Bargaining on the contract level is more inclusive because it defines the general relations of the parties for a specific period. It also defines their relative positions in terms of powers and restrictions. Like law generally, the contract is a compromise of groups jockeying for power, privilege, and position.

Grievance bargaining, on the other hand, is concerned with the daily operation and interpretation of the contract. Grievance bargaining may be considered as the judicial aspect of relations because it is concerned with the interpretation of the law. It is an important area of labor-management relations because, as many lawyers realize, the interpretation of the law is often as important as law itself.

In this section we shall study the process of grievance bargaining; contract bargaining will be considered in the following section. Grievance bargaining will be examined first and in greater detail because it is concerned with management-labor relations in the local work plant. The greater stress on grievance is justified, especially in the face of increasing industry-wide bargaining. In those plants covered by such argreements, grievance bargaining is the only area of local formal management and labor interaction.

Some students of labor deny that grievance is bargaining at all.[6] They conceive of it in the narrow executive and judicial sense, of enforcing the law and testing its obedience. Sociologically, however, grievance machinery is part of collective bargaining for a number of reasons. First, no law is so clearly defined that there cannot be struggles in its interpretation. Interpretation may turn out to be something contrary to the intentions desired by the lawmakers. In such cases, the court interpretation may almost have the power of legislation. Second, in the grievance process all activities tend to take on a precedence character. Thus, over a period of time a common practice takes on the aspect of law, and may later be included as law in the formal contract. Strategy and tactics during grievance sessions may be designed to prepare a case for prerogatives and limitations which should become part of the general contract.

Grievance bargaining characterizes the daily relations between labor and management in local work plants. Occasionally, collective bargaining groups meet to work out a point in the contract. Sometimes joint committees iron out points of conflict. In general, however, the grievance machinery which permeates much of the work plant organization is the day-to-day contact point of management and labor.[7] It is appropriate to begin the examination of grievance bargaining with the contact between the steward and a foreman.

STEWARD-FOREMAN BARGAINING

The Formal Process

Usually, the formal process of grievance bargaining is stated in the contract. The process itself varies somewhat with the size of the plant, but its general outlines are similar. When a worker is aggrieved he is usually supposed to report his complaint to his foreman (a tactical advantage for the company). The steward is then summoned, and efforts are made to settle the grievance immediately. If this cannot be done, the grievance is presented to a committee composed of higher plant managers and union grievance members. If no agreement is reached between them, the case is sent to an arbitrator or umpire for final decision.

Much of the behavior of stewards and foremen is also formalized or ritualized in grievance negotiations. Both the company and the union usually give a formal or informal course on grievance tactics to their respective officials. The foremen are trained primarily in the methods of handling and preventing grievances. The steward, on the other hand, is taught more aggressive tactics—how to spot grievances and how to win cases. Rules of how a good foreman or steward should behave are developed in handbooks.

[6] Neil W. Chamberlain, "Grievance Proceedings and Collective Bargaining," in Richard A. Lester and Joseph Shister (eds.), *Insight into Labor Issues*, The Macmillan Company, 1948.

[7] *Ibid.*, p. 81.

However, to win grievance cases participants must know something about the art of politics. Some foremen and stewards are very good politicians; others are very mediocre. In small plants if relations are amicable, if the union is accepted, and if there is no fundamental jockeying for power, grievance bargaining tends to correspond closely to the formal code. Whenever union or management is aggressive, a more dynamic pattern of bargaining evolves. The company tries to enforce a literal or "tight" interpretation of the contract, and the local wants a liberal or "loose" interpretation. Since the pattern of grievance bargaining is more clearly seen in dynamic situations, we shall elaborate that pattern.

Roles of the Steward

THE DETECTIVE

A steward plays a number of roles, sometimes emphasizing one role and sometimes another. His main role is that of detective. He should try to get around to see if the contract is being violated, and if workers have grievances arising from such violations. He needs to get acquainted with all new men in his department and find out if they carry union cards. Through observation, personal contact, and use of the "grapevine" he must secure information on all significant occurrences in his district. If he has a stationary job, and if the aggrieved parties must report to the foreman first, it is especially difficult in a large department to spot the incipient grievance and to get his defense set. The ambitious steward tries to get a job which gives him mobility. Failing this, he seeks permission to roam the plant one or two hours a day to inform himself on local grievances. Ordinarily, the contract states that the steward should not leave his job unless he is called. He is usually allotted (in the contract) an hour or two off the job to take care of union affairs.

An ambitious, active, inquiring steward may be considered dangerous by a foreman. The struggle of power may begin at this level. The foreman may do everything possible to demand good work performance of the steward and to restrict the latter's mobility to those cases in which he is officially summoned. The tactics of a foreman and a steward in such a situation were reported to us by a steward in an automobile plant in Detroit. The following is a wire recording of the interview:

There's a place where I'd say your average steward is—I'll say stupid. They don't use two hours [daily allotted to them in the contract]. When I don't use up my two hours one night, the next night I use up four hours. . . . Because I know throughout the GM family if most of us don't use those two hours, with the next contract we get—which they tried last time—they'll try to cut the time down to one hour.

As soon as management found out I was aggressive they put the heat on me.

O.K. they tell that foreman, "That guy doesn't leave the department until he's called." I had a hell of a time getting my system set up. I finally everytime I got called out I used my two hours and I go throughout the whole district. So I made a few contacts—I tell the guys, "If you work with me I'll work with you, see." Well they kept putting the thumb down on me. I couldn't get out of that department. Foreman was watching me all of the time. So I got my contract out—so I said, "John, tonight you call me at eight o'clock; Pete, tomorrow night you call me at 7:30." I not only used my two hours, I used two and a half to three hours. Then they said, "Jesus—you're using 2½ to 3 hours a night." I said, "Yep, I can't figure that out. Boy, there's a lot of grievances!"

Instead of fixing things up on the floor like, "You can't do this. Let's do it this way," I wouldn't do that. I'd say, "Nothing I can do about it" and fill out a lot of grievances. Then labor relations noticed all the grievances from me. Two big guys came down to see me. They says, "What's the matter?" I says, "Not a damned thing." They says, "Well, gees, you got more grievances than any other guy in the plant." I says, "I can't figure it out. Lots of this stuff could be settled on the floor if we'd cut out this baloney." I says, "Look right here, we got a little grievance down here right now. I don't want to use your valuable time. But, by God, you guys don't want to cooperate." They couldn't understand that and I told them. "My job is just like yours, as a matter of fact if it wasn't for us god-damn committee men, you guys would have a hell of a job. As long as you guys keep me away from my duty, you're going to get grievance after grievance after grievance."

That night, the foreman came up to me and said, "Well,—look, if you want to leave your department for 2 hours, it's all right as long as you turn in your time." I said, "That's good."

You see, it had to be that way. They were setting up a new department, new men being hired. I had to find out who the guys are, and introduce myself, and get them into the union.

This case illustrates the importance of the detective role to the steward. Unless he has mobility to ferret out the grievances, to get to know the men in his district, his effectiveness will be diminished. There is a jockeying for power on this basic level—to keep the steward from doing his best job and to exert pressure on the company to allow union activities free reign. Even more fundamental is the relationship of contract to custom. Every right and privilege in the contract is in danger of being abolished if the union doesn't show cause for its continuance. The reverse also holds. If either side can prove that a contract clause does not correspond to custom, there is danger that the clause may be removed. If, as in this case, the time allowed stewards for union activity were reduced, the detective role might be seriously impaired.

THE LAWYER

Another important role of the steward is his legal role. Not only must he know the contract in detail, but he should know how to interpret it. A good

steward carries a contract with him all the time. He constantly consults it, and when necessary shows it to the foreman or aggrieved workers. The foreman, of course, also shares the legal role with the steward. Aside from finding legal basis for action, the steward has to present the case to the foreman or higher officials. Many of the legal techniques of testimony, presenting evidence, examination and cross-examination may be used. Some stewards and foremen have a high capacity for this lawyer activity. The excitement and interest gained from this kind of legalistic give-and-take are often the only rewards stewards receive. Boredom of the job is relieved by involvement in the struggles of company and union. Each case is a challenge for the use of ingenuity. The following account (on a wire recording) by a steward illustrates the legal complexities involved in bargaining over some grievances.

This fella I'm telling you about got a really rotten deal with the company once. Well, he had an opportunity to do some carpentry work one summer and he took a week off. He contacted the supervisor, now that's something he shouldn't a done, and asked for a 90 day leave. The supervisor said, "I don't think you can get it but you come and work Monday and I'll see what I can do." Monday he told him, "I can't give you the time off because I can't find a replacement for you." This fellow makes a statement, "I'll find a replacement for you," and he walks off. Now we're not puttin' that in the minutes naturally. Management's contention was that he didn't notify them that he was going to leave.

So he takes off. Management was a little lenient, waiting eight days before they notified him that he's considered a voluntary quit. This fellow, instead of making a move right then waits several more days before he notified the union that the company notified him that he's out of work. So we filed a grievance.

We take our grievance down to the foreman, but he couldn't make a decision on a case like this. So we went to the general foreman. We pounded home the fact that this fellow is a good employee, was with the company for 15 years. We wanted to know why he'd fire a guy like this. He says, "It's not a fire, it's a quit!" We says, "Yeah, but the fellow wants his job back. You're the guy who can give it to him or not." "Well," he says, "I can't do it." That meant that he got labor relation's standing on the case.

Well, we pound labor relations. We use all our resources going on past practice. We brought up a case like this where a guy was fired even when he told management that he'd be back by a certain day. If this fellow here would have told the boss he wouldn't be in by a certain date, we'd had a good case. Now we had to lie like hell to get him back in. But after a lot of finagling we got him back all right. We really got management's crow on that one.

THE POLITICIAN

Playing a political role is almost an inescapable necessity for steward and foreman. Each of them is on the lowest rung of his political system. In a sense, they may be thought of as ward or precinct captains. Their

main duties are to act as listening posts, to organize opinion in favor of their respective causes, to root out sources of discontent, to help build a following for themselves or for some other person, to propagandize for a particular policy, to exert pressure on their own members and threaten the opposition, and to distribute favors or patronage.

Some of the techniques used in the political role are legal, some are sub-legal, and others are criminal or illegal. It may be assumed that any or all of these techniques will be used in different situations. Occasionally, foremen and stewards use their position to extort money for personal ends. Such a pirate sub-legal role is not uncommon in American industry. Its agents are rugged individualists who espouse any cause for personal advancement. Not infrequently they jump from one side to another seeking the best opportunity to ply their trade.

TACTICS AND WEAPONS

The tactics and weapons used by stewards and foremen in grievance bargaining depend upon their roles and orientations, the history of labor-management relations in the plant, and the wider strategy of the two groups.

Gaining Acceptance

Both foremen and stewards are taught that they are most effective if they get accepted as likable people who are reasonable to deal with. They are told to win each other's confidence, to act sincerely, and to be friendly. A steward relates how he gets acceptance by foremen.

Well, I go to the employee and get all the information from him. Then I'll say, "Now look, don't lie to me. If there's any lying let me do it. Now go ahead and repeat what you just told me." By the time he repeats it it's all a little bit different. So then I take notes and go in to the foreman and start talking to him. Naturally, each foreman I use a little bit different approach. Now there's one foreman who's very much of a fisherman. Well I go fishing with him for maybe twenty minutes before I go to work on a case. Now there's another who's a gentleman farmer. I garden with him a little bit, and so on down the line. I use each one different. I have one I can go in and hit the desk with my fist a couple times and he'll sit and shake. Another you couldn't scare— they're union haters. There's where lots of stewards are weak. They don't know how to handle different foremen. They go in and say, "According to the contract you gotta do this or you can't do this." The contract gives you very little ammunition or support. If you had to use your contract, you might as well leave the committeemen out and just forget about the union, because you have nothing there.

Establishing Dominance

A tactic frequently used by both sides is establishing and maintaining the initiative. The foreman is urged to anticipate grievances at their source. Many grievances, for example, may arise over accidents. Safety is usually

the foreman's responsibility. By repeatedly insisting on the use of safety devices (safety glasses, for instance), he may establish dominance. The more the foreman anticipates grievances, the greater the likelihood that the steward will lose interest in his responsibilities and let the foreman have a pretty free hand. The same tactic may be used by the steward. He may be alert for every picayune violation of the contract. At every opportunity he may jump the foreman until the latter gets into the pattern of consulting the steward before he makes any important decision.

Intimidation

Intimidation is usually a more useful weapon to the steward than to the foreman. Since the steward's job is usually protected by the contract, there is little that the foreman can do as long as a union exists. However, the security of the foreman is dependent on the coöperation he secures from those in his department. Foremen are rated by higher managers on their ability to settle grievances on the floor and on their ability to get out production. If the steward decides to push grievances up the channel for settlement, and if he can organize the department to sabotage the foreman's effort for high productivity, the latter's tenure is at stake. The "squeeze play" on the foreman usually "brings him around." This is a form of intimidation which works as long as management does not actively enter the struggle at the first-line level. If it does, a "squeeze" may be applied to the steward as a way to discredit his efforts. A steward relates how a foreman is dependent on the workers and the process they use to intimidate him:

A short time ago we had a lot of trouble with a certain foreman. He was an ex-committeeman by the way. He started out all right, was a good boy, but the guys took advantage of him. So he had to get back at them. He was making them toe the line . . . no quitting early, work from whistle to whistle, no sitting down, no horseplay, this and that. I told the committeeman there, "You do the same thing. Every time he does any work, even if he picks up a box, write a grievance, violation of paragraph 66, violation of paragraph 32, violation of paragraph so and so." The first thing you know grievances started mounting— finally had a pile like that.

Things got so bad that they called a meeting of the top committee. I told them that the guys naturally jump at a foreman when he gets that way. This foreman was removed from that department. He was moved to our department and it's his last chance. If he doesn't do good in this department out he goes. So I went to the guy and told him. "It's your last chance here and you know it. You cooperate with us and we'll cooperate with you. If you don't, we'll put the screws on you and out you go." Things are working out pretty good so far.

Indebtedness

A common technique of influencing an agent or officer is to get him in a state of indebtedness. Foremen and stewards may do each other favors which eventually lead to intimate and dependent relationships. Instead

of regarding each other as representatives of organizations, they come
to think of each other as people who have personal problems. If the relations of company and union are cordial, friendliness is no deterrent to
effective coöperation. If relations are tense or in a state of transition, friendliness and indebtedness may lead to greater eventual difficulties in grievance
bargaining. For this reason militant unions discourage friendliness with
management. They feel that the higher prestige of management may lead
to fawning on the part of union members. A steward's report illustrates a
tactic of indebtedness used by a foreman:

Two or three times the foreman came up to me and I noticed he had a
funny look on his face. Finally at five o'clock I says, "Hans, I'd like to get a
pass to go to the union meeting. I'll be back around 7:30 to pick it up. I'll be
back at work about ten o'clock." "Okay," he says. He didn't have to do it,
mind you. I was going on his better graces. So at 7:30 I asked,
    "You got my pass ready, Hans?"
    "Yeah," he says. "Come on in the office. Look!" he says. "You don't have to
punch out."
    Naturally I acted dumb and said, "Whad'ya mean? I gotta punch out."
    "No, that's all right, just go on and I'll take care of it."
    "Whad'ya mean take care of it?"
    "Why," he says, "you lose two or three hours every time you go out of here."
    "Yeah, I know that."
    "Well, that's three or four dollars every time you go."
    "Yeah, I know that." I played dumb as hell.
    "Look, you just go ahead. Just leave the card in the rack, don't punch it."
    I said, "No," and he got mad.
    I got back about 9:30. To get back you gotta take the card to the foreman and
he writes the time you get in on the back.
    He says, "Go ahead, I can okay this here."
    I said, "No, you better not."
    "Look," he said, "why don't you want me to do that?"
    "Do you really want to know? Maybe some of these days one of these guys
will be on the carpet. He'll call his committeeman and I'll come in here, and
I'll get the case, and maybe say to you,
    " 'Hans, what in the hell are you doing this for?' And you'll give me a song
and dance about how rotten the employee is. Finally, if I keep on bargaining
you'll say,
    " 'Look, for Christ sake, don't you remember the time when I okay'd your
card?' "
    I say, "For a lousy three or four dollars I leave some poor bastard idle." That
foreman got redder than a goddam beet.

The steward may do a foreman a good turn by urging high productivity
when the foreman is under the pressure of the plant manager. He may
give him a ride home, mow or water his grass. All this may be done in
friendliness, but it also affects grievance bargaining.

One of the weapons that a foreman can use effectively to win support among his workers is distribution of overtime work. Most contracts state that management shall "equalize hours as far as practicable." What is practicable is determined by the foreman. Therefore, grievance cases on equalization are very hard to win. The only way a steward can overcome this advantage of the foreman is to make the workers very conscious of the number of hours each of them works. Then they will insist that the foreman be just in distribution of overtime. Many so-called wildcat strikes are engineered by stewards as a protest to such unenforceable violations on the part of the foreman and company.

When overtime is distributed with an eye to getting loyalty, it is, of course, a form of patronage. Patronage is an accepted technique of gaining support in American culture. It is used both by the union and by management. Bribery is resorted to but rarely, excepting in racketeer unions and business, where it is systematic and rational.

CONTRACT BARGAINING

THE INTERMITTENT PROCESS OF BARGAINING

Contract bargaining is by its very nature an intermittent process. Every one or two years the executives of management and union meet to determine their relations for the next fixed period. Between the periods of actual negotiations much spadework may be done by both sides in the form of collecting data and preparing for negotiations. However, the actual process of contract bargaining is an intermittent process and must be analyzed as such. The period between negotiations may be considered one of relative accommodation, whereas contract bargaining is the power struggle which determines the nature of the coming accommodation. If this cannot be achieved, a period of conflict follows which is exemplified by the strike or lockout.

Area of the Process

Unlike grievance bargaining, contract bargaining involves total organizations. The entire union and the entire management organization are concerned directly or indirectly. Increasingly, outside agencies are being implicated. Management's freedom in bargaining at the local level is being restricted by employers' associations which seek solidarity and uniformity of relations with labor. The union local is also losing its freedom to the international. As industry-wide agreements spread, more local enterprises and unions are tied into single agreements. The bureaucratization of bargaining means that higher officials have augmented powers and that the rank and file of labor and management have smaller opportunity to exert influence.

Atmosphere of the Process

Contract bargaining is a serious affair. The agreements which are legis-
lated constitute the most important business of both management and
labor. At the bargaining table negotiators can alter any previous relationship and set new ones as well. Economic well-being, job security, relative
status and power positions are set by the conference. The conditions under
which the company must face the market are largely determined by the
costs of labor. These are things that cannot be taken lightly. Yet the day-to-
day atmosphere of negotiations may vary considerably. Barbash, commenting on this point says, "One kind of union negotiator comes to the collective
bargaining conference all set to thump the table, another makes his point
serenely; still others alternate between serenity and toughness, as the occasion demands. Sometimes the union bargaining committee is chosen to
represent the diverse temperaments that have their special purpose at a
negotiations conference. When the table thumper has issued his ultimatum,
the situation is 'rescued' from a state of impasse by the committee member
who specializes in 'pouring oil on troubled waters.' "[8]

Although union negotiators are chosen more for their bargaining ability
than are management negotiators, the latter also vary in their approach to
bargaining. Some are quiet and dignified, others are aggressive and dynamic.
Variations in the atmosphere of negotiations are associated with the type
of labor-management relations that have been established in different industries. Negotiations in the automobile industry are typically acrimonious;
those in the building trades tend to be more tempered.

STAGES OF COLLECTIVE BARGAINING [9]

Agreement on the final contract is the last stage in a series of steps. The
first step on both sides is to determine the kind of contract the parties desire
for the next period.

1. The Gathering of Ideas for the New Contract

In the case of the union, sentiment of the members on what is "wrong"
with the existing contract is gathered systematically. For example, grievance
cases may have come up which were lost. Plans are therefore made to
change the contract so that such cases may be won. Changes in wage rates
may have been made during the year which at first appeared reasonable but
turned out to be harmful in practice. An effort must be made to change the
rates in the new contract. On the other hand, certain clauses in the old
contract may have proved to be unexpected windfalls. Sentiment for their

[8] Jack Barbash, *Labor in Action*, Harper & Brothers, 1948, p. 102.
[9] Many of the ideas in this section have been inspired by reading Neil W. Chamberlain's *Collective Bargaining Procedures*, American Council on Public Affairs, 1944.

retention in the next contract is indicated. Thus, the proposals for the new contract usually reflect the frustrations of the old contract, the long-term desires of the membership, and certain other demands which the union believes it can secure.

The proposals for the new contract are often privately drawn up by the union officers. In many unions, contract proposals are discussed in open meetings of the membership. When the contract proposal reflects the general feelings of the membership, it is a vital sociological document which is an embodiment of public opinion among the workers. It also reflects the compromises of factions within the union.

Larger unions make some provision for regional or national meetings to gather the proposals of their locals. However, the more highly centralized the unions, the smaller is the probability that ideas of local groups will be represented. Where bargaining occurs on an industry-wide basis, sentiments of particular locals must be either compromised or ignored. This fact is one reason for strong home-rule sentiment in the larger democratic unions.

Contract proposals preoccupy the minds of management for a couple of months before negotiations begin. The experience of living with a particular agreement gives executives ideas about what they like and don't like in the contract. Efforts are made by intelligent managers to get the feelings of all supervisors on the shortcomings of the present contract and their suggestions for the new one. However, there is no compulsion in this matter and more frequently the board of directors or top line officials determine what kind of contract is needed.

2. Drafting the Proposal and the Counterproposal

A formal contract proposal or counterproposal, whether it is to be given orally or in written terms, is drafted by both sides before negotiations begin. In the local union the executive or contract committee usually drafts its first proposal. Anyone may be consulted during this process for ideas about how far the company will go in yielding to demands. When the proposal is prepared, it usually is submitted to the membership for ratification or amendment. Strong factions may attack the proposal as weak, with the result that demands are raised. Leaders must take these demands to the bargaining table whether they believe them capable of realization or not. Where bargaining is on an industry-wide basis, drafting is done by regional or national panels, and leaders are responsible to the international union.

By custom, the union at the first bargaining session submits its proposal to the company. In the meantime, company officials seek to anticipate what the union will demand. This is usually not difficult, because once the union submits its proposals to the membership the demands become known and there is little possibility of keeping them secret. With the union proposals in mind, a counterproposal is prepared by company negotiators. Not infre-

quently, executives of trade associations are consulted to make sure that the counterproposal will not deviate materially from the pattern desired by the industry. Indeed, associations often determine the exact content of the proposals.

3. The First Meeting

The first meeting of the joint negotiating committees is usually regarded as extremely important, for it may set the tone for all of the negotiations. Although the union proposal is regarded as an offensive instrument, the manner of its reception is often set by tradition. Many unions, for example, make eloquent, blue-sky proposals at the first session. They demand fantastic wages, hours, and working conditions and attempt to justify their position. Both union and management realize that the final contract will be much closer to the present one than the proposals. Unrealistic union demands flow from the political nature of the union. They arise to satisfy factions in the membership that they are out for everything possible. Thus, blue-sky proposals are either rituals or indications that the union will not be satisfied with ordinary concessions. From the presentation at the meeting and from the "grapevine," management must guess whether the "union boys are putting on an act" or whether "they really mean business."

At either the same or the following meeting, management usually submits a counterproposal. It is also regarded as an offensive weapon of great value, because it sets the attack to be used in future meetings.[10] An elaborate justification for the position is presented not only to contain union proposals but to put the union on the defensive. The company proposals are often as unrealistic and ritualistic as the blue-sky demands. They are made to secure a tactical advantage and to suggest to the union some of the concessions it must make.

4. The Bargaining Sessions

The actual conduct of future meetings depends upon a number of factors. Chamberlain suggests that among the most important of these are the composition of the representatives of management and union, the nature of their authority, and the manner of organization they represent.[11] Obviously, a committee of like-minded professional union bargainers who have complete authority to make a settlement will bargain differently from a local bargaining committee made up of representatives of different factions who have no authority to make a final agreement. Similarly, management's negotiators will vary in reference to these factors.

In addition to these considerations, bargaining will be greatly affected by the historical framework of union-management relations. That is, nego-

[10] How to Handle Collective Bargaining, National Foreman's Institute, 1944, p. 8.
[11] Op. cit., p. 26.

tiators' tactics will vary with the traditional motives which each group has and the motives they impute to the other side. Harbison and Dubin illustrate this point by contrasting the negotiations of the United Auto Workers union with General Motors and Studebaker.[12] In the case of General Motors, the corporation insists that managerial functions be protected at all costs. This is based on the corporation's conviction that the union's economic objectives would bring about the destruction of private enterprise and the undermining of the authority and status of management.[13] Union officials, on the other hand, believe that full production and employment cannot be achieved in the automobile industry unless government and the union exert social controls over the major policies of the corporation.

The structure of relations between the union and Studebaker are quite different.[14] Coöperation rather than antagonism characterizes their relations, because bargaining centers around problems rather than principles. The union operates within an atmosphere of security actively supported by company policies. Management, on the other hand, has its own prerogatives which are not challenged by the union. Both groups share in making and administering work rules. As a result, the balance of power between management and the union is rather stable.

Another important factor in conditioning bargaining is the type of labor-management pattern that exists in the industry in question. Three general patterns have been suggested.[15] The first is the *generating type*, represented by General Motors and the U.A.W., U.S. Steel and United Steel Workers, and others. These powerful management and union groups through their bargaining set the pattern of wages, working conditions, and conditions of employment in the entire industry. Thousands of other employers are influenced in their decisions by the pattern set by the leaders. These constitute the *satellite type* because their market climate is set by another labor-management pattern. The third type is the *semi-isolated*. Industries and unions in this category are not large enough or powerful enough to influence other groups. At the same time, they are not directly influenced by patterns set by the generating type. Relations between union and management are more or less self-contained.

In actual bargaining sessions the negotiators in the generating and in the semi-isolated patterns have greater independence in bargaining. Their sessions are more likely to be dynamic and strategic in nature. Sessions in the

[12] Frederick H. Harbison and Robert Dubin, *Union-Management Relations*, Science Research Associates, 1937, p. 65.

[13] *Ibid.*, p. 67.

[14] *Ibid.*, p. 133.

[15] See Frederick H. Harbison, Robert R. Burns, and Robert Dubin, "Toward a Theory of Labor Management Relations," in *Insight into Labor Issues*, edited by Richard A. Lester and Joseph Shister, The Macmillan Company, 1948, pp. 21-23.

satellite pattern will be more tactical in nature because its participants realize that their broad relations have been set. Advantages can only be gained on "fringe" issues such as holidays, pensions, vacations, etc.

BARGAINING TACTICS

To have true collective bargaining there must be a rough equality of power. When one party can dictate terms of an agreement, there is no chance for a bargain. For implicit in bargaining is the threat of the ultimate use of force. Where force is absent, concessions rest on the mercy of the opponent, and there is little mercy in collective bargaining. It follows, then, that tactics are useless when both parties are aware that a significant difference in power exists between them. Tactics are useful when power relations are unknown, and when there is an approximate equality of power.

Bargaining as an Art

Successful bargaining has been called an art because the ingredients of influence have not been scientifically analyzed. Bluffing, the using of facts, leaving the door open, retiring gracefully, pursuing an advantage, threatening to use force, laying a trap, and confusing the opponent are common tactics in bargaining. Some negotiators are more successful with some techniques than with others. Whatever methods are employed, effective bargaining certainly rests on the use of the right techniques at the right time. A knowledge of personalities, social situation, and market conditions is necessary for success in this area.

Reducing Disagreement

The process of collective bargaining is one of reducing the issues of disagreement. This is done by both parties as they come to concern themselves with specific issues rather than with the general contract. The conference chairman may propose that each point be taken up individually, or in a particular order. If this is done, a number of items may be dispensed with quickly. First, there tends to be a ready agreement to the traditional prerogatives of both groups which were embodied in the previous contract. Other items on which the parties are not wide apart are considered next and disposed of. When long and heated arguments ensue on an issue, progress may be made by postponing a decision on it and moving to another item on the agenda. In the meantime, each party may conduct a caucus and decide upon future concessions and tactics.

From Principles to Practices

Each party in the negotiations feels that it has some rights and principles which it must protect at all costs. For management these are its "prerogatives" and for the union, its "rights." Obstacles to agreement usually arise

when these prerogatives or rights are challenged as such. It is virtually impossible to settle controversy on principles. For example, union negotiators may argue that profits are too high. This is an area of decision in which management feels it should have complete control. A compromise on how profits should be distributed is impossible. The tactic that should be used to resolve the deadlock is to pass from principle to practice. In this case it would be to negotiate specific wages for specific jobs in the light of the company's ability to pay. Obviously, this is just another way of deciding upon the distribution of profits. Higher wages, when prices remain constant, come largely from profit. Men fight to protect semantic idols. In practice, the idol may be chipped away without their decrying it.

Good negotiators know this to be true. They avoid red-flag words which excite emotion and settle nothing. Such verbal substitution can be made as:[16]

Principle	Substitute
Management prerogatives	Management functions
Fire	Terminate employment
Strike	Work stoppage
Seniority	Length of service

These substitutions work well until they become stereotypes or emotive labels. Then new terms must be found that are devoid of emotional connotations.

Appeal to Facts

Almost all negotiators make use of economic data in the presentation or refutation of an argument. Charts may be made depicting trends in average wages in the industry, profit position, cost of living, prices, costs, and so on. How effective this practice is in influencing the opposing party is open to question. Arguments invariably develop as to the "validity" of the statistics. Accusations are made that the facts are "loaded" to prove a point.

Facts influence if men are rational and if they share common ends. When this is not true an appeal to statistics assumes the form of a rite or ritual. This does not mean that the ritual has no function. The presentation of data may actually serve to reduce the blue-sky demands. It may indicate that the group was concerned enough about the issue to have spent much time and money gathering facts. Such a concern with the subject shows, perhaps, that they will not yield easily on the issue. Moreover, the newspaper may print their data and bring the pressures of public opinion to their aid.

There are contests which can be influenced by statistics, but bargaining

[16] See Lee H. Hill and Charles R. Hook, *Management at the Bargaining Table*, McGraw-Hill Book Company, Inc., 1945, p. 258.

battles are not won with them. Facts and figures don't solve the ultimate problem of what is a "fair" distribution of profits and wages. Relative power determines this. At some stage, the balance of power is finally revealed. Depending upon the balance, concession or impasse results.

Impasses in Negotiations

Not infrequently bargainers cannot come to an agreement on certain issues. Unless they are to resort to force, a compromise must be arranged. Sometimes simple logrolling occurs. One party yields on one issue while the other party yields on some other issue. Many additional techniques may be tried to break the jam. The conference committee may be reduced in size with the hope that a smaller group can compromise more easily than a larger one. A cooling-off period may be suggested, or the intervention of a third party may be sought. The public may be impatient at the delay in settlement, especially when the parties are so close. However, both parties may feel that they have compromised too much already, and on this last issue the other side should yield. The status of the individual bargainers as well as the groups is at stake. Even to arbitrate may mean defeat.

Calling in the government or an outside agency to mediate may be interpreted as a sign of weakness by either side. Management may feel that calling in an outside agency is an improper delegation of their authority. Union leaders may feel that so-called impartial agencies are antilabor. In addition, much time is consumed by informing the third party of everything that has transpired. It is considered better to resolve differences than to have an unfair decision forced upon one.

When the agreement is finally decided, it usually must be submitted to the membership of the union for approval. When union negotiators feel that a bad contract is proposed, they may encourage the membership, via the grapevine, to reject it. When the negotiators believe they have made the best bargain possible and it is rejected by members, a new bargaining committee is appointed to resume negotiations. It usually follows that defeated negotiators are put out of office on the following election. If the contract is accepted by the rank and file, it is usually played up as a great victory. Management also likes to feel that it has won a victory. The bargainers of both groups shake hands, smile for the photographers, and suspend their struggles for another year.

UNION-MANAGEMENT COÖPERATION
VOLUNTARY COÖPERATION

Labor-management relations are said to go through three stages: opposition, toleration, and coöperation. Many people who regard interruption in production as "the labor problem" dream of the day when coöperation will

typify all labor-management relations. They seem unaware that some areas of coöperation already exist, among them the grievance and collective bargaining procedures. But this is not enough for them; they want to eliminate strikes; they want both groups to end the wastages of restrictive practices; they want both groups to promote the efficiency of the industry for their mutual welfare. Such "coöperation" has occurred, but it has been relatively rare.

The Economic Setting

Shister found, in surveying cases in which union-management coöperation had been successful in reducing unit costs, that such coöperation was rarely found in prosperous times or in prosperous industries.[17] General economic depression has been partly responsible for coöperation in reducing cost, lowering wages, or rationalizing production *and not the intellectual acceptance of the principles of union-labor coöperation.* The men's clothing industry is the classic case in point. In the 1920's costs in the industry were reduced by wage cuts, introduction of the piece-rate system, and elimination of restrictive rules. These concessions are usually made with the understanding that management too will cut costs by modernizing equipment, seeking new markets, and raising wages as efficiency increases.

Instances of coöperation are found when a unionized company is competing disadvantageously with nonunionized plants. It is also evident when an industry is adversely affected by competition from a substitute product. The railroad industry was stimulated to coöperative practices by the introduction of new transportation media such as planes, buses, and automobiles. A similar situation was found as demand shifted from cotton to silk and rayon.[18]

Elements of Coöperation

An obviously depressed economic condition, either generally or in a specific industry, does not necessarily lead to coöperation. Coöperation depends upon union objectives, workers' sentiments, union leadership, and management's attitudes.[19] The union objective may be to maintain wage rates as high as possible even though it may result in greater unemployment. The union may be opposed in principle to collaboration with employers. In addition, workers may be opposed to incentive systems or coöperation on the basis of sentiment alone, irrespective of the difference it may mean in the size of their pay envelope. The union leaders may or may not be able to educate the rank and file on the reality of nonunion competition

[17] Joseph Shister, "Union-Management Cooperation: An Analysis," in Lester and Shister, *op. cit.*, pp. 87-115.
[18] See S. H. Slichter, *Union Policies and Industrial Management,* The Brookings Institution, 1941, chaps. 17 and 18.
[19] Shister, *op. cit.*, pp. 91-105.

and on the difference of unemployment resulting from depression on the one hand and industrial rationalization on the other. Unemployment is unemployment. Obviously, coöperation cannot occur if management is antiunion. Full acceptance of the union is necessary to inaugurate union-management coöperation.

STIMULATED COÖPERATION

In general, the union and management prefer the system of bargaining periodically to an institutionalized system of coöperation. Management considers ordinary losses incurred by restrictive practices as constant costs of production. Unions feel that the possible wage losses incurred by non-coöperation are worth the price of independence. During national emergencies, however, the government feels that the nation cannot afford the luxury of these losses. Especially during war, government feels that highest production can be achieved only by the active coöperation of both parties. During both world wars the government stimulated the formation of joint labor-management committees to this end.

Labor-Management Committees

Early in 1942 the War Production Board suggested that labor-management committees be established to increase the output of war goods. Agreements were signed by representatives of the union, management, and the government stating that they would form committees whose purpose would be attainment of the highest production possible. These committees were in no way to be substitutes for the bargaining committees already existent. Their activities were numerous.[20] Suggestion systems were organized to find ways of improving production. Salvage and conservation programs were inaugurated, and improved systems of caring for tools and equipment were installed. Committees also encouraged improvement of the quality of work. Health, safety, and transportation facilities were instituted to decrease absenteeism and loss of man-hours. Housing, training, and other programs were jointly sponsored to the end that morale and production might be improved.

No doubt the work done by these committees was considerable. Management and union leaders did work *with* each other toward common goals. Although in many cases coöperation was nothing more than "window dressing," investment of time and energy in joint activities was on the whole worth while. However, with the cessation of the war and the withdrawal of stimulation from the government most of these committees collapsed. The relations between union and management that existed prior to the war soon returned. It is unlikely that widespread active coöperation

[20] See Clyde E. Dankert, *Contemporary Unionism in the United States*, Prentice-Hall, Inc., 1948, pp. 473-475.

such as existed during the war will return. A powerful government may encourage it, a totalitarian government may insist on it, but free unions and businesses will assume it only when they see no more profitable alternative.

INFORMAL COÖPERATION

Despite the attitudes that management and union leaders take on formal coöperation, a certain amount of informal coöperation is necessary if the enterprise is going to survive. In the first place, there is an economic interdependence which binds both groups in mutual endeavor despite divergences in their ideologies. But even more important than their symbiotic interdependence are the common sentiments binding them together.

Plant and Work Pride

One of the sentiments that all workers in a plant usually share is identification with the plant. Both managers and workers take pride in the product turned out and the plant they work in, or the prestige of the plant in the community. It is difficult to spend half of one's waking hours in a place and have no emotional involvement in it. Anti-management workers seem to derive as much pleasure from showing their families where they work as do pro-management workers. To stimulate this identification with the plant, many executives have inaugurated "family days." The workers' families first are conducted through the plant. They see where the family member works, and are then entertained and fed. All animosities are temporarily forgotten.

Function of the Holiday

Holidays are often observed both in the work plant and in the community. All workers, irrespective of their positions and roles in the organization, observe the rituals associated with the particular holiday. In fact, one of the functions of holidays is to provide areas of common ritualistic experience. As rites, they tend to underline or emphasize common ideals and values. This is especially the case when holidays are observed in the plant. Holidays are not observed for their religious values but rather for their hedonistic associations. For holidays in America are becoming less and less holy days and increasingly days "to have fun." An approaching holiday means primarily cessation from work and interruption of the common struggles and animosities.

The holidays most commonly observed in work plants are Christmas and New Year's. Celebrations vary in their elaborateness from playing appropriate music during lunch hour to having special programs. Not infrequently, managers use this season to give the annual bonus. Significantly, the bonus is given not only when it is most needed but at the time when good will is most likely to abound. Newspapers emphasize the joy and good cheer of the season. A typical report reads:

2,500 CHILDREN SEE SANTA CLAUS AT PRE-CHRISTMAS PARTIES
and Adults Are Feted, Too, at Affairs in Rochester

Christmas may be officially celebrated Dec. 25, but some 2,500 screaming, happy kids had a different answer yesterday as a flurry of pre-Christmas parties blanketed the Rochester area. And to prove that the festive holiday isn't solely for children, countless other parties, for adults only, were held in local hotels, hospitals and private homes.

Top afternoon crowd was counted at the Bausch and Lomb Co. children's party where nearly 1,800 youngsters and sons and daughters of plant employees, jammed their way into the auditorium to join in the merriment. Other local industries and veteran and fraternal organizations collaborated to make Saturday, Dec. 18 glow in every tot's memory.

A premature Christmas celebration was also observed at Whiting-Buick where 78 children of the firm's employees gathered to talk to Santa and to receive gifts. A dinner was followed by entertainment and dancing. One highlight was the presentation of the more than 100 bonus checks to the kiddies' fathers.[21]

Other holidays may be celebrated less elaborately, but their function is more or less the same. Patriotic holidays, especially, are observed by almost every group irrespective of status, race, religion, or other attributes.

Private Holidays

Occasionally, other opportunities for joint celebrations occur. A factory may want to celebrate an anniversary of twenty-five, fifty, or a hundred years in a community. Managers try to make the anniversary celebration take on the characteristics of a general holiday. For this reason they want everyone of importance in the community to participate in the program. Leaders from labor, business, government, and religion are asked to play a role. A presser in a clothing factory tells of a centennial anniversary dinner given by the company.

What a party we had yesterday at the Iroquois Hotel! Jesus, there must a been about 2,000 people in the ballroom. What a feed we had—turkey, chicken, salad, steak, pie—everything you could eat. And boy, there was everything to drink— wine, beer, whiskey, everything!

Everybody had a wonderful time.

All the big shots in the city were there. There was the mayor, the Bishop, the president of the company, the president of the International, newspaper photographers, and lots of other people. After the dinner, the mayor, Mr. — (president of the company) and Mr. — (president of the union) made speeches. . . . What did they say? Oh, I don't know, they talked about the company being in business for a hundred years . . . what a good name the company has . . . there's going to be lots of work ahead . . . we gotta keep up quality work . . . what a good union we got . . . season's greetings . . . and things like that.

[21] Rochester *Democrat and Chronicle*, December 19, 1948.

After the speeches there were drinks. Everybody was walking around drinking, visiting, and having a good time. The mayor, the Bishop, and the union big shots were drinking in a little room on the side. I went in there 'cause I was feeling a little rocky I guess. But they were very nice. They offered me a drink and I talked a while, and then joined the boys. . . . I'll bet that party cost the company more than ten thousand bucks.

Other private celebrations are held which, if successful, reinforce those few common sentiments that bind management and union together. Such coöperative strands as now exist are not sufficiently strong to overcome the widening breaches developing between these two groups. Genuine coöperative relations cannot be developed until the area of common sentiments is widened and buttressed with joint structures in which both groups make all major decisions which affect them.

SUMMARY

The House of Management and the House of Labor are locked together in a continuing power struggle. This is not to be decried but to be appreciated. Bargaining requires freedom. We have evidence of a democracy when management and labor can bargain freely with each other.

We have observed that political processes run through the social structure of industry. The political structures of management and labor touch during the negotiating of the contract and in the bargaining over grievances. Formal and latent organizations operate so that the political processes are simultaneously exposed and screened. Men who seek to administer and control these processes must learn to play the appropriate roles. Such roles require adaptability to the techniques of conflict, accommodation, and coöperation. If they are successful they may gain power and status. If they fail, others rise to take their places.

SUPPLEMENTARY STUDIES

FIELD OBSERVATION: DIRECT OBSERVATION OF A SELECTED WORK PLANT
(Continued)

In the work plant selected, set out:
The Power Structure of Management and Labor
  Describe:
1. The political structure of management.
2. The political structure of labor.
3. Major conflicts between union and management.
4. Tactics and weapons each structure uses.
5. Types of union-management coöperation.

LIBRARY: BOOKS AND ARTICLES

Bakke, E. W., *Mutual Survival*, Harper & Brothers, 1946.

Drucker, Peter, "Citizenship in the Plant," *Harper's Magazine*, December, 1946, pp. 511-520.

Drucker, Peter, "Why Men Strike," *Harper's Magazine*, November, 1946, pp. 385-395.

Harbison, Frederick H., and Dubin, Robert, *Patterns of Union-Management Relations. The UAW (CIO), General Motors and Studebaker*, Science Research Associates, 1949.

Labor Committee of the Twentieth Century Fund, *Partners in Production*, The Twentieth Century Fund, 1949.

Selekman, Benjamin B., *Labor Relations and Human Relations*, McGraw-Hill Book Company, Inc., 1947, Part I, "Transition in Labor Relations: A Social Change," pp. 1-44 also chap. 4, "Building Joint Relationships," pp. 45-74.

LIBRARY: NEWSPAPERS, PAMPHLETS, AND SONGS

Listen to some labor songs. An interesting album is Keynote Album 106, *Talking Union*.

Read or sing some of the union songs in *The People's Song Book*, edited by Waldemar Hille and published by Boni and Gaer, Inc., 1948.

Read some of the labor and management newspapers and magazines. Some of the most important are:

N A M News, published by the National Association of Manufacturers.

CIO News, published by the Congress of Industrial Organizations.

American Federationist, published by the American Federation of Labor.

Nation's Business, published by the United States Chamber of Commerce.

UAW-CIO Ammunition published by the United Auto Workers.

Read some pamphlets. The National Association of Manufacturers, 14 West 49th Street, New York 20, N. Y., has pamphlets and films available on request. Some interesting pamphlets are:

The Closed Shop, Information Bulletin No. 13.

Management Answers to Some Union Objections on Wage Incentives, Information Bulletin No. 15.

Preparing to Negotiate, Management Memo No. 2.

Should Labor Be Given a Direct Share in the Management of Industry?

Ten Basic Principles Essential to a Sound National Labor Policy.

National Labor Policy and Industrial Relations, speech by Caroll E. French.

Seniority, Management Memo. No. 1.

Employment Stabilization—Industry's Progress Toward Steady Work and Steady Pay.

The Congress of Industrial Organizations, 718 Jackson Place, N.W., Washington 6, D.C., publishes a number of pamphlets available for small sums. Among these are:

No. 93, *Political Primer for All Americans.*

No. 173, *CIO—What It Is and What It Does.*

No. 166, *Resolutions*, CIO Tenth Annual Convention, Portland, Oregon.
No. 158, *How Big Is Big Business?*
No. 168, *CIO's Two-Way Drive for Social Security*.

Laboratory: Experimentation in Labor-Management Interaction

Step 1. Select five persons who will represent management at the bargaining table. It may facilitate the conference to secure persons who have had supervisory experience in management positions.

Select five persons who will represent the union at the bargaining table. Union members or students of labor usually make good representatives.

Step 2. The situation is the annual bargaining conference over a new contract. The company is engaged in the manufacture of .... It contains (number) .... employees.

Step 3. Each side is dismissed for a caucus. Labor group decides upon demands. Management prepares a defense against anticipated demands. It seeks to maintain the present contract without change.

While each side is in caucus, the class decides to watch for the pattern of ideas and sentiments characterizing the management and labor members such as

Management	Labor
Cost	Security (standard of living, seniority, tenure, safety)
Profit	
Output	Recognition (grievance, suggestions, closed shop)
Competition (wages, hours, and working conditions in labor market)	
Efficiency (fair day's work, merit)	Opportunity (merit rating, promotion, job analysis)
Rating	Union rights (joint-consultation; information)
Management rights or privileges bestowed	

Step 4. Bring in both parties and practice the negotiating conference.
Step 5. Summarize the pattern of ideas and sentiments used by each side. Discuss with the class:

> What compromises were effected?
> How were compromises effected?
> Where was compromise impossible to attain? Why?
> How might a compromise have been reached?

Library: Moving Film

For the Record (19 minutes), record of the 1946 strikes of the C.I.O., their causes and outcome. Produced by Brandon Films.

Research Gaps

1. The influence of the latent and informal structure of sub-legal activities of the power structures of management and labor.
2. Evaluation of the processes fostering conflict and coöperation in management-union relations of a given work plant.
3. The bargaining relationships between foreman and steward.
4. Internal struggles for power within management; within the union.

CHAPTER XI

Status Organization of the Work Plant

THE UNIVERSALITY OF STATUS ORGANIZATIONS

THE CONCEPT OF STATUS ORGANIZATION

Work plant society is a balance of power between union and management organizations on the one hand, and a network of informal interacting groups on the other. How foremen, stewards, and other officials operate is a function of their work positions, social roles, and orientations. The work roles and orientations of people in these offices are set by their social positions in the groups in which they function.

In the section on informal social organization we concluded that social position is fixed both by formal criteria and by interpersonal relations. Thus, a foreman has formal power attached to his work position. His effectiveness, however, is dependent on his social position in the work group. If he is accepted, he has influence in addition to power. If he is not accepted, he has only naked power. We have just examined the organization and distribution of power in the contemporary work plant. In this chapter we shall focus our attention on how status is organized on a plant-wide basis.

The Distinction Between Status and Power

The status of a person may be defined as the position he occupies in an organization or group. It is convenient to think of people living in status situations. In the latter is included every component of social life that affects an individual's status or prestige in the group. Although it is easy to confuse a status situation with a power position, the two should be kept distinct. Perhaps an illustration will serve to emphasize the difference.

We may examine a chain of responsibilities in a government bureau. The supervisory structure in this bureau is, in our terminology, an authority or power organization. It also tends to be true that those positions with greater power have greater status. However, two people having the same formal authority may occupy different status positions. That is, they have unequal respect or prestige in the groups in which they participate. Thus, two chiefs of filing divisions may have the same amount of power in their sections, but one chief has higher status because he supervises the filing of records of executive conferences, whereas the other supervises the filing of wage records. Why such differences in prestige exist between two or more offices may not be apparent at first. Some of the factors that account for them are the traditions of the local situation, the personalities of the supervisors, and the class level of the people in the work groups.

The Importance of Status in the Work Plant

The satisfactions or dissatisfactions people get from their work depend on the status they have at work. For many people the work group is the

only group or one of the few groups from which they obtain personal recognition. For many workers it is one of the most important groups in which they seek recognition. It is reasonable, then, to regard the work plant as a social organization, such as a club, school, or lodge, in which people strive for status. Whether they recognize it or not, most workers are more sensitive of their status in the work society than in any other group.

The American Creed

Many Americans are verbal equalitarians. They are reluctant to admit that American society or the work society promotes inequalities. Furthermore, they deny that a person's social position is basic in establishing his economic position. In fact, they like to believe that a free society does not measure a man in social terms. They argue that what counts is what a man produces, not how much influence he has.

It is easily demonstrated that these are erroneous statements. In interviews with 120 workers, the authors asked the question, "Do people you work with have the same social background as you have?" The workers understood the question and answered it directly. Their comments were analyzed and classified in Table 9.

TABLE 9. Percentage in Various Occupational Levels Signifying Social Location of Work Associates

Occupational Levels	Same Social Background (Percent)	Reservations, or Different Social Backgrounds (Percent)	Total (Percent)
Professionals (16)	84	16	100
Owners, managers, and officials (22)	60	40	100
Clerical and kindred workers (17)	63	37	100
Skilled workers and foremen (19)	70	30	100
Semiskilled and operatives (25)	65	35	100
Unskilled workers (14)	58	42	100
Domestic and personal service workers (7)	44	56	100
Total (120)	64	36	100

Almost two-thirds of the workers believe their work associates have "backgrounds" similar to their own. That is, they believe they are operating in groups of status equals. Over one-third, however, feel that inequalities exist in their work group. Some differences according to occupational level are discernible. Highest agreement over similarity of status among co-workers is found among professionals (84 percent) and skilled workers (70 percent). Greatest inequality among work associates is felt by proprietors (40 percent), unskilled workers (42 percent), and domestics (56 percent). Although the number of cases in our sample is small, the data point to the fact that

workers are well aware of status differences in their work groups. The variations found in their responses reflect the fact that the range of social contacts on the job is larger for some occupations than others. Some jobs limit contacts to people who do exactly the same kind of work; other jobs expose their occupants to people of various skills and backgrounds. Proprietors, for example, usually associate with people of many status levels, whereas this is less true of skilled and semiskilled workers.

The beginning worker in a new job or department is keenly aware of the existence of a status structure and his position in it. He is on trial; he must find his place in the already existing structure. When he does not achieve this, he is even more sharply aware of the reality of the status organization. The older worker, on the other hand, has found his "place" in the group. If he finds that his status is satisfactory, he may soon be unaware that there are such things as "places." Even if his "place" is unsatisfactory, he may accommodate to it after a time. In fact, a position of higher status may make him uncomfortable. Such is the case with the maid who refuses to eat with her employer. It is also the case of the worker who refused to be promoted to foreman. He said, "We're all the same, and I just can't lord it over the other fellows. . . . Give it to somebody else."

Some Illustrations

Two case histories are presented which document the reality of a status organization in operation. The first is that of a girl who has just entered college after her first job experience.

Last summer was the first time in my life that I had ever worked for pay. The place was a large department store. I was put in hosiery. My first day was a hectic one. I tried to learn the job, become acquainted with the other clerks, find time for lunch, and become an expert on salesmanship the first day.

As the time went on, I became more settled in the routine duties of a salesgirl and began to notice what went on among the personnel.

A large department store hires many different types of people. The main floor consists mostly of high school girls. In the gown department and fur department are the older, more experienced women. Then, of course, there are the supervisors, floor walkers, stock people, and many others that make up the store. All these people belong to different cliques. The members are interested in their own welfare and not in the clerks as a whole.

The whole matter depends on the supervisor. For instance, in our store the supervisor was a very attractive woman of about forty years of age. She dressed perfectly and had a charming personality. Her one fault was intolerable. It was nationality prejudice. It seems that her ancestors came over on the Mayflower. She had a great dislike for Italians and Jews. Anything that went wrong was blamed on them. When one of the Italian or Jewish girls wanted a day off, they were refused, though the other clerks were granted days off for less serious

purposes than theirs. And so it went, those who had social prestige and those who had none, the haves against the have-nots!

Social snobbery on the job is one of the many faults we have in America. We may read and hear about American Democracy, but when we come right down to the facts, we haven't much.

A male college freshman discusses his irritations over a particular status situation:

It is very easy to say that there can't be such a thing as social snobbery. A job is a job and every person who has anything to do with that job should do it at his very best. This statement, however true it may be, is not always just so. I have had the experience where it has been entirely different.

A few years ago, I worked on a job that paid quite a bit per hour, but it was at the same time a dirty job. I worked with two other boys as a cleanup crew. One of the boys was from a family of about the same caliber in social standing as my family. The other boy was older than we were and he was from a better family. I didn't mean better in a sense of perfectness but his father was well-to-do for he had a good job as the president of a small factory. The three of us working together could have been almost excellent on the job. As it was, we were not working together, for the boy whose dad was rich had an exalted opinion of himself.

Our job as a cleanup crew was to keep the floors clean, bale scrap paper, and to keep the machines clean. We had decided to divide the work among ourselves and make it easier for us. The rich boy was very much turned against this idea for he didn't want to clean any of the machines when it was his turn. He shirked all his duties with a fear of getting a little dirt on his hands. He came to work in his suit of good clothes when we came in our overalls. I slowly took an attitude toward him which wasn't very nice but which I knew the other boys also took. When we were asked to do things out of our line of work, our friend, the rich boy, did not take his share, but we dropped our other jobs, finished what we were asked to do and went back and picked up where we had stopped.

The man who had charge of keeping us busy began to notice what was going on so he went to the boss about it. We found out that he had gone in and as we waited for his return we hoped that this wouldn't cost us a job. When he came out, he took us into a corner and explained the situation. The rich boy's father had done a lot of business for this particular company and had gotten his son the job there. Our boss was obligated to the boy's father for many things, and therefore, he was in no place or position to fire him. He could not and did not. We had to learn to get along ourselves and let our rich friend keep on at his usual rate of loafing. We were never friends, and I doubt if we ever will be. I only hope that someday for his sake somebody will be in a position to make him see the light.

There is snobbery over a job as long as one person, it only takes one, among the whole group of people has an exalted opinion of himself. People who are doing a job should do it with a feeling of helping somebody else and not just themselves.

These case histories are illustration of an informal status organization in operation. The members of small work groups gradually evolve a system of informal social placements. The formal organization also grants different degrees of recognition to workers. However, the informal and formal rankings need not correspond. The formal status structure grants recognition on the basis which managers believe to be important. They grant recognition, for example, to long and faithful service, to loyalty to the organization, and to obedience. This approval may be expressed by giving the worker a promotion, a raise, a dinner, awards, medals, plaques, or certificates. These sources of honor in formal management organization may in the informal groups make a worker a "stool pigeon," a "scab," a "climber," or a "rat." Status may be given to the worker who has resisted management, who has championed the "rights" of Department X, who challenges directives, and who tells the foremen to "go to hell."

CHARACTERISTICS OF STATUS ORGANIZATIONS

FORMAL AND INFORMAL STATUS ORGANIZATIONS

One of the best analyses of the status organization in industry has been made by C. I. Barnard. He suggests that this subject has not been given thorough consideration.

"This neglect appears not to be due to failure to recognize the importance of status in organizations, but rather to failure to recognize that status is systematic and that systems of status have a considerable degree of independence of other structural aspects of organization. Status systems are very closely related, for example, to systems of specialization, to systems of organization communication, and to systems of authority, so that differences of status have appeared to be incidental to these other structural aspects of organization and not to constitute a separate system. This view appears to be inadequate."[1]

The social organization which revolves around status is often extensive. Sometimes it is formally recognized and sometimes it remains on the unrecognized or informal level. Despite the hesitation in America to give status much formal recognition, most work plants have evolved some formal means to establish and maintain status. Barnard believes that these various means may be divided into several categories.[2] We have recombined them into four groups.

1. Ceremonies of induction and appointment. Here are included formal dinners, parties, and admonitions given to newly appointed officials. On

---

[1] C. I. Barnard, "Functions and Pathology of Status Systems in Formal Organization," in William Foote Whyte, *Industry and Society*, McGraw-Hill Book Company, Inc., 1946, p. 46.
[2] *Ibid.*, pp. 50-52.

the informal level such ceremonies may be less reserved. They take the form of joking, "razzing," giving gifts, and making speeches.

2. Symbols of status such as titles, name plates, union and company emblems, job titles, and special stationery.

3. Emoluments, perquisites, and privileges given to different status positions. These include better offices, bonuses, private secretaries, and private telephones. Such privileges may, in turn, become symbols of status.

4. Restrictions and limitation of behavior. Along with acceptance of the prerogatives which accompany increased status, prerogatives of previous status positions must be dropped. The president cannot go beer drinking in public places with his former cronies. These prohibitions are as much a part of the status structure as the prerogatives.

In general, the formal status structure of a work plant tends to correspond to the lines of authority in the organization chart. The president has the highest prestige, then the general manager, and so on down the line. Generally, the compensations associated with each position tend to correspond to the supervisory and prestige structure. This is patently clear in the case of military organizations, whose hierarchies are formalized in many ways including dress. Where there is not a direct correspondence of income, authority, and prestige, conflicts sometimes arise.

Such was the case in a telephone accounting office that the authors studied. A middle-aged woman (Bertha) had the job known as "district clerk." Bertha was an efficient worker whose advice was sought by everyone in the department. The other workers such as the typist, bookkeeper, and cashier gave Bertha deference. The authors were surprised to discover at a later date that Bertha had quit her position as the result of a salary row. An investigation revealed that Bertha's salary was exactly that of the bookkeeper, and both were already at the top levels of the salary scales. Because of her diligence and alertness, Bertha had made her job a "catchall." She had gradually taken over many responsibilities, especially some of her supervisor's. The latter, although she appreciated Bertha's worth, was unable to raise her salary above the official ceiling. When Bertha quit, a basic readjustment of job duties was demanded on the part of everybody in the department. Bertha's old job of district clerk continued to have considerable prestige, and many girls competed for it.

Such situations are not unusual in many work plants. The job patterns of a department interact in terms of status. Gradually, a status equilibrium arises that has considerable persistence.

Barnard believes that a status structure arises out of the different needs, interests, and capacities of the individuals in a work group. These are:[3]

1. Differences in the abilities of individuals to do different jobs. These differences may concern native capacity, formal or informal training, and work experience.

[3] *Ibid.*, pp. 53-62.

2. Differences in the comparative difficulty of various kinds of work. Obviously some jobs demand greater skill than others, and this provides the basis of selecting individuals of differing abilities.

3. Differences in the importance attached to various types of jobs. Some jobs are in greater demand in the job market and therefore are considered more important. Other jobs, such as the doctor, teacher, and pastor, are granted higher social prestige.

4. Differences in observable symbols of status. By this is meant that the existence of status symbols such as diplomas, stripes, and credentials makes it possible for people to identify those who presumably have ability and power.

5. The need for protecting the integrity of the person. Placing the person in a status scale prevents others from making demands that are either too small or too great. The foreman is not asked to make policy decisions for the company. Neither is he asked to sweep the floor. His position and that of others are protected by knowledge of their relative status.

Other factors omitted by Barnard are responsible for the rise and persistence of status structures. These depend on group rather than individual factors.

6. A "need" for personal recognition within groups. Once it attaches to a position or job, it becomes a part of tradition.

7. The intrusion of extra-plant values in the plant. Religious, class, ethnic, and ideological status differences in the community are transferred to the work plant.

Out of these forces, status structures arise. Some are extremely stable, others are unstable; some have little informal organization, others have a great deal; some are exemplified by great mobility between status levels, others are caste-like. It is this latter attribute that is of interest to us.

OPEN AND CLOSED STATUS STRUCTURES

When Americans acknowledge the importance of status they feel that its acquisition should be available to all. That is, they believe in an "open" or "free" status system. This ideology of social mobility has a powerful influence in most work plants, although its validity may be questionable. It is true that there are forces which tend to "solidify" or "freeze" the status structure operating simultaneously with forces that tend to unsettle the structure. No doubt the amount and ease of mobility varies in different segments of the work plant. Lynd suggests that there is less mobility on the plant floor than in the white-collar and managerial levels. Although mobility occurs on all levels, the white-collar ladder is longer and easier to climb. Whereas a clerk may aspire to a managerial post with some justification, the skilled worker has a smaller chance of becoming a manager.

There are several forces that tend to solidify and shatter the formal

status structures of work plants. Perhaps the strongest force in keeping the status structure open is the above-mentioned ideology of free mobility. Since workers believe in the free-mobility ideology, managers are constrained to put it in practice. This pressure cannot be resisted too long without impairment of morale. It is also reasonable to assume that if status circulation is unduly restricted, plant efficiency is lowered. An organization can absorb only so much "dead wood" and still function adequately. Only a limited number can be "kicked upstairs." "Shakedowns" are inevitable and "new blood" must be transfused into the system. The introduction of new machines demands changes in the technical organization and therefore in the status organization of the work plant. Cost accounting methods reveal inefficiencies that can be removed only by changing personnel. Whenever people are shifted the status structure is made more fluid.

The forces solidifying the status structures are many. The mere inertia of an organization makes changes difficult. Every status position becomes somebody's vested interest which is difficult to break. Barnard agrees that "the resistance to loss of status is in general stronger than the desire to achieve higher status."[4] Since this is true the organization must be protected against the disruptive tendencies inherent in the status system. The problem that the administrator faces is whether to replace inferior men who have knowledge of the local work situation with superior men who do not have this knowledge and who do not have the support of the workers in the local situation.[5] Gardner also suggests another obstacle to mobility: "In many cases the one who works hardest or is best at the lower level is not the one who can do the best at the next level. . . . The best mechanic or the most efficient operator does not always make the best foreman, the ability to handle a group does not develop naturally out of the ability to handle machines."[6]

The hierarchical nature of the business ladder means that fewer and fewer jobs are open at upper levels, so that there is less and less room for mobility. There are masses of workers who can climb in hourly rate but for whom there is no pathway to advancement. For many of them, their jobs lead to a blind alley. This situation is aggravated by the modern tendency to select college-trained people for administrative posts.

THE LEVELS OF PARTICIPATION

Whether a status structure is open or closed does not determine how the individual participates in that structure. In larger work plants we may classify workers as seeking recognition on two levels:

[4] *Ibid.*, p. 78.
[5] *Ibid.*, p. 76.
[6] Burleigh B. Gardner, *Human Relations in Industry*, Richard D. Irwin, Inc., 1945, p. 189.

1. Some people seek recognition mainly within the primary groups and are content with this source alone. This level is more typical of manual workers whose occupations do not give them many contacts with people outside of their immediate work groups. For them it is more important to bowl with the boys than to attend a shop conference on safety. Buying a gift for a work partner who is going to be married is more important than representing the factory on the Community Chest drive. Those people who obtain status satisfaction in the small, immediate work groups we shall call the "primaries."

2. Other people compete for status largely on the secondary level. That is, they desire status in the *work plant society* (in the general organization of either the plant, the union, or the community) rather than in their primary work groups. They seek broad recognition both inside and outside of the work plant. This widespread acclaim may be sought from occupational, professional, managerial, or union organizations. Recognition may also be sought as "leaders" in community-wide organizations, such as the Community Chest, Red Cross, Chamber of Commerce, and Safety Council. This level of participation is more typical of workers in managerial or white-collar jobs. We may call them the "secondaries."

A third level of status participation may be outlined. There are some people who seek recognition on *both* primary and secondary levels. They are dissatisfied with recognition from only one source. For want of a better term, we shall label them the "marginals."

A different social orientation probably characterizes each level. Those who seek status on the extremes of these levels do not understand each other. The "secondaries" may regard the "primaries" as gossipy, narrow, and mundane people. The "secondaries" are irritated by status problems on the primary level. This was the case when a manager asked a new man to organize the collection of Community Chest pledges in his department. Since the oldest worker was traditionally given this job, resistance to collections was encountered. Not uncommonly, the "secondaries" try to ignore "petty" status problems on the primary level. They feel that they cannot spend time with "mediocre people who count on small things so much."

The "secondaries" regard themselves as intelligent, rational, self-sufficient, resourceful, self-reliant people, whose energies benefit the work plant and the community as a whole. They feel they have the right to lead and to expect deference from those on the lower status levels. At the same time, they have status problems on their own primary levels. Even though these may be very important, they tend to verbalize them as "unimportant petty details."

If participation in formal organizations outside the work plant may be taken as a partial index of participation on the secondary status level, it appears that *the higher the socioeconomic level of the occupation the*

greater the secondary level of participation.[7] In a sample of over 400 workers we found a direct, positive relation between participation and occupational level. Table 10 reveals this relation. The mean social participation score for all workers is 23.6. White-collar workers tend to have scores above this figure and manual workers scores below it.

TABLE 10.   Social Participation Data by Occupational Levels

Occupational Levels	Mean Social Participation Scores	Number of Cases	Standard Deviations
Professionals and semi-professionals	28.5	70	20.0
Owners, managers, and officials	28.0	128	20.0
Clerical, sales or office	21.0	89	15.0
Skilled workers and foremen	19.7	82	15.0
Operatives and semiskilled workers	16.7	67	12.5
Unskilled workers and laborers	10.2	19	8.6
Total	23.6	455	9.5

Workers operating on the primary status level have attitudes toward those operating on the secondary level. The latter's constant, struggling, restless, dissatisfied, eager, manic behavior is regarded as almost inhuman. The "primaries" cannot understand why the "secondaries" do not participate in ball games, why they don't have a glass of beer with the boys and enjoy good fellowship. They regard the "secondaries" as "stuck up," proud, unbending, humorless, diffident people. The "primaries" are surprised when they see the "human side" of "secondaries." Grief occasioned by their children's misfortunes, laughter unexpectedly aroused, the rare participation in petty gossip elicits the comment, "Maybe he's a regular fellow after all."

The social psychology of the "marginals" is typical of marginal people in general. They have greater adjustment problems since they seek recognition from groups which are often antagonistic to one another. It is not unusual under these circumstances for both groups to suspect them. Workers sometimes become "marginals" when they seek to move from the primary to the secondary level of status recognition. Not infrequently they are charged with violating group loyalties, becoming climbers, and assuming "airs." Those who move from the secondary to the primary level of status recognition also have problems. Remarks about them may be, "The guy is slipping"; "He didn't have the stuff"; "The going was too rough for him"; "He had to find out the hard way who his friends are." The successful "marginal"

[7] F. S. Chapin has developed an objective technique of measuring social participation. One's score is based upon the number of organizational affiliations plus the nature of participation, such as committee member, officer, contributor. See his "Social Participation and Social Intelligence," *American Sociological Review*, April, 1939, p. 157.

is rather rare because he needs unusual social insight and skills. He is able to see the status problems on each level, appreciate them for what they are, and behave accordingly.

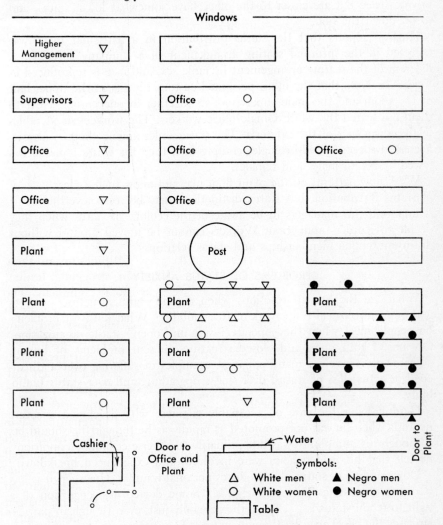

FIG. 41. Seating by Age, Sex, and Race in a Factory Cafeteria. (From E. C. Hughes, "The Knitting of Racial Groups in Industry," *American Sociological Review*, October, 1946, p. 514.)

THE ECOLOGY OF STATUS

Sometimes the status structure of a plant reflects itself in space. For example, if a work plant is a tall office building, a worker's status position roughly corresponds to the floor on which his office is located; the higher

the floor the higher his status. The parking lot may reflect the status structures. Those people who have private parking spaces close to the main entrance of the work plant have highest status. Those who do not have private space but are closer to the office have somewhat lower status, and so on down the line.

Hughes[8] reports that the status distribution in a particular plant was reflected in the informal seating arrangement in a company cafeteria. A diagram of the seating arrangement by rank, sex, and race is reproduced in Figure 41. Note that the office personnel customarily sits in the upper half of the room and the male supervisors sit together in one corner. Next to them are seated the white female office workers. The workers sit at tables in the lower half of the cafeteria. The status order among them is also reflected in space, the white males coming first, then the white females, followed by Negro males and females.

Work flow patterns on the plant floor may not allow such a clear pattern of status distribution, but status distinctions may be seen nevertheless. It is important for managers to be aware of the ecology of status when they decide to reorder production. Workers cannot be moved around without disturbing clique memberships and status relations.

PROBLEMS OF STATUS ANXIETY

What are the human reactions when a rigid status structure operates within an ideological framework of free mobility? What kinds of problems do people meet when they operate inside an "open" status organization? Obviously, both open and closed structures present problems of human adjustment. There are many poignant examples of suffering over a threatened or actual loss of status, over status upgrading, and over status immobility.

Gardner cites the case of a capable engineer who developed a severe neurosis when he was not promoted as rapidly as he thought he should be. Although his immobility was due primarily to adverse economic conditions, he felt that his inadequacies were involved, and experienced breakdown.[9]

Downgrading of status also produces personal traumas. However, it is less frequent because, as Barnard suggests, "Some degree of recognition of a right to retain status is . . . felt to be generally just, even though in particular cases the effect may be thought not so. The sentiments supporting conservation with respect to status are developed and maintained by rationalizations, ceremonies, and symbolism."[10]

Devices are therefore created to ease the downward mobility. These in-

[8] Everett C. Hughes, "The Knitting of Racial Groups in Industry," *American Sociological Review*, October, 1946, p. 514.
[9] Gardner, *op. cit.*, p. 181.
[10] Barnard, *op. cit.*, p. 79.

clude kicking a person upstairs, "retiring" others, shifting others to another plant, changing of job title, putting a person at the head of a new department whose status is unclear, making "temporary" arrangements, and others. The higher the status of the job, the more likely the utilization of these subterfuges when changes in status are involved.

Promotion and upgrading also precipitates adjustment problems. The recently promoted foreman sometimes has such difficulties. If he keeps up old friendships, he is accused of playing favorites; if he does not he is called "snooty," or "high-hat." Obviously his whole pattern of social relations changes when he becomes a supervisor, and his behavior must be adjusted accordingly. Under these circumstances it is understandable why some workers refuse promotions.

We may conclude, then, that status satisfaction depends on the worker's status expectations plus his history of status mobility. Thus, if the son of an unskilled worker becomes a skilled worker, he may be satisfied with the respect of his peers. On the other hand, if his expectations are higher, he may experience status anxiety and maladjustment.

THE SYMBOLS OF STATUS

Those who have status usually receive other rewards as well: increased influence, financial return, consultation, or the right to wear a badge. We are interested especially in the last reward, the right to have a symbol of status.[11]

Symbols of status arise for a number of reasons. In the first place, they help the newcomer to locate those individuals who should be awarded recognition. Especially in large groups with high membership turnover and secondary relations, symbols of status must be evolved to distinguish high- and low-status people. The symbols are, then, a form of advertising and a request for deference. Workers strive as much for the symbols of status as they do for the factors that underlie status. Not infrequently, managers underestimate the importance of status to others. Their preoccupation with salaries, wages, and other such items makes them unaware that many of the dissatisfactions of workers can be traced to their unwillingness or failure to grant status to lower-income groups. The Negro laborer, for example, might rather be called "mister" than receive a raise of five cents an hour. Sometimes a status symbol brings its bearer considerable inconvenience. In an earlier illustration we suggested that in many office buildings the symbol of status is the floor on which a person's office is located. Having to travel to upper floors every day is a considerable inconvenience. Yet workers would rather be inconvenienced than have their office relocated on a lower floor.

Different occupations and work plants evolve unique symbols of status.

[11] See H. Speier, "Honor and the Social Structure," *Social Research*, February, 1933. pp. 74-97.

However, some symbols are rather widespread. We shall attempt to list just a few of them. One of the most common is clothing. It is a well-known fact that people who work in their "going-out clothes" generally have higher status than those who wear occupational garbs. Thus, the white-collar worker has greater prestige than the worker in overalls. This factor of clothing may be carried to a ludicrous degree. In a small garage that the authors studied a wide gamut of clothing symbolized gradations of status. The owner worked in his "business" suit. The stock and order clerk wore no special uniform but had to remove his coat and worked in his shirt sleeves. The supervisor of the mechanics in the shop also removed his coat, but he wore a very nonfunctional piece of clothing, a white smock. The mechanics wore full-length blue jumpers, and the apprentices and cleanup men wore overalls or discarded clothing of darker hues. Although this hierarchy of garb was not formally instituted, it was nonetheless scrupulously observed. No one could presume to rise above his status by wearing the costume "inappropriate" to his job.

Uniforms, with some notable exceptions, indicate lower-status jobs. They are common among personal and domestic service workers, truck drivers, and public service workers. Some corporations have found the status struggle via clothing so intense that they have instituted uniforms to settle the question. But the uniform may also be used to signify the distribution of status. The military forces have, with the use of "gold braid," developed symbols to reflect both a status and a power hierarchy. The uniforms of the policemen, firemen, movie ushers, nurses, (academic robes of) college professors, and waitresses follow a similar pattern.[12]

The hours of work symbolize prestige position. Usually the later the worker arrives and the earlier he leaves his job, the higher his status. Whether he punches a time clock or not is also a matter of prestige. (It is interesting to note the rationalizations of office workers against installing time clocks.) The time of the lunch hour and the length of the lunch hour are other things around which status clings. Usually, the longer and later the lunch hour, the higher the status.

The places one dines or lunches also reflect status—whether on the plant floor, cafeteria, nearby restaurants, or downtown. The duration of the vacation, the opportunity to choose the time of year off, the number of vacations and holidays off, all are indicative of prestige rank. A winter Florida vacation reflects the acme of status.

Other things around the office reflect status. The size of the desk, the location of the desk, the display of a name plate, the private office, the size of the office, the number of secretaries, the proximity to the chief executive, the rug on the floor, paintings on the wall, private entrances, private telephone, reception room, or washroom, display of magazines—all are symbolic

[12] See Thorstein Veblen, *The Theory of the Leisure Class*, Modern Library, 1931, chap. 7.

of relative prestige. White-collar workers develop a great amount of ritual istic status behavior. One hypothesis that may account for this is that the work of white-collar people is not easily distinguishable. They are surrounded with paper, and all papers look alike to the outside observer. Therefore, other devices must be conceived to impress observers of the exact status position of the individual workers.

Some corporations have evolved elaborate systems of formal status symbols. With each job promotion the company may specify the use of an additional symbol, such as a secretary, a larger office, a larger desk, the use of a name plate, being listed in the company directory, a change in the title of the position. In the absence of such consciously erected symbols, workers informally create them and observe them as scrupulously as the formal symbols.

Of course, manual workers also develop status symbols. Many of their symbols are similar to those in the white-collar occupations. Some of these are the use of job titles, the location of the bench, and type of clothing worn on the job. Perhaps the most important sign of status is to be consulted by supervisors. No matter how well management has coördinated production, bottlenecks arise that can be solved only when the experience and skill of the workers are utilized. The frequency of consultation, therefore, is symbolic of status. Other things indicate prestige—for example, being called to mediate conflicts. Sometimes it is difficult to distinguish status symbols from the things that contribute to status. We shall now turn our attention to the factors which underlie status organizations.

GENERAL FACTORS UNDERLYING STATUS ORGANIZATIONS

Some factors which underlie the status structure in the community carry over in the status structure of industry. Among the most important of these are age, sex, race, ethnic background, class, occupation, and status background. How some of these factors operate is rather simple.

AGE AND WORK PLANT STATUS

Let us take the matter of age first. Traditionally, prestige has gone to the older worker, because he has had time to acquire skills. In an economy that was dominated by manual skills the old hand was the efficient and stable worker. Helpers and the apprentices were younger men who "knew their places." They had to wait patiently for the older worker to teach them new skills and allow them to do new jobs. They had to defer to the "masters," on whom they depended for mobility and acceptance. The literature of the guilds and the early craft unions is replete with data on the importance of age.[13]

[13] Henri Pirenne, "Guilds, European," Encyclopaedia of the Social Sciences, The Macmillan Company, 1930.

Age prestige still survives in American industry. The average age of the skilled worker is higher than for other laborers. The old-timer still looks down at the neophyte as a "young punk who doesn't know what the score is." He regards the newcomer with a mixture of anxiety and self-assurance. The old-timer is somewhat secure because he knows what "bugs" there are in learning a new job, how to save his energy, how to cut corners, how to loaf without being caught, how to shift blame or responsibility, what the pace of the work should be, and how to get along with the idiosyncrasies of his fellow workers.

The younger worker hopes to compensate for his lack of skill by using his abundant energy. The "cagey old-timers" who have control of the informal social organization admonish the younger worker to "take it easy" or "do it this way." The oldsters tend to receive the support of the foreman and supervisors because the latter do not want to disturb the prevailing work patterns. They feel it best not to alienate the dependable and stable workers on the job.

Recognition is formally given to age and its twin, length of service. Doddering old hands are frequently kept on the job because of their past "loyalty" to the company. They are given watches, awards, and testimonials as tokens for their service. Employers sometimes prefer older workers because (1) they already know the job, (2) they are more dependable and accept responsibility better than younger workers, (3) their greater family responsibilities make them cautious about losing time, moving to a new job, or "falling" for agitators.[14] Promotion preferences are usually offered to the older workers, and those who have longer length of service. The seniority rules in contracts between unions and managements are a formal recognition of the status of age.

However, the prestige of age is being undermined by the "accent on youth" and by the "leveling forces" operating in industry.[15] As skills become diluted by spreading automatic and semiautomatic machinery, reliance on skilled labor is decreased. It becomes easier to transfer from one job to another, from one plant to another, and from one department to another. This practice of "playing the job market" reduces seniority and age grading. As the "speedup" system spreads and jobs are broken down, the young men who can stand the pace of the machine are sought increasingly. They are in demand particularly during depressed economic conditions when a man of forty-five is "too old to work and too young to die."

Yet despite these forces certain jobs are still assigned by age groups. This tendency is seen in Table 11, giving the median ages of various occupational levels by sex.

Table 11 reveals that the youngest workers are found among the unskilled, semiskilled, and clerical workers. Those who are midde-aged predominate

[14] E. Wight Bakke, *The Unemployed Worker*, Yale University Press, p. 244.
[15] See the section of this chapter on "Leveling Forces in the Status System."

in domestic, protective, and other services, as well as in skilled and professional work. Farmers, proprietors, managers, and officials are the oldest workers. Oddly enough, except for protective service workers, who are in the old group for women but in the middle-age group for men, the general distribution of ages in the occupational levels is strikingly similar for both men and women. Also the differences between the median age of working men and women is not as great as is commonly supposed; 38.3 years for the men, 32.3 years for the women, a difference of six years.

TABLE 11.   Median Age of Men and Women by Occupational Level: 1940[16]

Occupation	Males	Females
Professional and semiprofessional	38.7	33.4
Farmers and farm managers	46.6	52.1
Proprietors, managers, and officials	44.5	44.3
Clerical, sales, and kindred workers	35.2	29.9
Craftsmen, foremen, and kindred workers	41.4	37.2
Operatives and kindred workers	34.0	31.1
Domestic service workers	38.7	33.6
Protective service workers	39.0	45.5
Service workers, except domestic and protective	38.7	34.2
Farm laborers and foremen	24.9	26.6
Laborers, except farm and mine	34.9	29.2
Total	38.3	32.3

Several factors may account for the age stratification in Table 11. They are:

1. The unskilled jobs are usually the heaviest jobs and are most efficiently done by young people.

2. Young manual workers usually enter the bottom of the occupational ladder. After a period of testing and apprenticeship some may move into semiskilled and skilled labor. Hence the low median age for laborers.

3. Clerical jobs not only are considered somewhat temporary for many young women workers, but they are also jobs which provide channels into semiprofessional, managerial, and supervisory levels; hence the comparative youth of clerical workers.

4. Domestic and service workers are limited in mobility. A great proportion who are Negroes and foreign born enter this level and remain in it; hence their middle-age composition.

5. Since professional work requires much time for formal education, and since skilled labor requires much experience, these occupational levels tend toward greater stability, and their members tend to be middle-aged.

6. Farmers, proprietors, managers, and officials are at the top of the occupational ladder. The fact that (a) time is required for upward mobility and (b) security is offered by these occupations makes people in them above average in age.

[16] *Sixteenth Census of the United States.* Vol. III, *The Labor Force*, Part I, Table 65, pp. 98-100.

It may be of interest to select specific occupations that are monopolized by younger and older workers for each sex. Tables 12 and 13 provide these data.

Young men predominate as: servants, soldiers, laborers in manufacturing, truck drivers, salesmen, stenographers, office machine operators, designers, dancers, athletes, teachers, and chemists. *Older men* dominate as: clergymen, veterinarians, conductors, postmasters, baggagemen, real estate agents and brokers, locomotive engineers, shoemakers, tailors, guards, watchmen, and boarding-house keepers.

Younger women take jobs as: bookkeepers, typists, cashiers, saleswomen, operatives in manufacturing, beauticians, elevator operators, waitresses, and bartenders. *Older women* may be found among: proprietors and managers in wholesale and retail trade, insurance and real estate agents, dressmakers, cooks, practical nurses, charwomen, and college professors.

In general, except for the very aged, the younger the age level of those in an occupation, the lower its prestige. Low status is tolerable for the young worker because the job is often considered temporary. Difficulties in adjustment are evident when the age of a worker does not correspond to the *age expectation* of his job. If the occupant is too young for the job, he must struggle to attain status, and to carry out the responsibilities attached to the job.

This happens not infrequently on college campuses where young, well-trained men are called to assume headships of departments. Older faculty

TABLE 12.   Median Ages for Males in Selected Occupations: 1940[17]

Older Workers	Age	Younger Workers	Age
Clergymen	45.6	Chemists, metallurgists	33.6
Veterinarians	50.1	Teachers	34.3
Conductor (R.R.)	53.2	Dancers, showmen, and athletes	32.5
Postmaster and officers	46.4	Designers and draftsmen	34.4
Proprietors, managers, officials in		Surveyors	33.9
general	45.0	Messengers	20.4
Baggagemen, expressmen, mes-		Office machine operators	28.4
sengers, railway mail clerks	45.8	Shipping, receiving clerks	31.4
Real estate agents and brokers	51.1	Stenographers, typists, secretaries	31.1
Locomotive engineers	53.3	Newsboys	17.2
Shoemakers and repairers	47.1	Other salesmen	32.1
Tailors and furriers	49.6	Attendants (filling stations, etc.)	26.8
Brakemen and switchmen (R.R.)	45.6	Truck drivers, deliverymen	32.7
Conductors (bus and street rail-		Painters	34.5
way)	45.3	Operatives generally	33.9
Dressmakers and seamstresses	47.3	Soldiers, sailors, etc.	23.8
Guards and watchmen	52.3	Servants	30.2
Boarding-house keepers	54.8	Farm laborers	30.3
		Laborers (manuf.)	33.2

[17] *Ibid.*, pp. 98-99.

members are reluctant to defer to younger and supposedly "inexperienced" colleagues. The latter resort to formal and bureaucratic devices to insulate themselves against the attempts of older members to demonstrate their status equality or superiority. Since this disturbs the organization, administrators sometime feel justified in keeping older people in high-ranking jobs. This in turn creates a new problem because younger men feel impatient about the blocks to upward mobility.

TABLE 13. Median Ages for Women in Selected Occupations: 1940[18]

Older Workers	Age	Younger Workers	Age
Farmers and farm managers	52.1	Bookkeepers, accountants,	
Proprietors, managers, officials		cashiers, ticket agents	30.9
(wholesale and retail trade)	45.3	Office machine operators	28.5
Proprietors, etc., in personal		Stenographers, typists, secretaries	28.2
service	47.7	Saleswomen	30.9
Insurance agents and brokers	44.4	Operatives, manufacturing	
Real estate agents and brokers	48.9	generally	29.2
Dressmakers and seamstresses	47.5	Barbers, beauticians, manicurists	29.5
Boarding-house and board-		Elevator operators	29.0
lodging-house keepers	51.4	Waitresses and bartenders	26.4
Cooks, except private families	42.4	Farm laborers	29.6
Practical nurses and midwives	46.3		
Charwomen, janitors	46.3		
College presidents, professors	41.2		

When workers do not advance rapidly enough, they may feel too old for the job. A supervisor of a newspaper told the authors: "Benny has been with the *Journal* for fourteen years now. He came to us as a messenger boy when he was almost twenty. He's still a messenger boy. He told us when he came that he wanted to become a reporter. Every now and then he does give us some news, but he'll never make the grade. Most of the boys feel sorry for Benny, even though he is hard to get along with. I told him to look for another job because he has no future here, but he claims that he can't find work and that the *Journal* needs him."

Sometimes old people are kept on the job "just to give them something to do." Being called "boy" and asked to do dirty jobs, dreaming of their past importance, having "to take stuff from the young punks" produces an embittered and often maladjusted personality. This whole area, the relation of age of workers to age expectation of the occupation, is an interesting problem which needs sociological investigation.

SEX TYPING AND JOB PRESTIGE

Every society exhibits a sexual division of labor. What is regarded as man's work and woman's work varies the world over. Western societies have

[18] *Ibid.*, p. 100.

traditionally assigned women jobs in and about the home and have resisted their entrance into the monetary work market. Yet women have gradually entered the job market to the point of actually dominating many occupations. Table 14 presents the proportions of men and women in selected jobs. Women are dominant as social and welfare workers, teachers, librarians, nurses, religious workers, office machine operators, demonstrators, milliners,

TABLE 14. Percentage of Males in Selected Occupations: 1940[19]

Occupation	Percent	Occupation	Percent
Locomotive firemen	100.0	Social and welfare workers	35.7
Piano tuners	99.1	Operatives (tobacco mfg.)	28.1
Conductors	99.1	Religious workers	25.4
Dentists	98.5	Teachers	24.6
Bakers	92.2	Operatives (apparel mfg.)	22.6
Purchasing agents	91.8	Laundry operatives	22.3
Proprietors (retail trade)	88.5	Demonstrators (sales)	17.4
Actors	59.3	Office machine operators	13.9
Laborers (laundry and dyeing)	58.8	Librarians	10.5
Operatives (cotton mfg.)	53.0	Boardinghouse keepers	9.5
Healers, medical social workers	51.4	Stenographers, typists, secretaries	6.5
Operatives (woolen industry)	50.3	Milliners	5.8
Servants, except private family	44.7	Housekeepers (private family)	0.8

and as operatives in tobacco manufacturing and apparel industries. Men and women are represented in equal proportions among actors, bookkeepers, accountants, ticket agents, servants, laborers in laundries, and operatives in textile mills. Women are greatly underrepresented among dentists, proprietors, bakers, conductors, purchasing agents, and many others.

However, the number of jobs women are entering has been increasing. Their invasion is being resisted by men, because women are often hired at lower wages and because women generally reduce the status of the jobs they enter. Women's work is regarded by men as "inferior" work; it is often simpler, lighter, more monotonous, and lower paid.

Women invade the job market during periods of crisis and prosperity. During World War II they not only replaced men in semiskilled jobs, but many became skilled workers such as welders, machinists, inspectors, and foremen. Their entrance into these jobs was facilitated by "breaking down" the jobs into simpler ones, and by introducing new methods of job instruction.

This has had the effect of further shattering the status system of industry. The fact that many women enter monetary work plants temporarily before marriage, or to "help out" the family, decreases the stability of the job market. These impermanent workers or "helper-outers" compete with men

[19] *Ibid.*, Table 58.

who want permanent jobs and a career. It is understandable, then, that men use every formal and informal device to keep women out of their jobs, or desert their jobs when women come in.

It may be, however, that the lowering of the male's status in the work world by the ingress of women is somewhat exaggerated. It is true that women do enter the labor market as routine workers, and do compete with men for some jobs. However, their very mobility and their willingness to accept lower pay has the indirect effect of upgrading the men. The women are, in a sense, replacing immigrant and rural laborers in the lower rungs of the occupational scale. Their invasion of the bottom has an effect of raising the other stable workers. This is particularly true in clerical jobs in which men hold positions of higher authority and pay by virtue of their stability.

The Status of the Woman Supervisor

Statistics do show, however, that more women are becoming a part of the stable labor force. Larger proportions of married women are working with the intention of remaining in the labor force. They, as well as unmarried career women, have become men's real competitors.[20] Both men and women do not want a woman to become their supervisor. Men, especially, feel that a woman supervisor lowers the status level of their jobs. Even where they accommodate to this situation their work associates jibe them about being dominated by women both at home and on the job.

The rationalizations that men make against having a woman supervisor are many. The most common is that women are too emotional to be supervisors; they cannot take their responsibilities impersonally; they hold grudges; they cannot take criticism; they are more autocratic and demanding than men.[21]

It is no doubt true that women supervisors do exhibit some of the behavior of which they are accused. But Gardner believes that this does not follow because of their sex but because of the new social role they are playing. Their behavior is more typical of new supervisors generally. Their alleged limitations are for the most part mythical and, where not mythical, the result of a difficult social situation and not of their peculiar or limited capacities.[22]

ETHNIC GROUPS AND STATUS

Ethnic groups compete for status both in the community and in the work plant. Some ethnic groups are mutually antagonistic because they are competing for economic and status advantages. In one section of the country

[20] Ralph C. Hurlin and Meredith B. Givens, "Shifting Occupational Patterns," *Recent Social Trends*, McGraw-Hill Book Company, Inc., New York, 1933.

[21] Gardner, *op. cit.*, p. 269.

[22] *Ibid.*

the Irish and English are antagonistic; in another, the Italians and Jews; in another, the Negroes and Mexicans.

Many employers who know this promote or diminish ethnic antagonisms, depending on their ends. For example, in order to keep production going smoothly, management may find it wise to segregate antagonistic groups. However, when the main issue is unionism, managers have promoted antagonisms among ethnic groups, with the hope that their attention might be diverted from economic coöperation to the status struggle.

It is common knowledge that the foreign born and those of other races generally have lower-status jobs than the native born and Caucasians. Census data reflect the lower socioeconomic status of foreign born and Negroes in the United States.[23] Table 15 contrasts the occupational levels of Negroes and whites by sex. Negro males exceed white males in the manual occupations by almost 25 percent. The greatest difference lies in unskilled labor, in which are found 14.5 percent of the white male workers, as contrasted to 41 percent of the Negro male workers. Negroes are overrepresented in farm work, domestic and service work, and in unskilled labor. The whites have larger proportions in professional, proprietary, clerical, skilled, and semiskilled labor.

TABLE 15.   Occupational Level of Negro and White in United States by Sex: 1940[24]

Occupational Level	Male		Female	
	White	Negro	White	Negro
Professional and semiprofessional	5.9	1.8	14.7	4.3
Farmers and farm managers	14.0	21.1	1.1	3.0
Proprietors, managers, and officials	10.6	1.3	4.3	.7
Clerical, sales, and kindred workers	13.9	2.0	32.8	1.3
Craftsmen, foremen, and kindred workers	15.6	4.4	1.1	.2
Operatives and kindred workers	18.8	12.5	20.3	6.2
Protective service workers	2.1	.5	—	—
Domestic and service workers	3.9	14.7	22.3	69.9
Laborers and farm laborers	14.5	41.0	2.1	13.7
No information	.7	.7	1.3	.7
Total	100.0	100.0	100.0	100.0

Similar generalizations hold true for women workers. White women have greater proportions of their totals in professional, proprietary, clerical, and semiskilled work, whereas larger percentages of Negro women are found in farm, domestic and service, and unskilled labor categories. About 45 percent of the white women are in the manual occupations, compared to almost 90 percent of the Negro women.

These census statistics need to be reinterpreted for their psychological and

[23] Cf. *Sixteenth Census of the United States.* Vol. III, *The Labor Force,* Part I, Table 64, p. 97.
[24] *Ibid.*

social meaning. Some jobs become associated with one race or another, e.g., a "white man's job" or a "Negro's job." Such expressions convey certain notions—that some jobs are the monopoly of specific groups, that the status of the job and the worker should be fixed, that normally each race should not compete for the same jobs, that jobs identify the status of the worker. Thus, in some work plants certain jobs are assigned to Negroes, others to native born, foreign born, old immigrants, or new immigrants, as the case may be. When these ethnic job expectations are threatened, conflict may ensue. Collins describes a strong ethnic status structure in a New England factory. The management and personnel officials were Yankee, the foremen Irish, and the workers of other ethnic backgrounds. When a Yankee was appointed foreman, a wildcat strike was called because management had violated the ethnic pattern of promotion. Only when management changed the job title did it succeed in giving the Yankee a job commensurate with the foreman's job.[25]

The Breakdown of Ethnic and Racial Job Statuses

A two-way process occurs in a breakdown of the ethnic job status structure. One phase is that of invasion. Jobs that traditionally "belong" to one group are invaded by foreign born and Negroes. This process is gradual, but its accumulated results are spectacular. For example, the Negroes have been invading industrial occupations for decades. Of course, they entered at the bottom of the ladder, but during war periods and prosperous times they climbed to jobs that require greater skills. As industry needs unskilled and skilled jobs less, and semiskilled jobs more, there is no other place for the unskilled Negroes and others to go but upward. Thus, the leveling forces of technology are throwing people of different ethnic groups and races together constantly.

The second phase in the breakdown of a status structure occurs during periods of economic depression and retrenchment. Pressure is then exerted on invaders to go back to their previous lower-status jobs. This is resisted violently both by those who have made the advances and by those groups below which are threatened by a backwash of competitors. Management has recognized but often underestimated the power of informal work groups to control their membership. Hughes has studied this process. He relates:

In a certain plant, Negroes were first hired in a department that, though dirty and smelly, and without prestige, has a very stable working force. The men in it, mostly elderly Poles, work in groups of three that produce as units and are paid so as to make teamwork the key to a good income. It was thought that these men would not have much prejudice and that the isolation of the department would allow the hiring of Negroes without much comment. Of several Negroes hired,

[25] Orvis Collins, "Ethnic Behavior in Industry: Sponsorship and Rejection in a New England Factory," *American Journal of Sociology*, January, 1946, pp. 293-298.

none stayed more than a few days. The management was disturbed, for it thought the Negroes were confirming the common opinion that they are unreliable. Interviews with these Negro men brought out a consistent and simple story. The workers in the department had practiced every obvious and subtle art to let the newcomers know that they would never learn (i.e., be taught) the work. Upon hearing all this an aged member of the management, now retired, snorted that no one had ever succeeded in 40 years in putting in that department any new man not chosen by the men already there.[26]

In this case, management apparently considered the statuses of the Polish and Negro workers to be roughly equal. It is possible that the Polish workers did not have feelings of racial animosity (status superiority feelings) toward the Negroes. Yet they realized that in management's eyes they were considered in the lowest status position. They were unwilling to accept management's low definition of their position.

The pattern of resistance to Negro workers is similar to that against accepting women employees as status equals. Personnel officers rarely admit a prejudice against employing Negroes in higher-status jobs. They rationalize that Negroes do not have the required skills, that they are incompetent, unintelligent, unskilled, and undependable. They complain that Negroes, foreign born, poor whites, and other groups have high rates of absenteeism, do not respond to financial incentives, refuse to be educated, are shiftless and irresponsible, and lack ambition. A superficial analysis supports this position. However, a further analysis reveals that Negroes and foreign groups represent a new and inexperienced labor force, as yet not acclimated to the patterns of modern industry. It is surprising that they do as well as they do, and not that they do badly. Wilson and Gilmore have shown that industries that appreciate this point of view have been able to integrate Negroes into their labor forces.[27]

Allison Davis has also investigated this problem.[28] He concludes that management has the attitudes, habits, and values of America's middle class. The foremen and administrators emphasize the values of middle-class culture, which include punctuality and responsibility. However, ethnic groups in lower social and economic levels do not respond to the same middle-class "virtues." The low income, the terrible pressure for physical survival, the responsibility of the family-clan for the individual, the practice of communal group living rather than individual living, the low physical level of health due to loss of sleep that results from inadequate housing, the lack of real rewards in the educational system, biological enjoyment compensating for the negation of pleasure in the work and social environment, and the lack of extended economic security—all serve to create a culture which is anti-

[26] Whyte, op. cit., "Race Relations in Industry," by Everett C. Hughes, pp. 113-114.
[27] L. Wilson and H. Gilmore, "White Employers and Negro Workers," American Sociological Review, December, 1943, pp. 698-705.
[28] "The Motivation of the Underprivileged Worker," in Whyte, op. cit.

thetical to middle-class rewards. The real "problem," some believe, is to change the social structure, to make the attainment of middle-class values possible. Whether this is desirable depends upon the social biases of the observers. Whether changes in our socioeconomic system will occur to enable middle-class values to become more widespread is finally a question which lies in the realm of national social policies.

Induction of Negro Workers in Industry

Frequently, Negroes are refused entrance into new occupations on the basis of status objections alone. The reasons workers give are: Negroes are dirty, ignorant, diseased, uncouth, and not fit for companionship. When racial contacts cannot be avoided, efforts are made to keep them at a minimum. Separate facilities are sometimes demanded, such as washrooms, dining halls, and locker rooms. Difficulties are also involved in union membership, for some of the older unions refuse membership to Negroes.

Gardner describes the process used to introduce Negroes into a particular department of a factory during the war.[29] When Negroes were to be moved in as underlings, sweepers, and janitors, no "social" preparations were considered necessary.[30] When the decision was made to move them in as operatives, preliminary discussions were held with union leaders, supervisors, and even workers. At first the "best type" Negro was selected—the "nice-looking" type with "white" features, who was clean and knew the "etiquette" of the race relations. The Negroes were introduced gradually and individually, so as not to produce much antagonism. As the war progressed, the "best type" was soon exhausted, and it was necessary to be less "discriminating" about the new recruits. They were introduced more rapidly and in larger numbers. The problems of assimilating them under the unusual pressures of war living were fraught with danger. The tensions wrought from long working hours, crowded washrooms, high production demands, and no vacations spilled over into race conflict. The frustrations produced by these abnormal conditions were directed toward the Negro. He was accused of avoiding the draft, holding down departmental quotas, stealing a white man's job, high absenteeism, and disloyalty. On occasion these tensions resulted in fights and riots. It took the greatest social skill on the part of personnel people and administrators to control these conflicts.

OCCUPATIONS AND THE PRESTIGE STRUCTURE

Occupation is perhaps the most important factor which underlies the status structure of both the community and industry. Status tends to accrue to occupations almost independent of the people in them. Many attempts have been made to classify occupations according to socioeconomic status.

[29] See Gardner, *op. cit.*, p. 259.
[30] *Ibid.*, p. 263.

One of the most popular is that of Alba Edwards used in the *Sixteenth Census of the United States*. Edwards' classification is somewhat abbreviated as follows:

1. Professional and semiprofessional workers.
2. Proprietors, managers, and officials.
3. Clerical, sales, and kindred workers.
4. Foremen, skilled, and kindred workers.
5. Operatives, apprentices, and semiskilled workers.
6. Unskilled workers and laborers.

This classification is based on skill, status, and economic position.

Other attempts have been made to rank specific occupations in a prestige scale.[31] The most ambitious and sophisticated approach has been by Maphaus Smith, who has ranked 100 common occupations.[32] It shows, as do most studies, that high prestige is accorded to the professionals, especially independent professionals. High status is also bestowed on large business owners or executives, and on people in supervisory capacities. Small businessmen and white-collar workers follow. People who work with people, paper, or ideas seem to form an upper-status group which is to be differentiated from the manual workers or the "working class." Thus a clerk on the plant floor often feels status superiority to a skilled manual worker. Our school systems are run by people of middle-class origins and they imbue students with the value and importance of white-collar jobs.[33]

One shortcoming of these studies of job rank is that they assume the general population agrees on occupational rankings. Some studies show that people in different occupations tend to regard the prestige ranking of specific jobs from different perspectives. In a study of the prestige ranks of thirteen common jobs William H. Form found that manual workers tended to rank their own jobs higher than clerical jobs. Clerical workers, on the other hand, ranked their jobs higher than manual jobs.[34] Apparently, there is some degree of job ethnocentrism at work.

It has been suggested that in a dynamic society the status of occupations may change with the passing of time. A study by Deeg and Paterson comparing the status of twenty-five occupations over a twenty-year period

[31] G. S. Counts, "Social Status of Occupations," *School Review*, January, 1925, pp. 16-17; G. A. Hartman, "Prestige of Occupations," *Personnel Journal*, October, 1934, pp. 144-152; H. C. Lehman and P. A. Witty, "Further Study of the Social Status of Occupations," *Journal of Educational Sociology*, September, 1931, pp. 101-112; F. Wilkinson, "Social Distance Between Occupations," *Sociology and Social Research*, January, 1929, pp. 234-244.

[32] "An Empirical Scale of the Prestige Status of Occupations," *American Sociological Review*, April, 1943.

[33] See W. L. Warner, R. J. Havighurst, and M. Loeb, *Who Shall Be Educated?* Harper & Brothers, 1944.

[34] William H. Form, "Toward an Occupational Social Psychology," *Journal of Social Psychology*, August, 1946, pp. 85-99.

indicated that only a little change occurred in the relative ranks of occupations. The results of their research are shown in Table 16. Except for the
slight decline in the rank of the farmer and the traveling salesman, and the
slight rise in the prestige of the insurance agent, there was no appreciable

TABLE 16.   Comparison of Social Status Ranks of Twenty-five Occupations Obtained
in 1925 and in 1946[35]

Occupation	Rank Order by Counts 1925	Rank Order by Deeg and Paterson 1946
Banker	1	2.5
Physician	2	1
Lawyer	3	2.5
Supt. of schools	4	4
Civil engineer	5	5
Army captain	6	6
Foreign missionary	7	7
Elementary school teacher	8	8
Farmer	9	12
Machinist	10	9
Traveling salesman	11	16
Grocer	12	13
Electrician	13	11
Insurance agent	14	10
Mail carrier	15	14
Carpenter	16	15
Soldier	17	19
Plumber	18	17
Motorman	19	18
Barber	20	20
Truck driver	21	21.5
Coal miner	22	21.5
Janitor	23	23
Hod carrier	24	24
Ditch digger	25	25

difference in prestige ranks over the twenty-year period. It may be noted that
rankers included only two manual jobs (farmer and machinist) in the upper
half of the list of occupations and only two white-collar jobs (insurance
agent and mail carrier) in the lower half of the list. The general white-collar,
manual worker status division is corroborated.

When workers are asked why certain jobs deserve more esteem or respect,
they tend to answer, "Men have respect, not jobs. Some jobs are more *impor-*

[35] M. E. Deeg and D. G. Paterson, "Changes in the Social Status of Occupations,"
Occupations, January, 1947, pp. 265-268.

tant than others, but all should be equally respected, for all are needed."
When pressed for reasons underlying the relative importance of jobs, they
usually reply that some jobs demand more *skill*, greater responsibility, or
longer training. Sometimes this is an objective fact, which can be proved
by direct observation or by job-evaluation techniques. Not infrequently,
however, no discernible reason can be found for status distinctions. One
concludes that tradition decrees that some jobs should have more prestige
than others; or that some jobs borrow prestige from association with
others. For example, two supervisors in a department store may have
similar jobs with equal pay and responsibilities. One may supervise the
kitchenware department, the other the jewelry department. The latter
usually has greater prestige because he associates with higher-status customers
and clerks. This "halo effect" is also seen in the personal servant's sense of
superiority over the yard servant. Sometimes even this tenuous basis for a
job's prestige cannot be found. One job is more honorable simply because
people say it is.

INCOME, PROPERTY, AND POWER

Income and property are fundamental factors underlying the status structure of work plants and communities. Contemporary Western culture is
materialistic, and it tends to measure social honor in economic terms. To
many people "success," status, and money are one and the same thing.
They tend to believe that the fact of wealth is more important than its
origin. With some notable exceptions, then, occupations which are associated with greatest monetary return also have the highest status. A "better
job" is a higher-paying job.

During and following World War II, manual workers were receiving more
money than many clerical, semiprofessional, and professional workers. Men
and women were abandoning white-collar jobs for manual ones, and younger
men and women began to train in larger numbers for manual jobs. The
traditional status superiority of the white-collar job was insufficient to maintain *all* of its occupants and to attract others. Manual workers are now
beginning to regard their jobs with a sense of superiority, and some white-
collar workers agree with them. As an auto worker from Flint, Michigan,
declared, "My son could'a had a job in the office, but he's comin' to work
with me in the plant . . . more money." Such a statement does not necessarily reveal a new status orientation, but it does reflect the tenuous nature
of status appeal in the face of reduced income. In the long run status tends
to parallel economic levels.

The independent businessman has received much prestige in the United
States. Owning and running one's own business has been an ideal toward
which many still aspire. No doubt many workers believe that more money
can be accumulated only if one works for himself. "You can't get rich

working for somebody else," is a popular expression. In addition, many feel that property brings the person independence. "To be one's own boss" is an American dream. In the small-business economy of the past many achieved this independent status. However, the proportion of independent workers has been constantly decreasing, both in business and in the professions. Yet the desire for independence survives as a middle-class virtue.[36]

In the white-collar suburb of Greenbelt, Maryland, the authors found that slightly over 42 percent of the heads of families desired to get into "independent" occupations. Although hesitant to express occupational choices for their children, they preferred them to choose the independent professions.

Since many workers realize that they cannot attain economic independence, they want jobs that give them more "freedom." Thus many dependent workers want supervisory jobs or "independent" jobs, which will give them freedom from supervision. "Bossing" denotes power over others, and non-supervision denotes freedom from domination. Both are highly desirable values, whose attainment brings status.

In a very real sense, workers who have a somewhat independent job feel superior to "scrub" bosses. They often remark, "Even the bosses take orders from lots of other bosses, but I don't have to take 'guff' from anybody, except from Mr. Black, and he never comes around." This attitude percolates down the ladder, and jobs are sought which have even the slightest amount of independence.

Next lower in status are jobs whose occupants are occasionally consulted. Although imparting advice is *not the same as having power*, it does mean that others are partially dependent on the worker. This is somewhat flattering to the ego. "I'm not the foreman, but the foreman can't run the place without me" is a common expression. The more the worker has a reservoir of picayune knowledge unknown to other workers and to the supervisors, the greater is the dependence on him, and the higher his general status. The worker who lacks authority, the worker who has no independence, the worker who is never consulted is usually on the bottom of the status scale.

We have named only a few general factors which underlie the status structure. The job of researcher or administrator in industry is to discover their *relative* importance, the ways in which they are related to each other, and how they relate to the special conditions in the work situation.

LEVELING FORCES IN THE STATUS SYSTEM

Many observers have felt that the contemporary trend toward the mechanization and rationalization of work patterns has removed "dignity" from the worker. The dissipation of skills and the large increase of semiskilled work

[36] Alfred M. Bingham, *Insurgent America*, Harper & Brothers, 1935.

has taken much of the "individuality" from the job. This diminution of individual differences reduces the differentiation which is basic to stratification in general and status stratification in particular. Many workers find themselves one of a mass performing the same routines, taking the same orders from the same supervisors, and receiving the same rate of pay. The new tendency, therefore, is to reward not skill or production (which is geared to the average worker) but length of service, regularity of work habits, good attendance, coöperation with management, making "contacts" on and off the job, and "good personality." Since many people satisfy these requisites, graduations of income and status become based more and more on *group* affiliation and *group* membership. The status of the individual becomes increasingly determined by the relative status of the group of which he is a member, rather than by the technical skill inherent in his work position.

When we appreciate the diminished chances of individuals to experience upward mobility in American industry, the greater importance of group position and group status becomes apparent. For example, a foreman may feel that there is little "sense in promoting a worker from the drill press to the milling machine, especially when that worker is doing a good job—and seems to be accommodated to it." The tendency is to bring in a new person from the outside, and start him afresh on the job. Drucker expresses this thought as follows:

> There is little chance for anybody below the executive level to find satisfaction in a job whose relation to reality is very obscure. For the great majority of automobile workers, the only meaning of the job is in the pay check, not in anything connected with the work or the product. Work appears as something unnatural, a disagreeable, meaningless and stultifying condition of getting the pay check, devoid of dignity as well as of importance. No wonder that this puts a premium on slovenly work, on slowdowns, and on other tricks to get the same pay check with less work. No wonder that this results in an unhappy and discontented worker—because a pay check is not enough to base one's respect on.[37]

"INDIVIDUALISTIC" REACTIONS TO BLOCKS IN UPWARD STATUS MOBILITY

How does the worker achieve status under the leveling influences on the job? We are interested here in two basic patterns of behavior: the individualistic and the group variety. Each type has subtypes which we shall examine.

Self-Improvement Response

The self-improvement reaction is very common to blocks in upward status mobility. Improve-yourself-and-some-day-your-chance-will-come has been the

[37] Peter F. Drucker, *Concept of the Corporation,* The John Day Company, 1946, p. 179.

traditional advice imparted to ambitious workers in America. Once this slogan meant that one should improve himself on the job—where he would obtain prestige and recognition, and eventually more income and authority. With the growing realization that jobs are "dead-end" jobs, the "improve yourself" adage has been reinterpreted to mean that the worker should train himself for another job, which offers greater promise of prestige, income, and authority.

Going to night school has been a favorite path of the ambitious status seeker. The purpose of getting additional training is motivated by the desire not only to learn but to gain favorable attention from supervisors. It is a way of informing authority of the strong desire to climb the supervisory ladder. At times business may encourage additional education by paying for it or by sharing some of its expenses. This act may soothe the worker. He thinks, "The company is interested in me, and when my chance comes I'll be prepared."

Many businesses have inaugurated training programs of their own. In such cases employees are given time off during working hours to attend school. Thousands of workers are annually given rudimentary training of one type or another. They jump at the chance to secure recognition as good students. Obviously, no more than a small proportion of trainees will secure job advancement and the recognition that goes with it. The higher the goals, the fewer the jobs, and the more numerous the candidates. Fortunately, many continue to feel that "Education is never wasted." Hope springs eternal that opportunity will come some day. The fact that a small proportion *are* upgraded and receive formal recognition keeps hope alive in many workers.

As a matter of fact, the training programs of many corporations serve a double purpose. For one thing, they drain off frustrations of many status seekers; for another, they serve to increase the transferability of the worker within the plant. It is "smart management" to train workers so that they may be shifted from one job to another as the market demands changes in the products.

Living-Beyond-Your-Status Response

Another individualistic or *middle-class response* to mobility blockages is for the person to try to improve his "social" contacts on the job. He tries to ingratiate himself with the foreman, become a "stool pigeon," and avoid association with "ordinary" men in his department. These acts are despised by the mass of workers as unfair. The worker who is "snooty," an "eager beaver," or the "foreman's pet" must be able to endure the status attacks of his fellow workers.

These individualistic responses are more prevalent among white-collar workers and petty managers and officials. They seek status by showing

superiors that they already belong to a higher-status level. The family budget is strained and manipulated to enable the breadwinner to display the style of life similar to that of his immediate status superiors. The worker may feel that he must buy a tailor-made, double-breasted suit, that it would be nice to join a book-of-the-month club, that he should serve Scotch rather than beer, that he should move to another section of town, that he should shift church membership or acquire impressive sterling tableware, or buy the Mrs. an expensive evening gown for the next dance.[38]

Petty supervisors and minor executives are especially concerned about the status attributes. The training they seek is often "personality development." "How to win friends and influence people" has much more appeal to lower white-collar male workers than courses in bookkeeping and accounting. Learning how to get along in the personality market,[39] making yourself well liked, developing a dynamic, expansive personality, making people feel comfortable, having savoir-faire are necessary (so the belief goes) to status acceptance and status climbing.

The Displacement of the Area of Status Struggle

The third type of adjustment to status blocking is to abandon hope of getting prestige rewards from the job. The individual seeks to excel and gain esteem in his off-job relationships in the work plant. The sources of status or gratification at work are many. Some arise from the informal interaction among the workers and others from organizations sponsored by management.

Many informal groups arise in which the individual can obtain some recognition. In them someone acquires the reputation of a cardsharp, another is lauded because he can defy the authority of the supervisor, still another has a knack of pacifying antagonists, another is a good storyteller or jokester, another is a good labor man, another is spokesman for the group. In this informal status structure many are willing to risk to achieve status. They do their work adequately, but their chief satisfactions derive from their status in the informal group.

Status may also be attained from company-sponsored after-work programs. Many businesses, offices, hospitals, and schools sponsor recreational programs for their employees. Baseball, basketball, bowling, and volleyball teams are established. All kinds of clubs are formed—camera, hiking, band, orchestra, choir, and others. Dances, banquets, and dinners are given. All these activities mean that contacts are multiplied and new social organizations are created. *The greater the amount and complexity of the social organization, the greater are the chances of active social participation and the larger the opportunities for personal recognition.* Since such organizations increase

---

[38] See Veblen, *op. cit.*, Chapter 4, "Conspicuous Consumption."
[39] C. Wright Mills, "The Competitive Personality," *Partisan Review*, September-October, 1946, pp. 433-441.

the "area of acquaintance" of the individual, they are an additional source of prestige. They make possible the anachronism of low income, little authority, little formal recognition, but plant-wide informal recognition.

"You pitched a fine game last night, Walt"; "Too bad you muffed that foul shot, Bill"; "Congratulations for being elected chairman of the local, Bob"; "How much did we make from the dance, Betty?" "That's a beautiful watch the company gave you last night, Pop"; "That's a beautiful snapshot, Dick"; "You've been chosen chairman of the flower committee, Mona."

Such statements reflect the existence of complex social organization and the operation of social prestige mechanisms.

The thesis has been suggested that these plant-sponsored activities are designed to drain off frustration arising from the blocks to status advancement.

Management may or may not consciously realize that its programs have this effect. Yet it is clear that tension is reduced and status demands are channelized.

Gardner reports an excellent illustration of this mechanism at work:

In another concern there was a large engineering staff with many young graduate engineers in the lowest-status engineering jobs. While these were good jobs and fairly well paid as compared to shop jobs, they were, nevertheless, at the bottom of the engineering hierarchy and advancement was often slow. Among the employees of the company a very active camera club was developed in which many of these young engineers participated, and there was a great deal of competition for recognition in the photographic exhibits and for positions as officers of the club. Through this club they apparently received the recognition which they felt was lacking in their jobs. As soon as they began to advance in the supervisory hierarchy or otherwise gain status on the job, they began to lose interest in the club, they found they did not have the time to compete in exhibits, and often would practically give up the hobby.[40]

Achieving status in the community is a less direct method of securing recognition on the job. Nevertheless, values which bring recognition in the community are transferred somewhat into the work plant. This is especially true when the plant is located in a small town or city. But even in the larger cities and communities this transference occurs, because many work associates live in the same neighborhood. Not infrequently they belong to the same church, send their children to the same schools, join the same clubs and lodges, eat and drink together.

Recognition in the community usually derives from participation in its social organizations. Recognition at work is given to the newly elected grand master of the lodge, the head of the World-Wide Service League, the parents of the school's valedictorian, the organizer of the Jay-Teen Club, the deacon of the church, and the head of the Parent-Teacher Association.

[40] Gardner, op. cit., pp. 179-180.

Conversely, a worker's status is lowered by a divorce in the family, appearance in court, having children expelled from school, mismanagement of lodge or church funds. These events provide much of the grist for gossip around the workbench or in the office.

THE GROUP RESPONSE TO STATUS-LEVELING FORCES

The second way workers compensate for loss of individual status is by seeking *group status* within the work plant. As industry corralled workers into teams, as it set up production lines, as it organized work, it forged groups of individuals who became interdependent by way of division of labor. The organization and socialization of workers resulted from the impersonal forces in capitalistic enterprise—from its drives toward rationalization, mechanization, and mass production. Consequently, the grievances, elations, salaries, aspirations, and general conditions of work became the same for many workers. Their frustrations, arising out of loss of skill, loss of prestige, blocked upward mobility, long hours, and often low wages, motivated them to organize for self-protection.

The earliest basis for such organization was economic. Almost all grievances and frustrations were submerged and allowed to find expression in economic terms. Where labor unions were formed, there was some effort to re-create some of the "fraternal" and status aspects of the ancient guilds. There was talk of "brotherhood," the bond of occupation, and the need for mutual aid and understanding. The main emphasis in organization was and still is, however, economic bargaining. Yet we should not ignore the noneconomic and status aspects of union and group organization. The history of trade unionism reveals a gradual growth in the interests and areas of bargaining. Increasingly, unions are providing their members recreational, cultural, and, more recently, political training. Although many of these activities (camps, picnics, recreation, counseling programs) are motivated by the desire to secure greater solidarity for economic struggles, they provide at the same time *another area for social participation, another opportunity for status achievement, and another avenue for status, economic, and political mobility*. To many life is given new meaning because a career, a faith, an ideology, an opportunity for recognition are now available.

The labor union operates within a group orientation. It is concerned with status of the workers as groups, in situations where groups are struggling for recognition, power, and wealth. Here we are concerned with group struggles for status and recognition.

Emergence of Group Status

The displacement of individual status striving by group status striving is not new in industrial organization. What is new is the greater emphasis on group status, and the efforts of management and labor to promote it. This is a difficult task because some of the group identifications have been lost

in the urbanization process. Hence, conscious effort must be exerted to make groups aware of themselves and to make them compete for status. Thus, not only must status be artificially induced, but the search for it must de directed in areas "that don't really count."

To illustrate: Company A inaugurates a recreation association. A league is created, prizes are offered, emblems are awarded, and publicity is distributed. The plant is divided into teams drawn from different departments. These departments may or may not correspond to any natural groupings that arise in the factory. More than likely, they represent arbitrary divisions created by the management to expedite production, processing, or servicing.

Department 26 wins the bowling championship. It hangs a banner as proof of this achievement. The workers in Department 26 have cheered the team, purchased their uniforms, fought over the scoring. Next year, the banner may be lost to Department 6. Preparations are then made to retrieve the banner and the lost status. The fact that one department is predominantly Negro, another foreign born, another native born may heighten the competition of departments and increase everyone's status awareness.

A status system built upon petty devices is a tenuous thing. The satisfactions derived from competition in recreation are secondary sources of status. We do not assert that status competition in the area of recreation is unimportant. We do assert that it is in the nature of a *substitute*, for our society demands that status be awarded mainly for economic progress. As we have shown, economic progress is now a matter of group pressure. Economic and status rewards are simultaneously derived from increased power.

The Management of Group Status

Many of the battles between organized employers and employees can only be understood as battles for income and *status*.

The public often does not understand why labor and management will not come to agreement on a wage scale, especially when they are so close to a settlement—often a matter of two or three cents an hour. This is especially the case during the strike, when both sides are losing and stand to lose more than they can possibly gain. Each side calls the other side "pig-headed," "unreasonable," and the "public" utters "a curse on both your houses." Although such impasses are tests of power and endurance, the antagonists would be better off to nurse their strength for a showdown on more important issues. Since they do not do this, it is reasonable to conclude that such battles are not motivated by economic reasons alone but by demands for recognition and status.

The continuous demands of organized labor also are motivated by the desire for greater recognition. The ceaseless demands for better working conditions, cleaner washrooms, higher pay, more effective grievance machinery, better promotion and security plans, protective devices, and special clothing may be sincere, but they are also attention-getting devices. Labor

is strongly motivated to be accepted as a social equal to management. The new "dignity" of labor is a concept which envisions labor as a copartner, equal in every way with management.

Labor is making a final assault on the last barrier to status equality, an assault on management prerogatives. Management has received perennial recognition because it has made the important decisions in industry. Labor leaders are pointing out that all men should participate in making decisions that affect their welfare. Management, on the other hand, says that decision making goes with ownership. It claims that labor is unfit technically and unjustified ethically to play the role of management.

However, to be master of one's destiny has been an endless source of gratification in America. Labor's demands may be interpreted as attempts to gain this kind of self-respect. Workers' skills may be in process of dilution. Workers may be easily replaceable, workers may be part of a productive machine, but workers want to feel and want others to know that they are an important part of industry. They are girding their power and organization to prove it.

CONCLUSION

Status has been traditionally conceived as an individual attribute. We have demonstrated that it must be considered as a group phenomenon. In fact, every work plant has a status organization somewhat independent from the supervisory and other organizations. Like other structures, status may be formally and informally organized; its structure may be rigid or fluid. In any case workers are much concerned about their status positions in their work groups. They are constantly trying to obtain those symbols which others will accord recognition.

One of the main attributes of the modern industrial system is its tendency to reduce the social differences among workers. Workers evolve many adjustments to this leveling process, the most important of which is the creation of pressure groups. Many workers and unions feel that when they get power equal with management, status equality will automatically follow.

SUPPLEMENTARY STUDIES

FIELD OBSERVATION: DIRECT OBSERVATION OF A SELECTED WORK PLANT
(Continued)

In the work plant selected, outline:
Status Organization
Report:
1. Status hierarchy.

2. Status symbols.
3. The rights and limitations surrounding the various status positions.
4. Status problems or grievances.
5. Relationships and adjustments demanded by the status structure.

FIELD OBSERVATION: CASUAL OBSERVATIONS

Observe workers in different occupations and make an inventory of role behavior which appears directly attributable to the status position occupied by the worker.

LIBRARY: BOOKS AND ARTICLES

Archibald, Katherine, "The Pattern of Status," *Wartime Shipyard*, University of California Press, 1947, pp. 110-127.

Barnard, Chester I., "Functions and Pathology of Status Systems in Formal Organizations," *Industry and Society*, William F. Whyte (ed.), McGraw-Hill Book Company, Inc., 1946, chap. 4, pp. 46-83.

Leopold, Lewis, *Prestige: A Psychological Study of Social Estimates*, T. Fisher Unwin, 1913.

Warner, W. L., and Low, J. O., "The Break in the Skill Hierarchy," *The Social System of the Modern Factory*, Yale University Press, 1947, pp. 66-89.

Whyte, William F., "Status in the Kitchen," *Human Relations in the Restaurant Industry*, McGraw-Hill Book Company, Inc., 1948, chap. 4, pp. 33-46.

RESEARCH GAPS

1. The organizing and disruptive effects of a status system within different work plants.
2. Determination of status-leveling forces within different work plants and union organizations.

CHAPTER XII

Class Organization of the Work Plant

THE PECUNIARY COMPLEX

EAVESDROPPING AROUND THE WORK PLANT

"The board of directors is wondering what management is up to. . . ."
"Tell those supervisors to watch out for the slowdown. . . ."
"In ten years, if things go right, I'll be making $8000. . . ."

"What do 'they' want, our blood?"

"It's 93¼ cents an hour, or we'll strike!"

"There's a reorganization scheme that may cut away our jobs."

"My job just ain't no more, a machine can do it better and *cheaper.*"

"I'd like to punch the efficiency expert in the nose, telling me I ought to turn out 300 more pieces."

"His record shows an efficiency rating of only 64½ percent."

"We must cut the costs of production!"

"If I get that raise, I'll buy a new Buick."

"I'm saving all of my raise; you've got to look out for a rainy day."

"It's amazing how low a guy will sink for a few lousy bucks."

"My bonus depends on getting the new organizations scheme operating in the plant."

"Don't you think Jim's become a little snooty since he got that last raise and a foreman's job?"

MONEY, THE MEASURE OF MAN

Any of the above statements might be heard around work plants today. Although they may at first appear disconnected and unrelated, one may note that the prevailing theme concerns itself largely with pecuniary and property values. A stranger in our society would stand back in wonderment to observe the almost pathological preoccupation we have with accumulating money and property. He would be inclined to state that the greatest zeal is not to be found in our religious life but in our economic enterprises. This materialistic zeal expresses itself in many different ways. We observe a person who has a passion to increase his income; there is another who wants to clutter his home with tawdry objects; here is one who, although rich, is still struggling to accumulate even more wealth.

Financial dissatisfaction is felt by most workers, from the top managers to the lowest-paid workers on the plant floor. All desire an increase of income —sometimes at the expense of each other, sometimes at the expense of the consumer. There is little ethics in this matter of pecuniary struggle and evaluation—the object is to get an advantage. Only a few people are resigned to their economic status. These tend to be the very poor and the very rich. The others seem possessed by a restless and endless search for the "goods" of life. Every increase in income is greeted by a determined drive for more; every saving is considered a sacrament, every expansion in material accumulation is a sign of success.

"Success" becomes the ever sought-for goal. Although success is ill defined, it concerns itself with getting an economic advantage. Success is measured by the income saved or the property accumulated. Preoccupation with success is a syndrome in our culture. Ubiquitous comparisons with others on income and property are constantly made. Such ever present questions insert themselves in many situations: Am I more or less successful in others'

eyes? In my own eyes? How do I measure up to the success of my friends, relatives, neighbors, and others? What are my chances for future wealth and security?

The answers to these questions are not difficult to find. The measurement of man's success and that of his organizations is achieved by applying this universal yardstick: the amount of income received and the amount of wealth accumulated. Everywhere we turn, both inside and outside of the world of work, we see the pecuniary yardstick being applied. Success is measured by the money or goods one has, or his ability to convert his property into money. Monetary success is considered so important that it is almost equated to moral stature.[1] And it is possible to measure this stature rather accurately, because the yardstick of money is capable of almost infinite subdivision.

Man's concern about his economic position makes itself felt in noneconomic areas of behavior. Many of his social attitudes and much of his collective behavior are anchored and related to relative financial level and to relative financial security. Status position becomes dependent more or less on the amount of income received and on its stability. Power over one's associates, family, and friends is likewise related to this financial position. Patterns of spending and consumption relate to economic level. The "worth" of institutions is measured by their financial stability or their moneymaking ability. Organizations are established to determine the credit ratings of men, the financial stability of business organizations and public corporations. Organizations such as the stock market are even built around the idea of estimating the future economic position of other business. A man's integrity is set by his credit rating when he enters a new community or when he attempts to set up a new business.

Much thought has been given to the sensitivity of modern man to the importance of money and economic position in his intimate and personal life. Yet he does not like to consider his character dominated by economic considerations. This conflict about the primacy of economic interests over other interests has been pointed out by Lynd.[2] Some current aphorisms reflect the deep-seated role that money plays in man's intimate life:

"Touch a man's pocketbook, and you touch his heart."

"Money is your best friend. Dollars will never let you down."

"Money talks."

"Remember the Almighty Dollar."

[1] In fact, in the Calvinistic code, economic success was interpreted as evidence of God's grace. This code still survives in American culture. See Max Weber, *The Protestant Ethic and the Spirit of Capitalism*, translated by Talcott Parsons, George Allen and Unwin, Ltd., 1930.

In Part Four, "The Social Adjustment of the Worker," we have explained how this code becomes a part of the workers' habits and attitudes.

[2] Robert S. Lynd, *Knowledge for What?* Princeton University Press, 1945, pp. 60-62.

"Never lend money to a friend."

"It takes money to make money."

"That man is as sound as a dollar."

"There isn't anything that money can't buy."

"Money isn't race-conscious."

"You can't live on good will."

"Money isn't everything, but it helps."

Aside from its overt importance, money is something very personal and intimate. Since it is so easy to compare people by this yardstick, a deep sense of privacy develops about it. The amount one makes is a matter of curiosity for others. It is considered improper and indiscreet to ask a man directly what his income is. Yet curiosity about the subject is considered legitimate, for many devices are utilized to pierce this veil of privacy. If an individual feels self-assured in terms of his economic position, he may boast of the size of his income, savings, and accumulation. However, he may hesitate to give his income if he is asked directly. He is suspicious of the inquirer. If he senses the possibility of an economic inferiority in a monetary comparison, he may work out a rather complex defense mechanism to keep his financial position a secret. Yet ordinary small talk and gossip is loaded with tangential statements, inquiries, and comments to glean bits of economic data about other people. An endless list of such statements can be made. Below are just a few:

"You can't support a home like his on peanuts, you know."

"He's breaking his back to maintain appearances."

"He only rents that house; he doesn't own it."

"He must have a separate income to afford that liquor bill."

"I understand that his folks had money."

"They drive a Buick, but the kids don't wear underwear."

This persistent interest, this preoccupation with money, may be termed the materialistic—or better, the pecuniary—complex. The complex manifests itself in a number of ways. There is, for example, a tendency for man to attribute to his social organizations the economic attributes that he himself possesses. This anthropomorphic tendency is witnessed in his interest in and reactions to the financial stability and growth of business organizations especially. A poor workman may become so identified with U.S. Steel, for example, that he glows with pride when the company nets large profits, when it plans a large expansion program; he grieves over the financial crisis the corporation is facing; he feels hurt that the government is attacking it. In short, he may tend to personalize business, the budget of the United States government, the policies of large corporations. He applies to business and to government the same economic motives for behaving as he does to himself and to other people.

These economic identifications are seldom recognized, let alone evaluated

by Western man. So ingrained is the materialistic complex in our culture
that he is inclined mistakenly to attribute it to a biological root. He would
suggest that it is "natural" for man to be preoccupied with economic
interests; that it is "natural" for economic organizations to reflect man's
original nature. Cultural anthropology has revealed that the habits of men
in different cultures show wide variations and that there is no justification

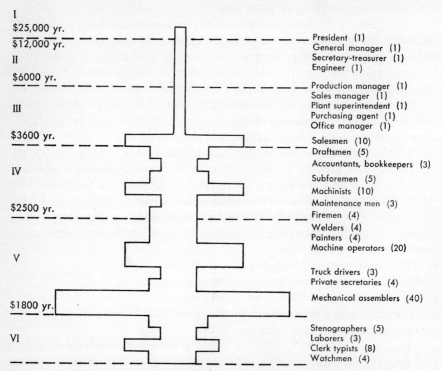

FIG. 42. A Profile of the Class Structure in the Midwestern Compressor Company. All
incomes are on a yearly basis; bonus is not added to income; Classes I, II, III also are
stockholders, but income from stock is not included. The lengths of the bars indicate
the relative number of people in the occupation.

in the belief that man is "naturally" acquisitive. Societies based on the
principle of use rather than on the principle of gain produce much different
economic motives.

THE CLASS STRUCTURE IN THE WORK PLANT

The locus of the economic struggle occurs in the social structure of the
work plant. It is therefore to be expected that the work plant has social
classes as does the community. The class system of a work plant may be
conveniently seen in its salary and wage schedule. In our terminology, those

who receive the highest incomes are in the highest class, and vice versa. Usually, high prestige and power are also accorded those who receive the largest returns. But this is not our concern here. We are focusing only on the economic aspects of social structure.

In large private work plants, those that form the highest class are either the owners or the managers. In cases of absentee owners, the managers make up the upper stratum. Since they have so much autonomous control, they may participate directly in the profits as well as draw salaries. Below the managers and owners are the minor executives, supervisory personnel, and clerical workers. Their incomes usually are in the form of salaries and bonuses. Below them are the wage workers, whose incomes vary reputedly with their skills and the demand for their skills in the labor market.

Figure 42 shows the class structure of a midwest industrial plant.

From this figure it is evident that there are several layers or strata of incomes. Where one stratum begins and another ends is a matter of decision on the part of the researcher. Since income groups are not necessarily segregated, the separation of classes is often arbitrary. If there are convenient breaks in the amount of income, or if several kinds of income are present, the classes may be divided at these points. In the illustration used here, the classes were drawn at breaks in the income continuum.

Classes I, II, and III are largely managerial groups who receive salaries, bonuses, and dividends. Class IV is made up of salaried and wage workers, as is the lowest class, VI. Class V is made up almost entirely of wage workers who also receive bonuses. The most important break occurs between Classes III and IV. Those in the first three classes are largely the managerial group, who receive highest incomes, and those below are dependent salaried and wage workers. Mobility between these two composite groups is negligible or even absent. Mobility among the individual classes is also small, the greatest being between IV and V. Most of the mobility occurs within the classes, and Class V, largely semiskilled workers, has the greatest amount of mobility.

FLUIDITIES AND RIGIDITIES

One should not conclude, however, that this class structure is solid or frozen. There is always some movement up and down the economic ladder, but it is generally restricted in volume and in range of mobility. Lynd and others have demonstrated that the class structure is usually composed of two separate substructures—roughly the white-collar "business" structure and the blue-shirt worker structure. Mobility up and down each structure is possible and recurrent, but mobility between structures is rare.[3] Thus, the chance for a low-paid clerk to become a member of management and

[3] Robert S. Lynd and Helen M. Lynd, *Middletown in Transition*, Harcourt, Brace and Company, 1937, chap. 2, "Making a Living."

participate in greater returns is higher than for a worker on the plant floor.

All kinds of obstacles, rules, regulations, and social organizations tend to block mobility in the class structure. For example, in the Midwestern Compressor plant, Negroes could never aspire to jobs higher than the maintenance and semiskilled levels. Assemblers might become skilled workers, but the latter could not climb into the white-collar or managerial class. Being a union leader or a shop steward may also block upward economic mobility. Union contracts, salary schedules, informal agreements, "traditional" wages or salaries tend to preserve the class structure.

On the other hand, the possibilities for a worker to increase his income within his respective class are relatively numerous. Rate increases and promotions constitute the largest economic incentive. This range of economic advance for the manual workers of United States Steel Corporation illustrates how the hourly wage worker may climb within the broad blue-shirt working class. The standard hourly wage scales for all steel-making subsidiaries of United States Steel were in 1947 as follows:[4]

Job Class O– 1	$1.09
2	1.13
3	1.17
4	1.21
5	1.25
6	1.29
7	1.33
8	1.37
9	1.41
10	1.45
11	1.49
12	1.53
13	1.57
14	1.61
15	1.65
16	1.69
17	1.73
18	1.77
19	1.81
20	1.85
21	1.89
22	1.93
23	1.97
24	2.01
25	2.05
26	2.09
27	2.13
28	2.17
29	2.21
30	2.25

The possibility of increasing his income gives the worker a real sense of opportunity. He can still "get ahead" even though there are blocks to his mobility into a "higher" class. Management has offered its workers addi-

[4] Robert Tilove, "The Wage Rationalization Program in U.S. Steel," *Monthly Labor Review*, June, 1947, p. 977.

tional income incentives with the hope of stepping up output. Such devices include the piece-price system, the group incentive plan, profit sharing, promise of bonus, prizes, and other monetary rewards. Yet these devices are limited in scope, for although management can try to stimulate production by monetary incentives, it must still attempt to maintain a "proper balance" of incomes among workers. The limits of each stratum are fixed formally by the organization, or informally in management's mind.

Management realizes, perhaps unconsciously, that equal-status jobs and equal-power jobs must have approximately the same incomes. When semi-skilled workers earn more than their foreman, when accountants make more than general superintendents, the social integration of the working force is jarred. There comes a point of diminishing returns when a disruption of the class system produces less rather than more production.

THREE PREVAILING MORES OF INDIVIDUAL BARGAINING

The tradition of individual bargaining is still very strong in America. Efforts are made by individuals to increase their income or bargaining position when they apply for a job and for promotions once on the job. Some of these efforts are permissive and done openly; others are considered "disloyal," and may be done only in a clandestine fashion. On the floor, there are at least three prevailing mores of pay and promotion.

1. Basically, a man should be paid for the *work* he does. The union slogan is equal pay for equal work. (2) An exception to this rule might be that older workers should receive higher rates for the same job, but even here there should be a limited difference between newest and oldest workers. (3) Promotions should be based on skill or merit primarily and age secondarily. These values give stability to the class structure.

Enforcement of the Bargaining Mores

Individuals who circumvent these basic conventions are generally condemned. Using direct measures such as bribing a "superior" to get an advance brings immediate and antagonistic reactions from fellow workers. In fact, any association with "superiors" in order to gain an economic advantage is suspect. This is known as using "pull," and the reaction of workers to it is violent. Whereas it is considered proper and even advisable on the part of white-collar, professional, and businessmen to seek "social" contacts with their superiors, manual workers regard such action on the part of their co-workers with scorn. The worker who is known as the foreman's "pet" spends an unpleasant life on the plant floor. All the techniques of social disapproval are applied. The subject is "razzed," is made the object of ribaldry and other types of jokes. He receives slurs on his character and may even be physically manhandled. The non-work relations with superiors are usually rather clearly defined. For example, a worker may send his foreman a Christmas card, contribute toward a birthday present, ask about the health

of his family, but he may go no further. Each work plant and different occupations may have slightly different codes, but they are nonetheless ubiquitous.

THE PROBLEMS RAISED BY GROSS INEQUALITIES

Workers are usually aware of where they stand in reference to others in regard to income. They may not know the exact incomes earned by people in other departments, but they do at least have an approximate idea. They know rather accurately how their incomes or rates of pay compare with others' in immediate departments. Often these small differences in pay are magnified to an inordinate degree. The workers will spend many hours trying to account for the fact that they do not receive as much as others. They will worry about whether they should approach the boss for a raise; whether they should "tell the supervisor off" the next time they meet; whether their chances of climbing in the plant are good or bad.

The administrators also worry about gross inequalities in incomes. Thus, in a library, all members of the staff were questioned on the salaries of their fellow employees. It was discovered that they knew the salaries rather accurately. This was true despite the fact that salaries were considered confidential and were never openly discussed. Many of the tensions in the library resulted in part from the generally known fact that the actual salaries did not conform to what the workers and the administration thought they should be.

Below is a table which compares two salary schedules—what the administration thought they should be and what they actually were. The theoretical schedule followed a designated and existing hierarchy of authority and responsibilities, whereas the actual salaries reflected a previously existing hierarchy:

Positions	Theoretical Salaries	Actual Salaries
Librarian	$4500	$4500
Chief of processing	4000	3000
Chief of service	4000	Vacant
Order librarian	3000	2530
Cataloguer	3000	3300
Circulation librarian	2800	2400
Readers' adviser	2800	2400
Reference assistant	2800	1980
Junior cataloguer	2500	Vacant
Accessions librarian	2500	3300
Circulation assistant	2200	1980
Circulation assistant	2200	1680
Periodicals librarian	2200	1560
Juvenile librarian	2200	1620
Janitors		1620
Student assistant	$.50 hr.	$.65 hr.
Student assistants (57)	$.40-.50 hr.	$.40-.65 hr.

The tensions did not arise from a feeling that salaries should be higher, but because the *relative* salaries were thought to be "out of line." For example, the chief of processing and the chief of service had lower salaries than their subordinates, the cataloguer and the accessions librarian. The newer workers felt that they had more training than older workers, and that they did more important jobs. Yet they received smaller salaries. Circulation assistants did the same jobs, yet their salaries differed. Student assistants got wage rates higher than was theoretically possible. Such situations are not uncommon causes of tensions in work plants. Let us turn to the importance that income and class position have for the workers in the plants themselves.

THE SIGNIFICANCE OF CLASS POSITION

CLASS POSITION AND IN-PLANT MOBILITY

The worker often feels that his future economic position in the plant is jeopardized by the limitations of his present income. To cite a seemingly insignificant illustration: Joe Doaks carries a sack lunch to work. No matter how good a lunch he has, Joe thinks he would "get farther" if he could afford to eat in the cafeteria, or perhaps in the rather "exclusive" restaurant a few blocks away. Why should this be so important to him? Obviously, he feels he cannot associate with people of greater influence if he eats his lunch on the plant floor. There is prestige to be gained and a greater chance for advancement if he can eat with "higher-ups" in the cafeteria or restaurant. But this is possible only if a high enough income is earned.

Upper-group workers may stop for a cocktail on the way home. Participation in such a drinking ritual again demands a high income. Membership in the social organizations of the "men of influence" in the plant likewise demands economic power. An illustration drawn from a conversation of a clerical worker in an optical company demonstrates this point.

I began to wonder how it was that some people became supervisors. I worked as hard as anybody else, yet I never got any place. I asked Joe, and he says, "It's all a racket; you've got to be a Mason. All of the Masons help each other out. Look at Bob, at Jim, and Bill. They're all Masons, and they haven't been here more than two years, yet they're supervisors." I tried to join the Masons when I found this out, but you can't join—you've got to be invited. So I asked my uncle to invite me. But things are not so simple. I started to hang around a bunch of Masons. I found out it costs seventy-five dollars to join. Then, there are dues. But that's just the beginning. You must do the things everybody else does. Thirty cents for every game of bowling, seventy-five cents for every glass of whiskey. And you've got to treat like everybody else. Of course, if you're a supervisor you can do these things—which I admit I enjoy. But how long can you stand it on a clerk's pay? I gave up the idea.

Thus, the way of life associated with higher classes inside and outside of the plant depends in part on economic power. It is no wonder that the aphorism so commonly repeated is, "You've got to have money to make money." Also, "It's who you know, not what you know, that counts."

CLASS POSITION AND STATUS

It is a common saying in work plants: "To get to the top, you've got to act like those at the top." One should belong to the "proper" social organizations such as lodges, country clubs, churches, and so on. One must be able to entertain one's "superiors," but this cannot be done if the home is in need of repair, if the furniture is shoddy and antiquated, and if the family is not dressed properly. The frustration that many feel arises from their lower-class position and their inability to match their style of living with that in the upper classes. A vicious circle is set up—social contacts are needed to raise one's class levels, yet class position makes it economically difficult to observe the style of life needed to make social contacts. This increases awareness of shortcomings in the lower classes, which serves, in turn, to augment feelings of insecurity and inferiority.

Many other things impinge on class position in the work plant. These are largely things that increase the status and power of the individual or group. Not only is a high level of income sought for its own sake, but a new job with higher income means that one may have a larger desk, a more spacious office, a private secretary, a longer vacation, more pleasant working conditions, and work that is less physically exhausting.

CLASS POSITION AND SECURITY

Another correlate of higher income is increased general security. A higher income usually puts one on a salary basis. A salaried person is not as quickly affected by fluctuations in business, by lower or higher profits, and by threats of unemployment. In a poll of Standard Oil workers, Stuart Chase reported that most workers prefer a steady job with moderate wages to an intermittent job with high wages. Other studies point in the same direction.[5] A dividend of higher-class position in the plant is the increased chance to participate in policy formation.[6] The opportunity to participate in the control of conditions that affect the individual's own economic well-being and status is highly prized by many workers. One of the greatest frustrations of low-income jobs arises from the fact that the worker's future well-being is not subject to his control. As one typist said in an interview, "More and more things happen to people, and they can't do anything about it." It is

[5] Stuart Chase, "A Generation of Industrial Peace," *Lamp*, October, 1946; C. Calkins, *Some Folks Won't Work*, Harcourt, Brace and Company, 1930.

[6] See Peter Drucker, *The Concept of the Corporation*, The John Day Company, 1946. Drucker points out how General Motors executives vie for membership on the "Sloan Committee," a group which has top decision-making power and status.

true that no worker is the absolute master of his own destiny. Nevertheless, the belief that one can control his destiny, even in small measure, is conducive to mental health.[7]

One of the prevailing beliefs of our society is that the individual is responsible for his economic position.[8] It is held that unemployment, high income, independence, and servitude are conditions for which the individual is largely answerable. This myth survives despite the fact that a continually smaller proportion of the workers are able to achieve an independent occupational status. The doctrine of personal responsibility in an impersonally directed world still lives. The drive of workers to secure economic strength grows more desperate as opportunity to gain security and self-direction lessens.

CLASS POSITION AND LIFE CHANCES

Although man may have created myths to support his beliefs that he is naturally an economic being, there is considerable evidence that many of the things he considers "good" are indeed dependent on his income and property. From birth to death, his chances of obtaining what he wishes depend on his success in the world of work, and this success is defined in monetary terms.

Certainly, the chances of staying alive constitute one of the basic life chances in our society. This seems to be dependent, in part at least, on income, as is indicated in Table 17.

TABLE 17.   Infant Mortality and Income[9]

Family Income	Deaths per 1000 Live Births
Under $450	167
$ 450–$ 549	106
$ 550–$ 649	117
$ 650–$ 849	108
$ 850–$1049	83
$1150–$1249	64
$1250 and over	59

Other studies point to the central place of income in determining life chances in American society. Not only does income affect one's chances of

[7] E. W. Bakke, The Unemployed Worker, Yale University Press, 1940.

[8] Witness the high proportion of people who want to own their own businesses. In a survey of occupational aspirations, 40 percent of the heads of families of Greenbelt, Maryland, elicited a desire to become independent businessmen and independent professionals. See William H. Form, "Status Stratification in a Planned Community," American Sociological Review, October, 1945, pp. 605-613.

[9] R. M. Woodbury, "Infant Mortality in the U.S.," Annals of the American Academy of Political and Social Sciences, November, 1936, pp. 102-104.

staying alive, but it also is directly related to the chances of becoming ill. The National Health Survey of 1935-1936 indicated that the number of chronic disabilities, the frequency of illnesses, the duration of illness, the amount of medical care received correlate directly with the amount of income received and the amount of property held.[10] In other words, the lower the income, the greater the chances of falling ill, the longer the duration of the illness, and the less available the medical care.

Despite the attempt to equate availability of opportunity in American society, basic life chances are still set by economic position. For example, the chances of getting education have been demonstrated as depending in large part on the income of the parents.[11] Even the chances of engaging in criminal behavior are related to economic position. Bowers demonstrated that the poorer areas of the city have the highest crime rates.[12] The residents of these areas are least able to hire competent legal aid. At the same time, such organizations as the Boy Scouts and Girl Scouts, which are supposed to act as deterrents to antisocial activity, are found in smallest numbers in the economically poorer areas of the city.[13]

Similarly, the chances of climbing the income and occupational ladder are related to father's income and occupation.[14] The National Resources Committee has demonstrated in a dramatic fashion the disproportionate distribution of such commodities as food, clothing, housing, transportation, household furnishings, recreation, reading matter, and autos to the various income classes.[15]

THE PSYCHOLOGICAL CORRELATES OF CLASS POSITION

We have pointed to the importance of class position in the work world. Class position is a dynamic and changing thing, for salaries and wages rise and fall in the work plant. They are subjected to constant pressure on the part of individuals and groups. There is an insistent effort to change the absolute or relative economic position of individuals and groups. It is important, therefore, to appraise the economic or class position of the worker over a period of time. Class position and changes in it are not important *per se*, but their social effects are. They are translated into general feelings

[10] "Illness and Medical Care in Relation to Economic Status," Bulletin No. 2, *The National Health Survey*, 1935-36, United States Government Printing Office, 1938.

[11] W. L. Warner, Robert Havighurst, and Martin Loeb, *Who Shall Be Educated?* Harper & Brothers, 1945.

[12] R. V. Bowers, "Ecological Patterning of Rochester, N. Y.," *American Sociological Review*, April, 1939, pp. 180-186.

[13] *Ibid.*

[14] P. E. Davidson and H. D. Anderson, *Occupational Mobility in an American Community*, Stanford University Press, 1937, chap. 7.

[15] *Consumer Expenditure in the U.S.*, United States Government Printing Office, 1939.

of well-being and insecurity, self-confidence and anxiety. The interest of the social scientist is on such social and personal meanings of class position. We shall discuss this subject in reference to these considerations: (1) the importance of relative class position of the worker or group of workers; (2) the significance of fluctuations in class position.

THE IMPORTANCE OF RELATIVE CLASS POSITION

If increases in income and the resulting increases in life chances were the *only* factors which motivated workers to work, many would not work so hard. This is true because rises and falls in income do not necessarily reflect themselves directly in proportionate changes in life chances. A difference in income of one or a few hundred dollars a year is of immense significance at the lower end of the economic scale. Every increase in income means greater personal comfort, appreciably better food, housing, clothing, better personal grooming, and so on. Many studies on consumption not only point this out but indicate the large changes in basic expenditure patterns that result from increased or decreased incomes.[16] These studies show that the increases in incomes do not bear a uniform relationship to increases in life chances. At the lower end of the economic scale, as income increases,

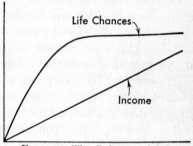

FIG. 43. The Relation of Life Chances to Income.

life chances probably rise faster. Then, as income continues to increase, there is a period of proportionate rise in life chances. Later increases in income indicate smaller proportionate rises in life chances. A diagram of the relationship would approximate the curves suggested in Figure 43. Obviously, with highly augmented incomes the rate of consumption must decline. In short, the style of living of moderately wealthy and extremely wealthy groups does not differ appreciably.

Yet despite this condition, workers in the highest income categories continue to work. People in the lowest categories continue to strive for minute increments in income. Obviously, the *relative* economic position becomes important under these conditions. The greater concern of workers over relative wage rates rather than the earnings themselves has been noted.[17]

The concern over relative class position is related to the area of prestige and status which was discussed in the preceding chapter. Our intent here is to indicate the role of economic position in this prestige world. There is a social meaning to impersonal economic arrangements of men. In fact,

[16] See materials on Engels' laws of consumption and criticism.
[17] See Bakke, *op. cit.*, chap. 1, "Workers' Goals."

as our industrial society grows in size and complexity, as it becomes more bureaucratic in nature, and as individual business units grow, money is more frequently used as a measure of general worth and becomes more important. The need for impersonal criteria in an impersonal world to gauge social approval increases rather than decreases, and new symbols of status must be created. Thorstein Veblen dramatically analyzed the nature of these symbols as directed toward invidious and conspicuous display. Display depends in large measure upon economic power. Frequently, then, personal economic security is considered less important than the ability to display superior relative economic position. Psychologically, the important question becomes: Is my income increasing or decreasing faster than that of those whose approval I expect and desire? Differences and changes in income are common measures of relative changes in social status.

Dreyfuss contends that the aim of many men in power is to accentuate rather than to gloss over income differences of people in similar occupations. Highly stratified income schedules are created, and employees are urged to climb the income ladder. Small income differentials are accentuated by giving similar jobs different names. Thus assistant and associate chief clerk may have very similar duties with an annual income difference of $100 a year. Such a situation serves to make workers more conscious of their relative income and status differences. Thus, the probability that they will collaborate in the economic struggle against a third party diminishes.[18] Simultaneously, the illusion of economic and status mobility is increased. The effect of all this will be one of endorsing and supporting the economic system that brings rewards and satisfactions. Wage systems and incentive schemes are also used for the purely utilitarian purpose of increasing work effort, income, and profit. Most of the literature on this subject concerns itself exclusively with the matter of comparative wages and incentive plans, and ignores the social and political meaning of income differences.[19]

FLUCTUATIONS IN CLASS POSITION

The social and psychological meanings of class position make themselves felt not only in invidious class situations but also in historical fluctuations in income and class position within the plant. Changes in class affect the individual's position in his family, work group, and community in an intimate, personal way.

It has been observed that Americans are reared in a culture that stresses individual economic achievement. The accepted explanation is that con-

[18] Carl Dreyfuss, *Ideology and Occupation of the Salaried Employee*, translated by Ernst E. Warburg, Columbia University Press, 1938.

[19] See, for example, John W. Riegel, *Wage Determination*, University of Michigan Press, 1937 (see Bibliography); C. W. Lytle, *Wage Incentive Methods*, Ronald Press, 1942; R. C. Smyth and M. J. Murphy, *Job Evaluation and Employee Rating*, McGraw-Hill Book Company, Inc., 1946.

tinued and applied effort will lead inevitably to upward economic mobility. American culture is extremely career-conscious. Since upward occupational and income mobility is envisioned, most people tend to regard their present economic status in the perspective of a career pattern. The approximation of the actual and expected patterns accounts in large measure for the attitude people have toward their jobs, toward their work associates, toward themselves, and toward their communities.

THE TYPES OF CLASS WORK HISTORIES

In this section we propose to examine several types of class work histories. The types of class experience are manifold. Abstractly, one may conceive of many of them. Out of the many possible, it may be convenient to list several ideal-typical patterns of class mobility:

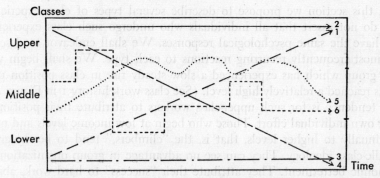

FIG. 44. Types of Class Work Histories.

1. Demonstrates a slow, steady progress from lower to higher levels.
2. Begins work career in upper-class position and remains on that level.
3. Starts work career in a lower class and remains on that level.
4. Demonstrates slow, steady deterioration of class position.
5. Exhibits regular fluctuation in class position between any levels.
6. Exhibits irregular fluctuation in class position on any level.
7. Shows plateau shifts in class position from any level to any other. (Many variations are possible in this type.)

Some of these types of class experiences are illustrated in Figure 44. No pretense is made that these patterns exhaust the logical as well as actual types. We seek only to set up hypotheses that different types of class experience will affect the workers' attitudes toward themselves, their work, and their fellow employees. Class experience may even affect their social and political participation in and outside of the work plant. The psychological and sociological components of a class experience may be very

similar even though the actual class positions differ. For example, a worker may fall from high to middle class, and another may fall from middle to lower class. Both may react to this situation in essentially the same way.

In a society that tends to be typified by insecurity in class position, which at the same time makes cultural demands for upward mobility, one may expect psychological repercussions of one type or another. Although it is difficult to predict exactly how a particular individual will react to a particular class experience, the researcher or personnel administrator will be wise to expect some kinds of reactions to different types of class experiences. Much of the workers' behavior may be better understood if his class experience is considered. It is odd that though almost all work plants gather class data in their application forms, few make use of them to guide personnel and administrative policies.

1. THE CLIMBERS

In this section we propose to describe several types of class experience. We do not assert that all individuals who undergo such class experiences will have the same psychological responses. We shall endeavor to describe the most frequently recurring reactions to each type. We shall begin with that group which has experienced a slow steady rise in class position until it has reached a relatively high level. (See class work history 1 in Figure 44.) The tendency is for such upper-class workers to attribute their position to their own individual effort. Those who begin at low income levels and move continually to higher levels, that is, the "climbers," tend to be driven by middle-class ideology. They can see no advantage in group organization for economic betterment. They attribute their "success" to hard work, ability, and initiative. Although they like to associate with those in the higher classes, they make verbal pretenses of being "democratic" or kindly disposed toward able, aggressive, and efficient individuals who are rising from the bottom. Overtly, their feelings of security tend to be rather strong, and their economic convictions tend to be rather conservative. They are inclined, however, to retain a highly developed work drive, even after the need is no longer evident. This may be in part due to the retention of earlier habits, but it also reflects some anxieties about falling and anxieties about reaching the higher-status levels. The following quotation from a steel mill superintendent illustrates the above:

I attribute my success to hard work, nothing more, nothing less. I don't believe I'm more capable than the ordinary man, but I've gone farther. I always tell my workers that any man who works by the clock will never get any place. I've never looked at the clock, as long as I've worked. I've put in extra time and I've done more than was expected. And I've been amply rewarded. I've always been able to hold my head high and look any man straight in the eye. My family has never lacked anything. It was difficult the first few years—skimping

and all; but we've always had enough to appear decent. And now we can afford some luxuries. I own a big home in a good section of town, my children are going to college, I have a responsible job, and I don't have to worry about another depression. In a few years, I'll be able to retire and do things that I've always wanted to do.

2. THE BRAHMIN

The second type we are concerned with is made up of those individuals who begin at the top of the class within the work plant and generally remain there. (See class work history 2 in Figure 44.) These people often have inherited a business which is stable and rather efficient. They may also be well-trained managers, most of whose work experience has been on that level. In either case, they are the best-paid workers in the plant.

The most important factor to remember is that these individuals form the upper class of the work plant, and they have had little or no experience on lower-class levels. The members of this group, like those who climbed, consciously and unconsciously believe in their inherent individual worth and ability. They differ from the "climbers" in one important aspect, namely, they have a greater feeling of security, both economically and socially. This feeling affects their relations with other members of the work plant. In the first place, their contacts with the lower-class workers tend to be fewer in number and less intensive as well. Contact with them is through intermediaries, often through the "climbers." There is not so much an antipathy toward lower-class workers as an air of impersonalness and even indifference. They share the attitude of the "climbers" that members of the lower classes are likely to be rather incapable, inefficient, indolent, and irresponsible. They are more ready to admit that they do not want to associate with members of the lower classes, and that the latter are unworthy of trust. Their attitude here is one of impersonal authority.

Toward the "climbers" there is a peculiar relationship. Often these two groups are indistinguishable economically. However, the "Brahmin" are usually better educated and come from higher-status groups. Thus, in their relationships with the "climbers" there tends to be a condescending air, or a strained appearance of equal social acceptance. Of course, this is what the "climbers" desire. To become ingratiated, they carry out with vigor the ideas of the "Brahmin" on the plant floor. However, since the social acceptance is rarely of a total nature, there is an antagonism in the relationship. This derives, in part, from the resentment on the part of the "climbers" of the self-assured attitudes of the "Brahmin." The latter seem more comfortable behind new large desks; they are sure that their personnel and technical plans will work out without a hitch; they do not show much concern about their economic and social future. This strong sense of security is native to this group and appears as a source of aggravation to those who have had

to exert themselves to reach the pinnacle of economic success. Below is a section of an interview which a student had with an executive of a rather large shoe factory:

Some of the young engineers and even some of the old-timers irritate me occasionally. My grandfather started this company, and my father is running it now. I imagine I'll have to carry on in a few more years myself. One of the first things I'll do is get rid of some of these eager-beavers. Half of my father's time is consumed turning down some of the "bright ideas" of the young squirt engineers and the suggestions of the old-timers who think they own the place. The old-timers are the superintendents, and they aren't so bad; but they annoy me with their eternal politeness. We couldn't really run the place without them, for they know how to handle the men in the shop.

It's a funny situation; the engineers are trained, but they have little experience; the old-timers have the experience but they don't have much native capacity. I've been raised in the shoe business, and I've had good training besides. I don't have to think of new ideas just to insure my security. A family enterprise such as this is good, because it is guided with balance and reason.

3. LOWER-CLASS NONMOBILES

The case of the lower-class worker who begins and remains on that level is perhaps least known. (See Figure 44.) Americans have been so concerned with upward economic mobility that they have failed to give much attention to the lower-class, nonmobile pattern in our society. As a matter of fact, this pattern is probably more dominant than any other. Davidson and Anderson made a study of inheritance of jobs—from fathers to sons. They found that occupational inheritance seems to be the rule rather than the exception. For example, they found that from 60 to 73 percent of the recorded regular occupations of sons fall upon or are adjacent to the level of their fathers' regular occupations.[20] Lack of occupational mobility implies in our society an absence of class mobility. Clark has shown that relative life earnings of various occupations tend to remain rather constant.[21] Earnings may rise and fall, but the relative earnings of occupations are likely to remain the same. Thus, unskilled labor and farm labor remained at the bottom of the income heap over the years.

The reactions of lower-class workers with no mobility in the work plant are of interest, because they also have been exposed to the myth of mobility. However, they are disinclined to believe it or give it much thought. Their primary aim is to make enough money to satisfy their immediate physical needs. They have submerged the notion that they will some day achieve wealth and security. They expect to work until their physical strength ebbs. Work is not attractive, but merely a means of self-support. Yet they feel a pride in their work—they feel that they *really* labor, and that they *really*

[20] P. E. Davidson and H. D. Anderson, *op. cit.*, p. 24.

[21] See H. F. Clark, *Life Earnings of Selected Occupations*, Harper & Brothers, 1937, Table 3, p. 7.

earn their money. Physical labor is the "real" labor upon which all workers must ultimately depend. They would like to "do something" to improve permanently their economic position, but their fatalism makes this difficult.

Part of a conversation with a worker of foreign origin reveals some of the typical attitudes:

You ask me what I want most out of life. Not much. My wants are few. Most of all I want to have my health and my strength, for without these, a man cannot work. All my life I've worked hard, and if God gives me the strength, I must continue. You see, I did not get much education, for my father was not one to do much for his children. I began working at the age of seven, and I know nothing but work. I only hope that I won't have to depend on my children for anything in my old age. Maybe I can even leave them something, who knows? But this is very hard. When I first came to America, I made only a dollar a day working, now I make almost nine dollars a day. But it's always the same for the workingman. I couldn't save my money then and I can't save it now. It costs more to live now. Yes, the union helped the workingman a little, but the worker is always the same. What do I do with my free time? I rest, for I tire easier now than I used to.

In the actual work plant, the "lower-class nonmobiles" are inclined to hold resentment against those who have "easier" jobs with more pay. A job is defined as easy if the physical exertion is small, or material production is lacking. The boss, foreman, or clerical worker does "nothing" and earns resentment.

Because of his job, the lower-class worker is exposed to the very first drops in production, and layoffs are common. In addition, he does not develop, as do other groups, a sense of loyalty to the firm, the boss, or even his work associates. He realizes that "his labor is worth so much an hour just about any place." Raises are few and far between, seniority has a limited meaning. If, therefore, he knows of another job that pays slightly more, he does not hesitate to move.

The lower-class, nonmobile worker "puts in his time." He does not do anything "extra," for extras are not rewarded. Patterns of ingratiation with those above tend to be limited, and are even frowned upon. He has, in short, adjusted to the notion of nonmobility. In this state of mind, he is inclined to resist innovations on the job which might be interpreted as "exploitative." New ideas, new techniques, new demands are resisted. This tends to produce, in management's thinking, the notion that these people are untractable, unreliable, independent, and unpredictable. For the lower-class, nonmobile worker has little to lose, and quits if the job becomes "uncomfortable."

4. THE SKIDDERS

The experience of class-falling is perhaps the most interesting and intricate one; yet it is the most difficult to understand. A "has-been" is in a

particularly difficult position, for he has to explain to himself and to others the reasons for his decline. If a long history of decline is noted, an elaborate defense mechanism must be created, for it is difficult in our society to avoid the feeling that the individual is not responsible for his position. The "slipping" worker in our culture feels guilty, and he needs to build up a complicated explanation of his position.

It is rare that an individual will openly and totally accept the doctrine of individual responsibility as applicable to himself, especially when he has fallen in class position. He would and does prefer an impersonal social explanation. Many of the workers interviewed blamed the depression for their economic fall. But such an "explanation" cannot be used indefinitely. Chance or fate may be introduced, as "I had just one bad break after another." Often, unscrupulous persons are blamed for the fall, as "My boss had it in for me," or "They are prejudiced against people of my religion or my nationality." Such explanations personalize the situation and become more socially acceptable.

The "skidder" is rarely one who takes his fall nonchalantly or with a high degree of fatalism. He tends to be a conspicuous person. He may borrow prestige from the past, alluding to his former association with the "big shots." He has the "inside" story of how decisions are made, and feels superior because of it. Some may refuse to talk about their past and continually attempt to regain favor in order to pursue the path of upward mobility. Frequently there is a disdain for the common worker and the individual may never identify himself with the class position of the work group in which he is employed.

On the other hand, an opposite reaction may be noted on the part of others whom we have called "skidders." These completely alienate themselves from their past and become assimilated to the lower-class position. They do not share in the typical fatalistic reactions of those whose entire history is in the lower class. They are more self-conscious, and they attempt to impart this feeling to others. They are frequently in the vanguard of political leadership in the unions and other workers' organizations. They are more class-conscious than their work mates, and they exert much energy to spur themselves and their fellows to organization and resistance. The following case history demonstrates this type of reaction:

My father was an engineer who made pretty good money. He wanted me to become an engineer, too. I suppose I would have become one if it weren't for the war—World War I, I mean. I left high school in my senior year to "join up." I saw all the action I wanted to. When I got back I went to work in my father's firm. But that's a long story. The firm got in a financial mess, my father died, and I looked for another job. With my inheritance I started an electrical appliance business. I lost my shirt in it. Then, I did some selling, and did pretty well in it for a while. I invested all of my savings in the company I was working for.

The depression soon liquidated that, and my job. I took all kinds of jobs, and now I'm an inspector of electric motors. That's a fancy title, but actually the job is easy and it doesn't pay much. I've been trying to stir the boys up to join the union. The fools don't know that you can't win unless you get organized as well as the bosses.

5. THE WANDERERS

A regularly fluctuating class experience may occur on any level—high, medium, or low—or between any levels. (See class work history 5, Figure 44.) This experience of fluctuation is perhaps rarer than most people are inclined to expect. It is true that our economic organization is characteristically unstable, and that periodicity in economic fluctuation may be discerned. But it is also true that all classes do not feel equally the repercussions of economic instability. The lower classes, especially those with the smallest economic reserves, feel the effects of economic instability more directly and more immediately. Their relative fall may indeed be smaller than that of the upper classes; nevertheless, their marginal living is sensitive to even the smallest changes.

Psychologically, we can anticipate at least three main types of reactions to the fluctuating-class situation:

a. Hope-springs-eternal reaction.

b. Ride-with-the-tide fatalism.

c. Confused, mixed, and alternating responses.

The Hopeful Pattern

Research is needed to discover which of these reactions is more recurrent on the different class levels and whether they arise out of different experiences. The hopeful reaction is an optimistic one. It entertains the belief that economic conditions will soon improve and the subject will rise in the economic scale. The feeling that the individual is not responsible for his temporary economic reversal is characteristic. Circumstances which are inevitable and uncontrollable are blamed for present plight. However, if one is persistent and optimistic, if one has faith in himself and in the system, he will see better times. It is the tenacious, diligent worker who will eventually find economic success and security.

It is probably true that the hopeful reactions recur more frequently at the higher and middle fluctuating levels. This may be because of the greater possibility of building economic reserves on the higher levels. The hope of eventual success breeds an optimistic individualism. The experience of "success" in the past suggests to some that it is possible in the future. "I did it before, I can do it again" is the typical reaction here. Above all, these optimists have faith in themselves and in the future of the economic system. Said a rather prosperous life insurance salesman in a heated political argument:

The trouble with you liberals is that you don't have faith in yourselves and in the economic system. Sure, life is tough, but those who are persistent will get there. Take Mr. Taylor, for instance. He's got a good business in that garage. He's got twenty men working for him. He's set now, but how do you suppose he got there? The other day when I sold him some insurance, he told me that he started in business fourteen times. He's been through bankruptcy five times. But did he quit or lose faith? No, he was building up experience. He doesn't have to work any more, but he does. He's naturally an energetic and nervous man. He'll retire in a few years and he won't have to worry about the future. Sure he's an independent cuss, but who wouldn't be after what he's gone through? You've got to give him credit, boy. He's not waiting for handouts.

The Fatalistic Pattern

The fatalistic pattern is more typical of the lower-class positions. It is essentially a do-nothing reaction that may have sprung from continued economic setbacks. Perhaps it reveals an acknowledgment that what happens to the individual is beyond his control. He refuses to fight or to falter, making the best of the situation. Emotional involvement is reduced by repeated and ineffective attempts to raise the class position. Such individuals tend to be "realistic" in the work situation. They refuse to participate in harebrained schemes, yet they tend to be somewhat opportunist, for they are bereft of extreme ideals. Consequently, they are usually "easy to get along with" for they accept things as they are, demanding, asking, giving, what is "within reason." Above all, they dissociate themselves from the upward-mobility mythology entertained by the hopefuls. Certainly their enthusiasm is never unbounded. A garrulous barber explained,

Oh, we barbers are used to this kind of thing. You know, barbers never make much money. At the union meeting, we decided to raise our price for hair-cuts to one dollar. There wasn't much fuss about it. We know that in a little while we'll have to lower our prices again, and it's better to lower them from higher prices than from lower prices. So we take things as they come, the good with the bad. . . . Yep, I've been barbering now for fifteen years. Just when I get enough saved to buy a good shop at a good location, a depression hits us. I suppose me and Jack will stay here the rest of our lives. I just hope my legs and hand hold out a few more years. You know your hands and legs are the first things that go on a barber—arthritis.

The Confused Pattern

The third pattern, which we've called the confused and mixed reaction, is really a combination of the hopeful and fatalistic reactions. But here the individual worker either has ambivalent reactions toward himself and the situation in which he is working or swings toward one pole or another, depending on external circumstances. The cultural impetus in our society is toward the direction of hope and faith, so we may presume that this is more recurrent.

The mixed reaction is perhaps the least adjustive psychologically. At one time the worker feels successful and optimistic, when his class position is considered "satisfactory." At another time he may feel pessimistic and unsuccessful. At one moment he feels identified with the upper classes, at another he may feel intense hatred. Ambivalent reactions may manifest themselves toward fellow workers, "superiors," or "inferiors." The worker's chimerical reactions may involve neurotic anxieties. His self-conception is murky and confused; he is not sure whether he is a success or a failure in his eyes or in the eyes of others. He does not appreciate whether he is responsible for his present class position or whether circumstances should be praised or blamed for it. This uncertainty may make itself felt indirectly at least in the social interaction with his fellow workers. Thus, many may regard him as an unpredictable and sometimes an irresponsible fellow. He may be dubbed "queer," "nervous," "untrustworthy," or "nutty" by his co-workers. A student reports a conversation with a work mate of his brother:

You know, your brother Jerry is a peculiar guy. He's been workin' at the [radio] plant with us now for four years. I know he's a pretty bright guy—he knows a lot about radio. But he can't forget that he once used to use that stuff he knows. After all, he does the same things like us—you know—assemble parts. He tried to start a union when he worked for Warner's, didn't he? Now, he's changed and he won't even join the union. What's he trying to do, become a foreman again? I tell you he's kind of peculiar. . . . You know, he talks down the union and then tells us that we're saps because we ain't radical enough. We know he ain't a stoolpigeon, but he's always stirring up some argument and he's talking all the time. He don't belong in a factory. He should 'a been a lawyer.

6. THE IRREGULARS

(See class work history 6, Figure 44.) Two sub-types exist among the "irregulars"; one is characterized by irregular fluctuation, the other by plateau shifts in class experience. The only difference is that the class experiences of the plateau type are of longer duration. Both types are abstractions which occur infrequently. Their very lack of trend and their absence of periodicity make even speculation about self-image and nature of class adjustment most unreliable. We shall, therefore, not attempt to describe any common patterns but recognize that the "irregulars" are characterized by a wide range of possible reactions.

SUMMARY

The description of the social structure of industry is completed. The formal, informal, power, status, and class organizations which characterize the work plant have been examined. The many roles which managers and workers play have been observed and a record of satisfactions and frustrations has been written.

After the full view of industrial structure has been observed, it should

no longer seem surprising that modern industry has problems of human relations in addition to technical and economic problems. The compelling task is to find ways and means of getting the whole organization to pull together. The business administrator must find a way to coördinate people to secure coöperation. The union leader has similar problems. The industrial sociologist is able to help both through research and advice. Two major problems of in-plant social structure are the problems of worker placement and of industrial morale and teamwork. We turn our attention in Part Three to these major administrative responsibilities.

SUPPLEMENTARY STUDIES

FIELD OBSERVATION: DIRECT OBSERVATION OF A SELECTED WORK PLANT
(Continued)

In the work plant selected, depict:

Class Organization
State:
1. The salary and wage structure.
   (If data are not available make estimates.)
2. Material evidences of differences in class positions.
3. Prevailing mores regarding pay.
4. Problems of gross or felt inequality.
   a. By individual workers.
   b. By groups of workers.
5. Ways pressure is exerted to relieve gross or felt inequalities.
   a. By individual workers.
   b. By groups of workers.
6. Suggestions for reducing tension or aggravation caused by gross or felt inequality.

FIELD INTERVIEWS: PLANNED

Discuss with a supervisor or union leader how workers put pressure on him to increase wage or salary rates. Find out how he handles requests or demands for more money.

FIELD INTERVIEWS: CASUAL

Discuss with a number of persons in different occupations how they believe workers increase their wage or salary in their occupation. It is particularly desirable to sample both union and nonunionized workers.

LIBRARY: BOOKS AND ARTICLES

Drucker, Peter F., "Who Should Get a Raise and When?" *Harper's Magazine,* March, 1946, pp. 215-223.

Gardner, Burleigh B., *Human Relations in Industry*, Richard D. Irwin, Inc., 1945, chap. 6, "Wages and Wage Systems," pp. 117-149.

Warner, W. L., and Low, J. O., *The Social System of the Modern Factory*, Yale University Press, 1947, chap. 6, "Wages and Worker Solidarity," pp. 90-107.

Research Gaps

1. Study of class work histories.
2. The effect of in-plant wage inequities upon morale and productivity.

Part Three

MAJOR PROBLEMS OF APPLIED
INDUSTRIAL SOCIOLOGY

The productive potential of a work plant depends upon both its technological and its social organization. The social organization is a moving pattern of social interactions activated by people. An empty plant at night has no social structure —only the possibility that on the morrow there will again be one.

Technological equipment stands ready to deliver when charged with inanimate energy, but human beings must daily re-create energy, ability, and purpose. The worker, to be most effective, must want to work. The construction of a satisfying social structure must be built upon such a foundation. This means that the responsibility for good human relations begins with the placement of a worker in a work position. It continues until the worker is intimately related to a work group and finally to the entire work plant society. The problem of worker placement is succeeded by the problem of industrial morale and teamwork.

The industrial sociologist, when engaged with applied problems, is usually working to improve worker placement or group collaboration. This task of building and repairing social structure to improve human relations is a difficult and delicate assignment. The two chapters in Part Three demonstrate that the industrial sociologist has just arrived at a new frontier, and he would be the first to admit that he has a long way to go before more precise skill is attained. However, there is no mistaking the certainty of direction. Advance must be made in this direction within industry or technological progress may be in vain.

CHAPTER XIII

The Problem of Worker Placement

JOB PLACEMENT IS SOCIAL PLACEMENT

Every placement of a worker is a social placement. This is true because the worker must take his place within a work group. If he is to achieve high levels of efficiency and personal satisfaction he must be able to perform the job well and to accept and be accepted in the work group. It is no accident that people seek to appraise the work placement of another by asking the familiar question, "Do you like to work there?" The job abstracted from its social meanings becomes a word which has no meaning in reality. For this reason it is preferable to speak of the *work position*.

THE WORK POSITION: ITS THREEFOLD ASPECTS

The work position refers to the place which the worker occupies within the work plant. This place is a component of technical, physical, and social correlates. The *technical* aspect refers to the techniques of work activity. These may range from very simple skills to highly complex ones. The

physical aspect of a work position includes the location and all of the physical objects which compose and surround a given work station. Even the view and the atmosphere must be included as part of the physical environment. The *social* factors of a work position are represented by those social demands which must be fulfilled by anyone who is to perform adequately in the position. For example, the position of a salesclerk demands a willingness and ability to service customers. This requirement is a part of the position regardless of the individual who assumes it. In addition, the worker in this position must report to a supervisor, who will give orders to be followed. It is essential that a demand to obey orders be acceptable to the worker.

In a very real sense the worker must find satisfaction in all of these component parts of his position. The technical, physical, and social correlates combine to mark his status in the work plant. They will determine what kind of work he does, where he works, under what conditions he works, and to a large extent the number and kind of people he will come in contact with.

THE WORK SITUATION AS A PATTERN OF RELATIONSHIPS

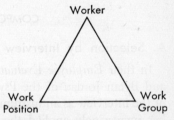

FIG. 45. Part-Whole Relationships of the Work Situation.

The work position is the basic structural unit of a work plant. When a worker assumes a position he takes his place inside a work situation. A work situation refers to a focalized pattern of social relationships involving a worker, a work position, and a work group. We may also see the work situation as a part of a larger context of relationships—departmental, division, or even company relationships. Figure 45 diagrams the triangular nature of the work situation. This pattern is a configuration of part-whole relationships which are interlaced in the work situation. To abstract one part and to consider that part separate from the configuration is to remove it from reality. This interrelatedness of the individual to a work position and a work group is well understood by Elton Mayo, who says, "The belief that the behavior of an individual within the factory can be predicted before employment upon the basis of a laborious and minute examination by tests of his technical and other capacities is mainly, if not wholly, mistaken. Examination of his developed social skills and his general adaptability might give better results. The usual situation is that after employment his relation to 'the team' will go far to determine the use he makes of such capacities as he has developed."[1]

[1] Elton Mayo, *The Social Problems of an Industrial Civilization*, Harvard University Press, 1945, p. 111.

SOCIAL PLACEMENT IS A PROBLEM OF
MATCHING WORKER, WORK POSITION,
AND WORK GROUP

The problem of matching men and women with jobs becomes a problem of identifying the salient qualities of the worker, the work position, and the group in reference to each work situation. The greatest attention has been given to the individual and the work position, the least attention to the group. This disproportionate emphasis cannot be explained by the lack of importance which the group plays in determining individual performance. It appears that the relatively early entrance of the psychologist to industrial study and the relatively late arrival of the sociologist have brought about this weight in emphasis. It is well to begin the appraisal with the individual worker and to examine the contributions of psychology and sociology to the study of selection tests and techniques.

COMPONENT 1: THE WORKER

A. Selection by Interview

In their *Employee Evaluation Manual for Interviewers* Richard A. Fear and Byran Jordan of the Psychological Corporation stress the importance of the interview as an instrument of measurement. They say that: "Industry has increasingly applied the concept of measurement to the solution of personal problems. Many progressive organizations today have adopted job rating for the establishment of wage rates, employment tests as an aid in the selection of new workers, and merit rating in the determination of employee efficiency on the job.

"In developing these new and important techniques, however, the potentiality of the interview as an instrument of measurement has been largely overlooked. Yet this basic tool represents the core of personnel procedures and, as such, will always play an important part in employee selection and upgrading."[2]

It might be added that the interview is indispensable not only in business but in many areas of social science, in law, in education, and indeed in all professions and occupations in which human relations and contacts are uppermost.

Within the work plant there are three major uses of the interview. These are employee selection and placement, employee counseling, and employee contact.

[2] Richard A. Fear and Byran Jordan, *Employee Evaluation Manual for Interviewers,* The Psychological Corporation, 1943, p. 3.

The use of the interview in employee selection and placement is our major concern in this chapter. In the following chapter, on morale and teamwork, reference will be made to the interview as an indispensable tool for employee counseling and employee contact. Most employee interviewing proceeds on the assumption that the best indication of what an individual will do in the future is what he has done in the past. Past performance is not, however, to be considered in terms of a single factor such as work experience but rather from the standpoint of the person as a whole.[3]

The interview is extensively employed not only in searching for *objective* data, such as education and occupational experience of an applicant for employment, but also to assemble subjective data or facts of inner experience. The interview may secure data regarding likes and dislikes, interest in work, occupational preferences, worries, grievances, ambitions and other motives, ideals, group and institutional loyalties, and such mental attitudes as those commonly generalized as "good will" or "unrest." In fact, the interview, skillfully used, has its greatest value in obtaining knowledge not about specific events but about an interviewee's own attitudes, feelings, and customary behavior. It is in general the most dependable means of ascertaining certain facts for which records and similar objective sources are least available, namely, facts about the interviewee's own attitudes and emotional reactions.[4]

THE INTERVIEW AS A MEANS OF REVEALING THE INDIVIDUAL'S DEFINITION OF A
    PROSPECTIVE WORK ROLE

The writers suggest that the applicant's own work role definition should be tapped through the interview. The conception of the role the individual thinks he would play within a given work position provides a useful measure of the kind of future behavior which may be expected. While it is recognized that there may be a large discrepancy between what an applicant says he thinks he would do and what he actually does when placed in the work position, it nonetheless follows that vital habits and attitudes may be correctly appraised.

A successful vice-presidential applicant for a large corporation conceived his future role as follows:[5]

To be successful in the position of First (Executive) Vice President I've got to be able to get teamwork and direct cooperation from all of my subordinates and my superiors which includes the President of the Company and the Board of Directors. I shall be acting as General Manager and the entire operation of the

---

[3] *Ibid.*, p. 7.
[4] Walter Van Dyke Bingham and Bruce V. Moore, *How to Interview*, Harper & Brothers, 1931, pp. 247-249.
[5] This man had occupied a closely related position when he made this role diagnosis.

company will be directly under my jurisdiction. I must consult with the Sales managers, production managers of each division, secretary and auditor of the company. I must approve proposals on major issues for the president, or on issues between department heads. I must see that proper personnel heads the major divisions of our business. I must have meetings of junior executive groups to explain company policies. I must help to arrange programs for sales conferences which involve all company personnel or production conferences, or research conferences. I must study plant improvements and pass on all appropriations or present major expenditures to our board for approval. I must keep posted on labor conditions, not only throughout the company, but throughout the country, as they may affect the operation. The branch and warehouse activities must be studied to avoid major inventory losses, etc., due to market conditions. I must maintain direct contact with our plants and branches to be properly aware of local conditions that enable us to more surely render major decisions. I must know the people in the plants, their general thinking relating to their jobs and to the company to properly work out a good employee-employer relations program. The same holds true for the sales organization, and certainly our white collar group. All of this will take time, and I shall have difficulty to keep up with these demands but all of these contacts must be maintained if I am to keep "alive" on my job to the conditions which should be considered in connection with policy making. More than anything else, I will have to reestablish confidence in our subordinate personnel, and even in certain of the executive group in their responsibility to carry out the functions of their positions to the best of their ability. This is an attitude which few had, due to the policy of certain individuals no longer with the company who insisted that everything had to be passed on by themselves, and it has killed a great deal of initiative on the part of the men.

The toughest part of my job is the responsibility for labor relations, and that means getting along with the labor men, especially Mr. Thomas, who is on the labor committee. Mr. Thomas is not the union president but an old-timer who helped organize the union in the plant. He is suspicious of anyone who represents management. He is a brusque, loud-talking man who carries considerable influence because of his aggressiveness and his seniority. If I can sell him on a proposal, I can get by all right; if I can't, there's trouble brewing in the plant. You have to be tough and firm with Thomas or he won't respect you. But you can reason with him, just so you don't get him started on his pet peeve which is rate setting.

My job requires that I try to see what the union wants and why they want it. Then, I have to try to show them what management wants and why management wants its provisions in the contract. I must be very cautious about making concessions because every contract must be justified to the Board. I must keep in touch with the President and Board chairman and when an important concession is to be made I must get their approval. That means I often have to work as hard or harder to sell a contract to the "top" as to the labor men. If I fail and a strike results, I usually take the blame.

I guess I'm the man in the middle. It wouldn't be so bad if I only had the President to deal with because he will usually go along with my recommendations. The Board chairman is a more determined man. He says, "Labor would

drive you out of the plant if you let them." He makes important concessions only when a strike is imminent. Sometimes he just says, "Let them go out. In a few days they will cool off and talk business." Sometimes it works, but we had a strike last year that really gave me trouble.

If I were to try to summarize what this labor relations job takes, I would say a tough skin, patience, and someone who can handle the Board chairman and Mr. Thomas of the labor committee.

AUGMENTING THE PREDICTIVE VALUE OF THE INTERVIEW

This self-analysis of a given work position exemplifies the possibilities of more accurate appraisal of an applicant. It should be noted that the individual role definition plumbs for behavior within a specific situation. It seeks out probable relationships to be established with persons and groups. As such it becomes more meaningful and therefore more valuable if the applicant has an opportunity to experience social contacts in the prospective work group. In the example of the new vice-president, the applicant had some experience in a closely related work position and was therefore able to prepare a relatively concrete definition of a vice-president's work position. The challenge to construct a prospective work role definition as a rehearsal of imagined work behavior is a promising lead into possible future behavior. This is true whether the applicant is familiar with the specific people he will work with or not. However, it is likewise true that if an interviewer is seeking to ascertain the pattern of social relationships an applicant is likely to establish in a work group he must maximize the opportunities for the applicant to make contacts in that group. If the interviewer seeks data which relate an applicant to the specific work group he will come to deal with, the interview will become a more valid measure of employee selection and placement.

CRITICISM OF THE INTERVIEW AS A SELECTION INSTRUMENT

A number of weaknesses inhere in the interview. Joseph Eaton has listed three of the more serious handicaps.

1. The nature, content, and length of the interview varies widely with each interviewer and his ability to draw out different candidates.
2. The interviewer who does the rating of the candidates is himself part of the oral test. He is occupied with thinking of responses to and asking new questions of the candidate. He is emotionally influenced by the candidate's reaction to him.
3. Individual interviews are not a good measure of a man's social behavior. The capacity to function well in the relaxing intimacy of most interview situations is not necessarily the same as capacity to handle more complex social situations involving many people, as well as conflict and cooperation with them.[6]

[6] Joseph W. Eaton, "Experiments in Testing for Leadership," *American Journal of Sociology*, May, 1947, pp. 523-535.

The interview has, we have noted, its greatest value in revealing *feelings and attitudes*. If the interview is utilized for this task it becomes but one and not the only selection instrument.

B. Selection by Psychological Tests

The question is then posed: What other tests of selection can be used to supplement the interview and insure against the subjective hazards that inhere within it? The traditional answer has been the psychological test which diagnoses for learning ability, mechanical aptitude, dexterity, and personality traits. The intelligence test is well known. The other tests, not so commonly recognized, are nonetheless part of a modern personnel selection program. Most of these tests have been of a pencil-paper type. The great advantage of such tests is the objective nature of their construction and scoring. When quantitative measures are carefully secured by the use of reliable and valid tests, human bias is almost completely removed from the test. Unfortunately, the variables which have been reduced to precise quantitative measures are not those which have demonstrated a very high correlation with successful job placement. Numerous studies have shown that inability to get along with fellow workmen and superiors is more frequent than inefficiency in causing discharge of workers.[7]

PSYCHOLOGICAL SCORES AND OUTPUT IN THE HAWTHORNE BANK WIRING OBSERVATION ROOM

The output records of the workers in the bank wiring observation room in the Hawthorne study were compared with their measured intelligence dexterity scores. Figure 46 compares output with intelligence and dexterity.

The records show that there was no direct relation between performance in the bank wiring observation room and capacity to perform as measured by either intelligence or dexterity tests. W9, the lowest producer, ranked first in intelligence and third in the weighted soldering scores. W2, the highest producer on the soldering test, ranked seventh in intelligence and seventh in output. W4 ranked last in the soldering test and shared first place with W9 in intelligence; yet he ranked fifth in output. W3 ranked relatively low on the soldering test but quite high in intelligence; W6, in contrast, ranked fairly high in the soldering test but low in intelligence; yet their outputs were equal. This, then, is evidence of the social forces which operated in the observation room in such a way as to restrict the perform-

[7] See for instance, J. N. Brewer, "Causes for Discharge," *Personnel Journal*, August, 1927, pp. 171-172. A recent report by Robert N. McMurry & Co. of Chicago shows that in a sample of 1167 young college graduate trainees in 247 companies, 42 percent (490) proved unsatisfactory or left their jobs before the end of one year, with resultant loss of $1,347,500 to the companies involved. Dr. McMurry feels the results show too much stress on academic record, high I.Q., and good appearance. More important is stability, industriousness, perseverance, loyalty, self-reliance, ability to get on with fellow workers, willingness to lead and take responsibility. *Business Week*, November 27, 1948.

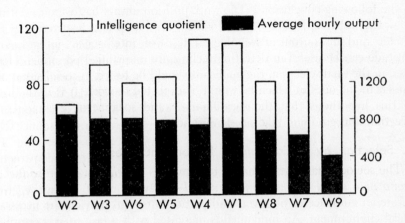

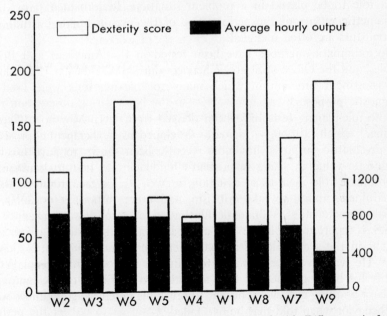

Fig. 46. Differences in Average Hourly Output Compared with Differences in Intelligence and Dexterity. (Reprinted by permission of the publishers from F. J. Roethlisberger and William J. Dickson, *Management and the Worker*, Cambridge, Mass.: Harvard University Press, 1939.)

ance capacity of the workers. However, in the relay assembly test room
where group relations were exceptionally good the researchers had found a
direct relation between tests of ability and output.[8] Research results point
to the following conclusions: The work position always has a group setting.
How the individual worker fits into the work group largely determines his
morale and his output. Psychological tests of intelligence, interest, and
aptitude can be useful in detecting technically unqualified personnel. However, in the final selection, the applicant should be tested in social situations
similar to the ones in which he would be expected to work. It is in the light
of this hypothesis that the sociodramatic and sociometric techniques of
selection and grouping take on significance.

C. Selection by Sociodramatic Performance Tests

The sociodramatic performance test involves *activity by an individual or
group in a social situation of simulated reality.* The test is usually given
before an audience of observers and participants who provide the necessary
social environment. An individual is presented with a task to be performed
or a role to be played in a problem situation. Performance ratings and
sociometric ratings of the performance of the person tested by the other
participants are often included.

Sociodramatic methods have been tested in the American and British
armies, and the Office of Strategic Services during World War II developed
an assessment program in which many role-playing tests were used for
diagnostic purposes.[9]

The role-playing tests have been derived from J. L. Moreno's "Psychodrama," which, although originally developed as a therapeutic procedure
for psychiatric purposes, has more recently been shown to have excellent
diagnostic value in sizing up a man's tendencies to take a dominant or
subordinate role in a social situation, as well as his tact, resourcefulness,
forcefulness, ability to take criticism, and other important personal and
social characteristics. A dramatic illustration of a role test as used by the
O.S.S. is reported as follows: The applicant was told that he had just been
caught in the secret files of a government department without authoriza-
tion. He was given ten minutes to think of a good way to explain and
justify his behavior. He was then subjected to a grilling cross-examination
under a blinding eye-level spotlight to break his defensive story and observe
his behavior when told that he had failed.[10]

[8] F. J. Roethlisberger and W. J. Dickson, *Management and the Worker*, Harvard
University Press, 1947, pp. 444-445.

[9] A description of the work of the Office of Strategic Services Assessment School may
be found in "A Good Man Is Hard to Find" (anon.), *Fortune*, March, 1946, pp. 92-95,
217, 218, 220, 223. See also Henry A. Murray and Donald W. MacKinnon, "Assessment
of O.S.S. Personnel," *Journal of Consulting Psychology*, March-April, 1946, pp. 76-80.

[10] Reported by Joseph Eaton, *op. cit.*, p. 531.

Less spectacular but equally penetrating were the many other improvisations in which one man was asked to play a role with another man in a dramatic situation usually involving conflict between the two men. The group was instructed as follows:

"Everyone at times finds himself in new and unfamiliar situations in which he has to exercise his ingenuity and resourcefulness. This evening we are going to place each of you in problem situations involving another man in order to discover how you can manage yourself. Two of you will be placed together to take these roles and you will be given certain facts. I want you to work out these situations in the most effective way you can. However, we do not want you to 'act' in the ordinary sense of the word, but we want you to be yourself and to behave as you yourself would behave in a similar situation in actual life. . . . We want to find out how you yourself as you are now tend to meet certain situations."[11]

With these instructions, an improvised role situation which had been hand tailored to fit the individuals was enacted. First one member of the team was assigned a role, and then a role was assigned to the man whom he was to play opposite. It was customary to place one man in his home or office to receive the second man as his guest. In every case each man was given a motive for the meeting.

TYPES OF ROLE-PLAYING IMPROVISATIONS

The role-playing episodes were planned in order to test out the reaction of candidates along lines about which the interviewer of a candidate felt some uncertainty. The 111 improvisation situations used in O.S.S. fall into seven types.

Type A. Personal criticism (one man is criticized for some fault or misdemeanor by the other)
  Briefing: (a) Person being criticized might be sent out and his critic told the nature of the charges against him and possibly how the interests of the critic were being adversely affected. (b) Critic might be sent out and the person being criticized told of some countercharge he might make.
  Test variables: Criticized person tested for reaction to failure, reaction to attack, resourcefulness, tendency to give excuses, persuasiveness, diplomacy, ability to counter-attack. Critic tested for tact, tolerance, ability to discipline a subordinate, forcefulness, resourcefulness, tendency to be severe, sympathy.
Type B. Interpersonal conflict of aims, goals, ideals
  Example: Partnership dissolution
  Briefing: One or both men might be sent out. Each man might be told the point of view and motives which he is to hold (to retain or break up their

[11] Percival M. Symonds, "Role Playing as a Diagnostic Procedure in the Selection of Leaders," *Sociatry*, March, 1947, p. 43.

partnership) and the reasons for holding it (criticism of the other person, for his own advantage or disadvantage of the other).

Test variables: Both persons tested for tact, social relations, forcefulness, resourcefulness, integrity, and ability to control temper.

Type C. Situations involving moral issues

Example: Stealing

Briefing: Man who was at fault is sent out; the other man accuses the first.

Test variables: Accuser tested for his tact, forcefulness, and tendency to be severe. The person against whom the charge was made tested for his reaction to attack, resourcefulness, tendency to give excuses.

Type D. Interview

Example: Prospective business manager

Briefing: Interviewee is always sent out and the interviewer told what he is to find out—that he is to determine fitness of the prospective employee.

Test variables: Interviewer tested for resourcefulness in questioning, reporting ability, ability to judge and to make a decision. Person being questioned tested for his social relations, resourcefulness, and ability to sell himself.

Type E. Rejection

Example: Position which goes to another man

Briefing: The rejected man is sent out and the other man told the nature and basis of the rejection.

Test variables: Rejected person tested for ability to accept rejection, persuasive powers, assertiveness, and resourcefulness. Person doing rejecting tested for tact, diplomacy, social relations, and forcefulness.

Type F. Intrapersonal conflict and decision

Example: Conflict of loyalties—whether to be loyal to employer or union

Briefing: Man not in conflict is sent out and man with the conflict kept in and told the nature of the conflict.

Test variables: Man in conflict tested for his resourcefulness, ability to make a decision, and assertiveness. Other person tested for persuasiveness and resourcefulness.

Type G. Authority-subordination

Example: Disagreeable order must be issued and enforced.

Briefing: Man in subordinate role is sent out. Man in authority is told about role he is to play.

Test variables: Person in authority tested for resourcefulness, firmness, social relations. Person in subordinate role tested for his ability to take orders, to play the subordinate role, and to report.

Each skit was allowed five minutes. When the skit was finished, observers and participants were urged to describe the behavior of the two participants and to compare it with their ordinary behavior. Diagnostic and therapeutic purposes may be served in this way at the same time.[12]

These sociodramatic performance tests indicate the wide scope of situational possibilities which may be constructed for test purposes. In England

[12] All of these improvisations are more fully described in *ibid.*, pp. 45-50.

the War Office Selection Boards have used this kind of test for making personality assessments of officers or officer candidates, to determine their suitability for various officer roles in the army. One example is a test of physical courage. Applicants were asked to climb a big oak tree. At a height of fifteen or twenty feet they had to jump from one of the branches two or three feet in the air to catch a suspended rope on which they could slide down. In addition to these tests of courage, many tests of leadership ability were constructed.

The U.S. Army ground forces also used sociodramatic tests. Every soldier in basic training was given the infantry infiltration test. Each soldier had to crawl a distance of several hundred yards through mud, wire entanglements, and ditches. Machine-gun bullets were fired a few inches above the crouching soldiers. Explosive charges were set off in close proximity. Highly realistic battle conditions were created. Soldiers who failed the test were considered unsatisfactory for combat units.

Sociometric ratings, "buddy ratings," were solicited from each student in the officer candidate course about all other students in his training company. The U.S. Marine Corps made a study of 185 second lieutenants who had been in combat. It was found that success in O.C.S. as measured by paperpencil tests, such as Personal Inventory Sheet, General Classification and Mechanical Aptitude Test grades, and final composite numerical O.C.S. grades was not significantly related to success in combat, as measured by the combat efficiency report of the commanding officers. However, a tetrachoric correlation of .42 was found between reports of senior combat officers and the buddy rating scores. A research report states, "The evidence thus far presented points strongly to the conclusion that the men themselves are more capable of picking their own leaders than are their instructors and training officers."[13]

TWO POTENTIAL USES FOR SOCIODRAMATIC PERFORMANCE TESTS IN INDUSTRY

These new tests have two different functions which enhance their usefulness. It is possible to use them not only for selection purposes but also for the training of employees and supervisors. Bavelas gives an example which illustrates the double-barreled nature of sociodramatic performance testing:

1. Select and send out of the meeting room two or three of the applicants (or trainees) for the foremanship.

2. Describe to the judges (or trainees) the situation which will be played out. It might be a situation in which a foreman has decided to have a talk with one of his men regarding excessive absenteeism. The details might be: (a) The

[13] "Validation of Officer Selection Tests by Means of Combat Proficiency Ratings," Progress Report No. 1, Medical Field Research Laboratory, Camp Lejeune, N. C., p. 10.

man has been employed for a year and a half and is a better-than-average worker; (b) up to three months ago his attendance had been very good; (c) a month ago he received a routine warning slip on his absenteeism, but the absenteeism continued; (d) the foreman has decided to do something about it; (e) the man's absenteeism is due to some very personal difficulties, and he would rather lose his job than talk about them to the foreman.

3. Select a member of the group to play the role of the worker. The examiner (or trainer) may play this role.

4. Call in one of the applicants (or trainees). Have him take his place at the desk and explain the problem to him. (It is usually important in a problem like this one to say nothing of the worker's resistance to revealing the reason for his absenteeism. Let the foreman applicant [or trainee] discover it for himself as he would in a real life situation.) Make sure he understands the setting and then start the action—"The problem is clear? Very well. You are in your office and you have asked Jack to come in. Here he is. He walks in and says, 'Did you want to see me?'"

5. The role taking begins. The foreman may try to discover the underlying cause or accept rationalizations from the worker. He may threaten when the worker refuses to tell him his real reasons for absence. He may fire him. He may say it doesn't matter. He may be completely blocked. Whatever the pattern of interaction, the role taking ends either by the man going back to his imagined place of work or by a signal from the examiner (or trainer).[14]

This role-playing situation has not been standardized, so it is simply a raw test. Yet it can be clearly seen that this kind of problem situation offers excellent possibilities not only of selecting qualified people but of training persons so that they may achieve qualified levels of performance. The training of supervisory personnel in supervisory relations is particularly important where supervisors have come to their positions on the sole basis of technical competence or seniority. For them sociodramatic performance tests become training standards. In this discussion the central problem is improved selection and placement. In the following chapter the emphasis is turned to training and group morale. This sequence is a logical one. For it is important to first build an organization with qualified personnel.

STANDARDIZING THE SOCIODRAMATIC PERFORMANCE TEST

The data on hand give promise that sociodramatic tests combined with sociometric ratings could be developed to locate with increasing accuracy those persons most likely to succeed or fail as workers or leaders in a specified group. The application of these techniques to industry constitutes a research frontier that challenges industrial sociology. The guiding principles which must direct such research are now fairly well established. Joseph Eaton presents the following principles:

[14] Alex Bavelas, "Role Playing and Management Training," *Sociatry*, June, 1947, pp. 183-191.

1. Criterion.—No research should be started without a clear definition of the criterion against which the test can be validated. . . .
2. Test Items.—The skill to be tested should be analyzed into as many components as possible. Sociodramatic tests should be constructed in such a manner that they contain measures of each component. They should involve the application of specific and typical technical, muscular, and social skills. They should be conducted in a social situation of simulated reality, with trained assistants and observer-raters.
3. Simplicity.—The tests must be kept as simple as possible to facilitate uniform and easy administration.
4. Scoring.—Each component of the test should be studied to discover the different alternative responses possible in the testing situation. Each response should be evaluated with respect to its significance and, if possible, be expressed in a numerical weight. This would improve the reliability of the judgments of those who score the tests.
5. Sociometry.—Sociometric ratings by all participants should be made use of.
6. Interpretation.—The final test results should be expressed in rough gradations, such as deciles or quartiles of the total tests population or in sigmas of the mean if the distribution is normal.[15]

There are very few sociodramatic performance tests ready for industrial application that have been constructed according to these guiding principles.[16] However, such development should be rapid in the near future.

The task of locating personnel that will perform efficiently, happily, and continuously in their work positions is not an easy one. To do this the search for better selection instruments must continue. Another promising attempt at improving the selection of supervisory personnel is the interactional chronograph invented by Eliot D. Chapple and Gordon Donald Jr., of the Chapple Company.

D. Selection of Supervisory Leadership by the Interactional Chronograph

The interactional chronograph method is designed to evaluate personality and temperament by measuring the promptness, frequency, and duration of the spoken reactions of persons in contact with one another. It is an objective method since it is based solely on observations of actual behavior of individuals. It examines the *time* element in interpersonal relations and yields a record which can be read by anyone. Chapple and Donald describe the development of their method as follows:

[15] J. Eaton, *op. cit.*, pp. 534-535. Professor Eaton served during World War II as a member of the Personnel Research Section, Adjutant General's Office, United States Army.

[16] For a major report on the research direction of future work see Urie Bronfenbrenner and Theodore M. Newcomb, "Improvisations—An Application of Psychodrama in Personality Diagnosis," *Sociatry*, March, 1948, pp. 367-382. Also useful is the section on improvisations reported by the staff of the Office of Strategic Services in *Assessment of Men*, Rinehart and Company, 1948, pp. 168-176. (Reprinted in *Sociatry*, April-August, 1948, pp. 27-36.)

. . . We developed a simple recording instrument. Essentially, it consisted of a moving tape, driven at a uniform speed, upon which lines were drawn continuously when keys were pressed down. When an individual started to act, say in initiating a contact, the observer would depress the key assigned to that person. When he stopped acting, his key would be released and the line would end. The blank space between the lines provided a measure of his inactivity. The same procedure was used for each person under observation. Once we started to use this recording instrument, we found that we were obtaining far more information about the relationships among the individuals observed than we could get in continuous observation with stop watch and notebook.

PERSONALITY TRAITS REVEALED BY VERBAL BEHAVIOR

We soon found that conversational contacts provided a convenient and easily controllable medium in which to take our personality measurements. This does not necessarily mean that the individual who speaks longest, soonest, or most often has the best—or for that matter the worst—personality for any specific purpose or job. It only means that men in contact with one another reveal, by the way they respond and react to each other, certain personality traits like initiative, resourcefulness, and social adaptability; that the relative degree to which they possess such traits affects in one way or another the time—and the timing— of their conversational (or other) contacts; and that we had developed a device to measure and record that time element.[17]

With the interactional chronograph the researchers found that every individual had a characteristic pattern which remained constant regardless of the person with whom he interacted, and this pattern was not affected by any attempts on the part of the subject to conceal or distort his natural interaction pattern.

After early experiments Chapple and Donald began to consider what specific personality traits, as revealed by chronograph measurements, might be appropriate for specific purposes or jobs.

INTERACTIONAL CHRONOGRAPH CURVES

Six curves were derived from the records. These were:
1. Activity curve—measures preponderance of the individual's activity to his inactivity.
2. Speed curve—measures the length of time between his starting one action and starting the next.
3. Subject's adjustment curve—measures the preponderance of his interruptions against his failures to respond.
4. Interviewer's adjustment curve—measures the interviewer's interruptions of the subject against the subject's failure to respond.
5. Initiative-dominance curve—records relative frequency of the subject's initiative and dominations relative to the other person's.

[17] Eliot D. Chapple and Gordon Donald, Jr., "A Method for Evaluating Supervisory Personnel," Harvard Business Review, Winter, 1946, pp. 200-201.

6. Free give-and-take—measures the frequency of the occasions when he is able to adjust without interrupting or failing to respond in consecutive exchanges.

EVIDENCE FOR VALIDITY OF MEASUREMENTS

These curves drawn from a standardized experimental interview proved to be of sufficient weight in the requirements for success as an executive to serve as an index of overall supervisory capacity. In one of a number of tests, the interaction measurements of the foremen, superintendents and general operating executives of an industrial company actually showed as potentially top-caliber supervisory personnel 92 percent of the men whom the company had already rated highest on the basis of their records and other criteria, and none of these rated lowest. This means that if the inter-actional chronograph had been used before the men were placed in their present positions, it would have foretold the kind of record they would make with a high degree of accuracy.

A NEW POSSIBILITY OF RELATING THE WORKER TO PERSONALITIES OF WORK GROUP MEMBERS

One of the possibilities of the interactional chronograph is the attack it permits on the problem of worker placement. This method embraces not only fitting the right man to the right job but also fitting him to the right group. The researchers point on that

All too frequently job placement ignores these two factors: (1) the differences in initiative, in drive, in speed, in adaptability, in emotional stability which a given job imposes on the person who fills it and (2) the added impact of the other people with whom the individual comes into contact—people who have their own personalities which modify the structure of the job itself. A common example is the subordinate placed in a position where considerable initiative should be exerted and yet reporting to a chief who feels it necessary to initiate all the contacts himself. If the subordinate has a good deal of drive and dominance, he and his chief will soon be at loggerheads, and the resultant effects on the organizational structure will be such as to warp it considerably from its original design.[18]

A Summary of Selection Methods Designed to Appraise the Pesonality Traits of the Worker

Four methods of analyzing individual performance and appraising personal qualities have been discussed. These were (1) interview with special emphasis on the individual's definition of a prospective work role, (2) psychological tests, (3) sociodramatic performance tests, and (4) the inter-actional chronograph method for appraising supervisory personnel. The newer approaches are seen to be efforts to secure measurements of personality

[18] *Ibid.*, p. 214.

within a social situation of simulated reality. The major difficulty in perfect-
ing these newer instruments is found in the troublesome problem of stand-
ardization. When each response can be evaluated in respect to its significance
and expressed in a numerical weight, new sociodramatic performance scales
and interactional scales will be available. These promise to increase the
accuracy of the predictions regarding work behavior which may be expected
from a given worker in a given work position. However, such increased
precision awaits more careful appraisal of the social demands made by
specific work positions inside specific work groups. Attention will now be
turned to these essential components of successful worker placement.

COMPONENT 2: THE WORK POSITION

The Content of the Work Position

The work position has been referred to as the place which the worker
occupies within the work plant. It is composed of technical, spatial, and
social demands by virtue of the organizational function to be fulfilled.
Work positions can and should be analyzed as integral parts of an organizational structure. Such analysis concentrates attention upon work positions,
not upon the men and women holding these positions.

Job description and analysis is well known to industrial psychologists and
personnel specialists. The aim of such study is to find out what a worker
does on each specific job and the demands, in terms of such factors as skill,
effort, and responsibility, that the job makes upon the worker. Good job
descriptions are needed in selection and placement, training, transfer, upgrading, and promotion, and in making wage surveys. They are also helpful
in connection with safety programs and wage incentive plans.[19]

A complete job description explains what the worker does, how he does
it, and why he does it. A complete job analysis lists those basic factors of
the job which distinguish it from other jobs. A fairly common set of job
factors which are examined for differences include skill, responsibility,
physical effort, and working conditions.[20] The assembly of job description
and job analysis data for a given job is ordinarily called a *job specification*.
When a new employee is hired it is considered that an excellent placement
has been made when the personal qualities of the employee match the
requirements of the job specification. The ideal placement requires that
reliable and valid measures of selection and job analysis have been used to
insure that the decision to place a worker on a given job is an accurate judg-

[19] Paul Pigors and Charles A. Myers, *Personnel Administration*, McGraw-Hill Book
Company, 1947.
[20] *Ibid.*, p. 222. For another list see also the excellent *Training and Reference Manual
for Job Analysis*, Bureau of Manpower Utilization, War Manpower Commission, June,
1944. This list includes responsibility, job knowledge, mental application, dexterity, accuracy, experience, training, physical demands (such as physical activities, working conditions,
and hazards), and worker characteristics required on the job.

ment of his future performance. There is reason to believe that most placements, even when made under the best known conditions, are not yet nearly as good as may be achieved when social factors are given greater consideration.

The Role of the Industrial Sociologist

The industrial sociologist must examine the instruments of selection and placement and ascertain the extent to which the social relationships of placement have been identified and measured. Industry and government are indebted almost exclusively to industrial psychology for the current levels of achievement in employment testing and placement. Industrial psychology has focused upon the individual worker and upon the individual job. Industrial sociology focuses upon the worker-in-the-group. The term "work position" is used deliberately to convey the notion of an organic relationship between the technical detail of the job and its interlocked social and physical environment which describes a setting for every job.

The description of the social character of specific jobs has lagged far behind technical description.[21] We have been taught during most of our lives to think about jobs as technical skills. Thus, an engineer is regarded as one who learns engineering techniques, a carpenter as one who has acquired specialized woodworking skills, and a physician as one who has mastered materia medica. Even the college professor is considered a person who reads books, talks about them abstrusely, and spends most of his time doing research within the confines of his office and laboratory.

The power of stereotypes and incomplete job descriptions to mislead student, vocational counselor, worker, and personnel director can be great, and enormously expensive. The tremendous waste due to labor turnover, transfer, and absenteeism may be partly accounted for by the ignorance of the social setting as men and jobs are improperly matched. Such recognition of the social skills necessary for work as does exist is usually expressed in statements like "You have to be able to get along with people in that job," or "She is good at that job because she has a pleasing personality," or "I like the job because it gives me a chance to get away from a desk and meet people." These folk observations reveal a sensitivity to the social characteristics required in some occupations but certainly do not describe the pattern of social relations which compose the social milieu within which each occupation is set. The social environment of every job requires unique adjustments from each person who undertakes the responsibilities of the work. It can be readily understood that these social environments are characterized by great diversity not only between occupations but within the same occupation. Moreover, widely different personalities are to be found in any given occupation.

[21] See Elton Mayo, op. cit., p. 20.

A Search for Common Social Factors in Work Positions

The scientific task requires a reduction of this complexity and the discovery of uniformity. Therefore, the question arises: Is it possible to find common social factors that underlie and characterize all occupations? This question narrows the search to the examination of the "social structure" of the work situation as found in the manifold varieties of occupations. The structural aspects refer to those characteristics of an occupation which exist by reason of the function that defines it. For example, the social status of an occupation such as is represented by a doctor, mechanic, or executive has meaningful connotation apart from any given individual who may work with these job titles. It must be clearly understood that attention is focused on the *job*, and no consideration is given here to the personality traits of any individual who is now or may be employed in a given occupation. The study that follows is not concerned with the reactions and adjustments of the individual worker as he performs his work. However, it is to be hoped that this concentration upon the social structure of the work position will make the matching of men and jobs a much more efficient process as the industrial sociologist of the future supplies sociometric profiles of jobs and the industrial psychologist furnishes personality profiles of potential workers.

An Illustrative Study: Specific Purposes and Methods

The purposes of this study are: (1) to identify the most important social factors which are common to work situations; (2) to construct a sociometric scale to measure the vocational social ability required by different occupations; (3) to make a social evaluation of jobs in a small industrial company; and (4) to prepare sociometric profiles of selected jobs. These purposes call forth the maximum of observational experience that can be brought to bear. The writer, D. C. Miller, has used his two years of experience within a large industrial plant of 35,000 workers, in which he had an opportunity to observe every kind of work behavior in the company preparatory to training workers and assisting in job evaluation. A year spent in examining job evaluations as presented by American industries to the National War Labor Board has been useful in widening the range of work behavior studied.[22] In determining the most important social factors of work and in judging their relative weight personnel directors, psychologists, sociologists, college deans, vocational counselors, college appointments officers, and vocational education directors have been consulted. The methods used in constructing the scale and evaluating jobs will be described under the appropriate section in the following pages.

[22] Assistant Supervisory Training Supervisor, Sperry Gyroscope Company, New York City, 1942-1944; Section Chief, Wage Analysis, Policy Appraisal Division, National War Labor Board, Washington, D.C., 1944-1945.

I. THE SOCIAL FACTORS OF THE WORK POSITION

In order to identify common social factors of work positions it is necessary to divorce arbitrarily each occupation from its technical function. When stripped of their usual referents, jobs which seemed wide apart suddenly reveal themselves in striking similarity. For example, let us consider such different occupations as represented by physician and barber. If we examine the nature of their social contacts, many similarities can be noted. Each has face-to-face contact with clients or patrons who seek a special service. Each may meet persons from all the different social classes of the community or each may have a special clientele. Each may have his own workshop and may be his own boss. Each must learn to avoid pressing his own political and social opinions on his clients. Although there are obvious differences in the technical work and in the social status, the point to be emphasized is that an analysis of social characteristics of each occupation reveals similarities where a comparison of jobs in terms of technical skills only accentuates the differences and hides these similarities.[23]

When observation is disciplined to seek out the social skills of jobs, so often screened from view by their technical and status connotations, then common social elements can be discovered. From a survey of many hundreds of jobs the following seven social factors were selected as the most important characteristics common to all jobs.

A. Scope of social contact
   1. Direct contact with customers or general public.
   2. Direct contact with working associates.
   3. Direct contact with both customers or general public and working associates.
   4. None or infrequent contacts.
B. Status range of social contacts
   1. Contact with business class, i.e., with those who address their activities in getting their living predominantly to *people* in the selling or promotion of things, services, and ideas.
   2. Contact with working class, i.e., with those who address their activities in getting their living primarily to *things*, utilizing material tools in the making of things and the performance of services.
   3. Contacts with both business and working classes.
C. Social demands when "off the job"
   1. No social entertainment "off the job" required.
   2. Entertainment of customers or influential persons required.
   3. Entertainment of working associates or influential persons expected.

[23] Interestingly, one friendship constellation of a small Vermont village which was studied by Lundberg and Lawsing centered about a physician and a barber. See George A. Lundberg and Margaret Lawsing, "The Sociography of Some Community Relations," *American Sociological Review*, June, 1937, pp. 318-325.

D. Social leadership
1. Secure disciplined and coöperative response from persons who are expected to so respond because of the authority vested in the position by the business institution.
2. Secure disciplined and coöperative response from persons who are themselves in positions of authority.
3. Secure coöperative response from persons for whom there is no predetermined or expected pattern of disciplined and coöperative behavior.
E. Size of work group directed
1. Direct or indirect supervision of a small group (less than ten).
2. Direct or indirect supervision of a group intermediate in size (ten to fifty).
3. Direct or indirect supervision of a large group (over fifty).
F. Social participation
1. Primary participation within the work group, i.e., face-to-face contact, characterized by intimate and personal association.
2. Quasi-primary or intermediate participation, i.e., face-to-face contact, characterized by formal association.
3. Secondary participation, i.e., characterized by impersonal association through communication devices.
G. Personal responsibility or social accountability
1. Number of people who report directly and indirectly to position.

These factors will be more thoroughly described as they are utilized in the sociometric scale which follows.

II. CONSTRUCTION OF A SOCIOMETRIC SCALE TO MEASURE VOCATIONAL SOCIAL
ABILITY

1. *The Social Evaluation of Jobs.* The second purpose of this study calls for a measuring instrument that will make possible a social evaluation of jobs. Such an evaluation must seek to delineate clearly the social nature of different jobs. If successful, it promises to be useful in the following ways:
a. Reorienting personnel and administrative policy with recognition of job analysis as social analysis. Such reorientation might involve selection, placement, and training of workers, wage and salary administration, supervisory methods, production planning, and job methods.
b. Building a new awareness of the social responsibility of different jobs.
c. Improving vocational guidance in schools and colleges.

It is only too clear that unless the social nature of specific jobs is better understood, waste in training and placement of workers will continue to be large. Personality analysis furnishes us with some data of fairly high predictive value. Thus, in placement work we often rely heavily on our estimates of the person, yet neglect or guess about the social nature of the job. Therefore, failure often results not because an unqualified person is placed but because that person is placed on the "wrong" job—very often a job which demands social abilities not recognized by the counselor or placement officer.

2. *Factors Common to All Jobs and How They Are Determined.* The seven social factors of work which have been identified are variable factors. When evaluated, they will give point values, or the relative social evaluation for each job. There are many social factors which are common to all jobs but it is believed the factors set out here are the most important. They have been drawn out of a process of observation, analysis, and comparison of a large number of different kinds of work. Consideration was given at all times to the conditions drawn out by the following questions:

a. What does the job require an employee to have?

b. To what does the job subject an employee?

Each job was evaluated on the basis of an average worker performing a fair day's work.

3. *Basic Social Skills.* These factors reveal four basic social skills. These are:

A. Ability to make vocational social contacts. This ability involves social acceptance in those social contacts which are required for successful performance on the job. Such ability may involve:

(1) Contacts with working associates, customers, or the general public.

(2) Contacts with business class, working class, or both.

(3) Contacts required or expected when "off the job."

Manifest Social Skills B. Ability to direct individuals and work groups. This factor involves *social leadership* or direction of others in such a way that coöperative response is obtained. Such ability may involve:

(4) Direction of non-supervisory subordinates, supervisory subordinates, or persuasive and consultative direction of others.

(5) Direction of individuals or groups of varying size.

C. Ability to coöperate with members of work groups. This factor requires ability to *participate* coöperatively within the work environment, and involves:

(6) Participation in work groups requiring intimate association, formal association, or relative social isolation.

Latent Social Skills D. Ability to assume personal responsibility for others. This factor involves *social responsibility* or accountability. It requires ability to *maintain self-confidence and effective direction* of the required job functions in the presence of latent or manifest pressure of individual or group demands.

(7) Job requires responsibility for (number of) persons who report directly or indirectly to position.

The identification of the significant social skills is a crucial determination for it is essential that the skills which "make" or "break" successful job performance be located. In this determination a recognition of the manifest and latent character of social skills is made. The skills that require ability to *gain social acceptance,* to *direct* others, and to *participate coöperatively*

are considered manifest skills. These skills are open to direct observation. Others may (and others commonly do) judge the extent to which habits of a particular individual conform to their expectations, based on their personal interpretations of the requirements of specific jobs. In other words, manifest skills are performed as overt behavior. Others are aware of their presence or absence.

Almost no scientific attention has been given to the ability to assume personal responsibility for others. As conceived here this skill is latent. Others cannot easily observe or judge the extent to which it is required on the job, nor can individuals be easily identified who possess it. For we are speaking here of the ability to maintain *self-confidence* and *effective direction* of the required job functions in the presence of actual or potential pressure of individual or group demands. As we examine a job which requires this skill we are concerned with such questions as: To what extent does this job require:

A person who can take criticism?

A person who can build resistance to the pressure of individual groups?

A person who can maintain physical and mental health in the midst of competitive and hostile social forces?

A person who can perform the functions of the job without seriously affecting his other social skills?

There are persons who can successfully meet the requirements of a job which calls out the manifest skills if personal responsibility for others is not demanded, but fail when asked to meet this demand. Others can carry various freights of personal responsibility but have breaking points nonetheless.

Each of these four basic social skills has been carefully examined in order to locate measures for the evaluation of the *intensity* of the skill called out in each specific job. The search for a quantitative statement has directed the choice of indexes which meet the criteria of clarity, objectivity, and ease of application. A description follows:

4. *Base Points.* Some social factors with varying minimum requirements are common to all occupations. These include willingness to work, and reasonable dress, health, and personal habits. The social evaluation of jobs is concerned only with characteristics above this minimum.

5. *Weighting of Social Factors.* The relative social evaluation of a job depends upon the extent to which the seven social factors are present in the requirements of the job. These factors are included in the four basic skills. Each factor is given a maximum weight of 100 except the last, which is permitted a maximum weight of 400. The scale includes a possible 1000 points with 600 allocated to the manifest skills A, B, and C., and 400 to the latent skill D. This weighting was made after consultation with a general

manager and a personnel director. No attempt was made here to strive for greater precision in the relative weights, for it is recognized that the factors are not completely independent and that there is overlapping.

Factors	Relative weight
A. Ability to make vocational social contacts	
1. Scope of social contacts	100
2. Status range of contacts	100
3. Social demands "off the job"	100
	300
B. Ability to direct individuals and groups	
4. Social leadership	100
5. Skill intensity for size of group directed	100
	200
C. Ability to coöperate with members of work groups	100
6. Social participation	100
	600
D. Ability to assume personal responsibility for others	
7. Direct responsibility for others, 25 points per person	
Indirect responsibility for others, 1 point per person	
Maximum equals	400
	400
Total points	1000

After the seven social factors were in final form they were pretested on a small group. After some revisions they were submitted to expert judges, who were asked to rank the different requirements of each factor in order of the relative social skills involved. Twelve judges were selected for this task, on the basis of two criteria: First, their experience gave them intimate acquaintance with a wide number of jobs, and secondly, their experience gave them an appreciation of the social skills involved. The list included three personnel directors, one college appointments director, one industrial arts director, one vocational counselor, one dean of men, one foreman, two ministers, and two sociologists. Working independently of one another, they agreed on the rank to be assigned the requirements with no factor showing less than 80 percent agreement. The factors are described and the point values are assigned according to the rank which each requirement received.

6. The Social Factors Described.

A. Ability to make vocational social contacts.
   (1) *Contacts with working associates, customers, or the general public.*
       Under this factor evaluate the extent to which the work requires dealing with others and the relative social skill involved.
Point Values:
         (a) Job requires few or infrequent contacts with people during most of the work time.

0-25   Examples: Night watchman, many writers and research workers, forest ranger.

    (b) Job requires direct contact with working associates during most of the work time.

26-50   Examples: Workers on assembly line, railroad crew, office workers.

    (c) Job requires direct contact with customers, clients, or general public during most of the work time.

51-75   Examples: Banker, foods demonstrator, many salesmen, waitress, most physicians and teachers, many retail clerks.

    (d) Job requires a large number of contacts with both working associates and customers or general public during most of the work time.

76-100   Examples: College president or dean, many managerial positions, public relations official, newspaper publisher and editor.

  (2) *Contacts with business class, working class, or both.*

Under this factor identify the class of people with which the job requires contact and evaluate the relative social skill involved. People may be considered belonging to the business class when they address their activities predominantly to *people* in the selling or promotion of things, services, and ideas. People of the working class may be considered as those who address their activities in getting their living primarily to things, utilizing material tools in the making of things and the performance of services.

Point Values:

    (a) Job requires contact with persons of the business class during most of the work time.

0-50   Examples: Office manager, accountant, most business executives.

    (b) Job requires contact with persons of the working class during most of the work time.

0-50   Examples: Social worker, shop foreman, shop mechanic.

    (c) Job requires a number of contacts with both business and working people during the work time.

51-100   Examples: Life insurance agent, public school teacher, many county and city officials, retail clerks.

  (3) *Contacts required or expected when "off the job."*

Under this factor determine whether successful job performance normally demands the entertainment of customers, working associates, or influential people during "off the job" hours. Evaluate relative social skill involved.

Point Values:

    (a) Job requires little or no social entertainment when "off the job."

0-32   Examples: Truck driver, retail clerk, office worker.

    (b) Job requires entertainment of customers or influential persons when "off the job." (Special expense account is often provided for such entertainment.)

33–66   Examples: Many salesmen, some executives.

   (c) Job carries expectation that working associates or influential people outside the work group will be entertained.

67–100   Examples: College president, college professor, lobbyist, most business executives.

B. Ability to direct individuals and work groups.

   (4) *Direction of non-supervisory subordinates, supervisory subordinates, or persuasive and consultative direction of others.*

   Under this factor identify the nature of the social responsibility and evaluate the relative difficulty in managing people under different definitions of authority.

Point Values:

   (a) Job requires the ability to manage subordinates who have no supervisory authority but who are directly responsible to the position.

0–24   Examples: Any supervisory job which has direct "line" authority over "workers."

   (b) Job requires the ability to manage subordinates who are supervisors themselves.

25–50   Example: Managerial positions which have direct "line" authority over supervisory subordinates.

   (c) Job requires the ability to persuade or guide others to buy products or follow instructions or advice when the respondents are not required to do so by any direct line of formal authority.

51–75   Example: Production planning engineer, personnel director, college teacher, salesman.

   (d) Job requires contacts which demand both the ability to persuade or guide others over whom the job has no formally invested authority and the ability to manage supervisory or non-supervisory subordinates through the use of line authority.

76–100   Examples: Y.M.C.A. director, Boy Scout executive, minister of a church which has a paid staff, college president.

   (5) *Responsibility for small, intermediate, or large groups of people as working associates or clients.*

   Under this factor identify the size of the group managed and evaluate the relative social skill involved.

Point Values:

   (a) Job requires direct or indirect supervision of a small group (less than ten) of people.

0–32   Examples: Straw boss, manager of small office.

   (b) Job requires direct or indirect supervision of a group intermediate in size (ten-fifty persons).

33–66   Examples: Foreman, teacher, lawyer.

   (c) Job requires direct or indirect supervision of a large group (over fifty).

67–100   Examples: Plant superintendent, college president, college teacher, physician, dentist, minister, corporation president.

C. Ability to coöperate with members of work groups.

    (6) *Participation in work groups requiring intimate association or formal association.*

        Under this factor identify the kind of social participation in work group which the job demands, and evaluate the relative social skill involved in the attainment of joint action.

Point Values:

        (a) Job requires relatively few social contacts of any kind during the work time.

0–19   Examples: Night watchman, janitor, writer.

        (b) Job requires intimate and personal association in daily face-to-face contact.

20–39   Examples: Railroad crew, workers in office and shop.

        (c) Job requires formal association within a large group with minimum of face-to-face contact but with greater use of letters, telephone, telegram, and memoranda.

40–59   Examples: Jobs requiring a high degree of technical or administrative planning and organizing, such as production planning executive, methods engineering superintendent, some office managers.

        (d) Job requires formal association in daily face-to-face contact.

60–79   Examples: Policy-making and educational functions such as are fulfilled by executives whose work load involves a large amount of conference. This requirement is a large part of the work of teachers, physicians, lawyers, and dentists.

        (e) Job requires a large amount of formal association both in face-to-face contact and also through the use of communication devices.

80–100   Examples: College president, many business executives, Y.M.C.A., and Y.W.C.A. directors.

D. Ability to assume personal responsibility for others.

    (7) *Personal responsibility for people who report directly or indirectly to position.*

        Under this factor identify the number of persons reporting directly or indirectly to position.

Point Values:

25 per   (a) Job requires responsibility for (number of) persons who report
person   directly to position.

1 per   (b) Job requires responsibility for (number of) persons who report
person,   indirectly to position or who are in position as members to bring
maximum   a critical influence to bear on the position.
400 points

Formal tests of the reliability and validity of the scale have been postponed until extensive studies of its strength and weaknesses have been revealed by applications. This is an exploratory study. This scale which purports to make a social measurement of jobs may be likened to those first efforts which were

made to effect job evaluation. If social measurement of jobs is feasible and useful there is much work yet to be done in building more precise scales. We shall be satisfied at this stage if the instrument can be widely applied

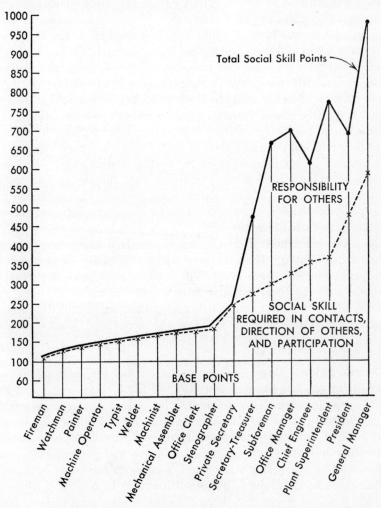

FIG. 47. Social Evaluation of Key Jobs—Midwestern Compressor Company.

to work situations and will reveal more clearly the essential social requirements of such situations. Our efforts are directed here to a demonstration of the discriminatory power of the present scale when applied to the job structure of a small industrial company.

III. A SOCIAL EVALUATION OF JOBS IN A SMALL INDUSTRIAL COMPANY

The industrial company which was chosen for application of the scale employs 180 persons. It will be referred to as the Midwestern Compressor Company. This company carries an office force of approximately 25 employees and a factory force of about 155. It is engaged in the manufacture of air compressors and power take-offs.

Before applying the scale, the researcher observed the work behavior of all employees in the company. This was done to assure that proper application of each social factor would be made when the jobs were evaluated. The coöperation of the general manager was solicited to make the ratings because of his intimate knowledge of the job structure. After training in the meaning of the scale and the application of each factor, the general manager was then asked to assign the proper weight to the relative social skill involved in each job. The researcher checked to see that the proper interpretation of the scale was made while the general manager made the evaluation factor by factor. All evaluations were referred to the jobs themselves and *not* to the individual currently filling them.[24]

The social evaluation of jobs in the Midwestern Compressor Company is shown in Figure 47. Here the total social skill points of each job have been plotted in the upper curve. The lower curve shows the social skill attributable to the three manifest skills: ability to make vocational social contacts, ability to direct individuals and groups, and ability to participate coöperatively. The difference between the upper and lower curves is a representation of the evaluated latent skill, the ability to assume personal responsibility.

The chart clearly shows that the greatest social skill is required by the general manager, and the least is required of the fireman. The social worlds of these two jobs are vastly different. The general manager has an office which averages five to ten telephone calls an hour. Conferences are many. The scope of contacts includes salesmen, government officials, customers, community leaders, plant and office officials, and sometimes workmen. Letters must be read and others written. Visiting customers and government officials must be entertained. Business trips must be arranged. Meanwhile, fourteen positions report directly to the general manager and indirectly the responsibility for 151 other persons is on his shoulders. In diametric contrast to this large range of frequent contact and responsibility, the night fireman maintains a solitary vigil at the furnaces. He sees no one except the night watchman, who stops occasionally during his rounds to exchange gossip. He eats his lunch alone. He has no responsibility for others on his job. Between these two poles, the general manager and the night fireman, rests the job structure with its varying options of association and responsibility.

[24] The author is indebted to Mr. S. V. Saginor, General Manager of "Midwestern" Compressor Company.

The range and intensity of the manifest skills required in the jobs of the company follow the rough outline of the growth curve. Approximately 160 workers are represented in the low tail of the curve within the area of non-supervisory jobs. The social skill demanded of the great bulk of workers is relatively low. The social skill required in a few of the jobs is relatively great. Perhaps the monotony of industrial jobs might be examined in this light. It may well be that it is not so much the presence of repetitive mechanical operations which is reducing the creative elements of so many industrial jobs, but the dearth of opportunities for stimulating and meaningful social contact.[25]

The contrast between those who carry responsibility for others and those who do not is shown in Figure 47. Jobs which make relatively high demands

SOCIAL FACTORS OF WORK SITUATION	T-Scores
	0 10 20 30 40 50 60 70 80 90 100
Scope of Social Contact	
Status Range of Contact	
Social Participation	
Social Demands "Off the Job"	
Direction of Others	
Skill Intensity for Size of Group Directed	
Responsibility for Others	

Fig. 48. Sociometric Profiles of Three Managerial Jobs.

for social skills also require assuming responsibility for others. This means that the jobs with high social demands require individuals who not only can handle people but also must be *responsible* for people.[26] It has been indicated elsewhere that this makes a dual demand on the nervous system. Satisfactory overt skills must be forthcoming as well as psychic strength to carry responsibility. In the chart, the responsibility for others is regarded as a superstructure which lets a weight down upon the individual, who must keep performing his daily contacts beneath it. Some individuals carry this weight lightly and well; others stagger irritably under it. For our purposes here it is desirable that this kind of description reveal more clearly the nature of the demands in the job and the kind of individual who is needed to perform satisfactorily on the job.

[25] See Elton Mayo and George Lombard, *Teamwork and Labor Turnover in the Aircraft Industry of Southern California*, Harvard University Press, 1944.

[26] The relationship between social skill and social responsibility shown in this company does not demonstrate a principle. It is possible for social skill and social responsibility to be uncorrelated. This is particularly true in highly authoritarian structures. In such instances authority may stand in lieu of social skill yet responsibility for others may be very great. This is not uncommon in military organization.

IV. SOCIOMETRIC PROFILES OF SELECTED JOBS

The final purpose of this study is to examine the social demands of selected jobs, through the use of sociometric profiles. The sociometric profile is an adaptation of the widely used psychological profile, which is a chart showing a *person's* place in a group on several different appraisals. The sociometric profile used here show a *job*, set in the job structure of this small industrial company and compared on several different social factors that are considered important and somewhat independent. The profile chart is made by laying off on graph paper a line which represents the mean of a group and other parallel lines which represent units of dispersion such as standard scores. Figure 48 is a sociometric profile chart on which have been plotted the ratings of three managerial jobs in the Midwestern Com-

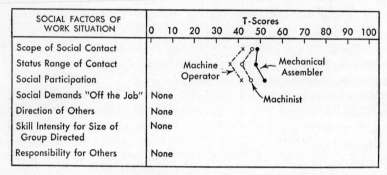

FIG. 49.   Sociometric Profiles of Three Factory Jobs.

pressor Company. The ratings of each job on all seven factors which make up the sociometric scale are shown in standard scores as expressed in T-scores using McCall's well-known T-Scale.[27] The McCall scale assumes a distribution ranging from -5σ to $+5\sigma$. Each sigma unit is subdivided into ten parts of $.1\sigma$ each so that the total scale has 100 points in all. This means that a score of 60 on any factor is 1σ above the mean and therefore comparable in standard units. Figure 48 shows that the general manager requires the greatest social skill. The scope and status range of contacts required in this job are great, as was described in the previous section. The president has to meet a wide scope of contacts but his status range is small since his contacts are usually with the business class only. In this company the president is also the vice-president of two other industrial enterprises and

[27] See E. F. Lindquist, *A First Course in Statistics*, Houghton Mifflin Company, 1938, pp. 133-134. The formula for T-scores is $T=\dfrac{10(X-M)}{S.D.}+50$ where X is a particular raw score in a given distribution and M and S.D. the mean and standard deviation, respectively, of the distribution.

divides his time between three interests. He carries direct responsibility for only five men who report to him in the Midwestern Compressor Company. Only in the social demands "off the job" are requirements greater than for the general manager. The plant superintendent services a limited scope and range of contacts for he does not meet customers, salesmen, or government officials. His job is to supervise eleven subforemen and maintain good labor relations with the 155 men on the factory floor. He stands on equal terms with the general manager in assuming the largest weight of responsibility for others. A high degree of skill is required in directing his group although he is greatly aided in having line authority to back all of his contacts. He hires and fires. He is the "boss" in the factory. For this reason his job requires less versatility than those of the president and general manager, both of whom must be successful in situations where they carry no formal authority, such as in contacts with potential customers and government officials. The plant superintendent has relatively light requirements in "off the job" activities. He is expected to entertain his foremen occasionally and also on occasion to accompany the general manager and president at lunch or dinner in the entertainment of customers or influential persons.

Figure 49 focuses attention on three job titles held by ninety-three men. These are the jobs of mechanical assembler, machinist, and machine operator. They carry similar social demands yet the differences between them are great enough to require careful placement of the men. The superintendent and general manager have both attested to the importance of teamwork in the tasks required of the mechanical assembler. One of the current jobs on which the mechanical assemblers are engaged is the assembly of portable machine shops. This work requires that teams of five to seven men work in and around a large truck assembling equipment which requires mechanical and electrical manipulation. The men must work in all kinds of work positions in proximity to one another. There must be almost automatic synchronization of function so that the work of each may supplement the work of the others in order not to waste time and effort. These men must be able to get along with one another. Anyone who disrupts good job relations hinders the efficiency of the group. Each person must be versatile. Changing work assignments require new group arrangements. New men are brought in and former members may leave, yet new work teams must form quickly to complete the task assigned. The plant operates on a profit-sharing plan and the men themselves are often resentful of any members who jeopardize their earnings through lack of coöperation and efficient workmanship.

The machinists work on machine tools such as lathes, grinders, and boring mills. They work in a more fixed position since their work is tied to a stationary machine. However, they are required to move about the

machine shop as they are assigned to different machining operations. They must be able to work around other machinists and machine operators. Thus, they must be able to get along with all the men in the machine shop.

The machine operator is assigned to one machine only. He has a stationary position and is not moved about the machine shop. His job therefore makes a lighter requirement for social acceptance and participation.[28]

The Relation of the Work Position to the Work Group

These examples demonstrate that it is possible to find common social factors underlying and characterizing all occupations and to measure the relative social skills required in different jobs. The *social evaluation of jobs* thrusts into bold relief the social requirements and responsibilities residual in the jobs. This emphasis is important in any job specification. It is hoped that as measuring instruments of social factors improve, the job specification will include an ever greater volume of social information.

This intensive examination of the work position "leaves out" the dynamic interrelations which are set into motion as workers perform their jobs and interact with other workers. Each work position is set within a work group and within a work plant society. The work situation which confronts the worker defines the characteristics and limits of social participation. Each new worker must learn that he is to play a *role* which will be defined largely by the persons who compose his work group. No placement procedure can expect to function at high efficiency unless it has taken into consideration the specific work group surrounding a given work position. This requirement is the third component of the work situation.

COMPONENT 3. THE WORK GROUP

The most difficult but most important aspect of social placement is correct group assignment. If a worker does not come to feel that he belongs in the group to which he is assigned he will not be a happy worker and in the long run he will not be a satisfactory worker. Even if his performance meets job standards his interaction with other workers is quite likely to be disruptive of either his morale or that of his work group and perhaps both.

The personnel function as it applies to group assignment is twofold in nature. First, the worker must be placed in the group within which he can play a work role that fits the group's expectation. Second, he must find himself attracted to the group, and the group, in turn, must at least accept him. Unless this condition of mutual acceptance is met, the placement of the worker is unstable. Dissatisfaction, grievance, and termination are products of poor social placement.

[28] Delbert C. Miller, "Social Factors of the Work Situation," *American Sociological Review*, June, 1946, pp. 300-314.

Group Definition of Role

The group definition of a given work role is made up of certain expectations. These must be fulfilled regardless of who the particular worker may be. A carpenter is supposed to wear a particular work costume including the proper kind of overalls, shirt, hat, and shoes. He is supposed to understand the use of certain tools. He joins the union and supports it by striking against his employer if the majority of the members of his local union vote to do so. He will not scab on his fellow workers. He will talk like his fellow workers, which means that he will not use big words or any words for that matter which the group does not understand. He will probably bring his lunch in a pail. He will tend to eat as they eat and he will not criticize them if they have different eating habits. He will listen to dirty stories and tell some of his own. He will probably vote the Democratic ticket and express political views in conformance with those of his associates.

A carpenter placed in a work group with these expectations is under great pressure to conform. Ideally his own definition of the work role will coincide with the group definition. The deviations from this ideal are the source of difficulty in placement. These deviations seem to be of particular importance in the case of supervisory and managerial appointments. The sad last words of outgoing administrators have often been, "I didn't know that was what they expected. If I had known . . ."

Two types of deviations may be analyzed as occurring in the role definitions held by a worker and his work group. The worker may be a subordinate or supervisor. (1) In either instance he may overevaluate and overplay the role which the group expects him to play. This results in the group's feeling a pressure to which its members will react in some way. Their reactions will depend largely upon their approval of the worker's or supervisor's motives. (2) If the worker or supervisor underevaluates and underplays his role, he will eventually come to feel the pressure of the group, which will demand changes to place the work role in conformance with their expectation. All of the social controls may be utilized to secure that conformity—ridicule, complaint, soldiering, insubordination, and others. These types of deviations from the ideal coincidence of individual definition of work role with the group definition cannot explain the many specific problems arising in this area of group assignment.

However, industrial sociologists have begun to identify the more important social factors which locate the work role definitions as made by workers in the innumerable work groups. Although the interaction patterns of many groupings that actually arise will not be subject to direct control, it is possible to improve the social placement of workers and to stimulate more cohesive work groups. These possibilities become more certain as the determinants of successful social placement and group collaboration are identified. Suc-

cessful social placement in a work position requires knowledge of the social factors operating to determine work role definition.

Social Factors Operating to Establish Role Definitions

Among the various social factors operating to establish role definitions within different work groups are: (1) ascribed status behavior of the work position; (2) informal code of the work group; (3) age; (4) sex; (5) marital status; (6) social background; (7) length of service; (8) race; (9) ethnic identity.[29]

1. ASCRIBED STATUS BEHAVIOR OF THE WORK POSITION

Every work position has an ascribed status. Ralph Linton, the anthropologist, has defined an ascribed status as one which is assigned to individuals without reference to their innate differences or abilities. When it comes to ascription of occupational status, we find that each occupation has a ranking within some family of occupations and within the range of all occupations generally. Whyte has discovered the status rankings ascribed to workers in the restaurant industry. The following is the usual hierarchy of ascribed status:

Owner
Manager
Assistant manager
Cost control superintendent
Food production manager
Chef
General kitchen superintendent
Hostess
Head waitress—if in superintendent capacity
Checker
Superintendent of countermen
Superintendent of dishwashers
Waitresses
Countermen
Food preparers
1. those who cook
2. salad
3. chicken preparation
    a. white meat
    b. dark meat
4. meat
    a. beef
    b. pork
       roasts
       frying

[29] Refer also to Chapter XI, "Status Organization of the Work Plant."

5. chicken cooking
6. vegetables
   a. parsley
   b. chives
   c. celery
   d. beans—green
   e. spinach
   f. carrots
   g. potatoes
   h. onions
7. fish
Runners
Dishwashers
Charwomen[30]

This hierarchy determines in advance the kind of status behavior which will be expected of each member who works within it. Any worker is expected to defer to those above him in status and to receive the respect of those below him in status. This deference expectation may display itself in many different ways. Whyte describes how a cook (high status) reacted to pressure from a runner (low status). The runner had tried to get the cook to prepare food faster. The cook made this comment, "That guy would try to come down in the kitchen and tell us what to do. But not me. No, sir. He came down here one day and tried to tell me what to do. He said to me, 'We're going to be very busy today.' I just looked at him, 'Yeah?' I said. 'Who are you? Go on upstairs. Go on. Mind your own business.' Can you beat that! 'We're going to be very busy today!' He never came down and told *me* anything again. 'Who are you?' I asked him. That's all I had to say to him."[31]

2. INFORMAL CODE OF THE WORK GROUP

Most work groups hold certain definite ideas as to the way in which an individual should conduct himself within the group. These ideas are connected chiefly with occupation, output, and supervision.

In the bank wiring observation group at Hawthorne, Roethlisberger and Dickson report that the workers had a very definite idea of how much work should be turned out. A member who turned out too much was called a "rate buster"; one who turned out too little a "chiseler." Moreover, a worker who told a supervisor anything that would seem to act to the detriment of a fellow worker was a "squealer."

This behavior is in essence no different from that which takes place in a

[30] Drawn from William F. Whyte, *Human Relations in the Restaurant Industry*, McGraw-Hill Book Company, Inc., pp. 33-46.
[31] From *Human Relations in the Restaurant Industry*, by William F. Whyte. 1948. Courtesy of McGraw-Hill Book Company.

schoolroom, whether it is occupied by students eight or eighty years of age. The students come to consider themselves part of an in-group under pressure imposed by an out-group composed of teachers and administrators. If a student works extremely hard for a high grade he is called a "greasy grind" or a "Phi Bete." If he tries to get a passing record by playing upon the ego of his teacher with techniques of flattery, he is called a variety of names ranging from "apple polisher" to "quill shooter." If he wants to be a "regular" guy he will try to give the appearance of one who is not working very hard and who positively will do no "apple polishing."

E. Wight Bakke has set down the definition of a socially respected industrial worker as made by the workers themselves. He says that "the socially respected worker 'has money in his pocket, has the cash to buy what he needs,' 'is thrifty and a man of foresight,' 'is prepared for a rainy day,' 'owns property,' 'is a good provider,' 'doesn't let his family down,' 'sees to it that his kids are educated,' and himself is a graduate of the school of hard knocks."[32]

Katherine Archibald confirms these observations through her own study of shipyard workers.

Though shipyard workers showed little interest in the broad issues of ethics, they respected definite commandments for the regulation of the familial system. A man was as good or bad as his practice of the family virtues; his acts possessed or lacked merit as they affected his family. The harshest words that one boss had for a member of his gang too often late to work were that he obviously had no regard for the security of his wife and children and was a poor provider. "His old lady sure ought to ride into him," the boss asserted, "losing money from his checks the way he does by being late about every morning—and him with four kids, too." . . . A discussion with a minister was reported at some length to me by a worker; out of pride in his own position. A minister asked me, he said, "how I could hope to be a Christian if I didn't go to church every Sunday and say my prayers at night. Well, I told him that being good to my wife and paying my gas bills on time was Christianity enough for me, and I didn't need to pray because I thanked God every day by working hard for the sake of my wife and kid."[33]

These illustrations convey the importance of the informal code in depicting the socially acceptable role as defined by the work group. Such characteristics constitute behavior expectations which must be fulfilled if the worker is to acquire full social acceptance.

So far in this discussion the demand has been shown to be twofold. The worker must play the role designated by the status ascribed to the work position he fills. In addition, he must play the role designated by the informal code of the group. When a new worker is to be fitted into a work

[32] E. Wight Bakke, The Unemployed Worker, Yale University Press, 1940, p. 15.
[33] Katharine Archibald, War Time Shipyard, University of California Press, 1947, pp. 224-225.

group these two demands will often loom larger in successful placement than the technical competence required for the work position. The need to get this social data and make them a part of the job description is obviously important. The social scientist must offer assistance in formulating the method and instruments necessary to systematize such data. Many factors need to be considered. Age is one that must not be ignored.

3. AGE

Age differentiates workers on the basis of status, interests, and physical energy. Each of these differences may be important in determining social participation in the group.

Thus Whyte found that a waitress over thirty might be quite a different worker in orientation from a younger waitress. In one large restaurant he observed four waitresses over thirty who ate together and saw each other outside of work. One of them had this to say:

"Most of these waitresses are younger than I am, and this kidding around that they do seems childish and boring to me. Of course, they are much younger, and you have to think you were young once yourself and just like that, although in my own case I don't think I ever was so flighty because I had lots of responsibility."[34]

4. SEX

Every anthropologist knows that sex differences have been common bases for differentiating the labor and the rights of members in social life. In our contemporary society sex differences do not cut so sharply the occupational roles as they formerly did but it is nonetheless true that they are far-reaching in work life.

Katherine Archibald describes the role of sex in the wartime shipyard:

Sex attitudes made up the tangled background of the male worker's point of view. Sex was his great avocational interest; whether bounded by the proprieties of marriage or unconstrained in the reaches of bachelor fancy, it was the spice of his existence, the principal joy of his social life. The largest part of shipyard conversation, beyond the routine of the day's necessities, was occupied with some aspect of the pleasures or the problems of sex; and shipyard jokes were broad and racy in the extreme. Emphasized in this interest was the sexual role of women, which influenced every association between the sexes and surrounded with an atmosphere of obscure emotionality each area of unfamiliar and unusual cooperation. The emphasis upon sex, moreover, as it evoked the biological distinctions between men and women, also reinforced the lines of social demarcation. Traditions supposedly governing the proper division of labor between men and women were linked with even more pro-

[34] From *Human Relations in the Restaurant Industry*, by William F. Whyte. 1948. Courtesy of McGraw-Hill Company.

foundly rooted traditions concerning divisions in biological function, and change in the structure of the former might seem to imply a threat to the latter's sacrosanct stability. . . . Thus, on my first day of work in the yards I was warned by the superintendent of my craft that any flirting with the men in the yards would result in dire consequences for me. "Remember what I told you," he called after me as I left his office; "give a man an inch and he'll take a mile, and if there's any funny business on the job, it'll be you who goes out like a light."[35]

In this description of "the proper division of labor between men and women" is evidence that sexual differences must be considered as an important factor in social placement wherever such differences matter in organizing work teams.

5 and 6. MARITAL STATUS AND SOCIAL BACKGROUND

The two factors of marital status and social background may be treated together for the significance of both in placement is that they may induce differentials in interest. Two waitresses indicate these differences. The first stresses the differences due to marital status, the second, those due to social background.

They've asked me to go down there but I wouldn't do it. I'm the oldest girl on this floor, so I could go down anytime. The trouble is, the girls down there are older, and they're a different type from us up here. A lot of those girls are married. They talk about different things. I just wouldn't fit in. And you know some of them, even if they are married, they go out. Some of those girls have asked me to go with them on dates, and I've refused. But if I was working down there with them, I couldn't refuse, could I? I'd be going out with them, and I'd get like them myself. . . .

There is one main division, I think. There are the girls who work here a long time, the professional waitress type. Then there are the other girls who aren't waiting on tables as a career. Those two groups talk differently, and I wouldn't feel at home in the first group at all. I feel uncomfortable when I am with those girls. You can even tell it down in the girls' rest room. Even when the girls are all mixed up, sitting on different sides of the room, you'll have two conversations going right across the room. The two groups will talk right across each other, and they just don't mix in.[36]

7. LENGTH OF SERVICE

The length of service which a worker has given to one employer is ordinarily regarded as the basis for certain rights and obligations. New workers are expected to wait their turn before being admitted to full status. Thus a work group made up of workers with considerable seniority will expect the new worker to earn the rights won by a long length of service.

[35] Katharine Archibald, *op. cit.*, pp. 18-20.
[36] From *Human Relations in the Restaurant Industry*, by William F. Whyte. 1948. Courtesy of McGraw-Hill Company.

They will expect the newcomer to defer to their greater knowledge of the work plant and its characteristic patterns. He will be expected to restrain any hopes for advancement until the seniority rights of older workers are recognized. The newcomers who appear as strangers to their long association may find it difficult to secure a place of acceptance in a well-knit group of older workers.

E. C. Hughes observed the informal organization of women workers in the polishing room of a certain work plant. He found that,

> The cliques in this room are not mutually exclusive and sharply defined. There is a central group, the "Old Girls," made up of young women of from twenty-two to thirty-three years of age and of an average length of service of about five years. The "Old Girls" eat in the cafeteria; each usually manages to eat with at least one or two of her clique fellows. Another group, also of long service, bring their lunches and eat in the lounge. But there is little association between them and the "Old Girls" clique. There are a number of smaller satellite cliques, each attached by at least one common member to the "Old Girls." It appears likely that a new girl may be sponsored into the organization through the satellite cliques. We observed one girl who was, when first interviewed, unfriendly toward other workers, a "lone wolf." Two months later she had been accepted. . . .[37]

8. RACE

The largest minority group in America is the American Negro group. If a Negro is to win a place in a white or mixed work group he must play the role which is expected. That role is most often prescribed as the part of an inferior who will willingly take the lowest-paid, most onerous jobs and will entertain no hopes of promotion to anything better. Katharine Archibald describes the relations of Negroes and whites at Moore Dry Dock, Oakland, California, which hired about 20 percent of Negro personnel in shipbuilding during the war years.

> On the hulls and in the shops, Negroes and whites cooperated in countless tasks, white shoulders straining beside black, and to a casual observer the relationships of the two races seemed miraculously free from tension. The slightest touch, however, revealed the impermanence of the surface calm and the depth of the hatred beneath. In most of the whites the hatred was basic, a deep-seated and strong-flavored aversion that was evident in almost every gesture or remark which was not retarded by the Negro's presence and supposed readiness to take violent revenge for insults. The Negro was seldom even named in all-white talk except in appellations of implied derogation and antagonism, the most common being the timeworn "nigger" and the more recent "jigaboo" or "zigaboo" frequently shortened to "jig" and "zig."[38]

[37] E. C. Hughes, "The Knitting of Racial Groups in Industry," *American Sociological Review*, October, 1946, p. 517.
[38] K. Archibald, *op. cit.*, p. 61.

Attempts of a tolerant white person to establish normal friendly relations with Negroes in the shipyard brought decisive cries of "nigger lover" and other group pressures so strong that patterns of avoidance became the only acceptable conduct. No white woman could safely talk with a Negro man at length on any topic without incurring the immediate and unequivocal reaction, "Well, when's the wedding going to be?"[39]

Such attitudes enforced social distance and created many solitaries. The solitary is a person who does not feel himself a part of any closely knit group. In the mixed group of white and Negro women workers which

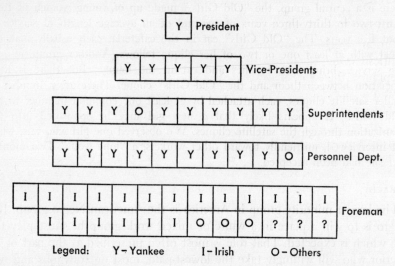

Legend: Y – Yankee   I – Irish   O – Others

FIG. 50. Job-Ethnic Hierarchy in a New England Factory. The non-Yankee at the superintendent level is a testing engineer. The non-Yankee member of the personnel group is a young Italian who does safety cartoons and acts as a general errand boy. (Adapted from Orvis Collins, "Ethnic Behavior in Industry: Sponsorship and Rejection in a New England Factory," *American Journal of Sociology*, January, 1946, p. 294.)

Hughes observed, "No Negro girl, no matter what her length of service, her production rate, or her personality, has found a place in the system of cliques of the white girls."[40]

Both Whyte in his observations of the Negro restaurant worker and Hughes in his study of the Negro factory worker report that attempts of Negroes to satisfy management's demands upon them often tend to further isolate them from the work group. The Negroes' job security rests precariously with management satisfaction. Management demands may force the Negro worker to violate the informal group code as regards production and in giving information to management representatives.

[39] *Ibid.*, p. 72.
[40] E. C. Hughes, *op. cit.*, p. 517.

All of these forces make the placement of the Negro difficult. However, it has been found that the manner in which Negroes are introduced into work groups is more significant in the success of Negro placement than are the generalized racial attitudes of the white workers concerned.[41] Mayo has reported that "we have indeed been surprised throughout this country during the war—East, Midwest, and California—by the ease with which colored people and others are absorbed into a working group if and when they have clearly 'made the team.' We are not prepared at this stage to make any generalizations upon a basis of so few instances; but as a tentative observation, the fact must give us pause."[42]

9. ETHNIC IDENTITY

Various work groups are marked by in-group attitudes tied to ethnic loyalties. When such in-group characteristics are determinants of social acceptance, the social placement of a new worker can proceed satisfactorily only in a clear recognition of the compulsive force of such attitudes. Orvis Collins spent six months working and observing within a New England factory. He found an informal ethnic system of job occupancy and of expectation in promotion. Figure 50 is a representation of the ethnic job hierarchy within this factory.[43]

The figure shows that there are two sharply defined areas. The management area is dominated by Yankees and the supervisory area by the Irish. These tightly drawn ethnic groupings have led to the expectation that Yankees will be hired for management and that newly appointed foremen will be Irish. This does not mean that a foreman, for example, must be Irish, but it does mean that when management appoints a non-Irish foreman it will be with the blessing of the workers and the other foremen. When Peters, a Yankee, was promoted to be subforeman to replace Sullivan, who had been "old country" Irish, all hell broke loose. A walkout materialized. A formal grievance was lodged with management and the workers returned to work. Social pressure in the tightly integrated work group mounted. Several days later Peters the Yankee failed to come to work. It was announced that Peters was ill and that his job would be filled by a man named MURPHY. Peters did not return to work!

Effectuating Successful Group Placement

The problem of social placement can be denied and the traditional practice of filling a job in terms of technical skills and personality traits can be continued. But it should be recognized that such practice ignores interpersonal relations and assumes that collaboration will take place without any

[41] Ibid.
[42] E. Mayo, op. cit., p. 110.
[43] Orvis Collins, "Ethnic Behavior in Industry: Sponsorship and Rejection in a New England Factory," American Journal of Sociology, January, 1946, p. 294.

further consideration. Yet successful group placement may very well be more important in getting quantity and quality production than any other consideration. In ever greater number management executives are saying, "We dare not leave the development of good working human relations to chance."[44] It can be predicted on what we know now that good personnel practice will in the future give most careful attention to the character of the constituent work group into which the new or transferred worker will be placed. Such placement may be assisted by a group description that will rest

STEAM LAUNDRY
Structure of Work Group Before Reconstruction

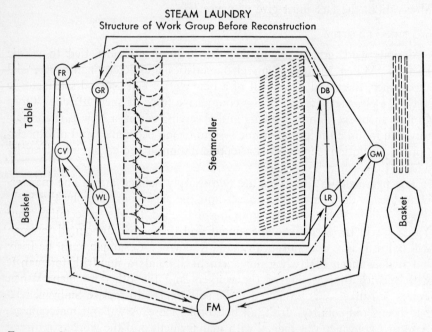

FIG. 51. Sociogram of a Work Group Before Reconstruction. (From J. L. Moreno, *Who Shall Survive? A New Approach to the Problem of Human Interrelations*, Nervous and Mental Disease Publishing Company, 1934, p. 318.)

side by side with the job description. That group description will list essential characteristics such as the leaders, the cliques, the solitaries, and the group norms. The group norms will be determined by the nine (or more) social factors which have been identified. These have been shown to be: (1) ascribed status behavior of the work position; (2) informal code of the work group; (3) age; (4) sex; (5) marital status; (6) social background; (7) length of service; (8) race; (9) ethnic identity.

In addition to these data the charts of interpersonal feelings of the work groups will make it possible to guide the induction and assimilation of the worker into a work group with a minimum of difficulty. Perhaps the first-

[44] S. V. Saginor, Vice-President of Robinson Clay Product Company, Akron, Ohio.

line supervisor as well as the personnel director may come to employ such charts with increasing frequency. The contributions of sociometry to social placement deserve our careful attention.

The Meaning of Sociometric Placement

Sociometry is the study of interpersonal feelings or relationships. For a long time management and labor alike have given lip service to an intangible factor called employees' feelings toward each other. Sociometry recog-

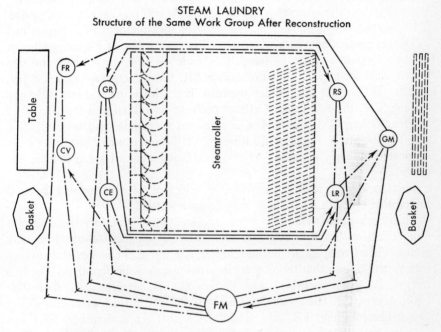

FIG. 52.   Sociogram of a Work Group After Reconstruction. (From Moreno.)

nizes that all work groups have a dynamic structure of feelings which lies under all of the formal and informal groupings. This underlying structure penetrates and encompasses the surface structure of groups. Neither can be separated from the other; in reciprocal relationship each exerts pressure and influence upon the other with the result that every sphere of human action is affected.

The network of interpersonal feelings is exposed by the use of sociometry tests which reveal the spontaneous feelings and choices that workers make. The spontaneous feelings within a person are shown by free choice. Feelings are divided into three classes:

    1. Attraction (like).

    2. Repulsion (dislike).

    3. Indifference (neutral feeling).

Such a test is commonly set up as a group preference schedule with the names of all work group members listed. Each worker in the group then indicates how he feels about working with the various members of his group by marking like, dislike, or indifferent.

A spontaneous choice test gives more information on whom the worker most likes to be associated with in work assignments. Ordinarily each person is asked to choose workers they would prefer to work with. (The test commonly seeks three or five choices from each worker.)

These choices can then be shown as sociograms or charts, which display in graphic form the interpersonal feelings of workers making up work groups. J. L. Moreno was a pioneer in the study of measurement of interpersonal feelings of participants in work groups. Figure 51 is one of his sociograms of a work group in a steam laundry. It is made up of seven workers and one forewoman. Stella, DR, and Philamina, LR, the feeders, reject each other. Myrtle, WL, reject the feeder opposite her, Philamina. Lillian, FR, and Rosalie, CV, the two folders, attract each other. Lillian and Rosalie reject Myrtle. Esther, GM, the shaker, is attracted to Rosalie and rejects Hilda, GR. Esther, Stella, Hilda, and Lillian reject the forewoman, but only Stella is rejected by her. Philamina, Myrtle, and Rosalie are attracted to the forewoman.

This sociogram reveals considerable rejection of the forewoman and some other crucial internal relationships of rejection.

This work group demands reconstruction. Some transfers will make it more effective. To this end DR and WL are assigned to another work group. Their replacement by newcomers RS and CE changes the psychological structure so that the new sociogram appears as in Figure 52. The two feeders, RS (new member) and Philamina, LR, attract each other. The two catchers, CE (new member) and Hilda, GR, attract each other. The two folders, Lillian, FR, and Rosalie, CV, attract each other. The two catchers are attracted to the two feeders opposite them. All the workers except Esther, GM, are attracted to the forewoman.[45]

THE RELATION OF SOCIOMETRIC CHOICES TO COÖPERATION AND PRODUCTIVITY

Since this early application of sociometry to a work group a number of additional studies have been reported.[46] Maria Rogers in her review concludes that "all of the studies of work situations made by sociometrists have revealed that liking, or attraction, between members of a group results in heightened cooperation; that repulsions between workers cause frictions

[45] J. L. Moreno, *Who Shall Survive?* Nervous and Mental Disease Publishing Company, 1934, pp. 318, 319.
[46] For a review and bibliography see Maria Rogers, "Problems of Human Relations Within Industry," *Sociometry*, November, 1946, pp. 350-371. Especially useful is the suggestive work of John H. Jacobs, "The Application of Sociometry to Industry," *Sociometry*, May, 1945, pp. 181-198.

CHOICES EXPRESSED BY CADET NO.............

FLYING CADETS	1	2	3	4	5	6	7	8	9	10	11	12	13	14	15	16	17	18	19	20	21	22	23	24	25	26	27	28	29	30	31
ELEMENT I																															
1		0	0	.5	.5	0	1	.5	1	0	0	0	0	.5	0	0	0	0	0	.5	-.5	1	.5	.5	0	.5	0	0	0	.5	.5
2	-1		0	.5	0	1	0	0	.5	-.5	0	0	0	-.5	0	0	0	.5	-1	-1	0	-1	-1	1	0	0	0	0	-1	-1	-.5
3	-1	-1		-.5	0	-1	0	0	.5	-.5	-.5	0	-.5	0	0	-.5	0	0	-1	0	-.5	.5	-.5	-1	0	0	0	0	0	-.5	0
4	0	0	1		.5	1	0	.5	0	0	0	0	0	-.5	0	-.5	0	0	-.5	0	-.5	0	-.5	-.5	0	0	0	0	0	-.5	0
5	1	1	1	.5		0	.5	0	1	0	-.5	1	0	0	0	-.5	0	0	0	-1	-.5	.5	-1	-.5	.5	0	0	0	0	-.5	-.5
6	1	1	1	.5	.5		.5	0	.5	0	0	0	-1	0	0	0	0	0	-.5	0	.5	-.5	.5	1	0	0	0	1	0	0	-.5
7	1	0	0	-.5	0	0		0	.5	0	0	0	0	0	0	0	0	0	0	0	0	.5	-.5	-.5	0	0	-.5	0	-.5	-.5	0
MORALE INDEX +.25 / ELEMENT II																															
8	-1	0	0	.5	0	0	-1		.5	.5	0	1	0	0	0	0	0	0	0	0	0	-.5	1	1	0	0	0	0	0	-.5	-.5
9	0	0	1	0	1	.5	.5	1		1	0	1	0	1	1	0	0	0	0	.5	0	1	.5	-.5	1	-1	0	0	0	-.5	0
10	0	1	0	0	0	.5	0	1	.5		0	-1	1	0	0	0	0	0	0	0	0	.5	.5	1	0	0	0	0	0	-.5	0
11	0	0	0	0	0	0	0	0	1	.5		1	0	0	0	0	0	0	-.5	.5	-.5	.5	-.5	-.5	0	0	0	0	0	-.5	.5
12	0	0	0	0	0	0	0	0	1	-.5	1		1	0	.5	0	0	0	0	0	-.5	.5	-.5	-.5	0	0	0	0	0	-.5	.5
13	0	0	0	0	0	0	0	1	.5	1	0	1		0	0	1	0	0	0	0	1	1	1	1	0	.5	0	0	1	-.5	0
MORALE INDEX +.50 / ELEMENT III																															
14	.5	0	1	0	0	0	0	0	.5	0	0	0	0		1	0	.5	1	1	0	-.5	1	.5	-.5	0	1	1	0	0	0	.5
15	0	0	0	0	0	0	0	0	.5	0	0	0	0	-1		0	.5	0	0	0	-.5	.5	-.5	-.5	.5	.5	0	0	0	0	0
16	0	0	0	0	0	0	0	1	0	1	0	0	1	1	.5		1	0	-.5	.5	1	.5	1	.5	0	0	0	0	0	0	.5
17	0	0	0	0	0	0	0	0	.5	0	0	0	0	.5	1	1		1	1	.5	-.5	1	-.5	-.5	1	.5	0	0	0	0	0
18	0	0	0	0	0	0	0	0	.5	0	0	0	0	1	.5	1	1		1	0	0	1	-.5	-.5	1	0	1	0	0	0	0
19	0	0	0	0	0	0	0	0	.5	0	0	0	0	0	1	0	1	1		0	-.5	.5	.5	-.5	1	1	0	0	0	0	.5
MORALE INDEX +.60 / ELEMENT IV																															
20	0	0	0	0	0	0	0	0	.5	0	-1	0	0	0	0	0	1	0	1		-1	1	0	-.5	1	1	1	0	-1	0	1
21	0	1	0	0	0	0	0	1	0	0	0	0	1	0	0	1	0	0	0	0		1	1	1	1	-1	0	0	0	0	.5
22	0	-.5	0	0	0	0	0	0	.5	0	0	0	0	.5	0	0	1	1	0	0		●	.5	-.5	.5	.5	1	0	0	1	.5
23	-.5	0	0	0	0	0	0	0	.5	0	0	0	0	0	0	0	0	0	0	0	1	.5		1	.5	-1	0	0	0	-.5	0
24	-1	1	0	-.5	0	.5	0	0	0	1	0	0	0	0	0	1	0	-1	-.5	-1	1	0	.5		.5	-1	0	0	-.5	-1	.5
25	0	0	0	0	0	0	0	0	1	0	0	0	0	0	1	0	1	0	1	0	0	1	.5	1		1	0	0	0	0	.5
MORALE INDEX +.40 / ELEMENT V																															
26	0	0	0	0	0	0	0	0	-.5	0	0	0	.5	.5	0	0	0	0	0	-1	-.5	.5	-.5	-.5	1		1	0	-1	0	.5
27	0	0	0	-.5	0	0	-1	0	0	-.5	0	0	0	.5	0	0	0	0	0	0	-1	.5	-.5	-.5	.5	.5		0	0	0	.5
28	0	0	0	-.5	0	0	-1	-1	-.5	-.5	0	-.5	-1	-.5	0	-1	0	0	0	0	-1	-1	-.5	-.5	0	.5	0		-1	-1	.5
29	.5	0	0	0	0	0	-.5	0	.5	0	0	0	0	0	0	0	0	0	0	1	0	1	-.5	-.5	0	0	1	1		1	.5
30	0	0	0	0	0	0	0	0	.5	0	0	0	0	0	0	0	0	0	0	0	0	1	-.5	-.5	0	.5	0	0	1		1
31	0	0	0	-.5	0	0	0	0	-.5	0	0	-1	-1	-.5	0	-.5	0	0	0	0	-.5	.5	-1	-.5	0	-1	0	0	-1	1	
MORALE INDEX +.18																															

CHOICES "RECEIVED" BY

FLYING TEAMS SOCIOLOGICALLY GROUPED	ELEMENT I	ELEMENT II	ELEMENT III	ELEMENT IV	ELEMENT V
	1–7	8–9	14–15	20–22	26–27
	2–6	10–13	16–17	21–23	29–30
	4–5	11–12	18–19	24–25	31–?
	3–				

FIG. 53. Pattern of Choices and Rejections of Flying Partners. (Adapted from Leslie D. Zeleny, "Selection of Compatible Flying Partners," *American Journal of Sociology*, March, 1947, p. 425.)

on the job, lowered morale, and limited productivity. In this context, the supervisor or immediate administrator must be considered a member of a group, for 'leadership' is a function of interpersonal relations, dependent on the give-and-take between the members of a group. It is relative to the group process."[47]

These findings thus stress the importance of selection by sociometric choice. Leslie D. Zeleny has demonstrated in a study of the selection of compatible flying partners that opportunities for cadets to express spontaneous choices and rejections with respect to flying partners provided a better basis for the selection of compatible flying teams than the method of random selection in use.[48] A "flight" of forty-eight cadet pilot observers in an advanced Army Air Forces flying school was studied. Since a cadet actually placed his life in the hands of his partner when the latter flew the aircraft, there was ample motive to make positive and negative choices of members in one's element and flight. Each cadet was permitted to express his feelings on a sociometric test about flying with each of the cadets in his flight and to make choices.[49] His sociometric test contained the following instructions.

1. If you would like to fly with a particular cadet in a flying team, encircle "yes" after his name. If you would like not to fly with a particular cadet in a flying team encircle "No" after his name. If you do not know how you feel about flying with a cadet encircle "I" for "indifferent." Remember, your choices may determine with whom you will fly the next few weeks.

2. Examine the name of each cadet after which "Yes" has been encircled; place a "1" to the upper right of the "Yes" following the names of the five cadets who are your *First Five Choices* as persons with whom to fly. (Do this now. Then read on.)

3. Examine the name of each cadet after which a "No" or "I" has been encircled; place an "L" to the upper right of the "No" or "I" following the names of five cadets who are your *Last Five Choices* in your flight as persons with whom to fly.

Each cadet was free to choose or reject as many persons as he wished in his flight of forty-eight cadets. His responses were of necessity based on limited acquaintance since the flight had been in the advanced school only a short time. However, at the very beginning of instruction it was customary for members of a flight to be listed in alphabetical order, divided into "elements" of five to seven cadets each, and assigned to a flight instructor. Teams were taken in pairs from the elements. This random method often created flying teams of a relatively low degree of compatibility, and the results can be seen in Figure 53, which shows the pattern of choices and

[47] M. Rogers, *op. cit.*, p. 364.
[48] Leslie D. Zeleny, "Selection of Compatible Flying Partners," *American Journal of Sociology*, March, 1947, pp. 424-431.
[49] *Ibid.*

rejections for thirty-one of the forty-eight cadets actually tested. This figure shows the reaction of each cadet to every other cadet and, especially important, the reactions within each *instructional element*. The verbal responses have been translated into mathematical symbols, as follows: Yes[1] (yes, a first, second, third, fourth, or fifth choice) = +1.0; Yes (no special choice) = +0.5; No = −0.5; I (indifferent) = 0.0; I[L] = indifferent and with some rejection = −0.5; No = −0.5; No[L] (no, a first, second, third, fourth, or fifth rejection) = −1.0. The degree of compatibility or morale among the cadets in each instructional element has been computed. This index is defined as the average of the units of intensity of the interpersonal choices and rejections in a group ($\bar{I}$) plus or minus the average deviation of the intensities from $\bar{I}$ (D).

$$C \text{ (compatibility index)} = \bar{I} \pm D.$$

When I equals the intensity of choices or rejections and N equals the numbers of persons in the group, then

$$C = \bar{I} \pm D, \text{ where } \bar{I} = \frac{\Sigma I}{N(N-1)} \text{ and } D = \frac{\Sigma(\bar{I} \sim I)}{N(N-1)}$$

Using this formula, five instructional elements show the following index numbers:[50] Element I = +.25; Element II = +.50; Element III = +.60; Element IV = +.40; Element V = +.18.

Element III has the highest morale or compatibility. However, this is not very high since an index number of almost +1.00 is possible. The random method of alphabetical selection carried out by administrative decision obviously does not bring high sociometric scores. *Much better compatibility could be attained by selection through sociometric choice.*[51] It was possible to select the most compatible teams within the elements. These have been indicated at the bottom of Figure 53. In actual practice a number of these

[50] Consider the compatibility of a flying team composed of the first two members of Element I; that is, selected at random, as was the practice. No. 1's response to No. 2 was one of rejection (−1), and the response of No. 2 to No. 1 was one of indifference (0). The compatibility index would be computed as follows:

$$\bar{I} = \frac{\Sigma I}{N(N-1)} = \frac{-1+0}{2(2-1)} = \frac{-1}{2} = -.5 \text{ unit}$$

$$D = \bar{d} = \frac{\Sigma d}{n}$$ where d represents the deviation of any one attitude from the mean of all the attitudes. The sign of the intensities is considered only in the relation of the distance of $\bar{I}$ from I.

$$= \frac{\Sigma(\bar{I} \sim I)}{N(N-1)} = \frac{.5+.5}{2(2-1)} = \frac{1}{2} = .5 \text{ unit}$$

$C = \bar{I} \pm D = -.5 \pm .5$ where the −.5 represents the average intensity of the interpersonal reactions and $D \pm .5$ represents the average deviation.

[51] For example, cadet No. 1 and cadet No. 7 have a compatibility index of 1.00.

recommended teams were used by flying instructors with satisfactory results.

This study explains the technique by which industry could match workers with groups in such a way as to maximize the efficiency and morale of both the worker and the group. If such a method seems at first startling and impractical to the reader it may be well to reflect upon the alternative. A continuation of selection and placement which is guided only by the technical skill of the worker and the location of equipment or office space denies the importance of social factors. Such a denial proceeds in the face of a growing research consensus. Perhaps Mayo put this consensus most convincingly when he wrote, "The fact that the United States has developed a successful series of tests for technical skills does not provide any extenuation for psychology. Within its narrow limits, this is useful and, indeed, excellent. But the general effect is to focus attention on technical problems and blind us to the importance of the problems of human cooperation— social skill. This blindness has unquestionably contributed to the advent of calamity."[52]

The problem of worker placement is so closely interrelated with the problem of group collaboration that the following chapter may be regarded as a continuation of the all-embracing search for more effective ways to build a stronger social structure in the work plant.

SUPPLEMENTARY STUDIES

LABORATORY: DEMONSTRATION AND INTERVIEW PRACTICE

The instructor explains the principles of good practice in employment interviewing. The writers especially recommend Richard A. Fear and Byran Jordan, *Employee Evaluation Manual for Interviewers*, The Psychological Corporation, 1943. After a few practice demonstrations using the Employee Evaluation Form for Interviewers, p. 40, all students may gain experience by pairing and practicing the employment interview.

LABORATORY: EXPERIMENTATION IN USE OF SOCIODRAMATIC PERFORMANCE TESTS AS AN EMPLOYEE SELECTION TECHNIQUE

Step 1. Two persons are selected and asked to wait outside the laboratory room.

Step 2. Explain to the student group that a stress situation such as might be found commonly in industry is to be simulated. The situation is that of a supervisor in a department of a retail store in which sales have been steadily declining although economic conditions have been good. The general manager suspects that the supervisor has been "too easy" in dealing with his

[52] E. Mayo, *op. cit.*, p. 20.

employees. The employees have been taking long lunch periods. There have been complaints of rudeness to customers, of keeping customers waiting, or engaging in horseplay on the job. The general manager has just sent a curt memo to the supervisor of the department that "this situation must be cleared up or ELSE."

Step 3. Select seven persons to represent employees. Get some possible roles as: (Class may select the roles they wish to see represented if desired.)

Sour Grapes	*The Climber*	*Lazy*
Has longer seniority than supervisor; wanted job of supervisor himself; doesn't believe supervisor knows how to handle the job.	Will do anything to please. He will use every trick to get himself ahead.	Doesn't want to be pushed to work any harder. He feels that he is working hard enough for the job.

Belligerent or Organizer	*Cynic*	*Hypochondriac*
The pay is "lousy," the working conditions are poor, and the big bosses only think about profits. Calls for steward if union is represented or threatens to form a union.	Doesn't think the supervisor means to do anything. Just the usual pep talk.	His health goes bad under pressure. There is too much pressure already. He cites his anxiety and ailments.

Open Role

The person plays any role he desires.

Step 4. Ask group: "What can happen here?" "What appeals may be made by the supervisor?" "What rewards and punishments will he employ?" "What consequences can be foreseen?"

Step 5. Brief the first person who is chosen to play the role of supervisor. Tell him the situation. Do *not* tell him that his "employees" have been given roles. Introduce supervisor and tell him to handle the situation. (If desired, one supervisor may be briefed to handle the situation in a belligerent manner while the second may be cast as one who tries to be very understanding and seek causes for the tensions in the situations. The casting of supervisors into roles protects their actions from personal criticism since it can be pointed out that they were merely practicing a role. Although this protects the ego of the "supervisors," it weakens the situation as a reality practice.)

Step 6. Role situation is practiced. The situation may be brought to a close by the supervisor or may be cut when deemed appropriate by the instructor.

Step 7. Get reactions from the supervisor. Ask him what he considered most effective and what he considered most ineffective. Ask him if he can diagnose the roles of his employees. Tell him what the roles actually were.

Step 8. Get reactions from the group.

Step 9. Repeat role practice with the second person (who is still outside) chosen to be the supervisor. Repeat steps 6, 7, and 8.

LABORATORY: EXPERIMENTATION IN THE EVALUATION OF SOCIAL SKILLS REQUIRED BY WORK POSITIONS

Study the scale on pp. 433-436. This scale purports to measure the social factors or skills required in various work positions.

Step 1. Prepare a detailed description of the kinds of social skills required on each of the following jobs commonly found in a college or university:

> Housemother
> Secretary to a department head
> Dean of men
> Teaching professor
> Research professor
> Department head
> President
> Mimeograph operator
> Librarian
> Football coach
> Janitor
> Director of athletics

Step 2. Using the job descriptions, identify the social factors involved for each of the jobs as indicated on the scale. Start with one job and go through the scale and make a record of the factor and the skill required. For example, on the first factor a night watchman would be identified as (1) (a) (*Contacts with working associates, customers, or the general public*). Job requires few or infrequent contact with people during most of the worktime.

If the night watchman were engaged in admitting college professors to a campus building, he would be identified as (2) (a) on the second factor, (3) (a) on the third factor. Skill factors (4), (5), and (7) are not required at all. On skill factor (6) the night watchman may be identified as (6) (a).

All jobs are so identified and a chart is prepared as follows:

Factor	1	2	3	4	5	6	7
Job A	(b)	(c)	(b)	(d)	(b)	(c)	(a)
Job B	(a)	(b)	(a)	(a)	(c)	(b)	(a)(b)
Job C	(b)	(a)	(a)	(c)	(b)	(a)	(a)
Job D etc.							

Step 3. Assign points from the range given, comparing the jobs on each of the factors starting with the first factor, *Contacts with working associates, customers, or the general public*, and examining all jobs with notation (a): Job requires few or infrequent contacts with people during most of the work time. After points are assigned for (a), go on to (b): Job requires direct contact with working associates during most of the work time. Assign points by comparing job descriptions and continue on through (c) and (d). Continue similarly with the other six factors. It should be noted that factor (7) carries a maxi-

mum of 400 points for *Personal responsibility for people who report directly or indirectly to position.*

When assigning points no analyst or committee member consults his associates, so each ranking represents a separate judgment.

Step 4. Average points of your group or class. The average of all points is taken as the official point rating of social skill requirements.

LIBRARY: BOOKS AND ARTICLES

Chapple, Eliot D., and Donald, Gordon, Jr., "A Method for Evaluating Supervisory Personnel," *Harvard Business Review*, Winter, 1946, pp. 197-214.

Eaton, Joseph W., "Experiments in Testing for Leadership," *American Journal of Sociology*, May, 1947, pp. 523-535.

Staff of the Office of Strategic Services, *The Assessment of Men*, Selection of Personnel for the Office of Strategic Services, Rinehart and Company, 1948.

Symonds, Percival M., "Role Playing as a Diagnostic Procedure in the Selection of Leaders," *Sociatry*, March, 1947, pp. 43-50.

Zeleny, Leslie D., "Selection of Compatible Flying Partners," *American Journal of Sociology*, March, 1947, pp. 424-431.

RESEARCH GAPS

1. Sociodramatic performance tests of determined reliability and validity to select work applicants having the appropriate social skills required in the work positions for which they have applied.
2. Diagnoses of social roles required in different occupations and work positions.
3. Refinement of scales for evaluating the social skills required by different work positions.
4. Role-playing techniques for the training of supervisors and stewards.

CHAPTER XIV

The Problem of Industrial Morale and Teamwork

THE WILL TO WORK IN INDUSTRIAL SOCIETY

Production of every good and every service rests upon human will and purpose. The industrial revolution profoundly affected the work and status relationships of almost all workers. Some changes accompanying the industrial organization of society are apparent in the emergence of large corporations, the growth of great cities, and the modern ways of living which automobiles, radios, and movies have brought about. But the emergence of a national and international market for goods has had many implications which are not so immediately discerned. In earlier centuries duties were owed to a small local community which was mainly self-supporting and engaged in production for use rather than for surpluses to be placed on a market for sale. The religious view of work which predominated considered that a man was "called" to his vocation. The idea was held that each man, in performing his task well, fulfilled an earthly stewardship before God. Each person could thus feel that he not only contributed to his own and others' well-being and security but also gained in personal worth. Out of this belief grew the further idea that every approved calling had *equal* worth in the eyes of men and of God. In such a society men carried a sense of moral worth and of economic justice.

With the industrial revolution came the large market. Workers left the land to enter the factory, store, and mine. Work became more and more regarded as a source of gains—as a commodity to be purchased by an employer when sales were brisk and to be removed when the market was bad. Karl Polanyi points out in *The Great Transformation*:

As the development of the factory system had been organized as part of a process of buying and selling, therefore labor, land, and money had to be transformed into commodities in order to keep production going. . . . Of the three, one stands out: labor is the technical term used for human beings, in so far as they are not employers but employed; it follows that henceforth the organization of labor would change concurrently with the organization of the market system. But as the organization of labor is only another word for the forms of life of the common people this means that the development of the market system would be accompanied by a change in the organization of society itself. All along the line, human society had become an accessory of the economic system.[1]

[1] Karl Polanyi, *The Great Transformation,* Rinehart and Company, 1944, p. 75.

Gradually the ethical norms were weakened. Work was stripped of its public and moral significance. Workers reacted to their new status by repudiating the idea of moral obligation to the employer or to the public. They came to feel that work was performed because of economic necessity, not because of a sense of participation in a joint project.[2]

As manual work became regarded as "inferior" work and subject to large insecurities it was shunned by all who could avoid it. Parents urged their children to seek education in order to get "good" jobs promising high security and status—i.e., white-collar jobs, especially the well-regarded professional and technical jobs. To escape the insecurities of manual labor the mass yearning became one of getting in the big money, acquiring large savings, or owning a business. This brief picture of changing work and status relationships brings us to our own time.

Every monetary work plant and in addition our schools, families, and churches are faced in the mid-part of the twentieth century with perplexing problems of motivation and morale. What is the meaning and intense purpose of life and work, people ask, and none of the answers seem satisfying. In recognition of human needs, many sincere attempts have been made by far-sighted industrial and labor leaders to establish industrial relations on a basis of partnership between management and labor. The emerging of new ethical concepts can be discerned. However, there is no complete promise that the root causes which impede this partnership are now under control. The intense depression of the 1930's stands as a painful reminder that the market can be a severe and discriminating element in differentiating the security and well-being of American workers. Yet the possibilities of rebuilding work relations so that human dignity and worth may be restored are to be found in the efforts by management, labor, and government to secure and stabilize high levels of employment. The rise of real wages to manual labor is another sign of amelioration.

These efforts to make a more stable economic order will doubtless continue with varying degrees of success. Meanwhile, on the inside of work plants men and women must be given opportunities to rediscover human dignity and worth. This is the central problem in establishing higher levels of coöperation. And to this end many industrial and labor leaders must find new thoughtways and new techniques for restoring community feelings. It is pertinent, therefore, to turn our attention to the process of establishing coöperative relationships.

[2] For an excellent discussion see E. T. Hiller, *Social Relations and Structures*, Harper & Brothers, 1947, pp. 497-514.

THE MEANING OF COÖPERATION

Coöperation refers to joint efforts expended by two or more persons engaged in attaining a common goal. Appraising the role of a person in every situation in which other individuals are interacting with him requires a twofold consideration. The first involves an indvidual's *powers* in the situation and the second is concerned with his *determination* or volition within the limits set by his powers.

Chester Barnard has explained that

In the millions of interactions that daily take place between men, these appraisals are not separate in any observable way in most cases. Nevertheless, they are so discriminated and separately expressed in numerous instances. The expressions of the first appraisal will be the answers to such questions as these: 'Who is he?' 'What kind of man is he?' 'What can he do?' The second appraisal is expressed in answer to such questions as: 'What does he want? What is he trying to do? What will he do?'

These appraisals implicit in human relations affect the behavior of persons in two ways in matters of purposeful conduct. What actually may be done by one person to establish satisfactory relationships with another person may be approached either by the attempt to *narrow the limitations* of the second person's choice, or to *expand the opportunities* of his choice.[3]

These alternatives suggest that behavior with reference to other persons may take the form of regarding such persons either as *objects* to be *manipulated* by changing the factors affecting them or as *subjects* to be *satisfied.*

The perspective in which people are viewed influences their action greatly. In the first case, factors external to the person may be applied in the belief that they will be effective in securing desired goals. The earlier belief that improved working conditions or financial incentives would automatically raise production and morale is an instance of this thoughtway. When persons are viewed as *subjects* to be *satisfied,* attention must be turned to the feelings and attitudes of individuals. It is *within* rather than from *without* the person that results are sought.

Barnard has made it clear that an understanding and operation of coöperative relationships within an organization must of necessity involve both of these views of persons. An organization must become both *effective* and *efficient.* It must both attain ends and satisfy personal desires. It is *effective* if it accomplishes its specifically desired ends; it is *efficient* if it satisfies the motives of those participating in the accomplishment of those ends.

[3] Chester I. Barnard, *The Functions of an Executive,* Harvard University Press, 1947, p. 39.

It is possible for an organization to be effective but not efficient, or efficient but not effective. The function of leadership is precisely to weld these two aims together. On this point Barnard says,

For the continued existence of an organization either *effectiveness* or *efficiency* is necessary; and the longer the life, the more necessary both are. The vitality of organizations lies in the willingness of individuals to contribute forces to the cooperative system. This willingness requires the belief that the purpose can be carried out, a faith that diminishes to the vanishing point as it appears that it is not in fact in process of being attained. Hence, when effectiveness ceases, willingness to contribute disappears. The continuance of willingness also depends upon the satisfactions that are secured by individual contributors in the process of carrying out the purpose. If the satisfactions do not exceed the sacrifices required, willingness disappears, and the condition is one of organization inefficiency. If the satisfactions exceed the sacrifices, willingness, persists, and the condition is one of efficiency of organization.[4]

The problem of securing coöperative effort can be seen as a demand to build a specific coöperative system both *effectively* and *efficiently*. To secure *efficiency*, organizations depend upon the motives of individuals and the inducements that satisfy them. To secure *effectiveness*, organizations must depend upon goals and the demands made to achieve them. These two requirements often furnish a setting of opposed facts and of opposed thought and emotions of human beings. It becomes the function of executive leadership to reconcile the conflicting interests and ideals which determine finally the *efficiency* and *effectiveness* of an organization. Therefore, the first questions we need to ask are, What do workers want? What do managers want?

WHAT DO WORKERS WANT?

There are many who believe this question of what the workers want is ridiculously simple. They are quick to reply, "All that most workers want is the almighty dollar!"

The social scientist recognizes in such folk expressions a large gap between popular thinking and the facts which come out of the research studies on worker motivation. The Western Electric researches show that *nonfinancial* incentives rank high among the needs which workers demonstrate are important to them. The sense of belonging to a group, of feeling important and being wanted are aims written large over these studies. Recently Joseph Shister and Lloyd G. Reynolds of the Yale Labor and Management Center interviewed 450 manual workers in a New England city. They asked those workers who had transferred to other jobs voluntarily in the previous eighteen months what the primary source of their dissatisfaction had been. Fifteen percent of them said they had been satisfied but had left for a

[4] *Ibid.*, p. 82.

better job. In the remaining 85 percent only 24 percent gave wages as the cause for quitting. The causes most commonly mentioned included interest in their job, fairness of treatment over matters not involving wages, physical characteristics of the job, independence and control, and their relations with fellow workers. When the interviewers turned to the group of workers who were satisfied with their present jobs only 15 percent of them mentioned wages.

Shister and Reynolds concluded: "As regards conditions on the job itself—We have succeeded in distinguishing things of major importance to the worker from those of minor importance. The three most important factors have to do with: (1) 'human relations' on the job—the degree of independence and control, fairness of treatment (including the wage aspect of this), and relations with fellow workers; (2) the intrinsic nature of the job, including both its physical characteristics and the degree of variety and interest which it affords to the worker; and (3) wages in an absolute or 'standard-of-living' sense."[5]

One after another the research studies continue to demonstrate that wages are seldom a major cause of satisfaction or dissatisfaction. They are seen to be *indicators* of satisfaction or dissatisfaction arising from such fundamental wants as security, chance to advance, being treated like a human being, and simple, genuine human dignity.[6]

Peter Drucker has pressed this point so far as to declare that *"wage rates are rarely an important cause of labor trouble in American industry,* except in a few areas of substandard wages. . . . Wage conflicts are effects and symptoms rather than causes, releases for tension and resentments built up in human rather than in financial relations."[7]

The large gap between folklore and science on the question of wages demands an explanation. How could management and the worker grow so far apart in understanding each other? The answer is that the modern industrial organization has outgrown its internal communication system and that special institutional channels of communication must be rebuilt to bring the workers' point of view to management and management's point of view to the workers. The area of ignorance which fills the schism is perhaps the most dangerous foe to coöperation. Drucker has explained that "by necessity management and worker look at industrial relations from different sides, from different angles of vision. What are obvious facts to management are completely beyond the knowledge, imagination, and experience of the worker and vice versa. What is of vital importance to the

[5] Joseph Shister and Lloyd G. Reynolds, *Job Horizons: A Study of Job Satisfaction and Labor Mobility,* Harper & Brothers, 1949, pp. 33-34.

[6] Elmo Roper, "What American Labor Wants," *American Mercury,* February, 1944.

[7] Peter Drucker, "The Way to Industrial Peace," *Harper's Magazine,* November, 1946, p. 386.

worker—so important that any violation of it must appear to him as a deliberate attack—is often something that has never even occurred to management."[8]

WHAT DO MANAGERS WANT?

Many persons believe this question of what managers want is also a simple one. The quick reply is that the managers want to drive workers as hard as they can to make fat salaries for themselves and fat profits for the company.

Again, the social scientist must turn to the research record to check this assertion. He finds that an evolution has taken place in modern industry, characterized by a shift of management from the owner-manager or founder-manager (a Carnegie, Rockefeller, Ford, Westinghouse, Wanamaker, or Armour) to the professional administrator of the enterprise (a Walter Gifford, Benjamin Fairless, C. E. Wilson). The loyalty of such professional administrators is directed toward the company as an institution in which they have invested their skill and effort. Salary return and professional satisfactions are their rewards. Their "interest in the enterprise tends to be more long-range than that of ownership, for the simple reason that stocks are apt to be more liquid than good jobs. . . . Being one of the less tangible assets of a company, good human relations has a greater appeal to the more permanent interest of management than to the often shorter-term interest of the owners. Then, too, the gap between the executive and the production worker is more easily bridged. Being the one who is judged by the community for the treatment of his employees, the manager is more sensitive to social pressures. He is also sensitive to the professional standards of the management group, which in the field of labor relations are rising rapidly."[9]

What do these professional managers want to achieve? E. Wight Bakke set out in 1946 to find an answer by interviewing sixty management leaders in nine major industrial centers. He concluded that the most common goals which management leaders sought included:

1. The economic welfare of the company. "The first objective of industrial relations, like that of every function of management, is the economic welfare of the particular company."

2. Relations with its own employees. "Industrial relations are primarily and basically a matter of relations between management and employees, its own employees."

3. Freedom to manage. "Industrial relations arrangements must leave unimpaired management's prerogatives and freedom essential to the meeting of management's responsibilities."

[8] Peter Drucker, "Citizenship in the Plant," *Harper's Magazine*, December, 1946, p. 513.

[9] Labor Committee, *Partners in Production*, The Twentieth Century Fund, 1949, p. 63.

4. Businesslike, responsible relations. "All parties to industrial relations should be businesslike and responsible."[10]

ATTAINING COMMON GOALS

Bakke summarized his study of labor-management relations with the following conclusion:

The basic issue in labor-management relations at the moment then, arises from the fact that each party is concerned with its *individual* survival. Its attention is focused on the means to that end. The leaders of each group are trying in every industrial negotiation and every political maneuver not merely to solve a specific problem. They are trying to solve it in a way that preserves their own structure of living intact. They are expecting peace on terms consistent with the maintenance of their own sovereignty. Preoccupied with that expectation and the effort to implement it, they have forgotten a very fundamental truth: that sovereignty in a democracy must be shared, not exclusively possessed by a particular group. Many have neglected the fact that partnership is essential to a democratic relationship in industrial as in political and family life; and that if one would be a partner, the other partner's interest must become one's own, at least to that degree which permits cooperative effort toward a common goal.[11]

Expert observers of industrial relations have come into close agreement on one point. This is that *no necessary and irreconcilable conflict* exists between the wage earner's loyalty to his union and his loyalty to the company in which he is employed.[12] Evidence that this kind of mutual loyalty can be developed is available in the history of peaceful relations between the clothing industry and the International Garment Workers Union, the Standard Oil Company and the oil workers, the Pacific Coast Pulp and Paper Industry and its unions, and many others. All work in labor relations takes time. It took almost thirty years to discover the way to build mutually satisfying relationships at Standard Oil; twenty years at American Cast Iron Pipe. But sincere efforts repay in results long before the industrial relations machinery is built.

When two parties fail to build good relations, it is not because of *irreconcilable interests* so much as the presence of *irreconcilable attitudes*. In these observations it is not assumed that conflict can be made to disappear in thin air. To the contrary, peace in democratic industrial relations proceeds as a mixture of hostility and mutuality or, as William Graham Sumner once said, as a state of antagonistic coöperation. Parties pursue their own interest but they respect the survival need of the other. To accomplish this, each comes to understand the job the other has to do, the convictions which

[10] E. Wight Bakke, *Mutual Survival—The Goal of Unions and Management*, Harper & Brothers, 1947.
[11] *Ibid.*, p. 80.
[12] Cf. Labor Committee, *op. cit.*, p. 145; E. W. Bakke, *op. cit.*, p. 80.

each carries regarding needs for good performance and how these motivate each to seek his own aims. Actions taken are appraised in full awareness of effects upon mutual goals rather than upon individual survival.

HUMAN RELATIONS ARE MORE THAN BARGAINING RELATIONS

The tenor of this discussion places attention upon bargaining relations between management and the union. But this focus is too narrow for the problem of group collaboration. The whole social structure of a work plant is involved in the day-by-day, hour-by-hour procession of human contacts that shape the lives of those who both labor and manage. Union and non-union employees, major and minor managers, foremen and supervisors make up a work plant community. In a very real way, all employees are, as Drucker put it, citizens in the work plant.

Labor-management leaders agree that "Once a real plant community has been developed by a number of successes in the solution of mutual problems, then there will come, slowly to be sure, a mature assumption of responsibility; a set of duties as well as rewards; a shop routine that is efficient because it is accepted; a sense of the dignity of work, because it is understood and granted a social status; a feeling of security that comes from playing a recognized role among one's fellows: a will to produce in behalf of a series of objectives that are chosen by a functioning, alert, cooperating, and profitable plant community."[13]

The problem of group collaboration as we see it is the problem of building good human relationships in all of the work groups which make up a work plant community. A study of how morale and teamwork may be built inevitably leads to individual as well as to group approaches. The remainder of this chapter discusses the various methods which may be utilized in building better work relations.

BUILDING MORALE THROUGH INDIVIDUAL APPROACHES

TRAINING FOR SUPERVISORY LEADERSHIP

It is a well-recognized fact from a series of research studies[14] that the first-line supervisor is more important than any other official in determining morale and efficiency within a work group. This recognition has led managers of business, labor, and governmental organizations to an awareness of the importance of their supervisors and has brought about changes in

[13] Labor Committee, *op. cit.*, pp. 130-131.
[14] Cf. John B. Fox and Jerome F. Scott, *Absenteeism: Management's Problem*, Harvard University Press, 1943; Elton Mayo and George F. F. Lombard, *Teamwork and Labor Turnover in the Aircraft Industry of Southern California*, Harvard University Press, 1944.

selection and training. A new kind of foreman has appeared in those companies which have come to select men who exhibit ability to handle people rather than those who show only high proficiency in the technical detail of a department. Unfortunately, ideal first-line supervisors do not appear in great numbers. Many must be trained in supervisory relations. Many must be trained to attain technical proficiency. Those who can combine both abilities through either experience or training are not easily produced. But the need for more socially responsive, technically competent supervisors is perhaps the truly great shortage affecting organized work effort.

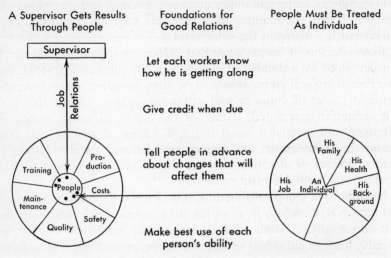

F<small>IG</small>. 54. The Foundations of Good Job Relations. (From the *Job Relations Manual*, War Manpower Commission, United States Government Printing Office, June, 1944, p. 20.)

Supervisory training in work relations is one way to raise the social awareness and social skills of supervisors. Continuous supervisory training is going on in those organizations which have appreciated that the major question of production is not what makes the worker more productive but what makes the worker more willing. Good supervision tends to bring willing, coöperative effort and with it high levels of production *under conditions of mutual trust and interest.*

The wartime efforts of Training Within Industry of the United States War Manpower Commission in their Job Relations Training Program indicate the way modern supervisory relations were taught in terms that every foreman could understand.

At the outset the foreman is led to see that "*good supervision* means that the supervisor gets the people in his department to do *what* he wants done, *when* it should be done, and the *way* he wants it done, because they want

to do it."[15] He is led to appreciate that people constitute the core of his responsibility.

Trainer: "I was in a group not long ago where one supervisor said, 'I make wire.' Did that supervisor make wire?"

Answer drawn from foremen: "No, he supervised a department in which many people worked together to turn out the wire."

Now step by step the foreman is led through the Foundations for Good Relations until he sees the relationships shown in Figure 54.

Through this blackboard chart he can picture each of his actions as affecting the job relations line between himself and the people he supervises. He comes to see that every action either strengthens or weakens that job relations line. He is taught to consider the effect of his actions on the individual, the group, and on production. A four-step approach to handling a problem is presented, and the supervisor uses his own problems in practicing this approach. He carries with him a card which reminds him of the method he should always practice. It reads:

How to Handle a Problem

1—GET THE FACTS
Review the record.
Find out what rules and plant customs apply.
Talk with individuals concerned.
Get opinions and feelings.
Be sure you have the whole story.

2—WEIGH AND DECIDE
Fit the facts together.
Consider their bearing on each other.
Check practices and policies.
What possible actions are there?
Consider effect on individual, group, and production.
Don't jump at conclusions.

3—TAKE ACTION
Are you going to handle this yourself?
Do you need help in handling?
Should you refer this to your supervisor?
Watch the timing of your action.
Don't pass the buck.

4—CHECK RESULTS
How soon will you follow up?
How often will you need to check?
Watch for changes in output, attitudes, and relationships.
Did your action help production?

Modern supervisory training is supplemented by films, slides, check lists, company bulletins, and newsletters which assist in the learning of the social

[15] *Job Relations Manual,* War Manpower Commission, United States Government Printing Office, June 1, 1944, p. 19.

skills of foremanship. The newer technique of role playing as described in the preceding chapter on worker placement is a promising development. Through role playing the foreman not only learns what to do in a specific situation but *how* to do it. A laboratory experiment of role playing is suggested at the end of this chapter.

In many organizations it is recognized that the foreman wants to feel he is a responsible and participating member of the management. Such organizations give their foremen opportunities to participate in conferences concerned with company policies and problems.

These management conferences shorten the communication lines between top management and the supervisor. Effectuating the social machinery to make these conferences work is a matter of group organization and will be discussed under group approaches to the building of teamwork. Meanwhile, three other methods of improving individual morale are of importance. The first of these is employee counseling.

EMPLOYEE COUNSELING

Most counseling programs now operating in industry came into being during the Second World War. Many of these have been eliminated or are operating with skeleton staffs. Counseling cannot yet be regarded as an established function within industry. This is not because counseling has not proved its worth but may be explained as:

1. The decline in the proportion of women workers, for whom most counseling programs were instituted.
2. The relatively high cost of well-trained counselors.
3. The growing feeling that the supervisor should learn to handle the counseling problems of his own department.

In spite of these factors hindering the growth of employee counseling many companies have continued to place confidence in the value of the services which counseling can provide. Two well-known companies long before the Second World War had established either counseling or psychiatric service for their employees. In 1922 the Metropolitan Life Insurance Company through its medical department offered psychiatric and mental health services. In 1925, R. H. Macy & Company began a mental hygiene program. In 1927 the Western Electric Company began the interviewing program which was described in Chapter III. These companies have discovered that the feelings and attitudes of employees are important in determining morale and productivity. Many companies have found that it *pays* to support counseling programs. Among the leading corporations of the country the following have adopted some form of the counselor plan.

AC Spark Plug Division
Allis-Chalmers Mfg. Co.
Bell Aircraft Corp.

Boeing Airplane Co.
Briggs Mfg. Co.
The Carborundum Co.
J. I. Case Mfg. Co.
Colt Patent Fire Arms Mfg. Co.
Curtiss Wright Corp., Airplane Division,
    Buffalo and St. Louis
Douglass Aircraft Co.
Eastern Aircraft Division
General Motors
International Harvester Co.
Lockheed Aircraft Corp.
Metropolitan Life Insurance Co.
North American Aviation Inc.
Oregon Shipbuilding Co.
Republic Aviation Corp.
Republic Drill and Tool Co.
Servel Inc.
Southern Pacific Co.
Sperry Gyroscope Co.
Twin Cities Ordinance
United States War Department
Vickers, Inc.
Warner and Swasey Co.
Western Electric Co.
Wright Aeronautical Co.[16]

Nathaniel Cantor found that counselors in the various companies accumulated widely different functions. Their duties fell into three classes: (1) providing information to the employee, such as interpretation of company policy; (2) gathering information for the personnel director to coordinate the departments' activities; (3) providing personal service to the employee through interviews. It is believed that the first two classes should not be attached to the counselor's duties, that the counselor should be free to devote his attention to the personal problems of employees. Cantor says, "The consultant has one job only: to help the employee find the solution to his own emotional problem in his own way and at his own tempo."[17] The end result is finally more satisfied and more productive employees. The feeling that the organization cares what happens to people is an industrial relation asset which can grow out of the operation of a professional counseling program. As such it is a personnel program that affects not only those who need help but all employees who regard the counselors as friends and

[16] Nathaniel Cantor, *Employee Counseling*, McGraw-Hill Book Company, Inc., 1945, p. 24.
[17] *Ibid.*, p. 66.

the interest of the organization as a sincere one. Figurę 55 shows how representative plants all over the country responded to a questionnaire sent to them by *Factory Management and Maintenance*. Their favorable impression of counseling is clearly indicated.

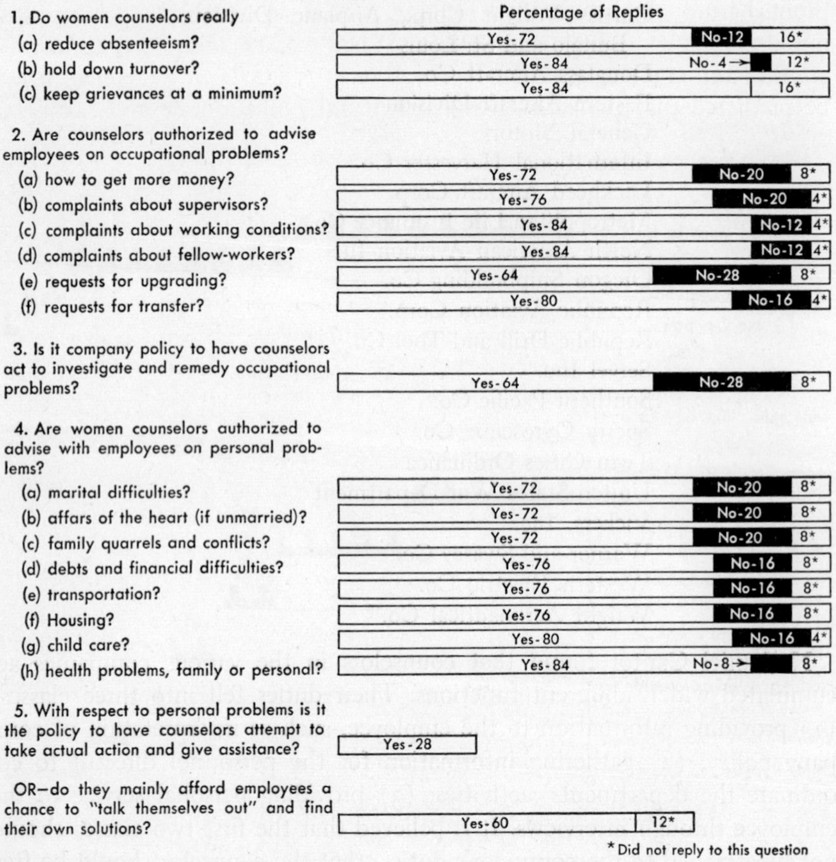

1. Do women counselors really
   (a) reduce absenteeism?
   (b) hold down turnover?
   (c) keep grievances at a minimum?

Percentage of Replies

Yes-72   No-12   16*
Yes-84   No-4→   12*
Yes-84   16*

2. Are counselors authorized to advise employees on occupational problems?
   (a) how to get more money?
   (b) complaints about supervisors?
   (c) complaints about working conditions?
   (d) complaints about fellow-workers?
   (e) requests for upgrading?
   (f) requests for transfer?

Yes-72   No-20   8*
Yes-76   No-20   4*
Yes-84   No-12   4*
Yes-84   No-12   4*
Yes-64   No-28   8*
Yes-80   No-16   4*

3. Is it company policy to have counselors act to investigate and remedy occupational problems?

Yes-64   No-28   8*

4. Are women counselors authorized to advise with employees on personal problems?
   (a) marital difficulties?
   (b) affars of the heart (if unmarried)?
   (c) family quarrels and conflicts?
   (d) debts and financial difficulties?
   (e) transportation?
   (f) Housing?
   (g) child care?
   (h) health problems, family or personal?

Yes-72   No-20   8*
Yes-72   No-20   8*
Yes-72   No-20   8*
Yes-76   No-16   8*
Yes-76   No-16   8*
Yes-76   No-16   8*
Yes-80   No-16   4*
Yes-84   No-8→   8*

5. With respect to personal problems is it the policy to have counselors attempt to take actual action and give assistance?

Yes-28

OR—do they mainly afford employees a chance to "talk themselves out" and find their own solutions?

Yes-60   12*

* Did not reply to this question

Fig. 55. The Opinions of Representative American Employers Regarding Counseling. (From *Factory Management and Maintenance*, March, 1944, p. 126.)

INCENTIVES

Financial incentives are usually successful only if other basic needs are felt to be secure. If a financial incentive is to succeed, a worker cannot feel that he is "working himself out of a job," "pushing up" the standard rate, or injuring the security of a fellow worker. Unless safeguards are provided, workers everywhere tend to repeat the restriction of their output which marked the Hawthorne bank wiring group.[18]

[18] F. J. Roethlisberger and W. J. Dickson, *Management and the Worker*, Harvard University Press, 1939; Charleton Bradshaw, "Sure, I Could Produce More," *Harper's*

Inevitably, the analysis of incentives soon leads to deeper underlying problems such as effects of mechanization on job security, the impact of a depression, or conflicts over the division of returns between wages and profits. Although financial incentives such as bonus, commission, and profit-sharing plans have had striking success in some plants they have raised many new difficulties in others. When workers are pitted against one another and come to feel that their job security has been weakened, it may be predicted that the incentive plan will not build morale and teamwork.

When a man takes a job in a factory, how much work should he turn out?

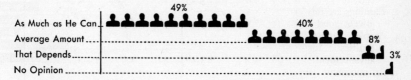

What do you think would happen if he turns out **more** than the average (addressed to those who said "average amount")?

FIG. 56. What the Worker Really Thinks About Productivity. (From *Factory Management and Maintenance*, January, 1946, p. 83.)

And it will not bring increased production. In Figure 56 the fears of workers are graphically demonstrated. Any incentive plan must come to terms with these hesitations.

Perhaps many managers who have introduced incentive plans have done so on the false assumption that more than anything else the worker wants more money. The take-home pay is important to the worker. He does want the share of the production which he has earned but not at the expense of year-around security on his job or the approval of his fellow workers.

In this sense there are probably no "individual" incentives. What exists

Magazine, May, 1947, pp. 396-340; Stanley B. Mathewson, *Restriction of Output Among Unorganized Workers*, The Viking Press, 1931.

TABLE 18. Morale Groups by Characteristics of the Job

Characteristics	Men			Women			Men High Women High C. R.[c] Col. 1 Compared with Col. 3	Men Low Women Low C. R.[c] Col. 2 Compared with Col. 4
	Percentage High Morale[a] 1.	Percentage Low Morale[a] 2.	Critical Ratio[b] Col. 1 Compared with Col. 2	Percentage High Morale[a] 3.	Percentage Low Morale[a] 4.	Critical Ratio[b] Col. 3 Compared with Col. 4		
1. Income is fairly certain	83	66	+2.83	93	90	—	−2.01	−3.93
2. Tenure is fairly certain	79	66	+1.95	83	75	—	—	—
3. Earnings are relatively good	85	64	+3.46	78	69	—	—	—
4. Ample opportunities for advancement	66	43	+3.28	42	15	+3.57	+3.02	+5.18
5. Advancement is relatively rapid	43	21	+3.28	24	9	+2.30	+2.49	—
6. Advancement on basis of merit	73	43	+4.34	47	22	+3.00	+3.23	+2.88
7. Competition is too intense	12	33	−3.52	5	2	—	—	—
8. Work possesses prestige	76	53	+3.42	63	58	—	—	—
9. Contact with many pleasant people	92	78	+2.80	94	74	+3.32	—	—
10. Reasonable freedom on the job	92	84	—[d]	89	85	—	—	—
11. Friends approve of job	91	79	+2.39	88	89	—	—	—
12. Employers are congenial	90	87	—	88	94	—	—	—
13. Family obligations can be satisfied	87	69	+3.01	83	69	—	—	—
14. Personal life is one's own	73	76	—	71	72	—	—	—
15. Family members approve of job	96	71	+4.98	85	92	—	—	−3.74
16. Work is healthful	80	63	+2.67	81	69	—	—	—
17. Working hours of right length	68	70	—	81	84	—	—	−2.19
18. Work is too fatiguing	3	14	−2.76	14	15	—	−2.38	—
19. Work is too monotonous	6	15	−2.05	11	25	−2.18	—	—
20. Work is in line with my abilities	88	70	+3.12	81	75	—	—	—

is a system of rewards and penalties which influences all workers. For this reason incentives gain meaning only as carriers of social values to a work group.

The personnel consulting firm McKinsey and Company urges that non-financial incentives should be the foundation of any well-rounded plan. Such a plan would emphasize better working conditions, better opportunities for advancement, and sound personnel policies.[19]

EMPLOYEE PRACTICES

Industry has adopted a large number of practices in the belief that they would help morale and increase worker productivity. Figure 57 shows the kinds of practices and the degree to which 1200 companies were adhering to them in September, 1943. The interest of the industrial sociologist is focused on the appraisal of their effectiveness. To what extent will they raise or lower morale? The Western Electric studies have shown that how workers regard these practices is more important than the presence or absence of the practices themselves. *What is of crucial importance in a given work plant is the extent to which the personality needs of workers are satisfied.* At this point the researcher must come to the assistance of the personnel administrator. What does research show is important for the morale of the worker?

JOB FACTORS ASSOCIATED WITH MORALE

The basic human needs of workers have been fairly well identified and were stated earlier, in the discussion of what workers want. The specific characteristics of the job which influence morale have also been studied.[20] In one study, 951 college-trained adults were measured on the Rundquist-Sletto morale scale.[21] A hundred men and a hundred women of the highest and a hundred men and a hundred women of the lowest morale were sorted out and their responses to various characteristics of their job were compared. Table 18 shows responses of these morale groups to twenty characteristics of the job.

[19] "Stores Turn to Incentive Plans," *Business Week*, June 29, 1946, p. 76. An outstanding discussion of incentives is that of Alexander R. Heron, *Why Men Work*, Stanford University Press, 1948.

[20] D. C. Miller, "Economic Factors in the Morale of College Trained Adults," *American Journal of Sociology*, September, 1941, pp. 139-156.

[21] E. A. Rundquist and R. F. Sletto, *Personality in the Depression*, University of Minnesota Press, 1936.

---

[a] Data represent those who answered "Yes."

[b] +C.R. indicates higher percentage in high-morale group; −C.R. indicates higher percentage in low-morale group.

[c] +C.R. indicates higher percentage among men; −C.R. indicates higher percentage among women.

[d] Values for critical ratios below 2.00 have been omitted as too far below a confidence level.

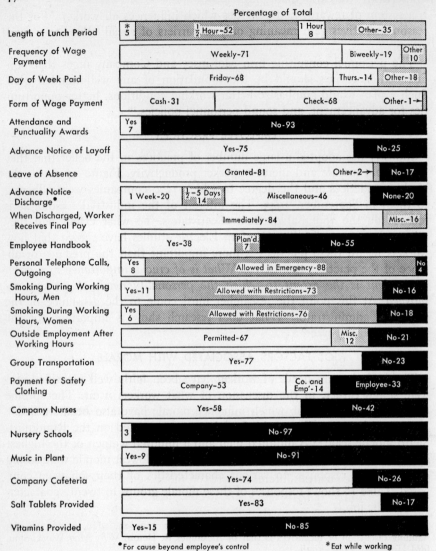

Percentage of Total

Length of Lunch Period	*5 — ½ Hour-52 — 1 Hour 8 — Other-35
Frequency of Wage Payment	Weekly-71 — Biweekly-19 — Other 10
Day of Week Paid	Friday-68 — Thurs.-14 — Other-18
Form of Wage Payment	Cash-31 — Check-68 — Other-1→
Attendance and Punctuality Awards	Yes 7 — No-93
Advance Notice of Layoff	Yes-75 — No-25
Leave of Absence	Granted-81 — Other-2→ — No-17
Advance Notice Discharge*	1 Week-20 — ½-5 Days 14 — Miscellaneous-46 — None-20
When Discharged, Worker Receives Final Pay	Immediately-84 — Misc.-16
Employee Handbook	Yes-38 — Plan'd. 7 — No-55
Personal Telephone Calls, Outgoing	Yes 8 — Allowed in Emergency-88 — No 4
Smoking During Working Hours, Men	Yes-11 — Allowed with Restrictions-73 — No-16
Smoking During Working Hours, Women	Yes 6 — Allowed with Restrictions-76 — No-18
Outside Employment After Working Hours	Permitted-67 — Misc. 12 — No-21
Group Transportation	Yes-77 — No-23
Payment for Safety Clothing	Company-53 — Co. and Emp'-14 — Employee-33
Company Nurses	Yes-58 — No-42
Nursery Schools	3 — No-97
Music in Plant	Yes-9 — No-91
Company Cafeteria	Yes-74 — No-26
Salt Tablets Provided	Yes-83 — No-17
Vitamins Provided	Yes-15 — No-85

*For cause beyond employee's control   *Eat while working

FIG. 57.   Guide to Personnel Practices. (From *Factory Management and Maintenance*, March, 1944, p. 130.)

Men

Significant differences between men of high and low morale show that three major considerations are associated with morale. These are (1) the social approval which the job holder feels he has acquired from his job; (2) the opportunity he feels he has for advancement; (3) the return he feels he is getting for his labor.

1. The importance of social approval is shown by the association of high morale when the men report that family members approve of their job, that their work possesses prestige, and that friends approve of their job.

2. Characteristics of advancement are associated with morale as shown by the responses to "advancement on basis of merit," "Ample opportunities for advancement," and "Advancement is relatively rapid."

3. High morale is associated with the feeling that there are satisfying rewards for the labor exerted. This is to be seen in the series including "Earnings are relatively good," "Family obligations can be satisfied," "Income is fairly certain," "Tenure is fairly certain," "Contact with many pleasant people," and "Work is healthful."

Although only a small percentage answered in agreement, significantly more low-morale men complained that competition is too intense, the work too monotonous and fatiguing.

Women

Women may need approval of their job, but our data do not reveal differences between high- and low-morale groups. Apparently, the college-trained women of the sample have jobs which they feel are approved. This is understandable since only 9 percent are working in manual activity.

The significant differences for women appear in (1) the characteristics of advancement and (2) satisfaction with the environmental conditions of their work. Associations with advancement are demonstarted in the affirmative answers of high-morale persons and in the denial of this opportunity reported by the low-morale persons. These statements reveal significant differences:

1. Of the items "Ample opportunities for advancement," "Advancement on basis of merit," and "Advancement is relatively rapid," it is interesting to note that the greatest difference between morale groups of women should occur on "Ample opportunities for advancement." Although the women are classified in high occupational classes, it appears that advancement is limited for many of them. Many women, doubtlessly, have seen less-trained men promoted over them since our culture has traditionally assigned most leadership roles to men. The struggle of the single or the married woman to hold her job in the face of increasing male competition may diminish the opportunities for advancement.

2. The rewards for labor which are associated with high morale are seen in "Contacts with many pleasant people," "Family obligations can be satisfied," and "Work is healthful." Associated with low morale among women (with a small percentage reporting) is a feeling that the work is too monotonous.

Men Compared with Women

Striking differences occur between men and women. Men have greater advancement opportunities but less security and tenure. Low-morale men also feel that they have less approval of their jobs by others than do women. Women are more satisfied with the length of their working hours than are the men but complain of the fatigue and monotony of their work more often than do the men.

SUMMARY

The examination of personal approaches to the problem of building morale has shown that workers are constantly evaluating their rewards and their satisfactions by comparing themselves with others who work or whose approval is important to them. It is inevitable that the problem of morale should become the problem of teamwork, for the individual worker simply does not exist apart from a work group, a family, a congeniality group, a community, or a nation. Increasingly, administrators and researchers are turning their attention to the worker in the group and are thinking more and more about group approaches to the building of teamwork.

BUILDING TEAMWORK THROUGH GROUP APPROACHES

When we approach the problem of teamwork our focus moves from the individual worker to the work group. The size of the work group may vary from two persons to thousands, depending upon the situation. The social researcher and the plant administrator will probably assume different perspectives and responsibilities as they work at the same problems. Both, however, must come to recognize that the problem of building morale and teamwork in a business organization breaks down into two parts. F. J. Roethlisberger has stated these as "(1) the daily problems of maintaining internal equilibrium within the organization, that is, maintaining that kind of social organization in which individuals and groups through working together can obtain human satisfactions that will make them willing to contribute their services to the economic objective of cooperation, and (2) the daily problems of diagnosing possible sources of interference, of locating sore spots, or liquidating human tensions and strains among individuals and groups, of spotting blockages in the channels of communication."[22]

DIFFICULTIES OF GROUP FORMATION

Research has clearly demonstrated that no external remedies can change a fundamental defect within the organization itself.[23] This finding has

[22] F. J. Roethlisberger, *Management and Morale*, Harvard University Press, 1947, p. 192.

[23] Elton Mayo and George F. F. Lombard, *op. cit.*, p. 2.

important consequences for all personnel practice. It gives the lie to any quick or clever programs which purport to revolutionize morale, training, or productivity. The social structure of a business organization is not a simple mechanism. It is made up of many different workers with many different needs. But one of the most fundamental of these needs workers share together. This is the deep-seated desire for close-knit association such as is implied by the "team." And yet in spite of the desire for such association good work teams do not just happen.

The Nature of a Work Team

Individuals must be welded together to form effective work teams. Individuals express a wide range of differences in today's highly differentiated society. Common purpose and sentiment are not easily developed. E. W. Bakke has caught and explained this with good humor. He asks,

What makes a team out of a crowd of individuals? Here they are in a plant or in a union. They've come from all sorts of social, political, religious, and economic backgrounds. They've been brought up in different ways. Some are polite, considerate, and respectful; others are swashbuckling, bigoted pirates, born a hundred and thirty years too late. Some are skilled, competent chaps who know what to do and how to do it; others are fumbling fellows with ten thumbs on their hands and solid bone for brain. Some of them are natural cooperators; others make the sparks fly whenever they come within sight of another person. The job is to take this bunch of varied individuals and weld them into a team.[24]

The team, when formed, is a group of persons who share common purposes and symbols. Individual effort and will are subordinated to group effort and will. A code of behavior develops and the group begins to exercise a discipline over its own members. Elton Mayo, who became so conscious of the importance of the group in his later studies, describes the way in which work groups come to support formal organization:

As a team begins to form, it takes over the task of maintaining communication with all its members. The need for administration is not done away with, but it can be less concerned with problems of achieving the intimate discipline necessary to promote the objectives of the organization—regular attendance, for instance. This function the team takes over for itself; and it is a function that, if management alone is concerned with it, leads almost inextricably to an ever complicating web of complaints, the settlement of one of which serves only to provoke the expression of another. Thus teams and administration, the relation among workers and their relations to their supervisors, support each other when there is a balance in administration among technical, operational, and human considerations; where there is no balance, the result is discord and inefficiency.[25]

[24] E. W. Bakke, "Teamwork in Industry," *Scientific Monthly*, March, 1948, p. 214.
[25] Mayo and Lombard, *op. cit.*, p. 2.

The Administrator's Problem

The business administrator who recognizes the importance of work teams must try somehow to make his entire department function as a unified group. This requires a high degree of social skill. The scarcity of administrators who possess such skill is great. Those who have it find that the conditions of modern industry make it most difficult to build work groups. Layoffs, voluntary and involuntary terminations, transfers, and promotions move workers about with such rapidity that bonds of human sentiment often do not have a chance to form or are constantly being broken.

The administrator must learn to build work teams in this kind of setting. How shall he go about it?

E. W. Bakke has examined the bonds of organization which provide the cohesion between members of a work group and has shown the kind of inadequacies which break down teamwork.[26]

FIVE BONDS OF ORGANIZATION

The bonds which hold individuals together are the same for a factory, an army, a football squad, or a union. They are (1) job specifications and requirements, (2) the communication system, (3) the status system, (4) the system of rewards and punishments, (5) the organizational charter. Each of these bonds will be illustrated by references to new research efforts which throw light on the organization of team work.

I. Job Specifications

The first requirement of teamwork is that each worker shall understand clearly what his job is and how it relates to the jobs of those with whom he works. Increasingly, companies have made job analyses and organization charts to show with definiteness what each worker is responsible for and what authority he has delegated to him.

Job specifications may be unwritten, but in any event they must be understood by all members of a work team. The manager especially must know what the requirements of workers in his employ are if he is to understand the effect of his actions upon their work. Labor relations are improved when managers can understand the responsibilities and pressures under which labor leaders must work. Union leaders, in turn, are probably more successful when they have a clear understanding of the manager's position.

In general, managers and union leaders have given close attention to job specifications, but it is not uncommon to find workers in all levels of an organization who are uncertain of their responsibilities or their authority. In the last ten years the lead-man position has been causing much difficulty in the factory. The lead man ordinarily serves a small group in the capacities

[26] Bakke, "Teamwork in Industry," *Scientific Monthly*, March, 1948.

of instructor, setup man, and worker. He is often made responsible for orders and productivity while at the same time being denied the authority of a supervisor to issue orders or command discipline. The lead man complains that his responsibilities are not matched by an equivalent measure of authority and that this causes him great difficulty. His role, he feels, is imperfectly defined. Management replies that since he may join a union he cannot be trusted too far with the authority of a supervisor.

This contradiction of function and authority is not uncommon at other levels of organization since informal, unwritten responsibilities often operate in the place of formally designated specifications. This may be seen in cases in which a "weak" man holds a responsible position by virtue of "pull" or seniority or some other reason besides merit and many of his responsibilities are simply taken over informally by others. This can also happen to a capable but timid worker when an aggressive fellow worker or manager invades and seizes responsibility and authority not formally designated to him. Bakke has listed four other major inadequacies:

1. The specifications neglect the definition of how a particular job is related to other jobs.

2. They fail to leave an area of freedom for the initiative and inventiveness of the worker.

3. The job specifications are not matched with the actual or potential abilities of the job holder.

4. Changes are made so frequently and perhaps arbitrarily that workers do not know what they are expected to do or how their jobs are related to those with whom they work.[27]

II. Communication System

A method of communication is the second essential for good teamwork. Information must constantly flow to workers explaining what must be done, how it must be done, and why it must be done. This kind of information must not only get down the line of authority but go up the line as recommendations and suggestions. An organization which has teamwork understands where it is going and why it moves in a given direction. No company is so big that it can afford to let its workers be cut off from information vital to technical or social needs of the organization. Alexander Heron calls on management to develop an *aggressive willingness* to *share* with employees important facts about their organization, its progress and its plans. Yet inadequacies in the communication system of industry are very common, for difficulties grow apace in larger units. Some of these inadequacies have been as follows:

1. The communication system which was otherwise satisfactory simply was not used to carry down the kinds of information needed and desired.

[27] *Ibid.*, p. 219.

Workers want to know about their company as a totality. They want to know how the company fits within the larger social and economic structure and how it is prepared to meet changing conditions.

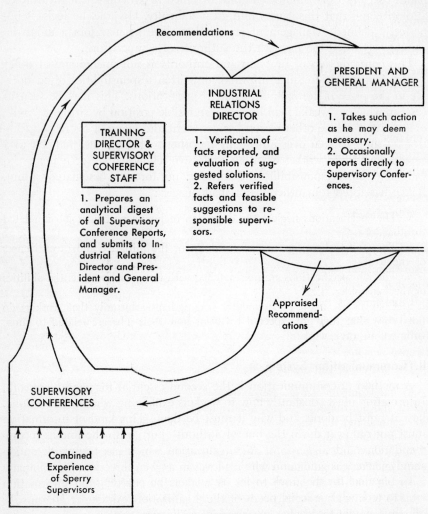

FIG. 58.   Supervisory Conferences as a Two-Way Channel for the Development of Policy and Procedures.

2. The communication system did not function to bring information up the line. The day-by-day reactions of workers, their suggestions, recommendations, and grievances provide top management with a valuable source of information with which to improve the *efficiency* and *effectiveness* of their organization. Everyone wants a chance to have his say. A channel must be

open, and interested leaders must be available to hear and listen if team-work is to be more than an empty word.

3. The communication line was not short and direct enough to carry information in either direction so that it came out as it was started. Distortion is common on long communication lines and misunderstandings may result.

4. Persons communicating information either lacked authority or had their position so poorly defined in the eyes of those who received the information that the messages were received with a lack of confidence and sometimes mistrust.

5. The communications were so designed that they did not inspire acceptance of them as sincere explanations. As a result they were often regarded as management excuses or efforts to conceal the underlying facts which workers wanted to know.

EFFORTS TO IMPROVE THE COMMUNICATION SYSTEM THROUGH SUPERVISORY CONFERENCES

Increasing attention is being given to these inadequacies in communication systems. Many companies are redefining supervisory training as supervisory conferences. Figure 58 shows the kind of two-way channel recommended to one large industrial company in order to open the largest possible flow of two-way information in the shortest possible time. The machinery suggested was based on regular and continuous conferences, with foremen, supervisors, and executives meeting in small groups of fifteen to twenty persons.

The writers of the report wrote:

As our Company grows, and as organizational distances increase, both vertically and horizontally, there is greater need to help the supervisor feel that he still counts, and that the "boss is still interested in him and what he hopes he can contribute to the company." *There is no more effective way to do this than through the frank exchange of ideas gathered in conference, pooled in conclusions, and hammered into recommendations.*

The channel for the development of policies and procedures becomes a two way channel only when there is recognition by management so that supervisors feel their recommendations have been received, appraised, and considered for action. That recognition is best when it comes from the highest responsible official. It would seem desirable in our Company for the Industrial Relations Director to prepare reports which can be read or sent to the Supervisory Conference Groups at frequent intervals preferably once every month. An occasional letter from the General Manager or President would do much to convince supervisors of management's sincere interest.[28]

[28] R. L. Witham, James H. Russell, and Delbert C. Miller, *Report on the Supervisory Conference Plan*, Sperry Gyroscope Company, 1942, pp. 45-46.

EFFORTS TO IMPROVE THE COMMUNICATION SYSTEM BY REDUCTION OF THE
  LEVELS OF AUTHORITY

The International Business Machines Corporation at Endicott, New
York, has pioneered in reducing levels of authority and thus reducing the
length of the communication line. Between 1940 and 1947 the company
doubled in size and was faced with all the inevitable difficulties of an expanding industry. In 1940 there were in the plant seven levels of authority
for those working in the main manufacturing departments. These were the
executive's assistant, superintendent, assistant superintendent, department
supervisor, foreman, assistant, and operator.

By 1947 the number of levels was cut to four by dropping the assistant
foreman and by making the superintendent the plant head in charge of all
manufacturing. This reduction still fell short of the company's policy of
seeking to establish but three levels in the factory. The company policy is
to support a structure composed of what it calls *management, manager,*
and *man.*

These changes have increased the number of men acting as foreman or
manager and have reduced section by section the number of workers supervised. Greater responsibility for human relations was given the foreman.
He was as far as possible to manage all the affairs of his own particular
section. He was to be selected not only for his technical and supervisory
ability but also for his qualifications as a human relations manager.

Richardson and Walker, who have appraised these changes in organization, have written: "These adjustments had the effect of increasing, or at
least retaining, the frequency and improving the quality of contacts characteristic of the smaller scale operations, and of simplifying the complicated
method of dealing with dissatisfied employees characteristic of large companies. The decreased number of dissatisfied employees, the marked increase
in plant productivity plus the testimony of supervisory personnel suggests
that human relations in the company had, during the same period, not only
continued satisfactory but had improved."[29]

III. The Status System

A third requirement of good teamwork is a status system which functions
in such a way that the worker's sense of justice is not violated. A status
system of some kind is bound to arise. The formal structure of an organization with its organization chart places people in positions carrying authority
over and obligations to others. Sometimes the actual organization of status
varies widely from the organization chart as workers informally compare
and evaluate one another. For teamwork, the informal status system should

[29] F. L. W. Richardson, Jr., and Charles R. Walker, *Human Relations in an Expanding Company*, Yale University Labor and Management Center, 1948, p. 31.

be consistent with the formal status system. The University of Washington has a procedure of "jury rating" to determine promotions of faculty members. A jury of five colleagues from the faculty submit their personal rating of a faculty candidate following a standardized scale. On the basis of their ratings and other considerations promotion is either achieved or denied. This procedure is based on the recognized importance of keeping the formal status structure consistent with the informal status system.

Violations of this principle cause teamwork difficulties. Some of the inadequacies which Bakke finds common to organizations include:

1. A confused structure of authority causing workers to be uncertain to whom they must look for guidance and formal approval.
2. An autocratic structure which denies any real sense of importance to all except those at the very top.
3. A violation of merit in the selection of persons relative to the performance expected within a given position.

IV. System of Rewards and Punishments

Teamwork requires satisfactions of attainment. Rewards range from simple praise—"Good work, Joe"—to monetary rewards and honorific titles. Punishments range from the ignoring of a worker to definite denial of advancement in status or money.

The system of rewards and punishments is one of the most important instruments of policy in determining good human relations within a work group. If it is to be effective, it must operate so as to be consistent with the view held by the people who are rewarded or punished. The failure of managers to take such a view results in many defects in the system. Some of these are as follows:

1. The system is not understood by all concerned; misunderstanding arises between worker and manager.
2. The system of distribution is without plan, and rewards and punishments are distributed arbitrarily.
3. Equal pay is not distributed for equal work; such maldistribution violates workers' sense of justice.
4. The system rewards in such a way as to induce conflict by rivalry among individual workers rather than to encourage coöperation in groups. This is done by wage systems which reward individual achievement rather than team accomplishments.
5. The system emphasizes economic reward at the expense of a desire of workers for social respect and self-respect.

V. The Organizational Charter

Bakke uses the concept of the organizational charter to refer to the picture that members of the team have of the team as a whole. The concept

is similar to Durkheim's notion of *"collective representations."* The reference is to the image which appears in the minds of a group as they reflect on the purposes, achievements, traditions, and symbols of the group. It is the picture that workers have who say, "I work for Boeing Aircraft Company" or "I am a member of the United Auto Workers of America."

The picture which workers have of different business organizations varies widely.

"FEMALE FACTORY HAND"

Recently the *New Statesman and Nation*, an English journal, published a letter from Pearl Jephcott, a "female factory hand" in London, England. Perhaps the picture is all too typical of the company image carried by industrial workers. She writes:

Three months ago I got a job as a general factory hand at A. Nons Ltd. I knew nothing of the firm except what it made; that it stood on a London by-pass among a batch of buildings with a 1938-ish look; and that a lot of girls were said to work there. Even now I don't know how many people Nons employ, though I'd estimate about five hundred. It's been as difficult to get casual information on that as on other factual points about our firm. What I have accumulated, however, is a plateful of theories on the standard industrial headaches. One stands out—the desirability of some measure of democracy at work for the unskilled female employee.

I've done three jobs in the three months. On job A I stood or sat at a runway. Boxes trundled along it, four to the minute. I did one of three things: inserted a couple of pieces of paper, thrust in a handful of shavings, or fixed the lid on. In job B a conveyor bore two species of boxes, old and new. I lifted off the latter. Job C is less complex. Only one kind of box sails along the belt. But it weighs 8 lbs. and has to be stacked into a pile 12 feet by 14 feet, behind me. I can see, and occasionally am near enough to talk to, one of six other stackers: and I can snatch disjointed bits of conversation with the girls and women who, at intervals, carry off the boxes on trucks to the delivery vans. In other words, I'm on a typical stock-room job. Most, not all of us, dislike "stacking." My mate, for example, a cautious middle-aged woman, finds it quite satisfactory—no interference, no hustle, and nothing in it to worry you.

We have a 44-hour week and regard the pay as reasonably good. The weekly £3 12s. I get is 2s. 5d. more than the average for women manual wage earners. The amenities, which are good too, we take for granted. The surroundings are light, airy, clean, gaily painted and not overpoweringly noisy except in certain spots. We have all the standard facilities—a first-rate canteen; nurses; hot water; music while you work; pension schemes. We see notices about cricket and tennis, but the only voluntary activity which has touched my mate or me was the Derby sweep.

This doesn't mean we have no sport at work. Any amount of banter, joking, bottom-slapping and robust, inhibited liveliness crops up among ourselves, and between us and any men engineers and electricians who, at rare intervals, come

into our orbit. Individuals burst into abrupt, strident snatches of song, "Cos I *love* my blossom," or "Ave Maria." No one frowns on this. It's part of the lustiness and bonhomie which sets us apart from schools and offices with their middle-class traditions of the solemnness of work. Moral disapproval seldom blights us. The youngster who larks about and upsets a truck isn't a "naughty girl." She's a "young fool." The compensations are obvious.

We are a presentable lot—our rig-outs as multi-coloured as the front gardens of the L. C. C. housing estate where some of us live. Slatterns are out of date. Perms, wedges, turbans and Max Factor mask the range of social strata which we represent. And they camouflage the fence that still divides us unskilled factory hands from the formally educated. My guess is that we are less literate and less socially civilized than our looks suggest. We don't admit it, but I fancy that we are conscious of social and intellectual inferiority. Some of us don't care for the people on the bus to see that we carry a factory overall; and we fairly often refer to the fact that for an office or shop job you need more brains and education than we have.

Our conversation shows up the intellectual level. The girls' talk hardly ranges beyond two themes, personal appearance and personal relations. The latter means fellows—mine, yours, hers. Even among the older women the only public event in the last three months which has fished talk out of the sea of personal and domestic affairs has been the Derby. Again, no one in a group of women in their 40s challenges the assumption that the new higher insurance contribution is just a Government racket to squeeze more cash from us. "Bet Attlee's feathering *his* nest all right." Another indication of limited interests is perhaps shown in the amount of mild innuendo on sex and the physical functions. Half a dozen girls of 19 or 20, if they feel like it, can work this up into an afternoon of sheer bawdiness.

It's partly the narrowness of our feminine factory world which charges our personal relations with such extreme significance. I'd say that on the whole these are good at Nons. The toilets don't produce any heavier crop of malicious gossip than is normal. The cluster of cronies who aren't having any outsider sitting on *their* bench (at the tea break) are amiable enough to other, equally exclusive sets. And we don't discriminate against other departments except for a generic sniff at the office staff. They are no better than us of course, but only about four of our girls have the nerve to go up to the office-frequented tennis club. And there are pointers to positive good will. Old hands show the most obvious of ropes to new ones for days on end. One of us has a financial crisis and there is a whip round for her, quick and quiet.

Few of us show positive feelings, either of attachment or dislike, towards the firm. Among the youngsters, the typical contented girl is satisfied by having good personal relationships (with the half dozen people she works beside), decent working conditions, and reasonably good money. She doesn't bother much what job she actually handles. She assumes that she will marry at about 21-23 (nine of the sixteen girls under 21 whom I've worked alongside in the three months are officially engaged) and that, if she should go back to work later on, it will be just a temporary measure to meet a financial emergency. In other words, her

contentment is based on immediate personal satisfactions. She has no conception of a continuing and ascending career, and no reasoned attachment to the firm.

The discontented girls demonstrate their emotions in cheek, casualness, unsocial behavior and the usual insignia of personal frustration. They are profoundly indifferent to "work"—the boring, petty jobs which don't give them a chance to vent their hostility on overcoming difficulties connected with it. The firm doesn't mean a rap to them. If they realize that a production drive exists, it's "Why work harder for no more pay?" (or for more than you need to buy those wedges on Friday?) Why work at all? Better get married.

Our attitude to trade unions is another disturbing feature. My mate, for example, generous, kind-hearted, and socially co-operative, has no sort of use for the official machinery of a Union—"only makes you discontented." The rest of us share her opinion apparently. We have no Union. Not only have we no Union and no shop stewards, but there is apparently no machinery by which we can get information about our firm. The foreman and the personnel manager are the two we know by name who must have the facts; but people like us, timid as we are about making new contacts even within our own social level, aren't going to any foreman with our questions. And we do need facts. Here are my mate and I, grown women, with the firm for three months, and we know less of the how and why of Nons than any visitor who gapes round of an afternoon. We know nothing of its history, war record, personalities, triumphs—the human story which, to quote our magazines, would touch our little womanly hearts. Profits, losses, experiments, difficulties—where the raw materials come from, where our two thousand boxes each day go off to—who knows? And, of course, we know nothing whatever of our firm's part in the production drive. Are we hitting our target? Have we got a target?

We shouldn't care if we did know? My hunch is that such an assumption underestimates our goodwill and our wits. If that's how management assesses us, I'd say it's too witless itself to realize what social and economic reforms, plus a couple of wars, have done to raise the level of the traditional female factory hand. I've another hunch, that we women are incurably altruistic. We've a passion to be useful—to a person. And some of us would extend this feminine vice from our private life to our job *if* we realized that anyone's well-being depended on us in the national economic crisis or even in A. Nons' unintelligible concerns.

Would it step up production? I can only speak of my own job. I couldn't shift a box *better* certainly; but I could do it a shade more quickly, and I should be much more likely to stay with the firm (and bring down those labour turnover figures) if I had a more intelligent conception of my part in it. What we need is some mental stimulant connected with our working life.[30]

Many industrial organizations have been concerned with attitudes like those of Pearl Jephcott. Some have made serious attempts to do something about it.

[30] Pearl Jephcott, "Female Factory Hand," *New Statesman and Nation*, September 11, 1948.

EFFORTS TO BUILD COMPANY UNITY AT JACK AND HEINTZ

The Jack and Heintz Company of Cleveland commanded nation-wide attention during World War II for its efforts to weld employees into a close identity with the company. President Bill Jack called his employees "associates" and the symbol JAHCO was devised to provide a name for the company which would be easily pronounced and easily reproduced. Soon JAHCO could be seen on the uniform of company work clothes and athletics teams. Bill Jack with his brown shirt, open at the neck, became a symbol of the attempt to reduce the status barrier between management and the worker. His messages over the public-address system were designed to secure increased group effort.

An excerpt from one of these talks, made on D-day, June 12, 1944, illustrates the attempt to strengthen the organizational charter by building stronger in-group ties.

We have one of the biggest jobs ahead of us that any management was ever faced with. I think you all know the policy of this organization—the production manager—the plant manager—the foremen—the supervisors—are carrying the torch for me in their daily activities. They know what I am trying to do in behalf of the associates of JAHCO and their families. I cannot do it myself. I must put it on to their shoulders. There will be and maybe have been many mistakes made and maybe there will be many mistakes made in the future but I wish and I hope and pray that these men who are heading up the various departments, who are doing the job and carrying on the work, will realize what toleration means—fair play—honesty, and don't forget—"Do unto others as you would have others do unto you." This is a big job and I'm trying to spread the doctrine of humanism in industry throughout the United States of America wherever it's possible. I'm fighting this fight for you and the members of your family and for every man and woman who is working for a living. If we are to be successful I must have your support—that means right from the top to the bottom. We must never forget that we have pledged to ourselves that "I will do my part." If you lay down on the job you are not only hurting yourself, you are not only hurting your fellow associates, but you may be hurting some of the boys who are over there as well. So do your best and that's all we can ask at any time.

. . . When we find a man in a department who may be qualified for something better than he is doing, it's up to the superintendent and it's up to the foreman to encourage that man—not discourage. Give him a pat on the back and push him into the job that he knows he's better qualified to do than the one he may be doing. For example, we may have certain men sweeping floors who may be good on one of a dozen things. He may be a plater—he may be a former policeman—he may have been a truck driver—he may have been many things that he may be advanced on with a lot of experience. So those are the type of men that JAHCO is going to need in the future. They are going to have to be drawn from our own people—to make the leaders for JAHCO in the years to

come. So let any superintendent, foreman, or whatnot in this organization—do not discredit a man when he feels that he has something on the ball and wants to put it to use. Because you must remember that there are a lot of people who are sincere in the JAHCO spirit and there isn't anything they wouldn't do to promote the JAHCO spirit. We must never let the JAHCO spirit get in a rut. The associates of this organization must find new ways and means among themselves of keeping the JAHCO spirit alive—keeping it to the forefront—initiating new things that will always help to improve the quality of the products of JAHCO and the morale of JAHCO at all times. When the associates of JAHCO are on the outside, let them recognize that if they do something that isn't according to Hoyle they are hurting the morale of the associates of JAHCO so, please, if you will bear those things in mind, I know that you will be practicing the slogan of "one for all and all for one."[31]

This address of President Bill Jack illustrates something of the art which is management. Behind the color and uniqueness of Bill Jack's personality can also be discerned the science of management. The bonds of organization represent the active forces which any manager must be in command of if he would build groups.

These five bonds of organization, (1) job specifications, (2) communication system, (3) status system, (4) system of rewards and punishments, and (5) organizational charter, are among the basic requirements for a stable social structure in the work plant. When implemented by well-conceived management policy and procedure, effective group formation is possible. This much is known, but many unsolved problems still stand between existing knowledge and practical attainment of the optimum human organization.

UNSOLVED PROBLEMS AWAITING RESEARCH SOLUTION

At present, social scientists know many questions they need to explore to increase their understanding of group formation. When Elton Mayo completed his last research, which was on the wartime problems of teamwork and labor turnover in the aircraft industry, he knew very clearly what kinds of research problems would need to be solved. He urged both researchers and managers to explore and find answers to the following questions:

I. The size of work groups.
   1. Where large numbers of people must work geographically together, what can be done in the organization of their work to stimulate the formation among them of small, effective groups?
   2. What should be the optimum size of a work group from the point of

[31] Rosewell Ward, *The Personnel Program of Jack and Heintz*, Harper & Brothers, 1946, pp. 18-21.

view of a situation as a whole, considering its technical, operating, and human needs together?

II. The building of new groups of workers around common experiences or interests, especially when the individuals concerned have already developed friendships.

1. To what extent can similarities of past experiences and of life outside the factory be used as a basis for the self-creation of teams?

2. To what extent should people who know one another and apply for work together be placed together irrespective of whatever untrained manipulative skills they may possess?

3. To what extent would the enthusiasm resulting from the social satisfactions thus maintained lead to a more willing interest in acquiring the new skills necessary to getting out production?

III. The preservation of work groups in loans and transfers of workers.

1. To what extent is it possible, when the organization of operations requires loans and transfers of workers, to transfer in groups those who on their regular assignments work together, and thus encourage human association in spite of a disorganization of operations?

IV. The selection by management, through acquaintance with its subordinates, of supervisors who can maintain effective communication with their workers.

1. To what extent can management select, as the persons through whom they make their communications to workers, the leaders of teams instead of, as so often happens, the highest producer, who frequently is not a member of the team at all?

2. Would selection of such leaders increase the likelihood that communications from management would be, in the first instance, acceptable to workers as coming from their recognized leader instead of from someone "outside the team"?

V. The use of group incentive payment plans.

1. To what extent can group incentive payment plans be administered to promote the formation of teams?[32]

These questions command inquiry in an area which demands all the research that can be marshaled. Industrial sociologists have just begun to seek answers to them. Mayo and his colleagues have come to certain conclusions based on their studies which provide a valuable orientation for future research.

SOME FUNDAMENTAL CONCLUSIONS

These conclusions may be stated as follows:

First, the desire of individuals for association in work with others is compelling and is sure to find some form of expression in either formal or informal organizations.

Second, working groups will vary in their attitude toward management

[32] Adapted from Mayo and Lombard, *op. cit.*, pp. 3, 29.

from hostile to coöperative and friendly. The usual attitude is one of being wary of whole-hearted coöperation.

Third, effective organization cannot be developed by leaving group formation wholly to circumstance or chance. First-line supervisors must be able to organize teamwork. The most effective supervisors have been able to help individual workers to solve these problems and become a part of a group, to adjust technical difficulties, and to handle for members of the group their contacts with others (inspectors, efficiency men, and the like) in the world outside the immediate work group.

Fourth, rapid changes of personnel disrupt the natural process of group association. Large movements of workers by transfer within the plant or by termination and recruitment outside the plant seriously weaken the best of efforts to build teamwork and improve productivity.[33]

THE RESEARCH STUDY OF HUMAN RELATIONS
IN INDUSTRY

FIVE TYPES OF RESEARCH STUDY

Five major types of research study are conducted by industrial sociologists as they seek to describe the social adjustments of workers or the functioning of work groups. The industrial researcher, depending upon the design of his project, may wish to:

1. Interview workers on the street, in their homes, at the union hall, at the Chamber of Commerce building, or in some other community organization outside the work plant.
2. Analyze industrial records such as application cards, merit rating forms, absence and turnover files, counselor reports, production and spoilage records, etc.
3. Observe work behavior as it normally proceeds in a work group or department within a work plant.
4. Observe and interview workers in a work group or department within a work plant.
5. Arrange work behavior within the work plant so that it takes place under controlled conditions; introduce given social factors and ascertain the effect upon some dependent variable such as production or morale.

The five different types of research study have been arranged in an order which indicates increasing difficulty of access to the kind of data ordinarily desired by the industrial sociologist. Some of the most needed studies fall within the first two types, which may not require any access to the work plant itself. Studies based on interviews or records usually inquire into some aspect of worker adjustment. Studies of 3, 4, and 5, which are based on observation and interviewing of workers, usually make work group behavior

[33] Mayo and Lombard, *op. cit.*, p. 28.

the focus of attention. Some projects call for a combining of some or all of these five types.

The initiation of research on work group behavior within a work plant poses the problem of establishing a research relationship with industry. A discussion of this relationship is necessary because of the special difficulties involved.

ESTABLISHING A RESEARCH RELATIONSHIP WITH INDUSTRY

Burleigh Gardner and William F. Whyte have aptly said, "Factories are social organizations with walls around them." There is no access without permission of management and the union. Furthermore, both parties may be reluctant to permit an outsider to come in and view their problems. There is a widespread suspicion that a researcher may stir up discontent in the worker's mind while probing for causes and effects of industrial and union policies.

Research in industry requires, therefore, fulfillment of certain conditions:

[1] The researcher must be able to get into industry.

[2] He must be able to establish and maintain relationships within the organization to be studied.

[3] He must have tools for collecting the pertinent data without interfering with his relationships.

[4] For anything more than superficial studies, there must be a continuity of research relationships with a given organization.

[5] To permit such relationships to continue and to allow for the possibility of experimentation, management must understand the research and take an interest in its development.[34]

Whyte and Gardner emphasize that when an observer (and this is especially true if the observer is a student) seeks entry into industry, the way must be carefully paved for him. Management and union leaders must have confidence in the research sponsors. The building of confidence requires time. It cannot usually be accomplished by a persuasive talk but must grow out of a more informal sort of relationship maintained over a period of time.

When access and permission to initiate research have been granted, the researcher has a decision to make in designing his project. He must decide whether he shall make observations with or without introducing changes into the situation. It is much easier to get permission to make studies if changes in personnel and working conditions need not be made. But this condition limits the area of research. Facility to experiment opens new

[34] Burleigh Gardner and William F. Whyte, "Methods for the Study of Human Relations in Industry," *American Sociological Review*, October, 1946, p. 506. Errors that can be made easily by the industrial researcher are described by Robert K. Bain, "The Researcher's Role: A Case Study," *Human Organization*, Spring, 1950, pp. 23-28.

possibilities. An illustration and discussion of experimental sociology in industry will clarify this point.

The Observation of Social Structure in Industry

When the industrial sociologist studies work behavior, it is likely that he will seek to describe the functioning of a work group, department, or plant. He knows that he must do field work.[35] The observer may gain acceptance through employment as a worker, going through the regular channels of

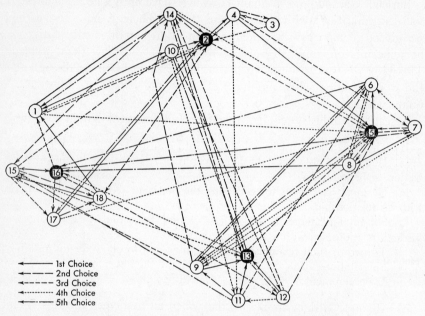

FIG. 59. A Sociogram Composed of Eighteen Workers.

employment and placement, or being placed on a selected job with the knowledge and permission of management and the union.

Inside the work plant the industrial sociologist most commonly employs the methods of direct observation and interview. He gives a great deal of attention to informal social structure. One of the newer approaches to the observation of informal social structure is sociometric analysis of the inter-personal relationships and of the communication networks that make a group an organic entity. Two applications of sociometric study were discussed in the last chapter when J. L. Moreno's work on the reconstruction of work groups in the steam laundry and L. D. Zeleny's work on the selection of compatible flying teams were described.

[35] George C. Homans, "The Strategy of Industrial Sociology," *American Journal of Sociology*, January, 1949, pp. 330-337.

An Illustration of Sociometric Analysis

At the University of Washington many studies are being conducted to measure interpersonal relationships in industry more objectively. One of these studies will illustrate one kind of attack on the basic problem of leadership role and group cohesion.[36] Figure 59 illustrates a sociogram or

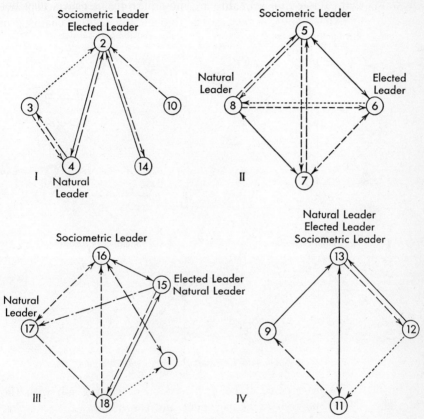

Fig. 60. Four Working Groups in Sociometric Arrangement, January, 1948.

chart of a work group of eighteen student workers. These eighteen workers were asked, "With what persons would you most prefer to work?" Each worker was asked privately to name five persons in order of his choice. It can be seen that the most important constellations are grouped around workers 2, 5, 13, and 16. These workers we have called sociometric leaders. The remaining workers were grouped around the sociometric leaders so that four working groups were formed. Each worker was placed in such a way as to maximize his likelihood of being in contact with the persons to

[36] This study was conducted by D. C. Miller, James Reilly, and Virginia Beagley.

whom he was most attracted. Figure 60 shows the four groups as they were constituted in January when they began to work together.

Each group was asked to elect a leader and to begin work on projects assigned to them. The elected leader is shown in each of the four groups. It should be noted that in only two of the four groups did the sociometric leader win election. This distinction is important. It demonstrates that the person whose qualities of personality are most pleasing to others may not

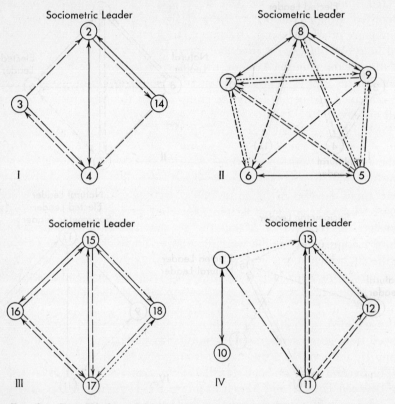

FIG. 61.   Four Working Groups in Sociometric Arrangement, March, 1948.

have in the eyes of those same people the leadership quality which they seek in the active direction of a group.

Another distinction is to be noted. The observation of these groups in active work demonstrated that the elected leader was not always the "natural" leader. We have called a worker a "natural" leader of a group when he provided the initiative and energy which moved the group forward. The natural leader could be relatively easily identified by the observers who watched the group activities. In two work groups natural leaders were not elected to leadership. In three work groups natural leaders were not

able to achieve the position of sociometric leader. This divergence seems to indicate that many persons of high ability, initiative, and dominance may be neither especially liked nor able to achieve popular election as a leader. It was our hypothesis that a leader who could secure his position simultaneously as the sociometric, elected, and natural leader would be able to build the greatest amount of cohesion. To test this hypothesis we made especially careful observations of group IV where worker 13 was the sociometric, elected, and natural leader. His group was a well-organized, coöperative, interested group. Number 13 showed by far the greatest initiative and dominance of any person in the group. His interaction score was the highest and he spoke longer at a time and interrupted more freely than any other member of the group.[37] At times the observers felt that he repeated himself unnecessarily and in some cases showed little discretion in speaking. Number 9 seemed inclined to hurry the group on but the other members seemed well satisfied.

To learn more about the nature of the interpersonal relations and the role of the leader a second measurement of sociometric choice was planned, to be given to the entire class three months after the initial formation of the four working groups. Since the eighteen members participated together three times a week in the classroom as well as within the small working groups, there was ample opportunity for every person to know one another. However, at the end of March the sociometric pattern demanded only minor readjustments in the working groups. These changes can be seen in Figure 61, which shows groups I, II, III, IV as they were reconstituted to maximize attractions. The correlation between the first and second sociometric choice tests was $r = .704$, indicating a fairly high degree of stability. The question of how persons could be regrouped to insure higher compatibility revealed that only three moves would be necessary. Number 10 was moved from group I to group IV, number 9 was moved from group IV to group II, and number 1 was moved from group III to group IV.

This second measurement revealed more clearly what had been happening between January and March in group III. Here, number 15, a woman, was obviously winning sociometric leadership in addition to her achievements as an elected and natural leader. Group III consisted of five members, all women. Number 15 was the determined "natural" leader and the elected leader. In addition, by March she had emerged as the sociometric leader. Number 15 might be characterized by her attempt to please all members of the group, to ask their opinions on nearly all moves. She opened the meetings, organized the material, and kept the records, but always asked for the opinion and decision of the group on all important issues. Number 17 was also a "natural" leader in the group but she achieved a slightly lower choice

---

[37] The qualities compare with those that E. D. Chapple has identified in leaders with the use of his interactional chronograph. See Chapter XIII, pp. 423-425 above.

status in the small group and a much lower rating from the total classroom population. In contrast, number 15 by March had secured the highest choice status in her working group and more choices than any other member on the total class preference test. Therefore, of these two natural leaders (15 and 17) in the same group, 15 has won leadership on her natural ability as well as ability to gain acceptance. It is apparent that her more democratic manner and discretion in speaking are most satisfactory to this closely knit group.

Thus, groups III and IV tend to validate the research hypothesis but group II as strongly contradicts it. Group II consisted of members 5, 6, 7, 8, all men. (See Figure 60.) Three different types of leadership were offered this group by three different persons. The sociometric leader is number 5, the elected leader, number 6, and the natural leader, number 8. There is no evidence that this separation of leadership was incompatible with group harmony. On the contrary, this group emerged in March as the most cohesive as measured by sociometric choice. More choices were given to members inside the work group than were given by any other group to its own members.

What does activity in these groups reveal about leadership? Our observations lead us to believe that leadership is a series of contributions to a group and that such contributions may be displayed by a number of persons. Leadership is shared activity regardless of the titles distributed to group members. There is good evidence that leadership activity should frequently shift within a group according to its goals. Carroll L. Shartle, in a ten-year study being conducted at Ohio State University for the Navy Department, is currently investigating the hypothesis that when goals are specific and when high-goal achievement is necessary over a short period of time, dominant leadership produces higher goal achievement than does leadership with low dominance. He is also testing the hypothesis that when goals are in general terms and require long periods for achievement, the attitudes of members toward the less dominant leadership is more favorable.

While these findings and hypotheses promise to shed light on the activity called leadership, this is not the time to recommend to business and government leaders that social scientists now know how to select the person who will be most effective in setting production records and in building harmonious teamwork. It is suggested that the research upon sociometric choice and leadership role continue. A repeating of this experiment might prove fruitful, especially under different work situations with different goals. We would urge that in addition to the test we used which asked for the five choices of persons each would prefer as working associates to include also a question seeking a reaction of like, dislike, or indifference to the prospect of working with each person in the population. A much tighter analysis of leadership status within the subgroups may be made if such data are gathered.

Meanwhile, we know enough now to question the common tendency in business to select "natural" leaders simply because they have high initiative and dominance to offer a work group. It may be that business has progressively eliminated socially conscious leaders from the executive and supervisory ranks because of failure to recognize them and appreciate their role in the productive process. Good human relations are built by leaders who appreciate the values of such relations. But more than this they must themselves have won acceptance in the groups they seek to motivate. Such acceptance involves liking and being liked; it involves ability, respect, and social consciousness. When an executive or union leader fails to possess all these qualities (and few indeed have them all!) he must rely consciously or unconsciously on other members of his group to provide for the deficiencies. Fortunately, there usually seems to be among the group members abundant pools of the very abilities which he lacks. A leader who recognizes this fact may by conscious direction lead his group to unusual achievement. The variety of ways in which human abilities in the group may be combined, and the possibilities of energizing latent resources among group members make the problem of leadership the many-sided, contradictory, perplexing, and yet challenging problem which it continues to be. Obviously, much more research work is needed to inquire into the dynamics of group interaction. The growing interest in group dynamics promises to add new knowledge to this area with increasing rapidity.[38]

It will be observed that the sociometric study just described entailed the moving of workers about so that the four groups could be composed of certain persons that the *researchers wanted in interaction*. This ability to experiment with new combinations is of great assistance to research when it is important to identify and isolate the effect of one variable upon another.

THE DEVELOPMENT OF EXPERIMENTAL RESEARCH OPPORTUNITIES

Gardner and Whyte describe the manner in which they have been working out research arrangements with industrial and business firms.

Their program involves the following five steps:

1. We make an intensive study of the problem situation.
2. On the basis of that study, we map out a course of action for management, which, we think, will improve that situation.

[38] The National Education Association and the Research Center for Group Dynamics at the University of Michigan hold yearly training laboratories at Bethel, Maine. For an account of their work see Leland P. Bradford and Dorwin Cartwright, *Training Laboratory on Group Development*, National Education Association and Research Center for Group Dynamics, Massachusetts Institute of Technology, 1947. Also by Bradford and Cartwright is *Report of the Second Summer Laboratory Session*, Bulletin No. 3, National Education Association and Research Center for Group Dynamics, University of Michigan, 1948. A third laboratory was held in 1949 and a report is forthcoming. See too Carroll L. Shartle, "Leadership and Executive Performance," American Management Association, 1949; reprinted from *Personnel*, March, 1949.

3. We communicate these recommendations to management in a form such that they can be understood and acted upon. This must be done primarily through informal conversations with executives. Written memoranda may be submitted also, but they are distinctly supplemental to the direct person-to-person relationship.

4. Management takes action along the lines agreed upon.

5. We follow closely every step of management action and make an intensive study of the resulting developments. If events follow the course we have anticipated we are in a position to observe just how and why these results were obtained. If the results are substantially different, then we are in a position to study the factors that accounted for the discrepancies and gain knowledge out of our own failures.[39]

It can be noted that the researchers make contact with a problem situation in the role of clinicians. After diagnosing the situation they work with management in such a way that *management introduces* the variables the researchers wish to study. When they have reached step 5 of their program an experimental design has been achieved and research is under way. This demand for the preparation of contact, the gaining of permission, and the designing of an experiment in a problem situation will not attract impatient researchers. Those who have believed that industry or a union could be treated like a laboratory which would gladly welcome the changes researchers wished to make will find themselves sadly disillusioned. Those who are willing to practice human relations can find alert managers and union leaders everywhere who are willing to assist capable researchers. To these administrators of experimental bent industrial sociology owes a growing debt. Together the administrator and researcher may be able to find basic knowledge about the formation and functioning of the work teams. Increasingly, both recognize that solutions to many problems of production and industrial organization await advances in the knowledge of group interaction.

SUPPLEMENTARY STUDIES

Laboratory: Designing a Schedule and Questionnaire for the Appraisal of an Industry or a Business

The following observation schedule for the restaurant and the accompanying waitress questionnaire were designed to enable an investigator to diagnose the social structure and social relationships existing in *any* restaurant. Make a similar set of research instruments for a selected class of work plants such as department store, grocery, factory, etc. It is suggested that the student select for his class of work plants the same business or industry he chose for his field observational studies of Chapters V-XII.

[39] Gardner and Whyte, *op. cit.*, p. 511.

This project requires ability to construct a single set of research tools that will be applicable to the variety of social structures which may be found in the many different work plants of a given business or industry.

OBSERVATION SCHEDULE FOR RESTAURANTS[40]
Delbert C. Miller and Sally O'Brien

Observer:

Date:

1. Make a diagram of the kitchen showing:
   a. relative position of workers
   b. job assignments
   c. groups
2. How many persons are employed in the kitchen?_____
   a. If it varies: peak hours_____slow hours_____ .
3. What is the seating capacity?_____persons.
4. What type of service does this restaurant have? (Check one.)
   a._____all booths
   b._____all counters
   c._____both counters and booths
   d._____cafeteria style
5. Is this restaurant part of a chain?
   a._____yes
   b._____no
6. What is the address of this restaurant?

   _____

7. Following are the possible job classifications in a restaurant. If this restaurant has such a job title at present, check.
   a._____hostess
   b._____checker
   c._____manager
   d._____owner
   e._____food production manager
   f._____chef
   g._____fry cook
   h._____countermen
   i._____counterwomen
   j._____vegetable preparers
   k._____salad makers
   l._____dishwasher·
   m._____head-waitress
   n._____waitress
   o._____general kitchen supervisor
   p._____cost control supervisor
   q._____supervisor of countermen

[40] Data drawn from W. F. Whyte, *Human Relations in the Restaurant Industry,* have suggested many of the items in this schedule.

r._____runners
s._____supervisor of dishwashers
t._____meat preparers
u._____assistant manager
v._____peelers
w._____pastry maker
x._____bus boy

Many times these jobs are combined. If such is the case, please note below.
For example—c and d are the same person.

a._____
b._____
c._____
d._____
e._____

M – Manager
SU – Supervisor
CH – Checker
CC – Cost control supt.
C – Customers
W – Waitress
B – Bartender
P – Pantry workers
K – Kitchen workers
R – Runners
D – Dishwashers
S – Service employees
W – Workers

8. Following are diagrams of various stages of growth of a restaurant. Please indicate below the stage this restaurant is in (as closely as possible).
   a._____

9. Status—rank the following using number one for the highest status.
   a._____peelers
   b._____salad maker
   c._____vegetable preparer
   d._____pantry girls or countermen
   e._____dishwasher
   f._____fry cook
   g._____chef
   h._____pastry maker
   i._____runner
   j._____meat preparer
   k._____hostess
   l._____checker
   m._____waitress
   n._____bus boy

10. The line of pressure. (Who initiates action for whom.) Start line with number one. (In both 10 and 11, one group may initiate action for several groups or one person may pass down authority to several groups. If this is the case, follow the example.)

     __3__ chef

     __4__ vegetable preparer

     __4__ meat preparer

  a._____fry cook
  b._____vegetable preparer
  c._____runner
  d._____meat preparer
  e._____waitress
  f._____pantry girl or countermen
  g._____dishwasher
  h._____salad maker
  i._____peeler
  j._____chef
  k._____bus boy

11. Formal line of authority. Start with number one.
  a._____general kitchen supervisor
  b._____waitress
  c._____dishwasher
  d._____manager
  e._____peeler
  f._____vegetable preparer
  g._____meat preparer
  h._____chef
  i._____fry cook
  j._____supervisor of countermen or pantry girls
  k._____runner
  l._____head-waitress
  m._____owner
  n._____hostess
  o._____supervisor of dishwashers
  p._____assistant manager
  q._____salad maker
  r._____bus boy
  s._____pastry maker

12. Fill in the charts at the end.

13. Owner
  a. Spends most of his time: (Check one.)
    1._____in office
    2._____in kitchen
    3._____in dining area
    4._____out of restaurant

b. Does he act in managerial capacity?
    1._____yes
    2._____no
c. Does he know the majority of the workers by name?
    1._____yes
    2._____no
d. Relationship between owner and supervisors: (Check one or more.)
    1._____he criticizes them in front of workers
    2._____he skips their position and gives orders or directions to workers
    3._____he upholds them in their decisions to workers
    4._____there is an informal, friendly relationship
    5._____is not clearly defined—alternates
e. Relationship between owner and workers: (Check one or more.)
    1._____he criticizes them in front of workers
    2._____he steps in and helps during rush hours
    3._____work tempo changes with owner's presence
    4._____is informal, friendly
    5._____formal
    6._____tense, dislike, distrust, or little communication
    7._____is not clearly defined—alternates

14. Manager
a. If owner is manager then skip this section.
b. Spends most of his time: (Check one.)
    1._____in office
    2._____in kitchen
    3._____in dining area
    4._____out of restaurant
c. In his relations with supervisors he: (Check one.)
    1._____sometimes skips them and gives orders to workers
    2._____criticizes them in front of other workers
    3._____upholds the supervisors' decisions to workers
d. In his relations with workers: (Check one or more.)
    1._____he criticizes them in front of other workers
    2._____he steps in and helps during rush hours
    3._____is informal, friendly
    4._____formal
    5._____tense, dislike, distrust, or little communication
    6._____is not clearly defined—alternates
e. Does he have an office he can use for conferences?
    1._____yes
    2._____no

15. Supervisors
a. They: (Check one.)
    1._____are working supervisors
    2._____help during peak hours
    3._____oversee workers at all times

    b. Relationship with workers: (Check one.)

        1._____criticizes them in front of other workers

        2._____is informal, friendly

        3._____formal

        4._____tense, dislike, distrust, little communication

        5._____is not clearly defined—alternates

    c. When he gives orders: (Check two.)

        1._____it is very clear as to what he wants done, by whom and when

        2._____workers are confused by his orders

        3._____workers resent his orders

        4._____workers accept his orders

16. Informal groups

    a. Basis of: (Check as many as you think are relevant.)

        1._____marital status

        2._____age

        3._____mating and dating desirability

        4._____education

        5._____social background

        6._____length of service

        7._____previous association

        8._____formal organization

    b. How many informal groups do you find?_____

17. Coöperation

    a. The workers: (Check one or more.)

        1._____help each other

        2._____give words or signs of encouragement

        3._____ignore the difficulties of others

        4._____place barriers in front of other workers to make it difficult for them

    b. Management tries to build coöperation by: (Check one or more.)

        1._____encouraging supervisors to listen to employee "gripes"

        2._____not having physical barriers or rules against it

        3._____by demanding it

        4._____recognizing informal groups

        5._____offering incentives

        6._____introducing new employees to workers

        7._____having group meetings

18. Communication

    a. Management has: (Check one.)

        1._____frequent contact with all workers (every day)

        2._____few, irregular contacts with all workers

        3._____frequent contacts with a small group of workers (every day)

    b. Workers (Check one.)

        1._____take their problems to supervisors

        2._____are not sure of the response they'll receive from supervisor

        3._____never discuss problems with supervisor

    c. Group meetings are: (Check one.)
       1._____held at regular intervals
       2._____held when need arises
       3._____never held
    d. Management and workers
       1._____get together socially on occasion (other than "Christmas Party")
       2._____never get together socially

19. Integration
    a. How many unassimilated workers do you see?_____
    b. How many "outcasts" do you see? (Workers that are avoided by others.)_____
    c. Management has:
       1._____a comprehensive program of induction that they follow with every worker
       2._____a partial program of induction that they follow with every worker
       3._____a comprehensive program of induction that they follow on certain jobs
       4._____no program at all of induction
    d. In your estimation the workers are:
       1._____well integrated
       2._____partly integrated
       3._____poorly integrated

20. Listed below are problems that are found in many restaurants. If you notice any of these please check. List any additional below.
    a._____crying waitress
    b._____shortage of food during peak hours
    c._____men in certain positions take orders from women and they resent it
    d._____there is a group of "old-timers" who have better communication with management
    e._____workers resist change of any kind
    f._____workers gripe between themselves, but don't go to management
    g._____supervisor usually tries to fix the blame on a worker (not the same one always, but the actual one at fault)
    h._____hostess overloads on waitress's station

21. List below any comments that you hear or any attitudes prevalent.

Group	Arrangement of Workers		Number in Group		Age Distribution			Race Distribution		
	Congested	Dispersed	Male	Female	–30	30–50	50–	White	Negro	Mong.
Peeler										
Dishwasher										
Runner										
Counterman or Pantry girl										
Chef										
Cook										
Vegetable preparer										
Waitress										

| Group | Uniform | | | | | | | | | | |
| | Color | | | | Sleeve length | | Collar | | Status decoration | | |
	white	blue	green	pink	to elbow	to wrist	V-neck	square	ric-rac	sleeve	collar
Peeler											
Dishwasher											
Runner											
Counterman or Pantry girl											
Chef											
Cook											
Vegetable preparer											
Waitress											

Groups	Formal contact points	Informal contact points	Pressure is dispelled by		
	with other groups	with other groups	joking	crying	"telling off"
Peeler					
Dishwasher					
Runner					
Counterman or Pantry girl					
Chef					
Cook					
Vegetable preparer					
Waitress					

WAITRESS QUESTIONNAIRE
Delbert C. Miller and Sally O'Brien

Interviewer:
Date:
1. Age: (Check one of the following.)
    a._____20-30
    b._____30-40
    c._____40-50
    d._____50-
2. You are: (Check any.)
    a._____single
        1._____live at home
        2._____live with girl friends
        3._____live alone
    b._____married
        1._____number of children
        2._____husband's occupation
    c._____widowed
    d._____divorced
3. Grade of school completed:_____
4. What are or were the occupations of your parents?
    a. Mother _____
    b. Father _____

5. How many children are there in your family?
6. How long have you been a waitress?
   a. How long have you worked in this restaurant?
   b. Number of years _____ Number of months _____
     Number of years _____ Number of months _____
7. List the other types of jobs that you have had.

8. What occupation would you like to be in? (No daydreaming.)

---

9. Check if you are a member of any of the following.
   a. National and/or regional organization
     1._____professional
     2._____recreational
     3._____educational
     4._____others
   b. Local organization
     1._____professional
     2._____recreational
     3._____educational
     4._____others
10. Have you ever been an officer or leader of a group of which you have been or are a member?
   a._____yes
   b._____no
   c. If yes, what? _____
11. Do you get together with the other workers here socially?
   a._____yes
   b._____no
   c. If yes, which other workers? (i.e., by their job titles, or duties)

12. Do you feel that your boss is:
   a._____very fair in his dealings with the workers
   b._____above average in his dealings with the workers
   c._____average in his dealings with the workers
   d._____below average in his dealings with the workers
   e._____very unfair in his dealings with the workers
13. Do you go to your boss with your problems of work?
   a._____yes
   b._____no
   c. If no, to whom do you go? _____

14. Do you feel that if the occasion arose you could go to your boss with a problem of a personal nature?
   a._____yes
   b._____no
15. Do you enjoy meeting people?
   a._____yes
   b._____no
16. Do you try to show your customers that you have the situation in hand, so they don't become restless?
   a._____yes
   b._____no
   c. If yes, what do you do? _____
   _____

17. How do you act with the majority of your customers?
   a._____laugh and joke with them.
   b._____talk to them—about other things than the menu or restaurant.
   c._____have as little conversation as possible.
   d. How would you prefer to act? _____
18. When you are under pressure, what do you do?
   a._____cry
   b._____yell, or talk loudly
   c._____laugh
   d._____become upset, but try not to show it
   e. List any other things you do.
19. Do your customers tip?
   a._____yes
   b._____no
   c. If your wages were increased to make up any loss you might suffer, which would you prefer—tipping or no tipping? _____
20. How do you feel about your work?
   a._____very happy
   b._____happy
   c._____satisfied
   d._____unhappy
   e._____very unhappy
21. In this question it would be appreciated if you would evaluate your feelings about your co-workers. Identify them by name, preferably, or by number. All information is confidential.

Name or Number	Like Them	Indifferent to Them	Dislike Them

FIELD: DIRECT OBSERVATION AND PLANNED INTERVIEWING

Using your newly constructed observation schedule and questionnaire gather data on two or three work plants for which it is designed. Make an interpretive report for each of the work plants you examined. The report might be one which would be designed for your district manager if such an assignment were given you. Attach all schedules and questionnaires.

If you decide not to construct your own research instruments, use the preceding observation schedule and questionnaire on two or three restaurants for which you gain entree to study.

LABORATORY EXPERIMENTATION: PRACTICE IN ROLE PLAYING AS A SUPERVISORY TRAINING TECHNIQUE

Step 1. Two persons are selected and asked to remain outside the laboratory.

Step 2. Describe the situation: "We are going to structure a stress situation such as any supervisor might meet. The situation involves a worker and a supervisor. The person outside will be briefed as follows:

" 'You are a supervisor. You have an employee who has been employed about one year. He was a good worker at first. Now he is falling down. First, you noticed lateness, then loafing on the job. His production is down. You have meant to speak to him but you were busy. This morning he came in late again. You decide that this is the time to have a showdown.' "

Step 3. Select a person to be the employee. Brief him as follows:

"You are a worker. When the boss jumps you, you are to say that nobody has ever said anything. You think that you are doing fine. Answer his questions but when he tries to make you give reasons for your low production say, 'I'm doing as well as anyone else.' "

Step 4. Ask audience, What may happen? Will supervisor lose his temper? Will he threaten to fire the employee? What can he do in this situation?

Step 5. Call in one of the persons from the outside. Have him take his place at the desk and explain the problem to him. (Say nothing about the worker's role. Let the supervisor discover it as he would in the actual situation.) Make sure he understands and then practice situation. The instructor says to him, "You are in your office. The employee walks in and asks, 'Did you want to see me, Mr.—?' "

Step 6. Practice situation. The situation should come to an end by the employee's returning to his place of work. If the situation does not come to an end naturally, the instructor may decide to "cut" it.

Step 7. Have the first supervisor return to the group. Summarize the action. Outline the events briefly on the blackboard. Do not encourage discussion at this point of how the supervisor role could have been done differently. Focus the attention of the group upon differences between what they have seen and what they should watch for in the next practice situation to follow.

Step 8. Call in the second person and brief in identical fashion. The person taking the role of the employee tries to repeat his previous behavior as consistently as possible.

Step 9. Practice situation. Sum up action of the second practice and review the first. The blackboard will now have two outlines, side by side, describing the action of two practice situations.

Before general discussion give each "supervisor" a chance to "save face" by evaluating his own practice. Ask the person who practiced the employee role to give his reactions to the two supervisors.

Step 10. Open a general discussion. Seek to get a consensus of what group considers preferred supervisory behavior.

Step 11. The instructor may request one or both of the original "supervisors" to practice situation again. If neither desires to practice the same situation, select a member of the group who has not yet practiced a role and have him play out the role as closely as he can to the group consensus.

Step 12. General discussion.

(Situations which confront a foreman, supervisor, or union steward may be suggested by the group and training sessions can go on as long as desired.)

Library: Books and Articles   •

Barron, Margaret E., "Role Practice in Interview Training," *Sociatry*, June, 1947, pp. 198-208.

Bavelas, Alex, "Role Playing and Management Training," *Sociatry*, June, 1947, pp. 183-191.

Cantor, Nathaniel, *Employee Counseling*, McGraw-Hill Book Company, Inc., 1945.

Homans, George C., "The Strategy of Industrial Sociology," *American Journal of Sociology*, January, 1949, pp. 330-337.

Lewin, Kurt, *Resolving Social Conflicts*, Harper & Brothers, 1948.

Lippitt, Ronald, *Training in Community Relations*, Harper & Brothers, 1949.

Richardson, F. L. W., Jr., and Walker, Charles R., *Human Relations in an Expanding Company*, Yale University Press, 1949.

Rogers, Carl R., *Counseling and Psychotherapy*, Houghton Mifflin Company, 1942.

Ward, Roswell, *The Personnel Program of Jack and Heintz*, Harper & Brothers, 1946.

Library: Films

By Jupiter (27 minutes), approaches the universal problem of improving the attitude of man toward man. Drives home story that courtesy is contagious. Produced by Wilding Pictures.

You Are Sperry (30 minutes). The war efforts of workers in the Sperry Gyroscope Company. Shows how the company tries to build group morale and teamwork around war goals. Produced for the Sperry Gyroscope Company, Brooklyn, N. Y.

Research Gaps

1. Sociometric analysis of work groups and the grouping of workers into efficient work teams.
2. Measurement of job security.
3. Measurement of employee morale.
4. Evaluation of democratic and authoritarian social structures in the work plant.
5. Assessment of the effect of various personnel programs on employee morale and group collaboration.
6. Carefully tested observation schedules and questionnaires for the appraisal of social structure and social relationships in different work plants.
7. Description of different kinds of leadership in various work groups and assessment of social cohesion.
8. Methods of planning for community life in a sociological sense within the work plant.

Part Four

THE SOCIAL ADJUSTMENT
OF THE WORKER

The social adjustments made by the worker begin with birth and end only with death. This section begins with the socialization of the child to the work patterns of American society. The school and the home provide early work experiences. The initial work period opens opportunities for the young worker to secure "paid jobs." As the worker begins to "make his own money" he learns about the adult world of work. After the termination of his formal schooling the transition from school to work is completed. The early years of struggle to get a secure, satisfying, well-paid job occupy the worker. As the later years of work life bring stability to many workers, deeper community roots are put down. Finally, the withdrawal from active work life marks the end of a career and eventually of life itself. A description of the many significant social adjustments imposed by the culture on the worker through this cycle of work life provides the content of this section.

CHAPTER XV

The Preparatory Work Period

EARLY EXPERIENCES IN WORK PLANTS

I. THE HOME

The Beginning of Socialization

The prospective worker begins his life in the family. During the first month of infancy, he might be described as a "looker-on" who has a generalized feeling that he has been set down into what William James once described as "one great, blooming, buzzing confusion."[1] The newborn babe is not a *person*; he becomes a person as he becomes a participating member of the group. Before he can participate, he must discover the group

[1] William James, *Principles of Psychology*, Vol. I, Henry Holt and Company, 1890, p. 488.

of which he is a part. He must make some sense out of the confusion—which is to say, he must find out what others are doing and what they expect him to do. Only in this way can he achieve a position in the group and thus become a person. The process by which the individual member of society becomes a functioning part of the group, learning to conform to group standards and traditions and coming to feel himself a part of the group, is called *socialization*.

Socialization may be defined as the process by which the human animal acquires a personality and thus becomes a social being. The newborn infant contains in its plastic, unformed, generalized original nature, which it has inherited, all the potentialities for social behavior. But at birth this bundle of protoplasm is innocent of all knowledge about the "important" things in his new world. He is born without belief, morals, or social awareness. He has no expectations of his own, and he is unaware that his parents "love" him and regard him as a "human being." He doesn't know that he is an object any different in kind from the crib, chairs, walls, or air that surround him. He has no idea what he looks like, and he doesn't care. He doesn't know where he came from or where he is going. He does not believe in God, unions, free enterprise, or brushing teeth. He has no "ambition" to be anything or anybody, but to remain warm, rested, and fed. His overwhelming need is to have some expression, if it is only sucking his thumb, for his restless energy effervesces in random activity. Although he does not know it, he, of all the animals possesses the greatest capacity for boredom.

Socialization begins with learning. Slowly, at first, and then with enlarging comprehension, a social world begins to form into *meanings*. The beginnings are marked by the awareness of others and the recognition of meanings which the others seem to attach to their conduct—and, indeed, recognition of meanings which the others assign to his own behavior. He learns to "smile" as others use smiles, to show friendly, happy feelings, and as he discovers that others expect him to "smile" in return. The process of discovering what is expected has been called by social psychologists "*defining the situation*." To become human it is essential that the infant recognize what meanings these older, bigger, and more authoritarian humans about him have put on the myriad of social situations which they have created. He is prompted to engage in this game because it brings him satisfactions in increased attention, recognition, and new experiences.

Sex differences and work roles are rather advanced discriminations, but between three and a half and six years of age the child becomes aware that one or both parents leave the home to work and that the household seems in some way regulated by the coming and going of those who work.[2]

[2] See John Dollard, L. W. Doob, N. E. Miller, O. H. Mowrer, and R. A. Sears, *Frustration and Aggression*, Yale University Press, 1939, p. 69. The writers say, "It seems that with increasing verbal control of its surroundings, say in the period between three and a half and six years of age, the child gains a conception of its parents and of how they live their lives."

Socialization Within the Home

The home may serve as a social center, a dormitory, a restaurant, a school, a church, a playground, a laundry, a repair shop and in many other capacities. As a center for the consumption of goods and services it takes on in many ways the functions performed in monetary work plants where goods and services are produced for sale. As a kind of many-sided work plant, the home provides the child with early opportunities to observe and participate in work activity. The mysteries of home appliances in an age of electricity are dispelled. The discipline of manual and craft labor is slowly instilled as the child is taught responsibility for the storage of his toys, the care of his clothes, and the cleanliness of his body. The girl begins her apprenticeship for homemaking by assuming responsibilities for dusting, washing dishes, and making beds. The boy may be given small hand tools so that he can imitate the parents' use of such tools which he has observed as they repair the house and its furnishings. The child becomes aware of those workers who service the home—newspaper boy, plumber, doctor, gas man, iceman, and grocery boy—and those who work in the community—policeman, grocer, sweeper, fireman, and storekeeper.

The person whose behavior provides the example for learning has been aptly termed a "model."[3] The workers whom the child observes become his models. He watches their behavior and then rehearses it in the world of fantasy or of play. This rehearsal involves a *taking of the role*, putting himself vicariously into the place of the worker, and imagining what the worker does and how he feels. Toys become objects which facilitate the taking of work roles in the play world. The play fireman, policeman, and doctor are roles that extract their content out of adult life. In this way the work habits and attitudes of fireman, policeman, and doctor are brought concretely into the personality, doubtless with considerable distortion but nonetheless real enough to influence occupational ambitions and goals.

Vocational goals are formed and developed essentially by this role-taking device. They become real to the child because they are experienced as real goals. It makes little difference whether adults conceive these choices to be mean or great. (Don't tell the child he won't want to be a policeman when he grows up, because *he knows now* that he wants to be a policeman.)

PRIMARY WORK MODELS

The earliest and most influential work models in a child's development may be spoken of as "the primary work models."[4] From them the child will acquire the earliest habits and attitudes which will serve to condition the later development of his personality.

[3] R. T. LaPiere and P. R. Farnsworth, *Social Psychology*, McGraw-Hill Book Company, Inc., 1942, p. 97.
[4] *Ibid.*, p. 99.

The mother ordinarily becomes the more influential model during the early years of the child, for it is she who devotes to him the greatest time and attention.[5] The child, tagging at her footsteps, watches the mother perform a wide number of work tasks. He sees her preparing and cooking food, setting the table, serving food, washing and storing dishes, cleaning house, dusting furniture, and washing, ironing, mending, and storing clothes. The child rehearses these experiences in play, and when the role of mother is assumed, the work skills are tried out in imitation of the model. See with what eagerness he plays house!

And those who make up the family of the child—father, brothers, and sisters—likewise serve as models, providing motivation for new social experiences. The father supplies new experiences for the child as he carries out his chores about the house. Often it is father who mows the lawn, fires the furnace, hoes the garden, tinkers with the family car, paints the kitchen, and repairs the house.[6] These tasks give the child some of his first opportunities to see and perhaps actually use hand tools and to make and repair wooden and metal things. Likewise, many other materials are introduced, such as stone, cement, fertilizer, paints, and varnishes. He observes the skills of many workmen and may be given a chance to learn some of them. A versatile and wise father can provide the child with a growing body of knowledge and experience as gardener, painter, carpenter, electrician, mason, fireman, and auto mechanic.

Older brothers and sisters also serve as models for the child during his later development. Life adjustment is expansive. No set pattern is adequate for long. Older brothers and sisters bring the life of the school to the home. Their talk of teachers, pupils, classrooms, and playgrounds furnishes the preschool child with guides and expectations to his next big adventure.

Father and a working brother or sister (or mother, if she works outside the home) bring the life of other work plants into the home. There may be talk of factory, office, and school. In this setting, the work world may often seem to the child more unreal than real. Yet it is in this atmosphere that attitudes are formed, aspirations found, and patterns of adjustment anticipated. The child craves growth and status. To have these, he must learn to live in work plants and to gain a more responsible work role. When he is ready for school, he will carry with him work habits that have been laid down in the home. The primary work models will have furnished by precept and example, but mostly in the unconscious way that is example, the roots of his habits of order, punctuality, care, and regularity—and even

[5] When the mother works, as may often be the case in a lower- or middle-class family, a "sociological" mother such as an older sister or grandmother may replace the blood mother as model.

[6] A father in a lower-class family is much more likely to construct and repair objects around the living quarters than is an upper-middle- or upper-class father. In the upper classes, construction and repair men are more commonly utilized.

more subtly, the roots of social skills which will determine so largely the range of achievement to which he may ultimately aspire.

II. THE SCHOOL

Socialization Within the School

When the child crosses the threshold of the school, he finds a new kind of world waiting for him. He sees a concentration of persons in his own age group. In a relatively short time he becomes a participating member in a society which soon discovers its own mutual interests, forms values, and learns to apply social pressures to those who will not conform. This society is sometimes reinforced and sometimes opposed by the classroom society, which includes the omnipresent teachers who have command of so many new and different kinds of expectations.

As teachers and pupils place themselves opposite one another, it may be said that two cultures come to coexist side by side in *symbiotic relationship*—i.e., each culture, although different, leans heavily upon the other for continual support. The "peer culture" is patterned to express the free-flowing rhythms and motivations of youthful energy—play and rest, fighting and friendship, realism and fantasy, rivalry and teamwork. The school culture is built by adults to make adults out of children—or course, all in good time. Teachers and principals, deriving their authority from the consent of adults, have their own rituals and expectations to impress upon the children's activities. It is their task to impose the "right," the "good," and the "useful" ways of life in such a way that the members of the peer culture like them or at least do not become actually antagonistic and rebellious to them.[7]

FIVE MAJOR FUNCTIONS OF THE SCHOOL

The school and the peer culture blend together, making an accommodation to each other, but the school culture seems always to dominate. Parents expect the school culture to dominate. Teachers are supposed to see to it that: (1) the pupil is trained to stay on the job and learn his lessons; (2) the pupil is trained to obey authority; (3) the pupil is encouraged to develop initiative and to rise socially; (4) the pupil is trained to develop character; (5) the pupil is trained to get along with his teachers and his schoolmates. Parents seldom realize what a large proportion of the influences upon personal conduct lie outside the classroom activities and are attributable to the family and play groups of the child. They hold the school responsible for the training of the child. Under this demand the school presses to achieve parental expectations.

1. The pupil is trained to stay on the job and learn his lessons. Within the classroom, routine and ritual press the child into more coercive patterns

[7] Willard Waller, *Sociology of Teaching*, John Wiley and Sons, 1932, pp. 103-119.

than he has yet experienced over sustained periods of time. Life moves by the clock—a great face which seems to determine how long reading will last, how long spelling will go, how long it will be before the joyful release from the hard seat to the freedom of the playground. Adults say these routines constitute discipline—the child must learn to stay on a job, to work hard, and to learn his lessons.

2. The pupil is trained to obey authority. Never before have things been so hard to get or has talking been so often denied. Individual wishes must now be subordinated to the common purposes of thirty to forty others. Talk and movement are everywhere circumscribed by routines, rules, and time. The smile or the frown of the teacher is the signal of approval or disapproval, reward or punishment. Violations of the rules bring more than penalties of denial; they focus the intent eyes of those thirty or forty others upon the individual, shaming him, ridiculing him, pitying him. These eyes are not like the eyes of parents, brothers, and sisters, who love and accept the person in his strength and in his weakness; these are the eyes of peers who are being taught to pit their wits against one another. Adults say that one must learn to listen, to obey authority, to learn to get along in a work group. And the time to learn these things, they say, is when a person is young. Some parents feel this so keenly that they select a military school for their child so that the importance of obedience may be more greatly emphasized.

3. The pupil is encouraged to develop initiative and to rise socially. Rivalry is stimulated within the school and the peer cultures.

Many parents, especially from lower- and middle-class homes, regard the school as a social elevator on which their children may rise to secure good white-collar jobs and to "have an easier time" than they had. If their children can only rise socially they feel that they have achieved a measure of success as parents.

The school is a social institution which responds to these cultural cravings, and for a significant minority of the children it offers a means to the fulfillment of parental aspirations. However, most children are trained by the home and neighborhood to occupy the social positions to which they are born. W. L. Warner, Robert J. Havighurst, and Martin B. Loeb in their book *Who Shall Be Educated?* point out that "the school offers some opposition to home and neighborhood training in the case of the lower class children but usually fights a losing battle over them. It supports and supplements the home and neighborhood training of middle-class children. It tends to democratize the training of upper-class children but loses many of these to private schools which give them a class education."[8]

The school can thus be observed as a social system which operates to

[8] Warner, Havighurst, and Loeb, *Who Shall Be Educated?* Harper & Brothers, 1944, pp. 56-57.

help preserve for the child the status level achieved by the parents and to help some children climb higher within the status system. It selects many lower- and middle-class children and helps them rise by giving them an opportunity to:

Associate with children of middle and upper social class.

Learn the social skills of middle and upper status.

Learn the vocational skills of middle and upper economic status.[9]

This function of promoting social mobility is the one best understood and most highly valued by the parents who charge the school to perform its rightful tasks.

The school responds to these urgings. In the classroom, patterns of competition are rewarded by letter symbols known as grades. The child is taught to become aggressive toward grades—getting them in much the same spirit as an adult who is encouraged to struggle for higher-paying jobs. The school pupil may be rewarded with such honors as silvered paper stars, special mentions, parts in plays, positions on athletic teams, and extra recesses for his achievements in grade getting. He is punished by numerous penalties or disapprovals in the school and in the home for his failures. He learns that he must climb the ladder of promotions if he is to be considered a "success" in school. He is taught that all the famous men and women worked hard and long to achieve success and if he will follow their example he too may reach the highest position in the land. Parents say that life is a struggle and that the child must learn to become aggressive and competitive in order to develop the initiative needed for success. They urge the school to sponsor these habits in the classroom, gymnasium, auditorium, and playground.

While these habits are being instilled it is considered that the school will develop the "character" and "personality" of the child.

4. The pupil is trained to develop "character" and "personality." In the school culture, educational achievement is set forth formally as the chief measure for differentiating between members, and rewards are to be distributed solely for such accomplishments as may be merited. Actually, other standards get more than passing attention. Adults charge the school with "character building and personality development." This means that classroom rewards and penalties may be distributed according to the teachers' estimates of the courtesy, cleanliness, honesty, regularity, and attentiveness demonstrated by the child. Thus, learning and "discipline" become twin objectives, and teachers are selected for their ability to "learn 'em and discipline 'em." Moreover, teachers may take into account, consciously or unconsciously, the racial, class, or power position of the child's parents. The behavior of the teacher may be unduly influenced by whether she is judging the behavior of a girl or a boy, and even by her belief that the child is

[9] *Ibid.*, p. 57.

good-looking or ugly. Usually, she accepts uncritically the main values of society and attempts to inculcate them into the students.[10]

5. The pupil is trained to get along with his teachers and his schoolmates. Whom the child associates with and how he learns to get along with others is determined by many influences that include the social position of the parents, the opinions of teachers, and the judgments of children within their own peer culture. From these influences and others the child gets a "reputation." Warner and his associates have found that "a child's reputation among other children stems from a variety of sources: from its actual behavior; from what other people, especially parents and teachers, say about the child, and the way they behave toward him; and also from what older people think and say about the child's family and their associates."[11]

As the child becomes increasingly aware of these bases of evaluation he takes more seriously the choices of friends which his parents have made for him. He avoids with special care those who his parents have warned are "inferiors." The school becomes a social center where the classroom, playground, and family activities of the child converge. Getting along with teachers and schoolmates is essentially a problem of finding one's place and achieving satisfactory adjustment within it. This does not always occur easily, for feelings of superiority and inferiority are involved. A good illustration is given by an elementary school teacher:

I'll give you an instance of the way they feel. You know I have this little club in my grade and in June I took a group of them to the state capital. When I first asked them to sign up, I had twenty-one to go but when they finally got around to going there were only twelve, and all but one of those twelve were my A section socialites. The only little girl from B section almost didn't go and she took weeks making up her mind. She came and said, "Well, I just think I would feel funny going with those other girls. You know I don't go to the same places they do. They don't ask me to their parties and we are just different. I think I would feel funny going with all of them." Well, I said to her: "Now Marion, I don't think I would feel that way. We are going to be together while we are there. I don't think you need to worry about it. I know all those girls are too well bred to be rude to you even if you don't go to the same parties they do. And you must remember that you are just as smart as they are and you dress just as nicely and you look just as nice all the time. I don't think you need to feel uncomfortable about it at all." She said: "Yes, Ma'am, I know, but they just don't feel that way about it."[12]

Somehow, some way the school is expected to offer democratic participation and yet not interfere with the status structure. In this context parents

[10] Warner and his associates have shown that teachers are recruited from middle-class backgrounds and may be expected to instill middle-class ideas and sentiments. See *ibid.*, pp. 101-105.

[11] *Ibid.*, pp. 84-85.

[12] *Ibid.*, p. 82.

charge the school to train the pupil to get along with his teachers and his schoolmates. The peer culture complicates the task even more by its wide range of values. In the peer culture where children are choosing their friends they decide who is good-looking, who plays games well, who is a good fighter, who is a leader, who is quiet, who is noisy, who is the teacher's pet, and a host of other judgments about each other. The playground as well as the classroom becomes an arena of competition. The intensity of the competition in the classroom is matched only by the intensity of rivalry on the playground. Fair play, loyalty, and sincerity are values highly esteemed, and each member takes the measure of the others and makes a rating on the basis of these values. In the classroom the rewards of achievement are furnished primarily by the approval of teachers and parents and only secondarily by the reluctant and often jealous respect of one's fellows. Grade getting and teacher approval in the classroom are accomplishments within the school culture; they are seldom regarded by a child's fellows as of his own making. On the playground the honors of success are granted by one's own age group.

Activity in the peer culture embraces a wider range of personality than does that of the classroom. The peer culture operates primarily through play and congeniality groups, which are small and intimate. In these groups there is complete participation, and the many facets of the personality are brought to light and evaluated by the group members. Complete participation makes what Cooley called the *primary group*. In contrast, the classroom group is usually large, and social relationships are more formal. Partial association is more often the rule in such *secondary* groups. If the child is to make a satisfactory adjustment to "school," he must achieve approval within both the peer culture and the school culture—and the more important of these is the peer culture.[13] Acceptance to the classroom is automatic upon fulfillment of adult requirements; acceptance in play groups is by way of peer choices. These groups have the power to make or break the status of any member. Peer groups select their leaders and assign the followers.[14] Thus status grows to have meaning in the social participation of one's own group. Failure to win acceptance or make good adjustments in the play groups may have far-reaching consequences. Indeed, many years later, the graduating youth may discover with some shock that monetary work posi-

[13] Meek says, "There is little we can do for him educationally until we have helped him achieve satisfactory status with his peers. Until he sees some solution for that problem, he is in no state to profit from the intellectual experiences the school offers." Lois H. Meek, *The Personal-Social Development of Boys and Girls with Implications for Secondary Education*, Progressive Education Association, 1940, p. 66.

[14] Warner, Havighurst, and Loeb say that results "demonstrate how class values and ideologies operate in children, just as they unconsciously and consciously do in the lives of their parents. Few, if any, of the children studied realized they were making class judgments about their peers. Most of their parents are only infrequently aware of the ever-present class bias in their judgments of their neighbors, friends, and fellow citizens." *Op. cit.*, pp. 86-87.

tions test different abilities and reward achievements by different standards from those he learned in the classroom. He may discover painfully that the *more important determiners are the kind of values which were dominant in the play and comradeship groups in which he failed to participate successfully*. Perhaps only then will he become fully aware that although the classroom provides status mainly through educational achievement, occupational success may derive from such social elevators as family name, reputation of schools attended, kind of friends, sex appeal, beauty, cultural tastes, special talents, or "personality." Numerous illustrations will be presented in the following chapters to show that class values and social elevators are of the greatest importance in the training of children from the moment of birth throughout their growth and, in fact, throughout their lives. We shall see that after a person's "reputation" is established certain rewards or handicaps follow him through his career. A "good reputation" will often aid him in securing jobs, surmounting obstacles, and securing status out of proportion to that which actual expenditure of energy and skills entitles him to.

THE SCHOOL IS A LIMITED WORK WORLD

It is significant, therefore, to recall that it is in the school that the child grows to youth, adolescence, and adulthood. From eight to twenty years this school work plant provides the largest volume of social experiences outside the family and community. Here the individual is subject to the judgment of his adult teachers as well as his contemporaries. The teachers provide models from which glimpses of life in the outer adult world are caught. These teacher models may seem unreal—not at all like parents or other adults in the community. Sometimes the impatient youth feels isolated, as if he had been forcibly walled off from a more exciting, more responsible role in the world of work.

Indeed, the shortcomings of the school are most often indicated in its failure to provide life experiences with adults in their work plants. This glaring failure is shared by the community, which increasingly denies jobs to its youth. The opportunity to participate in the jobs of other work plants has been slowly but steadily diminishing.[15]

This is occurring at a time when the developing child needs contact with an expanding area of work experiences. He needs *secondary work models*, i.e., people in various vocations whom he may use as examples for learning. But these people are working behind walls which have no ready access for

[15] Paul Landis, *Adolescence and Youth*, McGraw-Hill Book Company, Inc., 1945, pp. 317-318. Landis cites four reasons for the restriction of employment opportunities for youth. These are: (1) increasing shift of employment to large industrial organizations, with its consequent dependence on market conditions; (2) child labor laws; (3) growth of labor unions, whose emphasis upon seniority rights gives the established worker an advantage over youth; (4) general trend of American industry and agriculture to replace man power with machine power.

his random observations. The chemical engineer, the turret lathe operator, the junior executive, or even the farmer may be so very far away and so inaccessible that only the allusions of books can provide the shadowy details of the real worker. When the young man or woman is asked what kinds of vocations he has thought he might pursue at different times in his life, such sequences as the following often occur:

Young man: (1) Fireman; (2) Policeman; (3) Carpenter; (4) Druggist; (5) Doctor

Young woman: (1) Mother; (2) Nurse; (3) Teacher; (4) Private secretary; (5) Airline hostess

These sequences when carefully studied show two things: first, a high dependence upon available models, and second, an attachment to glamour models whose content is seldom experienced except through casual or vicarious contact. The latter fact was well illustrated recently by the voluntary attendance of 1800 pupils at thirty vocational seminars sponsored by a Seattle high school. The principal reports with dismay that the largest attendance was given to the glamour jobs of architecture, aviation, commercial art, dramatics, engineering, medicine, nursing, and office work. Far down the list in attraction were such occupations as the trades, teaching, and agriculture. Three hundred pupils, 90 percent of them girls, came into the seminar on office work. Forty boys and girls went to learn about a career in medicine. When it came to teaching, sixteen girls and ten boys showed up. Interest in following a trade is indicated by the seventeen out of 1800 who attended that session.[16]

The seriousness of the breakdown in work apprenticeship experience and of the urban isolation of secondary work models will be the occasion for frequent references during the succeeding chapters. For the moment it is pertinent to ask what opportunities for work experiences outside of the school are available to the child.

Although the opportunities for work are becoming fewer and less meaningful, the child may still find a work role for himself in the home. The home may be considered an enterprise requiring for its size relatively large amounts of both skilled and unskilled labor. There are many work tasks in its maintenance and operation in which the school child may share.

THE WORK ADJUSTMENT OF THE SCHOOL CHILD IN THE HOME

CHORES

The child's first work assignments in the home are called *chores*. Chores refer to a number of unskilled, routine tasks performed in the work plant, especially in such plants as the home and the farm. These tasks may include

[16] Seattle *Times*, March 12, 1947.

such maintenance jobs about the home as washing dishes, removing ashes, disposing of garbage, cleaning rooms, mowing the lawn, hoeing the garden, and repairing toys and furniture. About the farm, there are such jobs to be done as bringing in water, gathering eggs, feeding the chickens, "slopping" the pigs, milking the cows, separating the milk, and sawing wood. In the large family, there are always children to be put to bed, to be rocked to sleep; feet, knees, and hands to be washed.

The Louisiana Educational Survey reported that both boys and girls of all age levels share in doing household work. City children seem to contribute to the work of the home only slightly less than do town and country children. The most common types of help given by all children include doing the dishes, cleaning the house, and helping with younger children. Almost all children help with the upkeep of lawn and garden. Most of the eleventh-grade girls help at home with cooking and washing, and about one-third help with sewing. Household repair is performed by boys on all age levels. Nearly four out of five high school senior boys perform household repairs.[17]

These tasks express the burden associated with unskilled, repetitive work. But they represent work vitally necessary to the operation of the home. Parents have felt (and most still do!) that the chores represent an opportunity to train their children in the Puritan virtues of hard work, thrift, and the value of money. Many a child has received his first "pay" for his part in the work of the home. The Louisiana survey showed that over one-half of all school children were given some spending money every week by their parents.[18]

HOMEWORK

Chores represent the demand of the home for the sustained effort of the child; homework or outside study represents the demand of the school for worktime within the home. Homework refers to the periodic lesson assignments made by a teacher or teachers, requiring performance outside the classroom. These assignments constitute the main unsupervised activity for which the school holds the pupil responsible. It is this activity which tests whether the child learns to study effectively. Sustained mental effort is not easy; it is, in fact, one of the most demanding claims upon human energy. The complaint of the college teacher that many of his students do not know how to study can be matched by the cry of the plant manager that he can't find foremen who will "study" their jobs. Both laments are testimony for the difficulty of acquiring habits of sustained mental effort. Yet more and more occupations are requiring these habits.

[17] Henry Harap and Edgar A. Schuler, *Louisiana Educational Survey*, Section 4, "Home and Community," Louisiana Educational Survey Commission, 1942, pp. 25-30.
[18] *Ibid.*, p. 31.

Effective Thinking and Planning Is Required in Industry

The rise of staff jobs in industry and commerce requires more people who can deal with ideas. Even the factory floor has witnessed the removal of much heavy lifting, the reduction of human movement, and the ever growing importance of planning. The advance of industrial civilization might almost be measured by the number of seats, chairs, and stools that have been introduced into work plants during the last 150 years. Progress, as it were, has lifted man off his feet, placed him in a sedentary position, and demanded that brain tissue take dominance over muscle. The manual worker has watched the industrial tool designers, the production planners, and the method engineers slowly but surely strip away the manual skills required in the machining and assembly of goods. Human robots rather than "all-round mechanics" have been needed for the growth of highly repetitive jobs in many areas of manufacture. Yet there are reasons to believe that this stage may be only a transition in technological advance.[19] The growth of professional, semiprofessional, clerical, and service occupations seems to herald the direction in which more and more technologically displaced persons (both in industry and in agriculture) must seek their work. These occupations require a different adaptability—skills in handling the symbols of things, such as money, accounts, or blueprints, rather than manipulation of tangible goods. There are new demands made upon imagination, abstract thinking, versatility, and scheduling of work loads.

Planned Study in Industry Compared with Planned Scholarship

Systematic consideration of the arrangement of materials, the method of teaching a job, and the method of performing a job has been found measurably to increase industrial output. An example of systematic teaching is to be found in the Texas Company Refinery at Port Arthur. In October, 1943, job instruction training was given to the 1511 supervisors in this large refinery. Operation of the training plan resulted in every one of the 5000 employees being listed on departmental timetables. The plan indicated the progress of each employee, the number of employees who were prepared for jobs in the next department to which they could normally advance. Supervisors prepared over 10,000 job breakdowns, which were used to train employees so that they might learn the job step by step in the shortest time with least spoilage. The Texas Company reports the following results of the plan:[20]

[19] For a discussion of this point see Stuart Chase, *Men and Machines*, the Macmillan Company, 1929, p. 104.
[20] *The Training Within Industry Report*, 1940-1945, United States Government Printing Office, 1945, p. 147. For a national picture of results obtained, see Chap. 7, "Measuring the Results of TWI Programs," pp. 89-105.

Manufacturing costs reduced	20%
Accidents resulting in lost time reduced	75%
Minor accidents reduced	20%
Break in time reduced	40%
Scrap and rework reduced	20%

Can the value of efforts to improve methods of mental work be similarly demonstrated? Students who have been taught to read and write correctly, who have learned how to plan and budget time and how to take notes and prepare reports, have repeatedly been shown to "flunk out" less often and to have higher average marks than other students of equal ability.[21]

"One college student expressed with keen insight the problem of study when he said, 'Above all, the necessary thing and the one which must be developed and one which I think I am learning is the correct method of studying. It is possible to study hours and not master a thing, while if it were approached from a different angle, its facility of mastery would be amazing. The main thing is knowing your own limitations and gauging time, place, advantages, and benefits through cognizance of these limitations.' "[22]

The books which have been written on how to study are many. The rules are not particularly long or difficult.[23] Yet the failure to adjust to study is an old story in the history of school failure. Students themselves say:

"My bad habit is procrastination. This is, I think, a common failing. If I studied at the first opportunity that came along each day, studying would probably be easier."

"I tend to put off work until late at night and then lose sleep to do it."

"I don't get down to really studying until the best part of the term has passed."

"I have a tendency to study the easiest subjects first before proceeding to the more difficult ones."

"I have difficulty in planning a definite study schedule."

"I can't organize material in logical sequence."

"I can't find the important things to remember and pay too much attention to small details."

"When I have finished something, I quite often do not remember what I read."[24]

Transfer of School Skills to the World of Work

Poor study habits and lack of motivation are not only barriers to success in the school; they can be the stumbling blocks to success in business and

[21] Kenneth L. Heaton and Vivian Weedon, *The Failing Student*, University of Chicago Press, 1939.

[22] *Ibid.*, p. 58.

[23] For a list of rules that have been found helpful in increasing efficiency in study, see S. L. Pressey, J. E. Janney, and R. G. Kuhlen, *Life; A Psychological Survey*, Harper & Brothers, 1939, pp. 502-505; Mortimer J. Adler, *How to Read a Book*, Simon and Schuster, 1939.

[24] Adapted from Heaton and Weedon, *op. cit.*, pp. 65-71.

industrial plants. Ability to work independently and efficiently is rewarded in business as well as in the school. A foreman would put it like this: "There's a good worker. You don't have to keep telling Joe what to do—he can see what there is to be done, and goes ahead and does it." A senior executive appraising the work of a junior executive might say it more succinctly: "A damn' good man—he's got ideas, and he gets things done." Psychologists Pressey, Janney, and Kuhlen claim that continuing success on the job depends on the individual's ability to do three things: (1) to take care in a dependable manner of the routine work he is expected to do, (2) to get along with associates, and (3) to perform his functions with increasing effectiveness.[25]

In the very first jobs, the habits of the home and school will be taken into work plants and their economic worth will be appraised. In work plants where work is "paid for," new motives and new demands are introduced. And new work habits arise to blend with the old. We shall now turn our attention to these work habits as they are utilized in work positions of the monetary work market.

ENTRANCE TO WORK POSITIONS IN THE MONETARY WORK MARKET

"HOLDING A JOB"—ITS SOCIAL AND ECONOMIC DEFINITIONS

In the adult world any effort which does not receive a direct payment in money, goods, or services is not regarded in the same way as work which is so rewarded. Thus, the student or housewife is considered outside the market—indeed, more a part of the leisure class than of the population making up the labor force. However, any part-time or full-time worker in a factory, store, or office is said to be "holding a job," i.e., shouldering a part of the world's productive work.

This distinction was nurtured for many years by the traditional economists, who refused to consider students and housewives as producers of wealth. The economist likewise excluded merchants, sailors, carpenters, actors, and domestic workers as productive workers—in fact, any who failed to produce material wealth. Alfred Marshall was considered revolutionary when he first defined "labour as any exertion of mind or body undergone partly or wholly with a view to some good other than the pleasure derived directly from the work." He proposed that all labor be regarded "as productive except that which failed to promote the aim towards which it was directed."[26] This

[25] Pressey, Janney, and Kuhlen, *op. cit.*, pp. 601-603. Cf. Heaton and Weedon, *op. cit.*, pp. 58-83, 128-138, 158-197; in their analysis of the failing college student they find that among the factors that cause failure are inadequate study habits and skills, lack of vocational motivation, and poor social adjustment.

[26] Alfred Marshall, *Principles of Economics*, The Macmillan Company, 8th ed., 1930, p. 65.

point of view has since been accepted by economists and constitutes a base upon which to examine the economic operation of home, school, hospital, church, and service fields with the same standards as might be applied to factory, office, store, and insurance route. It is this perspective that the writers are trying to interpret in the social analysis of various work plants and in the adjustment of the worker to them.

Yet there remains in popular thinking economic and social differences between non-monetary work positions in such work plants as the home and school and monetary work positions in such work plants as the factory or store. As we have pointed out in an earlier chapter, these differences are largely explained by the identification of the *market*. The *market* is defined as a physical location characterized by buying and selling of goods and services, with prices determined according to the supply and demand for such goods and services. Unless the worker is hired in a labor market—which is to say, employed by an employer who can choose his workers from an available supply and pay them according to a competitively determined rate—his work assignment is not a "job." Ordinarily a boy or girl gets his first "job" only when a work assignment is secured outside the home or school. Getting a job is regarded as taking a step out into the adult world. Sometimes the skills required in these first jobs are very simple, yet the collective responsibility is often great. A large city newspaper would find itself much embarrassed if its newsboys failed to appear at their appointed time. It is not entirely "palaver" when the newspaper publisher tells his newsboys, "We are in business together."

Entrance into this job world provides status not alone because of the responsibility and monetary return but also because the great American legend regards every worker as launching on an upward course toward success. The very young worker is never regarded as "stuck" in a job; he is merely proving himself for the day when he may climb from the bottom to the top ranks of fame and fortune. Indeed, the worker can perform most distasteful work with adequate spirit if he knows that he is merely doing temporary work which will eventually lead to better things—and especially if he knows that his family and friends regard his present job as only a temporary step to a more responsible one.

The adjustment phase we are about to examine begins when the boy or girl finds his first part-time job while enrolled in school. This takes the young person into the initial period of work adjustment. It is called the initial period, since it marks the beginning of work behavior in the work market. This entrance into the work market is actually the second of a fivefold work pattern which the individual may live to experience. Since the five periods of work adjustment are knit together in most occupational histories, our first task will be to define and illustrate each period.

FIVE PERIODS OF THE LIFEWORK PATTERN

PREPARATORY, INITIAL, TRIAL, STABLE, AND RETIREMENT
PERIODS OF WORK ADJUSTMENT

In a full life, five spans of work adjustment bridge the beginning and end of working. These may be called: (1) preparatory, (2) initial, (3) trial, (4) stable, and (5) retirement. Figure 62 illustrates the lifework pattern of the typical worker. It can be seen that the initial, trial, and stable periods encompass most of the work adjustments made in the work market. These three periods represent what is often referred to as the "active work life." It should be noted that many work adjustments in the home and the community are part of the active work life. There are the manifold tasks of household maintenance, child rearing, and the "organization work"

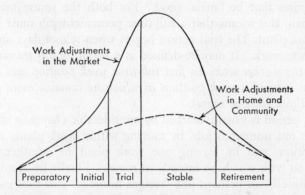

FIG. 62. Five Periods of the Lifework Pattern.

which the alert citizen and businessman find themselves obliged to undertake. The work adjustments of home and community are present in every one of the work periods. The preparatory period represents early experiences and adjustments in the home, school, and community as the young person develops physical and mental maturity. The end of life is marked by a retirement period which demands new adjustments in the home and community as the work position in the market place is relinquished.

The preparatory period has been discussed in this chapter. In the following chapters, each of the other four periods of the lifework pattern will be examined. Our attention will be focused especially on the three periods which make up the "active work life."

The worker begins his active work life when he accepts his first job in the work market. With this step, he enters the initial period—*a period of job impermanence beginning when the worker seeks his first jobs during his span of school enrollment and continuing until he has terminated his*

education. The worker accepts jobs knowing full well that he intends to fill them only temporarily. His main job is the completion of his education, and his life is oriented largely to the school. The part-time or full-time jobs which he takes are stopgaps for him. It is true that the young worker may perform them with conscientious and serious zeal, but such earnestness is almost always accompanied by the belief that the present job is only a stepping stone to a better job. He takes for granted that he is on a temporary job, although he may look forward to a permanent job with his employer at a later time.

Compulsory education laws place the accent upon the school as the main preoccupation of childhood and much of youth. Only when formal education is terminated does the young worker feel the demand for a permanent job. If he is to find a new orientation, he must discover a satisfying substitute for the status he had while permanently occupied in the school. His culture requires that he "make good." For both the young man and the young woman, this means that a full-time permanent job must be secured in some work plant. The trial period begins when school days are over and youth "goes to work." It may be defined as *a period of job transition beginning when the worker seeks his first full-time work position and continuing until he has secured a work position in which he remains more or less permanently (three years or more).*

The trial period is usually marked by considerable changing of jobs. The worker tries out numerous jobs by moving within work plants via transfer and promotion, and by leaving one work plant for another, seeking a work position with which he intends to remain. Finally he "finds himself," "steadies himself," or perhaps just "resigns himself," and thus enters into a period of stable work adjustment. The *stable period* may be defined as *a period of job persistence beginning when the worker finds a work position in which he remains more or less permanently (three years or more), and continuing until retirement, death, or until he enters another trial period.* Stability is most secure when the worker is satisfied that he is performing in his "chosen" occupation and within a given work plant in which he intends to remain during the rest of his work life.

Figure 63 summarizes some of the characteristics of the three periods of "active work life." The worker is shown progressing from the initial period, when he works only temporarily at the jobs he secures, to the trial period, when he "gets started" in earnest on a full-time job which he "tries out." The stable period is shown as a stage of job persistence when the worker has become relatively fixed in a given occupation and in a given work plant. The feelings and attitudes of the worker during these periods reflect the kind of adjustments which characterize each period.

A consideration of these three periods of active work life raises many questions. What are the first jobs which the worker finds? How do they affect his later work life? How does the school prepare for monetary work

positions? How does the worker get his first permanent job? Is there any order or plan by which workers get jobs and then progress? Can workers still climb from the bottom to the top? When does a worker become stable? What happens to the worker's outlook on life when he reaches the stable period? These and many other questions must be answered before we have

Periods of Work Adjustment	Initial Period	Trial Period	Stable Period
Nature of job	Part-time and summer employment	Full-time employment	Full-time employment
Mobility	High occupational and work plant mobility	High occupational and work plant mobility	Low occupational and work plant mobility
Worker's Occupational history is characterized by:	Job Impermanence	Job transition	Job persistence
Psychological components: I. Feelings of the worker	Worker feels that he is only working temporarily and that his performance on the job is secondary to his school life.	Worker feels that he is working at a job (1) in preparation for a more responsible job or (2) to find out if he wants to remain at his present job or work plant, or is merely (3) holding on until he can make a change.	Worker feels that he has found the job and the work plant in which he intends to remain, or finds himself unable to move from the job or the work plant.
II. Attitudes of worker and observers as described by common folk expressions	"Making some spending money" "Preparing himself" "Helping out" "Working temporarily"	"Getting started" "Moving around" "Trying to find out what he likes" "Staying until the first of the year" "It's a living for a while"	"A fixture" "Old-timer" "Intends to stick here" "He likes his job" "He's stuck in that rut"

FIGURE 63. Periods of Active Work Life.

completed an analysis of the lifework pattern. We shall not find that all workers are destined to gain stable work lives. All that can be said is that the normal thrust for a stable work life is a strain for that job (or occupation) which the worker conceives as "the job, or kind of job, I've always wanted." The worker may fail of his mark and accept a compromise for less than he aspired. He may stay on a job because of the necessity of

making a living although his work brings no satisfying reward except the means of livelihood. Yet the struggle for vocational satisfaction sets up tensions that are dynamic. When the "right" job cannot be secured, changes in jobs or changes in work plant dot the occupational history. Life histories are affected by larger social and economic changes as well as by the indeterminate forces of personal health and fortune. It should be understood, therefore, that the periods of the lifework pattern reflect the anticipated road of work socialization as the hopes and ambitions of young workers point toward the future. The road we have drawn constitutes the occupational segment of what Mannheim has called the *plan of life*.[27] The concepts of initial, trial, and stable worker are "constructed types"[28] to draw from reality the social and psychological characteristics of workers in three distinctive work situations. Before we conclude this section, a final type must be explored. This is the retired worker—the worker who has resigned from active life in the work market but whose work adjustments continue. We shall begin with an examination of the adjustment of the worker during the initial period.

SUPPLEMENTARY STUDIES

FIELD: PLANNED INTERVIEWS

Make one or more interviews of boys and girls in the preparatory work period. The best ages for interviewing are probably between twelve and fourteen years of age. For a comparative analysis it is very desirable to seek interviews with boys and girls from lower-, middle-, and upper-class families. The following interview form is suggested as a guide:[29]

Name _____   Interviewer _____
                                         Date _____
                                         City _____ State _____
A. Background
   Age _____ Sex _____ Grade in School _____
   Occupation of: Father _____
                     Mother _____
                     Brother _____   Sister _____
                     Brother _____   Sister _____
                     Brother _____   Sister _____

---

[27] Karl Mannheim, *Man and Society in an Age of Reconstruction*, Kegan Paul, Trench, Trubner and Company, Ltd., 1940, p. 56.

[28] Howard Becker, "Constructive Typology in the Social Sciences," in Harry E. Barnes, Howard Becker, and Francis Bennet Becker (eds.), *Contemporary Social Theory*, Appleton-Century-Crofts, Inc., 1940, pp. 17-46.

[29] The writers are indebted to Mr. Blair Bower for assistance in the construction of the interview forms suggested for the various work periods.

B. Job and Work
  1. What kinds of work have you done? Start with first jobs and tell me about these jobs.
    a. What was the job?
    b. How did you get it?
    c. What did you like and dislike about it?
  2. What do you do now?
    a. After school
    b. On week ends
    c. Last summer
  3. What kinds of work are you best acquainted with? List.
  4. Have you ever been to the place where your father works? Have you actually seen him at his work? Do you wish to do the same kind of work? Why or why not?
  5. Do you think your father likes his job? Does your mother think your father has a good job?
  6. What jobs have you thought you might like to do when you start to work? Start with the first choice you ever made and tell me of any choices you have made since then.
  7. What job do you think you would rather do now? Do you think there is a good chance that you will get such a job?

C. School and Work
  8. Do you think going to school will really help you get a job?
  9. Do your father and mother think it's a good thing for you to finish high school?
  10. Do you think going to school is about the same as working on the job? Why?
  11. Do you think the teacher really knows about jobs and what work is like in the outside world?
  12. What are the kinds of jobs that the gang you run around with want to do?
  13. What kind of jobs do members of your group do?

D. Home and Work
  14. Do you have homework to do? Do you spend much of your time at home doing schoolwork?
  15. Do you have chores or jobs to do around the house? Do you get paid for these or some allowance money?
  16. What kinds of work does your father do around the house? What kinds of work does your mother do around the house? On what jobs do you assist your parents? Do your parents like to have help or do they prefer to do the jobs themselves?
  17. What talk about work and unions have you heard around the house?
  18. What do your parents think you should do in planning for work and getting a job when you have finished school? What are your ideas about it?

E. Community and Work

Ask respondent for information which will enable you to scale social participation on the Chapin Social Participation Scale. This scale is reproduced below:

Name of Organization	1. Member	2. Attendance	3. Financial Contribution	4. Member of Committee	5. Offices Held
1.					
2.					
3.					
4.					

Scoring: Weights of 1, 2, 3, 4, 5 are assigned to each type of participation as indicated by the order at the top of the scale. For example, if a person belonged to 6 clubs or organizations, attended 5, contributed to 3, was a member of 2 committees, and was an officer in an organization, his total score would be 38. Tentative norms for the Social Participation Scale may be found in F. Stuart Chapin, *Experimental Designs in Sociological Research*, Harper & Brothers, 1947, p. 195.

LIBRARY: BOOKS AND ARTICLES

Hiller, E. T., *Social Relations and Structures*, Harper & Brothers, 1947, chap. 23, "Child Status," and chap. 24, "Youth and Adolescence."

Landis, Paul, *Adolescence and Youth*, McGraw-Hill Book Company, Inc., 1945.

Warner, W. Lloyd, Havighurst, Robert J., and Loeb, Martin B., *Who Shall Be Educated?* Harper & Brothers, 1947.

RESEARCH GAPS

1. The sequence of different jobs desired at various times by young persons in the preparatory work period.
2. Measurement of the area of contact with different work positions by young persons in the preparatory work period.
3. Study of chores.
4. Study of homework.
5. Description of group values demanded on the playground for boys and for girls.
6. Measurement of work habits and attitudes acquired from the classroom.

The Initial Work Period

SPECIAL CHARACTERISTICS OF THE
INITIAL WORK PERIOD

INITIATION TO THE WORLD OF WORK

A young worker describes his first job and the experiences he gained upon it in the following paragraph:

My first real job was that of a paper boy. The summer before I entered high school, when I was twelve years old, I fell heir to a paper route of nearly eighty customers. The route encompassed an area of about fifteen city blocks, and this was my work field for the next five years. As I mull over the countless ramifications of my accepting the role of paper boy, I am sure of one thing, namely, this early task stimulated my maturity over and above a normal rate of growth. For one thing, it inculcated in me a personal sense of responsibility. Those fifteen blocks were *my* work field. Those eighty customers were depending upon *me* to deliver their *Philadelphia Evening Bulletin*. For another thing, this assignment introduced me to status-consciousness. A great many people over the years came to know me, if not as Paul Whitworth, then as the evening paper boy. I was more than just another kid in the neighborhood; I was the paper boy—and I sensed that elevated status. I felt important when I walked down the street with some of my buddies, to have numerous adults and young people hail me with a friendly greeting or gesture. Again, my job as a paper boy, since it included not only delivering the papers, but also collecting for them at the end of each week, initiated me to money-changing and bookkeeping. And what was far more important, it forced me into a position where I had to learn to deal with people. There I was with eighty families—fifty of them permanent, the other thirty in constant flux—and no two of them were exactly alike. Where one liked an efficient and prompt paper boy, another preferred a slightly mischievous, impish one. Where one might insist on my never stepping out of my role as the paper boy, another was likely to invite my friendship. And it was always up to me to match their temperament if I was to get along with them well. Looking at this aspect of a seemingly simple job, I know that I gained a wealth of experience and practice in the all important art of getting along with people.

The life of Paul Whitworth, the paper boy, illustrates how the initial period introduces the young worker to a new social world and thereby opens the way to an expanding area of social experience. It is not that the young worker, as often alleged, will get a taste of "work" for the first time; it is rather that the habits and attitudes which he will encounter among his work associates place him in a social atmosphere that contrasts in marked degree with such familiar work plants as home and school. In the work world youth mingles with adults and watches the competition of men and women for livelihood and status. As his work experiences grow wider and his observations more acute, he will come to recognize the quiet de-

lights of adult achievement, the cruelty of compulsive striving, the apathy of those who accept miserable conditions of work and home life, the frustrations and jealousies of thwarted men and women, and the despair of defeated and broken persons.

Job contacts often provide the first intimate association with persons of differing social classes, races, and nationalities. This gives the young worker opportunities to gain new insights into the motives, goals, and life satisfactions of workers from varying cultural backgrounds. Within the work plant the status of the young part-time worker is no longer that of the school pupil standing on relative equality in a similar grade, but is now more often than not that of the lowest-status worker, who (he is often reminded) is the first to be laid off or the easiest worker to replace. Thus, the importance of worker status given by the home and community is attenuated by the lowly ranking of the young worker within the work group. Status is both given and taken away. This is shown by the following expression from a worker.

The ensuing summer I was offered a position as a water boy on a "thrashing run." In those days of few combines the farmers still banded together, exchanging work during the wheat and oat harvest season. For two summers I participated in this activity. Long will I remember the cry, "Water boy! I'm hot, dry, and mad." And then off on a trot I would go for the jug. When I did not come fast enough they would shout, "Water boy! If you can't get here any faster we can find plenty of bare-foot men standing around to take your job." You had to hustle for it was true that there were others who could replace you, for the labor supply was almost unlimited.

The demands of work are more compelling within the monetary work plants. The orders of the boss carry the authority of one who can provide or deny access to work and money. Everywhere the requirements of a business are dated with time limits. Jobs must be done right, and on time.

To find out how young workers react to their early work experiences, it is necessary to trace out the characteristics of the initial period. Such questions arise as: (1) When does active work life begin and how long does the initial period last? (2) What are the psychological and social effects of the initial period? (3) What are the first jobs that workers secure? (4) When do students work? (5) Do age and education affect job opportunities during the initial period?

Answers to these questions are now forthcoming, thanks to research surveys which have been published in recent years. In addition, the writers of this book have conducted surveys especially designed to find facts not heretofore available in the research literature.[1]

1. When does work life begin and how long does the initial period last? The initial period has been defined as a period of job impermanence, be-

[1] Such survey will be identified as the Ohio Industrial Diamond Survey.

ginning when the worker seeks his first jobs during his span of school enrollment and continuing until he has terminated his education. Ordinarily,
the first jobs are secured during the high school years. In many states, child
labor laws prohibit the employment of workers under sixteen years of age.[2]
Although many young workers not yet in high school secure spot jobs such
as passing bills or short daily jobs such as delivering newspapers, the greater
proportion get their first jobs while enrolled in high school. Workers failing
to achieve high school standing usually go to work directly without developing an initial job history.

The first initial job histories begin to appear at about fourteen years of
age. Most of these are completed by the time the student has reached
seventeen or eighteen years of age. Then, the high school student may take
his high school record to a work plant and apply for his first permanent
job. Thus begins the trial period of his work life.

If the young man or woman pursues a college education, the initial job
period may extend many more years. In our files of job histories reported
by college undergraduate students, there are some cases in which persons
twenty-four, twenty-five, and twenty-six years old have not yet emerged from
the initial period. Many graduate students will undoubtedly have even a
more prolonged initial period. Two occupational histories are given to
illustrate prolonged and wide experience that may be gained during the
initial period. The first is that of a college junior, a man twenty-four years
old; the second is that of another junior, a woman twenty-two years old.

We shall call the man by the fictitious name of Robert Baker. His occupational history is reproduced just as he presented it.

Occupational Description	Part- or Full-time Job	Years	Income	Place
1. Street-corner (not carrier) news-paper boy	Part-time	5	$18 weekly	Batavia, N.Y.
2. Pin-setter in bowling alley	Part-time 7 P.M.-1 A.M.	3	$14 weekly	Batavia, N.Y.
3. Clerk in jewelry store	Full-time	6 months	$12 weekly	Batavia, N.Y.
4. Bus boy, Aviation Terrace, LaGuardia Airport	Full-time	3 months	$33 weekly	New York City
5. Taxi dance hall barker	Full-time	3 weeks	$35 weekly	New York City
6. Carnival barker James E. Strates Girl Show	Full-time	2 months	$50 weekly	Pa., Ohio, N.Y., Ky.

[2] "20 states now have a basic sixteen-year minimum age for employment and this has
been the minimum for general employment in establishments covered by the Fair Labor
Standards Act since 1938." Social Work Yearbook, Russell Sage Foundation, 1949, p. 93.

Occupational Description	Part- or Full-time Job	Years	Income	Place
7. Nite-club entertainer	Full-time	4 months	$40 weekly	Principal cities in N.Y., Mass., and Ohio
8. Salesman, second-hand store pawn shop	Full-time	3 months	$25 weekly	Columbus, Ohio
9. Burlesque barker and entertainer, candy butcher	Full-time	6 months	$40 weekly	N.Y., Ohio, Pa., Ill., Tex., La., Col., Calif., Mass., and others too numerous to mention in allotted space
10. United States Army	Full-time	2½ years	$50 monthly	Too numerous to mention
11. Bartender in café	Full-time	1 month	$40 weekly	Batavia, N.Y.
12. Bell man in Powers Hotel	Full-time	2 days	Don't remember	Rochester, N.Y.
13. Counter man, Embassy Café	Full-time	2 weeks	$35 weekly	Rochester, N.Y.
14. Waiter, Catelli's Restaurant	Full-time	3 weeks	$35 weekly	Rochester, N.Y.
15. Counter man, Cohen's Delicatessen	Full-time	3 weeks	$35 weekly	Rochester, N.Y.
16. Bell hop, Roosevelt Hotel	Full-time	6 months	$100 weekly	Pittsburgh, Pa.
17. Bartender, Venice Café	Part-time	9 months	$20 weekly	Kent, Ohio

The occupational history of Jane Gordon (a fictitious name, but a very real initial job record) reveals unusually wide experience for a twenty-two-year-old woman.

Occupational Description	Part- or Full-Time Job	Years	Income	Place
1. Clerk in a grocery store	Part-time, 3 hrs. day and Sat.	3 months	$6 week	Sebring, Ohio
2. Clerk in J. C. Penney Store	Full-time 45 hrs. wk.	3 months	40¢ hour	Alliance, Ohio

Occupational Description	Part- or Full-time Job	Years	Income	Place
3. Put boxes together in box factory	Part-time, 4 hrs. day	3 months	40¢ hour	Alliance, Ohio
4. Secretary and bookkeeper in a filling station	Part-time, 3 hrs. day	1½ months	35¢ hour	Sebring, Ohio
5. Waitress in confectionery	Part-time 1½ hrs. day	2 months	40¢ hour	Alliance, Ohio
6. Waitress at Robin Hood Restaurant	Part-time 3 hrs. day	3 months	40¢ hour	Kent, Ohio
7. Served food in college cafeteria	Part-time 3 hrs. day	2 quarters	35¢ hour	Kent, Ohio
8. Punch-press operator	Full-time 8 hrs. day	3½ months	75¢ hour	Alliance, Ohio
9. Copy girl (office boy), newspaper, Cleveland *Plain Dealer*	Full-time 8 hrs. day	3 months	$26 week	Cleveland, Ohio
10. Waitress	Part-time 3 hrs. day	Present job	40¢ hour	Kent, Ohio

In contrast to these extensive initial histories we find many persons who have reached voting age without ever having had a job. A young man begins his occupational autobiography with this apologetic explanation: "It might seem funny to some people that a person could live twenty-one years without having a job that could be called a job, but such is my case. I don't know why—maybe it was because I was always under the protecting wing of my family."

2. What are the psychological and social effects of the initial period? These cases demonstrate the occupational extremes produced by the cultural forces set in motion within an advanced industrial civilization. Young persons over fourteen can find opportunities to work, but the longer the period of educational preparation, the greater the postponement of the trial job period. And in a very real way this postponement of entry into the trial and stable job world becomes a postponement of maturity. The adult world refuses to accept high school and college "boys" as men until they have shouldered full responsibility for themselves within a monetary work plant. It is a sociological truism that the personality incorporates attitudes reflecting the social values of the cultural environment. The young person cannot experience the satisfaction of feeling adult until he is considered adult by his family, his teachers, his neighborhood, and his community. Adults just out of earshot are saying:

"They look so young—and they are so irresponsible."

"You can't trust them to carry through a job."

"They never have had to work hard."

"They don't know how to handle responsibility."

There is no way of knowing whether it is the actual lack of full-time job experience or the attitudes of adults toward the school or college "boy" which affect personality most. Whatever may be the relative effect of these two factors, it can be said that together they create profound disturbances in the young person. They boil over in resentment against adults who refuse to recognize school-going youth as independent. Sometimes guilt feelings appear as the youth pictures himself as parasitic upon those who work and support him during his educational training. In some persons, superiority traits break out in "trying to be a man" to cover the lack of confidence born of inexperience. Perhaps for most youth some degree of frustration and dissatisfaction lives in the substrata of consciousness. Evidence of this is most aptly recorded in the large number of young people who drop out of school without achieving their educational goal. Among the reasons given by almost 11,000 Maryland youth who left school, lack of interest accounted for almost a fourth. About one in every six left because of a desire to earn his own money, although there was no lack of family funds to prevent his continuation in school.[3]

In a study of more than 30,000 young people made during 1938 by the Works Progress Administration in seven large cities, it was found that almost a third quit because they had no desire for further education. One out of every five boys said he left to earn his own money, although again there was no lack of family funds. One out of every eight girls said she left to earn her own money.[4]

There can be little doubt in the midst of these facts that the values of the culture as they define "useful work" play upon human pride and thus draw young persons into the work market. No wonder young people can take pride in "working" even though they are put on a simple, repetitive, or dirty job. They will make many compromises for the satisfaction of "holding down a job." They often mask their education and hide their capacities, knowing that the initial worker must ordinarily take the bottom of the ladder. Some do this in the hope that they may be able to build up experiences or extend their education, which will enable them, on some later day, to get a better job. Middle-class parents reinforce the hopes of the young worker by an assurance that an occupational ascent has begun or will follow. The child of working-class parents may view his initial jobs

[3] Howard M. Bell, *Youth Tell Their Story*, American Council on Education, 1938, p. 64.

[4] *Urban Youth: Their Characteristics and Economic Problems*, Works Progress Administration, United States Government Printing Office, 1939, pp. 10-11.

TABLE 19. Part-Time Employment After School or on Saturday Reported by Canton, Ohio, High School Boys, 1937–1938

Manufacturing and Mechanical Industries		Transportation, Trade, and Clerical		Domestic and Personal Service	
Auto mechanic helpers	10	Bill passers	13	Bellboys	1
Assemblers, electric	1	Ambulance drivers	1	Bus boys	3
Baker helpers	4	Bowling alley attendants	20	Caddies	8
Carpenter helpers	1	Butchers	5	Car washers	3
Contractor helpers	2	Cashiers	1	Dish washers	2
Craneman helpers	1	Chauffeurs	1	Dry cleaner helpers	4
Egg candlers	1	Collectors	1	Hat blockers	1
Electrician helpers	1	Dance hall attendants	2	Janitor helpers	18
Fly tiers	2	Delivery boys	26	Laundry workers	4
Furnace installer helpers	1	Dispatchers	1	Lifeguards	1
Gas driller helpers	1	Errand boys	2	Messengers	1
General repairmen	1	Gas-oil station attendants	36	Shoe shine boys	12
Garage helpers	6	General office clerks	3	Waiters	18
Grinder helpers	2	Haulers	14	Window washers	1
Ice-cream hustlers	1	Junk yard helpers	1		
Ice-cream makers	1	Magazine sellers	6	Total domestic and personal service	77
Inspectors	1	Mail clerks	5		
Laborers (steel mill)	4	Messenger boys	4		
Mechanic helpers	1	N.Y.A.	17		
Packers	2	Office boys	6		
Paper hanger helpers	1	Paper boys	283		
Pattern maker helpers	1	Parking lot attendants	5		
Plumber helpers	1	Salespeople helpers	24		
Printer helpers	8	Shipping clerks	4		
Radio service men	2	Skating rink attendants	4		
Record changers	1	Stockroom boys	18		
Sheet-metal helpers	1	Store salespeople	223		
Sign painters	1	Truck drivers	22		
Tinner helpers	2	Truckers and haulers	12		
Umbrella repairmen	1	Typists	1		
Upholsterer helpers	1				
Window shade makers	1	Total transp., trade, and clerical	761		
Shoe shop helpers	3				
Total manufacturing and mechanical industries	68				

Agriculture		Extraction of Minerals		Other Occupations	
Dairyman helpers	6	Coal shovelers	1	Athletic manager assistants	1
Farmers	2	Mine operators	1	Helpers at home	3
Greenhouse helpers	1			Instructors	1
Planters	1	Total extraction of minerals	2	Musicians	11
Vegetable trimmers	3			Photographers	1
Total agriculture	13			Theater ushers and assistants	36
				Miscellaneous	33
				Total other occupations	86

much differently. They often become a necessary contribution to the living needs of his family. In fact, his parents may demand that he work to buy his own clothes or satisfy other needs in order to relieve the burden on the family. In contrast, upper-class children are often removed from these common concerns and will customarily spend their summers in camp or in travel, and their after-school leisure will be preoccupied with sports or hobbies. They share with all members of their age group one basic requirement. This is the ever present need for spending money which is a compulsion upon teen-agers of all backgrounds as they try to keep up with the adolescent social world they create and live in. Jobs or allowances must begin to carry many new demands for money. What are the first jobs that

TABLE 20. Part-Time Employment After School or on Saturday Reported by Canton, Ohio, High School Girls, 1937–1938

Transportation, Trade, and Clerical		Domestic and Personal Service		Other Occupations	
Cashiers	5	Beauty parlor operators	2	Dancers and dancing	
Demonstrators	1	Dish washers	1	teachers	4
Errand girls	1	Housemaids	123	Librarian helpers	5
General office clerks	3	Waitresses	19	Models	1
Multigraph operators	1	Nursemaids	91	Musicians—music	
N.Y.A.	2			teachers	8
Secretaries	2	Total domestic and		Professional ball players	1
Stenographers	1	personal service	236	Miscellaneous	2
Stock clerks	2				
Store salespeople	132			Total other	
Telephone girls	1			occupations	21
Typists	1				
Total transp., trade, and clerical	152				

workers secure? This question opens the door to the occupational content of "active work life."

3. What are the first jobs workers secure? Job histories reveal clearly how sex differences influence job opportunities and job placement. A boy has a greater opportunity to find a part-time job and a much wider choice than a girl. Moreover, the boy probably finds (though it is doubtful he will be aware of it) that he is under greater social pressure to seek part-time work. A study of Canton, Ohio, High School undergraduates shows these sex differences clearly.[5] A sample containing 3062 boys in grades 9, 10, 11, and 12 indicates that 33 percent have part-time employment after school or on Saturday. The sample containing 2956 girls in the high school grades shows that only 14 percent have part-time jobs.[6] The part-time jobs which these

[5] Canton Board of Education and State Board for Vocational Education, "Canton Occupational Study," Canton, Ohio, Board of Education (mimeographed), 1938, p. 188.
[6] Ibid., p. 206. Respondents gave information about their part-time jobs in 1937-1938.

high school students secured are shown in Tables 19 and 20.[7] These jobs
are worthy of careful examination, for they demonstrate the nature of occupational diversity at the bottom of the ladder. Canton, Ohio, with a
population over 100,000 may be considered representative of a large industrial city with diversified industry. As a steel center, it has heavy industry;
as a fabricator of many commodities, it enjoys much light industry as well.
Moreover, it has a relatively large commercial center. It is revealing, therefore, to find that transportation, trade, and clerical fields hold by a very
wide margin the bulk of the part-time jobs which boys secure. Figure 64
lists the five most frequent part-time jobs held by high school boys. Job

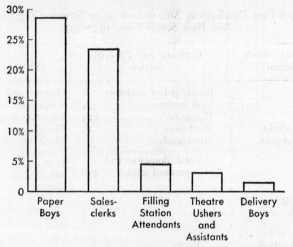

FIG. 64. Five Most Frequent Part-Time Jobs Held by High School Boys.

classifications of paper boy and salesclerk include one-half of the job opportunities. The other 50 percent is scattered over the remaining eighty-eight
classifications. Figure 65 shows the five most frequent part-time jobs held
by high school girls. Domestic and personal service hold most of the job
opportunities for girls, with housemaids leading the list. Girls, like boys,
also find opportunity as salesclerks. More than one-half of the girls find
their part-time jobs as salesclerks or housemaids.

4. When do students work? In the Louisiana Educational Survey over
1100 high school juniors were asked whether they worked for pay, and if
so, when they did their work. Roughly, eight out of every ten boys did
some work for pay, and three out of every ten girls received pay for their
work.[8] Figure 66 contrasts the part-time employment of high school boys

[7] Adapted from *ibid.*

[8] A survey made in the summer of 1946 showed that over 70 percent of all boys and
girls between the ages of twelve and eighteen earned at least a portion of their spending
money. See Virginia Richard, "Do They Know the Value of a Dollar?" *McCall's*,
November, 1946, p. 27.

and girls in gaining work experiences in monetary work plants.[9] The figure shows that high school students secure most of their jobs in the summer vacation period. More than half of all the boys (57.6 percent) work in the

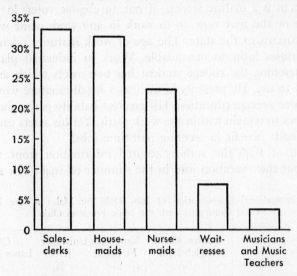

FIG. 65. Five Most Frequent Part-Time Jobs Held by High School Girls.

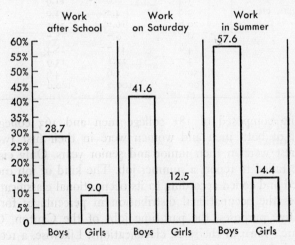

FIG. 66. Part-Time Work Reported by 1100 High School Juniors in Louisiana.

summer; only 14.4 percent of the girls report summer employment. Such data as are comparable from the Canton, Ohio, Occupational Study tend to show similar proportions for part-time workers in the high school levels.[10]

[9] The figure is adapted from data presented in Table 70, *Louisiana Educational Survey*, Vol. II, Section 4, Louisiana Educational Survey Commission, 1942, p. 164.

[10] The Canton study shows that 33 percent of the high school boys and 14 percent of the high school girls work either after school or on Saturday (year of 1937-1938).

5. Do age and education affect job opportunities during the initial period? College attendance ordinarily blocks out opportunity to engage in full-time work except in vacation periods. Yet by age eighteen in all states the young man or woman is a mature worker, if not an eligible voter, in the eyes of the law. He or she may now go to work in any work plant without permission of parents or the state. The age of work maturity opens up many job opportunities hitherto unavailable. Work in industrial plants is now possible. Therefore, the college student has two assets which an employer may be able to use. He presents himself as a legally mature worker and as one with above-average education. His greatest liability is the short working span he wishes to remain within the work plant. Yet his assets can be useful. Does he actually benefit in securing part-time jobs?

In the fall of 1946 the authors secured information from 343 college students about their vacation jobs in the summer of 1946. The sample was

TABLE 21.   Occupational Classification of Jobs Held by Males in the Initial Work Period Compared with the Male Force in Ohio

Occupation	Canton, Ohio, High School %	Kent State University Fr.-Soph. %	Jr.-Sr. %	Ohio Male Labor Force (1940) %
Professionals	1.3	0.0	11.9	6.0
Owners, managers, etc.	0.0	4.2	11.0	19.9
Clerical	29.8	16.7	27.5	13.8
Skilled	0.0	9.7	2.7	18.7
Semiskilled	14.6	41.7	28.4	26.0
Unskilled	3.7	22.1	13.9	15.4
Domestic	50.6	5.6	4.6	.2
Totals	100.0	100.0	100.0	100.0

a random one composed of 181 college men and 163 college women. Roughly half of both men and women were in their first two years of college; the rest were in their junior and senior years. Only eight in this entire sample failed to report a summer job. The kind of job each student held was listed and coded according to its occupational classification. Table 21 summarizes the occupational distribution in percentages for the men. For comparative purposes, the part-time jobs of the Canton, Ohio, high school boys are shown in the same classifications. Likewise, a record of the distribution of the normal full-time male working force of Ohio is given, using the data of the 1940 U.S. Census. With these statistics it is possible to assess the effect of age and education upon part-time job opportunities.

Figure 67 illustrates graphically some pronounced effects. College men are at an age when factory work is available to them. Their entrance into skilled, semiskilled, and unskilled jobs can be seen by examining the jobs held by college freshmen and sophomores. Only 18 percent of the high

school boys are working within these occupational levels, whereas 74 percent of the college freshmen and sophomores have gained entrance. These jobs pay relatively well, and college men are attracted to them. The high school boy finds his major field of employment within the domestic (51 percent) and clerical (30 percent) occupations. In contrast, only 5 percent of the

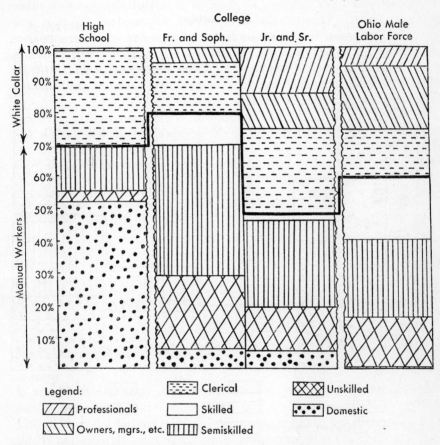

FIG. 67.   The Jobs Held in the Initial Work Period by Ohio High School and College Males; a Comparison with the Ohio Male Labor Force.

college men are found in the domestic occupations and 22 percent in clerical occupations. College men of junior and senior rank present some striking differences in their occupational picture. The increase of formal education seems to account for the 30 percent increase in jobs secured in the professional, managerial, and clerical classifications. With two or more years of college, higher-paid students can begin to bargain for good paying jobs in the white-collar area. This movement to white-collar jobs can be seen by observing the depth of the column from the top to the bisecting line.

Above the heavy line are white-collar jobs; below the heavy line, the so-called working-class manual jobs. The chart shows clearly that college men in their junior and senior years have secured a somewhat greater proportion of white-collar jobs (50 percent) than is held by the normal working force of Ohio (40 percent). However, it would seem that desire for higher pay

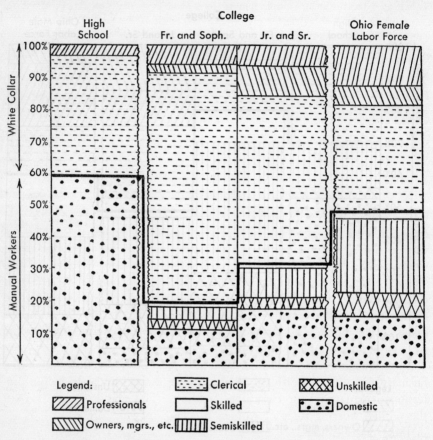

FIG. 68.   The Jobs Held in the Initial Work Period by Ohio High School and College Females; a Comparison with the Ohio Female Labor Force.

rather than status was the more compelling factor in the choices made by these applicants for initial jobs.

The initial job picture for college women is shown in Figure 68 and Table 22. It is clear that women are predominantly white-collar workers (75 percent), with the greatest number finding employment in clerical work (63 percent). Many of the same influences associated with age and education which applied to men can be seen in the job opportunities open to women. The major transition in jobs which can be identified between high school and college is the shift from domestic to clerical positions.

Whereas 60 percent of the high school girls did domestic work, only 14 percent of the college women were so employed. Of the high school girls, 38 percent secured clerical jobs, whereas 63 percent of the college women held such jobs.

TABLE 22.   Occupational Classification of Jobs Held by Females in the Initial Work Period Compared with the Female Labor Force of Ohio

Occupation	Canton, Ohio, High School %	Kent State University Fr.-Soph. %	Jr.-Sr. %	Ohio Female Labor Force (1940) %
Professionals	3.2	6.0	6.6	13.0
Owners, managers, etc.	0.0	3.0	9.8	4.3
Clerical	38.3	73.0	52.5	33.1
Skilled	0.0	1.0	1.6	1.3
Semiskilled	0.0	4.0	8.2	24.0
Unskilled	0.0	3.0	3.3	8.7
Domestic	58.5	10.0	18.0	15.6
Totals	100.0	100.0	100.0	100.0

The college women of junior and senior rank are able to find increased opportunity in the professional and managerial occupations. Seven more women out of every hundred were able to get into these brackets than were so able during the freshman and sophomore years. The junior and senior women display the same searching for higher-income jobs as the men do. This motive seems to draw the women into the semiskilled work of the factory and the higher-paid domestic work such as that of beauty parlor operator, etc. There is a 22 percent increase in these classifications over the freshman and sophomore years.

Most college women find their way into the "clean" occupations of the business class. Three-fourths of all the college women find jobs in the professional, managerial, or clerical occupations. This stands in contrast to the normal working force of women in Ohio, in which only one-half are in these classifications.

Both college men and college women have a greater range of job opportunity open to them, even as part-time workers, as their age and education are increased. By the junior and senior years, both can claim on the basis of their part-time jobs to have climbed into the "business class" (white-collar group) in greater proportion than is found in the full-time working population in Ohio.

SUMMARY

The five inquiries about the initial work period have shown that:

1. Many young people in both high school and college are searching for part-time jobs.

2. A majority of the high school boys, the college men, and the college women (in the reported studies) work in the summer vacation period. The high school girls seem to be the only group who fail to have a majority at work during summer vacation.

3. As age and education increase, opportunity for work increases, and this is recorded not only in more jobs but in a wider range of available jobs. This is particularly noticeable in the entry of college men and women into professional, managerial, and higher-paid clerical, and the skilled occupations.

4. Since most youth do not go to college, it is probable that a substantial number of young persons do not secure monetary work positions during the span of school enrollment.

THE CULTURAL EXPECTATIONS OF THE INITIAL WORK PERIOD

SOCIAL WEANING

The initial work period might be considered part of the *social weaning* process. The child's dependence upon the home must be broken. However, the habits and emotional ties which have so long provided a shelter for him are not easily unhinged. The child must be slowly prepared for the independence he must learn to assert, for there is no innate drive which will automatically direct him to such maturity. This is demonstrated by the following description given by a college man in his freshman year: "During the last two years in high school, I found that I would have to go to work in order to keep myself in spending money. How I hated the thought of going to work! The mere thought of going to work would send chills running up and down my spine. I had always helped in the garden at home and I always helped my mother clean house, but the thought of going some place else to work seemed different to me. I finally summoned up enough courage to start looking for a job."

INDOCTRINATION OF WORK VALUES

Maturity is acquired; its achievement is recognized when the social norms which define it are satisfactorily approximated. The index of achievement is made up of the opinions of interested adults who watch the progress of the young person. Their judgments will be expressed invariably in terms of cultural expectations. Some of the most compelling imperatives are:

1. You have to learn to accept responsibility.
2. You have to learn to work hard.
3. You have to learn to get along with people.
4. You have to learn the value of money.
5. You have to learn to hold a job and build a reputation for being a good worker.

These cultural expectations are indoctrinated into the child by the family and other institutions. The child hears his father and mother and his older brothers and sisters appraise the conduct of friends and outsiders in terms of these standards. The school reiterates and emphasizes them; the church gives its moral sanction to them.

THE CULTURAL BACKGROUND OF
TRADITIONAL WORK VALUES

ORIGINS OF TRADITIONAL WORK VALUES

Our traditional work values spring from a historic background which includes the experiences of survival on the frontier as well as a compelling interpretation of life called Puritanism. If we are to understand the patterns of work behavior expected of young people in our culture, we must examine the traditional work values. An understanding of the origins of these values will provide an opportunity to appraise their present usefulness. It will also help us to evaluate some of the conflicts and failures of the traditional values in modern life. The experiences of frontier life constitute the first source for explaining the cultural background of these work values.

Frontier Life

The frontier required hard work by everybody. Wright and Corbett put it: "Childhood was not long on the frontier, and youth was little different from manhood and womanhood."[11]

Children were important citizens. They lightened the labors of both men and women. And at fourteen a boy was given a rifle and assigned his loophole in the fort, where he stood shoulder to shoulder with the men. A boy's life or a girl's was filled with chores that were half work, half play. Getting in wood, making fires, feeding stock, and going to the mill were parts of the daily round and could themselves have filled any average day. But these were not all. Other tasks were the grating and pounding of corn, bringing water from the spring, and carrying clothes to and from the pond on wash days. There was the churning, the Saturday scrubbing and scouring with split brooms. . . . Children helped at all stages of woolen clothmaking from the shearing of sheep to the sewing of garments. . . . Girls were kept busy with skillet and spoon stirring and turning and mixing. They helped bake the johnny cake. They peeled turnips and potatoes. They helped with the washing at the pond or at the hollowed log trough and with the milking and churning. . . . At spinning, weaving, and knitting their fingers were as skilled and delicate as their brother's with his barlow knife.[12]

[11] J. E. Wright and Doris S. Corbett, *Pioneer Life*, University of Pittsburgh Press, 1940, p. 98.
[12] *Ibid.*, pp. 86-88.

Puritan Values

Life on the frontier made hard work a *necessity*; the influence of Puritanism made hard work a *virtue*. Puritanism may be described as a philosophy of life or that code of values which was carried to New England by the first settlers in the early seventeenth century. Any inventory of American traditions would have to commence with Puritanism. Miller and Johnson, in their comprehensive study of Puritanism, state:

Its role in American thought has been almost the dominant one, for the descendants of Puritans have carried at least some habits of the Puritan mind into a variety of pursuits, have spread across the country, and in many fields of activity have played a leading part. The force of Puritanism, furthermore, has been accentuated because it was the first of these traditions to be fully articulated, and because it has inspired certain traits which have persisted long after the vanishing of the original creed. Without some understanding of Puritanism, it may safely be said, there is no understanding of America.[13]

There are four values of Puritanism which have special reference to work. These might be described thus:

1. It is man's duty to know *how* to work and how to work *hard*.
2. Success in work is evidence of God's favor.
3. The measure of success is money and property.
4. The way to success is through industry and thrift.

Each of these values has left its mark on the passing generations of Americans. They live on in the tradition of America today. A study of them will enable us to understand the cultural expectations with which the young worker is ushered to his first work tasks.

1. It is man's duty to know *how* to work and how to work *hard*. "Root, hog, or die," was a common early American saying. James Truslow Adams says of this early pioneer period of American life, "It became deeply ingrained in our outlook on life that not only must a man work but that he must know *how* and that if he did not do either—work or know—it was his own fault. This, in the simplicity of our early frontiers, was to a large extent true, except for sheer physical or mental incapacity."[14] The low value which many early Americans placed on "schooling" (and some still do) sprang from the notion that all the practical education one needs for a job can be learned "out in life."

It is difficult for modern man to conceive of occupational choice limited to a few jobs. Yet in an agricultural civilization there were few pursuits other than farming. Franklin, in 1758, divided occupational groups into those who had a business, a trade, or a calling. Entrance into any of these

---

[13] Perry Miller and Thomas H. Johnson, *The Puritans*, American Book Company, 1938, p. 1.
[14] James Truslow Adams, *The American*, Charles Scribner's Sons, 1944, pp. 70-71.

groups could be attained with little formal schooling. Franklin himself
tells in his autobiography that at ten years of age he was taken from school
to assist his father in the business of "tallow-chandler and sope boiler." At
twelve, he signed indentures to serve as an apprentice printer until he was
twenty-one years of age. This was the accepted way of vocational training—
one learned a trade by "picking it up" on the job under the supervision of
an experienced worker.

In early America, all toil was honest and manual labor honored with
equal respect. The Puritans taught their children that all labor was honorable in the eyes of God. Franklin said, "He that hath a Trade hath an
Estate." And many an American father has continued to repeat this vener-
able wisdom to his son. The equal honor by which trade and calling were
held is understandable only in a society with an absence of rigid class lines.
"There are no classes in America," General Hugh Johnson used to assert.
"We are almost all middle class," James Truslow Adams declares. Adams
speaks of asking a young Frenchman what struck him most about the
American people. After a moment he replied, "I think it is the way that
every one looks you in the eye and takes it for granted that all are on the
same level."

Hard work and long hours were twin conditions of survival. To work
long hours became in itself a virtue. What American has not once or more
said (to quote Poor Richard), "Early to Bed, and Early to Rise, Makes a
man Healthy, Wealthy, and Wise!" Sometimes this virtue continued as a
value which guided behavior even when the need for survival was no longer
present. Hamlin Garland, in his autobiography, A Son of the Middle
Border, writes of his boyhood spent on a farm in Iowa in the 1870's. At
ten years of age, he was put behind the plow.

. . . It meant moving to and fro hour after hour, day after day, with no
one to talk to but the horses. It meant trudging eight or nine miles in the fore-
noon and as many more in the afternoon, with less than an hour off at noon.
. . . In truth, work would have been quite tolerable had it not been so long
drawn out. Ten hours of it even on a fine day made about twice too many for
a boy. . . . My father did not intend to be severe. As he had always been an
early riser and a busy toiler, it seemed perfectly natural and good discipline
that his sons should also plow and husk corn at ten years of age. He often told
of beginning life as a "bound boy" at nine, and these stories helped me to perform my own tasks without whining. I feared to voice my weakness.[15]

Young Garland arose at five o'clock in the morning, not, he says, because
he was eager to make a good record, but because his father believed in
early rising.

[15] Hamlin Garland, A Son of the Middle Border, The Macmillan Company, 1922,
pp. 86-88.

What did you gain by this disagreeable habit of early rising?"—this is a question I have often asked myself since. Was it only a useless obsession on the part of my pioneer dad? Why couldn't we have slept till six, or even seven? Why rise before the sun?

I cannot answer this, I only know such was our habit summer and winter, and that most of our neighbors conformed to the same rigorous tradition. None of us got rich, and as I look back on the situation, I cannot recall that those "sluggards" who rose an hour or two later were any poorer than we. I am inclined to think it was all a convention of the border, a custom which might very well have been broken by us all.[16]

This custom reminds the writer of a city school superintendent who took great pride in being at his desk at 6:30 A.M. and recommended that all ambitious teachers on his staff do the same. He transferred the early habits of his rural boyhood straightway to the urban setting irrespective of application to the tempo of city life.

Hard work and long hours endured without complaint, satisfaction in manual toil, pride in one's trade or calling—these, then, represent a core of frontier and Puritan values kept alive and transmitted to the passing generations. Even transition to an industrial civilization has not destroyed them. In the following pages these values will be found echoed again by modern youth as they go forth to receive their baptismals of work experience.

2. Success in work is evidence of God's favor. This is another Puritan belief which added further motivation for the necessity of working. Success in New England could not be achieved except by hard work and thrift, unless one was of the favored few. "If you did not work hard and were not shrewd, you did not achieve a rising scale of success, and, if you did not do that, you were evidently for some reason not in God's favor."[17]

Franklin said the same thing in *Poor Richard's Almanac* of 1758: "What though you have found no Treasure, nor has any rich Relation left you a legacy, *Diligence is the Mother of Good Luck*, as *Poor Richard* says, *and God gives all Things to Industry*."

Many have been the prayers to God asking for success in work. The early American said these prayers at his meals, at his bedside, and in his church. Prayer and hard work were considered the essentials of success. An all-seeing, omnipotent Power would surely hear and see and in His mercy reward honest toil. This is a powerful belief, and it guides many men and women about their work today. For some this belief rings out like a promise fulfilled; for others it remains a residue in the culture to be pulled out to justify the presence of poverty-stricken and unemployed workers. Economic depressions still bring out the accusers. "It's their (the unemployed's) own fault. They didn't work hard and they didn't save. Now they must suffer."

[16] *Ibid.*, p. 119.
[17] Adams, *op. cit.*, pp. 70-71.

The attempt of one employer to save his workers from immorality is recorded in his effort to translate hard work and God's favor into work habits for his employees. In 1822 he posted the following bulletin in his store:

Rules for Clerks

1. This store must be opened at Sunrise. No mistake. Open 6 o'clock A.M. Summer and Winter. Close about 8:30 or 9 P.M. the year round.
2. Store must be swept—dusted—doors and windows opened—lamps filled, trimmed and chimneys cleaned—counters, base shelves and show cases dusted —pens made—a pail of water and also the coal must be brought in before breakfast, if there is time to do it and attend to all the customers who call.
3. The store is not to be opened on the Sabbath day unless absolutely necessary and then only for a few minutes.
4. Should the store be opened on Sunday the clerks must go in alone and get tobacco for customers in need.
5. The clerk who is in the habit of smoking Spanish Cigars—being shaved at the barbers—going to dancing parties and other places of amusement and being out late at night—will assuredly give his employer reason to be ever suspicious of his integrity and honesty.
6. Clerks are allowed to smoke in the store provided they do not wait on women with a "stogie" in the mouth.
7. Each clerk must pay not less than $5.00 per year to the Church and must attend Sunday School regularly.
8. Men clerks are given one evening a week off for courting and two if they go to prayer meeting.
9. After the 14 hours in the store the leisure hours should be spent mostly in reading.[18]

"Griping" was not a trait of early Americans. They had their complaints about politics and morals, but complaints about personal hardships were not considered in good taste. Indeed, admission of such hardships might very well be taken as evidence that God's disfavor had been visited upon still another sinner. A friend of the authors' has an aunt living who has helped with all the manual work of the farm on which she lives. One day as she was riding the corn cutter she was thrown in front of the blades. One blade ripped into the lower leg, laying the flesh open from ankle to knee. More than twenty stitches were required to close the wide cut. She uttered not a word of pain. Throughout the entire period of recovery, she refused to speak about the accident or show the scar on her leg. It was a source of embarrassment to her for anyone to mention the incident. This behavior was part of a conviction, born of her early family training, that her suffering must be kept private—that, in fact, it was precipitated by

[18] Quoted from *"We" and Our Business*, Carson, Pirie, Scott and Company, 1927, p. 20.

evil forces which would not have beset her if she had been living a blameless life.

3. The measure of success is money and property. In an agricultural civilization, land is wealth and almost the sole form of wealth. In a country with abundant resources of cheap land, acquisition of land was possible, it was held, for anyone who worked hard. Adams says, "To rise meant to leave the wage class and to become a property owner, and property for the most part meant land. So, to rise socially, to be a successful American, and, in New England and where Puritan influence spread, to be one of the elect of God, you had to know the value of property. An odd complex thus developed of local patriotism, good citizenship, duty towards God, and the wisdom of the serpent, with success and moral virtue measured by money."[19]

The definition of success in terms of monetary values took a strong hold upon the American mind and still persists with remarkable vitality. On the factory floor, workers say, "If you're so smart, why ain't you rich?" In the community, the universal deference paid to the richest men of the town is a tribute to the superior shrewdness and industriousness attributed to them. Almost any American will tell you that it takes hard work to get to the top. This belief becomes thus related to the final Puritan value that has been singled out as of importance in understanding work values in our culture.

4. The way to success is through industry and thrift. It has been stated that a prime value among the Puritans was the belief that man had a duty to work hard. On the frontier there was always work to be done. Survival demanded it and the needs of civilization pressed for it. It must be remembered that the Pilgrims brought a civilization with them. The frontier cried out for strong men and women to work with driving vigor to turn a wilderness into a replica of Western civilization. There were endless resources of precious land, and its native treasures waited to be seized by whoever gave enough time and energy. Success could be claimed, it was said, by anyone who worked hard and saved his money.

"There are no Gains without Pains," Franklin said.

"If you were a Servant, would you not be ashamed that a good Master should catch you idle? Are you then your own master, *be ashamed to catch yourself idle.*"

"Drive thy Business, let not that drive thee."

"Sloth, by bringing on Disease, absolutely shortens life."

In these counsels, time becomes the taskmaster. Time is the most precious of all things. It provides the opportunity to do useful work and thereby to accumulate money.

Industry and attention to one's business is one virtue, but it must be coupled with frugality to win success. Poor Richard warns with wisdom that has been given by father to son for many generations: "You may think perhaps, that a *little* Tea or a *little* Punch now and then, Diet a *little* more

[19] Adams, *op. cit.,* pp. 70-71.

costly, Clothes a *little* finer, and a *little* Entertainment now and then, can be not a *great* Matter; but remember what Poor Richard says, *Many a Little Makes a Mickle.*"

"Beware of little expenses; Fools make Feasts and Wise Men Eat Them."

"*The first vice is running in Debt.* If you would know the value of money, go and try to borrow some; for, he that goes a borrowing, goes a sorrowing. Lying rides upon Debt's back."[20]

These precepts have been more than *The Way to Wealth* as Franklin saw it; they have remained as moral guides to Americans.

Work and success have been both man and God's goals. The motives for these goals were clearly understood by people of frontier and rural America. The way to them could be appraised in the tangible evidence of men's lives. Many of the industrious "proved" that hard work, perseverance, and frugality could take the lowest worker to wealth and power. It was implicitly understood that those who rose combined hard work with shrewdness. A persistent American belief has been that those who climbed to the upper ranks of wealth and power were rightly selected on the basis of intelligence as well as hard work. Only the critical few have become skeptical of this belief in modern times. The beloved sage of Emporia, the late William A. White, wrote shortly before his death of his new skepticism. He said, "I wish I could think that those who were well-placed in this town and country had really better brains than their less thrifty, less diligent and less prosperous brethren. I used to believe that way forty years ago, and it was a comforting faith. I confused the acquisitive faculty with brains. I mixed up hard work, prudence, and diligence with intelligence. I have had to surrender that prejudice. I know now that survival qualities in a competitive civilization are not the roots of human wisdom."[21]

This kind of heresy against a deep-rooted cultural value has not made many converts among the bright-faced, eager, middle-class American youths who are still hitching their wagons to stars. The triumph of aspiration, if not achievement, is told and retold by young workers in the following pages.

THE SOCIAL PSYCHOLOGY OF THE INITIAL WORK PERIOD

SOCIALIZATION TRANSLATES CULTURAL EXPECTATIONS INTO WISHES WITHIN THE PERSONALITY

The success of socialization is complete when the values of the group become attitudes in the personality. To be a nonconformist is to be self-reliant, says Emerson, but few individuals escape the force which our social groups exercise to compel conformity. In a contest between individuality

[20] These quotations are by Benjamin Franklin, taken from "Father Abraham's Speech" and forming the Preface to *Poor Richard's Almanac* for 1758.

[21] William A. White, "Emporia in Wartime," *New Republic,* April 13, 1942, p. 491.

and conformity, the strongest forces lie with conformity; for the group will provide its approval and praise for conformity and offer scorn and censure for nonconformity. *Thus the normal processes of socialization convert the cultural expectations of the initial work period into active wishes within the individual.* Five wishes normally arise as end products of the cultural expectations. These are the (1) wish for independence, (2) wish to demonstrate ability to work hard, (3) wish to determine ability to get along with people, (4) wish to have and manage money, and (5) wish to make a good job record. A description of each of these wishes will be illustrated by recent accounts of job experience in the initial period.

1. Wish for Independence

The young worker identifies working for pay as adult activity. The prestige of work hinges upon the dual promise of recognition as an adult (or being like an adult) and recognition as a productive worker—hence a useful member of society. The young worker drains out this prestige and mothers it like a precious possession. One young man of seventeen writes,

The first job I ever held was in an Isaly's Dairy store. I was quite young then, and I am sure my inexperience showed in my face, for the manager was quite reluctant to give me a job. I persisted, however, and succeeded in pestering the man to such an extent that he gave up in disgust and gave me a job. What a thrill! What an experience! My first job—I didn't actually need it, in fact, I battled with my parents for many months before I convinced them that I was capable of holding a job before they would even let me look for one. But convince them I did, and now I had my just reward.[22]

The feelings of responsibility and independence are illustrated by another college freshman, who says,

My first job consisted of several small jobs, each important in its own way. Although these jobs were "dirty jobs" and could be done by almost anyone, they had to be done, and so I was carrying responsibility for the first time in my life. This fact, my having some responsibility, was, I think, the most important fact concerning my job. Another was the fact that I was having to learn how to get along with people by myself—that is, without help coming from my parents.

Another young girl expresses her determination to work.

How well I recall my first job. It was the summer of forty-four and I was sixteen. When a girl reaches this age, it's time she was earning her own money during the summer months. Every girl and boy in the neighborhood had a job, that is, every girl and boy except me. Why didn't I have a job? My father didn't

[22] This is a student autobiography in the authors' collection. More than a thousand such papers were written by college men and women in their English courses at Kent State University during 1946. The experiences of these young people will be drawn upon at various times to illustrate the operation of social processes in the work experiences of youth during the initial work period.

approve. I couldn't let a little thing like my father stop me. If everyone else was working, I would work too. So I went to my high school principal. I knew he could help me with my troubles, and he did. He called my father. The following Monday I was behind counter twenty-three of the F. W. Woolworth Company selling ladies' underwear.

The ability to secure a job is regarded by young people as an achievement in maturity—especially if it can be done without "pull." One girl exclaims,

It was a wonderful feeling to know that I had obtained a position for the first time in my life without help from parents or friends. This thought alone seemed to be enough to spur me on.

The following picture of a boy's reaction to his first job provides many rich insights into personality reactions to work experience in the initial period.

On June 14, 1941, I graduated from the eighth grade. I was only thirteen years old, but decided that I wanted a job so I could earn my own money. My brother, who was only twelve at the time, and I rode out on our bicycle to the Coply Truck Farms. After we got to the truck farms, we hunted around for a farm that looked quite modern, as we wanted nice working conditions. We came to one farm where there were about ten boys working in the fields. I decided that we should get a job there because it wasn't too far away from the main road. We planned to thumb our way to work every morning, and we didn't want to walk from the main road. I walked over to the barn and told the man that I saw standing there that we were hunting for work. He asked me if we had ever had any farm experience. I told him that we worked two summers on my grandfather's farm. The man hired us and told us to report for work at 7:30 the next morning.

We reached home about an hour later and strutted into the house. My Mom asked us why we looked so happy, and we told her to wake us up at 5:30 in the morning from now on and to be sure and pack us a big lunch.

We walked the streets for the rest of the evening bragging about our job. The boys on the street envied us and also wanted to get a job. That night we went to bed quite early, as we were getting up at 5:30 in the morning. The morning came, we jumped out of bed, ate our breakfast, dressed, and were ready to go at six o'clock. We decided to leave early, as our job was about six miles away and we might have to walk if we couldn't get a ride. We left our house and got a ride from the very first car that we thumbed. He took us to within a half mile of the farm, and we walked the rest of the way. The boss said we were an hour early but that we should start to work as there was a lot to get done. We pulled weeds for nine hours in the hot sun, but we enjoyed it. The boss paid us a dollar each that day, and we felt very proud as we gave it to our mother. It was a feeling that one doesn't get very often.

Normal socializing forces sometimes fail to produce a desire for independence. In such instances, pressure rises outside the individual to push

him into the world of work. Some parents must encourage their sons and daughters to take their first steps into the work market, much as parent birds push their young from the shelter of the nest. One young man explains how he was pressed into his first job. He writes that his father told him, " 'You are a junior in high school, seventeen years old, and taking a course in business, so there is no reason why you should not get a job. The experience will be good for you.' My father was speaking in a tone of voice that meant only one thing—I had to find a job."

2. Wish to Demonstrate Ability to Work Hard

A second motive that can be detected as a strong force in the young worker's orientation is the determination to show others that he can work hard and to persevere no matter how hard the work becomes. Many times the summaries of initial job histories conclude with the statement, "My job taught me how to work hard." A girl's job history describes this feeling:

The first job I had was one I shall never forget, because while I worked, I learned many things which gave me a different outlook on life. I was only sixteen, and this was the first time in my life I had been away from my parents for any length of time. I was employed as a mangle ironer in the laundry of Ashtabula General Hospital at the rate of forty-five cents an hour. I had to get up at six o'clock every morning and be at work by seven. I thought I would melt, it was so hot. The mangle had a steam pressure of eighty-five degrees, and when I stood on the side where we folded the linen when it came through, the perspiration just ran down my face as if I had been crying. I had to stand up all day except during our half-hour lunch period. . . . That summer was well spent, in my estimation, even if I did lose nearly ten pounds and was on the verge of a collapse when I quit my job. I shall never forget the things I learned and the many friends I made while I lived in Ashtabula, and my parents know they can trust me anywhere now.

Sometimes the job requirements are not primarily physical demands but rather demands for endurance of boredom and monotony. This kind of hard work is commonly encountered. A typical job history describes reactions of a young worker in a factory:

I got my first job during the three-month period between my sophomore and senior years in high school. My father gave me the necessary "pull" to enable me to get the job. It was at the National Rubber and Machinery Company of Akron, Ohio, and my first job was operating a drill press. There were four thousand pieces to be drilled, and there were two holes to be drilled in each piece. On the machine was a square thing, which I learned was a jig, with a place just made to fit the piece I was to drill. All day long I stood at the drill press and drilled these little pieces. After a week of hard work I saw the pieces in my sleep, and after two weeks, I was finished at last. I never wanted to see another one of those pieces as long as I lived. But my jubilation at having finished

these four thousand pieces was short-lived. I was transferred from the drill press to the bench, where I was told I would be filing burrs off of castings. That sounded good for a change, so I went to the bench the next morning happy about the whole thing. But when I arrived at my place at the bench, my eyes almost burst from their sockets. There, piled in a monstrous heap, were the four thousand pieces I had just finished drilling. I stood there with my fists clenched and refused to file a single one of them. The boss was an understanding fellow and refused to fire me. He gave me a choice. I could file all of those four thousand pieces and be transferred to a milling machine, or I could file none of them and go back to the drill press with no chance of ever getting a job at another machine. So I filed burrs, and after another two weeks I was transferred to a milling machine. I have never regretted the lesson I received from my first job, and I know it has taught me the patience I need and will need all through life.

The young worker's desire to prove that he can do hard work is often short-lived, especially in the midst of very fatiguing or monotonous work. The belief of the initial worker that he will work only a temporary period induces him to accept all kinds of available jobs but does not guarantee his continuance, even during his available worktime. One young man accepted a job with a railroad repair crew. He says, "Of all the different jobs I have ever had, I think that work with the railroad repair crew was undoubtedly the hardest manual labor that I have ever been subjected to. At the end of my one day, I was certain that I would never again seek similar employment."

Another says of his work as a mason's helper, "I couldn't stand the thought of another two weeks like the last two. So I got my pay and quit. I immediately spent all my earnings for fishing equipment, and my father and I journeyed to Canada for a vacation."

A worker in a celery muck farm: "After a month of rawhiding, I was ready to quit. My mother now believed I should work the rest of the summer, but I didn't quite make it. Yes, someone might find some advantages in working on a muck farm, but my interests are found in other occupations."

A more determined or less enlightened muck farm worker says, "I worked at this job for several summers before I realized I could get easier spending money than that."

3. Wish to Determine Ability to Get Along with People

Rarely does any person admit that it is difficult for others to "get along" with him. Yet it is a source of great pride in the individual to prove to himself that he can get along with others. "I can get along with anybody," exclaims the executive, the clerk, and the drill press operator. Indeed, in the immense resources of egotism, the possibilities of self-deception seem unlimited. However, in the observance of *others*, most persons have ability

to judge readily and with considerable objectivity those who are "hard to get along with." And once such a label is pinned upon a worker, it may seriously impair his present and future chances for advancement. Young workers are warned by direct admonition and by the lessons of gossip that getting along with people is a very important qualification for success on the job.

A young man of eighteen tells about his first job experience on a paper route, which he assumed at twelve years of age. He says, "The most important effect that this job had upon me was the development of confidence in myself. Meeting people, speaking to them, doing business with them, selling my product to them—all these factors gave me confidence, made me more sure of myself in a world where self-assurance is a requisite second only in importance to ability."

An office boy describes his need for social savoir-faire.

I did not have one or even two bosses. I found that I had nearly twenty of them. And each one always had something for me to do. But I had been told that what I did for each one came in order of their importance in the department. Many is the time I would have three or four bosses ask me to do something all at one time.

For eleven months I worked side by side with people who were to me some of the most important people in the company. I met and came in contact with many interesting and important men and women. I have been told by the director of advertising at the firm that if I ever came back I would have a job waiting for me. It's worth thinking about.

Many young workers find their initial jobs send them into work situations where for the first time in their lives they come into intimate contact with adult men and women of the so-called "working class." They are certain that the workers they will meet will be so different that they will not be happy, or that they will be so self-conscious of their "higher status" that the workers will not be able to accept them.

A student accepting factory work reports: "My friends told me I would be unhappy there because the people I would meet working in a factory would be ignorant and not at all my type. I knew they were unfair in their statement after I met a few of my associates. They were not stupid, ignorant individuals. They were human beings making a living and not too 'proud' to work in a factory."

Another girl describes her work as a clerk in the five-and-ten-cent store. Of her fellow workers she says,

They were girls who had not graduated from high school and could not find other employment because of their lack of education. Most of them put on an appearance of superiority to counterbalance this lack. They dressed cheaply and without particular taste. Their talk was rough and vulgar, and most of them smoked and drank.

However, I feel that this type of girl was good at heart. I talked with all of them, and noticed that they were really sincere underneath the mask they put on. Some of them suffered from bad family conditions and others from poverty, which might have caused them to be what they were.

A young man found the way of customer coöperation difficult.

I did not like the job of clerking in the produce department. "The customer is always right," the boss said. That's what got into my hair the most. For example, we had bananas that were seconds, bruised a little, or fairly soft. We would put them into a basket and sell them for two cents a pound. We weren't supposed to pick out the better ones and leave the bad ones. They were to be sold as they came out of the basket, but some of the customers would argue if they saw that they were getting one that was soft. They would argue over one banana which sold for two cents a pound! If it had been rotten, it would have been different. But there were no rotten bananas in the basket. And if we gave all the better bananas to the customers that came first, the customers that came later would have to take what was left. I couldn't stand it, because I believe that all customers should be treated the same.

4. Wish to Have and to Manage Money

Money is the symbol of independence. It marks adulthood; it stamps the individual as an earner and as an important person. As one young worker put it, "Working gave me the status of a wage earner in the family." He explains, "That meant I was able to buy all my own clothes, to choose exactly what I wanted, and to pay for what I wanted. It meant I could see as many movies as I wished. I could go out at night as often as I liked and come in when I chose. I was released from many of the home tasks which I was previously asked to be responsible for. And above all, my family and my friends began to treat me like a man. . . ."

Money is not only a symbol of independence. It is also congealed power and respect. It buys goods and services when released. When accumulated, it commands deference. Parents and friends have often discussed money—how people get it, how they spend it, and the importance of saving it. The young worker comes to regard money as some powerful magic. He is warned that it has potentialities for good and evil. He is told that he must learn the *value* of money. It is little wonder then that the young worker approaches his first earnings with mixed feelings—pride in his reward, yet concern over its disposition. Even his fellow workers ask one another the questions he has heard raised in his own family: "Are you getting ahead?" "Are you able to put anything in the bank?"

A budding young magazine salesman, age eleven, tells how he reacted to the two dollars he received weekly. "Before I started selling magazines, I always wanted more money for ice cream and candy. Now that the time had come when I was making big money, I didn't spend a cent hardly. All

I wanted to do was to save money, and put it in the bank. Along with selling magazines, I hauled ashes and rubbish. Each week I made two to three dollars by doing this. In a year's time, I had $150 in the bank under my name."

A young tire worker in an Akron rubber company explains how he interprets money. "My job has taught me the value of money and not to spend it foolishly. When you have to put in so many hours to earn a certain sum of money, you are not apt to spend it as quickly and foolishly as if the money were given to you. Money doesn't go very far these days, as everything you buy is high. When you look at an object you have to buy, you think that it will cost a day's work or a week's work, etc."

Money saved is often regarded as the only permanent gain for working. It is sometimes considered the justification for continuing on a job which is otherwise unsatisfactory. As one young worker says of his clerical job in a downtown Cleveland store, "When I went back to school in September, 1943, I felt that although I hadn't gained much practical training on the job, my summer had been fairly well spent. I had saved a substantial sum of money and had purchased several United States War Bonds which I intended to cash in about seven years from now. This money should certainly be useful, especially since I hope to be married by then."

The use of wages for wanton spending strikes discordantly against the cultural norms and results in feelings of guilt. Placed against Puritan values, spending without some saving is the first sin (if not the original one). Some people learn the lessons of their culture by observation; others must test the cultural compulsions and find their lessons by experience. One college girl used her observations of people at an amusement park as a guide to experience.

Many people do not know the value of money. Before I worked at Summit Beach Park in Akron, I was one of these people. I worked during war times when money was plentiful and people just threw it away down at the park. I am not talking about those who would come down a few times during the season, but about those happy-go-lucky ones who would be there most of the week. The prices at the park were very unreasonable considering what a person got for his money. It was just like a slot machine. They can't be beat no matter how long you try. I believe in giving a person his money's worth. My boss and I had quite a few arguments in regard to this, but he always won, due to the fact that he owned the place and was strictly dogmatic about the whole deal.

Another young man who sins against the principle of saving tells of his repentance:

My first job was in the office of a local factory. In June of 1939 after one semester at Kent State University, I obtained this job with the idea of saving enough money through one summer to pay all my expenses through the coming

school year. All went as anticipated, that is, I saved money throughout the summer. I frugally deposited fifty dollars monthly into the bank. But when September came, I could not force myself to give up the life of plenty, financially, for one of want. I failed to enter college that fall. Since the die was cast, I immediately ceased all saving and started on a spending orgy. I bought a car, quite a few clothes, and started going out evenings more often. In fact, I seldom stayed home more than one night a week. As could be expected, the quality of my work was somewhat affected—it was much worse than usual. I was young (18) and had what I thought was plenty of money, so the pleas of my family to slow down a bit fell on deaf ears.

It took five years in the army plus the loss of numerous opportunities of obtaining a good job, because I was not a college graduate, to make me see the light. If I had given up that first job to return to college back in September of 1939, I probably would have been much better off.

5. Wish to Make a Good Job Record

A man's reputation is a prized possession. It is prerequisite for a man or woman who wishes to receive respect and material advancement. A job reputation is built on a twofold estimate: (1) what a man is as a total personality and (2) what a man can do. A young worker is aware as he starts his first job that he is on the threshold of his job history. "Making good" means convincing others of his individual worth; it means proving to himself that he is able to handle adult responsibilities. A good job record is a valuable asset. It can be traded in, as it were, in the bargaining for new jobs of higher pay and status. The poor job record is a stubborn liability that is not easily shaken off. It follows the holder wherever he goes and jeopardizes his search for a new start.

The young worker goes into his first jobs with the warnings and urgings of his parents, relatives, and friends ringing in his ears. "Make good!" they say. And as days on the job pass by, they keep on asking, "How are you getting along?" They "corner" work associates and again they ask, "How's the boy getting along?" This pressure to make good is revealed in the inner compulsions of the personality.

One young worker said, "Being a playground director taught me to be a more responsible person. I didn't realize what a complete child I was until I started working on the playground. From then on I was on my own and I had to make a success of my first job."

The pride of making a good job record is illustrated in some histories where the worker has climbed into more responsible jobs.

When I finished high school, the vocational director obtained a job for me as a sheet metal worker in a small shop. I had to start at the bottom, as most inexperienced help do. My hourly rate of pay was sixty-five cents. Being a small company, work was not always steady in some departments; therefore, I was continuously being moved from one kind of work to another. I did not object to the

practice because I was able to learn the grade as well as the business more completely. After I thought I knew enough about the production set-up, I asked to be given a better job working in the office where I could get more information on how the business was run through the front office. By luck, one of the men was leaving for the army in a few weeks, so I was given the opportunity of taking over his job. With the two weeks that he had left, I was given the brief fundamentals of the job. This job had no real title. It was a job that required taking care of the orders and shipments which were carried on between the superintendent's office and the shipping department. It was a job where I could learn enough about the business end so I could go on the road in a few years as a salesman. After working there for six months, I enlisted in the navy. When I returned after three years of service, I received a letter from my old employer stating that my old job was open for me whenever I wanted it. After I get a little more college experience, I'm going back and take a job as a salesman with this company.

The satisfaction of making good is illustrated in this Horatio Alger version of an initial job history:

My first job was at the Allen Theatre in Cleveland, Ohio. My working hours were from three o'clock in the afternoon until ten o'clock in the evening. I worked every day except Sunday, which was my day off. While working at this job, I attended school during the day and I managed to receive good grades in my studies.

I was fourteen years old when I began working at the Allen Theatre. I worked there for four years. During that time, I held the positions of usher, head usher, doorman, and head doorman. When I started as an usher, my duties were to escort the theatre patrons to their seats and to keep order in the theatre. Eight months later, I was promoted to the position of head usher; this position put me in charge of all ushers. I made sure that each usher performed his duties and was at his post at all times. A year passed and I found myself as the doorman of the Allen Theatre. My duties as doorman were to admit people to the theatre by taking their tickets and to render any necessary service to the theatre patrons. After a year as the doorman of the theatre, I was promoted to the position of head doorman. As the head doorman, I was in charge of all the theatre personnel. Whenever the manager and the assistant manager were absent from the theatre, I took full charge until their return.

Fourteen months later I was called to the army. This event interrupted a long and successful job. I hope I shall enjoy my future job or jobs as much as I enjoyed my first one.

Making good sometimes requires a search for a job which suits interests and abilities. The struggle of a young worker on initial jobs is depicted in the following account:

During the past six or seven years, I have had quite a few different jobs. Some of them were so bad I soon learned to hate them. There were a few in which I could not seem to get interested; there were some that I liked all right

but had to quit for different reasons. At any rate, no job seemed to stay with me for any great length of time. Of course, it was understood that I was just working during summer months and on Saturdays when I was in high school. Perhaps this accounts for the fact that my jobs were so numerous.

This habit of finding one job, working a few weeks, and then quitting stuck with me until I graduated from high school. I knew that soon after graduation I would have to go to the Army, but I decided to work awhile before they called me. I began to look around and finally landed a job at a bottling plant near my home. I had worked inside the plant for several days when my boss called me into his office. He explained to me that one of his truck drivers had quit a few days before and he needed another driver. He asked me if I wanted the job. I did not think it would appeal to me, but I said I would try it.

The very next morning I started driving the delivery truck. The minute I started out, I knew I would like it. This job was just what I had been waiting for. The working hours were good. The working conditions were excellent. I worked four and one-half days a week and made almost as much money in that one week as I had in a month previous to that. I literally fell in love with my new job.

I drove a truck for this same company for almost three months and then I was taken into the Army. That was the greatest blow of all—to have to quit a good job and go to the Army. Shortly after receiving my Army discharge, I started to school and did not try to get my old job back. However, it was the best job I ever had, and I probably will never forget how much I liked driving for that company.

These accounts from young workers in their initial period show how successfully the cultural compulsives can be translated into personality traits. The school and the home combine to stimulate ambition. The business employers and managers judge the success of the home and school on the ability of these agencies to produce the traditional work attitudes in youth. These traditional attitudes are not always forthcoming. In fact, there is a growing conviction that the home and school are failing increasingly in this responsibility. It is to this failure that the discussion is now turned.

THE FAILURE OF SOCIALIZATION TO INCULCATE TRADITIONAL WORK VALUES

CHANGING WORK ATTITUDES OF YOUTH

Socialization does not always succeed in transforming the cultural expectations into personal attitudes. Older adults often say, "I don't know what's got into young people today. They don't want to do anything that requires hard physical labor. You can't get them to accept responsibility, and they think it will kill them if you ask them to work more than eight hours a day. They spend their money like water and some of them are so discourteous you feel like taking a paddle to them. They all think that someone will take care of them."

CONTRADICTIONS IN WORK VALUES

These anguished complaints reflect a culture containing new values which have arisen in contradiction to the old. These cultural contradictions exist side by side in the same society. As persons strive to "belong" to the social groups in which they participate and to seek out recognition and prestige, they find ambiguous guides. They learn that:

1. You have to learn to accept responsibility. *But:* It takes a long time before you can get a job that calls for much responsibility.

2. You have to learn to work hard. *But:* A man doesn't have to risk his money and worry over a business, do hard physical labor, or work long hours in order to make a good living any more. There are lots of softer jobs which pay good money and you don't have to kill yourself. It is more important to get located right and make good contacts.

3. You have to learn to get along with people. *But:* You have to learn to be aggressive and push yourself or you won't ever get ahead. You have to step on some people's toes or you will never get things done.

4. You have to learn the value of money. *But:* Nobody gets rich these days by pinching pennies. If you want to make money, you must look and act as if you have money. The most important thing is to know the right people, belong to the right clubs, and get invited to the right social functions.

5. You have to learn to hold a job and build a reputation for being a good worker. *But:* You are not going to live your life in one company or one town. The way to get ahead is to keep moving around. You should be able to get a better job and more money on every move.

The existence of such contradictions results in a socialization of many differing work attitudes. Traditional work values have a strong hold over rural and small-town life. It is mainly in urban life that the conflict between traditional values and the new values is greatest. Young people are caught in this conflict, and many become confused as to what work role they should play. Some march on in conformance with the traditional values. Others turn to the new values and, with a feeling that they are wise in the ways of the world, assume work roles which aim for the big money.

In the following interviews the breakdown of Puritan values is clearly demonstrated. The first is that of a young woman; the second, of a young man. Both are eighteen years of age.

Glenda is a rather chic appearing brunette who works as an usherette for the Hamrick theaters. She usually works on Friday nights, and during the matinees. Sometimes she works additional nights, when usherettes are taken ill.

When the purpose of the interview was first explained, Glenda thought it was just a dodge to get acquainted and try to "get some strange stuff." She is a senior in high school, has considerable experience for an 18-year-old, and evidently

had been "propositioned" more than once. But when she understood that the manager had given his O.K. (the son is an old fraternity brother), she consented to talk while we were having lunch on me, Saturday noon. A very practical girl.

This is not the first job Glenda has held. She worked evenings in a small bakery before she was sixteen, and the money was paid in cash and without payroll deductions. It seems that was where she had her first experience with men. Unpleasant experience, that is. The boss evidently thought that, as long as the work was illegitimate, a few other things might as well be. She has also worked as a berry picker during summer vacations. The last job before this one was helping out in a variety store. She seemed to think the pay was pretty low, and she was not allowed to take over a counter herself. She ran errands for the regular clerks. The manager told her if she stayed on he would put her on a regular counter when she graduated and could work full time. That was about a year ago, and Glenda could not bring herself to stick it out so long.

The present job seems to please Glenda. She says boys and men occasionally try to get acquainted, but most of the time they just eye her and smile, or make appreciative noises among themselves. I asked her if this was unpleasant, and she said no, any girl likes to know she is something every man would like to get. But she said she resents having anyone "get an itch where I should be scratching." She thinks most of the men who come to theaters are either "pretty definitely" married or "strictly shmoos." As for the boys, they are just people to tickle her vanity temporarily. Not solid in the world as yet. Women are more likely to be fussy, she says, but on the whole there is no trouble from the public. The pay is satisfactory, she likes the snug fitting uniform, and she enjoys the sense of being in charge when people grope around in the dark, or when the house is packed and people stand in the foyer. She doesn't intend, however, to stay one day after graduation.

Glenda's future is all nicely blueprinted, as far as Glenda is concerned. No college for her. She has heard all about how college girls are left on the small end when it comes to making good marriage catches. And she knows that successful young men don't usually marry a girl under 20, and that they do marry smartly dressed, well groomed, cosmopolitan young women. She intends to go to beauty school just long enough to get all she needs in the way of care of face, hair, and figure. Then she will attend a model school to pick up what she needs on style and posture. After that, she hopes to land a job in the office of a fairly large plant, where she can hope to meet rising young executives, or perhaps really terrific salesmen with big futures.

I asked her, if she wanted such a job, why she did not plan to go to business college. Her reply was that the girls who have specialized training are stuck away in cubby holes and are expected to be devoted to the job. Besides, she feels that the average employer will hire a good looking, charming girl any day in preference to "a mechanical brain."

Altogether, it appears that Glenda has given considerable thought to the subject of ensnaring a productive male. Her father is a physician, but she does not want a professional man for a husband, any more than she wants a profession for herself. She wants a man who can entertain her and her friends, and be able to meet social appointments without mental reservations. Even a specialist,

she believes, is under more restraints than, say, a hotshot salesman. There is some indication, too, that she would relish the idea of entertaining customers and buttering the people who hand out promotions. In other words, she wants to be a social asset to an aggressive money maker, who in turn will be able to provide a gay and comfortable life for her.[23]

Charlie, the young man, shares many values with Glenda even though there are marked differences in their status aspirations.

Charlie works for Mr. Engstrom, who runs the grocery store four blocks from my home. He helps to put groceries on the shelf and mark the cans, after school. He also helps on Saturday, when his main job is delivering bags and boxes to the cars of customers.

I got Charlie into conversation one evening and asked, among other things, if it was a good job. He said, "Oh, sure."

"I suppose you plan on taking it up permanently?"

"Oh, no. Just kinda something to do. You know how it is."

"Oh, I see. You like to spend money."

"Yeah. Well, no. Not exactly."

I busied myself looking at a shelf of groceries, and then said, "No?"

"Well, I save money, too."

"Why?"

"I dunno—maybe I'll go to college some day. Or buy a car, if I decide to take an ordinary job."

"What do you have in mind?"

"Well, my older brother drives a truck. But I don't think I'd care for that, exactly. They say it's hard on the kidneys. I know a kid whose dad works in the packing house. He makes good money."

"Well, isn't that pretty hard work, pretty dirty?"

"Oh, sure. But he makes two bucks an hour. And he moves around once in awhile, and they always clean up before they come out. Punchy drove to get his dad once, and he looked just like a salesman, or something. Besides, they get wholesale on meat. And you know the old saying—people always eat."

"Do you think college would fit you for something better than any of that?"

"Well, that's a big question, I think. It all depends. My dad has a garage. He makes out fine, but he thinks I should get a job with a big company. Either that, or save my money and go at it the hard way, the way he did. But he thinks the big outfits will eventually be the whole cheese, you might say. On the other hand, I wouldn't know whether to be a chemist, or an engineer, or what."   •

"Isn't there anything you would like better than anything else?"

"Oh, sure, a doctor. But you have to have pull to get in. Letters from doctors, and all that. Besides knowing the right people afterward. It's a money racket, these days."

[23] This interview and the one following were obtained and written by Norman G. Hawkins, a graduate student in the Department of Sociology at the University of Washington.

I also sounded Charlie out on unions, as something to consider if he takes "an ordinary job." He seemed to think it was part of the game, like his father contributing to all sorts of worthy enterprises in order to maintain good will.

Then I probed into his background and got the following pattern:

When he was in junior high, they lived farther out, off the bus line. His father's business was located on the highway at that time. Instead of walking several blocks, he wanted to get a bike. His father, who seems to believe in thrift, said he could earn one. So Charlies got his first job, as a paper boy. He liked the work on the whole, but got the grocery job in order to get in out of the weather, and also because it had sort of a "grown up" appearance about it. He is a junior now, and has been at it since the rush season during August and September last year.

In order to try to get his feeling about status, I asked him, "Which do you consider more worth while, in the way of getting ahead in the world, this work you do, or your schooling?"

He said, "Oh, shucks. High school doesn't mean much. In fact, I'd say college doesn't mean too much. The guy that gets money is the one that figures the angles. And if you don't want money in particular, what difference does it make?"

"Well, would you like to make money?"

"Oh, not much. It gets to be a headache, after fifty or a hundred thousand. Naturally, anybody with any gumption likes to have things convenient, maybe a few luxuries. I like to travel. I've been up in B.C. and over on the peninsula, and east of the mountains. I went one summer to my uncle's place, back in Illinois. That was with my big brother. I'd like to go to sea once, too. And have money for a television set, and time to take in games and things."

"Do you intend to get married?"

"Well, that's another thing. This girl I'm going with. I think quite a lot of her. If we still feel the same next year, then we'll probably get married. As long as the job is decent and the pay is good, why break my neck for maybe the same pay in some office?"

"Then you don't feel that an education is an asset?"

"Oh, in certain lines, yes. Like a technician. Or if a man wants to be a teacher, or a politician, or some of them soft jobs like that."

"How about machine work, or something of that kind?"

"Oh, that's about like the doctors. Those boys have things pretty well sewed up. Dad could get me into the auto mechanic game all right, but it doesn't pay as good as some of the other ones. I kind of enjoy exercise, anyway."

"Do you get more exercise now than when you were a paper boy?"

"Oh, well. Some jobs are just for the drips. Like garbage collector. Even for six bucks an hour, you'd never catch me on the honey wagon. I mean he-man exercise."

In summarizing, I would say Charlie has found education tiresome and without connection with life as he sees it. He wants adventure, but he also wants the security and lack of responsibility that go with highly organized types of work. He doesn't want a lot of money as his father did, and he has the idea

that the easiest way is the best. He feels that a job is just a job, a means for getting the ordinary comforts of life.

THE DISORGANIZATION OF TRADITIONAL WORK VALUES

The motives and goals expressed by Glenda and Charlie strike discordantly upon the ears of those persons who have been socialized in the traditional work values. Moralists are quick to cry out that the home and the school are failing to do their duty. If, they say, parents and teachers taught their children as they were taught this "willful" and "irresponsible" behavior of modern youth would not occur. Their question is, "Why don't parents and teachers do something about it?"

The sociologist when asked to answer such a question attempts to direct attention to the influence of the total social environment upon a young person in our culture. He first turns to the reasons for the disorganization of traditional work values. He finds that a number of social forces have combined to frustrate the indoctrination of traditional values. The major forces operating to disorganize traditional expectations and to create new work values are: (1) manifold aspects of the industrial revolution; (2) the decay of the religious view of work; (3) the definition of formal education as vocational and professional training; (4) the growth of get-rich-quick opportunities and white-collar criminality; (5) the disappearance of social stability and confidence in long-run goals; (6) the disappearance of apprenticeship work experiences.

Major Forces Operating to Disorganize Traditional Work Values

1. MANIFOLD ASPECTS OF THE INDUSTRIAL REVOLUTION

The effects of the industrial revolution upon work motives and habits are far-reaching. Prominent cause-and-effect relationships may be identified.

	Cause	Effect
The industrial revolution:	1. Transferred an increasingly large number of persons from rural to urban life. Secondary group participation increasingly comes to predominate within the growing corporate structures.	Introduced impersonality and weakened the social controls supporting traditional work values.
	2. Replaced independent proprietorship with dependence upon an employer.	Brought about decline in motivation and sense of personal responsibility.
	3. Set work performance within highly specialized or highly routinized limits.	Weakened purposive effort as end product was obscured and the individual's part became unidentifiable.

4. Created an impersonal market in which demands for labor were subjected to extreme cyclical variations during which large groups of workers were exposed to economic insecurity and suffering.	Aroused feelings of insecurity and insignificance. "Nobody is indispensable."
5. Stimulated an increasingly restricted market as monopolistic practices of capital and labor multiplied.	Formed motives and habits in which attempts to gain by producing less rather than harder work and more production were seen to be rewarded.
6. Raised the standard of living by increased mechanization of work tasks.	Stimulated motive to reduce efforts of manual labor by "letting a machine do it."

2. THE DECAY OF THE RELIGIOUS VIEW OF WORK

The Christian view of work holds that all work and property belong to God. Man is the steward who is called to serve God through work. All work is of equal moral worth in His eyes.

This view placed each man in a position of duty to his fellow men as well as to his God. While it prevailed, a sense of moral worth and economic justice accompanied the distribution of work tasks.

Secular thinking has largely supplanted this concept. Distinct status rankings are now assigned to the occupational classifications which define "superior" and "inferior" work. The industrial revolution accentuated these status differentials as manual workers, particularly, were exposed to the insecurity and deprivation of economic depressions. A weakening of the moral view of work destroyed a sense of economic justice. Workers came to believe that they did not have a moral obligation to their employer.

3. THE DEFINITION OF FORMAL EDUCATION AS VOCATIONAL AND PROFESSIONAL TRAINING

The belief that each step reached on the educational ladder is at the same time a step taken toward a higher-status, better-paying job has stimulated greatly the aspiration for white-collar jobs. It explains why so many young people expect to avoid manual labor and why they often look with disdain upon workers engaged in manual labor.

4. THE GROWTH OF GET-RICH-QUICK OPPORTUNITIES AND WHITE-COLLAR CRIMINALITY

This is the country of bonanzas, rackets, and stock market fortunes. As Charlie said in his interview, "The guy that gets money is the one that

figures the angles." The widespread pattern of adult participation in get-rich-quick schemes ranging from chain-letter crazes to stock and land speculation has stimulated young workers to look for short cuts to "success."

5. THE DISAPPEARANCE OF SOCIAL STABILITY AND CONFIDENCE
   IN LONG-RUN GOALS

War, depression, and inflation shake the fabric of life plans and weaken confidence in long-run goals. This atmosphere places more value on what the worker can get now than on what he may attain later.

6. THE DISAPPEARANCE OF APPRENTICESHIP WORK EXPERIENCES

The urban child has become an economic liability. He is not wanted permanently in the work market until he is at least fourteen and preferably eighteen. There is but a limited range of work experiences open to him before that time. He is uncertain as to what occupation he shall follow for he understands what few of them entail. Within the rural environment his life as farmer would have been prepared for him by a long apprenticeship in which his work would be wanted and needed.

These and other forces have brought disorganization to traditional work values. Society shares a responsibility for the work habits and attitudes that it sees laid down in the young people. It is perhaps not so amazing that traditional values have become disorganized as that they have, in the midst of the forces recounted, held such continued vitality.

CULTURAL RATIONALIZATIONS

The traditional cultural expectations are never extinguished, even in the midst of their opposing contradictions. Morally, the traditional values are "right." They continue to bear down throughout the trial and stable periods of an individual's work life. Yet the culture does acknowledge that young workers may fail in their early efforts to mature as responsible workers. Thus, beside the expectations lie the cultural rationalizations. These enable the family, friends, and employer to soften the blows of failure. The individual, in turn, seizes upon these ready-made rationalizations to rebuild his ego defenses and start out again to seek his success in work. The most common rationalizations in the culture are:

1. "Youth are inexperienced; it takes time to learn a job."

2. "Youth are unstable; you can't expect them to bear down like an older worker. They have to sow their oats. They will settle down in time."

3. "Youth are not as strong as adults; you can't expect a growing girl or boy to work so hard. Some people are just not made for that kind of work. Anyway, you don't expect people to work so hard any more."

4. "Youth should not be expected to work on a temporary job like a person who works steady. It is not too important what you do on the first jobs."

5. "Youth should not be expected to work on all kinds of jobs; it isn't the kind of work or the atmosphere that's right for a young worker."

In these rationalizations the group acknowledges the imperfections of its members. It accepts the person with sympathetic understanding as its members recall their own past failures. Thus youth is prepared to embark again on the way to fame and fortune. For as Poor Richard says, "If you don't succeed at first, try, try, again," or as sophisticated youngsters say it, "Anyway, it's my life."

CONCLUSION

The initial jobs are more than experiences that provide job information and guidance for young workers. These jobs are entrances into the world of work. The work world is a social world in which individuals are tested. On this proving ground habits and attitudes of young workers are placed before the eyes of adults. Young workers are taught and watched by the older workers to see whether they meet the cultural expectations of work.

As each new worker goes to his test, the habits of many years go with him. The young worker has learned (or failed) to work in the home and in the school. His habits and attitudes derive from his experiences as a worker, a listener, and an observer. What he has done, what he has heard from his associates, and what he has seen others do coalesce into work habits which are taken with him to monetary work plants.

The transition from full-time occupation in the school to full-time activity within a monetary work plant is a change in cultural life so drastic as to induce marked changes in the personality. The study of this transition is the subject of the next chapter.

SUPPLEMENTARY STUDIES

Field: Planned Interviews

Make one or more interviews with youth in the initial work period. The best ages for interviewing are probably between sixteen and eighteen years of age. However, college students even through graduate standing may be considered in the initial work period and may properly be interviewed as in this period. For a comparative analysis it is very desirable to seek interviews with youth from lower-, middle-, and upper-class families. The following interview form is suggested as a guide.

Name _____ Interviewer _____
                                 Date _____
                                 City _____ State _____
A. Background
   Age _____ Sex _____ Grade in School _____

Occupation of: Father _____ Sister _____

Mother _____ Sister _____

Brother _____ Sister _____

Brother _____

Brother _____

B. Job and Work

1. What kinds of work have you done? **Start** with first jobs and tell me about these jobs.
   a. What was the job?
   b. How did you get it?
   c. What did you like and dislike about it?
   d. Why did you leave it?
2. What do you do now?
   a. After school
   b. On week ends
   c. Last summer
3. Have you been able to save any money? If so, what for?
4. What kind of job do you hope to secure when you are out of school? Do you wish this to be your regular occupation? If not, why not?
5. Do you think there is a good chance of getting the job you want? Why do you want that kind of job? What have you done along this line? How much have you watched this job? Where have you gotten most of your ideas about it?
6. How do you think people on a job get ahead?
7. Do you think you are going to have steady employment? Will you join a union? Why?
8. Do you think in the future there will be more money and more steady jobs for everybody?

C. School and Work

9. What differences are there between working and going to school? Look for such items as: free response of interviewee, nature of work, people, routine, freedom, authority.
10. Do you think going to school will really help you get a job?
11. Do your father and mother think it's a good thing for you to finish high school (or college)?
12. Which would you rather be doing now—going to school or having a real job? Why do you feel that way?

D. Home and Work

13. How do your parents feel about your working?
14. What talk about work have you heard around your house?
15. What do your parents think you should do in planning for work and getting a job when you have finished school? What are your ideas about it?
16. What about marriage?

E. Community and Work

   Ask respondent for information which will enable you to scale social participation on the Chapin Social Participation Scale. This scale is reproduced below:

Name of Organization	1. Member	2. Attendance	3. Financial Contribution	4. Member of Committee	5. Offices Held
1. _____					
2. _____					
3. _____					
4. _____					

Scoring: Weights of 1, 2, 3, 4, 5 are assigned to each type of participation as indicated by the order at the top of the scale. For example, if a person belonged to 6 clubs or organizations, attended 5, contributed to 3, was a member of 2 committees, and was an officer in an organization, his total score would be 38. Tentative norms for the Social Participation Scale may be found in F. Stuart Chapin, *Experimental Designs in Sociological Research*, Harper & Brothers, 1947, p. 195.

FIELD: CASUAL INTERVIEWS

On casual contact, talk about jobs with youth reveals a considerable body of information and insight into work habits and attitudes. Discuss work experiences with the young man or woman who is clerking or delivering your purchases. Ask young persons in your neighborhood what jobs they want. Discuss with parents the hopes they have for their youth.

LIBRARY: BOOKS

Hollingshead, A. B., *Elmtown's Youth*, John Wiley and Sons, 1949, especially chap. 11, "Jobs and Ideas of Jobs," and chap. 14, "Toil and Trouble."
Landis, Paul, *Adolescence and Youth: The Process of Maturing*, McGraw-Hill Book Company, Inc., 1945.

RESEARCH GAPS

1. Study of work experiences on the first job accepted from an employer.
2. Study of the sequence of jobs held by young persons in the initial work period.
3. Study of the work experiences of college students.

The Transition from School to Work

584

THE TRANSITION REQUIRES SOCIAL ADJUSTMENT

FROM STUDENT TO WORKER—A SHIFT IN FUNCTION AND IN STATUS

The transition from school to work is a movement which requires thousands of young work recruits to change each year from a non-monetary to a monetary work plant. For each individual this means that the life experiences offered by such social institutions as the home, school, church, and community are now to be supplemented by the experiences of money-rewarded work. But these supplementary experiences are more than mere additions, for the replacement of the monetary work plant for the school is not a simple substitution. Each new worker faces to a greater or less degree a different cultural environment in the work plant. To this new environment he must adjust if he is to secure his own livelihood. Quietly, but surely, the young worker comes to realize that he has inherited the status of a working adult. His dependence upon work activity is emphasized by the cultural expectation that he will now pay for his living needs. The discharge of this expectation carries the reward of adult status. New freedoms and new obligations result. To trace the impact of the social adjustments upon the young worker during the transition phase, the writers have elected to begin with a description of the new workers considered as a group. The number, age, sex, and education of these new work recruits are shown. Then the job preferences are examined over against the jobs the new workers actually secure in their first years of work life. Finally, the early work adjustments are analyzed to describe the way in which the individual worker must come to terms with his new world of work.

THE COMPOSITION OF THE NEW WORKERS IN THE LABOR FORCE

THE NUMBER OF YOUNG WORKERS IN THE LABOR FORCE

Between the ages of fourteen and twenty-four almost all young people begin working on their first full-time job. In 1940 the population of the United States included more than 26,000,000 persons between fourteen and twenty-four years of age inclusive. Although 10,000,000 of this group were still in school, 16,000,000 were out of school. Eleven and a half million were in the labor force.[1]

THE PROPORTION OF YOUNG WORKERS BY AGE GROUPS

Table 23 is an exhibit of the 1940 U.S. Census showing proportions of young workers by age groups.

TABLE 23. Percentage of Males and Females Fourteen Years to Twenty-four Years, Inclusive, in the Labor Force of the United States in 1940

Age	Population	Number in Labor Force	Percent of Population	Percent Total Labor Force
14–15	4,828,249	249,521	5.2	.5
16–17	4,892,170	1,029,291	21.0	1.9
18–19	5,018,834	2,645,289	52.7	5.0
20–24	11,587,835	7,670,549	66.2	14.5
Totals	26,327,088	11,594,650	44.4	21.9

The table shows that of the total population of fourteen- and fifteen-year-olds, only 5.2 percent are in the labor force. Twenty-one percent of the sixteen- and seventeen-year-olds are in the labor force. By eighteen and nineteen years of age, 52.7 percent are included, and the twenty- to twenty-four-year-old bracket contains 66.2 percent in monetary work plants.

On the average, 44.4 percent of the fourteen- to twenty-four-year-old group are in the labor force. The 11,500,000 workers from this section of the population constitute 21.9 percent of the entire labor force; or to put it more simply, one out of every five workers in the labor force is under twenty-five years of age.[2]

SEX DIFFERENCES REPRESENTED IN THE YOUNG WORKERS OF THE LABOR FORCE

Sixty-five percent of the young workers in this same group are males, 35 percent are females. Thus, men outnumber women almost two to one. In

[1] United States Census, 1940, Vol. III, *The Labor Force*, Part I, United States Summary, Table 5, "Employment Status of the Population by Age and Sex," United States Government Printing Office, 1943, p. 19.

[2] *Ibid.*, p. 19.

spite of the preponderance of men, the young women make up 31.4 percent of all the women in the labor force and the young men make up only 18.9 percent of the men in the labor force. These proportions can be explained, of course, by the fact that the male workers are an older group of workers. Table 24 shows the data.[3] Most of these young workers are unmarried. Only one male out of five is married and one female out of eight is married.[4]

TABLE 24. Employment Status of Young Workers by Age and Sex: 1940

Age	Male	Percentage of Total Males in Labor Force	Female	Percentage of Total Females in Labor Force
14–15	195,919	.5	53,602	.4
16–17	715,027	1.8	314,264	2.4
18–19	1,635,798	4.1	1,009,491	7.9
20–24	5,011,457	12.5	2,659,092	20.7
Totals	7,558,201	18.9	4,036,449	31.4

YEARLY INFLUX OF NEW WORKERS

The United States Employment Service Division estimates that 2,250,000 American youth reach the age of employability every year and about 1,750,000 of them enter the national labor market.[5]

AGE OF ENTRY

The Maryland Youth Survey showed that more than half the youth who ever had full-time jobs got them before they were eighteen years of age. The median age was 17.6 years.[6]

It is to the 1,750,000 new workers who annually enter the labor force that this chapter pays especial attention. They are an increasingly better-educated group of workers as they likewise become a somewhat older group. What kind of jobs do they want? What kind of jobs do they get? Are they happy with their occupational adjustments? For answers to these questions we turn to the new workers.

[3] Ibid.
[4] Ibid., p. 22.
[5] Howard M. Bell, Matching Youth and Jobs, American Council on Education, 1940, pp. 3, 25, 99. Estimates shown were prepared by the Employment Service Division of the Bureau of Employment Security in the Social Security Board. Davidson and Anderson say, "How large the annual crop of new workers is, and how it spreads itself over the field of occupations is not known in any detail." See Dewey Anderson and Percy E. Davidson, Recent Occupational Trends in American Labor, a supplement to Occupational Trends in the United States, Stanford University Press, 1945, p. 2.
[6] Howard M. Bell, Youth Tell Their Story, American Council on Education, 1938, p. 137.

THE ENTRANCE OF NEW WORKERS TO THE MARKET

TWO GROUPS OF NEW WORKERS, THE HIGH SCHOOL TRAINED AND THE COLLEGE TRAINED

Young workers can be divided into two groups, those with high school and those with college training. It is of interest and value to divide graduates from nongraduates in each group. In this discussion an occupational description of high school-trained and college-trained youth will be presented.

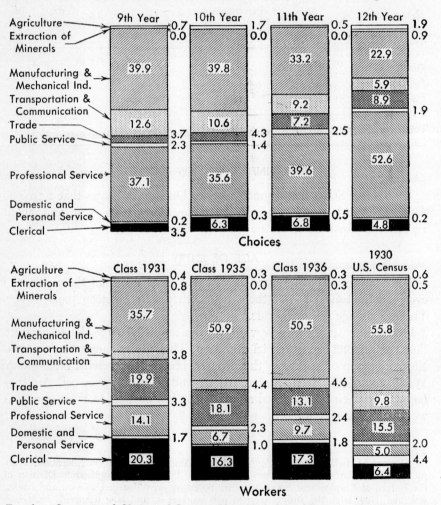

FIG. 69. Occupational Choices of Canton, Ohio, High School Boys in 1937. Percentage Distribution Compared with Percentage Occupational Distribution of Canton Male Graduates in 1931, 1935, 1936 Classes and Male Workers in 1930 U.S. Census. (The Canton, Ohio, Vocational Survey, Canton Board of Education, 1937.)

Differences which significantly differentiate the graduate from the non-graduate will be indicated. The opening discussion is concerned with the jobs which high school-trained workers want and the jobs they actually get.

The Jobs High School Youth Want and the Jobs They Secure

It is a well-documented fact that the occupational aspirations of young people are so high that only a relatively few can hope to find them fulfilled, especially in the early years of their work life. The home, the school, and the

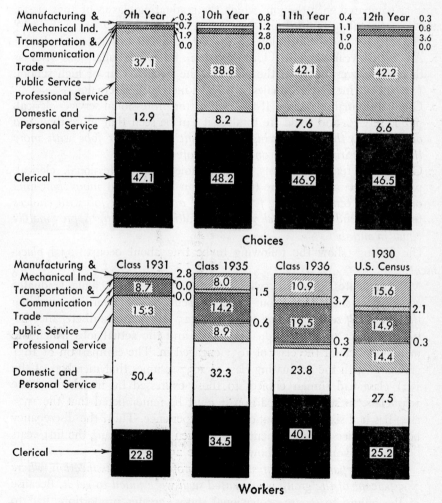

FIG. 70. Occupational Choices of Canton, Ohio, High School Girls in 1937. Percentage Distribution Compared with Percentage Occupational Distribution of Canton Female Graduates in 1931, 1935, 1936 Classes and Female Workers in 1930 U.S. Census. (The Canton, Ohio, Vocational Survey, Canton Board of Education, 1937.)

community awaken and stir the hopes of young people, who are led to aspire to the high-status, high-paying white-collar jobs. Many surveys are now available to show how the American dream of rising to the top has affected occupational choice. The Canton vocational survey shows very clearly the discrepancy between choice and fulfillment. This survey was initiated in December, 1937, when a questionnaire was sent to all the ninth-, tenth-, eleventh-, and twelfth-grade pupils in the Canton, Ohio, high schools and was filled in by 2062 boys and 2956 girls. Figures 69 and 70 reveal the difference between the occupational choices in the Canton high schools in 1937 as compared with the jobs which the graduating classes of 1931, 1935, and 1936 actually obtained.

The findings show the following to be true about occupational *choice*:
1. All twelfth-year students. The aspiration for white-collar jobs rises as there is progression from the ninth to the twelfth year of high school. (15 percent increase for males, 5 percent increase for females.)
2. Graduating male students. If the choices for professional service, clerical, public service, and trade are totaled, it can be seen that more than *two out of every three graduating males want white-collar jobs with more than half desiring a job in one of the professions.*
3. Graduating female students. If the choices for professional, clerical, public service, and trade are totaled, it can be seen that *more than nine out of every ten graduating females want a white-collar job with choices for clerical and professional work dominating and being approximately equal in number.*

The findings show the following to be true about occupational *placement*:
1. Male graduates. The jobs which Canton high school male graduates *actually get* show that about *one-half secure white-collar jobs* and *the the other half secure manual jobs.* Table 25 indicates the discrepancy between choices of 1937 graduating males and the actual jobs which the male members of the class of 1931 engaged in. The comparison of 1931 graduates with the graduating class of 1937 assumes that members of the 1931 class had similar choices to those expressed by members of the 1937 class. In such a comparison it must be remembered that the 1931 class has had six years of out-of-school experience. Thus, the discrepancy between choice and placement may be even greater during the first years of full-time work than is shown in Table 25.

The discrepancy is greatest in the professional classification where 38.5 percent of the group who wanted such work failed to get it. Because of the failure to secure professional status, greater proportions had to accept clerical and trade jobs and jobs in manufacturing and mechanical industries.
2. Female graduates. *Most female workers with a high school education in*

TABLE 25. A Comparison of the Occupational Choices of the Males in the Class of 1937 with the Actual Jobs on Which the Class of 1931 Is Engaged[7]

Occupational Classification	Occupational Choices 12th-Year Males, 1937 Percent	Occupations of Male Graduates Class of 1931 Percent	Percentage Differences Between Choices and Jobs Obtained[a]
Professional	52.6	14.1	−38.5
Public service	1.9	3.3	+ 1.4
Trade	8.9	19.9	+ 9.0
Clerical	4.8	20.3	+15.5
Transport. and communication	5.9	3.8	− 2.1
Manufacturing and mechanical industry	22.9	35.7	+12.8
Extraction of minerals	.9	.8	− .1
Agriculture	1.9	.4	− 1.5
Domestic and personal service	.2	1.7	+ 1.5
Totals	100.0	100.0	

[a] −indicates excess of choice over fulfillment.
+indicates excess of jobs secured but not desired by choice.

TABLE 26. A Comparison of the Occupational Choices of the Females in the Class of 1937 with the Actual Jobs on Which the Class of 1931 Is Engaged.[8] (Adapted from the Canton, Ohio, High School Survey, 1938.)

Occupational Classification	Occupational Choices 12th-Year Females, 1937 Percent	Occupations of Female Graduates Class of 1931 Percent	Percentage Differences Between Choices and Jobs Obtained[a]
Professional	42.2	15.3	−26.9
Public service	0.0	0.0	—
Trade	3.6	8.7	+ 5.1
Clerical	46.5	22.8	−23.7
Transport. and communication	.8	.0	− .8
Manufacturing and mechanical industry	.3	2.8	+ 2.5
Extraction of minerals	0.0	0.0	—
Agriculture	0.0	0.0	—
Domestic and personal service	6.6	50.4	+43.8
Totals	100.0	100.0	

[a] −indicates excess of choice over fulfillment.
+indicates excess of jobs secured but not desired by choice.
[7] Adapted from the Canton, Ohio, High School Survey, 1938.
[8] Adapted from ibid.

monetary work plants are white-collar workers. Table 26 indicates the discrepancy between choices of 1937 graduating females and the actual jobs on which the female members of the class of 1931 are engaged. The jobs which Canton High School female graduates actually get show that marriage removes an increasing proportion of workers from the monetary work plant to the home. This is shown in Table 26, in the classification "Domestic and personal service" where the survey researchers placed all housewives.

The discrepancy is greatest in "Domestic and personal service" but since this includes housewives, such discrepancy probably reflects a desired movement toward marriage as the females have grown older and approached the average age for marriage.

There is a marked discrepancy between the desire for professional jobs and ability to secure them. There is likewise a considerable discrepancy between desire for clerical work and placement in this classification. The marked discrepancy in the professional classification seems to represent a real block to professional aspirations. The block in the clerical classification does not seem to be as genuine as the figures indicate. Undoubtedly, some of the housewives were in clerical work before their marriage. Moreover, in the somewhat more prosperous years of 1935 and 1936 nearly as many as wanted clerical work secured it. It can be said that it is not too difficult for a high school girl graduate to secure clerical work if she desires it.

Other surveys have pointed out that a greater proportion of youth must be prepared to assume manual jobs than express preference to do so. The Maryland Youth Survey made in 1938 secured first-hand information from more than 13,000 youth. The report of the actual and preferred occupations of employed youth states that "More than five times as large a proportion of the employed subjects expressed a desire to do professional-technical work as were found to be employed in this field. More than four times as many youth wanted jobs in some kind of skilled labor as were found to be so employed. On the other hand, almost four times as large a number were found to be working in the semi-skilled occupations as preferred to be so employed."[9]

The Maryland Youth Survey is valuable for it includes information regarding the feelings of employed youth who have gained experience in different occupations and are in a position to evaluate their job satisfaction. The percentage of youth who preferred the occupational field in which they were employed is given in Table 27.

Howard Bell interprets the job satisfaction of these youth by saying,

In so far as the love of one's work is a part of one's enthusiasm for living, it is clear that about all that can be said for this younger generation is that they are a rather sorry and depressed lot. By what they voluntarily choose to say about

[9] H. Bell, *Youth Tell Their Story*, American Council on Education, 1038, p. 132.

themselves, it is evident that they don't like their jobs. With the single exception of those working on professional or technical jobs, more than half the youth in every occupational field expressed a preference for some other kind of work. In the semi-skilled group, which incidentally is one of the largest, about one in ten felt that what he was doing was exactly what he wanted.[10]

OCCUPATIONAL FRUSTRATION A NORMAL PRODUCT

Considerable frustration is indicated as a normal product of the transition period. Much aspiration must be beaten down to fit the realities of the occupational world. Many young people must permanently readjust their expectations as they search for their first full-time jobs; most will need to make such adjustments temporarily if not permanently. This scaling down

TABLE 27. Percentage of Youth Who Preferred the Occupational Field in Which They Were Employed[11]

Occupational Field in Which Youth Were Found to Be Employed	Percentage of Youth Who Preferred This Field
Semiskilled	10.7
Unskilled	13.6
Office-sales	35.5
Domestic-personal	36.6
Skilled	40.8
Managerial-farm owner	44.5
Professional-technical	91.2

of expectation is painful, especially after the individual has experienced years of conditioning that encouraged the building of high aspiration. A high school graduate drains off his resentments in the following letter to the editor of the Akron *Beacon Journal*. It is dated July 20, 1947, during a period of high employment levels.

DOES EDUCATION PAY OFF IN JOBS?

Editor *Beacon Journal*:

Graduation meant so much. "The world is yours, go out and take it; it awaits your knowledge and ability to make our country the best there is."

I've heard all these things many times in school and in public from fat and loud speakers. I looked for that day they were talking about when I would be eligible for the world, my country and what was said in many a speech.

I looked for the day when I would have a pleasant and decent job my 12 hard years of schooling called for. I thought a high school graduate had a place in this America, the place where things were booming and opportunities were a dime a dozen.

Now as I have stepped out into the cold and bleak world, all the talks and

[10] *Ibid.*, pp. 134-135.
[11] *Ibid.*, p. 134.

wonderful speeches are a shameful farce. I have studied hard; I stayed in school to finish because I knew graduates were in greater demand. I have taken subjects that I thought and my teachers thought would be assets to me and to my employer.

It's been over a month since school closed. I've tried employment bureaus, offices, large department stores and about every kind of small business in Akron and vicinity. Their belated answers were a displeased "I'm sorry" or "We have nothing that calls for your type of experience."

One person went so far as to ask why didn't I take a job as an automobile sander. Had I known when I was in the third grade a person was to offer me such a job today I would have quit school then and waited for the job.

Has 12 years of good schooling only that kind of work to offer? Must the graduates be *humiliated* and classed with the *unlettered, nongraduates*? [Italics are ours.]

Hasn't America, the land of milk and honey, an encouraging job to offer a person who wants to better himself and his environment? I don't expect to jump into a $50 a week salary, nor do I care if it is $25, just so I can say to people that my job was worth my education.

.......Dreamer

It is of interest to ascertain whether the young letter writer is average or unique when compared with other high school graduates who are making their first bid for a full-time job. The data gathered by the Canton Vocational Survey of 1938, the Youngstown Vocational Survey of 1938, and the Maryland Youth Survey of 1938 say the disappointed young man is no unusual exception. The years of 1937 and 1938 when these studies were being made were marked by relatively low production and employment in the United States. A later study made in Rochester, New York, enables us to look at 1941, when national income approached $100,000,000,000 and the labor market was developing scarcities.

The Rochester public schools made an attempt to find out what had happened to their high school students who had graduated or left school during 1940. In May, 1941, eleven months after the graduation of the 1940 class, a questionnaire was mailed. Out of 4815 recipients, 2738 returned the questionnaire, a 57 percent return. Nearly 40 percent of the boys and girls who replied to the questionnaire had either held no jobs or failed to report the number of jobs they had held during the year since they had left school.[12] The young people who succeeded in their search for work were not all employed for the full eleven months of the study. The average period of employment was about seven and one-half months for boys and about six months for girls. The jobs they secured are indicated in Table 28.

The data show that:

1. About one boy out of every five secured a white-collar job in the professional, managerial, or clerical fields.

[12] Howard C. Seymour and Carl E. Tremer, *We Left School a Year Ago*, Rochester Public Schools, 1941, p. 22.

2. The greatest opportunity seems to lie in semiskilled work in manufacturing. Approximately one out of three high school youth who find employment secure semiskilled jobs.
3. One girl in every four finds a white collar job in clerical work, which is the field offering the largest number of jobs to high school girls.

These data from the Rochester study of 1941 continue to reflect the conditions of occupational placement of youth in 1938 as shown by the Canton, Youngstown, and Maryland surveys. One fact emerges: There is limited opportunity for high school youth to secure white-collar jobs in the early years, at least, of their work life. There is reason to believe that this is

TABLE 28. Types of Occupation in Which Youth Were Employed in Each Group, May, 1941[13]

Occupation	Boys		Girls	
	Number	Percent	Numbers	Percent
Professional and semiprofessional	21	2.0	6	.5
Managerial and official	7	.5	1	—
Clerical and kindred workers	238	19.0	409	27.0
Skilled-manufacturing	116	9.0	13	1.0
Semiskilled	398	31.0	222	15.0
Unskilled	21	2.0	27	2.0
Service workers	61	5.0	112	8.0
Agricultural	19	1.5	1	—
No job or did not answer	385	30.0	681	46.5
Totals	1266	100.0	1472	100.0

true for a majority during their entire work life. Dr. Floyd Reeves says, "The stark fact is that our industrial civilization will provide white-collar jobs for less than half of those preparing for them."[14] The significance of this discrepancy between aspiration and achievement will be discussed in more detail in the next chapters on the trial and stable work periods. But an important question remains. Do the jobs which graduates secure reveal any tendency to differ from those secured by nongraduates?

High School Graduates Compared with Nongraduates on Occupational Distribution

The Rochester survey presents the following differences in occupational distributions based on the eleven-month follow-up of the graduates of 1940 and those who left school during that year without graduating:

[13] *Ibid.*, p. 17. Table has been adapted from Table 5 of the study.
[14] Floyd W. Reeves, in *Frontier Thinking in Guidance*, Science Research Associates, 1945, p. 10.

1. Of each ten employed girl graduates, *six* were engaged in sales and clerical occupations, *one* in personal service, and *three* in manufacture. Of each ten employed girl dropouts, *two* were engaged in sales and clerical occupations, *three* in domestic service, and *five* in manufacture. No other single observation of the entire study revealed so striking a difference between graduates and dropouts.

2. A similar, but much less marked, tendency was observed between dropout and graduate boys. Graduates were relatively more numerous in sales and clerical occupations and relatively less so in those of the service groups.[15]

The Rochester study recognizes that it is important to separate out those persons still in colleges, business schools, or other educational institutions in order to make an appraisal of *high school graduation*. The graduates who secure additional education will probably enter the labor market at higher levels. By eliminating this group the Rochester survey secured the employment status of youth not attending school. The comparison of graduates and dropouts is shown in Table 29. Two conclusions can be drawn:

TABLE 29.　Employment Among Youth Not Attending School[16]

| Kind of Work | Boys | | Girls | | Totals |
	Dropouts %	Graduates %	Dropouts %	Graduates %	
Clerical and sales	22.4	28.3	20.3	57.8	38.7
Service—domestic, personal, etc.	10.2	6.0	32.0	10.7	10.3
Manufacturing	62.8	60.1	46.9	30.4	47.7
Others	4.6	5.6	.8	1.1	3.3
Totals	100.0	100.0	100.0	100.0	100.0

1. Graduation from high school is a distinct advantage for the girl who wishes to enter into a sales or clerical occupation.

2. The *type of occupation entered into* by the boy who goes to work directly from high school seems to be little influenced by the fact of graduation from high school.

These discoveries regarding the occupational aspirations and occupational placement of high school-trained youth encourage a comparison with the college-trained youth. How do college-trained youth fare?

[15] Differences corroborated by the Youngstown, Canton, and Maryland surveys.
[16] Rochester Public School Survey, *We Left School a Year Ago*, p. 18; cf. Paul H. Landis, *Six Months After Commencement*, an analysis of the occupational roles of 133,651 graduates from Washington high schools, classes of 1934 through 1941, Youth Series No. 1, Bulletin No. 420, State College of Washington, Agricultural Experiment Station, Pullman, Washington, 1942.

The Jobs College-Trained Youth Want and the Jobs They Secure

A college education is presumed to be an elevator to higher-paying jobs in the upper socioeconomic classifications College undergraduates want jobs in the professions or seek managerial positions in business. Do college graduates actually secure such jobs?

The best answer to this question can be found in *The United States College Graduate*, a survey of 12,728 college graduates from 1164 institutions of higher learning made by *Time* magazine in 1940. These graduates

TABLE 30.   Type of Employment of Working Men and Women College Graduates Under Thirty Years of Age

Professions	Working Men Graduates Under Thirty	Working Women Graduates Under Thirty
Education	18.2	62.9
Medicine and dentistry	7.1	4.1
Sciences	12.6	2.5
Law	6.1	—
Government	6.3	5.0
Ministry	1.6	—
Arts	3.2	2.4
All other professions	—	1.7
Total professions	55.1%	78.6%
Business		
Manufacturing	15.6	—
Merchandising	11.7	6.9
Finance	10.8	3.3
Transportation and utilities	3.0	—
Farming	1.0	—
Production	1.6	—
Miscellaneous	1.2 All other bus.	11.2
Total business	44.9%	21.4%

are part of a sample believed to represent a "true cross section of all graduates," and "big enough to be statistically valid." Since we are concerned with the occupational distribution during the transition years it is pertinent to look at the type of employment which is secured by working graduates under thirty years of age. Table 30 gives the percentage distribution of young men and women college graduates in the various types of employment.[17] Although it is somewhat difficult to ascertain what specific job titles are included under manufacturing and merchandising, the evidence

[17] F. Lawrence Babcock, *The United States College Graduate*, published by *Time*, Inc., 1941, pp. 22-23.

is clear that college graduates do secure occupations in the white-collar classifications with a majority entering professional work. It becomes pertinent to ask what happens to the non-college graduate. Only a minority of entering college youth graduate. In a University of Minnesota sample of 1600 entering freshmen about 40 percent of the men and 45 percent of the women graduated. An investigation of the differences between graduates and nongraduates promises to give a broader picture of occupational adjustment.

College Graduates Compared with Nongraduates on Occupational Distribution

In 1937 the General College of the University of Minnesota set into motion a research program designed to find out the occupational and social experiences of 1600 college-trained adults who had entered the University of Minnesota in the classes of 1924, 1925, 1928, and 1929. These people ranged in age from twenty-three to forty-eight years with the median around thirty years. They had been out of school from one to twelve years. By questionnaire, information was obtained from 951 of these adults.

A general overview of the sample including both graduates and nongraduates shows that (1) 80 to 90 percent of the men are in professional, semiprofessional, clerical, skilled trades, or retail business; (2) about half of the women list no work except housewife. Of the women who work almost all are in professional, clerical, skilled trades, or retail business.[18]

Significant differences between graduates and nongraduates include the following:

1. Significantly larger proportions of graduates are found in the professions—roughly 50 percent of men graduates as contrasted with 15 percent men nongrads; and 33 percent women grads as contrasted with 6 percent nongrads.

2. Conversely, there are significantly fewer graduate men and women than nongrads found in clerical, skilled trades, retail business, semiskilled, minor clerical, and minor business occupations.

3. For women, significantly more nongrads than grads are housewives and list no other occupations.

Pace summarizes his comparisons by concluding: "The graduates were distinguished from the non-graduates chiefly by the fact that they were more likely to have professional jobs, a little—but not much—more income, and somewhat greater satisfaction with their jobs. In other areas of living there were few differences, or none at all, between the graduates and nongraduates."[19]

[18] Robert C. Pace, *They Went to College*, University of Minnesota Press, 1941, pp. 31-36. The figures above are from a mimeographed "Progress Report on the General College Adult Study" prepared by Dr. Pace in 1940.

[19] Pace, the "Progress Report" as cited, p. 51.

The Minnesota adult study showed that there is considerable discrepancy between *choice and actual occupation secured* by college-trained persons although a large proportion do secure white-collar jobs. Sixty-nine percent of the men and 58 percent of the women report that they had decided upon an occupation before entering the university. But only 49 percent of the men and 12 percent of the women who had so decided say that they are now in that occupation. It is evident that marked shifts in vocational choice have occurred, especially among those who did not graduate from the university. In fact, less than half of the nongraduates are likely to end up in the vocation on which they decided before or in college.[20]

CAUSES OF OCCUPATIONAL FRUSTRATION

It has been pointed out that occupational frustration may be regarded, not as abnormal, but as an expected end product of socialization within present culture patterns. The explanation of such a large volume of occupational frustration may be identified as a resultant of four major causes. These are:

1. Occupational expectancy based on social class membership.
2. Occupational expectancy based on educational achievement.
3. Breakdown of the moral valuations of work.
4. Pecuniary and status valuations of occupational and other life goals.

1. Occupational Expectancy Based on Social Class Membership

Veblen has shown that one pronounced effect of membership in a social class is the resulting expectation that the parents and the children will constantly strive to maintain their class standing and aspire, if only secretly, to the level above. "The motive is emulation—the stimulus of an invidious comparison which prompts us to outdo those with whom we are in the habit of classing ourselves. Substantially the same proposition is expressed in the commonplace remark that each class envies and emulates the class next above it in the social scale, while it rarely compares itself with those below or with those who are considerably in advance."[21]

Children during their long economic dependence on the family acquire many of the habits, tastes, and interests of their parents. Moreover, their status in their eyes and in the eyes of the community becomes almost automatically that of the parents. Both the child and the parents acquire a stake in either maintaining or elevating their status. Ambitious parents hope and plan for the class elevation of their children. In this projection of their aspiration middle-class parents tend to forget that they started their married life with less prestige as well as fewer material possessions. So the child is

[20] *Ibid.*, Cf. p. 96 in *They Went to College.*
[21] Thorstein Veblen, *The Theory of the Leisure Class*, Modern Library, 1934, pp. 103-104.

encouraged to expect that when he goes to work he will *start* where his parents are *now*.

This expectation has both subtle and deliberate roots. Indirectly, the child develops a desire to maintain his status and his standard of living as he experiences its rewards in prestige and comforts. The successful middle-class family provides a house, furnishing, food, auto, and recreation for its children. Personal tastes grow to match experiences. Soon, a myriad of habits and attitudes are laid down in the child demanding a level of expenditure which the child has not been responsible for. Many aspiring parents deliberately strive for the development of expensive tastes in their children. They encourage the boy to think he is entitled to *start in* where the father *has arrived* after years of work. The daughter may be urged to aim high for a "good" husband—one old enough and well established or from a family that will enable her to have a high social and economic standing.

In the upper classes this continuance of the parental standard of living is possible as the son inherits the business of his father (or the aid necessary to start his own business) and the daughter is married "well." The middle-income family in trying to imitate this upper-class pattern stores up impossible expectations and almost inevitable frustration for its children because it has no available surplus of wealth or property to provide such a transition. Lacking this economic surplus to provide an "easier life than they had" the parents rely on education to furnish the means of occupational elevation without, it is hoped, the necessity of either long or strenuous effort on the part of their child. This leads to a specific designation of education as vocational training and status elevation. More and more parents in wage-earning brackets are likewise looking to education as a way for their children to "escape working in a factory." For an overwhelming majority of parents and children educational progression has been defined as synonymous with occupational and income progression. In demanding that the school become an institution of both education and status elevation for such large numbers impossible expectations have been created. Let us examine this second cause of occupational frustration.

2. Occupational Expectancy Based on Educational Achievement

It is widely believed that each advance on the educational ladder is an investment which may be counted on to repay profits in the form of jobs with increasingly higher status, working conditions, and income. Thus education and industry are seen to be interlocked so that each grade in school corresponds with a job classification in industry. Each advance in education is believed to carry *pari passu* a future advance in the job world. For a substantial minority of our young people this promise can be realized in large part. For the majority the road is bound to be fraught with disappoint-

ment, if not forever, then at least in the early years of work life when waiting at lower levels is demanded.

W. L. Warner and J. O. Low, and Peter Drucker have shown that on the whole there has been a steady decline of skilled jobs and a decrease in the worker's chance to get ahead.[22] One result of this blocking of social mobility has been the use of union organization; another has been the increased use

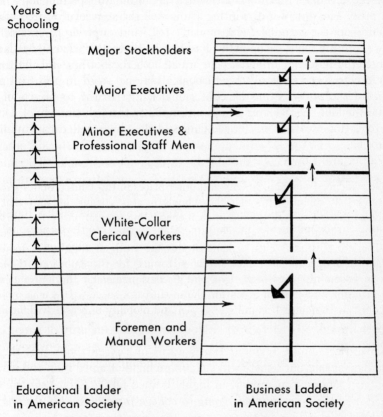

FIG. 71. Social Mobility in the School; Blocked Mobility in Business.

of the schools. The union is the worker's organization in which he seeks prestige as well as bargaining power. The school is seen to be the place where his child may climb upward and with hard work reach positions of power and prestige in the ranks of industry, business, and other social hierarchies. The school is made to take the place of the factory for the mobile and ambitious children of workers. This use of the school as a ladder to

[22] W. L. Warner and J. O. Low, *The Social System of a Modern Factory*, Yale University Press, 1947; Peter Drucker, *Concept of a Corporation*, The John Day Company, 1946.

occupational achievement is of course not limited to manual workers. The glorification of education rests in large part upon the expectation that anyone can rise in business by a rise in the number of school years completed.

Figure 71 is called "Social Mobility in the School; Blocked Mobility in Business."[23] The educational ladder on the left represents the years of schooling which may be obtained. The business ladder on the right represents the levels of advancement which are ordinarily present in a large enterprise. The downward pointing arrows tell the story of thwarted worker mobility on the manual, white-collar, staff, and supervisory levels. The arrows running from each of the business levels to the educational ladder indicate the tendency of those who are at both the bottom and the top of each level to speed their advance through additional schooling. The ultimate return of the arrows from the educational ladder to the top levels of the business ladder tell the story of upward mobility through the school. Unfortunately, this escalator is not an endless belt which will carry unlimited numbers.

Warner and Low claim that

The evidence from Yankee City and other places in the United States strongly indicates that mobility through the schools is also slowing up and that the higher positions tend to be filled in each succeeding generation by the sons and daughters of families who already enjoy high positions. The evidence from a great variety of studies clearly demonstrates the truth of this last statement.[24] While newer educational routes are being formed for the ambitious, the older ones are becoming increasingly tight, and it seems predictable that in time education may not be a certain route for those who seek success. It seems probable that our class system is becoming less open and mobility increasingly difficult for those at the bottom of the social heap.[25]

Harvard economist Seymour Harris warns in a recent book that there is a real danger that our society will yield more highly trained men and women than our economy can support in highly trained jobs. *"Those who are concerned over the large numbers going to college for professional reasons will find little consolation in this rise over the years from 1910 to 1940 of 24 per cent of employment opportunities for college trained personnel, in contrast to an expansion of 320 percent in college enrollments in regular sessions, and of more than 400 percent in the annual number of bachelor degrees and the disproportion promises to increase."*[26] He continues, "It is clear

[23] Figure 71 was suggested by Warner and Low, *op. cit.*, p. 184.

[24] W. L. Warner and Paul S. Lunt, *The Social Life of a Modern Community,* Yale University Press, 1941. Robert J. Havighurst, W. L. Warner, and Martin B. Loeb, *Who Shall Be Educated?* Harper & Brothers, 1944. See also Chapter XIX, "The Stable Work Period," for much evidence.

[25] Warner and Low, *op. cit.*, p. 185.

[26] Seymour E. Harris, *How Shall We Pay for Education?* Harper & Brothers, 1948, p. 3.

that the economic status of the educated man is likely to suffer relatively, though whether his loss will be absolute will depend upon the rate of economic advance."[27]

This description of the tightening of the older educational routes explains much occupational frustration and portends increasing pressure on the schools even as opportunities for occupational achievements through this route diminish. This stricture in our class system is all the more frustrating as workers in many fields carry a decreasing sense of worth and significance on the job. Much of this loss of human dignity can be traced to the breakdown of the moral valuations of work.

3. Breakdown of the Moral Valuations of Work

In Chapter XIV we discussed the far-reaching effects of the breakdown of moral valuations of work on teamwork and morale in industry. The earlier view that all honest toil is honorable and equal in God's eyes helped immensely to give satisfaction to all workers regardless of the monetary reward. As this Christian view lost meaning the status of work was ranked by the amount of education, income, level of living, and personal influence it afforded. Pecuniary and status valuations appeared in full force to replace the waning moral valuations.

4. Pecuniary and Status Valuations of Occupational and Other Life Goals

The importance of the job has been elevated so greatly that the link between a man's job and his community remains as almost the sole link holding him to a given community. Kinship, neighborhood, and friendship ties are all expected to be broken or left behind when a better-paying, more "interesting," or more "important" job offer beckons. Those who say good-by to the migrating worker repeat the cliché, "You've got to go where you can do your best." Doing one's best has come to mean "getting ahead" either in money or in status. How young people interpret getting ahead may be seen in a recent survey (1948) made at the University of Washington by one of the writers. Forty-two senior men were asked to state the salary they expected to make the first year and the salary they expected to make the tenth year. Their reply: median salary expected the first year, $2680; the tenth year, $5228. Every student expected a sizable increase in income within ten years. These figures show how life plans are projected as income elevators. Failure to achieve these aspirations brings to many the inevitable frustrations.

The status aspirations are indicated by the way young people rank occupations in social prestige. In 1925 Professor George S. Counts asked students

[27] *Ibid.*, p. 67.

to rank certain representative occupations. In 1946 M. E. Deeg and D. G. Paterson repeated the same investigation. The correlation (rho) between the two rankings is 0.97. The results are shown in Chapter XI, Table 16, on p. 369.

Deeg and Paterson say, "We are forced to conclude that the social status of occupations has changed very little in the United States during the past twenty-one years. . . . In America, the professions and 'higher' business occupations continue to receive high rank; the skilled trades, technical occupations and occupations in the distribution field are given intermediate ranks; and the semiskilled and unskilled occupations are given low ranks."[28]

High status and high income are coveted goals. They define the content of American "success."[29] Failure to achieve occupational goals in these terms places the worker in a position of personal failure. Even a moderate success may be viewed as a frustration. Fortunately, most of these ego wounds due to high aspiration are healed as compensatory or substitute goals are accepted. Organization work, family life, church activity, hobbies, and recreational outlets come to fill the off-the-job hours. Many of these activities give opportunities for leadership and growth which were not available in the work plant. In the midst of such "work" many a person comes to a larger stature. Those that fail to find an outlet for their energies in organized social life turn to the pleasures (and escapes) of commercialized recreations. The dance, the movie, and the beer garden are more than mere sources of entertainment. They become for many the motivation for work. Work is endured as reverie invites the future—"going to a dance tonight," "a movie Saturday," "a drive to the mountains Sunday."

It may be said, therefore, that the causes of occupational frustration are many; and that each new worker faces a range of adjustment problems in the transition from school to work. This new world of work will make many new demands upon him just as he presses his young hopes and ambitions upon it. In the transition each worker may have to grapple not only with new work conditions but with a reappraisal of his own career.

SUMMARY

An attempt has been made to show what jobs young people want and what jobs they actually secure during the first years of their full-time work life. It has become clear that there is a wide discrepancy between what young people have come to want as their lifework and what they actually are forced to take. The aspiration for professional and managerial positions is far in excess of possible fulfillment. It is difficult to evaluate the effects of

[28] Maethel E. Deeg and D. G. Paterson, "Changes in Social Status of Occupations," *Occupations*, January, 1947, p. 207.
[29] Cf. C. C. North and Paul K. Hatt, "Jobs and Occupations: A Popular Evaluation," *Opinion News*, September 1, 1947, pp. 3-13.

this striving. Only the college graduates as a group are able to approach fulfillment of their occupational hopes. The great remainder must discover how impossible it is to have the American success story repeated for them.

It may come as a shock that education was supposed to develop the individual as a person and that its vocational value was not of a blank check variety. In fact, if the new workers' opinions of the vocational value of an education were relied upon, the vocational valuations of the enrolled students might be adjusted downward. In the Minnesota study less than half of the non-graduates felt that their university training was helpful to them in getting jobs or gaining advancement. As would be expected, graduates rate the vocational value of their University work much higher than non-graduates. More than four fifths of the men graduates said that their university training helped them to get their first jobs and to gain advancement. However, out of their contacts with employers only one out of ten young adults report that employers demand college graduates only, and only one third of them say that employers prefer college graduates. In contrast, one fourth of these young adults said that among their fellow employees there was an unfavorable attitude toward college graduates.[30]

The high school graduate speaks with similar opinions when asked to give his estimate of the extent to which school training helped him on the job. Only one out of three high school-trained boys and girls in the Rochester study said his school training was of direct preparation or provided some training. One out of three estimated that his education helped in a general way only. One out of six said flatly, "School training was no help at all."[31]

The transition from school to work becomes a major adjustment in the life of the maturing person. The emphasis upon high aspirations in American society has led to occupational expectations beyond range of all but a minority to achieve. The vocational value of education has been so emphasized as to make it seem the major value, if not the sole purpose, of an education. This emphasis has built up many false hopes in American youth, who are encouraged to use the "successful" as models and to hide their eyes to the 60 percent of the nation's workers who make their living with their hands. Thus, in the transition period the private version of the great American dream becomes for many the American myth and youth learns to grapple with a bitter reality. In the process there is much to learn about the new cultural environment of the monetary work plant. For the patterns of home, school, and church have often developed the personality in directions opposed to the patterns which may be found in many monetary work plants. The early work adjustments which must be made in the transition from school to work are discussed in the next section.

[30] C. Robert Pace, the "Progress Report" as cited, pp. 30-50. Cf. *They Went to College*.
[31] Rochester Public School Study, *op. cit.*, p. 26.

THE EARLY WORK ADJUSTMENTS REQUIRED IN THE TRANSITION FROM SCHOOL TO WORK

The transition from school to work presents a twofold adjustment problem to the new worker. The work adjustments that face him in the monetary work plant involve modifications of past experience and new learning of both *technical and social skill*. He must learn to perform within a work plant society. There is reason to believe that for most new workers the more demanding adjustments are of a social rather than technical nature. This position is in contrast to popular observation, which focuses upon the technical requirements of jobs and almost ignores the social adjustments that must be made to perform specific jobs in different work plants. In this section we shall appraise the social adjustments imposed by demands for new work skills as well as for new social skills.

I. THE NATURE OF WORK ADJUSTMENTS IMPOSED BY NEW WORK SKILLS

Education and Experience Requirements

The study of the American Youth Commission under the title *Matching Youth and Jobs* is most often pointed to for the picture of job requirements that face new workers. During 1938 and 1939 the American Youth Commission and the United States Employment Service Division of the Social Security Board conducted a joint program of research into the needs of young people seeking jobs. A sample of some 2216 occupations in eighteen industries were studied. It is estimated that the sample represents approximately 70 percent of American workers. Two major inquiries were made of industrial and commercial employers concerning workers in the occupations selected. The first was, "What is the minimum amount of schooling required for successful performance on the jobs in your work plant?" The second question was, "How long a training period is required for the average worker to reach normal production on the job?" The answers to these questions are presented in Tables 31 and 32.

TABLE 31.   Minimum Educational Specifications of Employers in Hiring for 2216 Occupations in 18 Industries

Minimum Educational Specifications	Percentage of Occupations
None (requires ability to speak, read, and write English)	47.1
Some elementary school	7.8
Elementary school graduation	12.1
Some high school	3.8
High school graduation	20.2
Some college	2.5
College graduation	6.5

Table 31 shows that almost half of the jobs sampled require no education other than ability to speak, read, and write English. Slightly under thirty percent require high school graduation or college training.[32]

The on-the-job training required is shown in Table 32. More than two-thirds of the jobs required no training at all or training of a week or less. Less than 10 percent required as much as six months' experience.[33]

TABLE 32. Training-on-the-Job Required to Reach Normal Production on 2216 Occupations in 18 Industries

Training-on-the-Job Required	Percentage of Occupations
None	8.5
One week or less	59.0
More than one week, but not more than one month	11.2
More than one month but not more than three months	6.1
More than three months but not more than six months	5.6
More than six months	9.6

This study shows that the majority of jobs do not require high levels of either formal education or on-the-job training. The researchers conclude, "It thus appears that, for about 85 percent of the youth who will enter the labor market upon leaving school, their rendezvous are not with scientific laboratories, courtrooms, and pulpits, but with such unglamorous things as picks and shovels, filing cabinets, sales slips, and production lines."[34]

This conclusion indicates that most of the new workers will find that the greater adjustment to be made is a social rather than a technical one. It is largely the acquisition of social skills upon which success in the monetary work plant depends, whether success be measured in ability to achieve advancement or to secure the inner satisfaction of feeling at home in the work group.

[32] Howard M. Bell, *Matching Youth and Jobs*, American Council on Education, 1940, p. 56; cf. V. C. Fryklund, *The Selection and Training of the Modern Factory Worker*, Employment Stabilization Research Institute, University of Minnesota Press, 1934, p. 17.

[33] Bell, *Matching Youth and Jobs*, p. 58.

[34] *Ibid.*, p. 68. The researchers made a check study of 893 so-called beginner's jobs which required no previous experience. They found that the training required on the job was almost identical with that of the larger study of 2216 occupations. Only one exception needs to be noted. Only 3 percent of the assigned workers needed a job-training period of over six months before their productivity could be accepted as normal. This is in contrast to the 9.6 percent of the workers who need more than six months' training on the job in the larger sample. It is understood, of course, that these percentages relate exclusively to training on the job and do not include the months and years of study that are often necessary to achieve occupational efficiency in such occupations as are found in the professional, managerial, and skilled labor fields. See pp. 58-59 for a description of this check study of beginner's jobs.

II. THE NATURE OF WORK ADJUSTMENTS REQUIRED BY CULTURAL CONTRASTS BETWEEN THE SCHOOL AND THE MONETARY WORK PLANT

If social skills are important in work adjustments, then our inquiry might very well begin with an examination of the contrasting social characteristics of the school and the monetary work plant. The young worker must safely bridge these two social worlds. He would do well to stand within the school and to examine the work world which he proposes to enter. It would be best if for the moment he could forget about the technical skills he has to offer and would try to evisage only the salient social differences between the school and the new work plant which he may seek to enter.

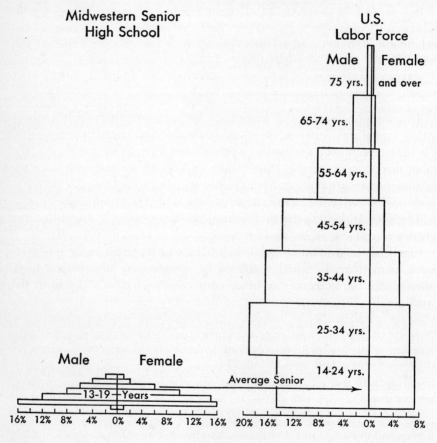

Fig. 72. Age and Sex Distribution of Midwestern Senior High School Compared with the Age and Sex Distribution of the United States Labor Force in 1940. (Source: High school population was drawn from Akron, Ohio, high school; United States labor force data was drawn from U.S. Census, Vol. III, *The Labor Force*, Part I, U.S. Summary, Table 5, "Employment Status of Population by Age and Sex for United States, 1940," p. 10.)

A. Differences Between the Social Base of the School and the Social Base of the Monetary Work Plant

There are marked contrasts to be observed between the social base of the school and the social base of the monetary work plant. The social base refers to those elements which characterize the social composition of the population. Three major differences in the social base have been selected to emphasize the contrasts between the school and the monetary work plant. These are (1) differences in age and sex composition, (2) differences in prestige differentials, and (3) differences in education.

1. DIFFERENCES IN AGE AND SEX COMPOSITION

It is impossible to specify all of the different kinds of social base for all school and work plants, but a few illustrations can be given which will exhibit the common contrasts between all such possibilities. Thus, on the left side of Figure 72 the social base of Midwestern High School is drawn. The name is fictitious but the data are drawn from a typical American high school. The age and sex composition reveals a population of approximately equal numbers of boys and girls between the ages of thirteen and twenty with the median age sixteen years. This is the base on which the social activity of Midwestern High School rests. To the right of Figure 72 the social base of the United States labor force is shown. The age and sex composition of the labor force based on the 1940 census reveals a population heavily weighted with males and with a small minority of females. The age range runs from fourteen years to seventy-five years and over, with the median male worker about thirty-eight years of age and the median female worker about thirty-two years of age.

The contrast here between the social bases of the school and the labor force means that the young worker will probably find himself in a work plant with a distinctly different kind of population. He will step from the youth to the adult world in one quick movement. This will not be the first time the youth has been brought into contact with adults for his family experiences alone have provided that opportunity. What is new is the commitment of his livelihood to this new world of adults, all of them, perhaps, strangers to him. Now he is on his own—he will make good or fail as he is tested against the standards of adults. A young woman worker explains her experiences.

My first job was with a receiving office of a department store in Cleveland. I felt uncomfortable on this job from the first because of the atmosphere and the people. Everyone there was at least ten years older than I was and all of them knew their work thoroughly. When I first started I felt as if I were corrupting the office rather than helping in it. The supervisor and the employees would explain something to me in a matter of fact, hurried way, and then expect me to remember it indefinitely. Being a lot older than I, they all became quite irritated

when something went wrong over what seemed to be trivial things to me. I was thoroughly unhappy there. I may have jobs that I will like even less than this one but I am going to try and avoid getting into a job where the people are so much older than I am.

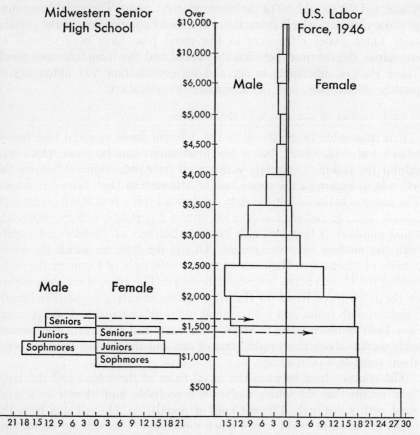

Fig. 73. The Average Entering Wage of High School-Trained Workers from Midwestern Senior High School Compared with Money Earnings Levels of Workers in the United States in 1946. (Source: High school population was drawn from Akron, Ohio, high school; percent distribution of urban and rural nonfarm civilian earners, fourteen years of age and over, by civilian money earnings from *Statistical Abstract of the United States*, United States Government Printing Office, 1948, p. 290.)

2. DIFFERENCES IN PRESTIGE DIFFERENTIALS

Midwestern High School is a senior high school of three grade levels. The population is divided into sophomores, juniors, and seniors in order to formulate proper curriculum offerings, but the students (and teachers, too) come to think of these levels as a kind of social hierarchy. Juniors have more prestige than sophomores and seniors are considered on the highest level

of status. In Figure 73, the social base of Midwestern High School is shown and the rankings of its students are given. In addition, the average entering wage of its students is shown. For comparison, the social base of wage or salary workers in the United States is placed beside the Midwestern High School base. The yearly wage levels of all workers who have no other income than their wage or salary payments are proportionately represented. These levels likewise reflect a kind of social hierarchy. Some of the highest levels require a lifetime of service. A young worker will probably take a place on one of the lower levels. The median yearly income of an Akron High School male graduate eighteen years of age was about $1680 in 1946.[35] For a male graduate this means that his income places him in the lowest third of the income distribution of male workers. This may seem a rude contrast with the social rank which he secured in the school, where, perhaps, after twelve years he achieved the highest rank of formal education obtainable within the facilities of the local community. Now inside the monetary work plant all of his honors become nothing but promises of future success. His educational background may sometimes seem to be more of a handicap than an advantage as he attempts to get along with his fellow workers. Moreover, his aspirations often race far ahead of attainment. A young man tells of his disappointment in seeking advancement in a small rubber factory.

Immediately following my graduation from high school, I secured a job with a small rubber factory in the northern part of Ohio. After being given the wonderful build-up that every graduate gets at his graduation exercises, I tried to give my first job all that it was humanly possible to give. But my first job gave me quite a set back on some of the ideas that I had built up in my short life.

The first three months on my job I was enthusiastic about my work. I tried to do my best. I thought that I had worked harder than any man in the factory. In two months I was able to produce my quota in an eight hour period. At the end of three months I asked for a raise. Two older men working the remaining two shifts on the same machine were making 40 cents an hour more than I was making. I was refused a raise. There was no union to go to and present my case. I began to see that it was a lost cause. So, at the end of five months of work, I quit my first and most hated job.

The woman worker is faced with still greater adjustments. As a graduating senior in 1946 she received an average of $1460 in yearly money earnings. In Figure 73 the disadvantaged position of the young woman graduate can be seen at the very beginning of her active work life. In the U.S. labor force she is in the minority. She lives in a man's world by reason of its large male population and leadership domination. Her opportunities for work positions are arbitrarily limited and she seldom has an equal chance to secure the higher wage levels. This fact is clearly shown in Figure 73 where money earning levels for men and women workers are compared.

[35] Based on a sample estimate.

3. DIFFERENCES IN EDUCATION

Figure 74 compares the number of years of education which the population of Midwestern High School has attained and the years of education
which the adult population of the United States (twenty-five years and

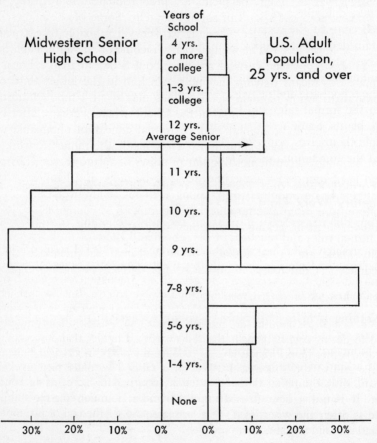

Fig. 74. Educational Attainment of Midwestern Senior High School Students Compared with the Educational Attainment of the Adult Population of the United States,
25 Years and Older, 1940. (Source: High school population was drawn from Akron,
Ohio, high school; United States adult population data was drawn from U.S. Census,
Vol. III, *The Labor Force*, Part I, "Characteristics of the Population," p. 40.

over) has achieved. The young worker who has attained senior rank in his
high school has lived in a relatively well-educated world. Nearly three out
of five of his adult contemporaries have never received any formal instruction
at the high school level. This puts him within the work plant in the anomalous position of one who has received much more education than the average

while occupying a lower rank than the average. This contrast can be observed as one examines the average educational achievement of the adult population of the United States.[36] In terms of behavior, this means the young worker must be careful not to flaunt his education. When he is within the monetary work plant, he may be told very early that "schooling is a good thing but it is not practical." "The only way to learn a job is on the job."

These differences in age and sex composition, in prestige, and in education which contrast the social world of the school with that of the work plant contain demands for social adjustments in the new worker. This is not yet the best place to stop for a detailed inspection. It is important that we first examine the differences which the individual discovers in the daily operation of the school and the monetary work plant. Some of these differences result from the formal rules and traditional practices which differentiate the two work plants. Some result from differences in interests and habits which the people themselves bring into the two plants. The formal differences arising from the functioning of the work plants are the first to be discussed.

B. Formal Rules and Practices Which Differentiate School and Monetary Work Plant

Four differences seem to mark off the most important contrasts between the formal rules and practices of the school and those of the monetary work plant. These are (1) differences in motivation, (2) differences in work schedules, (3) differences in authority, (4) differences in advancement.

1. DIFFERENCES IN MOTIVATION

Nothing is more noticeable to young workers than the motives which operate or fail to operate in the school and the monetary work plants. In the monetary work plant there is the reward of immediate payment, which gives a kind of continuous satisfaction. In the school there is no tangible reward, only the prospect that economic returns will accrue at a much later date. It is not a new observation that youth is impatient, and the older head is often the wiser head. One veteran in an American college in 1947 repeats the old wisdom as he says,

Several years lapsed between my graduation from high school and my entrance into college. I graduated from high school in nineteen-thirty-four. During those several years I had an opportunity to hold several jobs, some of these jobs were good and some of them were rather bad. After working at several jobs it is not hard to see the value of a college education.

Many students have come directly to college after graduation from high school, and have not yet learned the value of money. If many such students could earn their living for a few months, maybe they could appreciate what the

---

[36] Figure 74 reveals that only one out of four adults has received an education equivalent to high school graduation or above.

gains from college work can mean. There would be few of this group who would look to the immediate gains of work for pay and remain blind to the advantages that a college education can bring to them in the future.

Another worker describes in greater detail the work experiences which elevate the importance of education *after* the transition from school to work.

Before I can make a distinction between work at college and work for pay, I must give my progressive definitions of work. While attending high school I felt that work was something for someone other than me, and as far as school work was concerned, it completely stopped after the three o'clock bell. After I left high school and entered the highly competitive working-world, this conception was soon changed. I learned that I could expect from an employer no more than I gave him. The longer I earned my own living the more I realized that work should not be just a necessary evil or a means to an end, but rather it should be an enjoyable occupation. It should be an occupation in which all ability and ambition could be gainfully employed.

With the realization that my ambitions were not being achieved, the type of work that previously I had enjoyed became monotonous. I had advanced as far as my ability and education would permit. I found myself unprepared to meet the work world in the fashion which I wanted. I was caught in a trap that I had unwittingly set in high school.

A young college woman reveals her motivation to do college work as she profits from her initial job experiences. The reader should note how the hope of social and economic advancement becomes the leading motive for school-work at the college level. This hope seems to be important even though there may be small chances of its fulfillment.

This summer before I entered college I had the good fortune to be employed in a local department store. The hours were good. The pay was small but I didn't complain for I knew it was only a job for the summer months—I was going to college in the fall and start my training. I wanted to educate myself so that I would have a good profession in my future years—so I wouldn't have to smile at inane people all the time and have as my motto 'The customer is always right.'

Entering college in the fall, I found I had a different job than I had ever dreamed of having. Of course there were no more lovely pay days, but there is a certain reward when you get back papers marked "A," for you realize that day by day you are moving closer to your desired goal. Someday you will have a degree on your wall, security in your life, and a good profession—that is pay enough for your four years' work. Instead of being paid every week, you're paid all in one lump sum at the end of four years—in my mind that's worth working for.

A young man echoing the same hope is more blunt. "A student should have in mind that his education will, in later years, give him a better chance to make money and do so without having to work too hard. This is coming to be more true as years roll by."

Most of the above illustrations carry one thought: College work will be rewarded by the acquisition of a "better" job later on—by better, some mean more pay, some mean more prestige, some mean less physical or less repetitive work. All three of these characteristics were probably included by the student who said, "Work in college pays off for life and not just for the time being." The absence of a monetary reward in schoolwork is a puzzling lack to some, a bitter frustration to others. Work in our society is supposed to receive pay, or so we are taught to believe. Many students feel the lack of those psychological values which money brings. The following comments drawn from interviews express this feeling:

"Money makes you feel independent."

"Money makes you feel that your work was not in vain."

"Money makes you feel that work was for some one else; not just for yourself."

These comments indicate the importance of tangible reward in motivating human effort. The lack of such immediate reward is a major contrasting characteristic distinguishing the school from the monetary work plant.

2. DIFFERENCES IN WORK SCHEDULES

The student finds that his schoolwork is a relatively even flow of tasks assigned daily to him. They usually involve some variety and there is often considerable flexibility in the time granted for their completion.

The work plant into which the student graduates may conceivably approximate the work schedules he learned to follow in school. This is, perhaps, most true of many clerical jobs. But industry and commerce, unlike education, are subject to yearly, seasonal, weekly, daily, and in many businesses even hourly variations in the work load. Time assumes a new importance. Jobs must be done somehow, someway, within the time in which the work is needed. Cottrell describes the importance of time to the railroader.

All those who have direct responsibility for the actual operations of trains must carry a fine timepiece which will gain or lose not more than forty seconds in two weeks and which must be cleaned and regulated twice a year by a railroad watch inspector. A delay of thirty seconds in leaving a terminal calls for explanation, five minutes delay means investigation, and a half hour gives apoplexy to every official from the superintendent to lowest foreman. On single track roads where trains meet at passing tracks, thirty seconds delay means that one of the trains will be almost a half a mile from a passing track when the other reaches it, and that means delay of a second train, with possible misunderstanding and resultant disaster. . . . The technique of railroading itself makes it necessary to operate thousands of tons, moving at extremely high speeds with an accuracy greater than that maintained on many a factory assembly line.[37]

[37] W. F. Cottrell, "Of Time and the Railroader," *American Sociological Review,* April, 1939, pp. 190-198.

FORM 105 (R5)

OPERATION OBSERVATION SHEET   #2577

THE ████ COMPANY

SHEET *1* OF *1* SHEETS   "H" *Former Method*   DATE 8-28-43

PART NO.	64857
PART NAME	Point & Support
MODEL NO.	—
MACHINE NAME	Spotwelder
MACH. NO.	
OPERATION NO.	0531
OPERATION NAME	Spotweld point to support
TEMP. RATE	✓
BASE RATE	82 + 10%
OTHER PART NO.'S USING THIS OPERATION	
PERM. RATE	✓
CLOCK NO.	—
WORKER'S NAME	E. J. Bohinsky
DEPT. NO.	2300
DEPT. NAME	Machine Room

#	DESCRIPTION	UNITS 1	2	3	4	5	6	7	8	9	10	TOTAL MACH.	HAND	OCC. FACT.	LEVEL FACT.	ALLOW. TIME
1-	Place point on bottom electrode of Spotwelder with L.H.												074	1/1	115	.085
2-	Place cap on top of the point (Elemental Breakdown average of 10 pcs.)												054	1/1	115	.062
3-	Step on lever with R.F. and spotweld, then remove, inspect and place in tray in front of machine												073	1/1	115	.084
	Total average for breakdown												201			.231
	Production study (avg 10 pcs) Each												210	1/1	115	242
	" " (" " ") "												213	1/1	115	245
	" " (" " ") "												189	1/1	115	217
	Clean points average 1 time to 7 pieces (Each Cleaning)												118	1/1	115	136
	Allowances allowed in study															
	Salvage 7 pcs - (Re spotweld)															
	Sand off points everytime there is a scrap												1931			1.071
													4			4
	Total pieces on Study = 40															
	TOTAL												233			268

| TIME STARTED | TIME STOPPED | ELAPSED TIME | PIECES PRODUCED | | | | | TOTAL | 233 | | 268 |

(C) ALLOWED TIME PER PIECE	268 MIN.		(E) STANDARD TIME PER PIECE	292 MIN.
TOOL ALLOW. PER DAY (MIN.)	In study		(F) STANDARD HRS. PER 100 PIECES (EX1-67)	488 HRS.
HANDLING ALLOW. PER DAY (MIN.)	10 00			
PERSONAL ALLOW. PER DAY (MIN.)	30 00		(G) STANDARD PRODUCTION PER HOUR $\frac{100}{F}$	205 PCS.
MISC. PER DAY (MIN.)			COST PER 100 PCS. = (F×B.R.) = .488 × .902 = $.44	
" " " (MIN.)			STD. COST =	
TOTAL	40 00 + 440 = 9.1 %		TIME TAKEN BY W. E. Hudec	DATE 8/28/43	CALCULATED BY W. E. Hudec	DATE 8/28/43
		024 MIN.	FOREMAN'S APPROVAL E. M.	DATE	DATE EFFECTIVE
TOTAL	292 MIN.			

5M-9-45   — OVER —

FIG. 75. An Operation Observation Sheet.

In the factory the concept of an average day's work, sometimes called a quota or a bogey, has brought a measuring unit against which individual effort is gauged. The worker may find that each movement he is expected to make on the job has been timed including a "normal" amount for material and machine delays, fatigue and personal needs. A typical time

study of a machine operation is shown as Figure 75. This time study reflects the importance which is attached to time in industrial operations. Cost is a function of material and the time required to fabricate useful articles from it.

The differences in work schedules that pose contrasts between the school and the monetary work plant grow out of the relation of time to the activity. Learning, it is held, takes time and must not be forced. Educational efficiency is measured in the development of personality. In the monetary work plant the logics of cost and efficiency stress maximum output in units of time. In the store this means attention to merchandise turnover, in the factory it means monthly shipments, on the farm it means bushels of grain sold to the elevator. As long as effort is evaluated against tangible output, time becomes a strict discipline of monetary work plants, and work schedules usually make sterner demands upon the new worker.

3. DIFFERENCES IN AUTHORITY

Authority in the monetary work plant differs perhaps most significantly in the control which the employer or supervisor has in recommending merit increases and promotion. In the school the teacher has an analogous function of reporting a grade based on merit and recommending graduation. However, it is usually demonstrated that a stronger control rests in the hands of an employer for he holds the means of livelihood. He may upon cause fire the worker and thus remove him entirely from one source of livelihood.

There is likewise the social definition of the individual who has terminated his school life which is indicated by the expression "being on your own." The expectation that the young worker will provide for his own living needs and obligations means that his dependence upon the job becomes greater and therefore the control of his supervisor seems all the more compelling. "You must produce or *you're out*," the boss says to the new worker. One young worker described the exercise of authority which the bosses exerted over the crews working commercial celery fields: "The straw bosses were nothing but slave drivers. They were always inspecting everyone's work and blowing their 'top.' They didn't want the employees to talk because they said it slowed down production. All they wanted was more work done. They could 'pull' that slave driving because most of the employees were young school boys. Very few fellows protested because they were fired if they did so."

The increasing dependence upon the job for livelihood, status, and self-respect makes the control of the supervisor over his working subordinates more commanding than the control of a teacher over his students. Yet there are many new freedoms in the monetary work plant and the controls are implicit rather than explicit, so that the discipline of work behavior may *seem* less compulsive than classroom procedures. The monetary work plant

may offer more option in regard to dress, and such personal patterns as drinking, smoking, swearing, and horseplay. Moreover, the right of a free worker to quit his employment gives him considerable independence during labor scarcity. Life inside a monetary work plant offers new freedoms but it also demands acceptance of new responsibilities. One of these new responsibilities is accuracy and safety. The cost of a mistake in the schoolroom is usually a small reduction in the grade assigned to the performance. The cost of a mistake in business may involve the loss of time and money and endanger the life of the worker and his associates. One young worker explains how she learned the lesson of accuracy.

While employed as a stenographer for the warehousing section of the Cleveland Ordance Department located many miles underground in Cleveland Ohio, I came in contact with many people, mostly Army personnel.

The Warehousing Division handled all shipments of ammunition to be shipped to various exporting stations in the United States for shipment to our boys who were fighting overseas. It was my duty to see that any orders from the Washington Army Ordnance Plant located in Washington, D.C., which was headquarters for the rest of the Army depots located throughout the United States, the Detroit Arsenal, and the Arsenal located at Wright Field in Dayton, Ohio were carried out precisely. It was also my duty to record all the various railway yards in Cleveland that carried out the majority of our shipments and keep a definite record when we received munitions and when they were shipped out.

One morning I was very rushed for time and had several orders that were waiting to be typed out in detail. In rushing through with an order I typed the Cleveland, Cincinnati, Columbus Railway Company instead of the trucking company. A few days later we received a notice that the company located at Wright Field in Dayton, Ohio had received no such order. Much confusion resulted from that one mistake. New papers had to be made out and traced, and it also necessitated the fact that my immediate employer, Mr. Manning, had to go to Columbus Ohio to verify that the shipment of ammunition was ours. When he returned I thought he would be very angry with me but he wasn't. He emphatically told me regardless of how busy I was the next time to take plenty of precaution in what I was doing.

This case illustrates the implicit nature of the controls which operate in the monetary work plant. A production schedule is an impersonal demand. Accurate and safe work is a necessity in a work situation where the consequences of violation threaten life and security. It follows, therefore, that the controls of the monetary work plant are more demanding even when not formally imposed. It might be said that the production schedule becomes the taskmaster of the work plant as personal living expenses become the whiplash of daily work life. One young worker expresses the authority of the work plant by comparing his life to that inside of a prison. "I com-

mitted myself to the orders of a whistle that blows at exactly the same minute every day, week, and year. I felt that I was nothing more than a simple lever of a machine."

4. DIFFERENCES IN ADVANCEMENT

There is considerable difference between the school and a monetary work plant in the mode of advancement. In the school a series of tests are presented and the individual performance is constantly graded. The student may advance from course to course and from grade to grade at regular intervals provided he meets the standards, which are explained to him in advance. There are always new tasks, usually somewhat more difficult, to be sought and attained. Parents, teachers, and friends appraise the performance, and considerable recognition may be given the young learner. Certainly few performances receive wider or more generous publicity than do the activities of athletic stars.

In the monetary work plant job titles and wage or salary payments become the coveted goals of advancement. But there is seldom a one-way path to a given job title. The better-paying jobs are reached by means of education, experience, individual bargaining, "personality," "pull," or some combination of all these means. Therefore, the time required to go from a lower-paying to a higher-paying job is almost always an undetermined variable. The worker can only watch and by observing what his employers do in merit rating and promotion gain his estimate of the means effective for his own advancement. "Playing the game" usually resolves itself into a miniature power struggle. The worker pretends that better opportunities are being offered him elsewhere. He may, in addition, "pull strings," which means getting influential working associates to press the employer for his advancement. Social entertaining may prove an elevator to occupational advance. Sometimes an employer looks with favor only on those employees who take an active part in community life. Such participation is good public relations for the employer and he rewards his employees' contribution accordingly. Other elevators may include family background, a talent for entertaining, beauty or attractiveness, and the status of the schools attended.

It becomes apparent that getting ahead is a much more complex problem in the monetary work plant. Not only must the employee discover an effective way to improve his opportunities for advancement but he must also contest with his associates, who are likewise desirous of advance and employing such means as they have judged to be influential. The employer, thrown on the defensive, plays a "cagey game." He refuses to make promises but answers an employee's demands with suggestions of possibilities that await in the future. He points out the many deserving associates in his

employ and their record of service. He tries to convince his employee that he has already been well rewarded and to send him back to his job feeling that there is hope for advance in the future. In a multitude of such bargaining situations it is difficult to determine the relative merit, let alone the absolute merit, of the employee. Many employers refuse, especially for nonunionized salaried employees, to apply objective standards of measurement. Many even believe it is impossible to set up objective standards for the merit rating of employees. The result is that advancement becomes a mixture of merit and bargaining. It is this combination of elements which characterizes advancement in monetary work plants.

The young worker has been aware that other factors than merit have often influenced schoolteachers and administrators, but seldom has the contrast been so marked as in the monetary work plant. Indeed, in some industrial jobs advancement seems almost impossible. A young worker says,

I was disgusted at the thought that I might be resigned to working in the factory the rest of my life. I just can't conceivably see the sense of slaving for 30 years to reach the "esteemed" position of foreman of one of the shifts. Under the present system, it would be impossible for one without advanced technical training to advance beyond a foreman's job. That is all the common run of worker has to look forward to and for myself it is far too insufficient. Even if you did become a foreman, what then? You're just a flunky of the front office which keeps on your neck about production falling off. In turn, you pass the blame on to the workers and then no one likes you.

Another young worker describes his view of his job of stock trucker at Goodyear Tire and Rubber Company:

The thing I disliked most about my job was the fact that I had absolutely no chance for advancement. I was required to stay on that job or I had to transfer to another department and start at the bottom.

A trucker's job is one in which I could learn absolutely nothing. I did not advance in pay or position, and did not have any chance to show what I knew. A person with below average intelligence and without any ambition would have been well suited to this type of work. Not only was trucking a job that required very little thinking on the part of the worker, it was a job that required a lot of heavy lifting and tedious work. I like a job where I can show my intelligence and ability to learn.

These cases have been drawn from college students whose career expectations were such as to make them impatient with the lack of progress which they felt they were making. However, they are not unrepresentative of youth if the Maryland Youth Survey is an accurate guide to the attitudes of employed youth sixteen to twenty-four years of age. Of the 5828 employed youth interviewed, more than 85 percent believed that their jobs

either were dead-end jobs or offered but limited opportunities for advancement.[38]

SUMMARY OF DIFFERENCES BETWEEN SCHOOL AND MONETARY WORK PLANTS IMPOSED BY THE FORMAL STRUCTURE

We have traced four major differences between the school and the monetary work plant which arise because of differences in the social organization of these work societies. The differences in motivation, in work schedules, in authority, and in advancement have been discussed. In general, the monetary work plant can be characterized as securing motivation through financial rewards, putting tighter time limits on the work load of the individual, achieving somewhat greater authority and control as the worker becomes dependent upon the work plant for livelihood, and making advancement procedures a blend of merit and bargaining. The school, in contrast, relies largely upon nonfinancial incentives to motivate learners, imposes less tight time requirements over work scheduling, exerts heavy formal discipline but has a less compelling control over work behavior, and offers an explicitly patterned structure for advancement based largely on merit of performance.

These contrasts must be understood as generalizations based on the observation of work behavior in the two types of work plants. It must be admitted that wide deviations from these generalizations can be observed in certain individual cases. The importance of high or even passing grades in courses, the prestige of a dramatic role in a play, or the status of a football position can prove to be the most powerful of incentives. In so far as these become coveted goals, the authority of the teacher and school administrator becomes strong, work schedules are met with fierce pride, and even unscheduled work may be added to the work load. For those who have experienced the joy of classroom rivalry in the contest of alert minds, the tasks within the monetary work plant may present considerably less challenge, especially during the early part of the work history.

An appraisal of the differences between school and the monetary work plant must not focus upon the deviations but observe the modal populations in each of the two work plants. This is the view that has been taken as the differences described above were identified. These differences have been located in the *social base* and the *formal structure*. There are in addition *differences in values, habits, and interests* between the members of the school and the members of most monetary work plants. These grow out of the diverse social experiences and informal social interaction of the workers in the contrasting work plants. They emerge as behavior products differentiated by the characteristics of the social bases and formal structures of the two plants.

[38] Howard M. Bell, *Youth Tell Their Story*, American Council on Education, 1938, p. 131.

C. Value Differences Between the School and the Monetary Work Plant

Values refer to those activities which have common meanings for the members of a particular group. Values are objective counterparts of attitudes. In the home, school, and church characteristic patterns define the expected and "right" ways of acting from which arise the values of the group. Five contrasting patterns can be identified as associated with the school and monetary work plant. Figure 76 shows these contrasts with the values which emerge from them.

Patterns and Emergent Values Within the Non-Monetary Work Plants of Home, School, and Church	Patterns and Emergent Values Within the Monetary Work Plants of Factory, Office, and Store
1. Pattern: Nonoptional Membership. Value: Each person belongs permanently to the group.	Pattern: Optional Membership. Value: Each worker must be free to enter or leave employment of any employer; each employer must be free to accept or reject any worker (upon cause) from his employment.
2. Pattern: Sympathetic Coöperation. Value: Each person should try to help the other.	Pattern: Competitive Striving. Value: Every worker guards his self-interest if he wishes to hold his job or get ahead.
3. Pattern: Uniform Moral Code. Value: Each person should do what is considered right.	Pattern: Ethical Neutrality. Value: Each person should be free to lead his own life without dictation from his employer or fellow workers.
4. Pattern: Personality Growth. Value: Each person should have an opportunity to develop to his fullest capacity.	Pattern: Work Persistence. Value: Each person should learn to stick on a job.
5. Pattern: Status Devaluation. Value: Each person should be evaluated for what he is and what he can do as a person.	Pattern: Status Evaluation Value: Each person can be evaluated by his class, education, race, nationality, and religion.

Fig. 76. Contrasting Culture Patterns and Values Distinguishing the Non-Monetary Work Plants of Home, School and Church from the Monetary Work Plants of Factory, Office, and Store.

PATTERNS AND VALUES OF HOME, SCHOOL, AND CHURCH

The patterns and values of the home, school, and church represent the culture definitions which socialize personality in the preparatory and initial stages of work life. Five patterns characterizing these groups are (1) nonoptional membership, (2) sympathetic coöperation, (3) uniform moral code, (4) personality growth, (5) status devaluation.

1. *Pattern:* Nonoptional Membership. *Value:* Each person belongs permanently to the group.

In considering the nature of group identification during the early stages of socialization, perhaps the major characteristic is the fact of nonoptional membership. The individual has little or no choice in becoming a participating member of the family, school, or church. He is usually accepted automatically and is told that he belongs to the group. The group, in turn, accept him for what he is. As long as he conforms to the folkways and mores of the group he is secure in the knowledge that he will be considered a part of the group.[39]

2. *Pattern:* Sympathetic Coöperation. *Value:* Each person should try to help the other.

The family, public school class, and Sunday School class are usually small groups in which people get to know one another as total personalities. It is true that such groups are not without jealousies, rivalries, and sometimes bitter conflict, yet these behaviors fall outside the expected and approved modes of conduct. Sympathetic coöperation is encouraged by both precept and example. The group exerts considerable pressure to secure conformance to their value that each person should try to help the other person. Sharing, compromise, and tolerance are the traits which are rewarded by the esteem of one's peers and the regard of one's mentors.

3. *Pattern:* Uniform Moral Code. *Value:* Each person should do what is considered right.

Despite the changing morals of our time, the family, school, and church agree fairly closely on what is "right" personal behavior. The conventional code includes honesty, premarital chastity, respect for parents, consideration of others, temperance in food and drink, allegiance to marriage vows, respect for property, and willingness to work. These ways of behavior are among the traditional mores. A high degree of conformance is expected and the authorities of family, school, and church place pressure if necessary to secure conformance and employ various punishments to discipline young violators. A relatively uniform moral code is instilled in young people, and perhaps most successfully in middle-class society. Thus, "good" and "respectable" people come to agreement that each person should do what is considered right.

4. *Pattern:* Personality Growth. *Value:* Each person should have an opportunity to develop to his fullest capacity.

Deep-rooted in American culture is the belief that each person has capabilities irrespective of his origin of birth. Moreover, there is an equally strong belief that each person should have an opportunity to develop to his fullest capacity. This means access to education and work experiences that will open a way for an individual to demonstrate what he can do. Freedom of speech and action, the right of free inquiry, and the right to

[39] The problem of the minority group member is omitted from this discussion.

participate or be represented in decisions affecting personal welfare are ideals that have been set down in the legal guarantees of the Constitution.

In order to develop, the individual must have new tasks on which to try his skill. The school has developed a curriculum designed to feed succeedingly more difficult tasks to the learner at the fastest possible rate. The ideal atmosphere of the school is considered one in which each learner is mastering new skills and demanding more compelling tasks.

5. *Pattern:* Status Devaluation. *Value:* Each person should be evaluated for what he is and what he can do as a person.

American schools and churches are institutions with ideologies which play down the importance of status based on class, religion, nationality, or race. It is taught that privilege cannot be purchased inside the school or church and that each person should be evaluated for what he is as a person.

These five patterns attributable to home, school, and church represent democratic and religious ideals which are very real influences governing day-by-day behavior in these institutions. The contrasting patterns to be found in monetary work plants are not to be considered in complete antithesis. They should be regarded as patterns which do not necessarily replace American ideals but in many ways provide the opportunities for their fulfillment in adult life. At the same time the variations should not be lost sight of. The five patterns of the monetary work plant which have been identified are (1) optional membership, (2) competitive striving, (3) ethical neutrality, (4) work persistence, (5) status evaluation.

These may be regarded as emerging from the given social and economic organization of our society. Our economic life is dominated by private enterprise increasingly adapted to mechanized instruments of manufacture, communication, and transportation. The patterns described represent characteristic emphases of the economic structure in terms of work behavior.

PATTERNS AND EMERGENT VALUES OF THE MONETARY WORK PLANT

1. *Pattern:* Optional Membership. *Value:* Each worker must be free to enter or leave the employment of any employer. Each employer must be free to accept or reject any worker (upon cause) from his employment.

The pattern of optional membership gives the worker a basic freedom. Anything less would make him subservient to some form of compulsive behavior. Thus, optional membership gives him freedom to work where he pleases but it does not guarantee security. He knows that each employer is guaranteed the right to accept any worker or (upon cause) to reject him from his employment. He is told that he must prove he can perform the jobs assigned and that failure means complete rejection from the work group. If he succeeds, he still must understand that steady employment depends upon an impersonal force called the market. During times of good market employment is relatively steady but in times of bad or poor market

chances of employment are weakened and he must become accustomed to the fear of unemployment or its actuality.

2. *Pattern:* Competitive Striving. *Value:* Every worker guards his self-interest if he wishes to hold his job or get ahead.

At the school commencement exercises, the successful adults tell the youth that they are about to enter a world with great promise but one that is "cold" and sometimes cruel. The great mass of workers confirm the fact of a cold and sometimes cruel world by repeating the old saw, "It's every man for himself in business. People will walk all over you if you let them." Battered and cynical heads repeat, "You better look out for No. 1"; "the way to get ahead is to push yourself"; "You have to be a little crooked to make money."

These folk sayings reflect the pattern of competitive striving which is presumed to be the testing ground of ability and initiative. Every man is presumed to have an equal chance to get to the top in business and in the professions. Those who fail are said to lack either the necessary ability or initiative. Most important of these is said to be initiative. The man who plays it smart, makes the right contacts, and takes good risks is the man who is believed to be successful. A good businessman is presumed to keep his eye on the ledger and not to permit his emotions to become so dominating that he neglects business demands in his concern over the consequences of low wage rates, layoffs, and prolonged unemployment of his working associates.

3. *Pattern:* Ethical Neutrality. *Value:* Each person should be free to lead his own life without dictation from his employer.

The monetary work plant is considered a place where adults work and have their work behavior observed only by adults. Whether this be true or not for a given work plant, the pattern of ethical neutrality prevails. This means that there is common agreement that each person should be free to lead his own life without dictation from his employer as long as his work is maintained satisfactorily.

Just as the employer wishes to remain free from moral censure as his desire to make profits guides his business decisions, so the employee wishes no moral censure of his behavior as long as his habits do not interfere with his work. Thus, the monetary work plant supposedly does not regulate personal behavior in any way except as it exercises selection in its recruitment of workers. The result is that moral behavior of workers comes to reflect all the variations which are found in the local community. A large work plant necessarily pulls out workers from a wide range of economic position and family background. The attitudes, interests, and social habits of the workers display a far wider range of behavior than can usually be observed in a given home, school, or church. The young middle-class worker, particularly, is impressed by differences between his background and that of

the workers in a work plant drawing from all economic and social classes.

4. *Pattern:* Work Persistence. *Value:* Each person should learn to stay on a job.

The so-called challenging and interesting jobs are decidedly limited. Most work requires constant repetition and much of it requires hard manual labor. The monetary work plant requires considerable persistence. Young workers anxious to climb to better-paying and more challenging jobs are surprised to learn how long it may take to move from even the first rung of the ladder. Promotions and transfers are often regarded by the employer as expensive since the removal of a good worker means a replacement must be found and trained. The employer, therefore, often feels his economic interest is best served by workers who are willing to remain on a job. Workers who are impatient for advancement often become an irritation both to the employer and to their working associates.

5. *Pattern: Status Evaluation. Value:* Each person can be evaluated by his class, education, race, nationality, and religion.

Although our political, educational, and religious traditions play down the importance of status, it is nonetheless true that education, economic class, race, nationality, and religion are factors which accelerate or impede social and economic advancement depending upon the definition of what is desirable and undesirable identification. An individual's background and status in the community become predetermining influences against which his personal behavior is evaluated. Symbols of status (as discussed in Chapter XI) become important in providing tags which can be quickly interpreted and through which the status of the individual is evaluated. The clothes one wears, the car one drives, and the house one lives in become important determiners of one's status in the community and in the work plant. Thus, we speak of a pattern of status evaluation referring to the tendency to place emphasis upon background factors as a basis of "placing" the individual and defining behavior toward him.

Even those of low status often take great pride in the fact that they have discovered a group of individuals who have lower status than they. Anglo-Saxons parade their assumed superiority before the southern Europeans. The southern European may hold himself to be above the Jew or the Negro. Likewise, education and family status may be exploited to drain out feelings of superiority.

In the hiring of workers, in their vocational placement, and in their advancement, status usually plays some part. For there is a wide consensus, even though contrary to deep American traditions, that each worker can be and should be evaluated by his class, education, race, nationality, and religion.

Summary of Patterns Associated with Monetary Work Plants. Five patterns have been identified and have been claimed to be associated with

monetary work plants. These are (1) optional membership, (2) competitive striving, (3) ethical neutrality, (4) work persistence, (5) status evaluation.

If these associations can be solidly confirmed, the evidence will be discovered in the adjustments which young workers find themselves forced to make as they become a part of the transition from school to monetary work plant. There are almost no research data to discover these critical phases in the movement from the way of life that has been part of the graduating student to that which is to face him in the world of community and work plant. In order to seek such evidence our files of work histories were examined. These histories frequently show that the personality does feel the impact of the new cultural environment of a monetary work plant. A feeling of not quite belonging to this adult world replaces the assurance which the student carried with him in the school. Two reactions may mark the transitional phase of adjustment for the new worker. These adjustments are *culture shock* and *marginality*.

INDICATORS OF TRANSITIONAL ADJUSTMENTS

CULTURE SHOCK

Culture shock refers to the repulsion which the individual experiences as he comes into contact with a different culture. In our present study the concern is with the feelings and attitudes which the individual has as he makes the transition from the cultural environment of the school to the culture environment of a monetary work plant. A typical example of the frustration of an aspiring worker is found in the following work history.

When I returned home from the army I needed a job to fill in the idle time until I could continue my college education. I accepted a job in a small machine shop as an apprentice machinist.

During the first morning at work I was shown a drill press and taught how to operate it. My duties were to insert a metal part in a vice, then I moved a lever which drilled a hole in the metal part. My final task was to remove the part from the machine; then I was ready to go through the same operation again.

The monotony of endless repetition of the same motions over and over for the entire day was almost unbearable. I cannot understand why people are content to spend a large part of their lives on such a distasteful job.

After several days I began to talk to the men at various machines near mine. They seemed quite content with their jobs. They seemed to have the outlook that the job was easy as far as mental effort was concerned and the physical effort was not too great. They were making a decent wage and the method was of little importance to them.

I believe that a man should be interested in his work and its results, and that he should enjoy doing his job.

I do not enjoy monotonous tasks either manual or mental. Because of this I hope to become affiliated with a large industrial firm with a large foreign interest.

Another young worker is sickened by the lack of opportunity and future prospects of a laborer's job. He says,

The job to which I refer was one as a laborer in a sawmill. Unlike most saw-mills there was a large amount of skilled and semi-skilled labor in this one. The mill was one that would rip its own logs, kiln the wood, and produce its own goods. The number of different goods it had to produce was one of the reasons why I liked the job so well. For example, one lathe that I worked on turned out goods like cultivator spreaders, salt water fishing rod handles, and assorted wooden handles with various beaded grips. Among the more interesting handles was the hammer handle. This unit was turned out in one operation, oval on one end, round in the middle, and with the conventional oblong for the hammer head.

Another point that I liked about this work was that the men I associated with were of the highest calibre. I will admit that they were laborers, but they were good men. They were the kind that enjoyed doing honest work for their livelihood. A good day's work made them feel good. And in most cases, they really got their share of work there.

The variety of work there was fine, and the men with whom I worked were some of the best. Why then was it to be hated, one might ask. The answer to that question was easy to find.

As I sat one day, eating my lunch, I looked about me at the men with whom I worked. What a ragged and rugged looking lot! Some were big and some were small, some were old and some were young. Some had worked here for over twenty years. Some did not know what it was to do other work. They drove the same old car day after day, and they discussed the same old debts, the same old homes, and the same old troubles. It seemed to me that all of them were in a rut.

That is why I hated the job.

Another young man in the factory is shocked by the baldness of the jokes and the talk of his fellow workers. He says,

I started to work with the hope of advancement, and an increase in wages. The first job I was assigned to was operating a drill press for 55c an hour. The first week didn't go too badly because the time passed rapidly while I was learn-ing what I had to do to make the machine run more effectively. It wasn't very long until I hated to go into the plant. I lived until it was time to go home every night.

There were several reasons for my utter disgust and very bad state of mind. The one thing that I hated as much as the continuous pulling of the handle of the drill press all day was the conversation at lunch time. As soon as lunch time arrived the filthy conversation began. I didn't mind having a "joke" once in a while, but when I had them every day for lunch it was too much for me. I finally quit after a month, and was a much happier and contented fellow.

The feelings of a young girl reveal her sheltered background. She tells of her first job experience with a certain vague defensiveness.

When I was a Junior in high school I decided that I would like to get some kind of a job for after school and Saturdays. Mother and Daddy thought that I was entirely too young to work, but I was bound and determined that I was going to work. It wasn't difficult to find a job then as it was wartime, and most of my girl friends were working.

I noticed that most of the dime stores were looking for clerks to help part time. I was a little afraid to go in and apply for a job, but I finally got up my courage and entered the Woolworth store. I immediately located the floor-walker who directed me to the manager. The manager interviewed me and told me that he would call if he needed me.

I didn't think that he sounded very encouraging but sure enough the next day he called me. He told me to come down the following Saturday to begin work.

I was all excited and pleased. I could tell that Mother was a little disappointed that he had called, but she didn't say a word.

I got up at 8:00 the following Saturday and got ready for work. I was there in plenty of time so that the floorwalker could show me what I was to do.

The first day, in fact, the first week went along fine. I really enjoyed clerking and, at the same time, felt that it was a worthwhile experience. This was the first week, but as time went on, and I had worked for almost a month, I began to hate my job. The floorwalker, the manager, and even some of the other clerks began to get mean and sassy. I wasn't used to this and I couldn't take it very well. I also began to realize that I was working too hard for such a little bit of pay. It seemed as though each morning that Mother called me for work I just couldn't make it.

It was all right going to school and working there, but when it came time to go down to the store, I just couldn't make it. Mother and Daddy began to see that I wasn't satisfied with my job and insisted that I quit. It didn't take much persuasion to talk me into quitting a job such as that.

These work histories show that young workers are repelled by:
1. The routine of repetitive work.
   "The time clocks, the regimentation, the purely mechanical routine, all struck me as useless." (factory worker)
   "Feeding glass tubes into one of the smaller machines by yourself was sheer unadulterated hell. A machine is an inanimate thing which includes no sense of competition, cooperation, or workmanship." (glass worker)
   "I found myself after a few months becoming quiet and my senses dulled in everything I attempted to do." (rubber worker)
2. The fatigue of hard work.
   "The conditions under which I had to work were almost unbearable. I worked at the job for eight hours per day and when the day was completed I was dead tired. My body was filthy! Most laborers could not work at this type of work for any great length of time. If one worked there too long, he began to cough up blood and pieces of black graphite from the lungs." (laborer in steel foundry)

"The day would finally drag by and I was ready for a nice quiet evening and then a good night's rest. When the time for going to bed came I found myself hating to go to bed because I knew what the following morning was going to bring. Another minute-dragging eight hours appeared before me. I could see myself pushing a big load of bricks or carrying a hod of cement up three flights of newly constructed stairs. The prospect of another day kept me awake long after I had crawled into bed." (bricklayer's helper)

3. The commands of an authoritarian supervisor.

"The attitude of the employer was irritating. She had neither respect nor a kind word for the employees." (chef's assistant)

"Most of all I didn't like the boss's attitude. He had a high harsh voice, and demanded whatever he wanted done. He never had a smile. Just looking at him I got the impression that he hated the world and everything in it." (laborer)

4. Dishonest business procedures.

"We were told to represent ourselves as college boys working our way through the State University or some conservatory of music. We were told how to make some offers that seemed to give the subscriber more than he actually received. In everything you said you had to tell a falsehood. The sales organization was based upon the theory that if you do not take the dollar someone else will, and that you are always smarter or sharper than the customer. I became disgusted with the whole business." (magazine solicitor)

"I found that the higher ups approved a lot of things that were not entirely honest. I was disgusted with some of the things I saw but I learned it was best to keep my mouth shut.

"When I left the office, it was none too soon for me. I had originally planned to go into the business world, but now I am glad I have changed my mind. I have seen the business world and want no more to do with it." (bookkeeper)

5. Deviant personal habits of fellow workers.

"The first and only job that I have had was at the B. F. Goodrich Company. I was only sixteen years old when I began, and I wasn't very well acquainted with the rougher side of life.

"I came into contact with types of people and conditions that I never knew existed. Most of the people were southerners. The greatest majority came from West Virginia, Tennessee, and Georgia. These people had come to Akron at an early age seeking employment in the rubber shops. These southerners were the poorer class and had lived in poor conditions. This is probably why these people are so accustomed to such habits of life that I found.

"The language used by the men was quite shocking at first to me.

The men were very hot tempered. The very first night I worked one worker became angry at another and chased him around the department with a knife. I wasn't very used to happenings like that, so I learned that the best way to get along was to keep my mouth shut and my eyes and ears open." (rubber worker)

"I found that many business men are unmindful of their marriage vows. It proved very disgusting at times to see married men so free with their affections. I found many girls wearing a disguise of righteousness, but when one knew them they proved to be unfaithful and distrustful." (woman office clerk)

6. The insecurity of work.

"I looked around me, day after day, and saw men who were bent with age and tired of face—a tiredness which arises from a hopeless outlook on an almost negligible future. These men bore every mark of the shackles of life in a factory.

"Many jobs in factories can be learned in such a short time that no man who works at such a job can feel secure. This insecurity is one more factor which promotes dissatisfaction towards factory work, one more factor which tends to break a man's spirit, leaving him bent and soul-weary even though he remains an efficient cog in the industrial machine." (factory worker)

MARGINALITY

Professor Robert Park once described the "marginal man" as the "individual who through migration, education, marriage, or some other influence leaves one social group or culture without making a satisfactory adjustment to another and finds himself on the margin of each but a member of neither."[40]

The student who has terminated his education and has started on his first full-time job often falls into a marginal social position. Marginality refers here to the social position of a worker who is partially accepted by his working associates and partially accepted by his younger high school friends but who does not feel completely accepted by either. High school and college students leave behind them their clubs and classmates. If the worker moves from the community, former ties are rather completely shattered and he must begin to make a new group of friends. The social anonymity in which he may find himself is perhaps entirely new to him.

Zorbaugh reports that the world of furnished rooms in which so many single adults of the city live is in no sense "a social world." The roomer finds "his social contacts are more or less completely cut off. His wishes are thwarted; he finds in the roominghouse neither security, response, nor

[40] Robert Park in Everett V. Stonequist, *The Marginal Man*, Charles Scribner's Sons, 1937, p. 41.

recognition. His physical impulses are curbed. He is restless and he is lonely."[41] One of Zorbaugh's informants, a young woman from Emporia, Kansas, speaks of her experiences in Chicago. "They treated me as impersonally as though I had been a rag doll. . . . The city is like that. In all my work there had been the same lack of any personal touch. In all this city of three million souls I knew no one, cared for no one, was cared for by no one."[42]

If the young adult remains in the home community he has an alumnus status, and his emotional ties to his fraternity or clubs, and to the activities of the school, remain rather strong as long as his younger friends remain in school. His associates in his new work group, especially if they are older, may not accept him as a full-fledged equal. On the other hand, cut off from daily contact with the school, he finds fewer bonds to tie him to his younger high school friends. He may remain unadjusted between two worlds for some time. But the die has been cast, for slowly the younger friends of the school terminate their education and take their places inside monetary work plants. Eventually he too settles down in the trial world of his work life. Getting ahead on the job, the excitement of courtship, and finally the new roles and new responsibilities as husband and father become the predominant interests of the male worker. The young woman worker has been weighing the merits of life as career woman over against life as housewife and mother. These are the interests and problems of the trial work period. They stand as evidence that the transition from school to work is now complete. The trial period of work life becomes the discussion of the following chapter.

SUPPLEMENTARY STUDIES

FIELD: PLANNED INTERVIEWS

Make one or more interviews of young men and women in the transition from the initial to the trial work period. The best time for interviewing is during the first two years after the interviewee has left school to accept full-time work. For a comparative analysis it is very desirable to seek interviews with boys and girls from lower-, middle-, and upper-class families. The following interview form is suggested as a guide:

Name _____   Interviewer _____
                                          Date _____
                                          City _____ State _____

[41] Harvey W. Zorbaugh, *The Gold Coast and the Slum*, University of Chicago press, 1929, p. 82.
[42] *Ibid.*, p. 80.

A. Background

Age _____ Sex _____ Months Out of School _____

Occupation of: Father _____   Sister _____

                      Mother _____   Sister _____

                      Brother _____   Sister _____

                      Brother _____

                      Brother _____

B. Job and Work

    1. Tell me about the part-time and full-time jobs you have had. We would like you to start with your first job and tell us

        a. How did you get it?

        b. What did you do?

        c. What did you like or dislike about it?

        d. Why did you leave it?

    2. What job did you want when you were in school? Did you get that job? Do you still want that kind of job? If not, why not?

    3. What kind of job do you want now? Do you think there is a good chance of getting it? How long will you have to wait?

    4. How do you think people on a job get ahead? Do you save any money? If so, what for?

    5. Have you joined a union? Why? Do you think your union is a good union? Why?

    6. Is the company you work for a good company or not? Why?

    7. Have you found a group at work which shares your background and interests? Explain.

    8. What kinds of things or situations bother and worry your work associates? Do you worry over these things also?

    9. Do you think you are going to have steady employment? Do you think that there will be more money and more steady jobs for everybody in the future or that we will have booms and busts?

C. School and Work

    10. What differences are there between working and going to school? Look for free response.

        Suggest: People

                Routine

                Freedom

                Authority

                Nature of work

    11. Did you like it better when you were in school? Why?

D. Home and Work

    12. Are you married? If so, how has it changed your life? Has it changed your outlook on your job?

    13. If not married, what about marriage? How do you suppose marriage would change your outlook on your job?

E. Community and Work

Ask respondent for information which will enable you to scale social par-

ticipation on the Chapin social Participation Scale. This scale is reproduced below:

Name of Organization	1. Member	2. Attendance	3. Financial Contribution	4. Member of Committee	5. Offices Held
1.					
2.					
3.					
4.					

Scoring: Weights of 1, 2, 3, 4, 5 are assigned to each type of participation as indicated by the order at the top of the scale. For example, if a person belonged to 6 clubs or organizations, attended 5, contributed to 3, was a member of 2 committees, and was an officer in an organization, his total score would be 38. Tentative norms for the Social Participation Scale may be found in F. Stuart Chapin, *Experimental Designs in Sociological Research*, Harper & Brothers, 1947, p. 195.

RESEARCH GAPS

1. Types of cultural shock experienced by young persons entering work plants and subsequent adjustments made by them.
2. Measurement of the degree and extent of marginality as young persons adjust to work plant society.
3. Measurement of values as they interrelate in home, school, church, and industry. Determination of degree and extent of differences.
4. The social experiences of the job applicant including job searching, interview, waiting, and unemployment.

CHAPTER XVIII

The Trial Work Period

Career Orientation
   The Trial Work Period as a Social Experience
   Definition and Characteristics of the Trial Work Period
   Six Distinct Types of Career Orientation
      1. Ambitious
      2. Responsive
      3. Fulfilled
      4. Confused
      5. Frustrated
      6. Defeated
      Summary
The Cultural Background of Contemporary Workers
   The Finding of Occupational Goals
      1. The Apprentice Training Provided by the Family, School, and Community
            for the Contemporary Worker
            Contrasts Between the Agricultural and the Industrial Civilization
            Methods of Arriving at Lifework Choices
            The Process by Which Occupational Choice Is Made
            How Young Work Candidates Secure Their First Full-Time Jobs
            Conclusions Regarding Apprentice Training in the Contemporary Indus-
               trial Society
      2. The Cultural Expectations Impinging upon the Trial Worker
            The American Career Stereotype
            The Cultural Expectations of the Upper Class
            The Cultural Expectations of the Middle Class
            The Cultural Expectations of the Working Class
Career Patterns During the Trial Work Period
   The Occupational Mobility of Workers
   Horizontal Occupational Movement of Workers During the Trial Work Period
   Vertical Occupational Mobility of Workers During the Trial Work Period
The Social Psychology of the Trial Work Period
   The Strain of Occupational Achievement
   Aspiration Among Industrial Workers

635

CAREER ORIENTATION

THE TRIAL WORK PERIOD AS A SOCIAL EXPERIENCE

The trial work period can be defined arbitrarily as the first ten or fifteen years of the individual's full-time work experience. We might agree upon the age span of eighteen years to thirty-four years inclusive as that of the trial period. A precise section of work history would then be available for study.

However, it should be understood that the trial work period represents a type of social experience. It is during the trial period that the individual tries out jobs, tests his ability and interest, and sizes up his chances of advancement. The trial period becomes a struggle to find oneself and to place oneself in a relatively secure work position. For some, it is the climb to the desired vocational goal, to the career that has long been nourished in imagination and expectation. For others, it is a day-by-day struggle against insecurity and boredom. Yet all who participate in work must in varying degree live through a trial period. It will be but a very short period for some workers until a stable work life is achieved. For others, the trial period as a social experience will continue throughout the entire work life. Still

others will find that their work life is but an alternation of trial and stable work periods.

What must be recognized is that the trial period is merely a name for a social experience accompanying the work progression or career of a given worker. For purposes of study constructed types of work experience have been devised. These are the (1) preparatory, (2) initial, (3) trial, (4) stable, and (5) retired phases of the lifework pattern. The expected progression in the folkways of American class structure is a movement which carries the worker through the five types of work in the order named. Since there are many deviations in this lifework pattern, it becomes necessary to take a section from the life span when optimum conditions for studying the social experience of the trial work period are available. The age span of eighteen to thirty-four has been selected as the focus for such study.

DEFINITION AND CHARACTERISTICS OF THE TRIAL WORK PERIOD

The trial work period has been defined as the period of *job transition beginning when the worker seeks his first full-time job and continuing until he has secured a work position in which he remains more or less permanently (Three years or more)*. It is a period of high occupational and work plant mobility. The worker is trying to find and secure that "job" which satisfies his needs for expression, for security, and for recognition. Elmo Roper reported to the American Management Association that his experience in public opinion polling had shown that the average worker has four major wants, in this order: (1) security, (2) a chance to advance, (3) to be treated like a human being, (4) to feel important.[1] The trial work period commonly represents the personal struggles to find an occupation and a work plant where the worker feels these wants may be gratified.

Workers seldom look upon their first full-time jobs as those in which they will remain. More often the worker feels that he is working at a job in preparation for a more responsible one or to find out if he wants to remain at his present job or work plant; or he may be merely holding on until he can make a change. To secure information about the trial period the writers have examined the work histories of Ohio workers who make up a sample which matches the Ohio labor force in such characteristics as occupational distribution, age, and sex.[2] Interviews with workers in the states of Washington and Michigan have been conducted. All of these efforts have been centered upon the discovery of the nature of the occupational

[1] Address before the American Management Association, Conference on Manpower Stabilization, New York, Sept. 28, 1943. See also Elmo Roper, *American Mercury*, February, 1944.

[2] Delbert C. Miller and William H. Form, "Occupational Mobility and the Measurement of Occupational Adjustment," *Readings in General Sociology*, Robert O'Brien (ed.), Pacific Books, 1947, pp. 221-228; "Measuring Patterns of Occupational Security," *Sociometry*, November, 1947, pp. 362-375; "The Career Pattern as a Sociological Instrument," *American Journal of Sociology*, January, 1949, pp. 317-329.

Career Orientation	Ambitious	Responsive	Fulfilled
Character of Aspiration	Feeling of hope and confidence that higher occupational goals can be attained.	Feeling of acceptance with job progression which parents or relatives expect worker to follow.	Feeling of satisfaction upon attainment of desired occupational goal.

Career Orientation	Confused	Frustrated	Defeated
Character of Aspiration	Feeling of uncertainty regarding past and present work progress and indecision regarding further moves.	Feeling of being thwarted in occupational aspiration but desirous of moving toward another goal.	Feeling of resignation and hopelessness with work progress.

Kind of Work Progression	Rising	Repeating and Paralleling	Completed
Identified by:	Evidence of movement involving successive increase of income or status or both.	Evidence of acceptance of a job previously followed by a parent or relative. Evidence that steps are planned more or less in advance by others, usually parents or relatives.	Evidence that desired occupational goal was attained and the holder is now satisfied to remain in the occupation and at the level he has attained.

Kind of Work Progression	Erratic	Blocked	Regressive
Identified by:	Evidence of erratic horizontal and vertical occupational mobility.	Evidence that desired occupational goal was not attained and that holder is now unable, temporarily at least, to move to another goal.	Evidence of movement involving successive loss of income or status or both.

FIG. 77. Six Types of Career Orientation Found in the Trial Work Period.

progression, and the accompanying attitudes and roles which the worker exhibits.

SIX DISTINCT TYPES OF CAREER ORIENTATION

The types of career orientation which have been discovered among the workers in the eighteen-year to thirty-four-year span are attitudinal sets which may be distinguished as (1) ambitious, (2) responsive, (3) fulfilled, (4) confused, (5) frustrated, (6) defeated. Figure 77 illustrates these types. The figure also indicates the kind of work progression patterns which are commonly associated with the six orientations. These orientations and work progression patterns will be described.

1. Ambitious

The ambitious worker is one who has a feeling of hope and confidence that he can attain higher occupational goals. He usually seeks higher occupational goals in order to attain greater authority, status, or income.

The ambitious worker possesses a strong motivating drive that engages him in the competitive struggle to get ahead. Our culture smiles upon such behavior, stressing initiative and defining success as a job movement that progressively lifts the individual into positions of greater responsibility. Parents, relatives, friends, and teachers of middle-class society stimulate and encourage the young worker to fulfill the American career stereotype. One man told us:

It seems to me that I have always felt I had to make good. My father used to tell us that the people who live in the hilly north section of the county were poor because they were lazy and lacked ambition to get ahead. He said they could have good farms and a house as good as ours if they would save and work. He called the hill section people, "white trash." The thought of becoming "white trash" came to be more odious than the thought of being cast into Hell itself. It was unthinkable that anyone in our family should ever slip to the place where he would have to live in the hill section among such people.

I learned that I had to work hard. Every time that my father felt I was not working hard enough he would say, "You are getting more like that white trash every day you live." This would make me so mad that I did not dare to speak back. I resolved that I would show my father something about my ability to get ahead that would make him take back those words. I think that is partly the source of my ambition to make big money.

Figure 78 illustrates the work history of this man. It shows that he has successively occupied jobs as farm hand, telegrapher, army officer, bookkeeper, plant cashier, clerical assistant, purchasing agent, and secretary-

treasurer. His income increases from a no-cash basis to $600 a month. Measured against the standards of American tradition this man is a success. His is a work history of *rising*. Evidence of movement involving successive increases of income or status is commonly associated with the ambitious worker.

Figure 79 is another interesting work history exhibiting rising. It is a history of an ambitious Negro man who has lifted himself into a responsible position with the aid of a college and graduate education. After four years of experience in domestic and personal service work, educational back-

Case number C-17-1   Place of interview Warren, Ohio
SEX: Male X Female   Year born 1915
Marital status: S ___ M X W ___ Sep. ___ Div. ___
Father's regular occupation: Mother's occupation:
  Farmer   Housewife
Nationality: German   German
Education: Father   Mother   Subject
  Grade   8   8   8
  High   3
  College
  Professional
  Vocational   2

Occupational history:

	Occupational description	Part or full time	Yrs.	Income	City & state
1.	Farm hand	Full-time	3	none	Ravenna, Ohio
2.	Telegrapher	Full-time	2	$ 60 mo.	Champion, Ohio
3.	Bookkeeper	Full-time	1	$150 mo.	Columbus, Ohio
4.	Plant cashier	Full-time	1	$300 mo.	Cleveland, Ohio
5.	Accounting supervisor	Full-time	2	$500 mo.	Warren, Ohio
6.	Purchasing agent	Full-time	1	$550 mo.	Warren, Ohio
7.	Treasurer-secretary	Full-time	2	$600 mo.	Warren, Ohio

Interviewer: Mary Jones

FIG. 78. Occupational Data Sheet of an Ambitious Career as Shown by a Rising Work History.

ground enables the worker to assume supervisory and executive responsibility.

These work histories are records of job movement that lift the worker from one class position to another. In Chapter XII the significance of movement in respect to class position is discussed and the reader may wish to relate this material to the career orientations which are analyzed here.

The examination made of work histories in this chapter seeks to understand the kind of orientation which the individual worker may possess irrespective of his class or economic status. However, work histories which

show rising often involve movement from one social class to another. The ambitious workers often have the attributes which are described for the "climbers" in Chapter XII.

Case number 28   Place of interview Akron, Ohio
SEX: Male X Female   Year born 1916
Marital status: S   M X W   Sep.   Div.
Father's regular occupation: Mother's occupation:
    Barber (died 1917)   Laundry proprietor (died 1938)
Nationality: American Negro   American Negro
Education: Father   Mother   Subject
    Grade   8   4   8
    High   2   4
    College   4
    Vocational   1

Occupational history:

Occupational description (Last job first)	Part or full time	Yrs.	Income	City & state
1. Farm hand	Part	⅙	$6 wk.	Cadiz, Ohio
2. Paper boy	Part	3	$25–30 mo.	Cadiz, Ohio
3. Chauffeur and yard boy, private family	Full	⅙	$ 75 mo.	Akron, Ohio
4. Porter—Elks Club	Full	⅙	$100 mo.	Akron, Ohio
5. Janitor— Union Station	Part	½	$120 mo.	Akron, Ohio
6. Janitor— Goodyr. Tire-Rubber	Full	¼	$120 mo.	Akron, Ohio
7. Part-time Rec. Supvr. League Br.	Part	4	$ 720–1200	Akron, Ohio
8. Assist. Exec. Sec'ry League Branch Akron Urban	Full	2	$1500–1800	Akron, Ohio
9. Executive Secretary Omaha Urban League	Full	2	$2400–3600	Omaha, Nebraska
10. Executive Secretary League Branch Akron Urban	Full	1	$4500	Akron, Ohio

    Remarks:

                                        Interviewer: A. L. Herbert

FIG. 79. Occupational Data Sheet of an Ambitious Career as Shown by a Rising Work History.

2. Responsive

The responsive worker is identified as one who is fulfilling the career which others expect him to assume. The most common of all occupational patterns is that of the son following occupations on the same or adjacent socioeconomic level as that of the father. All research studies show that a majority of the recorded regular occupations of the sons fall upon or are adjacent to the level of their father's regular occupation on *all occupational levels*. The workers who "inherit" occupations in the same socioeconomic level are called responsive. Some may be characterized by strong motivating

drive as they feel compelled to match the achievement of their father. Others find that the circumstances of life lead them with less effort in almost automatic progression to their lifework. These latter cases are commonly observed among owners who plan that their sons will eventually assume the responsibilities of their business or professional practice. Both the final job and the intervening steps of education and apprenticeship may be planned out, and the worker is simply expected to fulfill his destiny by following the plan.[3]

One business proprietor told us:

My father told me when I was about five years of age that he expected me to take over the store someday. As I got older he talked with me about running the

Case number C-28-2   Place of interview Ravenna, Ohio
SEX: Male X Female   Year born March 28, 1914
Marital status: S___M X W___Sep.___Div.____
Father's regular occupation: Mother's occupation:
  Department store owner   Housewife
Nationality: Hungarian   Hungarian
Education: Father   Mother   Subject
  Grade   8   8   8
  High   4   4   4
  College   1
  Professional
  Vocational

Occupational history:

Occupational description	Part or Full time	Yrs.	Income	City & state
1. Worker for his father	Full	3	$25 wk.	Akron, Ohio
2. Auto salesman Chevrolet	Full	1	$50 wk.	Kenmore, Ohio
3. Opened his own auto repair business	Full	5	average $1500 yr.	Ravenna, Ohio

Interviewer: Caroline Havre

FIG. 80. Occupational Data Sheet of a Responsive Career as Shown by a Paralleling Work History.

store and he would take me with him to the store during after hours and on Sunday when he wanted to do some work. I was initiated into the mysteries of invoicing as soon as I could add and multiply numbers. When I was fourteen I was made a clerk. I continued to clerk during out of school hours until I was ready for college. My father had investigated the business training of numerous colleges and universities and he finally persuaded me to go to our state university. After I graduated I came back and became the assistant manager of the store when my father retired. When my father stepped out five years later the full responsibility of operating the store was turned over to me.

[3] The reader will recall the attitudes of the Brahmin in Chapter XII.

This repeating of the father's career may occur in different ways. In the case just described the worker eventually assumes the identical work position previously held by the father. However, another possibility is the paralleling of the father's occupation but in another work plant. This may happen when the young worker rebels at the prospect of inheriting his father's position. Sometimes he dislikes the type of work or the long years of waiting and desires the satisfaction of independent growth. Parents protect the social position of the family and assist "their boy" or "their girl" by way of financial support, the arranging of contacts, etc., until the son or daughter reaches an equivalent occupational classification within another work plant. Figure 80 is a typical illustration of this latter case of inheritance. This man began work as a clerk in his father's department store after one year of college. In an interview he told us he became discouraged after three years of work in the store because he felt he could not advance and was dissatisfied working for his father. He changed jobs and after a year as an auto salesman his father helped him with financial assistance to establish his own auto repair business, which he has operated successfully for five years.

Interesting cases for study are those of sons who are catapulted into positions of major responsibility at a relatively early age. Henry Ford II inherited the presidency of the giant Ford Motor Company in 1945 at twenty-nine years of age. Robert M. Hutchins attained the presidency of the University of Chicago at thirty-one years of age. The first repeated his father's career by assuming the identical position in the work plant, the second paralleled the career of his father, Francis S. Hutchins of Berea College.

Although these cases have involved sons of owners and professionals, responsive workers may be found also among clerical, skilled, and unskilled workers. Here the observable pattern is one of attitudes oriented in such a way that the son expects to continue in the occupation of the father. Bakke has pointed out that among working-class individuals one is regarded as successful when he has attained the sort of job and standard of living customary among his associates.[4] Therefore, the occupational expectation of sons and daughters seldom soars ahead of the standards attained by the father and other members in their social class. Where families have striven to provide children with the education and training that might equip them to climb from the working class the desire was commonly shared by the children *until they took their first job*. Once they have made a start as workers, ambition has become stifled and with each passing year the likelihood of advancement beyond working-class status becomes less probable. Bakke puts the orientation this way: "The best summary which characterizes the standards of many of those with whom we had contact was this, 'All that I ask now is a chance to pay my bills and be able not to worry.' "[5]

[4] E. Wight Bakke, *The Unemployed Worker*, Yale University Press, 1940, p. 20.
[5] *Ibid.*, p. 26.

Case number _C-27-2_   Place of interview _Akron, Ohio_
SEX: Male _X_ Female _____   Year born _1920_
Marital status: S _X_ M ___ W ____ Sep. ____ Div. ____
Father's regular occupation: Mother's occupation
  Dry cleaner   Seamstress
Nationality: English   Scottish
Education: Father   Mother   Subject
  Grade   6   6   8
  High   2   1   4
  College
  Professional   2
  Vocational   1

Occupational history:

| | Part or | | | |
Occupational description	full time	Yrs.	Income	City & State
1. Apprentice interior decorator	Part	2	$ 15 wk.	New York, N. Y.
2. Owner, decorating shop	Full	6½	$100 wk.	New York, N. Y.

Interviewer: _John H. Smith, Jr._

FIG. 81. Occupational Data Sheet of a Fulfilled Career as Shown by a Completed Work History.

Case number _C-33-2_   Place of interview _Akron, Ohio_
SEX: Male _X_ Female _____   Year born _1921_
Marital status: S ___ M _X_ W ____ Sep. ____ Div. ____
Father's regular occupation: Mother's occupation:
  Pattern maker   Housewife
Nationality: American   American
Education: Father   Mother   Subject
  Grade   8   8   8
  High
  College
  Professional
  Vocational

Occupational history:

| | Part or | | | |
Occupation description	full time	Yrs.	Income	City and state
1. Shipping clerk	Part	2	$ 15 wk.	Cleveland, Ohio
2. Cable splicer	Part	2	$ 20 wk.	Cleveland, Ohio
3. Flying squadron	Full	2	$ 30 wk.	Akron, Ohio
4. Superintendent production	Full	7	$150 wk.	Akron, Ohio

Interviewer: _Thomas Gisinger_

FIG. 82. Occupational Data Sheet of a Fulfilled Career as Shown by a Completed Work History.

3. Fulfilled

The fulfilled worker is characterized by a feeling of satisfaction upon attainment of a desired occupational goal. This worker may have been extremely ambitious in earlier stages of his work life when he was struggling to achieve his present work position. Now that he occupies that position, he wants nothing more than a successful tenure within it. The work history commonly associated is one that might be called *completed*. There is evidence of a work progression from less responsible to more responsible jobs. The fulfilled worker may seek more money and more prestige, but he is satisfied with his choice of occupation and has no ambition to move in any different direction. Figure 81 illustrates a case of the completed career. Here we find that specialized vocational training and a short apprenticeship lead to proprietorship of a decorating shop in New York City with a $100-a-week income. Figure 82 describes another worker with a completed career orientation. After completing a grade school education he began his first full-time work as a member of an in-plant training group called a flying squadron. After two years of such specialized vocational training he was appointed a plant superintendent and has served seven years in that capacity. He is satisfied that he has reached the highest job of which he is capable and he has no further desire or expectation of advancement.

4. Confused

The confused worker has a feeling of uncertainty regarding past and present work progress and indecision regarding future moves. The work history is commonly marked by evidence of *erratic* horizontal and vertical occupational mobility. Such histories are chronicles of floundering or of adventuresome floating. Two components seem to explain the apparent aimlessness of the patterns: Personality characteristics of the worker and the unstable nature of the jobs occupied. Such personal characteristics as desire for adventure or difficulty in getting along with people show up in high, erratic occupational mobility. Unstable jobs within semiskilled and unskilled classifications reveal still another frequent cause of high occupational mobility. Figure 83 is a work history which seems to reflect a picture of a person whose desire for adventure has driven him to many cities and states and into a wide variety of occupations. This worker is the proverbial "rolling stone." He has, in turn, been a streetcar conductor, a clerical worker, a taxicab driver, a secretary, an auto mechanic, a horse trainer, a construction mechanic, a rice grower, a ranch hand, and a farm overseer. For thirteen years he has been on the move. New York, Detroit, Memphis, Little Rock, St. Charles, and San Antonio have in turn been his residence. Even now, al-

though he has spent two years on the present job, it would be foolhardy to
predict that the worker has become stable.

Figure 84 is an occupational history of a young man thirty-two years of
age. He is a graduate from a leading university in the United States. All of
the jobs in his history have been assumed since his graduation. His history
seems to reflect two factors: personal difficulty in making social adjustments
and the impact of the war upon his work life. He is now enrolled in graduate

Case number C-33-2   Place of interview Chagrin Falls, O.
SEX: Male X Female   Year born 1912
Marital status: S____M X W____Sep.____Div.____
Father's regular occupation: Mother's occupation:
    Carpenter   Housewife
Nationality: English-Scotch   English
Education: Father   Mother   Subject
    Grade   8   8   8
    High   4   2 yrs. military academy
    College
    Professional
    Vocational   1½

Occupational history:

	Occupation description	Part or full-time	Yrs.	Income	City & state
1.	Streetcar conductor	Full	1	$ 95 mo.	New York, N.Y.
2.	Wrote out bills for lumber co.	Full	1	$100 mo.	New York, N.Y.
3.	Drove taxicab	Full	1	$600 mo.	Detroit, Mich.
4.	Took shorthand—typed letters	Full	1	$120 mo.	Detroit, Mich.
5.	Mechanic work on auto	Full	2	$500 mo.	Memphis, Tenn.
6.	Trained western saddle horses	Full	1	$150 mo.	Little Rock, Ark.
7.	Mechanic for road const. co.	Full	1	$200 mo.	Little Rock, Ark.
8.	Rice grower	Full	2	$250 mo.	St. Charles, Ark.
9.	General ranch work	Full	1	$180 mo.	San Antonio, Tex.
10.	Supervises farm	Full	2	$200 mo.	Chagrin Falls, O.

Interviewer: Donald Koerlin

FIG. 83. Occupational Data Sheet of a Confused Career as Shown by Erratic
Work History.

school preparing for college teaching. He thinks that he may be able to be
a better teacher at the college level but he is doubtful because he was unsuccessful as a high school teacher. His problem, he says, is finding a group of
people who think as he does. He believes that he would be happy if he
could become located in New York City.

Those two cases of *erratic* work histories seem to be explainable in
terms of particular personality characteristics. However, this is probably
only a part of the explanation. The struggle to find an emotionally secure
and satisfying place within work groups is a universal one. Most job histories
reveal evidence of this struggle in the patterns of vertical and horizontal
mobility or in the earlier shifts of educational training. It has been pointed

out that the intense specialization of our contemporary world has heightened the difficulty of finding one's "place." Moreover, secondary group life in large work groups may stifle emotional satisfactions even when the individual is thoroughly competent in the work position. Thus, the search for a

Case number C-35-3   Place of interview Seattle, Washington
SEX: Male X Female   Year born: 1914
Marital status: S__ M X W__ Sep.__ Div.__
Father's regular occupation: Mother's occupation:
  Insurance salesman   Social worker
Nationality: German   English
Education: Father   Mother   Subject
  Grade   8   8   8
  High   4   4   4
  College   4   5
  Professional
  Vocational

Occupational history:

Occupation description	Part or full time	Yrs.	Income	City & state
1. Typist	Full	1 mo.	$ 25 wk.	Chicago, Illinois
2. Cost clerk	Full	2 mo.	$ 20 wk.	Chicago, Illinois
3. Mail order clerk	Full	2 mo.	$ 22 wk.	Chicago, Illinois
4. History instructor	Full	6 mo.	$130 mo.	Brandt, S.D.
5. Book runner	Part	1 mo.	$ .50 hr.	Chicago, Illinois
6. History instructor (substitute)	Part	1 mo.	$ 10 day	Chicago, Illinois
7. History instructor	Full	6 mo.	$180 mo.	Colfax, Wisconsin
8. Material clerk	Full	3 mo.	$200 mo.	Chicago, Illinois
9. Checker	Full	1 mo.	$ 45 wk.	Chicago, Illinois
10. Invoice clerk	Full	18 mo.	$200 mo.	Chicago, Illinois
11. Auto part assembler	Full	1 mo.	$210 mo.	Chicago, Illinois
12. Fire extinguisher assembler	Full	1 mo.	$210 mo.	Chicago, Illinois
13. High school principal	Full	6 mo.	$240 mo.	La Manre, N.D.
14. Auto part assembler	Full	1 mo.	$210 mo.	Chicago, Illinois
15. Camera fitter	Full	2 mo.	$150 mo.	Chicago, Illinois
16. Cost clerk	Full	1 mo.	$ 40 wk.	Chicago, Illinois
17. Order picker	Full	2 mo.	$ 75 wk.	Chicago, Illinois

Interviewer: D. C. Miller

FIG. 84. Occupational Data Sheet of a Confused Career as Shown by Erratic Work History.

work position in which the individual feels competent technically and secure emotionally is not an easy one. The two case histories described here should in all probability be regarded as accentuated illustrations of this common search.[6]

[6] The reader will recall that other main types of reactions to fluctuating class histories were identified in Chapter XII. These were (a) hope-springs-eternal reaction, (b) ride-with-the-tide fatalism, and (c) confused, mixed, and alternating responses. In so far as the work history involves fluctuating movements between classes it will be useful to refer to Chapter XII for further insights regarding floundering work histories.

5. Frustrated

The frustrated worker feels that he has been thwarted in his occupational aspirations. He desires to move to another occupational goal but finds himself blocked. He is in an occupational rut. He knows he is blocked and is anxious to get out of his present job. The work history of the frustrated worker is identified by evidence that the desired occupational goal was not attained and that the worker is now unable to move to another goal. The case of a woman worker who has a *blocked* work history is shown in Figure 85. She is a woman who desired to teach home economics and completed

Case number C-11   Place of interview Seattle, Wash.
SEX: Male___Female X   Year born 1920
Marital status: S X M___W___Sep.___Div.____
Father's regular occupation: Mother's occupation:
  Bookkeeper   Housewife
Nationality: Irish   Scotch

Education:	Father	Mother	Subject
Grade	8	8	8
High	4	1	4
College			2
Professional			
Vocational			

Occupational history:

Occupation description	Part or full time	Yrs.	Income	City & state
1. Clerk and typist—coal yard	Part	1	$10 wk.	Kansas City, Kan.
2. Retail clerk—dry goods store	Part	2	$15 wk.	Tacoma, Wash.
3. Retail clerk—department store	Full	5	$42 wk.	Seattle, Wash.

Fig. 85. Occupational Data Sheet of a Frustrated Career as Shown by a Blocked Work History.

two years of college education. She and her mother moved to Tacoma, Washington, where she secured a position as clerk in a large department store in Seattle. She has worked there for five years. She often wishes she could have gone ahead with her career in home economics but she says she has the satisfaction of knowing that her mother is happy and will be well taken care of during the whole of her life.

6. Defeated

The defeated worker possesses a feeling of resignation and hopelessness with work progress. His most common reaction is to see himself as a failure.[7] His work history is commonly identified by a *regressive* work record involving successive loss of income or status or both. It may be that during the early part of the career there is upward movement, which becomes halted,

[7] Bakke, *op. cit.*, pp. 363-365.

and then the downward movement sets in. The "fall" may be small or great. These variations are not of significance to us except as they contribute to better understanding of the social adjustments of the defeated career.[8] What is of major interest is the emotional impact of the occupational descent and its ramifications in the social life of the worker and his family. A good illustration of the defeated career is found in Figure 86. This is a history of a man of thirty-five. He received his college training in engineer-

Case number C-97

Place of interview Akron, Ohio

SEX: Male X Female

Year born July 10, 1910

Marital status: S M X W Sep. Div.

Father's regular occupation:
  Engineer
Nationality: Scotch

Mother's occupation:
  Housewife
  Italian

Education:	Father	Mother	Subject
Grade	8	8	8
High	4	4	4
College	5	3	4
Professional		1	1
Vocational			

Occupational history:

Occupation description	Part or full time	Yrs.	Income	City & state
1. Retail clerk	Part	1	$ 5 wk.	Syracuse, N.Y.
2. Theater usher	Part	1	$30 wk.	New York, N.Y.
3. Bank clerk	Full	1	$40 wk.	New York, N.Y.
4. Attorney—specialization in corporate finance	Full	2	$75 wk.	New York, N.Y.
5. Law practice	Full	2	$27 wk.	Cleveland, O.
6. Truck driver	Full	1	$30 wk.	Akron, O.
7. Illness—unemployed		2		Akron, O.
8. General factory worker	Full	5	$58 wk.	Akron, O.

Interviewer: James F. Lavelle

FIG. 86. Occupational Data Sheet of a Defeated Career as Shown by a Regressive Work History.

ing but never engaged in engineering work. Instead, after two years as a bank clerk, he turned to law, received his degree and began practice as a specialist in corporation finance. Two years of fairly successful New York practice ensued. Then came the depression. The history shows a movement to Cleveland, Ohio, where the law practice continues but the weekly income is reduced by almost two-thirds of the previous income. After two years in Cleveland the shingle comes down and the worker accepts a job as a truck driver at $30 a week in Akron, Ohio. A year passes and a serious illness incapacitates the worker for one year. After another year of unem-

[8] The discussion of the "has-been" in Chapter XII may be recalled.

ployment he secures a job requiring general factory work. The worker told us:

The depression never gave me a chance. I was employed by a large law firm and was becoming fairly well known for my work in corporation finance. Then the bottom dropped out of Wall Street. I was laid off and after looking around for a while I decided to move the family to Cleveland where my wife's parents live. I was able to get a job as a law clerk at a measly $27 a week but that looked big to me then. That lasted two years but with the depression growing worse the old firm of Fairbanks and Cutter was doomed. I did not have a dime. After trying every law office in Cleveland I had to give up. I took a W.P.A. job as a truck driver. At first I hated every minute of it. And the family was miserable but it was a job and the $30 a week came in regularly. Business began to pick up and I tried to get back into law. My being on W.P.A. certainly didn't help. Even old professional friends seemed to turn up their noses when I came around to ask for a job. Then, just when I might have got a pretty good job I was crippled up and had to go to the hospital. When I got out I wasn't worth much for another year. By that time the World War had broken out. I made a last attempt to get back into law but it was no go. Anyway they were beginning to draft lawyers as non-essential so I went to work in the war plant. I have been making from $50 to $75 a week since. I can't say that I am happy but it is steady and we are getting ahead better than we ever did before. Of course, I should be pulling down big money in law now if the depression hadn't caught me. And then I had my operation on top of that. I've had my share of tough breaks. I had hoped my kids might have it better but I don't see much hope in this crazy world.

The depression, illness, and perhaps other forces have broken a career pattern which seemed established and secure. The early part of this career history may be fitted perfectly to the American career stereotype as the worker makes a successful progression into a professional career. But his skid into work life as a semiskilled worker runs counter to all social expectations and is regarded as "tragic." The worker suffers with the "shame" and self-pity of his "defeat" and his life outlook becomes profoundly affected.

Summary

Six types of career orientation have been presented as significant attitude sets of the worker in the trial work period. Only limited research has been done to trace out the full social ramifications of career histories. However, it is well known that important social effects can be observed to be associated with each type of career orientation. In the illustrations some of these effects have been suggested. In the latter part of this chapter an attempt will be made to find experiences which are common to the trial work period. In addition, the career patterns of workers will be examined in order to discover the nature of occupational mobility during the trial work period. Before this is undertaken it seems advisable to examine the cultural back-

grounds of young workers. In the light of the cultural background, the source of different career orientations can be partly identified.

THE CULTURAL BACKGROUND OF CONTEMPORARY WORKERS

THE FINDING OF OCCUPATIONAL GOALS

Individuals find their occupational goals through a compounding of work experience, observation, and expectation. Although the advance of scientific testing is notable, it is still true that trial and error is more often the process by which workers come to be placed in jobs rather than formal guidance. In fact, the more one studies case histories the more apparent it becomes that *accident* is the deciding factor in determining the occupation of a majority of workers. The *accident* of birth establishes family, race, nationality, social class, residential district, and to a great extent educational and cultural opportunity. This means that the family and its status provide rather definite boundaries within which the new individual will observe the work activities and participate in work life. For some persons, these boundaries enclose wide areas; for others, the scope of observation and experience is squeezed into narrow corridors. And as opportunity is diminished so too is expectation. The social world in which the work candidate lives can constrict occupational expectation as completely as it excludes opportunity. Therefore, many work possibilities never appear as possibilities in the thinking of the individual.

Occupational expectation is determined by technical, educational, and social influences. The status expectation of the family members, relatives, and friends profoundly shapes the choice of an occupational goal. The range of considered occupations is determined largely by the status expectations within the social class in which the individual finds himself. Figure 87 is a chart showing the vocational aims of high school students from the upper-, middle-, and working-class families of a midwestern town called Elmtown which was studied by A. B. Hollingshead. Note how vocational aims are related to class position of the family. In view of such facts it is understandable that when a young middle- or upper-class college graduate says that all he wants is a good job which offers opportunities, he is not telling you he will take any well-paying job which offers opportunities for advancement. What he is trying to say is that he will take any job which does not violate the expectations of his family and his friends within his social class. So it follows that occupational expectation is largely a reflex of social expectation determined by the class membership of the work candidate. Within the range of socially acceptable work the individual then builds expectations based on technical and educational considerations. Technical demands im-

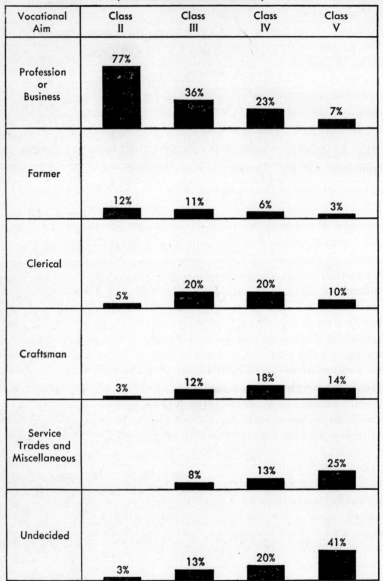

FIG. 87.   Vocational Choices of Elmtown High School Students from the Upper Middle, Lower Middle, Upper Lower, and Lower Lower Classes (Classes II, III, IV, and V, respectively). (Reproduced by permission from *Elmtown's Youth* by A. B. Hollingshead, published by John Wiley & Sons, Inc., 1949.)

pose the requirement of ability. Individuals appraise themselves to gain a feel for their competence to perform certain jobs. They evaluate the educational experiences which are required for the attainment of certain work positions.

The purpose of this section is to describe the cultural background as it operates to provide work experience, observations, and occupational expectation for the worker in the trial period. Two areas will be explored. These are (1) the apprentice training provided by the family, school, and community for the contemporary worker, and (2) the cultural expectations impinging upon the trial worker.

1. The Apprentice Training Provided by the Family, School, and Community for the Contemporary Worker

CONTRASTS BETWEEN THE AGRICULTURAL AND THE INDUSTRIAL CIVILIZATION

There is a marked contrast between the vocational training which the young man or woman received in the agricultural civilization and the vocational training which is received by youth for an industrial civilization. Appraised in terms of vocational adjustment, the training for the agricultural civilization was a superior one. It provided a limited education but an abundance of direct work experience which fitted the worker for his future occupational goal. This superiority was not one of conscious planning, but rather the result of certain factors in the work environment. Foremost among these factors was the coincidence of work plant and home. On the farm, there is no clear-cut line where family living and household work break away from the work of the fields and the barn. A person in a rural environment acquires the techniques of the job, the social role, and the appropriate social skills. He has many models available for his direction and guidance. From parents and neighbors the boy learns the man's life; the girl, the life of a woman. Life on and off the job is crystallized year by year in the folkways of the community, the technicways of the farm and home, and the ritual of the church.

Another factor simplifying vocational training in an agricultural civilization was the limited number of occupations. The older occupational situation was made up of a few established professions, some clerks and semiskilled workers, and a preponderance of farmers and proprietors, skilled and unskilled workers. With few occupations to prepare for, the problem of choosing a vocation was much less difficult. In fact, it was often taken for granted that the son would follow his father's trade and that the daughter would marry as soon as she reached her late teens. Moreover, except for the professions of law, medicine, and the ministry there were no very highly specialized occupations. The young man wishing to be a skilled tradesman would begin as an apprentice at a relatively early age, perhaps twelve or thirteen, and thus secure his vocational training inside a work plant rather

than a school. This had the advantage of placing him within an environment which indoctrinated both technical and social traits of the world he would of necessity live in. In this world the maturity that comes to the adult came soon to the child.

Contrast now the young American man or woman of, let us say, twenty years of age. A typical young person must contemplate the selection of a job among 29,744 occupational titles.[9] The resources he brings to that selection are to be found in fourteen years of educational training and such work experience as he was able to find in summer, after-school, and Saturday jobs. If a boy, his work experience, it will be recalled, was probably that of paper boy, sales clerk, filling station attendant, theater usher, or delivery boy. If a girl, her experience was probably that of sales clerk, housemaid, nursemaid, waitress, or musician.

Not only is work experience limited but so too is observation. Most work plans have no place for the young person under sixteen years, and many are not interested in offering any job to the school-going youth. There is a very good chance that our typical young person has never seen his father or mother (if she works outside the home) at work. The removal of the work plant from the home removed the models from young people. For the young person and for the adult, too, the world of working people tends to be walled off, inaccessible, and unobservable. Faced with this isolation young people are forced to choose their occupational goals on fragmentary experience, much of it reconstructed in the imagination and on second-hand information. This can be clearly seen from the following replies of 6000 high school youth as to the manner in which they arrived at their lifework choices (see Table 33).

TABLE 33. Methods of Arriving at Lifework Choices—High School Boys, Grades 9–12[10]

	No.	Percent
Through own observation and thought	1882	61
Parental advice	677	22
Through actual work experience after school or summer	247	8
Advice from others	180	6
Through reading	63	2
Through hearing lectures	13	1
	3062	100

METHODS OF ARRIVING AT LIFEWORK CHOICES

Table 33 shows that only 8 percent of all high school boys have derived their lifework choices by actual work experience, whereas 92 percent have

[9] For further discussion see William G. Campbell and James H. Bedford, "You and Your Future Job," Society for Occupational Research, Los Angeles, 1944, p. 2. The United States Employment Service in its published Dictionary of Occupational Titles, United States Government Printing Office, 1939, defines 17,452 distinct jobs and classifies an additional 12,292 alternate titles, a total of 29,744 occupational titles. The United States Census Report for 1940 lists over 20,000 different occupations.

[10] From "Canton Occupational Study," 1938, p. 178.

relied upon advice, observation, and reading. Among high school girls there is an even greater reliance upon advice, observation, and reading, as only 3 percent make their choices on the basis of actual work experiences (see Table 34).

TABLE 34. Methods of Arriving at Lifework Choices—High School Girls, Grades 9–12[11]

	No.	Percent
Through own observation and thought	2090	71
Parental advice	601	20
Through actual work experience after school or summer	95	3
Advice from others	134	5
Through reading	33	1
Through hearing lectures	3	negligible
	2956	100

These figures are one measure of how little opportunity exists for the trying out of jobs and coming to the choice of a lifework through actual work experience. For college-age people the situation is somewhat better but not strikingly so. Our cases show that a college student does get wider opportunities for employment, and as he finds more or less in accidental fashion that he has a certain ability in a job, he decides thereupon to prepare for that occupation. A large part of the current college population was greatly influenced by work experience gained in the army. Typical of scores of case histories is the following report by a young college man telling how he came to choose his lifework.

On September 7, 1939, I enlisted in the United States Navy. On November 11, 1939, I was sent to the Hospital Corps School, San Diego, California. After sixteen weeks of training in various classes, I was sent to the United States Naval Hospital, San Diego, California, for duty. I worked in several departments of the hospital; therefore, I gained an extensive view into the field of medicine. I soon became interested. After a few months of further training I was transferred to the United States Naval Training Station, San Diego, California, for more extensive work and training. At this training station I did work in the pharmacy laboratory, X-ray department, blood station, chemistry, and various other departments. On November 15, 1941, I went to sea. At sea, in close association with doctors, I really became interested in the field of medicine.

The first two years of the war, I was attached to different ships. I was then sent to Brisbane, Australia, for duty at a small seaplane base. There were no doctors at this base, only a chief pharmacist's mate and myself. We were responsible for the health and welfare of the men. There were several minor injuries and very few major injuries, but these gave the chief and myself an adequate opportunity to apply our practice.

On December 14, 1945, I was transferred to the merchant marine for independent duty aboard merchant marine vessels. Since there are no doctors aboard

[11] From *ibid.*, p. 200.

these vessels, I was placed in a position to act according to my own judgment. I liked this type of duty.

For the first time in my life, I had a reasonable amount of responsibility. It was necessary for me to study several medical and surgical books. In that last year aboard merchant vessels, I had no casualties.

Last August, in Seattle, I had a long talk with the examining doctor of the Board of Health. He advised me, because of my previous training and experience, to go to school and complete a course in medicine.

To become a doctor is now my ambition. I know this will be possible because I have a goal to study for and look forward to.

In this case history, experience and training have produced an occupational goal. Would this young man have found a desire for medicine without his war experiences? There is no way of answering, particularly without further information regarding his previous experiences. However, there is good reason to believe accident plays a large role. A case history which reveals very clearly this factor of accident follows:

Upon my graduation from high school in 1941 I was completely bewildered as to what I would do. All through four years of high school I took a college preparatory course. Should I enter college or should I work for a year to get enough money to finish all four years of my schooling instead of the two years I had money to pay for? Finally I decided to work for a period of a year.

My first job was that of an apprentice welder. I learned from the bottom up, and within four months I had a job as a regular welder. However, I decided that this job was not for me. Just when I was ready to quit, war broke out. Now I had to abandon my plans for college. I enlisted in the Marine Corps rather than be drafted.

As time went on I got to thinking more and more about what I would do when I was discharged from the service. I had been with Ernie Pyle for a few days (during the Okinawa invasion) and thought I would like to become a newspaperman. Talking it over with men on various papers I came to the conclusion that although I really liked that type of work there wasn't any money in it. I know also that the old adage goes something like this, "A man is happy in work he likes, no matter what the return." This is true but I thought I'd try the newspaper game for a while anyhow.

Upon my discharge, I came to Kent State. Enrolling in journalism, I found the work interesting but still didn't think it was what I wanted.

On a weekend (I hitch-hike home and back) I obtained a ride with a man from Pittsburgh who travels the Cleveland-Pittsburgh highway every Friday. He was an advertising man for "Coal Age," a McGraw-Hill Company publication. As we rode along our casual conversation got around to what each of us was doing, would like to do, etc. I said I would like to go into advertising, although up till that time I didn't know anything about it. He beamed and said, "That's funny, I just happen to be an advertising man." I could scarcely believe my ears.

He explained various phases of advertising to me in such an exciting and interesting way that I immediately became intrigued with the subject. Upon my return

to the campus I went to the library and read a few of the books I could find on the study of advertising. I have definitely decided to make my career in the field because it has a place for those with ideas and who can present a certain product to the public in such a manner that they will want to purchase it. The work is clean, and provides good pay to those who can turn out the things demanded by the consumers.

Since our first meeting almost six months ago, I have talked with the advertising man from "Coal Age" again, and I feel that he has helped me more to decide what I want to do than anyone else. In fact, he has offered me a job when I graduate from college.

In the case above we observe a young man who has twisted and turned upon the basis of likes, experience, and advice. His search for a high income level is apparent. Only occasionally in all of the cases does high altruism appear. A young would-be historian speaks out his desire to help the common weal as he says,

Man shall earn his bread by the sweat of his brow! Every child learns these words at an early age and as he grows older the problem they present becomes more complex.

Every one goes through that stage of "let's pretend" in which the ideal occupation is that of a policeman or an actor, but as the day approaches for this glamorous event to take place, no magic wand is waved to take the dreamer out of the drab life he leads. If he is a policeman or an actor at the age he expected to be one, the glamour is gone and the dream becomes just a way to make a living.

My life was a series of such fancy dreams, each of which became less glamorous with age. Farm hand, salesman, stevedore, cameraman, expeditor, truck driver, and soldier are some of the occupations to which I have been exposed and none of them have seemed to fit.

In 1944, I was in an Army rest camp in New Guinea. There was a portable library there and one of the books was a biography of Napoleon's life. There was nothing else to read one day when I wanted a book, so I took *Napoleon*. This was the book which decided the question of "daily bread" for me! I want to make history come alive for students. I want to make events stand out in flaming reality and bring the "hell of conflict" into the classroom. "Knowledge of past mistakes will prevent future mistakes."

If I can accomplish this "dream" I will be doing good for my fellowman and the "daily bread" will take care of itself.

Another case is presented to give one illustration of a young college woman who has sought to find her occupation. She says:

When I was but a small child my ambition was to become a nurse. My two playmates were easily convinced that nursing would be their life work, too. At one time we organized into what you might call a nurses' staff in one of the girl's playhouse, and delved into some very serious work.

After we were about ten years old I decided I would much rather be a school

teacher, but the other two girls disagreed and decided on other fields of work. In order to prepare for the vocation I had chosen (I had decided I would enjoy teaching commercial courses) I planned my high school courses accordingly. During my senior year I changed schools, and having enough credits to graduate I applied for a part-time job as secretary to the laboratory and X-ray staff in a hospital. There I became very interested in laboratory and X-ray work. I was allowed to participate in this work as well as my secretarial work because of the shortage of help. I was rather handicapped in the scientific work because I had majored in commercial courses in high school, but did learn enough to know that this work was very interesting.

At that time airline work was becoming very popular. When nursing requirements were no longer required for hostess work I changed all my plans and inquired about the other requirements that were needed. The airlines that are worth getting into require girls to be twenty-one. This was the only disadvantage I had come across. I have two or more years to wait and have decided to carry out my course in secretarial science although I have decided against teaching it. I do want to have a little more business experience after I leave college, but I am planning to go into the airlines when I am of age.

These case histories are typical of those we have studied, and indicate the circuitous process by which young people choose their occupations and begin their trial work period. If full samples are analyzed, the varieties of experience and motive may be shown. One sample of forty Ohio college men and women who had not decided definitely on an occupation were studied in 1946. When asked to write about "Occupations I have Considered Entering" they presented statements which revealed the following reason:

1. Found I "liked the work" as a result of work experience (11 in armed forces) 22
2. Desire for thrills, glamour, excitement, adventure, etc. 12
3. Desire for income 9
4. Desire for fame or to feel important 8
5. Influence of members of the family 8
6. Influence and/or advice from others than family members ... 8
7. Like the working conditions (including leisure, independence) 8
8. Length or expense of educational training 7
9. Childhood training or experience 6
10. Desire for security 6
11. Good chance for advance 6
12. Desire to help people 6
13. Special abilities or talents 5
14. General likes and dislikes such as "like to meet people" 5

                                                                              Total   116

It can be seen that each college student has listed an average of about three reasons which he himself recognized as a basis for considering his

occupational choice. In many cases one or more reasons were repeated as one tentative occupational choice after another was made.[12]

Another sample of 108 college students who had chosen an occupation were asked to write the explanation of "How I Came to Choose My Lifework." In these statements the same reasons come to the fore. For instance, a student preparing to become a physical education teacher said that "teachers are in great demand and always will be." One preparing to become a doctor said that there had been many members of the family in that profession and so he always had admired it, "and besides it offers complete financial security plus the satisfaction and joy of aiding afflicted persons." One preparing for the dentistry chose that profession as a result of army training as a dental technician. One preparing to become an elementary school teacher had a dislike for office and other work and liked children, besides believing teaching to be "one of the most important jobs in the nation." One preparing for the theater had from earliest childhood been influenced in that general direction by speaking in public, acting for company in the home, etc. One preparing to become a physical education teacher said that there "is not too much money in the profession, but it will provide a reliable source of income . . . and will provide honest, clean living." One planning to become an insurance agent had been influenced by his father's twenty-eight years of experience in that field and the realization that as an insurance agent he would be his own boss, have a good income, and have a high degree of security. One preparing for social or personnel work had been floundering in other jobs but had "humanistic impulses and drives" and had been found favorably inclined toward such work by an aptitude test taken in the Marine Corps. One chose teaching and coaching because it is interesting and useful and because "a person cannot be satisfied with a job merely because it pays good money." One was planning to become an electrical engineer because his father and his father's three partners needed one in their business. One planned to become a missionary because of his conversion at Pinebrook Bible Conference. One planned to become a salesman because he had liked meeting people in previous jobs; he likes to talk, and he likes to travel and meet people whereas he dislikes mathematics. One was planning to enter air conditioning because of a previous job on the railroad and advice from an electrical engineering friend of his father's who promised him a job after graduation.[13]

[12] From the personal files of the writers. For a review of the published studies which have analyzed the reasons given by students for choosing an occupation see Edward K. Strong, Vocational Interests of Men and Women, Stanford University Press, 1943, pp. 28 ff.

[13] The writers are indebted to David Moberg, Associate in Sociology, University of Washington, for assistance in compiling and classifying the data from these samples.

THE PROCESS BY WHICH OCCUPATIONAL CHOICE IS MADE

Is there any interpretation that can be made to explain the process by which these young persons come to make these choices? Edward K. Strong, Jr., is a psychologist who has devoted intensive study to vocational interest and guidance. He says,

How young people choose an occupational goal is largely unknown. Three possible explanations may be advanced with the thought that all three are probably involved in the choices made later in life, if not during grammar and high schools.

The first explanation is in terms of interests. Certain activities that are liked or disliked are identified with occupations, and so the occupations are liked or disliked. Thus liking mathematics and physics and disliking English is frequently interpreted as liking engineering; the reverse is interpreted as liking law. A great many early occupational choices are seemingly arrived at on this basis.

The second explanation is in terms of social prestige. A boy is continually asked, "What are you going to do when you grow up?" He must have a sensible answer and be able to defend it, or he "loses face." Any occupational choice is better than none under these circumstances. When defeated in argument he must name a new choice. Since his efforts are in the direction of making a good impression upon others, he tends to choose occupations with prestige value. . . . It would seem as though fairly stable choices are finally reached by first eliminating many occupations which are not liked or which fail to have the necessary prestige value and then choosing the best-liked occupation from the remainder.

The third explanation involves the preceding two but pertains primarily to the satisfactory adjustment of the personality to its environment. For example, the shut-in type selects opportunities which would never occur to the socially minded "good mixer." Acceptance must be viewed as ranging in individual cases from trivial to very complex considerations.

. . . All three of these explanations involve ability. Interests accompany satisfying activities; social prestige is not long maintained unless there is successful performance of a sort; one's personality traits are reflections in a rough sort of way of what one does well.[14]

We should like to add some sociological observations to this interpretation of the process by which young people choose an occupational goal. One characteristic is outstanding in the experiences of most of the case histories that have been cited. In their quest of a lifework there has been a vast amount of floundering, and chance experiences appear to have affected choices more than anything else. No single motivating influence underlies the majority of the choices made. It is the compounding of various experiences and influences which has finally crystallized into a *wish* for a certain occupation. Chance experiences undoubtedly explain the process by which most occupational choices are made. By chance experiences we are referring

[14] Strong, *op. cit.*, pp. 48 ff.

to those which are unplanned so far as the individuals themselves are concerned.

It has been pointed out in an earlier chapter that modern society is not giving much assistance to the planning and guiding of work experiences. The effect of a society characterized by intense occupational specialization is to guide *less* rather than *more* the process of "choosing" an occupational goal. Young people must adapt to an industrialized society which is relatively inhospitable to the school-going population. Employers do not seek or want the services of young people until they are adult except within a narrow band of clerical and unskilled occupations. In fact, child labor laws set up legal barriers. This walling off of work is not so much the result of intent as the product of an economic organization which relies on profitable efficiency as a criterion of success and survival. The girl or young woman is particularly handicapped as she becomes defined as a worker who does not intend to remain on the job, or who will not remain or who should not apply for "man's" work anyway. The boy or young man is told that he lacks experience or training and there is no way to introduce him to the job. Shut away from work experience, shut away from vital observation and contact with the workers in specialized occupations, the young man or woman relies on the crude factors of chance and circumstance to piece fragmentary experience into a career plan. If the result is an immature, self-seeking, floundering young worker, then the social forces surrounding employment must be held partly responsible. For a society that withdraws its work models and work experiences from its youth takes away the vital stuff upon which sound occupational goals are based. All the vocational testers and all the vocational guiders cannot put back what has been taken away. Their help is desperately needed but at best they can only cut down a part of the waste involved in improper job placement. As young men and women step out into the trial period, many are released to experiences which for the first time will give them an opportunity to make sound judgments regarding the occupation they are best suited by interest and ability to follow. It is not surprising, therefore, that 49 percent of the men and 12 percent of the women who had decided on an occupation before entering the University of Minnesota in 1924-1930 tell us some ten years later that they are not now in that occupation.[15] John R. Tunis reports that fifty percent of the 541 graduates of the Harvard class of 1911 are not, twenty-five years later, in the occupation they hoped to enter when they left Harvard with their degree.[16] In the light of these facts Strong has made an interesting discovery. He says he has found the question "What do you daydream of

[15] Charles R. Pace, "Progress Report of the General College Adult Study" (mimeographed), General College, University of Minnesota, p. 60a. See also C. R. Pace, *They Went to College*, University of Minnesota Press, 1941, p. 95.

[16] John R. Tunis, *Was College Worth While?* Harcourt, Brace and Company, 1936, p. 16.

doing fifteen years from now?" of great value for it "often discloses that the students' expressed desires represent quick ways of earning money which will make it possible to do something else later on. If the 'something else' is a possible vocation, it should be carefully considered as the real occupation to enter."[17]

The school, the community, and society must share in the difficulty of training and placing young people in the world of work. Of the three, society with its occupational specialization and its labor force regulations is the main block for it has all but destroyed apprenticeship as the agricultural-craft society knew it. In its place modern society has left unguided trial and error as the process of vocational training and placement to be borne by young people during the trial work period. It is interesting to compare in this connection the means by which young people secure their first full-time jobs.

HOW YOUNG WORK CANDIDATES SECURE THEIR FIRST FULL-TIME JOBS

If the Youngstown Occupational Survey of 1938 is representative of urban high school youth, it should be clearly demonstrated that "pull" is necessary for placement in the first full-time jobs.[18] The importance of sponsors can be seen in Table 35, which reports the means by which 1222 high school graduate boys and girls obtained their first jobs during the 1930's. At least nine out of ten jobs are secured with the aid of some personal influence. The aid of parents, relatives, friends, and neighbors enters in securing nine out of ten jobs for the boys and eight out of ten jobs for the girls.

TABLE 35. Means by which Youngstown High School Graduates Found Jobs During 1932, 1935, 1937

	Boys		Girls	
	Number	Percent	Number	Percent
Parents and relatives	309	44.3	195	36.1
Friends and neighbors	302	44.3	239	44.3
Principals and teachers	39	5.7	46	8.5
Church and lodge	19	2.8	9	1.7
Employment agency	13	1.9	51	9.4
	682	100.0	540	100.0

The aid of friends and relatives seems to play a lesser role in the first placement of college-trained workers. The University of Minnesota graduates and nongraduates who were trying to get their first jobs in the late 1920's and early 1930's report that they succeeded by direct application in

[17] Strong, op. cit., p. 452.
[18] The depressed labor market of the thirties must be considered in drawing generalizations. However, the general placement picture is probably shown in correct outline as high school youth seek employment in their local community.

about one-half of the cases. About one-fourth say they obtained jobs through the help of friends or relatives. Twenty percent of the graduates and 5 percent of the nongraduates say they secured their first jobs through the university employment office or some other university assistance.[19]

It is interesting to compare the San José workers with the high school and college graduates. Of 1119 workers in all age groups who reported, slightly over one-half had only their own effort to secure their first job in their regular occupation but one-third were assisted by relatives, friends, and teachers.[20] A comparison of these different groups suggests that the aid of friends and relatives is important in securing the first jobs in all occupational levels.

The explanation for the differences between high school- and college-trained youth probably lies in the fact that college-trained youth seek many more jobs outside their home community. Both employer and employee thus come to rely less on the help of friends and relatives, and employers look to their personnel organizations to recruit staff.

CONCLUSIONS REGARDING APPRENTICE TRAINING IN THE
CONTEMPORARY INDUSTRIAL SOCIETY

1. Opportunities for work experiences in monetary work plants are limited. More opportunities are available for males than for females.

2. Such work experiences as are available do not give opportunity to try out and to observe a wide range of occupations.

3. Work models have been continually removed from the direct observation of young people.

4. Most high school graduates secure their first full-time jobs through the aid of parents, relatives, and friends.

5. Most college-trained youth secure their first full-time jobs through direct application.

2. The Cultural Expectations Impinging upon the Trial Worker

The vocational aspiration of an individual has been viewed as a product of work experience, observation, and occupational expectation. The point has been made that each of these elements may be seen to vary with differences in the class position of the family and its members. In order to understand the attitudes and motivations of young people entering or living within the trial work period it is necessary to comprehend the cultural values within class groups. An analysis of these values within social classes reveals similarities and differences. Common to all classes is the American career stereotype.

[19] Charles R. Pace, *They Went to College*, University of Minnesota Press, 1941, pp. 94-95.
[20] Davidson and Anderson, *Occupational Mobility in an American Community*, Stanford University Press, 1937, Table 72, p. 137.

THE AMERICAN CAREER STEREOTYPE

The American career stereotype is a picture of a young, ambitious worker who may start his work life with no more than average intelligence but with high character, initiative, and hard work. With these qualities he is seen to climb from the lowliest of jobs and social background to the higher-paid brackets which spell social success. It is presumed that the way will be hard and long but that success will be inevitable. It is supposed that those who fail do so because of the lack of ability or ambition or both. Young Americans are encouraged to seize upon the career stereotype and incorporate it into their own personality as a model for their development of aspiration and character. Parents and teachers play up the cases of stereotype fulfillment found in historical, legendary, and contemporary life. There is reason to believe that these experiences are especially stressed within the middle class. Arnold Green has pointed out the nature of the social pressure placed on the middle-class child.

If the abstraction "ours is a competitive society" is translated into terms of what happens to the child born to modern middle class parents, it becomes quite relevant to the present discussion. Before the child has developed a real self-awareness he becomes a part of a process of invidious comparisons with other families: he uttered his first word two months earlier than the Jones' boy; he weighed so many pounds at the end of his first year. At Sunday School he received the Bible for perfect attendance; at public school his grades in arithmetic were higher than two-thirds of the other members of the class. He may take piano lessons in view of the day when Mrs. Smythe's pupils will be on public exhibition before the parents of the neighborhood. Everything he accomplishes or fails to accomplish becomes an inevitable part of the family's attempt to maintain or improve its standing in the community.[21]

An evaluation of the career stereotype has already been made in Chapter XVII. It was shown that the preferences for professional and technical employment far outnumbered the opportunities available and that much aspiration must be beaten down and out of many young work recruits. Our purpose now is to define the class differences which produce marked variations in the occupational outlook of young persons. It is most important to recognize that there are such differences. The career stereotype is so pervasive in the legendary literature of America and so well entrenched in middle-class society that it is often difficult to grasp the fact that many young people have been born and now live in social groups that define work life in widely different terms.

The cultural expectations of the social classes are projections of the common values derived from the work experiences and observations of the

[21] Arnold Green, "The Middle Class Male Child and Neurosis," *American Sociological Review*, February, 1946, p. 40.

family within a given social class. The term "cultural expectation" is used to refer to certain values which young members of the family or social class are "expected" to incorporate into their work goals and social roles. Many of these expectations may never be spoken; but they become real in the behavior of the family members. The values within the upper, middle, and lower social classes will illustrate these meanings.

THE CULTURAL EXPECTATIONS OF THE UPPER CLASS

We shall not be concerned here with a strict definition of upper class and its range of social characteristics. Classes will be regarded as social worlds within which a particular individual carries on most of his important relationships and within which an individual's personality structure tends to be laid down. The values or norms in upper-class society derive from social positions of high income, high status, or both. An upper-class father is often an owner-manager. He has a substantial ownership interest which gives him financial security apart from the income he receives from his position as manager. He devotes a large share of his time to maintaining his contacts with top executives in industry and government. He knows how important it is for the success of the business to maintain these contacts. He finds he must confer, lunch, and golf with these officials. Often he must travel long distances to attend conferences and to make speeches. He says that he is doing the most important public relations job for the company. He encourages his immediate working associates to make as many community and business contacts as possible and to train their subordinates to handle the details of running the business. He tells them that policy making and the maintaining of contacts is the real responsibility of top executives. Ample expense accounts are provided for travel and entertainment. He often expresses disappointment because he is so busy he cannot spend more time with his staff. He has long ago become isolated from the workers in the plant.

This picture of the upper-class father is that of a man who has a well-developed tendency to view his relations with others as connections useful to him in building the reputation and business of the company and in turn maintaining family status and power among friends in his upper-class social groups.

Bred in these values parents attempt to maintain for their children the high status they have won. The child feels early in life the social pressure which leads him to an assigned role. If the expectations are cast in the words of the parents they might be stated as follows:

1. "We expect our son to follow his father's business and he should begin to get some experience with the firm."

2. "If our son insists upon his own choice of a career we expect him to

secure a position which is socially acceptable to his family and comparable to the family status."

3. "We expect our son to remember that the social position of the family has been established by hard work and tradition. Only certain positions are worthy of that tradition."

4. "We expect our son to remember that the work position he chooses must bring an income sufficient to maintain high social status."

5. "We expect our son to maintain the social contacts he has with people in prominent families and keep in line with their thinking."

6. "We expect our daughter to recognize that a successful marriage with a socially eligible man is her most important goal in life."

7. "We expect our daughter to be particularly careful never to assume any work which would endanger her social position or lessen her chances of a marriage within a prominent family. (We encourage her to engage in philanthropic social work or community activity rather than enter the business world.)"

These cultural expectations of the upper class emerge as the guiding norms. Of course, variations about these norms exist in upper-class families, but the emphasis on maintenance of high status is almost universal.

THE CULTURAL EXPECTATIONS OF THE MIDDLE CLASS

Arnold Green has described the middle-class father as a person who has acquired a view of his relations with others as providing a means to an end.

The father's work takes him far from the place of residence, where most of his associates are only slightly less strangers to him than they are to his family. He is a white-collar worker. As a salesman, office worker, minor bureaucrat, or professional man, his job techniques revolve around manipulating the personalities of others, instead of tools. Since he has internalized the supreme middle-class value, individual success, he tries to use his associates, education, hobbies, intellectual interests, in terms of their possible value to his career. On the job he views himself not so much as functionally associated with others in a common purpose, as a self-contained unit establishing contacts with others. His work relations are not defined in fixed terms of status and role to the extent that they were in the past for he is on the move, or views himself in that way. He has, then, a well developed tendency to view his relations with others in terms of what he, as a mobile, displaced person can get out of them.[22]

This picture may be somewhat overdrawn but it most certainly approximates the set of attitudes common to middle-class workers. With such outlooks, middle-class parents transmit cultural expectations. Middle-class parents hold expectations regarding work roles of their children that may be identified as follows:

[22] *Ibid.*, p. 35.

1. "We expect our son and daughter to recognize that their job is an indication of social standing in the community."

2. "We expect our son and daughter to remember that they must start their work lives somewhere and that they can't be too choosy at first. However, the job should not be too far down the ladder. Our daughter should not accept 'manual work.'"

3. "We expect our daughter to remember that she will want to have a happy marriage and she ought to work someplace where she can meet eligible middle- or upper-class men."

4. "We expect our son to buckle down, work hard, and make a success."

5. "We expect our son to go to work for an individual or company which has a reputable standing in the community."

6. "We expect our son to get a job that is not dirty or involves the use of his hands. He should have a white-collar job. It should provide him with sufficient income to support his family, buy a home and a car, give his children a good education, live in a good residential district, and meet sound moral people."

7. "We expect our son to keep progressing and getting advancements. We are watching his job progress and expect him to build a good job record."

THE CULTURAL EXPECTATIONS OF THE WORKING CLASS

The working-class expectations are more immediate expressions of short-run goals. The working-class father is a manual worker. He is a factory worker, a skilled craftsman, or a laborer. He commonly moves from job to job but seldom changes his regular occupation. He tends to accept himself as stuck where he is. His concern is with finding a socially respectable and secure job. He knows it is not easy to keep the money coming in. There are always layoffs and quit slips to think about. He believes that the important thing is to keep his health and build up seniority when he finds a good job. He thinks the bosses are out for the profit and don't care much what happens to the workers. He says working people will never get any security or recognition unless all of them stick together. The working-class father therefore comes to view his relations with his fellow workers as associates who must unite and bargain together so that better conditions of work and security can be won.[23]

Cultural expectations of working-class parents may be stated as follows:

1. "We expect our son to recognize that a job means food and shelter for the wife and the kids. He should try to be a good provider."

[23] The desire for security can be overplayed. In his study of unemployed workers, Bakke says, "One would expect that among a group of unemployed, specifications of impressions would tend to involve dominantly those productive of economic insecurity. Such was not the case. Seventy out of every hundred suggestions for change dealt with changes which would remove barriers to realization of the other goal responses we have named. They were concerned with getting rid of conditions which kept them from functioning in a socially acceptable role, and that made them conscious of control by forces they could not master or understand." E. Wight Bakke, *op. cit.*, pp. 37-38.

2. "We expect our son to have a good time and be happy. A job is a way to eat but there is more to life than killing yourself in a factory. If you keep your health and your family is well that's the important thing."

3. "We expect our son to settle down and stick when he finds a good job. He should not try to go too far out of his class by being too choosy about his work or living too high. About all anyone can expect is to keep the pay checks coming in. The big shots have the top jobs sewed up."

4. "We expect our daughter to get married to a good provider and raise her children."

5. "We expect our son and daughter to stick with the union because that's the best way for working people to get ahead."

CAREER PATTERNS DURING THE TRIAL WORK PERIOD

The trial period has been defined as the period of job transition beginning when the worker seeks his first full-time job and continuing until he has secured an occupation in which he intends to remain during the rest of his work life. In research practice it has been our habit to regard any worker who has not remained for at least three years on a job as holding a trial job. A worker who has remained more than three years in a given work position has been regarded as on a stable job.

The assumption has been made that every worker enters the trial work period when he begins his search for his first full-time job. The early years of work life are observed to be years of testing when the individual may be called upon to make new adjustments as worker, marital partner, home-builder, and parent. The brunt of these adjustments may be best observed in the age span beginning around sixteen to twenty and continuing to about thirty to thirty-four years. The span eighteen years to thirty-four years has been arbitrarily selected in order to focus attention upon the age period when most workers will be struggling with common problems of adjustment.

It is always understood that the trial work period is meaningful only as it corresponds to a social experience. Therefore, some workers may be expected to achieve stability early in their work life and others late or not at all. What, then, is the history of workers when they embark on full-time work life? To gain insight into the meaning of these histories it is necessary to clarify the kind of mobility that can be observed.

THE OCCUPATIONAL MOBILITY OF WORKERS

The occupational histories of workers show two major types of mobility. These will be called horizontal occupational movement and vertical occupational mobility. *Horizontal occupational movement* refers here to any job movement which involves a transition from one work position to another work position. When we are interested in horizontal movement we examine

career patterns for the number of jobs held and the duration of each job. Such movement may be observed when a worker moves from (a) one job to another job within the same company (transfer or promotion), (b) one company to another company within the same local community, (c) one company to another company in another community. Therefore, horizontal occupational movement describes all job moves *without regard for their socioeconomic classification.*

Vertical occupational mobility refers to job movement between socioeconomic levels. A semiskilled drill press operator who assumes the work of a skilled turret lathe mechanic is considered as moving from a semiskilled to a skilled work classification, thus raising his socioeconomic classification. Obviously, vertical movement can be downward as well as upward on the socioeconomic ladder.

The recording of vertical mobility is weakened by the fact that it is difficult to establish the relative socioeconomic level of each job classification. Before any scale could have validity each occupation would need to be examined against such criteria as scale of living, occupation, income, wealth and savings, marital and family circumstances, social repute, schooling of parents and children, political character and influence, and, perhaps, recreational conditions. Since the degree of correlation between these conditions and given job classifications has never been determined with precision, no present scale of socioeconomic levels is entirely satisfactory. Research workers have made serious attempts to secure a good scale.[24]

The most widely known scale is that of Dr. Alba Edwards of the United States Census Bureau.[25] His scale lists the following "socioeconomic" classifications:

[24] D. Fryer, "Occupational Intelligence Standards," *School and Society,* September, 1922, p. 276. See also D. Fryer and E. J. Sparling, "Intelligence and Occupational Adjustment," *Occupations,* June, 1934, pp. 55-63; C. Burt, *A Study in Vocational Guidance,* Industrial Research Board Report No. 33, London, 1926; F. E. Barr, "A Scale for Measuring Mental Ability in Vocations and Some of Its Implications," M.A. thesis, Stanford University, 1918, reprinted by L. M. Terman in *Genetic Studies of Genius,* Vol. I, p. 66; E. S. Brussell, "A Revision of the Barr-Taussig Scale," University of Minnesota (unpublished); G. S. Counts, *The Selective Character of American Secondary Education,* University of Chicago Supplementary Education Monographs, No. 19, May, 1922; G. N. Kefauver, V. H. Noll, and E. E. Drake, *The Secondary School Population,* National Survey of Secondary Education, Bulletin No. 17, 1932, Monograph No. 4, United States Government Printing Office, 1933; R. O. Beckman, "A New Scale for Gauging Occupational Rank," *Personnel Journal,* December, 1934, pp. 225-233; F. Goodenough and E. J. Anderson, *Experimental Child Study,* University of Minnesota Press, 1931, pp. 234-244; Ethel Kawin, *Children of Pre-School Age,* University of Chicago Press, 1934, pp. 164-69.

[25] Alba M. Edwards, "A Social-Economic Grouping of the Gainful Workers in the United States," *Journal of the American Statistical Association,* December, 1933, pp. 377-387; Sixteenth Census of the United States, Alba M. Edwards, *Comparative Occupation Statistics for the United States,* United States Government Printing Office, 1940, p. 176.

1. Professional persons.
2. Proprietors, managers, and officials.
   a. Farmers (owners and tenants).
   b. Wholesale and retail dealers.
   c. Other proprietors, managers, and officials.
3. Clerks and kindred workers.
4. Skilled workers and foremen.
5. Semiskilled workers.
6. Unskilled workers.
   a. Farm laborers.
   b. Laborers, except farm.
   c. Servant classes.

Dr. Edwards defends his classifications by pointing out that each group has a somewhat distinct standard of life economically, and to a considerable extent intellectually and socially. Figures for 1940 are available for the major occupation groups showing wage or salary income and years of school completed. We have shown the medians for these socioeconomic groups in Chapter V. The figures when considered together indicate that the socio-economic groups so classified are arranged in the descending order of the social-economic status of the workers comprising them and that they do constitute a scale.

These groupings have been employed in classifying the gainfully employed workers in the United States in the 1930 and 1940 censuses. Most occupational research has followed either these classifications or a set very similar to them. Vertical mobility of workers will be recorded in terms of the Edwards scale in this chapter.

HORIZONTAL OCCUPATIONAL MOVEMENT OF WORKERS DURING THE TRIAL WORK PERIOD

There is no complete record of the occupational histories of the gainfully employed workers in the United States. The United States Census Bureau makes a survey once each decade to assess changes that have taken place within *occupational classifications*, but this record tells nothing about *individual work histories*. Very few institutions or associations have kept records of individual work histories *after* the individuals have severed their relationship with the institution. Most schools know very little about their graduates five or ten years after graduation. Business firms either destroy their terminated employee records or place them in their "dead" file and usually make no further follow-up. Social workers keep elaborate records on their active "cases" but seldom maintain follow-up records after their client has become rehabilitated. The result is an abundance of *cross-sectional* work records but a veritable absence of *longitudinal* histories. The study of work adjustment requires an ample body of continuous record following work histories from birth until death. Such histories are not now available. However, sample

studies enable us to begin the analysis of work life and the adjustment problems related to it. Most of these studies have been made by researchers who were interested in following up the careers of students who had graduated from high school[26] or from college.[27]

The research studies vary greatly in the number of years of follow-up and the care which was given in ascertaining experiences between the time of graduation and the terminal time used in the study. Despite the lack of continuous study of a given population there is a growing body of fact upon which to draw conclusions. Especially useful are the few studies which describe a sample of workers representative of the total labor force.[28]

Taussig and Joslyn's *American Business Leaders* has a comprehensive study of one occupational group, our outstanding business managers and owners. The writers will draw upon these published reports and their own research files to describe what is known about occupational mobility in the careers of American workers.

Davidson and Anderson have shown that young adults have relatively high horizontal occupational movement. When 466 San José respondents in the age group *twenty to thirty-four years* inclusive were asked how many different occupations they had followed for eight months or more, the results showed an average of three different occupations.[29] Figure 88 shows the percentage of different occupations specified for ages twenty to thirty-four years.

The recent study of Princeton graduates in the class of 1932 shows that

[26] Howard M. Bell, *Youth Tell Their Story*, American Council on Education, 1938; Herbert W. Benedict, *Canton Vocational Survey*, Canton Board of Education, Canton, Ohio, 1938; W. L. Richey, *Youngstown Occupational Survey*, Youngstown, Ohio, 1938; Don J. Bogue and H. Ashley Weeks, "Factors in the Occupational Adjustment of Male Youth in Whitman County, Washington," *Research Studies of the State College of Washington*, Vol. IX, 1941, pp. 119-133; Paul H. Landis, *Six Months After Commencement*, Bulletin No. 420, Agricultural Experiment Station, State College of Washington, 1942; Paul H. Landis, *Washington High School Graduates in Depression and in War Years*, Bulletin No. 463, Agricultural Experiment Station, State College of Washington, 1945; Howard C. Seymour and Carl E. Tremer, *We Left School a Year Ago*, Rochester Public Schools, Rochester, New York, 1941.

[27] John R. Tunis, *op. cit.*; Alvin C. Eurich and C. Robert Pace, *A Follow-Up Study of Minnesota Graduates from 1928 to 1936*, University of Minnesota, Committee on Educational Research, 1938; Walter J. Greenleaf, *Economic Status of College Alumni*, United States Government Printing Office, 1939; F. Lawrence Babcock, *The United States College Graduate*, The Macmillan Company, 1941; C. Robert Pace, *They Went to College*, University of Minnesota Press, 1941; Maitland Edey, "The Class of '32," *Life*, June 16, 1947, pp. 51-60.

[28] Percy E. Davidson and H. Dewey Anderson, *op. cit.*; William H. Form, "The Sociology of a White Collar Suburb: Greenbelt, Maryland," unpublished doctoral thesis, University of Maryland, 1944; Delbert C. Miller, and William H. Form, "Measuring Patterns of Occupational Security," *Sociometry*, November, 1947, pp. 362-375; W. H. Form and D. C. Miller, "The Career Pattern as a Sociological Instrument," *American Journal of Sociology*, January, 1949, pp. 317-329; Richard Centers, "Occupational Mobility of Urban Occupational Strata," *American Sociological Review*, April, 1948, pp. 197-206.

[29] Davidson and Anderson, *op. cit.*, p. 73.

after fifteen years out of college the average number of different jobs is 3.3 per graduate.[30]

The relatively high job movement of the trial work period contrasts with the more stable years of later work life. Davidson and Anderson report that workers in the age spans thirty-five to fifty-four years, and fifty-five years and over, have held an average of 4.1 different jobs in their lifetime.[31] This indicates that on the average only one more job move is made after thirty-five years of age. It can be said that there is *three times as much horizontal occupational movement before thirty-five years of age as after that age.* This finding must be considered as pertinent only to the San José population

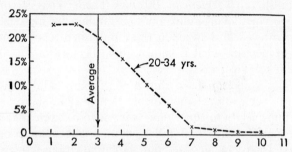

FIG. 88.   The Percentage of Different Occupations Followed for Eight Months or More for 466 Workers Between Twenty and Thirty-Four Years. (Reprinted from *Occupational Mobility in an American Community*, by Percy E. Davidson and Dewey Anderson with the permission of the authors and of the publishers, Stanford University Press, 1937, p. 73.)

of this study. The figures cited apply to the 1165 respondents twenty years of age and over. It must be remembered that the occupational mobility has been expressed in *average* terms. Actually there is a wide variation in the jobs held if individual careers are examined. Figure 88 shows that the trial period workers of San José have held from *one to ten* different jobs for eight months or more. One out of five says that he has never had more than one job. At the same time, one out of five says he has had five or more different occupations.

In the Princeton study all respondents have completed fifteen years of work life. One graduate reports fourteen different jobs during his trial work period. At the stable end of the range more than one out of four says he has been on one job only during his fifteen years.

These studies are among the very few to reveal the horizontal occupational movement of workers. They leave much to be desired. The San José study does not tell us about the job moves where the respondent had spent *less than eight months* on the job. It fails to give us a picture of work histories at the *end* of a given number of years but tells only about workers *within*

[30] Maitland Edey, *op. cit.*, p. 52.
[31] Davidson and Anderson, *op. cit.*, p. 73.

an age span. The weakness of the Princeton study appears in the unrepresentativeness of the sample. This is no fault of the researcher but grows out of the fact that Princeton graduates have family backgrounds which reflect higher income and educational level than is true of either the average young male worker of the United States or the average college graduate.

The picture of the trial work period does begin to emerge in spite of the lack of complete detail. It is a period of relatively high occupational move-

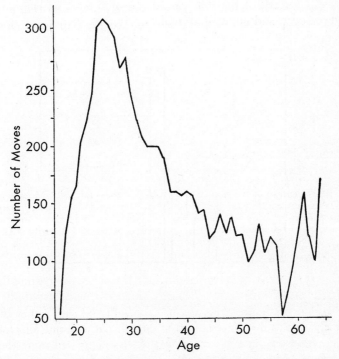

FIG. 89.   The Residential Mobility of 4103 Insurance Policy Holders by Age. (Adapted from Elon H. Moore, "Mobility of Insurance Policy Holders," *American Sociological Review*, February, 1938, p. 68.)

ment. Moreover, it is a period of high residential mobility. Elon H. Moore in an ingenious study of the mobility of insurance policy holders is able to demonstrate the current movement of people.[32] Moore used the 4103 active policies of an insurance company written by the company during the years 1922, 1923, 1924, and 1934. A check of the changes in the addresses of these insurance holders reveals their residential mobility. Figure 89 is a graph of the moves for each age group.

[32] Elon H. Moore, "Mobility of Insurance Policy Holders," *American Sociological Review*, February, 1938, pp. 63-77.

Moore states that, "The highest adult mobility incidence is found for ages 24-27, when nearly one in three annually change their residence. The later thirties reduce the mobility to one in six. In the forties, the ratio of the mobility falls to one in eight, while in the fifties, the average is nearer to one in nine. Throughout the years the heaviest mobility rates appear to be associated with social and job adjustment. If one accepts this hypothesis, then the process of adjusting appears greatest at about the age of 25 and—most stable . . . adjustment occurs in the fifties."[33]

The overall pattern of the trial period can now be described. Relatively high occupational and residential mobility is characteristic of this work

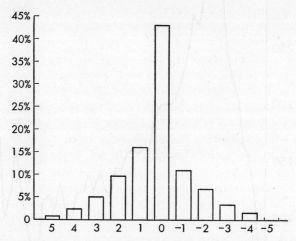

FIG. 90. Vertical Occupational Mobility of Workers Twenty to Thirty-Four Years of Age, for All Their Occupations Held for Eight Months or More. (Reprinted from *Occupational Mobility in an American Community*, by Percy E. Davidson and Dewey Anderson with the permission of the authors and of the publishers, Stanford University Press, 1937, p. 91.)

period. Manifold social adjustments are enforced as the demands of marriage and parenthood are encountered and new requirements of housing, transportation, and community life are met. The strains of these social adjustments will be discussed in the next section, on the social psychology of the worker. But one task must precede this discussion. The important facts of vertical mobility have not yet been explored. It has been assumed that the trial work period is a time of testing and of struggle to establish oneself. In America, workers have free choice of vocation and a large measure of educational opportunity. It is to be expected that there will be considerable movement up and down the ladder of socioeconomic levels. What do the work histories of young workers reveal?

[33] *Ibid.*, p. 68.

VERTICAL OCCUPATIONAL MOBILITY OF WORKERS
DURING THE TRIAL WORK PERIOD

When 466 San José workers in the *twenty-to-thirty-four-year age group* were investigated by Davidson and Anderson they reported 974 job moves in occupations they had held eight months or more. Figure 90 shows the steps moved *upward* and *downward* on the occupational ladder of socioeconomic classifications. A step is a movement upward or downward from the present regular occupation of the respondent. Job moves that were upward on the socioeconomic scale were reported by 36.1 percent of the respondents; 24.7 percent of the job moves were reported as downward. The largest percentage of moves, 39.2 percent, are on the same level. What, then, can be said about the upward movement of workers as they struggle for higher socioeconomic levels? The figures show that the mean number of steps moved is just slightly over one. The overall direction is very slightly upward (+.20).

The picture that emerges is one of *relatively little upward occupational mobility.* The climbing of the occupational ladder is apparently limited to rather few persons. Five to twenty-five more years of additional work experience does not alter this fact. A comparison among age groups twenty to thirty-four, thirty-five to fifty-four, and fifty-five years and over shows that they are much alike in the type of vertical movement their members have experienced.[34] The mean number of steps per change of occupation for all 1165 respondents in all age groups is +.19. It appears that *climbing or falling on the ladder of socioeconomic levels has not been a major factor in determining what classification the worker comes to occupy.* The writers sought to verify this finding in their study of a representative sample (276 cases) of the Ohio labor force. We set up the hypothesis that occupational careers of all workers tend to remain on the same occupational level from the first part-time job to the last job held. The problem was to determine whether the last job in the occupational career was related to the jobs held in the initial, trial, and stable work periods. Our desire was to attempt to measure the relationship along the historic route of job changes so that all jobs held by the worker were included.

To do this we first found the occupational distribution for the last job held. Then, taking each occupational level individually, we reconstructed the occupational distribution for all first jobs in the initial, trial, and stable work periods. Coefficients of contingency were computed showing 0.54 for the initial period, 0.71 for the trial period, and 0.87 for the stable period.[35] When we recall that the highest possible contingency coefficient for a

[34] Davidson and Anderson, *op cit.*, p. 91.

[35] Delbert C. Miller and William H. Form, "Measuring Patterns of Occupational Security," *Sociometry*, November, 1947, pp. 362-375.

7 × 7 table is 0.926, it is evident that strong and significant relationships exist.[36] These statistics support the hypothesis that job histories have a *strong internal strain toward consistency*.[37] Apparently, from the very beginning of the work career the job orientation paths are partially predetermined. People do not at any stage of their careers wander aimlessly and accidentally from one occupational level to another. Once started on an occupational level, a worker tends to remain on that level or an adjacent level. There are apparently social factors of education, occupation of father, "connections," and pressures that direct occupational choices along fairly predictable patterns.[38]

The trial work period can now be described as *a period of proportionately high occupational and residential mobility*. Occupational mobility is both horizontal and vertical. *The central tendency is toward high horizontal mobility with relatively little vertical mobility*. Vertical mobility in the San José age group twenty to thirty-four years was shown to be characterized by a very slight upward movement (less than one step) when the present regular occupation of each respondent was compared with all other jobs held for eight months or more. The direction and distance of the job moves appear to be less the result of a preconceived plan and more the product of impersonal social forces. Definite factors outside the range of individual option are seen to be directing the flow of workers from one occupation to another. In the next chapter, on the stable work period, careful attention will be directed at this finding and its validity evaluated over the lifework span. Meanwhile, there remains one major discussion of the trial work period. This period of work life was set out as a type of characteristic social experience. Our attention is now turned to the role of the person who is adjusting his life to the trial period.

THE SOCIAL PSYCHOLOGY OF THE TRIAL WORK PERIOD

THE STRAIN OF OCCUPATIONAL ACHIEVEMENT

The trial work period has been shown to have distinctive characteristics. It is a period which imposes new demands and adjustments upon young adults. The purpose of this section is to analyze and describe the nature of the stresses and strains which impinge upon workers during this work period and to describe some of the common reactions and adjustments.

There is always some hazard in trying to set out common patterns because variations are as real as central tendencies. It is probably true that no two persons have ever had identical lives. There are certainly many different experiences awaiting workers in the trial work period. Six quite different

[36] For a discussion of the contingency coefficient see G. U. Yule and N. G. Kendall, *An Introduction to the Theory of Statistics*, Charles Griffin and Company, 1937, p. 69.
[37] Cf. Davidson and Anderson, *op. cit.*, p. 96; p. 170.
[38] Cf. *ibid.*, pp. 94-102.

career orientations have been described. We have already spoken of those workers who will quickly find stable jobs and of those who will constantly move from job to job during their entire lifetime. Although these differences are recognized, there is no reason to halt the search for common experiences. It may turn out that there is far more similarity than has been supposed in the experiences of young adults in the first ten or fifteen years of their work life. We propose to examine and acknowledge important differences as we delineate common experiences. The aim of such efforts is to reconstruct crucial phases of experiences in the lives of young workers so that a greater understanding may be gained. Perhaps many students will come to understand themselves better and adjust more satisfactorily as they gain insight into the social factors conditioning early stages of full-time work behavior.

We may begin by repeating that there are wide differences among individual workers in occupational and social outlook and therefore in their occupational expectations. The cultural expectations of the upper-, middle-, and working-class families have been described. These not only condition the career pattern; they condition the social experiences of workers on and off their jobs. Before examining problems encountered in the trial work period it is well to set out how these class differences in cultural expectations are translated into the individual occupational aspirations of sons and daughters.

Individual concern with a career may be less than most middle- and upper-class groups are able to understand. Robert S. Lynd says:

> The business man still tends to point his life up the long slope of the future to a relatively distant goal; whereas the workingman and many white collar workers are accepting themselves as stuck where they are and forced to wrest such meaning as they can out of life on a dead-level. One emphasis on the future remains, however, even for the latter: the hope of sending the children to college. With this exception, if one represents the future as it feels psychologically to the businessman as a prolonged line sloping upward, it is probably safe to depict the sense of the future of a growing mass of workingmen as a horizontal line with incidental little waves of recurrent good times such as "getting out in the car *this* Sunday" and "going uptown to the movies *tonight*." The predominant time focus in the one case is relatively long, a matter of years; and, in the other short, from week to week or month to month. No research has been done on this cadence of life with regard to the future; but if, as seems likely, this differentiation is taking place, it presents a formidable disjunction in the American pattern of culture.[39]

Aspiration Among Industrial Workers

Since Lynd wrote down the above words, researchers have been uncovering facts to verify this hypothesis. Peter Drucker has made an intensive study of General Motors Corporation. He reports:

[39] Robert S. Lynd, *Knowledge for What?* Princeton University Press, 1945, pp. 92-93.

There is little chance for anybody below the executive level to find satisfaction in a job whose relation to reality is very obscure. For the great majority of automobile workers, the only meaning of the job is in the pay check, not in anything connected with the work or the product. Work appears as something unnatural; a disagreeable, meaningless, and stultifying condition of getting the pay check, devoid of dignity as well as of importance. No wonder that this puts a premium on slovenly work, on slowdowns, and on other tricks to get the same pay check with less work. No wonder that this results in an unhappy and discontented worker—because a pay check is not enough to base one's self respect on. Perhaps, the best way to sum up is by quoting a craftsman of the old school whom I met years ago. He had just decided to leave a well-paid job in the automobile industry. When I asked him why he was unhappy in Detroit, he said, "The whole place is on relief; even if they have jobs, they still behave and act as if they were unemployed."[40]

Drucker also explains that there is little chance to advance, that the worker is in effect *stuck*.

The extent to which the worker lacks equal opportunities to advance shows clearly in the way in which both management and labor look upon the worker's chances. There is an ever-growing tendency among plant managers to depend on outside sources rather than on the men in the plant for their supply of foremen and other junior executives. The degree of an engineering school or a college, or work in the clerical accounting or sales departments, today constitute the preferred qualifications for foremen and junior executives in many mass-production plants. . . . The worker shows his estimate of his opportunities in the demand for seniority as the basis for promotion instead of achievement. Even more revealing is the common belief of mass-production workers that the only chance for a smart man to advance today lies in work in the union and not in work in the plant. Finally, there is the fact that the mass-production worker, on the whole, does not want his children to follow in his footsteps; he is convinced that their best chance for social and economic advancement lies in avoiding work in a plant, by going to college; a glaring contrast to the pride of the old craftsman in his traditional and often inherited profession.[41]

Aspiration Among the Business Classes

It has been shown that the predominant beliefs of the business classes stand in marked contrast to those of industrial workers. The formula for success is confidently repeated—"work hard, be thrifty, watch your chances, the sky's the limit." Thus sons and daughters emerge from their upper- and middle-class families prepared for adult life with the conviction that they may climb the job ladder and reach its top rung even if they start at the bottom. Moreover, all who have the initiative and capacity, they are told, will succeed. These beliefs are embodied in cultural expectations carried by

[40] Peter F. Drucker, *Concept of the Corporation*, The John Day Company, 1946, p. 179.
[41] *Ibid.*, pp. 178-179.

the family and friends of the young worker. In fact, almost none of his school, church, or community contacts deny these expectations. On the contrary, leaders of American institutions will stimulate and encourage the career stereotype with promises of great reward. When the transition from school to work has been effected the competitive patterns of white-collar society goad the young worker on to fulfill his destiny. The imperative he hears comes to him with demands to "work harder," "work longer," "get around and meet people," "be clever," "get there first," "do the impossible," "watch your dress," "entertain," "put on a big front," "don't be afraid to push." Among the initiated the saying goes that "if the kid learns the ropes and learns how to get around he will make the grade." During the early years of trial work life the ambitious worker is seeking to learn and play this game which adults about him feel is the most important thing in the world.

In the midst of all the differences in occupational outlook and expectation which emerge from family and class motivations the young workers of the trial work period face common problems. One of these is finding a "line of work."

FINDING ONE'S WORK

The trial work period is seen to be a testing ground on which young workers try out their interests and capacities inside work plants. Each person is trying to find a place where both security and satisfaction may be his. This means he must find the kind of job on which he can perform adequately and on which he feels some degree of satisfaction. This dual demand requires a satisfactory *job* selection as well as *social placement*. He must be able both *to do the job and to fit into the social organization* of the work plant.

A. Problems of Job Selection

Common among the personal difficulties is the confusion over job selection. The individual faced with the demand to make up his own mind often finds himself bewildered as he tries to imagine which kind of job he should seek. This muddle often continues throughout the trial period, and work histories reveal the course of floundering careers. Even the best of vocational guidance may be of little help.

1. DIFFICULTIES ARISING BECAUSE OF CHANGE OF INTERESTS
WITH AGE AND EXPERIENCE

Sometimes an occupational choice which was satisfactory to a young worker during the early part of the trial period becomes a sour one as interests change with age and experience. A young chemist describes his shift to social work.

When I was nine years of age I decided I would become a chemist. At ten years of age I built my own small laboratory in the corner of the woodshed and performed most of the experiments my teachers made me repeat later in high school and college. I took every science and mathematics course in which I could enroll during high school and college. Then, just as I was about to be graduated the depression hit. My parents wrote me that the company for which my father had worked during the last thirty years was now bankrupt and my father was unemployed. The world I was taught to know seemed to have been turned upside down. I was taught that science had built a great country whose prosperity would grow undiminished if only science and technology progressed. As unemployment and suffering deepened I became more critical of the value of more science and technology in an economy which continued to stagnate. Upon graduation my search for a job as a chemist began. When I could not secure a job anywhere panic gripped me. I became angered that my years of training were not now wanted. I decided that social science knowledge was the great need of my generation and not technical knowledge. I decided to go back to college and begin to get an education which would enable me to feel that I was making a contribution to a far more important area of society. That's how I got started on the road that led me to become a social worker.

2. DIFFICULTIES IN CHOOSING A WORK PLANT

There may be conflict over choice of work plant even when there is satisfaction with the job. Workers will say, "The job and the money are O.K. but I don't like the company." There may be conflict as to whether to choose a large company or a small one, a highly rated work plant or a lower-rate work plant. Ambitious workers know that companies have different degrees of status in the minds of people who "count" to them. One of the ways to get ahead is to try to work for high-status companies or institutions. So the ambitious worker may seek employment in a large corporation, a big hospital, a famous office, a large university, a high-quality store, or a first-rate hotel. The price he may have to pay in competitive striving, in long years of waiting for advancement, and in low wage or salary brackets may seem unduly high. In smaller work plants the advantages of advancement, income, and social satisfaction may loom large. The weighing of advantages and disadvantages of different work plants may produce an unending conflict demonstrated by high occupational mobility between work plants.

3. DIFFICULTIES WHEN THE RANGE OF CHOICE IS LIMITED
BY AVAILABLE OPPORTUNITIES

For many workers there is almost no permissive choice of occupations or of work plant. They must take what they can get. In a small community the range of choice may be distinctly limited. Individual interests and desires may be subordinated to the few work opportunities. A coal miner's son may come to feel that he has been trapped from birth and there is nothing

he can do but go into the mine. His refusal to accept his "destiny" may involve him in real difficulties. The motion picture and the stage have illustrated the difficulties in which a striving coal miner's son became involved in Emlyn Williams' play entitled *The Corn Is Green*. Thornton Wilder's *Our Town* is equally effective in picturing the limited range of choice which may be open to the young worker in the small town.

B. Problems of Social Placement

Social placement often looms much larger than job placement. The new worker must "fit" with the work groups that he will be in contact with. He will be sized up quickly on the job as co-workers seek to find out who

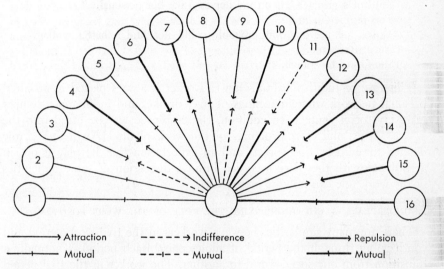

FIG. 91. The Sociogram of Judith. (Adapted from John H. Jacobs, "The Application of Sociometry to Industry," *Sociometry*, May, 1945, p. 196.)

he is and where he fits in with the functional relations of the work and the power, status, and class structures of the work plant. Fellow workers will soon find out who he is, what his job is, how he rates with management, what he has done, and what influence he is likely to have. Upon these terms he will be allocated his position in the work plant. He will learn about his fellow workers and what their status is relative to him and to each other. He will learn who his bosses are and the authority they have. He will be told how much influence each one has with his superiors. He will learn whom to seek out, whom to please, and whom to ignore. His fellow workers will, in turn, make their judgments about him, assign a status position, evaluate his sincerity and integrity, size up his motives and interests, and

come to some feeling of liking, disliking, or indifference about him.[42] A sociogram for a woman worker is shown in Figure 91. It is a graphic picture of the likes, dislikes, and indifferent responses of an employee named Judith toward her sixteen fellow office workers and of them toward her. Note that Judith dislikes two of her fellow workers and nine dislike her. She likes twelve of the sixteen girls but only six reciprocate with this choice. John H. Jacobs has reported that

> Judith is one of the oldest employees in the office. She tries to be extremely nice to all the girls, but has an alarming number of repulsions. One of the repulsions is mutual. The motivations for the repulsions should be noted:
> "Like her personally but she makes me nervous."
> "Too nervous. Works too hard at her machine."
> "Kind of a griper. Gets on my nerves. Like her personally."
> "Too temperamental."
> "Makes me nervous, but probably could not find a better worker."
> "She irritates me."
> "She gripes too much."[43]

This case of Judith illustrates how a worker is always placed in an interpersonal network wherein feelings of like, dislike, and indifference temper his every social contact. In addition, the employee will be fitted into the power, status, and class structures of the work plant. He will find a role defined for him by the workers and an expectation that he play it out in accordance with the place accorded him. A discussion of some difficulties of the work role can now be presented.

1. UNDERPLAYING AND OVERPLAYING THE ROLE OF THE WORK POSITION

There are many similarities between workers in the trial work period and youth going through the period of adolescence. Each period is normally a transition from one social world to another. The worker in the trial period has left behind his former dependence upon his parental home and the school and is seeking to gain status among older adults who have achieved the positions of authority in his work plant. He may alternately have feelings of inferiority and of superiority as he adjusts to this adult world. At one time he feels strongly the overwhelming advantage of the older, stable co-worker who has secured an entrenched position and status. The older worker not only may have experience and security to draw upon but may use the rights and privileges of his position as an asset in maintaining or improving his status. Yet in the daily conduct of business the younger worker may sense the advantage that he has in his energy, motivation, and new ideas. A sense of superiority may as quickly replace the feeling of

[42] John H. Jacobs, "The Application of Sociometry to Industry," *Sociometry*, May, 1945, pp. 181-198.
[43] *Ibid.*, p. 194.

inferiority. Now the older worker is conceived as one who has grown stale, has lost his drive, and will shortly be ready for retirement.

These feelings may alternate, and the young worker can be seen to both underplay and overplay the role of his position. He may apologize, appear weak and ineffectual in presenting his ideas, or simply remain silent or non-committal in conference. On another occasion he may overplay his role by acting in an overbearing manner, employing authoritarian command, and making haughty appraisals of his superiors. Some young workers fall into molds which have them constantly underplaying or overplaying the role in the position they occupy. The kind of mature balance which is so desperately needed in supervisory and executive positions may not be achieved by the young worker for some years and for many it may never be achieved. The older worker who finds himself in the trial period may seesaw interminably in his work role as he alternately enjoys hope and confidence and then suffers defeat and despair.

2. STRUGGLE FOR POWER, STATUS, OR CLASS POSITION

During the trial work period the young worker may feel a driving inner urge to climb into a higher power, status, or class position. The inner compulsion to make his mark is matched only in intensity by the pressure of competition which surrounds him. Ordinarily his work plant will contain many eager, intelligent, hard-working young colleagues who like himself are hoping and striving for recognition. Some want power, some want status, and some want class position—some want all these things. To refuse to meet the demands of competition is automatically to eliminate oneself from consideration. To accept such a fate is to condemn oneself to the guilt feelings which arise as friends speak of "what he might have been." To accept the competitive struggle is to take on a burden of stress and strain that offers no release except at the end of a far distant future. Moreover, the worker may have "no stomach" for the aggressive behavior which eliminates human sentiments for "success." It is not uncommon to see a young worker harassed with the personal conflict of a dilemma. He has the choice of defining his work as an activity satisfying for what it is and for the life it enables him to live inside and outside of the work plant—or of defining his work position as a temporary step on the ladder which leads to greater influence, recognition, or monetary reward. The first choice offers more leisure, more opportunity for varied experience, and more repose. The second choice offers prestige and influence purchased by harder work, limited leisure, and strict channeling of energy and nervous strain.

For most workers there is, in fact, no choice at all. The culture sets a standard of living which forces its people to strive for greater income with a subtle but driving desire. Richard Centers and Hadley Cantril tapped this social drive when they asked each adult in a national sample what his aver-

age weekly income was and then inquired, "About how much more money than that do you think your family would need to have the things that might make your family happier or more comfortable than it is now?" Their findings are shown in Table 36.

TABLE 36.   Income Satisfaction and Income Aspiration[44]

Weekly Income	Cases	Dis-satisfied	Satisfied	No Opinions	No. Specifying Some Additional Amount Wanted	Percentage Increase in Dollars Wanted	Actual Increase Wanted in Dollars[a]
National	1165	56%	32%	12%	581	86%	$ —
Under $20	163	68%	16%	16%	100	162%	16.20
$20–$29.99	170	72%	19%	9%	116	97%	24.25
$30–$39.99	207	67%	20%	13%	129	66%	23.10
$40–$59.99	310	54%	35%	11%	147	59%	29.50
$60–$99.99	191	43%	49%	8%	73	52%	41.60
$100 and over	124	20%	66%	14%	16	100%	100.00

[a] The dollars and cents "increase wanted" is a translation based on the percentage indicated—the mid-point of the income group concerned was used to construct this estimate. Ten dollars is used as the mid-point for the "under $20" group, while for the "$100 and over" group, no mid-point could be assigned, and thus $100 was used as a basis for calculation.

They report that: (1) Over one-half of the population is dissatisfied with its present income, and a large increase in income is generally desired by those who are dissatisfied. Less than one-third (32 percent) of the people are satisfied, and those dissatisfied want on the average an 86 percent increase over their present income. (2) The higher a person's income is, the more likely is he to be satisfied with it and the smaller is the *proportion* of present income desired in addition, except in the case of persons in the upper income group, where those who are dissatisfied want a relatively large increase.

These figures suggest that the strain for increased income will be great in the trial work period, for workers here are struggling with the heavy burdens of early work life on small incomes.

3. THE ROLE OF THE WIFE

The married worker brings his wife into the orbit of the work plant. Although spatially the work plant and its activities may be many miles removed from the home, there is no such separateness in feelings and atti-

[44] Richard Centers and Hadley Cantril, "Income Satisfaction and Income Aspiration," *Journal of Abnormal and Social Psychology*, January, 1946, pp. 64-69.

tudes. For hopes, fears, joys, and sorrows of the worker are imported into the home from the work plant. The wife usually becomes identified with the emotional problems created as her husband struggles with his work adjustments. If both of them work outside the home, then the freight of emotions may be largely made up of work problems. At any event, the wife may find herself under pressure to assume definite responsibilities if her husband is to climb the long ladder and gain the reward both hope for. She must be a homemaker, financial manager, mother, companion. If she is the wife of an aspiring professional or business man, she will become aware of the importance of her role as a hostess who makes the home or the club a pleasant and enjoyable place to entertain important business associates. She may sense the assets which the husband has when he can show off an attractive or companionable wife to advantage.

Home and work life may come to be caught up in one and the same pattern. The same competitive striving of the work plant is duplicated at the country club, with marked influence on the social structure of the work plant. The wife must make a place for herself and her husband within the woman's world. Her failure to impress the wives of the men for whom her husband works may prove a handicap to both. Each loses in a race which was important to them. Each is halted—the husband on the ladder of occupational ascent and the wife on the ladder of social ascent. Yet there are occasions when the strength of one helps the weakness of the other. Fortunate indeed is the "climber" who has an attractive, intelligent, and gay wife acceptable to the society of both men and women! She can "help him so much in his business."

4. EXTRA-WORK PLANT BURDENS

Life outside the work plant imposes increasing burdens on the worker in the trial period. As marriage and parenthood follow, the economic and social demands of the family bear heavily upon him. His income will probably be relatively small in comparison with future earnings. The family becomes in greater or less degree a financial strain. And this strain invariably becomes a stress which the worker carries into the work plant. Likewise, new emotional strains may thread through his work life. The worker may feel the compulsion to work harder and longer in order to secure promotion and increase his income. At the same time, the children seek the companionship of the parents and the father feels compelled to devote more time to them. His wife, too, caught in the isolation from adults because of her household and child care duties, may demand ever more companionship from her husband. She may press him to lend assistance with the tasks of household maintenance and child care. The male worker is caught between these irreconcilables and often finds no completely satisfactory solution.

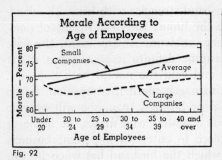

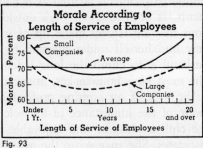

Fig. 92

Fig. 93

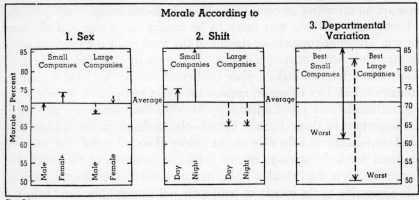

Fig. 94

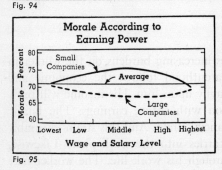

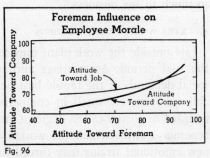

Fig. 95

Fig. 96

FIG. 92.   Morale According to Age of Employees.
FIG. 93.   Morale According to Length of Service of Employees.
FIG. 94.   Morale According to Sex, Shift, and Departmental Variation.
FIG. 95.   Morale According to Earning Power.
FIG. 96.   Foreman Influence on Employee Morale. (From Eugene J. Benge, "How to Learn What Workers Think of Job and Boss," *Factory Management and Maintenance*, May, 1944, p. 104.)

SYMPTOMS OF ADJUSTMENT PROBLEMS

The trial work period has been described as a span of work life which forces the individual to find his place in the work world. This means he must find a job whose duties fit his capabilities and his interests. It means he must find a society of workers in which he can find happy social placement. As the cultural patterns of power, status, and class act upon him and fill him with new wants, he must somehow reconcile his desires with the structure he has to live with. The burdens of family and community life must be shouldered and knit into work life in such a way that each supports rather than conflicts with the other. To surmount these demands and emerge confident and serene constitutes no small requirement. Obviously, there are those who can take all of these exercises in stride, but it is a commentary on industrial society that frustration, anxiety, and tension are widespread personality problems.[45]

EMPLOYEE MORALE AS A MEASURE OF ADJUSTMENT

These observations are borne out by studies of large groups of workers. Eugene J. Benge has made many studies of morale among workers. Some of his findings are shown in the following figures. Note that these figures show the relation of morale to age (Fig. 92), to length of service of employees (Fig. 93), to sex, shift, and departmental variation (Fig. 94), to earning power (Fig. 95), and to attitudes toward foreman or supervision (Fig. 96).

Benge draws these conclusions:

1. In small companies, morale rises with age; in large companies, it falls from age 20 to age 24, then rises with increasing years.

2. In large and small plants, morale falls off with each year of service until the eighth, then rises to a high point after the twentieth year.

3. The morale of employees in small companies is appreciably better than in large companies.

4. In both small and large companies, the morale of women surpasses that of men.

5. In small companies, the morale of the night shift markedly exceeds that of the day shift. In large companies, there is no difference as to morale between day and night shifts.

6. The morale variation from the best department to the worst is greater in big companies than in small.

7. In small plants, the middle bracket earners have better morale than the high and low earners; in large plants they have lower morale.

8. When the attitude of employees toward their foreman is good, they are likely to have good attitudes toward their jobs and even better attitudes toward

[45] Karen Horney, *The Neurotic Personality of Our Time*, W. W. Norton and Company, 1937.

their company. The converse is true; when employees feel dissatisfied about their foreman, they are likely to have poor attitudes toward their jobs and even worse attitudes toward their company.[46]

THREE COMMON MENTAL ADJUSTMENTS TO CAREER PROGRESS

The psychology of mental adjustment is complex and efforts to simplify it often seem naïve. However, there are three typical adjustments among normal people which can be identified and are useful to explain the reactions of persons to their own career progress. They are so common that the reader will undoubtedly recognize many examples of them. Figure 97 has been constructed to throw light on these adjustments. It shows three differ-

Observed Behavior	Criticism	Apology	Acceptance
Behavior Mechanism	Projection	Rationalization	Tolerance
Cultural Patterns	Cultural Critiques	Cultural Rationalizations	Cultural Defense

FIG. 97.   Three common mental adjustments to career progress.

ent levels of analysis. The first is the observed behavior encountered when workers feel dissatisfaction. These behaviors are identified as the *offering of criticism, the making of excuses and apology, or the accepting of present conditions*. Underneath these behavior products the common mechanisms of projection, rationalization, and tolerance can be recognized.

Projection refers to the transfer of blame from oneself to other persons. Thus, a worker may blame the foreman or the company for failing to promote him when the failure may be the result of inability or lack of motivation on the part of the worker himself. The ego receives its soothing balm by projecting the blame upon others. When dissatisfied workers seek to place the blame upon other persons, they can usually find that many criticisms have been made previously. Some of them may have originated in the immediate work group growing out of the interaction of the members as, let us say, between the workers and the supervisor. Others have derived from criticisms of contemporary social structure as exhibited, for example, in the arguments which attack current industrial organization. The argument that modern industry is autocratic in structure might be cited. This and other criticisms of such nature may be discovered in books written by learned men who have elaborated them in sound logic and with

[46] Eugene J. Benge, "How to Learn What Workers Think of Job and Boss," *Factory Management and Maintenance*, May, 1944, p. 104.

substantive research. Any social institution in a free society produces its spokesman and its writers who formulate criticism of this kind. These arguments filter down to all levels of society and appear in folk terms and folk logic among the masses of the people. The managers and the workers carry about an accumulated store of such stock critiques.

Some common *criticisms* made by workers of their managers or owners in contemporary plants include:

"The company is just out to drive the worker and make money. They don't have any feeling for the person."

"You can't trust any of the bosses. When the top man cracks the whip they have to fall in line whether they want to do the right thing or not."

"They pay you just what they can get you for and no more. If you want to get ahead you have to get another offer or threaten to quit."

"They talk about their merit rating scheme but the only way you can get ahead is through 'pull.'"

"You might just as well turn in your tools when you reach fifty. They want you while you are young. Then, when you begin to slow down they find some way to get rid of you."

"A fellow isn't allowed to think in the plant, let alone express his opinion of how he believes something should be done."

The managers have an equally great store of criticisms of the workers. Some common ones which might be heard around the manager's office of any modern industry include:

"They don't want to work anymore. Most of them are not interested in getting ahead. They just want a soft job."

"They don't understand the problems of managing a business. Costs just don't have any meaning for them. They don't consider the fact that we have to meet a pay roll and that pay roll depends on our ability to keep up with our competitors."

"They don't have any interest in their own work. You can't get it through their heads that it's quantity and quality of production that counts. All they want is more and more money. If you give them a nickel increase, they want a dime."

"They want all they can get and they try to get away with as much as they can."

"They are not loyal to the company. They quit when you need them most. And they have no gratitude for what you have done for them. All they want is more."

These beliefs or cultural criticisms are readily available for either workers or managers who wish to project the blame for their career problems upon others. This is not to say that the beliefs are either true or false. It is to point out that a person who wishes to project the causes for his failure may

find ample basis in the store of cultural criticism available in any work plant, whether it is factory, school, home, or hospital.

Rationalization is often described as the giving of good reasons in place of the *real* reasons for personal behavior in order to explain away an inner conflict. The making of excuses offers almost boundless opportunity for explaining away guilt feelings. When the worker is seen to be excusing or apologizing for his work performance he is seeking to diminish a conflict. Rationalization offers a satisfying outlet with which to defend the ego against private doubts and public assaults. When the person has secured excuses which are convincing to him as "real" reasons, his own responsibility for his dissatisfaction may be dismissed.

These reasons are not the real ones, but usually neither he nor his hearers can perform the operation necessary to uncover the ego wound which has now become so comfortably treated. The culture stands ready to offer the young worker a choice of rationalizations. For failures and frustrations of the trial worker there are many socially acceptable rationalizations. Some of the *common rationalizations* in the culture to justify changes in the work history include:

"You don't have to stay in one place all your life. You get ahead by moving around."

"You weren't learning anything new there. Anyway, they didn't give you a chance to show what you could do."

"You didn't work out on that job but it's nobody's fault. You are just not cut out for that kind of job."

"You didn't get enough money for that job. A guy has got to live."

"You are on your way up. You can consider yourself lucky to get out of that rut."

"You didn't have a stable job anyway. It didn't last but you got a whale of a lot of good experience."

"The whole gang that runs the place is crooked."

"They try to run your life."

"That's a lousy place to work. The fumes and dust would have taken years off your life."

The acceptance of disappointment or dissatisfaction is a third common reaction. The worker who failed to secure the rewards he had anticipated may accept his failure as a personal responsibility or at least with appreciation of the merits of the structure and with recognition of the difficulties involved in rewarding performances. This reaction has been called *tolerance*. The worker says in effect, "That's that." He defines the situation as one in which he had a fair trial. He may, therefore, defend the very procedure which took away his high hopes. He may draw upon the cultural tradition and ideology, which usually contains abundant reasons to explain the functioning of any institution. Some *defenses* of the cultural traditions within the work plant include:

"That is the way they have been rating people for a long time."

"Everybody has an equal chance."

"It's not easy to handle that many men and women. The supervisor is doing his best."

"You must remember the company has to make money to stay in business."

"The Big Boss has got an enormous job. You can't expect miracles."

"If things are too bad a person ought to get out instead of beefing all the time."

Through the three common mental adjustments most workers orient themselves to their disappointments and frustrations on the job. Workers may use the mechanisms of *projection, rationalization,* and *tolerance* in alternate fashion at different times. Sometimes workers can be seen to go through a complete cycle, which begins with a bitterness than can find no outlet except by blaming others. After a "cooling off period" the individual shifts the blame away from persons and onto certain "conditions." He realizes the source of the blame lies within him although he may never admit it consciously. Excuses come to his rescue and give him immediate relief from the hurt to his ego. Finally, he may come to acceptance of the situation if he defines it as one in which he was treated fairly and squarely according to the rules of the game.

The trial work period may loom as a large disappointment or as a grand conquest. Whether viewed as a success or failure most workers will attest to its strains. So many illusions must be broken, so many habits and attitudes must be re-formed that few indeed escape the tension and frustration of the early years of work life. Some of the most severe strains that can be placed on the worker are those growing from prolonged unemployment. Since the young worker in particular is prone to unemployment a brief discussion is included.

UNEMPLOYMENT: ITS SOCIAL AND PSYCHOLOGICAL CORRELATES IN THE TRIAL WORK PERIOD

UNEMPLOYMENT AND AGE

In the darkest days of the depression in 1932 nearly one-third of the men and women normally employed in industry were on the streets. During most of the decade 1930-1940 more than 10,000,000 persons were totally or partially unemployed. In 1937 an unemployment survey was conducted by asking those who were not working, or who were employed on emergency work projects, to register in a federal census. In response, 7,845,016 totally unemployed and emergency workers registered, and 3,219,502 who were working only part-time registered. Of the totally unemployed 75 percent were men and 25 percent were women. Hardest hit were the younger workers. *Over half* (51 percent) *were workers from fifteen to thirty-four years of*

age, with the largest single group between twenty and twenty-four years of age.[47]

Many of these younger workers had never been employed. In March, 1935, a month near the peak of the unemployment relief case load, there were 4,158,000 families with one or more workers registered for public assistance with the Federal Emergency Relief Administration. They included 6,513,000 workers, sixteen through sixty-four years of age. About 5,000,000 of these workers possessed previous work experience, but *nearly 1,000,000 never had been gainfully employed.*[48]

UNEMPLOYMENT AND OCCUPATIONAL CLASSIFICATION

Persons in every occupational group experienced unemployment. Examination of those registering during April, 1937, with United States Unemployment Service shows that production workers and physical laborers constituted more than half the men out of work and seeking employment. More than half of the women were service workers. Seventeen percent were clerical workers. Unemployed professional workers were among both sex groups. There were 3.5 percent men and 5.7 percent women in the professional or kindred occupations.[49]

UNEMPLOYMENT AND COLLEGE-TRAINED PERSONS

Students seeking their first full-time jobs found employment opportunities severely limited during the depression decade. In a representative sample of 10,146 college graduates drawn from the living graduates of 1000 colleges in the United States Babcock found that 2.1 percent of the men and 3.3 percent of the women listed themselves as unemployed or on relief in 1940.[50] These unemployment figures are remarkably low and show the college graduate to be favorably placed in economic life. However, if one moves a few years back and searches for the total work history, the depression status of college-trained persons darkens. Pace found among the 1000 college-trained persons from the University of Minnesota in 1937 that four out of ten men and three out of ten women interviewed said they had been out of a job at some time since leaving the university. He reports,

These proportions were the same for both the graduates and non-graduates. Although as many graduates as non-graduates had experienced unemployment the non-graduates were unemployed oftener and for longer periods of time. The

[47] *Final Report on Total and Partial Unemployment,* United States Government Printing Office, Vol. I, 1937, p. 2.

[48] *Workers on Relief in the United States* in March, 1935, Works Progress Administration, United States Government Printing Office, Vol. I, p. ix.

[49] *Survey of Unemployment Service Information,* United States Department of Labor, 1938, p. 45.

[50] F. Lawrence Babcock, *The United States College Graduate,* published by *Time* Inc., 1941, p. 19.

typical graduate who had been unemployed had been out of a job only once. Whereas the typical non-graduate who had experienced unemployment had been out of a job three times. The median period of unemployment for individuals who had been unemployed at some time since leaving the University was two months for the graduate men, four and a half months for the non-graduate men, nine months for the graduate women, and twelve months for the non-graduate women. . . . Asked, "What did you do when you were unemployed?" the following answers were typical.

"Found another job in a few days."

"Wore out shoe leather looking for a job."

"Wrote hundreds of letters and saw everyone I knew. I spent every day looking for a job."

"Stood in line at employment offices. Made out applications."

"Scoured the territory looking for a job."

"Found odd jobs."

"Looked for work and took advantage of my leisure by enjoying it."[51]

The 1940's have been years of war and reconstruction. Unemployment has dwindled to a minimum. However, the problem is not solved. In fact, W. I. King has estimated that on the average from 1,000,000 to 2,500,000 workers have been generally unemployed in the United States since the turn of the century.[52] Moreover, the threat of cyclical depression still hangs over the heads of the American people. Workers in or about to enter the trial work period must still reckon with the possibility of prolonged periods of unemployment.

REACTIONS OF WORKERS TO PROLONGED UNEMPLOYMENT

The first marked effect of unemployment, after the early efforts to get jobs have met with failure, is the loss of the sense of security. Most workers come to blame themselves, and a sense of inferiority and of blame develops. These feelings are further enhanced by reactions to relatives, friends, and neighbors. The wife and children may offer first sympathy and encouragement, but as unemployment continues they may begin to criticize the breadwinner for failure to contribute money to the family. The daily routines of the household are disrupted and the worker begins to feel in the way rather than the one who makes the household go. The children find many of their felt needs blocked by loss of money. Conflicts with wife and children appear to further intensify these feelings of insecurity. As one unemployed husband and father put it to a relief worker: "What do you think all these things do to me? They certainly don't add to my esteem and happiness. At times I boil inside, but mostly I just feel licked. I never

[51] Charles R. Pace, *They Went to College*, University of Minnesota Press, 1941, pp. 94-95. Cf. some data from college placement offices gathered by Mabel A. Elliot and Francis E. Merrill, *Social Disorganization*, Harper & Brothers, rev. ed., 1941, pp. 437-438.

[52] W. I. King, *Employment, Hours, and Earnings in Prosperity and Depression*. National Conference of Economic Research, 1923, p. 143.

imagined that the peace of my home and the control over my children depended on my job. *Why, the job just rules your life.*"[53]

Kimball Young has listed seven devices used by persons for meeting loss of economic security and morale. He says the individual:

1. May evidence extreme aggressive attitudes toward his situation.
2. May retreat from the situation losing in time his courage, ambition, and morale.
3. May retreat into fantasy thinking and acting.
4. Take to excessive alcoholic drinking or to indulgence in drugs.
5. Escape into illness, either mental or physical or both.
6. Find outlets in criminal and quasi-criminal behavior.
7. Commit suicide as a final gesture of despair and self-pity.[54]

Individuals and families employ different means of adjusting to the problem. Prolonged unemployment is a menace to mental health.

It is believed that the single person may encounter some personal problems more serious than the married man. One case of a well-educated bachelor is cited by Kimball Young. This man had once held a good position, but had lost his job and his savings. The social situation of this worker was described as: "Alone, belonging nowhere, frustrated at every turn, forced to live on charity against the principles on which he had been reared, sex starved, feeling utterly useless, it is no wonder that he is cowed and apathetic."[55]

SALUTE TO THE STABLE WORK PERIOD

The discussion of the trial work period is concluded. In the work life of an individual it is a social experience of struggle, testing, and mobility. Achievement and failure mark its course. The possibilities and limitations of self within the work plant community and within society are interlocked in a large set of relationships. If there is drama in work life, then this is the period when much of it is created. The satisfactions of achievement are exciting rewards. But achievement is no guarantee of a secure work life. Even during the mellowing years of the stable work period there is always the prospect of such social catastrophes as war and depression, sickness and accident to spring upon the unsuspecting worker and force him again into a trial work period. Risk, luck, and chance still wind their way through the strands of a career pattern. If the stable work period differs from the trial work period it is not that these three forces disappear but only that they have had a number of years to run their earlier course. Patterns of life

[53] Pauline V. Young, *Interviewing in Social Work*, McGraw-Hill Book Company, Inc., 1935, p. 162.

[54] Kimball Young, *Personality and Problems of Adjustment*, Appleton-Century-Crofts, Inc., 1940, pp. 619-620.

[55] Kimball Young, *op. cit.*, p. 618; cf. E. W. Bakke, *Citizens Without Work*, Yale University Press, 1939.

crystallize and set themselves in more stable forms. This period of work life has its own distinctive rewards and challenges. In the next chapter we shall discuss the social character of the stable work period.

SUPPLEMENTARY STUDIES

FIELD: PLANNED INTERVIEWS

Make one or more interviews of adult men and women in the trial work period. The best time for interviewing is during the age period twenty-five to thirty-five years of age. For a comparative analysis it is very desirable to seek interviews with adults from lower-, middle-, and upper-class families. The following interview form is suggested as a guide:

Name _____ Interviewer _____
                                              Date _____
                                              City _____ State _____

A. Background
    Age _____ Sex _____ Years Out of School _____
    Occupation of: Father _____
                        Mother _____
                        Brother _____   Sister _____
                        Brother _____   Sister _____
                        Brother _____   Sister _____

B. Job and Work
    1. Tell me about the part-time and full-time jobs you have had.
        a. How did you get them?
        b. What did you do?
        c. What did you like or dislike about them?
        d. Why did you leave them?
    2. What have these jobs meant to you? How long do you think you will be able to work on your job?
    3. What job did you want when you were in school? Did you get that job? Do you still want that kind of job? If not, why not?
    4. What kind of job do you want now? Do you think there is a good chance of getting it? How long will you have to wait?
    5. How do you think people on a job get ahead? Do you save any money? If so, what for?
    6. Have you joined a union? Why? Do you think your union is a good union? Why?
    7. What do you think of your company as a place to work?
    8. Have you found a group at work which shares your background and interests?
    9. What kinds of things bother and worry your work associates? Do you worry over these things also?

10. Do you think you are going to have steady employment? Do you think that there will be more money and more steady jobs for everybody in the future or that we will have booms and busts?

11. What explains why you are where you are today? If you had your life to live over would you have made any different decisions that would affect your work life?

C. Home and Work

12. Are you married? If so, how has it changed your life? Has it changed your outlook on your job?

13. If not married, what about marriage? How would marriage change your outlook on your job?

D. Community and Work

14. Ask respondent for information which will enable you to scale social participation on the Chapin Social Participation Scale. This scale is reproduced below:

Name of Organization	1. Member	2. Attendance	3. Financial Contribution	4. Member of Committee	5. Offices Held
1.					
2.					
3.					
4.					

Scoring: Weights of 1, 2, 3, 4, 5 are assigned to each type of participation as indicated by the order at the top of the scale. For example, if a person belonged to 6 clubs or organizations, attended 5, contributed to 3, was a member of 2 committees, and was an officer in an organization, his total score would be 38. Tentative norms may be found in F. Stuart Chapin, *Experimental Designs in Sociological Research*, Harper & Brothers, 1947, p. 195.

15. Would you agree that everybody would be happier, more secure, and more prosperous if the working people were given more power and influence in government, or would you say that we would all be better off if the working people had no more power than they have now?[56]

16. Which one of these statements do you most agree with? (1) The most important job for the government is to make it certain that there are good opportunities for each person to get ahead on his own. (2) The most important job for the government is to guarantee every person a decent and steady job and standard of living.

LIBRARY: NOVELS AND PLAYS

The following novels reveal attitudes and habits of work and other social traits as indoctrinated in different social classes.

[56] Questions 14 and 15 were asked by Richard Centers in his study. *The Psychology of Social Classes*, Princeton University Press, 1949, pp. 60-62. These questions draw significantly different response frequencies from white-collar and manual workers.

Churchill, Winston, *The Inside of the Cup* (dramatizes the struggle of a young clergyman against the control of his church by business interests)

Farrell, James T., *Studs Lonigan* (realistic description of a lower-middle-class youth who grows up in a section near the Chicago stockyards)

Ferber, Edna, *Come and Get It* (story of a chore boy who becomes a paper mill baron)

Morley, Christopher, *Kitty Foyle* (story of a working girl and her love of a Philadelphia upper-class man; contrasts the differences between the social backgrounds of the lower-middle and upper classes)

Schulberg, Budd, *What Makes Sammy Run?* (story of a Jewish boy who climbed to fame as a movie writer and producer)

Sinclair, Upton, *Oil* (story of the son of a wealthy oil man)

Wolfe, Thomas, *Look Homeward, Angel* (story of a young lower-class man in a newspaper office)

Wilder, Thornton, *Our Town* (a play describing the two neighboring families of Editor Webb and Doctor Gibbs)

LIBRARY: RESEARCH REPORTS

Pace, Charles Robert, *They Went to College,* University of Minnesota Press, 1941.

Babcock, F. Lawrence, *The United States College Graduate,* published by *Time Inc.,* 1941.

Bell, Howard M., *Youth Tell Their Story,* American Council on Education, 1938.

Edey, Maitland, "The Class of '32," *Life,* June 16, 1947, pp. 51-60.

RESEARCH GAPS

1. The social experiences of newly inducted workers.
2. Study of career expectations in different social classes.
3. Study of job sequences in the trial work period.
4. The significance of career expectation as compared with non-career expectation in establishing motivation and occupational attainment.
5. The social origins of career expectation.
6. The work partner role of the wife.
7. The distinctive social strains of the trial work period.

CHAPTER XIX

The Stable Work Period

DEFINING THE STABLE WORK PERIOD

The worker expects eventually to find a relatively stable work life. The American dream is fulfilled as the worker achieves a measure of occupational ascent, a family, an auto, a home, and a place in community life. A failure of the worker to fit this stereotype is believed to be due to his lack

of ability and initiative and he is therefore to be considered a personal failure or an eccentric. An analysis of the social backgrounds of workers as they arrive at the stable work period leaves little doubt that the traditional formula for success is in part, if not wholly, a gross oversimplification. In this chapter we shall seek to find out what workers are able to achieve occupational stability and why.

FOURTEEN DIFFERENT JOB SEQUENCES

Certainly, work life is not one experience. Many things happen to workers in different socioeconomic levels. The writers found fourteen different types of job sequences in 276 work histories representing the Ohio labor force. These types were discovered by identifying the initial, trial, and stable jobs occurring within the work history. An *initial job* refers to the before- or after-school jobs, summer full-time jobs, or jobs taken only as stopgaps until completion of education. A *trial job* refers to a job which was held less than three years, whereas a job held for more than three years is called *stable*. When work histories were examined and the sequence within each career pattern was determined, the fourteen sequences appeared as follows:

1. Stable.
2. Initial-Stable-Trial-Stable.
3. Stable-Trial-Stable.
4. Initial-Stable.
5. Initial-Trial-Stable.
6. Initial-Trial-Stable-Trial-Stable.
7. Trial-Stable.
8. Trial-Stable-Trial.
9. Initial-Trial-Stable-Trial.
10. Initial-Trial.
11. Trial.
12. Stable-Trial.
13. Initial-Stable-Trial.
14. Trial-Trial-Trial-etc.[1]

THE CHARACTER OF THE STABLE WORK PERIOD

It can be noted as one examines the career patterns of both young and older workers that there is a wide range of possible job histories. However, it can be equally demonstrated that for many workers the age span thirty-five years to sixty years becomes a stable work period. The worker finds a relatively permanent job and "settles down." He develops social roots in the work plant and in the local community. This period may be characterized by a relative absence of work tension, and the development of a feeling of

[1] In establishing these types of sequences, only the pattern is sought. This means that not every job is listed which may be in the work history; it is the sequence of jobs which determine the type or pattern.

belonging to the groups in which the worker participates. *The stable period may be defined as a period of job persistence beginning when the worker finds a work position in which he remains more or less permanently (three years or more) and continuing until retirement, death, or until he enters another trial period. Stability is most secure when the worker is satisfied that he is performing in his "chosen" occupation and within a given work plant in which he intends to remain during the rest of his working life.*

The stable period may be the result of freely chosen or constrained action. The worker may remain on a job because he is satisfied to make it

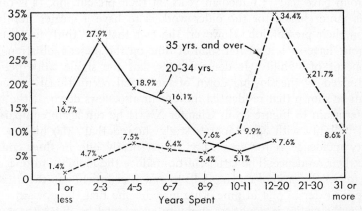

FIG. 98. Years Spent in Present Occupation by 749 Respondents Classified by Two Age Groups, Twenty to Thirty-Four Years of Age and Thirty-Five Years of Age and Over. (Reprinted from *Occupational Mobility in an American Community*, by Percy E. Davidson and Dewey Anderson with the permission of the authors and of the publishers, Stanford University Press, 1937, p. 81.)

a permanent one. On the other hand, he may remain on a job, hoping to move, but staying on because he cannot find an acceptable alternative. In either case, he probably becomes knit to the social life of the work plant and the community. Seniority or tenure gives him an increased measure of security. The family and the community exert pressures which dampen residential and occupational mobility.

Even if occupational stability is not achieved, the expectations of associates and of the community surround the mature worker and exert subtle but real pressures upon him. He is expected to marry and establish a home. He is expected to find the best job he is able to get and then make good. He is expected to send his children to school, to vote, pay his taxes, and participate in community life. He is expected, in short, to become a stable worker. The social forces which grip him tend to move him toward such a status. One bit of evidence is the decline in occupational and residential movement which the average worker experiences between thirty-five and sixty years of age.

Occupational and Residential Movement

Davidson and Anderson's study of occupational movement shows this tendency toward occupational stability in later work life. Figure 98 is a graphic representation of the time spent in the present occupation by 749 representative San José respondents. The first curve represents the respondents in the twenty to thirty-four-year age span; the second curve illustrates the group thirty-five years and over. The median years spent on the present job for the twenty to thirty-four-year group is 5.1; the thirty-five-year-and-over group have had 13.1 median years on their present job. It is obvious there is more chance for the older workers to have a greater number of years on their present job. However, the fact that the thirty-five-year-and-over group have such a greater span of time on the present job strengthens the concept of stability. It demonstrates that the stable work period is characterized by the slowing down of horizontal occupational movement.

It can be shown that residential movement also slows down. If the reader will refer again to Figure 89 in Chapter XVIII he can again compare residential mobility with age. Moore's study showed that "the highest adult mobility incidence is for ages 24-27, when nearly one in three annually change their residence. The latter thirties reduce the mobility to one in six. In the forties the ratio of moving falls to one in eight while in the fifties the average is nearer to one in nine. One may assume that the upward change found in the sixties is doubtless mobility occasioned by ill-health or made possible by retirement."[2]

These two studies indicate that a stable work period is probably experienced by large groups of workers. Many other indices, such as income, home ownership, marital status, and parenthood could be explored to find additional evidence for increased stability in the age group thirty-five years and over. The college graduate provides an interesting example.

The College Graduate: His Occupational Mobility

Let us look briefly at the college graduate and ascertain the characteristics of his work history in the stable work period. Babcock's study of the United States college graduate shows that occupational stability is achieved by the college-trained adults between thirty and forty years of age.[3]

Table 37 shows men working graduates classified by occupation into three age groups: under thirty years of age, thirty to thirty-nine years of age, forty years and over. Relatively small differences are observed between the second and third age groups (column III compared with column II). However,

[2] Elon Moore, "Mobility of Insurance Policy Holders," *American Sociological Review*, February, 1938, p. 67.

[3] F. Lawrence Babcock, *The United States College Graduate*, published by *Time* Inc., 1941, p. 24.

Our Table 37 is adapted from Babcock's Table N, p. 24.

there is evidence of considerable shifting about before the stabilizing years, thirty to thirty-nine, are reached. Only 13.6 percent change their classification after the ages of forty and over, but 33.6 percent alter their classification between ages under thirty and ages of forty and over (column III compared with column I). In other words, there appears to be 2½ times as much shifting about in different kinds of work before thirty years of age as takes place in the age bracket forty years and over.

The nature of this job movement can be understood if the occupational classifications are examined. If all men working graduates are considered, a

TABLE 37.   Positions Held by Men Working Graduates in Three Age Groups

Position Held	Age Groups—% of Total in Each			Occupational Change of Graduates 40 Years and Over When Compared with Graduates Under 30 Years (col. III–col. I)	Occupational Change of Graduates 40 Years and Over When Compared with Graduates 30-39 Years (col. III–col. II)
	I Under 30 Years	II 30–39 Years	III 40 Years and Over		
Executives and minor officials	11.3%	18.6%	21.9%	+10.6%	+3.3%
Professional workers and technicians	27.7	37.1	44.9	+17.2	+7.8
Proprietors and partners	2.8	5.5	7.2	+ 4.4	+1.7
Teachers	16.8	14.1	11.2	− 5.6	−2.9
Salesmen	7.1	6.6	4.6	− 2.5	−2.0
Skilled workers	11.8	7.0	4.0	− 7.8	−3.0
Clerical workers	18.7	7.3	3.4	−15.3	−3.9
Unskilled workers	2.8	2.2	0.4	− 2.4	−1.8
Farmers	1.0	1.6	2.4	+ 1.4	+0.8
Total	100.0%	100.0%	100.0%	00.0%	00.0%
				Change 33.6%	13.6%

total of 76.5 percent are found to be in the professional, proprietary, or managerial positions. Against these, there are 23.5 percent who work more or less in the ranks as clerical, sales, skilled and unskilled workers. Applying this breakdown of the occupational classifications to the three different age groups we find the following percentages:

	Under 30 Years	30–39 Years	40 Years and over
Professionals, proprietors and managers	59.6	76.9	87.6
Clerical, salesmen, skilled and unskilled	40.4	23.1	12.4

It can be seen that college men, to a degree that increases with age, are very likely to be employed in professional, proprietary, or managerial posi-

tions. The gravitation to these occupational levels begins to be stabilized by thirty to thirty-nine years of age for most college graduates. Although there is no further breakdown by age after forty, the weight of evidence indicates that there is relatively little vertical occupational mobility after that age.

Women working graduates follow the same general pattern except that they become stable in their occupations sooner than the men. This may be partly explained by the fact that women graduates are preponderantly engaged in teaching.

MARITAL STATUS AS EVIDENCE OF A STABLE WORK PERIOD FOR THE COLLEGE GRADUATE

Men graduates compose a married population by the time they reach forty years of age. Table 38 gives the marital status of men graduates by age groups. Only 9.2 percent are listed as single in the forty-year-and-over group. Although the under-thirty-year group is predominantly single (65.0 percent), the thirty to thirty-nine-year group and the forty-year-and-over group largely represent married workers. Women graduates present a somewhat different picture. At forty years and over, 40.8 percent have never married, 46.2 percent are married now, 13 percent are divorced, separated, or widowed.[4]

TABLE 38.   Marital Status of Men Graduates by Age Groups[5]

Status	All Age Groups	Under 30 Years	30–39 Years	40 Years and Over
Single	29.1%	65.0 %	22.6%	9.2%
Married	68.1	34.9	76.0	84.5
Divorced or separated	1.0	0.05	1.1	1.7
Widowed	1.8	0.05	0.3	4.6
	100.0%	100.00%	100.0%	100.0%

INCREASED INCOME AS EVIDENCE OF A STABLE WORK PERIOD FOR THE COLLEGE GRADUATE

Both men and women graduates can look forward to increasing incomes as they grow older. Table 39 shows the median earned income of men graduates as of 1940 by position held and by age group. Although these figures must be adjusted upward to compare with current levels (it is possible that they have doubled), relative differences are significant. The median income climbs from $1690 for men graduates under thirty years to $2590 for those thirty to thirty-nine years old and then goes to $4020 for those forty years and over. Women graduates find their incomes increase

[4] *Ibid.*, p. 63.
[5] From *ibid.*

but at lower levels. Women at forty years and over secure just about one-half (median $2060) what the men receive.[6]

TABLE 39. Median Earned Income of Men Graduates by Position Held and Age Group[7]

Position Held	All Working Men Graduates	Under 30 Years	30–39 Years	40 Years and Over
Executives and minor officials	$3460	$2080	$2900	$4840
Professional workers and technicians	$3090	$1880	$2940	$4320
Proprietors and partners	$3020	$1910	$2760	$4130
Salesmen	$2490	$1770	$2640	$3330
Skilled workers	$2200	$1810	$2350	$2780
Teachers	$1960	$1470	$2050	$3170
Farmers	$1900	$1560	$1770	$2560
Clerical workers	$1720	$1530	$1970	$2420
Unskilled workers	$1400	$1380	$1410	$1430
All positions held	$2620	$1690	$2590	$4020

Some Questions About the Stable Work Period

The stable work period is now placed in its structural setting. It is a work period of relatively low occupational and residential mobility. Stable workers are preponderantly married workers with incomes above the average in the community. They have acquired social roots inside a work plant and within a community.

How does life change for the stable worker? Does he have more economic and emotional security? Does he find greater strain or less? Does he grow more conservative in his thinking? Are there important differences between the lives of manual workers and those of white-collar workers?

These are questions for which we will seek answers. The initial task is to find out what similarity and difference can be observed in the work life of workers from various occupational classifications.

OCCUPATIONAL MOBILITY AND SECURITY

A work history, as we have conceptualized it, contains two interrelated factors; one is the amount of vertical mobility and the other is the amount of occupational stability and security as determined by a special analysis of the horizontal movements. In order to examine the relationship between these two factors we charted the changes in the initial, trial, and stable work periods against the occupational levels in which these changes occurred. The result is a gridlike pattern revealing the vertical mobility of a worker in a

[6] *Ibid.*, p. 35.
[7] *Ibid.*

given occupational grouping. An example of the charting for a single professional worker is shown in Figure 99.

R-19 began his work life with a part-time job as a soda jerk in a drugstore.
After finishing college his first job was teaching. After a brief trial on this
job he entered into a partnership with his uncle as an auto dealer (proprietor). Within two years he was back in teaching, holding the first such
job five years, and the second eight years—both stable jobs.

This chart portrays two kinds of changes: (1) changes in the tenure and
nature of work positions as described by the initial, trial, and stable jobs
within a work history; (2) changes in the occupational classification of the
worker as he moves vertically on the grid. This graphic device can be em-

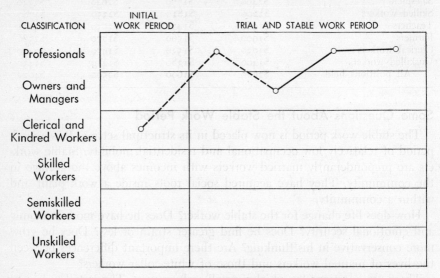

FIG. 99.   Work History of a Single Professional Worker.

ployed to exhibit the work life of groups of workers in each occupational
classification. The last job on which the worker is employed is always used
as the criterion to place him in an occupational grouping. The charts selected for such occupational groupings reveal modal patterns that distinguish the work histories of persons associated with different occupational
levels. The career patterns for the majority of workers in each occupational
level are reproduced in Figures 100 through 106, inclusive.

CAREER PATTERNS

Certain conclusions may be drawn from inspecting the varied career
patterns in each level. We shall comment only on the central tendencies.

1. Figure 100 shows that professional workers start their initial work on
many different levels, but soon move to the professional level without much

intervening experience in other occupations. Once they become professionals, only a few risk trying other jobs. Those who do, usually have trial jobs in the proprietary or managerial occupations, or both.

2. The proprietors, managers, and officials show histories of much vertical mobility in the initial and trial periods, but also show surprising stability in the stable period of their work lives (see Fig. 101).

3. Clerical workers (Fig. 102) exhibit some vertical movement before reaching the clerical level but little movement thereafter. An examination of the work histories of business owners and managers shows that in some

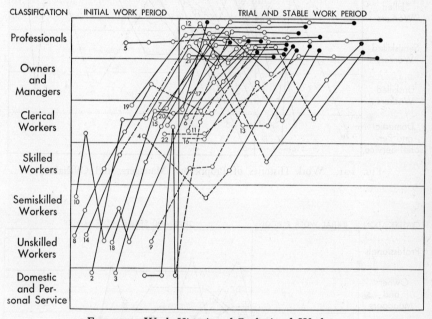

FIG. 100. Work Histories of Professional Workers

cases clerical work was a stepping stone. As far as we can determine here and on the basis of other research these cases of climbing are exemplary of a small minority, not a majority of clerical workers.[8]

4. The patterns for the skilled workers and foremen indicate that their work origins are largely in unskilled and semiskilled labor. When they become skilled workers and foremen they achieve a high degree of stability (see Fig. 103).

5. The semiskilled workers display some vertical movement, for many of them have had early jobs as personal and domestic service workers. Mobility above the semiskilled level, once it is attained, is rather infrequent (Fig. 104).

[8] See Davidson and Anderson, *Occupational Mobility in an American Community*, Stanford University Press, 1937, pp. 105-113.

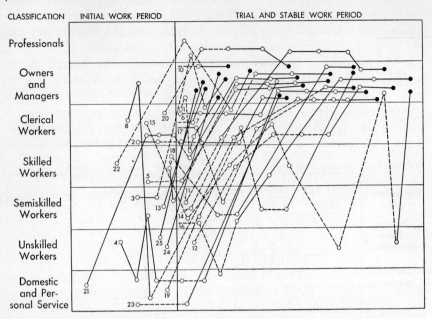

FIG. 101. Work Histories of Proprietors, Managers, and Officials.

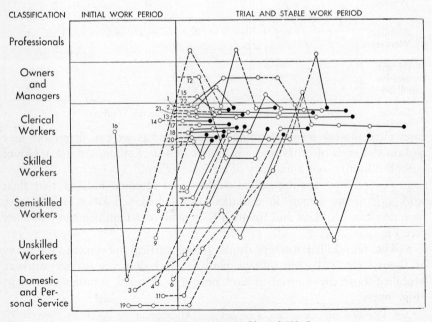

FIG. 102. Work Histories of Clerical Workers.

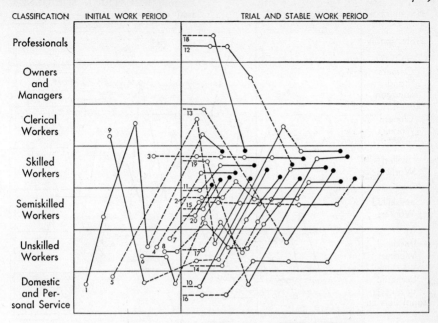

FIG. 103. Work Histories of Foremen and Skilled Workers.

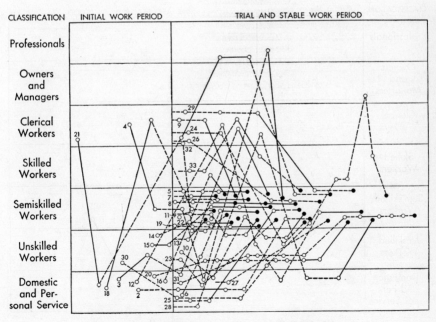

FIG. 104. Work Histories of Semiskilled Workers.

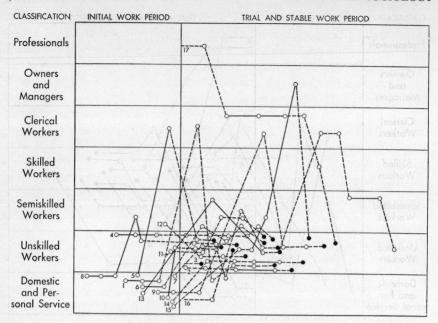

FIG. 105.   Work Histories of Unskilled Workers.

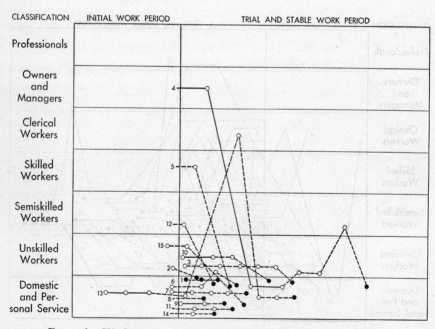

FIG. 106.   Work Histories of Domestic and Personal Service Workers.

6. The immobility of unskilled and domestic workers is pronounced. Many of them begin their work lives in domestic and personal service jobs. Some move to the unskilled labor classification and there remain; the others never budge from their beginning classification as domestic and personal service workers. Both groups experience many trial jobs and achieve only fleeting security (Figs. 105 and 106).

How do workers adjust to these job changes? What influences vertical mobility? Is there any way to measure the occupational security of workers? Some of these questions can now be answered; others will require further research efforts to produce the answers. Joslyn and Taussig have analyzed the work histories of business leaders. E. Wight Bakke has explored the social adjustments of the unemployed worker. William F. Whyte has investigated the restaurant worker, and W. Lloyd Warner and J. Low have presented their study of the factory worker. Logan Wilson has described *The Academic Man* and W. F. Cottrell *The Railroader*.[9] These resources and others will be drawn upon for such answers as can be given. We shall now turn to the problem of measuring the occupational security of different groups of workers.

MEASURING OCCUPATIONAL SECURITY

In the Ohio study each occupational history of 276 workers in the representative sample was plotted so that the actual sequence of initial, trial, and stable periods could be examined. It will be recalled that fourteen different types of job sequences were discovered and described at the beginning of this chapter.

Establishment of Career Families

These sequences have been combined into appropriate families. The families may be identified as stable, conventional, unstable, single trial, disestablished, and multiple trial. They represent different ways in which the career pattern may manifest itself. These classifications can best be understood by observing the associated job sequences which are shown in Figure 107. Each of the six career families defines a different kind of career movement. These are:

1. Early entrance into a stable job.
2. The "normal" job progression to a stable job.
3. Return to a trial job after attaining stability through the conventional pattern.

[9] F. W. Taussig and C. S. Joslyn, *American Business Leaders*, The Macmillan Company, 1932; E. W. Bakke, *The Unemployed Worker*, Yale University Press, 1940; William F. Whyte, *Human Relations in the Restaurant Industry*, McGraw-Hill Book Company, Inc., 1948; W. Lloyd Warner and J. Low, *The Social System of the Modern Factory*, Yale University Press, 1947; Logan Wilson, *The Academic Man*, Columbia University Press, 1942; W. F. Cottrell, *The Railroader*, Stanford University Press, 1940.

4. Beginning of the trial work period—mostly younger workers.

5. Return to a trial job after a quick attainment of a stable job.

6. Consecutive trial jobs with no stable job as yet attained.

It is our belief that each of these six career families distinguishes between important social experiences which stem from work activity. Many differences in cultural background, education, occupational outlook, age, and sex of worker may be associated with these career families.

Career Family	Job Sequence Associated	Major Defining Characteristics
Stable	Stable Initial–Stable–Trial–Stable Stable–Trial–Stable Initial–Stable	Early entrance into stable job
Conventional	Initial–Trial–Stable Initial–Trial–Stable–Trial–Stable Trial–Stable	The "normal" and "socially expected" job progression to a stable job
Unstable	Trial–Stable–Trial Initial–Trial–Stable–Trial	Return to a trial job after attaining stability through the conventional pattern
Single trial	Initial–Trial Trial	Beginning of trial work period—mostly younger workers
Disestablished	Stable–Trial Initial–Stable–Trial	Return to a trial job after quick attainment of a stable job
Multiple trial	Trial–Trial–Trial	Consecutive trial jobs with no stable job as yet attained

Fig. 107.   The Career Families Shown with Associated Job Sequences and Their Defining Characteristics.

What we wished to know in setting up a classification of career families was how various job sequences reflect occupational stability and security. Our assumption was that it would be more accurate to determine occupational security if we sought a measure which did not depend upon the worker's opinion. We wanted his *job history* to tell us about his own occupational security. The attempt to secure a measure of occupational security in this way required the setting up of an operational definition, i.e., it was necessary to assume that a worker on a job which he has held for less than three years is still relatively unstable and insecure. Either he may decide to quit or his employer may decide to remove him by transfer, promotion, layoff, or dismissal. We had to further assume that occupational stability was indicated when a worker remained more than three years on a given job and that this stability would likewise reflect a relatively high degree of

occupational security. These assumptions, once made, enabled us to examine work histories, find patterns, and make a determination of occupational security.

Distribution of Career Families

We wanted to know what occupational groups were relatively secure and which were relatively insecure. Everything needed to proceed was now

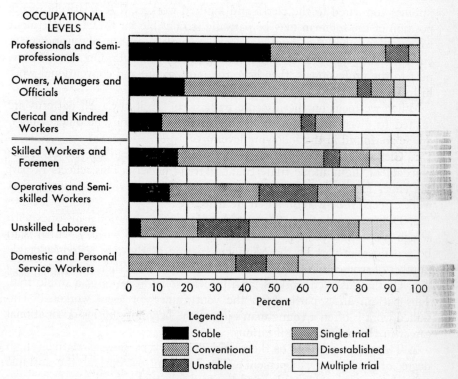

FIG. 108.   Distribution of Work Histories by Career Family.

available. Of the six career families, the *stable* and *conventional* might be regarded as reflecting a high degree of occupational security. The *unstable*, *single trial*, *disestablished*, and *multiple trial* patterns could be assumed to contain a high degree of occupational insecurity. Figure 108 presents the proportion of these six career families found for each occupational level in the Ohio sample.

Seventy-three percent of all white-collar workers (professionals, owners, managers, and clerical workers) are found to be in career families associated with occupational security. This is to be contrasted with the manual workers

(skilled, semiskilled, unskilled, and service workers), of whom only 46 percent are in secure career families.

The professional workers are the most secure, with 88 percent in the stable patterns, and the unskilled workers are the most insecure, with only 24 percent in the stable categories. Almost a linear relationship is noted—*the higher the occupational level, the greater the occupational security,* and vice versa. Only the skilled workers and foremen violate the general tendency. A larger proportion of their work histories is in the secure career families compared to the clerks and kindred workers. The relatively secure position of the foreman may be partially responsible for this. It is pertinent to point out that the reputed instability and insecurity of businessmen, entrepreneurs, and officials is not borne out by our data. On the contrary, next to the professionals, they have the most secure and conventional work histories.

When we focus on the insecure patterns to see if any such patterns are related to given occupational levels, certain associations become evident. These are found in the following levels:

1. Clerks have occupational histories showing a high proportion (22.8 percent) of the multiple trial (trial-trial-trial) pattern. This reflects in part the larger female representation of that stratum and their relatively short work careers, usually terminated by marriage.

2. Domestic and service workers likewise have occupational histories with a high proportion (29.2 percent) of the multiple trial pattern, which is to be explained in part by the temporary nature of the jobs. A considerable number of women also work in this classification until they marry.

3. Of the unskilled workers, 37.9 percent show histories of a single trial. This pattern arises partly from the youthfulness of these workers.[10] Unskilled work is often a young man's job at the beginning of his occupational career in the manual classifications.

4. The career patterns of the semiskilled workers show a relatively high degree of insecurity (54.1 percent). The dominant patterns are the unstable (alternating trial-stable-trial), and the multiple trial.

CAUSES OF DIFFERENCES IN THE SECURITY OF CAREER PATTERNS

The attempt to explain differences in the occupational security of workers introduces a number of questions. Are differences in occupational security in different occupational classifications due largely to the economic stability of the different kinds of work? Or are they due largely to the workers themselves as they vary in age and sex, and in motivation and outlook?

To test the effect of age, all workers who had more than ten years of

[10] See *Sixteenth Census of the United States,* Vol. III, *The Labor Force,* Part IV, pp. 671-672. The median age of male unskilled and semiskilled workers, which is approximately thirty-five years, is lower than that of any other occupational level.

occupational experience beginning with the first trial job were segregated from those who did not. Then the relative proportions of the older and the younger workers in the secure patterns were compared to determine whether age was influencing security. No single critical ratio for any occupational level demonstrated that such differences as were observed were due to the age factor.[11] However, the differences in each occupational level do indicate greater stability with workers of ten years or more full-time work experience. The appearance of all these small differences in the same direction indicates that the age factor cannot be completely ignored in accounting for security and insecurity exhibited within different occupational levels.

Although a considerable volume of research work has been done on measuring the intelligence of workers in different occupational classifications,[12] very little is known about the personality traits of workers in the classifications that we have used. One of the writers, D. C. Miller, has sought out relationships between occupational classifications and the morale of college-trained workers within them.[13] Adults of the highest and lowest morale were identified and their occupational classification was made. Approximately equal numbers of high- and low-morale persons were found among both men and women in professional work. Table 40 shows this fact. In contrast, it may be noted that executives and managers tend to exhibit high morale more often than low morale. It is suggested that the selective nature of the managerial and executive functions explains the predominance of persons with high morale. Management posts require energetic, optimistic personalities who believe that they can achieve goals set for themselves and their subordinates. In addition, the position of an executive in a social hierarchy is conspicuous, commands deference, and satisfies pride.

Low morale is exhibited by both men and women in such occupational levels as "Retail and skilled," "Agricultural," "Small proprietors, etc.," "Apprentices, etc.," and "Unskilled laborers." The number of cases is small and an association may not be demonstrated for each of the classifications. However, the cumulative differences do show more low-morale people at work in these lower occupational levels. This study suggests that there may be real differences in personality traits which distinguish workers in one occupational classification from another. Such differences could explain the

[11] The significance of the differences, $\dfrac{Diff.}{\sqrt{SD}_{(p1-p2)}}$ of the proportions between older workers and younger workers for each occupational level were: professional, 0.34; owners, etc., 0.69; clerks, 1.6; skilled, 1.3; semiskilled, 1.4; unskilled, 0.9; domestic and service, 1.2. For formula of critical ratios, see H. E. Garrett, *Statistics in Education and Psychology*, Longmans, Green and Company, 1938, p. 228.

[12] A number of studies are reported in the following section of this chapter.

[13] D. C. Miller, "Economic Factors in the Morale of College-Trained Adults," *American Journal of Sociology*, September, 1941, pp. 139-156.

variations observed in occupational security. However, until more is known it seems feasible to regard differences in occupational security as largely inherent in the nature of the jobs themselves. Workers, we believe, are secure when they find a job which has economic stability and provides certain social satisfactions. Workers exhibit insecure work histories when they are held within an occupational classification which denies either economic stability or the basic satisfactions of challenge and recognition.

TABLE 40.   High- and Low-Morale Groups of College-Trained Adults
(By Occupational Classification)

Minnesota Occupational Classification	Men			Women		
	Percentage High Morale N=100	Percentage Low Morale N=100	Critical Ratio	Percentage High Morale	Percentage Low Morale	Critical Ratio
I. Professional	33	33	—	20	23	—
II. Executives and managers	31	14	+2.94	14	8	+1.49
III. Retail and skilled	18	26	−1.37	12	23	−2.07
IV. Agricultural	1	1	—	5	7	—
V. Small proprietors, minor clerks, semiskilled	11	17	—	0	1	—
VI. Apprentices, etc.	4	5	—	0	0	—
VII. Unskilled laborers	1	2	—	0	0	—
VIII. Housewives	0	0	—	48	37	+1.58
No data	1	2	—	1	1	—
Combined classes (III & IV & V & VI & VII)	35	51	−2.31	17	31	−2.37

+C.R. indicates higher percentage with high morale.
−C.R. indicates higher percentage with low morale.

SUMMARY OF FINDINGS

Levels of security may be established for each occupational classification by using the proportion of secure patterns associated. Job security is associated with the white-collar workers. It is also associated with skilled workers and foremen. Job insecurity is associated with workers in the domestic service, unskilled, and semiskilled classifications. A ranking of the classifications from most secure to least secure establishes the following listing:

Professional and semiprofessional.

Owners, managers, and officials.

Skilled workers and foremen.

Clerks and kindred workers.

Semiskilled workers.

Domestic and personal service workers.

Unskilled workers.[14]

The stable work period can now be evaluated in the light of work histories ranging across all socioeconomic groupings of workers. It can be seen that a high degree of occupational stability and security is commonly achieved by workers in the professional, proprietary, and skilled classifications. Clerical, semiskilled, and unskilled workers find occupational stability and security much more elusive.[15]

How do workers come to occupy a position in these various socioeconomic classifications? What role does the father's occupation play in influencing the young worker? What is the effect of educational training? We shall turn our attention to these questions.

FACTORS AFFECTING OCCUPATIONAL PLACEMENT

FATHER'S OCCUPATION COMPARED WITH THE OCCUPATION OF HIS SONS AND DAUGHTERS

In 1927 Pitirim Sorokin analyzed the research studies which had been conducted on occupational inheritance up to that time. He sought to find out what relation existed between the occupation of the father and that of the son. On the basis of the available data he said a series of inferences could be made. Three of these are:

[1] Within present Western societies, children of fathers of the same occupation, and often children of the same family, are dispersed among the most different occupational groups.

[2] Each of the occupational groups at the present moment is recruited from the offspring of the most different groups.

[3] In spite of the dispersion among different occupations, the "hereditary" transmission of occupation still exists, and on the average it is still high enough. It is likely also that the father's occupation is still entered by the children in a greater proportion than any other.[16]

Since 1927 more research has been done and these influences can now be validated. Davidson and Anderson sought to determine the relations of family status to occupational careers of sons in their San José study of 1937. The respondents were asked to indicate their regular occupations and those of their brothers and fathers. Table 41 shows the level of regular occupation of 610 fathers compared with the level of regular occupations of all their 1547 sons. Respondents are thirty years of age and over.

[14] A full research report may be found in D. C. Miller and W. H. Form, "Measuring Patterns of Occupational Security," *Sociometry*, November, 1947, pp. 362-375; "The Career Pattern as a Sociological Instrument," *American Journal of Sociology*, January, 1949, pp. 317-329.

[15] Cf. Davidson and Anderson, *op. cit.*, pp. 80-81.

[16] Pitirim Sorokin, *Social Mobility*, Harper & Brothers, 1927, pp. 428-440.

These data show that the sons of fathers on any occupational level are distributed along the entire occupational range. For example, if one looks at the professional fathers (Table 41) of the San José sample, he can see that 24.7 percent of the sons became professional workers like their fathers before them. However, the other 75.4 percent of the sons are distributed in all the other occupational classes. Thirty-nine percent are found in the manual work classifications (skilled, semiskilled, unskilled). These findings and others[17] emphasize the fact that *"the children of fathers of the same occupation and often of the same family are dispersed among the most different occupational groups."*

TABLE 41.   Level of Regular Occupation of 610 Fathers Compared with Level of Regular Occupation of All Their Sons: Respondents Thirty Years of Age or Over

Level of Fathers' Regular Occupation	Number of Fathers	Number of Sons	Percentage of Sons Whose Regular Occupations Are on Level Indicated						
			Prof.	Prop.	Clerks	Skilled	Semi-skilled	Un-skilled	Total
Professional	31	77	24.7	10.4	26.0	18.2	11.7	9.1	100.1
Proprietors	300	794	15.2	32.2	12.7	15.2	10.7	14.0	100.0
Clerks	32	70	25.7	22.9	22.9	15.7	7.1	5.7	100.0
Skilled	127	295	6.1	13.6	14.9	42.0	16.6	6.8	100.0
Semiskilled	34	69	16.0	7.2	8.7	24.7	28.9	14.5	100.0
Unskilled	86	242	4.1	10.3	13.7	13.7	16.5	41.7	100.0
All levels	610	1547	12.7	22.6	14.2	20.7	13.4	16.4	100.0

If attention is focused on a particular occupational group making up today's labor force to find out what the father's regular occupation was, it will be discovered that a large body of evidence supports Sorokin's second inference: *"Each of the occupational groups at the present moment is recruited from the offspring of the most different groups."* An excellent demonstration of this statement is Taussig and Joslyn's study of American business leaders. In 1928 these researchers undertook the study of the social origins of major business leaders in the United States. They held that to be recognized as a leader the person must have occupied a position as a "major executive, partner, or sole owner in a business of such size as to be of more than local importance in its field."[18] They secured data for 7361 business leaders. Table 42 shows the occupation of the father as reported

[17] Cf. Richard Centers, "Occupational Mobility of Urban Occupational Strata," *American Sociological Review*, April, 1948. See also our Table 43, p. 721, which is from Centers' article, Table 1, p. 198.

[18] F. W. Taussig and C. S. Joslyn, *American Business Leaders*, The Macmillan Company, 1932, p. 6.

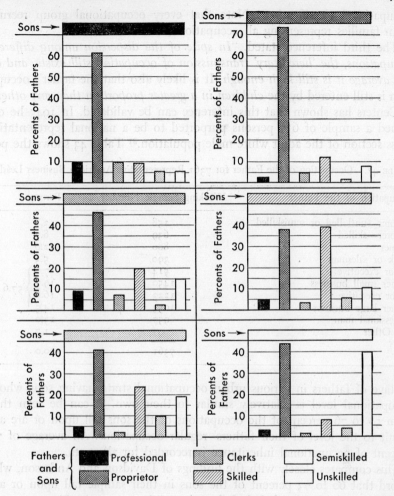

FIG. 109. Percentage Distribution of Fathers According to the Occupational Levels of Gainfully Employed Sons. (Reprinted from *Occupational Mobility in an American Community*, by Percy E. Davidson and Dewey Anderson, with the permission of the authors and of the publishers, Stanford University Press, 1937, p. 24.)

by each of the respondents.[19] This table reveals the diversity of occupational origins of business leaders. It should be noted, however, that the largest groups of leaders have followed in the footsteps of their fathers as they have assumed positions as owners or managers of business.

Davidson and Anderson show the social origins of occupational groups in their study. Figure 109 is a representation of 1547 workers in the various

[19] Taussig and Joslyn: *American Business Leaders*. Copyright 1932 by The Macmillan Company, and used with their permission.

occupational classifications. Note that every occupational group recruits from families representing all occupational classifications.[20]

The third inference stated, *"In spite of the dispersion among different occupations, the 'hereditary' transmission of occupation still exists, and on the average it is still high enough. It is likely also that the father's occupa*tion is still entered by the *children in a greater proportion than any other."*

Centers has shown that this inference can be validated. In 1945 he obtained a sample of 637 persons purported to be a national representative cross section of the adult white male population.[21] Table 43 shows the per-

TABLE 42.   Occupation of the Father for 7361 Representative American Business Leaders

Occupation of the Father	Working Sample Number	Percent
Laborer—unskilled or semiskilled	158	2.1
Laborer—skilled	639	8.7
Farmer	880	12.0
Clerk or salesman	390	5.3
Minor executive	514	7.0
Owner small business	1450	19.7
Major executive	1223	16.6
Owner large business	1053	14.3
Professional man	957	13.0
Other	97	1.3
	7361	100.0

(Owner small business, Major executive, Owner large business: 57.6)

centage of fathers in various urban occupational strata having sons whose occupational level is relatively similar to their own. It can be seen that from 58 to 76 percent of the occupations of the sons fall upon or are adjacent to the level of their fathers' regular occupations. An average of 71 percent of occupational inheritance is recorded for all strata.

This compares closely with the findings of Davidson and Anderson, who record that 60 to 73 percent of the sons in their sample fall upon or are adjacent to the levels of their fathers in regular occupation.[22]

The inheritance of the father's occupational level is strikingly shown in the study of American business leaders. Taussig and Joslyn have shown that the business and professional classes constitute only about 10 percent of the total of gainfully employed population, yet their contribution to the supply of business leaders is no less than 70 percent.[23]

Similarly, Professor Visher's study of 18,356 persons listed in *Who's*

[20] Cf. Centers, *op. cit.*, p. 203.

[21] *Ibid.*, p. 198. The writers have raised some critical questions about this research. See D. C. Miller and William H. Form, "Discussion of Centers' study of 'Occupational Mobility of Urban Occupational Strata,'" *American Sociological Review*, October, 1948, pp. 662-664.

[22] Davidson and Anderson, *op. cit.*, p. 24.

[23] Taussig and Joslyn, *op. cit.*, p. 241.

Who in America discloses that 69.6 percent had fathers who were business or professional men.[24] This close agreement with Taussig and Joslyn's figures is significant. "It does not seem too much to say that whether the field of endeavor be business, 'the professions,' the arts and sciences, or letters about 70 percent of the persons of superior talent in the United States have been drawn from classes constituting hardly more than 10 percent of the population. The manual laboring classes, on the other hand, constituting nearly half of the total gainfully employed population, have contributed no more than 10 percent."[25]

TABLE 43.   Percentages of Fathers in Various Urban Occupational Strata Having Sons Whose Occupational Level Is Relatively Similar to Their Own

Occupational Stratum of Father	Percent	Sons in Categories Included as Relatively Similar in Each Case
Large business	69	Large business and professional
Professional	64	Large business, professional, and small business
Small business	70	Professional, small business, white collar, and farm owners and managers
White collar	70	Small business, white collar, farm owners and managers, and skilled
Skilled manual	72	White collar, farm owners and managers, skilled, and semiskilled
Semiskilled	76	Skilled, semiskilled, unskilled, and farm tenants and laborers
Unskilled	58	Semiskilled, unskilled, and farm tenants and laborers
All strata	71	

How are these disparities to be explained? Are they due to an innate superiority of persons of the business and professional classes? Or to the greater privileges enjoyed by those who have excelled in family background, degree of schooling, wealth and influence of the family, and opportunities to make the "right contacts"? These questions are not easily answered. The subtle influence of many hereditary and social factors must be isolated and measured in order to secure facts which will permit conclusions. Although social and psychological sciences have come to agreement about the interrelatedness of hereditary and environmental conditions, there is no end yet to the controversy regarding the relative importance of nature and nurture.

Taussig and Joslyn say that, "As regards business leaders, the facts . . . strongly suggest even if they do not prove, that lack of native ability rather

[24] Stephen S. Visher, "A Study of the Type of the Place of Birth and of the Occupations of Subjects of Sketches in Who's Who in America," *American Journal of Sociology*, March, 1925, pp. 551-557.

[25] Taussig and Joslyn, *op. cit.*, p. 242.

than lack of opportunity is primarily responsible for the failure of the lower occupational classes to be as well represented as the higher classes."[26]

Davidson and Anderson contradict, "The data as a whole suggest that the occupational pyramid possesses an institutional character, that its marked stratification is due in large measure to forces related to an emerging from the occupational status of father's and family environments in which children are reared, and that these do not submit easily to other influences such as the school but tend to form certain patterns which become characteristic of the several occupational levels."[27]

The contrasting weight given to hereditary and social factors by these two sets of researchers can be discerned. Their interpretations invite us to look over the facts, for it is of utmost importance to secure a definitive answer if this is at all possible. If hereditary factors are correlated with social classes, then it must be recognized that personal and social effort can be of only secondary influence in fostering vertical occupational mobility. If social factors play a large role, then the promise of occupational ascent is brighter for large numbers of able persons in less privileged environments and social classes. To step between the jaws of this controversy is to accept a precarious assignment. However, there can be no escape from it if one wishes to find out how persons come to occupy given occupations during the stable work period. We shall begin by examining evidences of occupational differences in intelligence.

INTELLIGENCE AND OCCUPATION

On standard intelligence tests, adult occupational groups differ widely. *The average intelligence of the groups increases with socioeconomic status,* but with *considerable variation in each group.* Thus professional groups rank high, unskilled workers rank low, with considerable variation represented in each group so that the extremes tend toward the average intelligence scores of the community. To what extent do the differences between levels accurately reflect *hereditary factors* and to what extent are these differences due to *superior education and more stimulating environments* in which the persons of the upper levels move? If it could be completely demonstrated that standard intelligence tests tap only native intelligence and that native intelligence is a constant factor unchanged by environmental influences, we could proceed to announce that occupational differences in intelligence are due solely to heredity. Although intelligence tests represent outstanding achievements in psychological measurement, they measure responses that have been conditioned by a wide variety of cultural factors and individual experiences as well as heredity. Indeed, psychologists B. S.

---

[26] *Ibid.,* p. 264.
[27] Davidson and Anderson, *op. cit.,* p. 186.

Burks, F. N. Freeman, K. J. Holzinger, and others have shown that superior environments can raise intelligence scores an average of nine to ten points. Burks reports in a study of 204 foster children that the influence of variance in home environment is 17 percent. This leaves the residual variance in intelligence due to heredity at 83 percent of the total. *Home* environment is not a measure of all environment. Clearly the influence of variance in *total* environment is therefore greater than 17 percent. Murphy, Murphy, and Newcomb observe that in many communities the influence must be enormously greater. "The relative weight of variance in stock and of variance in environment will of course depend on the range within which each variable moves, e.g., the equalization of opportunity would make nature variance relatively more important than it now is, and an increase of inequality of opportunity would make it relatively less important."[28]

In an effort to probe further into the nature of occupational differences, researchers have turned to the comparison of intelligence scores of children with those of their fathers in various socioeconomic groups. A great number of studies show that children tend to reproduce similar average intelligence scores in accordance with the socioeconomic level of the father. The same tendency to wide variation at each level may be observed. Since in general there is also a high correlation between husbands and wives we may speak broadly of a family level of intelligence in relation to socioeconomic status.[29]

If a parent-child resemblance in intelligence could be discerned early in the child's life before the weight of social and cultural factors came into play, then it would be possible to measure a kind of "equalization of opportunity which would make nature variance more important." Unfortunately no valid infant tests of intelligence have been constructed. However, scores from standard intelligence tests at two years of age show a significant relation between the scores of children and the occupational classification of their fathers. The relationship at two continues upon testing for each succeeding age.[30]

These findings indicate that heredity is operating, but the influence of home environment and other cultural forces cannot be discounted even at these early ages. Both genetic and cultural forces are interacting but how are these influences intertwined?

Sociologists as well as psychologists have been vitally interested in this problem. Mapheus Smith has studied the relation of intelligence scores among university students and their fathers; 5487 records of undergraduate

---

[28] Gardner Murphy, Lois B. Murphy, and Theodore M. Newcomb, *Experimental Social Psychology*, Harper & Brothers, 1947, p. 43. The reader will find pp. 36-53 an excellent review of the literature.

[29] An excellent review of studies up to 1927 is that of P. Sorokin, *Social Mobility*, Harper & Brothers, 1927, pp. 292-297. Murphy, Murphy, and Newcomb, *op. cit.*, is an excellent source of reference for more recent work.

[30] Murphy, Murphy, and Newcomb, *op. cit.*, p. 47.

students at the University of Kansas during 1934-1938 were analyzed.[31] Table 44 shows the mean intelligence test percentile scores of the University students classified by occupation of father. Professor Smith reports that "the correlation between occupation and intelligence is shown to be as strong today as a generation ago. The 'white collar' occupational classes (professional workers, clerical workers, public service workers, and proprietors) clearly surpass the others. The children of fathers in occupations requiring more skill and training are superior to the children of those requiring less. . . . The data suggest that occupational differences in intelligence tend to be perpetuated. But whether the cause of the continuance is predominantly biological inheritance or such environmental factors as differential early stimulation, differential education, or differential motivation remains unclear."[32]

TABLE 44. Mean Intelligence Test Percentile Scores of 5487 University of Kansas Students Classified by Occupation of Father[33]

Occupational Class of Father	Mean Intelligence Percentile Score of the Student	
Professional	58.746	
Educators		64.031
Clergymen		61.129
Engineers		59.952
Lawyers		58.680
Other professional		58.544
Doctors		53.513
Clerical	56.215	
Other clerical		58.178
Clerical agents		55.280
Salespeople	55.280	
Sales agents		55.775
Salesmen		56.720
Public service	55.478	
Proprietors	53.342	
Manufacturing proprietors		56.690
Dealers		52.071
Bankers		50.796
Contractors		48.438
Skilled	51.469	
Foremen	50.071	
Semiskilled	47.543	
Farmers	47.344	
Domestic and personal service	47.323	
Unskilled	36.706	

[31] Mapheus Smith, "University Student Intelligence and Occupation of Fathers," *American Sociological Review*, December, 1942, pp. 764-771.

[32] *Ibid.*, pp. 769-770.

[33] *Ibid.*, pp. 764-771.

Clark and Gist made a follow-up study of 2423 students to discover the relationship between the measured intelligence of children and the occupation they later chose to enter.[34] At the time the tests were given in 1922-1923 the median age of the students was approximately sixteen; when the study was conducted, thirteen years later, the median age was therefore about twenty-nine. Table 45 shows the percentage of the 2423 in each of three I.Q. intervals by occupations. Here, again, the same positive relationship between measured intelligence and occupational level is demonstrated. The researchers state:

It appears that intelligence acts as a selective factor influencing occupational choice. More specifically it seems clear that in the environment from which this sample was taken, the professions and clerical vocations are attracting a larger proportion of young men and women with superior intelligence ratings than are the manual types of occupation, including farming. . . . Likewise in confirmatory significance is the fact that a large degree of overlapping occurs in the distribution of test scores among the various occupational classes. Each class draws both upon those having relatively high and those having relatively low scores, though in different proportions. No class can be said to skim off the cream, and only the cream, of mental ability as measured by the tests. The highest score in the entire sample, for example, was made by one classed as an unskilled laborer.[35]

We may summarize various implications of these data by explaining their significance for the individual and for the group. The Murphys and Newcomb speak for the individual:

We may say that neither a moron nor a person of average intelligence is likely to develop to a level of outstanding brilliance through improvement in environment, and conversely, a mind of distinctly high calibre is not likely to appear definitely inferior as a result of poor environment; but it is quite possible if not probable that, in general, slightly below average performance may be raised through environmental changes to somewhat above average performance. . . . Even if every street cleaner's son may not be a great engineer, he may perfectly well be a surveyor or a postal clerk; and a general raising of average I.Q.'s even five points may have far-flung consequences.[36]

The most significant implications for group differences grow from the observance of the wide variation in intelligence scores occurring in every occupational group. These variations make possible considerably more vertical occupational mobility than is now taking place in American life. Educational inequalities alone are holding down a large proportion of our population. The Pennsylvania study on education showed that if the students who ought to go on to college are those of the highest academic ability, the colleges are now getting only about half of the high school

---

[34] Carroll D. Clark and Noel P. Gist, "Intelligence as a Factor in Occupational Choice," *American Sociological Review*, October, 1938, pp. 683-694.

[35] *Ibid.*, pp. 693-694.

[36] Murphy, Murphy, and Newcomb, *op. cit.*, p. 53.

726 INDUSTRIAL SOCIOLOGY

graduates they ought to get. The other half go directly into jobs and their places in the college are taken by students with more money and less brains.[37]

There are quantities of human resources at every occupational level which are capable of occupational ascent. We have recorded the relation of measured "intelligence" with socioeconomic level. We leave the search

TABLE 45. Percentage of 2423 Persons in Each of Three I.Q. Intervals by Occupations[38]

Occupational Group	Number	Mean	Percentage in Each I.Q. Interval		
			Below 95	95–104	105 and Over
Total professional	365	102.82	32.60	33.97	33.43
Clerical	166	100.00	34.34	33.74	31.92
Teachers	207	99.28	38.17	31.40	30.43
Salespeople and proprietors	233	96.61	44.19	32.62	23.19
Skilled workers	131	96.18	45.80	32.83	21.37
Housewives	857	95.44	49.94	30.81	19.25
Semiskilled and unskilled	247	93.28	58.30	27.53	14.17
Farmers	345	92.75	58.84	29.85	11.31
Housekeepers and unemployed	79	91.39	63.29	31.65	5.06

here for factors associated with genetic or hereditary influences,[39] and seek to ascertain the explicit role of social and cultural background in determining the occupational level of workers in the stable work period.

FATHER'S INCOME AND EDUCATION COMPARED WITH EDUCATION AND OCCUPATION OF HIS SONS AND DAUGHTERS

Income and education along with occupation are interrelated factors which circumscribe the social background of an individual. From this background the individual acquires opportunities and outlooks which condition his future career pattern. The high correlation between father's and son's occupations has been demonstrated. Some of the influences which originate from the income and education of the father will be traced.

The father's income and education are also correlated with the occupational level attained by the son and daughter. This is understandable even without additional evidence since income and education are correlated with the Edwards occupational classifications and since the children are known

[37] Goodwin Watson, How Good Are Our Colleges? Public Affairs Committee, Inc., 1938, p. 9. Cf. W. L. Warner, R. J. Havighurst, and Martin B. Loeb, Who Shall Be Educated?, Harper & Brothers, 1944, p. 52.

[38] Adapted from Clark and Gist, op. cit., pp. 683-686.

[39] If the reader wishes to continue an investigation of physical factors related to occupation, see P. Sorokin, op. cit., pp. 215-333.

to stabilize in the level of the father or an adjacent level. At the professional, proprietary, and clerical levels an above average education is usually necessary. The status of the family in education and in income influences the attainments of the sons and daughters in a profound way.

How Family Status in Education and Income Influences the Occupational Attainment of the Children

Education plays an important role in determining occupational levels. The school is a selective agency which tends to eliminate those who cannot perform satisfactorily according to its standards or those who feel they cannot profit from its offerings. At the high school and college levels many persons are barred by the lack of financial support which is necessary. Still others acquire outlooks from their social backgrounds which diminish their chances of educational progress. College enrollment usually requires some

TABLE 46. The Relation of Parental Income to Full-Time College Attendance of Superior Milwaukee High School Graduates

Parental Income	Percent in College Full Time
$8000	100.0
$5000–$7000	92.0
$3000–$4999	72.9
$2000–$2999	44.4
$1500–$1999	28.9
$1000–$1499	25.5
$ 500–$ 999	26.8
Under $500	20.4

financial support and parental encouragement. Studies show that the socioeconomic status of the parents is a more deciding factor in the educational advance of their children than the ability of the children themselves. This was clearly shown by the Pennsylvania survey.[40] In this study 910 pupils with intelligence quotients of 110 or above were identified. It is generally believed that students with I.Q. of 110 or above are good college material. The researchers were interested to know how many of these 910 superior young people would secure a college education. They recorded the socioeconomic status of the pupils and ascertained their subsequent educational history. When this entire group of 910 persons was divided into two subgroups on the basis of socioeconomic status, it was discovered that the upper socioeconomic group contained 93 percent who graduated from high school and 57 percent that attended college. In the lower socioeconomic group 72 percent graduated from high school and 13 percent attended college. This

[40] Harlan Updegraff, *Inventory of Youth in Pennsylvania*, American Youth Commission, American Council on Education, 1936.

striking discrepancy is evidence of the fact that less educational opportunity was available to those from families of lower socioeconomic status although the students were equal in intellectual ability to those students who had higher status.[41]

The relation of parental income to the proportion of superior Milwaukee students who secure college attendance is shown in Table 46. These data were drawn from 1023 able students who graduated from Milwaukee high schools in 1937 and 1938. These students all had I.Q.'s of 117 or above. The pronounced relationship between parents' income and college attendance can be clearly seen.[42]

Helen Goetsch has also found that when those students who do secure college opportunities enroll in various curricula, family income is again a related factor. Table 47 shows how parental income plays a role in influencing choice of curricula undertaken by college students.

TABLE 47.   Parental Income and College Courses Pursued by Sons and Daughters

Curriculum	Median Parental Income
Law	$2118
Medicine and dentistry	$2112
Liberal arts	$2068
Journalism	$1907
Engineering	$1884
Teaching	$1570
Commercial	$1543
Nursing	$1368
Industrial Trades	$1104

These sets of figures are testimony to the high relationship between socioeconomic status and educational opportunity. However, it should not be overlooked that there is a substantial minority from lower positions in the social heap who are achieving social mobility through their education.[43]

It is now clear that opportunities for educational preparation at higher levels are dependent to a large degree upon the occupation and income of the family. Interwined with the opportunity provided by the family is the occupational outlook which the child acquires. This outlook is a function of expectation built and nourished within his social background. The educational background of the family becomes important in molding the expectations of the child. The reader has probably suspected that there is a high relationship between the education of the parents and the occupational

[41] Cf. Helen B. Goetsch, *Parental Income and College Opportunities*, Teachers College Contributions to Education, No. 795, Columbia University Press, 1940. See also our Tables 46 and 47, which are from Goetsch, Tables 26 and 27, respectively.

[42] *Ibid.* Reproduced in Warner, Havighurst, and Loeb, *op. cit.*, p. 53.

[43] Cf. Warner, Havighurst, and Loeb, *op. cit.*, p. 72.

aspirations and attainments of their sons and daughters. This relationship does exist and is illustrated in Table 48, based on the studies of the Ohio labor force by W. H. Form and D. C. Miller. A sample of workers representing the Ohio labor force by age, sex, and occupational distribution was studied in 1946. The male workers were asked to give their last school year completed and supply the same information for their fathers. The median years reported in the table show that higher occupational levels are filled with better-educated persons—for both the fathers and the sons. The rising level of education is recorded in the higher averages of the sons.

TABLE 48. Median Years of Education for a Representative Sample of 252 Ohio Fathers and Sons

Occupation	Median Years of Education: Fathers	Median Years of Education: Sons
Professional	11.0	16.0
Proprietary, etc.	9.2	13.4
Clerical	9.2	13.1
Skilled	8.0	11.2
Semiskilled	8.6	11.6
Unskilled	8.7	11.6

Some effects of social background upon occupational outlook can also be detected by examining the college expectations and attendance of young people from different social classes. Table 49 represents some research studies made by Warner, Havighurst, and Loeb in three different communities. The high school students in Hometown and Yankee City were asked whether they expected to enter college. When their answers were checked against their social backgrounds the striking relationship of expecta-

TABLE 49. College Expectations and College Attendance by Social Position in Three Different Communities[44]

Class	Percent of High School Students in Each Social Class Expecting to Attend College		Percent of High School Graduates in Each Social Class Attending College
	Hometown	Yankee City	Old City
Upper upper			
Lower upper	100	100	72
Upper middle	80	88	69
Lower middle	22	45	58
Upper lower	9	28	16
Lower lower	0	26	0

[44] Adapted from *ibid.*, pp. 59-66.

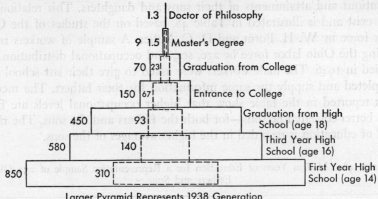

Larger Pyramid Represents 1938 Generation
Smaller Pyramid Represents 1910 Generation

Fig. 110.   A Comparison of the Number of People out of Every Thousand Who Reached Certain Levels of High School and College in Two Different Generations (1938 and 1910). (Adapted from data from biennial surveys of the United States Office of Education.)

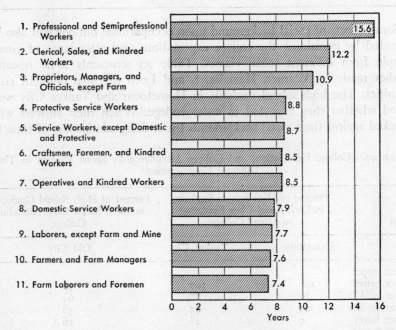

Fig. 111.   Major Occupational Groups Ranked According to the Median School Years Completed. (Adapted from *Sixteenth Census of the United States,* Alba M. Edwards, *Comparative Occupation Statistics,* United States Government Printing Office, 1940.)

tion and social class was disclosed. There were no upper-upper-class children in the public high school so there are no entries from this class. However, note that a range of 74 to 100 percent exists in college expectations. If the high school graduates of Old City are followed for a five-year period the percentages actually attending college can be found. The proportion who do attend college is shown to be directly related to class position.[45]

The amount of selection which takes place can be determined by looking at the figures for the number of young people who reach various levels of

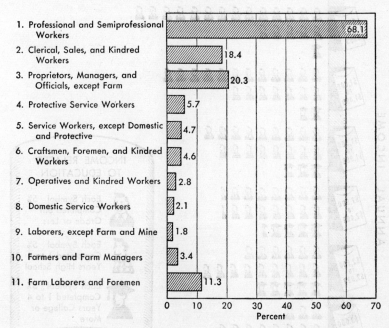

FIG. 112. Major Occupational Groups Ranked According to the Percentage of College-Trained Persons. (Adapted from *Sixteenth Census of the United States*, Alba M. Edwards, *Comparative Occupational Statistics*, United States Government Printing Office, 1940.)

the educational ladder. Figure 110 shows the number of people out of every thousand who reach high school and college levels. Two generations can be compared by observing those who reached given levels in 1938 and 1910. The increased number at all levels in 1939 indicate that high schools and colleges are less selective agencies than formerly. Both pyramids, however, continue to be striking exhibits of educational stratification. Because of the selective influence of the school and because of its role in providing much of the training necessary for occupational pursuits, it is to be expected that a high relationship between occupation and education could be demon-

[45] *Ibid.*, pp. 58-87.

strated. Figure 111 shows this relationship. The figure was devised to picture two kinds of educational ranking. Along the base the major occupational groups are ranked according to the median school years completed. The

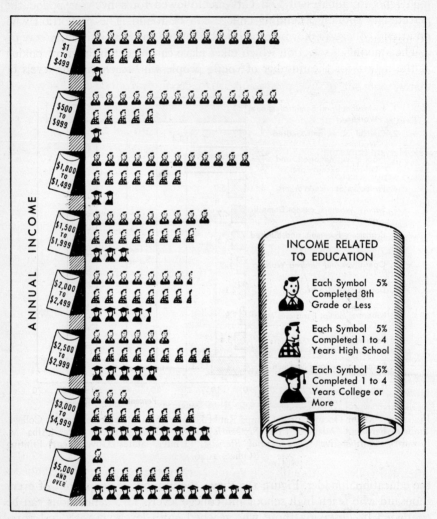

FIG. 113. Better-Educated Men Predominate in Higher-Salary Brackets. (From *Trends*, National Association of Manufacturers, January, 1946, p. 3.)

white-collar groups, professional, clerical, proprietary, and managerial workers, are shown to have the greater amount of formal education, but there is a pronounced gap between the professionals and the clerical-proprietary-managerial group. Manual workers including farm owners are shown to group together at a lower educational level. Speaking in averages, we can

say that manual workers constitute an elementary school-trained group, the proprietors, managers, and clerical workers a high school-trained group, and the professional workers a college-trained group. However, the averages are not sufficient guides to portray the total picture accurately. Each major occupation group has college-trained people within it. Figure 112 shows occupational groups and the corresponding proportion of college-trained persons in each group. The percentage of each group which has attended college one year or more is shown as a horizontal bar. Note that approximately one out of five proprietary, managerial, and clerical workers have

TABLE 50.   Median Earned Incomes of Men Working Graduates by Groups and Geographic Locations of Colleges Attended

Yale-Harvard-Princeton	$4700	$2400	$3740	$5580	4.7%
(1) Other "Ivy League"	3240	1900	2880	4640	5.8
(2) Twenty selected eastern colleges	3010	1760	2880	4270	5.1
(3) The "big ten" of the Middle West	2850	1830	2810	3970	11.9
Other New England and middle Atlantic	2580	1720	2600	4100	23.1
Other middle western	2360	1650	2330	3250	19.1
All other U.S. colleges	2310	1570	2470	3680	30.3
Total U.S. colleges	2620	1690	2590	4020	100.0

(1) Dartmouth, Cornell, Pennsylvania, Columbia

(2)

Amherst College	Hamilton College	Swarthmore College
Bates College	Haverford College	Trinity College
Bowdoin College	Hobart College	Tufts College
Brown University	Lafayette College	Union University
Clark University	Lehigh University	Wesleyan University
Colby College	Middlebury College	Williams College
Franklin and Marshall College	Rutgers University	

(3)

University of Chicago	University of Michigan	Purdue University
University of Illinois	University of Minnesota	University of Wisconsin
University of Indiana	Northwestern University	
University of Iowa	Ohio State University	

attended college. Although a large majority of the professionals attended a college it should be observed that almost a third have never received any college training. The large gap between the manual and white-collar groups in education is further indicated in the small proportion of the manual workers who have ever attended college.[46]

Education is definitely related to income received. This can be seen quite clearly in Figure 113, which shows that better-educated men predominate in the higher-salary brackets. Is education alone responsible for these remarkable advantages in income? To what extent are the incomes received by

[46] Data is from Alba Edwards, *Comparative Occupation Statistics for the United States*, United States Government Printing Office, 1940, p. 181.

college-trained persons due to the *prestige* of education? To what extent are they due to *influential connections* secured by family and friends? These questions are not easily answered but data indicate that the prestige of education and influential connections are intertwined with the income

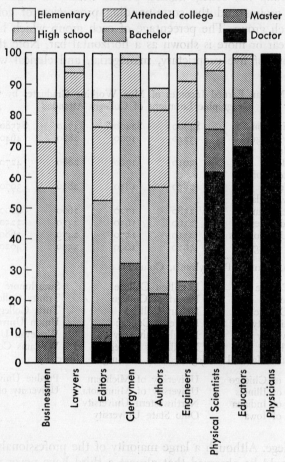

FIG. 114. Ranking of Occupational Groups in Educational Equipment. (From J. R. Shannon and Maxine Shaw, "Education of Business and Professional Leaders," *American Sociological Review*, June, 1940, p. 382.)

received and exercise a considerable influence apart from the increased productivity of the worker which is imputed to educational training. Table 50 is an interesting exhibit which casts light upon these influences. It shows the median earned incomes of men working graduates by groups and by geographic location of colleges attended. Here we see that Yale, Harvard, and Princeton graduate persons who are able to make higher incomes. Grad-

uates from these universities after forty years of age have incomes almost double those of other college graduates. Is this due to superior ability, superior education, or their predominantly upper-class social background?[47] This question cannot be answered with any degree of finality. However, a follow-up study of the process by which these graduates come to find their jobs would undoubtedly reveal the influence of "connections" and financial aid. Not much is known about these influences. However, Maitland Edey's recent study of the Princeton class of 1932 shows that 32 percent work for themselves, 63 percent work for others, 4 percent do both, and 1 percent list themselves as unemployed.[48] How did approximately one out of three get started in business or in a profession so that he became an independent worker? This information is not given. In a following section the relations of financial aid and influential contacts will be examined. Before this is done the relation of education to eminence should be recorded. It is generally known that education is related to superior performance in all levels of distinguished activity. The extent of this relationship is well demonstrated by Shannon and Shaw's study of the ten largest occupational groups in the 1938-1939 edition of *Who's Who in America*.[49] Figure 114 illustrates the educational background of eminent physicians, educators, physical scientists, engineers, authors, clergymen, editors, lawyers, and business men. The importance of higher education in the attainment of distinguished achievement can be clearly seen. Formal education has been shown to be related to occupational level, to income, and to eminence.

THE SIGNIFICANCE OF FINANCIAL AID AND INFLUENTIAL CONTACTS IN DETERMINING OCCUPATIONAL PLACEMENT

It is not easy to secure accurate information regarding financial aid and the role of influential contacts in determining occupational level. Some respondents will underestimate, some will overestimate the amount of importance of each factor. Some, in their pride, will consciously or unconsciously forget or ignore the help of these aids in their climb for occupational status. However, financial aid is often essential to proprietor and professional status. Influential contacts are often exceedingly useful if not absolutely necessary.

Davidson and Anderson found that a fourth of all their San José professional occupations have made use of initial capital during their occupational careers. The greatest need for financial aid appears in the proprietary and professional classifications, with one-third of the proprietors and one-fourth

[47] Warner and his collaborators have pointed out how colleges fit the status system of our society. W. L. Warner, Robert J. Havighurst, Martin B. Loeb, *op. cit.*, p. 71.

[48] Maitland Edey, "The Class of '32," *Life*, June 16, 1947, pp. 51-60.

[49] J. R. Shannon and Maxine Shaw, "Education of Business and Professional Leaders," *American Sociological Review*, June, 1940, pp. 381-383.

of the professionals specifying the use of financial aid in establishing themselves in their occupations.[50]

In their study of *American Business Leaders* Taussig and Joslyn asked the respondents if they had received the help of relatives or friends in establishing themselves. Eight out of a hundred said they had received help through *both* influential connections and financial aid. Thirty-one out of a hundred said they had help through *either* influential connections or financial aid. The remaining 61 percent said they had received no help. The range is well indicated by two contrasting replies to the questionnaire:

"I am at the head of a concern founded by my father over 25 years ago and which at his death I inherited. It is this fact, rather than training or technical education, which has placed me where I am. I have had to learn from the top down."

"Worked my way through college. Have never had any 'drag' or influence of any kind in my business career."[51]

These quotations reveal the contrasting possibilities of occupational mobility in America. The central tendency is more difficult to determine but tentative conclusions can be drawn.

The majority of respondents in all occupational levels disclaim the help of relatives and friends in establishing themselves. However, a substantial number in both the proprietary and the professional levels require some kind of assistance. If the financial support given to attain education, the financial aid to establish a business or professional practice, and the help of influential connections were all placed in the pan of a giant scale and weighed, there is ample reason to believe that the scale scores would be highly associated with family wealth or standing.

THE SIGNIFICANCE OF SOCIAL AND ECONOMIC CONDITIONS

After all the relationships of ability, education, family background, and influential connections are considered, it might seem that the factors responsible for determining a person's occupational level have been identified. In the longer view, however, it must be recognized that social and economic conditions existing within society may have a critical influence in orienting the course of a career. In war or warlike society military organization is paramount and calls forth the largest quantity of talent. At one time in history it is the church, at another time it is commerce or industry that challenges young people to come to its service. In times of expanding opportunity one may look for an increase in the number of distinguished men coming from the laboring class, and again, during periods of contrasting opportunity one would equally well expect the reverse. Joseph Schneider has shown that the definition of eminence tends to change with the existing

---

[50] Davidson and Anderson, *op. cit.*, p. 35.
[51] Taussig and Joslyn, *op. cit.*, pp. 170-171, 306-307.

historical scene. He points out that (1) the kind of eminence a person is likely to achieve is determined by his social origin; (2) it is not always easy to acquire fame in the same activity during different historical periods; (3) during periods of expanding opportunity many activities appear which either do not possess the prestige or appeal for the individuals born into the aristocracy and professions or else require skills the exercise of which is not yet restricted to particular groups in the population by imposition of professional standards.[52] These forces affect all occupational life. We have discussed in Chapter V the dynamic quality of work in modern life. The increased proportions of professional, clerical, and semiskilled workers are results of changes in technology. Accompanying these changes are redefinitions of the status or prestige of many occupations. Labor leaders are rising in status.[53] Occupational groups such as osteopaths, aviators, and radio announcers have appeared as new fields of professional and semiprofessional work. Real estate salesmen are trying to raise their status by claiming they are *realtors* —a professional title." Bankers have slipped somewhat in prestige since the thirties. Blacksmiths have lost their "place" in the economy and in the community.

William Graham Sumner pointed out in the famed *Folkways* that "luck" always seemed to play an important part in the affairs of men. To the individual, forces outside of his control often seem to be due to luck, some to good luck and some to bad luck. In trying to ascertain why a person or a group of persons comes to attain certain occupational levels one cannot dismiss the role of luck or chance. Sometimes chance operates on the individual level only. This is illustrated by the statement of an American business leader.

"Any analysis of a man's success must take two factors into consideration; luck and personality. The writer does not feel that he has any unusual abilities. In fact he thinks his abilities are not proportionate to his job. Luck has played a most important part in his career in that he met by luck two influential men who liked him more for his personality than any demonstrated ability. He has since tried to capitalize his opportunities by surrounding himself with capable men who would keep him from making too many errors in conducting a business for which he had no previous training."[54]

Chance seems real to many a group influence. One young man about forty told us: "I got out of college in the heart of the depression. There just weren't jobs enough for my class. Many didn't get decent jobs for years. I fooled around on a clerk's job at $20 a week for five years and was glad

[52] Joseph Schneider, "Social Class, Historical Circumstances and Fame," *American Journal of Sociology*, July, 1937, pp. 37-56. See also his articles, "The Definition of Eminence" and "The Social Origins of Famous English Men of Genius," *American Sociological Review*, December, 1938, pp. 834-849.
[53] C. Wright Mills, *New Men of Power*, Harcourt, Brace & Company, 1948.
[54] Cited by Taussig and Joslyn, *op. cit.*, p. 300.

to have it. Most of my class had the same experience except where the old man had a job waiting for his son. Most of us just had to take the brunt of the depression. If my class had graduated in '27 or '28 we would have gotten started and could have held on when the depression hit. It was just our bad luck to get out a few years later and then we were stuck."

THE EXPLANATION OF CAREER CAUSATION

TWO CONTRASTING THEORIES OF CAREER CAUSATION

If you ask a man or a woman what factors have been responsible for his or her success, the answer is usually a simple one. For example, business leaders say,

"Simply got into business I most enjoyed and went to it with all my energy and ability."

"Hard knocks, hard work, long hours, and constant plugging produced results."

"I'm just an average man, but I work at it harder than the average man."

"I was brought up in a small town where I learned that work was the normal lot of man, not a misfortune, as it is taught now."

"Every young man should choose the business in which he is intensely interested—in which he sees possibilities and in which he will be happy—and then stick to this one thing until he gets there. Keep his daily exercise in the outdoors—have plenty of fun and try to save half of his earnings for future investment."

"Everything else being equal, I believe that friendship is very important to getting ahead."

"Enthroned within the consciousness of every man who accomplishes much in service to civilization there is a SUPER-PERSONALITY who silently drives, who chides, who commands, but who rarely commends. This personality shapes the destiny of the individual. A man's wife may supplement and give greater power to such influence."[55]

These beliefs represent the conviction that personal motivation and hard work explain the career pattern and that occupational success can be attained regardless of social background. This kind of thinking might be called the *individual* causation theory of career patterns. In contrast, the network of interrelated social factors that have been demonstrated to be associated with occupational levels might become the basis of a *social* causation theory of career patterns. Such a theory would impute the origin and development of a career to those social factors that have been identified. We have shown a relationship between occupational level of a worker and (1) the father's occupation, (2) the intelligence of the worker, (3) the father's income and education, (4) financial aid and influential contacts,

[55] *Ibid.*, pp. 299-301.

(5) social and economic conditions. An accurate weighing of the facts will demonstrate that the social background of the worker is a base of opportunities and limitations. As opportunities are enlarged the *possibilities* of occupational mobility are increased. Personal motivation and work are necessary components to an enlarging career pattern. However, there is good evidence that the social backgrounds of workers are the crucial determiners in the *number* who are able to come into various occupational levels. The reservoir of human ability among all socioeconomic levels is greater than is generally assumed. The discounting of ability goes on because observers are unable to visualize the possible growth of millions of workers who if

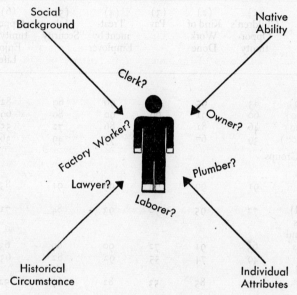

FIG. 115.   Equilibrium of Four Forces that Determine Occupational Level.

placed within the kind of social settings which have been shown to be correlated with the upper occupational classifications would acquire new outlooks, motivations, and work skills. Some interesting evidence to substantiate this position comes from Arthur Kornhauser's Chicago Attitude Study. He asked the following questions of his Chicago sample:

Do you feel that your children or those of your friends and neighbors have as much opportunity as they should have?
Do you like the kind of work you do?
Do you feel that your pay or salary is fair?
Would you say you are treated well by the people you work for?
Do you feel that there is any danger of losing your job?

Do you feel that you have as much opportunity to enjoy life as you should have?

Do you feel that you have a good chance to get ahead in life and become fairly well off?

The principal findings by income and typical occupational groups are summarized in Table 51. It is apparent that attitudinal responses to the above questions are correlated positively with income and occupation. A high correlation is indicated by the rather steep gradient from highest to

TABLE 51.   Comparisons of Groups on Personal Satisfaction Questions
Percent Satisfied vs. Dissatisfied on Following Questions

	(1) Children's Opportunity	(2) Kind of Work Done	(3) Pay	(4) Treatment by Employer	(5) Job Security	(6) Opportunity to Enjoy Life	(7) Chance to Get Ahead
Income Levels							
A (over $5000)	83	95	90	96	89	82	96
B ($2000–5000)	60	91	69	90	80	69	78
C ($1000–2000)	46	81	53	86	72	55	69
D (under $1000)	39	67	34	77	49	36	43
Occupational Groups							
Major business Executives	91	99	94	99	91	85	98
Engineers (professional)	72	95	70	93	84	71	92
Minor business executives and small owners	65	91	72	90	89	63	80
Office workers	49	74	55	92	82	63	87
Skilled manual workers	49	85	53	82	67	52	55
Unskilled and semiskilled	44	71	47	82	64	48	61

lowest groups. Kornhauser's conclusion is that "the figures tend to support the hypothesis presented earlier that the differences among socioeconomic classes are largely differences in contentment, life satisfaction, and personal adjustment."[56]

AN EQUILIBRIUM THEORY TO ACCOUNT FOR CAREER CAUSATION

Forces making for the location of workers at various occupational levels have been identified and described. *Social background, native ability, his-*

[56] Arthur Kornhauser, "Analysis of Class Structure of Contemporary American Society —Psychological Bases of Class Divisions," in G. W. Hartmann and T. Newcomb, *Industrial Conflict*, The Dryden Press, 1939, pp. 242-243.

torical circumstance, and *individual attributes* are the influences determining the career pattern of any person. These forces may be considered as intertwined and pulling upon each worker with different intensities at various times in his career. By the time a man or woman reaches thirty-five or forty years of age these forces often become equilibrated, and what the occupational history is from thirty-five years to sixty years is a fair index of whatever stability the worker will experience.

Figure 115 shows the resolution of forces that bring about stability in a career pattern. How these forces work themselves out for contemporary American workers will be described.

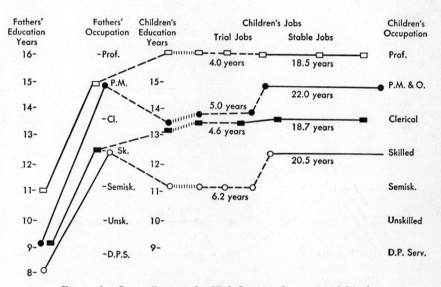

FIG. 116. Career Patterns for High-Security Occupational Levels.

PORTRAYAL OF CAREER PATTERNS

If occupational histories of a large number of workers in all occupational levels are analyzed, definite tendencies can be located. These tendencies reflect varying degrees of struggle for occupational stability and security. When the Ohio survey was made by the writers, the work histories were analyzed for the modal patterns. The professional, proprietary-managerial, clerical, and skilled workers have already been described as those having relatively high occupational security. The semiskilled, unskilled, and domestic and personal service workers are known to have relatively low occupational security as we have defined it. In Figures 116 and 117 modal career patterns of the major occupational groups are shown divided by their degrees of occupational security. These histories show the trial and stable jobs held

in each group. We have tried to suggest how the histories in each level may be affected by differences in such related variables as (1) the modal education of the fathers, (2) the occupation of the fathers, and (3) the years of education attained by their sons and daughters.

THE OCCUPATIONAL PYRAMID

It would be useful if all the research data including our own from the above could be brought together so that a rather complete picture of a typical worker in each occupational grouping might be presented. Unfortunately studies to date have not been sufficiently numerous to make a full

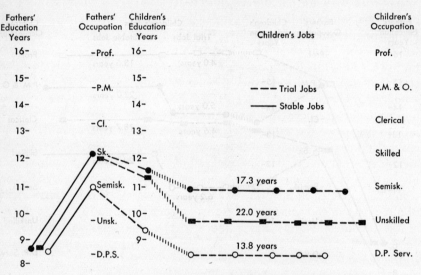

Fig. 117. Career Patterns for Low-Security Occupational Levels.

portrayal for the United States labor force. Those that have been reported include the work of Davidson and Anderson, Miller and Form, W. S. Woytinsky, and the United States Census researchers, especially that of Alba M. Edwards.[57] These writers do not give all the information that is desired but the social background of the labor force can now be drawn in outline. All agree that the socioeconomic levels of workers roughly form a pyramid composed of the unskilled workers at the base and ranging through levels of semiskilled, skilled and clerical, farmers, proprietors, managers, and officials, and professional persons. These groupings can be seen to be the result of institutional forces many of which have been described. The descrip-

[57] All of these studies have been cited except W. S. Woytinsky, *Labor in the United States*, Social Science Research Council, 1938; cf. especially Percy E. Davidson and Dewey Anderson, *Ballots and the Democratic Class Struggle*, Stanford University Press, 1943.

tion of the average characteristics drawn from the sources indicated provides a set of summarizing sketches.[58]

Professional Workers

The typical professional worker is a male, probably a teacher, lawyer, physician, or clergyman. He is born into an upper-middle- or upper-class family. His father is a business proprietor or manager who has received an above average education. He encourages the son to plan on going to college, which he does with the financial aid of his parents. The son enrolls in a professional curriculum and begins his specialized training. He may engage in part-time work for pay during college days, but upon completion of his professional schooling he moves directly into his professional career without floundering. During his first four years out of college he moves twice as he seeks a "good" firm or a "good" location for his professional practice. He finds what he wants for a permanent location and settles down in an urban community. At about twenty-eight or twenty-nine years of age he marries a college graduate of about twenty-five years of age who comes from an upper-middle- or upper-class family. He receives an income which permits him to live above the comfort level. However, he limits his family to one child. He buys his home and lives in the better, more modern residential area in the community. The rise and fall of business activity usually curtails his income but seldom forces him to move from his job or to another community. He is, in fact, one of the most stable workers, occupationally, of any group in the community. He has high prestige and is widely sought as a leader in community organizations. He takes pride in the fact that his child is getting every educational and social opportunity that is available to the home or the community. His child is healthy and likes all kinds of outdoor sports. His boy or girl looks forward to college, makes a good record, and graduates as he did. He watches his boy get established in a profession (or his girl marry a "good" professional man). He comes to know with finality, as he always really knew, that ability, hard work, and careful managing are responsible for individual success. He and his son unually vote Republican. Toward the end of his life, he looks back on a long career and a healthy life, satisfied that his contribution to society was substantial and that the future is safe in the hands of men like his son.

Proprietors, Managers, or Officials

The second group is composed of merchants, business managers, farm owners and managers, manufacturers, and government officials. There is such

[58] Data on size of family secured from *Recent Social Trends in the United States*, McGraw-Hill Book Company, Inc., 1934, pp. 685-686; data on age at marriage from Joseph K. Folsom, *The Family and Democratic Society*, John Wiley and Sons, 1943, pp. 129-131; data on educational expectation from Warner, Havighurst, and Loeb, *op. cit.*, pp. 58-72.

a wide range that it is a difficult group to typify. Yet certain characteristics can be singled out as defining the "businessman." The typical businessman is a manager with all or some ownership interests in the business with which he is associated. He comes from a home where his father was either a farmer or a business proprietor. The ownership or management of property has always characterized the occupational setting. Generally, his home is rated as an upper-middle- or upper-class home in the community. His father has an education above the average (some high school) but regrets that he did not get more. He encourages the son to plan on either a professional or a business career. His son usually decides on the business career and gets two years of college education. He makes his start in business and begins moving around to find better opportunities. Within five years he has moved to three different jobs but finally secures a "good" position as a minor executive with the help of a good friend of his father's. As he nears the end of this trial work period, he marries a college-trained woman who is from an upper-middle- or upper-class home. They limit their family to one or two children. He buys his home and lives in the best residential area of the city. His parents sometimes help him by loans or gifts to get started right. He joins clubs limited to higher-status groups and takes an active part in community life. His children are encouraged to participate in carefully selected groups in the neighborhood, in the schools, in the church, and in the summer camp. As he becomes a proprietor, his father helps him to get started with a business of his own by using family connections at the bank. He takes pride in the fact that the businessmen run the community. He is usually a confident man, but so many things seem to affect business that he is subject to fears. Depressions make it very difficult for the businessman and the high rate of mortality in some businesses put proprietorship in a precarious position. However, the above average proprietor has a high community standing, property assets, insurance policies, and savings which enable him to weather most economic disturbances. All in all he can count on more years of stable work life than can any other group of workers.

After his children are married and placed in the business class of some community, he can approach later maturity with general satisfaction that he has played an active part in managing his business, his home, and his community. He is convinced that there is plenty of opportunity for anyone to do what he has done, but it takes ability and hard work. He and members of his family vote Republican. They help support the Episcopalian or Presbyterian Church. They believe that any wealth they may have accumulated is a just reward for the work they have done. As grandparents they look with pride and anticipation to the day when their estate will be passed on to their children and their grandchildren. They have learned that money is important.

Clerical and Kindred Workers

The typical clerk is a male who is a salesman, bookkeeper, or store clerk. He comes from a lower-middle-class home. His father had some high school education and was employed as a skilled or clerical worker. He encourages his son or daughter to plan on finishing high school and to secure some college or business training. His youngster does enroll in college and at considerable sacrifice to the parents is able to get a year or two of college training. For his first full-time job the son is able to secure a clerical position. He changes jobs twice within the first five years, hoping to get a better-paying job. He is proud to be a member of the white-collar group. At twenty-five or twenty-six he marries a clerk from one of the offices in town—a young woman of twenty-four from a lower-middle-class family. He receives a lower income than his father but has higher status. He lives at a minimum comfort scale of living and feels that one child is all they can afford to raise. He finds that it is very difficult to manage their budget since their needs for clothing run high. He never seems to get ahead although his work is very stable. They rent their home in a middle-class section and are looking forward to buying a house in the future. He knows there is better money in the factory, but he prefers the associations he has in the office or the freedom he has on the road. He is trying to see that his child gets a chance to go right to the top and not remain a clerk all his life. He sees to it that his child understands the importance of education and plans to get a college education. He tells his daughter that it is important to get her education if she wants to marry well.

After his child is raised and educated he continues to plug away on his job. He is satisfied that the education which he gave his boy or daughter will give him or her a better opportunity than he had.

Skilled Workers

The typical skilled artisan comes from the home of a skilled or farmer father. He is a machinist, a carpenter, a foreman, or a painter. His background is usually identified as lower middle. His father finished the eighth grade and worked as an apprentice in a machine shop until he became a skilled machinist. He encouraged his son to get a good education but is proud when the son shows interest in skilled work. He does not force him to finish high school. He arranges with a friend who is a foreman in another department at the plant to get the boy started so that he can learn the machinist's trade. The boy starts at semiskilled jobs and is moved about on various jobs to build his skills. At the end of six or seven years he is promoted to a skilled job, where he remains most of his working life. At twenty-five years of age he marries a girl from a foreman's family. They have two children. They feel that they are quite fortunate. They have a steady job

which pays well and they are respected in their neighborhood. They have started to buy their home, a substantial house in a good working-class neighborhood.

They encourage their children to make the most of their educational opportunities. At home the children hear a good deal about the problems of labor and the importance of strong organization to protect the skilled worker against hard times. The children learn that skilled workers are the aristocracy of labor, an abler, better-organized group of workers who play a strong part in the political elections and mostly vote Democrat. After the children are married and the boy is established in a good trade, the skilled worker continues to take pride in the achievements which his skill makes possible. Under his hands new construction and new machinery are built. In war he likes to hear himself called a soldier of production. He feels that as long as he has a strong union back of him he has a security that he needs.

Semiskilled Workers

The number of semiskilled workers has grown with the mechanization of industry. A typical semiskilled worker is a male who operates a semi-automatic machine tool, drives a truck, or is an apprentice tradesman. He begins his working career on the farm or on the manual labor level and remains there all the rest of his life. He comes from a lower-middle-class home. His father was a farmer or skilled worker with average education, but the children did not like school too well and dropped out before finishing high school. The boy got his first job as a truck driver. He got tired of that after one year and went into the factory as a drill press operator. At twenty-five years of age he married a girl who lived in his neighborhood. They have had a rather difficult life. They have never had an income which permitted more than a minimum comfort level. They have two children and there has been more than an average amount of sickness. The doctor bills have always kept them nearly broke. They rent their house. They have thought of buying but their income is so uncertain they are afraid to undertake it. A layoff or unemployment can come any time.

They try to give their children the best they can but there are a lot of things the family simply cannot afford. They live in an old house and drive a second-hand automobile. Their children associate with some rowdies in the neighborhood but there is not very much they can do about it. They breathe a sigh of relief as well as regret as their children marry and start out on their own. Release from the financial burden of the children comes just in time because there is talk of giving men past fifty their quit slips. The semiskilled worker sees a strong union as his only hope of security. He votes Democratic because that party, he believes, gives labor more support. He says there is little hope for decent wages and working conditions unless labor sticks together and fights for its rights.

Unskilled Workers

The unskilled workers are the largest occupational group and include factory and farm laborers, domestic and personal service workers. The women predominate in domestic service but males are in the overwhelming majority in other types of unskilled labor. The typical unskilled worker comes from the home of skilled and semiskilled workers. His father received an eighth-grade education and became an apprentice on the semiskilled job. The son completes grammar school and receives a year of high school. He starts to work at fifteen years of age as an unskilled laborer. At twenty-three or twenty-four years of age he marries a girl twenty-two years old. They go to live in a rented house in the poorest residential section of the city. They have three children but their income is not sufficient to support them at the American Standard of Living. They have a great deal of sickness and are often in debt. They are not able to do much for the children except to keep them fed and clothed and get them to school. The children work at odd jobs whenever they can find anything to do. The father and mother will both work when the children can be left alone. Neither can find a job which they can hold for long. When layoffs and unemployment come the family draws on unemployment insurance as long as it can. When they have exhausted their insurance they go on relief. They cannot seem to get ahead. A good home, a new auto, or a substantial savings account is out of their reach. They feel that they are doing well if they keep their health and get along without going into debt. They believe something has to be done in this country to help the little fellow more.

THE OCCUPATIONAL CHAIN

A chain of cause-and-effect relationships is suggested by the stratified conditions that have been described. The social and economic status of the family associated particularly with the occupation, education, and income of the chief breadwinner exerts a strong and decisive effect upon the habits and attitudes and subsequent life patterns of its members. The links in the chain of cause and effect appear as follows:

1. The first job, obtained by and through the help of friends or relatives, dependent largely on the background, place of residence, occupation, and connections of the father.
2. Discovery of a "regular" occupation and the attainment of an occupational level at approximately that of the father, which somehow fixes the type of employment followed throughout the working life though not the specific jobs obtained.
3. The range of income associated with the employment secured on the occupational level attained.
4. The scale of living for self and family permitted by the occupational income received.

5. The place of residence and type of living permitted or encouraged by the occupation followed and the income received.
6. The consequent status or degree of prestige accorded by society to workers in this occupational level and living on this particular plane of well-being.
7. The degree of social and political influence wielded by the worker and his family.
8. The reflex effect of this status on the worker and his family, resulting in family attitude and conduct.
9. The consequent degree of health and personal and cultural attainments of the family, and their influence on the children.
10. As the cycle is renewed in the oncoming generation, the incentives, schooling, occupational training, and personal equipment of the children for competition in the industrial world and for the consumption of goods and services.[59]

THE SOCIAL BACKGROUND OF THE STABLE WORK PERIOD

Walter Pitkin has made a national slogan with his book *Life Begins at Forty*. Though a significant section of life is still to be lived after forty years of age, there is more reason to believe that the main outline of a person's life is fairly well drawn by forty or earlier. Indeed, if one is talking about occupational life, the probability of entering a given occupational level can be predicted for a worker with some degree of accuracy as soon as the father's occupation, income, and education are known. Even the first part-time jobs of the initial work period show a low but significant relationship with the regular occupation the worker will come to pursue. These relationships derive from uniformities that grow out of social background and do not take into account individual attributes, native ability, and historical circumstance. It takes some time for all of these influences to be tested out in the career of the worker. How long does it take? What stabilizing forces surround him as he grows in age and work experience?

By the time a man or woman is thirty or thirty-five years of age it is expected that the trial work period is about over and that the regular occupation has been entered. People say, "He should be pretty well set by now." This does not mean as he enters the stable work period that no further horizontal or vertical mobility will occur. Rather it implies a slowing down, a growing gravitation, a fixity within a given occupation and a given work plant. It was for this reason that in seeking an index of occupational stability and security we defined trial jobs as those held less than three years, whereas stable jobs were called those on which the worker spent three years or more. In Figures 116 and 117 the trial jobs and the stable jobs of the modal career patterns of workers in the Ohio sample were shown. Professionals, proprie-

[59] Dewey Anderson and Percy E. Davidson, *Ballots and the Democratic Class Struggle*, Stanford University Press, 1943, pp. 88-89.

tors, managers, clerical, and skilled workers were shown to have trial work periods of from 4.0 years to 6.2 years and then for each of them a long stable work period. For the semiskilled and unskilled laborer, the career pattern is characterized by a sequence of many trial jobs interspersed with an average of one stable job. For domestic service workers occupational stability does not usually occur at all. These patterns, it must be remembered, represent the typical job sequences for workers active now in the various occupational groups and not those who have completed their careers. Although occupational stability is not associated with all occupational levels or individual workers in equal measure, nonetheless certain stabilizing forces come to surround most workers and press them toward more stable career patterns.

FORCES STABILIZING CAREERS

1. Realization or Rationalization of the Trial Period Goal

During the trial period the worker has been looking for a job he likes— that is to say, a job which fits his interests, his ideas about good working conditions, and his wishes for recognition and security. As he changes jobs he usually comes closer to "what he wants." This ordinarily means that he has gotten started in the occupation he wishes to pursue and has found an acceptable company or work plant in which to work. It does not necessarily mean that ambition is now satisfied. Far from it. New needs give rise to new goals. Strivings for more prestige, more money, or more authority may serve as a driving motivation quickening the pace of life rather than diminishing it. But what is important in understanding the significance of the stable work period is the fact that the goals of the trial period do come to complete or partial fulfillment, and when this happens the rather frenzied mobility of the trial period is dampened.

Not all reach the goal they had earlier nourished in imagination and hope. But many of these persons defend their failure to attain the higher ranks and accept a more limited goal. The three mental adjustments described in the preceding chapter are common alternate modes of reaction. Some accept their achievements with tolerance, others defend their egos by rationalization and substitution, and still others relieve their frustrated feelings by projection of the blame upon other persons. Whatever the reaction, it is apparent that many make their peace (on their own reservations) with the work position they have attained. The reason for this is that other pressures have come to act upon them. Among these job seniority looms large.

2. Seniority

As a worker acquires seniority, he stores up advantages over his fellow workers. Sometimes these advantages are formally written out in provisions for increases in wage or salary, or security against layoffs and dismissal. At

other times they pile up as expectations in the minds of the worker's associates and in the mind of his employer. The prestige of experience displays itself in promotions, assignments to the better machines or offices, and other special privileges of many different kinds. Seniority becomes a kind of *insurance* against the risks of economic fluctuations which create unemployment in the work force. Moreover, as a worker increases his seniority within a given work position, routines often build habits which incapacitate him for further occupational movement. He becomes stamped in the habits of his work and finds his technical and emotional adaptability lessened. He "just wouldn't be happy doing anything else." If he does leave he may face the necessity of starting over in some other work plant in new duties without seniority. He may find himself engaged in competition with ambitious workers who are making their bids to attain higher work positions including his own. If you talk with him, he will tell you that "you think twice" before embarking on such hazardous occupational voyages.

3. Age

Age has a prestige which exhibits itself differently in various occupational pursuits. Young men may have unusual opportunities in a rapidly changing field of activity such as physics, aeronautics, and sociology. New enterprises —plastics, television, and prefabricated housing—may open new channels for young men and women. However, the upper levels of administration are not usually open to young men and women. Even the concept of "young" is redefined for administrative posts. A man of forty may well be described in such connection as "young." Advancing age can carry with it increasing prestige. As long as both younger and older men feel more confidence in the latter, it can be expected that older men will command respect and prestige that cannot be easily matched by younger men. Moreover, it is not uncommon to see older men and women accorded special rights and privileges. "You just don't talk to an older man like you do to a young fellow." Respect for age still survives in the culture in spite of the modern challenges of equal pay and deference for equal work. Therefore, age as a badge of experience and maturity gives certain advantages in many occupational pursuits. These advantages tend to stabilize career patterns of workers. Indeed, age acts also in a negative way to halt occupational movement. Conservatism, which often increases with age, is a psychological block which may diminish the willingness of a worker to change to a different work position and to assume new habits and risks.

4. Income

With advancing age and seniority income usually increases. Since the most common index of success in America is the pay envelope, the culminating rewards of ability, seniority, age, and experience are supposedly meas-

urable in the dollars and cents returned. In classical economic theory the worker earns what he produces. The pay check, it is assumed, reflects, therefore, the contribution of the worker to the company. From it he can ascertain his relative worth to his employer. He is pleased to find that he is usually considered more valuable and rewarded with a larger wage or salary as he builds up service. Income advancement often provides a sense of career progress in the stable period comparable to the occupational movements of the trial work period.

5. Marriage and Family

Financial burdens as well as financial rewards hold the worker in a more fixed position. As marriage and children add to the demands upon the family income, it is no longer possible to risk long periods of looking around for a new job or to assume the expenses of moving the family and furniture to a new locality. Many workers say it doesn't pay in the long run to move even though the new job would pay more.

It is also true that the financial burden of marriage and children can sometimes be bargaining assets which open new occupational opportunities and increase income. This may happen because the employer feels that marriage and children make the worker "more stable." He is more strongly motivated and takes the "rough going" better. Moreover, there is less chance he will seek amorous adventures that will complicate his business life.

When all of these assets are capitalized there remains still another appeal that can often be translated into increased income. This is the appeal to what Willard Waller called the pathos of marriage and parenthood. Implicit in the mores of monogamy is the belief that it is a good thing to marry and have children. The struggles which such responsibilities entail evoke in us a sympathetic, pitying, approving reaction. One who does such a good thing as marrying and rearing children deserves certain privileges. From then on, he is entitled to trade upon the pathos of the marriage relation in applying for a job, asking for a raise, or seeking promotion.

Thus marriage and children can be both reward and burden. In either instance the effect is to cause the worker to remain on the job and to diminish the possibility of moving either from his job or from his community.

6. Home Ownership

Most homeowners share their pleasure or burden, as the case may be, with their banker who holds the mortgage. To put it bluntly, they are in debt, and usually this debt runs into many thousands of dollars. Each month for ten, fifteen, or twenty-five years a payment must be made to the bank. In paying for his house, the worker in most instances is buying the most expensive consumers' good he will ever purchase. This good cannot be taken with him if he wishes to move. He is therefore faced with the neces-

sity of selling his house if he wishes to accept a job in another locality. The risk of loss sometimes is a large consideration. The employer and the worker both recognize that home ownership tends to "tie you down." The employer knows he can count upon his home-owning workers to think twice before leaving their jobs for others, especially in the out-of-town market. Some will be deterred by the financial difficulties and losses that may be encountered. Others will remain because of their pride in their houses. Therefore, the question, "Does he own his home?" gives additional evidence of the probable stability of the worker on the job and in the community.

7. Friendship Ties

We have spoken of financial rewards and burdens, of incentives and deterrents that keep workers stable on a job. Another equally strong set of pressures is contained in the emotional bonds which the worker has forged with his society. His friendships represent a part of himself. First they are actively shared, and then stored in the personality as memories. Some people will tell the worker that friendships are the most important possessions of life. Some of these friendships are in the plant and some are in the community. His wife and children share equally in some of his friendships and in addition have circles of their own. Cutting each one of these friendship bonds to live and work in another community requires family surgery of a painful nature. When people say, "They won't leave Toledo because all of their friends live here," they are speaking about a major resistance to mobility.

8. Institutional Ties

Related to these friendship ties are connections with institutions and organizations. The children must be taken from their "good" school. The family is agreed that they have never been happier in any church than their community church. The Masonic lodge to which the father belongs is the best in the state. The mother has held all the chairs in the local Eastern Star. And so it goes. These ties lash the family to the community and it is only with difficulty that they may be broken.

9. Identification with Work Plant and Community

The strongest emotional weld occurs when all of the emotional ties result in identity of the worker and his family with the work plant and the community. This merger of self with society is indicated when the worker speaks of "my company," "our city," "my club," or "my church." References to these organizations in conversations or in the newspaper are matters for emotional response. Praiseworthy references fill the person with pride; critical references evoke defensive reactions. Even the climate in the region, although insufferable, may be elaborately rationalized in order to impart a tolerable character to it!

All of these stabilizing forces operate either in totality or in part. Their action explains the decline in occupational and residential mobility which is associated with the years of work life that have been called the stable work period. However, the career patterns of many workers show that those forces are matched in intensity by disruptive forces. These disruptive pressures break career patterns into insecure and unstable modes of work life especially among semiskilled and unskilled workers.

FORCES DISRUPTING CAREERS

1. Cyclical and Seasonal Unemployment

The greatest menace to stable career patterns is cyclical and seasonal unemployment. The depressed economic market hits hardest at semiskilled and unskilled workers. These are the expendables. In contrast to the employment of executives, and specialists who are carried as overhead costs, the lower occupational levels are at the mercy of the sales chart and the profit margins of their employer. Full records on unemployment are not available, but such estimates as have been made confirm the opinion that unemployment never disappears and rarely falls much below 5 percent of the labor forces.[60] This would include workers out of work for short periods when changing jobs, and workers forced into longer periods of unemployment by seasonal and depressed market conditions. It would also include another form of unemployment which often has a very disruptive effect on the worker: technological unemployment.

2. Technological Unemployment.

Technological unemployment not only removes the man from his job but also forces him to change his job. A new machine or process can eliminate the need for skills which a worker has built up in the course of a lifetime. Unless he can learn new skills he may discover that he has become unwanted. Machine methods of coal mining and cotton picking are but two examples of the technological apparatus disturbing and threatening to disturb the work of millions of workers.

3. Sickness and Physical Disability

Sickness and accident are two additional perils to career patterns. Sickness can sap vitality and destroy initiative. Accidents can bring disability totally or in part. These misfortunes may injure the possibilities for a white-collar worker. A manual worker may be so incapacitated as to be unable to return to work. Unable to stand, unable to lift, or unable to keep up with his machine, he may have to shift to quite different work—if such work is available.

[60] J. Frederic Dewhurst and associates, *America's Needs and Resources*, The Twentieth Century Fund, 1947, p. 550.

4. Divorce

When the family is broken by divorce, the social and institutional ties of the worker are changed. Some of his former friends may blame him for his part in disrupting the marriage. As a consequence, he may seek to avoid them and even some of his associates. He may feel young and fancy-free again and desirous of building a new life for himself. In such a mood, the worker may wish to change his occupation or his community or perhaps both. He is potentially an unstable worker; at best, a less stable worker.

5. Chance Risks of Life

There are such risks of life as fire, theft, flood, tornado, implication in crime, war, business failure, and death of friends and relatives that can markedly change the social world of the individual. These risks must always be reckoned with in analyzing certain career patterns. They shake up the personal habits and attitudes of the worker and change his established ways of living. The fact of risks gives the lie to the belief that all men and women are free to choose and can guide their lives on whatever course they may wish. Many careers seem to have followed sets of changing pressures which have caused them to move more like bobbing corks than like well-directed vessels.

THE STABLE WORK LIFE IN PERSPECTIVE

The stable work period can be understood now as a social and cultural experience. Some social forces tend to anchor the individual to a given job and to a given work plant; others act like cross currents to jeopardize occupational stability and security. All workers as they enter into mid-work life are exposed to these forces and counterforces. Some emerge with lifelong histories of stability and security; others are caught in the disruptive forces and have work histories that reveal high occupational and residential mobility. Yet whatever may be the history of a given career there is a common set of cultural expectations and experiences which mark off the stable work period. These uniformities constitute the setting for the social psychological adjustments of the stable work period.

SOME IMPORTANT SOCIAL ADJUSTMENTS OF THE STABLE WORK PERIOD

REDEFINITION OF OCCUPATIONAL GOALS

When the worker has a job in the occupational classification which he hoped to attain it does not follow that his ambition has been satisfied. On the contrary, he will find that higher levels of income, status, and authority

beckon him to set up new goals. If he does not seek to better himself he is regarded as somewhat queer by both his employer and his associates. It is not human nature, they say, for a man to be satisfied when he could get so much more if he were willing to go after it. The cultural compulsion, being what it is, impels the worker toward new goals. He sets up alternate levels of aspiration. In general, his top level corresponds to the highest level of income and status which he can gain and still perform work which "interests" him. His lowest level is the maintenance of his present position, but with an aspiration toward the highest income level which he can attain. Neither of these aspirations can be held without effort. The press of ambitious newcomers from below and the demands and whims of bosses from above often act like a whipsaw on his emotions, filling him with frustration and anxiety. Sometimes he reflects with disillusionment upon the stable work period. He expected a kind of tranquil existence free from the strains that attended the trial period. Instead, the stable period is full of personal problems, some of them more demanding and more burdensome than any yet encountered. One of these problems is getting ahead and the common frustration of waiting.

THE FRUSTRATION OF WAITING

Competence, experience, and ability are not the only criteria for advancement. Equally necessary is the "opening." The "opening" is created when another worker is promoted, transferred, retired, dismissed, or overtaken by death. Sometimes these happenings do not occur within a given work situation for many years. Even when the opening is available it may not be filled if formal requirements which have been set up are not met. An example is the requirement of service. One university has set the following normal service minima for advancement up the academic ladder.

Rank	Wait
Professor	
Associate professor	6 years
Assistant professor	6 years
Instructor	3 years

An instructor waits three years before promotion to assistant professor. The assistant and associate professorships each require six-year waits before the coveted professorship is available.[61]

In business, formal requirements are not usually set. The waiting period is therefore often shorter for a given job. The employer says the wait depends on the man, not the job. However, the average length of time re-

---

[61] These waits are verified in actual university practice in Indiana University. See A. B. Hollingshead, "Climbing the Academic Ladder," *American Sociological Review*, June, 1940, pp. 384-394.

quired for promotion may be even longer where formal requirements are
lacking. In such work plants it is understood that promotion is not automatic or to be expected after any specified number of years. When promotion depends on the appearance of an opening the worker often feels
frustrated. He is aware of his ability to handle the more important job,
even before his employer concedes that he has the ability, but is faced with
the fact that he must continue to wait. He is thus denied an opportunity to
utilize his highest abilities and receive the rewards which he feels could be
his. Many of his fellow workers find themselves "caught" in the same way.
They tell one another that the "only way to get ahead is to quit and move
to another company." Many make such moves but others feel hesitant
about taking the leap. They say it would mean selling their houses and
moving their furniture. The children would have to be pulled out of school
and everyone in the family would have to cut his community ties. Anyway,
the other company has a reputation for driving its men and the president
is a hatchet man when it comes to trimming budgets. Moreover, if they
stay with their present employer they may get their promotion before too
long. All of them agree it is a problem to know what to do. It is irritating
just to have to *wait*.

FRUSTRATION INDUCED WHEN ABILITY EXCEEDS JOB SPECIFICATIONS

The frustration of waiting is heightened for a worker when his ability
exceeds the job specifications. Ordinarily, the worker finds the job doesn't
require what he believes is his full ability. Often he can be heard to say
that anybody with a grammar school education could handle his job. A
manual worker may put it more simply: "All you need for the job are strong
legs and a strong back." Arthur W. Kornhauser has suggested that

With respect to the problem of full utilization of abilities, certain interesting
psychological speculations grow out of the apparent facts concerning intellectual
qualifications for work. Intelligence is believed to be distributed through the
population in a manner approximately represented by the bell-shaped normal
probability curve. There is considerable reason to assume, on the other hand,
that the *requirements* for intelligence through the world of occupations conform
more nearly to the traditional job "pyramid"—i.e., that the great mass of jobs
are at low levels demanding little intelligence and that fewer and fewer jobs
occur as the higher levels requiring greater intelligence are reached. If this difference does exist between the distribution of intelligence and the distribution of
the occupational requirements and opportunities for the use of intelligence, it
follows that large numbers of people are forced to work at a level below that for
which they are intellectually equipped. On the assumption that this discrepancy
does exist, it may account for much industrial discontent of a continuing
character.[62]

[62] Arthur W. Kornhauser, *op. cit.*, p. 229.

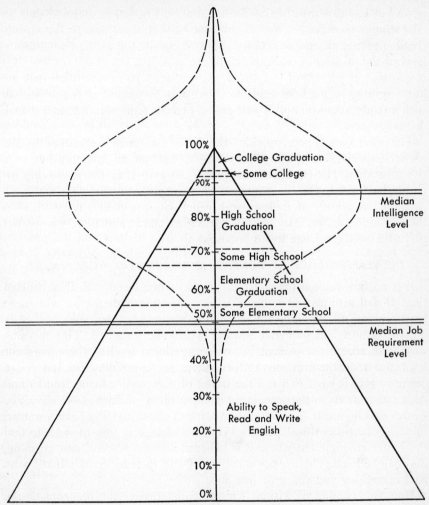

100%
— College Graduation
—Some College
90%

Median
Intelligence
Level

80% High School
Graduation

70% Some High School

Elementary School
60% Graduation

50% Some Elementary School

Median Job
Requirement
Level

40%

30%
Ability to Speak,
Read and Write
20% English

10%

0%

Fig. 118. The Job Requirements for Intelligence (Shown in Job Pyramid) Compared with the Distribution of Intelligence (Shown in the Bell-Shaped Normal Probability Curves). (Adapted from data on minimum of educational specifications of employers in hiring for 2216 occupations in eighteen industries, from Howard M. Bell, *Matching Youth and Jobs*, American Council on Education, 1940, p. 56.)

In Figure 118 this disparity between occupational requirements and native ability is illustrated. The pyramid of job requirements is constructed with the use of data gathered by the American Council on Education specifying the minimum educational requirements for 2216 occupations. Although the sample covers directly only about 28 percent of the gainfully employed population, it is believed to be representative of roughly 70 percent of all American workers. The median job requirement level is seen to

make but low demands for intellectual ability. Employers specified that no education was necessary for roughly one-half of their jobs if the worker could speak, read, and write English. In contrast, the median intelligence level of the population indicates ability to graduate from high school. This means that 50 percent of the American population could potentially assume jobs requiring high school graduation but only 20 percent of the jobs make such a requirement on ability and only 9 percent require college attendance or graduation.

The discrepancy here provides the basis for much frustration in the worker, especially in the highly routinized work of an assembly line or a clerical system. His frustration may not even stop after the promotion for which he waited. On the contrary, he may discover that the new work position has a body of routine work which challenges him no more than the previous position. His reward is a higher status and more money but no really large challenge to his potential ability.

THE REAPPEARANCE OF CONFLICT OVER LIFE AND WORK VALUES

It is not uncommon for the stable worker when faced with these frustrations to fall into a conflict between two opposing wishes. One wish is to keep pressing on, climbing toward the higher occupational goals and reaping the honors and monetary rewards which are promised. The opposing wish is to accept the present job or occupational level as the permanent level and to extinguish any further desire for climbing. The latter is a desire to take it easy, to avoid the welter of competitive living, and to find daily satisfactions in the acceptance of a personally defined *status quo*. The worker says he wants "a chance to do some of the things I've always wanted to do." Sometimes this desire gives rise to a change in jobs in order to find the better environment where it is believed a more peaceful and satisfying life may be lived. The worker tells himself and then his friends that "work isn't everything and you only live once."

How this conflict of wishes is resolved determines the *life plan* of the individual. Karl Mannheim considered the life plan as a form of self-rationalization, a mode of conduct by which behavior is guided by principles and directed toward personal goals. A life plan involves control over and regulation of personal impulses—the repression to a certain degree of immediate satisfaction of the impulses and wishes for the sake of the later social use of one's spiritual energies.[63]

A life plan grows almost unconsciously out of choices permitted by the cultural values. It is a fact of our culture that many values are mutually contradictory. To follow one value is to deny the other, yet both will continue to bear down upon the individual and exert pressure upon him. In our culture, for example, there is a demand that a man keep working and

[63] Karl Mannheim, *Man and Society in an Age of Reconstruction*, Kegan Paul, French, Trubner, and Company, Ltd., 1940, pp. 56, 104 n.

striving until he dies or retires. His employer and his associates tell him: "A man must keep driving himself at his work if he expects to get ahead. A man must work hard even to maintain his position. Any man can be replaced and it should be kept in mind that there are young men who are eager for advancement." "A man must keep producing more and more. You can't afford to slip now. If you lose out, you may never be able to secure as good a job. Perhaps there will be no job at all for you. Remember, many companies will not hire men over forty-five years of age."

In contrast, his family, his friends, and perhaps even his employer say to the worker: "You should learn to relax. No man should kill himself on the job. You should spend more time with your wife and children. You should get more exercise and recreation. You should participate in the community more."

The stable worker's dilemma can now be understood as these contradictions in cultural values induce personal conflicts. The life plan of any individual must grow out of some kind of orientation to these values. The contemporary worker is seldom able to completely insulate himself against the competitive pressures in which his work position is set. It has been said that the industrial revolution gave modern man the option of having more leisure, more babies, or a higher standard of living. He "chose" the latter and thereby committed himself to the pressures of competitive work, which often forces him to bear a freight of anxieties and misgivings.

ADDITIONAL STRAINS OF THE STABLE WORK PERIOD

A myriad of additional strains grow about the role which the stable worker is expected to play. He wants to have a good time and forget about his worries but he is told he must act his age and remember that he is setting an example for his children or the younger workers.

He wants to help the younger men and women along but he feels that he must protect his skills or these energetic "youngsters" will be in a position to push him out. He is told that he should be loyal to the company but his associates call him a "red apple" boy who is trying to push himself ahead at their expense. Fortunately, the stable worker has resources to pit against all of the anxieties and strains which beset him. Among these resources is a relative security of status and a set of interests and values ground out of life experiences. As he grows older he becomes increasingly able to withdraw from the status strivings of his younger days. Increasingly he is able to find inner satisfactions and is more comfortable alone with himself. E. K. Strong has charted the change of interests with age.

CHANGE OF INTERESTS WITH AGE

Strong studied 2340 men, most of whom were in professional and business occupations. The ages of his respondents ranged from twenty-five to fifty-five years. Each respondent was given the Strong Vocational Interest

TABLE 52.   Changes in Interests Between Ages Twenty-five and Fifty-five
Increases in liking for activities pursued alone or with few persons

	Critical Ratio[a]
Reading a book vs. going to a movie	5.2
Bible study	4.3
Reading *National Geographic Magazine*	4.4
Observing birds	4.9
Art galleries	5.3
Museums	3.8
Cabinetmaking	2.9

Decline in liking for and interest in physical activity	C.R.	*Decline in liking for change*	C.R.
Hunting	5.2	Dislike of changing actions	8.2
Tennis	5.9	Work in one place rather than change	5.8
Climbing along the edge of a precipice	6.5	Dislike of opportunity for promotion	6.7
Aviation	9.1	Methodical work	4.6
Reading sport pages	9.4	Playing safe vs. taking a chance	3.5
Driving an automobile	5.9		

Decline in liking for competitive or rivalry relations	C.R.	*Decline in liking work with mechanical objects*	C.R.
Being pitted against another	8.0	Making a radio set	4.8
Arguments	3.7	Repairing a technical wiring	4.4
Bargaining	2.7	Adjusting carburetor	4.7

Decline in liking for the company of many persons especially as it requires preparation and ritual	C.R.	*Decline in liking card games*	C.R.
Full-dress affairs	5.3	Poker	5.7
Entertaining others	2.3	Bridge	9.6
Nights spent away from home vs. nights spent at home	9.3	Solitaire	2.6
Many acquaintances vs. few intimate friends	4.6		
Belonging to few societies rather than many	2.7		
Picnics	3.4		
Smokers	3.8		

[a] The critical ratio is a measure of the significance of the difference between the two proportions. A critical ratio of 3.0 indicates that such a difference as has been observed could happen less than three times in a thousand by pure chance. A ratio of 2.5 would occur about once in a hundred by chance alone. In general, a ratio of 2.5 or above can be regarded as indicating a significant difference. All critical ratios apply to the differences observed between twenty-five and fifty-five years.

Blank, which had 420 items. The researcher concluded that change in interest does not take place uniformly from twenty-five to fifty-five. Fifty percent of the total change occurs between twenty-five and thirty-five, 20 percent between thirty-five and forty-five, and 30 percent between forty-five and fifty-five. There is little or no change from fifty-five to sixty-five.[64] An inventory of significant changes in interests between ages fifty-five and twenty-five is shown in Table 52.[65]

A major change in interest is the *increase in liking for activities pursued alone or with few persons.* This is shown in the liking for reading and quiet activities like observing birds and visiting art galleries and museums. This liking is accompanied by a decline in liking for physical activity, for competitive or rivalry relations, and for the company of many persons. There is a marked decline in liking changes of almost any kind. Mechanical objects and card games seem to fall out of the range of interests.

These changes in interest come gradually between ages twenty-five and fifty-five but as Strong points out they do not take place uniformly. They indicate effects of aging as seen in the changes in liking for physical activity. The growth of *conservatism* can be inferred from the many resistances to change.

FAMILY ADJUSTMENTS DURING THE STABLE WORK PERIOD

The stable worker is generally married and a parent. His home is an economic and social base which provides him and his family with restaurant and dormitory facilities as well as intimate social contacts. The degree to which these two functions are supplied varies widely among American families. In some, the home may be little more than a dormitory which houses the worker in the short span when he is away from his work. In others, it becomes the work plant, as in the case of a professional man who uses his house as an office.

The modern family is held together largely by the affectional bond. Stripped of many earlier functions, the family is a weakened social unit. The larger society is full of pressures that threaten to disrupt the affectional bond and lessen the last ties maintaining the family. The increased tensions which arise in the family affect the worker at home and in the work plant. When problems of family life come to preoccupy him, his performance in the plant usually suffers.

However, one major responsibility of the family becomes a central point of interest binding the parents together. The children must be reared and put through school. Unless the family income is large this requires some planning and sacrifice.

[64] E. K. Strong, *Change of Interests With Age,* Stanford University Press, 1931, p. 20.
[65] Reprinted from *Change of Interests With Age,* by Edward K. Strong, with the permission of the author and of the publishers, Stanford University Press.

In a family built about the affectional, recreational, and educational needs of its members, an emotional stability can be imparted to each member. This kind of stability can give the worker a great advantage in his quest for a happy and satisfying work life.

IDENTIFICATION WITH THE COMMUNITY AND SOCIETY

The stable work period is a time of social participation in the affairs of the community and society. Now, if ever, the worker comes to his greatest stature in his role as citizen.[66]

As he becomes recognized as a stable member of the community, more and more invitations to participate in the clubs and institutions of the community come to him. The encouragement of his children in school and in church requires his attention and perhaps participation in community organizations. A transfer of values takes place such that new motivation and aspirations are discovered. Perhaps he sees the emergent patterns of morality as a threat to his own marriage. As a parent he comes to see them as a threat to his conceptions of conduct for his children. The free thinking of younger days is turned into the conservative thought of tradition.[67] And as always in dynamic societies the parents become "old fogeys" in the eyes of their children—much to their own surprise!

GROWTH OF POLITICAL AND ECONOMIC CONSERVATISM

The conservatism in morality is matched only by a growing conservatism in political and economic belief. Murphy, Murphy, and Newcomb summarize research on age differences by concluding: "With increasing age somewhat relenting economic pressure and social competition render the average adult less sensitive to changing structures of society, so that less attitudinal adaptation takes place. Those in whom the fewest changes occur are, other things being equal, those upon whom changing structures impinge least urgently."[68]

This reluctance to sponsor change showed up in Strong's study, which revealed the strong dislike of those activities directly affecting changes in the habits of individuals as well as dislike for those persons who represent changes.[69] These conservative tendencies can be seen in voting behavior. In Table 53 the Republican voting preferences for the ten-year period 1936-1946 are shown. The Republican party is regarded as a conservative

[66] Lazarsfeld found that on each educational level older people were more interested in the political election of 1940 than younger people. Paul F. Lazarsfeld, Bernard Berelson, and Hazel Gaudet, *The People's Choice*, Duell, Sloan and Pearce, 1944, p. 44.

[67] Between the ages of seventeen and thirty there is a steady *decrease* in favorable attitude toward the church. Both fathers and mothers *increase* steadily in *favorable* attitude with advancing age. See Murphy, Murphy, and Newcomb, *op. cit.*, p. 921.

[68] *Ibid.*, p. 929.

[69] Strong, *op. cit.*, p. 74.

party and as such it commands greater votes from the population as age advances. It should be noted, however, that a *majority* of older persons as well as a *majority* of younger persons voted Democratic. The difference in conservatism is a matter of degree better understood as individual differences than contrasting group differences.[70]

TABLE 53. The Republican Party Preference by Age Groups, 1935-1946 as Shown by Surveys Made by the American Institute of Public Opinion[71]

Ages	1936[a]	1940[a]	1944[a]	1946[b]
21-29	32%	40%	38%	35%
30-49	35%	44%	49%	45%
50 and over	44%	49%	53%	51%

[a] Adapted from an analysis of American Institute of Public Opinion Surveys made by Eduard G. Benson and Evelyn Wicoff, "Voters Pick Their Party," *The Public Opinion Quarterly*, Summer, 1944, p. 169.
[b] The 1946 survey question was, "If a presidential election were being held today, which party would you vote for—the Democratic or Republican?" (Jan. and Feb., 1946, AIPO). See "The Quarter's Polls," *The Public Opinion Quarterly*, Spring, 1946, p. 132. The age group 15-88 years preferred the Democratic party with a 65% vote, the Republican party by a 35% vote.

AGING

The stable worker must face the fact of physical and mental decline as his age advances. Strength and skill grow with the organism to a peak in the twenties, and then move into a slow decline. However, the demands of everyday life are usually sufficiently within the limits of the decline to make it of relatively slight practical importance until well into the older ages. Susceptibility to illness and death vary with the years but there is evidence of the rise and the slow fall of the organism's vitality. Fortunately there is much evidence that mortality and morbidity may be lessened.[72]

Mental ability grows rapidly during childhood and adolescence reaching a peak between eighteen and twenty-one. Then a gradual decline sets in which continues until age fifty-five. The averages for the older ages are not strikingly lower. Ability to learn, as shown by tests of learning in actual situations, has a similar growth and then slow decline.

These facts do not imply that one's knowledge or understanding ceases

[70] Otto Pollak challenges the assumption that old people are more conservative than young on the same grounds. "A comparison of attitudes of people below and above the forties shows that more persons in the older groups are conservative. However, the numerical differences are so small that where majorities of the old reject a change so do majorities of the young. There seems to be no social conflict between old conservatives and young progressives in terms of large population groups opposing each other." "Conservatism in Later Maturity and Old Age," *American Sociological Review*, April, 1943, p. 175.
[71] AIPO survey results are based on the question, "Which party do you want to see win the presidential election this fall—the Republican or the Democratic?"
[72] Sidney L. Pressey, J. Elliott Janney, and Raymond G. Kuhlen, *Life: A Psychological Survey*, Harper & Brothers, 1939, pp. 125-160.

to grow after twenty-one, but rather that the *capacity* to learn no longer increases after that time. A person continues to learn but not more quickly. The accumulation of knowledge and experience and the maturing of judgment may continue. The maximum productivity of authors, inventors, and scientists is reached in the thirties if judged by books published. Some studies place the average age of the "master work" in the late forties. Leaders in business and politics are usually over fifty.

However, tests and records of accomplishment indicate a definite decline after sixty. Whether it be physical vitality or mental alertness, the range of individual differences is shown to be very great.[73] Certainly in mental alertness or eagerness to learn a man of sixty may be superior to the young man. However, the weight of the averages is to make such cases exceptions rather than typical. Finally the stable worker must bow out of active work life. If death does not intervene he will begin to talk about retirement. In many work plants retirement is mandatory at some fixed age. Increasingly, with the extension of private and public plans of retirement annuities, financial security for later maturity has been or is being provided. The life and problems of the retired worker are our next concern.

SUPPLEMENTARY STUDIES

FIELD: PLANNED INTERVIEWS

Make one or more interviews of adult men and women in the stable work period. The best time for interviewing is during the age period fifty-five to sixty-five years of age although interviews during the period of thirty-five to sixty-five years of age are appropriate. For a comparative analysis it is very desirable to seek interviews with adults from lower-, middle-, and upper-class families. The interview form suggested for interviewing in the trial work period, Chapter XVIII, is applicable to the stable work period.

LIBRARY: NOVELS

The following novels reveal attitudes and habits of work and other social traits as indoctrinated in different social classes.

Churchill, Winston, *A Far Country* (story of a corporation lawyer, a man who "sells his intellect" to get along in the world)

Dreiser, Theodore, *The Financier* (the rise of a bank clerk to a successful note broker)

Halper, Albert, *The Foundry* (realistic picture of all classes and individuals working in a foundry)

Halper, Albert, *The Little People* (depicts the lives of the employees of a huge department store)

Lewis, Sinclair, *Babbitt* (life of a real estate operator in a small city)

[73] *Ibid.*, pp. 161-219.

Lewis, Sinclair, *Main Street* (story of a doctor and his wife in a small town in Minnesota)

Marquand, John P., *The Late George Apley, Wickford Point, So Little Time,* and *Point of No Return* (describe the behavior of the top layers of New England society)

Sinclair, Upton, *The Jungle* (the story of a young Lithuanian who comes as a workingman with his family to America where he goes to work in the meat-packing industry of Chicago)

Walker, Charles R., *Bread and Fire* (excellent sociological novel of steel mills and labor conditions in steel towns)

Wolff, Maritta, *Night Shift* (a picture of work life in a small factory town in wartime; naturalistic treatment of boarding house, restaurant, hospital, factory, night club)

LIBRARY: RESEARCH REPORTS

Centers, Richard, *The Psychology of Social Classes*, Princeton University Press, 1949, chap. 10, "Sociological and Psychological Correlates of Class Consciousness: The Problem of Determinants," pp. 160-190.

Cottrell, W. Fred, *The Railroader*, Stanford University Press, 1939.

Donovan, Francis R., *The Woman Who Waits*, R. G. Badger, 1920.

Donovan, Francis R., *The Saleslady*, University of Chicago Press, 1929.

Donovan, Francis R., *The School Ma'am*, Stokes and Company, 1938.

Dreyfuss, Carl, *Occupations and Ideology of the Salaried Employees*, translated by Eva Abranovich, W.P.A. and Social Science Division of Columbia University, 1938.

Lastrucci, Carlo L., "The Status and Significance of Occupational Research," *American Sociological Review*, February, 1946, pp. 78-84.

Tunis, John R., *Was College Worth While?* Harcourt, Brace and Company, 1936.

Williams, Whiting, *What's on the Worker's Mind*, Charles Scribner's Sons, 1920.

Wilson, Logan, *The Academic Man*, Oxford University Press, 1942.

RESEARCH GAPS

1. Occupational and social adjustment of
   - a. Professional workers.
   - b. Managerial workers and proprietors.
   - c. Clerical workers.
   - d. Skilled workers.
   - e. Semiskilled workers.
   - f. Unskilled workers.
2. Long-ladder occupational careers.
3. Short-ladder occupational careers.
4. Forces which have disrupted careers.
5. Strains of family adjustments which affect work adjustment.
6. Degree and extent of waiting required for advancement.
7. Sociological factors in downward mobility.
8. Occupational and social adjustments of unstable careers.

CHAPTER XX

The Retired Work Period

THE CRISIS OF RETIREMENT

The worker must sooner or later face the fact that he is growing old. An early signal is the sensing of a decline in energy reserve. As a person grows older he becomes aware of the danger of leaving some things to other years. There is a recognition that he is slipping and that his preroga-

tives are being invaded by younger and more vigorous men.[1] Finally, unless he must be carried out to die, he comes to retirement from active work life. Retirement marks another crucial transition of status in the life history of the individual. Just as many years earlier there were large adjustments to be made in the transition to the trial work period, to marriage, and to parenthood, so now another crisis of life impends. In many cultures these crises tend to be the focus for ritual activities which have been called *rites-de-passage*. The importance of occupational status in our own society is so

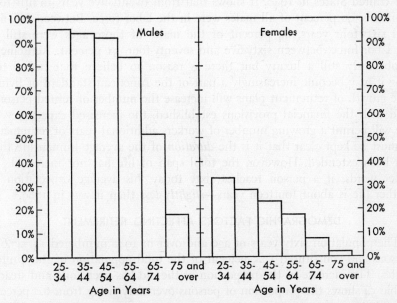

FIG. 119. Percentage of Males and Females Twenty-Five Years and Over in the Labor Force for the United States, 1940. (Adapted from *Sixteenth Census of the United States: 1940*, Vol. III, *The Labor Force*, Summary, p. 5.)

great that the severance of occupational connections certainly constitutes a transition of critical significance and is in many ways analogous to other major crises of life.

WHEN DOES RETIREMENT BEGIN?

The question of when retirement begins can be answered in many different ways. For the bulk of American workers there is no retirement. They either die on the job or suffer physical breakdown and are forced home to die. However, this picture is changing. With the inauguration and extension of the social security program a certain amount of old-age security has

[1] L. G. Lowrey, "Adjustment over the Life Span," in George Lawton, *New Goals for Old Age*, Columbia University Press, 1943, p. 9.

been placed under millions of workers who may draw upon their accumulated reserve at age sixty-five. Indeed, it has become customary to think of
retirement as beginning at the age sixty-five. It is to be expected that more
and more persons will retire (or be forced to retire) by that age. However,
such was not true in 1940 when the United States Census was taken. At
that time 51 percent of all males between the ages of sixty-five and seventy-
four were reported as gainfully employed. Figure 119 is a report of the
percentage of gainful workers among males and females of different ages in
the United States in 1940. It shows that from twenty-five years to fifty-four
years over 90 percent of all males were in the labor force. Between fifty-five
and sixty-four years, 84 percent of the males of those ages were still in
the labor force; between sixty-five and seventy-four, 51 percent. Retirement
is obviously still a luxury but there is reason to believe that before too
long it may become increasingly a part of the American standard of living.
The growth of retirement plans will increase the number of retired persons.
And with the financial provisions established, the increased expectancy of
life will permit a growing number of workers additional years of retirement.
It must be kept clear that it is the *duration* of the average human life that
has been extended. However, the total span of life has not increased. In
other words, if a person reaches sixty today, his average expectation of
further life is about fourteen years—*slightly less* than it was in 1789.[2]

DEMOGRAPHIC FACTORS AFFECTING RETIREMENT

The population sixty years of age and over in 1940 numbered 13,747,654
persons and constituted 10.5 percent of the total population of the United
States. The increase in the proportion of the old has been long and steady.
Table 54 shows the proportion of persons over sixty rising from 6.0 percent
in 1890 to 10.5 percent in 1940.

TABLE 54.   Increase in the Percentage of the Population That Is Sixty Years and Over[3]

Years	1890	1900	1910	1920	1930	1940
Percentage	6.0	6.4	6.6	7.4	8.5	10.5

A more extended analysis shows that in 1850, 2.6 percent of the population of the United States was sixty-five years of age and over; a steady increase brought the percentage to 6.5 in 1940. A projection into the future
shows that in 1980, 14.4 percent of the population will be sixty-five years
of age and over.[4]

[2] Joseph K. Folsom, *The Family and Democratic Society*, John Wiley and Sons, 1943,
p. 160.
[3] *Sixteenth Census of the United States. Population*, United States Government
Printing Office, 1943, Part I, p. 2.
[4] Louis I. Dublin, "Statistical and Social Implication in the Problem of Our Aging
Population," *Diplomatic*, October, 1941, pp. 227-237.

Death takes a heavy toll of those who survive into old age. Table 55 shows the rapidity with which the percentage of persons sixty years and over shrinks in each succeeding five-year period. Of the total population sixty years of age and over, 62 percent are in their sixties, 30 percent in their seventies, 7 percent in their eighties, and less than 1 percent in their nineties.

TABLE 55.   Percentage of the Population Sixty Years of Age and Over at Each Age Period[5]

Age	Population	Percentage
60–64	4,728,340	34.39
65–69	3,806,657	27.69
70–74	2,569,532	18.69
75–79	1,503,982	10.94
80–84	774,391	5.63
85–89	277,012	2.01
90–94	69,598	.51
95–99	14,463	.11
100 and over	3,679	.03
Total	13,747,654	100.00

Although death is an indeterminate, the average expectancy of life is a guide for assessing the average length of the retired work period. At sixty years of age the average expectancy for males is fifteen more years of life; at sixty-five years of age the average expectancy is twelve years.[6] These expectancies may be taken as the periods of social adjustment to be analyzed.

SOCIAL FACTORS AFFECTING RETIREMENT

Whatever may have been the incidence of retirement in the past, a combination of conditions now exists which will greatly increase both the number and the proportion of the population who willingly or unwillingly retire. The effect of old-age insurance provisions in the Social Security Act has already been mentioned. These and other retirement provisions, public and private, will enable millions to plan and to realize in part their plans for retirement.

Another powerful influence pressing older people into retirement is the economic competition set up in the labor force. This is being brought about by the changing nature of the country's age composition. As a result of the extension in the length of life, a marked decline in the birth rate, and a significant decrease in immigration, a large proportion within the active working years of twenty and sixty developed. Moreover, the total

[5] *Sixteenth Census of the United States. Population*, Part I, p. 3.

[6] *Statistical Abstract of the United States*, United States Government Printing Office, 1948, p. 81. The life expectancy for females at sixty years is seventeen years; at sixty-five years, 13.5 years.

number of men in the working age period twenty to sixty years increases by about 300,000 each year.[7] This means that there are more competitors for jobs. There are fewer dependent obligations per worker than ever before. For these reasons the movement toward earlier dismissal of older workers may be expected to increase. Many may find themselves in voluntary retirement well before the age of sixty. The following conclusions can be drawn from the data available on demographies and social factors affecting retirement:

1. Most workers do not retire. They either die on the job or suffer a physical breakdown on the job which leads to death.

2. There is a growing number of older persons in the population. The proportion of persons sixty-five years of age and over will more than double between 1940 and 1980.

3. Although the total span of life has not increased, the duration of the average life has been extended.

4. Increasing provision for old-age security has been made by public and private agencies.

5. Movement toward earlier dismissal of the older worker will increase.

6. The number of retired workers can be expected to increase *at an accelerating rate* for the next thirty years or more.

PERSONALITY CHANGES IN OLDER PERSONS

There are very wide differences among persons at sixty, sixty-five, or seventy. The variation in physical and mental traits is striking at the older age levels. However, progressive age changes follow patterns, many of which are well known. The decline in visual perception, hearing, motor ability, manual skill, and ability to learn new material is documented by careful experiments.[8] Many changes in attitudes have been observed chiefly by psychiatrists but have not been reduced to measurement and comparison by tests. There is rather general agreement that these changes are:

Worry over finances, attendant upon threatened retirement.
Worry over health.
Feeling unwanted, isolated, lonely.
Feeling suspicious.
Narrowing of interests, leading to introspection, increased interest in bodily sensations, and physical pleasures.
Loss of memory, especially for recent events and in the field of spontaneous recall.

[7] Elon H. Moore, "Preparation for Retirement," *Journal of Gerontology*, April, 1946, p. 203.
[8] Cf. *Social Adjustment in Old Age*, Social Science Research Council, 1946, pp. 143-144.

Mental rigidity.

Overtalkativeness, especially of the past.

Hoarding, often of trivial things.

Loss of interest in activity and increased interest in quiescence.

Feeling of inadequacy, leading to feelings of insecurity and anxiety.

Reduction of sexual activity but increased sexual interest, especially in the male; regression to earlier levels of expression.

Untidiness and uncleanliness.

Conservatism.

Inability to adjust to changed conditions.

Decreased social contacts and participation.[9]

Erich Rosenthal has prepared a digest of an account given by a Swiss psychiatrist who at the age of eighty, two months before his death, completed the description of his own experience in aging. Rosenthal writes,

At the age of 60, shortly before the outbreak of the first World War, he became really conscious of the mortal nature of human existence for the first time. He lost interest in his empirical studies and busied himself with philosophical problems. He withdrew from his family and his friends. His sleep was frequently interrupted by experiences of the past over which he felt guilty and by previous happy events of which his wishful thinking demanded a repetition. At his seventieth birthday he still enjoyed the honors shown him. In his last three years, however, he became indifferent toward praise or hostility. He also was often unable to see other people's arguments, was afraid of emotional upsets, and showed apathy for new names. He no longer was under a compulsion to write scientific articles; instead he enjoyed reading literature. He felt tired and was lazy without self reproach. He began to hate the usual recreational activities like movies, sports, and the theatre. He began to sift his correspondence and files and give things to people who might enjoy using them. Since he lived a full life he expected death quietly. After the death of his wife he felt a great need for affection. The affection of his children was not sufficient and he was sincerely grateful for any attention shown to him, wherever it might come from.[10]

THREE THEORIES ACCOUNTING FOR PERSONALITY IN OLD AGE

There are several theories to explain personality development and change in old age. The three most commonly held views may be labeled the *quantitative*, the *qualitative*, and the *regression* theories.

The quantitative view represented by Miles is that old age is a gradual decline in energy from the peak levels achieved in early maturity.[11] The

[9] *Ibid.*, pp. 144-145.

[10] Erich Rosenthal, reviewing C. Von Monakow, "Panegyrismus des Greisenalter," *Schweizer Archiv—fur Neurologie und Psychiatrie*, 1939, pp. 105-129. See *Social Adjustment in Old Age*, pp. 58-59.

[11] W. R. Miles, "Psychological Aspects of Ageing," in *Problems of Ageing*, edited by E. V. Cowdry, The Williams and Wilkins Company, 1939, p. 351.

difference between youth and age is seen to be a quantitative one. This view is useful in explaining differences in intelligence test scores which gradually decline from their peak in the late teens or early twenties.

The qualitative view conceives of old age as a reorganization or restructuralization so that youth is one kind of Gestalt or configuration and old age another. This theory is better suited to explain the feelings and attitudes of old age.[12]

A third view holds aging to be a regression to a level of personality prior to maturity. The regression is seen to go all the way back to infantile states. Regression, whether gradual or sudden in onset, is taken as a return to the individual's basic type of personality structure, "his reaction pattern."[13]

Lawton feels that more aspects of the aging personality are clarified by this third theory. He finds that the nature of personality maladjustment is the same whether in the child or the senescent. Such differences as occur are due to variations in physical, mental, and emotional capacities of the two age groups and therefore in activities and environment. He says:

The basic struggle of the late teens and early twenties, is for the boy or girl to orientate himself in an unfamiliar and unyielding world, to discover who he is and what he is good for, whom he is to love and be loved by. The theme of adolescence is exploration and goal finding. Maturity is the time of assimilation and achievement. One presumably has by that time completed the orientation process and proceeds to develop one's possibilities to the fullest and to realize the maximum from this development, maximum in terms of money, power, fame, and affection.

"Normal" old age is characterized by a constructive handling of limitations. It is the epoch when one faces the diminishment or total loss of those possessions so dearly won! Job, loved ones, friends, social prestige, health, looks. The great problem of old age is how to handle the frustration which assails one. Some of these must be accepted with as good a grace as we can muster. For other limitations we must devise substitutions which come as close to the real thing as possible.

The successful old person is one who has retained a maximum of the mental and spiritual possessions of maturity, and added to these the new insights and activities which are unique to old age. One grows out of life if he simply must, but he puts up a strong, good-natured battle every step of the way—that is the aim of "normal" senescence. The great need is to maintain one's integrity of personality, to keep the spirit independent if it is not always possible to do as much for the body or for the individual as a social unit.[14]

[12] Lawrence C. Frank, "The Ageing of the Personality," in *Social Adjustment in Old Age*, Social Science Research Council, 1946, pp. 116-117.

[13] G. V. Hamilton, "Changes in Personality and Psychosexual Phenomena with Age," in E. V. Cowdry (ed.), *op. cit.*, pp. 810-831.

[14] George Lawton, "Theories of Personality Changes in Old Age," in *Social Adjustment in Old Age*, Social Science Research Council, 1946, p. 110.

THE ROLE OF THE RETIRED WORKER

The retired worker may be fifty-five years of age or seventy-five years of age. He may be a person of great energy and intellectual alertness or an enfeebled person whose intellectual and emotional characteristics are more like those of a child. To understand the role of a specific retired worker it is necessary to know the *health* of the worker and the limitations imposed by various forms of illness and infirmity. The amount of *income* available may greatly influence the prestige, responsibility, and range of activities. His *employment status* will affect his activity. Some workers retire completely from active work life. Others work part-time or accept increasing unemployment as they grow older. Some retire voluntarily and some are forced into retirement. Whether the retired worker is a *proprietor of a household, living in the household of relatives, living in the household of nonrelatives,* or *living outside any family context* will greatly influence his role. If he is living with *recently married people, middle-aged people,* or *elderly people,* separately or all together in one household, his expectations and those of other members in the household will determine much of his conduct. Likewise, there is the question of his *relationship to the community.* Particularly in upper-income groups, we have the phenomenon of older people actually leaving the community in which they have spent their active working life and spending their retirement in resort communities. This produces a new social situation and contributes to the social isolation of the aged. The nature and continuity of community ties will condition social participation. These variables all stress the differences that may be expected in the adjustments of the retired worker. However great the differences, there are basic uniformities.

Anthropologists have found that old people have much the same wants in all societies and cultures. These may be summed up roughly as fourfold:

1. To live as long as possible, at least until life's satisfactions no longer compensate for its privations, or until the advantages of death seem to outweigh the burdens of life.
2. To remain active participants in personal and group affairs in either operational or supervisory roles—any participation, in fact, being preferable to complete idleness and indifference.
3. To safeguard or even strengthen any prerogative acquired in a long life, i.e., skills, possessions, rights, authority, prestige, and so forth.
4. To withdraw from life, when necessity requires it, as honorably as possible without too much suffering, and with maximum prospects for an attractive hereafter.[15]

[15] Leo W. Simmons, "The Position and Treatment of the Aged in Primitive and Other Societies," *American Anthropologist,* July-September, 1945, pp. 433-438. See also, by the same author, *The Role of the Aged in Primitive Society,* Yale University Press, 1945.

SOCIAL ADJUSTMENTS IN RETIREMENT

An understanding of adjustment problems of retirement requires an estimate of the personal factors influencing retirement. The preparation for retirement begins early in terms of the life pattern and should not be neglected too long for the development of attitudes, interests, and hobbies suitable for the older years of life. Forty should prepare for sixty quite as much as twenty prepares for forty. If at sixty the individual has brought forth no resources within himself, it is too late to provide them.

SHIFT FROM WORK PLANT TO HOME INTERESTS

There are a number of forces from within the individual which condition attitudes toward retirement. The specialization of industry has broken the

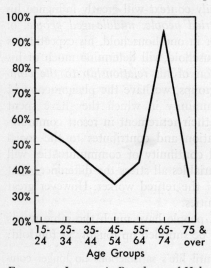

FIG. 120. Increase in Prevalence of Hobbies with Age as Shown by Percentage of Adults. (Adapted from E. S. Briggs, "How Adults in Missouri Use Their Leisure Time," *School and Society*, 1938, pp. 805-808.)

creative process of manufacture into so many small segments that the individual worker often has a relatively small part to play either in making or in providing the specialized service necessary for the final product. He cannot see how his work fits into the total organization. Still less frequently can he see or know what happens to the product or service. This denial of what Veblen called the "instinct of workmanship" often stores up frustrations. Many crave experiences denied to them in their day-to-day functioning in a limited field. Retirement offers the opportunity for following interests that bring more complete satisfactions. The increase in the prevalence of hobbies is one of the indications of the need and the release that is sought. Figure 120 shows the rising proportion of adults in the various age groups who reported a hobby in the Missouri survey of adult leisure. From the teens up to fifty years the number reported regularly decreases, but at fifty the trend is strikingly reversed until, by the decade sixty-five to seventy-four, 95 percent are so engaged. The drop thereafter could be explained on the basis of physical decline.[16]

[16] E. S. Briggs, "How Adults in Missouri Use Their Leisure Time," *School and Society*, 1938, pp. 805-808.

CHANGES IN STATUS

A second personal factor influencing attitudes toward retirement is the real or anticipated change in status which may result as the worker grows older. Some workers look forward to increases in status; other workers face the prospect of being pushed downward on the occupational ladder. W. S. Woytinsky has studied United States Census data to locate the shifts of workers as age advances. Figure 121 shows the percentage distribution of

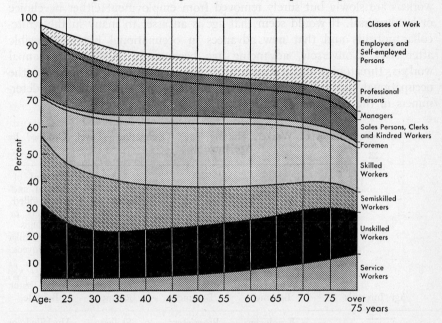

FIG. 121. Percentage Distribution of Male Workers of Different Ages in Nonagricultural Pursuits, by Class. (From W. S. Woytinsky, *Labor in the United States*, Social Science Research Council, 1938, p. 92.)

male workers of different ages in nonagricultural pursuits by classification of work in the United States for 1930. The principal significance of this figure is its indication of the probability of shifts from dependent to independent pursuits, from clerical occupations to managers, from semiskilled and unskilled labor to skilled trades, and, in the more advanced ages, from skilled labor to unskilled or service work.[17] Table 56 compiles the percentages of workers shifting their occupational level as they grow older. Columns 1, 2, and 3 show upward movements involving salary or wage earner, clerks, semiskilled and unskilled workers. Column 4 shows a downward movement of skilled and semiskilled workers to unskilled and service work. After sixty

[17] W. S. Woytinsky, *Labor in the United States*, Social Science Research Council, 1938, pp. 91-93.

years of age the most pronounced characteristics of the distribution of male workers are to be found in (1) the relatively high proportion of proprietary and professional workers and (2) the relatively high proportion of service workers (see Fig. 121). All other occupational groups show slowly declining proportions of workers after sixty years of age. This leads to the conclusion that the "business class" fares better than the "working class" when the retirement work period is entered after sixty years of age. Many proprietors and professionals continue to work; skilled, semiskilled, and finally unskilled workers are slowly but surely removed from employment either by choice or by dismissal. It would seem that age is an asset to many in the white-collar pursuits and that new advances in occupational life are possible after sixty. Conversely, advancing age becomes a liability for manual workers, threatening either dismissal or the necessity of "going down the occupational ladder." These changes in status become important determiners in the decisions of retirement.

TABLE 56. Percentages of Workers Shifting Their Occupational Level, Grouped by Age Intervals

Age Intervals	Percent of Salary or Wage Earners at 25 Years of Age Who Later Became:	Percent of Clerks or Salespersons at 25 Years of Age Who Later Became:	Percent of Unskilled laborers or Semiskilled Workers at 25 Years of Age Who Later Became:	Percent of Skilled and Semiskilled Workers or Perhaps White-Collar Employees at 35 Years of Age Who Later Became:
	Employers and Self-Employed Col. 1	Proprietors, Managers, and Officials Col. 2	Skilled Workers and Foremen Col. 3	Unskilled or Service Workers Col. 4
Before 35 years of age	8	14	15	
Before 45 years of age	10	23	19	2 to 3
Before 55 years of age	12	25	21	5 to 6
Before 65 years of age	15			10 to 12

REDUCED COMRADE RELATIONSHIPS

A third personal factor arises from the death and departure of contemporaries. This attrition in old friendships is frequently more difficult to endure than the loss of prestige or physical comforts. The effect of this social constriction may be quite different for different persons. One worker will find the work plant a lonely place without former associates and will

hasten to leave it as soon as he can. Another may find in his work the only real satisfactions of daily life and will desperately seek to cling to his work position.

REACTION TO PROBLEM OF SECURITY

A fourth factor involves the reaction of the aging person toward the problem of security during his remaining life. Security involves not only necessities but also maintenance of those items considered essential to an achieved standard of living. Persons who cannot anticipate an enjoyable life without the full budget on which they previously lived may be tied to their jobs long after they feel a desire to retire. However, those who look forward to retirement as a time of happy living with simple needs may even speed their retirement. There is always a danger that, as the time of retirement nears, the worker will delay his departure from work because his standard of living has continued to rise. The effect of inflation in reducing the purchasing power of accumulated reserves is another deterrent to retirement.

DECLINING HEALTH AND ENERGY

The health and energy available to the older worker are often of major significance in his decision to retire. In most fields of activity the normal decline which comes with the years may not prove to be of great consequence. The more important consideration is the older person's concern over his ability to continue his useful functioning at the level of competition on which he works. This concern is heightened by the recognized conditions of fatigue and marked decline in nervous energy, which produce a source of irritations. Retirement offers an escape from what is often a losing fight against a waning prestige caused by aging and competition from younger and more vigorous men. The mental and physical health of the worker often improves upon removal from areas of intense competition to activities in which differentials in prestige are of less concern.[18]

RETIREMENT ATTITUDES

Older workers may be retired (A) or not retired (a) if retirement is defined as separation from regular work at the usual occupation. Likewise, each older worker may be assumed to have a positive or negative attitude toward retirement. He either accepts the situation (B) or he does not accept it (b). If these items are considered simultaneously, four distinct groups may be identified.

[18] The writers are indebted to Elon H. Moore for his incisive analysis of forces affecting retirement. Cf. E. H. Moore, *op. cit.*, and his forthcoming book.

FOUR RETIREMENT ATTITUDE GROUPS

Group I (AB). Workers who have been separated from full-time work in their usual occupations (retired) and who either sought separation or have become reconciled to it.

Group II (Ab). Workers who have been retired but who have not accepted the situation.

Group III (aB). Workers who are still employed full-time in the usual occupation but who would retire if financial and other circumstances would permit.

Group IV (ab). Workers who are still employed and who wish to remain so, i.e., have a negative attitude toward retirement.[19]

Group I

Group I is a relatively large, heterogeneous group of workers which is rapidly growing. It includes workers who have looked forward to retirement and who made early financial preparations, and have sought separation from their work. These workers are commonly found among farmers, businessmen, and professionals, who have accumulated savings and built up annuities so that they might retire at some given age. It is to be expected that most of them will adjust with a minimum of difficulty to the retired work period. Ranging above average in education, they have a wider variety of interests which should provide satisfying leisure as well as opportunities for social participation and leadership in community life.

Group I also includes workers who have not sought retirement but who have made plans for it and have accepted their retirement as inevitable. They have recognized the possibility that chronic illness or disability may not permit them to work until they die. Some have become aware that they may be unwanted by industry when they grow older. Provision is made for these contingencies through voluntary participation or actual demands for a pension plan. Although their subsequent retirement was not voluntary, they have accepted the inevitable and become reconciled to their new social situation. These workers may have a lesser chance of successful adjustment. Their anticipation of retirement as a necessity rather than as an opportunity reflects an orientation to active work life rather than to a more leisurely existence. Ordinarily such persons would score low on scales of leisure participation and enjoyment.

This retirement group as a whole included 2.6 million males sixty-five years of age and over, who were classified as not in the labor force in the

---

[19] These groups have been suggested by Tibbitts and Pollak. They have worked out a research outline for future research. See Clark Tibbitts and Otto Pollak, "Social Adjustment to Retirement," in *Social Adjustment in Old Age*, Social Science Research Council, 1946, pp. 88-97.

1940 census. This means that about three male workers in every five over sixty-five years of age have accepted retirement.

Group II

In Group II are those workers who have lost their jobs but who remain in the working force. They refuse to accept retirement either because they have no financial provision for it or because they refuse to give up an active work life. This group included 182,000 males sixty-five years of age and over in 1940; i.e., four male workers in every hundred workers will not or cannot accept retirement although they are without employment. Perhaps this group is the most poorly adjusted. Bedeviled by economic insecurity or a poverty of leisure interests they walk restlessly between employment offices or rock nervously in their easy chairs hoping for a chance to get back to active work.

Groups III and IV

Groups III and IV include workers who are still employed. These groups were represented by 1.8 million males sixty-five years old and over in 1940. The male population totaled 4.4 million in the sixty-five-year-and-over age group. This means that 41 percent or two out of five male workers were still working in the age group sixty-five years of age or over.[20] Many of these workers will die on the job. It may be assumed that many workers would like to retire but are financially unable to do so (Group III). Those in Group IV do not wish to retire and thus far at least have been able to avoid it. Although none of these workers in Groups III and IV have experienced retirement from active work life, all have entered the retirement work period. Ordinarily, they are expected to retire or to be unable to continue at their work within a relatively short period of time. The adjustment of these workers depends on their own outlook toward work.

Probably most of these workers fall into Group III, i.e., they would like to retire but financially are unable to do so. For them work is a kind of forced labor which, as workers long accustomed to labor, they endure as a means to basic necessities. The workers in Group IV are perhaps well adjusted. Their choice is to work and they are happy with the opportunity to play an active role in the work plant.

It is obvious that any study of adjustment during the retired work period must take into account these retirement attitude groups. It is important to establish the economic status, occupation, education, cultural factors, and health of those who make up each group. This cannot be done as yet, but the Social Science Research Council has a subcommittee on Social Adjustment in Old Age charged with the responsibility of research

[20] Cf. United States Census, Vol. III, *The Labor Force*, p. 19.

which is now in progress.[21] It is possible and pertinent to describe some of the social and financial problems which are critical in the adjustment of the retired worker.

SOCIAL PROBLEMS OF RETIREMENT

The problem of retirement is usually thought of in terms of the gainfully employed. In the older age groups these are primarily males. For the gainfully employed retirement is often something of a crisis. Full unemployment comes all at once and is very often like a shock even when it is foreseen. Lifelong habit patterns are broken abruptly. The man (or woman) accustomed to full days of work is often unable to conceive of the vast amount of leisure time in a day not filled with employment. But retirement is a problem for the housewife as well as for the male worker. Her retirement is a gradual process during which the more strenuous household activities must be eliminated. These duties must then be transferred to another person or done poorly, a situation which entails a lowering of personal and domestic standards of cleanliness, diet, and recreational activities.

How well the individual adjusts to retirement depends first of all on the preparation in attitudes and pattern of life for a retirement experience. Whether one accepts retirement or frets at its limitations, clings to places and things with symbolic meanings or restlessly moves about from place to place, is frequently but a counterpart of experiences and reactions developed many years before retirement.

Perhaps the most useful test for the prediction of an individual's adjustment to retirement is found in the previous surrenders which have been made throughout life. All through life there is a series of surrenders. Every person must successively give up the satisfactions of nursing, childhood habits, adolescence, vigorous maturity, vocation, and lastly life itself. If the pattern of personality adjustment has been to resist the roles necessary for each successive adjustment, then it may be anticipated that real difficulties will appear at retirement. On the other hand, if the person has a history of adapting successfully to the adjustments of childhood, marriage, and parenthood, there is every reason to believe that the acceptance of his retirement role will be accomplished with tolerance and satisfaction.[22] The retirement of the worker from the work plant does not mean that he retires from work. On the contrary, he may fill his days with all kinds of work which

[21] Otto Pollak has completely reorganized and largely rewritten the mimeographed planning report on social adjustment in old age issued by the Social Science Research Council. See *Social Adjustment in Old Age*, Bulletin 59. Social Science Research Council, 1948, pp. 116-124.
[22] Moore, *op. cit.*, p. 206.

he enjoys. He may turn to gardening and raise a large share of the vegetables and fruit. His wife may continue to process the food he grows. Home repairs and remodeling may occupy much of his time. Some professional workers continue to write and to edit manuscripts. All of these activities may actually contribute to the income of the retired couple. We have seen how hobbies grow in importance as woodworking, painting, music, quilting, knitting, weaving, and reading occupy a large part of leisure.

Active community participation occupies the attention of many retired workers. Retired leaders of the community are often eagerly sought out to direct the Community Chest, to push the Red Cross drive, or to serve on the school board. Others find social opportunities in the church and in the growing number of Over Sixty clubs. These clubs provide much entertainment, in addition to a healthier and more alert outlook for those of advanced years. Older men take part in horseshoe pitching, bowling-on-the-green, old-time dancing, and other games and social diversions.

Travel is a luxury which is available to a growing number of retired persons. Trains, buses, and autos (trailers attached) are filled with many retired persons going to see new and interesting places. The sightseeing tours and cruises secure a large part of their income from older people.

One writer, after studying the adaptation of some fifty men and women to old age, concludes that three factors are of especial importance. Most important are strong or varied interests and activities; second is economic security or independence; and third is freedom from physical handicap.[23] The problems induced by economic insecurity in old age require special attention.

FINANCIAL PROBLEMS

The stoppage of the weekly wage or monthly salary brings acute financial problems to many older workers. In fact, the financial problems of retirement have overshadowed problems of personal and social adjustment.

There are four major sources of support for the retired worker. These are savings, pensions, relief, dependence on relatives or friends. Though some workers are able to accumulate savings sufficient for their old age, most have not been able to do so. Public and private pension plans are providing that financial support for most retired workers. The largest of such plans is the federal social security program. By the end of 1946 accounts were held by some 77,500,000 living workers aged fourteen years and over, or more than 71 percent of the population in that age group. In June, 1947, over 1,000,000 retired workers or their wives received benefits. The average benefit for a retired man was $25.00 and for a retired man

[23] F. Conkey, "Adaptations of Fifty Men and Fifty Women to Old Age," *Journal of Home Economics*, May, 1933, pp. 387-389.

and his aged wife $39.20. These sums are small and there has been considerable pressure to raise them.

Many workers cannot qualify for old-age insurance relief or assistance. The federal-state programs assisted 2,270,000 older persons in the country as a whole in June, 1947. This means that 214 persons out of every 1000 persons aged sixty-five and over received some financial help. The average payment was $36.04.[24] In addition, others receive pensions from places of previous employment or are given assistance by children or relatives or through local charities. The need for additional financial assistance or for nursing care often forces the worker to become dependent upon someone else. This raises the delicate problem of family relationships.

FAMILY RELATIONSHIPS

The structure of family relationships is first shaken by the new role of the retired worker. Retirement brings with it a change of role of the husband from the income producer, with all that this implies in the way of authority and independence, to a role of noncontributor to the family income. Cavan has suggested that a thorough inquiry into the effects of such a change in familial role should be twofold. It should ascertain the *role of the chief earner* with reference to the family members *before retirement*, especially in what fields he exerted authority, over what family members he exercised authority, the extent of his authority, the extent to which his counsel and advice were voluntarily sought by his family, and the amount of respect shown him in the family. The second part of the study should review changes in these same fields *after the loss of earning power.* Questions assuming importance would be: To what extent has the status of the chief earner been lowered? What compensations to a lowering of status has he found within or outside the family? What emotional reactions has he had? To what extent does the wife, as household manager, tend to assume the dominant role in the family? What type of personality is best able to resist loss of status? What type of family organization is best able to adjust to the change in the role of the chief earner?[25]

Answers to these many questions are not yet forthcoming. Research is in progress and considerably more knowledge may soon be available. When it is known how different living arrangements affect the retired worker, it will be possible to prescribe an optimum structuring of social relationships. We know that the dwelling must substitute for the work plant in retirement and that the line between living and working almost disappears. Living arrangements become especially important. Retired persons are

[24] Computed by Social Security Administration, Bureau of Old-Age and Survivors Insurance. See *The World Almanac*, 1948, pp. 457-458.

[25] Ruth Shoule Cavan, "Family Relationships of Old Persons," in *Social Adjustment to Old Age*, Social Science Research Council, 1946, p. 45.

distributed within four principal types of living arrangements: (1) as proprietors of a household, (2) living in the household of relatives, (3) living in the household of nonrelatives, (4) living outside any family household context.[26]

1. As Proprietors of a Household

The most common arrangement for males (but not for females) is that in which both husband and wife survive and maintain their own household. It often happens that whereas the retired couple are the proprietors other relatives or nonrelatives are present. In some cases the older person or couple is the actual proprietor but is dependent on the care of other people who largely manage the household.

2. Living in the Household of Relatives

Living with relatives usually means living with the children. The tendency is for a single person to live with the children or relatives, or in an institutional home. This means new adjustments for all the household in entertaining friends, and for the older person new problems of fitting in such activities as hobbies, maintaining church and club memberships, and enjoying other favorite amusements. These adjustments are particularly difficult if income must be provided by the relatives.

Dinkel has shown that conflicts between aged parents and their children are induced by differentials in cultural background. He reports some of the comments of the old people he interviewed.

A woman, 75 years of age. "I think they go too fast. They enjoy themselves and don't look out for the future. We never thought of that. These cars take an awful lot of money and all those movies and shows and all of that stuff."

A woman, 77 years of age. "Such a great number of young folks can't be satisfied a minute unless they have something exciting; some place to go and do. I think they're living beyond their means. All they think about is style. They have the latest to wear and have the latest furniture in their home. They're bound to have it regardless of means."

A man, 65 years of age. "I believe the movies have their place, but I have no use for drinking. That is the stepping stone to hell itself for a great many people. I've seen lots of it. . . . It's surely enough to scare anybody when you see boys and girls sitting up around the bar and drinking."[27]

The problems of two or three generational families within the same household is beyond the scope of this book. It must be sufficient to point

[26] Talcott Parsons, "The Situation of the Aged in American Society," in *Social Adjustment to Old Age*, Social Science Council, 1946, p. 32.

[27] Robert M. Dinkel, "Parent-Child Conflict in Minnesota Families," *American Sociological Review*, August, 1943, pp. 412-424.

out the incipient nature of parent-child conflict, which may explode and cause some of the most difficult adjustment problems of the retired worker.

3 and 4. Living in the Household of Nonrelatives or Outside Any Family Household Context

The older persons who live outside their own or their relatives' homes are those who have no relatives to take them in or who have been cut off from their family connections voluntarily or involuntarily. There is reason to believe that different adjustments would be demanded by this kind of arrangement. The communal aspect of such living presents many opportunities for group participation. At the same time many older people feel cut off from emotional ties—and carry the feeling that nobody really cares what happens to them.

These varieties of living arrangements stress the different roles which the retired worker may have to play. He may find himself an independent proprietor of a small house in which he and his wife live, a provider of a home for his children or a dependent of his children, or a ward of the state. In either case he can look back on a long life filled with many experiences. A central core of those experiences has been built up of innumerable strands of work relationships and areas of life influenced by his work. He can remember his father at his work, particularly how his father worked and what he thought about work. He can recall his school days and the chores he had about home. He remembers his first part-time jobs and how much money he was paid on some of them. The early years of struggle on his first permanent jobs come back to him as memories of successes and failures in the midst of marriage and parenthood. The middle years in good times and bad times stand out as rewards in the forms of a house, furniture, or a new auto or appear as painful memories of deprivation and unemployment. The retirement years can be seen as burdens and joys. Work and leisure have blended together. A lifetime of work is concluded.

SUPPLEMENTARY STUDIES

Field: Planned Interviews

Make one or more interviews of adult men and women in the retired work period. The best time for interviewing is during the first five years of retirement. For a comparative analysis it is very desirable to seek interviews with adults from lower-, middle-, and upper-class families. The following interview form is suggested as a guide:

Name _____ Interviewer _____

Date _____

City _____ State _____

A. Background

Age _____ Sex _____ Years in Retirement _____

Occupation of: Father _____

Mother _____

Brother _____ Sister _____

Brother _____ Sister _____

Brother _____ Sister _____

Son _____ Daughter _____

Son _____ Daughter _____

B. Job and Work

1. Tell me about the part-time and full-time jobs you have had.
   a. How did you get them?
   b. What did you do?
   c. What did you like or dislike about them?
   d. Why did you leave them?
2. Have you retired from full-time work life? If not, do you want to retire? If yes, did you want to retire? Where are you living now?
3. What have your jobs meant to you? What explains how you came to have the job you had when you retired?
4. What job did you want when you were in school? Did you get that job?
5. How do you think people on a job get ahead?
6. Did you join a union? Why? Do you think unions are a good thing or not?
7. What kinds of companies have you worked for? Do you think that business has treated you fairly or unfairly?
8. Since you have retired have you found a group who share your background and interests?
9. What bothers and worries other retired people that you know? Do you share these worries?
10. Do you think that there will be more money and more steady jobs for everybody in the future or that we will have booms and busts?
11. What explains why you are where you are today? If you had your life to live over would you have made any different decisions that would affect your work life?

C. Home and Work

12. Are you married? If so, how has it changed your life? Has it changed your outlook on your work during your life?
13. How do you spend most of your time?

D. Community and Work

14. Ask respondent for information which will enable you to scale social participation on the Chapin Social Participation Scale. This scale is reproduced on the following page:

Name of organization	1. Member	2. Attendance	3. Financial Contribution	4. Member of Committee	5. Offices Held
1.					
2.					
3.					

Scoring: Weights of 1, 2, 3, 4, 5 are assigned to each type of participation as indicated by the order at the top of the scale. For example, if a person belonged to 6 clubs or organizations, attended 5, contributed to 3, was a member of 2 committees, and was an officer in an organization, his total score would be 38. Tentative norms may be found in F. Stuart Chapin, *Experimental Designs in Sociological Research*, Harper & Brothers, 1947, p. 195.

15. Would you agree that everybody would be happier, more secure, and more prosperous if the working people were given more power and influence in government, or would you say that we would all be better off if the working people had no more power than they have now?[28]

16. Which one of these statements do you most agree with?
(1) The most important job for the government is to make it certain that there are good opportunities for each person to get ahead on his own. (2) The most important job for the government is to guarantee every person a decent and steady job and standard of living.

RESEARCH GAPS

1. Study of cases of gradual retirement from the work plant.
2. Work interests and schedules of retired workers in the home and community.
3. Frustrations of the retired worker.
4. Measurement of the extent of the four different retirement attitude groups.

[28] Questions 14 and 15 were asked by Richard Centers in his study, *The Psychology of Social Classes*, Princeton University Press, 1949, pp. 60, 62. These questions draw significantly different response frequencies from white-collar and manual workers.

Part Five

INDUSTRY, COMMUNITY, AND SOCIETY

Society is a great mirror in which the social organization of a people is reflected. The values by which and for which people live appear in any representative sample of their society. The community is a segment of the society differentiated only by its local individuality.

In the community, industry and all the other institutions meet and interact. The modern community is marked by an elaboration of economic institutions. Business looms as the most influential institution in setting of thoughtways and patterns of behavior. This dominant position of business is being threatened by the increasing power of labor organizations and the political state. Industrial society in the middle of the twentieth century promises material abundance but is consumed with conflicting group interests. Organization counts, and the individual increasingly has influence only in and through large organizations. This pattern has brought new forces to bear upon every worker and every work plant and, indeed, upon the entire fabric of society. In Part Five the impact of industry upon the community and upon society will be examined.

Industry and the Community[1]

[1] Many of the ideas in this chapter were stimulated by Samuel A. Pratt and Walter S. Adams, who participated in a seminar on industry and the community at Michigan State College.

INTERDEPENDENCE OF INDUSTRY AND COMMUNITY

AN INQUIRING OBSERVER IN A NEW COMMUNITY

Whenever an inquiring observer approaches a new community he asks several questions to orient himself to the locality. Driving from the railroad station, bus terminal, or airport, he asks his friend, taxicab driver, or new acquaintance, "What's the size of this place?" "What are the main businesses and industries?" As the informant provides answers, new questions are formulated. They might be, "What kind of people (ethnic-racial) live here?" "Who runs this place?" "What kind of newspapers do you have?" Depending upon his acuity and that of his informer, more pointed inquiries may be made. "What's the political situation here?" "Who runs the school board?" "How strong is labor?"

Armed with answers to these questions, the observer now knows how to talk, whom to associate with, and how to behave. He has asked the critical questions about the nature of industry and community relations. This chapter is not concerned with the occupational life of workers inside plants. Rather it seeks to analyze the ways by which the economic institution affects the daily activity of people. We want to know industry's relations with community institutions, organizations, and groups as work and life intertwine in schools, churches, governments, welfare agencies, informal cliques, and associations. There is a twofold relationship to be explored. Industry and labor influence directly or indirectly all the groups in the community. Industrial organization is, in turn, affected in its daily operation by the attitudes and activities of local groups. This interdependence of industry and community is intimate and organic in nature. Community institutions cannot function without an economic base, and business operations cannot occur without a minimum of coöperation from the community. The spatial pattern of industry dominates the distribution of housing and the transportation network. Some industrial and occupational patterns encourage close interaction of people in the community and others segregate people. On the other hand, the social composition (ethnic, class, religious, racial) of the community encourages certain contacts and discour-

ages others within the work plants of the surrounding area. Informal groups may arise out of work relations in the plant which evolve into associations and influence community behavior. At the same time, interpersonal relations established in neighborhoods and institutions may be transferred into industry with direct consequences on industrial operations.

Technological changes in the work plant upset established social relations in the locality. But the changing age structure of the area may in turn bring pressure for technological changes in the industries. Industries may band together to control the operation of local government, and the municipality may retaliate with burdensome and punitive taxes. These are just a few areas of industry-community relations which we shall explore.

PREVIOUS STUDIES

Sociologists have made many interesting community studies, but only a few have concentrated on the problem of industry-community relations. The typical study does not ignore the economic institution; on the contrary, it usually includes a check list of the number of businesses in the area, how many people they employ, their growth and decline. Other institutions are analyzed separately, and without regard for their relation to industry.

Several studies have concentrated on the problem of institutional interaction, especially on the relations of industry and government. Although the muckraking era stimulated thinking in this field,[2] they were still incomplete descriptions of the total system of institutional interaction. Indeed, to draw such a picture for any large community would be a gigantic task, as Charles Booth discovered in his famous *Life and Labor of People in London*.[3] Since a complete study cannot be made often, the student should at least have a broad conceptual framework to view industry-community relations. This we shall try to provide for him in the present chapter.

THE ROLE OF HISTORY

The relations between industry and its locality are best understood when particular communities are studied. Although a broad conceptual base is needed before an investigation for a community begins, particular circumstances in a given locale may require careful attention. Industry-community relations vary so much that the historical approach is a necessary part of a particular study.

Historical data are needed for at least two reasons. First, the history of given institutions becomes a factor in the future relations of those institutions. For example, if there has been a history of antagonism between the community and industry, this fact will continue to play an important part

---

[2] *The Autobiography of Lincoln Steffens*, Harcourt, Brace and Company, 1931, is the classic model in this field.

[3] The Macmillan Company, 1902.

in any new situation which may arise. The second reason for the use of historical materials is to establish social trends so that one may come to appreciate the meaning of current patterns and the possibilities of future development.

Communities are history-conscious. The library of almost every community contains a history of that community. It is usually a boastful legend of the gigantic growth and the present importance of the city. The "historians" who wrote them were untrained, and further, they produced the kind of document that the leading fathers wanted. Attention, therefore, was devoted to the genealogies and the achievements of the "best" families. The skullduggery, graft, and corruption were usually ignored. More important, the daily lives of the lower classes were neglected or ignored. Almost no effort was made to relate events, draw trends, and present a complete and honest picture. A few studies by professional historians and sociologists provide better guideposts to the scientific study of industry-community relations.[4]

ECONOMIC DEPENDENCE

The relationship between industry and community is clearly seen in the economic dependence of the community. Once an industrial pattern is established, many of the community routines revolve about it. This fact can be observed dramatically in one-industry towns. Cottrell describes how the social life of a town was largely governed by the railroad, its main industry.[5] When the railroad selected an area to build its shops, it stimulated the development of a town with a particular pattern. Mechanics, highly skilled in the metal trades, moved in. They built their homes, established their schools, and began training their children to become railroaders.

Soon other businesses were attracted to the town. Single men needed to be housed, so hotels were built. Special kinds of clothing, gear, and tools were needed by the workers, and stores came in to sell these commodities. Gradually all of the general community services were provided—economic, recreational, religious, and political. Large investments were made by businessmen and by the municipality, based on the notion that the town would be there forever. The town was proud of its railroad heritage.

Then the railroad switched from steam to Diesel engines. The stop at this town was no longer necessary to refuel, to repair engines, or to pick up passengers. The company withdrew its shops and services. All the loyalty it had asked of its employees in the past was now forgotten. The workers were left to shift for themselves. Large loans were outstanding on the

---

[4] Robert S. Lynd and Helen Merrell Lynd, *Middletown*, Harcourt, Brace and Company, 1929; Alfred Winslow Jones, *Life, Liberty, and Property*, J. B. Lippincott Company, 1941; W. Lloyd Warner and J. O. Low, *The Social System of the Modern Factory*, Yale University Press, 1947.

[5] William Fred Cottrell, "Death of a Railroad Town," unpublished manuscript.

municipality for the excellent educational system it had built. Businesses had large mortgages to pay off. Real estate prices started to go down. Houses were abandoned. A lifetime of savings by individuals and businesses was gradually liquidated. Churches withdrew their ministers, children were discouraged from going into railroading, and the railroad corporation became an object of hate.

The town began to look for a new economic base. It tried to struggle along on the old patterns. Young people began to leave, but old people had no place to go. Middle-aged workers, their hard-won seniority gone, had to begin life all over again—to learn new skills, or become dependent on the community. It has become clear that finding a new economic base will be impossible. The town is now faced with slow but certain death. At this date it is continuing to lose population and is taking on the appearance of a ghost town.

Other communities in similar situations have been more fortunate in finding a new economic base. Many northern Michigan communities lost their economic base when the timber supply was exhausted. Some towns turned to the tourist trade, others to truck gardening, and others to shipping.[6] But such adjustments are difficult to make for communities can change character only slowly. However as long as community facilities are supported, a town will continue to live. But industry of some sort is needed to provide the all-important foundation for such facilities. Too often the role of industry in providing an economic base for a community is taken for granted. Moreover, industry sets the spatial or ecological development of the community.

INDUSTRY AND THE ECOLOGICAL GROWTH OF THE COMMUNITY

How land is utilized for particular purposes depends in large measure on the pattern of industrial land utilization. The distribution of residences, the network of the transportation system, and the location of services largely hinge on the placement of industries.

LOCATION OF INDUSTRIES

Human ecologists and geographers have investigated the location of industrial and other activities in cities. Their explanations are generally economic in nature. They hold that since industry is dominant in economic power it decides directly or indirectly what land will be utilized for what purposes. Where industry itself locates is determined by forces responsible

[6] See D. L. Gibson, *Socio-economic Evaluation in a Timbered Area in Northern Michigan*, Michigan State College Agricultural Experiment Station, Technical Bulletin 193, June, 1944.

for its economic survival. Cities flourish where industries flourish, and the ecology of the city is largely set by the industrial use of land.

Ecological Factors Accounting for Plant Sites

According to traditional ecological theory, enterprises locate close to the resources they need. They move to areas that are strategically located in reference to raw materials, transportation facilities, markets, and labor supply. The more effectively managers weigh these factors in deciding upon plant sites, the more profitable (other things being equal) industry will be. When poor decisions are made, businesses must either move, become marginal, or perish.

Different industries, depending on their peculiarities, make different kinds of demands for city land use. Light industries, as jewelry manufacturing, clothing, and personal services, try to locate close to the geographic and population traffic center of the city. Heavier industries, as steel and auto, tend to concentrate farther out where land values are lower. Once large investments in building and equipment are made in an area, inertia to movement develops. Psychological inertia to mobility also grows, for once a pattern of location is developed it shows stability and persistence. In fact, the concentration of factories or services in an area may attract other enterprises.[7]

Community Factors Accounting for Plant Sites

Ecological explanations of industrial location tend to be theoretically true; that is, true when other factors are not operating in actual situations. Yet these other factors, usually social in nature, are of critical importance for both the location and the profitableness of business. We refer to the attitudes of the community and its institutions toward industry which affect favorably or unfavorably plant location and operation.

Many municipalities, for example, consciously interfere with the operation of natural ecological processes. Where land might be too expensive for an industry, the government may donate land without charge, reduce taxes, or even erase taxes for a number of years. In such cases, government not only subsidizes business but actually participates in locating it. Figure 122 portrays two types of appeals made by the local governments of two small communities seeking to attract more industry.

Other kinds of subsidization which affect location occur. When factories are unsuitably placed in reference to transportation of materials or of workers, the municipality may overextend its transit facilities, often at a considerable cost. Indeed, one city built an expensive and unnecessary open subway system in the guise of providing better commuter service. In reality, the

[7] See Noel P. Gist and L. A. Halbert, *Urban Society*, Thomas Y. Crowell Company, 1948, Part II, "Ecology of the City and Region."

FIG. 122.   Two Approaches to Industrial Subsidies.

actual motive was to tie related industries together by the subway railroad. It is perhaps unrealistic in this case and in many similar ones to speak of community as apart from industry. Often the "community" is merely an agency of industry. It is made to bear hidden ecological grants-in-aid as the extension of water, sewerage, and power facilities. To be sure, cities need industries to provide income for their citizens. But there is a difference when industries themselves bear the expenses of location and when the government gives a hand. An "economic" problem thus often becomes a social and political one, for how space is utilized is a question of social control and tradition, and not one of economics alone.

This fact is clearly brought out when cities participate directly in the competitive battles between businesses. Practically every large city has a number of legendary or real accounts of industries exerting pressure upon the local government to prevent competitive industries from settling in the locality. This restrictive practice is occasioned by the fact that wage scales may rise when new industries begin to compete for local labor.

Communities may influence the location of industries in other ways. The more services a city has—economic, recreational, religious, etc.—and the less incumbent it is on industry to provide them, the more likely it is that business will settle there. Business recognizes that municipal services are "free rides" from the taxpayers. When business must provide the services, as it does in a company or boom town, it is an expensive affair.

Although most cities impose some restrictions on industrial location, the dominant pattern is to attract businesses. The returns to the community in the form of pay rolls, taxes, and jobs are ample rewards for almost any sacrifices. However, most localities protect themselves minimally by imposing zoning laws. Other laws may be passed to abate noise, restrict pollution of the air and water, and prevent blight. Also high taxes may be imposed to run local government. If these laws become too restrictive, industry can put pressure on the community by threatening to locate elsewhere. By decentralizing or by only moving across the city boundary, enterprises can and do escape heavy taxes and other restrictions. Indeed, suburban decentralization of industry has brought serious financial problems to our cities, for the cities still continue to provide a wide range of services without receiving income in return.[8]

HOW INDUSTRIAL LOCATION AFFECTS DAILY LIVING

A thorough investigation of the implication of industrial location on the daily lives of people has not been made because much significant occupational and industrial information has not been subjected to ecological treatment. Before the implications of ecology can be appreciated fully maps

[8] *Our Cities*, National Resources Committees, United States Government Printing Office, 1937.

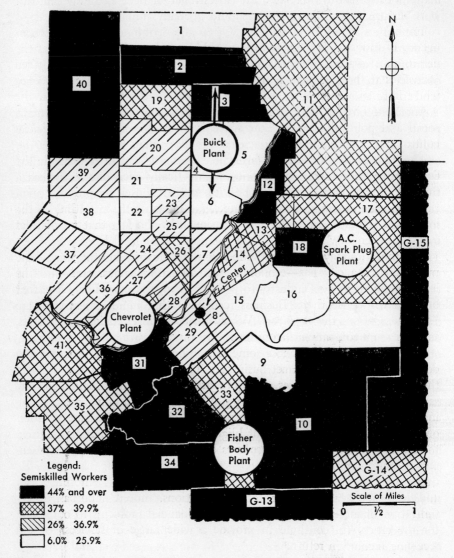

FIG. 123. The Four Major Factories of Flint, Michigan, Showing the Predominant
          Semiskilled Worker Residences Around Each Work Plant.

must be drawn which relate distributive characteristics of workers with their
work plant. Such social base maps of a community would show the distribution of occupational groups and characteristics like age, sex, race, and ethnic,
religious, and class identity. These data could then be examined for given
work plants and correlated with maps of community services and social
participation. Although sociologists have done extensive work in ecological

mapping, the field of occupational ecology has scarcely been opened and work plant ecology is even more sparsely worked.

The writers have prepared Figure 123 to suggest the possibilities of studying work plant ecology. The figure portrays by census tracts the residential distribution of male semiskilled workers in Flint, Michigan. From it we observe that these workers are not distributed evenly over the city. They tend to live around those plants which employ them.

Another ecological study of Flint shows that around each of its four main plants (see Fig. 123) low socioeconomic areas appear. Within a one-mile radius of each of these factories rents are lower than the average for the city.[9] The plurality of male workers in these mile circles are semiskilled workers employed in the neighboring plants. This fact points to the selective recruitment of industrial labor in the urban community.

The uneven distribution of rent and occupations in the city would seem to support the notion that the city is a number of local and self-contained industrial neighborhoods which are relatively isolated from one another. The lack of interaction among these neighborhoods reinforces the ideas, prejudices, and myths that each group has toward the others. An analysis of the isolation and communication patterns might also account for some of the tensions between industry and various parts of the community. Indeed, the generalization may be hazarded that the larger the city the less its different segments appreciate the lives, institutions, and culture of those in other areas. As a college junior remarked after a field trip through the factory section of her community, "Honest, Dr. Laing, it seems like I don't know anything about the city. I've lived here all my life but I've never been to the East Side actually. We've driven along Cedar Street lots of times, but we've never gone inside the area. I've heard of the rubber workers at home and all the trouble they cause, but I never really saw the conditions of their homes and neighborhoods. The trip this afternoon was a revelation! Wait till I see my dad tonight. We're going to have a long talk."

Many adults never have the revealing experience of this girl. They live their entire lives in one or two sections of the community. Their *job travel path is so short* or so uniform that differences in social patterns are not perceived.[10] Indeed, early training has so incapacitated their perception that they cannot see social differences even when exposed to them. Babbitt's reactions to the city on his job travel path illustrate this point.

And all the while he was conscious of the loveliness of Zenith. He admired each district along his familiar route to the office: The bungalows and shrubs and winding irregular driveways of Floral Heights. The one-story shops on Smith Street, a glare of plate-glass and new yellow brick; groceries and laundries and drug-stores to supply the more immediate needs of East Side housewives. The

[9] See John Kantner, *The Relationship Between Accessibility and Socio-Economic Status of Residential Lands, Flint, Michigan,* The University of Michigan Press, 1948, p. 24.

[10] Kate Liepmann, *Journey to Work,* Oxford University Press, 1947.

market gardens in Dutch Hollow, their shanties patched with corrugated iron and stolen doors. Billboards, with crimson goddesses nine feet tall advertising cinema films, pipe tobacco, and talcum powder. The old "mansions" along Ninth Street, S. E., like aged dandies in filthy linen; wooden castles turned into boarding-houses, with muddy walks and rusty hedges, jostled by fast-intruding garages, cheap apartment-houses, and fruit-stands conducted by bland sleek Athenians. Across the belt of railroad tracks, factories with high-perched water-tanks and tall stacks—factories producing condensed milk, paper boxes, lighting-fixtures, motor cars. Then the business center, the thickening darting traffic, the crammed trolleys unloading, and high doorways of marble and polished granite.

It was big—and Babbitt respected bigness in anything. . . . He thought of the outlying factory suburbs; of the Chaloosa River with its strangely eroded banks; of the orchard-dappled Tonawanda Hills to the North, and all the fat dairy land and big barns and comfortable herds. As he dropped his passenger he cried, "Gosh, I feel pretty good this morning!"[11]

The relation of the place of work to residence is important for it has an effect on the family, neighborhood, and community routines of the worker and his family. For example, when work and residence are in the same neighborhood, family members are likely to see more of each other. The fact that they may eat all three of their meals around the family table increases the opportunity for family activities. As the job travel path lengthens, the noon meal at home disappears and is replaced by the lunch which is carried to work or secured in a restaurant.

When the breadwinner must travel great distances to work, he comes to use the home as a dormitory but his food and recreational needs are satisfied elsewhere. He does not see his children during meals or after school. He becomes of necessity the week-end father. Thus, the length of the job travel path markedly affects family life.

If there is a change in the location of the work plant, whole sets of habits are threatened. The equilibrium of family routines, neighborhood, and community living is upset. Sometimes these changes are desirable and sometimes not. But there is always a disruption of habit patterns for the family as well as the breadwinner.

Engineers who recommend change in plant site are often unaware of the social implications of their activity. They cannot understand why men sometimes become disgruntled when operations shift to a clean new plant. This problem of adjusting plant location to residence is becoming particularly keen today because many industries are moving out to the fringe areas of the cities. This industrial decentralization is changing the routines of two groups: urban dwellers, who have to commute greater distances, and farmers, who as the work plant comes closer to the hinterland, turn to factory work to supplement their income, especially during the winter. Apart

[11] Sinclair Lewis, *Babbitt*, Bantam Books, 1946, p. 31.

from changing the social patterns of these two groups, rural-urban conflict in the informal organization of the factory is heightened.

IMPACT OF INDUSTRIAL ORGANIZATION ON COMMUNITY LIFE

Industry-community relations may be examined in two perspectives: first, the ways in which industry affects community relations, and second, the ways in which community structures affect industrial operations. We have been stressing that industry-community relations are in a constant state of dynamic interdependence. They constitute an interactional and continuous system of relationships. Thus, the social organization of industry and community is not composed of two discrete sub-organizations. As Arensberg so clearly points out, it would be erroneous to think of social organization of the community as something distinct from the technical organization of industry. Only by having a common set of concepts dealing with both organizations is it possible to trace the specific consequences of changes from one area to the other.[12]

In this section we shall examine how the structure of industry affects community life. Four areas of industry will be examined in this light: (1) the impact of technological change on institutional organization, (2) the influence of the supervisory structure in community organization, (3) the community programs sponsored by industry, and (4) the role of informal work groups in community associations.

TECHNOLOGICAL CHANGE

Work plant organization is human organization. In the factory, hospital, and department store, workers are arranged in such a way as to encourage the greatest amount of coöperative effort. The positions that men occupy in work organization to a large extent fix their social position at work *and* in the community. When there is a change in a worker's status in his work plant, this change tends to be quickly reflected in the community groups to which he belongs. Thus changes in work organization affect community organization as well.

Before the industrial revolution technical organization remained relatively stable. A balanced adjustment between work and community life was the rule. With the advent of industrialism, the chief characteristic of technical organization became change. Profit was derived not only by improving machinery but also by improving work organization. Indeed, technical and mechanical alterations in production forced changes in the organization of workers in the plant, and this, in turn, disturbed social patterns in the community.

[12] Conrad Arensberg, "Industry and the Community," *American Journal of Sociology,* July, 1942, p. 3.

Period	Technology	Form of Division of Labor	Form of Ownership and Control	Producer-Consumer Relations	Worker Relations	Structure of Economic Relations
IV The Present (1920–1945)	Machine Tools mass production, assembly line methods	Nearly all jobs low skilled; a very large number of routinized jobs	Outside ownership and control of the factory (tools leased)	Very few retail outlets; factory merely one source of supply for a chain of shoe stores	Rise of industrial unions, state supervised....no (or weak) unions	Center of dominance New York. Very complex financial producer and retail structure. Local factory not important in it
III Late Intermediate Period (approximately to World War I)	Machine Tools machines predominate; beginning of mass production through use of the machine (McKay)	A central factory with machines; still high degree of skill in many jobs	First small, and later, large local men of wealth own or lease the tools, and machines	National market and local capitalist; many outlets	Craft and apprenticeship (St. Crispin's Union)	Center of dominance local factory; complex hierarchy in local factory system
II Early Intermediate Period (approximately to the Civil War)	Machine Tools few machines first application (Elias Howe, etc.)	One man assigns highly skilled jobs to few men; highly skilled craftsmen ("letting-out" system)	Small, locally controlled manufacturers; tools still owned by workers, materials by capitalist, market controlled by "owner"	Owner and salesmen to the consumer regional market	Informal, apprenticeship and craft relations	Simple economic no longer kinship; worker subordinate to manager
	Hand Tools increasing specialization and accumulation of hand tools	Specialization among several families; a few highly skilled jobs	Local Control not all shoemakers need own all tools; beginning of specialization	Local buyer from several producer families sells products (no central factory)	Kinship and neighbors among workers	Semi-economic but also kinship and neighborliness
I The Beginning (early 1600's)	Hand Tools few, basic, and simple	All productive skills in the family, including making of shoes; a few cobblers for the local market	Local Control skills, tools, and materials owned and controlled by each family; or by the local cobbler	The family produces and consumes shoes and most other products	Largely kinship and family relations among workers	Very simple non-economic; the immediate family

FIG. 124. The History of the Differentiation of the Yankee City Shoe Industry. (From W. L. Warner and J. O. Low, *The Social System of the Modern Factory*, Yale University Press, 1947, p. 65.)

The general social effects of invention and technological change have been catalogued by Ogburn, the Rosens, and others.[13] For example, the auto has stimulated the growth of many established industries like steel, and has given rise to many new industries including refineries, filling stations, garages, auto parts stores, and hot-dog stands. In addition the auto has revolutionized the whole pattern of rural life. Indeed it is gradually erasing the distinctions between city and country. Horace Miner has been exploring the specific effects of inventions on rural life to determine more precisely the manner in which rural organization has been influenced by technological change.[14]

Technological Change and Community Solidarity

Warner and Low have presented a historical account of how changes in the technology of the shoe industry altered social relations both in the factory and the community.[15] Figure 124 shows that during the early factory period the skill hierarchy dominated workers' lives and largely fixed their status positions in the community. The hierarchy of crafts was at the same time a community age-grade system through which young men were expected to pass. Indeed the factories themselves were under the informal control of community traditions. Shoe manufacturers were accepted by all classes as leaders; and they felt a sense of responsibility toward the community.

The mechanization of shoe production largely destroyed the skill hierarchy *and* the age-grade system that accompanied it. Skilled workers became semiskilled, and semiskilled workers remained on that level. Young men could no longer anticipate an ascent into jobs requiring greater skills. They lost hope and security. The older people also lost security, status, and confidence in local leaders. Along with changes in production went a change in the structure of business ownership. Big city financiers assumed financial and directional control of local factories. Thus, the changes in occupational structure and financial control of the factories shattered the network of personal relations, loyalties, and obligations between the industries and the community.

This fact was not appreciated until a strike was called by the workers in a town that absentee managers considered unionproof and strikeproof. The managers were surprised at the amount of support the strikers received from small businessmen, churchmen, the police, and others. The reason for this was that the captains of industry were no longer the community

[13] William F. Ogburn and S. C. Gilfillan, "The Influence of Invention and Discovery," Chap. 3 of *Recent Social Trends*, McGraw-Hill Book Company, Inc., 1938; S. McKee Rosen and Laura Rosen, *Technology and Society*, The Macmillan Company, 1941.

[14] Horace Miner, *Agriculture and Culture*, University of Michigan Press, 1949.

[15] *Op. cit.*

leaders. They could not count on the support of local leaders. Consequently, the workers won the strike, and an industrial union became a part of the social fabric of Yankee City. Equally important, leadership in the factory, as far as the workers were concerned, passed from management to the union.

Technology and the Class System

One of the most important attributes of a community is its class system. Ordinarily, the composition of each class does not change rapidly. When changes do occur they usually arise from changes in social relations brought about by industrial change. Smith reports how shifts in the class system of a New England town were produced by the introduction of the stretch-out in a textile mill.[16] In this case the technical process of clothmaking was gradually altered, whereas the actual process of weaving remained essentially the same. Important changes were also introduced in the organization of workers, particularly by breaking down their jobs in the weaving process. In the early days a weaver had complete charge of the loom—cleaning it, loading shuttle bobbins in the creel, tying the ends of yarn together, picking out the flaws in the cloth, repairing the "smashes," and so on. With mechanical, material, and process improvements, the weaver attended more and more looms and spent less and less time on skilled work. The time he spent on *unskilled* work, however, grew so great that mills began to hire unskilled "specialists" to take over the weavers' routine operations. Consequently, weavers were expected to attend even more looms. Fewer weavers were needed, with the result that many had to become unskilled hands.[17]

Further, as mechanical improvements and labor rationalization expanded, the demand for college-trained technical specialists and supervisors also grew. The top managers were recruited increasingly from these college-trained technicians and decreasingly from mill operatives. Since the college-trained men had little or no contact with the workers either in the plant or in the community, the net result of all these changes was an emphasis on the *differences* between labor and management. There was a decrease in common goals and common participation in the community. Formal education replaced work experience as the main avenue into management. In this case, then, *class distinctions in the community were almost entirely a product of changes in industrial organization*. Political and social issues in the town were directly related to the organizational structure and changes in the industry.

Other studies are needed to assess the effect of speed-up, transfer and promotion, seasonal layoffs, mechanization, rationalization, quality controls,

[16] Elliot Dunlap Smith with Richmond Carter Nyman, *Technology and Labor*, Yale University Press, 1939.
[17] *Ibid.*, pp. 1-4.

and other industrial changes on family-community relations. No doubt such studies will further document the fact that modern industry has a tendency to shatter social relations both within itself and in the community. Each change creates more instability and insecurity, and the fractures spread throughout the entire society. This trend has not gone completely unchallenged. There have developed within the community and in the work plant organized and unorganized attempts to resist innovations.[18]

Resisting Effects of Technological Change

The rise of labor unions is often attributed to the unsettling effects of technological and organizational changes. Unions are fighting some industrial changes directly, attempting to soften the effects of others, and encouraging those which increase the security of the workers.

In such industries as building construction, which is by nature dynamic and unsettling, particularly strong unions have arisen. They have sought to minimize the effects of insecurity by controlling the recruitment of workers, setting the pace of work, resisting technological improvements, and establishing benefit funds.[19] These measures have fallen short of their goals because the industry is only part of a larger society which lacks stability. Increasingly, therefore, unions have been driven to participate in local and national affairs to widen their influence.

The specific changes that technology brings to the community are usually not anticipated by businessmen and industrialists. However, many businessmen realize the importance of having a favorable climate of public opinion in the community. They consciously and intentionally participate in local organizations to further their ends. In the following section we shall examine their participation.

THE SUPERVISORY STRUCTURE IN COMMUNITY ORGANIZATIONS

Formal power relations in industry are clearly specified by the supervisory ladder. Since the community is not as unilaterally organized as industry, its power relations are not easily seen. One of the problems of the sociologist is to investigate the power situation existing between industry and the community. At one extreme there is the company town in which the supervisory structure is also the power pyramid in the town. The other extreme occurs when industry confronts a hostile community, where businessmen lose their influence and the supervisory structure of industry is no longer the power pyramid of the community. Although there are great variations in the power situations existing between industries and communities, a historical trend may nonetheless be noted.

[18] See Benjamin M. Selekman, chap. 6, "Resistance to Shop Changes," *Labor Relations and Human Relations*, McGraw-Hill Book Company, Inc., 1947.

[19] T. N. Whitehead, *Leadership in a Free Society*, Harvard University Press, 1936, p. 161.

The power ladder in the industrial communities of the nineteenth century (and in many smaller industrial communities today) duplicated the supervisory hierarchy in industry. No important organization could function contrary to the wishes of business. The officers of local organizations were either business managers or their approved substitutes, and this situation was considered to be the normal state of affairs. Businessmen believed that they were natural leaders; that they knew what was good for the community; that what was good for business was also good for the community. Many people today still believe this, and in most places businessmen continue to dominate community organizations. In smaller communities, where both managers and workers participate in the same organizations, there can be no opposition to industry on any major issue. The power of the managers is carried over into town affairs. Resistance to management can be easily located, and those who resist can be summarily dismissed from their jobs.

The Lynds have documented how this type of business class control can exist today in a city of 50,000 people. The X family is a leading industrial family of Middletown. One man commenting on their power said,

If I'm out of work I go to the X plant; if I need money I go to the X bank, and if they don't like me, I don't get it; my children go to the X college; when I get sick I go to the X hospital; I buy a building lot or house in an X subdivision; my wife goes downtown to buy clothes at the X department store; if my dog stays away he is put in the X pound; I buy X milk; I drink X beer; vote for X political parties and get help from X charities; my boy goes to the X Y.M.C.A. and my girl to their Y.W.C.A.; I listen to the word of God in X-subsidized churches; if I'm a Mason I go to the X Masonic Temple; I read the news from the X morning paper; and if I am rich enough, I travel via the X airport.[20]

The fact that this pattern is more difficult to maintain in large cities may be accounted for historically. As communities grew in size common participation by the entire population in the same organizations tended to decrease. Consequently, the number of organizations that employers could control diminished, and this resulted in their partial withdrawal from active community participation and "responsibility." With expanding urbanization and the spread of the impersonal market, insecurity grew among the workers. They tried to meet this problem partly by organizing labor unions and by challenging industry's leadership in the community. As their power has grown, businessmen have shown a growing concern lest they lose out in the struggle to retain power in the community.

Whitehead has made a sophisticated but conservative case for businessmen to *reassert their leadership and assume major responsibility* in com-

[20] Robert S. Lynd and Helen Merrell Lynd, *Middletown in Transition*, Harcourt, Brace and Company, 1937, p. 74.

munity affairs.[21] He suggests that they use their "tremendous advantages" of natural dominance, organizational backing, legal knowledge, business skills, and physical resources to get sympathetic understanding of business problems by the local people.

No longer able to control local cliques and the multitude of new organizations, industry has now launched a double-barreled program. One part consists of adding a public relations department to their structures; the other part encompasses a broad community program including such things as student scholarships, athletic teams, youth organizations, community services, and many philanthropies. Both the public relations department and the community services are aimed largely at the manual and low-income workers.

COMMUNITY PROGRAMS OF MANAGEMENT AND LABOR

The size of the programs that industry will support in the community may vary with industry's need for good will and public support. Although some industries have a genuine and unselfish interest in the welfare of the community, this interest is heightened when they feel that they do not have all the public confidence they deserve. Whether secure or insecure, industry has been sold on the importance of good community relations. In general, the support of community programs by business has been generous.

The Welfare Approach

There are three broad areas of community life in which industry shows interest: welfare, education, and leisure. Welfare organizations such as hospitals, Community Chest, and research foundations are supported by private companies, individuals, and such business service organizations as Rotary, Kiwanis, and Lions.

Private charity was the typical pattern of business welfare in the past. If a company felt any obligation toward local inhabitants, it set up a special program of its own. It might dispense private relief in the form of Christmas baskets, or help to the handicapped, indigents, or unemployed. Money might be contributed to favored welfare organizations—such as settlement houses, sanatoria, or medical clinics. These private philanthropies have tended to disappear although some corporations still continue to support them.

One reason for the decrease in private philanthropy was that smaller companies found that they were unable to dispense welfare on a large enough scale to enhance their status in the large community. Their individual contributions were lost in the maze of welfare effort. To meet th s situation service organizations grew, such clubs as Kiwanis, Lions, and Rotary. Many small businessmen together might sponsor a wide range of welfare projects

[21] Whitehead, *op. cit.*, p. 172.

which could not have been undertaken by a small company. Thus in one
community a service club builds a swimming pool, in another it maintains
an old people's home, in another it sponsors an improvement association.
Whatever the project, these clubs feel that by helping the community they
help improve the status of business.

After World War I private businesses and business associations were
urged by social welfare workers to pool their contributions with those of
other organizations. Social workers pointed out that there was a lack of
coördination between the needs and resources available to different social
agencies. Some services had more money than they needed and others did
not have enough. They requested that *all* businesses, unions, and other
organizations aid in raising money, but that the social workers be permitted
to evaluate community needs and to disburse the funds. At first this program was resisted because the various businesses felt that they would remain
anonymous and therefore could not enhance their status. It was only when
businesses were permitted to use the fund-raising campaign to advertise the
size of their contributions that such city-wide organizations as Community
Chest gained acceptance.

Since most of the welfare activities of business were directed at the
poorer classes, unions also began to invade the welfare field. They considered business welfare a threat to union loyalty and allegiance. During
and following World War II the welfare activities of unions expanded
many fold. Many union leaders now feel that the problems of nonmembers
are not different from those of members. They have begun to consider
problems of the whole community as their general concern.

This attitude was formally expressed by Philip Murray, C.I.O. President
in 1945. He announced that the C.I.O. War Welfare Committee had
changed its name and had become the National Community Services. He
said its work would be to coöperate with public and private welfare agencies
on the community level.[22] Currently, the union is expanding welfare facilities to its members. Social workers and counselors are being added to
union staffs, credit unions are being instituted, and political organizations
are being sponsored in the city, state, and nation.

The U.A.W.-C.I.O. has a highly developed community action program.
It reaches out into farm groups, churches, fraternal organizations, youth
groups, health societies, and recreational organizations. The union is sponsoring Boy Scouts, Girl Scouts, and Campfire Girls to get these activities
organized broadly and democratically in contrast to troops "organized
around attendance at a particular church." The union has adjudicated disputes between factions on school boards, provided halls for all kinds of
community meetings, stimulated the formation of neighborhood improve-

---

[22] Mark Starr, "Role of Union Organization," *Industry and Society*, William Foote
Whyte (ed.), McGraw-Hill Book Company, Inc., 1946, p. 159.

ment groups, led drives for community playgrounds, and undertaken other activities of this nature.[23]

Professor Hart, who made a study of the role of the union in reducing community anomie in Windsor, Ontario, makes the following statement: "Instead of going inside Dean Donham's beautiful plants to find the more satisfactory and stabilized life, the worker, or at least the auto worker, has gone into the union hall. There within his union, he is finding his own ways of building a more satisfying social life; and when he looks out at the social chaos that is Windsor, he does not run for help into the Ford Plant or the Chrysler plant, rather he calls upon his union to undertake the job of cleaning up that social chaos and rebuilding the community along more satisfying lines."[24]

Influencing the Educational System

The interest that business and labor have in education is easily understandable. Apart from learning skills which will be useful at work, students also learn in the classroom attitudes toward business and unions. Schools generally play the role that industry wants them to play. They want to coöperate with business by teaching students the skills and attitudes which will enable them to "adjust" well in the world of work.

Industry's program for education takes many forms. In almost every school system enterprises donate medals to students for highest achievement in science, scholarship, or citizenship. Sometimes scholarships are offered to deserving pupils to enable them to continue their education.

The National Association of Manufacturers has prepared pamphlets, slides, charts, and films for use in the schools. A list of some recent publications include:

The American Triangle of Plenty.
America's Vocational Schools.
Jobs and the Woman.
Free Enterprise—Its Past and Future.
Guide to the Evaluation of Educational Experiences in the Armed Services.
Preparing for Industrial Work.
Industry Report to Veterans on Jobs.

These publications reveal the interests of business as it seeks to coöperate with education. Business above all else wants the schools to tell its story— the story of "free enterprise" and the "triangle of plenty." It wants the schools to emphasize "the American way." In the N.A.M. booklet Free Enterprise—Its Past and Future we find that management has dedicated itself to "serve veterans and youth—the enterprises of tomorrow—by keep-

[23] UAW-CIO Ammunition, February, 1949, p. 51.
[24] C. W. M. Hart, "Industrial Relations Research and Social Theory," Canadian Journal of Economics and Political Science, February, 1949, p. 73.

ing open the avenues of opportunity and assuring full competition in and ready access to every economic field." There is a review of "how free competitive enterprise has given the American worker the highest standard of living the world has known, provided consumers with constantly improved and lower-priced products, and prepared the nation to be the arsenal of democracy."[25]

Businessmen are disturbed when they feel the schools are failing to tell or slighting the "free enterprise" story. High school and college teachers are apprehensive that what they teach might not be well received in the business community. Sometimes businessmen are told that they have a responsibility to act as sentinels of democracy and to watch the schools in their community to see that the right kind of education is being given. They may form committees to explore the loyalty of teachers, the Americanism of the textbooks, and the conduct of their classes.

Businessmen have a second concern which motivates them to coöperate closely with school authorities. They are disturbed that the schools might not prepare a practical program of education. They want the schools to teach skills that will help students to make a living. Other things such as good citizenship (loyalty to prevailing sentiments) may be encouraged, but not too much of the taxpayers' money should be spent on non-useful frills.

Whenever possible, industry wants the public to assume the expense and burden of training for specific skills. Commercial, vocational, and business courses are constantly being added to the curriculum from grade school through college. Education assumes more and more of the burden of teaching young people how to care for golf greens, test cloth, make cheese, and write letters.

A college senior reports on the relations between industry and education in a western Massachusetts city.

The development of a machinist training program and extensive plans for enlarging the high school machineshop has been pushed by councilmen that are employees of the company. In 1935 an enlarged commercial course for stenographic and secretarial work was begun and has progressively grown. College preparatory courses stress pre-engineering courses such as math, chemistry, and physics (foreign languages, literature and English are only self perpetuating). After graduation, students are encouraged to enroll in the apprentice training course offered by the company. In 1940 a cooperative program was developed between the company and high school for training draftsmen. An adult machinist night school, established during the war, has been continued. The Chairman of the City Board of Education since 1935 is a high company official.[26]

When education fails to meet the practical goals of business, employers form citizen committees to put pressure on the boards of education. An

[25] *Trends*, National Association of Manufacturers, January, 1946, p. 23.
[26] From a report by Roger H. Stuart, student at Michigan State College, 1948.

interesting illustration of this kind of pressure occurred in Detroit where a committee of businessmen attacked the performance of the Detroit public school system. The newspapers took up the hue and cry.

SCHOOLS FAILING, EMPLOYER'S CHARGE

Detroit schools are grinding out another "lost generation." Ignorant of the three R's children are "sloughed off" upon a business world which rejects many of them as "unacceptable" and "unemployable."

Employment managers told the Free Press that up to 40 percent of the boys and girls leave school without mastering simple arithmetic.

One personnel executive said their handwriting is atrocious.

Their statements were made as the school board prepared to ask a record-breaking 1949-50 budget of $73,000,000. Three new board members will be elected this spring. . . .

Employers charge that youngsters are turned out with a "poor work attitude," lacking in responsibility toward the job and the employer. . . .

Blame for this is placed on the modern method of education in which emphasis is placed on stimulating the child's imagination, his wish to learn, power of analysis and sense of inquiry. . . .

"Children have flitted through school like a game," said one personnel expert. "School is work like any job. Pupils should be taught that they must produce. . . ."

More than one-third of Detroit public school students take the college preparatory course. They graduate with a smattering of cultural knowledge but no "saleable" training.[27]

Educators recognize the need to integrate the institutions of industry and education. They send children on field trips into the factories and businesses to expose them to the work world. Generally, business executives are happy to coöperate with the schools in this type of educational experience. Rarely, however, are labor leaders called in to address students on the role that unions play in work organizations.

Recently, some educators have been urging more intimate reciprocal relations between industry and education. Business-Industry-Education Days have been sponsored, wherein all teachers visit plants in the city and businessmen observe the schools in action. The thought is that each may learn the problems of the other. In this exchange, executives apparently have more self-confidence than teachers. Many of the latter are hard pressed to give their classroom activity a "practical slant." One kindergarten teacher in a middle-sized midwestern city commented anxiously, "Mr Yokely, the principal, talked to me after teachers' meeting last night. He said that the businessmen were going to visit the school pretty soon, and when they arrive, the children should be doing something practical. He definitely instructed that the children should not be playing on the playground, they

[27] Detroit *Free Press*, fourth in a series of articles by John Griffith, February 2, 1949.

should not be having recess, they must not be singing or doing art work. There really isn't much left for them to do. Do you have any ideas?"

This somewhat ludicrous situation illustrates the precarious position in which some teachers find themselves. Teachers on low salaries cannot afford to offend the business leaders of the community. They share with businessmen the desire that young people should get the best possible education for life, work, and citizenship. Teachers, however, tend to put more weight on the total growth of the personality. Art, music, creative writing, critical literature, and critical thought are believed to be among the elements which enrich living and stimulate independent growth. Businessmen often fail to be sympathetic to such a philosophy of education, at least as proposed for all of the young people.[28] In fact, the boards of education or trustees usually have a strong or even dominant representation of businessmen to assure a "practical" educational program.[29]

Union Challenge to Educational Control

Before the Wagner Labor Act compelled recognition of duly organized unions, educational institutions in the community were not greatly affected by labor unions. With legal recognition and accompanying respectability, unions began to put pressure on local school systems to abstain from anti-labor teaching. In the colleges they demanded that economics and other courses include the study of labor problems and issues. In some state colleges and universities labor and business cooperated in inaugurating schools of labor-management relations. Several state universities have in their extension teaching programs served the educational needs of union locals. Courses in labor economics, labor law, grievance procedure, and union organization have been taught by college personnel, often in the union halls. In Michigan the charge from big business that Marxian economics was being taught brought an end to this type of program. The attempt of the university to resurrect the Workers Educational Service was virtually boycotted by all the unions.

The *Michigan CIO News* reported on February 9, 1949:

**LABOR MAPS CLASS PROGRAM AS U. OF M. EMBALMS WORKERS
EDUCATIONAL SERVICE
Ruthven Says Requiem After 1 Pupil Attends GM-Patterned Courses**

Ann Arbor, Mich. A watered-down Workers Education Service was cancelled this week by the University of Michigan authorities after it was found that the program had been reinstated with complete disregard to the advice of the WES advisory committee that the program did not meet the needs of the workers.

[28] See Lynd and Lynd, *Middletown in Transition*, chap. 6, "Training the Young," for an account of the various kinds of pressure that business and other groups put on educational institutions from kindergarten to college.

[29] Cf. George S. Counts, *School and Society in Chicago*, Harcourt, Brace and Company, 1928, and *Secondary Education and Industrialism*, Harvard University Press, 1929; Jerome Davis, *Capitalism and Its Culture*, Farrar and Rinehart, 1935, p. 346.

Barney Hopkins, Michigan CIO secretary-treasurer said, "The University can now thank the General Motors Corporation and the Regents for smashing a program servicing more than 65,000 workers."

In announcing curtailment of the Service, University President Alexander Ruthven regretted that the "response of workers for whom the program was designed has not matched the efforts which the University has made to serve their needs."

But in union circles the failure of the program was attributed to the University's insistence on telling the workers what type of classes they should have and the by-passing of an advisory committee set up to supervise the WES.

Faced with such an unfavorable educational climate unions have understandably established separate educational programs of their own to teach union history, practices, organization, and sentiments. Public schools have not been willing or able to do for labor what they have done for business and industry.

Industry's Leisure Program for the Community

Business and industry are gradually expanding their influence in the sphere of leisure and recreation. Both labor and management have well-developed "intramural recreational programs" including such activities as photography clubs, athletic leagues, charm classes, picnics, and dancing. Important as these activities are, we are more interested in the recreational programs which take workers outside the plant and into the community. Recreational programs which do not involve the workers themselves but the leisure-time activities of others (especially the youth) are more important in the study of industry-community relations.

Industry's sponsorship of recreational and youth organizations takes many forms such as financial underwriting, organizational promoting, advertising certain activities, or coöperating with other agencies in establishing a recreational service. Among the many leisure activities sponsored by industry in American cities are:

Athletic teams of all kinds in city-wide leagues.

Youth "leisure" organizations such as Boy and Girl Scouts, and the Young Men's and Young Women's Christian Association.

Library and "educational" facilities.

Community services such as parks, playgrounds, and orchestras.

Managers are interested in the after-work activities of employees, because these activities may influence work performance, company loyalty, and company acceptability in the community. Athletic participation not only serves to maintain bodily tonus but may at the same time improve work performance. Playing also induces an *esprit de corps* which is easily transformed into company loyalty. The enthusiasm that the community has for athletic contests tends to create good will for the sponsoring industries.

Not all businesses are convinced that they should support recreational

"frills." Many employers, however, do not regard expenditure on an after-work program as a frill. The good will secured by supporting a Scout troop may bring greater returns than outright advertising. Building up company loyalty by supporting a bowling team may have the effect of repulsing approaches of labor unions. Satisfactions that workers derive from sports participation may provide an adequate substitute for a wage increase. Occupying the time of workers in a healthful program may be wiser than leaving them to their own resources, for one of the effects of a recreational program is extending informal supervision over a longer period of the day. All executives do not consciously plan leisure-time activities with these motives clearly in mind. Many of them have genuine interest in the welfare of their workers and the community. However, several motives may be satisfied by the same program.

Unions Invade the Field of Leisure

Union leaders generally believe that loyalty to the company threatens loyalty to the union. During working hours industry has control and attention of the workers. Only after the day's work can the union obtain the worker's interest. Since business meetings of the union local draw small and unenthusiastic audiences, recreational inducements are often provided. Cards, beer, bowling, and lottery are just a few of the attractions used.

Increasingly, however, union executives realize that the social functions of unions cannot be approached so haphazardly. They are planning activities to occupy the leisure time of their members. These often duplicate and compete with programs sponsored by employers. As a consequence both management and the union are offering athletic facilities, social clubs, specialized training, and credit unions. Both are supporting Scout troops, the Y.M.C.A., and other youth organizations. The union has one advantage over business in its programs. Since union officers know the social and cultural values of its members much better than do managers, the programs they offer are more in line with what workers want and understand.

For example, Local 195 of the U.A.W. in Windsor has opened an attractive and congenial bar in its union hall. The bar helps make the union hall a social center for its members. It helps strengthen their loyalty to the union.[30] This is a far cry from the feeling of middle-class businessmen, that drinking is not a good thing for workingmen, that workers should not spend their money on drink but on the essentials of life.

In the future we can expect the union to expand its welfare, educational, and leisure-time programs until they may overshadow those of employers. This has certainly been the case in Europe, where unions have evolved extensive programs for the workers and the community. Already, unions are expanding their local political activities to the point where they may chal-

[30] *UAW-CIO Ammunition*, May, 1949, p. 48.

lenge or destroy the business-class control of the municipality. Labor-oriented groups have already successfully challenged business domination of city government in Milwaukee, Minneapolis, Reading, Bridgeport, and other cities.[31] Advances that labor makes in the control of city government are more important than advances in any other area; for here they are dealing with the ultimate source of authority.

INFORMAL WORK ORGANIZATION

Work throws people together, and many kinds of groups are forged up and down the supervisory hierarchy. Many of these small work groups have such a remarkable degree of stability that they continue to operate as groups in community affairs. Warner found that the informal organization of workers was higher in some industries than in others: "Being a worker in a shoe factory modified the operative's social life in the community at large both qualitatively and quantitatively. He behaved differently from individuals in the community of comparable place in the social stratification. The effects of the shoe factories on the social lives of operatives demonstrate that these factories must be considered as social institutions."[32]

This means that the social ties at work lead people to bowl together, engage in ward politics, become cliques in the P.T.A. or the spark plugs of a charity drive. When this happens community participation reinforces the group ties that arise in industry.

A work clique in a community organization may have power and influence out of proportion to its size. In a large association a well-knit clique can usually secure its ends from the larger group. When the same clique operates in two different organizations, it does not function with two different sets of values. This means that the ends of one organization may be changed or deflected to conform to the purposes of another, as the clique carries its values from one organization to the other. In such instances the clique imbues the members of one organization with the values and purposes of another.

For example, church members are also workers, parents, business leaders, and citizens. Some church congregations contain within them influential cliques of persons from the business class, and others contain cliques of ardent unionists. Each clique has its own set of values and exerts an influence on the pastor and the congregation.

An illustration of this fact occurred during the General Motors sit-down strike of January, 1937. Flint pastors and ministers took different positions according to the composition of their congregations. Ministers in congregations which had no informally organized cliques of workers could ignore

[31] Harold Zink, *Government of Cities in the United States*, The Macmillan Company, 1939, p. 216.
[32] Warner and Low, *op. cit.*, pp. 217-218.

the strike issue or take any position on it. However, this could not happen
in churches whose membership contained cliques of union members. In
these churches, pressure was exerted on the ministers to favor the union's
side on the strike.

Another illustration serves to demonstrate how informally organized
work groups affect the operation of other organizations. A midwestern suburban community was composed of two dominant occupational groups:
college professors and business executives. The P.T.A. and the school board
of this community were split on educational policy for the local schools.
In general, college and business people took opposite sides in the struggle.
Although the business families outnumbered the college professors, the
latter won the school board election. This was possible because of superior
communication among the college faculty members. They belonged to one
institution, and were tied together with many formal and informal ties.
The business people were employed in many enterprises. Their contacts
with one another were less frequent and more formal in nature. They found
that they had to do more electioneering with less rewards for their efforts.
Although the college group had inferior formal or political organization
their superior informal organization was sufficient to bring victory.

In summary, we have seen that industry brings about changes in community relations when it changes its technological processes. Since the
supervisory structure of industry functions as a structure in community
affairs, businessmen have great power. In addition to this organizational
advantage, management has developed a complex associational program to
influence community behavior. Recently, labor unions have established
competing associations to obtain the sympathy of workers and the other
members of the community. Informally organized work groups often participate as groups in community affairs. The outcome of issues in the city or
the town depends upon the integration of work groups as they function
informally in the various organizations within the community.

INSTITUTIONAL PRESSURES ON
INDUSTRIAL OPERATIONS

Industry can bring pressures and influences to bear upon the various
institutions in the community. The community, on the other hand, also
has the power to influence industry and, indeed, to dictate the very terms
on which the survival of industry depends. When business feels no "interference" from the outside, either all sections of the community share its
values or business has a monopoly of local power. When the community
feels no "interference" from business, then such institutions as the church,
family, school, local government, labor organizations, professional and
fraternal societies have together the power to determine the course of the

community and the conditions under which local industries shall operate. An observer who wishes to appraise the relative pressures of the community organizations as opposed to those of local industry and its influential business leaders, has a difficult task. The interdependence of industry and community is particularly apparent when an attempt is made to separate the influence of each. Businessmen live and participate in the community, often side by side with white-collar and manual workers. However, the community does house many different institutions, each exerting its own peculiar influence in community life. This fact suggests one approach that may be used to determine how the community affects the conduct of business and union affairs. We may ask specifically, "How does each institution and formally organized group interfere with or enhance the aims and ends of the different industrial groups?" With this approach government, education, family, welfare, and religious organizations are analyzed for their effects on business. We shall first examine the impact of local institutions on work plants in the community. Later on we shall ascertain the effect that cultural influences arising from the different class, racial, ethnic, and religious groups in the city have on the operation of industry.

ECONOMIC FORCES IN THE COMMUNITY

It is an economic axiom that survival of industry depends on relations to other industries and to consumers. Altogether too frequently "other business" and "consumers" are thought of as impersonal entities that are won over or lost by economic performance alone. This is not a sociological fact because all relations, including economic, are also social relations. The importance of social relations to a business is more evident when it is dependent on the local market. The attitudes of its employees, consumers, related businesses, and the union often determine economic survival. These attitudes may range from sympathetic support to economic and social boycott. The dependence of a business on the good will of the component members of the economic institution is often taken for granted until the good will is suddenly removed.

INDUSTRY'S DEPENDENCE ON LOCAL GOOD WILL

During World War II a foreign film manufacturing company moved to a small New England town. Most of the film it produced was for government consumption. One small batch was defective and the government returned it to the company. Many employees insisted that the company merely repacked this film and sent it elsewhere, and the word spread from one locality to another. When the consumer market returned, the company did not find the local outlets it anticipated. As men were laid off, rumors of defective films and foreign connections of the company increased. Whether or not these rumors had any basis the fact remains that the company was

partially dependent for survival on the sentiments of the local people. When support was not forthcoming it could not weather the strain of transitional economic hardship.[33]

At times the survival of a company depends upon the attitude of other businesses and not its consumers. Warner reports a situation wherein the absentee owners of the shoe factories of Yankee City did not receive the support of the managers of locally owned factories.

"Big Mike" Rafferty was president of a small shoe enterprise. He had been a former mayor of Yankee City and publisher of *Hard Facts*, a weekly filled with his ideas about reputable citizens of the city. During the strike "Big Mike" repeatedly endorsed the strikers against the manufacturers. At one of the meetings during strike negotiations he berated the employers, "Why if I knew as much about the shoe manufacturing as you fellows are supposed to I'd be ashamed not to pay employees more money. . . . [Why don't] you manufacturers who make your money in Yankee City . . . sleep here too? If the union could be recognized in Boston [why] couldn't it be recognized in Yankee City?"[34] (Brackets are ours.)

These questions made a strong impression on the managers of the absentee-owned companies. It brought attention to the fact that local citizens *and businessmen* were supporting local laborers against absentee owners. The union won recognition and the strike. This illustration shows that one of the institutions that a business must adjust to is the economic institution itself.

THE ROLE OF LOCAL INFORMAL ORGANIZATION

Local industry and businesses are also dependent on the informal organization in the neighborhoods of the community. This is especially the case for retail business. Lundberg has shown clearly that the process of informal communication is vital in the buying process.[35] Each local neighborhood has one or more opinion leaders with high influence and prestige. The products they buy, the stores they patronize or do not patronize, the union policies they endorse or oppose become the patterns for a large number of followers or satellites. Since each class level or neighborhood has its own informal structure and leaders, influence does not flow uniformly from the top of the community ladder to the very bottom. Businesses that cater to only upper-class people or groups in the local community may not be tapping the real sources of influence in other sections of the community. In fact, they may be alienating those sources. Thus, the market is socially as well as economically organized. Those industries that appreciate the social

[33] Based on a student report by Ruth Bissett, Michigan State College, 1948.
[34] Warner and Low, *op. cit.*, p. 149.
[35] George A. Lundberg, "Marketing and Social Organization," Charles Coolidge Parlin Memorial Lecture, Philadelphia, 1945.

realities of the market in local neighborhoods and communities survive and profit. Those that do not may flounder or remain marginal.

GOVERNMENT EXERTS ITS POWER

The influence that local government has on industry's behavior should not be underestimated. During a crisis, such as a strike, the municipality can ignore the issue, join either side, or attempt a conciliation. Whatever its course, government purports to speak and act for the "public"; that is, for the mass of citizens who are not parties to the dispute. However, when government acts it invariably affects the relative positions of management and labor.

In some cases, government acts directly in the interest of business. During the Flint sit-down strike of 1937 the city manager reputedly called a secret meeting of the company men to outline a "back to work" campaign. The plan was launched under the title of "The Flint Alliance for the Security of Our Jobs, Our Homes, and Our Community."[36] The Alliance, which claimed a membership of 20,000 citizens and businessmen, condemned the strike, demanded forcible evacuation of the sit-downers, and insisted on the right of workers to return to work.

After a mass union demonstration the city manager and the police chief began organizing a civilian army "to repossess Flint for the forces of law and order." The manager told reporters, "The strikers have taken over this town and we are going to take it back. We have asked the state police and National Guard to keep order and have been refused; so we are going down there shooting."[37] All these local government activities in the name of the public did not work in this case. They demonstrate, however, how close the tie between government and industry can be.

Local Courts

The position of local courts is also critical during a strike. They may be called upon to protect the rights of labor or of property, as the case may be. Students of law recognize that courts have been and are affected in their decisions by current opinion. Historically, the courts have tended to buttress the most powerful groups in the community. As changes in the relations between groups in the community and nation have occurred, courts have tended to make decisions in accord with the new power alignment.[38] Whether or not the court will grant an injunction in the case of a strike depends upon the historical pressures put on it. This does not

[36] See "Industrial Conflict in Detroit," by Dwight W. Chapman, in *Industrial Conflict*, The Cordon Company, 1939; and Henry Kraus, chap. 6, "Counter-Attack," in *The Many and the Few*, The Plantin Press, 1947.

[37] Kraus, *op. cit.*, p. 241.

[38] Charles A. Beard, *An Economic Interpretation of the Constitution*, The Macmillan Company, 1923.

mean that judges are subject to pressure in all daily decisions, but it does mean that they are selected by those in power on an assumption that they will perform according to certain expectations. The political party and those who control it influence executive selection of judges. They also screen judicial candidates who run for election. To understand the operation of local courts, sociological studies focusing on the relations between political parties, labor, management, and the governmental structure must be made.

Tax Manipulation

The municipality can influence the economic and social position of business directly through its tax policy. The attitude of local government ranges from the one extreme of subsidy to the other extreme of burdensome taxes. The kind of decision that is made on the problem of taxes depends upon the power relations between industry and government, and on the attitudes that community leaders have toward certain businesses.[39]

It is not an accident to find businesses failing to carry their share of local taxes. Homeowners and other citizens often pay disproportionately high taxes when they cannot control the tax machinery. Vivid illustrations of this situation are found where large industries move to fringe areas of the city. There they escape paying taxes for schools, roads, and transit systems which the workers must have. At the same time, they make demands for local governmental services all out of proportion to the taxes they pay.

When business pays exorbitantly high taxes, the reasons for the antagonistic attitude of local government must be located. A discriminatory tax policy arises when business has not only lost local influence but antagonized those in control of the municipality. This is the case in the Gogebic and Mesabi Iron Range communities in the upper peninsula of Michigan and Minnesota.

In these towns the surface rights belong to the public and the underground rights to iron mining companies. The Range towns, although they contain only one major industry, are independent and not company towns. Since 1921 they have lacked nothing in the way of ordinary public facilities and utilities. Not infrequently over 90 percent of all funds to pay for these facilities come from taxation on mining properties. Wakefield, Michigan (4000 population), has an elaborate well-lighted boulevard, modern schools, and other major facilities. Like other towns it has taxed the mines while they were running full blast. No surplus money was allowed to accumulate in the city treasury, so as not to give the companies justification to ask for tax reduction.

Many people believed that every cent possible should be collected from

[39] Competing businesses may fight each other by trying to get control of tax policy machinery. Preferential and discriminatory taxes, though illegal, are often accomplished by various subterfuges.

the companies while they are still operating and that the town should retain a share of the wealth which, once removed, would never return. Although the town governments try to collect all taxes possible, they overlook violations of the mining codes.

The great corporations which took possession of the Mesabi around 1900 had only one aim—profits for stockholders. They introduced a predatory pattern in dealing with employees and with the State's heritage in ore. . . . The public gradually sided with labor in their sympathies, and the two groups together, through controlling government, gradually adopted the same predatory pattern of the mining companies. Their only weapon was taxation. Through taxation they could acquire not only poor relief for labor but subsidies for struggling business enterprises; not only the necessary conveniences for the public good, but luxuries. They found, through taxation, a way to reinstate beauty where industry had marred it, a way to bring culture and refinement in a locality where many nations had been mixed in a struggle for bread, a way to bring recreation and play to both unemployed youth and adults.[40]

INFLUENCE OF FAMILY SYSTEM

Many studies have analyzed the changes that modern industry and technology have made on family structure and relations. However, only a few people have investigated how industry's operations are in turn affected by the kind of family system prevailing in certain localities. Yet this direction of influence is very important because certain industries can flourish only when a "congenial" family system is in their vicinity. For example, highly seasonal enterprises need many workers during some seasons and very few in other periods. Marginal industries need a labor supply during lush years but will release workers in normal or depressed periods. Some industries need large numbers of women and children as workers, and others demand only men.

Such industries can operate successfully only in areas where family systems are characterized by great flexibility—families that can readily shift from one form of subsistence to another. Arensberg maintains that the location of the plastic industry in New England towns rests on the presence of such a family system. The immigrant family in New England showed remarkable solidarity despite the fact that some of its members were farmers and others were factory workers. When factory employment was high, sons, daughters, and wives became wage workers; when employment became scarce, the family shifted greater energy to farming.[41] Needless to say, such marginal-seasonal industries cannot survive where wives will not accept factory work or where children leave home early and set up separate households.

The rubber industry of Akron, which needs a flexible labor supply, is

[40] Paul H. Landis, *Three Iron Mining Towns*, Edwards Brothers, Inc., 1938, p. 112.
[41] Arensberg, *op. cit.*, p. 5.

aided by the mobility of "hillbilly" families from West Virginia which move in and out, depending on the needs of the industry. Zimmerman has documented the helplessness of people in stranded industrial towns whose family structure did not permit ready shift from urban to rural employment. Nor would these families supply labor to marginal industries when stable employment was available.[42]

In many other ways industry must take into consideration family structure and family needs. Businesses cannot move too far from the residences of the bulk of their workers for fear of interfering with family life. During the war many industries that located in rural and fringe areas found that workers would not trade time at home for high wages and excellent working conditions.

CHURCH, PROPERTY, AND LABOR

The influence of the church on industry and labor is of recent interest to industrial sociologists. The role played by this institution in local affairs is important because it is the only institution that relates itself to powers above those of mortal men. Utterances of church officials are hard to ignore because they presumably speak the word of God. They are supposed to provide men with a code of conduct which will guide them in everyday affairs. On occasion, therefore, church officials are called into labor disputes to use their influence in averting violence, promoting justice, and encouraging good will.

Such active participation in local labor disputes is the exception rather than the rule. Churchmen generally ignore local problems or deal with them on an abstract theological basis. As the Lynds observed in Middletown, "The gap between religion's verbalizing and Middletown life has become so wide that the entire institution of religion has tended to be put on the defensive. . . . It is timid in jeopardizing its foothold in the culture by espousing unpopular causes."[43]

Although churchmen tend to ignore local problems, their influence in the community should not be underestimated. Historically, they have sanctioned and underwritten the prevailing sentiments of business—hard work, the rights of property, duty, individualism, loyalty, and the inevitability of suffering. The church, besides being a powerful educative institution in its own right, sponsors community programs (Boy Scouts, fellowship leagues, parochial schools) which instill prevailing property sentiments.[44] This is true despite the fact that religions and denominations tend to be stratified on a class basis; the Episcopal Church (upper class),

---

[42] Carle C. Zimmerman and Merle E. Frampton, *Family and Society*, D. Van Nostrand Company, 1935, chap. 17, "Subsistence Adjustment in a Stranded Industrial Town."
[43] Lynd and Lynd, *Middletown in Transition*, p. 311.
[44] See Jerome Davis, *op. cit.*, chap. 19, "An Interlocking Control of Religion."

the Catholic (middle and lower class), and the Baptist (lower middle and lower) have all generally supported the *status quo*. Notwithstanding the variety of sophistication of religious appeals, most churches do not criticize specifically and directly the groups upon whom they eventually depend for survival.

Since about 1930, however, a small but vocal minority of religious leaders has urged churches to play a more direct and vigorous role in local affairs. Social action agencies have been formed, which take an active interest in management-labor relations. The Presbyterian Fellowship for Social Action, the Methodist Federation for Social Service, the Unitarian Fellowship of Social Justice are a few of the religious associations that are making critical studies of current local problems. In some cases they have corralled public opinion behind labor.

The Catholic Church has also developed a pro-labor wing to work within the communities and the labor unions. The Association of Catholic Trade Unionists is an organization which exerts religious influence within unions. Labor schools have been established in certain parishes, and Catholic universities have established institutes of industrial relations. Although most churches continue to support management or remain silent on labor issues, a realignment according to sympathies of parishioners seems to be increasing.

CULTURAL INFLUENCES ON INDUSTRIAL BEHAVIOR

The modern industrial city is a complex of sub-cultural groups. Different class, racial, ethnic, economic, and religious groups have distinctive values, sentiments, organizations, and behavior patterns. These groups must interact with each other, especially in the factories, market place, and other economic establishments. As the modern industrial system grows and expands into new areas, groups that have been segregated are often brought together. Some groups invade residential areas that have long guarded their racial or ethnic identity. Conflicts and accommodation between invaders and invaded invariably occur. Likewise, as the industrial system expands within a given area, it becomes more diversified, segregating people and reducing the area of common sentiments. Each group builds up a system of stereotypes and prejudices against the other, even as they are attempting of necessity to find a way of living together.

Businessmen often behave ruthlessly and aggressively in the face of cultural heterogeneity. Frequently they think, "Get the best man for the job, sweep away any impediment to production, reward the aggressive individual." These sentiments ignore the thought that cultural variations are real and that adjustments must be made in industrial operations where different cultural groups interact. Although cultural groups are rarely co-

terminous with communities, the latter are necessary to sustain and transmit cultures. Once the student knows which cultural groups are interacting in industry he can predict many of the adjustments that must be made in all the communities where these groups are found.

A COLONIAL SITUATION

Perhaps the most illuminating example of changes forced upon management may be found where capitalistic enterprises operate in colonial areas. These enterprises are often extractive industries which need an abundance of local unskilled laborers. Inexperienced managers in these instances try to operate much as they have at home. They introduce an individual wage system (itself an innovation of considerable magnitude), economic incentives for production, and threats of layoff and wage reduction. Of course, they find that these practices are not successful. Countless difficulties arise in the recruitment, direction, and retention of workers.

Hughes points out, "The natives themselves are often not accustomed to individual wage work, at least as a continued and sole means of getting a living. They may have worked only as members of communities, their tasks and rewards determined by their places in a social system. . . . The economic incentives do not bring in a labor supply. Industry departs from its mother-country practice of encouraging free movement of labor, and uses the police power instead."[45]

Other repercussions of such a system are evident. Native labor, though forced into industry, is not given the opportunity to climb in it. Executive, technical, and skilled workers are usually nonnative. They develop monopolistic job practices which are reinforced by racial and ethnic prejudices. Although such practices are continued only with tremendous economic and social costs, they nevertheless persist. Further, the more that natives embrace the ideology of the industrial system, the more anachronistic it appears to them. Racial or ethnic self-awareness, militancy, and inevitable conflicts are the results.[46]

Colonialism at Home

This situation has existed, though in less extreme form, in the industrial frontier communities of the United States. When New England industries moved into the southern Appalachian region and into rural areas, they brought with them a core of managers and technicians whose behavior toward the local population was not unlike that of industrial imperialists. These managers attempted to control the total lives of the workers,

[45] Everett C. Hughes, "Queries Concerning Industry and Society Growing Out of Study of Ethnic Relations in Industry," *American Sociological Review*, April, 1949, p. 215.

[46] Wilbert Moore, "Primitives and Peasants in Industry," *Social Research*, March, 1948, pp. 71-72.

kept out union leaders, provided a minimum of services, kept local people from climbing the supervisory ladder, and let the community flounder during depressed periods.

On the other hand industries do make easy accommodations to new cultural situations. In many southern regions the resentment and rebellion against Yankee employers has not been great. One reason for this is that the customs and traditions of the feudal plantation system, with its paternalistic responsibility and profitable control, already existed in the South. "Foreign" industrialists merely adopted the whole system into their operations— "Housing and village communities, Sunday schools and night classes, commissaries, sanitary regulations, child labor, working mothers, employment of whole families, physical and social isolation . . . were direct inheritances from the older order."[47] In other words, manufacturers continued the old social order within a new technological setting. They adopted or did not interfere with the local religious, political, and racial mores.

This feudal industrial pattern was in fact so well knit that labor leaders had to adjust to it if they were going to succeed in unionization. Only recently have union organizers modified their traditional practices to conform to southern customs. The use of folk and religious songs, identifying owners as Yankees, belittling the "dangers" of Negro competition, appealing to the traditional individualism of the natives are some of the newer techniques that organizers now feel they must use.

THE EFFECT OF COMMUNITY ORGANIZATION ON DAILY PLANT OPERATIONS

Technical operations within plants often are bottlenecked because of management's failure to take into account the social and cultural organization prevailing in the community. The basic consideration that is neglected is that the system of relations outside the plant is reinforced by the social relations within the plant. Changes in operations which alter the flow of work will sometimes disturb the established web of relations necessary for group collaboration.

Arensberg interpreted the causes of a paper mill strike with this hypothesis in mind. In this case after management had inaugurated an incentive scheme in the cutting room, disturbances followed which led to a strike by the paper machine crew. Management was mystified in trying to explain why the men in a seemingly unrelated department would walk out over an affair which concerned another department. Actually, the workers in these departments were tied together in a system of kinship, age patterns, and occupational prestige. "The company engineers . . . had reversed the customary pattern of authority by setting the juniors and inferiors to hurrying

[47] Harriet Herring, "The Outside Employer in the Southern Industrial Pattern," *Social Forces*, October, 1939, pp. 115-116.

up their seniors and superiors. The machine room men had struck against the disturbance of their community."[48]

Metropolitanized Algonac and Religious Holland[49]

The influence of community organization on plant operation may be seen by comparing the operation of identical plants in two different communities. In Algonac and Holland, Michigan, there is a company which owns plants in which cabin cruisers are built. The original plant is located in Algonac, a town of 2000 people located in the vacation-metropolitan hinterland of Detroit. Upper-middle-class suburban residents constitute the majority of the population. They want to keep Algonac a residential community—and thus discourage industries from settling there. The manual workers in or near the town are made up of Indians, French Canadians, native and foreign born—with their traditional antagonisms toward each other.

Apart from a small nucleus of older native workers, the majority of the plant employees are rather recent arrivals from other sections of the country. During the winter a number of Great Lakes sailors are employed, and their place is taken in summer by local schoolteachers. There is a strong union in the plant. The informal groups in the plant are based upon occupation, seniority, experience, and ethnic origin. Very few values and sentiments bind these groups and management together. The general work atmosphere is one full of bickering and tension. Management has had to deal with problems of strikes, high turnover, drinking in the plant, and absenteeism.

In order to escape some of these problems, especially the spread of unionism, the corporation purchased a plant in Holland, Michigan. Holland is a neat, clean city of 14,000 people. Its inhabitants are deeply religious Dutch descendants who take their callings seriously. When the corporation moved to Holland it sent a skeleton crew to build an organization similar to that in Algonac. The crew encountered several unexpected difficulties. The religious Dutch would not work on Sunday and the Seventh-Day Adventists would not work on Saturday. The imported Algonac foremen could not get obedience or coöperation when they swore at the workers. The Irish foremen were irritated at "the Stubborn Dutch," and the Dutch didn't like the blasphemous Irishmen. Not until local people became foremen did the sources of friction disappear.

Other changes in plant operations were necessary. At ten o'clock in the morning local workers stopped their machines for "coffee." This pattern was so strong that it was soon institutionalized. Workers also asked that the

[48] Arensberg, op. cit., p. 6.
[49] This section is based on a report by Willis D. Richardson, student at Michigan State College, 1949.

plant start operating earlier so they could spend more time with their families. This was done. Although an A.F. of L. union obtained recognition shortly before World War II, it was rather weak because many workers refused to join it on religious grounds. These brief descriptions indicate how the official everyday activities of management and union executives are invariably affected by the type of communities in which they operate.

THE PROBLEM OF RACE AND ETHNIC DIFFERENCES

Many ethnic and racial groups in American industrial communities constitute distinct sub-cultures. When members of these groups are recruited into industry, native American employers find that special problems arise and that special adjustments must be made to them. A period of acculturation for both groups occurs—managers find themselves changing their routines and minority groups slowly accept some of the values of management. During the early part of this transitional period the intermediary or the "go-between" makes his appearance. The go-between may or may not be the informal leader of the workers; he may or may not be their foreman. But he is always someone who understands the cultures of both groups. He interprets the aims and motives of each group to the other, and finds a path which is suitable to both.

Labor union leaders found very early that it was best not to change radically the behavior of immigrant workers. They were allowed to conduct union business in their native tongues. Union officers demanded that employers recognize the rights of workers to observe their special religious and other holidays.

During World War II a group of American Indians was employed in one of the navy yards. When the foreman complained that they were a sullen, unmanageable, and soldiering crew, a counselor was sent to investigate conditions. She located the chief in the group, found that he had had supervisory experience, and urged that he be given the job of the foreman.

"The Indians went to work with a will. The supervisor wisely ignored complaints that the Indians were loafers because they took their accustomed siestas, dozing in the shade. The work was done in unexpected ways, but results were, by highest production standards, excellent. Through utilization of established group leadership . . . the productivity of the group was released. . . . It seemed simpler to alter the procedures than to change the habits of the workers."[50]

A common phenomenon in American work plants is a system of ethnic job expectations. Management and labor officials have adjusted to this system rather unconsciously. When ethnic job expectations are violated repercussions follow. Collins reports that at Somerset, a New England

[50] Esther Boorman Strong, "Individual Adjustment in Industrial Society," *American Sociological Review*, June, 1949, p. 341.

factory, the job of foreman came to be a virtual monopoly of the Irish.[51] When a Yankee was promoted to replace an Irish subforeman, a short walkout materialized. Management was accused of discriminating against an Irish candidate. The union (a non-Yankee organization) allowed the grievance to be filed although it knew that there was no contractual support for this position. Subsequently, an Irish subforeman was named and relations between workers and management proceeded as formerly. It is significant that no such protests were made when Yankees were promoted to jobs within the hierarchy dominated by Yankees. Only when ethnic job expectations were violated did repercussions follow.

Similar problems are evident when management tries to bring into industries new ethnic and racial groups. Despite management's formal right to hire and promote, it often cannot do so and maintain production. This problem is especially acute when lower-status ethnic and racial groups are hired to mix with groups who consider their status to be higher.[52] Mexicans, Negroes, Indians, Orientals, and new immigrants have found much discrimination against them in industry by other racial and ethnic groups. Management and union leaders are inaugurating campaigns to reduce this practice, but progress is slow.

In this chapter we have endeavored to sketch out in broad outline some of the relations of industry to the community and to present some of the problems that need further research. Our preliminary analysis has shown that industry in a sense is responsible for the physical appearance of the community as well as its economic survival. But more important, the way industry functions influences the daily lives of the local inhabitants. Technological changes in production constitute the most dynamic source of change. Such diverse things as family life, class relations, and recreational patterns are influenced by changing production methods.

Apart from such changes that are unconsciously wrought, industrial managers are attempting to influence community relations directly. They have inaugurated community programs both for their workers and for others in an attempt to secure community approval. The union has launched similar programs to compete with those of management.

The community is not a purely passive agent. Its institutions also alter industrial life. Government, schools, the family, and the church play an important role in shaping community attitudes toward industry. In addition, the local sub-cultural groups in our cities make plant managers con-

[51] Orvis Collins, "Ethnic Behavior in Industry," *American Journal of Sociology*, January, 1946, pp. 295-297. See Chapter XIII, Figure 50, for the chart of ethnic job expectations.

[52] See Everett C. Hughes, "The Knitting of Racial Groups in Industry," *American Sociological Review*, October, 1946, pp. 512-519.

sider cultural heterogeneity before they act. In the following chapter, the broader impact of industry on society will be considered.

SUPPLEMENTARY STUDIES

FIELD: SURVEY OF LOCAL INDUSTRIES AND BUSINESSES

Make a survey of the kinds of industry and business operating in your community. In a small community it is desirable that such a survey be made by direct observation. In a larger community which cannot be actually covered by the observer such data as desired will probably be available to the local Chamber of Commerce. Another source is the United States Census.

FIELD: SURVEY OF LOCAL LABOR FORCE

Find out what the composition of the local labor force is. The state employment office in your town or city will probably have such information. A second source with less recent figures is *Sixteenth Census of the United States, Population,* Vol. III. The census contains labor force data on cities of 100,000 or more.

FIELD: STUDY OF THE OCCUPATIONAL COMPOSITION OF CERTAIN COMMUNITY BOARDS

Make a study of the occupations of:
1. Members of the local school board.
2. Members of the boards of your churches.
3. Members of the boards of local veterans organizations.
4. Members of the boards of certain local lodges.
5. Members of the board of the local chamber of commerce.
6. Members of the boards of certain local unions.

FIELD: PLANNED INTERVIEW

Interview the local officer in the state employment office in your town or city and find out what the local employment picture is. Discuss with him the relation of local industry to employment.

LIBRARY: FILM

The City (30 minutes), deals with three phases of city building as adapted to the prevailing industrial pattern. Contrasts planned and unplanned communities. Produced by the Museum of Modern Art.

LIBRARY: BOOKS AND ARTICLES

Arensberg, Conrad M., "Industry and the Community," *American Journal of Sociology,* July, 1942, pp. 1-12.
Jones, Alfred Winslow, *Life, Liberty, and Property,* J. B. Lippincott Company, 1941.
Landis, Paul H., *Three Iron Mining Towns,* Edwards Brothers, 1938.
Liepman, K., *Journey to Work,* Oxford University Press, 1947.

Lynd, Robert S., and Lynd, Helen M., *Middletown*, Harcourt, Brace and Company. 1929, chaps. 4-8, "Getting a Living."

Lynd, Robert S., and Lynd, Helen M., *Middletown in Transition*, Harcourt, Brace and Company, 1937, chap. 2, "Getting a Living," and chap. 3, "The X Family: A Pattern of Business Class Control."

Myers, Charles A. and Maclaurin, W. Rupert, *The Movement of Factory Workers*, John Wiley and Sons, Inc., 1943.

Walker, Charles, *Steeltown*, Harper & Brothers, 1950.

Warner, W. L., and Low, J. O., *The Social System of the Modern Factory*, Yale University Press, 1947.

RESEARCH GAPS

1. The ecological distribution of workers in the community for given work plants.
2. Social base maps showing sex, age, ethnic composition, etc., of different work plants.
3. The factors accounting for the reputation of a work plant in the community.
4. The occupational composition of community leaders.

CHAPTER XXII

Industry and Society

THE IMPACT OF INDUSTRY UPON SOCIETY

Industrial civilization has developed about a *machine technology,* a *market economy,* and an *industrial society.* The industrial mode of production has given rise to an economic organization that influences all parts of

society. Industrialism as a configuration of technology, economy, and business values emerges as a culture system, one of the most widely spread
systems in human history. No modern social institution has escaped the
influence of the economic organization of society. The school, the church,
the home, and recreational institutions are built upon human values arising
from the material framework of modern civilization. Industrial society,
therefore, refers to more than machines and markets; it refers to men and
institutions locked in the network of relationships dominated by business
mores and folkways. Industrial society has become a society in which social
relationships tend to be economic relationships.[1]

FOUR CONCENTRIC PATTERNS OF INDUSTRIAL SOCIETY

It follows that industry and society are almost indivisible. What affects
the economy will inevitably affect society and vice versa. We may conceive

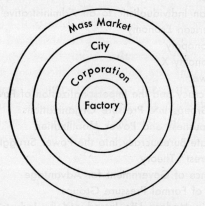

FIG. 125.   Four Concentric Patterns of
Industrial Society.

of industrial society as composed of four concentric patterns. Figure 125
shows these four patterns to be made up of the *factory*, the *corporation*,
the *city*, and the *mass market*.

The Factory

The hub is represented by the factory, which consists jointly of specialized machines or techniques, knowledge of processes and exchange problems, and a group of persons organized for work activities. The factory is
the most significant of all the various work plants of modern industrial
society for it contains the machines of production. The machine industries

[1] Thorstein Veblen has demonstrated this thesis brilliantly in *The Theory of Business
Enterprise*, Charles Scribner's Sons, 1927, and *The Theory of the Leisure Class*, B. W.
Huebsch, Inc., 1924.

are in a dominant position; they set the pace for the rest of the industrial system. It is this dominance of the machine process in industry which marks off the present industrial system from all other economies.

The Corporation

The corporation ties the work plant into the economic organization of society. Investors of stocks and bonds are invited from all parts of the nation and indeed from all ends of the earth. The only qualification for membership is possession of capital which may be hired for capital goods expansion. The pooling of capital enables the factory to employ mass-production techniques and the corporation to seek greater gains in ever larger markets. The private corporation has proved to be the most effective technique ever invented (outside of public finance) for the aggregation of wealth. The rise of the corporation has created a revolution in the relations of those who manage, those who work, those who own and control.

The workman's property in his craft or skill has all but disappeared with the growth of corporate enterprise. The industrial worker has become a worker without ownership of tools and with little need of skill. The owners have become increasingly separated from those who manage, and this separation of ownership and control has effected a radical shift in the property and power status of the absentee owners. With owners dispersed geographically and numerically, the managers have come to make the important decisions affecting the daily conduct of the business.[2] However, the major stockholders retain power over production, price, and wage policies.

The City

The city is the great labor center for the factory. The location of the factory has often determined the location of the city; it always has affected the growth of the city. Urban life is an old pattern but the rise of large cities paralleled industrial growth. The entire countryside became caught up in the "lure of the city."[3] More and more the sons and daughters of rural families migrated to the city. Work at a machine or in an office replaced work on the land. The new urban dweller became both a producer and a consumer, and the city came to regard him as part of both *labor* and the *market*. The range of his activities broadened to serve a growing number of business pursuits. Banking, publishing, retailing, utility, advertising, warehousing, clerking, transporting, educating, doctoring, and preaching became additional founts of enterprise. Paul Meadows has expressed precisely the correlation of industrial life with urban life. He says,

[2] Cf. James Burnham, *The Managerial Revolution*, The John Day Company, 1941.
[3] Arthur M. Schlesinger, *The Rise of the City, 1878-1898*, The Macmillan Company, 1933.

"Urbanization is the indispensable partner of industrialization, the measure of its growth, the mirror of its complexities, the interpreter of its values, and the matrix of its expansion."[4]

The Mass Market

A market is a meeting place for the purpose of barter or buying and selling. The local market in which goods are exchanged is a pattern of the early towns, but the long-distance market is associated with the commercial and industrial revolutions. Mass production requires mass markets. These markets are sought everywhere—in the country, village, town, city, nation, and in every part of the world. The economic organization of modern society is dependent upon these far-flung markets. Karl Polanyi traces out implications of this fact.

Ultimately, that is why the control of the economic system by the market is of overwhelming consequence to the whole organization of society; it means no less than the running of society as an adjunct to the market. Instead of the economy being embedded in social relations, social relations are embedded in the economic system. The vital importance of the economic factor to the existence of society precludes any other result. For once the economic system is organized in separate institutions, based on specific motives and conferring a special status, society must be shaped in such a manner as to allow that system to function according to its own laws. This is the meaning of the familiar assertion that a market economy can function only in a market society.[5]

Nineteenth-century society tried to make the market economy a self-regulating economy in which neither price, nor supply, nor demand must be fixed or regulated. Only policies and measures were in order that helped to insure the self-regulation of the market by creating conditions which make the market the only organizing power in the economic sphere. It was widely believed that such a system was "natural," allowing men freedom of choice, exercise of natural "instincts" and creative drives, and permitting expression of individual differences. It was not recognized that such a "natural" economic mechanism could be maintained only by some

[4] Paul Meadows, "The Industrial Way of Life," *Technology Review*, March, 1946.
[5] Karl Polanyi, *The Great Transformation*, Rinehart and Company, 1944, p. 57. It is interesting to compare another statement: "The outstanding discovery of recent historical and anthropological research is that man's economy, as a rule, is submerged in his social relationships. He does not act so as to safeguard his individual interest in the possession of material goods; he acts so as to safeguard his social standing, his social claims, his social assets. He values material goods only in so far as they serve this end. Neither the process of production nor that of distribution is linked to specific economic interests attached to the possession of goods; but every single step in that process is geared to a number of social interests which eventually ensure that the required step be taken. These interests will be very different in a small hunting or fishing community from those in a vast despotic society, but in either case the economic system will be run on non-economic motives." *Ibid.*, p. 46.

highly artificial stimulants in order to meet a situation which was created by the no less artificial phenomenon of the machine. Land, labor, and capital were called to the market like raw materials to function as agents of production. Wealth was created, but society was slowly splintered. Men failed to realize what the cohesion of society meant. The family, the neighborhood, and the community, in turn, were weakened by the endless churning of large population masses as mobility increased among all levels of society. The chief nexus between an individual and his community became the job. Kinship, neighborhood, political, religious, and recreational ties became secondary to the desire to increase personal wealth or status. Citizenship in the large city all too often lost meaning as special interest groups with distant leaders jostled for power. New personal freedoms were purchased by withdrawal from the permanent, intimate association of small groups and the acceptance of membership in large, specialized groups. The new urban dweller has been taught to keep his social roots shallow and his baggage light for he is supposed to be ready for the "better" job opportunity which will help him climb to greater fame or fortune. If he does not, the threat of some economic depression always hovers in the immediate background with dire warnings for those who refuse to "play it smart" and seize upon a more secure work position whatever the social sacrifice.

Industrial society in the twentieth century is now a highly interdependent unit. The influences of the factory, the corporation, the city, and the mass market spread out in all directions to affect every work plant and every worker. As we stand in the mid-part of this century almost every person is so exposed to the forces of industrialism that he shares with his associates a common sense of rapid change. One of the basic changes of our society is the transition from an individualistic to an administrative economy.

THE TRANSITION FROM AN INDIVIDUALISTIC TO AN ADMINISTRATIVE ECONOMY

THE SCOPE OF AMERICAN ECONOMY

Our economy is not one but many. It is made up of large private corporations and small corporations, independent proprietors, coöperatives, unions, associations, and public business of many different sizes and types. Although emphasis has been on trends centered around big business, there remain, of course, a large number of small businesses. The Department of Commerce defines a small business as one having annual net sales of less than $200,000 in wholesaling, net sales of less than $50,000 in retailing, a pay roll of 100 employees or less in manufacture. On this basis, there are 2,800,-000 little businesses in the country.[6] Most of these are concentrated in

[6] Stuart Chase, *Democracy Under Pressure*, The Twentieth Century Fund, 1945, p. 5.

retail trade and service industries. In addition there are more than 6,000,000 farm units. In 1935 there were fewer than 42,000 of these farm units on which more than five persons were gainfully employed.[7]

Yet in spite of the large number of concerns in these and other fields, a study by the National Resources Committee presents the estimate that "altogether little more than a third of the nation's economic activity is carried on by producing units engaging the activity of one to five persons. An almost equal proportion is carried on by a few hundred very large administrative units."[8] A measure of bigness is the frequency of combinations in which more than one industrial establishment is operated by a single central office. "In 1929—only about one-eighth of the manufacturing enterprises were of the plural unit type, but this small fraction accounted for about 48 percent of the wage earners, 54 percent of the value of the products and 50 percent of the value added by manufacture of all manufacturing enterprises."[9]

The student of the American economy must not lose sight of the large number of small businesses. This fact illuminates the psychology and values of our business civilization. Of this we shall have more to say later. But it is big business that is setting the pattern and shaping the course of the political state as well as the economy. The impact of industry on society almost implies big industry. The contrast between big business and little business can often be discerned as the contrast of monopoly and competition.

COMPETITION VS. MONOPOLY

The advance of science and technology has marched with large-scale production and the mass market. Business corporations capitalizing on these prime assets have grown in size and have moved through a series of progressive changes in their organization. The "most successful," which is to say, the big, corporations have come into such dominance that the whole course of economic organization has changed with them. Industrial capitalism represented the era when major corporations were managed by those who owned them in large part. Finance capitalism, a later development, is characterized by absentee owners and professional administrators. Modern economic society is now confronted with monopoly capitalism. This mature form of capitalistic development refers to the growth of corporations from large to giant structures whose absentee owners have by expansion, combination, merger, and the holding company succeeded in removing these

[7] Horace Taylor and Harold Barger, *The American Economy in Operation*, Harcourt, Brace and Company, 1949, p. 260.

[8] National Resources Committee, *The Structure of the American Economy*, United States Government Printing Office, 1939, Part I, p. 104.

[9] Alfred Bernheim and others, *Big Business: Its Growth and Its Place*, The Twentieth Century Fund, 1937, p. 3.

super corporations from the free market and the limitations of a competitive price and production policy.

Monopoly replaces competition when a business corporation either through its sole efforts or by collusion (or "coöperation") with others comes into command of the market to such an extent that it can administer price and production irrespective of supply and demand conditions within the market. In our society, the mass market has become subject to such wide fluctuations that monopoly has been a most desired goal of many business interests.

Just as much big business has embraced monopoly and administered prices to maximize its returns and protect itself against the fluctuating market, so too have agriculture, labor, and government. Each has built a structure of administrative controls seeking to strengthen its position in the economy. Free competitive enterprise has always been based on a presumption that large numbers of small sellers would operate in a self-regulating market. As such, free enterprise is being displaced step by step all over the world. In its place we can observe the rise of an administrative economy which Stuart Chase calls X.

THE COMING OF ECONOMY X

X is not socialism or fascism as the orthodox creeds prescribe. It is a pattern of centralized, collective controls. We can describe them as they appear in most countries.

FREE ENTERPRISE INTO "X"

A strong, centralized government.

An executive arm growing at the expense of the legislative and judicial arms. In some countries, power is consolidated in a dictator, issuing decrees.

The control of banking, credit and security exchanges by the government.

The underwriting of employment by the government, either through armaments or public works.

The underwriting of social security by the government—old age pensions, mothers' pensions, unemployment insurance, and the like.

The underwriting of food, housing, and medical care, by the government. The United States is already experimenting with providing these essentials. Other nations are far along the road.

The use of the deficit spending technique to finance these underwritings. The annually balanced budget has lost its old-time sanctity.

The abandonment of gold in favor of managed currencies.

The control of foreign trade by the government with increasing emphasis on bilateral agreements and barter deals.

The control of natural resources, with increasing emphasis on self-sufficiency.

The control of energy sources—hydroelectric power, coal, petroleum, and natural gas.

The control of transportation—railway, highway, airway, waterway.

The control of agricultural production.

The control of labor organizations, often to the point of prohibiting strikes.

The enlistment of young men and women in youth corps devoted to health, discipline, community service and ideologies consistent with those of the authorities.

Heavy taxation, with especial emphasis on the estates and incomes of the rich.

Not much "taking over" of property or industries in the old socialistic sense. The formula appears to be *control without ownership*. It is interesting to recall that the same formula is used by management of great corporations in depriving stockholders of power.

The state control of communications and propaganda.[10]

These characteristics exhibit themselves in various degrees in the major nations of the world. Incipient in some, they are well developed in others. The United States has adopted in some degree every item on the list.

Bigness, centralization, and *bureaucracy* are products of the forces which have developed in modern society. For better or for worse man as worker and as citizen must live with them and make them serve him. The economies and services of large-scale organization possess advantages too great to be given up voluntarily. As long as these advantages are desired, modern organizations will continue to be big, and bureaucracy the prevailing pattern in business, agriculture, labor, and government. Meanwhile a society in transition watches new groups rise to power and older groups fight to retain their earlier position of supremacy. A struggle for power among the powerful organized interest groups is an accompanying feature of the social transition.

THE STRUGGLE FOR POWER

THE RISE OF BUREAUCRACY AND THE IMPERSONALIZATION OF POWER

As enterprises grow in size, new forms of social organizations must be invented to control them. The historically recurrent form of organization best suited to do this is the bureaucracy.

Some characteristics of the bureaucracy are: (1) fixed and official jurisdictional areas ordered by rules, (2) a monocratically organized office hierarchy, (3) development of a record-keeping staff, (4) development of an expert staff in all offices. Thus the bureaucracy is a hierarchy of offices, a coördinated series of reciprocal responsibilities and duties.[11] This form of organization is not unique to Western culture, nor is it a new invention

[10] Stuart Chase, *The Road We Are Traveling*, The Twentieth Century Fund, 1942, pp. 95-96.

[11] H. H. Gerth and C. W. Mills, *From Max Weber: Essays in Sociology*, Oxford University Press, 1946, pp. 196-198.

of the last century or two. It was used in ancient and medieval times to organize armies, religious orders, and nations. The novel element today is the general application of bureaucratic principles in most of the institutions of modern society and especially in the economic organizations.

Bureaucracies simultaneously concentrate and delegate authority. They concentrate authority by giving fewer people at the top the right to make policy decisions, but delegate authority by distributing the actual execution of decisions to numerous functionaries. Thus a large enterprise is organized into units that have considerable vertical communication (communication flowing up and down) but not much horizontal communication between different segments on equal levels of authority. What this tends to do is to foster the self-consciousness of groups. Workers are made aware of their membership in a particular department, of their uniform pay level, of their restricted authority in the enterprise. It thus becomes a relatively simple thing to make the groups so formalized by the bureaucracy do other things. Since many workers are conscious of performing the same tasks as others, they can be organized rather easily to think in group terms. In conditions involving power relations, therefore, the tendency will be not to associate authority with individuals but with groups. The shift is from *personal to impersonal power,* from *informal, sympathetic relations to formal, contractual relations.*

FORMALIZATION OF GROUPS INTO PRESSURE ORGANIZATIONS

The greater the formalization of groups within enterprises and between enterprises the greater their chances of being turned into power-conscious and power-wielding groups. They will apply the same effective techniques of bureaucracies to organize themselves as industry has applied to itself. It should be emphasized that such tendencies occur within two areas. The first and most obvious area is within the enterprise. The self-bureaucratization tendency within industry and the problems that attend it are well known.[12] The second area of organization occurs among enterprises and among groups within those enterprises. That is, enterprises with similar problems and interests organize associations to "promote and protect their mutual interests" against associations of other enterprises. For example, wool manufacturers organize to protect their tariff against other groups who want it reduced. At the same time, different levels *within enterprises* band together "to protect and promote their interests" against other groups within the enterprises. Thus the workers in the wool enterprises organize unions against the employers in all the wool enterprises.

One measure of the extent of power groupings on a national scale is the presence of lobbies in Washington. The Temporary National Economic

[12] See Chapter X, "Power Organization: Interaction of Management and Labor."

Committee found more than 400 lobbies operating in Washington.[13] Stuart Chase has classified them into five groups:

The Big Three—Official business, labor, and farm organizations including such notables as The National Association of Manufacturers, the Chamber of Commerce, the American Federation of Labor, The Congress of Industrial Organizations, The Farm Bureau Federation, and The Grange.

Specialized Producers, such as cattlemen, publishers, citrus growers, broadcasting stations, telephone interests.

Professional and Occupational Groups, such as the bankers, insurance companies, advertisers, real-estate men, exporters and importers, doctors, teachers, lawyers.

Reformers, such as the conservationists and birth controllers.

The Governments in Exile, representing deposed monarchies, and overturned republics.[14]

These groups seek higher tariffs, subsidies, loans, escape from regulation, and so on. The objective is usually a direct subsidy for the interest itself or destruction of a competitor.

Out in the local community the struggle is waged with equal determination though the area of influence is smaller. The listing of the number of economic associations in Kansas City, Missouri shows the following:

> 42 functional business associations
> 15 professional associations
> 5 general city-wide business associations
> 10 general district business associations
> 81 labor union organizations
> 39 business associations having state, regional, or
>   national headquarters in the city
> _____
> 192 mutual aid organizations

This list of 192 "mutual aid" organizations gives us an impression of the extent of the organizing tendencies among economic groupings.[15] Almost two-fifths are labor unions and three-fifths are business associations. The designation "mutual aid" organization suggests an organization that is partly defensive in nature. It is true that they have been designed to protect their members, but the question should be raised, Against whom? Obviously if the associations are all engaged in "defense" against others, they are in reality collective bargaining agencies living in a political atmosphere. Thus labor unions are not the only collective bargaining organizations. Coöperatives, unions, trade associations, syndicates, and other such

[13] *Economic Power and Political Pressures,* T.N.E.C. Monograph No. 26, United States Government Printing Office, 1941.
[14] Stuart Chase, *Democracy Under Pressure,* The Twentieth Century Fund, 1945, p. 22.
[15] Noel P. Gist and L. A. Halbert, *Urban Society,* Thomas Y. Crowell Company, 1941, p. 432.

organizations are political collective bargaining organizations living in a house of power.

The trend of formalizing occupational groups and business associations into a power group is not a new development in European culture. The guilds and trading leagues of the Middle Ages are their forerunners, but not ancestors. The distinguishing feature or characteristic today is the tendency for functionally related groups to become broken up into rather autonomous groups. For example, it is not unusual for several "mutual aid" organizations, such as a managers' association, a foremen's association, factions of stockholders, labor unions, and perhaps even an organization of customers, to coexist in a particular enterprise. Each group is trying to manipulate the others to obtain as much of the economic or other returns from the enterprise as possible. One large employer reports that he must deal with twenty-three different unions. Some of the jurisdictional struggles between unions in the same plant wax with more bitterness than is exhibited against the employer himself.

GROUP SELF-CONSCIOUSNESS AND POWER MOBILIZATION

We have tried to show that rational, self-conscious contractual relationships obtain among the various economic groups today. The relatively little spontaneous give-and-take that characterizes the social contacts of such groups reflects the scarcity of common values outside of their economic struggles. Especially in the bargaining situation their practice is to use every known technique to seize an advantage and keep it as long as possible. Since most conflict situations require accommodations, each group tends to appraise itself in terms of its own strength and weaknesses, and the strength and weaknesses of its opponents. When the favorable opportunity to increase the strength of the organization presents itself, leaders of the pressure group strike out for advantage. They seek not only direct increases for the group but also advantage over their opponents.[16] In this way they arm themselves for a more successful assault in a future campaign. In the eighteenth century an accommodation of conflicting groups was supported by the sentiments and customs of the era, but today the equilibrium is more temporary and is defined by the power resources of the opposing groups. Figure 126 represents both formal and informal organizations which cluster about management and labor as they struggle for power. The owners as the investors and the public as consumers become interested parties. The newspaper, radio, community organizations, political party, and finally the government become active participants. Management and labor jockey for support of all these outside groups.

It is to be expected that self-conscious groups are more aware of power situations. They engage in purposive study to invent new techniques to (1)

[16] See E. T. Hiller, The Strike, University of Chicago Press, 1928.

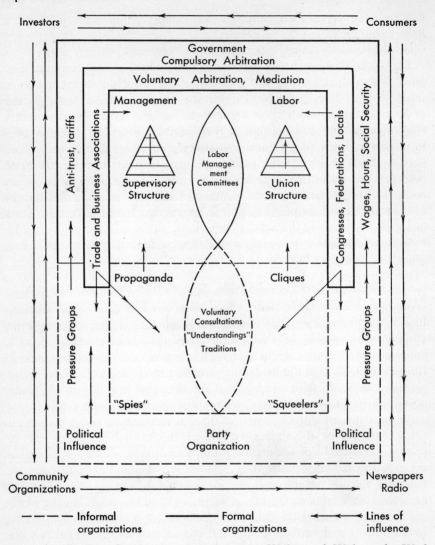

Fig. 126. The Formal and Informal Organizations Within and Without the Work
Plant Which Are Drawn into the Struggle for Power.

secure a stronger superordinate role or (2) work out more effective organizational methods to mediate their power struggles. It is not always easy to distinguish what techniques are invented to diminish the power of the opposition and what techniques are intended as genuine coöperation. Some techniques may be intended to do both. Some may be designed to achieve one end but actually achieve the opposite.[17] Since force, violence, and con-

[17] The reader might consult labor relations texts for some of these techniques. He also might consult Hiller, op. cit., and Robert Brady, Business as a System of Power, Columbia University Press, 1943.

flict have low verbal esteem in America, conflict groups hesitate to admit their intention to engage in political warfare. Euphemistic industrial relations programs are proposed to bring about "peace and understanding."

The reader is warned that many so-called "industrial relations programs" serve as propaganda fronts for conflict groups. To avoid being misled he should inspect every program in terms of its stated objectives and in terms of its actual operation. The participants in power struggles do this. In fact, they often become so suspicious of their enemies' programs that they grow to suspect any new plan or new idea. Merely scanning the newspapers and periodicals of labor and management groups will soon convince the reader that (1) the fuller intentions of certain management-labor programs are really devices to obtain a power advantage and (2) consequently there is distrust and apprehension on each side toward new ideas propagated by the other side.

Some management programs intended to weaken organized labor have often been entitled "Multiple Management," "Leadership in Industry," "Profit Sharing," "Community Relations," "Open Door Policy," "The Congressional System of Industrial Government," "Risk Participation," "Safeguarding the Right to Work," "Employee Counseling," "The American Plan," "The Mohawk Valley Plan," and others. We are not suggesting that all plans sharing these titles have been insidious devices of management to crush organized labor. On the contrary, some extremely sincere and effective things have been accomplished with plans having these titles. The names of programs or their published intentions are not significant, but the long-range intentions in reference to power relations in the future certainly are.

Obviously, both management and labor have some long-term plans. The plans of management groups are often simple; they are sometimes directed toward destroying organized labor but more often toward reducing its strength. On the other hand, organized labor in America generally does not entertain the idea of crushing business. Since destroying business would erase the source of labor's livelihood, the hidden motives of organized labor are aimed at reducing the power of management to hire and fire, sharing to a greater extent in the profits of industry, establishing better working conditions, weakening the authority of foremen and other managers. The most frequent title used for such programs is "Democracy Within Industry." The objective presumably is to "democratize" the power and income within the industry.

On the other hand, some programs have been aimed at mediating the obdurate type of conflicts developing between management and organized labor. These genuine fields of coöperation are resorted to when the other techniques do not work. The American Arbitration Association, the Conciliation Service of the Department of Labor, the National Mediation Board, management-labor committees, and fact-finding committees have operated with the ideology that both sides want a fair and impartial settle-

ment of their differences, that neither side is seeking a basic change in their power relations. Their techniques are basically aimed at mediating naked power struggles and trying to secure coöperation. We may look forward to more of these types of organizations within the next few decades.

ENTRANCE OF THE STATE BUREAUCRACY INTO THE POWER STRUGGLE

Another trend characterizing the power structure of modern industry is the entrance of a third and often the most powerful party into the struggle, namely, the local, state, or national government. This trend is a rather recent development arising around the turn of the century and growing spectacularly since 1932. The reasons have been manifold. One explanation suggests that the division of labor in modern society has become so extensive that any extended interruption in the operation of the basic industries can bring the entire economy to a standstill. In order to prevent widespread dislocation in the economy, a universal agency must insure that production continues. Thus any prolonged interruption in the mining of coal will in a relatively short period reduce the operations of the steel and transportation industries. When these two basic industries are crippled the entire economy suffers. The government must step in after a rather brief interval to bring about the reëstablishment of production. The same reasoning applies with less force to other industries. One is amazed by the number of overlapping governmental agencies that enter directly or indirectly into the operation and regulation of an industry such as coal.[18]

The "Public Interest" Theory

This explanation or argument for governmental intervention may be called the "public interest" theory. Members of the "new middle class" who are not directly involved with management or labor often urge this role for government. On the whole, the explanation is more inadequate than incorrect, for the "need" for government intervention existed before 1932, yet it was generally not forthcoming before that time. Moreover, if the interdependence of industry makes government intervention necessary in crises, a case could be made that every industry is essential to the economy and that the government should constantly intervene.

Obviously, other factors have been operating to induce government to intervene in labor-management relations. These other factors can only be assessed by appraising historical changes. In the past America has had two sovereignties—business and government. Business was sovereign over its domain; the government had no right to interfere in this domain excepting to legitimize the sovereignty of business. Repeatedly the courts proclaimed

[18] See John Bartlow Martin, "The Blast in Centralia No. 5," *Harper's Magazine*, March, 1948, pp. 193-220.

that government had no right of intervention in business affairs. They further ruled that many types of labor organizations and tactics were infringements of property rights.

It was not until labor unionism grew and became politically conscious, not until new laws were passed which sanctioned collective bargaining, not until the judiciary was restrained by new laws redefining the power or rather the limitations of property, that government "intervened" in management-labor relations. Of course the Great Depression, with which business seemed to be unable to cope, was the occasion of further governmental intervention. Gradually the two sovereignties were redefined, with government becoming more dominant. This does not mean that government has become more anti-business or more pro-labor. It means that government has formally established its right to enter the field of labor-management relations. Once in the field it can move in any direction.[19]

Using the Influence of Government for Advantage

When government intervenes, the immediate question arises, For whom will it intervene? It is almost impossible for even the most fair-minded mediating, arbitrating, or regulating agency to operate without prejudice or discrimination. Especially when dealing with suspicious, almost paranoid groups, no decision is considered a fair decision. To obtain a "fair" decision under these circumstances, the groups involved will attempt to influence the government and its agencies. This involvement of labor and business in government is another trend in the power relations of modern American industry.

Our history shows many attempts of business and labor to use government to further their individual ends. In general, propertied interests have historically been more successful in manipulating government for their own ends.[20] All kinds of techniques have been used by both management and labor to secure advantages over each other via governmental channels. We cannot go into an extensive discussion of the political roles of business and labor in America. This has been done adequately elsewhere.[21] We are concerned only with stressing the trends.

The political position of labor cannot be understood unless we take into account the two-party system in America. The strength and flexibility of

[19] Of course, there has always been some relation between economic and political institutions. How the present situation differs from that of the past is that government not only legitimatizes business but has entered into the conduct of business. In other nations of the world this "interference" is much greater than in the United States.

[20] Charles A. Beard, *An Economic Interpretation of the Constitution of the U.S.*, The Macmillan Company, 1925.

[21] Peter H. Odegard and E. Allen Helms, *American Politics*, Harper & Brothers, 1938, especially chaps. 8, 9, 10. V. O. Key, *Politics, Parties, and Pressure Groups*, Thomas Y. Crowell Company, 2nd ed., 1947.

this system have always been a source of amazement to foreign observers. It is generally agreed that the parties have not represented radically different programs over the years. The appeals of both the Republican and the Democratic parties have been made to widely divergent groups. It was inevitable that their general programs had to be conservative in reference to property. The result was that no consistent pro-labor legislation could be enacted.

From the beginning commercial and propertied interests in America have been able to control government to their own advantage. They achieved this primarily by dominating nongovernmental institutions. By controlling the educational institutions they were able to place into legislative and, particularly, judicial offices men who were indoctrinated with property and business values. It was not, as some would believe, a calculated conspiracy of the propertied to dominate the government and the economy. By presiding over the educational system, the press, and other institutions of communication, they indirectly and automatically determined the kind of people that would become legislators, executives, and judges. The latter naturally did "what was right."

With the extension of suffrage, some friends of labor hoped that labor's numerical dominance might give it control over the legislative bodies. Attempts were made to abandon the two-party system, and to form a labor party dedicated to promoting the best interests of this class. But labor parties, irrespective of their conservative or radical nature, generally failed to attract widespread labor support. American workers were mobility conscious. They did not consider themselves part of the laboring class. In fact, they regarded their position as temporary. One day, they too would be men of property, or at least their children would be. While awaiting that day, they were concerned only with the size of the pay envelope and what they could buy with it. With few minor exceptions in city governments, they never got into power.

This being true, it is understandable why the philosophy of Samuel Gompers held sway for so long a period of time. The essence of this philosophy was that labor should organize but not enter politics directly. Gompers urged that labor should first examine the records of legislators in either party, and vote for those who backed labor bills and vote against those who did not do so. In the meantime the usual techniques of a lobby should be used to secure influence in the legislative councils.

The Organizing of Formal Pressure Groups

The effect of following this advice was a gradual weakening of the informal monopoly that the commercial and business interests had over government. Thus those business interests that wanted favorable laws or political favors had to organize *formal pressure groups* for that end. When labor became organized into formal pressure groups, the era of informal monopoly of government by business came to an end. The struggles of management

and organized labor thus spread from restricted private affairs to public affairs in which the resources and power of government played important roles.

This is the stage in which we are today with one significant difference. Labor's traditional policy of "Reward your friends and punish your enemies" had been revised because of some of its shortcomings. The chief of these was that it was essentially an after-the-fact strategy. That is, after a candidate was chosen for office and sometimes elected, his performance had to be observed as to whether or not it suited labor. If not, and if labor was successful, the incumbent might be defeated for reëlection. His successor also had to be observed for his position on labor legislation. He too might be found to be antilabor after a period in office. To avoid this, labor has recently urged its members to attack this problem at the grass roots, namely, within the party organization, and especially in the local primary level. Some leaders of labor have urged their members to "take over" the Democratic party and make it a labor party. Perlman and others have suggested caution. This would be making a new labor party, and labor would lose its influence altogether.[22] Others have suggested that labor remain a pressure group within the party structure. This point of view has generally prevailed.

Since the New Deal, and especially since the end of World War II, labor has organized a number of associations to increase its effectiveness in the political realm. At times these groups have appeared as citizen non-labor groups, having the semblance of a party. The American Labor party in New York State, the Liberal party in the same state, and the Citizens' Political Action Committee fall into this category. Actually they tend to be organizations which can deliver labor votes to a major party who will choose candidates to labor's liking, or who will sponsor legislation favorable to labor. Since such groups can deliver the votes, which is always to the liking of a political party, they have had a modicum of success.

Other agencies of labor have been more direct and forthright in entering the field of politics. In 1945 the Congress of Industrial Organizations created the Political Action Committee and appropriated funds for political purposes. Some of its intentions were: to make labor more politically conscious, to educate labor to behave politically for its best interests, to support candidates in either party with financial and other resources, and to affect the policies of parties at their grass roots.

The American Federation of Labor has been more cautious than the C.I.O., but it too shows signs of entering politics more directly. In 1947 it appropriated money to educate its members on political candidates and political issues. These are signs that labor is being increasingly united in its political interests and activities.

The new techniques were effective, and they produced a reaction in management and conservative groups. By putting pressure on Congress,

[22] Selig Perlman, *Labor in the New Deal Decade*, Abco Press, 1945, pp. 29-36.

conservative groups succeeded in restricting the power of the labor unions. These limitations are presented in the Taft-Hartley Bill. The bill contains provisions that the union cannot use funds to back political candidates for office, it must publish financial statements, it cannot propagandize its members in a political sense, its officers must sign non-Communist affidavits before unions can use the services of the National Labor Relations Board, and other restrictions. In addition, business groups have used other devices to influence political parties and restrict the power of labor.

And the struggle goes on. Labor is now testing the constitutionality of some of the provisions of the Taft-Hartley Act. It is making this an issue in the coming campaigns, and management is meeting the challenge. Thus we see a struggle for power in the work plant, in the community, and in the general political institutions.

It is easy to become engrossed in the struggles of interest groups as first one and then the other gains advantage. Perhaps what is of most importance is not the temporary shifts of power relations which are established but the kind of society which is being formed. The analysis of social forces at work indicates that society as the cohesive fabric has grown weaker, less integrated, and less stable. This has happened while the nation has grown powerful, both economically and militarily. Why does this contradiction exist?

FOUR CONTRADICTIONS IN MODERN LIFE INTRODUCED BY INDUSTRIALISM

Cultural contradictions in modern society, as truly as pressure groups, splinter the social structure and divide men's minds. They make it increasingly difficult for the citizen to make up his mind as to what he should think, what he should want, and what he should do. Four contradictions may be singled out for analysis.

1. DEMOCRATIC IDEALS VS. CONCENTRATION OF ECONOMIC POWER

We believe in the democratic ideal of political equality—that each man is the equal of any other man in human right and human dignity. We believe that there should be equality between a man's political power and his economic power.

But we are faced with an intense concentration of economic power in the hands of relatively few persons and we believe that private individuals can run a business better than the government can. We believe, furthermore, that concentration of economic power in the hands of government men would be more dangerous to a free society than leaving such power in the hands of businessmen.

The American Republic was founded on the edge of a vast wilderness. Land was free to those who had the courage and initiative to go forth and claim it. Ownership and management of a farm was bought by hard work

and persistence. This easy entry into ownership encouraged widespread ownership of property and satisfied the economic ideal. We still believe that every worker should have the chance to go into business for himself. The image of a society of small manufacturers, merchants, free farmers, and artisans continues to keep alive the Jeffersonian ideal. In the America of 1820-1830, sixteen out of every twenty Americans owned their independent means of making a livelihood in the form of small property, mostly free farms. Most Americans could say, "What I work I own and what I own I work." One hundred years later an almost exactly opposite condition prevailed. Seventeen out of every twenty Americans were propertyless, and dependent for a livelihood upon the property owned by a small minority. This transference of ownership constitutes a revolutionary change in the entire fabric of society. Most men no longer "make a living"; they "earn a living." The corporation has replaced and is replacing the small businessman all along the business, agricultural, and industrial front. In this shift from a base of widespread ownership to a base of corporate business the relation between political power and economic power is drastically changed. Concentration of economic power has always been regarded as a threat to democratic institutions. We know that large-scale enterprise is here to stay. The private operation of such enterprise has been a mixed blessing. Higher levels of living have been accompanied by distribution problems causing widespread suffering. To transfer ownership to the government would not be a restoration of the Jeffersonian ideal. It would mean that government men would control the same corporate property which businessmen had controlled before. Our tradition has been one in which a free people have feared their government more than they have feared their businessmen. We have believed that businessmen were held in check by competition and the democratic processes, but that government men were eager to seize power and able to establish a coercion that would quickly destroy a free society. As the industrial and corporate growth has moved on, the question of business ownership vs. government ownership or regulation has become the major political question of the century. Americans are caught in a dilemma. Democratic ideals are threatened by the concentration of economic power, but the harnessing of such power by government threatens to strangle them. Moreover, we are badly prepared as a body of citizens to think our way clearly through this contradiction. Our psychology is provincial and our society is cosmopolitan. And here lies still another cause of cultural confusion.

2. PROVINCIAL FOLKWAYS VS. COSMOPOLITAN SOCIETY

We believe that the only way any man gets ahead is through hard work; we believe that competition determines price and quality and that big business has the same problems as little business except that big business has more and bigger

problems; we believe that anyone can understand what business and the nation are faced with by focusing attention upon the problems in the local community.

But society is now a vast world-wide network of interdependent forces which largely determines what local business conditions are and what local problems are. The initial generation of a change in conditions usually originates in a center or centers far removed from the local community. The forces generated tend to be different in kind and in magnitude from those arising in the local community.

Walter Lippmann in his analysis of public opinion differentiated between the "seen" world and the "unseen" world in which each person lives.[23] The "seen" world refers to the narrow and immediate pathway over which the daily course of personal life is run. The mental horizon tends to be limited to this "seen" world. Yet it is in the "unseen" world that the vast majority of influences over living are generated. The "unseen" world refers, of course, to the world-wide network of events which come into the local community and act silently upon it.

Men forget that for thousands of generations living has been going on in small communities where the personal relations of face-to-face contact have existed. Individual acts were judged in the arena of public opinion and the important values of life were determined in the concrete terms of the local event. In such a world, provincial thoughtways and folkways were largely insulated against outside forces.

Then, with the coming of industrialism, modern communication and transportation began to spread a multitude of new ideas and new ways of living. The strands of economic life began to draw all local communities into one interdependent economy. F. Stuart Chapin has found a cause for the many economic contradictions which have made it so difficult for the average person to understand the nature of the economic process. He says that throughout the whole of our economic life "there runs the principle of individual decisions and acts, each made independently of all the rest and arrived at on the basis of provincial habit systems trying to operate in a world network of communication."[24]

Some of these provincial habit systems in popular economic thinking may be identified. They gain significance as contrasted with the cosmopolitan thoughtways demanded by the modern economic structure. Let us take, for example, the conception of work. Stuart Chase likes to describe how his grandfather plowed the rocky New England fields for long hours each day. *Hard work* meant manual labor mixed with sweat. In contrast, modern life with its many white-collar tasks demands much sedentary or semisedentary activity. *Hard work* may come to mean concentration plus monotony. Grandfather snorts that the younger generation has forgotten how to work; the

[23] Walter Lippmann, *Public Opinion*, Harcourt, Brace and Company, 1922.
[24] F. Stuart Chapin, *Contemporary American Institutions*, Harper & Brothers, 1935, p. 5.

modern urban dweller replies that "it's so peaceful in the country" and that the old-timers never knew what nervous strain meant.

In his view of *business* it is not surprising that the average man carries a psychology of small business. The stores and services on Main Street represent BUSINESS to the bulk of Middletown's citizens. When the local merchant complains of *competition,* he speaks mostly of the prices and quality of products which the chain stores and other local stores are placing on the local market. In contrast, large corporate industry has largely discarded price competition and competes on quality, styling, or advertising of the product. Property in the nineteenth century meant land and buildings —i.e., real estate. Today the richest man in town may have his entire property locked up in a small box labeled "Stocks and Bonds." *Law* once meant that the local mores against crime had been written down, a far cry from the proliferation of economic and social regulations which municipal, county, state, national, and international agencies have pressed into legal form.

It is this contradiction between the thoughtways of provincial living and the imperatives of cosmopolitan society that causes much of the problem we call social change. Each small locality has been opened up to the drive and play of great forces generated in the large urban centers of society. These forces spread outward and act upon the local community. Provincial habit systems respond, and a myriad of individual acts and decisions take place. Almost immediately, their reverberations move back upon the urban centers. Chapin has likened this process to an alternating current which moves back and forth linking large and small communities of the nation into an endless chain.[25] In this process, contradictions between provincial and cosmopolitan habit systems are compounded and their consequences spread over the entire society. The irrationalities of a society which matches efforts to increase production with efforts to restrict production can be understood as a clash of habits as well as a clash of economic structures.

3. COÖPERATION VS. ISOLATION

A third contradiction appears as an opposition of coöperation and isolation.

We are drawn ever closer together. Modern technology, the threat of war, the promise of abundance all force men to recognize that this is "one world." *We believe* that men must coöperate or perish.

But society is divided into large interest groups, into classes, into regions, into racial and ethnic divisions. In the city, particularly, the person becomes dwarfed by large organizations and the impersonality of social contact. He tends to become isolated in the midst of frenzied attempts to get him to join and participate in organizations.

[25] *Ibid.,* p. 7.

Industrialism has set loose twin forces of opposition.[26] These are coöperation and isolation. Human relations have become both organized and
atomized, and this contradiction has strengthened and weakened social
structure simultaneously. We can observe that society is in an unceasing
process of organization and disorganization.

Modern economic organization requires a very high degree of coöperative
activity. The need for coöperative activity becomes particularly clear if our
industrial society is compared with a peasant society. In the peasant society
almost everybody works at the production of the same things. The subsistence economy of such a society consists of numerous and almost identical
units all engaged on the same tasks. Moreover, the contacts are very slight
as the individual peasant plows, sows, and reaps his harvest without any
outside coöperation. In contrast, each producer in an industrial society turns
out a different product, but he does it, not alone, but by close association
with many others. The producers of automobiles, steel, glass, cement, and
cloth must somehow get along with one another in order to insure that the
right proportions of goods are produced. As John Strachey has said, "Men
cannot live by tin cans alone." Thousands of different goods and services
are needed to keep our economy in operation. Without a proportionate
flow of goods, the whole economy would come to a halt or be destroyed.
Legend has it that "for want of a nail, a shoe was lost; for want of a shoe,
a horse was lost; for want of a horse, a king was lost; for want of a king,
a kingdom was lost."

Much of the tremendous quantity of coöperative relationship in our
society is bought as men are tied by salaries and wages into large-scale
organizations. In the place of group in-feeling based on custom and sentiment all too often there is only the impersonality of a contractual relationship mediated by a specialized skill or money income.

We have shown how the city with its large population masses is a product
of the industrial economy. The transformation of community life into
urban patterns has brought a fragmentation which isolates the individual
while at the same time placing him in a fast-moving stream of human
contacts. The mobility of the urban dweller tends to rip out his community
ties (if he lives within a community long enough to develop them). The
size of the city makes it difficult for him to see and know people who wish
to lead the political and social agencies. He is more apt to read about them
or hear about them if he has developed an interest in them. Social stratification builds status walls that make access to some persons all but impossible. Entire strata of people live their lives beyond the daily horizon of
other dwellers. In such a society the individual comes to realize that he
counts for little unless he is organized within a group. When he is organ-

[26] Cf. Paul Meadows, "Human Relations in Industrial Civilization," *Technology Review*, April, 1947, pp. 341-348.

ized in a group he may find that group ends distort individual purpose and morality. In this contradiction, coöperation and isolation are both real and far apart.

4. SYMPATHY VS. AGGRESSIVENESS

The fourth contradiction singled out for analysis pits two human sentiments against one another.

Modern man is lonely. He seeks companionship, affection, love. *He says* that his religion calls all men his brothers.

But everywhere men compete aggressively and sometimes ruthlessly with one another for money, status, mates, and power. The pattern of competition is encouraged in the school, in the work plant, in the church, and in the home. The child is taught as was the father that the future belongs to those who have drive and who are willing to push themselves.

The loneliness of modern man is brought about by a convergence of many different forces. Science has shattered much of the comforting religious belief he once held. J. H. Randall has written:

It swept man out of his proud position as the central figure and end of the universe, and made him a tiny speck on a third-rate planet revolving about a tenth-rate sun drifting in an endless cosmic ocean. . . . Purposes gave way to mathematics, human will and foresight to immutable and inflexible mechanical order. Throughout the whole vast windy stretches of infinity, in stone and plant and animal, nowhere a being who felt and suffered, loved and feared and hoped, who thought and knew. Man was alone, quite alone, in a vast and complex cosmic machine. Gone were the angelic hosts, gone the devils and their pranks, gone the daily miracles of supernatural intervention, gone even was man's imploring cry of prayer.[27]

Modern man has had to rediscover what he could believe in to give purpose to living. The threats of war and depression beating down daily on his personal security have driven him to find some "ways to relax nerves" and capture an elusive "peace of mind." The loosely knit ties of kinship and community life tend to sterilize emotional life and focus it upon the small family. A man or woman who fails to establish himself within a family is left with poor emotional substitutes in the large city. Casual, exploitative relationships of dalliance replace the interwoven ties of marriage. Spectator amusements provide vicarious enjoyments which stimulate but seldom feed and satisfy man's basic biological and social needs. The poet Wystan Hugh Auden in his book *The Age of Anxiety* expresses the anxious frustrations of modern life through a shipping clerk named Malin:

[27] John H. Randall, *The Making of the Modern Mind*, Houghton Mifflin Company, 1926, pp. 226-227.

But the new barbarian is no uncouth
Desert-dweller; he does not emerge
From fir forests: factories bred him;
Corporate companies, college towns
Mothered his mind, and many journals
Backed his beliefs. He was born here. The
Bravura of revolvers in vogue now
And the cult of death are quite at home
Inside the city.[28]

Men in the midst of modern life have sought more purposeful ways to live with one another. Generous impulse is still alive in the conduct of human affairs, but opposed against the desire for sympathetic identification with persons and groups are respectable patterns of aggressiveness and sometimes ruthlessness. Veblen has pointed out that wherever the institution of private property is found, the economic process is marked by a struggle between men for the possession of goods. Such a struggle carries far beyond the subsistence level of living, for the motive that lies at the root of ownership is emulation. The possession of wealth confers honor and brings the holder satisfaction or dissatisfaction as he compares himself with others.[29] Veblen said that pecuniary emulation through invidious comparison becomes the basis of esteem. As such, property or wealth in some amount becomes necessary in order to have any reputable standing in the community. There is no limit to the property desired, for the process of invidious comparison is dynamic. A person desires as much wealth as those have with whom he classes himself. When this is gained he desires more. "The invidious comparison can never become so favorable to the individual making it that he would not gladly rate himself still higher relatively to his competitors in the struggle for pecuniary reputability."[30]

In our society material accumulation is roughly equated with honor. The pattern of aggressive behavior is approved for career climbing. It is "one against all" and "may the best man win." If this aggressive pattern must ride down human sentiment in order to gain material advantage, then sentiment must go. "Business is business," after all. So it follows that even as sympathy and the desire for human response is ground down in business contacts, the need for a more satisfying emotional life remains.

As the four major contradictions are surveyed, it becomes apparent that social and psychological problems have been stirred up in the train of influences which have accompanied the industrial way of life. Industry is intimately tied to the most subtle nuances of daily living. We are drawn

[28] Reprinted by permission of Random House, Inc. Copyright 1947 by W. H. Auden.
[29] This notion is thoroughly analyzed in Chapter XII. "Class Organization of the Work Plant."
[30] Thorstein Veblen, *The Theory of the Leisure Class*, The Macmillan Company, 1924, pp. 31-32.

to reflect upon the future. Will industry continue to dominate institutional life? Will cultural patterns assume more consistent and less contradictory forms? We do not know the answers to these questions but we can follow some trend lines and make some speculations.

THE FUTURE RELATIONSHIP OF INDUSTRY AND SOCIETY

Sociologists are wary of long-range forecasting. The forces which move through modern society are fluid, and manifold possibilities of social change present themselves. However, there are ways to discern the future which surpass idle speculation. When the social scientist wishes to discover probable social developments in the proximate future, he begins by selecting

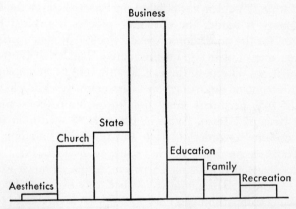

FIG. 127. A Suggested Ranking of American Institutions by Power and Influence in 1900.

those prime factors which seem to be most instrumental in causing current changes in the social segment he is examining. He isolates and measures the trend of such factors over a period of time in order that the rate of change may be carefully determined. He must then make an estimate of what such a conjunction of the prime factors will bring in the way of new social changes.

Among the prime factors acting on American society are:
1. The advances of technology applied to manufacturing, transportation, and communication.
2. The declining rate of population growth.
3. The closing of the frontier.
4. The increasing urbanization of society.
5. The ideological conflict of state socialism, democratic socialism, and democratic capitalism.

Our purpose is not to develop an appraisal of these forces but to direct attention to them as we make a brief examination of the changes in American institutions.

POWER STRUCTURING OF AMERICAN INSTITUTIONS IN 1900

American institutions may be viewed in relation to their power structuring. Such a view reveals their relatively uneven influence over American life. If we turn to the beginning of the twentieth century we find an institutional power structure in which business institutions dominate. Figure 127 is a heuristic diagram which purports to suggest the relative ranking of institutions in terms of their power and influence on American life. In this

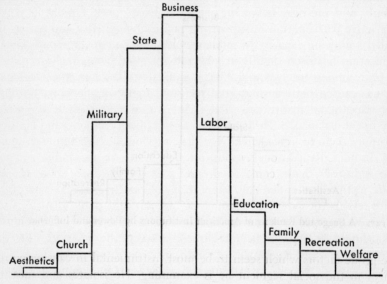

FIG. 128. The Power Structuring of American Institutions in 1950.

figure the prominent position of business dwarfs the remaining institutions which lie about its base. In 1900 private business was relatively free from political regulation. Businessmen made the important decisions affecting the economy and the society. They became the established social leaders and set the values in most American communities. The school, state, church, recreational and aesthetic institutions were largely controlled by boards of businessmen or lived by their philanthropy. The family was drawn ever more tightly into the orbit of the business institutions as economic self-sufficiency was replaced with an economic dependence upon those who owned factories, offices, and stores.

INSTITUTIONAL STRUCTURE IN 1950

In 1950 a change in the relation of American institutions may be observed. Figure 128 shows the prominent rise of the political state into a new level of power. The state so increased its power during the fifty-year interval that it now threatens to rival the long-established dominance of business institutions. Government men (who are very often former businessmen) began to make the more important decisions regarding the over-all direction of the economy. The 1950 government appropriations calling for an expenditure of $46,000,000,000 give government men a large organization with great national powers and responsibilities. The military organization by reason of the world power struggle has grown to a huge peacetime establishment. The threat of an atomic war gives the military organization an enhanced authority and prestige. Labor organizations have grown rapidly in power. Their active participation in supporting political candidates and parties has revealed a growing capacity to influence elections and governmental policy.

Education has risen slightly in power as the state increasingly recruits its staff from among teachers and college graduates. However, the ideological scare has caused both business and the state to throw increased restraints about educational institutions. The slight rise of education hangs precariously in the balance. Such institutions as the family, church, and aesthetic institutions seem to have remained at their previous level or to have suffered slight declines. Recreational institutions, led by the movie, radio, and television industries, have come to occupy a larger place of influence, and welfare institutions under state support are obviously growing. The overall picture reveals the power dominance of business and political institutions. The largest question confronting institutional life is the kind of relationship which should be or will be established between the political state and business institutions. Russia with state socialism, Spain with state capitalism, England with democratic socialism, and America with democratic capitalism are the major political-economic amalgams that are present in the world today. The United States with its democratic capitalism is confronted in the world scene with a powerful Russian state which represents state socialism. The external power struggle between these great states is affecting the organization of society even as internal forces act upon the development of political and economic institutions in each nation.

Many writers have regarded the society of 1950 as in a state of transition. The search for a stable society must go on, and great forces only partly understood and still less controlled will grind away until a new stability is achieved. This particular transition stage in human history is different from all others. For the first time technological advance has accomplished the miracle of abundance. Men no longer need to starve. The machine on the farm and in the factory can produce a tremendous quantity of food and

living commodities so that Americans and, in time, all peoples can live in comfort and security. A Utopia of abundance has a material base that will pass an inventory in terms of machines, men, and materials. Against the promise of this material Utopia looms the threat of war and internal strife. Both are real and both are possible. H. G. Wells said many years ago that the world is caught in a race between education and catastrophe.

TWO CONTRASTING STRUCTURES FOR 2000 A.D.

In 2000 A.D. two possible forms of institutional structuring may be envisioned. Figures 129 and 130 attempt to show these possibilities. The structuring of these two hypothetical societies is a study in contrast. Figure

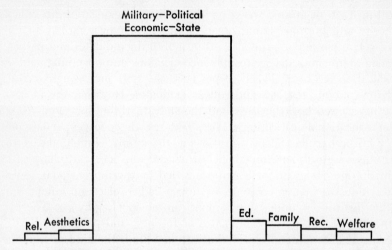

FIG. 129. A Possible Power Structuring of American Institutions in 2000 A.D.— Option A.

129 represents a society in which economic and military security is threatened. As a result, the military, political, and economic institutions have lost their separate identity and are now merged in one all-powerful state. All other institutions defer in complete subservience to the state. Labor organizations have been abolished by state edict.

Figure 130 pictures a completely different society—one in which the economic struggle has almost ceased. Men have turned to a struggle for status and prestige in educational, ethical, and recreational institutions. Leisure-time activity predominates and status must be won in the institutions which enrich human living. The family and aesthetic institutions have secured a position of much greater importance, but economic and political institutions have declined to a low level of importance. Automatic machinery has cut labor demands in the manufacture and distribution of goods so

drastically that very little time or skill is required to service the economic needs of society. Labor organizations have all but disappeared as the line between owner and worker has become less meaningful. The political state has become greatly simplified by the cessation of economic struggles, which has removed its manifold responsibilities as an umpire. The coördination function is one of interrelating the ethical obligations of the person to society in conjunction with his educational and recreational growth. The ethical, educational, and recreational institutions share this large responsibility.

It must be admitted that human imagination in the middle of the twentieth century is strained by these two contrasts in the structuring of

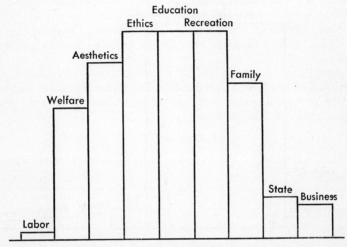

FIG. 130.   A Possible Power Structuring of American Institutions in 2000 A.D.—Option B.

institutions. The revolutionary changes suggested by Figure 130 may seem beyond belief. The writers hasten to disclaim any great concern with their success in forecasting hypothetical societies. What is most important is the fact of social change in institutional structuring. To grasp the significance of a changing relationship between institutions is to open the mind to new interpretations of current life and to pose new possibilities in the future. The relationship between industry and society has changed, is changing, and will continue to change. The student of industrial sociology never forgets that all of his observations and interpretations of industry take place within a changing society. If he shuts his eyes to the larger context he loses perspective as researcher, teacher, or citizen. The interrelationship between industry and society is not the ending but the beginning of industrial sociology.

SUPPLEMENTARY STUDIES

LIBRARY: BOOKS AND ARTICLES

Arnold, Thurman, *The Folklore of Capitalism*, Yale University Press, 1937.

Brady, Robert, *Business as a System of Power*, Columbia University Press, 1943.

Chase, Stuart, *Democracy Under Pressure*, The Twentieth Century Fund, 1945.

Chase, Stuart, *The Road We Are Traveling*, The Twentieth Century Fund, 1943.

Davis, Jerome, *Capitalism and Its Culture*, Farrar and Rinehart, 1935.

Mannheim, Karl, *Man and Society in an Age of Reconstruction*, Kegan Paul, Trench, Trubner and Company, Ltd., 1942.

Meadows, Paul, "Human Relations in Industrial Civilization," *Technological Review*, April, 1947, pp. 341-345.

Meadows, Paul, "The Industrial Way of Life," *Technological Review*, March, 1946.

Polanyi, Karl, *The Great Transformation*, Rinehart and Company, 1944.

Veblen, Thorstein, *The Theory of the Leisure Class*, The Modern Library, 1934.

LIBRARY: FILM

Productivity: Key to Plenty (20 minutes). The technological revolution which caused an increase in productivity and a higher standard of living. Produced by Encyclopaedia Britannica Films, Inc.

RESEARCH GAP

An empirical determination of the power structuring of contemporary American institutions.

Glossary

absenteeism—rate at which regular work force fails to report to work.

argot—conventionalized slang of a work group.

ascribed status—status assigned to any person occupying a position irrespective of his individual or innate peculiarities.

big boss—(colloquial) high supervisory official, usually president, manager, or owner.

bureaucracy—a form of organization in which offices are rationally arranged in reference to each other in respect to function and authority.

business class—people who work with ideas, paper, and other people.

career expectation—wish that an occupational sequence may be achieved at some future time.

career families—closely related types of career patterns grouped together because they have dominant common attributes.

career hierarchy—the arrangement of related jobs in an ascending order of importance of power, status, and returns.

career orientation—see **orientation**.

career pattern—sequence of jobs that follow some orderly development.

career plateauing—situations where career climbing is intermittent rather than continuous; where changes in authority, status, and economic returns are spasmodic rather than gradual accretions.

chores—a number of unskilled, routine tasks performed in a work plant.

class organization—organization of workers in terms of their salary or wage levels in a plant.

class position—the salary or wage position occupied by a worker within a work plant.

cleavage—tendency for social distance to develop among interdependent units of an organization. See **segmentation**.

collective bargaining—process by which union and management try to reach agreement on wages, hours, working conditions, and other relations between the two groups.

communication distortion—the tendency for information flow to become partial, altered, or confused as it proceeds either up or down the line.

communication organization—the channels along which orders, reports, rumors, and information of any sort travel.

communication system—all the channels of information flow considered in their interrelational sense.

control organization—groups such as cost control, rate setting, and inspection which supply the basis for management's evaluation and control of the operation of the work plant.

counseling—the process of helping a person through interviews and other devices to solve his problems and to improve his planning.

demography—the quantitative study of the social attributes of a population, such as age, sex, race, mortality, morbidity, and mobility.

distortion—see **communication distortion.**

ecology—the study of the distribution of groups and social forms in *time* and *space*, and the forces accounting for this distribution.

effective organization—an organization which accomplishes its specifically desired ends.

efficient organization—an organization which satisfies the motives of participants while they try to attain the ends of the organization.

ethos—see social atmosphere of work plant.

fawning—the use of ingratiating devices to secure "pull."

filtered information—the altering of orders or reports in the flow up and down the job hierarchies according to the individual definition of the work situation. See **communication distortion.**

first line—the lowest level of management or supervision concerned with actual production or servicing.

formal organization—system of consciously coördinated activities of two or more persons to achieve group goals.

functional organization—the arrangement of units and departments in a work plant in terms of the operations or services each performs in reference to other units and departments.

functional relationship—a relationship that grows out of interdependence or from division of labor.

grapevine—(colloquial) informal channels of information flow which operate outside the line of communication.

grievance—charge on the part of workers or union that contract regulations have been violated or ignored by employers or their representatives.

griping—(colloquial) constant complaint about the work situation which is not primarily motivated to change the situation but acts as a therapeutic release device to displace or channelize frustration.

horizontal occupational movement—any movement from one work position to another without regard to socioeconomic status.

horizontal work groups—those groups in a work plant society that are regarded as containing members whose jobs have roughly the same amounts of status, authority, skill, and perhaps economic income.

House of Labor—all formal and informal organizations found in labor unions and among non-supervisory workers generally.

House of Management—all formal and informal organizations found among the supervisory workers generally.

ideology—system of ideas and emotions out of which arise specific verbal

patterns in the form of myths, folklore, clichés, legends, slogans, and stereotypes.

induction—socialization of a worker to a new work position or work group.

industrial sociology—study of work groups and work relations, the role the worker plays in such groups, and the social organization of work society.

industry—generic term often referring to manufacturing concerns especially but also referring to all enterprises of a type or combination of businesses.

informal code of work—proscriptions and prescriptions of behavior both explicit and inferred which are necessary for acceptance in the nuclear or satellite work group.

informal organization—network of personal and social relations which are not defined or prescribed by formal organization.

initial work period—a period of job impermanence beginning when the worker seeks his first temporary jobs during his span of school enrollment and continuing until he has completed his education.

institution—a need and the culture surrounding it, including dominant attitudes and behavior patterns, symbolic and utilitarian culture traits, and written or oral codes that specify conduct.

interactional chronograph—an instrument constructed to measure promptness, frequency, and duration of verbal responses in interviews and other fixed social situations.

international union—an organization in which all union locals of a craft or industry in the nation or adjoining nations are represented to fix and execute common policies or agreements.

jargon—the technical or secret vocabulary of an art, trade, profession, or special group.

job—any definite work assumed calling for technical behavior.

job hierarchy—the arrangement of jobs in ascending order of authority, status, and economic returns.

job placement—fitting the person to his work position; technical, physical, and social placement of the worker.

job protection devices—those activities or attitudes adopted by individuals or groups to deter others from undermining their power, status, and financial position.

job specification—job description and job analysis data for a given job.

job travel path—the route people take to work.

labor force—all those people who are gainfully employed and willing to be gainfully employed, including unpaid family workers on farms.

line—hierarchy of authority and function in the formal organization of the work plant.

line of pressure—the transmission of work pressure from one worker to another along the chain of operations required to produce a good or service.

line organization—segment of work plant that is concerned with carrying out of actual production or service.

management—any and all work positions which are primarily concerned with formally coördinating the work of individuals, groups, and organizations.

management organization—the supervisory hierarchy including the staff organizations.

marginality—state of partially participating in two groups or cultures, and not totally accepting the values of either and being totally accepted in return.

morale—the state in which the individual subordinates his own interests and desires to those of the group, so that consensus and group goals may be most readily achieved.

nuclear work group—group in which workers operate in face-to-face social interaction on the job.

occupational chain—the linkage of social, economic, educational, occupational, and cultural factors that determine the way of life of succeeding generations for various segments of the society.

occupational culture—set of customs, myths, rituals, and beliefs which a craft or work group acquires and transmits as tradition.

occupational security—feeling of assurance that job performance meets satisfactory standards for the given occupation.

organizational charter—the images that members of a group have of the symbols, traditions, purposes, and achievements of the group.

orientation—direction of attention and aspirations.

path to work—see job travel path.

peer communication—flow of information horizontally among equals in a work plant.

peer culture—the complex of customs, symbols, traditions, beliefs, and other things that are distinctive of an age or status group; the culture that a peer group does not share with other groups in the society.

placing—process by which a newcomer finds out where he fits in terms of the functional relations of the work and the status system of the work plant society.

plant manager—high line official who is primarily and directly responsible for the production or service function of the organization.

political organizations—structures which deal with acquisition of and contest for power, opposed to executive organization, which administers agreements reached.

power organization—the arrangement of individuals and groups in terms of their ability to secure obedience from others.

preparatory work period—early experiences and adjustments in the home,

school, and community that occur before gainful employment and have a bearing on behavior in future work situations.

profession—relatively high-status job which requires prolonged and specialized training as prerequisite to practicing. Usually higher formal education is considered essential. Occupational egocentrism tends to be high.

psychodrama—a training technique wherein members of a group reënact their roles or those of others before a trainer or observer.

"pull"—(colloquial) unearned influence which a worker has secured with those in higher jobs which he uses for private advantage.

rank and file—members of a union who are not officers; ordinary union members.

rest period—officially determined lengths of time when work is interrupted to alleviate the effect of fatigue or boredom.

riding—(colloquial) efforts to disconcert a fellow worker by resorting to quasi-serious or humorous complaints and accusations.

role—the part played by the person in the group or social situation.

satellite work group—any group related to the work plant society in which the worker participates outside of his nuclear work group.

segmentation—process inherent in all larger organizations in which smaller units tend to become independent of and antagonistic toward other units or the whole organization; a process of cleavages developing within an organization.

sentiment—emotionally toned ideas or convictions which are protected and furthered.

short-circuiting—the practice in work plants of disregarding the formal channels of information flow along the hierarchies.

social base—the dominant demographic and social characteristics of a particular group, institution, or population.

social behavior—behavior in response to the presence or activity of others, or that which reflects or incorporates the behavior of others.

social atmosphere of work plant—culture traits and patterns that influence worker's pace, work outlook, sentiments, and culturally observable acts.

social class—a socioeconomic grouping of the population which tends to exhibit similar social and cultural habits and characteristics; sometimes a general status group.

social factors of work position—factors which define the social environment of a job.

social organization—system of enduring relations among persons and groups that give unity to the structure as a whole.

social placement—see **job placement.**

social process—regular patterns of human interaction existing in groups, such as coöperation, conflict, competition, arbitration, etc.

social skill—capacity to adjust to new groups and situations, as well as the ability to understand and manipulate people and groups.

social structure—a static view of relatively stable social relations and social organization existing in a situation or institution.

social system—complex pattern of social relations considered as a *whole* because each part is interdependent with all others.

social weaning—the process by which the child's dependence on his family and home is gradually weakened until he asserts a relatively independent and mature status.

socialization—the process by which the person becomes a part of the group by learning and accepting its standards, values, and traditions.

societal group—any group which the worker belongs to as a member of a local community.

sociodrama—carrying on the psychodrama in a group setting.

sociograms—charts depicting sociometric relations among group members.

sociography—mapping of social relations.

sociometric placement—arranging work group in conformity to results of sociometric choices and tests.

sociometric profile—a graph which compares the scores of a worker with others on several closely associated social characteristics or scales.

sociometry—method of studying interpersonal relations in terms of attraction-repulsion patterns existing among group members.

sociotechnical behavior—social behavior which is necessary to perform technical aspects of the job.

stable period—a period of job persistence beginning when the worker finds a work position in which he remains more or less permanently (three years or more). Stability is increased when he performs his work position within a given work plant in which he intends to remain during the rest of his working life.

staff organization—segment of work organization that is concerned with planning and providing such specialized services as sales, finance, engineering, personnel, public and labor relations.

status anxiety—feeling of apprehension arising from concern over relative work position, expressing itself in worry and anxiety over recognition, status, or advancement chances.

status expectation—wish that the work position be given an anticipated amount of status or recognition.

status hierarchy—a ranking of jobs or positions in status levels from lowest to highest.

status organization—how the social and prestige positions of a work plant are arranged in reference to each other.

status symbols—any article, object, activity, or other device associated with a job or worker to which the group agrees to give deference.

status system—the interrelations of all prestige and positional elements in a group or organization.

style of living—the particular mode of living which the work position tends to establish for a worker.

supervisory hierarchy—the arrangement of supervisory positions in a work organization in order of formal power and authority.

symbiosis—a relation in which groups coexist side by side in accommodative relationship, but remaining at the same time discrete entities that do not share a common social life.

technical behavior—that part of the worker's behavior required solely in the technical operations of a given work position.

technical organization—the arrangement of relations between persons and groups in a work plant that are determined by the productive or service requirements of the plant.

top management—highest officials in the plant organization who fix and direct policy.

trial work period—a period of job transition beginning when the worker seeks his first full-time permanent job and continuing until he has secured an occupation with which he intends to remain during the rest of his working life.

turnover (labor)—rate at which labor supply is lost or rate needed to replace labor supply.

union locals—small units of the union organized along craft or industrial lines in particular communities.

values—ends or objects toward which desires, attitudes, and behavior are directed; anything capable of being appreciated.

vertical occupational mobility—change of occupation to either a higher or lower socioeconomic level.

vertical work groups—those groups in a work plant society that are regarded as containing members whose jobs vary in the amount of skill, authority, honor, and income attached to them.

wage hierarchy—ranking of jobs in order of the wages or salaries associated with them.

work—totality of technical and social behavior associated with a job.

work clique—informal association of workers usually in the nuclear or satellite work group who are bound to each other primarily by social relations.

work culture—those folkways, mores, traditions, rituals, skills, knowledge, ideas, and attitudes that prevail in an occupation and in a work situation.

work ecology—the placement of workers in the sociopositional sense; i.e., the study of the distribution of co-workers and the patterns of work relations that are affected by work location.

work field—refers to a service or marketing area which is treated as a unit

by an employer for canvassing, soliciting, and distributing a product or service.

work flow—the movement of materials from one worker to another or the way that work operations fit into each other in production or servicing.

work group—any group related to the work plant society.

work model—a worker whose technical and social behavior provides a learning example for another person.

work plant—the building, machinery, apparatus, fixtures, etc., employed in work operations.

work plant community—a number of permanent local and larger groups within a work plant tied together by interdependence and common interests.

work plant security—feeling that job performance is satisfactory not only in regard to occupational requirements but also in regard to the social demands of the work plant society.

work plant society—an abstract term that connotes the complex of interrelationships existing among work groups within a work plant.

work-play—innovations introduced in and about the work activity which tend to decrease boredom, strain, or anxiety by increasing social interaction within the work group.

work position—refers to the definite place which the worker occupies within the total pattern of the work plant community. His position is based on his job and his duties, physical location, contact with other people and objects, circumscribed round of activities, and the way he fits into the activities of others.

work pressure—imposed or self-imposed demands for increased application of effort to increase output or maintain a set tempo of work.

work relations—social interaction among workers within the work plant society.

work role—the part played by the worker in the work group.

work route—the path of work activity the worker takes as he moves about the plant in his job performance.

work situation—the complex of formal and informal social and technical requirements which confront the members of a work group as they meet daily problems on the job.

work station—the physical location in a work plant where the worker is placed to perform his job.

working class—people who work with their hands primarily in making and servicing things.

APPENDIX: OUTLINE FOR THE
ORGANIZATIONAL ANALYSIS AND RECONSTRUCTION
OF SOCIAL STRUCTURE IN THE WORK PLANT

(Prepared for use by the professional sociologist or
for training of the graduate student)

Part I: Analysis

Describe the social structure of the work plant by analysis of the type parts shown in the left column. Watch for tension and adjustment points that may be present. The most frequently occurring tensions are indicated in the right column. Record the nature of such tensions as may be associated with the appropriate structural part. Avoid any discussion of suggested changes since it is important to restrict examination to analysis of the entire structure before planning a program of organizational reconstruction. Part II provides a suggested outline for reconstruction after analysis is completed.

Elements of Work Plant Structure | Common Tension and Adjustment Points

I. Industry-Community Relationships

1. Brief history of community
   a. "Reputation" of the community

   Discrepancies between community standards and plant standards

2. Brief history of company with the community
   a. "Reputation" of the company
   b. "Reputation" of the union

   2.1 Hostility of community directed the work plant
   a. Hostility directed against the workers or groups of workers (charges of "undesirables," "striking at expense of community prosperity," etc.)
   b. Hostility directed against the owners or managers (charges of "labor haters," "monopolists," discriminate against workers, dump factory wastes in rivers, etc.)

3. Social contacts of workers in the community

   3.1 Hostility of work plant directed against the community
   a. Hostility of workers toward the community (charges of "unfriendly," dis-

Elements of Work Plant Structure	Common Tension and Adjustment Points
	criminates in housing, credit, schooling of children, etc.)
	b. Hostility of owners or managers toward community (charges of "lack of understanding," "unsympathetic," discrimination in taxation, access to facilities, and harmful governmental regulation, etc.)
4. Status of workers in community	4.1 Discrepancies between role and status achieved in plant as compared with the community (*Ex.:* Low status in work plant in contrast to higher status in community organizations may induce dissatisfaction)

II. Culture Content of Work Plant

1. Material culture
   Invoice culture traits
   Identify culture complexes and core traits

2. Physical and social atmosphere	2.1 Dissatisfaction with physical conditions and services, particularly differential facilities for different groups of workers and supervisors
3. Jargon and argot	3.1 Bewilderment and frustration from failure to understand or to communicate
4. Folkways, mores, rules	4.1 Discrepancies between mores and rules
5. Social myths about work	5.1 Disillusionment about equity in pay advancements, etc.
6. Public values and ideals	6.1 Discrepancies between ideals and actions
7. Style of life induced	7.1 Conflict in different styles of life: supervisory vs. worker, conflict in work plants between workers who hold puritan values of hard work and those who hold "group norms" of work and think bosses are no better than they are

Elements of Work Plant Structure	Common Tension and Adjustment Points
8. Cultural integration Content of culture uniformities, specialties, and alternatives Contradictions between culture patterns in the work plant	8.1 Lack of meaning or purpose for work; no sense of belonging 8.2 Confusion of motives and rewards

III. Grouping and Contacts

1. Make a rough floor plan of the work plant showing arrangement of workers at their *work stations.* Show *work* routes.	1.1 Inadequate definition of work routes and work stations 1.2 Differences in the estimated time to arrive at the work station and to leave the work station, in reporting to work, in rest periods, in other allowed time, in cleaning up and leaving work

2. Describe size and number of separate work groups	2.1 Discrepancies between the work group desired by the worker and the actual work group in which he has been placed
	   a. Physical and Social isolation from other workers
	   b. Conflicting values or attitudes produced by heterogeneous work groups
	2.2 Differences in the estimated number of individuals deemed necessary for the project as judged by workers, or as judged by superiors

3. Identify the kind of interaction Primary Quasi-primary Secondary	3.1 Improper social placement; i.e., placement on job either demanding social skills not possessed by the worker or lacking the social skill for which the worker desires expression 3.2 Differences in the judgments of supervisors and of workers as to effect of social interaction on worker efficiency
4. Describe the workers: list age, sex, and background; indicate where they live and some of the characteristics	4.1 Strains produced in getting to and from work because of poor roads, traffic congestion, length of time in travel, etc.

Elements of Work Plant Structure	Common Tension and Adjustment Points
of their *paths to and from work*	
5. If customer contacts, describe	5.1 Tension over ritual and etiquette of super-ordinate—subordinate relationship induced in seller-buyer contacts
IV. Formal Structure of Management	
1. Describe the chain of command showing line and staff	1.1 Inadequate definition of the chain of command causing confusion in the authority and responsibility relationship
a. Examine "span of control," i.e., number of subordinate executives or supervisors reporting to a single individual	1.2 Span of control is too great to give direction needed; span of control is too short to develop self-reliance and initiative in the supervision leadership
2. Describe the segmentation of the structure Time Space Divisional, sub-divisional, and departmental Breaks between supervisory levels Breaks between line and staff	2.1 Certain segments claim they are not being used or that their functions have been usurped by other segments
	2.2 Blockage of action by superior officials or coördinate officials in other segments
	2.3 Blockage of action caused by difficult job conditions, lack of parts, inadequate tools, complicated procedures, etc.
	2.4 Differences in the estimates of quantity or quality of work that was expected by supervisors and/ or workers on successive shifts
	2.5 Tensions over values, hours of work of different work groups such as office, shop, etc.
V. Communication	
1. Communication structure down the line	1.1 Lack of adequate channels for communication down the line
a. Order-issuing procedures and contacts of supervisors and employees Use of bulletin boards	1.2 Failure of structure to deliver information to supervisors and employees a. Inadequate definition of re-

Elements of Work Plant Structure	Common Tension and Adjustment Points
Use of public address system	sponsibility for delivering communication
Use of newspaper	1.3 Dissatisfaction with slowness or manner of communication from the top or any other position in the chain of command
Use of conferences	
b. Effects and defects of communication	
Down the Line	
Blockage	1.4 Misinterpretation of the meaning of communication induces tension
Distortion	
2. Communication Structure up the Line	2.1 Lack of adequate channels for communication up the line
a. Procedures	
Access to Supervisors	2.2 Social distance maintained by supervisors blocks access
Grievance Procedure	
Suggestion Box	2.3 Dissatisfaction with grievance procedure
Personnel Department Channel	
b. Effects and defects of communication	2.4 Ideological resistances to criticisms and reports
Up the Line	
Filtered Information	
Short-circuiting	
Deliberate Blockage	
3. Coördinate status or peer communication. Describe:	3.1 Fragmentary or distorted horizontal communication causes misinterpretation
Work flow contacts	
Rest period contacts	
Lunch group contacts	
Transportation contacts	
Dormitory contacts	
4. Oblique communication, describe:	4.1 Inability to achieve confidence and rapport
Contacts with staff and service	4.2 Secret sharing induces jealousy and charges of favoritism
Operation of grapevine (overt medium)	
Secret Sharing (covert medium)	

VI. Work Flow

| 1. Diagram the main stream of work flow | 1.1 Defects in the technological arrangement of the work plant, restricting movement of workers, |

Elements of Work Plant Structure	Common Tension and Adjustment Points
	inducing strained body posture, etc.
2. Diagram the tributaries of work flow	2.1 Lack of supplies, equipment, transportation, storage, etc.
	2.2 Limited labor force available to do varying jobs which must be done; tensions arising in the ensuing competition among departments for more workers
3. Mark the points where action originates and chart the line or lines of pressure	3.1 Excessive demands placed on any part of the main flow of work
	3.2 Pressure applied by various tributaries on each other to get the various jobs done in order that any particular tributary may go ahead
4. Describe the manner in which pressure is transferred or absorbed	4.1 Pressure transferred from person to person by delegating jobs to others, trying to speed up the work pace of others, projection of blame to others, etc.
	4.2 Pressure absorbed by working faster, crying, joking, laughing, rationalizing, etc.
5. Describe human relations problems and tensions induced	5.1 Frictions between work positions under greatest pressure
	5.2 Fears due to dangers of inadequate safety devices, toxic substances, dangerous materials, etc.
	5.3 Conflicting definitions of performance standards a. Sense of unjust work load
	5.4 Inadequate job performance inducing greater burdens on work associates
VII. Work Positions and Work Roles of Managers	
1. List the work positions and analyze the work roles which are observed a. Patterns of Routine Behavior	1.1 Differential judgments of desirable standards in managerial performance a. Differences in formulating or executing policies

Elements of Work Plant Structure	Common Tension and Adjustment Points
b. Exceptional Behavior	b. Discrepancies alleged between managerial ability and authority
	1.2 Conflicts over qualifications desired in the selection, assignment, and promotion of supervisory leaders, specialists, and workers
	1.3 Ambiguity and inconsistency in managerial roles exhibited by one or more managers
2. Examine the manner in which workers with authority exercise their power or influence over their work associates	2.1 Authoritarian, arbitrary, and/or unreasonable exercise of authority
3. Indicate any real or potential cleavages and conflicts a. In the line b. In the staff c. Between line and staff	3.1 Promotional and status conflict between managers and supervisors 3.2 Staff influence is contested or ignored by line officers

4. Describe the informal organization of managers
a. Talk patterns
  Who talks
  Amount of talk
b. Sociometric patterns
  Cliques
  Lunch Associations
  Recreation Associations
  Club and Lodge Associations
  Clique of Managers Wives
	4.1 Exclusion of some managers from informal group because of personality, social background, or other considerations
	4.2 Demands that managers affiliate with social clubs or otherwise maintain a standard of living beyond economic means
	4.3 The conflict or ostracism of one or more of the wives of the supervisors by the other wives

VIII. Structure and Operation of Union Local

1. Chain of command a. Line b. Staff	1.1 Inadequate definition of responsibility and authority a. Overlapping of responsibilities and authority b. Inadequate delegation of responsibility

Elements of Work Plant Structure | Common Tension and Adjustment Points

2. Segmentation of the structure

2.1 Certain segments claim they are not being used or that their functions have been usurped by other segments

3. Work positions and work roles
   a. Patterns of routine behavior
   b. Exceptional behavior

3.1 Differential judgments of desirable standards in leader performance
   a. Differences in formulating or executing policies
   b. Discrepancies alleged between managerial ability and authority

4. Exercise of power and influence

4.1 Authoritarian or autocratic control and behavior of union leaders, steward over union members
   a. Worker-steward resentment
   b. Union leader-steward resentment

5. Cleavage and conflicts

5.1 Group cleavages
   a. Between line and staff
   b. Between full-time leaders and part-time leaders and workers
   c. Between college trained leaders and rank and file leaders
   d. Between those with ideological and those with pragmatic conceptions of trade unions
   e. Between local leaders and international representatives

6. Relations with union members

6.1 Members display hostile or half-hearted attitudes toward the union and participation in it

7. Relations with management

7.1 Union is not recognized by management as socially desirable or necessary

IX. Informal Group Structure

1. Kinds of technical, sociotechnical, and social behavior in which the worker engages

1.1 Discrepancy between managerial-supervisory goals based on cost and efficiency and worker goals and satisfactions
   a. Refusal of workers on the job to conform to technical, sociotechnical, and social behavior expectations of the managers

Elements of Work Plant Structure	Common Tension and Adjustment Points

2. Talk Patterns
Who talks
Amount of talk
Content of talk
    Interest subjects
    Avoidance subjects
    Patterns of ideas and sentiments
	2.1 Discrepancy between group standards and individual patterns
	  a. Worker talks too much, especially ego-centered talk
	  b. Worker introduces topics not the concern of the group
	  c. Worker refuses to participate in lunch group, adhere to group standards of work, group standards of behavior toward supervisors, etc.
	  d. Group refuses participation to worker

3. Sociometric Patterns Cliques Car pools Lunch association Recreation association Interpersonal relations and feelings Reciprocal behavior patterns such as job trading, helping one another, etc.	3.1 Clique antagonisms 3.2 Work position isolates worker shunting informal group participation

4. Initiation, ceremonies, and rituals
  a. Naming
  b. Hazing
	4.1 Changes in rituals resisted

5. Work play such as gambling, horseplay, practical joking, singing, joking relationships, etc.	5.1 Suppression of these activities resisted
6. Conflicts such as fighting, "politicking," and sabotage	6.1 Individual rivalries contesting for popularity, prestige, or power in the work group
7. Informal group code a. Social controls to enforce the code	7.1 Violations of the informal group code "rate buster," "chiseler," "stealer"
8. Race and ethnic relations	

9. Coöperative and conflict behavior evidenced between formal and informal organization	9.1 Conceptions of:
	  a. Fair day's work
	  b. Just wage
	  c. Safe or desirable tools, equipment, etc.

Elements of Work Plant Structure	Common Tension and Adjustment Points
X. The Power Structure of Management and Labor	
1. The political structure of management	1.1 Cleavages with formal supervisory structure
2. The political structure of labor	2.1 Union factionalism
3. Major conflicts between union and management	3.1 Major differences in interest, worker rights, management prerogatives, etc.
	3.2 Conflicting Values and Role Expectations of Union Leaders and Managers in contact with one another a. In grievance bargaining b. In collective bargaining
	3.3 Lack of Communication channels between management and the union
4. Tactics and weapons each structure uses	4.1 Conflicts over strategy and tactics such as work stoppage, use of press and radio, etc.
5. Types of union-management coöperation	
6. The play of external forces Public opinion Government Community pressure Newspapers	6.1 Bias and partiality of external groups
XI. Status Structure of Work Plant	
1. Status hierarchy	1.1 Discrepancies between formal status and informal status a. Seniority vs. ability b. Position or pay vs. ability or function
2. Status symbols	2.1 Discrepancy between status position and the status symbols rewarded or assumed by the worker
3. Rights and limitations surrounding various status positions	3.1 Inadequate or ambiguous definition of status rights and limitations resulting in tension over use of particular tools, rooms, seating arrangements, etc.

Elements of Work Plant Structure	Common Tension and Adjustment Points
4. Status problems and grievances	4.1 Violations between status position and the status rights and privileges assumed
	4.2 The exploitation by particular individuals of their status, such as burdening lower status persons with disagreeable jobs, preferential treatment of those with higher status
5. Relationships and adjustments demanded by the status structure	

XII. Class Structure of Work Plant

1. The salary and wage structure	1.1 Discrepancies between workers' expected standard of living and his economic return
	1.2 A wage incentive system which sets worker against worker in violation of group standards
2. Material evidence of differences in class position	
3. Prevailing mores regarding pay	3.1 Lack of relationship between skill and responsibility on job required and wage return
	a. Within wage structure of plant
	b. In comparisons of wage structures of other plants
	3.2 Violation of merit in administration of wage system
4. Problems of gross or felt inequality	4.1 Discrepancies between individual's subjective evaluation of his effort and the recognition received in pay
a. By individual workers	
b. By groups of workers	4.2 Differentials in living facilities provided
	4.3 Misunderstanding or lack of information of wage system
5. Way pressure is exerted to relieve gross or felt inequalities	5.1 Threats, fawning, organizing, striking, slow-down, sabotage, stealing
a. By individual workers	
b. By groups of workers	

Part II: Reconstruction

Carefully review the tension and adjustment points that have been identified in the analysis.

Prepare a suggested program of organizational reconstruction designed to eliminate or reduce tension to a minimum. Review adjustments required in each of the twelve elements of the work plant structure.

The procedure suggested is illustrated.

1. Describe tension or adjustment point
   a. The nature and context in which tension is located
   b. The origin and history of the tension
   c. Pragmatic or ideological resistance to adjustment. (May be impossible to proceed farther.)
2. Suggested change for remediation
   a. Nature of change
   b. Resources required
      Personnel
      Material
      Time
3. Social repercussions expected from change
   a. Probable
   b. Possible
4. Suggested procedure for introduction and monitoring of change
   a. Introduction of change
   b. Monitoring of change
5. Suggested research design to assess effects of proposed change
   a. Design
   b. Instruments of measurement

Index

INDEX OF NAMES

Adams, James Truslow, 558, 559, 560, 562
Adams, Walter S., 789
Allan, Douglas M., 176 n.
Allbutt, T. E., 100-101
Anderson, H. D., 398, 671, 672, 675, 702, 717, 719, 722, 742
Archibald, Katherine, 446, 447-448, 449-450
Arensberg, Conrad M., 10, 819, 823-824
Auden, W. H., 851-852

Babcock, F. Lawrence, 692, 702
Bakke, E. Wight, 10, 11, 230-231, 446, 467-468, 481, 643, 667 n., 711
  bonds of organization, 482-488
Barbash, Jack, 328
Barnard, C. I., 145, 149, 152, 347-349, 350, 354, 464-465
Bavelas, Alex, 421-422
Beagley, Virginia, 497 n.
Bell, Daniel, 76
Bell, Howard, 592-593
Benge, Eugene J., 687-688
Berle, Adolf A., Jr., 149
Blumer, Herbert, 10
Booth, Charles, 791
Bowers, R. V., 392
Breckinridge, S. P., 128
Brown, George, 10 n.
Burks, B. S., 723

Calverton, V. F., 74
Cantor, Nathaniel, 473
Cantril, Hadley, 683-684
Centers, Richard, 683-684, 720
Chamberlain, Neil W., 328 n., 330
Chapin, F. Stuart, 28, 230, 352 n., 848, 849
Chapple, Eliot D., 10, 423-425, 499 n.
Chase, Stuart, 4-7, 390, 835-836, 838, 848
Clark, Carroll D., 725
Clark, H. F., 398
Collins, Orvis, 451, 825-826
Conover, William, 11
Cooley, Charles H., 68-69, 527
Corbett, Doris S., 557
Cottrell, W. Fred, 116, 615, 711, 792
Counts, George S., 603-604

Davidson, P. E., 398, 671, 672, 675, 702, 717, 719, 722, 742
Davis, Allison, 10 n., 366
Deeg, M. E., 368-369, 604
Dewey, John, 97-98
Dickson, William J., 44, 55, 57, 78, 276, 445
Dietz, Walter, 11
Dinkel, Robert M., 783
Donald, Gordon, Jr., 423-425
Donato, Pietro di, 119-120, 124-125
Donham, Wallace B., 37
Dooley, C. R., 11
Dreyfuss, Carl, 394
Drucker, Peter F., 208, 214, 372, 466-467, 469, 601, 677-678
Dubin, Robert, 10, 331
Dunlop, John T., 231

Eaton, Joseph, 415, 422-423
Edey, Maitland, 735
Edwards, Alba, 129, 136, 137-138, 368, 669-670, 726, 742

Fairchild, Henry Pratt, 8
Fear, Richard A., 412
Ford, Henry, II, 643
Form, William H., 10, 368, 729, 742
Fox, John B., 11
Franklin, Benjamin, 558-559, 560, 562-563
Freeman, F. N., 723
French, John R. P., 25 n.

Gardner, Burleigh B., 10, 163, 198-199, 210, 214, 350, 354, 363, 367, 375, 495, 501-502
Garland, Hamlin, 559-560
Gilmore, H., 366
Gilson, Mary B., 49-50, 76, 79
Gist, Noel P., 725
Goetsch, Helen B., 728
Golden, Clinton S., 234
Gompers, Samuel, 235, 844
Green, Arnold, 664, 666

Hallberg, Robert M., 300 n.
Hansen, A. T., 303 n.
Harbison, F. H., 10, 331

883